Communicating
NUTRITION

The
Authoritative Guide

BARBARA J. MAYFIELD, MS, RDN, FAND

EDITOR

FOREWORD BY ELLIE KRIEGER, MS, RDN

eat right. Academy of Nutrition and Dietetics

.eat® right. Academy of Nutrition and Dietetics

Academy of Nutrition and Dietetics
120 S. Riverside Plaza, Suite 2190
Chicago, IL 60606

Communicating Nutrition: The Authoritative Guide

ISBN 978-0-88091-017-0 (print)
ISBN 978-0-88091-018-7 (eBook)
Catalog Number 017020 (print)
Catalog Number 017020e (eBook)

The views expressed in this publication are those of the authors and do not necessarily reflect policies and/or official positions of the Academy of Nutrition and Dietetics. Mention of product names in this publication does not constitute endorsement by the authors or the Academy of Nutrition and Dietetics. The Academy of Nutrition and Dietetics disclaims responsibility for the application of the information contained herein.

All FNCE® attendees submit a photography waiver as part of the registration process, which gives permission to the Academy to use their likenesses.

10   9   8   7   6   5   4   3   2   1

For more information on the Academy of Nutrition and Dietetics, visit www.eatright.org.

Library of Congress Cataloging-in-Publication Data

Names: Mayfield, Barbara J., editor. | Academy of Nutrition and Dietetics, issuing body.
Title: Communicating nutrition : the authoritative guide / Barbara J. Mayfield, editor.
Description: Chicago, IL : Academy of Nutrition and Dietetics, [2020] | Includes bibliographical references and index. | Summary: "Written and reviewed by experienced nutrition communicators and educators, this authoritative guide provides the knowledge and skills needed to develop and deliver all types of communication in a variety of settings. Students, interns, and practitioners alike will find this to be an indispensable resource. The book's 42 chapters are presented in 8 sections, each with an opening showcase featuring a communication success story and applied advice. Highlights of the chapters include guidance on: Writing and interpreting scientific research Developing science-based messages Addressing misinformation Customizing communications to various audiences Delivering effective presentations Mastering media interviews Using social media, websites, videos, and demonstrations Communicating in business settings - and much more! Theoretical background for best practices in nutrition communication is addressed throughout to help build foundational knowledge and skills. This is rounded out with "words of experience," hands-on strategies, and real-life stories in every chapter, along with objectives, checklists, and key takeaways"-- Provided by publisher.
Identifiers: LCCN 2020015839 (print) | LCCN 2020015840 (ebook) | ISBN 9780880910170 (paperback) | ISBN 9780880910187 (ebook)
Subjects: MESH: Health Communication--methods | Nutritional Physiological Phenomena | Health Education--methods | Nutritional Sciences--methods
Classification: LCC RA423.2 (print) | LCC RA423.2 (ebook) | NLM WA 590 | DDC 362.101/4--dc23
LC record available at https://lccn.loc.gov/2020015839
LC ebook record available at https://lccn.loc.gov/2020015840

CONTENTS

PART I

Nutrition Communication Is Built on a Firm Foundation: Professional, Science-Based, Audience-Focused

SECTION 1: Communication Forms the Foundation of Professional Practice

SECTION 2: Nutrition Communication Is Science-Based

SECTION 3: Nutrition Communication Is Audience-Focused

PART II

Nutrition Communication Is Designed and Delivered with Excellence

SECTION 4: Designing and Delivering Presentations

SECTION 8: Designing and Delivering Professional Communications

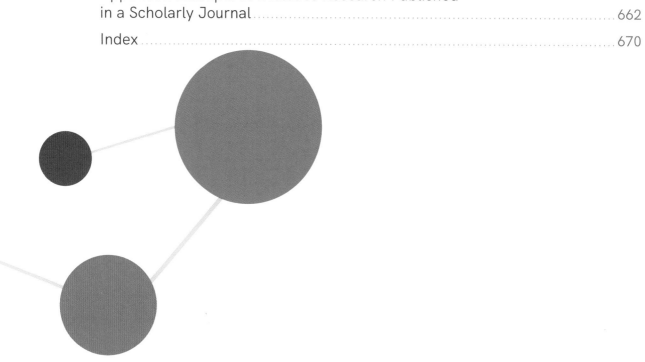

CONTRIBUTORS

Lucille Beseler, MS, RDN, LDN, CDE, FAND
President, Family Nutrition Center of
South Florida
Coconut Creek, FL

Susan T. Borra, RDN
Former Chief Health and Wellness Officer,
(Retired) Food Marketing Institute
Arlington, VA

Nicci Brown, MS, RDN
Nutrition Communications Specialist,
Academy of Nutrition and Dietetics
Foundation
Chicago, IL

Anna Busenburg, RDN, CSP, LD, CLC
Neonatal Dietitian, Cincinnati Children's
Hospital Medical Center
Cincinnati, OH

Carol Byrd-Bredbenner, PhD, RD, FAND
Distinguished Professor of Nutrition,
Rutgers University
New Brunswick, NJ

Anne Elizabeth Cundiff, RD, LD, FAND
Registered Dietitian, Author, and Podcast
Host, AE Huebert Consulting
Waukee, IA

Kristin Cunningham, MHA, RD, LD
Dietitian, Washington University in St Louis
School of Medicine, Inflammatory Bowel
Disease Center
St Louis, MO

Melissa Joy Dobbins, MS, RDN, CDCES
CEO, Sound Bites Inc
Chicago, IL

Lynn Dugan, MS, RDN
Founder, Nutritionist/Chef,
MyPlate2Yours, LLC
Glen Ellyn, IL

Tatyana El-Kour, MA, MS, RDN, FAND
Health and Nutrition Coordinator, Action
Against Hunger, Syria Mission
Damascus, SY

Ann Gaba, EdD, RD, CDN, CDCES, FAND
Assistant Professor and Internship Director,
City University of New York Graduate
School of Public Health and Health Policy
New York, NY

Devon L. Golem, PhD, RD, LDN
Founder and CEO, Institute of Continuing
Education for Nutrition Professionals
Cary, NC

L. Suzanne Goodell, PhD, RDN
Associate Professor in Nutrition,
North Carolina State University
Raleigh, NC

Laura Goolsby, MS, RDN, LDN
Clinical Coordinator-Master of Science
in Nutrition with Distance Learning
Internship, Keiser University
Lakeland, FL

Lori Greene, MS, RDN, LDN
Instructor, University of Alabama
Tuscaloosa, AL

Ardyth Harris Gillespie, PhD
Retired Community Nutritionist, Cornell
University; Co-Leader, Harrisdale
Homestead Food Education and
Research Center
Atlantic, IA

Angie Hasemann Bayliss, MS, RDN, CSP
Co-Clinical Nutrition Manager, University
of Virginia Health System
Charlottesville, VA

Jen Haugen, RDN, LD
Author, Speaker, Kitchen Consultant
Austin, MN

Erin E. Healy, MS, RDN
Consultant and Instructor, Booz Allen
Hamilton and Framingham State University
Framingham, MA

Janet Helm, MS, RDN
Executive Vice President, Chief Food and
Nutrition Strategist, Weber Shandwick
Chicago, IL

Alice Henneman, MS, RDN
Extension Educator, Emeritus, University
of Nebraska-Lincoln
Lincoln, NE

Mindy Hermann, MBA, RDN
President, Hermann Communications
Somers, NY

David H. Holben, PhD, RDN, LD, FAND
Professor and Gillespie Distinguished
Scholar; Director, Office of Food and
Nutrition Security, University of Mississippi,
School of Applied Sciences
University, MS

Jill Jayne, MS, RD
Founder and CEO, Jump with Jill
Pittsburgh, PA

Becky Jensen, MS, RDN, LN
Nutrition and Dietetics Internship
Program Director, Instructor, South
Dakota State University
Brookings, SD

Lisa Ann Jones, MA, RDN, LDN, FAND
Nutrition Communications Consultant
Woolwich Township, NJ

Lori A. Kaley, MS, RDN, LD, MSB
Program Manager, University of
New England
Portland, ME

Sonja Kassis Stetzler, MA, RDN, CPC
President/Founder, Effective Connecting
Charlotte, NC

Heidi Katte, MS, RDN, CD, FAND
Program Director, Dietetic Technician
Program, Milwaukee Area Technical College
West Allis, WI

Carolyn Lagoe, PhD
Associate Professor, Nazareth College
Rochester, NY

**Roberta Larson Duyff, MS, RDN, FAND,
FADA**
Food and Nutrition Consultant/Author,
Duyff Associates
St Louis, MO

Trinh Le, MPH, RD
Content Strategist, Fitbit
San Francisco, CA

Arielle "Dani" Lebovitz, MS, RDN, CSSD, CDE
Author, Speaker, Experience-Based
Educator, Experience Delicious LLC
New Windsor, NY

Shelley Maniscalco, MPH, RD
Founder and President, Nutrition
On Demand
Arlington, VA

Donna S. Martin, EdS, RDN, LD, SNS, FAND
School Nutrition Director, Burke
County Public Schools
Waynesboro, GA

Rachel Meltzer Warren, MS, RDN
Owner, RMW Nutrition
Jersey City, NJ

Katie McKee, MCN, RDN, LD
Health and Wellness Director, Dairy Max
Lantana, TX

Amy R. Mobley, PhD, RD
Associate Professor, Health Education
and Behavior, University of Florida
Gainesville, FL

Carolyn O'Neil, MS, RDN, LD
President, ONeil Nutrition Communications
Atlanta, GA

Rachel Paul, PhD, RD
Founder, Rachel Paul Nutrition LLC
San Francisco, CA

Virginia Quick, PhD, RDN
Director, Didactic Program in Dietetics,
Rutgers University, School of Environmental
and Biological Sciences
New Brunswick, NJ

Betsy Ramirez, MEd, RDN
Food and Nutrition Communications
Consultant/Adjunct Professor
Lewisburg, TN

Sylvia Rowe, MAT
President, SR Strategy, LLC
Washington, DC

Rosanne Rust, MS, RDN, LDN
Nutrition Communications Consultant and
Freelance Writer, Rust Nutrition Services
Meadville, PA

**Martine I. Scannavino, DHSc, RDN, LDN,
FAND**
Allen Chair, Department of Nutrition,
Cedar Crest College
Allentown, PA

Jaime Schwartz Cohen, MS, RD
SVP, Director of Nutrition, Ketchum
New York, NY

Jo Ellen (Jodie) Shield, MEd, RDN, LDN
President and Editor-in-Chief, Healthy
Eating for Families, Inc
Kildeer, IL

**Kayle Skorupski, MS, RDN-AP, CSG, CNSC,
FAND**
Assistant Professor of Practice, University
of Arizona Nutritional Sciences Department
Tucson, AZ

Ilene V. Smith, MS, RDN
Principal, I ON FOOD
New York, NY

**Marianne Smith Edge, MS, RDN, LD, FAND,
FADA**
Founder/Principal, The AgriNutrition Edge
Owensboro, KY

Virginia C. Stage, PhD, RDN
Associate Professor, East
Carolina University
Greenville, NC

Milton Stokes, PhD, MPH, RD, FAND
Director, Global Health and Nutrition
Outreach, Bayer Crop Science
St Louis, MO

Barbara Storper, MS, RD
Executive Director, FoodPlay Productions
Hatfield, MA

Cheryl D. Toner, MS, RDN
Director of Food Sector Engagement,
American Heart Association
Herndon, VA

Evelyn Tribole, MS, RDN, CEDRD-S
Co-author, *Intuitive Eating*
Newport Beach, CA

Liz Weiss, MS, RDN
Podcast Host and Blogger, Liz's
Healthy Kitchen
Lexington, MA

Wendy H. Weiss, MA, RD
Nutrition and Health
Communications Specialist
River Vale, NJ

Elizabeth Yakes Jimenez, PhD, RDN, LD
Research Associate Professor, Departments
of Pediatrics and Internal Medicine,
University of New Mexico Health
Sciences Center; Director, Nutrition
Research Network, Academy of
Nutrition and Dietetics
Albuquerque, NM; Chicago, IL

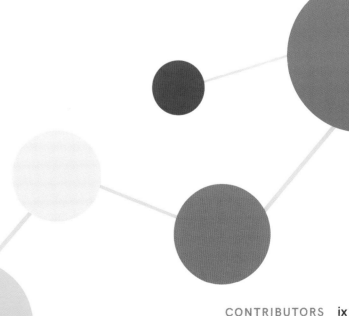

REVIEWERS

Susan E. Adams, MS, RD, LDN, FAND
Assistant Professor, Nutrition Programs,
La Salle University
Philadelphia, PA

Franca B. Alphin, MPH, RDN, CSSD, LDN, CEDRD
Associate Professor Family Medicine and
Community Health, Director of Student
Health Nutrition Services, Duke University
Durham, NC

Rachel Baer, MS, RDN, LD
Nutrition Communications Consultant
Atlanta, GA

Neva Cochran, MS, RDN, LD, FAND
Nutrition Communications Consultant
Dallas, TX

Connie Diekman, MEd, RD, CSSD, LD, FAND, FADA
President, Academy of Nutrition and
Dietetics, 2007-2008, Food and
Nutrition Consultant
St Louis, MO

Judith L. Dodd, MS, RDN, LDN, FAND
Assistant Professor, Sports Medicine and
Nutrition, University of Pittsburgh
Pittsburgh, PA

Jennifer Doley, MBA, RD, CNSC, FAND
Regional Clinical Nutrition Manager
and Dietetic Internship Director,
Morrison Healthcare at Carondelet
St Mary's Hospital
Tucson, AZ

Linda S. Eck Mills, MBA, RDN, LDN, FADA
Owner, Dynamic Communication Services
Bernville, PA

Leia Flure, MS, RD, LDN
Marketing and Communications
Coordinator, University of Illinois Extension
Urbana, IL

Teresa Fung, ScD, RD, LDN
Professor, Department of Nutrition,
Simmons University
Boston, MA

Barbara J. Ivens, MS, RDN, FAND, FADA
Principal, Nutrition Information Exchange
Newaygo, MI

Deanne K. Kelleher, MS, RDN
Academic Specialist, Michigan State
University
East Lansing, MI

Michelle L. Lee, PhD, RDN
Associate Professor and Graduate
Coordinator, East Tennessee State University
Johnson City, TN

Kevan Mellendick, PhD, RDN, CSSD, CSCS
Medical Service Corps, US Navy

Marisa Moore, MBA, RDN, LD
Marisa Moore Nutrition, LLC
Atlanta, GA

Christine M. Palumbo, MBA, RDN, FAND
Principal, Christine Palumbo Nutrition
Naperville, IL

Denise Pickett-Bernard, PhD, RDN, LDN, IFMCP, IFNCP
Owner, Dr Dee Nutrition
Roswell, GA

Laura Poland, RDN, LD
Owner, Dietitian In Your Kitchen
Westerville, OH

Diane Quagliani, MBA, RDN, LDN
President, Quagliani Communications, Inc.
Western Springs, IL

Shelley A. Rael, MS, RDN, LD
Registered Dietitian Nutritionist,
ShelleyRael.com
Albuquerque, NM

Alice Jo Rainville, PhD, RD, CHE, SNS, FAND
Professor of Nutrition and Graduate
Coordinator, Eastern Michigan University
Ypsilanti, MI

Kenrya Rankin
Sensitivity Reader/Editor,
Luminous Prose, LLC
Washington, DC

Alexandra Oppenheimer Delvito, MS, RD, CDN
Vice President, Pollock Communications
New York, NY

Lona Sandon, PhD, RDN
Associate Professor and Program
Director, University of Texas
Southwestern Medical Center
Dallas, TX

Jean Storlie, MS, RD
President and Owner, Storlietelling LLC
Golden Valley, MN

Elizabeth M. Ward, MS, RDN
Nutrition Consultant and Author
Reading, MA

Kathleen Zelman, MPH, RDN
Director of Nutrition, WebMD
Marietta, GA

FOREWORD

As a nutrition professional, you will have amassed a wealth of knowledge about food and health. But what good is it if you can't communicate it effectively? If there is no one around to hear you, there is the possibility of our nutrition communication reaching nobody. No matter your focus in our vast profession, your impact depends on how well you get your message across. Whether you are speaking, writing, posting, counseling, instructing, demonstrating, pitching, presenting, creating recipes, developing infographics, photographing images, or producing videos, the end goal is the same: getting through to people in a way that sparks understanding and change.

With so much noise to overcome, that task can seem more challenging than ever. A health journalist I know once described a popular social media influencer as "not burdened by science." I chuckled at his witty description at the time but couldn't shake it out of my head because it got to the core of what I see as our greatest challenge as communicators. As credentialed nutrition experts, we are beholden to the science, which evolves at a glacial pace compared to the lightning speed of news today. We can't—and don't want to—grab people's attention with shiny trinkets of misinformation, lofty promises, or fear mongering, yet we have to compete in an environment where that is commonplace. It is a challenge for sure, but one I know we are up to, and keeping a good, sharp set of communication skills is essential to meeting it.

Perhaps the most important tool of all is listening. Little did I know as a loquacious child the wisdom of my grandfather's words when he'd tell me that God gave me two ears and one mouth for a reason. It's almost counterintuitive—we have so much knowledge we eagerly want to share, so it's tempting to just start downloading information. But when we listen first, finding out what our audience needs, what motivates them, what confuses them—when we understand their resources, concerns, constraints, and ideas—we open the door to genuine, meaningful connection, and we can tailor our messages so they truly penetrate. That's the first step of any good communication cycle, which is essentially formatted like the instructions on a shampoo bottle: 1) Listen. 2) Create message. 3) Repeat.

While it might seem like some people just have a natural knack for communicating, much of it is a learned and practiced skill. I can tell you that firsthand. I have always enjoyed public speaking and writing, but I cringe when I look back at my early work—when I read the dense wordiness of my first magazine articles, watch my deer-in-the-headlights expression during television interviews, and read the vague instructions I wrote into my early recipes. But no one starts out a communications expert: You get there by stepping into the ring and keeping at it, integrating the tools of the trade and building your skills along the way. This comprehensive text, filled with the insights of the best in the business, is your trusty companion for doing so. Turn the page and start the journey.

ELLIE KRIEGER, MS, RDN
Award-winning cookbook author, columnist, and television personality

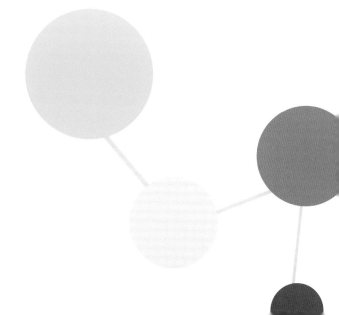

PREFACE

"Education is not the filling of a pail, but the lighting of a fire." —WILLIAM BUTLER YEATS

Nutrition professionals have a passion for going beyond acquiring knowledge of food and nutrition to sharing that knowledge with others—a passion for *communicating nutrition*. Achieving this desire requires expertise in the art and science of nutrition communication. *Communicating Nutrition: The Authoritative Guide* provides expert guidance—based on evidence and experience—to communicate effectively.

An Idea is Born

The Academy of Nutrition and Dietetics identified a need for a nutrition communication text based on requests from educators and practitioners for resources on this topic. A book published by the American Dietetic Association on this topic called *Communicating as Professionals* went out of print in the early 2000s. Since then, there has not been a book published on the topic of nutrition communication. Although there are books about nutrition counseling and nutrition education, they have a different focus, purpose, and scope. The Academy of Nutrition and Dietetics determined to fill this gap with a comprehensive book that spoke to both future nutrition professionals and to those already in the field.

One contributing author described the authors' collective opinion about the need for this book: "This is the book we wish we would've had as a reference and guide to prepare us for our careers and the many ways we communicate."

Reflecting on the origin of my contribution to this book, I realize it began when I took Purdue University's nutrition communication course as an undergraduate more than 40 years ago. While enrolled in this course, I realized that communicating nutrition was to be my primary objective, no matter my practice setting. Over the next two decades, I built on the knowledge and skills learned in that class and derived great career satisfaction through a variety of communication experiences: speaking, writing, and media.

When the professor who designed Purdue's nutrition communication course retired, my former department invited me to fill the position. It was like a dream come true, being able to teach my favorite course and pass on to future nutrition professionals the ability and desire to communicate nutrition. For 32 semesters, together with hundreds of students, we learned and practiced the art and science of nutrition communication. What we learned is captured in this text. Long after graduation, former students consistently recognize the importance of their knowledge and skills in nutrition communication to their career success in a variety of settings.

Soon after I retired from teaching, the Academy of Nutrition and Dietetics approached me about using my experience to lead the development of a book to fill the void in resources about nutrition communication. This felt similar to my invitation to teach—it was an opportunity not to be missed. This time, the reach would be to an exponentially larger audience of not only future nutrition professionals but also fellow practitioners and educators. I accepted the challenge.

Collaboration Brings the Idea to Life

If there is one thing that teaching has taught me, it's that I do not know everything—no matter my level of expertise. Therefore, if I was going to take on writing this book, it would not be alone. By design, this book has been a collaborative effort from its inception to its completion:

- During development, we solicited the input of educators and practitioners to determine its depth and breadth.
- We invited the participation of other credentialed food and nutrition professionals to serve as writers and dozens volunteered. In the end, 57 authors contributed to the writing. Each one wrote from their unique knowledge and experiences creating a truly authoritative guide.
- We enlisted dozens more credentialed food and nutrition professionals to serve as peer reviewers of the book. With their input, the original manuscript was revised and improved.
- Once we had a good working draft, we invited educators to pilot sections of the book in their classes. Over several semesters, dozens of students read the book and provided feedback along with their instructors. This feedback provided insight into how to best utilize this resource as a textbook, not only in programs with dedicated nutrition communication courses but in those where the subject is covered in multiple courses.
- Additional experts in copy editing, book design, and publishing helped bring the book to completion.

The expertise and enthusiasm invested in this project cannot be measured but is evident on every page.

The Book Takes Shape

This book is divided into eight sections split into two parts. The first part establishes the foundation of nutrition communication and the second part focuses on the design and delivery of nutrition communication via a variety of channels. Each section opens with a Showcase that illustrates a real-life nutrition communication example that sets the stage for the topics covered in that section.

Part 1: Nutrition Communication Is Built on a Firm Foundation: Professional, Science-Based, Audience-Focused

The first part of the book provides the basis for what sets effective nutrition communication apart, and how it is supported by three foundational pillars: (1) the professionalism of the registered dietitian nutritionist (RDN), who is credentialed, ethical, and knowledgeable in both nutrition and communication; (2) the scientific evidence-base for nutrition messages; and (3) its focus on the audience, addressing their needs, culture, and preferences.

- Section 1 orients the reader to nutrition communication and sets the stage for the remaining chapters. It serves as a review of communication theory put into the context of nutrition science. It establishes the importance of communication for both the dietetics student and the practicing nutrition professional.
- Section 2 establishes the rationale for communicating accurate, current, science-based messages. Students and practitioners alike will learn how to read and interpret research in their communication. Properly citing references, both orally and in writing, is a critical skill along with avoiding plagiarism. Professional ethics related to communication is also addressed.
- Section 3 sets the stage for designing audience-focused communication. Models for message development are described along with practical strategies. The importance of a needs assessment is established, and techniques for completing one are described. An overview of behavior change theories used successfully in nutrition education and communication is provided along with examples for their practical use. Tailoring messages to audiences based on culture, gender, age, and generation is discussed. The section culminates with how to write communication goals, learning objectives, key message points, and how to outline and organize a message.

Part II: Nutrition Communication Is Designed and Delivered with Excellence

With the foundation of insuring that the communicator is professional and prepared—their message is supported by scientific evidence and has been tailored to meet the audience's needs—the second part of the book focuses on how nutrition communication is designed and delivered to be most effective: engaging the audience, presenting information meaningfully and memorably, and motivating positive lifestyles. All types of nutrition communication are described with practical strategies for excellence in design and delivery provided.

- Section 4 focuses on traditional oral presentations, breaking down the parts of an effective presentation as well as effective presentation skills and tools.
- Section 5 covers several channels used effectively by nutrition communicators including writing, video, food demonstrations, and food photography.
- Section 6 explores the wide variety of channels that effectively reach large numbers of people via mass media.
- Section 7 investigates a number of topics that are often overlooked but can make or break the success of any form of communication endeavor.
- Section 8 is primarily for the practicing nutrition professional, covering topics related to business and professional communication.

Application and Education

This book is for both credentialed food and nutrition professionals seeking to expand their knowledge and skills in nutrition communication and for future professionals building foundational knowledge and skills. Equipped with the guidance contained in this book, nutrition communicators can reach any audience, through any channel, with accurate, well-crafted messages that meet audience needs and improve lives.

Speaking on behalf of all of the authors, reviewers, editors, and designers, it has been our privilege to create this book. May it be a valuable resource that you turn to often and may it ignite your passion for communicating nutrition

BARBARA J. MAYFIELD, MS, RDN, FAND
Editor

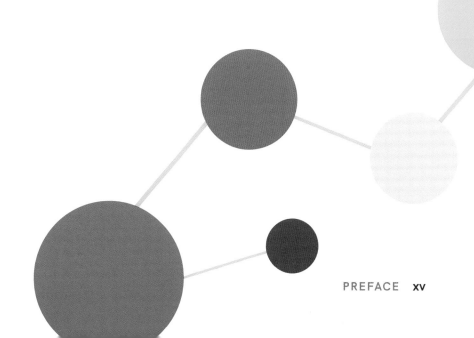

ACKNOWLEDGMENTS

Communication is a collaborative endeavor. Creating a book requires extensive collaboration from start to finish. From its inception, throughout development, until its completion, this book is the result of countless individuals who contributed in numerous ways. I would like to acknowledge everyone who helped bring this book to life.

You, the reader, are first. Without an audience, communication doesn't exist. A book is no exception. Therefore, I wish to thank the food and nutrition students and colleagues who inspired the need for this text. All current and former audience members of the author team, whether students or fellow nutrition professionals, contributed (largely unknowingly) to every word. This book is because of you and for you, our audience.

This book would also not exist without the editorial and financial support of the Academy of Nutrition and Dietetics. The Academy recognized the need, spearheaded its creation, and was instrumental in every stage. I am grateful for the privilege of working alongside the Academy's dedicated staff throughout the process, which began in 2016, when Betsy Hornick, MS, RDN, Manager of Acquisitions and Development at the Academy, contacted me after learning about the nutrition communication class I had taught for many years at Purdue University. This springboarded into a publishing contract where I would serve as editor-in-chief for this Academy book on nutrition communication. Betsy and I collaborated closely from the book's inception to its completion: developing the initial surveys to identify topics, authors, and reviewers; creating a table of contents and outline; and then working through development, peer review, revision, and pilot testing. I also had the pleasure of collaborating with Erin Fagan Faley, Manager of Production and Digital Content Development, who took over the production phase and skillfully managed the copyediting, design, proofreading, indexing, and finally taking this book to print, along with the help of graphic designer and Production Specialist, Alison Staffin. Betsy, Erin, and Alison, you are my superheroes.

I extend my deepest gratitude to the entire author team, listed by name on pages vii to ix, who contributed their expertise without financial compensation out of their dedication to our profession and as a gift to all future and current food and nutrition professionals. It was my honor to work alongside them and count them as both colleagues and friends.

Working behind the scenes, with their only recognition on pages x to xi, is our team of reviewers. I would like to express my appreciation to each of them for strengthening the book's content and writing. Like the authors, they contributed their expertise and dedication to enhancing our collective skills in nutrition communication as a service to their profession.

Finally, I wish to thank all of the family members and friends of the above individuals who supported and encouraged this project. We welcomed seven new babies among the authors' families, along with numerous job changes and other life and national events that were navigated while writing, reviewing, editing, and bringing this book into being.

Yes, communication is collaborative. Thank you, Academy. Thank you, authors. Thank you, audience.

MEET BARBARA J. MAYFIELD

Barb Mayfield has been communicating nutrition throughout her career. As you read her career story below, Barb invites you to reflect on your journey and the varied and valuable contributions you have made, are making, and will make, as you find your unique voice.

Barb's journey as a nutrition professional began at Purdue and was profoundly inspired by her favorite course, nutrition communication. She continued her education at Cornell, where she was inspired and mentored by her coauthor for Chapter 1 and where she investigated the role of sender-receiver interaction, leading to a lifelong interest in nutrition communication.

Barb's early work as a registered dietitian included a private practice, an unconventional position in the early 1980s. She focused on communicating evidence-based information using audience-centered approaches even before those phrases were coined as best practices. A stint in long-term care allowed Barb opportunities in the only setting of her career that included clinical and food-service. Communicating effectively with staff, residents, and family was the key to making changes and achieving positive outcomes and centered on creating articles and in-services.

Community nutrition and nutrition education formed the centerpiece of Barb's career, with 20 years in the Special Supplemental Nutrition Program for Women, Infants, and Children (WIC) program. Highlights included developing a curriculum for preschoolers that was implemented in all 50 states and creating trainings for staff that enhanced support for breastfeeding, parent-infant bonding, addressed childhood obesity, and promoted family meals. Concurrently, Barb worked with families as an early intervention specialist and provided nutrition education resources and training via her company, Noteworthy Creations, Inc.

Barb's experiences as a nutrition communicator led to her invitation to return to Purdue to teach. For 16 years she served on the Nutrition Science faculty, teaching future nutrition professionals to be effective nutrition communicators. She continued to create resources and trainings throughout this time reaching audiences of all ages with evidence-based, audience-centered nutrition information.

Upon her retirement from teaching, Barb took her work in new directions with unprecedented opportunities to reach even greater numbers of current and future nutrition professionals—online via her LLC, Nutrition Communicator, and via the pages in this book.

No matter your current or future work setting, you have the opportunity to share your knowledge and skills with unique audiences utilizing every available channel.

Go forth, be heard, and make a difference!!

ALL THE BEST,

Barb

SECTION

Communication Forms the Foundation of Professional Practice

Nutrition Communication Is an Art and a Science

Sylvia Rowe, MAT, and Cheryl D. Toner, MS, RDN

Sylvia Rowe, MAT

Cheryl D. Toner, MS, RDN

For more information on bridging science for consumers, see the Showcase on pages 142 to 143.

Communication Is A Team Effort

The digital age is undoubtedly challenging with the evolving ways that we relate to and communicate with one another. This ageless challenge, layered with unique issues related to science, nutrition, and food production, necessitated the formation of the International Food Information Council (IFIC) and IFIC Foundation. Both organizations are dedicated to building a bridge between communication and the science of nutrition and food safety.

IFIC's core competencies—convene, connect, and communicate—were understood to be interrelated, and still are today, such that communication is futile if the right people and issues are not connected in the process.

Many paths can be taken to build a successful communications career, and we believe that a diversity of backgrounds enriches nutrition communication efforts. Sylvia, with a background in journalism and issues management, built an IFIC team that included not only well-qualified registered dietitian nutritionists (RDNs) as the nutrition experts but also experts in food science, journalism, food regulation, public health, and public relations. Joining the team as an RDN with little formal communications experience, Cheryl learned that nutrition expertise is enhanced and leveraged for greater effect when partnered with the perspectives and skills inherent in complementary fields.

Building Diverse Perspectives into Practice

Our different viewpoints and expertise created fertile ground for the IFIC team to address a wide swath of nutrition-related scientific evidence, as well as appreciate the broad context from which it emerged and in which it impacted the world. We excelled at building diverse coalitions and creating broad-reaching initiatives designed for a wide range of audiences. One of IFIC Foundation's hallmark initiatives under Sylvia's leadership was "Improving Public Understanding: Guidelines for Communicating Emerging Science on Nutrition, Food Safety, and Health" (www.foodinsight .org/Improving_Public_Understanding). Because the Harvard School of Public Health and IFIC Foundation worked in partnership, we were able to convene a more diverse advisory group than could have been achieved independently and to produce a resource that was deemed credible and meaningful to target audiences. Round tables held around the country involved more than 60 nutrition researchers, food scientists, journal editors, university press officers, broadcast and print reporters, consumer groups, and food industry executives. The guidelines were published in the *Journal of the National Cancer Institute*[1] and highlighted in the *Journal of the American Medical Association* and the *New England Journal of Medicine* and are still utilized today as a teaching tool for responsible health communication.

> "While humans make sounds with their mouths and occasionally look at each other, there is no solid evidence that they actually communicate with each other." —SOURCE UNKNOWN

The Importance of Research and Systems Thinking

A primary way in which IFIC supports nutrition communicators in building a bridge between science and consumers has been through media and consumer research. *Food for Thought*, an analysis of media coverage on nutrition and food safety issues, provided a platform for our work with nutrition communicators.[2] We utilized these findings to raise consciousness in media coverage about the importance of and need for context, such as to whom research results matter and in what situations. Bringing scientific context to consumers through the media is part of building a bridge of understanding.

Consumer research is another essential building block on the bridge between science and consumers. The now-signature IFIC *Food and Health Survey* (www.foodinsight.org/2018 -food-and-health-survey) and numerous other consumer research programs at IFIC provide an important listening tool for nutrition communicators. From these research programs, the IFIC staff has built robust programs for communicators, including tool kits, professional conference presentations, media training workshops, speakers' bureaus, and continuing education. "It's All About You!" is a particularly salient communications program example, built upon extensive consumer research by a coalition of diverse stakeholders (see Figure 1). The Dietary

Guidelines Alliance, convened by IFIC, designed the research to "listen" first in order to reach the consumer more effectively. Importantly, the work of the alliance and the strategy of utilizing qualitative and quantitative research to inform messaging were sustained throughout four cycles of the US Dietary Guidelines for Americans. IFIC's multidisciplinary approach supported our ability to deliver resources to and encourage science-based nutrition messaging from a range of nutrition communicators. Connecting consumer and media research with communicators facilitates more effective two-way communication through better understanding of both nutrition science and the consumer.

FIGURE 1 "It's All About You!" campaign logo, Dietary Guidelines Alliance

The Dietary Guidelines Alliance

It's
All
About
YOU

Choose MyPlate.gov

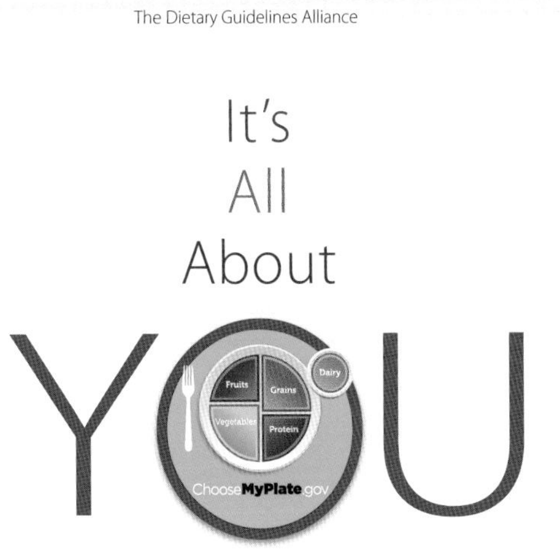

Reproduced with permission from the International Food Information Council Foundation. Mathews J. It's All About You! International Food Information Council Foundation website. Published June 6, 2014. Accessed July 17, 2019. https://food insight.org/ItsAll AboutYou[3]

Fast forward to today, and we see enduring evidence for the importance of broad expertise and perspectives in the marriage between nutrition and communication. The definition of nutrition is evolving with not only scientific advancement but also a convergence of issues formerly seen as unrelated, such as linking sustainability with dietary patterns. Dietitians are trained to think beyond the nutrients in foods—to understand and apply food, sensory, and behavioral sciences to our care for individuals, our oversight of food production, and our communications to the public. Today, however, anyone working in the food world must also be aware of food supply chains, agriculture, and the environment. A systems approach, such as depicted in Figure 2, is espoused by many as the key to better understanding our food, the environment it comes from, and the drivers of consumer food choices and eating behaviors.[4] A National Academies consensus committee looked at ways research may be utilized to improve how we communicate and asserted that a systems approach to science communications research may be necessary to tackle the complexities of the field.[5] With a broad view of the nuanced and complex factors inherent in food and food choices, we can leverage complementary expertise and better communicate with the public.

FIGURE 2 **Understanding systems science: A visual and integrative approach**

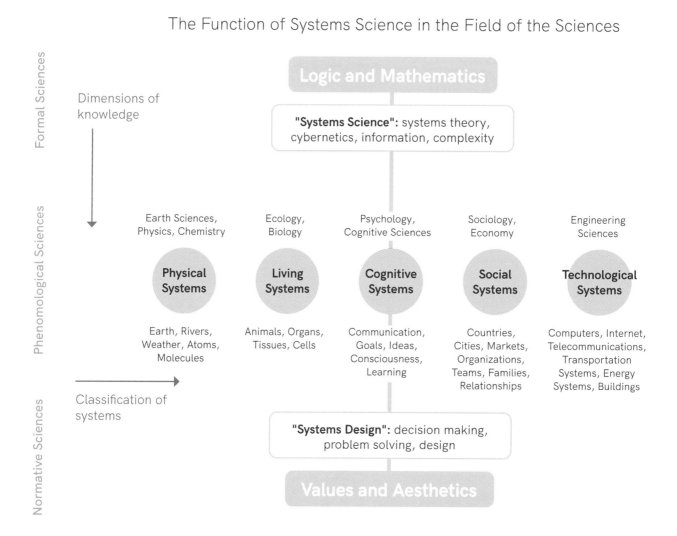

The Function of Systems Science in the Field of the Sciences

Adapted with permission from John Wiley & Sons, Ltd. Hieronymi, A. Understanding Systems Science: A Visual and Integrative Approach. *Syst. Res.* 2013;30:580-595. doi:10.1002/sres.2215[4]

Listen and Learn

The art of nutrition communication requires understanding scientific principles and diverse areas of science, including communications science, and an expanded view of the multiple factors affecting food and eating. We must first, therefore, listen. Ultimately, this fosters two additional elements of successful communication: to develop a narrative around an issue and to have empathy for the audience.

The needs and demands of the nutrition communication field are vast and complicated, best traveled with friends and colleagues who challenge us to view the science and the issues through different lenses, all focused on the ultimate goal of positively impacting the lives of the public through food and nutrition. We both live this reality as we each pursue consulting, academic, and professional service interests, connecting to share ideas and collaborate from time to time on projects related to our shared passion for communication. We hope that you will join us in the challenging and rewarding field of nutrition communication, with respect for the value of diverse backgrounds and broad thinking as a way to cultivate approaches that truly speak to consumers.

REFERENCES

1. Fineberg H, Rowe S. Improving public understanding: guidelines for communicating emerging science on nutrition, food safety, and health for journalists, scientists, and other communicators. *J Natl Cancer Inst.* 1998;90(3):194-199.
2. Wellmann N, Borra S, Schleman J, Matthews J, Amundson D, Tuttle M. Trends in news media reporting of food and health issues: 1995–2005. *Nutr Today.* 2011;46(3):123-129. doi:10.1097/NT.0b013e31821a9da4
3. Mathews J. It's all about you! International Food Information Council Foundation website. Published June 6, 2014. Accessed July 17, 2019. www.foodinsight.org/ItsAllAboutYou
4. Hieronymi A. Understanding systems science: a visual and integrative approach. *Sys Res Behav Sci.* 2013;30(5):580-595. doi:10.1002/sres.2215
5. National Academies of Sciences, Engineering, and Medicine. *Communicating Science Effectively: A Research Agenda.* National Academies Press; 2017. doi:10.17226/23674

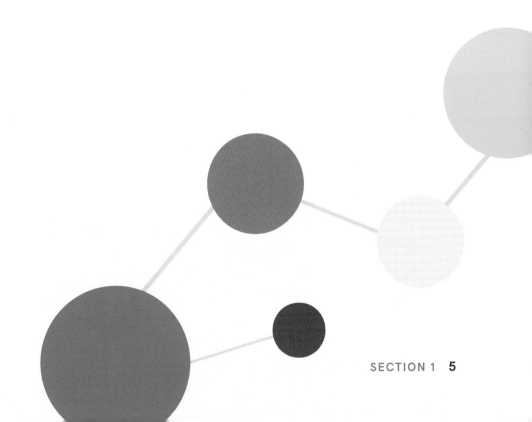

Communication Is the Essence of Nutrition Practice

Barbara J. Mayfield, MS, RDN, FAND
and Ardyth H. Gillespie, PhD

"The role of communication in nutrition practice is so pervasive that its importance could be overlooked. Communication knowledge and skills must not be taken for granted. Being an effective communicator is essential for effective nutrition practice."

"You cannot not communicate."

—PAUL WATZLAWICK

Introduction

Communication is a universal experience that begins with a baby's first cry. It develops through language acquisition, learning to read and write, and throughout life as a person interacts with others in an increasingly complex world. Communication is an essential life skill that includes not only words but also body language, facial expressions, and tone of voice. People communicate through spoken and written words, illustrations, videos, and even silence. As Hybels and Weaver succinctly state in *Communicating Effectively*, "To live is to communicate."[1]

Nutrition professionals communicate about nutrition, food, and health with diverse audiences to meet a multitude of needs. Eating is a universal experience, but what, where, when, and how people eat varies widely. Health is a universal concept that is also deeply personal. Effective communication is audience-focused. It is accurate and evidence-based. It is creatively delivered and requires expertise in the subject matter *and* communication.

This chapter answers four questions:

- What is nutrition communication?
- What is the role of communication in nutrition practice?
- How do models and theories enhance nutrition communication?
- How is nutrition communication both an art and a science?

This opening chapter provides foundational knowledge of nutrition communication concepts that will be discussed throughout the book. Food and nutrition professionals communicate with diverse audiences in a wide variety of settings and applications, which are introduced here and addressed in future chapters. Note that the focus of this book is primarily on communicating with people via group settings or via media channels rather than counseling and direct patient care; however, the foundational principles are similar and widely applicable.

This book will serve as a guide in combining nutrition knowledge with the art and science of communication. Credentialed food and nutrition professionals who build expertise in nutrition communication will maximize the impact of their messages.

What Is Nutrition Communication?

The study of nutrition communication begins with building a working definition. Consider what the term *nutrition communication* means. How is it defined? Definitions will vary based on experiences, but the meaning is intuitive. Read on to learn more about nutrition communication.

Nutrition Communication Is Self-Explanatory

Nutrition communication is just what it says it is—communication about nutrition. Though obvious, the term deserves further definition in a book dedicated to its study.

Fully defining *nutrition communication* requires first appreciating its origins—the science and art of communication. When communication principles and theories are applied to the field of nutrition and dietetics, the result is nutrition communication.

COMMUNICATION TERMS TO KNOW AND USE

Understanding nutrition communication requires familiarity with a core set of communication terms, which are listed in the Terms to Know box. The bolded words are generic terms used in communication literature. These are followed by their definition and then more specific terms that are used throughout this text. These more specific terms are synonyms or are specifically related to nutrition communication and are followed by examples.

DEFINITIONS BUILD FROM GENERAL TO SPECIFIC

The definitions that follow progress from general and all-encompassing to increasingly specific.

Communication is ... the act of transmitting or exchanging information, thoughts, or ideas (as in nonverbal, verbal, or written messages) between a sender and one or more receivers. The term is also used for the message itself, for the means used for transmitting messages, and for the field of study concerned with the interchange of ideas and messages.[2]

Science communication is ... "the use of appropriate skills, media, activities, and dialogue to produce one or more of the following personal responses to science (the AEIOU vowel analogy): Awareness, Enjoyment, Interest, Opinion-forming, and Understanding."[3] This definition focuses on outcomes and is intended to promote further research and evaluation of science communication.

Health communication is ... "the study and use of communication strategies to inform and influence individual and community decisions that enhance health," as defined by the Centers for Disease Control and Prevention (CDC) and the National Cancer Institute.[4] In health communication, the same principles apply for groups as for individuals; however, different strategies are employed.

Nutrition communication is ... communication about food and nutrition for the purpose of developing a platform for inquiry and exchange of ideas or to influence knowledge, understanding, attitudes, decision-making processes, or behaviors. A related term is *nutrition education*.

How to write goals and objectives is covered in Chapter 15.

Nutrition education is ... "any combination of educational strategies, accompanied by environmental supports, designed to facilitate voluntary adoption of food choices and other food- and nutrition-related behaviors conducive to health and well-being. Nutrition education is delivered through multiple venues and involves activities at the individual, community, and policy levels."[5]

The words used in each term above imply *why* communication is taking place. The next section explores the varied reasons for nutrition communication.

Nutrition Communication Fulfills Varied Goals and Purposes

Nutrition communication is designed to address a perceived need or interest. A variety of terms may be used to convey the reasons for nutrition communication: *purposes*, *goals*, *outcomes*, and *objectives*. Each has a slightly different meaning; however, they may be used interchangeably.

- **Purposes** for nutrition communication may include building awareness, education, promotion, inspiration, motivation, entertainment, forming a relationship, or building a platform, among others. A purpose is a broad statement and is more general than goals, outcomes, or objectives. It helps create goals, which will then lead to outcomes or objectives.
- A **goal** contains more detail than a purpose statement. Goals can relate to a particular program, a series of events or delivered messages, or an individual message. Goals can be written from the perspective of what the nutrition communicator will accomplish or what the audience will achieve.
- Desired **outcomes** or **objectives** are specific measurements that indicate whether the goal was achieved. They are written from the viewpoint of what the audience members will learn, engage in, or demonstrate.

In subsequent chapters, a variety of nutrition communication purposes, goals, and desired outcomes will be discussed. Box 1.1 on page 10 provides an example of how these terms work together. Note the use of the word *strategies* in the objective. Throughout the book, strategies for achieving specific chapter objectives will be described. Likewise, audiences need to know how to accomplish a goal.

TERMS TO KNOW

Sender		The person or group of people who initiate communication. The sender conveys ideas or information to one or more other individuals.
	Specific term:	Nutrition communicator
	Examples:	Speaker at a nutrition conference, author of an article, organization promoting a health or nutrition campaign
Receiver		The person or group of people to whom the transmitted information is directed.
	Specific term:	Audience
	Examples:	Attendees of a nutrition class or conference, subscribers to a health or nutrition resource, target audience of a health campaign
Message		The ideas or information transmitted from sender to receiver.
	Specific term:	Main idea(s) are called key messages, which are succinct summaries of main concepts.
	Examples:	Annual National Nutrition Month slogan
Channel		The means through which the message is conveyed.
	Specific term:	Varies depending on type of media used (written, verbal, visual)
	Examples:	Verbal and written messages sent via articles, blogs, websites, videos, presentations, illustrations and images
Feedback		The response sent back to the sender from the receiver about the message via the same or a different channel from the original message.
	Specific term:	Evaluation, data collection
	Examples:	Evaluation survey (formal), body language such as confused expression (informal), answer to icebreaker question designed to evaluate audience knowledge (formal), raising hand to indicate understanding (informal), comments on blogs or social media posts
Environment		The physical, social, and emotional context in which a message is transmitted, including external and internal environments.
	Specific terms:	Context, physical setting, social group, cultural background, emotional state
	Examples:	Meeting room, auditorium, community center, park, restaurant, family gathering, club meeting, group of friends vs crowd of strangers, calm vs stressed
Interference or "Noise"		Any physical, social, mental, or emotional hindrance to a message being transmitted clearly and completely.
	Specific terms:	Internal or external barriers
	Examples:	Preoccupation, multitasking, personal beliefs and biases
Predisposition		A frame of mind rooted in a person's values, beliefs, knowledge, and past experiences that inclines the person toward certain patterns of selective perceptions, interpretations, feelings, and actions when presented with any particular situation or stimulus.
	Example:	Negative childhood experience with broccoli

Purposes, Goals, and Objectives Work Together

Purpose:	To motivate
Goal:	Motivate the audience to prevent food waste
Objective:	Audience members will describe four strategies they plan to implement to prevent food waste. (This is considered a behavioral intention.)

GOALS FOR NUTRITION COMMUNICATION

The National Academies of Sciences, Engineering, and Medicine Committee on the Science of Science Communication identified five goals for communicating science.[6] These goals served as inspiration for generating the goals for nutrition communication listed below. Think of these as categories of nutrition communication goals.

- Increase appreciation of science and the role of food and nutrition in health and well-being.
- Influence individual or collective decision-making processes related to food, nutrition, and health.
- Improve knowledge, attitudes, and behaviors related to food, nutrition, and health.
- Engage change agents in collective inquiry, analysis, reflection, and innovation. Change agents are those in a position to influence others, such as parents, educators, other professionals, including those in industry, government, academia, and more.
- Inspire creative thinking, goal setting, behavior change, and long-term improvements in health and well-being.

What are other nutrition communication goals? The goals for nutrition communication may seem to be the same as the overall goals for nutrition practice. This is because nutrition cannot be practiced effectively without communication. Communication is the essence of nutrition practice.

What Is the Role of Communication in Nutrition Practice?

The role of communication in nutrition practice is so pervasive that its importance could be overlooked. Communication knowledge and skills must not be taken for granted. Being an effective communicator is essential for effective nutrition practice.

Communication Is Essential to Nutrition Practice

The Academy of Nutrition and Dietetics describes registered dietitian nutritionists (RDNs) as "food and nutrition experts who translate the science of nutrition into practical solutions for healthy living. Working in a number of areas, RDNs advance the nutritional health of Americans and people around the world." The tagline used for RDNs is "Optimizing the Public's Health Through Food and Nutrition."[7] To "translate science into practical solutions" and "advance nutritional heath" requires more than nutrition knowledge; it requires communication knowledge and skills.

"If you can't communicate, it doesn't matter what you know."

—CHRIS GARDNER, *THE PURSUIT OF HAPPYNESS*

An Academy of Nutrition and Dietetics practice paper[8] describes the role of communication as follows:

> *RDNs must actively take steps to position themselves as reliable sources of science-based food and nutrition information and communicate through a variety of new media and traditional channels. RDNs are uniquely qualified to evaluate and interpret nutrition research within the context of the body of science, and appropriately translate the findings into positive and practical food and diet advice for the public.*

EVERYTHING INVOLVES COMMUNICATION

Nutrition professionals use communication skills in every aspect of their career, and over the course of a career, nutrition professionals will participate in a wide variety of nutrition communication activities. Even on a daily basis, nutrition professionals are engaged in communication in numerous ways, from writing emails and meeting with colleagues to creating and delivering science-based messages to various audiences. Those who excel at communication are often sought to fill job vacancies and are generally more effective in all they do. Communication skills are recognized as a critical skill for all professionals, including those in health care, education, and business.

COMMUNICATION SKILLS ARE HIGHLY SOUGHT BY EMPLOYERS

The importance of preparing health care practitioners and other professionals with communication knowledge and skills has been recognized by numerous organizations and agencies. For example, the Institute of Medicine, in their report titled, *Who Will Keep the Public Healthy?*, identified communication as one of eight new competency areas for public health practitioners in the 21st century.[9] In the decade since, communication education has become a mainstay in public health academic programs and continuing professional education.

The National Institutes of Health published a series of special issue papers presenting the role of communication science in nutrition.[10] Collectively, these papers recognize the value in taking a multidisciplinary approach to promoting optimal nutrition through the use of communication science. In addition to their extensive knowledge of food and nutrition science, nutrition professionals also need to expand their communication knowledge and skills to effectively promote optimal nutrition.

In a broader context, employers are seeking candidates with soft skills (interpersonal or people skills) in addition to the technical skills specific to a job function. Surveys of employers consistently rank communication at the top of desirable skills in new hires. These skills include written and oral communication, listening, and presentation skills, among others.[11] A CareerBuilder survey found that 52% of employers said recent college graduates lack interpersonal skills, 41% reported a lack

of oral communication skills, 40% pointed to a lack of leadership skills, and 38% said new graduates need better written communication skills.[12] No matter what the professional setting, strong communication skills are essential to success. Poor communication can be costly and can inhibit professional growth and advancement.

POOR COMMUNICATION LEADS TO NEGATIVE OUTCOMES

Research on the economic and health impact of poor communication among care providers indicates a great need for improved communication skills in health care settings. A qualitative study of communication challenges was undertaken in seven hospitals of varying sizes and locations. The economic costs were derived from wasted physician time, wasted nurse time, and increase in patient length of stay. Costs associated with medical errors, patient or staff satisfaction, and other negative outcomes were not included, making the estimates only a portion of the total economic burden. Poor communication among care providers was estimated to cost a 500-bed hospital more than $4 million in lost revenue per year. The total economic impact of communication inefficiencies for all US hospitals was estimated to be over $12 billion annually.[13]

Researchers have also studied the impact of poor written communication in health care settings. A narrative literature review of 69 research articles found that poor written communication occurs between caregivers as well as between caregivers and patients. Common negative outcomes include compromised patient safety, patient dissatisfaction, discontinuity of care, and inefficient use of resources. The authors recommend improved content and timeliness of written communication in health care.[14]

Poor communication is also recognized as costly in the business sector. Data collected from 400 US corporations with 100,000 or more employees indicate the total estimated economic burden resulting from employee misunderstandings is $37 billion annually. The average cost per company is more than $62 million annually. This data set indicates that companies with leaders who are considered highly effective communicators had 47% higher earnings over a 5-year period compared to companies with leaders with poor communication skills.[15]

No matter the setting, poor communication has a significant negative impact. In health care, the impact leads to both poorer economic and health outcomes. Poor communication also results in decreased productivity and reduced patient and caregiver satisfaction. Improved communication skills can save time and money and result in improved health and well-being.

Nutrition Communication Takes Many Forms

Nutrition communication occurs in many different settings and through a variety of channels. These can be grouped into several categories that form the basis for the major sections within this book.

PRESENTATIONS TO VARIED AUDIENCES

Nutrition communicators present to all sizes of groups, from small, intimate groups to audiences of thousands. Audiences can consist of employees and staff, students and interns, clients and patients, community leaders and members, children, and various professionals. Section 4 of the book is focused on the knowledge and skills needed to design and deliver effective oral presentations.

An effective presentation has a logical, well-organized structure designed to present well-written key messages with supporting evidence and meaningful illustrations. It has a strong opening and closing that capture the audience's attention and inspire taking action. To enhance the presentation and help deliver the content in an engaging way, graphics and other media, such as videos, can be included.

Effective nutrition communicators enlist a variety of audience participation techniques to engage the audience, enhance learning, and promote behavior change. These include facilitated discussions and other activities to promote audience engagement. Effective nutrition communicators learn and master presentation skills to excel at message delivery. The skills covered in Section 4 are transferable to other types of communication, such as videos, demonstrations, and webinars.

WRITING, VIDEOS, FOOD DEMONSTRATIONS, AND PHOTOS

Section 5 of the book is focused on the knowledge and skills needed to design and deliver effective communication via writing, video, food demonstrations, and food photography. Communicating in writing is a major form of nutrition communication and a great way to reach large audiences. Most types of communication are based on writing, making these skills essential for communication success. For example, most verbal and visual messages are based on a written plan or script.

Video is one of the fastest growing channels for nutrition communication, but one for which very few nutrition professionals have received any training. This section includes a chapter covering how to create video, whether independently or working with a professional.

Communicating with food is an effective form of nutrition communication that includes culinary demonstrations and food photography. Food demonstrations are a multisensory way of communicating about food and nutrition that are entertaining as well as informative. Food photography is considered an essential feature of print and online recipes as well as articles about food and nutrition. Photos can help teach how to prepare a recipe, show the ingredients, suggest portion size, or simply entice the reader. Photos are also critical to the "shareability" of an online article or social media post[16]—without a photo, a nutrition-related article cannot effectively be shared on social media sites, such as Instagram or Pinterest, and is less likely to garner high engagement on Facebook and other online social platforms.

TRADITIONAL AND NONTRADITIONAL MEDIA CHANNELS

Section 6 of the book is focused on the knowledge and skills needed to design and deliver effectively via mass communication channels, including traditional and newer channels. Channels covered in this book include newspapers; magazines; social media; web-based communication, such as blogging; online courses and webinars; and shows and interviews for television, radio, and podcasts. These channels can reach hundreds of thousands of people, which means effective communication skills have the potential to influence and inspire widespread change.

This section will build the knowledge and skills for being the host or the interviewee. Roles may be reversed, but the principles and best practices are the same. With strong media skills, nutrition professionals expand their reach and influence and serve as a source of credible, science-based information in an era where nutrition misinformation is pervasive.

Principles for communicating through today's mass media channels will prepare the nutrition communicator for the channels of the future.

COUNSELING AND DIRECT PATIENT CARE

One of the primary forms of communication common to nutrition professionals is counseling and direct patient care in the clinical setting. Although this area of nutrition communication is outside the scope of this book, and excellent counseling resources are available, the communication principles covered in this text are in harmony with counseling communication principles. These include audience-focused communication, cultural competence, and ethics. While the examples in this text don't directly apply to counseling, much of the content does. However, an effective counselor will not approach an individual patient in the same manner as a nutrition communicator approaches a diverse audience.

How Do Models and Theories Enhance Nutrition Communication?

Theories are used to explain how something works. They may be commonly associated with academic settings; however, all people have mental maps that help them negotiate their social and physical worlds. Theories help to simplify reality by identifying priorities and predicting responses. Practitioners who use theories—consciously or not—find the application of theories can enhance their practice. Especially in a complex or multifaceted situation, a theory can help to:

- sort through the details;
- articulate a purpose, goals, and objectives;
- clarify a message;
- provide a platform for work; and
- contribute further to the body of theory.

Theories emerge from practice as well as research and are validated as they are articulated, tested, and refined. From this perspective, "there is nothing so practical as a good theory."[17]

Social and Behavioral Science Theories Inform Nutrition Communication

Nutrition communication theory builds on a number of social and behavioral science theories. These include basic communication theories and models, such as the sender-receiver model of Shannon and Weaver[18] and the theory of metacommunication, which encompasses "communication about communication,"[19] as well as the verbal and nonverbal interactions between people. It also involves theories and models for developing messages, including those described in Chapter 10, and behavior change theories, which are described in Chapter 12.

In the 1980s, selected theories were applied to understand how to more effectively communicate nutrition messages, especially through mass media. These theories were organized into a nutrition communication model[20,21] for their application in practice and research.[22] This model was grounded in the concept that communicators make better communication decisions when they respond to audience inputs. This includes recognizing that an audience's lifetime of experiences with food and nutrition predisposes how they engage in the communication process. By understanding the reasons behind individual responses at various stages of the process, nutrition communicators can develop more effective messages.

This conceptual model has been updated and expanded through research and experience to serve as a framework for planning and evaluating nutrition communication. The updated version is illustrated in Figure 1.1 on page 14. The nutrition communication framework recognizes the importance of building relationships among all parties involved: between communicators and audience members, among audience members, and between communicators.

Communication Is a Relational Activity

Communication is more than a message; it is a relational activity. In fact, communication has both instrumental and relational dimensions. The instrumental or task-oriented dimension includes the message and the channel.[23] The relational dimension includes all of the human interactions that enhance or impair effective communication between and among communicators and audiences. Metacommunication is one of the foundations of relational communication. It examines interactions among people and defines communicator-audience relationships through verbal and nonverbal cues. The first principle of metacommunication is "one cannot *not* communicate."[19]

Developing messages is further described in Chapter 10.

Read more about behavior change theories in Chapter 12.

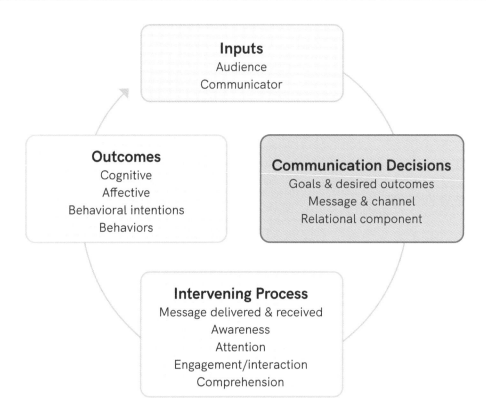

Understanding the relational dimension of communication reveals strategies for building relationships. This is important because building relationships has been demonstrated to enhance nutrition communication program outcomes.[24]

Relationships can be developed in all types of communication encounters and settings, from communicating one-on-one to navigating multiple layers of relationships in both professional and public contexts. Although it might be easier to think about building relationships in face-to-face encounters, relationship building can occur via mass or social media channels as well—for example, when social media visitors comment on posts or when online education participants interact via discussion boards. Relational communication may be particularly important when there are multiple layers of communicators and audience members, as it creates the social context for learning from and valuing the perspectives of others. One example is Cooking Together for Family Meals, described in the Words of Experience box.[25]

Building and maintaining relationships is a critical component of effective communication regardless of the setting, timing, or channel. A relationship will form between the communicator and the audience, no matter how the message is delivered:

- face-to-face, to a group, or to a wide internet or television audience;
- once, or in a series of messages, as described in the Words of Experience box; or
- verbally, in writing, or visually.

Even a single encounter can have a powerful effect. Food and nutrition professionals likely already use strategies for building relationships. How can relationships with colleagues, teachers, mentors, students, clients, and other intended audiences be built?

This book explores what makes nutrition communication effective, and an essential component of effective communication is building relationships. Chapter 3 introduces the concept of connecting with the audience, which is further developed in later chapters. The next section examines the components of the nutrition communication framework—each of which involves people. Consider how these interactions between people form and build relationships that can help or hinder the communication process.

A Conceptual Framework Guides Understanding and Designing Communication

Illustrated in Figure 1.1, the nutrition communication framework provides a guide for understanding, designing, and evaluating nutrition communication. To explain this framework, four main concept areas will be discussed: inputs, communication decisions, intervening process, and outcomes. Underlying all the activities and interactions is the concept of relational communication previously discussed.

INPUTS

Communication inputs consist of what the audience and the communicator bring to the communication process. These must be taken into account at the onset of communication design. See the orange box in Figure 1.1.

Audience Inputs Audience members are not blank slates to receive messages; they have a lifetime of experiences and relationships that predispose how they filter any message as they receive it and how they respond. Predisposition is a frame of mind rooted in a person's values, beliefs, knowledge, and past experiences that inclines that person toward certain patterns of selective perceptions, interpretations, feelings, and actions when presented with any particular situation or stimulus—such as a nutrition communication. A person will harbor a range of topic-specific predispositions relating to food and dietary practices. As members of society, people's predispositions toward particular situations or stimuli will tend to be similar to those of others in the same social category, culture, and subculture, with exceptions resulting from individuals' personal experiences, such as positive or negative experiences with a particular food. Other inputs include their aspirations and current situation.

Drawing from behavior change theories, Terms to Know on page 187 summarizes key influencers of diet and health behaviors, which are inputs that can influence how an audience responds to a message and considers changing behavior. Understanding the constructs of behavior change models can be useful in making evidence-based communication decisions.

If direct engagement to assess audience inputs is not possible, use other sources to find out about an audience. Formal approaches like needs

WORDS OF EXPERIENCE

Relational Communication in Practice: Cooking Together for Family Meals

by Ardyth Gillespie, PhD (in collaboration with Kathleen Dischner, Holly Gump, Suzanne Gervais, and the CTFM Leadership Team)

This program was developed by a leadership team that included frontline educators, professional nutritionists, and academic professionals and researchers.

Relationship building occurred among team members, between team members and audience members, and among audience members:

- Building communication competence *among* team members and drawing upon knowledge about audience predispositions provided a rich context for developing an innovative approach to improving food decision making and behavioral outcomes.
- Team members built relationships *with* families and *among* families participating in the series of workshops by (1) inviting participants to select which foods to prepare at the next workshop, (2) sitting around the table to eat the foods they prepared and discussing their experiences, and (3) continuing discussions and experiences among family members at home after each workshop.
- Communication was fostered *within* each family during the workshop and encouraged the exploration of family food decision making together at home.

Each of these sets of relationships created the context for effective communication and behavior change.

assessments, formative evaluation, and research and evaluation literature can provide information about an audience. Section 3 in this book covers strategies for learning about an audience.

Communicator Inputs Communicators need to be aware that they also harbor predispositions rooted in their past professional and personal experiences with food, nutrition, and communication as well as perceptions about an intended audience. These, in addition to professional goals, influence message framing, content selection, and delivery strategies, affecting how messages reach and are received by members of an intended audience.

The congruences of communicator and audience inputs are potential areas for developing relationships between communicator and audience or could serve as barriers to communication. For example, a primary reason for hiring paraprofessional educators, who are from the audience being served, in programs such as the Expanded Food and Nutrition Education Program (EFNEP), the Supplemental Nutrition Assistance Program's Education Program (SNAP-Ed), or the Special Supplemental Nutrition Program for Women, Infants, and Children (WIC) is the similarity in their predispositions and current situation to those of the people they will teach or mentor.

Influences that are often outside the communicator's control, such as policy and resource constraints, can also affect how a message can be developed and delivered. Some aspects of this situational context can be manipulated, such as the time and place for receiving the message(s).

COMMUNICATION DECISIONS

Decisions include determining the communication goals and desired outcomes, framing and designing the message content and delivery, and developing the relational component. See the red box in Figure 1.1 (page 14).

Goals and Desired Outcomes Articulating communication goals and desired outcomes is the first decision in developing nutrition communication for a target audience. What is the purpose for the communication? How will the audience members expand their ways of thinking? What will they think about, know, or do as a result? As much as possible, engage an audience in this step to obtain more relevant goals and achievable outcomes.[26]

Communication Design Communication design decisions include both instrumental and relational components. The instrumental or task-oriented component includes the content of the message as well as the background (the evidence base), how the message is treated (eg, with logical arguments, humor, or satire), the organization of the message, which channels (mass or interpersonal) are employed, and the delivery strategy. The

relational component involves the audience inputs during the planning stages and decisions about audience engagement and interaction during the intervening process—when the communication is delivered and received.

Decisions about the overall strategy and the apparent source of the communication may influence both the relational and the instrumental (message) components. Audience members may respond differently depending upon their impression of the source of the communication. Factors such as perceived trustworthiness, expertise, and the relationship between communicator and audience all influence variations in response. For example, an audience member in a community program for limited-resource audiences may respond differently to a peer educator, a credentialed nutrition professional such as an RDN, or a university faculty member.[27]

INTERVENING PROCESS

The intervening process includes everything that happens between initiation of communication and outcomes. This includes communication delivery and how well the communication is received. Receiving the message involves the audience being aware of the message and attending to it, and also varying levels of audience comprehension, participation, and engagement. Involvement with the communication process determines the level at which the audience comprehends or understands the message. During the intervening process, the communicator and audience ideally interact, taking advantage of relational communication. This can take the form of formal or informal feedback, discussion, or many other types of interaction. Interaction enhances the audience's receipt of the message and potentially leads to more positive outcomes.[21] See the blue box in Figure 1.1.

OUTCOMES

The desired outcomes selected at the beginning of communication planning can be in the cognitive, affective, behavioral intention, or behavioral domains. Behavioral intention is considered a precursor to actual behavior change, so it may be valuable to evaluate.[28] See the green box in Figure 1.1.

Evaluating all aspects of the process helps explain why desired outcomes were or were not achieved. It is best to plan an evaluation strategy while designing the communication to capture the most useful data. The ideal outcome is for the audience to accurately understand a message due to positive influences in the intervening process. Partial understanding can lead to misunderstanding and negative outcomes. Full and accurate understanding is more likely to lead to achieving the desired outcomes in the cognitive, affective, and behavioral domains. To summarize the nutrition communication planning process outlined by this framework:

- Assess audience and communicator inputs. When direct contact is not possible before the program, learn about the audience by other methods.
- Set realistic goals with members of the audience.
- Plan methods to evaluate the intervening process both during and after the program.
- Plan communication using the most applicable theory, data, and guidelines available.
- Use the best art of communicating within your own communication style. Add innovation and creativity while maintaining accuracy and meeting the communication goals.
- Evaluate the communication process and how well program objectives were achieved.

Theories continue to evolve as they are articulated and tested. The next section of this chapter discusses how nutrition professionals can play an important role in this evolution through their practice.[26]

How Is Nutrition Communication Both an Art and a Science?

Nutrition communication relies on the acquisition of knowledge in nutrition and communication science, as well as learning and practicing the creative and artistic application of skills in communication design and delivery. The effective nutrition communicator achieves both the art and the science of nutrition communication.

Responsible Nutrition Communication Is Evidence-Based

Nutrition communicators draw upon scientific theories and research in food, nutrition, and health as well as in the field of communication to develop message content and delivery approaches. Evidence accumulates through program evaluation and research. As theories of practice are articulated and tested, they can become scientific theory. In nutrition communication, the evidence base includes knowledge generated through practice as well as previously established evidence-based research. Just as research informs practice, practice informs research. As illustrated in Figure 1.2, the integration of research and practice builds theory.[29]

FIGURE 1.2 **Practice as well as research contributes to theory**

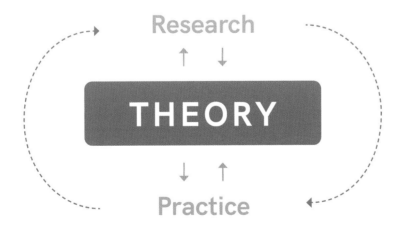

Improving practice, informing research, enhancing theory

Adapted with permission from Brun J, Gillespie AH. Nutrition education research: past, present, and future. *J Nutr Educ*. 1992;24(5):220-221.[29]

Nutrition communication applies a number of social and behavioral science theories. The nutrition communication framework in Figure 1.1 (page 14), which guides nutrition communication development and evaluation, is informed by peer-reviewed and published theories and research and is an example of practice informing research and research improving practice.

Research on communication in the sciences is a recognized need. As stated in *Communicating Science Effectively: A Research Agenda*: "Substantially more research is needed to help science communicators determine which approaches to communicating are effective for whom and under which conditions for achieving specific communication goals."[6] Nutrition communicators can contribute to research by following evidence-based practice, completing evaluations, and sharing outcomes. What is learned not only helps improve subsequent communication but also has the potential to contribute to nutrition communication theory.

Nutrition Communication Requires Skill and Creativity

Using evidence-based science for content, competent nutrition communicators can use the art of nutrition communication to employ specific creative skills to design and deliver effective messages. Both soft skills and hard (or technical) skills are needed.

SOFT SKILLS FOR NUTRITION COMMUNICATORS

Soft skills is a term that encompasses interpersonal or people skills and other personal attributes that enhance a person's ability to communicate and relate to others successfully. These are the soft skills employers list as most needed in today's workplace[30]:

- Communication—speaking, listening, writing
- Courtesy—etiquette, gracious, respectful
- Flexibility—adaptability, lifelong learner, teachable
- Integrity—honest, ethical, moral
- Interpersonal—personable, empathetic, patient
- Positive attitude—enthusiastic, encouraging, confident

Soft skills will be further discussed in Chapters 2 and 3.

See Chapter 22 for more information on writing skills.

- Professionalism—businesslike, well-dressed, poised
- Responsibility—accountable, resourceful, self-disciplined
- Teamwork—cooperative, collaborative, supportive
- Work ethic—showing initiative, self-motivated, hardworking

Research on the contributions of soft and hard skills to success finds that 85% of success can be attributed to soft skills and 15% to hard skills.[30] Soft skills contribute to relational communication. These skills can be employed in the workplace, but they are also applicable to success in all aspects of day-to-day life.

HARD (TECHNICAL) SKILLS FOR NUTRITION COMMUNICATORS

Nutrition communicators need technical skills, including research, presentation, writing, culinary, photography, and other skills. Many of these skills require not only basic knowledge and practice but also ongoing education to keep up with the evolution of technology.

Research skills include skills in accessing scientific research, identifying credible sources, reading and interpreting research, clearly communicating science, properly referencing sources, and adhering to ethical standards. Section 2 of the book establishes the foundation for building these essential skills. Evidence-based practice requires that credentialed nutrition professionals can access and translate scientific knowledge.

Presentation skills include skills needed for planning as well as delivering presentations. Section 4 of the book focuses on these skills; it addresses how to organize a presentation, effectively use visual aids (including presentation software), lead discussions, engage audiences with interactive strategies, and effectively use body language and vocal variety to convey messages effectively. Section 7 of the book offers additional skills in moderating an educational session, managing an audience, and answering audience questions.

Writing skills are the focus of Chapter 22 as well as several additional chapters related to specific written channels, such as newsletters, magazines, blogs, professional journals, and books. The characteristics of effective writing and ways to improve writing skills are addressed.

Other skills employed by nutrition communicators include video creation, food demonstrations and related culinary skills, and food styling and photography.

Proficiency in some skills—such as writing, listening, and speaking—is necessary for all credentialed nutrition professionals. However, other skills—such as video production, photography, media interviews, and book writing—can be further developed based on need, interest, and aptitude.

CREATIVITY ENHANCES SKILLS AND IMPROVES EFFECTIVENESS

When technical skills are performed with creativity, the nutrition communicator is blending the art and science of nutrition communication. Being creative means being novel and exploring new ideas; it can encourage critical thinking and promote problem solving. Creative approaches to communication can enhance audience attention and promote long-term memory.

This book is dedicated to exploring an in-depth approach to both the art and the science of nutrition communication. Take the challenge to build and add new skills to your professional nutrition foundation.

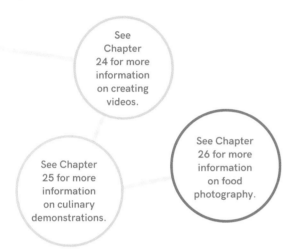

See Chapter 24 for more information on creating videos.

See Chapter 25 for more information on culinary demonstrations.

See Chapter 26 for more information on food photography.

KEY POINTS

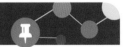

Communication Is the Essence of Nutrition Practice

1. Nutrition communication is communication about food and nutrition for the purpose of developing a platform for inquiry and exchange of ideas or to influence knowledge, attitudes, decision-making processes, or behaviors.

2. The role of communication in nutrition practice is so pervasive that its importance could be overlooked. Communication knowledge and skills must not be taken for granted. Being an effective communicator is essential for effective nutrition practice.

3. Nutrition communication applies a number of social and behavioral science theories, which enhance an understanding of how nutrition communication works, including the important dimension of relational communication. Conceptual models integrate multiple theories and apply them to practice and everyday life.

4. Nutrition communication relies on applying evidence-based knowledge in nutrition and communication science, as well as learning and practicing creative and artistic skills in communication design and delivery. The effective nutrition communicator practices both the art and the science of nutrition communication.

REFERENCES

1. Hybels S, Weaver R. *Communicating Effectively.* 5th ed. McGraw-Hill; 1998.
2. Collins English Dictionary. Communication. Accessed April 25, 2018. www.collinsdictionary.com/us/dictionary/english/communication
3. Burns T, O'Connor D, Stocklmayer S. Science communication: a contemporary definition. *Public Underst Sci.* 2003;12:183-202.
4. What is health communications? Centers for Disease Control and Prevention Website. Published 2011. Accessed November 5, 2017. www.cdc.gov/healthcommunication/healthbasics/whatishc.html
5. Contento IR. *Nutrition Education: Linking Research, Theory, and Practice.* Jones and Bartlett; 2007.
6. National Academies of Sciences, Engineering, and Medicine. *Communicating Science Effectively: A Research Agenda.* National Academies Press; 2017. doi:10.17226/23674
7. Academy of Nutrition and Dietetics. Registered dietitian nutritionists: optimizing the public's health through food and nutrition. Accessed November 5, 2017. www.eatright.org/~/media/eatright%20files/rdn-optimizing-the-publics-health-through-food-and-nutrition.ashx
8. Quagliani D, Hermann M. Communicating accurate food and nutrition information. *J Acad Nutr Diet.* 2012;112(5):759.
9. Institute of Medicine. *Who Will Keep the Public Healthy?* National Academies Press; 2003.
10. Johnson-Taylor W, Yaroch A, Krebs-Smith S, Rodgers A. What can communication science tell us about promoting optimal dietary behavior? *J Nutr Educ Behav.* 2007;39:S1-S4.
11. Graduate Management Admission Council. Employers seek communication skills in new hires. Published 2014. Accessed November 7, 2017. www.mba.com/us/the-gmat-blog-hub/the-official-gmat-blog/2014/aug/employers-want-communication-skills-in-new-hires.aspx
12. Elliott M. 5 skills college grads need to get a job. *USA Today.* May 3, 2015.
13. Agarwal R, Sands D, Schneider J. Quantifying the economic impact of communication inefficiencies in U.S. hospitals. *J Healthc Manag.* 2010;55(4):265-281.
14. Vermeir P, Vandijck D, Degroote S, et al. Communication in healthcare: a narrative review of the literature and practical recommendations. *Int J Clin Pract.* 2015;69(11):1257-1267.
15. Grossman D. The cost of poor communications. *Holmes Report.* July 16, 2011. Accessed November 7, 2017. www.holmesreport.com/latest/article/the-cost-of-poor-communications

16. Ordenes F, Grewal D, Ludwig S, DeRuyter K, Mahr K, Wetzels M. Cutting through content clutter: how speech and image acts drive consumer sharing of social media brand messages. *J Consum Res.* 2018;45(5):988-1012. doi:10.1093/jcr/ucy032
17. Lewin K. Forces behind food habits and methods of change. In: *The Problem of Changing Food Habits: Report on the Committee on Food Habits, 1941–1943.* National Research Council; 1943:35-65.
18. Shannon C, Weaver W. *The Mathematical Theory of Communication.* University of Illinois Press; 1949.
19. Watzlawick P, Bavelas J, Jackson D. *Pragmatics of Human Communication: A Study of Interactional Patterns, Pathologies, and Paradoxes.* Norton; 1967.
20. Yarbrough P. Communication theory and nutrition education research. *J Nutr Educ.* 1981;13:S16-S27.
21. Gillespie A, Yarbrough P. A conceptual model for communicating nutrition. *J Nutr Educ.* 1984;16:168-172.
22. Gillespie A. Communication theory as a basis for nutrition education research. *J Am Diet Assoc.* 1987:S44-S52.
23. Keyton J. Relational communication in groups. In: Frey L, Gouran D, Poole M, eds. *The Handbook of Group Communication Theory and Research.* Sage; 1999:192-222.
24. Gillespie A. Nutrition communication program: a direct mail approach. *J Am Diet Assoc.* 1983;82(3):254-259.
25. Gillespie A, Sung G-J. Enhancing interdisciplinary communication: collaborative engaged research on food systems for health and well-being. In: O'Rourke M, Crowley S, Eigenbrode S, Wulfhorst J, eds. *Enhancing Communication and Collaboration in Interdisciplinary Research.* Sage; 2014:148-170.
26. Gillespie A. The evolution of community nutrition in the U.S. *J Community Nutr.* 2003;5(4):195-208.
27. Rogers E. *Diffusion of Innovations.* 5th ed. Free Press; 2004.
28. Fishbein M, Ajzen I. *Predicting and Changing Behavior: The Reasoned Action Approach.* Routledge; 2015.
29. Brun J, Gillespie AH. Nutrition education research: past, present, and future. *J Nutr Educ.* 1992;24(5):220-221.
30. Robles M. Executive perceptions of the top 10 soft skills needed in today's workplace. *Bus Commun Q.* 2012;75(4):453-465.

Nutrition Professionals Are Effective Communicators

Barbara J. Mayfield, MS, RDN, FAND
and Sonja Kassis Stetzler, MA, RDN, CPC

"Effective communicators are made, not born. To become effective communicators, competent food and nutrition professionals must learn how to communicate skillfully and put that learning into practice."

> "Communication is not a personality trait but a series of learned skills. Communication in medicine needs to be taught with the same rigor as other core clinical skills."
>
> —SUZANNE KURTZ, JONATHAN SILVERMAN, JULIET DRAPER, JAN VAN DALEN, FREDERIC W. PLATT IN *TEACHING AND LEARNING COMMUNICATION SKILLS IN MEDICINE*, 2ND EDITION

Introduction

Effective communicators are made, not born. To become effective communicators, competent food and nutrition professionals must learn how to communicate skillfully and put that learning into practice. This learning begins during academic training and continues throughout the course of a career.

This chapter answers three questions:

- What are the Academy of Nutrition and Dietetics Communication Competencies and Performance Indicators?
- What are the characteristics of successful communicators?
- How can a nutrition professional improve communication effectiveness?

Credentialed food and nutrition practitioners learn and demonstrate communication-related competencies during academic training and in supervised practice, giving them the base they need to use these important skills throughout their careers. To successfully master all of the competencies, practitioners must first know what they entail, then create a plan to develop skills in areas that align with their career goals, and, finally, strive to attain excellence in practice. Once the practitioner is in the field, effective communication skills are enhanced through experience as well as continuing education covering the latest communication knowledge, skills, platforms, and strategies.

Successful communicators acquire and expand the basic and advanced knowledge and skills necessary for effective communication. They also learn to present themselves as credible, compelling, and continually improving. Nutrition communicators never stop learning and growing.

Consider where you are on your journey as a nutrition communicator. What knowledge and skills do you need to acquire or develop? As you study this chapter, determine where you are and where you want to go as you continue through the remaining chapters of this book. Never stop learning and growing as a nutrition communicator.

What Are the Academy of Nutrition and Dietetics Communication Competencies and Performance Indicators?

The Academy of Nutrition and Dietetics has established standards for dietetics students and interns who are studying at accredited universities as well as for credentialed nutrition and dietetics practitioners who work in a variety of careers.

The Commission on Dietetic Registration (CDR), the credentialing agency for the Academy of Nutrition and Dietetics, has developed the Essential Practice Competencies for CDR Credentialed Nutrition and Dietetics Practitioners to provide overarching validated standards for two credentials, the Registered Dietitian (RD) or Registered Dietitian Nutritionist

(RDN), and the Dietetic Technician, Registered (DTR) or Nutrition and Dietetics Technician, Registered (NDTR).

Practice competencies define the knowledge, skill, judgment and attitude requirements throughout a practitioner's career, across practice, and within focus areas. Competencies provide a structured guide to help identify, evaluate, and develop the behaviors required for continuing competence. Unlike entry-level competencies, which focus on preparation and evaluation for minimum competence upon completion of an ACEND [Accreditation Council for Education in Nutrition and Dietetics] education program and during early years of practice, the essential practice competencies are intended for use throughout a nutrition and dietetics practitioner's career.[1]

The core competencies designed by CDR encompass a range of knowledge, skills, judgments, and attitudes that apply across the board to practitioners regardless of their work setting or experience. Communication skills are interwoven among the many CDR core Essential Practice Competencies, as they are foundational skills upon which advanced competencies can be built.

Within CDR's practice competencies, numerous performance indicators include communication skills as components of practical skill sets. Communication in all forms, whether verbal, written, digital, or any other, is necessary for food and nutrition professionals to effectively perform in today's work environments. No matter where practitioners work—in a clinical setting, private practice, the community, public health, management, teaching, communications, marketing, or research—their work involves communicating with others.

Accreditation Council for Education in Nutrition and Dietetics Defines Communication Knowledge Requirements and Competencies

ACEND is the accrediting agency for education programs preparing students for careers as RDNs or NDTRs. ACEND assures the quality and continued improvement of nutrition and dietetics education programs and is a reliable authority on the quality of these programs.[2] The ACEND accreditation standards are published for Didactic Programs in Dietetics (DPDs),[3] Coordinated Programs (CPs),[4] and Dietetic Internships (DIs).[5]

Key communication skills start at the undergraduate level, where students in accredited DPD programs build core knowledge in multiple domains. Within each domain, specific knowledge requirements for RDNs (KRDNs) are delineated. Figure 2.1 (see page 24) lists domains and the KRDNs within each domain that relate to nutrition communication and are covered in this book.[3]

The knowledge requirements for DPD programs prepare students to enter supervised practice and further develop communication knowledge and skills. The competencies for RDNs (CRDNs) related to communication, and covered in this book, for CPs and DIs are listed in Figure 2.2 (see page 25).[4,5] Students in CPs and DIs receive additional academic training and experiential learning, which build on the KRDNs listed in Figure 2.1.[3] Other general competencies not listed also apply to nutrition communication, such as incorporating critical thinking skills in overall practice.

Practicing RDNs apply the expected competencies, the skills of a professional and respected dietetics practitioner, to their work daily. Students who successfully achieve these knowledge requirements and competencies are prepared to work in all types of traditional and nontraditional settings. Accredited programs cover these KRDNs and CRDNs in diverse ways.

Communication Is Covered in Diverse Ways

The curriculum and learning activities provided to dietetics students in accredited programs are designed to "ensure the breadth and depth of requisite knowledge needed for entry to supervised practice"[3] in undergraduate programs, and to "ensure the breadth and depth of requisite knowledge and skills needed for entry-level practice as a registered dietitian nutritionist"[4,5] in supervised practice programs. Communication knowledge requirements and competencies are covered in various courses and experiential learning experiences. No specific sequence of courses is required, as long as the curriculum logically builds from introductory to advanced-level knowledge and skills.

In preparation for writing this book, the Academy of Nutrition and Dietetics Publications, Resources, and Products team administered two online surveys in the spring of 2017 to help determine the breadth and depth of content for

Scientific and Evidence Base of Practice: Integration of scientific information and translation of research into practice

KRDN 1.1 Demonstrate how to locate, interpret, evaluate, and use professional literature to make ethical, evidence-based decisions.

KRDN 1.2 Use current information technologies to locate and apply evidence-based guidelines and protocols.

Professional Practice Expectations: Beliefs, values, attitudes, and behaviors for the professional dietitian nutritionist level of practice

KRDN 2.1 Demonstrate effective and professional oral and written communication and documentation.

KRDN 2.2 Describe the governance of nutrition and dietetics practice, such as the Scope of Practice for the Registered Dietitian Nutritionist and the Code of Ethics for the Nutrition and Dietetics Profession; and describe interprofessional relationships in various practice settings.

KRDN 2.5 Identify and describe the work of interprofessional teams and the roles of others with whom the registered dietitian nutritionist collaborates in the delivery of food and nutrition services.

KRDN 2.6 Demonstrate an understanding of cultural competence/sensitivity.

Clinical and Customer Services: Development and delivery of information, products, and services to individuals, groups, and populations

KRDN 3.2 Develop an educational session or program/educational strategy for a target population.

KRDN 3.3 Demonstrate counseling and education methods to facilitate behavior change and enhance wellness for diverse individuals and groups.

Adapted with permission from Accreditation Council for Education in Nutrition and Dietetics of the Academy of Nutrition and Dietetics. *ACEND Accreditation Standards for Nutrition and Dietetics Didactic Programs.* ACEND; 2017.[3]

Scientific and Evidence Base of Practice: Integration of scientific information and translation of research into practice

CRDN 1.1 Select indicators of program quality and/or customer service and measure achievement of objectives.

CRDN 1.2 Apply evidence-based guidelines, systematic reviews, and scientific literature.

CRDN 1.4 Evaluate emerging research for application in nutrition and dietetics practice.

Professional Practice Expectations: Beliefs, values, attitudes, and behaviors for the professional dietitian nutritionist level of practice

CRDN 2.2 Demonstrate professional writing skills in preparing professional communications.

CRDN 2.3 Demonstrate active participation, teamwork, and contributions in group settings.

CRDN 2.4 Function as a member of interprofessional teams.

CRDN 2.10 Demonstrate professional attributes in all areas of practice.

CRDN 2.11 Show cultural competence/sensitivity in interactions with clients, colleagues and staff.

Clinical and Customer Services: Development and delivery of information, products, and services to individuals, groups, and populations

CRDN 3.3 Demonstrate effective communications skills for clinical and customer services in a variety of formats and settings.

CRDN 3.4 Design, implement, and evaluate presentations to a target audience.

CRDN 3.5 Develop nutrition education materials that are culturally and age appropriate and designed for the literacy level of the audience.

CRDN 3.6 Use effective education and counseling skills to facilitate behavior change.

CRDN 3.7 Develop and deliver products, programs, or services that promote consumer health, wellness, and lifestyle management.

CRDN 3.8 Deliver respectful, science-based answers to client questions concerning emerging trends.

Adapted with permission from the Accreditation Council for Education in Nutrition and Dietetics of the Academy of Nutrition and Dietetics. *ACEND Accreditation Standards for Coordinated Programs* and *ACEND Accreditation Standards for Dietetic Internship Programs*. ACEND; 2017.[4,5]

inclusion in the entire book. Dietetics educators were surveyed via the Nutrition and Dietetic Educators and Preceptors listserve and by phone interview. Dietetics practitioners were surveyed via dietetic practice groups (DPGs) with a greater representation of RDNs working in the area of nutrition communication than other practice areas, such as Nutrition Entrepreneurs and Dietitians in Business and Communications. Both surveys also asked RDNs about dietetics education regarding communication.

About half (51%) of the 144 dietetics educators who completed the first survey represented undergraduate education programs (including both DPDs and CPs), 30% represented supervised practice programs, and 15% represented graduate programs. The remaining educators were in allied health professional education. The 15 educators who participated in phone interviews represented a higher percentage of graduate and supervised practice programs than in the survey.

The educators' survey asked, "How does your program cover the ACEND standards related to communication?" The overwhelming majority of respondents (81%) stated that communication standards were covered in multiple courses rather than a dedicated course. A similar finding was revealed in the survey completed by 551 dietetics practitioners. A comparable question was posed: "As an undergraduate student or dietetic intern, did you take a course focused on nutrition communication?" Less than 13% of the RDNs stated that they had. Other responses mentioned that nutrition communication was addressed in multiple courses (25%), there was limited coverage included in courses related to nutrition counseling (23%), or there was no coursework that covered nutrition communication (39%).

In the phone interviews with educators, very few reported having a dedicated course for nutrition communication. Several were working on creating one, especially at the graduate level. Courses that addressed nutrition communication included general communication courses, technical writing, community nutrition, counseling and education, nutrition education, health education, and life cycle courses. Many described communication as being covered in modules within these courses. Regardless of whether nutrition communication was covered in one course or multiple courses, educators agreed that a single

text that addressed knowledge requirements and competencies could be used throughout the curriculum to cover this topic.

Committee on Dietetic Registration Defines Performance Indicators for Professionals

Professionals' ability to communicate—and communicate well—is directly related to their success, no matter where they work. Because effective communication is such an important skill set, CDR includes communication-related learning outcomes throughout the performance indicators. Figure 2.3 lists examples of CDR's Performance Indicators that include communication skills.[1]

This Book Meets Entry-Level and Advanced Practice Standards

Because the target audience for this book includes both entry-level and advanced practitioners, content is included that is applicable to both audiences.

Take, for example, these three related outcomes:

- KRDN 3.2: the knowledge requirement to develop an educational session or program or educational strategy for a target population that is expected for the DPD student
- CRDN 3.4: the competency to design, implement, and evaluate presentations to a target audience for the CP student or DI participant
- 9.4: the competency for the practitioner to teach, guide, and instruct a variety of individuals, groups, or populations

All are related to increasing skills for developing educational programs and presenting to target audiences. Section 3 of this book covers both introductory and advanced-level knowledge and skills for understanding and customizing communication to target audiences. Section 4 covers the skills of developing and presenting educational sessions. At the undergraduate level, the student is expected to be able to prepare a lesson for one target audience. The practitioner is expected to be able to prepare and present to a variety of audiences. Credentialed food and nutrition practitioners are

FIGURE 2.3 **Examples of performance indicators spheres and competencies**

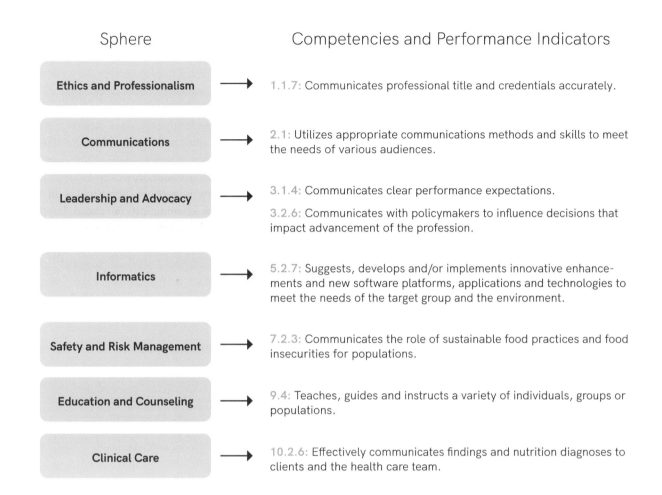

Sphere	Competencies and Performance Indicators
Ethics and Professionalism	1.1.7: Communicates professional title and credentials accurately.
Communications	2.1: Utilizes appropriate communications methods and skills to meet the needs of various audiences.
Leadership and Advocacy	3.1.4: Communicates clear performance expectations. 3.2.6: Communicates with policymakers to influence decisions that impact advancement of the profession.
Informatics	5.2.7: Suggests, develops and/or implements innovative enhancements and new software platforms, applications and technologies to meet the needs of the target group and the environment.
Safety and Risk Management	7.2.3: Communicates the role of sustainable food practices and food insecurities for populations.
Education and Counseling	9.4: Teaches, guides and instructs a variety of individuals, groups or populations.
Clinical Care	10.2.6: Effectively communicates findings and nutrition diagnoses to clients and the health care team.

Adapted with permission from Commission on Dietetic Registration. *Essential Practice Competencies for the Commission on Dietetic Registration Credentialed Nutrition and Dietetics Practitioners*. Published 2015. Accessed April 6, 2020. https://admin.cdrnet.org/vault/2459/web/files/FINAL-CDR_Competency.pdf[1]

known for their subject matter knowledge and expertise. No matter the work setting, successful practitioners stay highly committed to continued development and improvement in both their subject matter and communication knowledge and skills. The knowledge and skills acquired by professionals are gained through a culmination of evidence-based study, learning through experience, and learning through peers. The next section explores additional characteristics necessary for success.

What Are the Characteristics of Successful Communicators?

Successful nutrition communicators possess more than the required knowledge and skills; they demonstrate specific characteristics that transform their work from adequate to outstanding. The characteristics (further described on the next page) are grouped into three broad categories:

- characteristics that build credibility,
- characteristics that enable a communicator to be compelling, and

To read more on persuasive communication, see Chapter 10.

- characteristics that demonstrate a communicator's commitment to excellence and improvement.

These three categories of characteristics parallel the ethos, pathos, and logos that Aristotle suggested are essential for persuasive communication. Excellence is timeless.

Successful Nutrition Communicators Are Credible

A communicator must be perceived as credible before an audience will pay attention, listen, and trust the message. A communicator's credibility is built on more than academic degrees; it derives from the audience's perception of the communicator as believable. Professionalism and integrity build credibility. Communicators who exhibit these qualities will be highly respected and will have greater influence and impact.

PROFESSIONALISM

Successful nutrition communicators display a high level of professionalism. This refers to conduct in the workplace and is demonstrated by high standards, appropriate workplace behaviors, and a positive attitude, which reflects well on the individual as well as the individual's entire profession.

Varying standards for professionalism exist because it can be exhibited in a variety of ways, depending on the context. The Center for Professional Excellence at York College of Pennsylvania conducts an annual national survey about professionalism in the workplace among recent college graduates. Figure 2.4 lists professional and unprofessional attributes and behaviors.[6-8] Depending on who is asked and who is being described, the top qualities describing professionalism vary, but overall they share many common attributes and behaviors. Notably, communication skills consistently appear in the top five qualities.

FIGURE 2.4 **Qualities describing professional and unprofessional behavior**

Career development professionals at colleges and universities describe students:	
Top 5 qualities of professionalism:	**Top 5 qualities of being unprofessional:**
- Prepared - Communication skills - Appearance - Ambitious - Polite	- Disrespectful - Lack of communication skills - Lack of ambition - Appearance - Entitlement

Employers responsible for hiring new graduates describe new hires:	
Top 5 qualities of professionalism:	**Top 5 qualities of being unprofessional:**
- Work until a task is completed competently - Interpersonal skills including civility - Appropriate appearance - Punctuality and regular attendance - Communication skills	- Inappropriate appearance - Poor work ethic - Unfocused - Apathetic - Sense of entitlement

Recent graduates in the workplace describe qualities associated with a coworker:	
Top 5 qualities of professionalism:	**Top 5 qualities of being unprofessional:**
- Focused (not distracted by technology) - Punctuality and regular attendance - Humble - Diligent - Communication skills	- Disrespectful - Irresponsible, distracted - Not ambitious, lazy - Always late, absenteeism - Lack of communication skills

Figure created based on information from:
Polk-Lepson Research Group. National Professionalism Survey: Career Development Report. 2014.[6]
Polk-Lepson Research Group. National Professionalism Survey: Professionalism in the Workplace. 2013.[7]
Polk-Lepson Research Group. National Professionalism Survey: Recent Graduate Study. 2015.[8]

Professionalism is also perceived by clients, patients, and other audiences. These perceptions can be formed based on a phone conversation, website view, or social media post. An impression of professionalism—or lack thereof—can be made long before face-to-face contact occurs. Demonstrating respect, humility, focus, competence, and communication skills in all settings promotes professionalism and credibility.

Professionals dress appropriately for the work setting. A polished look signals confidence and garners respect from clients, coworkers, and other audiences. Surveys on professionalism consistently find wearing professional and appropriate attire and footwear is essential for getting hired and being perceived as competent.[6-8] Appearance plays an even greater role in many settings where nutrition communicators work. Later chapters will discuss appropriate dress for media work and presentations.

INTEGRITY

Professionals are reliable—they do what they say they are going to do. They uphold strong ethical standards, have a high degree of integrity, and are trustworthy. Professionals also realize when the work they have been asked to do falls out of their scope of practice[9] and refer the work to others who have expertise in that particular domain.

Integrity is an essential component of building credibility and trust. An Australian-based study of dietitian-client relationships found that key values attributed to dietitians included honesty, reliability, and integrity. These attributes, supported by credentials and enhanced by communication skills, resulted in a trusting relationship.[10] As soon as a practitioner loses the trust of a client or audience member, credibility is lost as well.

Fiske and Dupree researched how various communicators are perceived by the public and found that communicator credibility requires both expertise and trust. Combinations of perceived competence and warmth, which is defined as being friendly and trustworthy, have been assessed for various professionals. Researchers and scientists are perceived as competent but cold. Teachers, doctors, and nurses are perceived as competent and warm.[11,12]

Public perceptions of all four combinations of competence and warmth are distinct. People who are considered cold and incompetent are viewed with disgust. Those who are warm and

incompetent are viewed with pity. Those who are competent and cold are viewed with envy. Those who are competent and warm are viewed with pride.[12]

Honesty and integrity are fundamental standards of ethical conduct. Food and nutrition professionals adhere to a code of ethics established by the Academy of Nutrition and Dietetics and the CDR.

Successful Nutrition Communicators Are Compelling

Credibility is critical for success, but alone it is not enough. In order for communicators to be highly successful, they must be compelling. Compelling communicators are able to capture an audience's attention amid competing messages. They are more than interesting; they are captivating and inspiring. Being compelling does not require a show-business persona or mastery of sales techniques. A compelling communicator is genuine and authentic, demonstrating perspective and empathy, enthusiasm, and a positive attitude.

PERSPECTIVE AND EMPATHY

Professionals display a high degree of empathy and presence, characteristics of emotional intelligence. They are able to self-regulate their emotions and have a high regard for the emotions and needs of others. They listen well without interrupting, consider all viewpoints before making a decision, and recognize when their personal bias comes into play.

Listening is defined as "the active and dynamic process of attending, perceiving, interpreting, remembering, and responding to the expressed (verbal and nonverbal) needs, concerns, and information offered by other human beings."[13] In verbal communication, many people focus on what they are going to say rather than interpreting what they are hearing. True listening goes beyond understanding the words one is hearing and involves understanding the feelings and motives of the speaker. By suspending a personal perspective, individuals can gain insight into other points of view and communicate more effectively.

POSITIVITY

Successful nutrition communicators have positive attitudes and are positive role models for those whom they lead. Barbara Fredrickson, a

Chapter 9 is devoted to the Code of Ethics and putting it into practice as nutrition communicators.

researcher and distinguished professor of psychology at the University of North Carolina as well as the author of the book *Positivity*, has found that "positivity produces success in life as much as it reflects success in life."[14] Her research has also found that people who experience more positive emotions than negative emotions are able to see the bigger picture, build better relationships, and thrive in their career and life.

Research in neuroscience has revealed that emotions are contagious. People would much rather be around positive people than negative people. Leaders who exude positive attributes such as trustworthiness, empathy, and connectedness find that those who work for them report feeling more calm, creative, and innovative.[15] But, rudeness and other negative attitudes and behaviors are also highly contagious, resulting in a cascade of negative consequences.[16] Bottom line: Spread positivity, not negativity.

ENTHUSIASM

A communicator who expresses enthusiasm when speaking or writing may be perceived by an audience as more credible, believable, and worth supporting. Enthusiasm also demonstrates that a communicator cares about the audience. Having the audience's best interests at heart and showing commitment to their well-being raises a communicator's credibility and enhances an audience's trust.

> "No one cares how much you know until they know how much you care."
>
> —THEODORE ROOSEVELT

Successful Nutrition Communicators Are Continually Improving

Successful nutrition communicators refuse to be stagnant. They challenge themselves to continually get better at what they do. The four characteristics that propel improvement are curiosity, creativity, collaboration, and commitment.

Successful communicators are curious. They are continually seeking to learn and trying out fresh, new approaches. They are teachable and willing to learn from mistakes and take advice. Successful communicators are creative. They deliver messages with imagination. They are willing to stretch themselves rather than settle for doing things "the way we've always done it." Successful communicators work well with others, accepting new perspectives. They work hard and follow through on their commitments.

CURIOSITY

Successful nutrition communicators are lifelong learners, taking advantage of advancements and new knowledge constantly becoming available. Humans are naturally curious. More important, though, is what humans do with their curiosity. Curiosity can lead down a path to ideas, solutions to difficult problems, and the opportunity to make an impact or change something to make it better. An openness and desire to incorporate new ideas, theories, and skill sets can prepare practitioners for successful outcomes.

Learning new skills and incorporating new ideas sets practitioners up for developing a competitive advantage and for becoming thought leaders in the field. The ability to connect the dots and create new insights from new knowledge provides value to clients, customers, and employers.

CREATIVITY

According to John Medina, a molecular biologist in human brain development and the author of *Brain Rules*, people's attention spans last about 10 minutes.[17] Effective communicators need to be aware of how they structure their content as well as how to deliver it creatively. How can an audience's attention be sustained? Medina offers three suggestions:

1. Change the way content is delivered and break presentations into 10-minute segments.
2. Human brains process meaning before details. To capitalize on this, provide an overall concept first, then add in the details to help an audience make sense of the main idea.
3. Let an audience know the game plan at the beginning of a presentation. The communicator is playing the role of a guide, using verbal communication, and audiences prefer to know where they are going.

Notice if audiences lose interest in a straight lecture after 10 minutes. Structure content to include a change in delivery at approximately 10 minute intervals. This could include an interactive activity, a demonstration, or a story that relates to the concept being presented. Stories generally make an emotional connection with an audience and are memorable. All of these creative approaches will be described further in later chapters.

An audience's attention can also be held with creativity in how a message is delivered. See the Words of Experience box for creative approaches from the authors' experiences in which costumes were employed to create interest and teach.

A little creativity or a novel idea, combined with insight into how a particular audience best receives messages, will enable both the communicator and the message to be more memorable.

COLLABORATION

Success in today's world depends on an ability to work well in groups. According to the American Management Association's "Critical Skills Survey," 71% of top corporate managers rated the ability to work in groups a critical factor in career advancement.[18] Characteristics of an effective team member include listening well to others, contributing and sharing ideas and information, supporting the efforts of others, and successfully working through conflict. All of these traits involve communication, and successful nutrition communicators strive to be effective team players.

It is not uncommon for practitioners to work on virtual teams or to work remotely. Without the ability to read body language, being an effective team player in these circumstances requires a heightened awareness of other nonverbal communication skills, such as interpreting tone of voice, and using clear and concise messaging.

COMMITMENT

Commitment, exhibited by a strong work ethic, is another attribute highly valued in the workplace. It involves the dual characteristics of initiative and perseverance. A person with a strong work ethic gets the job started and keeps going until completion.

Initiative is a highly desirable trait because it not only leads to higher-quality work but also reduces the stress associated with waiting until the last minute. Research suggests 20% of people are chronic procrastinators.[19] The other 80%

Dress Up for Creativity

by Sonja Kassis Stetzler, MS, RDN, CPC, and Barbara J. Mayfield, MS, RDN, FAND

Sonja writes: Many years ago, while working in hospital food service management, we were looking for ways to further our reach in the community. An idea struck me—become the "Calorie Clown." I borrowed a clown costume from my mom (who had made a couple for a Halloween party years before), purchased and learned a few magic tricks from a local magic shop, and piloted my "Calorie Clown" program in several kindergartens and first-grade classrooms to teach the students about good nutrition. It was a hit with both the students and the community. The message about good nutrition was simple enough for the children to understand, and it was delivered in a way that was memorable.

Barb writes: As a young dietitian I visited schools, community groups, and fairs each year to promote National Nutrition Month. Our local dietetic association had a "Nutribird" costume that helped us spread the annual messages and was well loved. More recently, I learned the value of a good costume when teaching nutrition communication at Purdue. Students often incorporated costumes when giving community presentations and food demonstrations, and these always added excitement and interest. Even in presentations to adult audiences and professional groups, making a point with a pair of silly glasses, or a theme hat, or a sash depicting an award can make a point in a fun and creative way.

Don't be afraid to dress up!

Barb and Sonja dress up to creatively engage with their audiences.

procrastinate on occasion. Getting started is the solution for everyone.

Once started on a project, food and nutrition professionals with a strong work ethic do not give up until the work is completed. They will undoubtedly encounter delays and difficulties, but they persevere to the end. Those who persist in any given endeavor often surpass those who may be considered more talented or educated but fail to exhibit the same grit.

"Grit is living life like it is a marathon, not a sprint."

—ANGELA DUCKWORTH, AUTHOR OF *GRIT*

Professionals have grit. *Grit*, as defined by Merriam-Webster, is "firmness of mind or spirit: unyielding courage in the face of hardship or danger."[20] In other words, professionals are not afraid to try new approaches, and if they are not successful, they learn from their trials. Learning from mistakes can be thought of as "failing forward."[21] Professionals persevere through obstacles that occur in the pursuit of their goals and look for solutions rather than quitting.

"Success—the real success—does not depend upon the position you hold, but upon how you carry yourself in that position."

—THEODORE ROOSEVELT

How Can a Nutrition Professional Improve Communication Effectiveness?

Communication effectiveness is built upon a strong foundation formed during undergraduate education, graduate study, and supervised practice. Upon entry into the workforce, the food and nutrition professional must continue to seek opportunities to continue learning and practicing communication skills. These include training and experiences within the work setting and continuing education provided through CDR-approved channels, such as conference sessions sponsored by local and state Academy of Nutrition and Dietetics affiliates and online webinars. Books, TED talks, and online courses also offer opportunities to hone communication skills. Organizations such as Toastmasters International (more details later in this section) and one-on-one communication coaches and mentors also can help to build communication knowledge and skills.

Establish a Foundation of Coursework

In order for dietetics students to become proficient with communication skills, dietetics curriculums in colleges and universities throughout the country require communication courses. Even though people communicate their entire lives, formal study of communication can improve these skills. Communication skills in the 21st century include not only speaking and writing but also interpersonal communication, intercultural communication, small-group and organizational communication, and digital communication.

Communication courses as part of undergraduate degrees can serve as foundations for subsequent study in graduate programs. Dietitians who wish to pursue careers with public relations firms, in nutrition communications consulting, or in marketing may benefit from advanced communications courses.

Feedback from supervisors during internships can provide valuable information about areas of improvement. Knowledge about communication theories and processes is valuable in counseling or coaching patients and clients, as well as in knowing how to build positive work environments, positively managing conflict with others, monitoring self-perceptions, and understanding different communication styles. To advance in any career, good communication skills are essential.

Take Advantage of Continuing Education Opportunities

As mentioned earlier in this chapter, the opportunities to enhance communication skills can be seen throughout current performance indicators and the guidelines set up by CDR. Many communication-related continuing education programs offered through CDR can be found online (www.cdrnet.org/go/and/cdr/cpe_search.cfm). CDR offers a continuing professional education (CPE) database of live and self-study programs that have been approved for continuing education credits.

Many local and state Academy of Nutrition and Dietetics affiliates offer continuing education at their monthly and annual meetings. One of the best ways to influence the topics and types of continuing education programs is to join or lead the program planning committee. Each state affiliate is set up differently with regard to how their continuing education events are planned. There may be opportunities for those holding an elected office at the district, state, or national level to obtain CPE credits, as participating in an elected office often requires the development of leadership and professional development skills.

Many DPGs, such as Dietitians in Business and Communications and Nutrition Entrepreneurs, also offer continuing professional education credits in communication-related topics. These educational offerings are offered mainly through webinars, self-study courses, or regional meetings. In addition to the CPE opportunities, involvement with DPGs can offer leadership, communication, and professional development opportunities as well as a chance to expand a professional network.

Take Advantage of External Opportunities

Outside organizations like Toastmasters International, the National Speakers Association, and the National Communication Association offer learning opportunities and mentoring from more seasoned professionals in the speaking and communication world and can open opportunities for networking and speaking opportunities outside of dietetics.

Many cities where medical universities are located have an Area Health Education Center that offers continuing education for those in medical fields. Courses offered through Area Health Education Centers programs, such as the TeamSTEPPS training,[22] can be beneficial in improving communication skills. See the resources section at the end of the chapter for website addresses for these organizations and opportunities.

Work with a Coach or Mentor

Another option to improve communication skills is to work with a coach or mentor. Ongoing work with a coach may involve finding a core message for a presentation, organizing supporting material for a presentation, developing a stronger voice, displaying more confident nonverbal body language, and overcoming fear.

Some DPGs (eg, Nutrition Entrepreneurs and Dietitians in Business and Communications) offer mentoring programs as a benefit for their members, and some credentialed food and nutrition practitioners have entire businesses built around mentoring other professionals in these areas. Consider seeking out a mentor who has experience in nutrition communications to further develop these skills.

Continually Learn and Practice Skills

Lifelong learners continue to work on developing their communication skills. Communicators' mindfulness about the messages they are sending and how they are sending them will improve over time, with continued practice and with feedback. As Daniel Coyle writes in *The Little Book of Talent*, "Practice is transformative, if it's the right kind of practice. The key to practice is to reach. This means to stretch yourself slightly beyond your current ability, spending time in the zone of difficulty called the sweet spot."[23]

Additionally, Coyle suggests setting a "smallest achievable perfection," or SAP. By this, he means to look for a small improvement that can be made with 100% consistency. Small improvements consistently made over time have been shown to result in major successes.

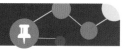

KEY POINTS

Nutrition Professionals Are Effective Communicators

1 The Academy of Nutrition and Dietetics has set Communication Competencies and Performance Indicators so that practitioners develop and build upon skills that are essential to successful dietetics practice.

2 Three overarching goals for successful communicators are building credibility, developing and delivering compelling messages, and continually improving. Credibility is built by demonstrating professionalism through integrity and work ethic. Compelling messages are conveyed by displaying empathy and positivity with clients and coworkers and enthusiasm for food, nutrition, and health. Continuous improvement involves remaining curious, being creative, and collaborating in efforts to maintain excellence in delivering nutrition messages.

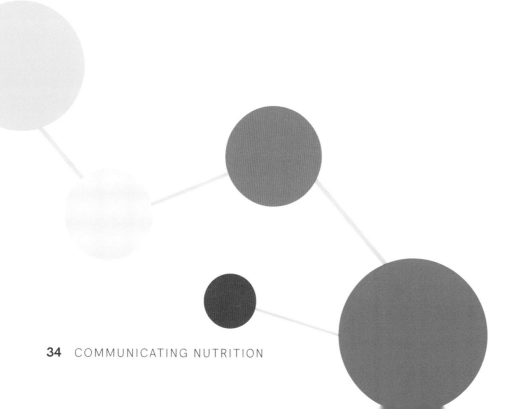

RESOURCES

ACEND Accreditation Standards:
www.eatrightpro.org/resources/acend/accreditation
-standards-fees-and-policies/2017-standards

CDR Essential Practice Competencies:
https://admin.cdrnet.org/vault/2459/web/files
/FINAL-CDR_Competency.pdf

CDR Continuing Professional Education (CPE)
database: www.cdrnet.org/go/and/cdr/cpe_search.cfm

Toastmasters International: www.toastmasters.org

Toastmasters International—find a local club:
www.toastmasters.org/find-a-club

National Speakers Association: www.nsaspeaker.org

National Communication Association:
www.natcom.org

TeamSTEPPS Training: www.ahrq.gov/teamstepps
/index.html

REFERENCES

1. Commission on Dietetic Registration. *Essential Practice Competencies for the Commission on Dietetic Registration Credentialed Nutrition and Dietetics Practitioners.* Published 2015. Accessed April 6, 2020. https://admin.cdrnet .org/vault/2459/web/files/FINAL-CDR _Competency.pdf
2. Academy of Nutrition and Dietetics. Accreditation Council for Education in Nutrition and Dietetics. Published 2017. Accessed November 13, 2017. www.eatrightpro.org /resources/acend
3. Accreditation Council for Education in Nutrition and Dietetics of the Academy of Nutrition and Dietetics. *ACEND Accreditation Standards for Nutrition and Dietetics Didactic Programs.* ACEND; 2017.
4. Accreditation Council for Education in Nutrition and Dietetics of the Academy of Nutrition and Dietetics. *ACEND Accreditation Standards for Coordinated Programs.* ACEND; 2017.
5. Accreditation Council for Education in Nutrition and Dietetics of the Academy of Nutrition and Dietetics. *ACEND Accreditation Standards for Dietetic Internship Programs.* ACEND; 2017.
6. Polk-Lepson Research Group. *National Professionalism Survey: Career Development Report.* Polk-Lepson Research Group; 2014.
7. Polk-Lepson Research Group. *National Professionalism Survey: Professionalism in the Workplace.* Polk-Lepson Research Group; 2013.
8. Polk-Lepson Research Group. *National Professionalism Survey: Recent Graduate Study.* Polk-Lepson Research Group; 2015.
9. Academy of Nutrition and Dietetics. Scope of practice. Accessed May 15, 2018. www.eatrightpro .org/practice/quality-management/scope-of -practice
10. Cant R. Constructions of competence within dietetics: trust, professionalism and communications with individual clients. *Nutr Diet.* 2009;66:113-118.
11. Fiske S, Dupree C. Gaining trust as well as respect in communicating to motivated audiences about science topics. *Proc Natl Acad Sci.* 2014;111.(suppl 4):1-5.
12. Arthur M. Sackler Colloquia of the National Academy of Sciences. *The Science of Science Communication II: Summary of a Colloquium.* National Academies Press; 2014.
13. Purdy M, Borisoff D. *Listening in Everyday Life: A Personal and Professional Approach.* 2nd ed. University Press of America; 1997.
14. Fredrickson B. *Positivity.* Three Rivers Press; 2009.
15. Goleman D. *Social Intelligence.* Bantam Dell; 2006.
16. Foulk T, Woolum A, Erez A. Catching rudeness is like catching a cold: the contagion effects of low-intensity negative behaviors. *J Appl Psychol.* 2016;101(1):50-67.
17. Medina J. *Brain Rules.* Pear Press; 2008.
18. American Management Association. AMA 2010 critical skills survey. Published 2010. Accessed November 18, 2017. www.amanet.org/news/ama -2010-critical-skills-survey.aspx
19. Jaffe E. Why wait? The science behind procrastination. Association for Psychological Science website. Published 2013. Accessed November 19, 2017. www.psychologicalscience .org/observer/why-wait-the-science-behind -procrastination
20. Merriam-Webster. Grit. Accessed November 18, 2017. www.merriam-webster.com/dictionary/grit
21. Maxwell JC. *Failing Forward.* Thomas Nelson; 2007.
22. Agency for Healthcare Research and Quality. TeamSTEPPS. Accessed May 15, 2018. www.ahrq.gov/teamstepps/index.html
23. Coyle D. *The Little Book of Talent.* Bantam Dell; 2012.

CHAPTER 3

Effective Nutrition Communication Is Strategically Designed

Barbara J. Mayfield, MS, RDN, FAND
and Sonja Kassis Stetzler, MA, RDN, CPC

"Successful communication creates a sharing of ideas and feelings, resulting in an audience that attends to, engages with, and takes action on the message communicated in the manner intended by the communicator."

> "The two words *information* and *communication* are often used interchangeably, but they signify quite different things. Information is giving out; communication is getting through."
>
> —SYDNEY J. HARRIS

Introduction

Effective nutrition communication is not an accident. It is strategically designed by creating and executing a plan. Effective communicators evaluate the entire process as well as the outcomes. Lucky breaks can happen, but the old adage holds true: Luck occurs when hard work and preparation meet opportunity. Nutrition communicators who appear to succeed simply by throwing something together have likely spent time in the trenches, learning from mistakes and honing their craft.

Well-designed nutrition communication follows an evidence-based strategy and focuses on three key elements: the audience, the message, and the channel. The design and delivery of effective nutrition communication follow organized and systematic approaches. The audience and other experts are involved in the design process as well as in delivery and evaluation. The entire process has clearly defined goals.

This chapter answers four questions:

- What is our focus?
- What is our strategy?
- Who is involved?
- What defines successful communication?

The answers to these questions provide the foundation for the remaining sections in this book. Nutrition communicators who apply the principles set forth in this chapter will more effectively achieve their communication goals.

What Is Our Focus?

Designing effective nutrition communication requires a multipronged focus. The nutrition communicator must focus on the audience, the message, and the channel simultaneously and consider how each of these factors influences decisions in the other areas. When communicating, practitioners must consider to *whom* they are communicating, *what* and *why* they are communicating, and the *way* they are communicating. An additional area of focus, which is covered briefly in this chapter, is evaluation.[1]

The following sections consider each area of focus as well as what is involved when designing nutrition communication.

Audience: To *Whom* Is the Message Being Communicated?

Communication requires both a sender and a receiver. The receiver of communication is generally referred to as the audience. The size of an audience may range from one person to many. For example, a nutrition counselor typically has an audience of one person in each session, whereas a media spokesperson may have an audience of millions for an interview. Audiences can be specifically defined, such as elderly people with hypertension or pregnant women with limited resources. Audiences can also be generally defined, such as adults in the viewing area or potential patients of Memorial Hospital. A starting point for designing communication is to define the audience.

See Chapter 38 for more information on evaluation.

Refer to Chapter 1 for a review of the basics of communication theory.

Designing audience-focused nutrition communication is described in detail in Section 3 and involves knowing the audience so that the messages to be communicated and the channel(s) for delivering the communication can be tailored to their needs and preferences. Communication that is designed to match the needs and preferences of the communicator, not the audience, may be ineffective. When this takes place, the receiving audience may question whether the sender understands what they need. Although other factors determine decisions regarding message content and delivery, knowing the audience is central to all decisions for effective communication.

Once an audience is defined, the next step involves learning about them and accounting for their culture, socioeconomic status, literacy and health literacy, and other details. Learning about their needs, concerns, interests, values, beliefs, and preferences informs the design and delivery of the communication. This book, for example, has two target audiences:

- nutrition and dietetics practitioners already in the field and
- future nutrition and dietetics practitioners, currently enrolled in accredited educational programs at the undergraduate, graduate, or supervised practice level.

How is this book designed for both audiences? The initial development was informed by surveys and interviews with educators involved in a variety of dietetics education programs, as well as with practitioners in the field. This information directed the breadth and depth of content included, as well as an emphasis on the practical application of knowledge. Authors and reviewers throughout the writing process represented both practitioners and educators. Chapters underwent further pilot testing with students and practicing nutrition and dietetics professionals before final revision.

Effective nutrition communication resonates with the audience because it is designed for them. Although the nutrition and dietetics professionals and students this book targets are a diverse group made up of unique individuals, the book will only be effective if each reader feels that it meets his or her needs in a relevant and meaningful way. As described later in this chapter, incorporating the active involvement of the audience into any communication design strategy increases a project's likelihood for success. Build the active involvement of the audience into any communication design strategy.

Message: *What* Is Being Communicated and *Why*?

A message is a piece of information, bit of content, or an idea communicated from one person or group of people (the sender) to another person or group of people (the receiver or audience).[2] Messages vary in scope and purposes: "HELP" written in the sand seeks a rescuer; a text asking where and when to meet elicits directions; a billboard or phone app listing nearby restaurants promotes businesses and serves hungry travelers; a novel entertains; and a position paper from a professional organization provides evidence-based guidelines. Messages can be long or short, written or spoken, or even conveyed in art or music. A message is *what* the sender wants to convey and is created with a strategic purpose, the *why* of the communication.

Determining the purpose for communicating is the first step in creating the message. It lays the foundation for the message development and strategy. Is the intent to teach an audience new information? If so, then the goal is to convey the information clearly, accurately, and in a way that is interesting to the audience. If the purpose is to influence an audience to change a behavior or to take a particular action as a result of the communication, the goal will shift toward advocacy, and the communication strategy will reflect this goal. Determining the purpose of the communication and creating measurable objectives are also beneficial in measuring the success of the communication. Did the audience understand the information that was conveyed? Did the audience change a behavior or take action?

Messages compete for attention. The average consumer is exposed to tens of thousands of messages every day. Consider how often people check their mobile devices and how many messages bombard readers on screens, on signs and package labels, and through speakers in public places or through earbuds. The sheer volume of messages can be overwhelming. How does anyone create a message that stands out and makes a difference? An effective, well-developed message—accurately and creatively conveying information or an idea—is attended to, is understood, and results in the desired outcomes, as illustrated in the framework for planning and evaluating nutrition communication (see Figure 1.1 on page 14).

Message development is covered throughout this book. Nutrition communicators need knowledge and skills to convey messages that are grounded in science, in contrast to messages that confuse the public with misinformation or opinions presented as facts. The research basis for developing evidence-based messages is described in Section 2, as well as ways to effectively communicate science. Nutrition communicators also need to tailor messages to match each audience—using words and images they understand, matching their needs and concerns—rather than using the same message for everyone. Developing messages that are audience-focused is covered in Section 3. Finally, nutrition communicators need expertise in crafting and modifying messages that can be delivered through a variety of channels. The remaining sections focus on effective delivery of messages and cover specific strategies and principles of message design.

Channel: *How* Is the Message Being Communicated?

Messages reach an audience through a channel. *Channels* are any visual or auditory mediums through which a message is transmitted. Channels come in the following forms:

- speech, including nonverbal expressions
- electronic or digital, as in webinars, social media posts, and videos
- written, such as articles, memos, and handouts
- visual, such as illustrations, props, and photographs
- auditory, such as radio broadcasts, podcasts, or recorded books

The best choice for a particular communication is determined by the audience, the message, and channel availability.

Effective nutrition communication generally employs multiple channels in order to maximize reach and meet the diversity of audience preferences.[1] For example, effective presenters not only speak with skill and confidence but also utilize visual aids, provide written support (such as handouts), and encourage social media sharing, which reinforces the message with the primary audience as it is shared with others. A public health communication campaign may include posters, transit signs, social media, traditional media, group sessions, brochures, and a website. Individually, each type of communication is limited in reach and effectiveness. Collectively, they make a greater impact.

Choosing channels that match an audience's channel usage and preferences will increase the potential for a message to reach its intended audience. Using the wrong channel can result in missing the target audience or not reaching them effectively. For example, young children who are nonreaders will respond more positively to images and hands-on activities than to wordy handouts or text-laden slide presentations. Similarly, audiences with low literacy skills prefer visually rich presentations and handouts using pictures in place of words. Some audiences prefer videos, and others prefer to read. An older audience may prefer a lecture, and a younger audience may prefer a discussion. If in doubt about which channels to select, ask the audience.

Also consider channel availability and affordability. If a facility is not equipped with a projector or does not have internet access, select a channel that doesn't require their use. Having a "low-tech" channel ready for delivering a message, such as a presentation and discussion supported by handouts, is always a smart strategy. Affordability considers both development cost and ongoing cost. Creating a quality video may cost more than a one-time presentation; however, the video can be shown multiple times at little to no additional cost. A written document may be cost-prohibitive if printed in full color yet cost little to share electronically.

Communication channels will continue to evolve with advances in technology. But, these new channels will continue to involve media that enlist people's visual and auditory senses. Part II of this book covers all major categories of communication channels commonly employed by nutrition communicators, including speeches, facilitated discussions, video, food demonstrations, social media, blogging, media interviews, and professional writing. New channels will utilize the same principles for design and delivery used by current channels.

What Is Our Strategy?

Following a process for identifying and assessing an audience, researching and creating a message, and selecting and utilizing one or more channels will yield a successful outcome for the delivery of nutrition messages. The best planning approach aligns the message, audience, and channel with available resources.

Plans may differ in titles or descriptions for various steps, but the overall process for designing effective nutrition communication remains consistent in these recommended planning practices[1,3]:

- Assess the audience and tailor the communication to their needs and preferences.
- Create a message that is meaningful to the audience and that is evidence-based, current, and accurate.

Examples of evidence-based approaches to designing and delivering programs are described in Chapters 10, 16, and 37

Additional planning models are described in Chapter 10.

- Select appropriate channels and optimize their effectiveness.

The following describes a best practice in designing and delivering nutrition communication, followed by a description of acceptable shortcuts when resources are limited.

Best Practice: Nutrition Communication Development Strategy

The Nutrition Communication Development Strategy (see Figure 3.1) outlines 10 critical steps required to design effective communication. The steps are selected from best practices described in health communication literature.[3-5]

This strategy is briefly introduced in this chapter; more detailed descriptions of each step follow in later chapters, as noted in Box 3.1.

FIGURE 3.1 **Nutrition communication development strategy**

The Nutrition Communication Development Strategy uses 10 steps that occur both concurrently and in sequence to identify what, why, when, and how to communicate and to whom.

Audience
1. Identify Audience
2. Conduct Needs Assessment

Message
3. Identify Purpose and Key Message
4. Research Message
5. Write and Organize Message

Channel
6. Identify Channels
7. Plan Strategies
8. Practice, Pilot, Revise
9. Present, Publish
10. Evaluate

Adapted with permission from Nutrition Communicator, LLC. Design concept by Barbara J. Mayfield, MS, RDN, FAND, and Sonja Kassis Stetzler, MA, RDN, CPC. Design by Jen Chapman Creative.

While learning about and going through the steps individually, keep the entire process in mind in order to understand the interrelationships among the steps.

Effective communication includes three focus areas—audience, message, and channel—that are identified and designed in concert. A communicator's entry point may be the audience, the message, or the channel, depending on the situation. Make it a rule not to proceed past the step of identifying the message or the channel without also identifying the audience.

Use the list in Box 3.1 as a helpful checklist to guide nutrition communication development strategies. See the resource list at the end of this chapter to access a detailed worksheet describing the steps.

The Words of Experience box on page 42 illustrates the value of completing steps 1 and 2 in the development strategy, identifying and assessing the needs of the audience.

BOX 3.1 Nutrition Communication Development Strategy: 10 Steps

Step 1: Identify Audience. The steps that follow are dependent upon *whom* the message is developed for. The audience may be familiar or new to the communicator. The audience may extend an invitation or be approached. To complete this step, describe the audience and the setting in which communication will occur. (Chapter 10)

Step 2: Conduct Needs Assessment. Learn about an audience so that the communication provided meets their needs and preferences. (Chapter 11)

Step 3: Identify Purpose and Key Message. Determine the overall purpose of the communication (to educate, to persuade, to motivate, and so on). Select an appropriate message based on factors outlined in Chapter 10 and the needs assessment. This step includes identifying the purpose, the single overriding communication objective, learning objectives, and key message points. This step is initiated along with step 1. (Chapters 10 and 15)

Step 4: Research Message. Seek current and accurate information about the topic to provide the evidence base for the message. This step occurs with step 3. (Chapter 4)

Step 5: Write and Organize Message. Determine the information that is to be communicated. The order in which the substance of the message is presented begins with an understanding of what the audience already knows and cares about, and follows a logical sequence. (Chapter 15)

Step 6: Identify Channel. This step is likely completed simultaneously with earlier steps. Even if the channel is selected along with step 1, it is critical that the choice is based on what is learned in completing steps 2 through 5. Confirm that the medium selected for delivery fits the audience, the message, and the available resources. (Part II covers steps 6 through 10.)

Step 7: Plan Effective Communication Strategies. Plan how messages will be presented and supported with activities, illustrations, examples, visual aids, Q&A, and audience involvement. Also plan for marketing, testing, and evaluation.

Step 8: Practice, Pilot Test, Revise. Now it is time to put it all together. Allow time for practice or pilot testing and revision. Review with peers as well as potential audiences. Then practice, pilot test, and revise some more.

Step 9: Present, Produce, or Publish. The work is completed.

Step 10: Evaluate. This may be listed as the final step, but it is actually incorporated throughout the process and helps inform future communication projects. It involves formative as well as summative evaluation to determine how well objectives were met. (Chapter 38)

Acceptable Practice: Smart Shortcuts

While it is ideal to follow all 10 steps listed in Figure 3.1 and Box 3.1, lack of resources such as time, money, and personnel may limit the ability to do so. Effective communications can still be developed by using practical shortcuts

Know Your Audience

by Sonja Kassis Stetzler, MA, RDN, CPC

Years ago, I had a client who was a marketing manager for a well-known beverage company and sought my help with his public speaking skills. He regularly made sales presentations to groups and wanted to gain an edge over his competition. He knew his purpose—to persuade his audience. I gave him a homework assignment to analyze his audiences. Who were they? What mattered most to each audience member?

When he came back for his next session, he had discovered he had four different audiences he delivered presentations to: high school athletes, college athletes, athletic directors, and parents of the high school athletes. This knowledge led him to new insights with his presentations.

In further analysis, he found the high school athletes valued sports celebrities and would purchase whatever beverage their favorite celebrity athlete in their chosen sport endorsed. The college athletes most highly valued performance and whatever beverage could give them a competitive advantage. The athletic directors valued athletic performance and were also motivated by money and rewards, such as being able to obtain more coolers for their team. Lastly, the parents of high school athletes were mainly interested in whether it was safe for their children to drink the beverage. They wanted to know if the ingredients used in the beverage were safe and if the beverage would help keep their child hydrated.

By understanding each of his target audiences, my client was better able to craft his message to answer the question, "What's in it for me?" He was able to tap into what each audience valued and was able to tweak his presentations to tap into their concerns. As a result, he became more effective in delivering his presentations.

to streamline the design process without short-changing the result.

The first shortcut is to continually collect information that helps to assess main audiences. This shortens the length of assessments.

The second shortcut is similar to the first. Continually collect information to stay current on the topics that are communicated about most often. This shortens the time investment in content research. Save resources that might be used for future programming in a filing system that allows for the quick location of ideas and information.

A third strategy is to reduce the length of time spent getting started. Procrastination prevents the highest-quality work. Getting started early and breaking up the design process into practical and doable amounts gets the job done well. Prioritize and put each step into a calendar.

A fourth approach is to manage one's workload by accepting only as many projects as can reasonably be accomplished—and declining invitations that can't be adequately fulfilled. Another idea is to adapt preexisting material that is suitable for a specific audience and situation. This can be handled by briefly sharing the content and approach with one or more representatives of the audience and confirming that it is appropriate.

The step of assessing an audience is too often skipped. If time and resources are limited, don't eliminate or avoid this step. Instead, complete an abbreviated assessment with as few as three to four well-selected questions. If the actual audience is unavailable or difficult to assess, use a similar convenience sample. This could include the next three scheduled clients, friends or neighbors, fellow members of organizations or groups, or social media contacts. Choose people that closely match the target audience when possible. At the very least, gain as much information as possible from a contact person for a presentation. Keep in mind that time and resources invested in a needs assessment pay dividends in all subsequent steps.

If it is not possible to assess an audience thoroughly prior to communicating with them, try to build in a mechanism to assess and involve them as part of the communication. For example, open a presentation with an interactive activity that allows the audience to share knowledge, concerns, or practices related to the topic. Be prepared to adapt, both in terms of content and in terms of delivery, based on what this activity reveals. For example, at the start of a program about increasing calcium in the diet, a practitioner could ask the audience about their customary intake of dairy foods. If it turns out there are many people in the group who avoid dairy due to allergy, lactose intolerance, or personal preference, the practitioner may need to emphasize alternative sources of calcium more than was originally planned.

One shortcut that should not be taken is reducing adequate research of a topic area. Practitioners should limit their communications to subjects they are well versed in and refer other topics to those with more knowledge. No practitioner is expected to be an expert about every food and nutrition topic.

Acceptable shortcuts in designing the delivery approach most often mean searching for available programs that have already been developed for similar audiences and topics. In addition to building a library of content resources for creating original programming, build a library of ready-made program materials and resources that can be drawn on regularly. Be sure to give credit to the originator of any ideas used.

Allow enough time to have a minimum of one trial run or pilot test of any program. Every audience deserves a practiced, if not polished, performance. Recording a practice presentation and critiquing the content and delivery can be done alone, with others, or even virtually at a distance. Make sure to keep all communications within the allotted time out of respect for the audience. A practice run will help to avoid going too long or not being long enough.

Most programs are delivered multiple times, so take the opportunity each time to gather feedback to make improvements and assess outcomes. Evaluations can be simple and brief and should never be omitted. If there is no opportunity to ask the audience or contact representatives for feedback, at least record some personal impressions of what went well and what could use improvement. Save these thoughts where they will be available the next time a similar program comes along.

Each time the steps in the program design process are followed, the knowledge and experiences gained inform future work and streamline the process for new programs. Effective nutrition communicators are constantly learning and improving.

Who Is Involved?

Communication is created by people, for people. When the design, delivery, and evaluation of communication is deliberately undertaken as a collaboration of all parties involved, there is much greater likelihood that the communication will be effectively received and result in the outcomes desired.

Collaborating to Communicate

Collaboration is defined as two or more parties working together cooperatively to achieve a desired outcome. It doesn't require that all parties agree on everything; in fact, compromise and building consensus where disagreements exist may result in communication that reaches a more diverse audience. To strategically design effective nutrition communication, consider three sets of people to involve: audience members, other professionals, and broader communities and organizations that interface with the audience or with the topic of the communication.

Building relationships offers an important facet of effective communication. The more an audience feels connected to the communicator and the more the communicator feels connected to the audience, the more effective the communication will be. Setting an intention to build a connection with an audience needs to be built into the entire communication design and delivery process. An audience that has collaborated on what is communicated and how it is communicated will be a more receptive audience. The message will resonate, and the channel will be one the audience uses and readily engages with.

WORKING WITH AUDIENCE MEMBERS

The audience is the most important group to collaborate with during the design and delivery process. They are in the best position to report what they need, what concerns them, what motivates them, what turns them off, and how they want to receive what is being communicated. In general, audiences want to be heard and are willing to share their thoughts and opinions if they are approached in a nonthreatening way. An audience that feels a specific piece of communication has been created *with* them rather than *for* them is more likely to hear the message and take action.[6]

For more on giving credit to a source, see Chapter 8.

Methods to assess an audience, such as involving them during the delivery of communication and eliciting feedback, are covered in depth in later chapters.

This book involved the audience throughout its creation. The audience was surveyed and interviewed prior to determining the content and approach. Audience members served as authors and reviewers, pilot tested the content in academic and practice settings, and provided feedback.

WORKING WITH OTHER PROFESSIONALS

Other professionals can contribute to the success of communication design, delivery, and evaluation in multiple ways. They can put nutrition communicators in contact with audiences they want to reach. Professional peers can assist with needs assessments, such as helping develop survey questions, providing access to audience members, or helping lead focus groups. They can serve as content experts, help find research and other types of information, and review communications for accuracy and clarity of scientific concepts. Other professionals may serve on a planning team or be called upon to act in a consultant role.

An example of this collaboration is how this book was created. The variety of perspectives and skills represented by the dozens of contributors resulted in a text with greater breadth and depth than one written by a sole author. In the same way, working within a collaborative team or soliciting input and feedback from other professionals throughout the design, development, and delivery of a nutrition communication project or program enhances the effectiveness.

WORKING WITHIN COMMUNITIES, ORGANIZATIONS, AND OTHER GROUPS

Audience members belong to various groups. They are part of families, neighborhoods, and any number of work-related, social, philanthropic, and faith-based organizations. Recognizing and

FIGURE 3.2 **The social-ecological model**[a]

[a] Adapted from reference 7.

engaging the communities and organizations they participate in helps create and deliver a message that is more readily accepted and put into practice. A useful model for identifying the various individuals and groups that influence the members of an audience is the social-ecological model illustrated in Figure 3.2.[7] Consider how other people at various levels may influence how a message is received and acted upon. Involve them in the design and delivery of messages as appropriate.

Audience members are influenced on multiple levels that involve many other people, social norms, organizational structures, and public policies. Practitioners should involve key leaders and other stakeholders who hold an interest in the work they are involved with. These colleagues could provide the resources needed for a successful communication campaign or endeavor. Potential stakeholders can be found at any of the levels surrounding the individual.

The interpersonal level includes audience members' families, friends, health care providers, and colleagues. These are people audience members come into direct contact with and can influence beliefs, attitudes, and behaviors surrounding food, nutrition, and health. Accounting for these relationships during the development and delivery of communication can improve outcomes.

The organizational and community levels include health care systems, worksites, professional and civic organizations, faith communities, and educational institutions. Working within the community of the audience can help shape the environment in which the audience lives, works, and plays in ways that enhance changes in attitude and behavior.

At the policy level are federal and state program goals and policies, such as Healthy People Goals and the US Dietary Guidelines for Americans. The policy level also includes professional associations and organizations that are involved in the topic being communicated. These organizations may conduct research, promote education, or publish position statements regarding the topic. Obtaining endorsements or demonstrating collaboration with these groups provides credibility and helps spread the message.

This book is the result of the Academy of Nutrition and Dietetics performing a market analysis and determining a void in textbooks and resource books covering nutrition communication. The Academy of Nutrition and Dietetics was involved in every step of the design and development of this book and was responsible for the book's publication and distribution. The book's credibility is strengthened and enhanced by the endorsement of the Academy of Nutrition and Dietetics.

Effective Teamwork

Designing effective communication for an audience is rarely a solo activity. Collaborating with others to develop and deliver communication requires teamwork. Participating in group projects does not end with graduation; working in teams is the norm in the workplace and in professional and community organizations. Students and practitioners alike work collaboratively to create messages, programs, and campaigns.

Learning to work effectively in teams enhances communication success. A popular saying describes teamwork as a way to divide the tasks and double the success. Teamwork can add greatly to the effectiveness of any communication endeavor, but it can also be the source of much frustration if handled improperly.

A team is defined as a task-oriented group whose members may differ in expertise and who are working together to achieve a common goal.[8] Characteristics that differentiate successful teams from unsuccessful teams include the following:

- clear purpose and goals
- trust
- effective communication
- accountability
- the ability to successfully work through conflict
- positive recognition of individual and team efforts toward goal achievement

To accomplish particular tasks or goals, teams are formed in many contexts, such as organizations, professional organizations, classrooms, and even virtually, drawing together members from around the world.

Teams also share leadership among members, and members may take on specific roles within the team. For example, members can play a task role to ensure that the team's work is completed on schedule. Task-related behaviors include initiating discussions, seeking information and input, and supplying information and opinions. Members may also take on relationship roles, which are characterized as supporters, encouragers, and harmonizers within the team. An effective team has members in both task roles and relationship roles, which provides a balance in team members' behavior and increases the team's effectiveness.

At times, conflict may occur among team members, but this is not necessarily negative. Conflict arises from differing opinions, positions, or interests pertaining to reaching the team's goal. Teams in which there is no conflict may experience groupthink, where no one in the group voices disagreement, everyone appears to agree, assumptions go unchallenged, and faulty decisions are made.

The following are guidelines for a functional and effective team[8]:

- Clarify goals and objectives so that team members have a clear understanding of the purpose and mission of the team.
- Create a climate where communication is open and constructive and members freely share ideas. The communication climate also allows for critical evaluation of ideas so that the best ideas are brought forward.
- Manage conflict productively. Diverse opinions and disagreements focus on issues, not personalities, and respect for team members is maintained.
- Delegate tasks. Although a strong leader may be designated to singularly lead a team, team members sometimes share leadership responsibility.
- Self-centered communication, disruptive conflict, and efforts to undermine a positive climate must be discouraged.

Factors predicting effective group performance have been studied in research using varying sizes of teams performing a variety of tasks.[9] Factors that might be expected to predict performance, such as individual intelligence or group cohesion, were not predictive. The most significant factor was "social sensitivity," measured using the Reading the Mind in the Eyes test. (A link to this test can be found in the resource list on page 49.) This test measures a person's ability to determine the mental state of another person from looking at that person's eyes. The other two predictive factors were taking turns equally in group conversations and having more female group members. (Women overall score higher on social sensitivity.)

Further research found these same factors predicted group performance in online teams communicating via text as well as in face-to-face teams.[3] Those with high social sensitivity were able to "read between the lines" as well as read the mind in the eyes. These measures of group effectiveness are referred to as *collective intelligence*.[9,10] Similar factors contribute to positive interactions between communicators and audiences, as will be seen in the exploration of the components of successful communication.

What Defines Successful Communication?

Successful communication creates a sharing of ideas and feelings, resulting in an audience that attends to, engages with, and takes action on the message communicated in the manner intended by the communicator.

This chapter opened with the three key factors that are the focus of communication: the audience, the message, and the channel. Each factor contributes to achieving the desired outcomes that define success, described next.

Communicator and Audience "Connect"

Successful communication begins and ends with the audience. Effective communicators know their audience because they have thoroughly assessed the audience's needs, concerns, interests, and behaviors. The communication is designed accounting for what the audience already knows and what is important to them. Effective communicators prioritize what the audience needs and connect what is communicated to the audience's values and concerns. Business owners have different concerns from parents, who have different concerns from an elderly audience. Successful communication resonates with the audience.

The more an audience perceives the communicator to be someone who understands them and can reflect their needs and concerns, the greater the communication success. An effective communicator intentionally tunes in to the audience's thoughts, values, emotions, and feelings throughout the communication process: during the assessment and planning phases and during delivery. A communicator's awareness and responsiveness enables a connection with the audience at a level that allows a free-flowing two-way exchange—successful communication.

Social neuroscience provides insight into these human connections by researching the pathways people's brains use when they communicate with others. Two neurological responses examined in social neuroscience research are empathy and Theory of Mind (ToM). These terms are often mistaken as synonyms, but each represents specific ways people's brains help them understand others.[11,12]

Empathy refers to the ability to understand the feelings of others and to share their emotions and sensations (such as pain, fear, embarrassment, and reward). Empathic responses activate the same regions of the brain that are activated during first-person experiences of the same emotion or physical sensation.[13] ToM describes the cognitive ability to infer another person's mental state. It is sometimes referred to as mentalizing or cognitive perspective taking.[14,15] Research suggests that ToM, empathy, and related prosocial behaviors, such as compassion, can be enhanced through training[13,16] and can increase a communicator's effectiveness when delivering a message to an audience. Strategies to enhance the connection with an audience are in Sections 3 and 4.

When an audience feels a connection with the communicator and believes that the message meets their needs and concerns, they are motivated to pay attention and to engage, and ultimately are more likely to take action regarding the message. Nutrition messages are designed to result in positive behaviors, not simply increases in knowledge or positive attitudes. An audience taking action to adopt positive behaviors and create a healthier lifestyle is the ultimate desired outcome of most nutrition communication messages and programs. This process may take time, and the effective communicator gears messages to an audience's readiness for change.

An essential yet often overlooked element in motivating an audience to take action lies in understanding the audience's attitude toward the content they are receiving. Audiences who are already in agreement with a message will appreciate new information that validates and reinforces their beliefs. Audiences who start out indifferent to a message are more likely to take action when the message is personalized and offers them a reason to care. For audiences who disagree with a message, finding common ground and acknowledging both sides tends to decrease resistance.

Message Is Clearly Understood

Successful communication is accurately and clearly conveyed. It is necessary for the words, expressions, and examples to be meaningful to the audience and for the audience to clearly understand the sender's intended message. A successful message results in the desired outcomes and objectives set forth during the communication design process.

If a message is misunderstood, it is largely the fault of the communicator. True, an audience may be hard of hearing, or may be distracted, or may make incorrect assumptions, but even in these instances, the communicator needs to take the lead in correcting or preventing these problems:

- For an audience that can't hear, use amplification and subtitles.
- For a distracted audience, gain and maintain their attention through effective attention-getters and engagement.
- Prevent incorrect assumptions through completing a needs assessment and asking good questions.

Don't blame the audience for not following the message—it is the nutrition communicator's responsibility to clarify the message. Use words they understand, provide illustrations that are meaningful, and check for understanding. Make sure the audience "gets it." Pay attention to the feedback they convey and respond appropriately.

Communication that is successful resonates with the audience. Most audiences want and need an intellectual connection, which provides new and current information, and an emotional connection, which personalizes the information and shows how they can benefit from what they have heard. Data and facts provide the intellectual connection that is made with an audience, while stories provide an emotional connection.

Channel Is Effective

Successful communication utilizes one or more channels that are well selected for the audience, the message, and the situation. The channels selected are affordable to both sender and receiver. They are appropriately and skillfully used. They are effective in reaching the intended audience

Taking action for behavior change is further discussed in Chapter 12.

Message development is the focus of Section 3.

Chapter 38 discusses evaluating effective communication.

and allowing the audience to provide feedback.

The choice of channel takes into consideration many factors. To be successful, the channel must be one that the audience uses and prefers. Find out from the audience how they prefer to receive information. Use multiple approaches as appropriate. As will be explored in Sections 3 and 4, audiences represent many different learning styles and preferences. Each channel will match some people's preferred style and not others'. Utilizing several channels increases the opportunity to be successful.

The channel must be properly used. Each type has guidelines for best practice that will be described as each channel is covered later in the book.

KEY POINTS

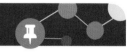

Effective Nutrition Communication Is Strategically Designed

1. Well-designed nutrition communication follows an evidence-based strategy and focuses on three key elements: the audience, the message, and the channel. These elements consider *whom* is being communicated to, *what* is being communicated and *why*, and the *way* something is being communicated.

2. The design and delivery of effective nutrition communication follows an organized and systematic approach outlined in the Nutrition Communication Development Strategy. The three focus areas—audience, message, and channel—are determined and designed in concert.

3. When the entire design, delivery, and evaluation of the communication process is deliberately undertaken as a collaborative effort, there is much greater likelihood that the communication will be effectively received and will result in the outcomes desired. Collaboration involves the audience, other experts, and communities and organizations related to the topic or audience.

4. Successful communication creates a sharing of ideas and feelings, resulting in an audience that attends to, engages with, and takes action on the message communicated in the manner intended by the communicator.

RESOURCES

Nutrition Communication Development Strategy:
www.nutritioncommunicator.com/resources

Reading the Mind in the Eyes test:
www.questionwritertracker.com/quiz/61/Z4MK3TKB
.html

Social Intelligence Test:
http://socialintelligence.labinthewild.org/mite

REFERENCES

1. Noar S. An audience–channel–message–evaluation (ACME) framework for health communication campaigns. *Health Promot Pract*. 2012;13(4): 481-488.
2. Lucas S. *The Art of Public Speaking*. 10th ed. McGraw-Hill; 2009.
3. Schiavo R. *Health Communication: From Theory to Practice*. 2nd ed. Jossey-Bass; 2014.
4. National Collaborating Centre for Methods and Tools. Developing health communication campaigns. Published 2007. Accessed May 23, 2018. www.nccmt.ca/knowledge-repositories /search/75
5. Community Tool Box. Section 1: developing a plan for communication. Published 2018.Accessed May 23, 2018. https://ctb.ku.edu/en/table-of -contents/participation/promoting-interest /communication-plan/main
6. Food Insight. Message making 101: creating consumer-friendly messages. International Food Information Council Foundation website. Published 2009. Accessed January 24, 2018. www.foodinsight.org/Message_Making_101 _Creating_Consumer_Friendly_Messages
7. McLeroy K, Bibeau D, Steckler A, Glanz K. An ecological perspective on health promotion programs. *Heal Educ Behav*. 1988;15(4):351-377.
8. Renz M, Greg J. The nature and uses of small groups. In: *Effective Small Group Communication in Theory and Practice*. Allyn and Bacon; 2000:18.
9. Woolley A, Chabris C, Pentland A, Hashmi N, Malone T. Evidence for a collective intelligence factor in the performance of human groups. *Science*. 2010;330(6004):686-688.
10. Engel D, Woolley A, Jing L, Chabris C, Malone T. Reading the mind in the eyes or reading between the lines? Theory of Mind predicts collective intelligence equally well online and face-to-face. *PLoS One*. 2014;9(12):e115212.
11. Kanske P, Bockler A, Trautwein F, Singer T. Dissecting the social brain: introducing the EmpToM to reveal distinct neural networks for empathy and Theory of Mind. *Neuroimage*. 2015;122:6-19.
12. Hein G, Singer T. I feel how you feel but not always: the empathic brain and its modulation. *Curr Opin Neurobiol*. 2008;18:153-158.
13. Bernhardt B, Singer T. The neural basis of empathy. *Annu Rev Neurosci*. 2012;35:1-23.
14. Schurz M, Radua J, Aichhorn M, Richlan F, Perner J. Fractioning Theory of Mind: a meta-analysis of functional brain imaging studies. *Neurosci Biobehav Rev*. 2014;42:9-34.
15. Singer T. The neuronal basis and ontogeny of empathy and mind reading: review of literature and implications for future research. *Neurosci Biobehav Rev*. 2006;30:855-863.
16. Jankowiak-Sinda K, Rymarczyk K, Grabowska A. How we empathize with others: a neurobiological perspective. *Med Sci Monit*. 2011;17(1):RA18-24.

SECTION 2

Nutrition Communication Is Science-Based

Nutrition Communicators Address the Global Challenge of Misinformation

Tatyana El-Kour, MA, MS, RDN, FAND

The Conflict

On a mission to one of the informal settlements in North Lebanon, I met Angham (name has been changed), a wonderful 8-year-old Syrian child, who rushed to help me carry a food stove and some food items. She saw onions in my hands and started screaming: "I hate onion!" I paused, looked her in the eye, and felt her sorrow. I knew she had a story to tell that went beyond the onion itself. She didn't spare a moment. She was crying and whispered in my ear: "I loved my father very much. He always took me with him everywhere." I could feel Angham's pounding heart. "That day, I went with him to buy some onions when a missile hit him." She paused. "He was killed before my eyes!" I froze for a moment. For Angham, the notion that her father would not have been killed should he not have gone to buy onions prevailed. At that moment, I thought to myself: *What evidence could I draw on now?* Angham knew that onions were good for her, but what she did not know is how to trust her struggle and make meaning of this experience, so I embarked on a journey with her to discover what meaning an onion could bring to her life.

Angham learned to make meaning of her experience despite the association of onions with her father's death. Empowered by science, Angham learned how cooking *mujaddarah*—a dish made of rice, lentils, onions, and vegetable oil—is nutritious and economical and preserves

Photograph provided by T. El-Kour. This image has been altered to protect the identity of the child pictured with the author.

family values, culture, and tradition while allowing her to socially integrate in a place far away from her own.

Across the globe, nutrition professionals encounter clients and consumers who have beliefs and experiences that prevent them from having a healthy relationship with food and eating, and that keep them from making positive changes to improve their health and well-being. Effective nutrition communicators are able to provide empathy and understanding along with scientific evidence to overcome these challenges, whether they work in settings of conflict and displacement due to war or in more peaceful settings where the conflicts and confusion stem from other sources, such as misinformation in social media or negative personal experiences.

The Challenge

In my work in global health and nutrition, misconceptions and misinformation are common, especially among women and girls around the areas of overweight, obesity, and anemia prevention, putting females at risk for micronutrient deficiencies and multiple failed attempts to manage both anemia and weight appropriately. Current global public health efforts regard this challenge as an obstacle to maternal and child health, as well as psychosocial well-being. Evidence suggests that unhealthy weight fluctuations affect reproduction. Additionally, multiple pregnancies and inadequate birth spacing—a phenomenon most prevalent among Arabs and Arab refugees—put women at greater risk of micronutrient deficiencies, overweight and obesity, depression, and chronic diseases later in life.

While the challenge is global in nature, it is of special importance to the Arab world—home to 400 million people—with modern conflicts, widespread revolts, and the region facing the largest refugee crisis in recent history. Nearly half of the Arab population is female, and half of them are under 25 years of age.[1] The 2017 World Health Statistics report showed that at least one-third of Arab females are either overweight or obese (in Bahrain, Kuwait, and Saudi Arabia, the prevalence is even higher), and nearly one-third of females suffer from iron deficiency anemia.[2]

The Opportunity

Interventions are designed to be corrective in nature, but traditional approaches have limited everyday engagement with women and girls. However, high utilization of smartphones by Arabs and by the refugee population alike offers a unique opportunity for using digital technology to support female engagement, access, and participation in sharing credible nutrition information and advocacy.[3] Food and nutrition misconceptions and misinformation are closely linked with one's cultural identity and should not be regarded as an obstacle to health, but rather as a source of potential. Evidence shows that mobile communication platforms, such as WhatsApp, are very popular among female Arab refugees residing in both Lebanon and Jordan.[4] Highest preference was given to apps allowing for voice recordings—compared to texts and images—due to minimal literacy efforts required to produce and share them. Voice recordings are regarded as a replacement for female gatherings.

A New Solution

Mobile technology is seen as a potential solution to address issues, such as protracted crises and problems of food access, availability, and affordability, while accounting for culture, literacy levels, and social integration needs. This solution takes advantage of the widespread adoption of mobile technology featuring applications with voice note capabilities. The high usage of mobile technology within the female Arab population allows for improved access to sustainable and credible information while involving women and girls as collaborators and as sources of inspiration and innovation.

Countering food and nutrition misinformation with science-based evidence is enhanced when the everyday talks of women and girls are used for shaping public health and nutrition interventions. Steps include the following:

- Train field teams on using mobile apps instead of, or in conjunction with, other nutrition communication tools.
- Work on analyzing the content of voice mails to identify the most common topics.
- Break down topics to thematic areas and contexts by location and time to allow for targeted correction of misinformation per area while identifying best times to communicate the message.
- Apply qualitative and quantitative methods of analysis to transform voice note content into a big data source that the public can use.
- Develop a mobile web interface to generate data visualizations and maximize the use of analysis to empower women and girls to make informed decisions. With these advances, women and girls can lead discussions and guide governments and humanitarian and development agencies in understanding their struggles with

how misconceptions come into play and what drives misinformed practices within the social, cultural, material, political, and displaced contexts in which they are immersed.

Defining Success

Success is when making a difference meets the evidence-based mind-set. Success is about making meaning of life experiences. It is about connecting scientific innovation with experiences, struggles, and most important, failures. Success is about continuously learning new ways to stand out and be outstanding. It is about identifying personal attributes, understanding unique values, and collaborating on implementing science-based approaches. While reading and studying this section, which is focused on establishing a firm foundation of science-based nutrition communication, consider the far-reaching applications of translating research into practice.

REFERENCES

1. United Nations, Department of Economic and Social Affairs, Population Division. *World Population Prospects: The 2017 Revision.* United Nations; 2017. Accessed April 16, 2020. https://esa.un.org/unpd/wpp /publications/Files/WPP2017_KeyFindings.pdf

2. World Health Organization. *World Health Statistics 2017: Monitoring Health For the SDGs, Sustainable Development Goals.* World Health Organization; 2017. Accessed April 16, 2020. www.who.int/gho /publications/world_health_statistics/2017/en/

3. Internews. Lost: Syrian refugees and the information gap. 2013. Accessed April 16, 2020. www.internews .org/sites/default/files/resources/Internews_Lost_SyriaReport_Nov2013_web.pdf

4. Talhouk R, Mesmar S, Theime A, et al. Syrian refugees and digital health in Lebanon: opportunities for improving antenatal health. *Proceedings of the 2016 CHI Conference on Human Factors in Computing Systems.* 2016:331-342. doi:10.1145/2858036.2858331

Nutrition Communicators Access Scientific Research

Carolyn Lagoe, PhD and
Kayle Skorupski, MS, RDN-AP, CSG, CNSC, FAND

"Scientific research is more accessible than ever, if a practitioner knows how and where to find it."

"Getting information off the internet is like taking a drink from a fire hydrant." —MITCHELL KAPOR, FOUNDER OF LOTUS

Introduction

Scientific research is more accessible than ever, if a practitioner knows how and where to find it. The internet has made it relatively easy to locate nutrition research, but navigating the different search methods and the vast amount of nutrition information available can be overwhelming. This chapter will introduce nutrition communicators to a variety of ways to find nutrition information, guidelines, and research.

This chapter answers three questions:

- How and where can nutrition professionals find nutrition information and guidelines?
- How and where can nutrition professionals find scientific research?
- How can nutrition professionals teach consumers to find credible nutrition research?

This chapter will help nutrition communicators identify reliable resources for data on the internet, as well as increase their knowledge and ability to use databases and search engines as tools for finding nutrition and health information. This knowledge and skill is transferable to engaged consumers, allowing nutrition communicators to, in turn, teach these techniques to others.

Chapter 5 addresses specific criteria for identifying credible information sources.

How and Where Can Nutrition Professionals Find Nutrition Information and Guidelines?

Because the internet provides a vast amount of information, nutrition communicators must know where to find credible, evidence-based, and up-to-date guidelines to use when communicating with audiences. What follows are some internet sources for health information, statistics, and health-related goals and guidelines for nutrition communicators to use. All websites mentioned are listed in the resources section at the end of this chapter.

Sources of Health Information on the Web

The internet is home to many sources of health information. Nutrition communicators must know which websites are reliable sources of information to use in their communications and to share with their audiences.

One website that provides a wide variety of resources is Healthfinder, hosted by the Office of Disease Prevention and Health Promotion (ODPHP), within the US Department of Health and Human Services. The site offers information on health conditions and diseases, nutrition and physical activity, pregnancy, doctor visits, everyday healthy living, and parenting.

The US government also provides a health resources website where the public can find answers to medical questions, as the site offers the ability to search Medline Plus. Medline Plus is the National Institute of Health (NIH) website for the public; it is produced by the National Library of Medicine, the world's largest medical library. This source provides information about diseases, conditions, and wellness issues in language the public can understand. The site also provides health resources and information, including links to pages about specific conditions, resources for seniors, general health information, and health insurance information. Resources for people with disabilities are available from the National Council on Disabilities (NCD), National Disability Rights Network (NDRN), and the Office of Special Education and Rehabilitative Services (OSERS). Health resources for Native Americans, including information about health care benefits and services as well as health issues in specific populations, are located here, as well as caregiver resources from the federal government and state and local resources.

Additional information can be found on the NIH's Health Information website. Here visitors can find information regarding health information lines, a health services locator, NIH clinical trials, wellness tool kits, science education resources, community resources, and much more.

Health information for women can be found on the US Department of Health and Human Services Office on Women's Health website. Located here are easy-to-access fact sheets, as well as infographics that nutrition communicators can use on topics such as breastfeeding, fitness, and nutrition. The health information website from the National Center for Complementary and Integrative Health is a source for information about alternative, complementary, and integrative health care. Visitors can search by topic and find information about how to be an informed consumer, safe use of complementary medicine, and how to find a provider.

Disease-specific health information is also available online. The National Institute of Diabetes and Digestive and Kidney Diseases Health Information site includes information on diabetes, digestive diseases, kidney diseases, weight management, liver disease, urologic diseases, diet and nutrition, blood diseases, and diagnostic tests. Other sources for disease-specific health information include the American Diabetes Association and the American Heart Association.

Sources for Health Statistics

Many websites provide health-related statistical information.

The World Health Organization (WHO) website provides country-specific global statistics such as total population, gross national income, life expectancy, and total expenditure on health. Additional information is available on child malnutrition, nutrition, risk factors, and mortality and burden of disease.

The Centers for Disease Control and Prevention (CDC) has a website dedicated to providing data and statistics by health condition, such as arthritis, cancer, and heart disease, as well as tools, resources, and links to related organizations. The CDC's National Center for Health Statistics website provides information on population surveys, vital records, and FastStats. FastStats offers quick access to statistics on topics of public health, and readers are given links for publications that include the presented statistics. A webpage on obesity and overweight is also available, which provides up-to-date statistics regarding overweight and obesity prevalence in adults and children in the United States, in addition to links to historical data.

The USA.gov Data and Statistics website contains census data and statistics, census survey results, links to federal agency program statistics, and links to state and local government data and statistics.

The Health Information and National Trends Survey collects cancer-related information about the US public. Various iterations of this survey examine information pertaining to health communication, social networks, risk perceptions, tobacco use, and food and medical products. The data are freely available and can be downloaded from the National Cancer Institute's website.

The County Health Rankings and Roadmaps website allows a viewer to search for state and local statistics and rankings via the Explore Health Rankings section as well as to review recommendations in the Take Action to Improve Health section. Take Action to Improve Health provides strategies and guidance for planning and resources to connect with possible partner organizations. Local and state statistics allow better understanding of the needs of the local population and can help guide presentations, allowing the practitioner to connect with audiences. Knowing how to access and use this information is vital for needs assessments.

See Chapter 11 for information about needs assessment.

Sources for Health-Related Goals and Guidelines

Several websites are sources of health-related goals and guidelines. Some are for overall health, such as ChooseMyPlate website and the Dietary Guidelines website, which can guide both professionals and the public. Others are for disease-specific guidelines, which can be found on sites of organizations such as the American Diabetes Association and the American Heart Association.

The WHO website provides nutrition guidelines for infants, children, and adults, as well as information on initiatives such as the Baby Friendly Hospital Initiative.

Health-related goals can be accessed on the HealthyPeople website hosted by the ODPHP, which houses the Healthy People 2020 initiative. The DATA2020 Search function allows users to explore data and technical information related to the 2020 goals. Also available are the Leading Health Infographics (LHI) and the Midcourse Review Interactive Infographics, which may be useful to nutrition communicators in their presentations and communications. The site also houses information about planning for the Healthy People 2030 initiative.

The ODPHP's Health.gov site is home to the US Dietary Guidelines for Americans. Here the guidelines can be explored in detail, with information that can be easily adopted by nutrition communicators to help communicate and educate about federal guidelines. The ChooseMyPlate website from the US Department of Agriculture helps disseminate the dietary guidelines. This website provides information for specific audiences on the food groups, as well as guidelines for overall healthy eating and physical activity. The site also includes videos that showcase how individuals and families have used ChooseMyPlate to help meet their goals.

WORDS OF EXPERIENCE

Using County Health Statistics to Guide Community Outreach and Engagement

by Kayle Skorupski, MS, RDN-AP, CSG, CNSC, FAND

Previously I worked as the director of food and nutrition at a rural critical access hospital. In this position, I played many roles, including coordinating community outreach and education and disseminating education to the local community. With limited resources, it was important that we undertook initiatives and events that would be relevant and impactful for the community and the hospital.

We utilized data to help determine our focus for our first initiative. We reviewed hospital admission information, looking at trends in chief complaints. The hospital admissions data showed that uncontrolled diabetes was a common admit diagnosis. I also searched for information specific to our county through the County Health Rankings and Roadmaps website (www.countyhealthrankings.org). This site provides information regarding health in a community: length of life, quality of life, heath behaviors, clinical care, social and economic factors, and the physical environment.

The county health rankings helped me compile statistics that supported making diabetes our first effort. The statistics that supported the need for our first initiative included quality of life, diabetes prevalence, adult obesity, physical activity, access to exercise opportunities, and access to clinical care, as well as social and economic factors.

Armed with this information, we garnered support from the hospital senior executives to initiate a monthly diabetes patient support group. With the assistance of our nurse case manager, we started holding the support group, which included group discussions, education sessions, and healthy snacks with recipes. We received feedback that encouraged us to continue to investigate other ways we could engage the public and also benefit the hospital—through the use of relevant data and statistics.

The CDC's Healthy Weight website presents information on healthy eating, losing weight, preventing weight gain, and physical activity. There are guidelines for managing specific diseases, including nutrition and physical activity recommendations.

The American Diabetes Association's Nutrition Therapy Recommendations for the Management of Adults with Diabetes, which were published in the journal *Diabetes Care*, are also online. These discuss the goals of medical nutrition therapy for those with diabetes.

The American Heart Association, in collaboration with the American College of Cardiology, published the Guidelines on Lifestyle Management to Reduce Cardiovascular Risk in the journal *Circulation,* and they are also online. These guidelines discuss dietary patterns, intake of sodium and potassium, and physical activity.

How do nutrition communicators use health data to develop and deliver messages and programming? See the Words of Experience box for a real-life example.

How and Where Can Nutrition Professionals Find Scientific Research?

Academic sources such as professional journals, academic databases, search engines, and web-based resources can be used to identify research pertaining to nutrition and communication. Let's examine each of these sources in greater detail.

Professional Journals

Professional journals span a wide variety of topics relating to food, nutrition, health, and nutrition communication. Journals range in their area of focus, and they can be useful resources to provide professionals and the public with vital developments in different areas.

When determining whether a professional journal is a quality source, researchers should look for several characteristics, including having an editorial board of experts, being peer-reviewed, and welcoming feedback in the form of letters to the editor. Reputable journals include publications from professional nutrition organizations such as the Academy of Nutrition and Dietetics, the Society for Nutrition Education and Behavior, and the American Society for Nutrition.

Peer-review is one hallmark of a trustworthy journal. The peer-review process involves the evaluation of submitted articles by experts in the field. Authors and reviewers are not aware of who is evaluating and being evaluated (referred to as blinded). To determine whether a journal is peer-reviewed, researchers can look up whether the journal has been designated as "refereed" in the Ulrich's Global Serial Directory. If the journal is refereed, an icon that looks like a referee jersey will appear next to the journal name (see Figure 4.1). If researchers are unsure about a journal, they should seek guidance from a reference librarian or choose articles from journals they know to be trustworthy.

There is no single approach to determining journal quality, and journals can be ranked using different proxy measures. These measures include (but are not limited to) total number of citations

FIGURE 4.1 **Referee icons indicating peer-reviewed journals in Ulrich's Global Serial Directory**

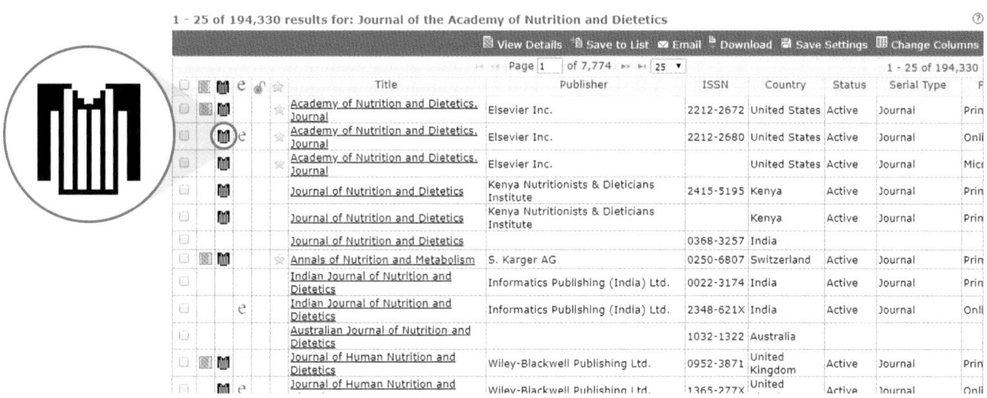
1 - 25 of 194,330 results for: Journal of the Academy of Nutrition and Dietetics

View Details | Save to List | Email | Download | Save Settings | Change Columns

Page 1 of 7,774 | 25 | 1 - 25 of 194,330

Title	Publisher	ISSN	Country	Status	Serial Type	F
Academy of Nutrition and Dietetics, Journal	Elsevier Inc.	2212-2672	United States	Active	Journal	Prin
Academy of Nutrition and Dietetics, Journal	Elsevier Inc.	2212-2680	United States	Active	Journal	Onli
Academy of Nutrition and Dietetics, Journal	Elsevier Inc.		United States	Active	Journal	Mic
Journal of Nutrition and Dietetics	Kenya Nutritionists & Dieticians Institute	2415-5195	Kenya	Active	Journal	Prin
Journal of Nutrition and Dietetics	Kenya Nutritionists & Dieticians Institute		Kenya	Active	Journal	Prin
Journal of Nutrition and Dietetics		0368-3257	India			
Annals of Nutrition and Metabolism	S. Karger AG	0250-6807	Switzerland	Active	Journal	Prin
Indian Journal of Nutrition and Dietetics	Informatics Publishing (India) Ltd.	0022-3174	India	Active	Journal	Prin
Indian Journal of Nutrition and Dietetics	Informatics Publishing (India) Ltd.	2348-621X	India	Active	Journal	Onli
Australian Journal of Nutrition and Dietetics		1032-1322	Australia			
Journal of Human Nutrition and Dietetics	Wiley-Blackwell Publishing Ltd.	0952-3871	United Kingdom	Active	Journal	Prin
Journal of Human Nutrition and	Wiley-Blackwell Publishing Ltd.	1365-277X	United	Active	Journal	Onli

per year, total number of citations over multiple years, and impact factor. The impact factor is the number of times an average article in a specific journal has been cited within a given year. It is used to measure the rank of a journal by calculating the number of times its articles are cited.

Predatory journals can also be a problem for those seeking to access credible scientific research. These journals tend to prey on scholars by engaging in a pay-to-play system in which authors' submissions are published for payment without regard for the scientific rigor of an investigation. It can be a challenge to recognize these journals. Most predatory journals do not have an editorial board composed of experts in the field and often do not subject submitted articles to peer review. A helpful guide to identify predatory journals can be found in the resources list at the end of the chapter.

For more on predatory journals, see Chapter 41.

Nutrition and dietetics journals with high impact factors include the *Journal of the Academy of Nutrition and Dietetics*, *Journal of Enteral and Parenteral Nutrition*, *American Journal of Clinical Nutrition*, and *Journal of the International Society of Sports Nutrition*.

Members of a professional association usually receive copies of the association's journal, such as the *Journal of the Academy of Nutrition and Dietetics*. Some of the Academy of Nutrition and Dietetics dietetic practice groups have access to other journals. For instance, the Academy of Nutrition and Dietetics Hunger and Environmental Nutrition practice group receives the *Journal of Hunger and Environmental Nutrition* as a member benefit. Journals are also available via libraries, especially academic and medical libraries, as both hard copies and electronically. In addition to these methods, one of the most commonly used means to access research articles is through academic databases.

DATABASES

A variety of academic databases are available covering issues related to health, nutrition, and communication:

- PubMed is a popular reference source used to search for academic literature covering health, medicine, nursing, communication, and social sciences.
- CINHAL is one of the largest nursing and allied health databases available and provides relevant information regarding nursing-based nutrition interventions.

- The CAB Abstracts database covers applied life science literature, including animal and veterinary sciences, entomology, dairy sciences, farming, agricultural economics, and food and nutrition.
- Scopus is a more general database that spans science, technology, medicine, social sciences, and humanities.
- AGRICOLA is a database created and maintained by the US Department of Agriculture's National Agricultural Library. It indexes journals, magazines, conference reports, theses and dissertations, books, and book chapters.
- ERIC stands for the Education Resources Information Center, and it is sponsored by the Institute of Education Sciences of the US Department of Education. It is a digital library of education research and information.
- Databases such as PsycInfo, PsycARTICLES, and Communication and Mass Media Complete focus on social science and humanities issues and may be useful for nutrition communicators who are researching nutrition-related social science, communication, and humanistic issues.

Scientific Search Engines

Search engines can also be useful resources to access scientific literature. Google Scholar is one of the most popular search engines. This bibliographic database allows users to search for literature in multiple disciplines and formats. Similar to academic databases, Google Scholar provides advanced search functions in which users can search for articles using various indicators such as title, author, topic, search terms, and year of publication.

Science.gov is a search engine that provides access to information about the results of federally funded research. In 2018, the site had the power to search over 60 databases, 2,200 scientific websites, and 200 million pages of federal science information.

Evidence Analysis Library

The Evidence Analysis Library (EAL) is a resource available to members of the Academy of Nutrition and Dietetics (www.andeal.org). Nonmembers can subscribe to this service for a monthly or annual fee. The EAL is a hub for reliable and credible evidence-based content that is used to advance knowledge and practice. The site provides resources for applying evidence-based research in practice settings, including systematic reviews on over 40 topics and evidence-based nutrition practice guidelines with over 400 recommendations. Two additional evidence analysis libraries are available from Cochrane Library and the Joanna Briggs Institute (JBI).

Other Web-Based Resources

Certain social media platforms, such as Researchgate and Academia.edu, can be used by scholars and the public to collect and review scientific data reports. Scholars use these sites to connect with others who have similar, divergent, or complementary research interests. The sites are used as platforms to post and disseminate published and unpublished research in researchers' respective fields. Google Scholar also has a social network function in which scholars can make personal profiles, tag their existing research, and connect with coauthors or others with similar research interests.

How Can Nutrition Professionals Teach Consumers to Find Nutrition Research?

Nutrition communicators are not the only individuals who can benefit from accessing credible scientific research. When feasible, nutrition communicators can empower consumers to identify and appropriately utilize scientific research.

Finding Reliable Research from News Articles and Web Posts

Health news articles and web posts currently serve as a primary method for consumers to seek out information related to health issues. However, recent work has noted that this can be problematic because of journalistic reporting practices.[1] These problematic practices include:

- inaccurate secondary summaries of existing research,
- the tendency to report on unique findings instead of consistent trends or meta-analyses, and

- the lack of follow-up that takes place after reporting on a single study (even if consistent evidence is identified that goes against the originally reported findings).

Given these issues, it is important to encourage consumers to go beyond secondary summaries of health-related research. If consumers have questions about findings from research investigations published in popular press articles, they should be encouraged to speak with their health care providers, including physicians and registered dietitian nutritionists (RDNs). Consumers can also retrieve reliable research using academic databases.

An additional concern is the use of native advertising to promote nutrition products in print and digital outlets. Native advertising is a type of advertisement or product promotion that is similar in aesthetic form and feel to the outlet or website it is embedded within. For instance, if an advertisement is published in the *New York Times*, its design will mirror that of the traditional paper format. This approach can make it difficult for a consumer to distinguish between actual news stories and the presentation of sponsored content.

Locating Where Reliable Research Is Published and Listed

Locating reliable scientific research can be easy or challenging, depending on the resources available to the individual who is searching. For example, it can be relatively easy for individuals who are affiliated with an academic or government institution that provides free use of scientific databases but challenging for those without these options or who are blocked from accessing certain articles by paywalls. In these cases, researchers or consumers seeking access to these databases should utilize services offered by their local public library. Consumers can use Google Scholar to explore the digital holdings of libraries they have affiliations with (including their local library). Users must add their library on Google Scholar using the scholar settings function.

Consumers can also retrieve information via Medscape. Medscape is available to all readers through a free registration; it provides up-to-date information on a wide variety of health topics, including public health and family medicine.

To search for articles more effectively and efficiently, use the controlled vocabulary and subject headings the database recommends. For example, Medline and PubMed use *medical subject headings*, otherwise known as MeSH terms. MeSH is the National Library of Medicine's controlled vocabulary, used for both indexing articles and searching for articles. For instructions on using MeSH terms, see the National Library of Medicine link in the resources list.

BOOLEAN OPERATORS AND NESTING

Boolean operators are words used to define the relationship between the terms in your search. The most popular Boolean operators are AND and OR and NOT. They should be used based on the purpose of the search and the discretion of the searcher. A search using the AND function collects articles that *must* include all criteria specified. A search using the OR function provides alternate search terms that can be used to search for and find an article. Often, the AND and OR functions are used in tandem to find the most relevant articles on a specific issue. NOT allows users to exclude certain terms from the search.[2]

These Boolean operators can be used in combination with parenthesis, called *nesting*, which allows users to group words together in the Boolean string. Much like in a mathematical equation where the first step is to solve what is in parenthesis, nesting uses the same mathematical logic and runs the parenthetical search before the others.[2] See Figure 4.2 for examples of Boolean operators and nesting.

EXACT PHRASE AND WILDCARDS

Searching for a term like *mass media* will return results for the words *mass*, *media*, and *mass media* all together. Placing *mass media* in quotation marks limits the results to the exact phrase *mass media*.[3]

Some searches are for words with multiple spellings or words that have a similar root word. Some search engines use different symbols (called wildcards), but most use a question mark in place of a single letter that can be altered; for example, *?ffect* could return results for *affect* and *effect*. When a longer string of letters is unknown, users can use an asterisk to indicate that multiple strings of letters may be included in the search results. *Communic** would return results for *communication*, *communicating*, and *communicative*.[3] See Figure 4.2 for examples of wildcard and exact phrase searches.

Scientific Database Article Search Checklist

Identify the general topic to explore further by searching the literature.

Brainstorm possible subject headings, keywords, and exact phrases to use as search terms to identify articles. Consider Boolean operators, nesting, and wildcards to use.

Using the search terms, find articles that are representative of the topic.

After finding a few representative articles, look at the subject headings, keywords, and exact phrases used in those articles to see whether the original search terms should be modified or updated. Consider new or additional Boolean operators or wildcards to help narrow or expand the search.

If search terms are modified or updated, rerun the search and review the results for relevant articles.

Review the reference lists of the most relevant articles for additional article leads.

Review the reference lists of the most relevant articles to identify authors that commonly publish on the subject.

FIGURE 4.2 **Tools for effective use of search terms**[a]

To find information related to mass media campaigns focused on nutrition for women, a search might begin with a combination of terms related to nutrition, communication, mass media, and campaigns.

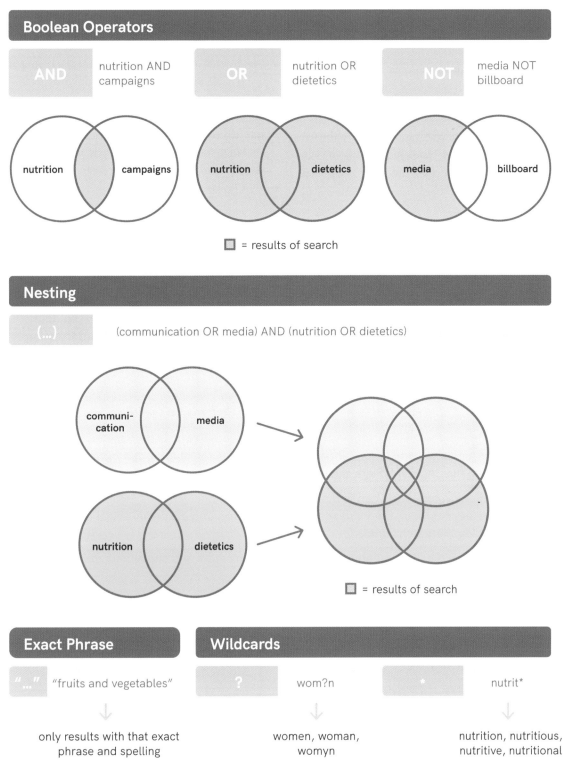

Boolean Operators

| AND | nutrition AND campaigns | OR | nutrition OR dietetics | NOT | media NOT billboard |

nutrition / campaigns

nutrition / dietetics

media / billboard

☐ = results of search

Nesting

(...)   (communication OR media) AND (nutrition OR dietetics)

communi-cation / media

nutrition / dietetics

☐ = results of search

Exact Phrase

"..."   "fruits and vegetables"

↓

only results with that exact phrase and spelling

Wildcards

?   wom?n

↓

women, woman, womyn

*   nutrit*

↓

nutrition, nutritious, nutritive, nutritional

[a] Adapted from reference 3.

Refer to the Scientific Database Article Search Checklist (see page 62) for guidance on completing a scientific database article search.

Search Smart

Try mixing and matching combinations of subject headings and keywords until the most useful terms are identified. Also, look for authors who frequently publish in the area and search for them. Look for lists of other relevant articles, which some search engines provide. After initially searching with these terms, review relevant abstracts. Review the keywords embedded within relevant papers to determine whether modifications should be made to the original search key terms; this will improve the ability to identify relevant articles.

If the initial keyword searches are not returning the desired research or are not returning enough research, there are two options. Modify the keywords and search functions (AND or OR) to see what iterations yield the most relevant results. Or, consider using the Abstract category instead of the Search Term or Keyword category to identify relevant literature. Often, the Abstract category will yield more relevant results than other approaches.

Effective nutrition communicators should use reliable resources for data on the internet and share these resources with consumers. The remaining chapters in this section will assist communicators and audiences to determine which sources are credible, to read and interpret scientific literature, and to clearly communicate science, ethically and with proper credit given.

KEY POINTS

Nutrition Communicators Can Access Scientific Research

1. Nutrition professionals can find health information and guidelines through multiple sources on the web. These sources include Healthfinder.gov, the Health Information website of the National Institutes of Health, and the site for the National Center for Complementary and Integrative Health.

2. Sources for health statistics include the Centers for Disease Control and Prevention, the USA.gov Data and Statistics site, and the County Health Rankings website.

3. Information for health-related goals and guidelines can be found on the World Health Organization website. Information can also be found at the Healthypeople.gov website and the ChooseMyPlate site provided by the US Department of Agriculture.

4. Nutrition professionals can find research in professional journals, academic databases (eg, PubMed), the Evidence Analysis Library, and academic social media platforms (eg, Research Gate).

5. When searching for research, nutrition communicators and consumers must consider sources and appropriate keywords.

RESOURCES

Academia: www.academia.edu

Academy of Nutrition and Dietetics—
Evidence Analysis Library: www.andeal.org

American Diabetes Association: www.diabetes.org

American Diabetes Association—Nutrition Therapy Recommendations for the Management of Adults with Diabetes: care.diabetesjournals.org /content/36/11/3821

American Heart Association: www.heart.org

American Heart Association—
2013 AHA/ACC Guideline on Lifestyle Management to Reduce Cardiovascular Risk: circ.ahajournals.org/content/129/25_suppl_2/S76

American Psychological Association—PsycARTICLES: www.apa.org/pubs/databases/psycarticles/index.aspx

American Psychological Association—PsycINFO: www.apa.org/pubs/databases/psycinfo/index.aspx

CABI—CAB Abstracts: www.cabi.org/publishing-products/online-information-resources/cab-abstracts

CINAHL Plus: https://health.ebsco.com/products/cinahl-plus

Centers for Disease Control and Prevention—Data and Statistics Page: www.cdc.gov/DataStatistics

Centers for Disease Control and Prevention—Healthy Weight: www.cdc.gov/healthyweight

Centers for Disease Control and Prevention—National Center for Health Statistics: www.cdc.gov/nchs/index.htm

Centers for Disease Control and Prevention—National Center for Health Statistics—Obesity and Overweight: www.cdc.gov/nchs/fastats/obesity-overweight.htm

County Health Rankings and Roadmaps: www.countyhealthrankings.org

Data and Statistics About the United States: www.usa.gov/statistics

EBSCO Information Services—Communication and Mass Media Complete: www.ebsco.com/products/research-databases/communication-mass-media-complete

Google Scholar: https://scholar.google.com

Health Information from the government: www.usa.gov/health-resources

Health information and National Trends Survey: https://hints.cancer.gov/data/default.aspx

Identifying predatory or pseudo-journals: www.ncbi.nlm.nih.gov/pmc/articles/PMC5493175

National Center for Complementary and Integrative Health—Health Information: www.nccih.nih.gov/health

National Center for Biotechnology Information—PubMed: www.ncbi.nlm.nih.gov/pubmed

National Library of Medicine: Using MeSH Database: https://www.nlm.nih.gov/mesh/mbinfo.html

Office of Disease Prevention and Health Promotion—Food and Nutrition/Dietary Guidelines: https://health.gov/our-work/food-nutrition

National Institute of Diabetes and Digestive and Kidney Diseases—Health Information: www.niddk.nih.gov/health-information

Office of Disease Prevention and Health Promotion—Healthy People 2020: www.healthypeople.gov

Office of Disease Prevention and Health Promotion—US Department of Health and Human Services: www.healthfinder.gov

ResearchGate: www.researchgate.net

Science.gov Alliance: www.science.gov

Scopus: www.scopus.com

US Department of Agriculture—ChooseMyPlate: www.choosemyplate.gov

US Department of Health and Human Services—National Institutes of Health—Health Information: www.nih.gov/health-information

US Department of Health and Human Services—Office on Women's Health: www.womenshealth.gov/printables-and-shareables/resource/fact-sheets

World Health Organization—Guidelines on Nutrition: www.who.int/publications/guidelines/nutrition/en

World Health Organization—The United States of America: www.who.int/countries/usa/en

REFERENCES

1. Dumas-Mallet E, Smith A, Boraud T, Gonon F. Poor replication validity of biomedical association studies reported by newspapers. *PLoS One.* 2017;12(2). doi:10.1371/journal.pone.0172650
2. Boolean operators and nesting. Library of Congress website. Accessed July 29, 2019. https://catalog.loc.gov/vwebv/ui/en_US/htdocs/help/searchBoolean.html
3. JSTOR Support. Searching: truncation, wildcards and proximity. JSTORE website. Accessed July 29, 2019. https://support.jstor.org/hc/en-us/articles/115012261448-Searching-Truncation-Wildcards-and-Proximity

Nutrition Communicators Identify Credible Sources

Nicci Brown, MS, RDN
Alice Henneman, MS, RDN
Katie McKee, MCN, RDN, LD
and Amy R. Mobley, PhD, RD

"Credentialed food and nutrition practitioners are uniquely positioned to teach consumers to discern the difference between credible and questionable nutrition information."

> # "Everyone is entitled to his own opinion but not to his own facts." —DANIEL PATRICK MOYNIHAN

Introduction

Food and nutrition professionals understand the importance of communicating sound science. The public may not. With many people using the internet as their primary source of news and information,[1] it can be challenging for consumers and patients to determine if the information and recommendations they find are evidence-based. Nutrition communicators can help the public understand how to identify credible sources.

This chapter answers five questions:

- What defines a credible source?
- What professional organizations are credible sources?
- What is disclosure and why is it important?
- How can a questionable source be identified?
- How can nutrition professionals teach consumers to discern the difference between credible and questionable sources?

This chapter is a guide to distinguishing fact from fiction in health and nutrition communications. Consumers are more confused than ever.[2] The job of the nutrition communicator is to provide them with the facts and leave the fake news behind.

What Defines a Credible Source?

Identifying a credible source is about asking the right questions. As with nutritional assessment,

it takes time to collect information and evaluate whether it is credible. Evaluation often starts with five questions: Who? What? Why? When? How? Knowing more about who the communicator is, what agenda may be present in communication, and how information is presented can be the best tools in deciding whether or not a source is credible.

Credentials and Training: Reputable vs Fake

Registered dietitian nutritionists (RDNs) work toward their title with the goal of becoming credible food and nutrition experts. In order to become dietitians, they pursue science-based coursework and complete internships focused on a variety of supervised practice settings, including patient care (hospital and outpatient settings), public health and community nutrition, media and communications, and other settings where education about food, nutrition, and health may be delivered (such as schools and fitness or wellness centers). As described in Chapter 2, RDNs complete a program accredited by the Accreditation Council for Education in Nutrition and Dietetics (ACEND). It is how they earn their credentials. Many (but not all) states also recognize the value in the profession by providing a license to practice. In a world where many people can call themselves a nutritionist, it is the responsibility of credentialed nutrition professionals, such as RDNs, to educate the public and other health professionals about the profession, its members, and how credentials benefit patients, clients, and consumers.

ETHICAL STANDARDS

Just as one may look to members of the Academy of Nutrition and Dietetics for a credible nutrition expert, those seeking a credible journalist can rely on the Society of Professional Journalists.[3] Ethical journalists seek to accurately report a story. It is about being both accurate and fair. Like nutrition and dietetics practitioners, journalists study ethics and practice adhering to a code of ethics.

Many media jobs do not require a degree, but attending journalism school offers distinct advantages for those in the field, including experience in writing and producing well-researched and well-written pieces, leadership roles in student-produced publications or media, and, often, internship experience. The role of the journalist has changed with the rise of the internet, and the need for credible, reliable sources is more important than ever. With so much misinformation available, it is important for those reporting the news to be fair and accurate.

It is the role of the nutrition and dietetics practitioner to review the headlines and help consumers understand the facts. Often headlines are misleading, and consumers may only read the first few lines of an article. Nutrition communicators need to be able to find reliable, credible information and share it with consumers.

HISTORY OF BEING A CREDIBLE SOURCE

> "The key question is how do they know? If it's not clear, you should be skeptical."
>
> —TOM ROSENSTEIL, EXECUTIVE DIRECTOR, AMERICAN PRESS INSTITUTE

With so many different voices in the media, it can be overwhelming to know exactly who is speaking. It is possible to identify major broadcast news networks, newspapers that have stood the test of time, and institutions that share science. It may be more difficult to evaluate independent journalists, experts, and individuals with a message to share. Identifying a credible source comes down to what that source reports and how it cites information. The American Press Institute gives five key features to assess the credibility of a news story[4]:

- content type
- cited sources
- vetted evidence
- interpretation, including any writer bias
- completeness

The reader should be clear on whether something is a story, an opinion, or an advertisement. Knowing which sources are cited and how the evidence is collected and evaluated is important, too, as is seeing whether the source has a track record of providing credible stories. It may be necessary to do a little research on the writer's previous work. The sources cited may need to be evaluated for credibility. Organizations with credibility are reviewed later in this chapter. It's important for a nutrition communicator to review the actual studies that may be mentioned in the stories and interpret them for the public. For example, journalists often confuse correlation and causation.

RED FLAGS

In the media and on the internet, it can be difficult to find a credible source. More and more people use an internet browser search box or their social media feeds to get news and information. Nutrition is a particularly hot topic, and much of the information on the internet about nutrition can be misleading for patients, clients, and consumers.[5] See Figure 5.1 for some common cautionary red flags to be aware of when reading health and nutrition stories.

In an age when there are many so-called experts, it is more important than ever to seek out reliable information.

Which Professional Organizations Are Credible Sources?

Professional organizations that promote facts and sound science are credible. Consider the following credible sources.

FIGURE 5.1 **Health and nutrition story red flags**

One-sided story

Credible journalists seek accuracy and fairness. If a story is one-sided, it may be more opinion than fact.

Ads disguised as news

Credible journalists research and write stories. Advertising sells something. Disclosure can help clarify whether or not a source is being paid to sell something.

Unsound science

It is important to evaluate a scientific study. If the piece has misinterpreted the science, written an attention-grabbing headline with little regard to fact, or made an overreaching claim about the science, it should not be regarded as a quality source.

Credible News Sources

The American Media Institute has a full list of professional journalism organizations.[6] A few standouts from that list include the following:

- American Press Institute (www.americanpressinstitute.org)
- National Association of Broadcasters (www.nab.org)
- National Newspaper Association (www.nnaweb.org)
- National Press Club (www.press.org)
- Society of Professional Journalists (www.spj.org)

Sound Science

Nutrition and dietetics practitioners communicate evidence-based information. Finding the best resources for sound science is essential. These are some credible sources:

- Academy of Nutrition and Dietetics (www.eatright.org)
- Cochrane Library (www.cochranelibrary.com)
- Nutrition.gov (www.nutrition.gov)

Credentialed nutrition professionals must understand and interpret nutrition science as it applies to their clients and the public. They must also focus on sharing knowledge in a responsible, unbiased, and credible way. Using quality sources that are credible is the first step in providing sound information to patients, clients, and consumers.

Clues to Credibility

Context and content are two ways to better understand a source. A few clues to the credibility of written communications can be found in what is shared and how the writer shares it. Here are a few items credible writers share:

- who they are (and where they work)
- where they obtained their information
- whether the content was sponsored

Transparency is key in evaluating the quality of a source.

What Is Disclosure and Why Is It Important?

A conflict of interest (COI) is defined as "a conflict between the private interests and the official responsibilities of a person in a position of trust."[7] COIs may include personal, professional, institutional, or financial situations. An example of a financial COI related to public health is the resignation of the director of the Centers for Disease Control and Prevention, Brenda Fitzgerald, MD, for not disclosing purchases of tobacco and drug stocks that could clearly interfere with her US leadership role in US public health and disease prevention.[8] A COI may still affect a person's judgment or actions even if the conflicts are fully disclosed.

The practice of full disclosure related to a COI, even if it is only remotely possible, has

Chapter 9 is devoted to ethical practice and the Code of Ethics.

become increasingly important as the public and the scientific community have begun to further scrutinize research, media reporting, and corresponding nutrition content. Further, the increased access to various forms of technology for nutrition information places a greater burden on

WORDS OF EXPERIENCE

Translate the Science

by Katie McKee, MCN, RDN, LD

Before I became an registered dietitian nutritionist (RDN), I worked as a writer, editor, and reporter for many years. The communication and investigation skills I learned as a journalist serve me well as a dietitian working in nutrition communications. Being clear and concise is helpful in all fields. Writing for a lay audience is a valuable skill when it comes to much of what we do—translating the science. An effective media interview is one where the speaker is clear, concise, compelling, and credible.

For many of us, when we train to become RDNs, we learn the science and how to apply that science to practice but may not learn to communicate that science clearly to consumers. If we appear on a news segment or are quoted in an article, we may get lost in the science and not share clear calls to action for our audience. Avoid getting caught up in technical jargon. Adapt the science for a consumer audience. Sometimes we have to get out of our own way. I'll share a secret: An interviewer is looking for a few key items—great quotes, clear calls to action, and an awesome introduction.

As a journalist, I think about a compelling headline. As an RDN, I think about being a credible source and sharing the science in the most compelling way. It is important to talk about evidence-based recommendations in a consumer-friendly way. Like many other things, it takes a bit of practice and planning. Before an interview, know the key messages, have the evidence to support those messages, and identify key takeaways. A message map, a basic document that helps organize key thoughts into distinct messages and supporting points, is a great tool to help prepare. The communicator's job has been done when the interviewer shares exactly what was intended. A clear, concise, compelling message will make the science simple and inspire an audience.

an individual to evaluate the validity and trustworthiness of the content. Disclosure of potential conflicts of interest should be transparent and readily accessible in many circumstances, as will be described later. The Academy of Nutrition and Dietetics Code of Ethics for the Profession[9] includes several guiding principles regarding the importance of disclosing potential conflicts of interest, especially as a responsibility to clients and the profession.

Partnerships, Consulting, and Grant Money

Nutrition and dietetics professionals may be responsible for securing outside support or may be approached to consider receiving sponsorship for a conference, a meeting, an event, a journal publication, endorsements, or a partnership.[10] When considering collaborating with an outside group, such as for sponsorship of a meeting, consulting on a project, or applying for grant funding, a practitioner should consider various COIs and disclose any that arise. These disclosures may include a practitioner's employer, partners, or collaborators. For example, if a practitioner works, consults, or partners with an industry trade group that promotes a certain food or product, the affiliation with that group should be disclosed so that the relationship is transparent. Nutrition and dietetics groups face further scrutiny when they partner with outside organizations for funding, especially if those organizations include foods, supplements, or related products that may not appear to completely support health or that promote claims not fully based on science.

In nutrition science research and grant settings, consumers, health professionals, and researchers are paying more attention to the types of sponsorships and funding sources and to the published outcomes. A previous research review indicated that nutrition science studies that were funded by industry groups typically did not include unfavorable results, thereby raising the question of whether or not the research was potentially biased or if the industry group was not supportive of publishing negative results.[11] Other studies, including a systematic review conducted by an Australia-based research group and a retrospective study of nutrition-practice research quality, did not find such clear associations between industry funding and nutrition research findings.[12,13] However, scrutiny over funding sources continues, and sound science, regardless of sponsorship, is essential.[13]

Disclosure on Social Media

Social media platforms present a unique and important challenge to disclosing potential conflicts of interest in the nutrition field. Because communication venues often limit the amount of text or information that can be shared, it may not be obvious or possible to determine who the original source of information is and if there may be a potential COI. Nutrition and dietetics professionals should consider COI disclosure when seeking information for treating or educating patients and clients, "friending" patients or clients, or discussing treatment with a patient or client on social media.[14]

Consequences of Failing to Disclose

While the attention to disclosing COIs appears to have originated in the field of medicine, the field of nutrition and dietetics is not exempt.[15] The disclosure of COIs is important to provide credibility to the profession among the vast public access to nutrition information and misinformation. COIs can take many different forms. For example, a personal COI can occur when an individual is involved in the hiring or direct supervision of a family member, while a professional COI can occur when an individual endorses a product or service using a work affiliation. Personal COIs can also embody financial COIs, which may be the most common—and most concerning—type. This could include accepting monetary compensation for a service or to endorse a product. For example, a dietetics manager could accept an undisclosed amount of money to evaluate a new formula for nutrition services and then, in return, adopt the use of that formula for his or her hospital worksite. Often, to avoid this, employers will have clear guidance on these types of practices and prohibit receipt of monetary gifts or goods, or at minimum, limit the amounts to a specified annual dollar amount.

Many organizations and worksites have policies in place to continually monitor potential COIs. Failing to disclose a conflict of interest can call a professional's credibility into question because it may indicate that someone is being untruthful, is hiding something, or to a lesser extent, may not realize that a COI even exists. Worse, failing to disclose a COI could cause an individual to lose his or her job. This is different from a situation when COI disclosures are required but then are not clearly cited or published, such as by an editor within a journal publication of a research study where a COI exists. Regardless, to avoid potential negative consequences, nutrition professionals should consider all potential COIs and clearly disclose them up front.

How Do You Identify A Questionable Source?

The 2018 Edelman Trust Barometer Global Report conducted a poll of more than 33,000 people in 28 countries. Its results indicated that the average trust in search engines and social media platforms decreased in 21 of the 28 countries studied in the past year. The steepest decline, reported from 2017 to 2018, was in the United States, with an 11% decline in trust for these platforms vs a range of 1% to 8% decline in the other 20 countries.[16]

Globally, there was uncertainty over legitimate vs false information (referred to as "fake news" in the survey). The survey found 63% agreed that "the average person does not know how to tell good journalism from rumor or falsehoods" and 59% agreed that "it is becoming harder to tell if a piece of news was produced by a respected media organization."[17]

The Edelman report indicated that globally, 65% of the public received news through such platforms as search engines and social media.[16] The internet allows almost anyone to be an instant news source, making it even more difficult to identify trustworthy sources. Following are some ways to help filter fact from fiction.

Media and Social Media Can Be Credible—or Questionable

Researchers at Massachusetts Institute of Technology's Media Lab analyzed some 126,000 stories passed along via Twitter more than 4.5 million times by about 3 million people from 2006 to 2017. The researchers checked whether the stories were true or false using information from six independent fact-checking organizations that exhibited 95% to 98% agreement on the classifications of the stories as true or false.[17]

Chapter 29 has more on social media disclosure.

> ## "Falsehood flies, and the Truth comes limping after it."
> —JONATHAN SWIFT

The study found that falsehoods spread faster, farther, deeper, and more broadly than the truth. False news tended to be more novel than the truth, suggesting people were more likely to spread unusual news.

Humans also appeared to be responsible for the speed of its spread. Researchers looked at internet robots (bots), programs that run automated tasks over the internet. For example, search engines such as Google and Bing use bots to collect information in their results pages. Though bots have a neutral origin, they also can be used to cause problems, such as creating spam. However, one surprising finding of the study was that bots accelerated the spread of true and false news at the same rate—indicating that the faster spread of false news was from humans.

In general, false news was 70% more likely to be retweeted than the truth. In a study by computer scientists at Columbia University and the French National Institute, 59% of the links on Twitter are shared without being read by the people sharing them.[18]

Clues to Question a Source

The Edelman report found that 66% of those interviewed agreed news organizations were more concerned with attracting a big audience than with their reporting, 65% agreed accuracy was sacrificed to be the first to break a story, and 59% agreed news was overly focused on supporting an ideology rather than informing the public.[16] Here are some clues to help gauge the accuracy of breaking and other news.

Does the headline appear to be clickbait or sharebait? Beware of headlines, especially those on the internet, that may be designed to make people want to click on them or—possibly without even clicking on them—share them. If a claim sounds too good (or too bad) to be true, it probably is. Common claims such as rapid weight loss or dire consequences if a certain food is eaten are examples.

Is the author selling something? Check what type of testing was done to assure the information or product is safe and does what the claims promote. Also, what are the author's qualifications for being knowledgeable in this area? Further guidelines on identifying whether a claim has been tested by a rigorous scientific method and examining the credentials of the author are given later in this chapter.

Do the facts appear to be "cherry-picked"? Even a reference from a credible source may not give the total story or the latest information. Are only references with positive outcomes given? Or, are only supportive facts from a reference given? Are they slanted to give a positive spin on a topic?

Is fear-based marketing used? This can be a red flag to dig deeper into the information or the product being sold. While fear has been shown to influence consumer behavior by persuading people to do certain things to avoid a negative outcome, research by Dunn and Hoegg[19] demonstrated fear also can influence consumers to like a brand. Their study found that consumers who experienced fear while watching a scary film felt a greater affiliation with a soft drink brand they consumed during the movie than those watching films evoking happiness, sadness, or excitement. The researchers explained that fear can create the motivation to form an attachment to something, even a soft drink, that might relieve that negative state. The takeaway: Look beyond a fearful situation or marketing claim and assess whether being influenced by fear leads to the best outcome.

Correlation Doesn't Equal Causation

In the 1950s, several experts believed ice cream caused polio because polio cases and ice cream consumption both peaked during the summer.[20] While there was a correlation between these two occurrences, one didn't cause the other. A correlation between two variables occurs when one variable either increases or decreases proportionally in relation to changes in the other variable. A correlation may aid in identifying causes for further investigation, but it can't determine with certainty the cause for something. What was the real cause of polio? The polio virus is more likely to cause disease in the warmer summer months.

Another common example of correlation is when people selling an item use anecdotal evidence based on only their personal experience or other limited experience. For example, it is common to hear, "I (People) lost weight after I (they) began eating _____ or stopped eating _____." But, the specific food may not have caused the weight loss; rather, eating fewer calories did.

To help determine a possible cause rather than a correlation—whenever it is possible to do so—researchers compare the results of one group whose members receive a certain treatment to those of a control group whose members aren't given the treatment. Neither group knows which treatment they are receiving. The gold standard in controlled studies is a randomized controlled trial, a double-blind study where the subjects are randomly assigned to groups and neither the subjects nor the researchers know which group is receiving the treatment until the results have been analyzed. Another benchmark of credibility is whether the results have been published in a peer-reviewed scientific journal. A peer-reviewed article has been examined by experts with credentials in the article's subject matter—that is, the author's peers—to determine whether the article represents a sound piece of research.

The levels of evidence illustrated in the evidence-based medicine pyramid provide a way to visualize the quality and quantity of evidence available on a topic (see Figure 5.2). The highest and least common levels of evidence are at the top of the pyramid. Filtered information resources appraise the quality of studies and often include recommendations for practice. For unfiltered information, the reader must take on the role of reviewing the validity and reliability of the information.[21]

For more on research design and methodology, as well as responsible research reporting, see Chapter 6.

To learn how to translate research to the public, refer to Chapter 7.

To learn about writing articles for peer-reviewed publications, see Chapter 41.

FIGURE 5.2 **Levels of evidence pyramid**

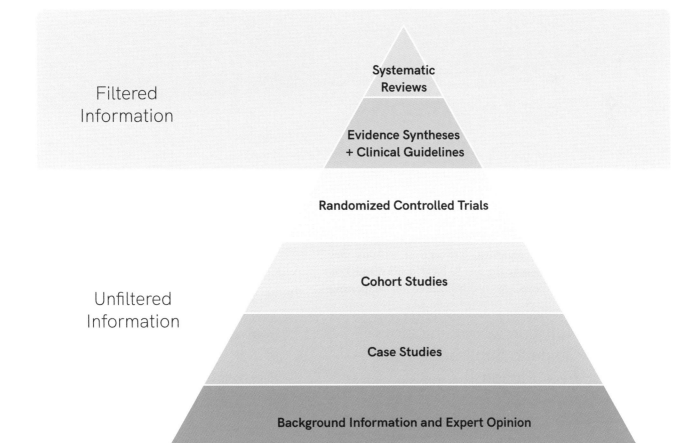

Filtered Information

Systematic Reviews

Evidence Syntheses + Clinical Guidelines

Randomized Controlled Trials

Unfiltered Information

Cohort Studies

Case Studies

Background Information and Expert Opinion

Adapted with permission from Tufts University. Community Health 30. Tufts University Library website. Updated February 21, 2019. Accessed July 30, 2019. https://researchguides.library.tufts.edu/c.php?g=454103&p=3102416[22]

Appropriate Credentials Don't Guarantee Ethics

Members of the Academy of Nutrition and Dietetics must complete one of several approved educational experiences in ethics every 5 years to maintain their credentials as RDNs. Here are several examples of less-than-ethical information given by health professionals who appear to be believable[23]:

- A health professional with expertise in one area gives advice in another area outside his or her area of training. Example: A physician with no or limited training in nutrition advocates specific nutrition practices even when there is no current body of evidence to support them.
- People trained in health and nutrition make statements based more on ideology than on scientific facts and surround certain types of foods with a "health halo." Example: A food is described as more nutritious because of the way it is grown even when there is no or limited research base to support the claim.
- Trained scientists find only a correlation in their research yet give a public health recommendation to avoid a certain food. Example: A recommendation is made to give up a certain food when people eating the food exhibit more of a certain characteristic—such as overweight or obesity—than those who don't eat the food. This recommendation is made without examining other factors that might have caused these results, such as total caloric intake. Perhaps people who ate that food were more likely to eat other higher-calorie foods. Making a recommendation to avoid a food would be premature without a randomized controlled trial that factored in other possible variables.

Nutrition Communicators' Guide to Separating Fact from Fiction

Before sharing a social media post, giving a talk, writing an article, or engaging in a new promoted practice, check it through the fact-vs-fiction filters in the Words of Experience box. These summarize the pointers given in the How Do You Identify a Questionable Source? section of this chapter.

Fact-vs-Fiction Filters for Information Sources

by Alice Henneman, MS, RDN

Filter 1. Did you read the complete social media post and article it refers to before sharing it? An enticing headline may be hiding less-than-accurate information. Read the full article and refer to the actual published studies if they are referred to in it.

Filter 2. Does a claim sound too good or too bad to be true?

Filter 3. Is the author selling something? Check the author's credentials and science-based proof in support of what is being sold.

Filter 4. Do the facts appear to be cherry-picked, slanted, or from older research that may no longer be valid?

Filter 5. Is the research conclusion founded on correlation or causation?

Filter 6. Is a recommendation based on a limited number of individual, personal, anecdotal experiences?

Filter 7. Does the person's degree or expertise qualify that person to offer advice in that given area?

Filter 8. Is the advice slanted toward a "health halo" around a topic, or is there science-based information to back up a claim?

Filter 9. Is the recommendation based on limited research before sufficient research is conducted to provide a definitive conclusion?

Filter 10. Did the experimental design eliminate other possible causes?

How Can Nutrition Professionals Teach Consumers to Discern the Difference?

Credentialed food and nutrition practitioners are uniquely positioned to teach consumers to discern the difference between credible and questionable nutrition information. In fact, this may be one of the greatest responsibilities that RDNs have and could be a motivating factor for a nutrition professional to pursue a career path in nutrition communications.

The weight loss industry is a $66 billion industry,[24] and these companies often invest in advertising to sell their weight loss products and solutions. Sometimes, these products and solutions are not evidence-based or are misleading. This presents an opportunity for credentialed food and nutrition practitioners to debunk myths, help prevent consumers from wasting their money on gimmicks and fads, and protect the public from potentially harmful or life-threatening weight loss "solutions."

Examine the Website

One key way nutrition professionals can educate the public on how to discern the difference between credible and questionable nutrition information is to help them examine the website where the information is found. Consumers can consider these questions:

- Does the site URL end with *.gov*, *.org*, or *.edu*? These sites tend to have more credible information, although a *.com* site isn't necessarily questionable. It may require a higher level of scrutiny to be deemed credible.
- Is the site a large, well-run site or associated with a larger business? For example, is it a major news network site or a questionable news site?
- If it's a blog, is it maintained by credentialed and appropriately trained health care professionals, such as by an RDN?
- What is the site's or author's motive and purpose? Are they trying to sell something? Is the information full of ads or other clickbait?

Examine the Author

Once a consumer has assessed the trustworthiness of the website, the next step is to assess the credibility of the author.

Consumers can consider these questions:

- What are the author's credentials? Do the credentials align with the topic of the article? For example, nutrition experts will almost always have the credentials RD (registered dietitian) or RDN.
- What is the author's title? Does the author even have a title? A title indicates a person's job function, such as department manager, clinic supervisor, and so on.
- Is the article sponsored or paid for by a partner organization?
- What is the author's background? Is the author an educated expert or a self-proclaimed expert? For example, someone who lost 20 pounds may claim to be able to help others do the same, but everyone is different, and personal experiences do not make qualified experts. Just because a person had heart surgery doesn't mean that person can perform it!
- Is the author selling something or being paid to promote a product or service? While this does not necessarily discredit the message, it is important to be aware of the author's motivation for sharing information. Credible authors will disclose this information, such as noting a service they are selling, a paid relationship they have with a company whose product they are promoting, or affiliate links to other services or products. This can include:

    - diet plans or diets that include meal delivery;
    - supplements, such as vitamins, powders, and protein shakes;
    - books, including cookbooks and diet books;
    - consultations; and
    - endorsements for specific products (such as foods, beverages, or supplements) or services.

Examine the Claims

When evaluating an article, consumers should learn to explore the claims the author makes. The fact-vs-fiction filters (see page 74) can be just as useful to consumers as to professionals. Also, encourage clients to question material and do a bit of simple internet research on the author and topic before accepting the information as fact.

Share the list of red flags of junk science from the Bellows and Moore,[5] shown in Figure 5.3, with clients and followers to help them identify misleading claims and false information.

Increased access to various forms of technology, as well as increased interest in and availability of nutrition and health information, may make it difficult for consumers to identify and interpret accurate nutrition information, whether it is in online articles, books, talk shows, podcasts, or videos. Therefore, it is even more important that RDNs position themselves as credible and reliable sources of nutrition information and work to communicate and provide these resources and recommended strategies to consumers. In doing so, RDNs need to ensure that they are utilizing credible sources themselves, following professional ethical guidelines, and clearly disclosing any potential conflicts of interest that may impact their ability to objectively review, interpret, and communicate nutrition information to various audiences. Further, RDNs should use credible tools and best practices in educating consumers on how to evaluate nutrition information and its sources.

FIGURE 5.3 **10 red flags of junk science**[a]

Claims that sound too good to be true

Lists of "good" and "bad" foods

Dire warnings of danger from a single product or regimen

Dramatic statements that are refuted by reputable scientific organizations

Recommendations that promise a quick fix

Non-science-based testimonials supporting the product, often from celebrities or highly satisfied customers

Stating that research is "currently underway," indicating that there is no current research

Recommendations based on a single study

Simplistic conclusions drawn from a complex study

"Spinning" information from another product to match the producer's claims

[a] Adapted from reference 5.

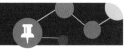
Nutrition Communicators Identify Credible Sources

1 Finding a credible source is about asking the right questions. It takes time to collect information and evaluate whether it is credible, beginning with five questions: Who? What? Why? When? How? The answers can reveal who the communicator is, what the agenda may be, and how information is presented, helping to clarify whether or not the source is credible.

2 Professional organizations that promote accurate news and sound science are credible. Clues to credibility can be found in what is shared and how it is shared. This includes content, context, and transparency.

3 The practice of full disclosure related to conflicts of interest has become increasingly important as the nonprofessionals and the scientific community have begun to further scrutinize research, media reporting, and corresponding nutrition content.

4 With the advent of the internet, anyone can now be an instant news source, making it even more difficult to identify trustworthy sources. Unfortunately, falsehoods spread faster, farther, deeper, and more broadly than the truth. Therefore, before anyone, professional and public alike, purchases something, shares a social media post, gives a talk, writes an article, or engages in a new promoted practice, he or she should consult the fact-vs-fiction filters. See the Words of Experience box on page 74 for a review of these filters.

5 Credentialed food and nutrition practitioners are uniquely positioned to teach consumers to discern the difference between credible and questionable nutrition information. In fact, this is perhaps one of the greatest responsibilities that RDNs have and could be a motivating factor for nutrition professionals to pursue a career path in nutrition communications.

RESOURCES

Identifying fraud and misleading claims: http://extension.colostate.edu/docs/pubs/foodnut/09350.pdf

Evaluating health information: www.ucsfhealth.org/education/evaluating_health_information

How to evaluate health information on the internet: https://ods.od.nih.gov/Health_Information/How_To_Evaluate_Health_Information_on_the_Internet_Questions_and_Answers.aspx

Communicating nutrition research: www.todaysdietitian.com/newarchives/0518p38.shtml

Finding and evaluating online resources: https://nccih.nih.gov/health/webresources

REFERENCES

1. Mitchell A, Shearer E, Gottfried J, Barthel M. Pathways to news. Pew Research Center website. Published 2016. Accessed January 30, 2019. www.journalism.org/2016/07/07/pathways-to-news

2. Consumers are confused about food and health. Food Executive website. Published 2018. Accessed January 30, 2019. www.foodexecutive.it/en/health-and-wellness/2910-consumers-are-confused.html

3. SPJ code of ethics. Society of Professional Journalists website. Accessed April 19, 2018. www.spj.org/ethicscode.asp

4. Rosenstiel T. Six questions that will tell you what media to trust. American Press Institute website. Accessed April 19, 2018. www.americanpressinstitute.org/publications/six-critical-questions-can-use-evaluate-media-content

5. Bellows L, Moore R. Nutrition misinformation: how to identify fraud and misleading claims. Colorado State University Extension website. Published 2013. Accessed January 30, 2019. http://extension.colostate.edu/topic-areas/nutrition-food-safety-health/nutrition-misinformation-how-to-identify-fraud-and-misleading-claims-9-350

6. Professional journalism organizations. American Media Institute website. Accessed April 19, 2018. https://americanmediainstitute.com/journalism-resources/professional-journalism-organizations

7. Merriam-Webster. Conflict of interest. Accessed April 12, 2018. www.merriam-webster.com/dictionary/conflict_of_interest

8. CDC director resigns over financial conflicts of interest. *US News & World Report*. January 31, 2018. Accessed April 12, 2018. www.usnews.com/news/news/articles/2018-01-31/cdc-director-resigns-over-financial-conflicts

9. Academy of Nutrition and Dietetics Commission on Dietetic Registration. Code of ethics for the nutrition and dietetics profession. 2018. Eatright website. Accessed June 27, 2018. www.eatrightpro.org/-/media/eatrightpro-files/career/code-of-ethics/codeofethicsdieteticsresources.pdf

10. Nestle M. Food company sponsorship of nutrition research and professional activities: a conflict of interest? *Public Health Nutr.* 2001;4(5):1015-1022.

11. Lesser LI, Ebbeling CB, Goozner M, Wypij D, Ludwig DS. Relationship between funding source and conclusion among nutrition-related scientific articles. *PLoS Med.* 2007;4(1):e5. doi:10.1371/journal.pmed.0040005

12. Chartres N, Fabbri A, Bero LA. Association of industry sponsorship with outcomes of nutrition studies: a systematic review and meta-analysis. *JAMA Intern Med.* 2016;176(12):1769-1777. doi:10.1001/jamainternmed.2016.6721

13. Myers EF, Parrott JS, Cummins DS, Splett P. Funding source and research report quality in nutrition practice-related research. Gluud LL, ed. *PLoS ONE.* 2011;6(12):e28437. doi:10.1371/journal.pone.0028437

14. Decamp M. Physicians, social media, and conflict of interest. *J Gen Intern Med.* 2013;28(2):299-303. doi:10.1007/s11606-012-2251-x

15. Lucas M. Conflicts of interest in nutritional sciences: the forgotten bias in meta-analysis. *World J of Methodol.* 2015;5(4):175-178. doi:10.5662/wjm.v5.i4.175

16. 2018 Edelman trust barometer: the employer advantage. Published January 2018. Edelman Holdings website. Accessed September 20, 2018. www.edelman.com/sites/g/files/aatuss191/files/2018-10/Edelman_Trust_Barometer_Employee_Experience_2018_0.pdf

17. Vosoughi S, Roy D, Aral S. The spread of true and false news online. *Science.* 2018;359(6380): 1146-1151. Accessed September 22, 2018. http://science.sciencemag.org/node/706797.full

18. Gabielkov M, Ramachandran A, Chaintreau A, Arnaud Legout A. Social clicks: what and who gets read on Twitter? Paper presented at ACM SIGMETRICS/IFIP, June 2016; Antibes Juan-les-Pins, France. Accessed September 22, 2018. https://hal.inria.fr/hal-01281190/document

19. Dunn L, Hoegg JA. The impact of fear on emotional brand attachment. *J Consumer Res.* 2014;41(1):152-168. doi:10.1086/675377

20. FreakonomicsVideos. Correlation vs. causality: freakonomics movie. YouTube. Published August 2011. Accessed September 22, 2018. https://youtu.be/lbODqslc4Tg

21. Evidence-based practice research: levels of evidence pyramid. Walden University Library website. Accessed September 22, 2018. https://academicguides.waldenu.edu/healthevidence/evidencepyramid

22. Tufts University. Community Health 30. Tufts University Library website. Updated February 21, 2019. Accessed July 30 2019. https://researchguides.library.tufts.edu/c.php?g=454103&p=3102416

23. Chin, ML. Going behind the headlines: when food and facts collide. Calorie Control Council website. Published November 2015. Accessed September 21, 2018. https://caloriecontrol.org/going-beyond-the-headlines

24. U.S. weight loss market worth $66 billion: commercial chains pace strong growth in 2017. MarketResearch website. Accessed April 2018. www.prnewswire.com/news-releases/us-weight-loss-market-worth-66-billion-300573968.html

Nutrition Communicators Read and Interpret Research

Virginia C. Stage, PhD, RDN
and L. Suzanne Goodell, PhD, RDN

"Becoming skilled at critically evaluating scientific literature and staying current with evidence-based research related to practice are critical habits for career success."

> "Good, sound research projects begin with straightforward, uncomplicated thoughts that are easy to read and understand." —JOHN W. CRESWELL

Introduction

Research serves as a foundation for nutrition and dietetics.[1] Research enables discoveries that benefit the profession through the identification of emerging or existing health problems, evaluation of new interventions for acute and chronic diseases, and provision of evidence for the development of new policies, among other things.[2]

A registered dietitian nutritionist (RDN) has the opportunity to be recognized as *the* nutrition expert. To achieve this, an RDN must be viewed as the primary communicator of up-to-date, evidence-based nutrition and dietetic-focused research to the lay public.[3] This responsibility is harder than it seems; it requires practitioners to be skilled at critically reviewing scientific literature and translating the findings accurately in an understandable way for patients, clients, and other audiences.

This chapter answers three questions:

- What are the basic research principles nutrition communicators need to understand?
- What are the best strategies to use for reading and understanding scientific research?
- How can nutrition and dietetics professionals interpret nutrition research accurately?

Becoming skilled at critically evaluating scientific literature and staying current with evidence-based research related to practice are critical habits for career success. The purpose of this chapter is to provide information important for understanding basic research concepts, research terminology (see the Terms to Know list below), and strategies for how to critically review a scientific research article.

⌖ TERMS TO KNOW

Abstract	A short summary of a scientific research article, typically presented in a single paragraph.
Analytical research design	A type of quantitative research study that seeks to test a hypothesis related to the research problem and attempts to answer *why* and *how*. Examples of analytic research designs include experimental studies (randomized controlled trials and quasi-experimental studies) and observational studies (cohort, case-control, and cross-sectional).
Analyzing data	The process of "taking data apart" to examine individual responses, then "putting it back together" to summarize responses from participants. Researchers will typically represent data in tables and graphs, while using text to explain answers to research questions.

Callout	A letter, word, number, or symbol identifying a table or graph. A callout draws the reader's attention to a table or graph presented in an article and indicates when the reader should reference a table or graph.
Case report	A type of quantitative research study that reports the characteristics of a single person in a specific place and time related to a specific disease or condition. This type of study is often used to identify patterns of a disease or condition.
Case series	A type of quantitative research study that reports the characteristics of more than one person in a specific place and time related to a specific disease or condition. This type of study is often used to identify patterns of a disease or condition.
Case study	A type of qualitative research that focuses on a specific program, event, or activity involving an individual.
Causal inference	The practice of drawing a cause-and-effect conclusion about two or more variables.
Code	A label applied to qualitative data by a researcher during data analysis.
Conclusion	The part of a scientific article that ends the discussion. This section may also be called "Implications" or "Application."
Confounding factor	A variable in a research study that is hard to measure or difficult to separate from the effects of other measured variables in the study.
Cross-sectional study	A type of quantitative research study that only collects data at one point in time.
Data analysis	*See* analyzing data.
Data collection	The process of collecting data that involves identifying and selecting individuals who will be included in the study, obtaining permission to collect data from individuals, and finally, actually collecting the data.
Dependent variable	The measured characteristic or attribute of participants that is considered the outcome being studied.
Descriptive research design	A type of quantitative research study that collects data at one point in time; examples include case reports, case series, and cross-sectional studies.
Discussion	The part of a scientific article that describes the key findings of a scientific study and compares, contrasts, and thoroughly discusses new study findings in the context of previously published research on the same topic.
Evaluating research	Occurs after the report has been completed and involves the critical analysis of the research by peer or public review.
Experimental research design	A quantitative research design typically used to compare the effectiveness of two or more treatments, interventions, or practices. This research design is considered the gold standard of quantitative research because it uses the practice of random assignment (a procedure where study participants are randomly assigned to a treatment or intervention group or to a control group).
Focus groups	A qualitative data collection method that uses group interviews led by a moderator. The goal of a focus group is to collect data about a small group of people with characteristics relevant to the research question.
Graph	A method of communicating research findings of a scientific research study. A graph, also known as a figure, is used when a visual presentation of data is more effective than words to convey a result.

Continues ▶

Grounded theory	A type of qualitative research design that seeks to understand a process, action, or interaction among a group of participants. A grounded theory study typically results in the presentation of a theoretical model.
Hypothesis	The researcher's prediction about the outcome of each research question.
Independent variable	The characteristic or attribute of the participant that influences the dependent variable.
Independent *t* test	*See t* **test**.
Introduction	The part of a scientific article that provides background information to help readers better understand the context of the article's methods and results. Generally, this section also describes the study population, location, and time frame.
Instruments or instrumentation	Tools for measuring, observing, and documenting quantitative data.
Interview guide	A method used to collect data in qualitative or mixed methods research designs. In one-on-one interviews, an interviewer asks one participant a series of open-ended questions about the research question, using an interview guide. The goal of the interview is for the participant to share details and examples about the subject being studied.
Interview	A qualitative data collection method that involves meeting one-on-one with study participants to gather information.
Literature review	A document that is written to summarize and synthesize scientific research on a specific topic. Strong reviews typically discuss what is known and what is not known about a specific topic.
Mean	A common statistic reported in quantitative research studies to describe the average value of responses to a single question.
Methods	The part of a scientific article that describes how the researchers conducted a study. Methods should describe the tools, techniques, and processes used by researchers.
Mixed methods	The practice of using a combination of qualitative and quantitative research methods to answer a research question.
Model	A graphical representation used in qualitative research to convey a specific concept or set of constructs. A model should help the reader better understand the research problem being studied.
Moderator	A trained individual who conducts a focus group. Focus groups are similar to one-on-one interviews in that a moderator asks a group of participants a series of open-ended questions about the research question, using a moderator guide.
Moderator guide	A protocol used by qualitative researchers when conducting a focus group.
Original research	A research article written by researchers who collected and analyzed data. Also known as *primary research*.
Paired *t* test	*See t* **test**.
Participant	An individual who has consented to participate in a research study. Data are collected from participants in order to answer the research question(s). Also known as a *subject*.
Pearson's correlation coefficient	A type of statistic that is used when researchers are exploring the association between two variables.

Peer-reviewed journal	A type of journal that contains scientific research articles that have been reviewed by people with credentials in the article's field of study prior to publication. Also known as a *refereed journal*.
Phenomenology	The study of objective experiences. Also known as a *phenomenological approach*; a type of qualitative research that seeks to understand the commonalities of a lived experience among a group of individuals.
P value	Also known as a *probability value*; used to determine whether the results observed are likely to reflect real differences between the groups being studied (ie, intervention vs control).
Quasi-experimental research design	Research designs that are experimental in nature but lack randomization or a control group.
Reporting research	The construction of a written report that communicates the findings of the research study, including its strengths and weaknesses, and that can be shared with the public.
Research design	Specific procedures used by researchers to collect, analyze, and report research in quantitative and qualitative research studies.
Research problem	A description of the issue, controversy, or concern being studied by the researcher. A research problem often can be connected to a specific gap in knowledge or a dilemma that needs to be addressed.
Research process	The steps a researcher follows when conducting quantitative and qualitative research.
Research purpose	A statement that clearly communicates the major focus or intent of a research study.
Research question	A specific question a researcher seeks to answer through the research process.
Results	The part of a scientific article that provides a detailed overview of the data actually generated by the study. The results section should not interpret the data.
Rich description	A term often used in qualitative research to describe presentation of the data that highlights the multifaceted complexities of the people, places, things, and situations being studied.
Saturation	The most common method qualitative researchers use to determine sample size. Saturation can be defined as learning nothing new after an additional round of collected data is analyzed.
Secondary research	A research article written by researchers who analyzed data that had already been collected.
Setting	The location where a study took place.
Significance level	A specific value set by researchers at the beginning of a study. The level represents the probability of rejecting the null hypothesis given that it is true. Significance levels of .05 or .01 (particularly in clinical studies) are common. For example, .05 indicates there is a 5% risk of concluding a difference exists when there is no actual difference.
Standard deviation	A common statistic reported in quantitative research studies. A standard deviation is often paired with the mean to show how the variables are distributed around the mean.
Statistics	Mathematical procedures used to analyze data in a quantitative study.
Structured abstract	A type of abstract that uses specific subheadings, like "Objectives," "Methods," "Results," and "Conclusion."
Table	A method of communicating research findings of a scientific research study. A table organizes and presents statistical results that are not easily listed in the text.

Continues ▸

Tertiary research	Scientific research that combines original and secondary sources to draw an overarching conclusion about the research problem.
Thematic analysis	A type of qualitative analysis that focuses on organizing key ideas that emerge from single or multiple forms of collected data.
Theme	A theme is a description of bigger trend(s) found within coded data in a qualitative study.
Theory	A set of ideas that attempt to explain the research problem.
Transcript	Verbatim, or word-for-word, documentation of what was said in an interview or focus group.
Trustworthiness	The method qualitative researchers use to express the quality of their research.
t test	A type of statistic used when researchers are exploring the differences between two groups. An independent *t* test is used when the two groups of individuals being compared are different (eg, comparing nutrition knowledge between two different classes). A paired *t* test is used when the two groups of individuals are the same or are related (eg, comparing nutrition knowledge at the beginning and end of a class).
Unstructured abstract	An abstract type that follows the same outline as a structured abstract (eg, objectives, methods, results, conclusion) but does not list specific subheadings.
Variable	A characteristic or attribute of individuals in a research study. To qualify as a variable, the characteristic or attribute must vary among participants and be measurable.

What Are the Basic Research Principles Nutrition Communicators Need to Understand?

Even if they are not nutrition researchers, it is likely that practitioners have conducted research, even if only on a personal level. Think about making a big decision, like deciding which college or university to attend for undergraduate studies. A large amount of information about the institutions would be collected first to help make the decision. Did the university offer degree programs of interest? Where was the university located? What was campus culture like? How much was tuition, and did the institution offer financial assistance? Determining answers to these questions likely involved a variety of resources, including the university's website, discussions with an admissions counselor,

and maybe even a visit to each campus as a way to gather more direct information about what a student's experience would be like. Throughout the process, advice was likely sought from parents, teachers, and maybe even other students who were attending or had attended the university.

Personal research can be similar to scientific research on a basic level. In the end, the decision about where to attend undergraduate studies was based on the information (data) collected. Ultimately, the problem-solving skills developed as a prospective student, for example, are generally the same skills that will be applied to understanding a research problem. Of course, the actual process of conducting scientific research is much more structured and rigorous in nature. Conducting formal research may not be an RDN's career choice, but it is nevertheless important to understand how to read scientific research in the field in order to effectively apply the information to practice. Before learning how to effectively read a scientific article, it is necessary to start with basic research concepts and the overall research process.[1,4,5]

The Research Process

The research process is a series of steps used to collect and analyze information about a specific topic (see Figure 6.1). At its most basic level, research consists of seven steps[6]:

1. Identifying a research problem
2. Reviewing the existing literature
3. Specifying the purpose for the research
4. Choosing a research design
5. Collecting data
6. Analyzing and interpreting data
7. Reporting and evaluating the outcomes of the research

This process is similar to the scientific method. Applied today, the research process includes a few more steps and is presented in a more cyclical fashion. The cyclical organization demonstrates how a good research study often generates more questions than it answers. Next we will briefly review each of the steps.

Step 1: Identify a research problem All research studies begin by identifying a research problem. This helps focus the study on a specific issue. Researchers should also justify the need for studying the problem by describing gaps in current understanding of the problem and the importance of filling in these gaps by conducting more research.

FIGURE 6.1 **The research process cycle**

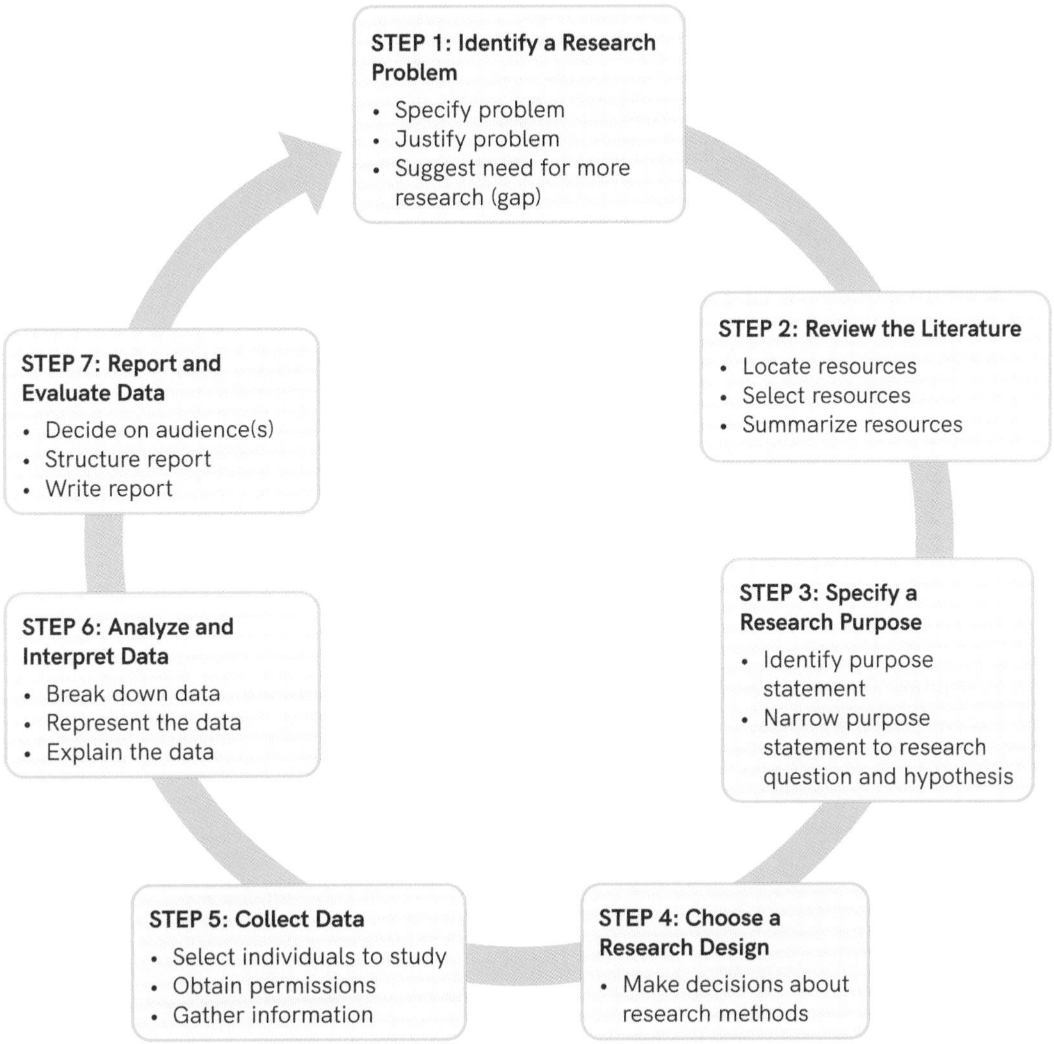

STEP 1: Identify a Research Problem
- Specify problem
- Justify problem
- Suggest need for more research (gap)

STEP 2: Review the Literature
- Locate resources
- Select resources
- Summarize resources

STEP 3: Specify a Research Purpose
- Identify purpose statement
- Narrow purpose statement to research question and hypothesis

STEP 4: Choose a Research Design
- Make decisions about research methods

STEP 5: Collect Data
- Select individuals to study
- Obtain permissions
- Gather information

STEP 6: Analyze and Interpret Data
- Break down data
- Represent the data
- Explain the data

STEP 7: Report and Evaluate Data
- Decide on audience(s)
- Structure report
- Write report

Adapted with permission from Creswell, JW., *Educational Research: Planning, Conducting, and Evaluating Quantitative and Qualitative Research*. Loose-Leaf Version. 5th ed. ©2015 Pearson Education, Inc.[6]

For example, Nansel and colleagues[7] conducted a study to investigate the impact of an educational intervention on the diet quality of children with type 1 diabetes who were also considered picky eaters. As an example, these researchers concisely described the research problem: "Children who are picky eaters typically demonstrate persistent food refusal and poor diet quality."

Step 2: Review the literature This step in the process requires the researcher to review the literature on the topic by locating books, peer-reviewed journals, government documents, and other indexed sources. The result of this process is a document called a literature review. Sources should be carefully selected and summarized in writing prior to beginning the research study. These types of summaries look similar to an abstract but put more emphasis on the study's methods and results. This step helps educate the researcher about current understanding on the topic and what research may still be needed to fill the gaps in knowledge.

For example, Nansel and colleagues[7] described family-based educational programs as an effective approach to reduce picky eating among children. However, they also described a lack of understanding around the influence picky eating behaviors may have on the success of an intervention. Put simply, their question was this: Will the impact of a family-based nutrition education program differ between picky and non-picky eaters?

Step 3: Specify a research purpose The third step requires the researcher to specify a research purpose, which is a single statement that clearly communicates the major focus or intent of a research study. Often the research purpose will be followed by an even more narrowed research question (a specific question a researcher seeks to answer through research) or hypotheses (a researcher's prediction about the outcome of each research question).

Step 4: Choose a research design Before researchers collect any data, they must make a series of decisions about how, when, where, and from whom they will collect data. Research designs provide researchers with specific procedures for data collection (step 5), analysis (step 6), and reporting (step 7) that will guide the overall research process. The research purposes, question(s), and hypotheses will also guide these decisions. More details about specific research designs in quantitative and qualitative research are in the next section of this chapter.

Step 5: Collect data The process of collecting data (commonly known as *data collection*) involves identifying and selecting individuals who will be included in the study, obtaining permission to collect data from them, and finally, actually collecting the data. The last step will vary greatly depending on the study's research objective.[6]

For example, a researcher might collect quantitative data by administering a standardized survey like the Child Feeding Questionnaire used by Nansel and colleagues,[7] or researchers could take a qualitative approach by conducting a series of in-depth individual interviews with the parents of picky and non-picky eaters.

Step 6: Analyze and interpret data During or immediately following data collection, the researcher will begin analyzing and interpreting the data. Analyzing and interpreting data involves taking data apart to examine individual responses, and putting it back together to summarize responses from participants. Researchers will typically represent data in tables and graphs, while using text to explain answers to research questions. The last step in the research process involves reporting and evaluating research.

Step 7: Report and evaluate data Research reporting involves the construction of a written report that communicates the findings of the research study, including its strengths and weaknesses, that can be shared with the public. Evaluating research occurs after the report has been completed and involves the critical analysis of the research by peer or public review.[6]

Qualitative vs Quantitative Research

Researchers can categorize their findings in several ways. They can categorize by methodology type—qualitative, quantitative, or mixed methodologies—using a combination of qualitative methods and quantitative methods to answer a research question (Figure 6.2). Understanding this type of categorization requires the researcher know how the data are collected and analyzed as well as how the results are reported.

FIGURE 6.2 The research process through quantitative and qualitative research

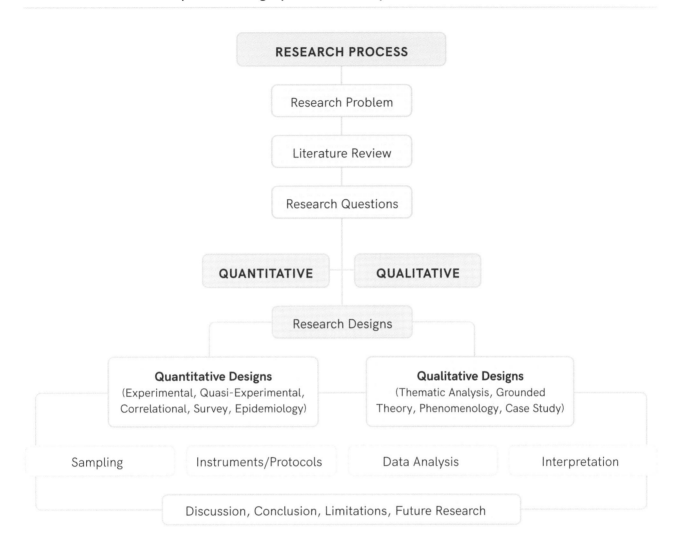

Adapted with permission from Creswell JW. *Educational Research: Planning, Conducting, and Evaluating Quantitative and Qualitative Research*. Loose-Leaf Version. 5th ed. ©2015 Pearson Education, Inc.[6]

Qualitative researchers traditionally approach data collection through open-ended questions; they focus on words, not numbers, and they report their findings with themes, models, or rich descriptions (a presentation of the data that highlights the multifaceted complexities of the people, places, things, and situations being studied). Qualitative research does not start with testing a research hypothesis; rather, it focuses on a broad research question.

In contrast, quantitative researchers typically approach data collection through questions that will lead to closed-ended or numerical data; they focus on numbers, reporting their findings with frequencies and statistics. While quantitative research may include a broad research question, the focus of the work is typically on testing hypotheses that the researchers generated before data were collected.

Less common are research articles that present both qualitative and quantitative research. It is likely that both methodologies will be described in less depth than if they were presented in separate articles. This is because scientific research articles typically have limits on space and length, and researchers must make critical decisions to provide the details most relevant to the research question. In these mixed methods articles, qualitative and quantitative research should complement each other.

For example, Perrin and colleagues used mixed methods to observe human milk–sharing communities on Facebook.[8] In this study, they quantified the number of interactions and types of interactions between Facebook users in milk-sharing groups. In part, they counted the number of times a mother asked for human milk for their child. To support the quantitative data, the researchers also qualitatively analyzed these interactions to describe the reasons the interactions occurred (eg, a mother was sick and couldn't produce milk). In this example, the qualitative research helped explain and support the quantitative research.

Common Qualitative Methodology and Terminology

The most common type of qualitative methodology found in nutrition research is thematic analysis. Other common types include grounded theory, phenomenology, and case studies. While each methodology has unique characteristics, some methods and techniques are used across all four methodologies.[9]

The two most common types of data collection methods in qualitative research are one-on-one interviews and focus groups. In one-on-one interviews, an interviewer asks one participant a series of open-ended questions about the research question, using an interview guide. The goal of the interview is for the participant to share details and examples about the subject being studied.[9]

For example, Dev and colleagues[10] assessed child-care providers' perceptions of their use of controlling feeding practices at mealtime. In the research article, the researchers described their use of interviews to ask child-care providers about their personal beliefs and habits. They were able to obtain rich descriptions about child-care feeding practices from their participants because they employed one-on-one interviews as their data collection method.

Focus groups are similar to one-on-one interviews in that a moderator asks a group of participants a series of open-ended questions about the research question, using a moderator guide. Like in an interview, the goal of the focus group is for participants to share as many details as possible about the subject being studied. The benefit of having multiple participants in a focus group is that they interact with one another through discussion that might provide the researcher with

more examples for each question. The types of questions asked in an interview or focus group are based on the qualitative methodology used (eg, thematic analysis, grounded theory, phenomenology) and the research question being studied.[11]

When interviews and focus groups are methods of data collection, the final data set typically includes a verbatim (word-for-word) transcript of what was said. Researchers often audiotape or videotape interviews and focus groups so that a transcriber can prepare a transcript later. Researchers read, reread, make notes on, and analyze transcripts to determine the findings of their study. Qualitative research articles often indicate that the authors coded the transcripts as part of the analytic process. This means the researchers read through their data and developed ways to label and organize participants' quotes. The use of codes (eg, labels) is analogous to the use of hashtags on social media. By labeling quotes from transcripts with codes, researchers can later search for quotes by code, just like a person could go to Instagram and search for photographs based on a hashtag.[11]

When qualitative researchers write articles about their work, they must distill their coded data into something meaningful and succinct. Traditionally, researchers present their qualitative findings using themes, theories, or models.[11] Whereas a code is a short label on part of the data, a theme is a description of bigger trends found within the coded data.

For example, Dev and colleagues[10] transformed their coded data into three categories (barriers, motivators, and facilitators), with each category representing three clear themes. The barrier themes included controlling feeding practices work, misconceptions, and fear of negative parental response. These themes are more complex than what would be found in a definition for a single code, and they answer the research question in a way that a code might not be able to do.

When trying to integrate qualitative research findings into one cohesive outcome, researchers may use theories to explain their work. Researchers may apply their findings to an already existing theory (eg, the theory of planned behavior), or they may create their own theory unique to the research question and target audience. Because theories are more complex than themes, researchers often create visual representations of theories to support their explanations and demonstrate processes or linkages. These visual representations of theories are called models. Of note, in some articles, researchers simply present themes, without integrating the themes to form a theory. Depending on the goal of the research, this is an acceptable and appropriate way to present findings. Only presenting themes does not inherently mean that the research is less rigorous, less complex, or less meaningful than research that is presented with a theory or model.[11]

Qualitative research differs from quantitative with regard to sampling. In quantitative research, sample size is typically determined before beginning the study through a power calculation or some other statistical justification. Data are then collected and analyzed. In contrast, in qualitative research, data are collected and analyzed simultaneously. After each round of data collection and analysis, qualitative researchers evaluate whether they have collected sufficient amounts (and depth) of data to cease data collection. The most common way qualitative researchers determine sample size is through saturation. Saturation can be defined as learning nothing new after an additional round of collected data is analyzed.[9] Therefore, when qualitative researchers write about sample size determination, they often discuss how they determined saturation.

The strength of scientific literature hinges on the quality of the research conducted and the ability of the researcher to communicate the findings clearly. Many words can be used to express the quality of research. In qualitative research, authors often express the quality of their research by describing how they strengthened the trustworthiness of their data and results. When researchers include details about trustworthiness in the description of their methods, they are trying to convey why they believe a reader should have confidence in their research work. They've taken steps to make sure their findings are true reflections of the answers to their research question in their target population.[9,11]

Common Quantitative Methodology and Terminology

Quantitative studies in the field of nutrition and dietetics fall in two basic categories: descriptive and analytic. A descriptive research study collects data at one point in time; examples include case reports, case series, and cross-sectional studies.[12] Often descriptive studies are useful for monitoring change over time, as with the National Health and Nutrition Examination Survey (NHANES), a cross-sectional survey administered by the Centers for Disease Control and Prevention (CDC) that is designed to assess the health and nutritional status of adults and children in the United States every 2 years.[13] Similar to a qualitative research study, a descriptive quantitative study is hypothesis-generating and seeks to answer *what*, *who*, *where*, and *when*. An analytic research study seeks to test a hypothesis related to the research problem and takes it a step further than a descriptive study by attempting to answer *why* and *how*. Examples of analytic research designs include experimental studies (randomized controlled trials and quasi-experimental studies) and observational studies (cohort, case-control, and cross-sectional studies).[12]

The strongest quantitative research design is the randomized controlled trial (RCT), an experimental design. Experimental research designs are typically used to compare the effectiveness of two or more treatments, interventions, or practices. This research design is considered the gold standard of quantitative research because it uses the practice of random assignment (a procedure where study participants are randomly assigned to a treatment or intervention group to a control group). Research designs that are experimental in nature but lack randomization or a control group are called quasi-experiments. While these designs do involve the use of a treatment or intervention, they are weaker in drawing causal inferences (that is, drawing cause-and-effect conclusions about two or more variables) from the study's findings compared to an RCT. It is possible other unmeasured variables may play a role in explaining the study's findings. The presence of these confounding factors (variables that are hard to measure) must be considered as potential limitations when interpreting the results.[12]

As with qualitative methodologies, each quantitative methodology has unique characteristics, but common methods and techniques are used across all designs. After identifying a research problem, researchers must consider what variables they will study. A variable is a characteristic or attribute of the individuals being studied. Variables must be measurable and must vary among participants.

For example, Nansel and colleagues[7] aimed to test whether pickiness influenced the ability of a nutrition education intervention to impact diet quality in youths with type 1 diabetes. Pickiness, age, and diet quality were important variables in the study because all are measurable and would likely vary between study participants. However, the presence of type 1 diabetes would not be considered a variable since it would not vary; as part of the criteria to participate, all participants would have type 1 diabetes.

The most important variables in any study are the dependent and independent variables. The independent variable is the characteristic or attribute of the participant that influences the dependent variable. The dependent variable is the measured characteristic or attribute of a participant that is considered the outcome being studied. The dependent variable is what is influenced by the independent variable(s).

Returning to the example, Nansel and colleagues[7] theorized that pickiness (the independent variable) would influence diet quality (the dependent variable). In this example, the intervention is also considered an independent (treatment) variable since it influenced the outcome (diet quality).

Researchers collect quantitative data using a variety of instruments to measure variables. Instruments are tools for measuring, observing, and documenting quantitative data. For example, researchers might use an instrument or survey (eg, a set of questions about nutrition knowledge or attitudes), they might gather observational data using a checklist (eg, observation of physical activity in preschool-aged children), or they might collect anthropometric (eg, height or weight) or clinical data (eg, hemoglobin A1c, blood pressure, lipid panel). The choice of data collection method depends largely on the type of data needed to answer the primary research question.

Once the data have been collected, the quantitative researcher will analyze the findings using mathematical procedures called statistics. As with qualitative analysis, quantitative data analysis requires the researcher to break down the larger data set into smaller parts to answer the primary research questions and hypotheses. Two simple statistical procedures involve comparing groups (eg, independent or paired *t* test), such as might be found in an experimental design, or relating scores, such as in a correlational design (eg, Pearson's correlation coefficient).[6]

Other common statistical terms in the data analysis or results section of a scientific research article are *mean*, *standard deviation*, and *P value*. A mean typically reports the average value of responses to a single question.

For example, Fildes and colleagues[13] reported the average age of the children in their study as 3.9 years. A standard deviation is often paired with the mean to show how the variables are distributed around the mean. In the example, children were an average age of 3.9 years with a standard deviation of 0.3 (reported as 3.9 ± 0.3). This finding means that children's ages ranged between 3.6 and 4.2 years, indicating some children were younger and some were older than the average of 3.9 years.

A *P* value, or probability value, is used to determine whether the results observed are likely to reflect real differences between the groups being studied (ie, intervention vs control).

For example, Fildes and colleagues[13] observed significantly higher changes in vegetable intake in a group of children whose parents were receiving mailed instructions on how to increase vegetable exposure for their preschool-aged children, compared to the control group of parents receiving no intervention. Researchers reported the *P* value as $P < .001$.

Most researchers agree that a *P* value of .05 or less is statistically significant.[12]

What Are the Best Strategies to Use for Reading and Understanding Scientific Research?

What qualifies as a research article? A research article is a paper written by researchers who either collected and analyzed data (original or primary research) or analyzed data that had already been collected (secondary research). While scientific research articles will describe other research that has been done on the topic in their introduction, their main focus is to present new analyses. Scientific literature can be read to keep up with current developments in the field or to find more information about a specific topic relevant to a particular practice. Either way, being able to understand a nutrition research article is an important skill set for RDNs to develop. RDNs must be able to critically review scientific literature and integrate the evidence into their daily practice. Key questions to ask of every scientific research article are these: "What are the practical implications of this research?" "What is the potential effect of these findings on my patients?" "How can I apply this knowledge to my setting or practice?"[3,15] It may also be useful to have conversations about "hot" research topics with researchers, scientists, and other health professionals within the field of nutrition to gain additional perspective.

Scientific research articles are the best source of evidence-based, rigorously evaluated information to inform practice.[1] Most scientific articles include the following basic sections: abstract; introduction and background; methods; results; and discussion and conclusion. Some scientific journals may also include an application or implication section to allow authors to discuss how findings can be applied in practice. Using the organization provided by each of these sections, authors will typically provide background on the work that has been accomplished in the area, justify why the topic of the current study is important, describe the methods used, present the results, and provide a discussion of the findings and limitations of the study.[16] The type of information generally included in each section is discussed next. Also see Box 6.1 on page 94 for a quick overview on common information included in each section of most scientific articles.

Abstract

The abstract is an excellent starting point for beginning to critically read and understand a scientific research article. It is a short summary of the article, typically presented in a single paragraph. Think of the abstract as a type of advertisement for the article. A strong abstract will grab a reader's attention and encourage further reading. Good abstracts are written in an accurate, comprehensive, and compelling manner. Since the role of an abstract is to summarize, they are generally very short. Most journals limit abstracts to 150 to 250 words. Two types of abstracts are common in nutrition research: structured abstracts and unstructured abstracts. A structured abstract uses specific subheadings, like Objectives, Methods, Results, and Conclusion. An unstructured abstract usually follows the same outline but does not list specific subheadings.[2]

Introduction and Background

The purpose of the introduction in a scientific article is to provide background information to help readers better understand the context of the article's methods and results. Generally, this section also describes the study population, location, and time frame. Depending on the type of article and field of study, the length of the introduction will vary. For example, a research brief published in the *Journal of the Academy of Nutrition and Dietetics* may have a shorter introduction than a research paper. Introduction sections should include a discussion of prior studies and justify why the new study is novel and needed. If these areas are not addressed in the introduction, check the discussion section instead. Most introduction sections will also highlight keywords or terminology important to the study; however, some papers may also address these words in the methods.

Regardless of format and length, the introduction should always end by stating the importance or significance of the study and the specific objectives or hypotheses addressed in the article.[2] When stating a research question and related hypotheses, some authors will predict what they think they will find. For example, in the article "Sugar Restriction Leads to Increased Ad Libitum Sugar Intake by Overweight Adolescents in an Experimental Test Meal Setting,"[17] the authors hypothesized that "participants would consume a greater amount of ad libitum sugar in the sugar restricted condition than in the exposure condition."

However, in some articles the authors simply state the purpose or the general question they seek to answer. This approach is also common in qualitative research studies, since qualitative research is hypothesis-generating (the findings help inform new hypotheses) rather than hypothesis-driven. Regardless of the approach used, the research question should be clearly stated and answered in the results section later in the article.[16]

Methods and Data Analysis

A methods section describes how the researchers conducted the study. Strong methods sections provide enough detail to allow other researchers to duplicate the study. For this reason, the methods section can be the most difficult to follow. To make it easier to understand, think of the methods as consisting of five main parts: study design, subjects, setting, intervention or instrumentation, and data analysis. The methods section should begin by clearly communicating the study design, subjects (ie, the study population), and setting (ie, the location and time frame) used in the study. If study population, location, and time frame were not addressed in the introduction, they should appear here. For example, in an experimental study, the methods section should describe both the experimental and the control groups. In a survey study, the methods section should discuss the survey instrument used and, if applicable, details on the development of the survey and the steps taken to ensure the tool was a valid method of assessment for the population being studied.[2] In original studies, the methods section should include detailed information about the population sample, how participants were recruited, and any relevant inclusion and exclusion criteria (ie, reasons why participants were eligible or not eligible to take part in the study).

Details related to the study's intervention or instrumentation, including how data were collected, should also be described. Depending on the study design, this might include a description of the intervention (eg, a nutrition education program), survey or interview techniques, specific laboratory methods, measurement and assessment tools, or physical assessments (eg, anthropometrics like height and weight).

For example, if the authors said they measured the nutrition knowledge of fourth-grade children attending public schools in eastern Tennessee, they should describe the measure in detail. What content was assessed (eg, knowledge of food groups vs specific nutrients and their function in the body)? Was the tool used previously validated for use in fourth-grade children living in eastern Tennessee? If not, what steps did the authors take to create the tool and assess its ability to measure nutrition knowledge among fourth-grade children consistently (reliability) and accurately (validity)?[16]

If the study is a secondary analysis, at a minimum, the article should describe who collected the original data, how the data were collected, how the data were acquired for secondary analysis, and the role the authors of the current study played in data collection. The last component of a good methods section will describe methods used for data analysis. The keyword here is *methods* to analyze the data; the actual results of the analysis should not be presented until the results section.[2]

Results, Tables, and Figures

The results section of a scientific article provides a detailed overview of the data actually generated by the study. The results section should not interpret the data; this is saved for the discussion section.[4] Typically, the results section begins by describing the sample of participants included in the study. This description should include the sample size and the participants' demographic information (eg, sex, age, ethnicity, or race). The key component is the specific outcomes of the statistical analyses described in the methods section. Results are typically presented in text and visual forms. Text is used to explain key points of the results, while tables and figures are used to communicate further detail about the study's findings. It is a good idea to use visual approaches to communicating results when possible.[2] Presenting data visually allows for the author to simplify complex information that is difficult to convey concisely using just words.[18]

Tables and figures are an important way to communicate study findings. Tables will organize and present statistical results that are not easily listed in the text. Graphs, also known as figures, are used when a visual presentation of data is more effective than words to convey a result. If an image is used, the intent should be to convey information, not simply to be decorative. Some journals limit the number of tables and graphs allowed for a single article. For these reasons, the information presented in a table or graph will have been carefully selected to highlight the most important details about the study. Information reported in the text should not be duplicated in a table or graph. However, it is important to draw the reader's attention to each table or graph presented in an article by using a callout (a letter, word, number, or symbol identifying a table or graph) that indicates when the reader should reference the table or graph.[2]

Tables and graphs should provide enough detail that the reader can understand the information being communicated without the article's text.[2] Follow these guidelines for clear and helpful tables and graphs:

- Table and graph titles are brief but clear about the content presented.
- Table rows and columns within a table are accompanied by a descriptive label, and when applicable, by units or sample sizes (often designated by N for the number of participants).

- For highlighted statistics, tables and graphs provide a confidence interval, *P* value, or other measure of uncertainty (eg, standard deviation or standard error for a mean).
- Tables include detailed footnotes. Asterisks (*) or other, similar symbols are used to convey further meaning.
- Tables and graphs use consistent fonts, spacing, and number of decimal points.

When interpreting data in tables and graphs, read all labels, headings, and footnotes carefully. If the authors discuss differences between groups, look for information on statistical significance (*P* values).[4]

Discussion, Conclusion, and Applications

The discussion section of an article typically begins by reviewing and summarizing the key findings of the new study. The key findings presented should match the objectives or hypotheses that were presented in the introduction.[2] The paragraphs that follow should compare, contrast, and thoroughly discuss the new study's findings within the context of those found in prior studies. When findings differ, the authors should propose reasons for these differences and offer interpretations for the new findings.[16]

For example, in a study by O'Reilly and colleagues[17] on sugar intake among adolescents, the authors compared their findings with those of the prior literature by stating, "Findings from previous studies support the notion that restriction of certain foods is causally linked to overeating of the restricted food when it becomes available." The authors used these prior findings to provide additional support for their finding that restricting sugar intake among overweight adolescents may result in increased consumption when high-sugar foods were made available again.

At the end of a discussion section, at least one paragraph should be dedicated to a description of the study's limitations to identify potential problems that may impact the validity or accuracy of the study's findings.[2] For example, if a study did not use random assignment to create groups for comparison, it may be difficult to determine cause and effect. Limitations cited in this study included short-term exposure to the diets being studied and unmeasured confounding variables (ie, did sugar restriction *really* cause overweight

adolescents to consume more high-sugar foods or was it something else that the researchers did not measure, like boredom due to an isolating experimental laboratory environment?).

Authors should clearly state their conclusions to clarify what their data can and cannot explain about the research problem. Specifically, readers should be alert for overstated findings (eg, statements in the study conclusion that make findings seem stronger than they are or that are not supported by the research data).[4] For example, a study may show that a nutrition education program was successful in significantly increasing children's fruit and vegetable consumption in one elementary school in rural North Carolina. With this finding in mind, the authors might conclude that the program was successful and should be expanded across the state of North Carolina, and potentially across the United States. However, this conclusion would be inappropriate and overstated because of the small sample size and limited geographic region of the study.

The study's overall conclusion is stated in the final paragraphs of the discussion section. The appropriateness and focus of the conclusion will vary by discipline and journal, but, in general, the conclusion section will include new theories that emerged from the analyses, implications or application of the study findings (eg, the impact of findings on nutrition education policy), and future research. An adequate number of references should be cited to provide support for the discussion; this is typically considered 20 to 40 references, depending on the amount of research that has been published on the topic. However, this can vary. Overall, the author should provide enough evidence, along with corresponding references, to justify or support the claims made throughout the article.[2]

Strategies for Understanding and Critically Reading a Nutrition Research Article

RDNs should be able to evaluate the overall quality of a scientific research article and whether or not the study's weaknesses limit the ability to apply the findings in practice.[1] If the meaning is not clear at any point, keep reading for further details and focus on the bigger picture of the study.[4]

This section will critically review one research article, "Prevalence of and Differences in Salad

BOX
6.1
Common Information Included in Each Section of an Article

Section	Content
Abstract/Summary	Summarizes the article using keywords
Introduction/ Background	Provides essential background information
	States the purpose, objective(s), research question(s), and hypotheses of the study
Methods	Identifies the study design (such as an experimental design in a quantitative study or a phenomenological approach in a qualitative study)
	Describes the source population (including selection methods, eligibility criteria, and—if applicable—recruiting methods), the setting, and the dates of the study
	Defines key exposures, key outcomes, and other variables
	Explains how data were collected
	Describes how the required study size was estimated (such as a sample size calculation in a quantitative study, or a description of how saturation was reached in a qualitative study)
	Discusses ethical considerations (such as which research ethics committees approved the project, whether an inducement was offered, and how informed consent was documented)
	Describes the methods used for analyses (including a description of statistics used in quantitative studies, or approaches to coding or theming in a qualitative study)
Results	Describes the study population's characteristics such as age, sex, ethnicity, and race; this description should also include the sample size (sometimes using a flow diagram to show the number of individual participants at each stage of the study)
	Reports relevant results (using tables and figures when possible)
Discussion	Summarizes key findings and how they relate to the study's purpose and objectives (research questions or hypotheses)
	Discusses the limitations and strengths of the study
	Provides a conservative and well-supported interpretation of the results, states how the new study fits with other relevant evidence (such as previous studies), and discusses the generalizability of the study (the populations to which findings might reasonably apply)
End Matter	Acknowledges the contributions of each author, the assistance by people who did not meet authorship criteria (if any), the sources of funding, and potential conflicts of interest (if any), if requested by the journal
	References

Adapted with permission from Jacobsen KH. *Introduction to Health Research Methods: A Practical Guide*. Jones & Bartlett Learning; 2012.[2]

Bar Implementation in Rural Versus Urban Arizona Schools," by Blumenschine and colleagues,[19] published in the *Journal of the Academy of Nutrition and Dietetics*. This article presents results from a study that compared the prevalence of school-lunch salad bars and differences in implementation in urban and rural schools in Arizona. The step-by-step process used in this example can be followed when critically reviewing other scientific research articles. To help support understanding and critical reading of other articles, Figure 6.3 presents a series of questions to use when reading each section of a research article. Keep in mind when reading the example, that this is only one article, and the discussion of each section will look different from reviews of other articles.

Before even starting to read a scientific article, the first thing to consider is the source of the article. Was it published in a peer-reviewed journal, a type of journal that contains scientific research articles that have been reviewed by people with credentials in the article's field of study prior to publication, also known as a refereed journal? Was it a published document on a website? Was the document written and published by the government? A peer-reviewed scientific article is accepted as being the most reliable source of information because it has undergone a rigorous review by experts in the field prior to being published. Although it is important to double-check, most reputable academic journals are peer-reviewed.[16]

Once it has been established that the article is from a reputable source, learn more about the type of research study being described. Does the article present primary, secondary, or tertiary research (research that combines original and secondary sources to draw an overarching conclusion about the research problem)? Is the study quantitative or qualitative? Did the study use an experimental or nonexperimental research design? What are the independent and dependent variables being studied? Often, the answers to many of these questions can be determined by reading the title.

Now it is time to read the full article. As previously described, research articles generally have the same general structure, including an abstract, introduction, methods, results, and discussion or conclusion. Many articles also include an applications or implications section to describe how the article findings can be applied.[2] The example article follows the standard structure by presenting

information under the following major headings: Introduction and Background, Methods (Analysis), Results, Discussion, and Conclusion. While it is important to know the major sections of a scientific article and what to expect in each section, when reading an article for understanding it may be easier to read it in a slightly different order: abstract, introduction, discussion, methods and data analysis, results, and conclusion. This out-of-order approach to reviewing a scientific article will provide an overview of the study (abstract), key background information (introduction), and the key findings (discussion) before getting into the details of the methods and results.

It is generally a good idea to begin with the abstract. Well-written abstracts can provide a good overview of a study, but don't rely on them to provide all of the necessary information. Sometimes abstracts can be misleading, only presenting the findings that were significant or that supported the study hypothesis.[4] For this reason, it is important to read the full article. In the example article, the structured abstract is divided into eight components according to journal standards: background, objective, design, participants and setting, main outcomes measured, statistical analyses performed, results, and conclusions.

Next, read the introduction for a review of the literature. As previously described, the goal of the introduction is to provide a summary of other research findings on the topic of study and to discuss any unanswered questions or areas of needed research. Blumenschine and colleagues[19] began their research article with a review of prior research related to fruit and vegetable consumption among adolescents and the school food environment in rural locations. The authors then narrowed their focus by more closely examining the literature on the use of salad bars as a method to improve fruit and vegetable intake among adolescents.

The authors make a point to clearly say that "no studies have examined differences in salad bars across metro vs non-metro areas in the US." At the end of this paragraph, the authors state the study's hypothesis: "It was hypothesized that prevalence of salad bars would differ between urban and rural settings, with urban schools having a greater prevalence of salad bars and fewer challenges in salad bar implementations."[19] The independent variable is the location (rural vs urban), while the dependent variables are the prevalence

Find the full text of "Prevalence and Differences in Salad Bar Implementation in Rural Versus Urban Arizona Schools" in the Appendix starting on page 662.

FIGURE 6.3 Checklist of questions for understanding and critically reviewing qualitative and quantitative research articles

	Qualitative	Quantitative
Title of the study	◎ Does it reflect the central phenomenon being studied? ◎ Does it reflect the people and site being studied?	◎ Does it reflect the major independent and dependent variables? ◎ Does it express either a comparison among groups or a relationship among variables? ◎ Does it convey the participants and site for the study?
Problem statement	◎ Does it indicate an important issue to study? ◎ Does the author provide evidence that this issue is important? ◎ Is there some indication that the author located this issue through a search of past literature or from personal experience? ◎ Does the research fit a qualitative approach? ◎ Are the assumptions of the study consistent with a qualitative approach?	◎ Does it indicate an important issue to study? ◎ Does the author provide evidence that this issue is important? ◎ Is there some indication that the author located this issue through a search of past literature or from personal experience? ◎ Does the research fit a quantitative approach? ◎ Are the assumptions of the study consistent with a quantitative approach?
Introduction and background	◎ Has the author provided a literature review of the research problem under study? ◎ Has the author signaled that the literature review is preliminary or tentatively based on the findings in the study?	◎ Are the studies about the independent and dependent variables clearly reviewed? ◎ Does the review end with how the author will extend or expand the current body of literature?
Purpose and research questions	◎ Does the author specify both a purpose statement and a central research question? ◎ Do the purpose statement and central question indicate the central phenomenon of study, the people involved, and the place where the study will occur? ◎ Are subquestions written to narrow the central question to topic areas or foreshadow the steps in data analysis?	◎ Does the author specify a purpose statement? ◎ Is the purpose statement clear, and does it indicate the variables, their relationship, and the people and site to be studied? ◎ Are either hypotheses or research questions written? ◎ Do these hypotheses or questions indicate major variables and participants in the study? ◎ Do the purpose statement and hypotheses or research questions contain the major components that will help a reader understand the study? ◎ Has the author identified a theory or explanation for the hypotheses or questions?

	Qualitative	Quantitative
Data Collection	○ Has the author taken steps to obtain access to people and sites?	○ Does the author mention the steps taken to obtain access to people and sites?
	○ Has the author chosen a specific purposeful sampling strategy for individuals or sites?	○ Is a rigorous probability sampling strategy used?
	○ Is the data collection clearly specified and is it extensive?	○ Has the author identified good, valid, and reliable instruments to use to measure the variables?
	○ Is there evidence that the author has used a protocol for recording data?	○ Are the instruments administered so that bias and error are not introduced into the study?
		○ Are the methods written with enough details that they could be duplicated by other researchers?
Data analysis and findings	○ Were appropriate steps taken to analyze text or visual data into themes or categories?	○ Are the statistics chosen for analysis consistent with the research questions, hypotheses, variables, and scales of measurement?
	○ Was sufficient evidence obtained (including quotes) to support each theme or category?	○ Is the unit of analysis appropriate to address the research problem?
	○ Did the findings answer the research questions?	○ Are the data adequately represented in tables and graphs?
	○ Were the findings realistic and accurate? Were steps taken to support this conclusion through verification?	○ Do the results answer the research questions and address the research problem?
	○ Were the findings represented in the themes or categories so that multiple perspectives can be easily seen?	○ Are the results substantiated by the evidence?
	○ Were the findings presented in narrative discussion or in visuals?	○ Are generalizations from the results limited to the population of participants in the study?

Adapted with permission from Drummond KE, Murphy-Reyes A. *Nutrition Research: Concepts and Applications*. Jones & Bartlett Learning; 2018.[4]

of salad bars in studied schools and the implementation challenges experienced. Remember, the independent variable is the predictor, or the variable that is theorized to influence the dependent variable (or the outcome) in the study. In this study, the authors examined the influence of school locale (the independent variable) on the prevalence of salad bars and the challenges faced when implementing them in the school setting (the dependent variable).

Next, read the discussion for context and limitations. While it might seem counterproductive to skip to the discussion sections of an article right after reading the introduction, the discussion will quickly help to identify the key findings of the study (from the author's perspective) and may serve as a reminder of some of the methods or limitations of the study. For a practitioner who is new to research and critically reviewing scientific literature, it can be easy to get lost in the details of a results section. Reviewing the discussion and conclusion first will give a general idea of the author's main takeaway messages from the article.

The discussion section in the example article by Blumenschine and colleagues[19] starts by re-reviewing an overview of the study purpose. This is followed by a brief summary of the study's key finding: "Results demonstrated that no significant differences exist in the prevalence of salad bars between urban and rural Arizona schools." The following three paragraphs represent the main body of the discussion, where the authors answer the primary research questions or hypotheses and compare and contrast results with those in prior literature published in the area. Within these paragraphs, the authors are careful to point out results in their study that are inconsistent with their a priori hypotheses (eg, "The adjusted prevalence of salad bars was not significantly different across locales, contrary to our expectations of rural inequalities") and those that are consistent (eg, "The results of this study are consistent with those of VanFrank and colleagues who report no statistically significant differences").

A discussion section will conclude with an examination of the study's limitations. For example, Blumenschine and colleagues[19] acknowledge their study was limited by its nonrandomized, cross-sectional study design (an observational study that collects data from one sample at one point in time). Only 36% of schools in Arizona were included in the study, meaning the authors' ability to generalize findings to the larger population of Arizona schools or to schools beyond the state was limited. Some studies will also point out strengths. Blumenschine and colleagues highlight one of their study's strengths as having a large sample size.

Finally, the discussion section will conclude with a brief overview of the main take-home message (eg, "No significant differences in prevalence of salad bars were observed … but school nutrition managers at rural schools that never had salad bars reported cost and food waste barriers more often than those at urban schools"[19]) and the need for future research (eg, "Researchers might consider investigating methods to address cost and waste concerns in rural areas"[19]).

Reading the methods and data analysis next will help to clarify the process the researchers used to execute the study. As discussed previously, thinking of the methods section as five main parts—research design, setting, participants, intervention or instrumentation, and statistical analyses—will make it easier to understand.

Research Design In the first sentence of the methods section of the example article, Blumenschine and colleagues[19] describe their research design as a secondary analysis of data that were obtained from a web-administered survey that was distributed over the 2013–2014 academic year to school nutrition managers in Arizona via email. Despite the secondary nature of the study, the authors still describe the design of the original study, including a detailed description of how participants were contacted and recruited for inclusion in the study.

Setting In the second paragraph, the authors describe the setting for the study. This study was particularly interested in examining schools in both rural and urban locations, so the authors provide a detailed description of how they classified rural vs urban locales used in the study.[19]

Participants In this study, the focus was more on a specific setting vs a specific population of subjects. Therefore, a discussion of subjects was not provided. However, in other articles that aim to study outcomes in a specific group of people, participants would be described in detail.

Instrumentation While this study did not implement a specific intervention, it did use a survey to collect data. Therefore, the authors next provide a detailed description of their instrumentation, being careful to point out the number of items in their survey (68 items), the method of development (a review of the literature and previously published survey tools on the topic), a brief description of how the survey was evaluated (content experts judged the face validity of developed items), and a citation for additional published information on its development. To provide further detail about the content of their survey, the authors describe specific survey questions ("Have you ever had a self-service salad bar for students in your school?") and response options (eg, yes or no). Providing this additional detail is important not only for understanding what the researchers actually asked participants but also for providing context when reading the results and revisiting the conclusions of the study.

Data Analysis Finally, strong research articles should provide a description of the data used in the analysis. This description usually has its own subheading (eg, analysis, data analysis, statistical analysis) and is almost always the last paragraph of the methods section. Blumenschine and colleagues[19] begin their data analysis paragraph by describing how their data were "cleaned" (ie, examined for errors that might have been made when entering data). The authors also describe participants who were removed from the data set for not meeting the inclusion criteria ("52 schools were excluded because they did not meet standards for rural or urban classification"). Finally, the authors end the data analysis subsection by describing how basic descriptive and generalized estimating equation models were used to compare urban and rural differences in the presence and implementation of salad bars. It can be challenging to understand the specific terms, such as statistical lingo like *generalized equation models*, or overall descriptions provided in a data analysis section. Here is a tip: If the study is quantitative and goes beyond basic descriptive analyses, the statistical analyses will likely result in P values. In fact, it is not uncommon to see the statement "Statistical significance was assessed at $P < .05$." If something like this appears in the methods section, look for P values in the results to help determine if the analyses that were used resulted in significant outcomes.[4]

Next comes understanding the actual data generated by the study, which are found in the results section. The results section often follows a logical order, with tables and graphs showing the results visually and text highlighting and explaining the

visual data. The first paragraph typically provides basic demographic information and other information important to understanding the background of study participants (eg, pretest data).

In the example article, Blumenschine and colleagues[19] describe some sample characteristics related to the schools in text ("596 surveys were included in this study with 462 [77.5%] surveys from urban schools and 134 [22.5%] surveys from rural schools"); additional details are provided in a table. While reading through the results, make sure to keep the study's research question and hypotheses in mind. The next few paragraphs directly address the study's hypothesis ("Salad bar [will] differ between urban and rural settings, with urban schools having a greater prevalence of salad bars and fewer challenges in salad bar implementation"). The authors use two tables to compare differences between rural and urban schools. For each comparison, P values are provided. With the exception of cost of produce and food waste, no significant differences were observed.

After reading an entire paper, look back at the study's conclusion and critically think about whether or not the study's findings support the hypothesis. The authors stated, "No significant differences in prevalence of salad bars were observed … but school nutrition managers at rural schools that never had salad bars reported cost and food waste barriers more often than those at urban schools." The authors also stated the need for future research: "Researchers might consider investigating methods to address cost and waste concerns in rural areas." Do the findings presented support the conclusion and the need for future research?

How Can Nutrition and Dietetics Professionals Interpret Research Accurately?

The media often use the latest nutrition research study to create sensational headlines. It is only later, if ever, that the public finds out those research findings were misrepresented or misinterpreted and that the findings were blown out of proportion. This is just one example of why it is so important that nutrition and dietetics professionals be able to accurately interpret nutrition research.

Consider the Strength of the Evidence

Before considering integrating the findings of a new scientific study into practice or communications, consider the overall strength of the evidence presented in the scientific article and in the field as a whole. Imagine a research problem as one large brick wall. The wall represents understanding of a research problem, such as childhood obesity. Each new study that is conducted adds a new brick (which in this analogy is new knowledge) to the wall. It is through the accumulation of findings from many research studies, such as these, that a broader, deeper understanding is gained of the multifaceted problem that is childhood obesity.

Very few studies present groundbreaking findings. The majority of studies will, at best, demonstrate that a specific hypothesis is more or less likely to be correct. For this reason, it is quite reasonable to conduct a study that is considered "unoriginal" since the depth of understanding of a research problem is dependent on the literature containing multiple studies that address a question is similar ways.

With this in mind, practical questions should be, "Does this new research add to the current knowledge about this topic in any way?" and "Does this new study move the field forward in this area of research?" These are more specific ideas to consider[20]:

- Does the study use a bigger sample size, does it use a longer time frame, or is it a larger study overall compared to prior studies?
- Is the methodology used in the new study more rigorous than that in prior studies? Or does the study address specific methodological limitations or criticisms of prior studies?
- Is the population being studied different from those in prior studies in any way (eg, different ages, sex, ethnic groups)?

Unfortunately, the answers to these questions are not straightforward. It is important to learn to assess the common strengths and weaknesses in research. Remember, there are no perfect studies. Researchers do their best to balance strengths and weaknesses, and practitioners should do the same when critically reviewing scientific research articles. The more practitioners learn and read about scientific research in nutrition and dietetics, the more their critical thinking skills will be sharpened around these subjects.

Consider Statistical Significance vs Clinical Significance

As previously described, most researchers consider a P value of less than or equal to .05 as statistically significant. The .05 value is more formally called a significance level. A significance level represents the maximum risk the researcher is willing to take that the differences observed are due to chance. In other words, researchers who choose a significance level of .05 are willing to take the risk that 5 out of 100 times, the differences they observe will be due to chance. Some researchers will set a significance level that is stricter, such as .01 or .001. These levels are more common in studies where researchers want to be more confident in their results, such as in clinical trials.[6] Statistical significance may be able tell whether or not the findings were due to chance, but it does not tell if the findings were clinically significant.[4] Clinical significance means that the differences between two groups are big enough to have practical meaning on an individual level. Statistical significance is concerned with population differences and can be observed with even very small differences between groups when sample sizes are large. For example, a .1 serving increase of vegetables may result in a statistically significant finding in a study sample of 15,000 adolescents. But practically, and from the perspective of a dietitian working one-on-one with a client, a .1 increase in vegetable intake may not be notable. When planning a study, statistical significance should be evaluated, but achieving clinical significance should be the goal.[21]

Understand Limitations

While many scientific journals use a peer-review process to ensure published studies are high quality, all research studies will have limitations. Science is rarely perfect; therefore, authors are expected to recognize the limits of the scope and impact of their work. Every good scientific research article will include a short section at the end of the discussion that addresses study limitations. The three areas often highlighted are weaknesses related to methodology, generalizability, and applications of the findings to real-world settings (otherwise known as *scope*).[22]

Numerous limitations can occur related to methodology, including sample size (small vs large sample sizes), lack of prior research (limited literature to help lay a foundation for understanding the research problem), data collection instruments, and use of self-reported data. Take a research methods course or consult a research methods textbook to learn more about the intricacies of these limitations. Such discussions are beyond the scope of this text, but it is important to know that these methodological limitations can directly impact how the study's findings can be generalized and applied.

For example, almost all research studies have a limited sample population. Therefore, caution should be taken with extrapolating research findings to other sample populations. For example, if a study is conducted in normal-weight, White, middle-income adults, don't assume the findings apply to obese, non-White, low-income adults. Before trying to apply a study's findings to a group outside of the sample population, ask why it would be appropriate to do so and think about what assumptions are being made.

Finally, in the limitations or the future research sections, researchers will often discuss the scope of their study and the types of research questions that were not answered. For nutrition and dietetics professionals, it is just as important to understand what a research study doesn't say as what it does say. If a practitioner understands a study's scope, the chances of misrepresenting its findings are much lower.[22]

While limitations are not ideal, they do occur. Researchers should acknowledge limitations, describe each in detail, and justify why they could not be overcome using other methods. Strong limitation descriptions will also assess the impact of each limitation as it relates to the overall findings of the study, and how new research may be needed to overcome the limitations experienced and further understand the research problem. Acknowledging that a study has limitations does not devalue the study or its findings. On the contrary, it demonstrates that the researcher has thought critically about the study's limitations, their potential impact, and how they can be generalized and applied in a real-world setting.[22]

Look for Potential Sources of Bias

Bias is anything that can influence the findings of a study. Despite the study design selected (eg, RCT vs quasi-experimental design), researchers should aim for the groups to be as similar as possible with the exception of the difference being examined in the study. Participants in each group should receive the same explanations, have the same contact with nutrition and dietetics professionals, and be evaluated using the same outcome measures. Different study designs may require different steps to reduce bias. In an RCT, one way to work toward avoiding bias is to select participants from the same or similar populations and randomly assign them to different groups. In a quasi-experimental design (nonrandomized), randomization would, of course, not be used. In this case, bias may be present, and critical analysis skills must be used to decide if the baseline differences between study groups are likely to produce bias. Are the differences between groups great or small? Are these differences likely to invalidate any differences observed between groups?[20] Other sources of bias might arise from errors related to nonresponses from participants, errors in measurement, or errors in the processing of data.[23] Even for practitioners who are not researchers, or who are not interested in pursuing research as a career, it is important to learn to look for potential sources of bias in any scientific research article. In advancing in an academic and professional career, this practice will get easier!

KEY POINTS

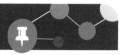

Nutrition Communicators Read and Interpret Research

1 Understanding and interpreting research requires an understanding of the research process. All research studies, whether qualitative, quantitative, or mixed-method, follow these seven steps[6]:

1. Identify a research problem.
2. Review the existing literature.
3. Specify a purpose for the research.
4. Choose a research design.
5. Collect data.
6. Analyze and interpret data.
7. Report and evaluate the outcomes of the research.

2 Most scientific articles include the same basic sections. To better understand the key points of a research article, novice readers may want to read the article in this order: abstract, introduction and background, discussion, methods, results, and conclusions.

3 Before applying a research article's findings to an area of practice or responding to a media request on the findings, evaluate the study's overall quality and its limitations.

RESOURCES

Elsevier Researcher Academy
(series of training/information videos):
https://researcheracademy.elsevier.com

CAT (Critically Appraised Topic)
Manager App:
www.cebma.org/resources-and-tools/cat-manager-app
This app can help you evaluate the trustworthiness of scientific articles published in academic journals.

Center for Evidence-Based Management
scientific article appraisal checklists for quantitative and qualitative studies:
www.cebma.org/resources-and-tools/what-is-critical -appraisal

How to Read a Clinical Research Study (video):
www.youtube.com/watch?v=Gz_gu7pPB7s

How to Read a Qualitative Research Study (video):
www.youtube.com/watch?v=vn5qhORY7fY

REFERENCES

1. Van Horn L, Beto J, eds. *Research: Successful Approaches in Nutrition and Dietetics.* 4th ed. Academy of Nutrition and Dietetics; 2019.
2. Jacobsen KH. *Introduction to Health Research Methods: A Practical Guide.* Jones & Bartlett Learning; 2012.
3. Harris JE. Research publications: the perspectives of the writer, reviewer, and reader. In: Van Horn L, Beto J, eds. *Research: Successful Approaches in Nutrition and Dietetics.* 4th ed. Academy of Nutrition and Dietetics; 2019:558-567.
4. Drummond KE, Murphy-Reyes A. *Nutrition Research: Concepts and Applications.* Jones & Bartlett Learning; 2018.
5. Glore S. Show me the science. *J Am Diet Assoc.* 2001;101:186.
6. Creswell JW. *Educational Research: Planning, Conducting, and Evaluating Quantitative and Qualitative Research.* Loose-leaf version. 5th ed. Pearson; 2015.
7. Nansel TR, Lipsky LM, Haynie DL, Eisenburg MH, Dempster K, Liu A. Picky eaters improved diet quality in a randomized behavioral intervention trial in youth with type 1 diabetes. *J Am Diet Assoc.* 2018;118:308-316. doi:10.1016/j.jand.2017.10.012

8. Perrin MT, Goodell LS, Allen JA, Fogleman A. A mixed-methods observational study of human milk sharing communities on Facebook. *Breastfeeding Med.* 2014;9(3):128-143. doi:10.1089/bfm.2013.0114

9. Creswell JW. *Qualitative Inquiry and Research Design: Choosing Among Five Approaches.* 2nd ed. Sage; 2008.

10. Dev D, McBride A, Spiers K, Blitch K, Williams N. "Great job cleaning your plate today!" Determinants of child-care providers' use of controlling feeding practices: an exploratory examination. *J Am Diet Assoc.* 2016;116(1):1803-1809. doi:10.1016/j.jand.2016.07.016

11. Goodell LS, Cooke NK, Stage VC. The basics of qualitative research. In: Drummond KE, Murphy-Reyes A, eds. *Nutrition Research: Concepts and Applications.* Jones & Bartlett Learning; 2017:243-284.

12. Boushey CJ, Harris J. Building the research foundation: the research question and study design. In: Van Horn L, Beto J, eds. *Research: Successful Approaches in Nutrition and Dietetics.* 4th ed. Academy of Nutrition and Dietetics; 2019:8-31.

13. National Center for Health Statistics. National Health and Nutrition Examination Survey (NHANES). Centers for Disease Control and Prevention website. Accessed April 18, 2018. www.cdc.gov/nchs/nhanes/index.htm

14. Fildes A, Jaarsveld HM, Wardle J, Cooke L. Parent-administered exposure to increase children's vegetable acceptance: a randomised controlled trial. *J Am Diet Assoc.* 2014;114:881-888. doi:10.1016/j.jand.2013.07.040

15. Strauss SE, Richardson WS, Glasziou P, Haynes RB. *Evidence-Based Medicine: How to Practice and Teach EBM.* 3rd ed. Elsevier/Churchill Livingstone; 2005.

16. Dunifon R. How to read a research article. Cornell Cooperative Extension. Published 2005. Accessed April 23, 2010. https://cpb-us-e1 .wpmucdn.com/blogs.cornell.edu/dist/f/575 /files/2015/12/How-to-Read-a-Research -Article-1tweh7l.pdf

17. O'Reilly G, Black DS, Huh J, Davis JN, Unger J, Spruijt-Metz D. Sugar restriction leads to increased ad libitum sugar intake by overweight adolescents in an experimental test meal setting. *J Am Diet Assoc.* 2017;117:1041-1048. doi:10.1016/j.jand.2017.03.025

18. Nicol AAM, Pexman PM. *Displaying Your Findings: A Practical Guide for Creating Figures, Posters, and Presentations.* 2nd ed. American Psychological Association; 2013.

19. Blumenschine M, Adams M, Bruening M. Prevalence of and differences in salad bar implementation in rural versus urban Arizona schools. *J Am Diet Assoc.* 2018;118(3):448-454. doi:10.1016/j.jand.2017.09.004

20. Greenhalgh, T. How to read a paper: assessing the methodological quality of published papers. *BMJ.* 1997;315:305. doi:10.1136/bmj.315.7103.305

21. Browner WS, Newman TB, Cummings SR, Hulley SB. Estimating sample size and power: the nitty gritty. In: Hulley SB, Cummings SR, Browner R, Browner WS, Grady D, Newman TB, eds. *Designing Clinical Research: An Epidemiological Approach.* 2nd ed. Lippincott Williams & Wilkins; 2001:65-91.

22. Price JH, Murnan J. Research limitations and the necessity of reporting them. *Am J Health Educ.* 2014;35:66-67. doi:10.1080/19325037.2004.1060 3611

23. Kirkpatrick SI. Nutrition monitoring in the United States: sources of data. In: Van Horn L, Beto J, eds. *Research: Successful Approaches in Nutrition and Dietetics.* 4th ed. Academy of Nutrition and Dietetics; 2019:153-189.

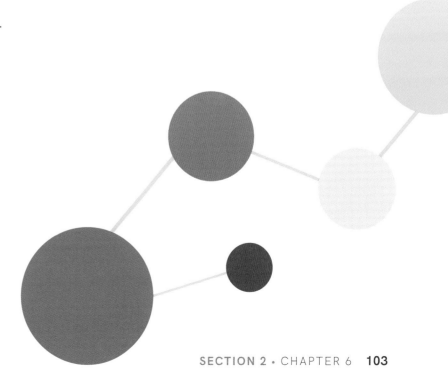

CHAPTER 7

Nutrition Communicators Clearly Communicate Science

Lori A. Kaley, MS, RDN, LD, MSB
and Rosanne Rust, MS, RDN, LDN

"Effective nutrition communicators are challenged with staying up-to-date on scientific evidence and providing sound nutrition advice that is interesting and easy to follow, in a way that helps consumers understand how the information applies to their health."

> "Scientists are from Saturn, the public is from Cleveland. Our challenge is to translate science to the public."
> —INTERNATIONAL FOOD INFORMATION COUNCIL

Introduction

One of the most challenging aspects in the field of nutrition communication is the sheer abundance of misinformation that exists regarding nutrition and health. It is important for nutrition communicators to keep in mind that the majority of the general population does not have formal education or experience in the natural sciences; thus they are not familiar with the intricacies of how the human body digests, metabolizes, and utilizes foods and nutrients.

Credentialed food and nutrition professionals have the background and training to critically review nutrition research studies and translate findings into practical nutrition guidance for audiences of all types. Clearly communicated science is essential to support the development and maintenance of healthy lifestyle behaviors, including food selection, meal and snack preparation, food safety practices, and cooking and eating habits that will help promote optimal health and prevention of chronic disease for all people.

This chapter answers three questions:

- How can nutrition research findings be put into context?
- How can nutrition research results be presented simply and accurately?
- How can nutrition data be presented in a meaningful way?

Effective nutrition communicators are challenged with staying up-to-date on scientific evidence and providing sound nutrition advice that is interesting and easy to follow, in a way that helps consumers understand how the information applies to their health. Learning to respectfully address misinformation in a diplomatic way, without turning off the audience to evidence-based messages, forms the basis of this chapter, which will provide the understanding and tools to take on the challenges of communicating credible, science-based information to the public.

How Can Nutrition Research Findings Be Put into Context?

The role of the nutrition communicator is to put research findings into context—in other words, to explain what results mean in relation to the bigger picture of health and nutrition. Context promotes understanding by:

- illustrating how research findings fit into the ever-evolving nature of research;
- relating findings to the broader topic and recognizing what is known (and unknown) about the subject;
- recognizing variability between individuals, including health status and lifestyle factors;
- accounting for the role of the environment; and
- discussing practical applications, such as usual dietary intake and dose.

Recognize Research Is Evolving

Each research study is just one step in the ever-evolving research process.[1] The research process is cyclical, and a good research study will usually generate more questions than it answers. Figure 6.1 on page 85 describes the research process cycle and how each study can only ask a finite set of questions within a specific group of subjects. Additional studies will take the research questions a step further, continuing to build upon the body of knowledge on a topic.

Nutrition communicators can play a critical role in helping consumers understand that findings from one nutrition research study add new information to a collective body of knowledge, and that one study is only a part of a bigger research process cycle, not necessarily the final answer. It's the totality of the research on a particular topic that gives it more weight. Clearly communicating that the research process is cyclical and develops gradually over time, building a body of evidence, can be an important answer to the public's outcry that nutrition scientists can't make up their minds.

A comprehensive description of each of the different types of research studies appears in Chapter 6, which categorizes research by how data are collected and analyzed as well as how results are reported. In evaluating where one research study may fit within the totality of research on a topic, consider that observational or correlational types of research studies are often conducted as exploratory or initial research. Observational research designs include cohort, case-control, and cross-sectional studies. Once variables have been identified and defined through observational research, more rigorous experimental types of research studies may be conducted to build upon the associations found and better delineate causality. Experimental research designs include randomized controlled trials (RCTs) and quasi-experimental studies. The gold standard of clinical trials and an example of an experimental research design is the RCT, which has typically been used to investigate medical drugs, therapies, and devices. Appropriately conducted RCTs are able to demonstrate cause and effect.

In the field of nutrition, the RCT experimental design may be used to successfully ascertain the effect of a single food component, such as a vitamin or mineral, but for determining the impact of an overall diet, its application can be limiting and impractical. Unlike drug research, where it is possible to isolate one chemical or substance, nutrition research presents unique challenges because nutrients and phytochemicals are not eaten in isolation. This makes it challenging to determine which food or nutrient is causing an outcome since there are numerous combinations of foods and nutrients. In addition, there are both practical and ethical considerations to having human beings consume a specific diet in a controlled environment over an extended period of time. This quandary leaves nutrition researchers utilizing other types of research and research designs to determine the effect on human health of a variety of foods, food components, and dietary patterns. In general, cohort studies provide valuable information about the link or associations between lifestyle factors and disease. A cohort study is an observational research design in which a large group of people are studied over a long period of time to determine the relationship between their characteristics; lifestyle choices, including dietary intake; and the prevalence of specific health outcomes.

As a nutrition communicator, take care when choosing the language to describe the results of a study. While the details of specific types of studies may not be appropriate for a general audience, it is important to make it clear that not all research studies can demonstrate cause and effect, and, most often, the results can only demonstrate an association or relationship.

Examine the Body of Knowledge on the Topic

When a new study is published, a key step in interpreting the results is to determine where this new information fits within the context of the existing body of knowledge on the topic. Look for key information in the introduction and conclusion sections when reviewing articles. Generally, this is where journal article authors will identify why they pursued their study and how the information presented fits into the current body of knowledge.

The media may portray a new study as contradicting the currently held belief on a topic, particularly for food- and nutrition-related topics, which are typically of high interest to the public. For example, think about conflicting information reported on the health benefits vs the health hazards of coffee. Use the questions outlined in Figure 6.3 on page 96 to understand and critically review each new study for the strength and relevance of the evidence presented. Then, help others understand that recommendations are not based on just one study but rather on a collective body of evidence gathered over time. Explain that although a single study may appear to contradict the body of knowledge on a topic, it does not undo the existing body of knowledge but rather adds to it. This is how studies fit into the research process cycle.

Research studies have nuanced variations in that they answer different questions and provide different findings that all fit within a certain body of knowledge. Pay particular attention to systematic reviews and meta-analyses on topics of interest, as these studies compile data and analyses from a collection of published research studies to provide a summary of findings, in the case of the systematic review, or to develop a single conclusion with greater statistical power than the individual studies, in the case of the meta-analysis.

The US Dietary Guidelines Advisory Committee (DGAC) Scientific Report[2] that is published every 5 years is an example of a systematic review of the latest body of evidence on food and nutrition topics based on the existing body of knowledge. The DGAC Scientific Report is used to inform the Dietary Guidelines for Americans that provide nutrition recommendations to promote the health of Americans through federal food and nutrition programs as well as help Americans make healthy choices for themselves and their families. This makes the Dietary Guidelines for Americans a useful science-based tool for understanding the current body of knowledge on key nutrition topics, including food and nutrient recommendations and healthy dietary patterns. These types of studies can provide nutrition communicators with the strength of the scientific evidence on which to base their professional opinions and practice.

Explaining research findings involves more than simply summarizing the key points found in a research study. Put those findings into context and tell a story that is relatable for an audience, including how the results fit into their everyday life. If the study results differ from previous research findings, explain why that may be based on the broader research context. Discuss the study's limitations and suggest the need for future studies that will build upon the data.

Consider Individual Differences

When putting research findings into context with regard to individuals vs populations, it is essential to examine characteristics of the study's subjects, such as age, gender, health status, and lifestyle factors, to determine whether the research findings can be extrapolated to other individuals. Keep in mind that lifestyle factors can include a wide variety of attributes, which may or may not be directly studied or controlled for as part of the research process. Lifestyle can include type of occupation, education level, economic status, family, emotional support system, religious affiliation, cultural identification, health status, sexuality, habits (eg, dietary intake, physical activity, stress modification), and so on. Review the demographic characteristics of the study population as well as the lifestyle variables addressed in the study so that communication of the study findings can be placed within the appropriate context.

A challenge with communicating nutrition research, especially related to study findings for specific conditions, is that others who do not have a health condition may try to apply this information to themselves unnecessarily. For example, there has been a dramatic increase in the number of gluten-free food products available, in part due to consumer demand. This demand has been fueled by celebrity books, media reports, and social media posts suggesting that gluten may be the cause of diffuse symptoms such as bloating, fatigue, weight gain, and more. This is further compounded because when people start paying attention to their diet and eating better, which may include consuming gluten-free foods, they tend to feel better and may attribute this to removing gluten from their diet. Unfortunately, self-diagnosis and lack of knowledge about gluten and other food components only perpetuates the cycle of spending time, money, and effort following a restrictive diet unnecessarily. In this situation, a nutrition communicator can share science-based messages on how it is essential for individuals with diagnosed celiac disease to consume a gluten-free diet for their lifetime to alleviate symptoms and promote well-being, as well as those with gluten intolerance and sensitivity. With regard to other conditions, nutrition communicators can clarify that research findings either do not exist or are very limited to support

See more about the research process cycle in Figure 6.1 on page 85.

the need for other individuals to follow a gluten-free diet for any length of time. Widespread attention to diet fads or trends can take the focus away from evidence-based dietary advice that can impact real risk.

From a population standpoint, chronic diseases, including obesity, cardiovascular diseases, diabetes, and cancer, may each require unique medical treatments, yet the overall dietary recommendations to both manage and prevent these diseases are comparable. Likewise, the research findings that generate nutrition and lifestyle recommendations from different health organizations may look different from the outside but on the whole are quite similar when applied to a population. Where individual differences are considered is through medical nutrition therapy with individual clients or patients, in which the RDN assesses an individual's overall health, nutrition, and lifestyle factors and communicates individualized guidance with the consistent goal of improving health and reducing risk.

Consider Environmental Factors

The environment is the conditions or surroundings in which an individual or population group lives, works, learns, and plays. Environment can include population density, urban vs rural location, access to healthy foods, stable housing, neighborhood safety, quality of education, laws and policies, public parks and green spaces, opportunities for physical activity, and water and air quality.

Research on the determinants of health looks at how the communities in which people live, work, learn, and play impact health. This includes how communities are designed and built, as well as a variety of social and economic factors. Accounting for the specific characteristics of the environment in which studies are conducted is important to provide appropriate context for the findings.

Consider the Dose and the Total Diet

When evaluating clinical research studies on food ingredients and their findings, consider if the amounts or "dosages" of the experimental treatment used are realistic. In particular, review the amounts of individual food components or additives as well as the relationship of those food components to the total diet. Ask the following questions about the amount or dose of the experimental treatment in human studies:

- If the dose of the experimental treatment being studied elicits an effect that is favorable or desirable, is it an amount that is attainable in a typical diet?
- If the response elicited is unfavorable, was the treatment dose higher than an amount that would be found in a typical diet?
- If there was no effect or response, was the treatment dose strong enough and in an amount that would be found in a typical diet?

Even in animal studies, the dose matters. An experimental dose given to a rodent can be hundreds of times the human dose of the substance, because often these studies are seeking the threshold in which a negative result occurs (such as tumors in rats). Studies with results that can be applied to real-life settings are practical and form the basis for evidence-based recommendations that are useful to nutrition communicators.

Practitioners need to take care when translating findings from animal studies to humans, even when the animals used in the studies are mammalian (ie, monkeys, rats, mice). While the studies using animals may pave the way for developing studies in human cell lines or in humans if it is ethical to do so, there are significant differences between animals and humans. There are times in animal studies when dosages of experimental treatments are much higher than would be consumed either in proportion to a typical animal diet or in a human diet.

How Can Research Results Be Presented Simply and Accurately?

First and foremost, nutrition and health research results must be presented accurately and without bias, judgment, or interpretation. Summarize the results as clearly and simply as possible, highlighting the main findings of interest to an audience.

Describe Research Methodology and Terminology Simply

The first step toward being able to describe research methodology and terminology simply is to have a solid understanding of the different types of research methodology and terminology that are used in studies. Chapter 6 provides these descriptions. An effective nutrition communicator can describe key research terms in ways that lay people can easily understand. A strategy to support the nutrition communicator in developing this skill includes the following tactics:

- Create a list of key research terms and their meanings to become familiar with how the terms are used.
- Develop an understanding and a vocabulary, and practice describing these terms to others.
- Effective nutrition communicators are challenged with staying up-to-date on scientific evidence and providing sound nutrition advice that is interesting and easy to follow, in a way that helps consumers understand how the information applies to their health. Figure 7.1 provides examples of simple words and phrases to use in describing research.

Translate Results and Conclusions Accurately

Research results should be neither overstated nor understated. Describing results accurately and clearly reflects that the type of research used can generate the outcomes reported. A common error in translating results is confusing causation with correlation or association. A specific type of study is needed to assign causation, such as a randomized trial that uses an experimental research design. Correlational types of studies that demonstrate significant results find relationships, associations, and links between variables and health outcomes. The fundamental issue here is that often the popular press reports study results implying causation, when in fact the study only showed a correlation. It is rare for a single research study to provide clear evidence that an independent variable causes an effect on the dependent variable. Instead, most nutrition studies are designed to show correlation—where two or more variables are related or correlated or have an association or are linked. This is where language such as "may lead to" or "suggests that" is more accurate than saying "caused by" when interpreting results.

Another issue in accurately describing results is giving anecdotal evidence too much credence. *Anecdotal* refers to self-reports or personal accounts that are not based on facts or research. All too often in the public, and even within the medical community, anecdotal evidence becomes accepted as evidence of causation. An example is drinking cranberry juice for the prevention and amelioration of symptoms of urinary tract infections (UTIs) in women. For many years, without the benefit of scientific evidence, health care providers recommended that women who experience the symptoms of a UTI or have recurrent UTIs not only drink plenty of fluids but incorporate cranberry juice specifically. In 2016, a RCT was published, demonstrating that women with recurrent UTI who drank 8 oz/d of the treatment cranberry juice had a 40% reduction in the incidence of recurrent UTI.[3] The scientific evidence in this study supports the anecdotal evidence. However, there are many other examples of anecdotal evidence that are not supported by science.

Research study conclusions typically provide the context for how results are significant within the larger body of knowledge on the topic and are of relevance to the audience. The conclusion not only summarizes the main topics studied but synthesizes key points on how the results found in the study either support or contradict the original hypothesis statement. Conclusions should not introduce new information, but they often identify areas for future research. They can provide a memorable closing message about the study.

Practitioners' colleagues and clients may call on them for professional expertise on nutrition information presented by a research study reported by the media. Practitioners must be comfortable reviewing original scientific articles rather than relying on news articles or what others are stating in the lay media when making their own professional conclusions regarding the information. A professional opinion can be offered with the clarification that it is based on anecdotal or correlational evidence rather than conclusive cause-and-effect evidence. In some cases, it may be enough to simply state that the

See Chapter 6 for more on research terms.

FIGURE 7.1 **Choose words carefully**

Instead of	Say
additional	added, more, other
adversely impact	hurt, set back
advise	recommend, tell
anticipate	expect
a number of	some
apparent	clear, plain
appropriate	proper, right
approximate	about
ascertain	find out, learn
assist, assistance	aid, help
associated with	linked, aligned
benefit	help
comply with	follow
component	part
comprise	form, include, make up
constitutes	is, forms, makes up
contains	has
delete	cut, drop
demonstrate	prove, show
determine	decide, figure, find
disclose	show
discontinue	drop, stop
disseminate	give, issue, pass, send
due to the fact that	due to, since
eliminate	cut, drop, end
establish	set up, prove, show
evidenced	shown
evident	clear
facilitate	ease, help
frequently	often
function	act, role, work
has a requirement for	needs
identical	same
identify	find, name, show

Instead of	Say
impacted	affected, changed
implement	carry out, start
indicate	show, write down
indication	sign
initial	first
initiate	start
it appears	it seems
it is essential	it must, it needs to
magnitude	size
maintain	keep, support
methodology	method
modify	change
monitor	check, watch
necessitate	cause, need
numerous	many
objective	aim, goal
parameters	limits
participate	take part
provide	give, offer, say
relationship	link, connection
relative to	about, on
represents	is
requirement	need
selection	choice
solicit	ask for, request
subsequent	later, next
sufficient	enough
utilize, utilization	use
validate	confirm
variable	factor
warrant	call for, permit
with reference to	about
with the exception of	except for

evidence is not strong enough to form an opinion. Practitioners' voices are needed—sharing information can move others to seek practitioners out as a trusted source for science-based food, nutrition, and dietetics information.

Carefully Address Disagreements and Misinformation on Controversial Topics

Some amount of controversy seems to be the norm when it comes to topics in food and nutrition. Superstitions and rumors, personal beliefs that have an emotional bias, and outdated information are not always in alignment with the current scientific evidence on a topic. There are times when the body of knowledge on a topic is inconclusive or the evidence from studies is mixed. One example is the impact of menu labeling in restaurants on consumer behavior.[4] Since this is a fairly new practice, there are some studies that show that consumers are aware of the posted information and use it to purchase lower-calorie choices, whereas other studies have not been able to demonstrate this effect.

Inconclusive or mixed results are still valuable and usually point to the need for more research. Nutrition communicators should emphasize this as well as examining the results in context. In the case of calorie labeling in restaurants, the context may pertain to certain populations (eg, adults vs children), to specific environments (eg, low-income vs higher-income neighborhoods), or to the type of chain restaurant (eg, a traditional fast-food restaurant vs a full-service restaurant). Opponents of menu labeling argue that the scientific evidence has been inconclusive. At the time of this writing, studies on the impact of calorie labeling were only completed in select cities, counties, and states since federal menu labeling legislation went into effect in May 2018.

There are many controversial nutrition-related topics, and dealing with misinformation will continue to create challenges for nutrition communicators. Some topics are sensationalized and are met with an emotional response, especially when they relate to children, safety, and health risks. Just a few examples include whether genetically modified food components are safe, whether the saturated fats from dairy

products and coconut oil promote heart health, and whether desired health benefits can be achieved from supplementation vs consumption of a whole food or dietary pattern. Nutrition communicators can state what is known on a topic and take the opportunity to respectfully present a professional opinion backed by available scientific evidence. Box 7.1 offers some practical tips for debunking misinformation.

Refer to Chapter 36 for further discussion on how to answer questions about controversial topics.

 ## Why Can Misinformation Be So Difficult to Correct?

Research findings can get lost in translation, resulting in confusing or misleading information communicated to public. It may seem obvious to simply correct the misinformation, but researchers have found that certain cognitive factors can make misinformation resistant to correction.[5] In many cases, rejecting a widely held belief is cognitively more challenging than simply accepting the truth.[6] Some practices to help frame communications around misinformation include the following:

- Avoid repetition of the myth and reinforce the correct facts. Provide real-life examples and application when possible.

- Keep the facts simple and appropriate for the audience. This can help to prevent backfiring or making it easier for people to just continue believing misinformation.

- Consider whether the content may be threatening to the values or cultural beliefs of an audience. Affirm personal values and concerns to help increase receptiveness to the facts.

In some situations where there is pervasive misinformation, it may be more appropriate to ignore the misinformation and provide a direct behavioral intervention to help facilitate a desired outcome, such as choosing to eat more fruits and vegetables regardless of how they are grown or if they are processed, such as canned or frozen.

How Can Nutrition Data Be Presented Meaningfully?

For data to be useful, they must be understood. Translating nutrition science to meaningful, relatable messages that are easy to grasp and understand is the purview of nutrition communicators. Presenting data visually is a way to help others quickly understand the key messages the data depict.

Represent Data Visually

The familiar saying that a picture is worth a thousand words certainly applies to effectively communicating scientific data. Data can be visualized graphically (using x and y axes, where the x-axis is horizontal and the y-axis is vertical) or for more complex data with charts or tables. The goal in communicating data is for the information to be accurate but easy to understand and meaningful to the user. Presenting the most relevant data in a visual way can help the reader understand complex results. The key is to determine who the audience is and then what the most salient points are, or what will be the most useful information to the audience—then cull those details and display them visually. The visual representation of data in graphs, tables, charts, and figures highlights relevant relationships and significant results, rather than writing out the information.

It is important for nutrition communicators to use modern technology to deliver science information. Although typically not used in peer-reviewed journal articles, infographics have become a popular way to visually display data and messages together in a one- to two-page format. An infographic includes simple, short written messages and displays pertinent data pictorially, including numerical data that are usually put into a context that the reader can understand. Quality infographics include references for the sources of data and information provided.

Figure 7.2 lists guidelines that nutrition communicators can use to develop visually appealing data presentations that are easy to read and understand. General guidelines for creating graphs or charts are followed by more specific guidelines for text, arrangement of elements, color use, and lines.

How to Choose the Type of Graph or Chart to Use

There are several basic types (with multiple variations) of graphs and charts that are useful for presenting data clearly and concisely. Some programs, such as Microsoft Excel, allow the user to present the same data in different types of graphs and charts; this can be useful for deciding which style presents the data most clearly. The following is a list of basic graphs and charts and the types of relationships within the data that they demonstrate.

- **Pie chart:** Shaped like a pie or a circle, the pie chart is used to show the proportions of the individual components to the whole. The individual components add up to 100%. See Figure 7.3 on page 115 for an example of a pie chart.
- **Column chart:** Uses the height of the bars on an x- and y-axis graph to show levels of and comparisons between discrete groups. Figure 7.3 contains an example of a column chart.
- **Bar graph:** A horizontal column chart on an x- and y-axis graph that is useful when the labels describing the discrete groups are lengthy. A depiction of a bar graph is included in Figure 7.3.
- **Line graph:** Plotted on an x- and y-axis graph to show the trend of data over a time period. Figure 7.3 includes an example line graph.
- **Mixed graph that includes bars and lines:** Plotted on an x- and y-axis graph to show levels of and comparisons between discrete groups with trends over time. See Figure 7.3 for an example of a mixed graph.
- **Scatter plot chart:** Plotted on an x- and y-axis graph to show the relationship between two different variables and to understand distribution of the data when there are many different data points. A sample scatter plot chart is included in Figure 7.3.
- **Bubble chart:** Plotted on an x- and y-axis graph and similar to a scatter plot chart; includes a third set of data as indicated by the size of the bubble. See Figure 7.3 for an example bubble chart.

FIGURE 7.2 **Data visualization checklist**

Data Visualization Checklist

by Stephanie Evergreen & Ann K. Emery
May 2016

This checklist is meant to be used as a guide for the development of high impact data visualizations. Rate each aspect of the data visualization by circling the most appropriate number, where 2 points means the guideline was fully met, 1 means it was partially met, and 0 means it was not met at all. n/a should not be used frequently, but reserved for when the guideline truly does not apply. For example, a pie chart has no axes lines or tick marks to rate. If the guidelines has been broken intentionally to make a point, rate it n/a and deduct those points from the total possible. Refer to the Data Visualization Anatomy Chart on the last page for guidance on vocabulary and the Resources at the end for more details.

	Guideline	Rating
Text Graphs don't contain much text, so existing text must encapsulate your message and pack a punch.	**6-12 word descriptive title is left-justified in upper left corner** Short titles enable readers to comprehend takeaway messages even while quickly skimming the graph. Rather than a generic phrase, use a descriptive sentence that encapsulates the graph's finding or "so what?" Western cultures start reading in the upper left, so locate the title there.	2 1 0 n/a
	Subtitle and/or annotations provide additional information Subtitles and annotations (call-out text within the graph) can add explanatory and interpretive power to a graph. Use them to answer questions a viewer might have or to highlight specific data points.	2 1 0 n/a
	Text size is hierarchical and readable Titles are in a larger size than subtitles or annotations, which are larger than labels, which are larger than axis labels, which are larger than source information. The smallest text - axis labels - are at least 9 point font size on paper, at least 20 on screen.	2 1 0 n/a
	Text is horizontal Titles, subtitles, annotations, and data labels are horizontal (not vertical or diagonal). Line labels and axis labels can deviate from this rule and still receive full points. Consider switching graph orientation (e.g., from column to bar chart) to make text horizontal.	2 1 0 n/a
	Data are labeled directly Position data labels near the data rather than in a separate legend (e.g., on top of or next to bars and next to lines). Eliminate/embed legends when possible because eye movement back and forth between the legend and the data can interrupt the brain's attempts to interpret the graph.	2 1 0 n/a
	Labels are used sparingly Focus attention by removing the redundancy. For example, in line charts, label every other year on an axis. Do not add numeric labels *and* use a y-axis scale, since this is redundant.	2 1 0 n/a
Arrangement Improper arrangement of graph elements can confuse readers at best and mislead viewer at worst. Thoughtful arrangement makes a data visualization easier for a viewer to interpret.	**Proportions are accurate** A viewer should be able measure the length or area of the graph with a ruler and find that it matches the relationship in the underlying data. Y-axis scales should be appropriate. Bar charts start axes at 0. Other graphs can have a minimum and maximum scale that reflects what should be an accurate interpretation of the data (e.g., the stock market ticker should not start at 0 or we won't see a meaningful pattern).	2 1 0 n/a
	Data are intentionally ordered Data should be displayed in an order that makes logical sense to the viewer. Data may be ordered by frequency counts (e.g., from greatest to least for nominal categories), by groupings or bins (e.g., histograms), by time period (e.g., line charts), alphabetically, etc. Use an order that supports interpretation of the data.	2 1 0 n/a
	Axis intervals are equidistant The spaces between axis intervals should be the same unit, even if every axis interval isn't labeled. Irregular data collection periods can be noted with markers on a line graph, for example.	2 1 0 n/a
	Graph is two-dimensional Avoid three-dimensional displays, bevels, and other distortions.	2 1 0 n/a
	Display is free from decoration Graph is free from clipart or other illustrations used solely for decoration. Some graphics, like icons, can support interpretation.	2 1 0 n/a
Color Keep culture-laden color connotations in mind. For example, pink is highly associated with feminine qualities in the USA. Use sites like Color Brewer to find color schemes suitable for reprinting in black-and-white and for colorblindness.	**Color scheme is intentional** Colors should represent brand or other intentional choice, not default color schemes. Use your organization's colors or your client's colors. Work with online tools to identify brand colors and others that are compatible.	2 1 0 n/a
	Color is used to highlight key patterns Action colors should guide the viewer to key parts of the display. Less important, supporting, or comparison data should be a muted color, like gray.	2 1 0 n/a
	Color is legible when printed in black and white When printed or photocopied in black and white, the viewer should still be able to see patterns in the data.	2 1 0 n/a
	Color is legible for people with colorblindness Avoid red-green and yellow-blue combinations when those colors touch one another.	2 1 0 n/a
	Text sufficiently contrasts background Black/very dark text against a white/transparent background is easiest to read.	2 1 0 n/a

Continues ▸

FIGURE 7.2 **Data visualization checklist** *(continued)*

Lines

Excessive lines—gridlines, borders, tick marks, and axes—can add clutter or noise to a graph, so eliminate them whenever they aren't useful for interpreting the data.

Gridlines, if present, are muted
Color should be faint gray, not black. Full points if no gridlines are used. Gridlines, even muted, should not be used when the graph includes numeric labels on each data point.

2   1   0   n/a

Graph does not have border line
Graph should bleed into the surrounding page or slide rather than being contained by a border.

2   1   0   n/a

Axes do not have unnecessary tick marks or axis lines
Tick marks can be useful in line graphs (to demarcate each point in time along the y-axis) but are unnecessary in most other graph types. Remove axes lines whenever possible.

2   1   0   n/a

Graph has one horizontal and one vertical axis
Viewers can best interpret one x- and one y-axis. Don't add a second y-axis. Try a connected scatter plot or two graphs, side by side, instead. (A secondary axis used to hack new graph types is ok, so long as viewers aren't being asked to interpret a second y-axis.)

2   1   0   n/a

Overall

Graphs will catch a viewer's attention so only visualize the data that needs attention. Too many graphics of unimportant information dilute the power of visualization.

Graph highlights significant finding or conclusion
Graphs should have a "so what?" – either a practical or statistical significance (or both) to warrant their presence. For example, contextualized or comparison data help the viewer understand the significance of the data and give the graph more interpretive power.

2   1   0   n/a

The type of graph is appropriate for data
Data are displayed using a graph type appropriate for the relationship within the data. For example, change over time is displayed as a line graph, area chart, slope graph, or dot plot.

2   1   0   n/a

Graph has appropriate level of precision
Use a level of precision that meets your audiences' needs. Few numeric labels need decimal places, unless you are speaking with academic peers. Charts intended for public consumption rarely need *p* values listed.

2   1   0   n/a

Individual chart elements work together to reinforce the overarching takeaway message
Choices about graph type, text, arrangement, color, and lines should reinforce the same takeaway message.

2   1   0   n/a

For more support, check out:

AnnKEmery.com/blog
StephanieEvergreen.com/blog
Stephanie Evergreen's books, *Presenting Data Effectively* & *Effective Data Visualization*

Score: _____ / _____ = _____ %

Well-formatted data visualizations score between 90-100% of available points. At this level, viewers are better able to read, interpret, and retain content.

Data Visualization Anatomy Chart

Confused by the terminology? Review the anatomy charts below for illustration of what's what.

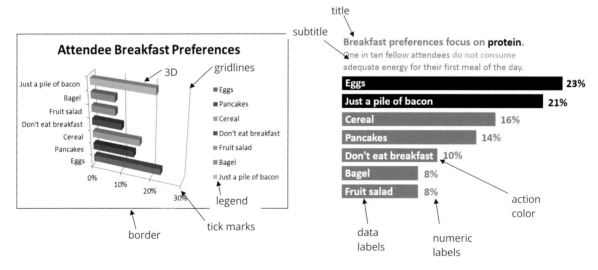

FIGURE 7.3 **Examples of charts**

PIE CHART

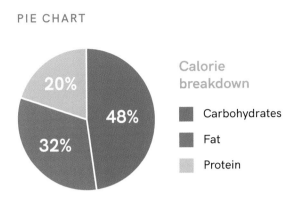

Calorie breakdown

■ Carbohydrates
■ Fat
■ Protein

COLUMN CHART

Cholesterol per Menu Item

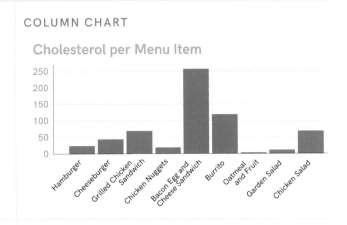

BAR GRAPH

Healthy Eating Index component scores

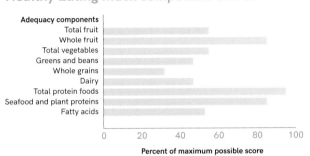

LINE GRAPH

Diet low in fruits

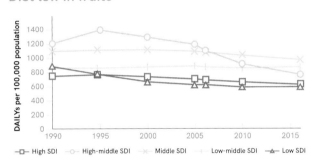

MIXED GRAPH

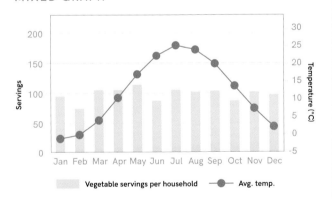

SCATTER PLOT CHART

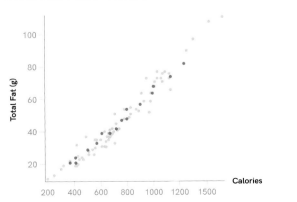

BUBBLE CHART

Scientific evidence for popular dietary supplements

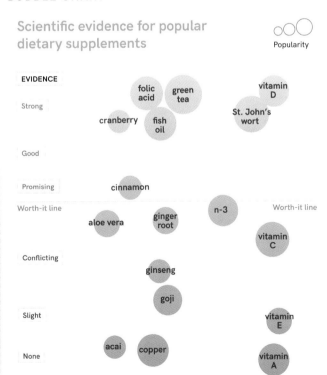

How to Represent Data Visually to Make a Point

When figuring out how to represent data visually to make a point, there are three main steps to consider:

- Identify the target audience.
- Determine the key points or most vital pieces of information to communicate to the target audience.
- Make the data as interesting and visually appealing as possible for that audience.

Gain an understanding of how an audience prefers to receive information. Use the tips and guidelines provided in Figure 7.2 to help create presentations of the data that get the desired point across. Use colorful and bold graphics to highlight key messages and black and white to create contrast when presenting text in charts and graphs. Keep any written content short and simple, and use font styles, font sizes, and contrasting colors that are easy to read. Make judicious use of graphics and images to enhance but not clutter the display. Present data accurately and include references. References can be in a small font and placed at the very bottom or along the sides of the data presentation. Make the data interesting by visually representing how the data relate to the audience; use examples, colors, and visual images that provide meaning and context.

KEY POINTS

Nutrition Communicators Clearly Communicate Science

1 The role of the nutrition communicator is to understand the context within which research findings make sense and can be applied, and to use this understanding to share the results of research studies in ways that tell a story and engage an audience.

2 Research results must be presented accurately and without bias, judgment, or interpretation. Summarize the results as clearly and simply as possible, highlighting the main findings of interest to an audience.

3 Data can be more meaningful when presented using visually appealing graphics and highlighting essential messages. Understanding the audience will help the nutrition communicator to select relevant messages and present them in ways that are easy for the audience to understand.

REFERENCES

1. Florida International University Libraries. Research methods help guide. FIU libraries website. Accessed April 21, 2018. http://libguides .fiu.edu/researchmethods/welcome
2. US Department of Health and Human Services and US Department of Agriculture. *Scientific Report of the 2015-2020 Dietary Guidelines Advisory Committee*. Published February 2015. Accessed April 23, 2020. https://ods.od.nih.gov /pubs/2015_dgac_scientific_report.pdf
3. Maki K, Kaspar K, Khoo C. Consumption of a cranberry juice beverage lowered the number of clinical urinary tract infection episodes in women with a recent history of urinary tract infection. *Am J Clin Nutr.* 2016;103:1434-1442. doi:10.3945/ ajcn.116.130542
4. VanEpps E, Roberto C, Park S. Restaurant menu labeling policy: review of evidence and controversies. *Curr Obes Rep.* 2016;5(1):72-80. doi:10.1007/s13679-016-0193-z
5. Lewandowsky S, Ecker U, Seifert C, Schwartz N, Cook J. Misinformation and its correction: continued influence and successful debiasing. *Psychol Sci Public Interes.* 2012;13(3):106-131. doi:10.1177/1529100612451018
6. Chan M, Jones C, Hall-Jamieson K, Albarracin D. Debunking: a meta-analysis of the psychological efficacy of messages containing misinformation. *Psychol Sci.* 2017;28(11):1531-1546. doi:10.1177/0956797617714579
7. Evergreen S, Emery A. Data visualization checklist. Evergreen Data website. Published 2016. Accessed May 12, 2018. http://stephanieevergreen.com/updated-data -visualization-checklist

Nutrition Communicators Properly Reference Sources

Milton Stokes, PhD, MPH, RD, FAND
and Heidi Katte, MS, RDN, CD, FAND

"Properly referencing sources serves many purposes, foremost establishing the credibility of the message and of the nutrition communicator."

> "Giving credit where credit is due is a very rewarding habit to form. Its rewards are inestimable." —LORETTA YOUNG

Introduction

Communication—of all types—builds on the body of knowledge about a topic. Effective and ethical communicators clearly convey sources of information for ideas that are not original or are considered common knowledge. Properly referencing sources serves the dual purpose of (1) giving credit to the source and (2) providing audiences with necessary information to locate references for additional context and further exploration.

Although giving credit where credit is due is a simple-sounding practice with a presumably simple corresponding process, adherence to this practice is less than perfect. One reason is that citing references can be tedious. Proper citation often depends on an oversight authority, such as a classroom professor or assignment editor, who requires citations and follows through to assure the citations are completed with accuracy. When presenting ideas in writing, exploring concepts in research, or conducting a literature review in preparation for a scholarly paper or presentation, a writer must indicate the sources from which the information, ideas, and words are derived. Failure to indicate sources properly can be considered plagiarism. This mistake is becoming increasingly common. According to the Pew Research Center, "…most college presidents (55%) say that plagiarism in students' papers has increased over the last 10 years."[1]

This chapter covers how to properly reference sources to avoid plagiarism and to promote evidence-based practice. It answers three main questions:

- How is proper credit given to a source, and why?
- How can plagiarism be avoided?
- What are strategies for giving credit when a full reference is not needed?

Properly referencing sources serves many purposes, foremost establishing the credibility of the message and of the nutrition communicator.

How and Why Is Attribution Given to a Source?

Giving proper credit is essential to demonstrate credibility for content, to acknowledge the source, to provide audience members with references for further study, and to avoid plagiarism. Citing sources properly requires adherence to the established rules of a selected style guide or assignment authority. Additionally, whom the author is writing for plays a role in determining if citations are required. For example, an article written for a trade publication requires citations, but one written for other mass media sources may not. Nutrition practice is evidence-based, which often separates credentialed food and nutrition professionals from other information sharers. Credentialed professionals find the science and translate it for the public to promote the public's understanding and application of the information. Properly attributing sources gives proper credit and establishes the credibility of the information, often encouraging the audience to search for more.

Writers should be aware that there are numerous citation styles. Though they may have some things in common, each citation style has very clear rules that differentiate it from other styles. Learning a specific citation style is akin to learning another language. Writers are often frustrated when they are asked to use a new and unfamiliar citation style. But, improperly citing or failing to cite sources can lead to negative, and potentially serious, consequences, such as punishment (in a classroom or in a courtroom) or reputational damage.

The requirement to cite original sources is not always clear. Is the thought or idea culturally inculcated—that is, is it accepted as common knowledge? Earth orbits the sun. Humans breathe air. Water sustains life. Common knowledge comprises information known to most people or known to groups who share characteristics. But what about a more specific piece of knowledge, such as the number of calories in a gram of carbohydrate or fat? While the number of calories in a gram of fat was discovered by a scientist, has been published in peer-reviewed, scholarly literature, and is taught in college textbooks, is it still necessary for professional food and nutrition communicators to cite the source of this information? It is helpful to ask: When does information penetrate the realm of common knowledge? And how does information become common knowledge? While these questions speak more to abstract theories of knowledge, communicators would be wise to follow the adage: When in doubt, cite your source.[2]

The form of the citation depends on the communication medium. Academic papers adhere to specific citation styles, whereas oral communication requires explicit mention of the scholar or originator of the idea, word, or phrase. Refer to Figure 8.1.[2,3]

Describing the Source of Information in Professional Writing and Speaking

In writing, it is standard to cite an information source—that is, to embed language in copy so that readers can identify source material and locate it independently. Academic material produced for a professional audience adheres to a formal style guide as set forth by an editor or publisher or by a school's governing body. What follows are examples of citations that follow the American

FIGURE 8.1 **General guide to understanding written plagiarism**

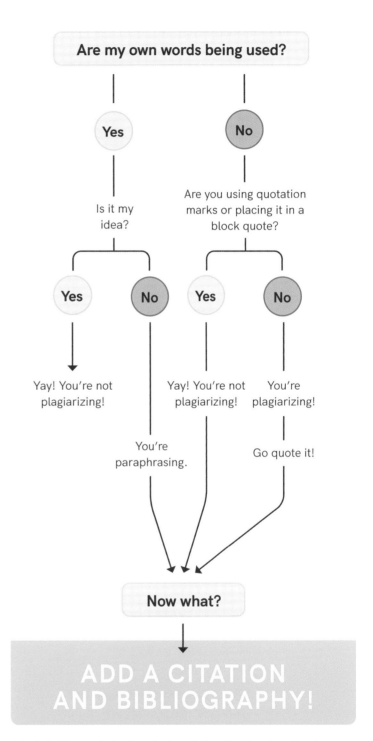

Adapted with permission from Indiana University. Overview: How to Recognize Plagiarism: Tutorial and Tests. Accessed April 23, 2020. https://plagiarism.iu.edu/overview/shouldDo.html.[6]

Medical Association (AMA) style, which is used by publications of the Academy of Nutrition and Dietetics, including the *Journal of the Academy of Nutrition and Dietetics*. For more information on using the AMA style, visit the Purdue Online Writing Lab website listed in the resources section at the end of the chapter.

CITING AN ARTICLE FROM A PEER-REVIEWED JOURNAL

A complete print journal reference includes the authors' surnames and initials, the title of the article (and subtitle, if included), the abbreviated name of the journal set in italics, the year, volume number, issue number, part or supplement number, as needed, and inclusive page numbers. The latest edition of the AMA style manual encourages authors to use a digital object identifier (DOI) over a URL in a reference. The DOI goes at the end of the citation; it is not followed by a period so as to be clear for the reader what punctuation is included in the DOI.

Journal Example:

Blumenschine M, Adams M, Bruening M. Prevalence of and differences in salad bar implementation in rural versus urban Arizona schools. *J Acad Nutr Diet.* 2018:118(3):448-454. doi:10.1016/j.jand.2017.09.00

CITING A BOOK

A complete reference to a print book includes the authors' surnames and initials, the chapter title (when cited), the surname and initials of book's authors or editors (if applicable), the title of the book (and subtitle, if any), volume number and volume title (if more than one), edition number (if not first), name of the publisher, the year of publication, and the page numbers (if a specific chapter is cited).

Book Examples (Full Book and Chapter in a Multiauthored Book):

Drummond KE, Murphy-Reyes A. *Nutrition Research: Concepts and Applications.* Jones & Bartlett Learning; 2018.

Gilbride JA, Byham-Gray L. Bridging research into practice. In: Van Horn L, Beto J, eds. *Research: Successful Practices in Nutrition and Dietetics.* 4th ed. Academy of Nutrition and Dietetics; 2019:570-591.

CITING A WEBPAGE

A complete reference for a webpage includes the authors' names, if provided (may use the name of the organization posting if no author is provided), the title of the specific item or article cited, the name of the website, the published date or updated date, the date the information was last accessed, and the URL without a period at the end.

Webpage Example:

US Department of Agriculture. MyPlate message toolkit for professionals: vary your veggies. ChooseMyPlate website. Published 2017. Accessed January 26, 2018. www.choosemyplate.gov/vary-your-veggies-0

CITING IN AN ORAL PRESENTATION

Oral communication presents citations differently, as they are highly dependent upon the audience and context. The speaker provides an indication that signals to listeners the source of ideas, words, or phrases. While there is no formal citation style guide for oral presentations, the speaker should strive to offer basic details for members of the audience who may wish to locate the original source. This information can be presented in a statement such as, "The following quote from the US Secretary of Agriculture," or the source may be provided in writing in an accompanying slide show or a supplementary handout, such as listing a URL in a slide or printed materials.

Here is a comparison of how a research study could be cited for three different audiences in an oral presentation.

Example 1: Speech to Peers

Blumenschine and colleagues at Arizona State University examined whether there was a difference in prevalence between rural and urban schools in implementing self-service salad bars as an approach to increase fruit and vegetable consumption. Their findings were published in the Journal of the Academy of Nutrition and Dietetics *in 2018.*

Example 2: Media Interview for Consumers

One of the proposed ways to increase the amount of fruits and vegetables schoolchildren eat is to provide self-service salad bars. Researchers from Arizona State University examined whether there was a difference between urban and rural schools in Arizona in their likelihood to have salad bars.

Example 3: Classroom Lecture to College Students

Your reading assignment is from the Journal of the Academy of Nutrition and Dietetics *from 2018, by Blumenschine and colleagues, titled "Prevalence of and Differences in Salad Bar Implementation in Rural Versus Urban Arizona Schools." For our next class, read the article and prepare to discuss barriers to salad-bar implementation.*

Citation and Style Guides

Different style guides are used for different subject areas. Modern Language Association (MLA) format is primarily used for English and humanities. American Psychological Association (APA) format is used for behavioral sciences. AMA or Scientific Style Format (SSF) are used primarily for medical and health sciences. Journals and organizations may specify which style guide they follow; for example, the Academy of Nutrition and Dietetics uses AMA format. Refer to the Purdue Online Writing Lab's citation guide listed in the resources section at the end of this chapter for more information about AMA style.

Giving Credit to Images, Figures, and Other Visual Representations

Just as with written and oral communication, illustrations and photographs require acknowledging the source properly. AMA does not have a style for citing visuals but does insist that a credit line be present.

Appearing below or near the image should be the following information: indication of permission or information on licensing; artist or author name; image title (if any); publication name or website; volume, issue, and page number (if in print); published date or updated date; access date (if from a website); and URL without a period at the end (if from a website).

Example 1: Photograph and Credit Line

Reproduced under the Pixabay License. DBreen. Vegetables. Published May 23, 2015. Accessed August 6, 2019. https://pixabay.com/en/users/dbreen-1643989

Example 2: Cartoon and Credit Line

Reproduced under the Pixabay License. GraphicMama-Team. Chef. Published May 30, 2016. Accessed August 6, 2019. https://pixabay.com/illustrations/chef-character-cook-gourmet-1417239

Example 3: Pie Chart and Credit Line

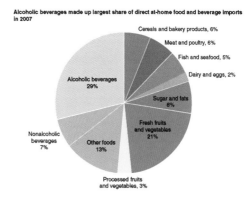

Reproduced from US Department of Agriculture: Economic Research Service. Alcoholic beverages made up largest share of direct at home food and beverage imports in 2007. USDA.gov website. Updated July 6, 2015. Accessed August 6, 2019. www.ers.usda.gov/data-products/chart-gallery/gallery/chart-detail/?chartId=62245

How Can Plagiarism Be Avoided?

Practicing proper citation skills requires discipline and consistency. It is important to give proper credit when using another's work. Most writers learn about and practice proper citation in a higher education setting. A typical college course syllabus or student handbook includes instructions on citation and sets clear expectations to avoid plagiarism. The rising incidence of plagiarism is likely related to easy access to information. In one study, 40% of students reported that access to internet materials contributed to cheating.[4] Violations may yield steep penalties, including failed grades for assignments, dismissal from a course, and erosion of trust; those working in higher education take this issue seriously.

Examples of Plagiarism

BOX 8.1

Direct plagiarism	Word-for-word transcription of a section of someone else's work without attribution and without quotation marks
Self-plagiarism	Submission of previous work, or mixing parts of previous works, without permission from all professors or assignment editors involved; also includes submission of the same piece of work for assignments in different classes or work settings without previous permission from all professors or assignment editors
Mosaic plagiarism (also called patch writing)	Borrowing phrases from a source without using quotation marks, or finding synonyms for the author's language while keeping to the same general structure and meaning of the original
Accidental plagiarism	Neglecting citations, misquoting sources, or unintentionally paraphrasing a source by using similar words, groups of words, or sentence structure without attribution

Adapted with permission from Office of the Dean of Students, Bowdoin College. The common types of plagiarism. Bowdoin College website. Accessed May 4, 2018. www.bowdoin.edu/studentaffairs/academic-honesty/common-types.shtml.[7]

Beyond college, the penalties for plagiarism can also be severe, including irreparable damage to a professional's reputation. Since communicators are expected to adequately cite material, complying with proper citation styles boosts credibility—and conversely, violation undermines it.

Plagiarism Defined

According to the *Oxford English Dictionary*, plagiarism is "the practice of taking someone else's work or ideas and passing them off as one's own."[5] The work taken from someone else could be verbatim language or patchwork pieces from multiple sources commingled into a work and presented as original.

For example, when leading a group for cancer patients, a practitioner creates a handout that includes a list of recommendations written by the American Cancer Society but fails to list the source. This would make it appear that the practitioner was the originator of the list. The practitioner might even include his or her name and contact information on the handout, inadvertently adding to the belief that the practitioner wrote the list. When a patient then gives the handout to a friend or family member, the potential for incorrect attribution spreads. Someone might even put the list in another publication and list the practitioner as the source. This oversight is plagiarism, and it also destroys credibility. Providing the correct source establishes a strong evidence base and gives the reader a source for obtaining additional information (in this example, from the American Cancer Society's website).

Online and print tools are available to help students and professionals understand plagiarism, learn about the common types of plagiarism, and read practice cases.[6] See the resources section for examples. Box 8.1 describes some examples of types of plagiarism.

Common Reasons for Plagiarism

There are several reasons why nutrition communicators may fail to properly attribute information and ideas originated by others.

Lack of Understanding The communicator did not understand the definition of plagiarism or know how to properly cite information sources. In some instances, such as in higher education settings, students accidentally plagiarize themselves by using part of a paper or assignment from one course to fulfill the requirements of another. For example, as graduate students advance through study, they may find themselves more deeply involved in a single topic and perform more and more research on that topic, resulting in the growth of their original work. Instead of citing themselves or other appropriate scholars, students may recycle their original manuscripts.

Pressure from Work or School Professors and work supervisors set performance targets for students and employees through course syllabuses and establishment of annual work goals. However, priorities may not always align, and competing demands may threaten a person's ability to meet the expectations of content creation. In some cases, content creators may take shortcuts, such as skipping citations, leading to plagiarism.

Possible Cultural Differences In some cultures, copying ideas and words directly is considered acceptable. International students may need instruction regarding plagiarism if they are not familiar with the rules of plagiarism in Western cultures.[8]

The Ease of "Copy and Paste" Copying and pasting original content is easier with modern technology. While writers may intend to rework or put quotes around pasted content, this may be overlooked or it may be inadequate, and plagiarism can be the result. According to a 2011 survey by the Pew Research Center, 89% of respondents believed computers and the internet played a major role in plagiarism trending upward.[1]

Intentional Plagiarism In this instance, the content creator is aware of the definition of plagiarism and chooses to plagiarize.

Preventing Plagiarism

College professors and professional communicators may choose to train students and employees on why plagiarism is problematic and then provide formal education and resources aimed at plagiarism prevention. Resources on plagiarism can come from many sources (like librarians) and be delivered in many forms, such as a printed style guide or a tutorial on plagiarism presented on the web. The tutorial might help viewers learn about, for example, when to use direct quotes and when to paraphrase ideas.

 A Series of Unfortunate Events

by Heidi Katte, MS, RDN, CD, FAND

All semester, Pete has had challenges in his business development and management course. His work traditionally has been the bare minimum. When a large project is assigned, he finds it challenging and isolates himself from his instructor and peers. As a result, he has limited references and resources for completing the project. How is he to start? Where does he find the information? Why is this so difficult? How does he organize his ideas, let alone his reference tools used for development? After much procrastination, he frantically completes the project at the last minute. The project has some original, creative ideas. After closer review, the instructor notes the dates of the projected project do not meet with the described business plan. The instructor realizes that something is not right. After further examination, the instructor determines the issue: The paper is plagiarized! What next for Pete?

Each educational institution has its own policies and procedures for dealing with plagiarism, which can range from a firm conversation with the instructor regarding the unethical practice of plagiarizing to expulsion from the institution.

The moral of the story is to spend the time to prepare and properly cite resources. This applies in both an academic and a professional setting.

Some educational programs offer students and faculty access to plagiarism detection software that is part of companion software tools supporting the course. Simple document scans yield snapshots of the likelihood that the submitted work existed beforehand; however, the tool only recognizes material that has already been scanned and made available to its database. In other words, documents that are not scanned would not be detected through such a software program. At the very least, writers could use free online tools to scan their own work to see if they have unintentionally plagiarized; this would also add to the database available to others working to detect plagiarism. Consider the story in Box 8.2 as an example of what could happen if appropriate steps for preventing plagiarism are not taken.

What Are Strategies for Giving Credit When a Full Reference Isn't Needed?

Evidence-based practice, founded on sound science, establishes the credibility of the dietetics profession. When communicating, whether in writing or orally, clearly indicate that the sources are research-based. Lay audiences do not expect a full reference or need as much detail about a reference as a professional audience, but they still desire the assurance that the information is from a credible source. If asked, practitioners should be able to provide complete references.

Descriptions of Sources When Writing for Lay Audiences

A health club newsletter is one example of where a practitioner might say that "recent research" or "research from XYZ" supports the benefits of consuming chocolate milk after working out due to

 WORDS OF EXPERIENCE

Communicating Source Material in Consumer Content

by Toby Amidor, MS, RD, CDN, FAND

It is important to let consumers know where information is obtained. Whether it is a research study, a nonstudy reference (like the US Dietary Guidelines for Americans or a government website), or a quote from a fellow registered dietitian nutritionist (RDN), the source of the information must be included in a way that consumers recognize. Here are examples of how to communicate the source from a research study, website, or quote.

Example A: Referencing a study

In a 2015 article I wrote for the FoodNetwork.com HealthyEats blog, titled "Cooked vs. Raw: Some Veggies Like It Hot," I discussed some vegetables that have higher nutrient values when cooked versus raw. For carrots, I discussed a study from the *Journal of Agricultural and Food Chemistry*. As readers will not want to read through long paragraphs explaining the study in detail, I gave the main idea in one line and linked to the abstract URL so readers could get more information if they chose.

Example B: Referencing a nonstudy document

In a 2018 article I wrote for the FoodNetwork.com HealthyEats blog, titled "Does a Plant-Based Diet Mean Eating Vegetarian?" I provided numerous facts from the US Dietary Guidelines for Americans. I referenced them as the "latest 2015-2020 Dietary Guidelines for Americans," with the specific date of the guidelines, to let readers know it uses current and relevant data. In cases where I mentioned specific appendixes in the guidelines, such as the new alcohol appendix, I linked to that URL.

Example C: Quoting experts

In a 2018 article in *US News & World Report* titled "Are You at Risk for a Social Media-Induced Eating Disorder?" I quoted fellow dietitian Heather Mangieri, RDN. How publications reference RDNs can vary. In this article I described the expert as "Heather Mangieri, a registered dietitian and nutrition consultant who specializes in disordered eating. In her book, *Fueling Young Athletes*, she shares stories of people who have orthorexia." Some writers will list full credentials after the expert's name (ie, MS, RDN), while others may prefer to write out the credentials (ie, registered dietitian). It is also important to include a few words on the expert's area of specialty and name any relevant publications (articles, books, and so on). If the publication allows it, further refer the reader to the expert's website, which I always try to do.

Toby Amidor, MS, RD, CDN, FAND, communicates with consumers as a best-selling author, a nutrition expert at FoodNetwork.com, and through her blog at tobyamidornutrition.com.

the contribution of glucose for refueling muscle glycogen and protein to support muscle recovery. Including a reference at the end of the article (or within the article using a hyperlink) provides credibility while avoiding detail within the text that might not interest a lay audience. Practitioners should begin or end an article with their name and credentials to identify themselves as a credible source. Review the Words of Experience box for examples of how one dietitian-author cites material.

Descriptions of Sources When Speaking to Lay Audiences

When speaking to a lay audience, it is good practice to begin with introductions in which the speaker is established as a credible source based on his or her education and credentials. This will set the stage for the audience to believe that what the speaker says is supported. Establish that the information the speaker is sharing is evidence-based by stating the source orally. For example, when presenting to a cardiac rehabilitation support group, explain that "according to the American Heart Association's [statement, recent publication], the incorporation of whole grains in the diet will assist with cholesterol reduction and management." If providing a handout, practitioners can include a URL or reference for the audience to find more information.

In summary, when communicating nutrition information to all types of audiences, whether it is in a written document, an online post, or an oral presentation, the speaker must accurately indicate the source of the information.

KEY POINTS

Nutrition Communicators Properly Reference Sources

1. Carefully select sources to provide the evidence base for communication, and properly cite all sources.

2. Do not take credit for the work of others, and do not let plagiarism result in expulsion from school or discrediting a professional nutrition credential.

3. When communicating nutrition information, correct indication of sources is required. This informs the audience that evidence-based nutrition research is being used, credits the source, and reflects the integrity of a nutrition professional's work.

RESOURCES

How to Recognize Plagiarism: Tutorials and Tests www.indiana.edu/~academy/firstPrinciples /certificationTests/index.html

Neville C. *The Complete Guide to Referencing and Avoiding Plagiarism*, 2nd ed. Neville C. *The Complete Guide to Referencing and Avoiding Plagiarism*. 2nd ed. Open University Press/McGraw-Hill Education; 2007.

Using the AMA Style, Purdue Online Writing Lab https://owl.english.purdue.edu/owl/resource/1017/01

REFERENCES

1. Parker K, Lenhart A, Moore K. The digital revolution and higher education: college presidents, public differ on value of online learning. Pew Research Center website. Published 2011. Accessed May 4, 2018. www.pewsocial trends.org/2011/08/28/the-digital-revolution-and -higher-education

2. What is common knowledge? In: *Academic Integrity at MIT: A Handbook for Students*. Accessed October 11, 2018. Academic Integrity at MIT website. https://integrity.mit.edu/handbook /citing-your-sources/what-common-knowledge

3. What is plagiarism? A guide to catching and fixing plagiarism. EasyBib website. Published 2017. Accessed May 4, 2018. www.easybib .com/guides/students/research-guide/what-is -plagiarism

4. Dordoy A. Cheating and plagiarism: student and staff perceptions and Northumbria. *Proceedings of the Northumbria Conference—Educating for the Future.* 2002:1-6.

5. Oxford English Dictionary. Plagiarism. Accessed May 4, 2018. www.oed.com/view/Entry/144939?redirectedFrom=plagiarism#eid

6. How to recognize plagiarism: tutorials and tests. Indiana University website. Published 2017. Accessed May 4, 2018. www.indiana.edu/~academy/firstPrinciples/overview/shouldDo.html

7. Office of the Dean of Students, Bowdoin College. The common types of plagiarism. Bowdoin College website. Accessed May 4, 2018. www.bowdoin.edu/studentaffairs/academic-honesty/common-types.shtml

8. Plagiarism resources. University of Connecticut Library website. Accessed May 4, 2018. https://lib.uconn.edu/about/get-help/writing/plagiarism-resources

Nutrition Communicators Adhere to the Code of Ethics for the Nutrition and Dietetics Profession

Martine I. Scannavino, DHSc, RDN, LDN, FAND
and Mindy Hermann, MBA, RDN

"It is essential to practice in a manner that reflects the profession's Code of Ethics as it applies to communication."

"Aspire to decency. Practice civility toward one another. Admire and emulate ethical behavior wherever you find it. Apply a rigid standard of morality to your lives; and if, periodically, you fail—as you surely will—adjust your lives, not the standards." —TED KOPPEL

Introduction

"Ethics refers to well-founded standards of right and wrong that prescribe what humans ought to do, usually in terms of rights, obligations, benefits to society, fairness, or specific virtues."[1]

Ethics in practice is dynamic and reflects societal changes. The Academy of Nutrition and Dietetics and the Commission on Dietetic Registration (CDR) have established a Code of Ethics (Academy/CDR Code of Ethics) to guide the nutrition professional through the process of ethical decision-making in all practice settings. The Academy/CDR Code of Ethics applies to nutrition professionals who are credentialed by CDR and all members of the Academy of Nutrition and Dietetics (regardless of credential status).[2]

This chapter answers three questions:

- What ethics principles are foundational to nutrition communication?
- Which ethics principles are of greatest concern in nutrition communication?
- How can nutrition professionals promote ethical practice and practice ethically?

The first section of this chapter will outline the ethics principles that are foundational to nutrition communication. These principles and their corresponding standards lay the groundwork for practicing ethically in the role of nutrition communicator. The next section provides a more in-depth discussion of the ethical principles of greatest concern to the nutrition professional as it relates to nutrition communication. The final section presents how the nutrition professional can practice and promote ethical practice. This content, along with the additional resources provided at the end of the chapter, can support nutrition professionals in their quest to practice and act ethically when providing nutrition information to the public.

What Ethics Principles Are Foundational to Nutrition Communication?

The Academy/CDR Code of Ethics applies to all nutrition professionals in all areas of practice.[2] Nutrition professionals serve as communicators in almost all that they do. However, there are times when communication is the central responsibility of the nutrition professional. In these instances, it is essential to practice in a manner that reflects the profession's code as it applies to communication.

The Academy/CDR Code of Ethics for the Nutrition and Dietetics Profession 2018 is built on the four fundamental principles of bioethics: nonmaleficence (do no harm), autonomy (informed consent and decision-making), beneficence (a duty to do good), and justice (fair and equal treatment for all).[2,3] These principles are the foundation of four guiding principles of the Academy/CDR Code of Ethics:

- competence and professional development in practice (nonmaleficence)
- integrity in personal and organizational behaviors and practices (autonomy)

- professionalism (beneficence)
- social responsibility for local, regional, national, and global nutrition and well-being (justice)

The four guiding principles are supported by 32 standards (see Figure 9.1). Ethical decision-making in practice is the core of effective nutrition communication. When communicating to the public, nutrition and dietetics professionals accept responsibility for the information and messages they share as well as the consequences of those messages.

According to Kathleen Gennuso, DHCE, MSBLE, of the Institute of Consultative Bioethics (written communication, October 30, 2018):

Ethics is usually defined as the systematic exploration of questions about how to act in relation to others. The questions relate to what is believed as right or wrong action, or the good of life. Ethics is usually taken to mean the overall way of viewing the world in a moral sense. Values describe the way that moral framework is put into practice in relationships with others and in how policy is interpreted and developed.

Every individual has some kind of personal code of ethics or moral (values) stance that is reflected in and influences everything they do. People can never be value neutral; therefore, it is important to be clear about how personal values affect both individuals and those they encounter.

According to Gennuso (written communication, October 30, 2018):

A framework for sound ethical decision-making includes the following steps:
- *gathering the facts,*
- *defining the ethical issues,*
- *identifying the affected stakeholders,*
- *identifying the consequences,*
- *identifying the obligations,*
- *considering one's own character and integrity,*
- *thinking creatively about potential actions, and*
- *checking a "gut feeling."*

FIGURE 9.1 **Excerpt from the Academy of Nutrition and Dietetics and Commission on Dietetic Registration Code of Ethics for the Nutrition and Dietetics Profession (2018)**

eat right. Academy of Nutrition and Dietetics

**Code of Ethics
for the Nutrition and Dietetics Profession**

Effective Date: June 1, 2018

Commission on Dietetic Registration
the credentialing agency for the
eat right. Academy of Nutrition and Dietetics

Preamble:

When providing services the nutrition and dietetics practitioner adheres to the core values of customer focus, integrity, innovation, social responsibility, and diversity. Science-based decisions, derived from the best available research and evidence, are the underpinnings of ethical conduct and practice.

This Code applies to nutrition and dietetics practitioners who act in a wide variety of capacities, provides general principles and specific ethical standards for situations frequently encountered in daily practice. The primary goal is the protection of the individuals, groups, organizations, communities, or populations with whom the practitioner works and interacts.

The nutrition and dietetics practitioner supports and promotes high standards of professional practice, accepting the obligation to protect clients, the public and the profession; upholds the Academy of Nutrition and Dietetics (Academy) and its credentialing agency the Commission on Dietetic Registration (CDR) Code of Ethics for the Nutrition and Dietetics Profession; and shall report perceived violations of the Code through established processes.

The Academy/CDR Code of Ethics for the Nutrition and Dietetics Profession establishes the principles and ethical standards that underlie the nutrition and dietetics practitioner's roles and conduct. All individuals to whom the Code applies are referred to as "nutrition and dietetics practitioners". By accepting membership in the Academy and/or accepting and maintaining CDR credentials, all nutrition and dietetics practitioners agree to abide by the Code.

Principles and Standards:
1. **Competence and professional development in practice (Non-maleficence)**
2. **Integrity in personal and organizational behaviors and practices (Autonomy)**
3. **Professionalism (Beneficence)**
4. **Social responsibility for local, regional, national, global nutrition and well-being (Justice)**

Find the full text of the Academy of Nutrition and Dietetics and Commission on Dietetic Registration Code of Ethics at www.eatrightpro .org/-/media/eatrightpro-files/career/code-of-ethics/coeforthenutritionanddieteticsprofession.pdf

Box 9.1 illustrates the obligations a practitioner must taken into account when considering the ethics of a dilemma.

There are specific Academy/CDR Code of Ethics principles and standards that are foundational to ethical practice when communicating with the public, as well as with other health care professionals. The following numbered code principles serve as a guide to these principles and standards.

Code Principles for Evidence-Based Information

The nutrition professional is charged with communicating nutrition information to the public that can be trusted as being truthful, accurate, and nonbiased. The Academy/CDR Code of Ethics provides language to guide the decision-making process in this realm.

CODE PRINCIPLE 1: Competence and Professional Development in Practice (Nonmaleficence)

Eight standards support this first principle; each is integral to competent and ethical practice (see Figure 9.1). Central to these principles is the commitment to evidence-based practice. Principle 1 is aligned with the bioethical principle of nonmaleficence, which translates to "do no harm"—refraining from subjecting patients or clients to ineffective or unproven treatments.

For the nutrition communicator, treatments encompass information provided to the lay population as well as to other health professionals.

Obligations for Consideration in Ethical Dilemmas, at a Glance

Duty—Fulfilling Duty and Using Power Appropriately

Who are the potential players?

- An individual
- Family, friends, church, community
- Organization—coworkers, employees, boss, stockholders, customers, suppliers
- Industry, society, future generations
- The law

Honesty

What are the foundational constructs?

- Be truthful.
- Avoid deceit.
- Maintain integrity.
- Form trusting relationships.

Do No Harm—Avoid or Minimize Injury

What must be considered?

- Actual harm vs potential harm (physical harm, economic harm, and psychological harm)
- Serious harm vs minor harm
- How many were harmed (humans vs animals vs plants)
- Harming the disadvantaged, vulnerable, or powerless

Respect for People and Their Rights

How can this be ensured?

- Everyone has a right to be respected as a human being and as an individual, and to be treated with dignity and a sense of worth, regardless of personal situation, culture, or behavior.
- Apply standards of confidentiality.

Self-Determination

What must a person do?

- Allow others to make their own choices, and do not force personal values or opinions on another.
- Ensure individuals are aware of all the options available in any given situation, and their possible consequences, and that they have access to resources to enable them to choose freely and fairly.
- Apply appropriate use of power—this empowers both follower and leader.

Reproduced with permission from K. Gennuso, DHCE, MSBLE, of the Institute of Consultative Bioethics (written communication, October 30, 2018).

Therefore:

- the information communicated must be evidence-based and within the practitioner's area of competence (Standard 1.a.);
- the practitioner must promote and provide unbiased information that is valid and supported by scientific evidence (Standard 1.c); and
- practitioners must assess their professional abilities, acknowledge personal limitations, and accordingly, work within their scope of practice (Standards 1.f and 1.g).

CODE PRINCIPLE 2: Integrity in Personal and Organizational Behaviors and Practices (Autonomy)

Standard 2a "Disclose any conflicts of interest, including any financial interests in products or services that are recommended. Refrain from accepting gifts or services which potentially influence or which may give the appearance of influencing professional judgment."

Standard 2e "Provide accurate and truthful information in all communications."

CODE PRINCIPLE 3. Professionalism (Beneficence)

Standard 3d "Refrain from communicating false, fraudulent, deceptive, misleading, disparaging or unfair statements or claims."

Code Principles for Respect for Individuals

CODE PRINCIPLE 1: Competence and Professional Development in Practice (Nonmaleficence)

Standard 1g "Act in a caring and respectful manner, mindful of individual differences, cultural, and ethnic diversity."

Cultural competence is central to this principle's standard. The ethics of cultural competence has been identified by Paashe-Orlow[4] as having three essential principles:

1. acknowledgment of the importance of culture in people's lives,
2. respect for cultural differences, and

3. minimization of any negative consequences of cultural differences.

To practice ethically, nutrition professionals must persistently work to build cultural competence. Cultural competence exists on a scale known as the cultural competence continuum.[5] As the term implies, this area of professional development requires ongoing commitment and attention to gain and maintain proficiency. In simple terms, it is a lifelong commitment to be a culturally competent practitioner fulfilling the ethical responsibility to "act in a caring and respectful manner, mindful of individual's differences, cultural and ethnic diversity."[6] In the quest to be culturally competent, a practitioner is never done.

Cultural competence is covered in more depth in Chapter 13.

CODE PRINCIPLE 3: Professionalism (Beneficence)

Standard 3h "Communicate at an appropriate level to promote health literacy."

When designing messages or communicating information to the public, the nutrition professional must be cognizant of the target audience to whom the message or information is directed. The nutrition professional's ethical obligation to communicate at an appropriate level to promote health literacy goes beyond providing effective messages to target populations. This standard challenges nutrition professionals to ensure that their message meets the criteria for "incorporat[ing] a range of abilities: reading, comprehending, and analyzing information; decoding instructions, symbols, charts, and diagrams; weighing risks and benefits; and, ultimately, making decisions and taking action" outlined by the National Institutes of Health.[7]

Code Principles for Using Credentials Appropriately

The nutrition professionals who are credentialed by CDR represent the profession to the public every time they write their credentials on a document, webpage, blog, newspaper article, or any other form of communication. Maintaining the credential through the mandated hours of continuing education, which align with a practitioner's individual professional development portfolio and are reinforced with practice experiences, is what makes nutrition professionals experts in their field. Bearing the credential of registered dietitian nutritionist (RDN) informs the public that the individual providing information is the food and nutrition expert. The Academy of Nutrition and Dietetics provides guidance on expert practice criteria through the Academy of Nutrition and Dietetics Standards of Practice (SOP) and Standards of Professional Performance (SOPP), "which can be used by credentialed nutrition and dietetics practitioners to assess their individual performance needs."[8]

CODE PRINCIPLE 1: Competence and Professional Development in Practice (Nonmaleficence)

Standard 1h "Practice within the limits of their scope and collaborate with the interprofessional team."

CODE PRINCIPLE 2: Integrity in Personal and Organizational Behaviors and Practices (Autonomy)

Standard 2c "Maintain and appropriately use credentials."

It is imperative that nutrition professionals carefully enter into the process of self-evaluation, assess their ethical compass, and seek development and mentorship to achieve a higher level of ethical practice. Ethics means "… the continuous effort of studying our own moral beliefs and our moral conduct, and striving to ensure that we, and the institutions we help to shape, live up to standards that are reasonable and solidly-based."[1]

Which Ethics Principles Are of Greatest Concern in Nutrition Communication?

Numerous ethics principles govern practice in nutrition communication. The growth and ubiquitous nature of newer forms of communication, namely social media, enhance the power of nutrition professionals to reach more people more rapidly. They also make professionals more vulnerable to lapses in ethics principles. When using social media, nutrition professionals must remember that they are governed by the same code of ethics that guides all other aspects of practice and helps them avoid mistakes and misjudgments involving ethics, professionalism, transparency, and disclosure.[9]

Within the principles of the Academy/CDR Code of Ethics, there are several standards that pose the greatest concern in nutrition communications (emphasis added in italics).

CODE PRINCIPLE 1: Competence and Professional Development in Practice (Nonmaleficence)

Standard 1c "Assess the validity and applicability of scientific evidence *without personal bias*."

Standard 1f "Recognize and exercise professional judgment *within the limits of individual qualifications* and collaborate with others, seek counsel, and make referrals as appropriate."

Standard 1h "Practice within the *limits of their scope* and collaborate with the inter-professional team."

Nutrition communicators who have established themselves as resources for information, translation, and interpretation can be called upon to comment in areas that are tangentially but not directly related to nutrition. Nutrition professionals in communications must be able to separate issues within their professional scope from those that are better addressed by other professionals. For example, a nutrition professional who has expertise in basic nutrition and nutrition for families may be called upon to comment on sports nutrition. An ethical decision would be to refer the request to a colleague who practices in that area, as outlined in principle 2:

CODE PRINCIPLE 2: Integrity in Personal and Organizational Behaviors and Practices (Autonomy)

Standard 2a "Disclose any *conflicts of interest*, including any financial interests in products or services that are recommended. Refrain from accepting gifts or services which potentially influence, or which may give the appearance of influencing professional judgment."

All formats, including blogs, podcasts, tweets, social media, shared video, and shared photos, require transparency because the reader, listener, or viewer may not realize that the communicator and the company whose products are mentioned have a relationship.[10] This does not mean that nutrition professionals cannot serve as consultants or participate in events where they receive meals, fees, or promotional products. Knowing how the "when" and "where" affect the "why" is a matter of judgment.[11]

Box 9.2 lists the types of activities requiring disclosure if the nutrition professional is associated with a company, commodity board, or association.

Conflicts of interest and their disclosure are among the most critical ethics considerations in nutrition communication. Material connections—that is, any relationship that involves money, sponsored travel, product samples, meals, or other items of value received from a company or association, as well as promotion of self-published materials—can bias the nutrition professional and create the appearance of personal gain from promoting a particular product. This type of relationship must be disclosed in clear language.[12] Box 9.3 lists examples of disclosure hashtags and statements. While not mandated by law, appropriate use of these terms supports transparency.

Nutrition professionals who write books that do not go through a peer-review process for scientific accuracy, including books for consumers and self-published books, need to disclose that the views and interpretations in the books are their own. Any sponsored nutrition communications must be tagged prominently and on the same page as the communication, using terms that define the relationship between the nutrition professional and the company or organization.

Example 1 A nutrition communicator receives pasta sauce samples from a company that hopes the communicator will write a blog post about the products. Accepting the samples may bias the nutrition professional to communicate an opinion or endorsement without fairly considering other products. The nutrition professional's blog post should clearly state his or her relationship with the company directly on the blog page and in easy-to-understand language. For example, "Company X provided me with samples; the opinions expressed in this blog post are my own." Readers might miss a disclosure that appears on a different page of the website.

Example 2 A nutrition professional who works as a spokesperson for a snack product independently mentions the product in a blog post and links the post to various social media outlets without being asked or paid separately by the producer of the product. Even though the post was not paid for directly, the nutrition professional must disclose the spokesperson relationship in the blog post and any related social media.

Types of Activities Requiring Disclosure If A Practitioner Is Associated with a Company, Commodity Board, or Association

Creating recipes

Receiving product samples for mentioning on social media

Hosting a Twitter chat

Contributing an editorial

Communicating as an editorial board member

Serving as a spokesperson

Mentioning products during a media appearance

Traveling to a meeting or conference, with expenses paid, and communicating about particular subject matter

Sample Disclosures

Hashtags	Statements
#client	Support provided by Company X
#spokesperson	
#consultant	Consultant for Company X
#advisor	
#sponsored	Board member for Company X
#samples	
#ad	Products for recipe development provided by Company X
#endorsement	

Example 3 A Food & Nutrition Conference & Expo (FNCE) exhibitor pays a nutrition professional for books and a book-signing session at FNCE. The nutrition professional must disclose the relationship in any social media posts that refer to the book signing.

Example 4 A professional in nutrition self-publishes a book on diets. When speaking to consumer audiences on the topic, the nutrition professional should disclose that the book is self-published and reflects the author's point of view.

Standard 2d "Respect intellectual property rights, including citation and recognition of the ideas and work of others, regardless of the medium (eg, written, oral, electronic)." The nature of media in general and social media in particular encourages the sharing of information. However, while they may be easily accessible on the internet, written materials, graphics, photographs, audio broadcasts, and video clips are protected by copyright, which also protects the person who

Chapter 8 provides more information about avoiding plagiarism.

created them; that person does not need to register a copyright to be protected.[13] Facts and ideas can be used, but exact language is protected, and permission must be requested and granted before reposting in any format, including social media.[14] Similarly, nutrition communicators also have a right to protect their own work.

A 2017 article in the *Journal of the Academy of Nutrition and Dietetics* elaborates on the legal and ethical aspects of copyright and plagiarism, which is copying without attribution[15]:

- If the content creator does not post a copyright notice that forbids content sharing, the content can be shared and linked to, with links preferable to verbatim reposting.
- The 1976 Copyright Act allows exemptions for fair use of short excerpts. Longer quotes should be limited in length, set apart with quotation marks, and attributed to the original author.
- Photos cannot be reproduced without permission from the creator or from the journal in which a photo appeared. The article encourages nutrition professionals to become familiar with fair use and, for photos, Creative Commons licensing when sharing content created by others.

Box 9.4 summarizes courses of action to respect the copyright of reproduced works.[14]

Standard 2e "Provide accurate and truthful information in all communications." The drive to communicate in a timely and compelling way can invite shortcuts—reading just headlines rather than full articles, relying on a study abstract only, or repeating the interpretation of another communicator rather than reviewing the original research. Accuracy suffers as a result. Communicators need to be wary of disseminating nutrition misinformation put forth by pseudo-experts, particularly in formats such as Twitter that encourage brief messaging.[15]

Nutrition professionals who receive gifts, fees, and other material items can appear to others to be presenting only one perspective rather than a balanced summary of the available science. This may not be the case, but it's important to be transparent about these relationships. In addition to fully disclosing the relationship, communicators should only endorse products that they have tried and validated.

BOX 9.4 Respecting the Copyright of Reproduced Works

Type of Material	Course of Action
A copyrighted comic in a PowerPoint presentation	Request permission; be prepared to pay a fee.
Reposting another author's blog post	Notify the author; payment may be requested.
A picture of a food product in a social media post	None; generally, no action is required if reposted from a company website.
Reposting a recipe and photo	It is professional courtesy to notify the author or photographer; permission may be required for the photo.
Adapting a recipe	It is professional courtesy to acknowledge the original source even if changes in ingredients are made; recipe introduction and instructions must be rewritten.
A government graphic on a website	None; works of the US government or its agencies are considered to be in the public domain and can be used without charge.
Facts from a magazine article	Reposting of widely-known facts is generally considered fair use; less-known facts require permission.

Standard 2h "Respect patient/client's autonomy. Safeguard patient/client confidentiality according to current regulations and laws." Protection of private patient or client information is a priority for nutrition professionals. In their various communications, nutrition professionals must safeguard information that could be used to identify a particular individual, including name, address, diagnosis, and photos. Any testimonials require written consent from the patient or client, including how that person will be identified.

A privacy policy on a website or blog discloses the type of visitor information that is collected, how it is used by the website or blog owner, and whether internet cookies have been employed to tag visitors. As with private patient or client information, visitor information must be protected. This is especially important for nutrition and dietetics practitioners who are monetizing their blogs and websites by receiving payment for particular services, such as by displaying third-party ads.[9]

CODE PRINCIPLE 3: Professionalism (Beneficence)

We can further look at four of the most important aspects of Code Principle 3.

Standard 3b "Respect the values, rights, knowledge, and skills of colleagues and other professionals."

Standard 3c "Demonstrate respect, constructive dialogue, civility, and professionalism in all communications, including social media."

Standard 3d "Refrain from communicating false, fraudulent, deceptive, misleading, disparaging, or unfair statements or claims."

Standard 3f "Refrain from verbal/physical/emotional/sexual harassment."

Communications in general and social media in particular enable both good and bad behavior related to civility. Respect for colleagues, other professionals, and other communicators involves calling out and giving credit for good work by others, acknowledging in print and presentation the contributions of collaborators and coauthors, and respecting varying but scientifically supported alternate points of view. The flip side involves choosing words of disagreement carefully, addressing ideas rather than people, supporting arguments with science-based facts, and avoiding combative language. Stay away from posting negative comments on social media about colleagues or other professionals—these comments can spread through social media and may be picked up by local or national news media, casting the author of the public comments in a negative light. See Figure 9.2 on page 137 for guidelines to address messages with professional civility.[16]

How Can Nutrition Professionals Promote Ethical Practice?

According to the Academy of Nutrition and Dietetics, nutrition professionals "have voluntarily adopted the Academy/CDR Code of Ethics to reflect the values and ethical principles guiding the dietetics profession and to set forth commitments and obligations of the dietetics practitioner to the public, clients, the profession, colleagues and other professionals."[17]

The description of the Academy/CDR Code of Ethics stresses the importance of customer (public) focus, integrity, and, importantly, science-based decisions derived from the best available research and evidence. A 2015 ethics article in the *Journal of the Academy of Nutrition and Dietetics* presents the following adaptation of steps for ethical decision-making[18]:

Step 1 State an ethical dilemma. Identify the components of a particular situation that represents a potential ethical dilemma. Is this an ethical issue? Or, alternatively, is it a communication problem or a legal matter?

> Example: A local news outlet reaches out to a nutrition communicator who has a strong media presence for comments on camera about a local health professional providing potentially unsafe diet guidance.

Step 2 Connect ethical theory to the dilemma in practice.

> Response to the news outlet requires consideration of damaging vs protecting reputations, basing comments on scientific evidence and disclosing any biases.

Step 3 *Apply the Academy/CDR Code of Ethics to the issue and ethical decision-making.*

Code principles and standards that apply in the local news outlet examples from Steps 1 and 2 in this situation include:

- Standard 1a: "Practice using an evidence-based approach within areas of competence, continuously develop and enhance expertise, and recognize limitations." *Is the nutrition communicator qualified to speak?*
- Standard 1b: "Demonstrate in-depth scientific knowledge of food, human nutrition, and behavior." *Can the nutrition communicator apply evidence-based information when responding?*
- Standard 1c: "Assess the validity and applicability of scientific evidence without personal bias." *Can the nutrition communicator comment independent of her or his feelings for the professional in question?*
- Standard 1e: "Make evidence-based practice decisions, taking into account the unique values and circumstances of the patient/client and community, in combination with the practitioner's expertise and judgment." *Can the nutrition communicator incorporate scientific evidence of potential harm?*
- Standard 2a: "Disclose any conflicts of interest, including any financial interests in products or services that are recommended." *Does the nutrition communicator have a relationship with a company that provides products or services in the area in question?*
- Standard 2e: "Provide accurate and truthful information in all communications." *Can the nutrition communicator speak truthfully at all times?*
- Standard 2f: "Report inappropriate behavior or treatment of a patient or client by another nutrition and dietetics practitioner or other professionals." *Does the nutrition communicator have enough evidence to report*

the other professional? What other avenues exist outside of the media for reporting potentially harmful behavior?
- Standard 3b: "Respect the values, rights, knowledge, and skills of colleagues and other professionals." *Is the other professional practicing within the scope of his or her profession?*
- Standard 3c: "Demonstrate respect, constructive dialogue, civility, and professionalism in all communications, including social media." *Can communications remain positive?*
- Standard 3d: "Refrain from communicating false, fraudulent, deceptive, misleading, disparaging, or unfair statements or claims." *Does the nutrition communicator have all necessary information to avoid making false statements?*

Step 4 Based on the scenario presented in Steps 1 and 2, select the best alternative and justify the decision. Consider cultural influences, values, and standards of practice.

Decide why or why not to accept the request, and be able to support the rationale for the decision.

Step 5 Develop strategies to successfully implement the chosen resolution from the local news outlet examples presented in Steps 1 and 2. Use the Standards of Professional Performance as a guide.

Comment only within the scope of practice as defined by the Standards of Practice and Standards of Professional Performance. If strategies are not clear, turning down the request, and explaining the rationale, may be the best course of action.

Step 6 Considering the scenario with the local news outlet from Steps 1 and 2, evaluate the outcomes and determine how to prevent a similar occurrence.

FIGURE 9.2 **Pledge of professional civility and guiding principles**

Professional Civility

New media communications — from engagement with consumers on social media platforms to discussions among fellow practitioners on private listservs and forums — provide an unprecedented ability to share information and perspectives. These are exciting opportunities for nutrition and dietetics practitioners, but with them come challenges, including reconciling social media best practices, principles of the code of ethics and professional courtesies and conduct.

To help foster camaraderie among our professional community and encourage constructive engagement among peers, *Food & Nutrition Magazine*® — published by the world's largest organization of food and nutrition professionals, the Academy of Nutrition and Dietetics — has developed a voluntary Pledge of Professional Civility, guiding principles and related resources:

The Pledge of Professional Civility

- I pledge to demonstrate respect to my colleagues and all others.
- I pledge to support constructive dialogue and positive engagement.
- I pledge to discourage the public belittling of my colleagues, even when we do not agree.
- I pledge to model professional conduct in all my public communications and actions.

Guiding Principles

The following represents basic tenets that any professional — irrespective of expertise, area of practice or personal values — should adopt as principles of conduct in public forums, including social media.

1. **Demonstrating respect:** The science and profession of nutrition and dietetics is an evolution of research, practices, culture and understanding. There are times when colleagues may not agree, and issues about which there may never be unanimity. Still, it is never beneficial for the profession when health practitioners publicly criticize their peers on forums or social media. As a vehicle for engagement and connection, social media should not be used for disrupting fellow colleagues' engagement with their communities. Practitioners who feel compelled to question the content of a fellow colleague should encourage respectful expression of opinions, especially when we do not agree, and to recognize that it is an individual's choice whether to engage in further conversation.

2. **Encouraging constructive dialogue**: When professional discussions do unfold on digital forums, attention should focus on the issue or topic at hand and never belittle a participant or his or her character, intelligence, culture or opinion. Constructive dialogue and amicable discourse foster greater insight and understanding, even if one's opinion or position on a matter ultimately remains unchanged. Whereas public antagonism and divisiveness dishonor the profession, and are a disservice to the more than 100,000 professionals who hold the RDN or NDTR credentials, positive engagement among peers demonstrates professionalism to both consumers and other health practitioners — and sets an example for future food and nutrition professionals.

3. **Discouraging public belittling of colleagues**: Professional peers should not encourage the humiliation or harassment of other professionals by "liking," retweeting or sharing content that is discourteous or disrespectful. Further, colleagues who witness the public harassment or humiliation of a fellow colleague, even one with whom they may not agree, might consider extending support to that colleague. Every individual has a right to participate in social media and should be able to do so without the threat or fear of being ostracized by one's own colleagues and fellow members whose opinions or perspectives may be different.

4. **Modeling professionalism**: RDNs and NDTRs are not only recognized experts in nutrition and health, but also colleagues in a distinguished profession that is more than 100,000 strong. Just as in work environments and professional settings, the words used, messages expressed and behaviors demonstrated on new media communications platforms not only reflect the competencies and conduct of the individual, but the values and credibility of the entire profession. Therefore, it is crucial that strong examples of personal conduct and professional behavior be set for fellow and future practitioners.

Reproduced with permission from Professional Civility. *Food & Nutrition Magazine*. Accessed July 8, 2020. https://foodandnutrition .org/professionalcivility[6]

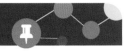

Nutrition Communicators Adhere to the Code of Ethics for the Nutrition and Dietetics Profession

1 It is essential to practice in a manner that reflects the profession's Code of Ethics as it applies to communication.

2 The nutrition professional is charged with communicating nutrition information to the public that can be trusted as being science-based, truthful, accurate, and nonbiased.

3 Conflicts of interest and their disclosure are among the most critical ethics considerations in nutrition communication.

4 The actions and communications of the nutrition professional must be beyond reproach. When in doubt, consult the Academy of Nutrition and Dietetics and Commission on Dietetic Registration's ethics educational resources or reach out to a mentor for guidance.

RESOURCES

Academy of Nutrition and Dietetic and Commission on Dietetic Registration Disciplinary and Ethics Complaints Policy: www.eatrightpro.org/-/media/eatrightpro-files /practice/disciplinaryandethics-complaintspolicy.pdf

Academy of Nutrition and Dietetics and Commission on Dietetic Registration Code of Ethics for the Nutrition and Dietetics Profession: www.eatrightpro.org/-/media/eatrightpro-files/career /code-of-ethics/coeforthenutritionanddietetics profession.pdf

Centers for Disease Control and Prevention Health Literacy Guidance and Tools: www.cdc.gov /healthliteracy/developmaterials/guidancestandards .html

Ethics Case Studies: Impact of Social Media: www.eatrightpro.org/-/media/eatrightpro-files/career /code-of-ethics/socialmediaethicscasestudy.pdf

Ethics Education Facilitators' Guide Handouts: www.eatrightpro.org/-/media/eatrightpro-files/career /code-of-ethics/facilitators-guidehandouts.pdf

Ethics Education PowerPoint Presentation: www.eatrightpro.org/-/media/eatrightpro-files/career /code-of-ethics/facilitatorsscript.pdf

Ethics Reading List: www.eatrightpro.org/practice /code-of-ethics/ethics-education-resources

Institute of Consultative Bioethics: www.icbioethics.com

Markkula Center for Applied Ethics. Making an Ethical Decision: A practical tool for thinking through tough choices (the Ethics APP): www.scu.edu/ethics-app

REFERENCES

1. Velasquez M, Andre C, Shanks T, SJ, Meyer MJ. What is ethics? Markkula Center for Applied Ethics at Santa Clara University website. Published 2010. Accessed June 1, 2018. www.scu.edu/ethics/ethics-resources/ethical -decision-making/what-is-ethics

2. Academy of Nutrition and Dietetics; Commission on Dietetic Registration. Code of ethics for the nutrition and dietetics profession. Eatright website. Published June 1, 2018. Accessed May 17, 2018. www.eatrightpro.org /-/media/eatrightpro-files/career/code-of-ethics /coeforthenutritionanddieteticsprofession.pdf

3. Beauchamp TL, Childress JF. Principles of biomedical ethics. *Oxford Univ Press.* 2008;6(1995):39-64. doi:10.1016/S0033 -3182(95)71674-7

4. Paasche-Orlow M. The ethics of cultural competence. *Acad Med.* 2004;79(4):347-350.

5. Cross TL, Bazron BJ, Dennis KW, Isaacs MR. *Towards a Culturally Competent System of Care: A Monograph on Effective Services for Minority Children Who Are Severely Emotionally Disturbed.* CASSP Technical Assistance Center; 1989.

6. Academy of Nutrition and Dietetics; Commission on Dietetic Registration. Code of ethics for the nutrition and dietetics profession. Eatright website. Accessed July 30, 2019. www.eatrightpro.org/-/media/eatrightpro-files /career/code-of-ethics/codeofethicshandout.pdf

7. Clear communication. National Institutes of Health website. Accessed April 26, 2018. www.nih.gov/institutes-nih/nih-office-director /office-communications-public-liaison/clear -communication

8. Academy of Nutrition and Dietetics. Standards of practice. Eatright website. Accessed April 28, 2018. www.eatrightpro.org/practice/quality -management/standards-of-practice

9. Helm J, Jones RM. Practice paper of the Academy of Nutrition and Dietetics: social media and the dietetics practitioner: opportunities, challenges, and best practices. *J Acad Nutr Diet.* 2016;116(11):1825-1835. doi:10.1016/j.jand .2016.09.003

10. Helm J. Ethics in action: ethical and legal issues related to blogging and social media. *J Acad Nutr Diet.* 2013;113(5):688-690.

11. Boyce B. The balance of professional ethics. *J Acad Nutr Diet.* 2017;117(7):1120-1123. doi:10.1016/j. jand.2017.01.019

12. Palmer S. Dietitians' food industry relationships: what is ethical and what is not? *Today's Dietit.* 2015;17(3):44.

13. Goedert PC. A plain-English guide to copyright. Barnes & Thornburg LLP website. Accessed May 1, 2018. www.aallnet.org/wp-content/uploads /2017/12/ChapterLeadershipLegalTraining2016 -17.pdf

14. Cochran N, King D. Dietitians on social media: promoting and protecting your work. *Today's Dietit.* 2015;17(10):50.

15. Peregrin T. Clearing up copyright confusion and social media use: what nutrition and dietetics practitioners need to know. *J Acad Nutr Diet.* 2017;117(4):623-625. doi:10.1016/j.jand.2017 .01.015

16. Professional Civility. *Food & Nutrition Magazine.* Accessed July 8, 2020. https://foodandnutrition .org/professionalcivility

17. Academy of Nutrition and Dietetics. What is the code of ethics? Accessed April 25, 2018. www.eatrightpro.org/practice/code-of-ethics/what -is-the-code-of-ethics

18. Fornari A. Approaches to Ethical Decision-Making. *J Acad Nutr Diet.* 2015;115(1):119-121. doi:10.1016/j.jand.2014.10.026

SECTION 3

Nutrition Communication Is Audience-Focused

Creating a New Nutrition Conversation with Consumers:

A Timeless Approach to Consumer-Focused Messaging

Susan T. Borra, RDN, and Shelley Maniscalco, MPH, RD

Susan T. Borra, RDN

Shelley Maniscalco, MPH, RD

A "New Nutrition Conversation" Is Born

Between standard headlines ("What Diet Is Best?"), concerns of the day ("Are You a Glutton for Gluten?"), and focus on "superfoods" that offer eternal promise ("Kale, Anyone?"), there is no shortage of information and, certainly, not a scarcity of food and nutrition data. The focus on nutrition and health in the marketplace has steadily grown over many decades. This is great news for the dietetics profession, but it also creates a responsibility and mandate for dietitians to help manage nutrition *misinformation* and to stand out as *the* relevant and compelling nutrition source for audiences everywhere. Of course, it's easier to be captivating and provocative when there isn't a professional obligation to be science-based—which is what we are competing with in the messaging environment. So dietitians need tools, based on tried-and-true marketing techniques, in our proverbial tool belts.

What's the first rule of marketing and communication? That's right: Know your audience. In fact, it was the search for the bridge between this golden rule and how, as a profession, we communicate with consumers about *what*, *why*, and *how* to implement healthful eating behaviors that began the journey that became the topic of this showcase.

The need for a new conversation with consumers about nutrition was our eureka moment. It was born out of questions such as: What if we could *think differently* about how we talk to consumers about nutrition? What if we talked *with* consumers versus *at* them? What if we had an approach, grounded in consumer research, to guide how we talk about healthy eating that meets them *where they are*?

In the early 2000s, these questions led us, while at the International Food Information Council (IFIC), to conduct consumer research designed to create a "New Nutrition Conversation with Consumers."[1] While we called this conversation new when it was in development, this approach is still just as relevant, if not more so, today.

Universal Truths

Several rounds of qualitative and quantitative consumer research guided all aspects of development of our "New Nutrition Conversation with Consumers," and what we found can guide dietitians in learning to create messaging and tips that transcend the noise and resonate with an audience on any nutrition topic.

First, consumers need different levels of messaging that speak to them broadly *and* specifically. This is a complement of high-level, directional messaging coupled with actionable tips to guide what to *do*. Information conveyed must be simple, positive, practical, and consistent. To be most actionable, how-tos must be positive, short and simple, personalized, specific, and manageable; they must provide the payoff; and they must talk food and fun.[2]

Presenting the Message Development Model

To evolve our nutrition conversation with consumers, we adapted a marketing model from Wirthlin Worldwide, a market research firm that is now part of Harris Interactive, to create a model that informs message development. The model is pictured and fully described in Chapter 10 (see Figure 10.1 on page 149). It consists of five steps, all focused on the audience, that begin with qualitative research and end with quantitative research. Here's a brief overview of the five steps:

1. **LEARN** what an audience knows and feels, and learn about their motivators and barriers.

2. **DEVELOP** initial message concepts based on what was learned in Step 1.

3. **RETURN** to the audience to assess whether the message concepts resonate with the audience.

4. **REVISE** and create the final messages based on information from Step 3.

5. **TEST** the messages with the target audience for validation. Return to Steps 3 and 4 to rework messages if needed.

Putting Learning into Practice: *You* Can Use the Message Development Model

Consumers will continue to be exposed to nutrition and health information—whether from friends and family, school, the internet, or trusted health professionals. Dietitians are experts in nutrition and well equipped to become proficient in reaching consumers with compelling messaging by using the Message Development Model approach.

In our respective professional experiences, we have applied this in many ways and settings, from communicating with consumers about the US Dietary Guidelines for Americans and MyPlate to helping consumers enjoy more meals together, as a family, at home.

We've learned that it's the process of going through these steps that strengthens messaging, not the money that is spent or even the scope at which it is implemented. It isn't necessary to have access to a vetted consumer panel or a big organization budget. The important part is following the steps, formally or casually, to focus on the audience; generate qualitative learnings (via interviews, focus groups, in-home observations); iteratively refine message concepts; gut-check messages along the way; and, finally, quantitatively validate with the targeted audience.

We'll end with our top five tips to keep in mind!

1. Tips are not one-size-fits-all; personalize whenever possible.
2. Positive messages about food, nutrition, and health work best.
3. If messages are not resonating, go back to an earlier step in the process; the goal is to have messages that truly work in the end.
4. Regardless of your timeline, network of contacts, or available budget, the most important part is talking *with* the audience.
5. You can do this!

> For a review of qualitative and quantitative research, refer to Chapter 6.

REFERENCES

1. Borra ST, Kelly L, Tuttle M, Neville K. Developing actionable dietary guidance messages: dietary fat as a case study. *J Am Diet Assoc.* 2001;101:678-684. doi:10.1016/S0002-8223(01)00170-5
2. Borra ST, Kelly L, Shirreffs M, Neville K, Geiger C. Developing health messages: qualitative studies with children, parents, and teachers help identify communications opportunities for healthful lifestyles and the prevention of obesity. *J Am Diet Assoc.* 2003;103:721-728. doi:10.1053/jada.2003.50140

Effective Messages Are Created with and for an Audience

Barbara J. Mayfield, MS, RDN, FAND
Lisa Ann Jones, MA, RDN, LDN, FAND and
Melissa Joy Dobbins, MS, RDN, CDCES

"Messages must be tailored to an audience in order to meet the audience's needs. Effective messages resonate with the audience. They use understandable language, address feelings as well as facts, and are realistic and inspirational."

> "It's easier for people to see it your way if you first see it their way." —DAN ZADRA

Introduction

Effective messages are created *with* and *for* an audience. The goal is audience-focused (also known as audience-centered) communication. Picture a target with the intended audience in the bull's-eye.

Stephen R. Covey, DRE, MBA, in *The 7 Habits of Highly Effective People*, described this need for having a target: "Begin with the end in mind."[1] This means the end goal must be identified before starting to plan. This certainly holds true when composing messages. Without a target audience, and desired outcomes tailored for them, there is no way to determine if a message has hit its mark. Maintain a focus on the target—the audience—throughout the process of creating and communicating a message.

Section 3 of this book is devoted to designing communication with an audience focus, including how to create messages with and for an audience; how to conduct a needs assessment to learn about an audience; how behavior change models help to understand and motivate audiences; how to understand and work with audiences of different cultures, ages, life stages, and generations; and how to utilize all of this knowledge to tailor messages to target audiences so that communication goals and learning objectives can be met.

This chapter answers three questions:

- Why must messages be tailored to the audience?
- How can models help to develop more effective messages?
- What are best practices for developing messages?

Developing an effective, audience-focused message begins with understanding the audience, proceeds with selecting and focusing the purpose and overall content of the message, and results in crafting a message that connects with the audience and is clear, concise, and compelling.

Why Must Messages Be Tailored to the Audience?

Short answer: to stand out. According to the American Marketing Association, the average consumer is exposed to up to 10,000 brand messages each day.[2] That equates to about 500 messages every waking hour! In addition to advertising, people are inundated with personal messages, work-related messages, entertainment, news, and even road signs and menus. With all that competition for an audience member's attention, a message must stand out from the noisy crowd. A message that stands out meets a need ("Aha! I need that information!") and resonates with the audience ("I understand—that message is meaningful to me").

Messages Must Meet an Audience's Needs

One of the most important components of message development is determining how to meet an audience's needs. Every audience has different needs and expectations. Identifying, understanding, and analyzing an audience are necessary to ensure that the audience's specific needs are met. Answering the following questions can be a useful brainstorming tool[3]:

- **Who** is the audience?
- **What** is important to this audience?
- **Where** will the message be delivered?
- **When** will they receive and share the message with others?
- **How** will the message be perceived and used?
- **Why** do they care about the message or topic?

Later in this chapter, as the various models for developing messages are described, note that assessing the audience is one of the initial steps in each one.

Messages Must Resonate with an Audience

Once an audience's needs have been assessed, messages can be designed that will resonate with them. What does it mean for a message to *resonate*? It implies a level of trust and agreement with the message and communicator, as well as evoking an emotional response, all of which could lead to taking action.

Many things influence whether a message resonates with an audience. Questions to ask while designing messages include these:

- How might the relationship between communicator and audience impact the way the message is perceived?
- Are the words used in the message easily understood?
- Does the message address emotions in addition to facts?
- Is the message realistic and inspirational?

In other words, is the communicator connecting with the audience, as well as being clear, concise, and compelling?

CONNECT WITH THE AUDIENCE

Recall from Chapter 1 that communication is more than just message transmission—it is a relational activity. Chapter 3 discussed how and why communication is successful when the communicator and audience connect. Connection involves shared understanding, empathy, and trust. When a communicator and audience are similar and in

a close relationship, connecting can be easily accomplished. However, when communicators and audiences differ in various ways, connecting can be more challenging. Consider how these factors and the messaging that results can promote or inhibit a connection with an audience[4]:

- **Differences in value** (equality and certainty): A message created in a participative environment including audience solicitation and involvement is considered *equality* messaging. Equality messaging includes supportive statements that mutually benefit the communicator and audience and permits audience members to consider alternative opinions. *Certainty* messaging implies that the communicator's message is correct, and the audience should agree with the message being sent. Certainty messaging is generally created without audience feedback or participation.
- **Differences in power** (upward, downward, and lateral messages): If the audience is made up of like-minded peers with the same knowledge level, the communicator will compose *lateral* messaging. If the message is targeted to an audience of laypeople with less knowledge about the subject area, the communicator may compose *downward* messaging. If the audience is high-powered superiors who may have more knowledge about the subject area than the communicator, *upward* messaging may be composed. For an audience that is mixed in power, a messaging combining upward, downward, and lateral content may be composed.
- **Social distance** (stranger, acquaintance, friend, enemy): Messages often change based on how the communicator is socially connected with the audience. A related factor is whether the delivery setting is formal or informal. How well the communicator knows an audience impacts both the message and its delivery.

When the communicator accounts for these differences and seeks to identify common ground by getting to know an audience and their needs, connecting with the audience becomes possible and communication that resonates with the audience can be achieved.

The process of determining an audience's needs is the focus of Chapter 11.

USE WORDS THE AUDIENCE UNDERSTANDS

Effective communication begins with words and messages that an audience can understand and relate to. Therefore, make sure to avoid jargon and unfamiliar or complex terminology. Simple, clear language helps an audience quickly understand and apply the information.

Word choices will vary depending upon audience characteristics. In the book *Leading Through Language*, author Bart Egnal[5] points out that jargon is useful when everyone is in the same industry or group but becomes a problem when it obscures or confuses. For example, a presenter would use medical terminology during a speech to health care professionals but common, everyday terms with the general public. Even a term as simple as *nutrient-dense* can be confusing or meaningless to an audience, whereas *nutrient-rich* could convey the point more clearly.

ADDRESS FEELINGS, FEARS, AND EMOTIONS

While it is necessary to communicate evidence-based information, it is also important to share more than just facts. By creating messages that incorporate facts and also address emotions, a communicator will be able to connect with the audience on a deeper level. This connection fosters trust and confidence in the content being shared.

Consider the example described in the Words of Experience box. Notice that learning about an audience's fears is essential for the nutrition communicator to provide information in a way that acknowledges and addresses their fears.

Pam McCarthy, MS, RD, has expertise in "emotion-based messaging and influence principles" to drive behavior change. She shares three simple facts from the Touching Hearts, Touching Minds—WIC (Well Informed Consumer) research project.[6,7,8]

- Telling people to do something because it's good for them doesn't change behavior.
- Educating people about nutrition and food does not translate into behavior change.
- Providing factual nutrition education materials does not equate to being a successful nutrition counselor.

WORDS OF EXPERIENCE

The Fear Factor

by Melissa Joy Dobbins, MSN, RDN, CDCES

As a certified diabetes educator for the past 20 years, I've seen firsthand how fear can keep people from taking action, and how facts alone aren't usually enough to empower someone to move beyond the fear. When I worked in a high-risk obstetrics clinic, one of my tasks was to teach group classes for pregnant mothers to learn how to inject insulin in their abdomens. None of my patients were particularly excited about this, but one mother was especially distraught. She did not say anything, ask any questions, or answer any questions. All she could do was cry. With the assistance of a counselor, we eventually were able to get her to open up. When she finally spoke, she said, "My grandmother went on insulin and died." She wasn't afraid of the needle; she was afraid of dying.

This experience spurred our health care team to adjust the class curriculum to include a focus on fears, feelings, and questions in order to better understand and support our patients.

A diagnosis of diabetes or another health condition may bring a great deal of fear, anxiety, and unfamiliar territory. If these feelings aren't addressed and acknowledged, it's difficult for people to hear any practical information about diet, exercise, medications, or other health goals. Knowledge may be power, but beliefs are powerful too.

This research project discovered the following:

- People are feeling machines that think, not thinking machines that feel.
- Rational thought is important, but feelings are more important than facts.
- Behavior change is more likely to happen when a communicator speaks to people's feelings and highlights the emotional benefits of taking action along with logic and fact.

Recognizing the importance of addressing emotion in messages is often overlooked but is not new. Consider that emotion was one of the three cornerstones of Aristotle's theory of persuasion more than two millennia ago.[9] Audiences are responsive to emotion-based messages.

BE REALISTIC AND INSPIRATIONAL

An ultimate goal of nutrition communication is to inspire an audience to take action. Therefore, messages must go beyond simply educating. When recommendations are both realistic and inspirational, the audience is more likely to act on the information. People achieve more when a task is both attainable as well as aspirational, and they achieve the highest levels of performance when a task is challenging yet possible.[10]

Words That Resonate

by Melissa Joy Dobbins, MS, RDN, CDCES

Interview with Stacey Baca, WLS-TV, ABC 7 Eyewitness News Chicago

In this live TV interview on produce and pesticides, I provided information that resonated with the viewers.

1. I was real and relatable, helping viewers feel a connection with me.

2. I used words the audience understood, avoiding technical terms such as *phytochemicals* and using more familiar terms such as *antioxidants*, *vitamins*, and *minerals*.

3. I addressed feelings in addition to facts. I acknowledged the fear of pesticides and reassured viewers that the health benefits of fruits and vegetables far outweigh any small exposure to pesticides. I explained that they can decrease their exposure by washing all produce (including organic) before eating.

4. I was realistic and inspirational. I let viewers know that canned, frozen, dried, and juices also count as servings of fruits and vegetables, not just fresh produce. I shared a simple, tasty recipe for viewers to try at home.

Consider messages that are realistic as the foundation and inspiration as the icing on the cake. A clear, inspiring call to action is key to creating messages that resonate with an audience. See the Words of Experience box for an example of tailoring messages that resonate.

Creating messages that meet an audience's needs, resonate with the audience, and promote knowledge gains and changes in attitudes and behaviors is best achieved by following evidence-based approaches. What are these approaches? Chapter 1 introduced the framework for planning and evaluating nutrition communication (see Figure 1.1 on page 14). Message creation is predominantly part of the communication decisions component, but it relates to all other components in the framework. Chapter 3 introduced the Nutrition Communication Development Strategy (see Figure 3.1 on page 40), where Steps 3 through 5 cover message design and development. This chapter will introduce four additional models that can serve as frameworks for message creation.

Building on this foundation, Chapter 11 will describe how to conduct needs assessments, a necessary first step and a component of each model. Understanding and promoting behavior change is the focus of Chapter 12, which introduces theories of behavior change. Chapters 13 and 14 provide assistance in learning more about an audience and effectively reaching different audiences with a message. The final chapter in this section walks through the steps to create communication goals, learning objectives, and key message points. Evaluation of impact will be presented in Section 7, Chapter 38.

How Can Models Help to Develop More Effective Messages?

Models provide a road map that communicators can follow to develop effective messages. This chapter discusses four evidence-based approaches that complement those introduced in Section 1:

- the Message Development Model created by the International Food Information Council,
- social marketing theory,
- logic models, and
- the PRECEDE-PROCEED model.

These four approaches have many similarities, but each one provides unique perspectives to help nutrition communicators develop effective messages tailored to the target audience. In situations where fully following each step in a model is unrealistic, use their principles as a mind-set for planning.

As mentioned previously in this chapter, the earliest recorded model for crafting effective messages was written by Aristotle two thousand years before these modern models were developed.[9] He suggested that for messages to be persuasive, they must contain three qualities: ethos, pathos, and logos. Ethos is the speaker's credibility: The communicator must be perceived as believable. Pathos is the emotional appeal of the message: The communicator must connect the message to the audience's feelings. Logos is the message being presented as a logical argument: The communicator must provide logical evidence to support the message. Modern models provide further guidance in creating effective nutrition communication for all types of audiences and purposes.

The International Food Information Council Message Development Model Provides Five Steps

The first model to be examined was introduced in the section showcase preceding this chapter, Creating a "New Nutrition Conversation with Consumers." The International Food Information Council (IFIC) designed this model to describe a process for developing consumer-oriented messages.[11] The IFIC Marketing Model, also known as the Message Development Model, is illustrated in Figure 10.1. The background and five steps are summarized below. For more background on the model, review the showcase.

INTERNATIONAL FOOD INFORMATION COUNCIL MODEL BACKGROUND AND RATIONALE

The IFIC Message Development Model came out of IFIC's research about how consumers perceive and make decisions based on food and nutrition messaging.[11] This work emphasizes the importance of having a conversation with consumers rather than talking at consumers. By listening to consumers, communicators can learn not only what consumers are thinking about food and nutrition but why consumers think what they do.

The sheer volume of nutrition messages and the often conflicting information they contain contribute to consumer confusion. Myths are prevalent, leaving consumers unsure who or what to believe. To overcome consumer confusion, IFIC designed the Message Development Model to create messages using consumer input throughout the process. Their research found consumers respond best to positive messages that are short and simple, personalized when possible, results-oriented,

FIGURE 10.1 International Food Information Council marketing model (message development model)

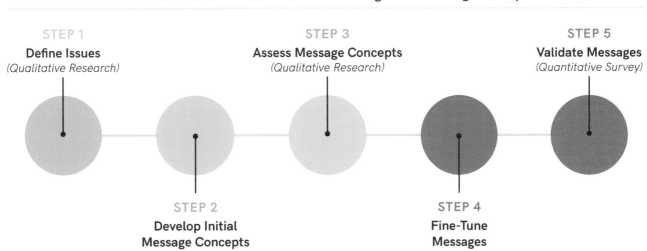

STEP 1
Define Issues
(Qualitative Research)

STEP 3
Assess Message Concepts
(Qualitative Research)

STEP 5
Validate Messages
(Quantitative Survey)

STEP 2
**Develop Initial
Message Concepts**

STEP 4
**Fine-Tune
Messages**

Adapted with permission from the International Food Information Council. Food Insight. Message making 101: creating consumer-friendly messages. International Food Information Council Foundation website. Published October 15, 2009. Accessed September 17, 2019. https://foodinsight.org/message-making-101-creating-consumer-friendly-messages[12]

practical and realistic to put into action, and *fun*. The IFIC Message Development Model is most often used in crafting messages for lay consumer audiences. It can be applied to all types of messages delivered through any type of channel.

FOLLOW ALL FIVE STEPS TO CREATE EFFECTIVE MESSAGES

As illustrated in Figure 10.1, the Message Development Model consists of five steps.[12] Each one is described here.

Step 1: Define the issues This step focuses on simply talking with a specific audience and conducting formative, qualitative research to learn more about them—what they know, what they feel, what motivates them, what gets them stuck, and so on. The idea is to go beyond the obvious and the practical. Go beyond demographics into psychographics. Observe and listen to the audience, explore their lifestyles, and find out what makes them tick at a deeper level.

This step occurs via a needs assessment, which examines the target audience and message content and tells the communicator what motivates the audience and what issues need to be addressed.

Step 2: Develop initial message concepts Armed with the information collected in Step 1— what drives an audience and what they know and feel about a given topic—a communicator is equipped to develop initial message concepts. This is an educated guess on motivating concepts and language based on what has been learned so far. Consider what behavior should be encouraged. Consider how to craft a message based on what motivates the audience and what their perceived or actual barriers are. Finally, think about the words being used and how the message may be received and understood by the audience.

Messages are based on the answers to these questions: What knowledge does the audience need? What attitudes and behaviors need changing? What concerns and problems (often referred to as pain points) need to be addressed or overcome?

Step 3: Assess message concepts Often, communicators stop there. They craft messaging based on what they know about their audience and march forth to put these messages into practice. Implementing these last three steps will allow for further targeting, fine-tuning, and validating of messages

for increased acceptance. In this third step, take the message concepts back into qualitative research to get a valuable read on whether they resonate with the audience, how the audience interprets what is being said, and what the audience is called to do.

Some of the questions to ask audience members in Step 3 include the following:

- What does this message mean to you?
- Does this message motivate you?
- Does this message fit with other things you value or want in life?

And, in terms of self-efficacy, ask yourself:

- Does the message entail a behavior change that's within the audience's repertoire of skills? Or do additional skills need to be learned?

Steps 1 and 3 can be accomplished using various data collection methods such as surveys, interviews, and focus groups.

Step 4: Fine-tune messages The audience's reaction to message concepts—what worked, what didn't, what was close but not quite—provides the information to refine messages to have the desired impact. Typically, at this stage, words are being tweaked here and there. If the message does not seem to resonate, it's a good idea to go back to Step 2 and develop new message concepts.

Step 5: Validate messages The first four steps of the Message Development Model employ qualitative research, which is instrumental in obtaining the depth and richness of knowledge necessary to create meaningful and relevant consumer messaging. However, qualitative research typically involves studying a limited number of consumers. This is where Step 5 proves valuable. Utilize a quantitative approach to target an audience on a larger scale to ensure that receptiveness to the nutrition message extends beyond the initial sample and speaks to a greater number of individuals. Even in settings where this step is not formally completed, it can be possible to track feedback such as social media comments and shares.

Social Marketing Theory Promotes Positive Change

Social marketing uses business marketing principles to sell or promote positive behaviors instead of products. It is most widely used in public health. Examples of campaigns built using social

See Chapter 11 for how to conduct a needs assessment and suggested information to obtain.

See Chapter 11 for descriptions of how to collect audience data.

marketing theory include the TRUTH antismoking campaign, the VERB physical activity promotion, and the Got Milk? campaign to promote drinking milk.[13] Of these three, the Got Milk? campaign also qualifies as commercial marketing, which has the purpose of generating sales. Social marketing generates societal benefits, such as improved health and safety.

A consensus definition of social marketing created by the International Social Marketing Association, the European Social Marketing Association, and the Australian Association of Social Marketing is this: "Social Marketing seeks to develop and integrate marketing concepts with other approaches to influence behaviors that benefit individuals and communities for the greater social good."[14]

SOCIAL MARKETING BACKGROUND AND RATIONALE

Social marketing originated in 1969 with a paper titled "Broadening the Concept of Marketing," published in the *Journal of Marketing*.[15] Drawing on many disciplines, social marketing expanded rapidly during the 1970s and continues to grow and evolve.[16] The guiding principles of social marketing include the following[13,14,16,17]:

- a focus on behavior change
  - Social marketing asks: What is the problem to address?
- promoting behavior change to achieve measurable behavioral objectives
  - Social marketing asks: What action will best address the problem?
- a basis in audience insight and research
  - Social marketing asks: What do people know, think, feel, and do?
- using audience segmentation to target and tailor interventions
  - Social marketing asks: Who is being asked to take action to address the problem? If more than one audience is targeted, messages and interventions are tailored to each one.
- a foundation in behavioral theory
  - Social marketing asks: What constructs explain behavior and motivate change?
- the concept of "exchange"
  - Social marketing asks: What motivates consumers to engage with an intervention and voluntarily exhibit a

behavior (the "cost") in exchange for the perceived value (or benefit) offered in return?
- employing two or more *P*'s in the "marketing mix"
  - Four factors are most commonly included: promotion, product, price, and place. Social marketing defines or creates the promotion (the message), the product (the idea or promoted behavior), the price (what the product "costs"), and the place (where the behavior takes place). Other potential *P*'s are policies and people.
- consideration of competition
  - All behaviors have competing behaviors. People have choices of how to act. Competing behaviors are considered and minimized by the intervention. Social marketing asks: How can the benefits of the desired behavior compete effectively with the perceived benefits of alternative behaviors?
- a systematic and rigorous planning, implementation, and evaluation process

Research on the effectiveness of using social marketing principles in programs aimed at changing nutrition behaviors has found that programs that incorporate more of the social marketing benchmarks described result in better outcomes.[18]

USING SOCIAL MARKETING PRINCIPLES TO DEVELOP MESSAGES

Social marketing principles can be used for developing messages that motivate change in all types of communication, not just large public health campaigns. As in other effective approaches, social marketing is focused on the audience and behavior change. Social marketing principles that enhance an audience focus are its emphasis on audience segmentation, analyzing the physical and social environment, exploring competing behaviors, and examining the exchange of costs and benefits.

Consider this example of a school nutrition director creating messaging to promote increased consumption of the fruits and vegetables offered in school lunch:

See Chapter 15 for guidance on how to write objectives.

See Chapter 11 for more information on conducting audience research.

See Chapters 13 and 14 for insights on specific audiences based on culture, age, and life stage.

See Chapter 12 for more about behavior change theories.

See Chapter 37 for more on marketing principles applied to nutrition communication.

See Chapter 38 for more on formative, process, and outcome evaluation.

- The problem behavior is plate waste.
- The behavioral objective is increased selection and consumption of fruits and vegetables.
- Audience analysis might identify differences between students at different grade levels, suggesting targeted messages for different audience segments.
- Product positioning could support message success by placing fruits and vegetables in a more desirable location in the serving line.
- If competing food choices are deemed more convenient or desirable, fruit could be served sliced and messaging could promote selection and consumption with slogans such as "Fresh fruit slices—fast, fun, and fabulous!"
- Vegetables could be promoted with fun vegetable characters given names voted on by the students.
- By making fruit and vegetable consumption fun and popular, the "cost" is reduced and the benefit is enhanced. Research has demonstrated the potential benefits of marketing fruits and vegetables to schoolchildren.[19,20]

Figure 10.2 illustrates two examples of marketing fruits and vegetables to schoolchildren. The first one emphasizes variety, and the second example promotes the farm-to-school initiative.

An emerging approach to marketing health messages and services is health marketing, which is very similar to social marketing. It is defined by the Centers for Disease Control and Prevention (CDC) as "*creating, communicating*, and *delivering* health information and interventions using customer-centered and science-based strategies to protect and promote the health of diverse populations.[21] For more information, see the resources section at the end of this chapter.

Logic Models Illustrate Planning, Implementation, and Evaluation

A logic model serves as a graphic illustration and conceptual framework that assists with every aspect of program design, delivery, and evaluation. Logic models also serve as useful tools for communicating with stakeholders and others about a program. They are considered systems models, which describe how interdependent components work together and help illustrate the entire process.[22]

LOGIC MODEL BACKGROUND AND RATIONALE

Logic models were developed in large part as a response to the Government Performance and Results Act (GPRA) of 1993. They serve to demonstrate and ensure effective program design and

FIGURE 10.2 School nutrition programs promote fruit and vegetable intake using social marketing principles

Left: Reproduced with permission from Jeanne Reilly, NDTR of Windham Raymond Schools in Maine. Right: Reproduced with permission from School Meals that Rock. Carrollton City Schools Nutrition Program. www.facebook.com/CCSNutrition

management. Federal agencies, the Cooperative Extension program, and nonprofit agencies are among the most common users of logic models.

See Figure 10.3 for an example of a logic model layout.[22] Notice how the model visualizes the entire program process, showing connections and logical relationships between program inputs (resources), program outputs (activities and participation), and program outcomes (short-, medium-, and long-term outcomes or impact). Although they may appear linear, logic models describe a very dynamic process and can be illustrated using various formats.

On the left of the logic model is the situation. This is the problem or issue to be addressed. After writing a succinct statement describing the situation, the writer sets priorities, which in turn leads to identifying the desired outcomes, listed as short-term outcomes (often knowledge gains and

behavioral intentions), medium-term outcomes (generally behavior changes), and long-term outcomes (societal impact). Once the desired outcomes have been determined, the steps to achieve the outcomes are delineated. This includes listing the available inputs needed (what is invested) to accomplish the program outputs (what is done and who is reached). At the bottom of the model are lists of assumptions (beliefs that influence program decisions) and external factors (such as cultural, political, and environmental influences).

MESSAGE DEVELOPMENT WITHIN THE LOGIC MODEL FRAMEWORK

The task of creating a logic model assures that all of the interrelated parts of a program are thoroughly considered. Logic models can assist with message development, delivery, and evaluation. The logic model depicted in Figure 10.4 depicts

FIGURE 10.3 **A logic model example**

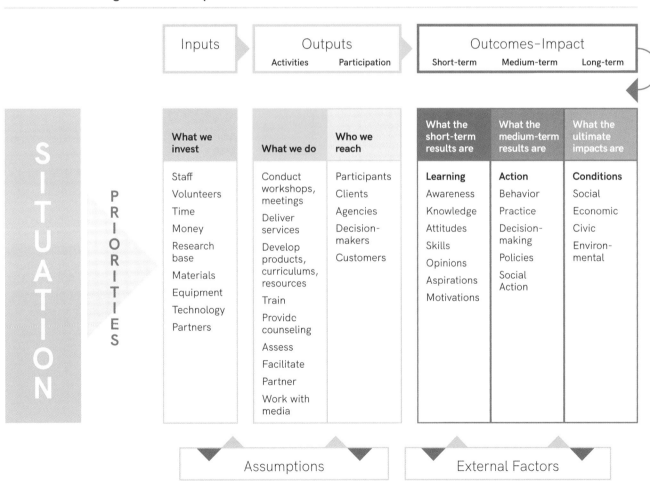

Adapted with permission from Taylor-Powell E, Henert E. *Developing a Logic Model: Teaching and Training Guide*. University of Wisconsin-Extension; 2008. Accessed September 17, 2019. www.alnap.org/system/files/content/resource/files/main/logic-model-guide.pdf[23]

a nutrition education program for senior adults. It is based on this situation:

Older adults who make healthier choices live longer and better lives. Diet and exercise play the most important roles in determining the quality and length of life for the elderly. Older adults, especially the very old, consume inadequate amounts of key nutrients. Low-income adults tend to have poorer diets than their higher income peers.[23]

The topics covered and the delivery channels are listed in the activities column. The audience is listed in the participation column. The desired outcomes are listed in the far right three columns. Messages are selected or created to accomplish program objectives and match the program design. An example of an appropriate message comes from the ChooseMyPlate.gov Older Adults page: "Add sliced fruits and vegetables to your meals and snacks. Look for presliced fruits and vegetables on sale if slicing and chopping is a challenge."[24]

The PRECEDE-PROCEED Model Provides a Planning Framework

The PRECEDE-PROCEED model is a type of logic model used for designing health education and promotion programs with the goal of changing behaviors and improving health and quality of life.

PRECEDE-PROCEED BACKGROUND AND RATIONALE

The model was developed in two parts: The PRECEDE part originated in the 1970s, and the PROCEED part was added in 1991. PRECEDE and PROCEED are acronyms that stand for the constructs in the model. The model is illustrated in Figure 10.5.[25]

The letters in PRECEDE stand for **P**redisposing, **R**einforcing, and **E**nabling **C**onstructs in **E**ducational/Environmental **D**iagnosis and **E**valuation. This represents the process that *precedes* a

FIGURE 10.4 **Logic model example of a nutrition education program for seniors**

Inputs	Outputs		Outcomes–Impact		
	Activities	Participation	Short-term	Medium-term	Long-term
Community-based nutrition educators Agency partners who collaborate Campus-based specialists that support county educators Research base Funding and other resources that support this program	**Educational sessions:** • Presentations • Learn-while-you-wait • Games and interactive learning activities • Posters, print materials **Topics:** • Eating more fruits and vegetables • Storing and handling food safely • Portion sizes • Choosing healthy snacks • Balancing food with physical activity	Low-income seniors at senior dining sites and senior housing sites	**Short-term changes we expect:** Participants increase their knowledge about the importance of choosing nutritious foods. Participants increase their knowledge about food handling safety. Participants think differently about their food choices. Participants plan to make nutrition-related behavior changes, including physical activity.	**Medium-term changes we expect:** Participants eat more fruits and vegetables. Participants handle foods safely. Participants read labels. Participants control portion size. Participants choose more healthy foods. Participants engage in appropriate physical activity.	**Long-term changes we expect:** The elderly enjoy healthier lives.

Adapted with permission from Taylor-Powell E, Henert E. *Developing a Logic Model: Teaching and Training Guide.* University of Wisconsin-Extension; 2008. Accessed September 17, 2019. www.alnap.org/system/files/content/resource/files/main/logic-model-guide.pdf[23]

program or intervention. It begins with the desired outcome and works backward to create an intervention. All four phases of PRECEDE are diagnostic, assessing the:

- social,
- epidemiological,
- educational and ecological, and
- administrative and policy factors related to the issue.

The letters in PROCEED stand for **P**olicy, **R**egulatory, and **O**rganizational **C**onstructs in **E**ducational and **E**nvironmental **D**evelopment.

This describes how to *proceed* with the implementation and evaluation of the intervention. The four phases of PROCEED are:

- implementation,
- process evaluation,
- impact evaluation, and
- outcome evaluation.

The PRECEDE-PROCEED model promotes the participation of the entire community in every phase. It recognizes that health is an individual and community issue and is best addressed in the context of community.

FIGURE 10.5 **The PRECEDE-PROCEED model**

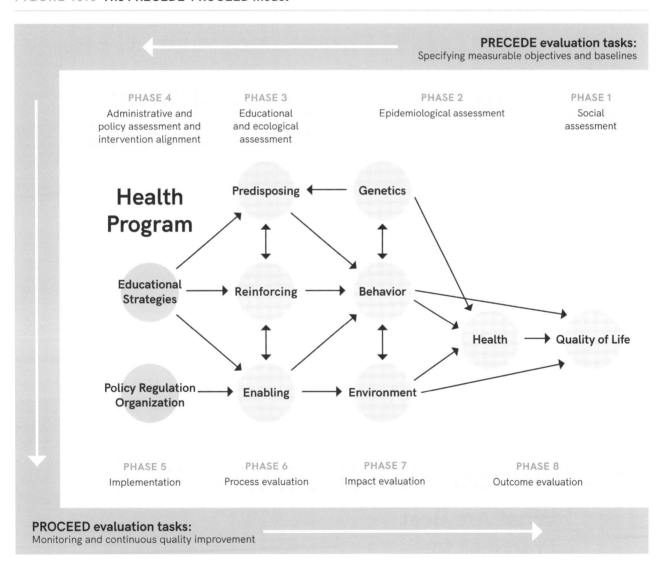

This model is featured in the The Community Tool Box, a service of the Center for Community Health and Development at the University of Kansas. It was adapted from the fourth edition of *Health Promotion Planning: An Educational and Ecological Approach* by Lawrence Green and Marshall Kreuter.[25] The fourth edition of this book is out of print. A new fifth edition is being published by Johns Hopkins University Press, with an expected release date in 2020. Adapted with permission from Lawrence Green and Marsall Kreuter.

MESSAGE DEVELOPMENT USING PRECEDE-PROCEED

The constructs of the PRECEDE-PROCEED model can assist communicators in developing messages that promote desired behavior changes. During the diagnostic PRECEDE phases, assessing factors that predispose, enable, and reinforce behaviors can help communicators design messages that account for different factors:

- Predisposing factors describe what motivates the audience—their knowledge, attitudes, beliefs, and readiness to change.
- Enabling factors are those that enable audience members to take action. These include supportive policies, the availability of resources, and the accessibility of services.
- Reinforcing factors are those that help individuals sustain changes in behavior, including perceived benefits, incentives, social support, and praise.

During the implementation and evaluation PROCEED phases, understanding environmental factors (policy, regulations, and organizational factors) that influence behavior change can direct message implementation, revision, and evaluation.

An example of a program designed with this model is PeerNET, which stands for peer nutrition education team. It was developed to equip dietetics students to be peer educators to fellow college students via individual and group instruction. Students were involved in development, training, implementation, and evaluation.[26]

The four models described in this chapter are considered planning models. Each one provides a helpful framework for designing and evaluating communication for education and behavior change. They complement the nutrition communication framework introduced in Chapter 1 and illustrated in Figure 1.1 on page 14. Use one or more of these models to inform and organize communication decisions and develop effective messages for target audiences.

What Are Best Practices for Developing Messages?

Many decisions factor into message development. Following best practices for developing messages can streamline and ensure the success of the planning process. Keep the following fundamental practices in mind while reading the remaining chapters in this section.

Work with the Audience

This best practice seems obvious for audience-focused communication, but it is all too often ignored. It can seem more expedient to develop messages based on communicator expertise and assumptions about the audience, but successful communication is based on the input and involvement of the audience.

This best practice includes working with the organization or target audience in message creation and begins with conducting a needs assessment. It can also include a message development brainstorming session. Start by asking:

- What are the messaging needs?
- Will there be one audience or multiple audiences?

If the answer to the second question is more than one, messages will need to be tailored to each group, ideally collaborating with members of each audience.

Throughout the message development process, involve the audience. Recall from the earlier discussion about the IFIC model that the audience is involved several times:

- to develop a tailored message,
- to gain their understanding of the proposed message prior to finalizing, and
- to determine if the message achieved the desired result.

Identify a Purpose

Once the communicator knows the audience and assesses audience needs, it is time to identify the purpose for communicating. Is the intent to inform, to persuade, or to take action? When identifying a purpose, make sure it addresses the audience and their needs. The messages developed must support the communication goals.

Throughout message development, communicating *with purpose* must remain a top priority. Whether crafting key messages or creating more developed messages with an introduction, supporting evidence and examples, and a closing or call to action, keep the underlying purpose in mind.

See Chapter 11 for more best practices for needs assessment.

Select the Content of the Message Based on Needs

What specific content needs to be communicated to achieve the purpose of the message? This involves selecting the topic, the depth of coverage, and illustrations or examples to support the message.

Conducting a needs assessment will help dictate the message topic. When selecting a message topic, identify one that is timely and relevant and addresses what the audience needs most. Topic selection may be initiated by an audience inquiry or by a newsworthy issue that prompts further investigation. The needs assessment will include researching current issues, news, and research as well as surveying potential audience members about potential topics that are already identified or that they request. Questions that can help identify timely topics include the following:

- What are examples of current nutritional problems? Which ones apply to the audience?
- What are some new areas of research? Which research topics are of interest to the audience and address audience needs and concerns? How can the research results be conveyed to the audience in ways they will understand and find useful?
- What are trending topics in the news? Find out if the audience has misconceptions about any of these topics that need to be corrected or clarified.

Keep in mind that the topic will need to be narrowed so that the message does not get lost and the audience takes away nothing. After narrowing the topic, think about how it can be further tailored for an audience. Is it an audience of professional peers or a lay audience? The answer to this question will dictate the depth and breadth of the topic coverage.

Other important considerations are of a more personal nature. Does the audience care about the topic? If not, is it possible to create an awareness of need? Are *you* knowledgeable and passionate about the topic? If not, the audience will be able to tell and the message won't be perceived as authentic. Refer to Box 10.1 for a handy checklist summarizing the main points for narrowing a topic.

Narrowing a Message Topic

Ways to effectively narrow a topic:

- Identify and address verified problems and concerns.
- Seek to share current news and research, addressing misconceptions and confusion.
- Determine what the audience needs to know versus providing what is nice to know.
- Focus on topics that match your expertise and interests.
- Address the audience's main concerns.

Communicate with Brevity and Clarity

While developing a message, strive to communicate with brevity and clarity. For most types of communication, aim to develop no more than three to five key messages. For each key point, provide supporting evidence and examples that are meaningful to the audience. Incorporating concrete examples to support each concept helps bring the message to life and increases audience comprehension.

Information that is thought out and well organized will be easier for an audience to understand and apply.[27] On the contrary, information that isn't succinct or clear may cause an audience to tune out. Communicating in a brief and clear manner can be a challenge, but it is extremely important nonetheless. Here are a few specific tips for brevity and clarity:

- Share only the most important information given the available space or time frame. Aim for only three main ideas or points.
- Prioritize content to share the most important information first and in an order that flows well.
- Use positive, active language for the specific call to action.
- Keep words and sentences short and simple. Use culturally appropriate terms. Avoid jargon or technical terms and abbreviations.

Chapter 15 provides additional guidance and a more in-depth discussion on writing key messages.

Promote Taking Action

In the refining stage, consider whether the message will motivate the target audience to act. If not, keep refining until the message delivers the appropriate impact. Once the message is refined to ensure action, test it with internal and external audiences. For example, bloggers can interact with and assess their audiences through comments received on their blog or social posts. This feedback is an effective way to continue to hone and tailor their message. The audience's responses can be incorporated into future or final messages. Over time, messages should be routinely reviewed to ensure relevance and to reflect current trends.

Since an ultimate goal of nutrition communication is to help audiences take action, messages must be positive, practical, and actionable. An audience must be able to apply the information to their situation and feel empowered to take steps toward realistic and sustainable behavior change. If information is too vague or unrealistic, it will be difficult to put it into action. For example, instead of making a vague recommendation to "eat more vegetables," share this specific tip from the MyPlate Message Toolkit: "Brighten your plate with vegetables that are red, orange, and dark green. They are full of vitamins and minerals. Try squash, tomatoes, peppers, or collard greens. They not only taste great but are good for you, too!"[28]

Figure 10.6 shows the World Health Organization (WHO) Strategic Communications Framework, which includes six principles of effective communications—namely, that messages should be: (1) accessible, (2) actionable, (3) credible, (4) relevant, (5) timely, and (6) understandable.[29,30] The purpose of this framework is for "communicating to and with audiences as health decision makers who use WHO communications products to make a range of health decisions," including individuals, health care providers, policy makers, communities, international organizations and stakeholders, and WHO staff. We've provided a checklist for evaluating messages, whether they are being created or have been retrieved from another source.

The remaining chapters in this section provide the tools and direction to create audience-focused communication. These principles for creating effective messages apply to all types of nutrition communication described throughout the remainder of the book. Whether creating one line of copy, a social media post, an article, a presentation, a video, or any type of program, intervention, or campaign, an audience focus—determined through a needs assessment and ongoing audience involvement—is essential for communication to be effective.

FIGURE 10.6 **World Health Organization principles for effective communications**

The World Health Organization (WHO) framework is organized according to six principles to ensure communications are:

- accessible,
- actionable,
- credible and trusted,
- relevant,
- timely, and
- understandable.

WHO strives at all times to ensure these principles are at the core of its communication activities and are reflected in the full range of materials and activities: social media messages; web-based fact sheets, feature stories, commentaries, infographics, and Q&As; intranet content for WHO staff; press conferences, news releases, and media advisories; videos; visibility and outreach activities, and so on.

Adapted with permission from the World Health Organization. WHO principles for effective communications. World Health Organization website. Accessed September 17, 2019. https://www.who.int/communicating-for-health/principles/en[30]

Message Evaluation Checklist

Effective messages are created with and for an audience. Every message should be …

_____ **Targeted** to an audience.

_____ **Easily understood,** with an appropriate reading level and word choice for the target audience.

_____ **Relevant** and meaningful to the audience, meeting their needs.

_____ **Supported** with accurate evidence and meaningful examples.

_____ **Focused on more than facts** by addressing feelings and fears.

_____ **Grounded in behavioral research,** utilizing behavior change and social marketing theories to understand and influence behavior change.

_____ **Realistic,** with recommendations that are practical and achievable.

_____ **Inspirational** to motivate and instill positive beliefs, attitudes, and behaviors.

_____ **Positive** to emphasize possibilities over threats.

_____ **Actionable,** with specific steps to take.

_____ **Concise,** brief, and to the point.

_____ **Clear,** with key messages that are evident, logically presented, and well explained.

_____ **Compelling** so that the audience is motivated to achieve the desired outcome.

KEY POINTS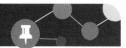

Effective Messages Are Created with and for an Audience

1 Messages must be tailored to an audience in order to meet the audience's needs. Effective messages resonate with the audience. They use understandable language, address feelings as well as facts, and are realistic and inspirational. Tailored messages achieve maximum effect.

2 Several models are available to help communicators develop effective messages. Models provide standardized and proven frameworks, steps, or benchmarks to follow. Models described include the International Food Information Council (IFIC) Message Development Model, social marketing, logic models, and the PRECEDE-PROCEED model.

3 Best practices for developing messages follow a process that keeps the audience's needs top of mind to ensure the delivery of effective messages. In short, the process includes identifying the purpose of the message, selecting a topic based on the needs assessment, and creating positive, practical, actionable messages that are clear and concise.

RESOURCES

Cook J, van der Linden S. Facts versus feelings isn't the way to think about communicating science. *The Conversation.* Published July 5, 2017. https://theconversation.com/facts-versus-feelings-isnt-the-way-to-think-about-communicating-science-80255

Emotion-based messages and materials:
- https://www.jneb.org/article/S1499-4046(10)00050-3/pdf
- https://wicworks.fns.usda.gov/wicworks/Sharing_Center/MA/HeartoftheMatter/postinterventionethno.pdf

Health marketing, from the Centers for Disease Control and Prevention: www.cdc.gov/healthcommunication/toolstemplates/WhatIsHM.html

Five tips for creating powerful key messages for a business: www.huffingtonpost.com/catriona-pollard/5-tips-for-creating-power_b_9775472.html

Developing effective educational materials using best practices in health literacy: www.joe.org/joe/2015august/tt2.php

World Health Organization Strategic Communications Framework for Effective Communications: www.who.int/mediacentre/communication-framework.pdf

MyPlate Message Toolkit: www.choosemyplate.gov/myplate-message-toolkit-professionals

REFERENCES

1. Marcum D. The 7 habits for sales leaders: begin with the end in mind. Franklin Covey website. Published 2014. Accessed January 22, 2018. https://resources.franklincovey.com/a-sales-training-blog-by-franklincovey/begin-with-the-end-in-mind-the-7-habits-of-highly-effective-sales-leaders

2. Veiga J, Saxon J. Why your customers' attention is the scarcest resource in 2017. Research World website. Published February 20, 2017. Accessed September 13, 2019. https://www.researchworld.com/why-your-customers-attention-is-the-scarcest-resource-in-2017

3. Hart G. The five W's: An old tool for the new task of audience analysis. *Tech Commun.* 1996;43(2):139-145. http://geoff-hart.com/articles/1995-1998/five-w.htm

4. Dubois D, Rucker DD, Galinsky AD. Dynamics of communicator and audience power: the persuasiveness of competence versus warmth. *J Consum Res.* 2016;43(1):68-85. doi:10.1093/jcr/ucw006

5. Egnal B. *Leading Through Language: Choosing Words That Influence and Inspire.* John Wiley and Sons; 2016.

6. Mind. Touching Hearts, Touching Minds–WIC. website. Published 2008. Accessed January 24, 2018. https://www.jneb.org/article/S1499-4046(10)00050-3/pdf

7. McCarthy P. *Getting to the Heart of the Matter: Post-Intervention Ethnographic Report.* Published May 19, 2010. Accessed May 1, 2020. https://wicworks.fns.usda.gov/wicworks/Sharing_Center/MA/HeartoftheMatter/postinterventionethno.pdf

8. Colchamiro R, Ghiringhelli K, Hause J. Touching Hearts, Touching Minds: using emotion-based messaging to promote healthful behavior in the Massachusetts WIC program. *J Nutr Educ Behav.* 2010;42(3):S59-S65. doi:10.1016/j.jneb.2010.02.004

9. Aristotle, Kennedy GA. *On Rhetoric: A Theory of Civic Discourse.* 2nd ed. Oxford University Press; 2006.

10. Locke EA, Lathan GP, eds. *New Developments in Goal Setting and Task Performance.* Routledge; 2013.

11. Food Insight. Message making 101: creating consume-friendly messages. International Food Information Council Foundation website. Published October 15, 2009. Accessed September 17, 2019. https://foodinsight.org/message-making-101-creating-consumer-friendly-messages

12. Food Insight. Message making 101: creating consumer-friendly messages. International Food Information Council Foundation website. Published October 15, 2009. Accessed January 24, 2018. http://foodinsight.org/Message_Making_101_Creating_Consumer_Friendly_Messages

13. Smith W. Social marketing: an overview of approach and effects. *Inj Prev.* 2006;12:38-43. doi:10.1136/ip.2006.012864

14. The ISMA, ESMA, AASM consensus definition of social marketing. Published October 5, 2013. http://i-socialmarketing.org/assets/social_marketing_definition.pdf

15. Kotler P, Levy S. Broadening the concept of marketing. *J Mark.* 1969;33(1):10-15. doi:10.2307/1248740

16. Dibb S. Up, up and away: social marketing breaks free. *J Mark Manag.* 2014;30(11-12):1159–1185. doi:10.1080/0267257X.2014.943264

17. Stead M, Gordon R, Angus K, McDermott L. A systematic review of social marketing effectiveness. *Health Educ.* 2007;107(2):126-191. doi:10.1108/09654280710731548

18. Carins J, Rundle-Thiele S. Eating for the better: a social marketing review (2000–2012). *Public Health Nutr.* 2014;17(7):1628-1639. doi:10.1017/S1368980013001365

19. Hanks A, Just D, Brumberg A. Marketing vegetables in elementary school cafeterias to increase uptake. *Pediatrics.* 2016;138(2). doi:10.1542/peds.2015-1720

20. Sharps M, Robinson E. Encouraging children to eat more fruit and vegetables: health vs descriptive social norm-based messages. *Appetite.* 2016;100:18-25. doi:10.1016/j.appet.2016.01.031

21. Centers for Disease Control and Prevention. What is health marketing? Published 2011. Accessed June 5, 2018. https://cdc.gov/healthcommunication/toolstemplates/WhatIsHM.html

22. Taylor-Powell E, Jones L, Henert E. *Enhancing Program Performance with Logic Models.* University of Wisconsin-Extension; Published 2003. Accessed May 1, 2020. https://fyi.extension.wisc.edu/programdevelopment/files/2016/03/lmcourseall.pdf

23. Taylor-Powell E, Henert E. *Developing a Logic Model: Teaching and Training Guide.* University of Wisconsin–Extension; Published 2008. Accessed September 17, 2019. www.alnap.org/system/files/content/resource/files/main/logic-model-guide.pdf

24. US Department of Agriculture. Older adults. ChooseMyPlate website. Published 2017. Accessed June 6, 2018. https://choosemyplate.gov/older-adults

25. Community tool box. Section 2: PRECEDE/PROCEED. Published 2017. Accessed January 26, 2018. http://ctb.ku.edu/en/table-contents/overview/other-models-promoting-community-health-and-development/preceder-proceder/main

26. Horacek T, Koszewski W, Young L, Miller K, Betts N, Schnepf M. Development of a peer nutrition education program applying PRECEDE-PROCEED: a program planning model. *Top Clin Nutr.* 2000;15(3):19-27. doi:10.1097/00008486-200015030-00004

27. Niebaum K, Cunningham-Solo L, Bellows L. Developing effective educational materials using best practices in health literacy. *J Ext.* 2015;53(4). https://joe.org/joe/2015august/tt2.php

28. US Department of Agriculture. Vary your veggies: MyPlate message toolkit for professionals. ChooseMyPlate website. Published 2017. Accessed January 26, 2018. https://choosemyplate.gov/vary-your-veggies-0

29. World Health Organization. *WHO Strategic Communications Framework for Effective Communications.* Published 2017. http://who.int/mediacentre/communication-framework.pdf

30. World Health Organization. WHO principles for effective communications. World Health Organization website. Accessed September 17, 2019. https://www.who.int/communicating-for-health/principles/en

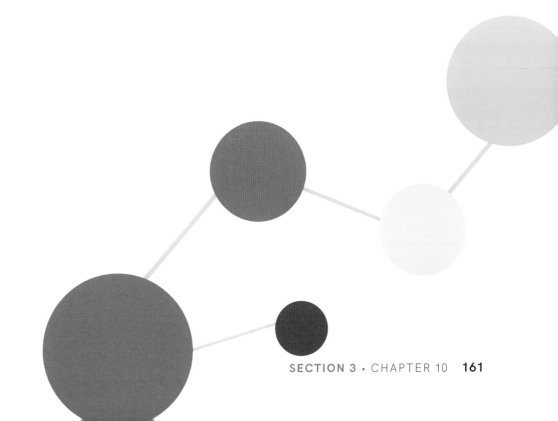

A Needs Assessment Is Essential for Audience-Focused Communication

Barbara J. Mayfield, MS, RDN, FAND
Becky Jensen, MS, RDN, LN
Carolyn Lagoe, PhD and
Virginia Quick, PhD, RDN

"Needs assessments are essential for effectively and efficiently creating nutrition communication.... The biggest mistake a communicator can make regarding needs assessments is not completing one. Focus groups and surveys are two approaches to collecting information about an audience."

"If you want to create messages that resonate with your audience, you need to know what they care about."

—NATE ELLIOTT, MARKETING TECHNOLOGY ADVISOR

Introduction

Audience-focused communication is effective because it:

- addresses needs,
- recognizes values and beliefs,
- provides relevant information, and
- answers questions.

Audience-focused communication requires an accurate picture of the audience and situation.

Needs assessments are essential for effectively and efficiently creating nutrition communication. As seen in the message development models described in Chapter 10, assessing the audience is the first step in developing messages and allows the communicator to focus on the audience. *Audience assessment* is a term that can be used for this process as well.

This chapter answers three questions:

- What is the purpose of a needs assessment?
- How are needs assessment data used to drive decisions?
- How is a needs assessment conducted?

Needs assessments can range from casual, quick-and-dirty approaches to more formalized data collection for research purposes. This chapter will describe best practices for completing needs assessments, including smart, effective shortcuts when resources are limited. The biggest mistake a communicator can make regarding needs assessments is not completing one.

What Is the Purpose of a Needs Assessment?

A needs assessment is a data collection and analysis process that provides information about an audience and is used to direct all aspects of communication planning and implementation, including determining desired outcomes, message development, and delivery channels and approaches. It helps prevent the communicator's message from missing the mark and wasting valuable resources. An often overlooked benefit of a needs assessment is the involvement of the audience. This demonstrates the communicator's interest in their needs and opens up channels of communication between the audience and the communicator.

Informs About an Audience Through Data Collection and Analysis

To reach an audience with a message, a communicator must know and understand the audience, including what knowledge, skills, and resources the audience has and what they need. Collecting this information can be done in a variety of ways, which will be described in the section How Is a Needs Assessment Conducted? That section also lists the specific types of information collected.

The overriding purpose for collecting information about the audience is to determine gaps that exist between what the audience currently has and what they need. Examples include not knowing how to read a nutrition label, wanting to learn about meal planning, or misunderstanding the difference between hypoglycemia and hyperglycemia. Closing those gaps and providing for the audience's needs is possible after analyzing the data collected.

Prevents Missing the Mark and Wasting Resources

Trying to reach an audience without a needs assessment could result in a waste of time and resources. A needs assessment identifies what is needed so the communicator can tailor and target messages. A needs assessment also provides baseline data that can be compared with outcome data to measure the effectiveness of a program or message.

Most communicators do not have the luxury of unlimited time or resources. Making the best use of available resources requires the knowledge that a needs assessment provides and helps determine priorities and best approaches to take. A needs assessment is a worthwhile use of resources. Even with limited time and small budgets, allocate a portion to conducting a needs assessment.

Involves the Audience and Demonstrates Interest in Their Needs

When a needs assessment is conducted in such a way that the audience is actively involved and engaged in the process, it demonstrates to them the communicator's concern for their needs and recognition of their resources and strengths; it goes a long way to build trust and mutual respect. If the audience has a say in what needs are addressed and how they are addressed, they will be more likely to attend to messages and support initiatives. In contrast, if the audience is left out of the decision-making process, they may be less likely to buy in to efforts to promote learning or behavior change. Consider the widespread use of online surveys to gauge an audience's interests, beliefs, and preferences. Not only do online surveys collect information, they demonstrate that the originator cares about the audience.

Community-based participatory research (CBPR)[1] is an example of involving the audience directly, not only in conducting needs assessments but also in developing the communication or interventions that result from the data collected. More information on CBPR can be found in the resources section at the end of the chapter.

No matter what method is used, audience participation in the needs assessment process leads to audience support of the resulting communication.

Creates a Connection Between Communicator and Audience

The purpose of any communication is to reach an audience with a message. A needs assessment provides the ideal opportunity to form meaningful connections with an audience and begin the dialogue. A well-conducted needs assessment engages the audience and invites them to openly and honestly share what they need, what they want, and how they plan to respond to the message. The communicator can use the needs assessment to determine the audience's perspectives and priorities as well as to create awareness of other possibilities for implementing positive change. The needs assessment can be a first step in bringing about change as the audience recognizes problems, potential solutions, barriers, and resources.

A needs assessment also informs the communicator about the audience's preferred methods and styles of communication, demonstrating what methods work best for delivering messages as well as for collecting baseline information and later feedback. Audience members may prefer to read, meet in person, or watch a video. They may prefer to respond to an online survey or have a phone interview.

A needs assessment allows for misunderstandings to be identified and corrected. Audiences that perceive the communicator is fully and nonjudgmentally listening will be more forthcoming with information as well as more receptive to the delivered messages.

A communicator who omits the needs assessment step will fall prey to the mistake of creating communication that is the same no matter the audience. People don't respond as well to one-size-fits-all communication as they do to tailored communication. Being audience-focused requires a needs assessment. The next section describes how needs assessment data are used to drive decisions.

How Are Needs Assessment Data Used to Drive Decisions?

Needs assessment data are valuable for making several decisions related to effective communication. For instance, they can be used to determine what topics are communicated, how to focus the coverage of these topics, the depth and breadth of coverage, and the best channels for delivering a message. Making the message meaningful to the audience through the proper use of understandable words and examples is made possible by a needs assessment. If the questions asked in the needs assessment remain unanswered, further assessment should occur.

Help Focus the Topics Covered

The topic of a message is chosen based on several factors, all of which can be determined from a needs assessment. First, the topic addresses a documented need of the target audience, such as health concerns and behaviors or health goals that are unmet. For example, an audience may consist of people with a high risk for heart disease or cancer and who don't consume the recommended amount of fiber. Rather than communicating everything there is to know about heart disease and cancer, a message could focus on the benefits of fiber for lowering the risk for these chronic diseases.

A second factor in focusing a topic is based on what new information and research may be unknown or confusing to the audience. The role of the nutrition communicator is to provide current information in ways an audience can understand and use. The needs assessment can assist the communicator in learning what the audience knows about a topic as well as what they don't understand. That knowledge allows the communicator to further focus the topic to address what the audience needs to know. In the example about fiber, the audience may know the difference between insoluble and soluble fiber but may not know about the advantages of fiber for promoting a healthy gut microbiome. An audience appreciates learning new information that they can put to use.

A third factor in focusing a topic is based on what the audience is interested in and deems

WORDS OF EXPERIENCE

Please Don't Talk to Us About Eating Disorders!

by Barbara J. Mayfield, MS, RDN, FAND

In the nutrition communications course at Purdue University, the students conduct needs assessments in preparation for creating presentations to groups. One semester, a set of partners who were former gymnasts chose to present to a group of young gymnasts in the local area. Through secondary data collection, as well as their own experience, they determined that eating disorders and body image were their top choices for what to cover with the group. Before conducting their onsite surveys and interviews, I insisted that they open their topic choices to the group to allow them to indicate whether they were interested in these topics or in something else.

Through their needs assessment, the students found out that not only were the young gymnasts not interested in those topics, they were adamantly against hearing another presentation about them. It turned out that everyone who spoke to the group talked about those topics and they were tired of it. Instead, they wanted to learn how to make fun, healthy snacks.

Consider what would have happened had the students gone in and done a talk about eating disorders or body image. How would they have been received?

Instead, the partners designed a fun, engaging, and informative presentation that met the group's interests and needs and was very well received.

important. The needs assessment can help the communicator build interest in a topic, but if the audience expresses limited interest, the communicator is better off selecting a topic that interests the audience because it will more likely garner attention and acceptance. In the fiber example, if the communicator learns that the audience isn't interested in the role of fiber in preventing chronic disease but is interested in maintaining a healthy weight, the communicator can refocus the topic to cover fiber's role in weight management.

The Words of Experience box above has an example of a needs assessment that identified a program topic an audience did *not* want.

Help Determine Appropriate Breadth and Depth

Another important consideration is the allowed length of a presentation or article. Within any given spoken or written communication, the communicator can only present so much content. This necessitates determining how much breadth and depth of the communication can be covered. The broader the topic, the more limited the depth. The narrower the breadth, the greater the depth of coverage. When deciding whether to choose more depth or more breadth about a topic, the most important determinant is the audience—their current knowledge, their need to learn more, and their interest in aspects of the topic's breadth and depth.

See Box 22.8 on page 353 for a list of readability tools.

A needs assessment reveals what an audience already knows so that new information can build on existing knowledge. It also indicates what information is most needed based on their knowledge, behaviors, and skills. Their education level and experiences help determine the appropriate depth. An important consideration is what information is "need to know" versus "nice to know." It is tempting to share all the information about a subject, even when audiences won't use it or don't care to know it.

Help Decide Channels to Use

The nutrition communicator has numerous channels to pick from to deliver a message. Which ones to use should not only be based on what is available and what the communicator is comfortable with but should also consider the channels the audience uses most. Does the audience prefer in-person communication or online channels? Do they prefer to read or watch a video? Matching audience preferences may stretch the communicator to learn new skills, but the payoff is an audience that engages, learns, and takes action on the message. Make sure that a needs assessment includes finding out preferred channels and learning strategies. An audience is best served by employing multiple channels whenever feasible, because doing so accounts for differences in audience preferences and provides multiple opportunities for audience engagement and learning.

Help Select Words and Examples to Use

Audiences respond to messages that are written in language that is familiar and understandable. At times, new words or jargon are needed to convey information. When that is the case, clearly explain the new terms and put them into practical examples the audience can relate to.

Additionally, be sure to determine what reading level is appropriate for an audience. If the audience varies in education level, match the reading level to the lower end of the range. Those who can read at a higher level will not find the information too simple if it is new and useful.

How Is a Needs Assessment Conducted?

A needs assessment should be conducted prior to all nutrition communication endeavors. The formality and method may vary depending on the platform and approach used to communicate with an audience. A formal needs assessment requires several steps. Nutrition communicators need to identify target audiences, consider what information is most important to gather from audience members, and decide which data collection approach will generate the most useful information. This section will address some of the most important issues to cover with target audience members, the most common quantitative and qualitative approaches to needs assessments, and different sampling methods to use when recruiting participants. This type of approach can be especially useful when designing programs, interventions, or mass media campaigns to reach target audience members. Less formal approaches to needs assessments will also be covered. These are ideally suited for bloggers and digital strategists.

Identify the Audience(s) to Assess

When conducting a needs assessment, the sample recruited should be similar to (and ideally representative of) the larger population the message is targeting. Depending on the resources available, information can be collected through formal and informal approaches. Informal and formal approaches may differ in their sampling methods, recruitment procedures, research methods used, and approaches to analysis.

Prior to recruiting participants, nutrition communicators need to determine whether they will use probability or nonprobability sampling procedures. Probability sampling involves the use of random selection procedures to minimize bias in a sample. Nutrition communicators can use these approaches to enhance the likelihood that demographic, psychographic, and other personal characteristics of a sample are in line with those of the broader population that will ultimately be served by the program. Alignment between these entities will enhance the likelihood a program addresses issues that are most relevant to target populations.

Not all types of nutrition communication are supported with the time and funds required to complete probability sampling. When this is the case, nonprobability sampling procedures may be used. Convenience sampling is one example of a nonprobabilistic sampling procedure; it occurs when a nutrition communicator collects data from individuals who are easy (or convenient) to reach. This may include conducting focus groups with individuals who frequent a local community center, sending a survey to a popular listserve, or gleaning insights from comments on blogs or social media posts.

When the right questions are asked, convenience approaches can provide important and relevant formative information for nutrition communicators. However, nutrition communicators must recognize that bias likely exists in the sample and that information acquired cannot be generalized to the broader population. Instead, types of bias should be considered, and nutrition communicators should try to account for this through modification of assessment efforts. For instance, a survey sent through social media might yield a greater proportion of responses from younger individuals than the broader population a program might reach.[2] If this is the case, additional steps should be taken to identify and sample older members of the focal population. Nutrition communicators must also acknowledge that unrecognizable bias is likely to exist in the sample and data despite their best efforts to minimize it.

Informal feedback is another approach that can be used for nutrition programs. Feedback can come from colleagues, coworkers, community stakeholders, and members of the target population. Getting feedback and learning from the experiences of other nutrition communicators can

enhance the quality and impact of the communication endeavor.

Not all nutrition communication will warrant this type of needs assessment. Informal approaches to learning about an audience can also be helpful. These can be used to garner feedback from audiences in a more relaxed manner and may be used to support popular press articles, infographics, social media posts, blog articles, and other digital content. In these circumstances, a modified approach to assessment could be used. Regardless of the circumstance, learning as much as possible about a target audience can help inform the distribution of information. This may include identifying facts and relevant statistics about a target audience's demographics, preferences, psychographics, and other key indicators to learn more about who is being addressed. (Refer to the next section: Determining Information to Collect.)

When using digital communication platforms, it may also be useful to generate additional information about a target audience by directly engaging with them. After content is disseminated through digital platforms, explore the comments and responses provided by interactors. What trends appear in the responses? What did interactors respond to favorably? Where do they still have questions? Interacting with audiences through comments can be a great method to target, tone, and tailor messages to be as directly connected to the needs of audience members as possible.

When disseminating information via digital platforms, past audience behavior can also be used to inform future communications. Google Analytics is a useful tool to help communicators learn more about audience behavior. It can be used to provide website traffic reports that provide information on sessions (site visits), average visit duration, and quality of user visits.

Determine the Information to Collect

The next stage in the needs assessment process is determining what information to collect. Arguably, this is one of the most difficult steps in the process. It is important for nutrition communicators to have a holistic understanding of the audiences they are working with; however, limited time and resources are available to capture this data. It is best to have a focused and prioritized list of what information should be obtained in the assessment. Nutrition communicators should also have an understanding of what they plan to do with the information gathered.

Based on the problem the communication will address, what information is needed from the target audience? What information is absolutely critical to the success of the communication? What information would be helpful but is not crucial? It is important to begin an assessment with a list of informational needs and wants. For instance, understanding existing knowledge levels within an audience is essential to executing messages focused on enhancing knowledge and encouraging behavioral action. By contrast, understanding the prevalence of certain personality traits among members of an audience may not be vital to the success of the communication. Next we will look at variables that are frequently examined through needs assessments.

ASSESS AUDIENCE KNOWLEDGE

Knowledge refers to the amount of accurate information an individual possesses about a person, event, topic, or behavior. A needs assessment can examine both objective and perceived knowledge to learn more about the audience.

Objective knowledge can be measured by asking target audience members questions about the focal issue or behavior that have clear correct or incorrect answers. The set of questions assessing objective knowledge must also holistically represent the focal phenomenon. For example, when examining knowledge levels about eating disorders in general, queries should not focus on one single disorder.

Possessing a deep understanding of target audience members' knowledge will enable nutrition communicators to develop more effective and tailored approaches to communicating information. If a needs assessment demonstrates that a substantial percentage of target audience members lack knowledge in a specific area, the communication should focus on improving knowledge in addition to possibly altering attitudes and behaviors.

Perceived knowledge refers to how well audience members *believe* they understand key issues, problems, or phenomena. Exploring perceived knowledge may include asking questions such as, "How well do you believe you understand [focal issue]?"

Assessing perceived knowledge in addition to objective knowledge can be especially important

when exploring topics that are not well understood among the public. Special communications approaches may need to be used if trends demonstrate that substantial gaps exist between perceived and actual knowledge pertaining to nutrition issues.

ASSESS AUDIENCE ATTITUDES, VALUES, AND BELIEFS

Attitudes, values, and beliefs are cognitive variables that represent personal orientations toward issues, events, behaviors, and more. Each of these variables can directly or indirectly influence actions taken.

- Beliefs are ideas that individuals consider to be true. They can be based on personal experiences and norms within a culture or society.[3] Beliefs can be spiritual, moral, or intellectual.
- Values are long-lasting beliefs about what is important. Values typically move beyond individual actions and behaviors.[4] Instead, they may lead to general conduct in the interest of achieving specific goals. For example, if a person believes that money is the key to a happy and stable life, it is likely that generating income will be an important personal value.
- Attitudes are an individual's overall evaluation of behaviors or phenomena. They are formed by an individual's beliefs about the positive and negative outcomes that may result from engaging in a behavior.[5,6] Attitudes help people determine whether they consider an object to be good or bad, fun or boring, healthy or unhealthy, and so on.

It is paramount for nutrition communicators to have an understanding of the beliefs, values, and attitudes of target audience members. A communication is likely to fail if it directly advocates against the beliefs and values of the target audience. Communication approaches should acknowledge the cognitive dispositions of audience members, and programs should be designed to account for these needs. Ultimately, beliefs, values, and attitudes all contribute to an individual's likelihood of partaking in a behavior.

ASSESS AUDIENCE BEHAVIORS AND PRACTICES

It is also important to consider current behaviors among audience members when determining how to design a program. Past behavior is associated with future behavior.[7] Nutrition communicators may need to address audience members differently based on whether the purpose of the communication endeavor is to encourage behavioral maintenance or behavioral change. Future intentions to engage in specified behaviors should be considered as well.

Behavioral intent is an individual's inclination or likelihood of partaking in an action in the future. Although there is not a one-to-one correlation between intentions and behaviors, research has shown that intentions are associated with future behavioral engagement.[8] For instance, individuals might intend to exercise three to five times a week, but this may not always occur due to a number of factors, including time, energy, and work stressors. However, intent presents some degree of initial interest in pursuing a particular course of action. This initial interest or intention may lead to enhanced likelihood of success in the future.

Nutrition communicators will need to address audiences differently depending on whether or not they already intend to partake in a specified behavior in the future. It will likely be easier to engage an individual who has expressed an intention to change a behavior than one who has not expressed any intention to do so.

ASSESS AUDIENCE MOTIVATORS, BARRIERS, AND READINESS TO CHANGE

When collecting information on the needs of target audience members, it is important to consider factors such as motivators, barriers, and readiness to change.

Motivators are intrinsic and extrinsic variables that are likely to encourage achievement of objectives in target audience members.

- Intrinsic motivators are characteristics internal to individuals, such as a strong sense of duty, personal responsibility, or interest in the task itself.
- Extrinsic motivators are external or environmental factors that facilitate action. Examples of extrinsic motivators include social pressure, competition, cultural approval of the behavior, or physical incentives.[9]

Barriers are obstacles that may preclude an individual from fulfilling the focal objective. These can include time, money, social connections, knowledge, resources, and personal concerns. For instance, some cultural groups are less likely to seek out care from medical professionals. Part of this mistrust stems from historical medical mistreatment of underserved groups throughout the United States.[10] With an understanding of barriers, nutrition communicators can design messages and approaches that are sensitive to the needs of their target audience.

Readiness to change is another important factor to consider when conducting a needs assessment. This refers to an individual's cognitive position with respect to behavioral change, which influences how a communication should be targeted and tailored toward a specific group.[11]

ASSESS AUDIENCE DEMOGRAPHICS

Demographics and psychographics are also key variables to consider when conducting a needs assessment. Demographics are personal characteristics, such as age, gender, race, ethnicity, income, marital status, education, and geographic location. When designing a program, consider the role demographics can play in engaging audience members. Awareness of trends can help ensure that communications are as closely tailored to the target populations as possible.

Nutrition communicators should not completely generalize audiences and make sweeping recommendations; audience needs may differ depending on the social and demographic groups audience members belong to. For instance, when addressing issues such as caloric intake, different recommendations and messaging may appeal to younger adults versus older adults.[12]

OTHER FACTORS

Based on the topic and nature of the nutrition communication, additional factors that might be important to include are participant learning styles, preferred channels, and other psychographics. Learning styles refer to the methods that audience members use to recognize, acquire, and interpret information. Although individuals tend to express preferences for visual or auditory learning, more evidence is needed to show that individuals have specific aptitudes for different learning styles.[13] Given this, it is best for planners to focus more on information channel preferences than on directly targeting learning styles when developing communications approaches.

See Chapter 12 for more on behavioral intent.

Readiness to change is a key variable covered in the stages of change model addressed in Chapter 12.

Communication channels refer to specific methods of information distribution. Channels include digital media, face-to-face communication, and mass media. When determining what channel or channels to use to reach target audience members, it is important to consider what methods of communication audience members use, trust, and prefer. Approaches to communication may be based on audience preferences *and* the focal topic. For instance, some programs may encourage community opinion leaders to advocate for a specific behavior or practice to promote health. Programs often use a combination of interpersonal and mass-mediated approaches to disseminate information.

In addition to attitudes, other psychographics to consider are goals and desires. Understanding the goals and desires of a target audience is valuable information to help that target population. It is important for nutrition communicators to consider what goals and achievements the target audience members wish to achieve. Many individuals have goals regarding improved health. If feasible, aligning program goals with target audience goals can be an effective way to gain interest from community members and enhance participation.

Secondary vs Primary Data Collection

Imagine being tasked with painting a picture representing a particular community or target audience. The canvas, paint brushes, and paint are provided. Where to begin? If the wrong kinds of color are used or the wrong objects depicted, the picture may end up looking nothing like the target audience.

Additional information on data sources is in Chapter 4.

Data collection is key in determining how to "paint a picture" of a target audience. It is essential that the data collected are credible, accurate, and reliable. Depending on the target audience in question or the problem being addressed, there may be an abundant amount of information available or there may be very little information. In either case, setting some limits or criteria on what and how much data will be collected and analyzed is crucial. Communicators should consider time and resources available when selecting methods for collecting secondary data, primary data, or a combination of both.

Secondary data, frequently referred to as *existing data*, are collected by another entity or for another purpose. Examples include census data, published research data, and data collected for the National Health and Nutrition Examination Survey. Primary data, sometimes referred to as *new data*, are collected by the person or group conducting the assessment.[14] Examples include conducting a focus group with potential audience members or circulating a survey.

SOURCES AND USES OF SECONDARY DATA

Starting data collection with secondary sources is generally recommended because it saves time and may yield adequate information to fully address the objectives of the needs assessment. There are a lot of different places to find relevant and credible data, depending on the focus. National and state indicator data may be easier to access than local information about a community (ie, the number of grocery stores in a certain area). The Centers for Disease Control and Prevention (CDC) lists sources of community-level indicators on its Public Health Professionals Gateway website (www.cdc.gov/stltpublichealth/cha/data.html).[14]

However, secondary data may not always be useful for nutrition communicators communicating through media channels such as articles, blogs, and social media. When a communicator has a consistent audience (also known as followers), it's always important to continue to get to know the audience specifically and not generalize high-level, secondary data to tailor communications. For example, using something like the International Food Information Council (IFIC) Food and Health Survey[15] may be helpful in understanding overarching trends but not necessarily the specific values and needs of a particular audience.

PRIMARY DATA COLLECTION

After gathering secondary data, identify any specific gaps in knowledge that are important to better understand a target audience. The following key questions[16] are important to address before proceeding with primary data collection:

- What is known, and what still needs to be learned?
- How will the information be collected?
- Who will be asked?
- What will be asked?
- Who will collect the data?
- How will the data be compiled and reported?
- What actions will be taken based on the data?

Primary data collection methods and tools vary, and there are strengths and limitations for each of the methods.

Surveys The most common quantitative testing and evaluation method used in nutrition communication projects is surveys, which can be disseminated in a variety of formats to obtain quantitative data. Questions can come in the form of multiple choice, ranking, checklist, Likert scales (agree or disagree), open-ended, or alternate responses (yes or no). A large number of respondents (usually 100 or more) are usually recruited to complete surveys. Surveys are commonly used in planning and assessment to obtain baseline and tracking information on knowledge of or attitudes and behaviors toward and behavioral intentions of a selected target audience.

For example, collecting data on target audience members' knowledge, attitudes, or behaviors toward eating fruits and vegetables at the beginning of program or message development can provide valuable insight. Once the nutrition program is in place or messages have been disseminated, surveys can also be used to assess usage or awareness of materials and even changes in health behaviors related to eating more fruits and vegetables. In this example, both a pretest and posttest can be used to measure changes in behavior and learning among the target audience, which can help control for some confounding variables at baseline.

As another example, a nutrition blogger who is focused on healthy eating for weight management might send out an annual survey to blog followers (the audience), asking how they have used the information from the blog and whether they have changed their behaviors and achieved weight loss. The survey can also include open-ended questions to help tailor future blog content, such as, "If you haven't lost weight since you started following this blog, what type of content and material would be useful to you?"

Most surveys are developed and customized to the research questions under investigation; however, some measurements may be adapted from other existing, reliable, and validated instruments.[17] For the blogging example, the National Cancer Institute's fruit and vegetable screener, a reliable and validated measure, could be incorporated into the survey to assess changes in the usual fruit and vegetable intake of participants from pretest to posttest.

To counter low response rates, many individuals employ incentives for surveys. Incentives can be paid prior to completion (prepaid); paid after completion of the survey (postpaid); lottery based, in which case the respondent has a chance to win the incentive; or participation based, in which case every respondent receives the incentive. Researchers have found that providing incentives can be effective at increasing participant response rates for general population surveys in all communication modes[18-21]; however, there is some concern about reliability due to the incentives exerting undue influence.[22] To achieve more representative samples and higher survey response rates, a best practice to follow is to spend more money on other aspects of the survey (eg, pilot testing, graphic design) rather than relying on incentives. Box 11.1 shows the various types of survey formats along with the advantages and disadvantages[23] of each type.

Interviews Interviews can be conducted to better understand an audience member's attitudes, thoughts, and opinions on a topic (eg, in an in-depth interview) or to assess the understanding of materials (eg, through a survey) or messages of a project (eg, through a cognitive interview) during project planning. Both in-depth and cognitive interview techniques have similar formats and can be conducted one-on-one with select individuals that represent the target audience. During cognitive interviewing, respondents are led through a survey or message and asked to paraphrase items; discuss thoughts, feelings, and ideas that come to mind; and suggest alternative wording for messages. For more detailed information on cognitive interviewing, see the resources section at the end of this chapter.

During interviews, the interviewer uses open-ended questions and probing of responses to obtain better insight into how the individual responds to a topic. Before the interview, an interview guide is developed that includes a list of questions and topics, arranged in a logical order, that need to be covered during the interview. A trained interviewer will use this guide as a tool to guide the formal interview. The guide will give the interviewer flexibility to follow other pertinent, yet unforeseen, topics not in the guide that may arise during the interview. Often, interviews are digitally recorded or a skilled note taker is present to allow the interviewer to focus on the conversation rather than be distracted by jotting down the interviewee's answers.

Advantages and Disadvantages of Various Survey Formats

Survey Format	Advantages	Disadvantages
Mail	• Convenient for participants • Can reach diverse populations that are hard to reach	• Inappropriate for participants with limited literacy skills • Low response rate that may require extensive and expensive follow-up • Data entry of responses leaves room for error
Telephone	• More appropriate for participants with limited literacy skills • Leaves less room for error because the interviewer enters responses directly into the computer • May be easier for participants to talk about sensitive issues	• Unable to sample participants who do not have telephones • Difficult to get participants to answer a phone call if they believe the survey is part of a solicitation call • Lack of availability of phone numbers (ie, cell phones unlisted)
In-person	• Can be used with all literacy levels • Useful with difficult-to-reach populations (eg, homeless, rural) • Interviewer can clarify questions for participants, leading to more complete responses	• Can be more expensive than self-administered or telephone surveys • Inappropriate for topics that are sensitive, threatening, or controversial, as participants may not respond truthfully
Online (web-based)	• Eliminates data entry and limits data reporting errors • Convenient for participants with internet access • Useful for complex surveys because computerized skipping patterns can be used	• Inappropriate for audiences with limited literacy skills or those not comfortable with computers • Requires participants to have access to a computer and the internet

Adapted with permission from Drummond KE, Cooke NK. How to develop and use surveys in research. In: Drummond KE, Murphy-Reyes A, eds. *Nutrition Research: Concepts and Applications.* Jones and Bartlett Learning; 2018:351-385.[23]

Interviews typically last from 30 minutes to an hour, depending on the number of topics to be addressed, and can be held in a variety of settings. Face-to-face interviewing has the advantage of giving the interviewer the ability to observe nonverbal cues of the interviewee. Telephone interviews, on the other hand, may be more convenient for both the interviewer and interviewee, but the interviewer will need to pay close attention to verbal intonations to make up for the inability to observe nonverbal cues. Usually, 10 interviews are conducted per audience segment to be addressed[24] (eg, if the project is on family meals with teens, 10 parents [target audience] and 10 teens [secondary audience] are interviewed). After the interview, the data collected are qualitatively analyzed using various thematic and coding schemes.

Interviews can be useful for sensitive topics that people might feel hesitant to discuss in groups. For example, if the topic is body image and disordered eating in athletes, talking with athletes individually versus in a group will likely provide more personal and insightful data. Even though interviews do not allow for interaction among group members, like in a focus group (discussed next), it can lead to richer detail and insights on the topic.

Interviews can be used at any stage of planning or implementation of a variety of communication modes. For example, a nutrition and dietetics practitioner in the process of developing a social marketing campaign promoting fruit and vegetable intake among young adults in the community may use interviews to inform messaging for the campaign. To ensure that the nutrition communication strategies

Refer to Chapter 6 as well as the resources section at the end of this chapter for more on qualitative research methods.

for the social marketing campaign resonate with the nutrition and dietetics practitioner's intended audience, semistructured interviews might be conducted among a handful of young adults, which can give further insight into the lifestyles of young adults in the community. The nutrition and dietetics practitioner's findings help refine the messaging of the campaign to better address young adults' barriers to eating fruits and vegetables. See Box 11.2 for tips for interviewers.

Focus Groups Unlike interviews, the focus group approach encourages discussion among group members, which tends to stimulate ideas that would not have been available otherwise.[24,25] The dynamic interplay generated by group members provides rich, descriptive information from the respondents' point of view and is particularly useful when seeking to discover respondents' meanings and ways of understanding.

Focus groups are led by a trained moderator and usually are limited to 6 to 10 participants to allow for meaningful group conversation.[24] Focus group participants are chosen based on certain characteristics or demographic information such as age, race or ethnicity, sex, and income. Often a screener or questionnaire is given to participants beforehand to ensure that the appropriate target audience is being recruited for the messages or programs that are being created.

Trained moderators use a guide with a series of questions to stimulate discussion. In focus groups, as in interviews, it is important for the moderator to not reveal his or her own opinions either verbally or through facial expressions or other body language. At times, the moderator may need to unobtrusively guide focus group members back to the discussion questions to keep them on track while still allowing members to talk freely and share their attitudes, thoughts, and opinions.

Focus group sessions usually last 90 minutes to 2 hours and can be held in a variety of settings; one common venue is a conference room that can accommodate the group comfortably. The number of focus groups needed depends on the magnitude of the program and number of distinct target audience segments.[24] As a general guideline, at the point where no new information is being gathered, researchers can decide that the number of focus groups held is sufficient. For more detailed information on focus group interviews, see the resources section at the end of this chapter.

BOX 11.2 Interviewer Tips

Allow enough time so the interviewee does not feel rushed.

Provide nonverbal reinforcement, such as nodding your head, so the interviewee knows you are listening.

Encourage the interviewee to provide specifics about what they are sharing.

Use the following prompts when you notice the interviewee appears to be having difficulty thinking aloud: "Tell me what you're thinking." "What are you thinking about right now?"

Carefully listen to what the interviewee wonders aloud about or mentions to allow further probing later on.

Instruct the note-taker, when applicable, to record any nonverbal actions the interviewee displays (eg, fidgeting, appearing distracted, change in tone of voice) that may influence their responses.

Adapted from Shafer K, Lohse B. How to conduct a cognitive interview: a nutrition education example. National Institute of Food and Agriculture website. https://nifa.usda.gov/sites/default/files/resource/how-to-conduct-a-cognitive-interview.pdf[26]

Web-based (online) focus groups are similar in format to in-person focus groups, except instead of gathering at a facility, members and the moderator log on to a private conferencing platform to conduct the focus group. The moderator posts questions and members respond. Some advantages to using web-based focus groups over conventional focus groups are that they are more convenient for respondents (since they can participate from home), they can reach a more geographically diverse population, and they are less expensive to conduct. However, some limitations to using web-based focus groups over conventional methods are that the moderator cannot always observe nonverbal reactions of members, group dynamics are muted or lost, and the members must have access to a computer and internet service to participate.

Regardless of which format is chosen for focus groups, they can be used by nutrition and dietetic practitioners during the planning and early implementation stages of program planning or even when testing a specific message or approach. For example, suppose a nutrition communicator wanted to develop nutrition messages for low-income parents with young children but was unsure of what nutrition topics and delivery methods would be of specific interest to the audience. Focus groups involving people from this demographic would help the communicator to identify topics that resonated with them, as well as nutrition communication approaches that would enable and motivate parents to positively change health behaviors for themselves and their children.

Observations In some instances, visual observation is an appropriate method of evaluating behavior, describing events, or noting physical characteristics in a natural setting. In nutrition projects, this method can be employed to allow a nutrition and dietetics practitioner to observe how individuals or groups respond to certain messages or learning activities.

The observations can be either direct or indirect. In direct observations, the observer watches for interactions, processes, or behaviors as they occur. During indirect observations, the observer watches the results of the interactions, processes, or behaviors.[27] An example of direct observation is when nutrition communicators are observed to determine whether they are delivering nutrition messages with knowledge and expertise. On the other hand, an example of indirect observation is when students are observed in a school cafeteria to determine whether they are more likely to choose healthier food items after participating in a nutrition education program.

The three ways of collecting observation data are:

- recording sheets and checklists—including both predetermined questions and observations;
- observation guides—listing interactions, processes, or behaviors to be observed; and
- field notes—open-ended narrative data that can be written or dictated onto a digital recorder or recorded in a voice recording app.[27]

The type of data collection method will vary depending on the focus of the observed evaluation, timing of events, and resources available. Either way, advantages of observation include being able to collect data where and when an event or activity is occurring and not having to rely on people's willingness or ability to provide the information. However, some disadvantages include

the susceptibility to observer bias (eg, subjective evaluations) and the expense and time-consuming nature of observations compared to other data collection methods.[27]

Photovoice An innovative method for collecting information about an audience is Photovoice.[28] "Photovoice is a process in which people—usually those with limited power due to poverty, language barriers, race, class, ethnicity, gender, culture, or other circumstances—use video and/or photo images to capture aspects of their environment and experiences and share them with others."[28] It is a qualitative method of assessment that involves the audience members themselves in capturing the images and videos to describe their situation and needs.

There are advantages to using this method of data collection:

- It describes the community (or situation) from the viewpoint of those who live there.
- It enables recording of strengths, challenges, and concerns.
- It promotes dialogue about key issues.
- It is relatively easy to use.
- Images can be understood regardless of cultural or language barriers.

However, there are also disadvantages:

- Analysis of images can be complex due to the volume and criteria for inclusion and exclusion.
- Photo release permissions may be required.
- Photography development and presentation of images can be costly.[29]

Tips for effectively using Photovoice are provided by the Community Tool Box[29] (see the resources section at the end of the chapter).

Regardless of the approach used to complete a needs assessment, it is essential to get to know an audience in order to tailor a message to their needs and select examples that relate to their life experiences. Chapters 12 through 14 will assist communicators in tailoring a message to an audience's beliefs, intentions, values, life stage, and more. When an audience is actively engaged in a needs assessment, the communicator will hear stories that can be used to illustrate messages and key points. Getting to know an audience translates into knowing what its members need and how to communicate with them. Complete a needs assessment!

Chapter 12 discusses how audiences change behaviors.

Chapters 13 and 14 talk about audiences of various cultures and age groups.

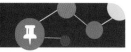
A Needs Assessment Is Essential for Audience-Focused Communication

1 A needs assessment is a data collection and analysis process that provides information about an audience and is used to direct all aspects of communication planning and implementation, including determining desired outcomes, message development, delivery channels, and approaches.

2 Needs assessment data can be used to determine what topics are communicated and how to focus the coverage of these topics. A needs assessment can also determine the depth and breadth of topic coverage, the best channels for delivering a message, and ways to make the message meaningful to the audience through the proper use of understandable words and examples.

3 Several variables can be assessed to create audience-focused communication including audience knowledge, attitudes, past behaviors, goals, desires, barriers, and motivators. Variables assessed should be based on the informational needs of the communicator and should shed light on the projected challenges and opportunities encountered with the audience. These data can be captured through various means, including surveys, focus groups, and interviews.

RESOURCES

Tool kit for conducting community assessments: http://ctb.ku.edu/en/assessing-community-needs-and -resources

Community-based participatory research: http://ctb.ku.edu/en/table-of-contents/evaluate /evaluation/intervention-research/main

How to conduct a cognitive interview: A nutrition education example guide: www.au.af.mil/au/awc /awcgate/usda/cog_interview.pdf

Guide to designing and conducting focus group interviews: www.eiu.edu/ihec/Krueger-FocusGroup Interviews.pdf

Tips for effectively using Photovoice, provided by the Community Tool Box: http://ctb.ku.edu/en /table-of-contents/assessment/assessing-community -needs-and-resources/photovoice/main

For more on evaluating qualitative research, see Cooke NK, Goodell S, Stage VC. How to evaluate qualitative research. In: Drummond KE, Murphy-Reyes A, eds. *Nutrition Research: Concepts and Applications*. Jones and Bartlett Learning; 2018:301-315.

REFERENCES

1. Community tool box. Section 2: community-based participatory research. Published 2017. Accessed June 1, 2017. http://ctb.ku.edu/en /table-of-contents/evaluate/evaluation /intervention-research/main

2. Smith A, Anderson M. Social media use 2018. Pew Research Center website. Published March 2018. Accessed August 17, 2018. www.pew internet.org/2018/03/01/social-media-use-2018 -acknowledgments

3. Immigration Advisers Authority. Personal beliefs, values, attitudes. Accessed August 17, 2018. https://iaa.govt.nz/for-advisers/adviser-tools /ethics-toolkit/personal-beliefs-values-attitudes -and-behaviour

4. Bergman MM. A theoretical note on the differences between attitudes, opinions, and values. *Swiss Political Sci Review.* 1998;4:81-93. doi:10.1002/j.1662-6370.1998.tb00239.x

5. Human M, Quick BL, Payne L. Community college students' health insurance enrollment, maintenance, and talking with parents intentions: an application of the reasoned action approach. *J Health Commun.* 2016;21:487-495. doi:10.1080 /10810730.2015.1103327

6. Fishbein M, Ajzen I. *Belief, Attitude, Intention and Behavior: An Introduction to Theory and Research.* Addison-Wesley; 1975.

7. Ouellette JA, Wood W. Habit and intention in everyday life: the multiple processes by which past behavior predicts future behavior. *Psycho Bull.* 1998;124(1):54-74. doi:10.1037/0033-2909.124.1.54

8. Sheeran P. Intention-behavior relations: a conceptual and empirical overview. *Eur Rev Soc Psychol.* 2002;12:1-36. doi:10.1080/14792772143000003

9. Seifert CM, Chapman LS, Hart JK, Perez P. Enhancing intrinsic motivation in health promotion and wellness. *Am J Health Promot.* 2012;26(3):1-12. doi:10.4278/ajhp.26.3.tahp

10. Adams LB, Richmond J, Corbie-Smith G, Powell W. Medical mistrust and colorectal screening among African Americans. *J Community Health.* 2017;42(5):1044-1061. doi:10.1007/s10900-017-0339-2

11. Prochaska JO, Velicer WF. The transtheoretical model of health behavior change. *Am J Health Promot.* 1997;12(1):38-48. doi:10.4278/0890-1171-12.1.38

12. US Department of Health and Human Services and US Department of Agriculture. Appendix 2: estimated calorie needs per day, by age, sex, and physical activity level. In: *2015–2020 Dietary Guidelines for Americans.* 8th ed. December 2015. Accessed June 18, 2018. https://health.gov/dietaryguidelines/2015/guidelines/appendix-2

13. Pashler H, McDaniel M, Rohrer D, Bjork R. Learning styles: concepts and evidence. *Psychol Sci Public Interest.* 2008;9(2):105-119. doi:10.1111/j.1539-6053.2009.01038.x

14. Data & benchmarks. Centers for Disease Control and Prevention website. Reviewed August 30, 2017. Accessed January 16, 2018. https://cdc.gov/stltpublichealth/cha/data.html

15. Food Insight. 2017 food and health survey: a focus on 50+. International Food Information Council Foundation website. Published May 5, 2017. Accessed August 17, 2018. https://foodinsight.org/2017-food-and-health-survey

16. Ladjahasan N. Preparing for a collaborative community assessment. Iowa State University Extension and Outreach website. Published January 2001. Accessed January 16, 2018. https://store.extension.iastate.edu/product/1086

17. Auld G, Baker S, McGirr K, Osborn K, Skaff P. Confirming the reliability and validity of others' evaluation tools before adopting for your programs. *J Nutr Educ Behav.* 2017;49:441-450. doi:10.1016/j.jneb.2017.02.006

18. Cobanoglu C, Cobanoglu N. The effect of incentives in web surveys: application and ethical considerations. *Intl J Mark Res.* 2003;4(4):1-13. doi:10.1177/147078530304500406

19. Deutskens E, Ruyter KD, Wetzels M, Oosterveld P. Response rate and response quality of internet-based surveys: an experimental study. *Mark Lett.* 2004;15(1):21-36. doi:10.1023/B:MARK.0000021968.86465.00

20. Heerwegh D. An investigation of the effects of lotteries on web survey response rates. *Field Methods.* 2006;18(2):205-220. doi:10.1177/1525822X05285781

21. Singer E, Ye C. The use and effects of incentives in surveys. In: Massey DS, Tourangeau R, eds. *The ANNALS of the American Academy of Political and Social Science.* Sage; 2013:112-141.

22. Singer E, Couper MP. Do incentives exert undue influence on survey participation? Experimental evidence. *J Empir Res Hum Res Ethics.* 2008;3:49-56. doi:10.1525/jer.2008.3.3.49

23. Drummond KE, Cooke NK. How to develop and use surveys in research. In: Drummond KE, Murphy-Reyes A, eds. *Nutrition Research: Concepts and Applications.* Jones and Bartlett Learning; 2018:351-385.

24. Borra S, Shelley G, Tuttle M. The art and science of consumer communications: using consumer research to create nutrition and health messages that work. In: Monsen E, Van Horn L, eds. *Research: Successful Approaches.* 3rd ed. American Dietetic Association; 2008:353-361.

25. Hartman J. Using focus groups to conduct business communication research. *Intl J Bus Comm.* 2004;41:402-410. doi:10.1177/0021943604267775

26. Shafer K, Lohse B. How to conduct a cognitive interview: a nutrition education example. National Institute of Food and Agriculture website. Accessed May 1, 2020. https://nifa.usda.gov/sites/default/files/resource/how-to-conduct-a-cognitive-interview.pdf

27. Data collection methods for program evaluation: observation. Northwest Center for Public Health Practice website. Accessed October 10, 2019. https://www.nwcphp.org/docs/data_collection/data_collection_print.pdf

28. Community Tool Box. Section 20: implementing Photovoice in your community. Accessed January 16, 2018. http://ctb.ku.edu/en/table-of-contents/assessment/assessing-community-needs-and-resources/photovoice/main

29. Centers for Disease Control and Prevention. *Community Health Assessment and Group Evaluation (CHANGE) Action Guide: Building a Foundation of Knowledge to Prioritize Community Needs.* US Department of Health and Human Services; 2010.

Use Behavior Change Theories to Create Effective Communication

Carol Byrd-Bredbenner, PhD, RD, FAND
and Virginia Quick, PhD, RDN

"Designing nutrition communications with behavior change theories in mind takes the simple act of educating consumers about a topic to a new level—one that moves people beyond the mental processes of acquiring information to actually applying information to improve health and well-being."

> "There is nothing so practical
> as a good theory."
>
> —KURT LEWIN, FOUNDING FATHER OF SOCIAL PSYCHOLOGY

Introduction

Behavior change theories can be used in all forms of communication—from blogging for a large audience to personal consultations with one patient. Designing nutrition communications with behavior change theories in mind takes the simple act of educating consumers about a topic to a new level—one that moves people beyond the mental processes of *acquiring* information to actually *applying* information to improve health and well-being. Behavior change theories help nutrition communicators more effectively and efficiently motivate audience members to adopt and perform many health-protective practices. And, these nutrition communicators are more likely to reach their own goals—healthier audiences!

This chapter answers five questions:

- What are behavior change theories?
- How does behavior change progress?
- Which factors influence behavior change?
- What decision-oriented behavior change theories are used in nutrition communication?
- What are effective strategies for using behavior change theories?

What Are Behavior Change Theories?

Behavior change theories, sometimes called behavior change models, offer explanations about why people behave as they do. They also describe how nutrition communicators can encourage new and improved health behaviors. Each theory is composed of several constructs that together explain why a behavior is performed or predict how behavior change will occur. Constructs, sometimes called concepts, are the key ideas or building blocks of a theory.[2] Constructs can include an individual's attitudes about health, value placed on likely outcomes from engaging in certain behaviors, or confidence in the ability to perform a behavior, among other things.

The most useful behavior change theories tell a logical, clear story about how their constructs influence health behavior practices and changes. Theories often have an illustration diagramming how constructs are related to each other and how they influence health behaviors. Health professionals who understand how behavior change progresses and how constructs affect health behaviors are equipped to create communications that more successfully promote behavior change. For example, a magazine writer might teach readers about all the benefits of eating more fruits and vegetables (a behavior change construct called outcome expectations) or tell a story about successfully overcoming obstacles to make a behavior change so as to build readers' confidence that they, too, can reach their goals (a construct called self-efficacy).

How Does Behavior Change Progress?

People progress through a series of changes as they take steps to modify health and nutrition behaviors. The nutrition communicator's goal is to enable and inspire listeners or readers to move through these stages of change to achieve improved health and well-being and prevent disease.

Several different stage-based theories explain the progress of behavior change, including:

- the transtheoretical model,
- the precaution-adoption process model,
- the integrated change model,
- the model of action phases, and
- the health action process.

These theories may differ in name, terminology, and explanations, but they all emphasize that health behavior change starts with a lack of awareness of the need for change, moves on to intending to change behavior, and ultimately results in performing and maintaining a new behavior.[3-5] Two key, commonly used, stage-based theories are the transtheoretical model and the precaution-adoption process model.

Transtheoretical Model (Stages of Change Model)

The transtheoretical model is also called the stages of change model. This model has five stages (see Figure 12.1).[4]

Precontemplation

Individuals in this stage are not considering a behavior change in the next 6 months because they are unaware, disengaged, or discouraged. For example, patients who discover their fasting blood glucose is too high after their annual checkup were not previously aware of a need to change their diet or exercise level. Precontemplators who don't try to change even after learning their blood glucose levels are high may not realize how

FIGURE 12.1 **The transtheoretical model**[a]

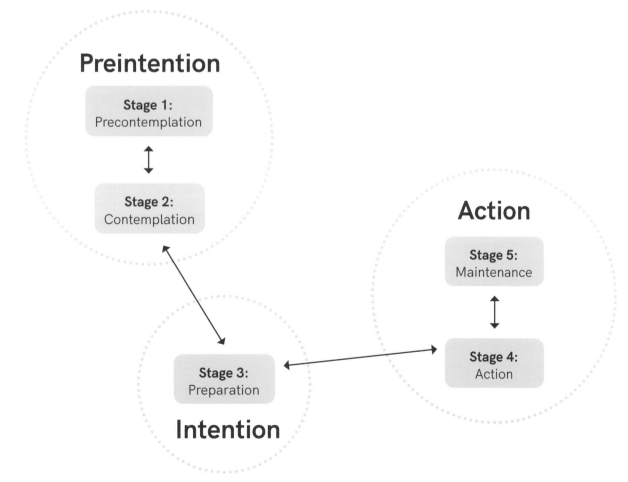

[a] Adapted from references 3 and 4.

important it is to make changes ("No worries, my whole family has high sugar"). Others may feel changing is too hard ("It is so much work to read food labels") or that the change doesn't apply to them ("I feel fine"), is threatening ("I don't want to give up chocolate"), or is not a priority ("I'm too busy right now"). Discouraged precontemplators have tried changing but got so frustrated they gave up and disengaged with the issue.

Contemplation

Individuals in this stage are considering a behavior change, usually in the next 6 months. Contemplators may think and learn about the behavior change and get the opinions of friends or family members. They may consult experts by chatting with them or reading information posted online. They consider the positives and negatives of their current behaviors and compare them with the new behaviors they are thinking about adopting. In the contemplation stage, the disadvantages of changing to the new behavior outweigh the advantages. Negatives may include potential embarrassment ("What will my friends think?"), anxiety ("I love soda—not sure I can give it up for water"), financial burden ("Healthy foods are so expensive"), time and effort costs ("I don't have time or energy to prepare healthy meals at home"), and competing priorities ("It's more important to get the kids to school on time than for me to eat a healthy breakfast"). As the advantages of a new health behavior— such as feeling more energetic, having less pain, or discovering healthy foods can be affordable and delicious—begin to outweigh the negatives, contemplators are ready to progress to the next stage. Chronic contemplators, however, are stuck in this stage—they may have fully analyzed the pros and cons of the new behavior and value its benefits but are unable to commit to a time to move forward and actually change. Nutrition communicators can help contemplators progress to the next stage by writing or talking about the benefits of a new behavior and offering ideas that help them get past common obstacles to change. For instance, if the goal is to promote increased consumption of whole grains, the communication might describe the many benefits of fiber and provide delicious solutions to avoid that "tastes like cardboard" complaint many express about whole grains.

Preparation

In this stage, individuals plan to change soon, usually in the next month. They continue to appraise the benefits of and barriers to changing, consider their abilities to change, make plans to change, and gain self-confidence in their plan to change. Some even start making small changes, such as joining a walking club, trying calorie-free flavored waters, or taking a supermarket tour. Successfully moving through this stage requires determination, energy, self-confidence, and skills to overcome barriers that may sidetrack progress (eg, envy of friends, inconvenience of finding healthy food options at work). To help those in this stage move forward, communicators could give how-to advice to help readers or listeners develop a new skill needed to make a change. To boost fruit and vegetable intake, for example, the communication could build consumer's confidence in their ability to choose the best-quality fresh produce by providing shopping tips or a simple recipe the whole family will love.

Action

Those in the action stage have changed their behavior during the past 6 months enough to reach thresholds that experts agree are likely to improve health and reduce disease risk. For instance, most health experts recommend limiting sodium to 2,300 mg/d, total dietary fat to 35% of energy, and leisure time or screen time to an hour or two daily. As individuals move through this stage, their feelings about the benefits of the new behavior grow increasingly strong and positive. Their confidence in performing the new behavior increases as they become more skillful at overcoming impediments to progress. By sharing strategies readers or listeners can use to track their progress or reward themselves after reaching a goal, nutrition communicators can help those who are in the action stage stay on target.

Maintenance

Those who reach this stage have changed their behavior long enough (usually 6 months) for it to be a natural part of their lifestyles. During this stage, individuals work to keep practicing the new behavior and not revert to previous practices. To protect new behaviors, nutrition communicators can offer insights that help individuals at this stage think about the progress that they made so far or effectively manage situations that tempt them to backslide.

Precaution-Adoption Process Model

The precaution-adoption process model[5] is similar to the transtheoretical model but differs in that it:

- does not state time frames for when a change will be made or practiced,
- divides unaware and unengaged precontemplators into two different stages, and
- acknowledges that some individuals decide to not change.

Compare Figure 12.1 with Figure 12.2 to see the similarities and differences.

Progressing Through the Stages

There is considerable variation in the time it takes people to move from one stage to the next. It usually takes many weeks or months to advance from stage to stage, with some stages taking longer than others. Individuals who once decided not to change may not always feel that way—they could change their minds in the future and move onward through the stages.

Movement through the stages is not always in a forward direction. Sometimes individuals return to a previous stage because circumstances change or motivation declines. For example, when the weather is too hot or cold, people may return

FIGURE 12.2 **The precaution-adoption process model**[a]

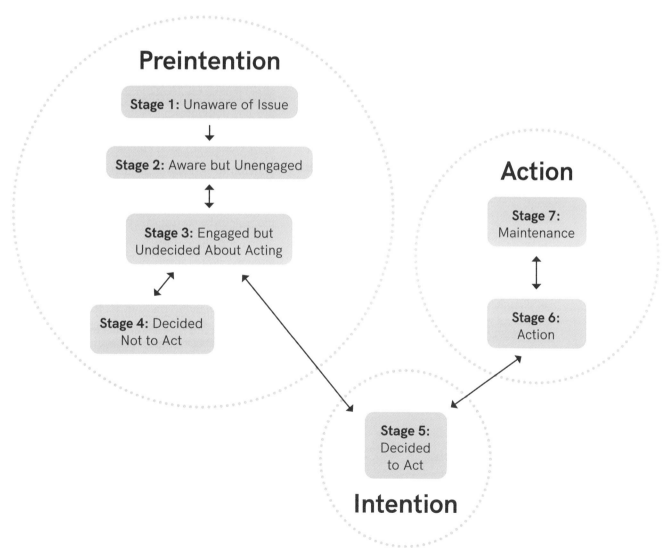

[a] Adapted from references 3 and 5.

to the preparation stage as they develop new strategies to exercise indoors. If stress at work or home rises, it may interfere with the changed behavior, perhaps causing a person who has been eating healthy meals for almost a year to revert to grabbing chips and soda from the vending machine for lunch. Regardless of where people are in the stages of change, nutrition communications can promote forward movement by skillfully incorporating behavior change influencers in their messaging.

In considering how the stages of change model can be used in communications intended for large groups, start by thinking about the intended audience of the communication and how much they likely know and are already doing. Figure 12.1 can help nutrition communicators assess which stage of change an audience is in and tailor their messages accordingly. Use Figure 12.3 for ideas for questions to use to assess readiness to change.

Getting detailed information on groups of people can be a challenge. So, it's often helpful to think about the audience as either not engaging in a behavior (they are in a preaction stage)

Chapter 11 describes methods for assessing an audience.

or engaging in a behavior (they are in the action or maintenance stage). For instance, a fact sheet being written for someone who is thinking about starting to exercise would contain very different information from one intended for an elite athlete. For those considering an exercise program, communicators could write about the benefits of exercising, how to get started—such as setting small goals or finding an exercise buddy—and ideas for boosting readers' confidence that they have what it takes to begin exercising. In the case of those already in the action or maintenance stage of exercise, communicators may offer advice that helps readers stick to their goals, find new ways to reward themselves for their healthy behavior, and exert control and cope with situations (eg, bad weather) that threaten their ability to keep up their exercise routine. In cases where communicators know little about the audience, it is often helpful to focus on the needs of people in the preaction stages. That's because as many as 80% of people with a given problem behavior are in one of the preaction stages.[6-9] See Box 12.1 for information on moving from knowledge into practice.

FIGURE 12.3 **Sample questions nutrition communicators can use to help determine an audience's stage of change**

Does the audience eat *five or more servings of fruits and vegetables* daily?*	Transtheoretical Model Stage	Precaution-Adoption Process Model Stage
Answer: No		
Why?		
1. Do not know that current diet is negatively affecting health	Precontemplation	Unaware of issue
2. Know current diet is negatively affecting health but haven't thought about why or how to change it	Precontemplation	Aware but unengaged
3. Do not want to change diet	Precontemplation	Decided not to act
4. Do not practice this behavior right now, but intend to start in the next 6 months	Contemplation	Engaged but undecided about acting
5. Do not practice this behavior right now, but intend to start in the next month	Preparation	Decided to act
Answer: Yes		
How long has the behavior been practiced?		
1. Less than 6 months	Action	Action
2. More than 6 months	Maintenance	Maintenance

* To adapt this question for other daily behaviors, replace the italicized words with words that describe another behavior, such as "drink 3 cups of milk," "limit soft drink intake to 8 ounces or less," "eat four servings of whole grains," and so on.

Although the precaution-adoption process model does not specify a time frame for engaging in an activity, those proposed by the transtheoretical model may be useful in determining when a behavior will be practiced or for how long a behavior has been practiced.

Put Knowledge of Stage of Change into Practice

Choose an audience for a nutrition communication (eg, older adults, pregnant women, athletes). Search the literature to identify health behaviors many of them need to change (eg, eating more vegetables or whole grains, consuming less fat or salt). Which stage of change are they likely in for each behavior identified? Explain the reasons for identifying that stage.

Which Factors Influence Behavior Change?

A behavior change influencer is exactly what it sounds like—it's something that influences behavior. By understanding how to influence behaviors, nutrition communicators are better able to create oral and written messages that help individuals and groups move through stages of change to achieve their health goals. Some of the influencers will be familiar, such as knowledge that helps people understand a nutrition concept, whereas others may be less familiar, such as messages that build the audience's self-efficacy and perceived control. Gaining expertise and confidence in using an array of these influencers helps communicators create nutrition messages that are more varied, engaging, effective, and memorable.

Behavior change influencers fall into three main groups or *spheres of influence*: personal, social environment, and physical environment. These are analogous to the social-ecological model shown in Figure 3.2 on page 44. The spheres are constantly interacting with each other, with changes in one simultaneously causing changes in the others—a concept called *reciprocal determinism* (see Figure 12.4). This section looks at key influencers of health and dietary behavior in each sphere that help individuals move through stages of change to achieve their health goals. As will be shown in the next section, these influencers are constructs in many behavior change theories.

Personal Sphere

An individual's intellectual, psychological, and physical resources are all part of his or her personal sphere and exert a strong influence on whether a person changes a behavior. By gathering information on the target audience's personal

FIGURE 12.4 Reciprocal determinism: The constant interaction of a person's behavior and the spheres of influence (physical environment, social environment, personal), and the effects caused by these interactions[a]

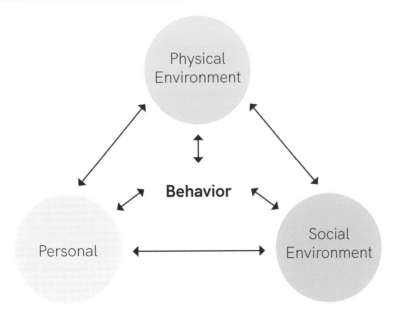

[a] Adapted from references 10 and 11.

sphere characteristics and considering how these characteristics likely impact the audience's intellectual, psychological, and physical resources, nutrition communicators can create more personalized messages. When a communication is perceived to be "just for me," the message is more likely to be read or listened to, rated as attention getting, and perceived as important. That is, personally relevant messages promote active thinking, which enhances message retention and behavior change.[12,13] The personal-sphere behavior change influencers are described below.

Nutrition communicators who are aware of their audience's personal intellectual, psychological, and physical resources can prepare messages that build on positive aspects of these and lessen negative aspects. In preparing to write a blog post, a nutrition communicator might discover that compliance with celiac disease treatment is highly dependent on attitudes toward following a restrictive diet.[14] By knowing this, the blogger is better able to help readers change their behavior by incorporating concepts aiming to improve attitudes toward managing the disease, perhaps by describing quick, easy ways to locate gluten-free foods in the supermarket or strategies for planning ahead to stay gluten-free when away from home.[14,15] Including a self-check quiz could further improve attitudes by building readers' confidence in their ability to apply the strategies in the blog post.

ATTITUDES

Attitudes are beliefs, feelings, and values about a health condition (eg, heart disease, overweight) or behavior (eg, eating less fat, not eating meat, taking supplements). The degree to which attitudes affect behavior change depend on how important the individual believes performing the behavior is to improving a health condition (outcome expectations), strength of emotions associated with a health condition or behavior (eg, anger about a diagnosis, feeling happy about exercising with friends), and value placed on the pros and cons of a health condition or behavior.[4] For example, the upside of being overweight and not dieting might be that a person can continue to eat as much as desired or not exercise at all. The downside of not losing weight might be feeling sweaty and out of breath when walking to class. Pros of losing weight could be feeling better and worrying less about health problems.

Cons might be the stress of dieting and dread of eating new foods.

OUTCOME EXPECTATIONS

Beliefs about how performing a health behavior is likely to positively and negatively affect a health condition. This includes perceptions about how severe the physical, emotional, social, or financial consequences of a health condition or health behavior likely will be. Those who believe a condition will lead to severe negative health results (heart attack, cancer) are more likely to engage in health protective behaviors than those who feel risks are not severe.[16] Outcome expectations also include beliefs about susceptibility to a negative health condition. Individuals who perceive they are at risk for a condition (eg, type 2 diabetes) are more likely to change associated behaviors, especially when the expected outcomes are important to them, than those who do not perceive themselves as at risk.[16]

INTERNAL RESOURCES

Internal resources are knowledge, abilities, and skills related to health and health behaviors.

Knowledge Knowledge is understanding of a health condition and how personal health behaviors affect its development and severity, such as how health behaviors (eg, increasing fiber intake or exercising) impact high blood lipid levels. Knowledge is an important internal resource because people with more nutrition knowledge tend to eat healthier diets than those who are less well informed.[17-19]

Abilities and skills These involve the capacity to make health-related decisions and carry them out, such as identifying lower-fat items from a restaurant menu and then ordering them. Knowledge, abilities, and skills develop through schooling, media exposure, and prior experience with or exposure to things (eg, food products, exercise equipment), activities (eg, following special diets, joining online support groups), institutions (eg, health clubs, insurance companies), and individuals (eg, nutrition writers and broadcasters, health care professionals, coaches, teachers, friends, family) related to a health behavior. Observational learning is a way of gaining knowledge that occurs through watching others and is especially important during childhood.

Personal characteristics An array of personal characteristics can affect implementation of knowledge, abilities, skills, and response to behavior change:

- **Mind-set:** mental health status and emotional state. Mind-set affects the ability to put knowledge into action.[20,21] Positive emotions build capacity for making health protective changes, whereas mental disturbances or negative emotions reduce it.
- **Personality:** thinking, feeling, and behavioral characteristics that are enduring (eg, openness to new experiences, conscientiousness, extroversion, agreeableness, and neuroticism). Positive personality characteristics (eg, conscientiousness, agreeableness) can support behavior change, whereas neuroticism and aversion to new experiences may deter it.[22] Resilience, or how people view life and use their resources (eg, money, knowledge, skill, self-esteem, social support system) to bounce back from adversity and protect their health, is another personality characteristic that supports health behavior change.
- **Biology:** physical and intellectual factors that moderate health and behavior change. Some factors cannot be altered (eg, life stage, genetic background) and some can (eg, physical health status, addictions). Biology can affect health and response to behavior changes. For example, genetic predispositions, such as a family history of heart disease, may affect health status and how a person's body responds to dietary behavior changes.
- **Lifestyle:** typical way of life, habits, and use of resources (eg, time, energy, money, skills, knowledge) that reflect personal values.

PERSONAL AGENCY

Personal agency is one's perceived and actual capacity to influence factors affecting a behavior (eg, social and physical environments). It includes the following:

Perceived control This relates to beliefs about the ability to control and manage oneself and environmental conditions so that it is possible to perform a specific behavior.

Self-efficacy Self-confidence in the ability to control and manage oneself and environmental conditions to perform a specific behavior, and to successfully manage resulting consequences as well as temptations trying to derail intended behaviors is part of self-efficacy.

Self-regulation Control of behavior and emotions using self-monitoring, self-appraisal, self-contracting and goal setting, planning ahead, self-reward and reinforcement, self-instruction, social support, and physical environment restructuring factor into self-regulation. Examples include daily tracking and evaluation of energy intake or making a contract with oneself to walk 10,000 steps daily, tracking progress, and rewarding oneself with an appointment for a pedicure after fulfilling the contract for a week. Self-instruction could be talking oneself through a situation (eg, "There are so many high-fat foods at this party! I am going to position myself near the fresh veggie tray so that I can keep my calorie intake under control"). Getting a friend to go for walks can provide the social support needed to continue to practice a behavior. Restructuring the environment might include keeping fewer snack foods on hand at home or purposely using hallways at work where there are no vending machines.

Coping capacity The ability to recognize useful coping strategies and utilize them to successfully manage behavior performance and ensuing psychological, emotional, and environmental consequences is part of coping. For instance, someone may feel guilty after eating more than planned. To actively and appropriately cope, individuals may recruit friends to promote a positive mind-set and help them renew efforts to achieve their dietary goals.

SOCIAL NORMS

These are societal rules that define "appropriate" thoughts, feelings, and behaviors and put pressure on people to believe and behave in a certain way. Social norms include these facets:

Social expectations Beliefs about how important others (eg, friends, families, colleagues) expect one to behave and one's motivation to conform to expectations are social expectations. In some families this means to eat dinner together every day. Teens wanting to please their parents will try to comply with parents' expectations. Communications that help those in authority (eg, parents, work supervisors) learn to effectively express their expectations can enable them to convince others to perform desired behaviors.[23,24]

Perceived norms Perceived norms are beliefs about how others behave, which may or may not accurately reflect the real world. For example, many college students mistakenly believe most of their peers frequently drink large amounts of alcohol, when in reality only a small percentage of students binge drink. Social marketing campaigns have tried to educate this audience about the facts in an attempt to shift this perception.

Social Environment Sphere

The social environment sphere includes interactions with others, such as family, friends, colleagues, and institutions (eg, educational, religious, political, and cultural groups). Key social environment factors affecting health behaviors are described in this section. The Terms to Know box provides a brief summary of these factors.

The strength of the effect of the social environment on a target audience's health choices needs to be considered at all stages of nutrition communication development. Understanding the target audience's social environment helps ensure the messaging is sensitive, is respectful, and effectively equips them to apply the messaging to the realities of their social environment. For example, in preparing to pitch a magazine article, a savvy nutrition communicator would find out who the typical reader is as well as review

For more on culture, see Chapter 13.

Put Knowledge of the Personal Sphere into Practice

Using the audience you researched in Box 12.1, think about each of the personal factors as they relate to the selected audience and the health behaviors they need to change. For each personal factor, describe what information could be shared with this audience that could help them adopt a new behavior. Hint: Recall the example of the blog post about celiac disease. Which personal factors were suggested as possible ways to help improve attitudes?

previous editions to judge the writing level and tone of articles.

Let's say a nutrition communicator decides on a magazine targeting lower-income women who have graduated from high school, have young kids, and are interested in do-it-yourself projects. The communicator's research discovers that the social environment characteristics of women like these tend to include tight food budgets, frantic mealtimes because of picky eaters (especially when it comes to vegetables), and busy schedules that make it hard to find enough time to spend with their kids.[25] The communicator decides to pitch an article on home gardening because it would be an economical way to add vegetables to the household food supply, would provide opportunities for fun family time throughout the summer, and would get kids involved in growing vegetables, which increases the chance that these picky eaters would eat these foods.[26] By relating home gardening to the realities of the readers' social environment, the magazine writer is able to help readers incorporate new behaviors that can help their family's health.

CULTURE

Culture is socially transmitted knowledge, behaviors, beliefs, values, attitudes, hierarchies, and roles that distinguish members of one group from others. Culture also includes the degree of acculturation to the prevailing culture. For instance, new immigrants' behaviors are likely to reflect values, beliefs, and practices of their country of origin, whereas those who have lived in a new country for a long time tend to have values, beliefs, and practices more like those of their new home. Basic or staple foods and preferences are often the last characteristics to change among immigrant groups.[27] Cultural groups may be based on ethnicity, race, and religion as well as social networks.

SOCIAL SUPPORT

Social support includes emotional support, aid (eg, Supplemental Nutrition Assistance Program [SNAP] benefits, counseling), information (advice, suggestions), and constructive feedback provided by family, friends, or professionals (eg, nutrition and dietetics practitioners, legal aid advisors, religious leaders, psychologists).

Social (In)equality

The distribution of wealth, opportunities, and privileges in a society are part of social equality. Social

Social environment sphere	Interactions with others and institutions
Culture	Socially transmitted knowledge, behaviors, beliefs, values, attitudes, hierarchies, and roles that distinguish members of one group from others
Social support	Emotional support, aid, information, and constructive feedback provided by others
Social (in)equality	The distribution of wealth, opportunities, and privileges in a society
Economic environment	Overall purchasing power resulting from employment, income, expenses, prices, and economy
Political environment	Laws and regulations that affect behaviors and options

equality is when all people in a society have equal status, equal legal rights (eg, freedom of speech, right to vote), and equal access to education, health care, job opportunities, police and fire protection, and other social programs. Social inequalities (eg, lack of affordable health insurance, prejudicial treatment) adversely affect physical and mental health and can present significant barriers to protecting health and making health behavior changes.[28]

ECONOMIC ENVIRONMENT

Overall purchasing power resulting from employment, income, expenses, prices, and economy (eg, recession) play a role in the economic environment. Purchasing power affects the type and amount of food that can be purchased, quality and safety of housing, availability of transportation, and access to health care, as well as many other goods and services that affect health and the ability to make health behavior changes.

POLITICAL ENVIRONMENT

The political environment includes laws and regulations that affect (promote, restrict, modify) behaviors and options. Laws requiring restaurants to post calories on menus may promote healthier food choices among patrons. Laws restricting sales of alcohol to minors limit access to these beverages. Taxing cigarettes or junk food at a high rate may change behaviors by reducing purchases. School nutrition policies dictate the types of foods that can be sold at school.

See Box 12.2 for ideas about applying knowledge of personal sphere factors. See Box 12.3 for ideas about applying knowledge of social environment factors.

Put Knowledge of the Social Environment Sphere into Practice

Choose a nutrition-related magazine article that aims to help people make a dietary behavior change. Who is the audience for the communication? Think about the audience's characteristics. Hint: Use the home gardening example at the beginning of this section and Box 12.2 to describe the audience's social environment characteristics. Search the literature to discover nutrition-related problems typically faced by this audience. How does the article address the audience's social environment characteristics and their typical nutrition problems? Now, think about the social environment factors and describe another way the article could address them.

Physical Environment Sphere

The physical environment sphere comprises the external surroundings and conditions in the natural and built environment that affect behavior. The physical environment prompts individuals to act in certain ways. The physical environment may present *barriers* to health behaviors (eg, limited access to accurate information, unsafe neighborhoods that deter playing outside), provide *facilitators* to health behaviors (eg, easy access to effective communications promoting behavior change, a school gym that is open in the evening for parents to be active with their kids), and offer *cues to action* (eg, a reminder postcard from a health professional, a bowl of fruit on the table as a signal to eat it as a snack). Access to high-quality physical environment factors frequently depends on the economic environment. Key physical environment factors affecting health choice are as follows.

- **Information environment:** information availability and accessibility, information sources (eg, nutrition professionals vs nonexperts), media channels (eg, television, internet, advertising), information quality (accuracy, completeness, clarity), and tone (positive, threatening) used to present the information.
- **Health behavior–specific environments:** vary depending on the health behavior. For dietary behavior, the environment includes food availability and accessibility in the home and community, feeding styles used by parents, mealtime rituals, body image norms, and nutrition information. For physical activity, the environment includes supports for physical activity (eg, equipment, parks, sidewalks) and deterrents (eg, energy-/time-saving conveniences, high traffic area).

- **Technological environment:** access to technological advances, such as new products (eg, medications, fat substitutes), new manufacturing methods (eg, those that reduce cost or reduce pollution), and new information dissemination methods (eg, internet).
- **Health care environment:** availability, quality, and accessibility of health care professionals, facilities, medications, and educational and social programs (eg, Special Supplemental Nutrition Program for Women, Infants, and Children [WIC]).

The Terms to Know box on page 189 summarizes these physical environment factors. And see Box 12.4 for ideas about how to put knowledge of physical environment factors into practice.

What Decision-Oriented Behavior Change Theories Are Used in Nutrition Communication?

Stage-based theories explain *how* behavior changes and behavior change influencers (or behavior change theory constructs) promote movement through the stages of change. A remaining question is *why* a behavior changes. Many decision-oriented health behavior theories have been developed to offer explanations about why people behave the way they do and propose why behavior change may occur. These theories describe how behavior change influencers are related and can help nutrition communicators identify the behavior change influencers within each sphere (personal, social, environment) to address. There are many decision-oriented theories; those most commonly used in health promotion and nutrition communications are described in this section.

Box 12.4 Put Knowledge of the Physical Environment Sphere into Practice

Using the audience that was targeted in the nutrition-related magazine article you analyzed for the Box 12.3 activity, search the literature to discover what their physical environment might be like. For example, do they live in areas where it is easy to access a wide array of foods? How much access do they have to nutrition information? Where are they getting most of their nutrition information? What is their health care environment probably like, especially with regard to nutrition education programs? What social environment and physical environment factors support or deter the behavior promoted in the article? Now, describe three ways nutrition communicators could take the audience's physical environment into account when designing nutrition messages for them. If it wasn't acknowledged, describe how it could have been.

Health Belief Model

The health belief model[16] proposes that a person's behavior is determined by the interactions between internal resources (eg, knowledge, life stage, personality), perceived threat (disease susceptibility and severity), outcome expectations (benefits), barriers, self-efficacy, and cues to action (see

Physical environment sphere	External surroundings and conditions in the natural and built environment that affect behavior
Information environment	Information availability and accessibility, information sources, media channels, information quality, and tone used to present information
Health behavior–specific environment	Aspects of the environment that affect a particular health behavior
Technological environment	Access to technological advances
Health care environment	Availability, quality, and accessibility of health care professionals, facilities, medications, and educational and social programs

Figure 12.5 on page 190). For example, if a man's parents both had heart disease, he may feel that he is very likely to develop heart disease (perceived susceptibility). If his parents died from heart disease complications, he might be even more concerned (perceived severity). If he had observed that his aunt who ate a healthy diet and exercised did not have heart disease complications, he may believe that those behaviors could really make a difference (perceived benefits). He may want to make changes, but he believes healthy foods cost too much and that he does not have time to exercise (perceived barriers). If he believes he is able to make the changes (self-efficacy), he may be more likely to actually change behaviors than if he does not believe he is capable of performing the new behavior. Although he may be influenced by susceptibility, severity, benefits, barriers, and self-efficacy, he may not change his behavior until there is a cue to action, such as being diagnosed with high blood pressure.

Not all people who need to make changes, like the man just described, experience life events that signal change is needed. That's where nutrition communicators play a vital role. These communicators can use the health belief model to help people make important, even life-saving, behavior changes. Using the heart disease example above, the communicator could provide information about heart disease that builds readers' knowledge about this health condition, helps them gauge their susceptibility to the disease, and encourages those at risk to seek medical advice because early intervention can ease its severity. Communicators could also help the audience learn what to

expect from making disease-preventative dietary and physical activity changes as well as strategies for overcoming barriers that might get in the way of these behavior changes. By including simple, easy-to-implement behavior change goals and ideas that cue the audience to stay on track with their goals (eg, put sneakers by the door to remember to walk after dinner), the communication can promote feelings of self-confidence.

Theory of Reasoned Action, Theory of Planned Behavior, and Integrated Behavioral Model

The theory of reasoned action was created first, then extended to become the theory of planned behavior, and enhanced again to become the integrated behavioral model (Figure 12.6 on page 191).[29] The integrated behavioral model proposes that intention to perform a behavior is the result of interactions between attitudes, personal agency, and social norms, all of which can be affected by internal resources. It further proposes that actually performing a behavior is the result of intention to perform the behavior as well as attitudes toward the salience of the behavior, social and physical environment barriers, and internal resources of knowledge, skills, and habits. For example, if a teenage girl feels positively about eating fruits and vegetables (experiential attitude) and believes the pros of eating fruits and vegetables outweigh the cons (instrumental attitudes), she may have a very positive attitude toward eating fruits and vegetables. However, she may perceive that her friends don't eat fruits and vegetables (social norms) and that she will be considered very "uncool" if she eats fruits and vegetables (social expectations). She also may feel she has no control (perceived control) over the shopping and food preparation at home or the foods available at school or in the local corner store. All of these factors, attitudes, social norms, and expressions of personal agency interact to influence this teen's intention to eat fruits and vegetables.

Intention to behave is a strong predictor of whether a person will perform a behavior. Even if intention is strong, other factors influence whether a behavior will occur. Let's say the teenage girl has a positive attitude toward eating fruits and vegetables and believes her friends eat these foods and want her to also eat them, and that her mother is willing to purchase more produce—all of these are supportive of eating more fruits and vegetables. If the family cannot afford to buy what is available at the grocery store (environmental barrier), doesn't know how to prepare these foods (internal resource), or thinks eating these foods isn't very important (salience of behavior), it will be difficult to turn intentions into actual behavior.

Nutrition communicators can use the integrated behavioral model to promote intention to behave and behavior change. Using the goal of increasing fruit and vegetable intake as the example, a website article could promote positive feelings toward eating fruits and vegetables by describing how these foods help with weight control and skin health. Worries about taste could

be eased with creative, easy-to-prepare recipes accompanied with beautifully styled photographs. The communication could address concerns about prep time, cost, and spoilage by including creative tips for using canned or frozen vegetables. To help those concerned about how friends might react to their eating fruits and vegetables, communicators could provide coping strategies to counteract potential negative reactions. To overcome other roadblocks, such as getting kids to try new fruits and vegetables, communicators could help parents develop strategies for introducing new foods and offer effective approaches for helping parents engage children in making healthier choices.

Social Cognitive Theory

Social cognitive theory was originally called social learning theory. Reciprocal determinism is a key premise of social cognitive theory: This theory proposes that people's behavior, personal characteristics, and social and physical environments constantly interact to influence each other (see Figure 12.4 on page 183).[10,11] This theory also proposes that people can restructure their environments to make it easier to perform a healthy behavior or not perform an unhealthy behavior (eg, smoking, eating fried food often). This restructuring can be achieved by individuals or a group of people who work together toward a common goal. According to this theory, optimally effective behavior change programs address all spheres of influence and promote behavior changes with these constructs:

FIGURE 12.5 **Health belief model**[a]

[a] Adapted from reference 16.

outcome expectations, self-regulation, self-efficacy, internal resources gained through observational learning, and environmental facilitators (eg, providing tools and resources that help people make behavior changes).

Social cognitive theory is frequently used by nutrition communicators to facilitate behavior change. Review the heart disease and fruit and vegetable examples given previously to demonstrate how the health belief model and integrated behavioral model, respectively, can be used in nutrition communications. Consider how a written communication on reducing sugar-sweetened beverage intake directed to mothers of preschoolers could be designed to include the social cognitive theory behavior change constructs. See Box 12.5 for ideas on how to apply knowledge of the various decision-oriented behavior change theories.

What Are Effective Strategies for Using Behavior Change Theories?

So, which theory is the best one to use? No one theory consistently outperforms others when it comes to predicting or explaining behavior. Nor have numerous studies led to a consensus on which theory is most useful. However, the

 ## Put Knowledge of Decision-Oriented Behavior Change Theories into Practice

Take a close look at each of the decision-oriented theories discussed (the health belief model, the integrated behavioral model, and social cognitive theory). How are they similar? How are they different? How are they related to the stage-based theories? Using the magazine article you selected for the activity in Box 12.3, compare the constructs used in the article to the behavior change theories. Which behavior change theory is most like the one used in the article? If a behavior change theory was not used, what would need to change to include all the constructs from one of the behavior change theories discussed? What stage of change was the writer targeting? What evidence helps to determine the stage of change?

nutrition communications and interventions that most effectively help people make changes to improve their health are guided by health behavior theory and the target audience's personal, social environment, and physical environment spheres of influence and stage of change.

A current challenge in the field of health behavior change is that commonly used theories

FIGURE 12.6 **Integrated behavioral model (an extension of the theory of reasoned action and theory of planned behavior)**[a]

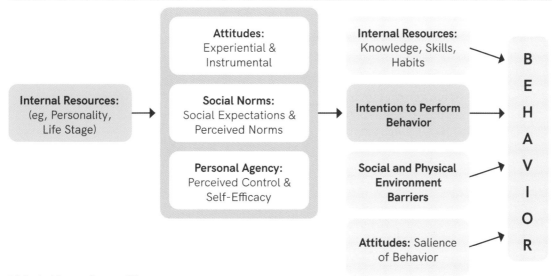

[a] Adapted from reference 29.

do not integrate the *how* of stage-based models with the *why* of decision-oriented models. Few efforts have been made to incorporate ideas from stage-based and decision-oriented theories despite the potential such a combination offers for advancing health behavior change and intervention development. The polytheoretical framework in Figure 12.7 is one attempt to merge a stage-based theory with key constructs from the most commonly used decision-oriented models.[30] It streamlines the work of nutrition communicators by providing a more holistic, unified view of health behavior change theories and the multitude of factors affecting health behavior change. Additionally, it shows how nutrition communicators can leverage behavior change influencers to help readers and listeners move more efficiently through the stages of change to achieve their health goals.

By enhancing the precaution-adoption process model, the polytheoretical framework describes both the how and why of behavior change and places change within the context of multiple spheres of influence. The framework proposes that cues to action from the physical and social environments as well as internal resources help individuals become aware of and engaged with a health behavior issue so they can move through the three preintention stages. Internal resources, outcome expectations, attitudes, social norms, personal agency, and culture influence movement from Stage 3 to intention. It further proposes that personal agency, attitudes, and cues to action from the physical and social environments affect movement from Stage 5 to action. Notice how some constructs directly affect movement through the stages, whereas others affect other constructs that affect movement through the stages. For example, outcome expectations affect attitudes and social norms. Or, social norms affect attitudes and personal agency.

The polytheoretical framework provides a road map that helps nutrition communicators boost the effectiveness of their messaging by targeting and tailoring it to their audience's stage of change. For instance, for those in a preintention stage, it is more helpful to develop their knowledge, abilities, skills, and positive mindset than it is to focus on other constructs. Once individuals are engaged with a health issue, nutrition communications can facilitate movement toward intention by helping them become aware of the outcomes they can expect, develop positive attitudes toward the behavior, weigh the pros and cons of changing with the goal of tilting the balance to the pro side, realize the importance

How to read Figure 12.7

1. Review the key.

2. Identify the three stages-of-change groups. Follow the double line arrows and move from preintention to action. Notice that the arrows go both ways.

3. Find the individual stages of change. Notice how they move from Stage 1 to Stage 7 and that the arrows go both ways.

4. Find the two main constructs that affect movement through the preintention stages. Think about why these constructs likely affect these stages.

5. Find the five main constructs that affect the intention stage. Consider why these constructs tend to affect the intention stage.

6. Find the two main constructs that affect the action stage. Think about why these constructs affect this stage.

Key

Large dotted-line ovals: stage-of-change group (preintention, intention, action)

Small solid-line oval: individual stage of change (eg, Stage 1: unaware of issue)

Rectangle: behavior change construct

Double-line double-head arrow: major path through stage-of-change groups

Wide-dashed arrow: main constructs affecting preintention

Narrow-dashed arrow: main constructs affecting intention

Dotted arrow: main constructs affecting action

FIGURE 12.7 **A polytheoretical framework merges the stage-based precaution-adoption process model with key constructs from the most commonly used decision-oriented theories[a]**

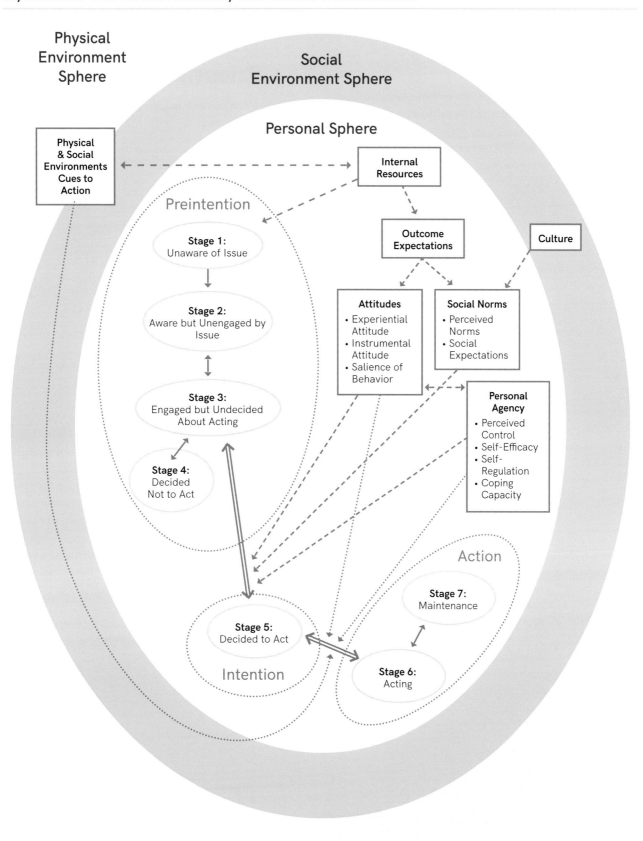

[a] Adapted from reference 30.

Put Knowledge of Health Behavior Change Theories into Practice

Think about a health behavior that many students on a local college campus need to change. Which constructs from the three spheres (ie, personal, physical environment, and social environment) seem to influence the behavior? Where are students likely to be in the stages of change? How could their stage placement be confirmed? Which behavior change influencers could be used? Why would they be used? For each of the behavior change influencers, write one sentence demonstrating the use of the behavior change influencer in a nutrition communication for this audience. For example, to help them develop self-efficacy or improve their attitude toward a behavior, what could the communication say?

Where Are *You* in the Stages of Change for Using Behavior Change Theories?

Changing any behavior can be a challenge—such as even starting to use behavior change theories in nutrition communications. Take another look at Figure 12.3 (page 182), and change the question to: "Do you use behavior change theories in your nutrition communications daily? Which stage of change are you in?" If it is a preintentional stage, review this chapter again to gain the internal resources needed to change some health communications behaviors. Go over Boxes 12.1 through 12.6 again. Review some of the resources at the end of the chapter. Critically analyze some nutrition communications written by others. Which behavior change influencers were used? Which could have been used in the communication?

In the intention stage for using behavior change theories, think about why the theories could be used and write some goals. Which behavior change influencers could be tried first? Which upcoming communications could they be used in? How will the effectiveness of these behavior change influencers be determined?

Take it slowly—try using one behavior change influencer at a time, and try using it in several communications and in numerous ways. Keep going until all of the behavior change influencers can be used skillfully and confidently in a variety of communications and with different audiences.

If you are in the action stage, congratulations and keep up the good work! Remember, by applying behavior change theories, nutrition communicators can be more successful in helping audience members achieve their health goals.

of the behavior change to health, and reflect on how social norms affect their behaviors to effectively use positive aspects of their social norms while minimizing the negative ones.

Nutrition communicators can help individuals move toward the intention stage by building perceived and actual capacity to influence factors affecting the behavior (personal agency). This can be achieved by presenting approaches individuals can use to control their behavior and environments and building self-confidence in the ability to change the behavior, self-regulation skills that support change, and effective methods for coping with change. To promote movement to the action stage, effective nutrition communications focus on attitudes and personal agency as well as methods for effectively using cues to action in the physical and social environments. See Box 12.6 for more information on putting health behavior change theories into practice.

Chapter 15 describes how to write goals.

Refer to Chapter 38 for potential approaches to evaluating effectiveness.

KEY POINTS

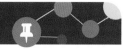

Use Behavior Change Theories to Create Effective Communication

1 Nutrition communicators who design their messages with behavior change theories in mind can more effectively and efficiently help clients adopt and perform many health protective practices.

2 Behavior change theories offer explanations about why people behave as they do and describe how nutrition communicators can encourage new and improved health behaviors.

3 Stage-based behavior change theories explain how health behavior change progresses through a series of stages, starting with a lack of awareness of the need for change, then moving on to intending to change behavior, and ultimately resulting in performing a new behavior. Two commonly used stage-based theories are the transtheoretical model and the precaution-adoption process model.

4 Behavior change influencers in the personal, social environment, and physical environment spheres of influence facilitate progress through stage-based theories. Personal behavior change influencers are an individual's intellectual, psychological, and physical resources. The social environment sphere includes interactions with others, such as family, friends, colleagues, and institutions. The physical environment comprises the external surroundings and conditions in the natural and built environment that affect behavior.

5 Decision-oriented behavior change theories offer explanations about *why* people behave the way they do and propose *why* behavior change may occur. These theories describe how behavior change influencers are related and help identify the behavior change influencers within each sphere of influence to address. The most commonly used decision-oriented behavior change theories are the health belief model; the closely related theory of reasoned action, theory of planned behavior, and integrated behavioral model; and social cognitive theory.

6 Nutrition communications and interventions that most effectively help people make changes to improve their health are guided by behavior change theory and the target audience's personal, social environment, and physical environment spheres of influence and stage of change.

7 The polytheoretical framework merges the concepts of stage-based and decision-oriented behavior change theories to describe the how and why of behavior change and places change within the context of multiple spheres of influence. This framework provides a road map that boosts the effectiveness of nutrition communications by targeting and tailoring it to their audience's stage of change.

RESOURCES

Glanz K, Rimer B, Viswanath K, eds. *Health Behavior: Theory, Research, and Practice.* 5th ed. Jossey-Bass; 2015.

Davis R, Campbell R, Hildon Z, Hobbs L, Michie S. Theories of behaviour and behaviour change across the social and behavioural sciences: a scoping review. *Health Psychol Rev.* 2015;9:323-344. doi:10.1080/17437199 .2014.941722

REFERENCES

1. Lewin K. *Field Theory in Social Science: Selected Theoretical Papers.* Cartwright D, ed. Harper & Brothers; 1951.
2. Glanz K, Rimer B, Viswanath K. The scope of health behavior and health education. In: Glanz K, Rimer B, Viswanath K, eds. *Health Behavior: Theory, Research, and Practice.* 5th ed. Jossey-Bass; 2015:3-22.
3. Schüz B, Sniehotta FF, Mallach N, Wiedemann AU, Schwarzer R. Predicting transitions from preintentional, intentional and actional stages of change. *Health Educ Res.* 2009;24:64-75. doi:10.1093 /her/cym092
4. Prochaska J, Redding C, Evers K. The transtheoretical model and stages of change. In: Glanz K, Rimer B, Viswanath K, eds. *Health Behavior: Theory, Research, and Practice.* 5th ed. Jossey-Bass; 2015:125-148.
5. Weinstein N, Sandman P, Blalock S. The precaution adoption process model. In: Glanz K, Rimer B, Viswanath K, eds. *Health Behavior: Theory, Research, and Practice.* 4th ed. Jossey-Bass; 2008:123-148.
6. Prochaska J, Norcross JC, Fowler JL, Follick MJ, Abrams DB. Attendance and outcome in a work site weight control program: processes and stages of change as process and predictor variables. *Addict Behav.* 1992;17:35-45.
7. Sandoval W, Heller K, Wiese W, Childs D. Stages of change: a model for nutrition counseling. *Top Clin Nutr.* 1994;9:64-69.
8. Wright J, Whiteley J, Laforge R, Adams W, Berry D, Friedman R. Validation of five stage of change measures for parental support of healthy eating and activity. *J Nutr Educ Behav.* 2015;47:134-142. doi:10.1016/j.jneb.2014.11.003
9. Hildebrand D, Betts N. Assessment of stage of change, decisional balance, self-efficacy, and use of processes of change of low-income parents for increasing servings of fruits and vegetables to preschool-aged children. *J Nutr Educ Behav.* 2009;41:110-119. doi:10.1016/j. jneb.2008.09.007
10. Viswanath K, Finnegan J, Gollust S. Communication and health behavior in a changing media environment. In: Glanz K, Rimer B, Viswanath K, eds. *Health Behavior: Theory, Research, and Practice.* 5th ed. Jossey-Bass; 2015:327-348.
11. Petty R, Wegener D. The elaboration likelihood model: current status and controversies. In: Chaiken S, Trope Y, eds. *Dual Process Theories in Social Psychology.* Guilford Press; 1999:41–72.
12. Garg A, Gupta R. Predictors of compliance to gluten-free diet in children with celiac disease. *Int Sch Res Notices.* 2014:1-9. doi:10.1155/2014/248402
13. Ludvigsson J, Card T, Ciclitira PJ, et al. Support for patients with celiac disease: a literature review. *United Eur Gastroenterol J.* 2015;3:146-159. doi:10.1177/2050640614562599
14. Skinner C, Tiro J, Champion V. The health belief model. In: Glanz K, Rimer B, Viswanath K, eds. *Health Behavior: Theory, Research, and Practice.* 5th ed. Jossey-Bass; 2015:75-94.
15. Spronk I, Kullen C, Burdon C, O'Connor H. Relationship between nutrition knowledge and dietary intake. *Br J Nutr.* 2014;111:1713-1726. doi:10.1017 /S0007114514000087
16. Wardle J, Parmenter K, Waller J. Nutrition knowledge and food intake. *Appetite.* 2000;34:269-275. doi:10.1006/appe.1999.0311
17. Asakura K, Todoriki H, Saski S. Relationship between nutrition knowledge and dietary intake among primary school children in Japan: combined effect of children's and their guardians' knowledge. *J Epidemiol.* 2017;27:483-491. doi:10.1016/j.je.2016.09.014
18. Ferrer R, Green PA, Oh AY, Hennessy E, Dwyer LA. Emotion suppression, emotional eating, and eating behavior among parent-adolescent dyads. *Emotion.* 2017;17:1052-1065. doi:10.1037/emo0000295
19. Ferrer R, Mendes W. Emotion, health decision making, and health behaviour. *Psych & Health.* 2018;33:1-16. doi:10.1080/08870446.2017.1385787
20. Huang I-C, Lee JL, Ketheeswaran P, Jones CM, Revicki DA, Wu AW. Does personality affect health-related quality of life? A systematic review. *PLoS ONE.* 2017;12:e0173806. doi:10.1371/journal.pone.0173806
21. Higgs S, Thomas J. Social influences on eating. *Curr Opin Behav Sci.* 2016;9:1-6. doi:10.1016/j.cobeha .2015.10.005
22. Reicks M, Banna J, Cluskey M, et al. Influence of parenting practices on eating behaviors of early adolescents during independent eating occasions: implications for obesity prevention. *Nutrients.* 2015;7:8783-8801. doi:10.3390/nu7105431
23. Martin-Biggers J, Spaccarotella K, Hongu N, Alleman G, Worobey J, Byrd-Bredbenner C. Translating it into real life: cognitions, barriers and supports for key weight-related behaviors of parents of preschoolers. *BMC Pub Health.* 2015;15:189.
24. Appleton K, Hemingway A, Saulais L, et al. Increasing vegetable intakes: rationale and systematic review of published interventions. *Eur J Nutr.* 2016;55:869-896. doi:10.1007/s00394-015-1130-8
25. Popovic-Lipovac A, Strasser B. A review on changes in food habits among immigrant women and implications for health. *J Immigr Minor Health.* 2015;17:582-590. doi:10.1007/s10903-013-9877-6

26. Smith B, Smith PM, Harper S, Manuel DG, Mustard CA. Reducing social inequalities in health: the role of simulation modelling in chronic disease epidemiology to evaluate the impact of population health interventions. *J Epidemiol Community Health.* 2014;68:384-389. doi:10.1136/jech-2013-202756

27. Montano D, Kasprzyk D. Theory of reasoned action, theory of planned behavior, and the integrated behavioral model. In: Glanz K, Rimer B, Viswanath K, eds. *Health Behavior: Theory, Research, and Practice.* 5th ed. Jossey-Bass; 2015:95-124.

28. Bandura A. Health promotion by social cognitive means. *Health Educ Behav.* 2004;31:143-164. doi:10.1177/1090198104263660

29. Kelder SH, Hoelscher D, Perry C. How individuals, environments, and health behaviors interact. In: Glanz K, Rimer B, Viswanath K, eds. *Health Behavior: Theory, Research, and Practice.* 5th ed. Jossey-Bass; 2015:159-182.

30. Corda K, Quick V, Schefske S, DeCandia J, Byrd-Bredbenner C. Toward a polytheoretical framework for health behavior. *Am J Health Stud.* 2010;25:211-230.

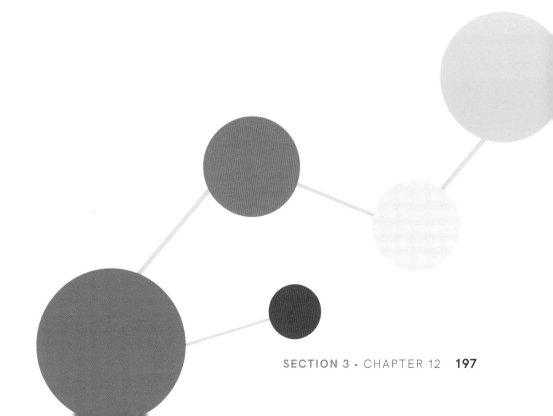

CHAPTER 13

Effective Nutrition Communication Is Tailored for the Target Culture

Roberta Larson Duyff, MS, RDN, FAND, FADA

"Culture: It cannot be measured. It's mostly invisible. Yet it guides behavior, communication, and social interactions, including perceptions, values, and decisions that impact nutritional well-being, health, and quality of life."

> "The essence of cross-cultural communication has more to do with releasing responses than with sending messages. It is more important to release the right response than to send the right message." —EDWARD T. HALL

Introduction

Culture shapes nearly everything in life, including food, lifestyle, health decisions, and behavior. It affects how an individual perceives and is perceived by others. It impacts how a nutrition communicator encourages and supports others to make healthful food and nutrition decisions for their lives. It determines how—*and if*—someone communicates.

Effective nutrition communicators reflect the theories, strategies, and skills shared throughout this book. They also value and embrace diversity, choosing the best communication platform (traditional, digital, in-person) for their target audiences, tailoring their messages and interaction accordingly, and reflecting their cultural competency.

Reasons for becoming culturally competent lie in the *biocultural* nature of nutrition itself, notes Diva Sanjur. While the consequences of food consumption are *biological*, impacting health over a lifetime, the nature of food intake—what people eat, how, when, where, and how much—is influenced heavily by *social, economic, political,* and *cultural processes*.[1] Cultural competence has a personal benefit for nutrition communicators, as it broadens and enriches their work and their own lives.

This chapter answers three questions:

- What is culture, and what attributes help define the many cultures a nutrition communicator may encounter?
- How can nutrition communicators effectively learn about cultures, including their own, and become culturally competent?
- What must be considered for effective, culturally sensitive nutrition communication?

First, some definitions: *cross-cultural, intercultural, multicultural*. Though these terms are often used interchangeably, they differ both in their meaning and use. *Cross-cultural* and *intercultural* generally refer to interactions among cultures or individuals within cultures. *Cross-cultural* is commonly used in work settings and typically refers to ethnicity or nationality. *Intercultural* often has a broader meaning that includes cultural groups related to gender, religion, and race; it's also academic terminology. *Multicultural* generally refers to attributes accorded to cultural diversity.[2]

What Is Culture and What Are Its Attributes?

Culture: It cannot be measured. It's mostly invisible. Yet it guides behavior, communication, and social interactions, including perceptions, values, and decisions that impact nutritional well-being, health, and quality of life.

Culture Defined

The term *culture* often brings to mind the arts, literature, and perhaps fine cuisine. While attributes (eg, food, garments, religion, language, and social habits) reflect culture, the definition is far more complex. In the context of this chapter, *culture* refers to the cumulative and commonly held characteristics that distinguish one group of people from another.

A group's culture encompasses its shared attributes—such as its values, attitudes, behaviors, and beliefs—and its shared knowledge, folklore, learned patterns (norms), and tendencies. For an ethnic or geographic group, culture is transmitted from one generation to another by communication and modeling. It evolves with both the times and the environment, or locale.

Norms are learned behavior patterns, or a system of rules, that are common within cultures and are shaped by members' values, attitudes, and beliefs. Simply stated, norms are why individuals within a culture typically do what they do in given situations. For example, a prayer of thanks before a meal is a norm in many religious cultures. Whether to use a spoon, fork, chopsticks, or fingers—and how to hold them—depends on cultural norms, as does the gender of the person who shops and prepares food for the family. And consider: Do people slurp their soup as a gesture of satisfaction, converse during a meal or remain quiet, or eat alone or only with others of their gender? These behaviors often reflect cultural norms. Individuals typically follow the cultural norms by which they were raised. Norms can change, for example when social, environmental, or health conditions change.

MODELS OF CULTURE

Because the concept of culture is abstract, many models make its complexities more tangible and understandable. Two models—the iceberg model and the onion model—are starting points for insights into the definition of culture. Each underscores the hidden and often overlooked aspects that underlie behavior. Yet neither model fully depicts all its complexities.

Iceberg model Visualize an iceberg. About 10% is visible; the remaining 90% hides below the waterline. The iceberg model aptly conveys some concepts of culture: what's obvious, conscious, and explicit, and what's hidden, unconscious, and implicit (see Figure 13.1).[3]

Even people with limited exposure to a culture can see and appreciate its visible features, such as its food, artifacts, social traditions, gestures, language, and arts. Sometimes called a *tourist viewpoint*, the observable is simply the "tip of the cultural iceberg"—easy to identify and differentiate.

Most aspects of culture, however, are hidden, often deep beneath the surface. They represent the values, norms, thought patterns, assumptions, beliefs, hierarchies, notions of time, gender roles, class, status, health practices, and communication patterns, for example, that underlie behavior and directly influence what's above the waterline. Being hidden, however, they're often difficult to know and understand and far harder to impact or change—even by those who are part of the culture.

What does the iceberg model imply for nutrition communicators? It represents the idea that it is not possible to judge or understand a food or health behavior by first and obvious impressions. A communicator must probe to understand *why*, *when*, *who*, and *how*—or what is below the waterline—before judging food- and health-related behavior. Rice in many Asian meals became a mainstay to satisfy hunger, for example: The *why* was to satisfy hunger when other foods were in short supply.

FIGURE 13.1 **Iceberg model of culture**[a]

The visible parts of culture …

traditional foods, cooking methods, housing, arts, literature, clothing, artifacts, type of language, recreation, others

Conscious (can be perceived and changed)

The hidden parts of culture …

values, beliefs, attitudes, gender roles, social class and structure, body language, communication style, conversation pattern, perceptions, bias, learning style, taboos, spirituality, worldview, nature of relationships, sense of time, approaches to problem solving and decision making, space perception, personal incentives, thought patterns, many others

Unconscious (difficult to perceive and change)

[a] Adapted from reference 3.

Food deserts in many low-income areas are the *why* that determines what's available to buy—and, so, to eat. Cultural background is the *why*, *when*, *who*, and *how* that influences how people view nutrition, their health, and their food decisions. And when cultural conflicts or misunderstandings arise, the causes may stem from a collision of what's hidden in two or more different cultural "icebergs."

Onion model Now visualize culture as an onion with several layers surrounding its core. In the onion model, the outermost layer represents the most observable aspects of culture: its symbols and artifacts, each carrying its own meanings (see Figure 13.2). The next layer represents the heroes (patterns) of a culture. The layer further inside encompasses the rituals and practices of a culture. The inner core, hidden by other layers, represents the values on which all other layers of a culture are built.[3]

What's the takeaway for nutrition communicators? The deeper the layer, the less visible the aspects of culture. Values, at the innermost core, can't be seen directly, yet they influence other aspects of that culture. Communicators must understand, respect, and take that into account for effective nutrition communication.

DEMOGRAPHICS OF CULTURE

Cultures and their subcultures (cultures within cultures) are identified broadly by similarities they share—both obvious and hidden, as just noted. These attributes relate to and often result from demographics, some changeable, others not. In other words, being of the same ethnicity doesn't necessarily equate to being of the same culture.

Multidimensional An individual's cultural identity is multidimensional, determined and influenced by many factors, including (1) age, race, and ethnicity (all three often visible to outsiders), which can't be changed; (2) education, geographic location, income level, lifestyle preferences, and so on (perhaps invisible), which can be influenced or changed; and (3) the situational and historical context of the social, cultural, and political events in someone's life.[4]

Subcultures, often determined by different economic or educational levels, ethnicities, religions, geographic regions, or generations, exist within dominant cultures. As examples, the cultural characteristics (including food behavior) of refugees fleeing a crisis differ from those individuals immigrating for educational or professional

FIGURE 13.2 Onion model of culture[a]

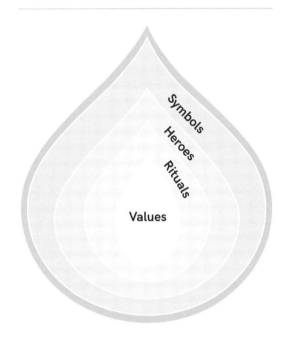

[a] Adapted from reference 3.

reasons, and people who are religiously devout may be more diligent with their faith's dietary practices than those with a secular identity with that faith.

Often overlooked are the cultural differences among the wealthy, middle class, and impoverished. As noted by R. F. Payne in the *Framework for Understanding Poverty*,[5] behavior, attitudes, and values about money aren't the only ways people differ. Perspectives on food, time, possessions, and socialization are among other attributes impacted by income level and social class. For example, having *enough* food is a priority for those in poverty, while the *quality* of food tends to matter more among the middle class, and the *presentation* of food (how it is served) tends to matter most to those with wealth. Economic status also plays a role in a culture's access to supermarkets; the availability of fresh produce, cooking equipment, and time for food preparation; and cooking skills.

The multidimensionality of culture affects how a person sees and lives in the world and, as significantly, how the world perceives that person. Those dimensions affect the person's food and health values, options, and behavior. Effective cross-cultural nutrition communication requires knowing, understanding, and reflecting the norms and behaviors of its subcultures.

Individual Cultural identity isn't static, nor is the cultural identity of one person the same as that of another, even within the same culture. Just as it's important to recognize the shared values, attitudes, beliefs, and norms of a subculture, communicators must be open to the uniqueness of individuals.

Consider the cultures that *you* were born into: your nationality, ethnicity, religion, and race. Now list other cultures of which you are a part, perhaps characterized by your lifestyle choices, the region where you live, and whether it's urban, suburban, or rural. Your economic status, educational level, social class, gender, and occupation also place you in unique subcultures, as do the generation of your birth, whether you're a grandparent, parent, or child, a worker or college student, in the military, and so on.

Even these cultural identities evolve or may be discarded over time. For example, as people enter adulthood, most discard teen or student cultures and embrace the attributes of work and often parenting cultures. With acculturation, second-generation immigrants differ not only from new immigrants but also from generations that follow. These cultural

shifts significantly impact attitudes, knowledge, and behavior related to food and health.

With all this stated, all people, regardless of cultural identity, are individuals. They may or may not be characterized by common group norms or attributes, or as part of a cultural melting pot or salad bowl (see Box 13.1).[6] When we remember that people in apparently homogeneous groups have diverse qualities, it's easier to resist the temptation to resort to stereotypes in cross-cultural communication.

SIX DIMENSIONS OF CULTURE

Being aware of a culture's generalized tendencies sheds light on effective, impactful, and comfortable cross-cultural interactions. Consider how to apply Hofstede's Six Dimensions of Culture[7] to nutrition communication—in person, with groups, and through targeted media:

1. **How people within a culture deal with inequality** Some cultures accept hierarchical direction, power, and authority more readily; others are characterized by a greater sense of equality, allowing for more interaction and shared decision-making.

For perspectives about age and generational cultures, see Chapter 14.

BOX 13.1 Nutrition Communication: Beyond the Melting Pot and Salad Bowl[6]

Historically, the melting pot was a metaphor for the assimilation of diverse populations, especially immigrants during the late 19th and early 20th centuries, into a common US culture. Now often criticized, this concept assumed that different cultural values and norms were relinquished to create a more homogeneous, mostly Euro-American society. Back then, food and nutrition professionals typically helped a very diverse population, including those of Black and Indigenous descent, adapt to norms of mainstream culture.

As the value of diversity gained attention in later decades of the last century, the salad bowl paradigm took its place, celebrating many cultural identities and their contributions to a diverse US society. So then, food and nutrition professionals

were encouraged to gain a deeper understanding of the cultural norms, practices, traits, and values of diverse populations, including Asian American, Latino or Hispanic American, and Middle Eastern American immigrants. The salad bowl metaphor was challenged too. Even with that understanding, cultural differences often were compared to the norms and values of a White-dominant reference culture.

Another cultural metaphor was introduced more recently. It's of an organism in an environment of diverse cultures that evolves as a whole, while retaining cultural boundaries and unique elements. That requires a higher level of cultural competence among food and nutrition communicators.

Arguably these metaphors provide different ways to view culture and shape nutrition communication. However, none focuses on individuals within a culture. Cultural competence, addressed in this chapter, and effective cross-cultural nutrition communication extends to viewing each person as an individual.

2. How those within cultures or communities are connected Where individualism is the norm, people tend to be more self-focused, valuing personal choice, personal obligations, and direct personal expression; they tend to take less responsibility for those outside their core group. Group-focused cultures put more value on relationships, loyalty, and group obligations and tend to avoid confrontation.

3. How they deal with unknowns Rules, predictability, and acceptance of fate, offering relief from stress and failure, are more common in some cultures. In cultures that positively anticipate unknowns and risks, people tend to prefer fewer rules and accept differences with less anxiety.

4. How those within a culture see progress toward outcomes Some cultures are more comfortable with slower steps to long-term results, while others typically want immediate results and benefits.

5. How cultures achieve outcomes Competition, ambition, and success are key drivers in some cultures, while collaboration, negotiation, and harmony are key drivers in others.

6. How people view happiness and control of their lives Some cultures tend to view life more positively, with optimism and indulgence, while other cultures tend to be more restrained, reserved, and more likely to be pessimistic.

COGNITIVE STYLE OF CULTURE

Culture impacts how people seek, perceive, process, and recall information. Referred to as cognitive style, it impacts learning, decision-making, and social interactions—another consideration for nutrition communication. Here is what we know about cognitive style and culture:

- Some cultures and subcultures place more value on abstract information, seeking more theory and explanations of why and when.
- Others expect more concrete information (facts, details, and context about who and what) before springing into action.
- Others are okay with surface-level processing.
- Absolute truth is valued by some; probability of truth by others.[8]

Cognitive style isn't the same as intelligence or learning style.

Culture and Communication Styles

Among other avenues, culture is communicated through language. Shared languages—spoken and written, actions, and silence—are common attributes of cultural identity. Linguistics, which includes language use, nonverbal cues, context (high and low), and direct and indirect styles, distinguishes the communication of one culture from another.[9,10] Arguably, culture influences language, and language influences culture.

LANGUAGE USE

Mastering a culture's spoken and written language—whether it be Arabic, Mandarin, Farsi, Spanish, Urdu, or any other language—is an obvious cross-cultural communication skill. After all, words matter. So does the manner of expression.[11]

The way language is used conveys far more than its literal meaning. Paralanguage, or elements of speech (accent, tone, pitch, rhythm, volume, and speed), as well as syntax, style, spelling, vocabulary, and dialect, transmit meaning, as does social context. Even pacing and pausing (silence and long pauses), taking turns between sender and receiver, and interruptions during conversation "talk."

Just as it's hard to read nonverbal cues, reading the subtle meanings of language usage in a culture other than one's own is challenging; it is challenging for outsiders and even for those who are fluent.

It is important to understand that before nutrition communicators accept what they *think* they hear or read in a language other than their native language, they should verify the message with a trusted cultural informant, a topic discussed later in this chapter.

NONVERBAL CUES

"Actions speak louder than words." It's a common saying. Nonverbal cues convey meaning that may differ from the spoken word.[12] Even if the "right" words are expressed, verbal and nonverbal messages that aren't in sync can result in miscommunication.

Intended or not, facial expressions, eye movements, eye contact, gestures, touch (haptics), personal proximity (proxemics), and body positions (commonly referred to as body language) convey *implicit* meaning, as do voice quality, or the elements of speech (pitch, tone, rate, and volume). [12]

The meanings behind a nod, a wink, or a thumbs-up may seem universal. Yet, the same nonverbal signals can express very different messages. A nod could mean agreement in one culture and "I'm listening" or "No, but I'm being polite" in another. A wink could invite romance in some cultures but reflect rudeness in others. A thumbs-up means okay in some cultures, while an okay sign with the thumb and forefinger may be perceived as vulgar, offensive, a curse, or simply zero (worthless) in others. A smile may cover embarrassment or show sarcasm rather than expressing humor or empathy as some might perceive.[12] Direct eye contact conveys equality, trust, and attention in some cultures, while averting eye contact shows respect in others, such as among some Indigenous people in America.[13]

Cultures also differ in their use of body movements and how they view proximity (intimate space, personal space, social space, public space), touching (who touches whom, when, and how), and certain postures (eg, crossed arms, slouching, legs spread, ankles crossed, towering). Gender, age, and social rank typically factor in.[12]

Misreading gestures, facial expressions, and other body language, ignoring them, or missing their nuances can lead to confusion, ambiguity, uneasiness, and misdiagnosis of health issues, and may even ignite conflict. The bigger the cultural gap, the more challenging it is to read nonverbal language.[12]

Take note: Nutrition communicators must learn to read nonverbal cues and use appropriate cues, especially when they don't share a cultural or linguistic background with their audience. Again, strive for cultural competence and rely on a trusted cultural informant.

Please note that different from nonverbal cues, American Sign Language (ASL) is the predominant language for deaf and hard of hearing people in the United States, as well as several other English-speaking and non-English-speaking countries. Many other sign languages, such as French Sign Language, Auslan, and Indo-Pakistani Sign Language, are used throughout the world, and use of sign language may also vary across communities within a particular country.

HIGH- AND LOW-CONTEXT COMMUNICATION

High-context and low-context are two communication modes that also describe communication styles.[10] Context refers to the amount of information transmitted through relationships, situations, and physical cues. How do high- and low-context

communications differ? What might that mean to a nutrition communicator?

High-context communication relies heavily on implicit messages—nonverbal messages, voice tone, silence, personal status, shared experience, personal history, social situations, and relationships—and less on verbal interactions. Face-to-face communications are often favored.

Cultures and individuals with close personal connections, developed over an extended period of time, tend to use high-context communication. As a result, people tend to know what others think and do without explicit communication. They share similar experiences and expectations, expecting that others can "read between the lines." They rely more on oral, rather than written, communication; for example, food-related behavior is learned through longtime familial experience, not through explicit talk. Relationships, mutual understanding, and nonverbal communications are more important than precise words. Silence may be comfortable. Disagreement tends to feel more personal. Cultures in and from some parts of Asia, Africa, and the Middle East tend to be high-context.[14] Talk with your cultural informant (discussed on page 210) to better understand the communication mode of your audience.

Low-context communication relies on explicit, precise, and often detailed spoken and written dialogue. It's the opposite of high-context communication. Background information, beliefs, and expectations are clearly stated and detailed to make sure they're heard and understood. Nonverbal communication, such as gestures, environmental cues, and unspoken moods, are often overlooked or missed. Silence may be uncomfortable. Disagreement tends to be taken less personally.

Low-context communication is more common in cultures and among individuals with widespread connections. Because relationships are often short-term (not developed over time), compartmentalized, and task-focused, spoken and written communication typically requires more context, direction, and details. Written communication, such as paper documentation, print material, and emails, is often more important. Cultures with mostly western European roots, such as White-identified groups in the United States, Canada, and Australia, tend to be low-context.[14]

To some degree, every culture—and every individual—conveys messages using both modes. And some situations and environments require

For more about body language and nonverbal communication, see Chapter 21.

more high-context communication while others need more low-context communication. Family relationships, for example, are typically high-context since family members generally share many common experiences. Business agreements or nutrition counseling often require low-context communication.

Effective cross-cultural communication requires observing, listening, and being aware of the level of context and seeking clarity and help from a cultural informant. Low-context communicators often fail to value or take time to build and maintain the relationships needed with high-context listeners or speakers. Detailed background information and focused directives may seem too direct, abrupt, and condescending to high-context cultures and result in misunderstanding. Conversely, high-context communicators may fail to provide enough information for low-context communicators.

DIRECT AND INDIRECT COMMUNICATION

There's yet another way to look at cross-cultural nutrition communication: Is the communication style of the target culture direct or indirect?[9] What may happen when one style meets another?

Direct (linear) communication Direct communication gets straight to the point. It's explicit and relies mostly on words, much less on context. Points and subpoints are sequentially shared in a straight line to the bottom line, or endpoint, but with only the amount of information others need. With direct communication (written or spoken), both the sender and receiver want to get to the point quickly without deviating. Those who communicate in an indirect manner may perceive this style as abrupt, rude, aggressive, or insensitive.

Indirect (circular) communication Rather than stating things outright, indirect communication suggests the key point or points. It's implicit and relies mostly on context surrounding often unstated points. Information (verbal and nonverbal) and stories provide a rich context that ultimately gets to the main point, once all the context is shared. With circular communication, the speaker tries to make the point or points with a broad amount of relevant information and perhaps stories and personal anecdotes, often letting others infer meaning. To direct communicators, stories and context may be perceived as wasting time, disorganized, or lacking in clarity.

Nutrition communicators must know their own communication style and that of the receiver. Skip the urge to judge or ignore the context or story of indirect communicators. Instead, be patient, listen, and learn from its richness. Similarly, refrain from being judgmental or dismissive of direct talk. Either way, find ways to adjust messages to the communication style of the audience. As a side note: Sharing stories is a communication strategy used today to market a product, capture reader interest, or convey information to mainstream audiences, too.

Perceptions of Culture

Knowing one's own cultural identity is one thing—however, cultural competence goes beyond *just* memorizing cultural attitudes, beliefs, values, and behavior, which can lead to assumptions and can oversimplify the fluidity of cultures and their diversity.[15] The ability to perceive other cultures in an informed, nonjudgmental way is quite different.

ETHNOCENTRISM VS ETHNORELATIVISM

Becoming culturally competent is a process. Bennett's model of cultural competence, or stages of ethnorelativism, offers a framework that reflects progress. It addresses how awareness, knowledge, skills, and attitudes (respect) with regard to different cultures develop along a continuum,[12] from a self-focused and limited view (ethnocentrism) to increased sensitivity to and respect for differences, while honoring commonalities (ethnorelativism) among cultures.[16] See Figure 13.3 (page 206).

An *ethnocentric perspective* is seeing one's own culture—for example, food beliefs, decisions, and practices—as the normal, right, and often superior way ("my way is best"). This view is culturally blind, meaning that the viewer sees others, including their food behavior, through the viewer's own cultural lens. This perspective typically stems from a limited exposure to other cultures with little context for others.

For nutrition communicators, food and health preconceptions derived only from one's own standards, customs, norms, and values limit intercultural sensitivity, food experiences, and the ability to interact and communicate effectively.

In contrast, an *ethnorelative perspective* acknowledges and values how differently others think, act, and feel about many things, including food and health behavior. Typically requiring cultural interaction over time, this perspective is a learned ability to experience one's own culture within the context of others.

With this perspective, nutrition communicators are better able to position healthy eating messages within the cultural context of the target population and make food-related norms of other cultures a comfortable part of their own.

GENERALIZATIONS VS STEREOTYPES

"Jorge eats tamales *and* he is a Mexican, not *because* he is Mexican." The subtle difference may seem unimportant; the difference in meaning is significant. Overgeneralizing often leads to inaccurate, inappropriate, and potentially damaging stereotypes.

Broad brushstrokes (generalizations, stereotypes, or unconscious bias) cannot accurately or fairly define a culture. So, are generalizations good or bad? That depends. What about

stereotyping? And how is it possible to overcome unconscious bias?

Generalizations can be a starting place They provide a basic awareness of the normative patterns and attributes of a culture and its subcultures. Generalizations can open the door for curious minds and serve as a launchpad to learn more. They're a basis for comparing, not judging, and provide context for anticipating, sorting, and understanding new information, gleaned from another culture.[17]

Overgeneralizing, however, leads to misrepresentation. Consider: No single Latino* or Hispanic culture exists for Puerto Rican, Mexican, Guatemalan, or Cuban immigrants to the United States—even if they all speak Spanish. Similarly, whether their roots are in Africa, Asia, Europe, or the Middle East, the cultures of those with deep

---

* Although Merriam Webster recognized the term Latinx as an inclusive term in 2018, *Communicating Nutrition* follows the *AMA Manual of Style*, 10th edition, in using "Latino or Hispanic" as the preferred term for this ethnic group. However, as a nutrition communicator, it is important for you to know the preferences of your audience. In some cases, Latinx may be more appropriate, and, when possible, more specific terms such as Mexican American or Cuban American are often preferred.

FIGURE 13.3 **From ethnocentrism to ethnorelativism: Six stages of the Bennett model of cultural competence**[a]

Where do you fit in M. J. Bennett's six-stage model of cultural competence? That depends on your experience with the target culture and its ethnic or religious background, social status, economic level, gender orientation, and age. The Bennett model suggests that those who accept, then adapt, and eventually integrate with another culture can communicate with it more effectively.

STAGE 1 **Denial** Individuals in this stage don't recognize cultural differences, perhaps due to little or no contact or experience with those from a different cultural background. Communicators have no context for adapting a nutrition message.

STAGE 2 **Defense** Individuals see cultural differences, but these differences are threatening to the individual's own sense of identity or reality. Communicators may use defense mechanisms, such as negative stereotyping, a belief in superiority, or denigrating one's own culture to idealize another, to neutralize differences.

STAGE 3 **Minimization** Individuals recognize cultural differences but think that similarities outweigh differences. Communicators may assume similarity without exploring existing differences and may try to change another's behavior to fit their own expectations.

STAGE 4 **Acceptance** Individuals recognize and value cultural differences and do not see them as positive or negative. Communicators may disagree with cultural differences but not because of ethnocentrism.

STAGE 5 **Adaptation** Individuals see the culture or world through a different lens and develop cross-cultural communication skills. Communicators adapt their behaviors and messages to better interact with others.

STAGE 6 **Integration** Individuals value and respect diversity and identify themselves (their values and behavior) in relation to other cultures. Communicators integrate their values and behavior with that of others instead of limiting themselves to their original culture.

[a] Adapted from reference 16.

historical roots in the United States differ dramatically from those of first-generation Americans.

Stereotypes are a "stopping place" They're generalized, fixed notions that consciously assume that everyone is the same. For example, "She eats rice because she's Asian—all Asians eat rice." Another example is ageism, stemming from beliefs in some cultures that older people are of less value than younger people, or the opposite in many Asian cultures. More often negative than positive, stereotypes often stem from preconceptions, conscious or unconscious bias, or a historical or contemporary prejudice.[17]

Stereotypical viewpoints resist new information about a culture, situation, group, or person. That in turn can interfere with communication. Often patronizing, stereotyping also can lead to unrealistic expectations, inappropriate behavior, inaction, conflict, and discrimination.

UNCONSCIOUS BIAS

Unconscious bias is stereotyping that's hidden in one's own "cultural iceberg."[18] These biases may not be compatible with someone's conscious values and beliefs. For example, someone may believe in being "healthy at many body sizes" yet have an unconscious bias toward an overweight airline passenger in the next seat.

Conscious or not, positive or negative, bias isn't limited to racial or ethnic groups or to those who are impoverished or economically elite. It may also extend, for example, to those with athletic proficiency, high or low intellectual ability, physical or mental disabilities, or a different gender orientation or physical appearance.

Everyone has unconscious biases that are learned in childhood and that impact perceptions. That said, with an open mind and self-awareness, biases can be unlearned or minimized. Cultural immersion, cultural informants, and trusted relationships with socially different individuals and groups help break down biases. Taking time to know each other makes all the difference for effective nutrition communication!

How Can Nutrition Communicators Become Culturally Competent?

Imagine needing to work with a team comprised of people from different cultures and perhaps different parts of the world. This chapter has already explored several questions: Why might people on the team react, think, and behave differently? Why might some interactions feel comfortable and others uncomfortable? Now, how might barriers to cultural competence be overcome?

Cultural competence isn't the same as knowing about a culture. And, while such competence appreciates other cultures, it does not appropriate them (see Box 13.3 on page 217). Instead, cultural competence is an ability to view values, norms, and behaviors as unique aspects of a culture—not

FIGURE 13.4 **From cultural knowledge to cultural competence**

Progress toward cultural competence can be described as a continuum. Where do you fall along the continuum?

CULTURAL KNOWLEDGE Knowing some characteristics, values, beliefs, lifestyles, problem-solving strategies, and norms of the target culture; for example, knowing its foods and food beliefs, behavior, and restrictions; knowing about access to food and health services and about health issues and practices

CULTURAL AWARENESS Openness to changing attitudes, biases, and perceptions when interacting with a target culture; for example, becoming aware of healthy foods and food preparations that are unfamiliar

CULTURAL SENSITIVITY Awareness of cultural differences and similarities without judgment and without conveying that one way or one type of advice is right or superior; for example, holding back advice on food practices until learning more

CULTURAL COMPETENCE Readiness to communicate and function effectively with a target culture that may have different values, attitudes, and norms from one's own; for example, having the ability to respect cultural food norms and provide appropriate guidance

as attributes of *all* people within a culture (see Figure 13.4). It's recognizing cultural similarities and differences without designating them as right or wrong, good or bad. It requires wisdom and a willingness to understand another culture, to know what's good in it, and to recognize the reasons "why it is what it is." Until that context is known, trying to "improve" a food behavior is unwise and arguably unethical.[19]

Culturally competent nutrition professionals understand the following[20]:

- relevant cultural norms, values, worldviews, and practicalities of everyday life
- cultural variations in family relationships
- culturally specific health beliefs and practices
- sociodemographic facts
- cultural food behavior (including foods commonly avoided or restricted)
- cultural attitudes about health care professionals and when to consult them
- physical, biological, or psychological differences among ethnic and racial groups (or other cultural groups)
- prevalence of diet-related health conditions in a culture or subculture
- impact of food habits and preferences on willingness and ability to follow nutrition advice

To begin the journey toward cultural competence, nutrition communicators must first know themselves. Engage with other cultures deeply, with an open mind. Rely on trusted cultural informants. Develop relationships; always show respect. And carry a desire for and commitment to cross-cultural communication.

Self-Awareness

Being aware of one's own culture and cultural interactions is a first step toward effectiveness as a nutrition communicator in diverse environments. After all, it's not just an audience that has a culture; a communicator does too—in fact, more than one. Much is hidden, even from a member of a given culture. Since people live their cultures every day, they may take them for granted or view them as norms for all. Understanding one's own cultural identity helps to:

- recognize cultural norms, traditions, and rituals (including food behavior) that may seem odd, uncomfortable, or unhealthy to others;

- detect and overcome culturally imposed biases, perceptions, prejudices, and assumptions that could affect and interfere with cross-cultural interaction and communication; and
- communicate in a nonjudgmental way.

When communicators can talk comfortably about their culture, others may feel more comfortable sharing theirs. Communicators who can recognize that others may have a bias toward them may better understand the impact of bias toward others.

See Figure 13.5 to assess your cultural self-awareness.

CULTURAL IMMERSION

Travel, festivals, restaurants, books, study, and more: These "tourist visits" reveal obvious aspects of a culture, above the cultural iceberg's waterline. While valuable, they generally don't disclose beliefs, values, and social dimensions that underlie a culture's norms and behavior.

The best teacher is cultural immersion, or active participation through firsthand experience, attentive awareness, and participation in a culture's daily life. Living or working abroad or in a different region or culture actively engages a person with an unfamiliar community, its members, and its daily life. Immersion teaches implicit aspects of a culture.

Even if it is not possible to live or spend an extended time in an unfamiliar culture, participation is still possible—not just with tourist eyes and ears and not in a drop-in, drop-by visit:

- Go beyond so-called tourist sites and events. Interact with many different people and experiences: food markets, neighborhoods, family gatherings, religious events, and other encounters that are important to the culture. Food shopping and preparation is an obvious opportunity.
- Observe, describe, and assess a situation or behavior within its cultural context, not through a personal cultural lens. See Box 13.2 on page 210.
- Ask open-ended, nonjudgmental questions. Listen attentively with both ears and eyes, rather than just waiting for a turn to talk. Listen for silence too.
- Suspend judgment and negative comparisons. After all, "It's not right; it's not wrong; it's just different."

FIGURE 13.5 **Cultural self-awareness assessment**

Cultural competence starts with self-awareness. After each statement, indicate where you fit on the continuum.

AWARENESS		CULTURAL COMPETENCE			
		Less ⟵ ⟶ More			
		Never	Sometimes/ Not Very Well	Fairly Often/ Pretty Well	Always/ Very Well
Value diversity	I view human differences as positive and a cause for celebration.				
Know myself	I have a clear view of my own ethnic, racial, and cultural identity.				
Share my culture	I am aware that in order to learn more about others I need to understand and be prepared to share my own culture.				
Am aware of areas of discomfort	I am aware of my own discomfort when I encounter differences in race, religion, sexual orientation, language, and ethnicity.				
Check my assumptions	I am aware of the assumptions I hold about people of cultures different from my own.				
Challenge my stereotypes	I am aware of my stereotypes when they arise and have developed personal strategies for reducing the harm they cause.				
Reflect on how my culture informs my judgment	I am aware of how my cultural perspective influences my judgment about what are "normal," "appropriate," or "superior" behaviors, values, and communication styles.				
Accept ambiguity	I accept that in cross-cultural situations there can be uncertainty and that uncertainty can make me anxious. It can also mean that I do not respond quickly and take the time needed to get more information.				
Am curious	I take any opportunity to put myself in a place where I can learn about differences and create relationships.				
Aware of personal privilege or of opportunities from my demographic or culture	When working with others who don't share my level of opportunity or privilege, I recognize that I may not be perceived as unbiased or as an ally.				

Adapted with permission from Central Vancouver Island Multicultural Society. Cultural competence self-assessment checklist. Accessed February 8, 2019. www.coloradoedinitiative.org/wp-content/uploads/2015/10/cultural-competence-self-assessment-checklist.pdf[21]

- Take time to learn about cultural norms, attitudes, and beliefs. That includes food, health, and health-related behaviors.
- Observe nonverbal behaviors. Try to follow those norms appropriately when interacting with others.
- Establish trust to participate in a culture, not just be a spectator.
- Engage mindfully. Even if these attempts aren't perfect, they need to be sensitive to cultural taboos and differences.
- Rely on cultural informants (discussed next).
- Take time for self-reflection. Experiential learning takes time and patience, questioning and observation, and open-mindedness.

CULTURAL INFORMANTS

Whether communicators are already immersed in a new culture or getting ready to do so, their best ally and resource is someone with extensive knowledge of and experience in the deeper aspects of both the target culture and the communicator's own.

What attributes do good cultural informants possess? Where are informants found? The right informants don't need to be food or nutrition experts but should be those who:

- know the target culture or subculture (and perhaps the language) well, ideally because it's their own;
- work comfortably with the communicator;
- can be trusted to reliably interpret what the communicator observes and experiences;
- are trusted and respected by the target culture;
- share willingly, objectively, and immediately; and
- acknowledge what they don't know.

Be cautious: Being a member of a dominant culture doesn't mean being a well-qualified informant for a subculture. For example, no cultural informant can speak for all Latinos or Hispanics, all Blacks, or all Indigenous people. In addition, the degree of assimilation and generational differences can impact and alter a person's insights and knowledge.

A cultural informant can be a colleague, friend, or a new contact developed by networking with the target culture. The member interest groups (MIGs) of the Academy of Nutrition and Dietetics (see www.eatrightpro.org/membership /academy-groups/member-interest-groups) are one source for cultural informants who are well informed about food and nutrition issues.

As a cultural informant, a sensitivity reader can be an invaluable asset in your effective food and nutrition communication. See Box 13.4 on page 218.

RELATIONSHIP BUILDING

Never underestimate the value of relationships! That's a truism for effectively communicating with anyone.

As you enlist the time, energy, and resources of those from other cultures—including cultural informants—ensure that your relationships are reciprocal. They aren't beholden to assist you. Although they may not be paid, they shouldn't be asked to do for free what you are being paid to do, nor can your relationships be forced on those who have less actual or perceived power in your interactions. These relationships must work toward a beneficial outcome for all.

Communicators must initiate connections, engage, and nurture relationships within other cultures as they do within their own culture:

- Start with people and organizations who are familiar. Too often, opportunities for cultural connections get overlooked.
- Experience new and unfamiliar places and situations, even if it feels uncomfortable or

BOX 13.2 Don't Judge—DIVE![22]

How do you react to a new, uncomfortable, or confusing situation or cultural setting? How do you make sense of what you see and hear? How do you make a fair judgment before trying to communicate? The DIVE tool, adapted from a 1970s model by Janet Bennett, is a useful way to appraise a situation or encounter first, before it's misinterpreted.

Describe Just the facts! Objectively describe what you observe verbally and nonverbally.

Interpret Generate explanations. Acknowledge what you know and don't know, as this can impact your perspectives.

Verify Check your interpretation with your cultural informant.

Evaluate Determine what is implicit in the culture based on what you know, and what you think should be communicated or done.

awkward—perhaps a faith-based setting, a cultural event, or a community outreach site. An open, nonjudgmental encounter usually receives a sincere welcome. Bring someone along if that will feel more comfortable.

- Read, listen, observe, question. Become educated about the culture and its issues. Asking questions shows interest, eases conversation, and indicates care. Try to understand a situation from another's point of view. Being highly informed isn't required for thoughtful, curious, and respectful discussion.
- Skip the urge to make assumptions. Probe for a rationale if disagreeing with a point. Once the context is understood, the situation or point of view often makes sense. See Box 13.2 on page 210.
- Earn trust over time. Remember that others may need to overcome their perceptions and cultural stereotypes about you, the communicator. Once trust is established, you may be able to openly address misperceptions about one another's cultures.
- Be authentic in order to find common ground as well as unique differences. Share your culture as you learn about theirs.
- Take risks. Accept and learn from cultural mistakes and miscommunication. They're inevitable. See them as learning experiences. Apologize for being insensitive or offensive, rather than letting mistakes become barriers to continued relationships.
- Stand up for others. Speak up on their behalf. Caring builds trust and motivates others in the target culture to listen and act on nutrition messages.

What Are Effective Strategies for Culturally Focused Nutrition Communication?

"The most important thing in communication is *hearing* what isn't said," as Peter Drucker once stated. That's key to effective, equitable, understandable, and respectful cross-cultural nutrition communication that can motivate a target culture to healthy food and lifestyle practices.

In fact, providing culturally and linguistically appropriate services and communication is being recognized as key to eliminating disparities in health and health care. That requires cultural competence on the part of those working with the target population.[23]

Collaborate with the Culture

"It takes a village!" Effective nutrition communication comes from collaboration with the target culture: its community, professionals, and grassroots organizations, which understand how their culture impacts food and health behavior. Partnering creates "buy-in" from the culture, expands the reach and capacity for initiatives, and helps a nutrition communicator focus on the right goals, the right strategies, and the right tactics.

An effective team informs about implicit cultural attributes; differences within subcultures; their food, nutrition, and health issues; and the underlying meanings of words and images. It also can identify the right communication channels (traditional media and social or digital media) and help communicators access community resources and stakeholders. To build partnerships, follow these steps:

- Develop foundational knowledge first, as noted in the discussion of cultural immersion earlier in this chapter. Know the trusted digital and print sources, community agencies, and libraries used by the community and its cultures. Identify events and places where people gather. For example, check community organizations that serve immigrants and refugees, faith-based groups, food pantries, and local government agencies for local resources.
- Develop a go-to network of cultural informants with members of the target population: trusted community nutrition and health representatives, community leaders, media, and other stakeholders, such as tribal leaders in Indigenous communities. Enable all on the team to play active roles.
- Collaborate to identify and prioritize food and nutrition issues and health risks, and develop communication strategies to address them. No matter how much research a communicator does, a team likely knows resources, tactics, and nuances that haven't been found.

See Who Is Involved? on page 43 to read more about collaborations.

Engage a Cross-Cultural Communication Team

by Roberta Larson Duyff, MS, RDN, FAND, FADA

Who's on a team? Over the years, cross-cultural communication skills have played essential roles in my professional and volunteer work. The prerequisite for success has always been the expertise and engagement of cultural informants, insights from the target audience, and an unstated openness. In each endeavor recounted here, members of our cross-cultural team were recognized for their valued efforts, insights, and guidance, and we were careful to be mindful of reciprocal benefits to them. Besides national conference and print recognition, these advisors were among the first to have these nutrition education resources created with their students and families in mind.

Rely on the expertise of grassroots leaders.
Several years ago, a colleague and I received a national Head Start grant. We were tasked with developing multicultural resources (children's books, hands-on activities, music, and a leader's guide) for early childhood programs, which we titled *The Foods I Eat … The Foods You Eat*. The goal: to use food experiences as a context for starting young children on a journey to cross-cultural awareness, respect for differences and sharing of similarities, and pride in their own cultures. We relied on on-site interviews, focus groups, cultural informants, and field testing in urban and rural areas, tribal towns, and communities of the target culture. Together the team informed the project about food and food behaviors, cultural norms and taboos, learning styles, graphics that reflected culture without stereotyping, and ways for educators to involve the program's hands-on learning and books with the different cultures of children and their families.

The cross-cultural communication team members were our "teachers" and sounding boards for creating nutrition education resources where children could find themselves and their cultures, while respectfully learning with and about others. Food provided the perfect learning context!

Embrace the creativity of the target population. In a US Department of Agriculture Team Nutrition project, meant to create low-literacy nutrition resources for food stamp (since renamed SNAP [Supplemental Nutrition Assistance Program] food benefits) recipients, teens in the target audiences became key members of our "creative group." These teens, who were involved in after-school or community arts initiatives, included young people who had previously dropped out of school, become parents as teens, belonged to gangs, or been incarcerated. Also, as the teens came from families receiving food stamps, they were better able to create healthy eating messages and graphics that spoke to their communities. Together with professional graphic designers, we probed their food-related issues; guided the nutrition content, words, and graphics; and took the project to completion.

The youth on our cross-cultural communication team were the brains behind these successful nutrition education resources designed for food stamp offices throughout the nation. The six community programs and the young artists that created the graphics and messages received national attention.

Partner with colleagues from the Academy of Nutrition and Dietetics member interest groups (MIGs). As a lifelong volunteer with AFS intercultural youth exchange and as a dietitian and host mom to several foreign-born Muslim teens, I'm often tasked with coleading national webinars that prepare non-Muslim host families for fasting practices and Iftar celebrations during Ramadan. Ramadan practices impact host-family food dynamics and challenge exchange students, especially when Ramadan falls during school days or during the long, hot days of late spring and summer when the time (sundown to sunrise) for nourishing meals and fluids is short.

While our foreign-born Muslim exchange students are cultural informants themselves, also working with an imam and with registered dietitian nutritionists from the Academy of Nutrition and Dietetics Religion MIG as part of a cross-cultural communication team provided relevant and practical insights and guidance to share with host-family orientations. I later teamed with these individuals on a related topic as a copresenter for a webinar offered to Academy of Nutrition and Dietetics members.

- Empower others—perhaps prominent community members—to take the lead and share credit as appropriate.

Refer to the Words of Experience box for lessons learned from cross-cultural collaboration.

Adapt the Communication Plan to the Culture

An effective communication plan—developed and implemented with a team—respects and supports cultural values, beliefs, knowledge, and practices. To develop a plan:

- Craft and conduct a needs assessment with the team. Identify the nutrition and health needs of the target culture, where and how they access food and health care, food taboos and restrictions, practices of folk medicine, trusted authorities, communication channels, their support mechanisms, and so on. Be aware of common health risks.
- Use insights and data gleaned from the assessment. Set realistic and achievable objectives with the communication team. Be aware of unconscious biases or cultural generalizations.
- Use communication strategies, resources, and messages that are culturally appropriate and relevant and that match the culture's communication style, discussed earlier. The low-context, direct style used by some people may be ineffective, even abrupt or brash, to those accustomed to high-context, indirect communication.
- Check with community agencies, health organizations, and cultural informants for culturally specific nutrition resources available to a particular audience. For global work, international organizations such as the Food and Agriculture Organization of the United Nations can provide country-specific nutrition education resources. For example, more than 100 countries have developed food-based dietary guidelines adapted to their nutrition situation, food availability, culinary cultures, and eating habits. Many have published food guides with graphics and messages similar to MyPlate; among them are the Japanese "spinning top" food guide, Qatar's "seashell" food guideline, and China's healthy-eating pagoda.

- Assess and adapt communications to the learning style of the audience and its culture. What cognitive style, addressed earlier, distinguishes the target audience? Are they concrete learners who thrive with experience, or are they abstract learners? Would storytelling work? While culture may impact learning style, all learners are individuals who process (acquire, retain, and apply) information in their own way. Individuals may be visual learners, auditory learners, kinesthetic learners, or multimodality learners.
- Identify the communication channels best suited to the target culture. Presenting nutrition messages in stories may be effective for those who learn indirectly through oral communication. Although social media is pervasive, it has limits. For example, people with fewer resources may not have access to a home computer or to software that detects and downloads attachments. Some people limit smartphone use to manage the expense. Tactics such as podcasts, blogs, other digital media, cooking demonstrations, shopping tours, and print material are discussed in other chapters.
- Organize focus groups and pilot projects to test the waters. Pretest communication tactics, language and literacy level, approach and design, and messages. Gather feedback; revise.
- Evaluate. With a communication team, determine how to measure or define success against agreed upon objectives. For more about evaluation, refer to Chapter 38.

Overcome Communication Barriers

Miscommunication—caused by language differences, ethnocentrism, prejudice, cultural assumptions, stereotyping, unconscious bias, contextual misunderstanding, and differences in norms, values, and viewpoints—and cultural appropriation are major barriers to working effectively across cultures; see Figure 13.6 (page 214) and Box 13.3 (page 217). Many of these issues are addressed earlier in this chapter.

To overcome cross-cultural communication barriers, consider the information presented in Figure 13.7 (page 215).

For the whys, hows, and uses of needs assessments, see Chapter 11.

To create targeted messages, see Chapters 10 and 15.

See Box 3.1 on page 41 for the steps in a nutrition communication strategy.

FIGURE 13.6 **Barriers to cross-cultural communication**

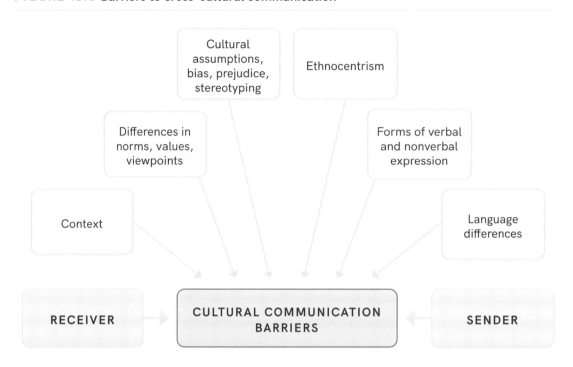

Go Beyond Simple Translations

Need to communicate in a different language? *Translations* are generally used to change written words into another language. *Interpretations* produce a spoken equivalent between two languages.[24]

When you need to communicate in another language, basic translations are rarely enough. Cultural context and relevancy matter. For example, a direct translation of a food guide doesn't reflect the foods typically purchased, prepared, and eaten by the target culture. Translating or interpreting tips for using Nutrition Facts labels, freshness codes, or unit pricing make no sense to recent immigrants accustomed to shopping in "wet" markets filled with unprocessed, fresh ingredients.

Translating and interpreting require somewhat different skills. Both require an ability to accurately and clearly convey explicit and implicit meanings. Being bilingual doesn't necessarily make someone a good translator or interpreter.

WRITTEN TRANSLATIONS

Good translations require more than language ability, literal or verbatim versions, and proper grammar and language use. Culturally appropriate symbols, graphics, pictures, and design, and perhaps equivalent expressions need to convey the same meaning and intent. Some translations require a software program for their writing system with the right font, diacritical marks (marks above or below a letter that indicate pronunciation), alphabet, or characters. Placement of diacritical marks must be correct, as they convey meaning.

Consider these tips for clearly understood and reliable translations:

- Engage a qualified, professional translator, preferably one trained in health issues and related vocabulary. As in English, good writing and editing, as well as proofreading for spelling, grammar, punctuation, and word usage, are essential skills. Good translators understand regional differences, dialects, slang, and idioms in both languages. The American Translators Association certifies translators (with the ATA-CT credential) for many foreign languages. Know that different writing systems—for example, Arabic, Vietnamese, and Russian—require technical abilities with the target alphabet, script, or characters. And, if respelled phonetically in the English alphabet, a single word may have multiple spellings; that happens when Mandarin characters are respelled in Pinyin (the English alphabet).
- Provide the translator with a clear version in English to remove guesswork. Avoid figures of speech, idioms, and words or phrases with connotations.

FIGURE 13.7 **Overcoming cross-cultural communication barriers**

Linguistic differences and unfamiliar accents Even if people share a language, differences in language usage (tone, speed, and volume, for example), accents, and pronunciations can cause miscommunication. Especially for those listeners with English as their second language, homophones (eg, ate/eight, here/hear, no/know, flour/flower, knead/need, weigh/way, buy/bye/by, wok/walk) and homonyms (*fast* meaning either "speedy" or "not eating," *right* meaning either "correct" or a direction) cause confusion. Be aware of different meanings for some English words in other languages; as an example, the English word *preservative* sounds like the French word *préservatif*, which means "condom."

TIP: Speak slowly, simply, and clearly. Check for meaning. For written communication, use visuals and perhaps basic vocabulary and simple sentence structure. Get help from a cultural informant, if needed.

Jargon, idiomatic expressions, and slang that are unfamiliar and differ from literal meanings

TIP: Use plain English; for example, use the word *chances* instead of *risks*, and say "what you eat and drink" instead of "food intake." If confusing terms are inadvertently used, rephrase with simpler, unambiguous wording.

Humor that's misinterpreted, perhaps confusing, and possibly offensive

TIP: Speak and write in a positive tone without trying to be funny.

Topics that are taboo, off limits, or emotionally difficult for the target population

TIP: Learn about the culture before communicating. Ask a cultural informant to help avoid or address difficult topics and to review the work before presenting it.

Assuming sameness or universal behavior or values, including literacy level and information retention (eg, "We *all* care about __, so __.")

TIP: Listen to understand, not to preach or defend nutrition advice or a point of view. Try to understand how messages mesh with the values and norms of the target culture specifically. Stay flexible; try a different learning style if needed.

Attempting to impose conformity without addressing individuality (eg, "What's best for everyone is what's best for an individual.")

TIP: Remember that everyone in a culture is an individual.

Assuming understanding, without checking for meaning

TIPS: Know that "yes," "maybe," or a nod can mean many things, including "no," "I hear you but don't understand," or "I'm being polite." Avoid questions with "yes" or "no" answers, such as "Do you understand?"

Whether spoken or written, use the "teach-back" technique to check for understanding. Ask listeners to rephrase. Write down critical information, perhaps numbers, to ensure understanding. Provide premade information sheets, perhaps in the native language if receivers can read. Use stories and examples when possible.

Ask listeners to explain what a word means to them before using it. Words may have connotations that differ from what's intended; for example, the words *power* and *action* may remind some people of threats in their life experiences.

Communicate at the appropriate literacy level. Graphics are important for those who cannot read English. After all, meaning comes from more than words.

Talking louder or speaking too fast, even when English is the shared language

TIPS: Adjust tone and style. Talk slower, not louder, especially when the content and context of the message is unfamiliar. Take turns talking and listening to check for understanding.

Misperceived or misunderstood spoken language, expressions, and connotations, as well as nonverbal cues or graphic elements

TIPS: Ask a cultural informant for help. In spoken language, learn to read and appropriately use nonverbal gestures. Be especially cautious of physical space and touch; ask permission before using touch as a caring gesture.

- Be clear about the right reading level of the translation for the target audience. Also, mainstream translations, as in "broadcast Spanish," may not work for everyone. For example, the word *orange*, for the fruit, translates to *naranja* for many who speak Spanish, but Puerto Ricans typically say *china*.
- Validate the translation with native speakers, even if it was done by a skilled translator or if you are skilled in the translated language. Think of it as peer review, best done by one or more nutrition experts who are native speakers. Not only do they know the subject matter, they also know the language nuances of their culture.
- Double-check for accuracy by translating back to English from the target language. For example, taking this step would clarify that the Spanish *intoxicado* doesn't mean *intoxicated*, but instead means "ingesting something that made one sick."
- As an aid for food shopping, have the translator put English words in parentheses after the translated wording. That way a non-English speaker can find the right items in the supermarket. That's especially important for buying infant food and formula, foods without allergens or gluten, or medications and supplements.
- Design for the target culture. Be aware of symbolism in certain images, colors, and shapes. Make sure graphics are culturally relevant and appropriate. Avoid images that suggest stereotypes, such as sombreros in Spanish translations. Some graphics, such as chopsticks placed upright in a rice bowl, are considered socially insensitive.
- Consider side-by-side translations with English on one side—but only if the imagery, design, and space work for both. Some languages use more words or characters than English for the same message. For example, Spanish often takes 20% more space.
- Don't trust a translation app. It can be a useful survival tool for tourists, perhaps to find a bathroom or taxi, order from a menu, or make a purchase, but for nutrition or health messages, an app translation could result in a convoluted message.

ORAL INTERPRETATIONS

Many skills required for good translations apply to interpreting spoken language. Skilled oral interpreters are proficient in both languages (and perhaps dialects), are able to work under stress during the interaction, and are culturally competent in the cultures and linguistics of both the speaker and the target audience. They are good listeners and speakers, able to interpret accurately without their own agenda and committed to confidentiality. Being trained in health, perhaps nutrition, is an asset. Interpreters certified by professional and government agencies often have a higher level of proficiency (as established by the National Council on Interpreting in Health Care) than simply being bilingual.

Can family members serve as interpreters? Not always. Family dynamics and issues of personal or family privacy can be problematic. Even if family members are bilingual, they may lack the knowledge and training to adequately interpret food, nutrition, and health issues. However, with an interpreter, they can provide clarity and follow-through.

When working with a qualified interpreter:

- Meet beforehand. Review the goals of the interaction, the key points and content, any technical terms, phrasing and pacing, and any written materials. Ask about appropriate greetings, protocols, how someone should be addressed, and the correct way to pronounce names. Learn basic words or phrases.
- Use visuals and written materials when possible. Check ahead to make sure they are culturally appropriate and match the audience's literacy level. Write out numbers.
- Speak slowly, speak clearly, pause appropriately. One or two sentences at a time is enough. This gives the interpreter enough time to share important information.
- Use plain English and simple sentences with just one or two ideas. Avoid figures of speech, idioms, professional jargon, and words or phrases with connotations.
- Be aware of body language. An audience will "see" what communicators say as they talk; use appropriate nonverbal cues to convey meaning. (Check ahead to avoid offense or misunderstanding.) Watch listeners to check for comprehension; direct—or indirect—eye contact may not indicate understanding.

⬤ Cultural Appreciation, Not Appropriation[25]

Global and regional cuisines are trendy topics for culinary classes, recipe development, blogs posts, and social media posts. Although often unintentional, communicators addressing cultural topics can unintentionally engage in cultural appropriation—or more accurately *mis*appropriation—especially when addressing foodways derived from other cultures.

Cambridge Dictionary defines *cultural appropriation* as "the act of taking or using things from a culture that is not your own, especially without showing an understanding or respect for this culture." Cultural appropriation is typically carried out by members of a more dominant (privileged) group who, for their own benefit, adopt or take elements of a culture (eg, cuisine or food traditions) from those who have been systemically marginalized or oppressed. This practice is often seen as offensive and degrading. For example, adapting a culture's recipe for a clean eating article or blog may be misperceived as degrading the traditional version as dirty.

Words matter! Although different from cultural appropriation, even the word *ethnic* (eg, ethnic food, ethnic cuisine, ethnic restaurant) may be misperceived because the term groups minority or less dominant cultures as "other" or "different." As it relates to food, *ethnic* is an outdated term: the category is too large to have meaning. In truth, every food and cuisine (in fact, every person) is ethnic! Ethnicity is shared cultural heritage.

So, can you write, talk, and share recipes as an outsider to a culture? Yes—if you take the time to be well-informed, to communicate with respect and proper context, and to give credit where due. Know that cultural exchange differs from appropriation. Exchange results in mutual sharing and lacks the characteristic power dynamic.

To honor regional and global foodways and reduce the chance of cultural appropriation, take time to identify a topic's context and complexities. Avoid overgeneralizing cultural, regional, and familial foodways. Refer to the Academy of Nutrition and Dietetics's cultural competency materials and find information from Member Interest Groups. And ask yourself the following questions:

- Am I celebrating the topic and respecting its origins, or am I trying to *own* it?
- Am I jumping on a trend bandwagon, or am I genuinely interested in the food's historical and cultural connections?
- Have I sought original sources and engaged a knowledgeable cultural informant?
- Have I sought and gained an understanding of the history and context of the food or topic?
- Have I given credit where due, acknowledged the origin of a food or custom, and placed the topic in its proper context, perhaps in a recipe headnote? (For example, instead of "Mexican hummus," you might write "Fiesta Bean Spread, inspired by Mexican flavors and Middle Eastern hummus.")
- Have I unintentionally used any terms (eg, "healthier" or "cleaner") that are perceived as detrimental, inflammatory, or falling out of favor or that have lost their meaning?
- Will any communities be negatively affected or confused by the intentions of my topic?
- Could my own status within those communities be impacted by my work?

Skilled interpreters probably can read nonverbal cues well.
- Talk directly to the audience, not the interpreter. If the cultural practice requires speakers to avert their gaze, the interpreter should do so also.
- Keep a positive facial expression. Skip humor, word plays, and idioms; they don't translate easily.

- Avoid modifying an English word or phrase to create a word or phrase in the target language. This could create a word that isn't intended. For example, adding the letters *ada* to the English word *embarrass* in an attempt to express this same sentiment in Spanish leads to an embarrassing mistake, because "embarrassada" sounds like the Spanish *embarazada*, which means "pregnant"!

Conversely, some non-English words sound like English but have different meanings.

- Check for understanding to avoid misinterpretation, but not with a yes or no question. For example, "Did I understand correctly *that* …?" (not "Did you understand?").
- For group presentations, provide visuals such as slideshows in the target language. Give the audience enough time to hear and see. If two screens are available, provide one in English and one in the translated language, especially for a different writing system, such as Mandarin or Arabic.

Why a Sensitivity Reader Is a Valued Cultural Informant[a]

As a nutrition communicator, you frequently address audiences from cultures that are different from yours. Even with the best intent and careful work, avoiding cultural inaccuracies, misrepresentations, or problematic language can pose challenges. Not only do words, phrases, and themes need attention, so do illustrations and images.

A sensitivity review (sometimes called diversity reading) can help prevent you from accidentally introducing potentially offensive material due to unconscious bias, overgeneralizing, lack of knowledge, or even the misguided application of good intent. When communicating about a culture that isn't your own, especially an often marginalized demographic, a sensitivity review is as important as your nutrition content review.

Sensitivity readers are commonly used with fiction writing when authors write about groups they don't belong to. But these readers are also valuable assets in developing and writing content for nonfiction books and other forms of health and nutrition communication. As cultural informants, sensitivity readers can help ensure accurate representation and point out unintentionally insensitive or incorrect portrayals of race, sexuality, gender, religion, physical and mental disabilities, and other demographic portrayals. So much that's hidden in the cultural iceberg analogy may be unknown to you—sensitivity readers can lower the water level. (See Figure 13.1 on page 200.)

If you are working with a professional publication team, your editor may enlist the skills of a sensitivity reader. Cultural informants who are members of the potential audience may provide important informal feedback, too, especially for self-published or consumer information. Even if you are part of the target audience, review by one or more sensitivity readers can be invaluable. The reason? Even within a cultural group, each person has their own individual experiences and viewpoints that make up their unique cultural identity.

To engage and work effectively with sensitivity readers, consider the following:

- Involve more than one sensitivity reader if possible, as each reader has different experiences. A single reader may not have all the answers you need or represent all subgroups within a culture.
- Identify readers who have both academic knowledge and personal experience with the target culture, if possible.
- Nurture and respect your relationship, as you do with other cultural informants.
- Like translators and interpreters, recognize that sensitivity readers provide professional services. Address appropriate compensation or reciprocity with them at the start.
- Learn with an open mind as you work together. Their guidance will help ensure trust in you from your target audience.

[a] Note that this chapter was reviewed by a sensitivity reader.

Effective Nutrition Communication Is Tailored for the Target Culture

1 Culture shapes nearly every food, lifestyle, and health decision and behavior. Effective cross-cultural communication requires understanding of and respect for the target culture. Tailored nutrition communication is more effective than "generic" messages for a mainstream audience.

2 The term *culture* refers to the cumulative and commonly held characteristics that distinguish one group of people from another. Cultures and their subcultures are defined by far more than ethnicity, nationality, and race; gender, age, and social status are among the demographics that contribute to cultural identity. Everyone is an individual within his or her culture.

3 Some cultural attributes are obvious; most are hidden. Cultural competence requires an awareness and understanding of hidden cultural values, attitudes, and norms. Culture impacts social interactions as well as cognitive and communication styles.

4 Becoming culturally competent is a process, progressing from ethnocentrism to ethnorelativism. While generalizations may lead to further learning, stereotyping, prejudice, and unconscious bias are barriers to cross-cultural communication.

5 Learning about cultural differences starts with an awareness of one's own culture. Although travel, reading, and research provide insights, cultural immersion and cultural informants can reveal hidden attributes. Effective cross-cultural communication comes from building trusted relationships and cultural competence.

6 Effective cross-cultural nutrition communication depends on collaboration with the community, professionals, and grassroots organizations that understand how the target culture impacts food and health behavior. In English or another language, culturally appropriate nutrition communication must reflect concepts and imagery that's accepted and understood by the target culture. When communicating in a different language is necessary, qualified translators and interpreters are invaluable.

RESOURCES

Books

Brown-Riggs C, Jones J. *Diabetes Guide to Enjoying Food of the World.* Academy of Nutrition and Dietetics; 2017.

Payne RK. *Framework for Understanding Poverty: A Cognitive Approach.* 6th ed. aha! Process; 2019.

Contento IR. Working with different population groups. In: *Nutrition Education: Linking Research, Theory, and Practice.* 3rd ed. Jones & Bartlett Learning; 2016:438-466.

Cultural Competency for Nutrition Professionals. Academy of Nutrition and Dietetics; 2015.

Durbala P, Kurko MJ. *Academy of Nutrition and Dietetics Pocket Guide to Spanish for the Nutrition Professional.* 3rd ed. Academy of Nutrition and Dietetics; 2018.

Goody CM, Drago D. *Cultural Food Practices.* American Dietetic Association; 2010.

Hurn B, Tomalin B. *Cross-Cultural Communication: Theory and Practice.* Palgrave Macmillan; 2013.

Klinger SM, Brogan K. *Hispanic Family Nutrition: Complete Counseling Kit.* Academy of Nutrition and Dietetics; 2016.

Substance Abuse and Mental Health Services Administration. *A Treatment Improvement Protocol: Improving Cultural Competence.* US Deptartment of Health and Human Services; 2014.

Swihart DL, Martin RL. *Cultural Religious Competence in Clinical Practice.* StatPearls [Internet]. US National Library of Medicine, February 17, 2020. www.ncbi.nlm.nih.gov/books /NBK493216.

Professional Groups

Academy of Nutrition and Dietetics Member Interest Groups (MIGs): www.eatrightpro.org /membership/academy-groups/member-interest -groups

International Affiliate of the Academy of Nutrition and Dietetics: https://eatrightinternational.org

Other Resources

Center for Medicare Education, Developing culturally appropriate Medicare education materials: [issue brief]. 2001;2(4).

Eliot C, Adams RJ, Sockalingam S. Communication patterns and assumptions of differing cultural groups in the United States: www.awesomelibrary.org/multiculturaltoolkit-patterns .html

Food Insights: Chapter 27: cultural competence in a multicultural world. Community Tool Box website. Published 2017. https://ctb.ku.edu/en/table-of -contents/culture/cultural-competence

Food and Agriculture Organization of the United Nations: Food-based dietary guidelines. www.fao.org /nutrition/education/food-dietary-guidelines/en

Georgetown University National Center for Cultural Competence: https://nccc.georgetown.edu

Godoy M. Why Hunting Down "Authentic Ethnic Food" Is a Loaded Proposition: The Salt: What's on Your Plate. www.npr.org/sections/thesalt/2016/04 /09/472568085/why-hunting-down-authentic-ethnic -food-is-a-loaded-proposition

Health Information Translations website: healthinfotranslations.org

Health Resources and Services Administration. Culture, language, and health literacy: https://hrsa .gov/cultural-competence/index.html

McCann S. The Cultural Appropriation of Food: Groundviews blog, Sound Ground, www.solid-ground .org/cultural-appropriation-of-food

University of Washington, "Cultures": ethnoMED. ethnomed.org/culture

US Department of Health and Human Services, Think cultural health: https://thinkculturalhealth .hhs.gov

US Department of Health and Human Services, Office of Minority Health. National standards for culturally and linguistically appropriate services in health and health care: a blueprint for advancing and sustaining CLAS policy and practic: Published April 2013. www.thinkculturalhealth.hhs.gov/pdfs /EnhancedCLASStandardsBlueprint.pdf

REFERENCES

1. Sanjur D. *Social and Cultural Perspectives in Nutrition.* Prentice-Hall; 1982.
2. AFS Intercultural Programs. Intercultural learning terminology. *Intercultural Link*. 2012. Accessed May 8, 2020. https://afs.org/education /intercultural-learning-for-afs-and-friends
3. AFS Intercultural Programs. Concepts and theories of culture. *Intercultural Link*. December 3, 2015. May 8, 2020. https://afs.org/education /intercultural-learning-for-afs-and-friends
4. Arrendondo P, Toporek E, Brown S, et al. Operationalization of the multicultural counseling competencies. *J Multicult Couns Devel*. 1996;24:42-78. doi:10.1002/j.2161-1912.1996 .tb00288.x
5. Payne RK. *A Framework for Understanding Poverty: A Cognitive Approach.* 6th ed. aha! Process; 2019.
6. Setiloane KT. Beyond the Melting Pot and Salad Bowl Views of Cultural Diversity: Advancing Cultural Diversity Education of Nutrition Educators. Society for Nutrition Education and Behavior Journal Club webinar. April 9, 2018.
7. Hofstede G. *Culture's Consequences: Comparing Values, Behaviors, Institutions, and Organizations Across Nations.* 2nd ed. Sage Publications; 2001.
8. Timm JT. The relationship between culture and cognitive style: a review of the evidence and some reflections for the classroom. *Midwest Educ Res.* 1999;Spring:36-44.
9. Liu M. Verbal communication styles and culture. *Oxford Research Encyclopedia.* Published November 2016. doi:10.1093/acrefore /9780190228613.013.162
10. Hurn B, Tomalin B. *Cross-Cultural Communication: Theory and Practice.* Palgrave Macmillan; 2013.
11. Matthews, Peter. *Concise Oxford Dictionary of Linguistics.* Oxford University Press; 2007.
12. Knapp ML, Hall JA, Horgan TG. *Nonverbal Communication in Human Interaction.* 8th ed. Cengage Learning; 2013.
13. Portland State University. Multicultural Topics in Communication Sciences and Disorders. The Navajo Culture. Accessed July 23, 2020. www.pdx.edu/multicultural-topics -communication-sciences-disorders/the -navajo-culture
14. Hurn B, Tomalin B. *Cross-Cultural Communication: Theory and Practice.* Palgrave Macmillan; 2013: 22-23.
15. Stein K. Navigating cultural competency: in preparation for an expected standard in 2010. *J Am Diet Assoc.* 2009;109(10):1676-1688. doi:10.1016/j.jada.2009.08.019
16. Bennett MJ. Towards ethnorelativism: a developmental model of intercultural sensitivity. In: Paige M, ed. *Education for the Intercultural Experience.* Intercultural Press; 1993:21-71.

17. AFS Intercultural Programs. Generalizations & stereotypes. *Intercultural Link*. 2011. Accessed May, 2020. https://afs.org/education/intercultural -learning-for-afs-and-friends

18. University of California, San Francisco, Office of Outreach and Diversity. Strategies to address unconscious bias. Accessed February 8, 2019. https://diversity.ucsf.edu/resources/strategies -address-unconscious-bias

19. Sanjur D. *Social and Cultural Perspectives in Nutrition*. Prentice-Hall; 1985:321-321.

20. Goody CM, Drago D. *Cultural Food Practices*. American Dietetic Association; 2010.

21. Central Vancouver Island Multicultural Society. Cultural competence self-assessment checklist. Accessed February 8, 2019. www.colorado edinitiative.org/wp-content/uploads/2015/10 /cultural-competence-self-assessment-checklist.pdf

22. AFS Intercultural Programs. Tools to suspend judgment. Published 2016. Accessed May 8, 2020. https://afs.org/education/intercultural -learning-for-afs-and-friends

23. US Department of Health and Human Services, Office of Minority Health. National standards for culturally and linguistically appropriate services (CLAS) in health and health care. Accessed May 2, 2020. https://thinkculturalhealth.hhs.gov/assets /pdfs/EnhancedNationalCLASStandards.pdf

24. ILR skill level descriptions for translation performance. Interagency Language Roundtable website. Accessed February 8, 2019. http://govtilr .org/Skills/AdoptedILRTranslationGuidelines .htm

25. Redmond M, Al Bochi R, Brown-Riggs C, Ray K. Global Appreciation or Cultural Appropriation? Avoiding Insensitive Pitfalls on Food Blogs. Presented at: Food and Nutrition Conference and Expo, October 28, 2019; Philadelphia, PA.

CHAPTER 14

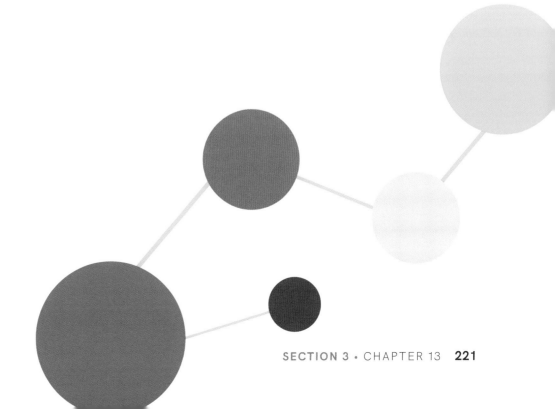

Effective Communication Is Tailored for Different Ages

Barbara J. Mayfield, MS, RDN, FAND
Arielle "Dani" Lebovitz, MS, RDN, CSSD, CDE
and Kristin Cunningham, MHA, RD, LD

"Nutrition communicators who demonstrate a desire to understand the interests and needs of their audience—even if they are not in the same age group, life stage, or generation—will have a greater likelihood of connecting with the audience, fostering a positive environment, and achieving their communication goals."

> *"Intellectual growth should commence at birth and cease only at death."* —ALBERT EINSTEIN

Introduction

Effective nutrition communication is audience-focused. However, communicators are challenged with understanding and accounting for the multitude of ways audiences differ. Chapter 13 explored the importance of understanding cultural differences. This chapter examines tailoring communication based on age and stage of life. Assessing an audience's age-related or life stage–related knowledge and cognitive abilities, values and worldviews, experiences, skills, and more enables the nutrition communicator to design and deliver messages that resonate with an audience and meet its members' unique needs.

Nutrition communicators who demonstrate a desire to understand the interests and needs of their audience—even if they are not in the same age group, life stage, or generation—will have a greater likelihood of connecting with the audience, fostering a positive environment, and achieving their communication goals. Make it a goal to follow the advice of Theodore Roosevelt: "No one cares how much you know until they know how much you care."

This chapter answers four questions:

- How can nutrition professionals communicate effectively with children of various ages?
- How can nutrition professionals communicate effectively with adults of various ages and stages of life?
- How can nutrition professionals communicate with adults of different generations?
- How can communication be adapted to fit the audience and setting?

Experienced nutrition communicators understand the most effective means of reaching their target audience is by having a greater understanding of the audience's needs and values. A well-designed nutrition communication plan considers not only age but also developmental stages, life stages, and generational cohorts. This chapter provides a road map for age-appropriate, life stage–appropriate, and generationally appropriate strategies for effective communication.

How Can Nutrition Professionals Communicate Effectively with Children of Various Ages?

Nutrition communication with children has tremendous potential for lifelong impact.[1] Consider how the habits formed in childhood may persist into adulthood, not to mention that health in childhood impacts lifelong health.[2-5] Well-crafted messages can provide foundational knowledge of food and nutrition, promote positive habits, and build healthy attitudes about food, eating, health, and body image. However, a common mantra is a reminder that "Children are not miniature adults."[6] Not only do they have different needs for nutrition messages, they have different capabilities for learning.

Tailor Goals and Strategies to Child Development

Understanding children's development at various ages is critical for determining how to effectively communicate with an audience of young people. Figure 14.1 (page 222) identifies trademarks of each developmental stage, communication goals, and strategies for effectively communicating with children of preschool age through high school age.

Translate Principles into Practice

As children progress from preschool through high school, several hallmarks of development inform strategies for effective communication. These hallmarks include a progression from concrete to abstract thinking; a transition from learning primarily through active, multisensory approaches to interactive, discussion-based learning; and a shift from viewing the teacher as a trusted authority and guide for discovery-based learning to a more self- and peer-centered focus for motivating and directing learning. The activities in Box 14.1, each intended to reinforce the concepts of MyPlate, illustrate the principles identified in Figure 14.1 put into practice by age of participants.

How Can Nutrition Professionals Communicate Effectively with Adults of Various Ages and Stages of Life?

Effective communication with adults recognizes the existence of predictable and evidence-based similarities as well as differences. Adult audiences share several core characteristics that are important to account for when designing communication. Additionally, adult audiences exhibit age-related

FIGURE 14.1 **Effective communication with children of various ages**[a]

	Preschool Audiences	Elementary School Age Audiences (Grades K-5)	Middle and High School Age Audiences (Grades 6-12)
Trademarks of the developmental stage	• Short attention span • Eager to learn • Able to categorize and classify items • Advance when challenged just beyond current level of mastery	• Curious • Trust and respect adults • Concrete thinkers • Progressively gain more independence throughout this span of years	• Interest in body image • Strongly influenced by peers • Less trustful of adults • Value independence • Beginning to think more abstractly
Communication goals	• Meet multiple learning styles • Engage the senses • Allow all students to contribute • Capture attention with fun, positive, and motivating style	• Allow children to share their own ideas and understandings about health • Deliver content in a manner that meets the developmental needs of the age group • Provide clear instructions for activities, worksheets, and other assignments	• Provide skill-building opportunities • Focus on motivations that are meaningful to adolescents • Include opportunities for self-directed learning • Encourage critical thinking • Address all viewpoints related to health with respect and sensitivity
Strategies for effective communication	• Role-play • Songs • Stories • Food preparation • Gardening • Sorting • Movement • Play • Games	• Experiments • Taste tests • Demonstrations involving food • Movement • Contests • Characters • Computer games	• Media literacy activities • Focus on choices made when eating out • Taste tests • Debates • Research to examine the validity of popular nutrition claims • Produce short, informative videos for peers

[a] Adapted from references 7 through 11.

and life course–related differences over the span of adulthood, not to mention a myriad of individual and cultural differences. Food and nutrition professionals who understand and recognize these similarities and differences will more successfully communicate with adult audiences.

Understand the Adult Learner

Adults seek to learn new information to meet a perceived need and focus their attention on messages that help them solve problems and achieve goals. A primary way adults learn is through life experience. An effective communicator identifies needs, assists adults in processing experiences, and provides options for solving problems. In considering communication with adult audiences, recognize that adults generally seek to be a partner in learning rather than a passive recipient.

The study of adult learning is grounded in several adult-learning theories, including

---

BOX 14.1

Translate Principles into Practice—A MyPlate Example[12]

Preschool Audiences

The nutrition communicator sets up a play grocery store and restaurant using food and drink images as groceries and menu items. Each child is assigned a role; options include grocery store shoppers, employees, cashiers, restaurant employees, and restaurant chefs. The store is organized by MyPlate food groups to make it easier for the children to identify which items belong in each food group.

When playing the role of shopper, the student will fill a shopping bag with one item from each food group. Shoppers check out with the cashier and deliver the groceries to the restaurant. Chefs prepare the meal by arranging the items on a plate and delivering it to the table. Restaurant employees set the tables with place mats, silverware, and napkins and bus tables by removing dishes and returning food items to the store. Grocery store employees restock the shelves by returning the foods to the proper areas. Roles rotate after each round. This activity addresses many principles outlined in Figure 14.1, including categorizing items, allowing all students to contribute, and engaging children through role-play, sorting, and play.

Elementary School Age Audiences

The nutrition communicator sets up a MyPlate Parfait Buffet for children to construct a parfait containing one ingredient from each MyPlate food group. Sample ingredients include yogurt (dairy group), cereal (grains group), carrot shreds (vegetables group), blueberries (fruits group), and sunflower seeds (protein group). This activity can integrate many skills: measuring, following or writing a recipe; handwashing; food safety; food tasting; and food photography. It addresses many of the principles outlined in Figure 14.1, including working independently, engaging children through taste tests, and food demonstrations.

Middle and High School Age Audiences

Participants evaluate popular diets using MyPlate. The nutrition communicator displays advertisements for popular diets from media sources, such as print, television, YouTube, or a billboard image. The students work in small groups to evaluate one diet, researching details of the diet on the internet or using documents provided by the communicator. They compare the diet to the concepts of MyPlate. The students also consider the role advertising plays in the diet's popularity.

Each group selects and addresses a few questions from the National Association for Media Literacy Education's "Key Questions to Ask When Analyzing Media Messages,"[12] such as, Who paid for this?, Who might be harmed by this message? And how credible is this (and how do you know)? Groups share their findings and perspectives, with guidance from the nutrition communicator. This activity addresses many of the principles outlined in Figure 14.1, including abstract thinking, skill building, self-directed learning, sharing viewpoints about health topics in a respectful environment, engaging youth through media literacy activities, and using research to examine the validity of nutrition claims.

andragogy,[13] experiential learning,[14] self-directed learning,[15] multiple intelligences,[16] and transformative learning.[17] The characteristics of adult learners described in the following paragraphs are based on Malcolm Knowles's assumptions about adult learners as well as the work of others.[13,18-20]

CHARACTERISTICS OF ADULT LEARNERS

Self-directed Adults no longer depend on teachers to determine what is important to learn. Adults decide what is important to them, based on not only their values and priorities but also on their current situation in life. The effective communicator finds out what is important to the audience before developing nutrition messages.

Experts on themselves Adults have a wealth of life experience that impacts learning. Past experiences can serve as either barriers or motivators to learning and change. Food and nutrition professionals are the subject matter experts, but to be effective, communicators need to honor adults as the experts about themselves.

Skeptical Adults need to validate information and try it out for themselves before accepting it as truth. Encourage adult audiences to ask questions and search for the answers. Provide them with reputable sources to locate the evidence they need as well as the means to apply it to their situation. For example, if an audience believes fresh vegetables are always more nutritious than frozen or canned, provide resources that explain the facts, rather than just stating that their belief is incorrect. Help them use this knowledge to make the best purchasing decisions.

Pragmatic and problem-centered Adults seek information that is immediately useful to solve their problems. Provide adult audiences with practical and realistic action steps to put information into practice to meet current perceived needs.

Internally motivated Adult learning is voluntary and based on internal motivators. Learning is one of many demands competing for an adult's attention. If learning doesn't meet an adult's perceived needs and lead to desired results, he or she may decide to opt out of the learning situation.

Autonomous Not only do adults decide what they will learn, they take responsibility for what they do as a result of that learning. The effective communicator provides audience members with potential solutions, assists with problem solving, and then allows audience members the autonomy to determine what to do with that knowledge.

Use Effective Approaches to Adult Learning

Effective approaches to adult learning take into account the characteristics just described. The following principles are based on the writings of Jane Vella,[21] Joye Norris,[22] and Patricia Cranton,[20] among others. These educators provide the following useful insights into how to communicate effectively with the adult learner:

- Needs assessments involve the full participation of the adult audience.
- Prior experience and learning is acknowledged and built on.
- Learning takes place in a warm, welcoming environment that promotes feeling safe to learn and participate.
- Mutual respect exists between teacher and learners and among learners. Open dialogue and active listening are encouraged and practiced.
- Learning is sequenced and reinforced, encompasses all learning styles, and promotes desired feelings and actions as well as knowledge.
- Adults use open-ended questions to learn by doing and reflecting.
- Learning is relevant and immediately useful.
- Engagement of learners in partner and small-group interactions and activities promotes learning.
- The teacher or communicator assumes the role of facilitator, coach, or mentor, not lecturer. In fact, the communicator is a colearner—building an authentic relationship with the audience and thus allowing learners to also be coteachers.

Effective approaches for presenting messages and promoting learning will be further described in Part II of this book, Nutrition Communication Is Designed and Delivered with Excellence.

With the knowledge of these adult learning principles, the communicator can now focus on potential differences within and between adult audiences based on life stage and chronological age. Figure 14.2 illustrates four stages of adulthood.

	Young or Emerging Adulthood (Age 18–30)	Early Adulthood (Age 30–40)	Middle Adulthood (Age 40–64)	Late Adulthood (Age 65+)
Understanding life stage	• Leaving family of origin • Becoming independent—advanced schooling or training • Entering the workforce • May include marriage and parenthood	• Settling down • Increasing responsibilities • Main period for parenthood • Establishing a career • Busy schedule	• Career is set • Generally more financially stable • Children leaving home or already "empty nesters" • Caretaking of parents may begin, or parental loss • Greater time for leisure, eating out • Planning for retirement	• Retirement • Volunteering • Grand-parenting • Relationships important • Recognition that life is finite • Sense of purpose
Health orientation and concerns	• May be motivated by convenience, price, and feelings over health	• Motivated to provide well for family, to have healthy children, and to be a role model	• Motivated to maintain youthfulness	• Motivated to maintain health and avoid or manage disease and age-related concerns
Nutrition communication goals	• Knowledge focused on current needs • Independent food choices • Promote healthy, cheap, and convenient foods • Build skills in food preparation	• Knowledge of child nutrition and development • Promote family meals and teach meal planning • Family-friendly food choices that are affordable, quick, and healthy	• Knowledge of nutrition to promote health and avoid disease • Healthful, economical, and pleasurable meal preparation at home and eating out	• Knowledge of nutrition to maintain health and avoid age-related concerns • Easy meal plans and food preparation for one or two people
Effective strategies	• Demonstrate empathy • Provide choices and alternatives • Make healthy eating delicious and the easy choice • Teach ways to save on food • Food tasting and demonstrations • Make it fun and entertaining • Be available on their time—online or on demand	• Demonstrate empathy • Tailor information to ages of children • Discussions and problem solving, parents sharing • Make healthy eating delicious and the easy choice • Teach ways to save on food • Provide tools, tips, recipes • Food tasting and demonstrations • Make it practical and useful • Provide child care as well as convenient timing	• Demonstrate empathy • Connect information provided to health concerns • Make healthy eating delicious and the easy choice • Teach ways to save on food • Food tasting and demonstrations • Make it worthwhile • Fit their schedule	• Demonstrate empathy • Target health concerns • Acknowledge limitations (vision, mobility, chewing, etc) • Make healthy eating delicious and the easy choice • Teach ways to save on food • Accommodate long-standing preferences • Food tasting and demonstrations • Daytime or early evening programs

[a] Adapted from references 23 through 25.

The ages and stages are general composites intended to describe common traits.

Definitions and age ranges vary considerably. Some authors and researchers define adulthood as starting after age 21. Parenthood may occur earlier, later, or not at all. Adults who do not have children do not share the same challenges as parents, but they still tend to be more settled, responsible, and busier than people in the young-adult stage that comes first. Midlife, or middle adulthood, may begin earlier or extend later and is often broken into early middle age and late middle age. Many adults do not consider themselves seniors or place themselves in late adulthood until age 70 or 80.

Keep in mind that each audience and audience member may or may not match these generalizations. The communication goals and strategies listed are useful guidelines based on the traits common to each life stage.

A common challenge in communicating with adults is motivating them to engage with the message or program because of the many demands competing for their attention. The Words of Experience box illustrates how parents can be motivated to participate in a program by the desire to provide for the needs and interests of their children.

How Can Nutrition Professionals Communicate with Adults of Different Generations?

Cultural, socioeconomic, and demographic information, such as age and gender, provide important insights for the creation of content for nutrition communication. However, effective communicators should also consider needs, values, attitudes, and methods of communication from a generational perspective. This involves understanding an audience's generational *cohort segments*, which are

 WORDS OF EXPERIENCE

Reaching and Teaching Parents by Reaching and Teaching Children

Barbara J. Mayfield, MS, RDN, FAND

I worked as a nutrition educator in the Special Supplemental Nutrition Program for Women, Infants, and Children (WIC) for 20 years. A pillar of this program, and my favorite part of working for WIC, was providing nutrition education to participants. However, enticing parents of young children to attend classes was an ongoing challenge. As noted in Figure 14.2, parents are busy. They are motivated to solve parenting struggles and become positive role models, but they need convenient educational opportunities that offer child care. Parents find it difficult to participate in classes if their children are distracting them.

As a young parent myself at the time, I noticed that parents showed up in droves for programs at my children's schools that were for the children, but not for programs for the parents themselves. I wondered … might our WIC programs be more successful if we geared them toward children instead parents? We tried it, and yes, parents were much more willing to attend a class where their children were learning and having fun. This insight led to Kids Club being born in our small, local WIC program.

At our Kids Club classes for children, parents sat around the perimeter of the room, observing and participating. Parents learned along with their children. Not only did the parents learn about food, nutrition, and health, they learned positive ways to interact with their children, as well as fun games, stories, and songs.

From that humble beginning in the late 1980s, a US Department of Agriculture grant allowed me to develop materials for WIC programs across the country to offer classes for children. Listed in the resources section at the end of this chapter is a link to several of the lessons.

groups of people who share similar historical or social life experiences. Understanding generations is helpful for effective message creation, curation of content from respected sources, and delivery via preferred channels.

The defining moments of a generation shape an age group and can include wartime efforts, technological advancements, social unrest, and political environments. These defining moments have long-lasting effects, forming perceptions that influence the ideals, mindsets, behaviors, beliefs, motivations, desires, and priorities of generational cohorts and future cohorts.[26]

Thoughtful consideration of these unique cohorts aids practitioners in crafting audience-focused nutrition messages, garnering respected supportive content, and providing education via preferred channels that will result in both increased knowledge and positive changes in behavior.[27-29]

Understand the Generations Living Today

Communicating effectively with an adult audience requires understanding the influences of the age group, life stage, and generation to which the audience belongs. Over time, all generations experience the ages and stages of adulthood. However, they experience them in the context of different historical events, including shared experiences and enduring consequences.[26]

Exploring motivations and expectations from a generational perspective provides insight on audience needs based on their life experiences. Cohorts span a significant time frame, ranging from 15 to 20 years, which groups people into generations that share formative experiences.[26] Note that individuals are not defined solely by their life experiences and not everyone in the same cohort segment holds the same beliefs and ideals, but understanding the subtleties of generational values and motivations is beneficial.[26] Recognizing and distinguishing behaviors, attitudes, and beliefs across generations helps nutrition communicators more effectively and efficiently deliver targeted messages.[30-34]

THE TRADITIONALIST OR SILENT GENERATION (BORN BEFORE 1946)

Traditionalists came of age during the Great Depression, World War II, and postwar efforts. The backdrop of severe economic hardship and wartime efforts heavily influences their financial considerations, respect for authority, and trust in institutions.

BABY BOOMERS (BORN 1946 THROUGH 1964)

The return of soldiers after World War II led to a significant increase in birth rates and financial resources, which contributes to the descriptive label of the baby boomer cohort. Coming of age during economic prosperity, the Vietnam War, social rights movements, and the era of sex, drugs, and rock n' roll results in baby boomers questioning authority and being less concerned about saving money.[30,35]

GENERATION X (BORN 1965 THROUGH 1980)

Generation X (Gen X), often called the MTV generation, grew up in a time when child welfare was of low priority. With both parents working and focusing on their careers, divorce rates soared. As a result, children came home to empty houses and cared for and entertained themselves, and thus the term *latchkey kid* was coined.[36] Gen Xers are independent, are wary of authority, desire a strong balance between work and their personal lives, and are motivated by opportunity.

GENERATION Y OR MILLENNIALS (BORN 1981 THROUGH 1996)

Millennials, or Generation Y, are shaped by the internet, technology, and economic challenges.[30] Millennials came of age during a surge of technological advancements and easily accessible information. They are known for their ability to multitask; they remain connected 24/7; and they are often less economically independent due to debt.[37] Millennials desire instant gratification, are team-oriented, and look for work that they find meaningful.

GENERATION Z, HOMELAND GENERATION, ZOOMERS (BORN 1997 THROUGH 2012)

The generation born in and after 1997 has been called many names, including Generation Z, the iGeneration, postmillennials, and the homeland generation. This cohort is still being closely studied for further understanding as they come of age. Preliminary observations show that it is shaped by a decade of war, including the terrorist attacks on

Employ a Needs Assessment to Understand Generations[30,31,33,38,41-44]

In order to influence an audience, a communicator must identify and understand that audience. When conducting a needs assessment (see Chapter 11), consider the following questions from a generational perspective:

- What are the wants and needs of the audience members? Think about their values, goals, priorities, worries, and concerns from a generational perspective as well as their current age and life stage.

  Example: Older baby boomers, who are now also senior adults and concerned with their health, may be interested in information about staying hydrated while minimizing frequent nighttime urination. Find out what myths this generation has been taught about hydration, such as that caffeine is dehydrating, and share evidence-based guidance to help them overcome this common concern.

- To what method of teaching do they best respond? Consider the potential preferences of each generation.

  Example: Those from the traditionalist generation are more familiar with lecture-style, face-to-face presentations and favor that approach over an online format that might be preferred by members of Generations X, Y, or Z. Traditionalists may also have age-related vision or hearing impairments and learn better with live demonstrations and large-print handouts.

- What mediums or outlets are perceived as trustworthy or credible sources? Understand where audiences retrieve their information from in order to select the appropriate medium to reach them.

  Example: Generation Z may trust the opinions of their peers and appreciate on-demand, real-time engagement of social media, while traditionalists may rely on information presented in local newspapers and on television news stations. Each generation will likely gravitate toward the most prevalent information sources available during their early adulthood.

9/11; economic recession; and rapid technological advancement.[30,38,39] More uniquely diverse and the first generation of digital natives, having never lived without the internet, members of Generation Z are socially aware, value fiscal responsibility, and are reliant on technology.[38,40,41]

Remember, these generational profiles are a broad introduction to each cohort, helping to identify and explain the implications of social change and values associated with their formative experiences.[39] These characterizations are best used as a general reference. Effective nutrition communicators identify the values and needs of each unique audience. See Box 14.2 for examples of how to use a needs assessment to understand generations.

Health concerns one might attribute to generations are largely age-related. In other words, as a generation ages, their health concerns age as well. There may be some differences in health practices or concerns that are generational, which are likely related to practices and treatments that became prevalent during a generation. Keep in mind that someday Gen Z will be senior citizens and baby boomers will only be a memory.

Communicate Effectively Across Generations

Understanding generational traits and values helps communicators craft meaningful messages that are sensitive to needs and behaviors beyond those related to age. Communicating to different generations simultaneously presents a special challenge because each audience carries its own set of unique expectations and perspectives. To develop communications, minimize assumptions and use information on cohort segments as a general road map for content development.

Figure 14.3 (pages 230 to 231) identifies traits and values of each generational cohort and strategies for effective communication.

For a nutrition communicator, preparing presentations for a varied audience may seem daunting, but understanding and using the recommended strategies can help to prepare and manage expectations. For example, understanding that baby boomers and millennials question authority, a communicator may need to provide additional resources the audience can relate to from trusted sources.[44] The addition of trusted resources may also positively influence members of Generation X, who are wary of authority.[45] Because the resources that are trusted may vary by generation, understanding an audience from a generational perspective can help a communicator plan accordingly.

Employ Effective Communication Strategies

Maximize success when communicating and working across generations by considering the following:

Needs assessment Use the findings from a needs assessment to help shape a communication's style, tone, and strategy.[28,29]

Traits and experience Be aware of generational traits and life experience. Encouraging cross-generational collaboration has many advantages and opportunities to optimize message delivery and behavior change.[46] For example, both baby boomers and millennials appreciate the opportunity for teamwork and active participation, creating an optimal environment for audience engagement, community building, and reciprocal mentorship.[28,43,44,45,51]

Values Utilize what is known about the values and behaviors of each cohort to support communication efforts. Keep the audience engaged by finding opportunities to create shared values.[29,42,43]

Formality Always be respectful and match formality standards. Traditionalists may prefer formal salutations such as *Mr* or *Mrs* and their last name, while a baby boomer may be more receptive to the personal nature of using his or her first name. When in doubt, ask![30,42,43]

Authority Understand the audience's opinions about authority and communicate with that in mind. Generation X is wary of authority and prefers an informal communication style. When working with members of this generation, consider their motivating factors, such as family and personal life, and share information prioritizing that angle.[43]

Communication Consider multiple strategies that motivate and empower each unique audience. Develop a communication approach to meet these needs. For example, millennials prefer a collaborative approach with discussion and immediate feedback. To reach this population, a panel discussion with a Q&A session may be more effective than a lecture-style presentation.[28,29,42,43]

Recognition Acknowledge or provide incentives for each intended audience based on its values. As shown in Chapter 1, communication is a relational activity, and interaction is possible throughout the process. Understanding what motivates a generation can aid in establishing a process for communication that continuously provides for positive interaction, via a means available to the target audience, keeping participants interested and feeling valued.

For example, traditionalists have a desire to feel appreciated. A communicator can use this information to thank an audience for coming or to praise audience members for contributing, whether they are correct or incorrect.[30,43] Recognition programs are especially notable for nutrition education program development. Identifying motivating factors for an audience, such as certificates or small rewards for traditionalists, baby boomers, and millennials, or a monetary incentive for Generation Z, can greatly influence positive outcomes among participants.[39,42,46,48,52]

Channels Deliver messages via varied channels, or mediums for communication, as described in Chapter 1, and develop partnerships with trusted organizations and brands to maximize reach.[28,29,42]

Flexibility Be flexible. If one thing is not working, try something else.

Refer to Chapter 11 for how to conduct a needs assessment.

How Can Communication Be Adapted to Fit the Audience and Setting?

As discussed throughout this chapter, effective communication is tailored to fit an audience, which includes consideration for each unique setting. The setting can influence message delivery and set the tone. Recognizing the nuances of presenting in various locations or via various online channels will help guide the planning process and prepare for success. Begin by identifying the audience, location or medium, and available resources. Collaborate with site staff to maximize the effectiveness of a communication.

Learn as much as possible about the audience and setting in advance of the presentation. Be prepared to adapt activities, as even the most well-thought-out plans can fall through due to circumstances beyond a communicator's control. Flexibility is the key to preventing disasters.

Refer to Chapter 33 for more on logistical planning.

FIGURE 14.3 **Effective communication with generational cohorts**[a]

	Traditionalists (Born Before 1946)	Baby Boomers (1946–1964)
Traits and values	• Loyal • Dedicated • Hardworking • Patriotic • Responsible • Respect authority • Desire to feel appreciated • Motivated by tokens of recognition	• Optimistic • Competitive • Hardworking, work-centric • Team-oriented • Emphasize integrity • Question authority • Desire to make a difference • Motivated by personal recognition, promotions, or monetary rewards
Strategies for effective communication	• Formal and respectful • Recognize experience • Interactive with small amounts of information at a time	• Semiformal • Focus on process • Collaborative and team-oriented—make an emotional connection
Mediums for effective communication	• Formal social gathering • TV news stations (eg, NBC, CBS, Fox) • Local newspapers • Billboards • Magazines • Direct mail • Telephone • Internet	• Social and recognition events • Face-to-face conversations • TV • Internet • Targeted social networks and blogs • Email • Direct mail
Partnerships for communication	• Health care providers • Nursing homes • AARP • Leisure activity tie-ins such as recreation centers, libraries, community gardens, faith-based organizations, trusted websites (eg, Yahoo, Google, AOL)	• Health care providers • Community involvement • TV (eg, Weather Channel, Discovery Channel) • Trusted websites (eg, Google, Yahoo) • Magazines (eg, *Parade*, *People*, *AARP*)

[a] Adapted from references 30-34,38,40,41,43,45,47, and 48.

Generation X (1965–1980)	Generation Y/Millennials (1981–1996)	Generation Z (1997–2012)
• Independent • Pragmatic • Resourceful • Self-reliant • Entrepreneurial • Wary of authority • Desire work–life balance • Motivated by family and resources	• Global perspective • Tech-savvy • Connected 24/7 • Multitaskers • Innovative • Question authority • Desire work that has meaning • Motivated by awards and bonuses	• Socially aware • Tech-savvy • Connected socially 24/7 • Self-starters • Multiscreen users • Conscious of authority • Desire for transparency and trust • Motivated by monetary rewards and job security
• Informal • Focus on results • Direct, consistent feedback	• Informal; social • Focus on involvement and collaboration • Facilitate discussion and participation with immediate feedback	• Informal; personal • Focus on personalization and customization • Information on-demand; real-time engagement
• In-person networking and social events • Word of mouth • TV • Internet • Social networks and online chats • Email • Direct mail • Games • Cell phones	• Interactive experiences • Word of mouth • TV • Internet • Social media (eg, Facebook, Twitter, Instagram) • E-learning, podcasts, blogs, video games • Text, email, and instant messages • Direct mail catalogs • Visual multimedia communication with humor, irony, truth	• Interactive and personalized messaging via the internet with opt-in for more information • TV • Social networking (eg, Facebook, Twitter, YouTube, Instagram, Pinterest, Snapchat) • Mobile optimized messaging • Key is engagement and connecting through images
• Health care providers • Schools • Trusted websites (eg, Google) • Magazines (eg, *People*, *Parents*, *Parade*)	• Event sponsorships and electronic media • Web marketing (eg, e-cards, banner advertisements, pop-ups, sponsorship content) • Connect through parents and grandparents • Trusted websites (eg, Google, YouTube) • Magazines (eg, *People*, *American Baby*) • Nontraditional TV platforms (eg, Netflix, Hulu, Apple TV)	• Partner with trusted brands or respected celebrities • Social networking and peer-to-peer engagement • Mobile apps • Trusted websites (eg, YouTube)

School and Extracurricular Settings Reach Children and Youths

Nutrition education geared toward youths occurs in a variety of settings. Presentations that take place during instructional time in a K–12 classroom may be more formal, while other youth settings allow for more casual interactions with young audiences. Thoughtful consideration of each unique setting and the resources available can maximize the effectiveness of message delivery.

YOUTH NUTRITION EDUCATION SETTINGS

Look for the following settings:

- Early childhood centers: preschools and child care centers
- K–12 schools (during dedicated classroom instructional time): elementary classes, as well as secondary-level classes in family and consumer sciences, health, physical education, science, culinary skills, life skills, and nursing
- K–12 schools (outside of dedicated classroom instructional time): cafeteria, health fair, school garden, and gymnasium
- After-school programs: schools, child care centers, and recreation or community centers
- Other settings: farmers markets, summer camps, community gardens, and food banks

Audience considerations include:
- Access data provided by the US Department of Education, such as the National Center for Education Statistics Common Core of Data (for public schools) and Private School Universe Survey (for private schools), both of which make demographic statistics for schools available to the public.[52,53]
- To learn more about the audience at a nonschool site, it may be useful to obtain information for a school located geographically near the site.

Academic and Professional Settings Are More Formal

Nutrition communication in academic and professional settings targets adult audiences in a more formal atmosphere than most other settings. Everything from the communicator's dress to choice of delivery channels, word choice, and supporting evidence provided will reflect the formality of the setting and the education level and experience of the audience.

ACADEMIC AND PROFESSIONAL SETTINGS

You can find these settings at the following:

- Seminars and symposiums on university campuses
- Medical round tables
- Professional meetings, workshops, symposiums, and conferences
- Online versions of the aforementioned, such as webinars and video conferencing, which are discussed at the end of this section

Audience considerations include:
- University faculty: Consider the disciplines represented.
- Medical professionals: Consider the specialty areas represented and type of degree, such as medical doctor (MD), registered nurse (RN), physical therapist (PT), or occupational therapist (OT).
- Nutrition, health, education, and business professionals: Consider the disciplines represented.
- For all audiences: Consider the purpose of the gathering.

Community and Recreational Settings Are More Casual

Communication should be adapted to serve each distinct setting within the community. There are numerous recreational settings and situations in which nutrition communicators may be asked to speak, each with a unique audience demographic. Community settings tend to be more casual, with topic and tone tailored to serve the needs of the audience.[44]

COMMUNITY AND RECREATIONAL SETTINGS

Community and recreational settings include:

- Community center
- Town hall meeting
- Fitness center
- Faith-based organization
- Independent or assisted living facility

Understanding Cultural Differences and Effective Communication Strategies for Children Makes All the Difference

by Arielle "Dani" Lebovitz, MS, RDN, CSSD, CDE

A few years ago, I had the opportunity to volunteer at two orphanages and a school in Lusaka, Zambia. During that period, I worked as a health and fitness specialist for the US Air Force, but my passion was working with children, so I was excited to travel across the globe to put my education and experience to good use.

Prior to my trip, I spent time getting to know my soon-to-be audience from a socioeconomic and cultural perspective. The average life expectancy of Zambians at that time was 40.9 years; 64% of the population lived below the poverty line; and 10% (1.2 million) were orphans. Before the trip, I took time to correspond with site staff to learn more about the kids I would interact with—their ages, interests, values, and needs. I collected books to help create a children's library, school supplies for use outside of school

hours, and sports equipment such as jump ropes and Frisbees for free play. We collected donations for what proved to be the most important and sought-after item—footballs (soccer balls in the United States)—which we purchased in the country to support the local economy.

Flexibility was the key to our volunteer work. We initially spent time reading the books and interacting with the new sports equipment. However, all the children were focused on the Africa Cup of Nations because the Zambian team was in the tournament, so we adapted our education to their interests.

We spent our time talking about how foods help us grow healthy and strong to play our favorite sports, sang songs and cheers related to football, and taught new skills and played games with footballs. The Zambian team, the Copper Bullets, lovingly referred to as the "Chipolopolo Boys," won the Africa Cup of Nations for the first time in history during our visit. The kids were highly engaged in our education because they learned new skills related to something they were sincerely interested in that was relevant to their everyday lives.

Preparing for our trip by understanding the children's cultural backgrounds and needs, and then adapting our approach based on their passion for football, helped us connect with the kids in a meaningful and long-lasting way.

- Library
- Farmers market
- Retail store
- Park
- Public health event or health fair

Audience Considerations include:

- Consider members of the community who frequent the setting; consider the varying demographics, including age, education, and socioeconomic status. Site staff are a valuable resource for insight on the audience profile.
- For all audiences, consider the purpose of the gathering with respect to values and interests.

Workplace Settings Have Unique Opportunities and Challenges

Nutrition communications in workplace settings have unique opportunities and challenges as audiences may vary in formality, education, and interest. Whether educating a group of sheet metal workers on an assembly line or executives as part of a corporate wellness program, effective communicators match the environment and audience needs to set the tone. For worksite wellness, flexibility is key—tailor education to the employees of each worksite.

WORKPLACE SETTINGS

You can find workplace setting at the following:

- Businesses and offices, both small and large (eg, a dry cleaner, a power plant, a Fortune 500 company)
- Hospitals or doctors' offices

Audience Considerations include:

- For employees of a worksite, consider demographics and occupation.
- Site staff are a valuable resource for insight on an audience profile.

Online Settings Allow for Greater Flexibility

Online settings for health communication provide an opportunity to target a wide variety of audiences. With the emergence of e-health for patient-provider communication in addition to webinars and podcasts, online venues may be formal for academic or patient education or casual for a community audience. The formality of communication is determined by the purpose and should be tailored for the intended audience.[54] Refer to Chapters 29, 30, and 31 for more information about online communication.

This chapter has explored how to communicate effectively with all audiences from preschoolers to senior citizens as well as how to examine the various settings in which audiences are reached. Understanding audience characteristics common to the ages, life stages, and generations represented allows nutrition communicators to tailor messages in meaningful ways that address each audience's unique needs, values, and experiences. The Words of Experience box on page 233 illustrates how knowing an audience from multiple perspectives is essential. In addition to assessing factors related to age, consider cultural influences and behavior change constructs that serve as motivators and barriers to learning and change.

KEY POINTS

Effective Communication Is Tailored for Different Ages

1. Well-designed nutrition communication is tailored to the audience by assessing age-related or life stage–related knowledge, cognitive abilities, and values. By understanding different needs and capabilities for learning, educators can craft effective messages that both increase knowledge and influence positive changes in behavior.

2. Nutrition communication with children has tremendous potential for providing foundational knowledge of food and nutrition, promoting positive habits, and building healthy attitudes about food, eating, health, and body image. Understanding children's development at various ages is critical for determining how to effectively communicate with young audiences.

3. Adults seek to learn new information to meet a perceived need, focus attention on messages that help them solve problems and achieve goals, and learn through life experience. An effective communicator identifies needs, assists adults in processing experiences, and provides options for solving problems.

4. When developing messages for people of different generations and across generations, consider the unique needs and values of each cohort segment. Recognizing behaviors, attitudes, and beliefs from a generational perspective is helpful for crafting and delivering targeted messages, but these characteristics do not define individuals and are best used as a loose guide.

5. Tailoring communication to an audience includes consideration for each unique setting. The setting can influence message delivery and set the tone. Recognizing the nuances of presenting in various locations helps guide the planning process and prepare for success.

RESOURCES

Lessons for preschool audiences:
www.nutritioncommunicator.com/kids-club-lessons
-and-songs

REFERENCES

1. Nagle G, Usry L. Using public health strategies to shape early childhood policy. *Am J Orthopsychiatry.* 2016;86(2):171-178. doi:10.1037/ort0000088

2. Telama R, Yang X, Viikari J, Valimaki I, Wanne O, Raitakari O. Physical activity from childhood to adulthood: a 21-year tracking study. *Am J Prev Med.* 2005;28(3):267-273. doi:10.1016/j.amepre.2004.12.003

3. Anderssen S. Promoting healthy weight in school children: what does the HEIA study teach us about effective interventions? *Br J Sports Med.* 2013;47(8):469. doi:10.1136/bjsports-2013-092470

4. Graybiel A, Smith K. Good habits, bad habits. *Sci Am.* 2014;310:38-43. doi:10.1038/scientificamerican0614-38

5. Croft C. *Prenatal and Childhood Nutrition: Evaluating the Neurocognitive Connections.* Apple Academic Press; 2015.

6. Rundell J. Children are not miniature adults. *Psychiatry.* 2000;63(2):150-152.

7. Contento I. Working with diverse population groups. In: *Nutrition Education: Linking Research, Theory, and Practice.* 2nd ed. Jones and Bartlett Publishers; 2011:393-416.

8. Contento I, Balch G, Bronner YL. Nutrition education for school-aged children. *J Nutr Educ Behav.* 1995;27(6):298-311.

9. National Association for the Education of Young Children. 12 principles of child development and learning that inform practice. NAEY website. Published 2009. Accessed November 30, 2017. https://naeyc.org/resources/topics/12-principles-of-child-development

10. Fairbrother H, Curtis P, Goyder E. Making health information meaningful: children's health literacy practices. *SSM—Popul Heal.* 2016;2:476-484. doi:10.1016/j.ssmph.2016.06.005

11. Wilson DM. Developmentally appropriate practice in the age of testing. *Harvard Educ Lett.* 2009;25(3). Accessed November 30, 2017. http://hepg.org/hel-home/issues/25_3/helarticle/developmentally-appropriate-practice-in-the-age-of

12. National Association for Media Literacy Education. The core principles of media literacy education. NAMLE website. Published 2007. Accessed January 16, 2018. https://namle.net/publications/core-principles

13. Knowles MS, Holton EF III, Swanson RA. *The Adult Learner: The Definitive Classic in Adult Education and Human Resource Development.* Elsevier; 2005.

14. Brookfield S. *Adult Learning: An Overview in the International Encyclopedia of Education.* Tuijnman A, ed. Pergamon Press; 1995.

15. Mirriam S, Caffarella R. *Learning in Adulthood.* 2nd ed. Jossey-Bass; 1999.

16. Gardner H. *Multiple Intelligences: The Theory in Practice.* Basic Books; 1993.

17. Mezirow J. *Transformative Dimensions of Adult Learning.* Jossey-Bass; 1991.

18. Cercone K. Characteristics of adult learners with implications for online learning design. *AACE J.* 2008;16(2):137-159.

19. Northwest Center for Public Health Practice. Effective adult learning: a toolkit for teaching adults. http://nwcphp.org/training/opportunities/toolkits-guides/effective-adult-learning-a-toolkit-for-teaching-adults

20. Cranton P. *Understanding and Promoting Transformative Learning: A Guide to Theory and Practice.* 3rd ed. Stylus Publishing; 2016.

21. Vella J. *Learning to Listen, Learning to Teach.* Jossey-Bass; 2002.

22. Norris J. *From Telling to Teaching.* Learning by Dialogue; 2003.

23. Holli B, Beto J. *Nutrition Counseling and Education Skills for Dietetics Professionals.* 6th ed. Wolters Kluwer, Lippincott, Williams, and Wilkins; 2014.

24. Contento IR. *Nutrition Education—Linking Research, Theory, and Practice.* Jones and Bartlett; 2007.

25. Medley M. Life satisfaction across four stages of adult life. *Int J Aging Hum Dev.* 1980;11(3):193-209. doi:10.2190/D4LG-ALJQ-8850-GYDV

26. Pew Research Center. The whys and hows of generations research. Published September 2015. http://assets.pewresearch.org/wp-content/uploads/sites/5/2015/09/09-3-2015-Generations-explainer-release.pdf

27. Berkowitz E. *Essentials of Health Care Marketing.* 2nd ed. Jones and Bartlett Learning; 2006.

28. Schiavo R. *Health Communication from Theory to Practice.* Jossey-Bass; 2007.

29. Yale D, Carothers A. *The Publicity Handbook.* 2nd ed. McGraw-Hill Education; 2001.

30. Williams KC, Page RA. Marketing to the generations. *J Behav Stud Bus.* 2011;5:1-17. doi:10.18394/iid.80342

31. US Department of Health and Human Services, Centers for Disease Control and Prevention. Audience insights: communicating to boomers (1946–1962). https://cdc.gov/health communication/pdf/audience/audienceinsight_boomers.pdf

32. US Department of Health and Human Services, Centers for Disease Control and Prevention. Audience insights: communicating to teens (aged 12–17). https://cdc.gov/healthcommunication /pdf/audience/audienceinsight_teens.pdf

33. US Department of Health and Human Services, Centers for Disease Control and Prevention. Audience insights: communicating to the responsible generation (aged 64–84). https://cdc.gov/healthcommunication/pdf /audience/audienceinsight_adult.pdf

34. US Department of Health and Human Services, Centers for Disease Control and Prevention. Audience insights: communicating to moms (with kids at home). https://cdc .gov/healthcommunication/pdf/audience /audienceinsight_moms.pdf

35. Wilcox D, Cameron G. *Public Relations: Strategies and Tactics.* 9th ed. Allyn and Bacon; 2008.

36. Howe N, Strauss W. The next 20 years: how customer and workforce attitudes will evolve. *Harv Bus Rev.* 2007;85(12):41-52. doi:10.1002/9781118687932.ch26

37. Levenson AR. Millennials and the world of work: an economist's perspective. *J Bus Psychol Spec Issue Millenn World Word.* 2010;25(2):257-264. doi:10.1007/sl0869-010-9170-9

38. Tulgan B; RainmakerThinking. *Meet Generation Z: The Second Generation Within the Giant "Millennial" Cohort.* Published 2013. Accessed October 1, 2017. http://rainmakerthinking.com /assets/uploads/2013/10/Gen-Z-Whitepaper.pdf

39. Dimock M. Where Millennials end and Generation Z begins. Pew Research Center website. Published January 17, 2019. http://pewresearch.org/fact-tank/2018/03/01 /defining-generations-where-millennials-end-and -post-millennials-begin

40. Turner A. Generation Z: technology and social interest. *J Individ Psychol.* 2015;71(2):103-113. doi:10.1353/jip.2015.0021

41. Schneider J. How to market to the iGeneration. *Harvard Bus Rev.* May 6, 2015. Accessed October 1, 2018. https://hbr.org/2015/05/how-to-market -to-the-igeneration

42. 10 tips for communicating across generations. *Forbes.* Published 2013. https://forbes.com /pictures/lmj45miil/navigating-the-new -workplace/#6bf837e943a9

43. Beekman T. Fill in the generation gap. *Strateg Financ.* 2011;93(3):15-17.

44. National Institutes of Health. *Making Health Communication Programs Work.* Accessed May 4, 2020. www.cancer.gov/publications/health -communication/pink-book.pdf

45. Lancaster L, Stillman D. *When Generations Collide: Who They Are. Why They Clash. How to Solve the Generational Puzzle at Work.* HarperBusiness; 2003.

46. How to manage different generations. *Wall Street Journal.* Accessed May 4, 2020. http://guides.wsj .com/management/managing-your-people/how -to-manage-different-generations/#

47. Millennials on Millennials: a look at viewing behavior, distraction and social media stars. Nielsen website. Published March 2, 2017. Accessed May 4, 2020. http://nielsen.com/us/en /insights/news/2017/millennials-on-millennials -a-look-at-viewing-behavior-distraction-social -media-stars

48. Keeter S, Taylor P. The Millennials. Pew Research Center website. Published December 10, 2009. Accessed May 4, 2020. www.pewresearch.org /2009/12/10/the-millennials

49. Thomas Y, Srinivasan R. Emerging shifts in learning paradigms—from Millennials to the Digital Natives. *Int J Appl Eng Res.* 2016;11(5):3616-3618.

50. Howe N. Millennials: a generation of page-turners. *Forbes.* January 16, 2017. https://forbes .com/sites/neilhowe/2017/01/16/millennials-a -generation-of-page-turners/#18b6bb461978

51. Knight R. Managing people from 5 generations. *Harv Bus Rev.* September 25, 2014. https://hbr.org/2014/09/managing-people- from-5-generations

52. US Department of Education. National Center for Education Statistics website. Search for private schools. Accessed January 14, 2018. https://nces.ed.gov/surveys/pss /privateschoolsearch

53. US Department of Education. National Center for Education Statistics. Common Core of Data. Accessed January 14, 2018. https://nces.ed.gov /ccd/

54. Katz SJ, Moyer CA. The emerging role of online communication between patients and their providers. *J Gen Intern Med.* 2004;19(9):978-983. doi:10.1111/j.1525-1497.2004.30432.x

Write Goals, Objectives, and Key Message Points to Focus and Organize a Message

Barbara J. Mayfield, MS, RDN, FAND
and Lori Greene, MS, RDN, LDN

"Goals, objectives, and key messages provide direction to communication. They answer the questions: 'Why is this communication important?' and 'What does it hope to accomplish?'"

> "Clarity of vision is the key to achieving your objectives." —TOM STEYER

Introduction

Effective communication has a clearly defined purpose and focus. Without these, communication may ramble meaninglessly, go in circles, and lead nowhere. Communication is literally pointless without a key message.

Equipped with knowledge about an audience and a well-selected topic based on the audience's needs, the nutrition communicator is prepared to focus the communication and write key messages, which also serve to organize the message content. Additionally, the communicator may determine learning objectives for the audience to achieve as a result of receiving the communication.

This chapter answers three questions:

- What are the purposes of writing goals, objectives, and key messages?
- What are the structures of goals, objectives, and key messages?
- How can key message points organize a message and form an outline?

No matter what type of communication is designed and delivered, writing key messages and learning objectives follows the completion of a needs assessment and precedes communication development and delivery.

What Are the Purposes of Goals, Objectives, and Key Messages?

A journey without a map lacks direction. Goals, objectives, and key messages provide direction to communication. They answer the questions: "Why is this communication important?" and "What does it hope to accomplish?" The specific purposes for goals, objectives, and key messages make it clear that all are vitally important.

Goals Are Written with the End in Mind

A goal is the outcome, reference point, or end result someone is trying to achieve.[1] Writing a goal puts into words what a person seeks to accomplish. In general, goals focus on the big picture, or the overall outcome. Goals take a long-term view.

In nutrition communication, goals can encompass a variety of areas. A communicator might state a goal of becoming a more effective speaker, having a video garner a million views, or having an audience's health parameters improve after participating in a program.

In the context of crafting messages, this chapter will focus on goals describing the desired result of an audience receiving a message. What should an audience know? What should an audience feel? What should an audience do? Writing the answers to these questions describes the destination a communicator has in mind for an audience.

Consider this example of a community nutrition program that is creating a message to promote breastfeeding. An overall goal could be an increase in the incidence of breastfeeding. Three potential goals that answer the questions "Why is this message important?" and "What does it hope to accomplish?" are:

- The expectant mothers will know breastfeeding promotes health for mothers and babies.
- The expectant mothers will value breastfeeding as a positive choice.
- The expectant mothers will be prepared to initiate breastfeeding at birth.

If meeting goals is the destination, objectives are a way to measure progress toward that destination. Before writing objectives, writing a list of goals or even one overall goal can be a useful first step. Writing learning objectives provides a route to meet the goals.

Learning Objectives Focus on the Audience

A learning objective is a statement of the knowledge, emotions, or skills a participant will know, feel, or be able to demonstrate after receiving a message or at the end of instruction. Learning objectives are more specific than goals and focus on a single learning outcome. Multiple learning objectives together may help an audience reach its end goal.

Creating learning objectives has several purposes. First, objectives identify what the nutrition communicator wants to accomplish. They help the communicator decide what aspects to focus on and what is extraneous. When it is necessary to cut content to meet space or time limits, objectives help to take away information that doesn't fulfill an objective and retain essential information.

In addition to identifying the communicator's desired outcome, objectives tell an audience what they will gain.[2] Learning objectives define for the audience what they will learn and how they will be able to use the knowledge. For this reason, it is critical that the message adequately covers what the learning objectives promise. If the audience perceives that a message did not deliver on the promised objectives, they may be disappointed.

Learning objectives are also essential for evaluating the success of a communication because they provide a tool for measuring outcomes.

Without them, how will a communicator know what to measure?

Lastly, learning objectives may be an expectation of the organization for which a practitioner is communicating. Nutrition communicators creating content for professional presentations, webinars, or self-study materials are required to submit learning objectives in order for an educational program to qualify for continuing education credits. At the undergraduate and graduate school levels, instructors are required to write learning objectives for their courses. As described in Chapter 2, defined outcomes, referred to as knowledge requirements, competencies, and performance indicators, have been established for all levels of training and practice.

Each purpose for writing objectives is beneficial for a different reason. Learning objectives are focused on the audience and what its members will take away from the communication. Write them well, deliver on what is promised, and measure their success.

A common mistake when writing learning objectives is for communicators to write them from their own perspective, addressing what they intend to teach. Compare the wording of these two statements:

Instructional objective: The instructor will describe health benefits of breastfeeding for both mother and baby.

Learning objective: The audience will be able to describe three or more ways that breastfeeding benefits the health of the mother and three or more ways it benefits the health of the baby after receiving the message.

The first statement is worded as an "instructional objective" and describes what information will be conveyed. The second is worded as a learning objective and describes what the audience will learn.

Key Messages Provide Clarity and Focus

A key message is a main idea or point a communicator is trying to convey. A well-written key message is clear and succinct. It is easy to understand and remember. The purpose of key messages is to provide clarity and focus to communication.

The title of each chapter in this book is a key message. This chapter is titled Write Goals, Objectives, and Key Message Points to Focus and

Chapter 38 addresses how to evaluate success using learning objectives as an important tool.

Organize a Message. It concisely summarizes the content covered in this chapter. Using a key message for the title more effectively helps the reader learn the content than using a title such as "Goals, Objectives, and Key Messages," which tells the topic but nothing more.

Think of key messages as the main ideas that help the audience achieve each learning objective. For example, consider a learning objective related to breastfeeding stating that the expectant mothers receiving the communication will be able to demonstrate proper positioning of an infant at the breast. A potential key message for this objective is: "For all breastfeeding positions, place baby tummy to mummy." This key message could then be followed with supporting evidence for why positions that place a baby's tummy against the mother ensure that the baby's head is properly aligned, along with descriptions of various positions and more detail. This key message conveys a unifying feature of all nursing positions and a distinct difference from how a baby is held when bottle feeding. It is short and easy to remember, which will be important when a new mother is presented with her newborn shortly after birth and wonders how to initiate breastfeeding. Strive to write one key message for each learning objective.

What Are the Structures of Goals, Objectives, and Key Messages?

Goals, objectives, and key messages should be crafted with their purposes in mind. This section will describe the format or structure of each and tips for creating ones that will achieve their intended purpose.

Goals and Objectives Are SMART and Motivating

Goals define the desired outcome and serve as the starting point for writing learning objectives and key messages. Goals that are written along with objectives can be more general. Goals that are used alone require more specificity.

A popular strategy for writing effective goals and objectives is referred to as SMART. This well-known acronym stands for five characteristics of a well-written goal: specific, measurable, achievable, relevant, and time-bound or trackable. (See Figure 15.1 for a description of each characteristic.)

FIGURE 15.1 **Description of SMART goals and objectives**

S	**Specific**	Target a specific area of improvement (who, what, and where).
M	**Measureable**	Quantify or suggest an indicator of progress (how many, how much, to what quality standard).
A	Achievable	Make goals and objectives attainable with the resources available and within the time frame set.
R	Relevant	Ensure that achievement of the objective is meaningful (eg, of importance to an organization or project goal).
T	Time-bound	Specify when the result(s) can be achieved.

The origin of the SMART approach is attributed to George T. Doran, a management consultant, in an article written in 1981.[3] The words used may vary between versions of this acronym, but the intended meanings are similar.

The goal stated previously for the breastfeeding promotion message was to increase the incidence of breastfeeding. When written as a SMART goal, this statement could be worded as follows:

The incidence of breastfeeding at birth among women enrolled in the community program will increase by 4% over 12 months.

SMART goals are not only for program generated communication; they can be used by communicators in all settings. Let's apply this example to a communicator blogging about the benefits of breastfeeding to an audience of expectant parents. A SMART goal could be worded as follows:

More than 80% of new parents reading the series of breastfeeding blog posts will report initiating breastfeeding at birth.

A second, less commonly used model for writing goals is the ABCD model.[4] The letters in this model stand for *audience, behavior, condition,* and *degree.* An ABCD goal specifies:

- who the learning *audience* is (Who?),
- the desired *behavior* (What?),
- the *conditions* under which the behavior will occur (How?), and
- the *degree* to which the audience will exhibit this behavior (How much?).

The sample goals above meet the ABCD criteria as well: The audience is the *women enrolled in the program* or *readers of the blog,* the behavior is *breastfeeding,* the condition is *at birth,* and the degree is *a 4% increase* or *80% of the readers.*

Goals and objectives are intended to motivate action to bring about the desired results. Both SMART and ABCD goals and objectives include a means to evaluate whether they were achieved. Where goals are not always written with this degree of specificity, learning objectives are designed to be specific and measurable.

Learning Objectives Are Measurable and Descriptive

A learning objective is descriptive, measurable, and created with the success of the learner in mind. Chapters 3 and 10 discussed the importance of knowing an audience. Chapters 11 through 14 provided tools and resources to learn about an audience. Knowing the audience is critical when writing learning objectives. Remember, the focus is on the audience or the learner and not on the instructor or creator of the message. If a communicator doesn't consider the audience when creating objectives, the audience may walk away having gained very little.

A well-written learning objective contains three key components:

- a carefully selected verb;
- a subject, which typically is a noun; and
- specific criteria to allow for the evaluation of success after the instruction.[5]

It is imperative that the communicator select these three key components carefully and with the learner in mind.

- Choose an appropriate verb and noun that reflect what the audience should know as a result of receiving a message.
- Choose a verb that can be assessed (eg, *describe, explain, list*). Verbs such as *understand* or *learn* are too broad.
- Consider knowledge the audience already has and skills they may already possess, if any, related to the topic.

Next let's look at a tool that can help communicators to select an appropriate verb for a learning objective.

THE COGNITIVE DOMAIN AND BLOOM'S TAXONOMY

Benjamin S. Bloom, with other college and university examiners, created a taxonomy of educational objectives. Today, this classification system is referred to as Bloom's taxonomy,[5] which goes from lower-level to higher-level learning objectives. The authors found that most learning objectives fit into one of three domains: cognitive, affective, and psychomotor. The original cognitive domain was published in 1956.[6] In 2001, David R. Krathwohl, one of the original contributors to the taxonomy, revised the cognitive domain of Bloom's taxonomy classification system.[6] This chapter will be using the revised version of the cognitive domain.

Most learning objectives fall into the cognitive domain, so this aspect of Bloom's taxonomy will be referred to most often. The cognitive domain contains six major classes, starting with remembering as the lowest-level class and advancing to *creating*, the highest-level class, as seen in Figure 15.2. It is important to use multiple levels when creating objectives and not just stay within one domain or one class within one domain. It is recommended that multiple objectives are created, advancing in skill throughout the delivery of a message.

Using the example of a mother receiving a message regarding breastfeeding:

- The first objective may be: "The expectant mother (learner) will be able to recall at least three benefits of breastfeeding." This objective falls in the class of remembering.

- The second objective may be: "The expectant mother (learner) will be able to identify (or select) at least two of the proper breastfeeding positions." This objective is higher-level knowledge, found at the applying level.

Note that both of these cognitive-domain objectives include a verb (see Figure 15.2), subject, and criteria for evaluating the objective.

THE AFFECTIVE DOMAIN

The second domain in Bloom's taxonomy is the affective domain. The affective focuses more on emotions and feelings. There are five classes or

FIGURE 15.2 **Bloom's taxonomy verbs**[a]

CLASS	VERBS				
Remembering	Choose	Label	Name	Recognize	Show
	Define	List	Omit	Relate	Spell
	Find	Match	Recall	Select	Tell
Understanding	Classify	Demonstrate	Illustrate	Outline	Show
	Compare	Explain	Infer	Relate	Summarize
	Contrast	Extend	Interpret	Rephrase	Translate
Applying	Apply	Construct	Identify	Model	Select
	Build	Develop	Interview	Organize	Solve
	Choose	Experiment with	Make use of	Plan	Utilize
Analyzing	Analyze	Conclude	Divide	List	Test
	Assume	Contrast	Examine	Assess motive	
	Categorize	Discover	Function	Relate	
	Classify	Dissect	Infer	Simplify	
	Compare	Distinguish	Inspect	Survey	
Evaluating	Agree	Deduce	Rate	Opine	Select
	Appraise	Defend	Influence	Perceive	Support
	Assess	Determine	Interpret	Prioritize	Value
	Choose	Disprove	Judge	Prove	
	Conclude	Estimate	Justify	Rate	
	Criticize	Evaluate	Mark	Recommend	
	Decide	Explain	Measure	Rule on	
Creating	Adapt	Construct	Estimate	Maximize	Solve
	Build	Create	Formulate	Minimize	Suppose
	Change	Delete	Happen	Modify	
	Choose	Design	Imagine	Originate	
	Combine	Develop	Improve	Plan	
	Compile	Discuss	Invent	Predict	
	Compose	Elaborate	Make up	Propose	

[a] Adapted from reference 5.

levels within the affective domain: *receiving* (attending), *responding, valuing, organization,* and *characterization* by value or value complex.[7]

An example of a learning objective within the affective domain may be: "The expectant mother (learner) will be able to explain, to at least one friend, her choice to breastfeed her baby." This learning objective is at the valuing level in the affective domain. It would pair well with the objectives created from the cognitive domain.

Figure 15.3 lists the classes within the affective domain and verbs that can be used in creating objectives within this domain. The resources section at the end of the chapter includes useful websites that also provide helpful tools for determining appropriate verbs for affective learning objectives.

THE PSYCHOMOTOR DOMAIN

The third domain is the psychomotor domain, which focuses on physical skills and may include coordination, strength, speed, and fine and gross motor skills. The classes within the psychomotor domain are *perception* (awareness), *set* (readiness to act), *guided response* (imitation), *mechanism* (basic proficiency), *complex overt response* (expert), *adaptation* (ability to modify), and *origination* (ability to create new patterns).[8] Depending on the topic of instruction, it may be difficult to create a learning objective that fits within this domain. This is acceptable as long as the learning objectives that are developed still cover more than one domain and different classes within a domain.

An example of a psychomotor learning objective for a breastfeeding mother may be: "The breastfeeding mother (learner) will be able to react to her baby's feeding cues to ensure proper timing and positioning of breastfeeding." This learning objective falls under the category of guided response within the psychomotor domain. In planning objectives within this domain, refer to Figure 15.4 (page 244) and check the resources section provided at the end of this chapter for key verbs to help create strong psychomotor learning objectives.

Effective learning objectives are created with the learner in mind. They should cover multiple domains within Bloom's taxonomy and different classes within the cognitive, affective, and psychomotor domains. Learning objectives should be created with an appropriate verb, a subject, and

FIGURE 15.3 **Affective domain verbs**[a]

CLASS	VERBS				
Receiving	Ask	Follow	Identify	Point to	Sit
	Choose	Give	Locate	Reply	Use
	Describe	Hold	Name	Select	
Responding	Answer	Conform	Label	Read	
	Aid	Discuss	Perform	Recite	
	Assist	Greet	Practice	Tell	
	Comply	Help	Present	Write	
Valuing	Complete	Explain	Initiate	Justify	Select
	Demonstrate	Follow	Invite	Propose	Share
	Differentiate	Form	Join	Report	Study
Organization	Adhere	Compare	Identify	Organize	
	Alter	Defend	Integrate	Prepare	
	Arrange	Formulate	Modify	Relate	
	Combine	Generalize	Order	Synthesize	
Characterization (internalizing values)	Act	Influence	Propose	Revise	Verify
	Discriminate	Listen	Qualify	Serve	
	Display	Modify	Question	Solve	

[a] Adapted from reference 7.

criteria for evaluating the success of the learner. Use the tool in Figure 15.5 to create objectives and to check to ensure key parts of an effective learning objective are included.

Key Messages Are Succinct and Memorable

A well-written key message is clear, succinct, and memorable and captures the main idea of a communication in an easy-to-say and easy-to-understand statement. A complete declarative statement makes a powerful and effective key message.

Which of the following makes a better key message?

- Breastfeeding benefits mother and baby.
- Benefits of breastfeeding for mother and baby

Although the second item may serve as a title or heading, it is not as effective as a key message.

The first item is a better key message. Making *benefits* a verb rather than a noun creates a complete declarative statement and a stronger key message.

Write key messages with the audience in mind. If it is certain that everyone in the audience is a potential breastfeeding mother, the message could be worded "Breastfeeding benefits you and your baby." In fact, that message could be considered relevant for both the mothers and fathers in the audience.

Key messages can be written using straightforward wording or more creatively using rhyming words, alliteration, or other methods that capture attention or reinforce memory. For example, the key message using the rhyming words *tummy* and *mummy* enhances memory. An example using alliteration is: "Breastfeeding benefits babies." Within one particular piece of communication, strive for key messages that follow a similar pattern or style. Whether a message is crafted to be clever or straightforward, be clear. Never sacrifice clarity.

FIGURE 15.4 **Psychomotor domain verbs**[a]

CLASS	VERBS				
Perception (awareness)	Choose Describe	Detect Differentiate	Distinguish Identify	Isolate Relate	Select
Set	Begin Display	Explain Move	Proceed Show	State Volunteer	
Guided response	Copy Follow	React Reproduce	Respond Trace		
Mechanism (basic proficiency)	Assemble Calibrate Construct	Dismantle Display Fasten	Fix Grind Heat	Manipulate Measure Mend	Mix Organize Sketch
Complex overt response (expert)[b]	Assemble Calibrate Construct	Dismantle Display Fasten	Fix Grind Heat	Manipulate Measure Mend	Mix Organize Sketch
Adaptation	Adapt Alter	Change Rearrange	Reorganize Revise	Vary	
Origination	Arrange Build	Combine Compose	Construct Create	Design Initiate	Make Originate

[a] Adapted from reference 8
[b] Key verbs for the complex overt response class are the same as for mechanism class, with adverbs or adjectives added to indicate the performance is faster, better, more accurate, and so on.

FIGURE 15.5 **Tool for creating objectives**

	Domain	Class	Verb	Subject/ Noun	Evaluate/ Measure
Example objective: The learner will be able to recall at least three benefits of breastfeeding.	Cognitive	Remembering	Recall	Breastfeeding	Three benefits
Objective:					

The number of key messages is determined by the content needing to be covered, with more content needing more key messages. However, to enhance memory, the total number should be minimized. To accomplish this, combine similar content so that the number of key messages does not exceed what can be easily learned and remembered. The human brain's active or working memory most easily recalls up to three main points[9,10] and struggles with remembering more unless a memory trigger, such as a mnemonic device, is used.

For example, for four key ideas related to breastfeeding, a communicator could come up with realistic messages that start with the letters that spell the word *baby*. With this word for a memory aid, it becomes more plausible for someone to recall all four points:

Breastfeeding has many benefits.
Any mother can learn how.
Babies are born to breastfeed.
You can do it, yes you can!

Key messages may be better received if they are written with positive rather than negative language. This is referred to as positive versus negative framing of messages.[11-13] For instance, instead of saying, "Avoid smoking while breastfeeding," say, "Be smoke-free when you breastfeed." Research indicates that positive framing is often, but not always, preferred or more effective. For this reason, pilot-test message concepts with target audience members, as recommended by the International Food Information Council (IFIC) Message Development Model. Along with assessing other aspects of a message, such as understandable word choice and relevance to the audience, assess whether the audience will better receive and be more likely to act on messages with positive or negative framing.

For more on the IFIC Message Development Model, see Chapter 10.

Single Overriding Communication Objectives Convey the Big Idea

In addition to writing key message points, write a single overriding communication objective (SOCO). Think of it as the *big* key message. There will be just one SOCO for a communication endeavor but several key messages. SOCOs make an effective closing statement for a presentation or written article. They are effective when introduced and repeated earlier as well, but make it a point to end with the SOCO.

Effective key messages and SOCOs say what needs to be said. Be brief but be complete. They may be more than one sentence if necessary. In the story featured in the Words of Experience box on page 246, the SOCO is two independent clauses (ie, essentially two complete thoughts that could stand alone as sentences) separated by a semicolon. Whether long or short, well-written SOCOs are remembered.

Well-Written Single Overriding Communication Objectives Stick

by Barbara J. Mayfield, MS, RDN, FAND

One semester in our nutrition communication class, I added a bonus question to a quiz to see whether students could recall any of the single overriding communication objectives (SOCOs) shared in recent student presentations. If a student remembered another student's SOCO, both students received bonus points. Out of all the student presentations, only one student's SOCO was remembered, and it was recalled by over half of the class more than a week after being shared in the presentation. Interestingly, it was about the same topic as our example: "Breast milk is the gold standard; mothers should use it, not refuse it!"

How Can Key Message Points Organize a Message?

Armed with key messages and a SOCO, the practitioner is ready to organize a communication. A well-organized message is easier for the communicator to develop and deliver and easier for the audience to receive. One of the best ways to organize a particular communication is by creating an outline. Outlines are a useful tool no matter what type of communication is created. In fact, if a particular form of communication is routinely created, developing an outline template can save time and improve the finished product. An outline provides structure, organization, and a logical flow.

Outlines Have a Predictable Structure

Outlines provide an organized structure for the information being communicated. They help the communicator present the information logically and help the audience have a clear idea of what is being communicated. An outline is often used to create the titles and headings used.

The most common outline format is the alphanumeric outline structure. Main, or first-level, headings use roman numerals. The next, or second-level, headings use capital letters. Third-level and fourth-level headings use Arabic numerals and lowercase letters, respectively. See the website listed in the resources section for examples and descriptions of this and other popular approaches to creating outlines.

Well-written outlines use their predicable structure to organize the information so that each heading at the same level has the same level of significance. Each subordinate heading should also share the same level of importance with other subordinate headings of the same level. Subordinate headings describe more specific components of the more general headings that precede them. At any given level, there must be at least two subordinate headings.

All headings of a particular level should follow a parallel structure. As described earlier, the chapter titles for this book, which are the first-level headings in the outline created for the book, are key message points. All second-level headings in the book's outline, which became the main headings within each chapter, are written as questions. The third-level headings are key message points that serve to answer these questions. The fourth- and fifth-level headings are subtopics. These subtopics should also use parallel language. For example, in this section, the first words of the subheadings are nouns (*outlines*, *key message points*, and *an outline*), followed by a descriptive purpose, as in the heading: "Key Message Points Organize an Outline." This subheading helps answer the question: How can key message points organize a message?

Consider the various outline structures that could be created for blog posts, nutrition lesson plans, webinars, or newsletters. Creating a template with each of the desired components forms a structure that helps create content and gives the message a logical organization; this, in turn, helps the audience receive and understand the message.

Key Message Points Organize an Outline

Key message points are an ideal approach to organizing an outline. By creating an outline using key messages, the communicator has a visual test of how well the key messages were selected. If an important concept was left out, an additional key message can be written. If two key messages overlap too much, one can be omitted, or they can be combined.

As stated previously, each chapter title in this book is a key message. Within the outline for each chapter, key messages are featured. Prior to writing a single chapter, the entire book was outlined. The outline comprised 42 pages of text. All authors were aware of the content covered in each chapter, allowing for cross-referencing between chapters and building of content while avoiding excessive repetition.

In the same way that a topic sentence organizes a paragraph, key messages organize an outline by clearly stating what content is covered in a specific section. As an outline becomes more detailed, supporting evidence, examples, and additional information can be listed in the sections in which they will be covered to support a key message.

An Outline Provides a Logical Flow

An outline tells a story. A complete and detailed outline includes an opening that introduces the story and helps both the communicator and the audience know where they are heading. It also includes a closing that wraps up the story, ideally with the SOCO—a strong, memorable statement that sums up the main point. Within the body of the outline, the key messages are listed in a logical order, with information that goes together being grouped together.

This logical flow allows the communicator to tell the story in an easy-to-follow way. Relationships between ideas presented are clear because an outline describes how topics are interrelated. The audience doesn't get lost because there are no diversions from the main story. To learn more about creating outlines, visit the website provided in the resources section at the end of the chapter.

Effective nutrition communicators write goals, objectives, and key message points to focus a message and an outline to organize a message. Use the checklist provided to create audience-focused communication based on what has been presented in Chapters 10 through 15.

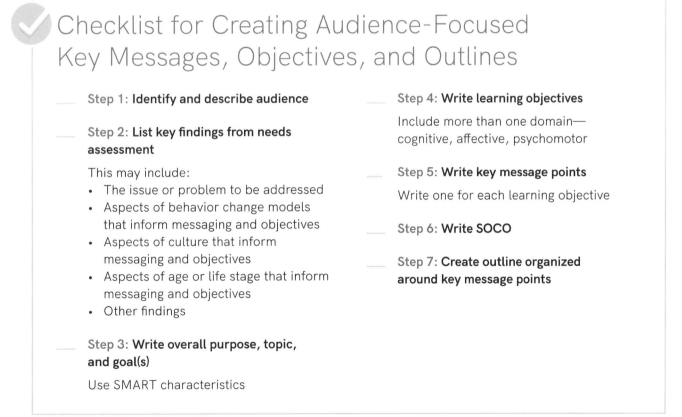

Checklist for Creating Audience-Focused Key Messages, Objectives, and Outlines

___ **Step 1: Identify and describe audience**

___ **Step 2: List key findings from needs assessment**

This may include:
- The issue or problem to be addressed
- Aspects of behavior change models that inform messaging and objectives
- Aspects of culture that inform messaging and objectives
- Aspects of age or life stage that inform messaging and objectives
- Other findings

___ **Step 3: Write overall purpose, topic, and goal(s)**

Use SMART characteristics

___ **Step 4: Write learning objectives**

Include more than one domain— cognitive, affective, psychomotor

___ **Step 5: Write key message points**

Write one for each learning objective

___ **Step 6: Write SOCO**

___ **Step 7: Create outline organized around key message points**

KEY POINTS

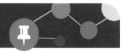

Write Goals, Objectives, and Key Message Points to Focus and Organize a Message

1 Goals, objectives, and key messages provide direction to communication. They answer the questions, "Why is this communication important?" and, "What does it hope to accomplish?" The specific purposes for goals, objectives, and key messages make it clear that all are vitally important.

2 Goals, objectives, and key messages should be carefully crafted with the learner in mind. A communicator should use the tools available to create these, such as the SMART strategy and Bloom's taxonomy.

3 An outline is used to provide structure, organization, and a logical flow to any type of communication. A well-organized message is easier for a communicator to develop and deliver and easier for an audience to receive.

RESOURCES

Three domains of learning: cognitive, affective, and psychomotor: https://thesecondprinciple.com/instructional-design/threedomainsoflearning

Bloom's revised taxonomy: cognitive, affective, and psychomotor: www.astate.edu/dotAsset/7a3b152c-b73a-45d6-b8a3-7ecf7f786f6a.pdf

Iowa State Center for Excellence in Teaching and Learning—revised Bloom's taxonomy: www.celt.iastate.edu/teaching/effective-teaching-practices/revised-blooms-taxonomy

How to write an outline: https://owl.english.purdue.edu/owl/resource/544/1

REFERENCES

1. Heath C, Larrick R, Wu G. Goals as reference points. *Cogn Psychol.* 1999;38:79-109. doi:10.1006/cogp.1998.0708
2. Moss C, Brookhart S, Long B. Knowing your learning target. *Educ Leadersh.* 2011;68(6):66-69.
3. Doran GT. There's a S.M.A.R.T. way to write management's goals and objectives. *Manage Rev.* 1981;70(11):35-36.
4. Heinrich R, Molenda M, Russell JD, Smaldino SE. *Instructional Media and Technologies for Learning.* Merrill; 1996.
5. Anderson LW, Krathwohl DR. *A Taxonomy for Learning, Teaching, and Assessing.* Allyn and Bacon; 2001.
6. Bloom BS, Krathwohl DR. *Taxonomy of Educational Objectives: The Classification of Educational Goals, by a Committee of College and University Examiners. Handbook I: Cognitive Domain.* Longmans, Green; 1956.
7. Krathwohl DR, Bloom BS, Masia BB. *Taxonomy of Educational Objectives: The Classification of Educational Goals. Handbook II: Affective Domain.* David McKay; 1964.
8. Simpson EJ. *The Classification of Educational Objectives in the Psychomotor Domain.* Gryphon House; 1972.
9. Cowan N. What are the differences between long-term, short-term, and working memory? *Prog Brain Res.* 2008;169:323-338. doi:10.1016/S0079-6123(07)00020-9
10. Cowan N. The magical number 4 in short-term memory: a reconsideration of mental storage capacity. *Behav Brain Sci.* 2001;24(1):87-114.
11. Aki E, Oxman A, Herrin J, et al. Framing of health information messages. *Cochrane Database Syst Rev.* 2011;12. doi:10.1002/14651858.CD006777
12. Mikels JA, Shuster MM, Thai ST, et al. Messages that matter: age differences in affective responses to framed health messages. *Psychol Aging.* 2016;31(4):409-414. doi:10.1037/pag0000040
13. Notthoff N, Carstensen LL. Positive messaging promotes walking in older adults. *Psychol Aging.* 2014;29(2):329-341. doi:10.1037/a0036748

SECTION 4

Designing and Delivering Presentations

Make Nutrition Come Alive!

Barbara Storper, MS, RD, and Jill Jayne, MS, RD

Barbara
Storper, MS, RD

Jill Jayne, MS, RD

Section 4 focuses on how to design and deliver effective presentations. This showcase features two registered dietitian nutritionists who are not afraid to use their creative talents in communicating nutrition to audiences of children. Each one has a unique story, but both encourage all nutrition communicators to bring their own passions and creative energies into their work … to make nutrition come alive!

FOODPLAY: Making Good Eating Great Fun!

Barbara Storper, MS, RD

Wonder how to turn kids on to healthy eating habits? That's been my life's work!

It started when I was an intern getting my master's in nutrition and was asked to give a lecture on nutrition to an inner-city school in Brooklyn. A lecture … on nutrition … to 400 kids … in Brooklyn? Oh, no, how boring! Then I thought, if advertisers could be successful getting kids to eat their food products, why couldn't we use similar techniques to get kids to go for healthy foods?

I wondered what could be as powerful as exciting television commercials. What is engaging, inspiring, motivating, and—most importantly for kids—fun? Live theater! Filled with motivating characters, amazing feats of juggling, music, magic, and audience participation—live theater could be a great way to make nutrition come alive! Luckily, juggling was one of the best things I learned in

college, and with food, there were so many things you could juggle. When I juggled and ate an apple, for example, kids would follow me around gleefully, kind of like I was the Pied Piper!

When FOODPLAY was born, it was a goofy script and some props and costumes bought at the local thrift shop. But, the amazing thing was that the auditorium full of elementary school children loved the show, and the food service staff was amazed to see that the kids went for the healthier options! Since that first Brooklyn show, FOOD-PLAY has reached over five million schoolchildren around the country and been performed by professional troupes of actors from New York to California and most states in between. We've been honored with 10 national nutrition and media awards plus an Emmy Award for "Best Children and Youth TV Special" when made for TV!

We've seen that using theater and the arts is an amazing and effective approach for health education. They are used throughout the world, from puppetry performances in Indonesia to radio soap operas in Nigeria, as a safe, nonthreatening, and deeply engaging way to bring health messages to various audiences. The unique opportunity that theater and the arts can provide is a nonthreatening approach to health messages—one that can deeply engage participants in a personal way and go directly to the heart and soul of a person, the place where making decisions about health and improving behaviors often takes place.

What I've learned is that we as a profession may need to find other ways to help our clients,

families, and especially kids improve their nutrition—other than saying, "Eat this; it's good for you!" Food is related to so many things—family, culture, memories, agriculture, environment, health, and, of course, taste. We need to connect the dots of these elements to reach and engage the hearts and minds of the people we work with, and using the arts is a great way to do so. Whatever way we each can bring what we love, our own passion, to our work, the better for everyone. Whether it's singing, dancing, reading, writing, cooking, gardening, rapping, painting, or loving fresh food—let's bring our joy into the game. It makes a big difference!

Are You Ready to Rock?!

Jill Jayne, MS, RD

Jump with Jill is a music-based health program for kids that makes nutrition education rock. I started the world's only rock and roll nutrition show because I believed that music could connect kids with the important topic of nutrition. If advertisers and pop stars could do it, so could we.

Jump with Jill celebrates healthy habits by transforming nutrition education into a live concert. It was born out of my credentials in nutrition and my experience as a musician. I'm a registered dietitian nutritionist with a master of science degree in nutrition education from Teachers College Columbia University, and a bachelor of science

FOODPLAY's Top 10 Strategies to Turn Kids on to Healthy Habits

by Barbara Storper, MS, RD

1. Find out where kids are at and start there!
2. Live it, don't preach it!
3. Make connections relevant to their world.
4. Show, don't tell!
5. Empower kids with consumer skills to see through media messages.
6. Make healthy food irresistible—attractive, accessible, and affordable!
7. Have fun—when you have fun, they'll have fun!
8. Promote diversity.
9. Get kids involved—growing, cooking, choosing, tasting.
10. Bring your passion—be a positive force for change!

Reproduced with permission from www.foodplay.com.

degree in nutritional sciences and theater from Penn State University. But I'm actually more famous for my former life as a mainstream recording artist with my rock band.

Jump with Jill was born out of attempts to please our record label. While signed to a development deal, we wrote nearly a hundred songs in a year. The label liked none of them. As an overachiever, I had never been told I was bad at anything. I didn't take the news well and started to seriously consider the unsolicited advice that I needed to pick either music or nutrition as my career. Instead, I showed my label representative the songs I had developed for my nutrition education master's thesis project for an after-school program in New York City public schools. He told me without hesitation to immediately dedicate myself to these pop songs about healthy eating and exercise.

The debut album for Jump with Jill was followed with an intense national tour. We applied the principles of running a successful rock band—finding partners to book the show, promoting the appearance, and structuring a strong song list. Our audiences of young children were experiencing the first rock show of their lives, so we carefully crafted the volume, content, and effective use of out-of-classroom time.

Jump with Jill uses singable mantras to make healthy habits memorable. Each song is focused on one healthy behavior that turns a broad goal like being healthy into a specific and actionable behavior that is the hook of the chorus, like eat vegetables ("Eat Superpower Vegetables!"), enjoy fruit ("Enjoy Nature's Candy!"), and exercise regularly ("Compose the Beat of Your Body!"). I use the verses to tell the story and script dialogue to set up the concept.

I use many different musical genres to enhance our storytelling and rely on the sounds that relate to the behaviors for instrumentation. For example, we have a Celtic song about drinking water that features tuned water glasses as the lead instrument and a Latin song about breakfast that features a cereal box as a maraca, a pan as a clave, and cereal bowls as agogo bells. My final process is thinking about how the songs will be performed live, looking for strategic places for the audience to move and sing along with the performers. Exercising while learning about the importance of exercise? It's kinesthetic learning in action.

We bring the full-scale technical production to each location; it includes the set, lighting, microphones, sound system, and meticulously costumed kid-appropriate rock-star team Jill and DJ. Jump with Jill energizes and engages audiences by making healthy choices behaviorally focused and so irresistibly catchy that you need to shake it.

Over the past decade, the Jump with Jill show has been performed over 3,000 times for a million kids in six countries. But, you don't need to start taking vocal lessons and go on a world tour to communicate effectively with your audiences. You have an equally unique story that brought you into this field in the first place. Hold that fire within you when you give your presentations and shine it on your audiences. They might be there to hear about the science, but they will only remember it if you deliver it with passion.

CHAPTER 16

Create High-Impact Presentations

Barbara J. Mayfield, MS, RDN, FAND
and Heidi Katte, MS, RDN, CD, FAND

"Effective presenters do not mimic other speakers; they convey messages using their own unique and authentic style. Effective presentations captivate and transform an audience by empowering and inspiring them to expand their knowledge and take action."

"There is no one way to give a great talk."

—CHRIS ANDERSON, *TED TALKS: THE OFFICIAL TED GUIDE TO PUBLIC SPEAKING*

Introduction

The audience has been identified, the objectives determined, and the key messages crafted. Now it is time to put it all together into a presentation an audience will pay attention to, engage with, and act upon. It is time to master the art of rhetoric, or what Chris Anderson, the head of TED, calls *presentation literacy*,[1] the art of speaking effectively.

What sets an effective presentation apart from a mediocre one? There is no one formula to follow but a variety of tools to employ. This chapter, and the ones that follow in Section 4, provide time-tested tools to design and deliver effective presentations. Effective presenters do not mimic other speakers; they convey messages using their own unique and authentic style. Effective presentations captivate and transform audiences by empowering and inspiring them to expand their knowledge and take action.

This chapter answers three questions:

- What is the purpose of a presentation?
- How is the content organized and presented for learning and application?
- How can understanding the way the audience learns determine presentation design and delivery?

The content in this chapter and the rest of this section focuses on effective presentations. While studying, consider how the same principles can be applied in numerous other communication contexts: videos, demonstrations, and even blogs and literature or article presentations using text along with supporting graphics. A valuable message must be designed and delivered effectively.

What Is the Purpose of a Presentation?

A presentation, as with any form of communication, is designed and delivered to make a point. A presentation communicates one or more key ideas to an audience in a way that resonates, inspires, and spurs action. The message has value to the audience. A presentation delivers that value in the form of key points and supporting evidence. It solves a problem or meets a need. The message is presented in ways that are meaningful to the audience, using methods that enhance memory and employing strategies that motivate the audience to pay attention, learn, engage, and take action.

Present Key Points and Supporting Evidence

Chapter 15 described how to write key message points and a SOCO—a single overriding communication objective; in other words, the *big* idea—and how to organize a message with an outline. This chapter goes a step further. It will discuss how to craft a message to powerfully and effectively present it so that the idea is shared with audience members and accurately forms the intended meaning in their minds. Sound far-fetched? This goal is actually quite possible. Neuroscience has been able to demonstrate using functional magnetic resonance imaging (fMRI) that mutual understanding can in fact happen between speakers and listeners.[2]

To accomplish this sharing of ideas requires the creative and effective use of language, non-verbal communication, visual aids, and audience

BOX 16.1

Analogies for Illustrating the Foundation of a Presentation

A thread or rope	Thread and rope are analogies for any conceptual tool used to "tie things together," making the concepts presented into a cohesive theme or message.
A journey	This analogy works well for a presentation in which the speaker takes the audience on a journey, such as the progression from diagnosis to successful treatment of a disease.
A story	Telling a real or fictional story puts a face on a message in a relatable way that is more memorable than presenting straight facts and information. Consider the seven basic plots: overcoming the monster, the quest, voyage and return, comedy, tragedy, rebirth, and rags to riches.
A narrative arc	The construction of a story plot is often composed of five parts: (1) exposition—in which characters and the problem or conflict are introduced; (2) rising action—a series of events that creates a rise in suspense, illustrating the characters' struggles; (3) climax—the point of greatest suspense and the turning point, describing how the characters overcome difficulties and hurdles to solve the problem; (4) falling action—the release of tension as events unfold, leading to the ... (5) resolution—when the characters succeed in overcoming or solving the problem or conflict.
The problem-solving spectrum	A presentation based on solving a problem may address a situation by including one or more parts of the problem-solving spectrum, which begins with recognition of the problem, followed by a definition of the problem, then puts the problem into the broader context, solves part of the problem, and potentially solves the whole problem. Make it clear from the outset what the expectations are for how far the presentation will take the audience in solving the problem.
A through-line	This is the unifying theme that holds all parts of a story together. No matter which analogy is used, it is essential to have a solid foundation.

participation strategies that create meaning—meaning that is not only understood but put into practice. However, before determining what visual aids to use or selecting activities for an audience to apply the information, the communicator must first establish a solid foundation upon which to build a presentation.

A solid foundation, or unifying theme, successfully ties the entire presentation together. The SOCO and key message points fit it like a glove. Any element added to the presentation enhances and builds on the theme. Every word, example, and visual aid helps fulfill the presentation's purpose. Many analogies can be used to illustrate this foundation; see Box 16.1 for common

examples.[1,3-5] Each one represents something that connects key points and conveys the SOCO so that an audience understands, remembers, and achieves the desired outcomes.

Once an overall foundation or theme is established, the structure of the presentation can be built. Creating an outline puts this structure on paper. Various methods can be used for organizing a presentation and are described later in the chapter. Whichever method is selected, the purpose remains: to present the key points along with supporting evidence. Supporting evidence includes examples, facts and statistics, illustrations, research studies, survey results, observations, personal stories, and more. What is chosen should be based on what will be most meaningful to an audience and what will make the best case to support the big idea. There is no need to tell everything about a topic. Almost always, the well-known axiom holds true: Less is more.

In determining specific content to present to support key points, follow this process:

- Begin with a brainstorming session to list as much as possible related to the topic. Compile research notes, other credible sources, and even personal experiences to make a complete list of potential content.
- Cluster data, ideas, and insights into themes. Step back from the list and organize it under the key points. If something doesn't fit a key point, remove it.
- If there are gaps, do further research for additional supporting evidence and examples. Consider the viewpoints of the audience. Does the presentation include information that will answer their questions, fit their values, and address common beliefs, objections, and misconceptions?
- Finally, get rid of what is unnecessary. Ask: What's the story? What does this mean? What should people take away? Cut anything that distracts. If there are three examples, pick the one that works best. It's always an option to provide an audience with a list of additional resources. A good presentation will encourage them to explore the topic more on their own.

At this stage in presentation development and design, beware of the temptation to share every piece of information with an audience. Review the list again; it is likely it still has too much content to reasonably share given the time constraints of a presentation or the needs and interest capacity of an audience. The purpose of a presentation is *not* for the presenter to look smart by sharing all he or she knows; rather, it is an opportunity to help an audience feel smart by gaining information in ways they can understand and put to use.[6]

Refer to Chapter 3 page 47 for a review of empathy.

Present Information for the Three *M*'s of Maximum Impact

For maximum impact, a message must be meaningful, memorable, and motivating. Each of these *M*'s plays a role in presentation effectiveness.

MEANINGFUL

Meaningful messages are understood by an audience. Meaningful learning occurs when new information is connected to an audience's pre-existing knowledge, using words and context they understand, and is provided to match their needs.[7-9] It is based on D. P. Ausubel's assimilation theory of meaningful learning,[7] which explains that an audience derives meaning from a message by connecting it to what they currently know and understand. When information is presented for meaningful learning, it allows audience members to organize their knowledge, integrate new information, and create connections between related concepts and ideas.

Neuroscience provides evidence for ways that meaningful learning produces structural changes in the brain.[9] Decision making and problem solving rely on strong neural connections. As greater understanding forms, learners are able to apply knowledge in novel situations.

If information is not connected to prior knowledge, it is no more than learning a sequence of numbers, as in a phone number, no more than pure memorization. Therefore, when communicating, it is essential to determine what the audience members already know so that new information can be presented in a way that connects it to their previous knowledge, using words they understand, and making it relevant to their life experience.

If audience members have no idea *why* they need to learn something and if they can't put it into context, it won't be meaningful to them, and it won't be attended to or remembered. However, when information is presented in ways that *are* meaningful to them, they will become interested and seek to learn more.[6] Making messages meaningful requires empathy. In other words, consider and try to understand an audience's perspective. The more that is known about an audience, with understanding of what the people in the audience want and need, the more likely that a presentation will reach and teach them.

MEMORABLE

Messages must not only be meaningful, they must be memorable. Communicate in ways that assist audiences in storing knowledge in long-term memory, where it can be retrieved and used, not only in the present but into the future.

Memory is characterized as having three components: sensory memory, working (or short-term) memory, and long-term memory.[10] The first component is learning through the senses. The senses of sight (visual) and sound (auditory) are employed most in traditional learning. Information is represented through two basic forms: descriptions and depictions. Descriptions can be printed text or symbols that are seen or spoken words that are heard. Depictions are photographs, illustrations, maps, models, graphics, videos, and so on.

Working memory has a limited capacity for storing and processing these descriptions and depictions of information. The cognitive load theory suggests that working memory is affected by both the total load of information presented and the complexity of information presented.[11] Working memory is also distracted by unnecessary, extraneous information. Effective communication does not overload the information processing and storing channels, but it reduces extraneous processing and manages essential processing.

Building on the importance of meaningful messages, long-term memory requires prior (internal) knowledge in order to understand text and images presented as external information.[10] It requires knowledge of the language used, object recognition, and conceptual knowledge. Learners build mental models from words and pictures. When these two modalities of combining words with pictures are involved in learning, a stronger mental representation is developed.[11]

Effective communication is designed to be meaningful to an audience, providing supportive information to bridge what is learned to what is known. Additionally, the audience is provided with guided practice to apply their knowledge to real life.[12] As knowledge is repeatedly put into practice, it becomes rooted in memory.

How humans communicate can enhance or detract from memory-making capacity. This chapter describes various approaches to presenting information that utilize multiple modes of learning and enhance understanding and memory.

MOTIVATING

The third *M* that conveys a characteristic of effective messages is *motivating*. In addition to being meaningful and memorable, a message must motivate an audience. Motivating messages resonate with an audience's values, interests, desires, and beliefs; motivating messages meet an audience's needs and solve their problems.[5]

A message that elicits an emotional response also motivates taking action. As Paul Zak, a neuroscientist, has learned in his research: "Narratives that cause us to pay attention and also involve us emotionally are the stories that move us to action."[13] Zak and colleagues are credited with the discovery that the release of oxytocin produces the feeling of trust, and a good story promotes oxytocin production.

What makes a "good story"? One that enables the audience to see themselves in the plot.[13] Therefore, writing a story or message that resonates with an audience requires the communicator to know what the audience wants and needs. An audience assessment can provide the communicator with the information needed to design a presentation that motivates learning and behavior change. Including factors related to behavior change in an audience assessment can provide the communicator with the information needed to design a presentation that motivates learning and behavior change.

See Chapter 11 for more on audience assessment.

Chapter 12 provides descriptions of factors that influence audience members to change behavior.

Present Content Using Strategies That Promote Attention and Engagement

An audience's attention span lasts about 10 minutes.[14] To overcome this challenge, the effective communicator employs the tool of contrast. Michael Port, in *Steal the Show*,[3] describes three types of contrast:

- structural
- emotional
- delivery

Structural contrast occurs when varying approaches are used to deliver content. Rather than conveying all of the information through the use of graphs and research statistics, include a story, an illustration, a demonstration, or an audience participation activity.

Emotional contrast occurs when approaches are varied in ways that lead the audience to experience differing emotions. Serious moments are balanced with joyful ones. Examples of this are using a joke to lighten the mood before or after presenting serious research results, or telling a moving story to illustrate the main idea along with providing straightforward statistics.

Delivery contrast involves the use of vocal variety, movement while presenting, variations in timing, and gestures. Structural and emotional contrast will be achieved using the techniques covered throughout this section.

However, gaining and maintaining attention is not enough for maximum impact. Audience engagement and full participation moves learning beyond remembering in the cognitive domain and beyond receiving in the affective domain. The more fully audience members participate in and engage with the learning process, the more they learn, the stronger the memory, and the greater the likelihood that they'll adopt desired behaviors.[15] Chapters 19 and 20 are devoted to methods that engage the audience during a presentation. This chapter explores how active participation helps make a presentation meaningful, memorable, and motivating. The first step is determining the overall structure of a presentation.

How Is Content Organized and Presented for Learning and Application?

When organizing content for a presentation or any type of communication, maintain focus on the overall goal, the SOCO and key message points, and the learning objectives, as described in Chapter 15. Select content and organize it based on the needs of an audience and not on a best guess of what they want and need. Figure out what they know and what they need to know. This knowledge will allow for meaningful connections between concepts and ideas in ways the audience can

understand. The structure of a presentation can help the presenter to make meaningful connections with the audience as well as help them put knowledge into practice. One of the most important gifts to give an audience is help in giving structure to the knowledge being presented. Structure makes connections; it paints the big picture and provides context. Structure enhances meaning.[16]

Organize Concepts Using Strategies That Promote Logical and Meaningful Connections

Having generated a list of ideas to present and an overall theme or through-line for a presentation, it is time to organize those ideas using a method that helps both presenter and audience make logical and meaningful connections. In this section, a variety of methods for organizing content will be described, with practical applications. The example of a presentation about food safety will illustrate how the same concepts can be organized in a variety of ways. Try out these methods and see which one(s) work best.

No matter what method is chosen to organize the content of a presentation, make sure it answers the *why*, *what*, and *how* questions: *Why* is this important? *What* does the audience need to know? *How* can the audience use the information? Recognize that before an audience is ready to learn *how* to do something, they need to know *why* to do it.

IDEA CHARTS

An idea chart uses a hierarchy, as in an organizational or ancestry diagram. See Figure 16.1 for

Chapter 21 will provide detailed examples of using delivery contrast.

See Chapter 15 for a refresher on taxonomies of educational objectives.

Chapter 11 covers needs assessment.

FIGURE 16.1 **An idea chart for a presentation about food safety**

FIGURE 16.2 **A storyboard about food-borne illness**

The problem	The cause	Conditions that promote the problem	Four principles that prevent the problem
Food-borne illness	Common pathogens	FAT TOM (food source, acidity, temperature, time, oxygen, and moisture)	CSCC (clean, separate, cook, and chill)

an example of using this technique to structure ideas presented about food safety. The main idea is at the top and subordinate points are illustrated below, in a pyramid shape. Ideas are grouped into categories, with lines depicting connections. For example, below each of the four main steps in Figure 16.1, subtopics can be added in the order to be presented.

STORYBOARDS

A storyboard uses a series of boxes in which key messages and images are sketched to describe the "story" of a presentation. This method is useful for planning a series of slides or a video. An example is illustrated in Figure 16.2.

In this example, the presentation begins with an overview of the problem of food-borne illness—its severity and magnitude. This is followed by a discussion of the most common food-borne pathogens. The third topic is the conditions that promote the growth of harmful microorganisms, which are abbreviated using the acronym *FAT TOM*: *food source, acidity, temperature, time, oxygen,* and *moisture*. This is followed by the four food safety principles that prevent food-borne illness: clean, separate, cook, and chill. Keep in mind that fully illustrating the presentation would require more than four boxes in the storyboard.

THREE ACTS

The three acts strategy can be used to structure a presentation with or without a dramatic plot. Without a storyline, consider the acts as three parts of a presentation: Act 1 establishes the situation,

Act 2 describes the problem or conflict, and Act 3 resolves the conflict or solves the problem.

The three-act structure is more commonly used with a story. In Box 16.1, a story or narrative arc was described in five parts (or acts), but stories can also be conveyed in as few as three acts. Stories can be from real life, or they can be made up. For example, a factual story can describe an actual food safety incident, or an imaginary story based on common food safety situations can be utilized.

Using a relatable food safety scenario:

- Act 1 can set the stage: "One morning a hungry student found three slices of leftover pizza in a box on her desk...."
- Act 2 can introduce the threat of food-borne illness: The story continues by depicting the student contemplating whether or not to eat the pizza and the reasons why or why not. This act might end with the student seeking help from a fellow student, accessing notes from a class on food safety, or going online to find answers.
- Act 3 can demonstrate how to use food safety principles to prevent a food-borne illness. After the student finds accurate answers to the dilemma of "to eat or not to eat," the story culminates with proper disposal of the pizza and the student heading off to the dining hall for breakfast.

PROBLEM SOLVING

A problem-solving organizational structure presents problems along with solutions. One or more problems are conveyed in turn and then solved. The more dramatic and compelling the depictions of the problems and solutions, the more impactful the presentation will be.

- For a youth audience, various food-borne illnesses could be depicted as evil villains, and the food safety measures could be portrayed as superhero characters coming to save the day.
- For a lay audience, typical food safety situations could be described, and audiences could select the proper course of action from a list of choices. As choices are discussed, food safety principles could be emphasized.
- For a professional audience, the use of compelling statistics and actual occurrences of food-borne illnesses from news reports could be described, and the audience could determine what measures might have prevented the incidents.

COMPARE AND CONTRAST

An organizational structure of compare and contrast works well when it is appropriate to discuss ideas that differ between two or more situations. For the food safety scenario, strategies could be compared between commercial kitchens and home food safety. How are they different and how are they the same? Another comparison could be food safety at home vs on the road (eg, packing lunches, picnics, bringing food home from a restaurant).

Other examples include comparing the evidence from observational vs experimental studies or comparing and contrasting ways to incorporate more of something in the diet vs reducing something in the diet. An example from this text is this very comparison of ways to organize and present information.

NUMBERED LIST

A numbered list is a simple and effective way to present information. Numbering provides structure where there may not be a hierarchical order. The numbers may designate importance, as in Top 10 lists, with number 1 being the highest, or each numbered item may have equal significance. In the food safety scenario, four components of food safety are listed and described. Each one is equally important. A numbered list provides structure and

order, alerting the audience that reaching number 4, for example, means this particular part of the presentation is almost finished.

TIMELINE

Presenting information chronologically provides a logical sequence to follow and is a useful structure when the information has a past, present, and future orientation. Examples of using a timeline include describing nutrition throughout the weeks or trimesters of pregnancy or during the first year of life for the infant. An example with the food safety scenario could take the audience through the stages of a food-borne illness, beginning with how the food became contaminated and describing how the illness spreads through cross-contamination, improper handling, cooking (or chilling) to improper temperatures, or improper storage. The timeline could be revisited to illustrate how the outcome of the story could be changed with preventive strategies employed.

MODULAR OR SECTIONAL

Information can also be presented as chunks of related information. These chunks can be referred to as modules, sections, parts, or many other names. This book is broken into sections. A reader can begin anywhere in the book and find references to helpful information in other chapters. For modular organization to work well, each section needs to be clearly labeled and described.

MIND MAPS

A mind map organizes the ideas to be presented with the central idea in the middle and subordinate ideas coming out in a circular fashion, as illustrated in Figure 16.3. A mind map works well when the information presented does not logically flow into a linear organization. The mind map assists the presenter in thinking through the connections that exist between concepts so these connections can be described to the audience.

CONCEPT MAPS

Similar to a mind map, a concept map provides a visual tool for organizing ideas and illustrating connections between concepts. This technique was developed by Joseph Novak and his research team at Cornell University in the 1970s.[17] Concept maps are considered a structured conceptualization technique.[18]

Concept maps can be used for illustrating an audience's current knowledge of a topic and visualizing relationships among concepts and themes. They can be generated from audience assessment data using software that applies multidimensional scaling and cluster analysis. This makes them a useful tool for both audience analysis and program planning.

Concept maps can be depicted in various ways. See Figure 16.4 on page 264 for an example. It shows a concept map related to food safety based on input from two sources: the brainstorming of colleagues and ideas from focus groups with audience members. The concepts depicted illustrate the issues of concern raised by both groups and how they relate to each other.

Concept mapping allows for systematic organization of information from potential end users and ensures that the content in the program uses language that is familiar to the end users.[18] Armed with the results of a needs assessment, the communicator lists knowledge concepts to be taught, taking into consideration audience needs, apprehensions, and concerns. Communicators design communication to meet audience needs and program goals and objectives.

Consider how to present the ideas in Figure 16.4 to promote logical and meaningful connections. Clearly, the ability to cook is an audience concern related to food safety. Therefore, it would be helpful to discuss how to practice food safety during food preparation, building both the audience's food safety knowledge and their cooking skills. While presenting, the communicator can further assess the audience's experiences with food-borne illness and use them to illustrate concepts and make the message meaningful. Interactions with the audience can assist the communicator in interpreting motivation for change. In the end, a well-organized presentation strategically connects the interrelationships among concepts identified using concept mapping.

Finally, concept maps can be used as a learning tool for an audience. Audience members can create concept maps to help them organize their knowledge and demonstrate understanding of the interrelationships between ideas. Students can generate lists of concepts learned in a lecture or a reading and draw a concept map to depict relationships and connections between ideas.

Present Content for Meaningful Learning

Recall that meaningful learning occurs when audience members connect new information to prior knowledge, when they understand the language used to convey the message, and when the information is relevant and useful.

As described in Chapter 12, constructs known to influence knowledge acquisition and behavior change can be applied to identify logical and meaningful connections. What are the audience's or participants' intrinsic motivators? A skilled presenter selects examples that draw the listener in, provide meaning, and connect emotionally with the audience.

"Information is not knowledge."

—ALBERT EINSTEIN

FIGURE 16.4 **Concept map of food safety for program planning**

Creating relevant and useful content can be a challenge because meaning and relevance differ depending on the person. What words does the audience understand? What context is meaningful? Answering these questions when preparing a presentation is critical, but there may still be some surprises from participants, no matter how much preparation is done. There are likely to be audience members at opposite ends of the knowledge and interest scales, with some audience members who know a fair amount about a topic and show great interest and others who are ambivalent or uninterested. How can a presentation be designed to meet the needs of people at the extremes as well as those somewhere in between?

Lee LeFever in *The Art of Explanation*[6] suggests imagining a scale from *A* to *Z* to represent the knowledge and interest level of an audience about a topic. The letter *Z* at the far right represents the level it is hoped an audience will achieve, as described in the goals or learning objectives. The letter *A* represents no knowledge or interest in the topic. Audience members may be at any point along the scale. For audience members at the left side of the scale, it is critical to begin by explaining why the topic is important and building context before moving into more depth about the topic or explaining how to put the knowledge into practice.

A common error is assuming the audience knows more than it does. A nutrition professional may be at the *Z* end of the scale, and likely surrounded by others at this level, making it natural to present messages based on a higher level of knowledge and interest. However, to reach audience members at the *A* end of the scale, it's important to build the content step by step, moving from explaining big-picture concepts to going into greater detail and depth. Don't worry that this will bore those who are more knowledgeable; in general, starting with big-picture concepts promotes confidence in what they know and serves as a welcome review.[6] When the basics are presented in such a way that they establish what is agreed on about the topic and provide needed context, the entire audience benefits. To leave a portion of the audience behind is a disservice to all.

The inability of a presenter to take the perspective of an audience has been dubbed the curse of knowledge, which means the more knowledge a person has, the harder it can be to see things from the viewpoint of someone with little knowledge.[19] To be effective requires empathy and recalling what it was like to be a novice. A major way to overcome the curse of knowledge is to use words and examples that are familiar to the audience.

SPEAK THE AUDIENCE'S LANGUAGE

After years of studying science and nutrition and being surrounded by people who understand the citric acid cycle, also known as the tricarboxylic acid (TCA) or Krebs cycle, it is easy to speak a technical language and expect other people to understand it. Remember, unless the audience are professionals, they will not have the same scientific background. For a message to have meaning, it must be relatable. An audience must understand a presenter. A presenter must speak an audience's language.

What is the language of an audience? How can a presenter know? Chapter 11 described how to complete an audience assessment. Use it to learn which words the audience knows and uses and which words are new or confusing. If it is not possible to do a needs assessment prior to a presentation, consider other methods to learn about an audience. Perhaps it is possible to have one-on-one contact with audience members who will be returning for a group session. Pay attention to the words they use and the examples they provide. For a brand-new audience, ask questions within a presentation. Watch for body language and facial expressions that indicate confusion or lack of understanding. Use interactive techniques that get the audience talking. Pick up on their word choices and build on them.

Practice making substitutions for common nutrition jargon. Rather than saying *ingest* or *consume*, say *eat*. Instead of *cardiovascular*, say *heart*. Replace the phrase *adipose tissue* with *fat*. If an accurate meaning requires the use of jargon, teach the audience words they need to know and reinforce the definitions in a handout.

CONNECT NEW KNOWLEDGE TO WHAT IS KNOWN

Presenting content for meaningful learning involves connecting knowledge to what is known. To do this, a presenter must know what an audience already knows. A needs assessment can provide this knowledge before a presentation. During a presentation, asking questions and engaging in interactions with the audience clearly shows what the audience knows. Questions and activities also provide opportunities to help an audience connect new knowledge to prior knowledge.

While learning how much or how little the audience already knows, don't be intimidated by a lack of knowledge or by a greater depth of knowledge than expected. Learn from participants. It may turn out that an audience member who claimed to understand something a certain way has misunderstood the content. It takes a skilled communicator to walk the line of explaining information effectively, opening listeners to learning new information, and avoiding arguments over controversial information. A presenter's job is to effectively disseminate accurate and relevant information. Communicators who know their audience will make meaningful connections and open audiences to listen and learn.

MAKE IT RELEVANT AND USEFUL

Information that is personally relevant to a communicator may or may not be relevant to a particular audience. Again, knowing an audience is the first step. Listen to their concerns. Listen to their stories. To prompt audiences to share their stories and concerns, ask questions and seek elaboration. Consider an example of a presentation for a diabetes support group. Prompts to learn their concerns and stories could include the following:

- Describe how you learned you had diabetes. What helped you make sense of your disease?
- Tell about a time when you had to explain diabetes to someone else. What helped that person understand it better?

Chapters 19 and 20 cover a multitude of techniques for audience interaction.

- Describe a time when you experienced an episode of high or low blood sugar.
- What is the most frustrating aspect of living with diabetes?

Pick up on examples audience members use and incorporate them into your presentation. Take advantage of the opportunity to share a variety of ways to apply the information. For example, in a presentation about diabetes management, find out what audience members currently know and do. This could happen during a needs assessment, by asking audience members to complete a preassessment prior to the presentation and going over their responses during it, or by interspersing questions throughout a talk. Examples of information that might be sought include whether they have misconceptions about consuming sugar and other carbohydrates, or what strategies they use for meal planning.

To make a presentation meaningful, what is presented and how it is presented must be relevant and meaningful to the audience. An audience that never cooks is not interested in substituting ingredients in a recipe or learning how to fry meat without added fat. An audience that eats out wants to learn how to make healthier choices from a menu.

After determining which examples will be relevant, design experiences to help audiences apply the information. Audience interaction allows ideas to be shared and audience members to learn from one another. Discussions have the potential to create an even greater number of concepts relevant to participants. Information becomes tangible and applicable to their lives.

Provide Content in Context That Is Meaningful to an Audience

Context is the setting in which words and ideas are given meaning. An audience eats food, not nutrients. Talking about food gives context to the nutrients an audience is learning about and, ultimately, eating. Providing context helps the audience see the big picture (the forest) without getting lost in the details (the trees). What are ways to provide meaningful context?

Behavior modification theories can be applied to provide context. For example, the health belief model (see Figure 12.5 on page 190) takes into consideration perceptions that something is

Chapter 18 provides ideas for the effective use of visual aids in presentations.

"Content is king, but context is the kingdom."

—TONY O'DRISCOLL, *LEARNING IN 3D: ADDING A NEW DIMENSION TO ENTERPRISE LEARNING AND COLLABORATION*

going to turn out a certain way relating to one's health. When delivering a message, help participants recognize whether they have barriers to learning information based on these perceptions. Everyone in the audience has a reason for being there. Help audience members acknowledge their needs and attend to the information presented as a means to meet their needs.

Visual aids are another approach to help an audience understand content by providing context. Visual aids can illustrate relationships between concepts or show real-life examples that audience members can relate to.

Even without visual aids, the use of visualization techniques can provide context and meaning. This strategy invites participants to imagine putting the information into practice in their lives. The presenter sets the stage and audience members fill in the context that fits their situation. To use the food safety example, the audience can be asked to imagine a trip to the store and to think about how they would select food, transport the food home, and store it safely.

Activities built into a presentation for the audience to practice applying their knowledge are useful for providing context. When audience members see how to apply information in real life, it becomes practical and useful. Select examples that fit the audience or provide a means for the audience to create an example during the presentation. Many strategies can be used to put information into context.

The final section of this chapter will set the stage for the remaining chapters in Section 4, which describe specific approaches for designing and delivering presentations. To be equipped to select the optimal presentation approaches for an audience, a presenter must first develop an appreciation for how that audience learns.

How Can Understanding the Way an Audience Learns Determine Presentation Design and Delivery?

There are numerous strategies for describing the variety of ways in which people prefer to learn, process information, adopt habits, and engage with others. These include various learning styles, personalities, and tendencies. Audiences are diverse, making it impractical to tailor a presentation to only one style of learning, engagement, or strategy for behavior change. Therefore, become aware of the variety of audience preferences and then use a variety of approaches, as all members of an audience can benefit from employing multiple learning strategies.

Communicate to Multiple Intelligences and Learning Styles

One of the best known schemes for describing the variety of ways learning occurs is based on the theory of multiple intelligences, introduced by Howard Gardner, a Harvard professor of cognition and education.[20] He identified eight types of intelligences. See Box 16.2 for a list of Gardner's learning styles and suggested teaching approaches to match each type of intelligence. Every person has all of them but prefers learning via some over others. For instance, some people prefer to learn and process information presented visually, while others prefer to learn and process information presented verbally. Does this mean a presenter needs to match teaching approaches to the learning style preferences of individual learners? No. Research supports presenting information in ways that assist all members of an audience to employ multiple ways of learning and processing information. In fact, the more intelligences employed when learning, the more is remembered, and learning itself is better.[21]

A similar approach, which focuses on how information is received and processed, is known as VARK, which stands for *visual*, *auditory*, *read/write*, and *kinesthetic*. It was developed by Fleming and Mills of Lincoln University in New Zealand.

 ## Gardner's Multiple Intelligences and Recommended Teaching Approaches

Multiple Intelligence Category	Recommended Teaching Approaches
Verbal/linguistic	Spoken and written words: reading, listening, speaking, writing
Logical/mathematical	Problem solving, structured learning
Visual/spatial	Visual aids and images
Bodily/kinesthetic	Movement and note-taking, concrete experiences
Musical/rhythmic	Songs, patterns, and rhythms
Interpersonal/relational	Discussions, brainstorming, collaborative learning
Intrapersonal/introspective	Reflection, independent work
Naturalist	Science and nature, learning through classification

Their research confirms the work of others and led them to this conclusion[22]:

> *It is simply not realistic to expect teachers to provide programs that accommodate the learning style diversity present in their classes, even if they can establish the nature and extent of that diversity.... [So,] the most realistic approach to the accommodation of learning styles in teaching programs should involve empowering students through knowledge of their own learning styles to adjust their learning behavior to the learning programs they encounter.*

The VARK website is listed in the resources section at the end of the chapter.

Another scheme is David A. Kolb's model of learning styles and experiential learning,[23] (see

FIGURE 16.5 **Kolb's model of learning styles and experiential learning**

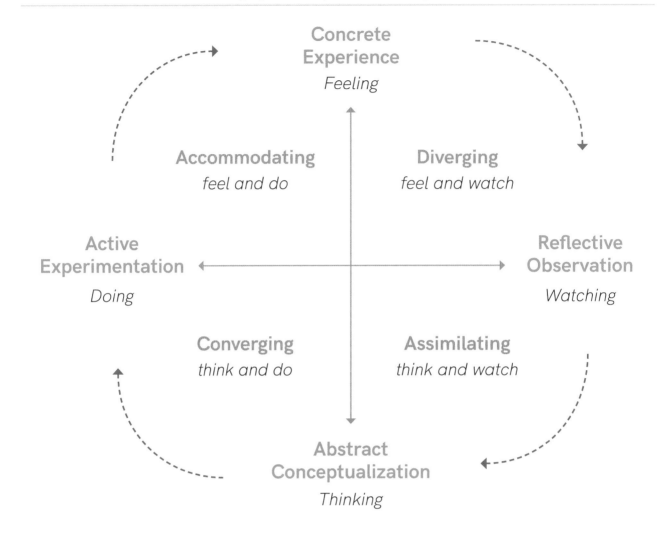

Figure 16.5), which illustrates another way to look at how people experience learning. His four-quadrant model is divided by a vertical line and a horizontal line. The vertical line places how a person perceives or thinks about things on a continuum, from sensing or feeling learning experiences to analyzing experiences logically. The horizontal line is a continuum representing how new information is processed. On one end is watching and reflecting and on the other is jumping right in and acting immediately, then reflecting later.

As illustrated with the arrows in the figure, learners cycle through the stages from first experiencing a learning event, then reflecting on their learning, followed by thinking in new ways about what was learned, and finally putting their knowledge into action in new ways.

When the two kinds of perceiving and processing information are put together, this makes up Kolb's four-quadrant learning style model.

IMAGINATIVE LEARNERS

Imaginative learners ("feel and watch") perceive information by feeling and process it reflectively. They strive to connect with information on a personal level. Educational activities they learn best with include films to trigger reflection, demonstrations, questions to prompt thinking, brainstorming, puzzles, observations, and games.

ANALYTIC LEARNERS

Analytic learners ("think and watch") perceive information abstractly and process it reflectively. They think through concepts and pay attention to expert opinions. They thrive in traditional lecture settings and enjoy discussions, debates, readings, and journals.

COMMONSENSE LEARNERS

Commonsense learners ("think and do") perceive information abstractly and process it actively. They apply theories to practice and are avid problem solvers. They like to learn how things work and want to put knowledge to immediate use. They like making graphs and charts, drawing, doing case studies, and completing writing activities and worksheets.

DYNAMIC LEARNERS

Dynamic learners ("feel and do") perceive information concretely and process it actively. They learn by trial and error and are enthusiastic about learning and trying new things. They like change and taking risks. They want hands-on activities, action plans, developing products, videos, skits, and simulations. They like working in the field.

Other learning style schemes and indexes have been published, such as the one by Richard Felder and Barbara Soloman of North Carolina State University, listed in the resources section along with links to a variety of assessment tests about learning style preferences. Keep in mind that these describe preferred ways of processing information and learning. All people benefit from being exposed to a variety of presentation methods that challenge them to learn in a variety of ways using all modes of learning.

Communicate to Different Personalities and Tendencies

Another approach to describe how people perceive the world and engage with information and with others is by identifying psychological or personality type. This approach originated with Carl Jung's theory of psychological types and was expanded by Katherine Cook Briggs and her daughter Isabel Briggs Myers. The famous Myers-Briggs Type Indicator (MBTI) assessment was first published in 1946 and has been widely used for more than seven decades to determine a person's psychological or personality type. The types are derived from 16 possible combinations of traits, including one of each trait in the following four pairs[24]:

- Extraverted (E) vs Introverted (I)
- Sensing (S) vs Intuition (N)
- Thinking (T) vs Feeling (F)
- Judging (J) vs Perceiving (P)

It is important to note that people are rarely 100% one trait or the other, but rather are somewhere in between, with a tendency to one trait more than the other. The website for the MBTI assessment is listed in the resources section.

In addition to having different learning styles and personalities, audiences are composed of people with different tendencies regarding what motivates them to take action. An approach to characterize these tendencies was developed and described by author Gretchen Rubin.[25] Rubin's Four Tendencies are currently being investigated as a potential approach to understanding patient compliance in clinical settings.[26] Each tendency is characterized by an inclination to be motivated by internal and external expectations. An example of an internal expectation is meeting a self-imposed goal. An example of an external expectation is meeting a deadline set by a boss. See Figure 16.6 (page 270) to see how each of the four tendencies responds to expectations.

The *upholder* is motivated by both external and internal expectations. The *questioner* is motivated by inner expectations but not outer expectations. The *obliger* is motivated by outer expectations but not inner expectations. The *rebel* is motivated by neither. This is a simple way to characterize each tendency and the recommended approach to promote positive behavior change for each[25]:

- **Upholder:** "I can do the things I want to do, and I can do the things I don't want to do."

  Provide clear expectations and a schedule with deadlines.

- **Questioner:** "I'll comply—if you convince me why."

  Provide clarity and justify expectations.

- **Obliger:** "You can count on me, and I'm counting on you to count on me."

  Provide outer accountability.

- **Rebel:** "You can't make me, and neither can I."

  Provide information, consequences, and choice.

A nationally representative sample of US adults with a mix of gender, age, and household income demonstrated that about 41% of respondents were obligers, 24% questioners, 19% upholders, and 17% rebels.[25] A URL for the quiz is in the resources section.

As with the intelligence and learning styles, use personality types and tendencies to help explain

FIGURE 16.6 **Rubin's Four Tendencies**[a]

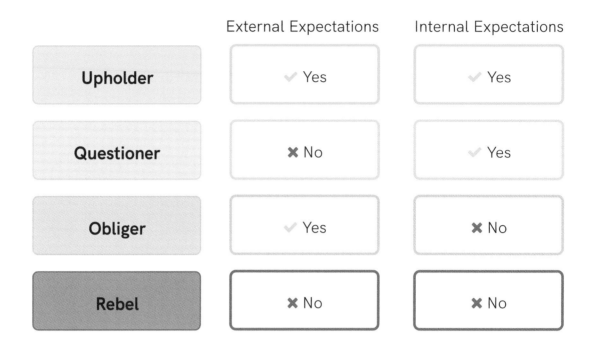

	External Expectations	Internal Expectations
Upholder	✓ Yes	✓ Yes
Questioner	✗ No	✓ Yes
Obliger	✓ Yes	✗ No
Rebel	✗ No	✗ No

[a] Adapted from reference 25.

and motivate learning and behavior rather than stereotyping or typecasting anyone into various categories. Above all, presenters must not assume that an audience shares their own preferences. As Abela wisely points out in *Advanced Presentations by Design*,[5] "Unless you consciously consider the kinds of personalities that are likely to be in your audience, you will end up designing your presentation so that it satisfies your own personality type only." It's natural to convey information in a way that is personally preferred, but try to communicate in ways that encompass all preferences.

Communicate in Ways That Promote Active Engagement

Long ago, Confucius said, "I hear and I forget. I see and I remember. I do and I understand." This statement is still considered as true today as it was 2,500 years ago. Learning takes place by doing.

A more recent version of this concept is found in Edgar Dale's Cone of Experience,[27] first developed in 1946 and illustrated in Figure 16.7. Various adaptations of this figure are often cited for the importance of providing active and multimedia learning experiences. Dale, a distinguished professor at the Ohio State University, described the cone as a "visual metaphor of learning experiences," warning, "You will make a dangerous mistake, however, if you regard the bands on the cone as rigid, inflexible divisions."[28]

The percentages frequently listed for retention of information are not from Dale; he makes no claims to empirical research in his books, but rather bases his work on theory and observation. The numbers are attributed to the National Training Laboratories Institute, but original research is not available to provide evidence.[29]

As in the previous discussion of learning styles, this model is most useful as a reminder of the importance of conveying information through a variety of strategies and approaches to maximize learning. Chapters 18 through 20 explore these concepts and strategies in more detail. This chapter summarizes key principles for including application experiences as an essential component of effective presentations.

A DIALOGUE APPROACH

One effective strategy for active engagement is the dialogue approach to adult learning.[30] This approach encourages communicators to design a learning task to incorporate four parts, each beginning with the letter A.

FIGURE 16.7 **Edgar Dale's Cone of Experience**[a]

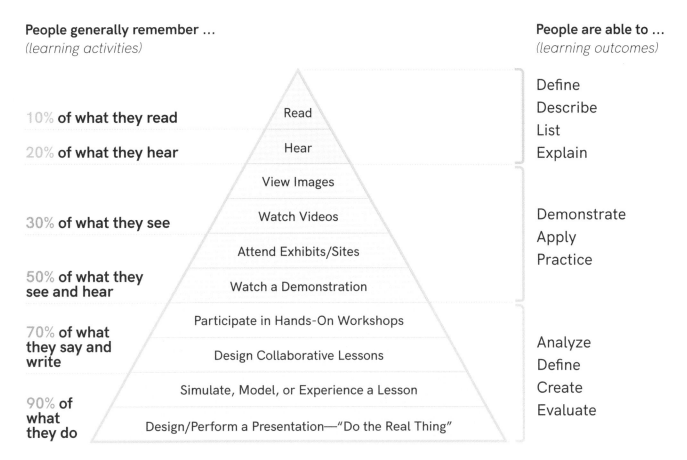

People generally remember ...
(learning activities)

People are able to ...
(learning outcomes)

10% **of what they read** — Read

20% **of what they hear** — Hear

Define
Describe
List
Explain

View Images

30% **of what they see** — Watch Videos

Attend Exhibits/Sites

50% **of what they see and hear** — Watch a Demonstration

Demonstrate
Apply
Practice

70% **of what they say and write** — Participate in Hands-On Workshops

Design Collaborative Lessons

90% **of what they do** — Simulate, Model, or Experience a Lesson

Design/Perform a Presentation—"Do the Real Thing"

Analyze
Define
Create
Evaluate

[a] Adapted from reference 27.

Anchor The topic is anchored in the audience members' lives. The topic is given relevance and meaning.

Add New information is provided in the presentation.

Apply The audience participates in an application activity to practice using the information.

Away The audience takes learning into the future with practical action steps.

PROVIDE PRACTICAL, ACTIONABLE STEPS

Recall from Chapter 14 that adult learners favor practical learning experiences that help them solve problems. Application experiences take knowledge and put it into practice in real-life situations. This means that in a presentation about food safety, the audience members don't just learn the importance of using a thermometer; they are instructed in how to calibrate a thermometer and insert it properly in food, and then they practice calibration and demonstrate proper insertion.

Adult learners appreciate application methods that are presented as easy-to-implement steps. Show and tell audience members how to do something, and then have them participate through guided practice. People are much more likely to take action if they have successfully practiced the activity in a safe environment. Recall the concept of self-efficacy from Chapter 12. When audience members are given opportunities to practice a behavior, often referred to as mastery experiences, their confidence in their ability to perform the activity is increased, as is their likelihood for further learning and adopting desired behaviors.[31]

In a presentation, incorporate one or more opportunities for application. If time or space is limited, choose to cover less content to allow ample time for application.

OFFER SUGGESTIONS AND OPTIONS

Chapter 14 addressed the fact that the adult learner is self-directed and internally motivated. Rather than telling an audience what to do, provide suggestions and options from which they can make their own choices. In a presentation about using legumes as a protein source, keep in mind that some audience members may prefer legumes rather than an entrée, whereas others may prefer to add legumes to casseroles; another person may prefer to add them to salads, another to soups, and someone else may use them in baked goods, such as brownies. Within any of these recipe options, provide legume options as well: black beans, red beans, navy beans, pintos, and more. When it comes to food, the options are endless.

Audience involvement, which is covered in later chapters, provides opportunities for the audience to suggest options. Audience members often take advice and suggestions from other audience members before they take the presenter's advice. There is power in positive peer influence.

When designing content to include in a presentation, consider the variety of options that can be shared that will resonate and appeal to an audience.

ALLOW FOR AUTONOMOUS DECISION MAKING

Finally, adults take responsibility for their learning. When audience members are given autonomy

> ## "People don't resist change, they resist being changed."
>
> **—PETER SENGE, PHD, DIRECTOR, CENTER FOR ORGANIZATIONAL LEARNING, MIT SLOAN SCHOOL OF MANAGEMENT**

in learning and decision making, they are more likely to make new healthy behaviors permanent habits.[32] With well-designed application experiences, well-selected options to pick from, and assistance in problem solving, audiences will be able to solve problems in ways that meet their needs. An effective presentation makes a difference because the audience not only learns but applies the learning to their lives. Provide the means for this to take place.

From the opening of a presentation to its closing statement, the effective communicator incorporates strategies that help the audience attend to the message, make sense of the message, store it in long-term memory, and apply it in their lives. The chapters that follow will present many approaches to delivering information and helping an audience put it into practice. Each strategy is grounded in research and practice. Additional background will be shared in each chapter.

Chapter 17 describes effective strategies for presentation openings and closings.

Chapter 18 describes the effective use of visual aids to enhance learning.

Chapter 19 introduces the effective use of facilitated discussions.

Chapter 20 describes several approaches for eliciting audience participation.

Chapter 21 describes how to be an effective presenter.

KEY POINTS

Create High-Impact Presentations

1 A presentation is designed and delivered to communicate one big, important idea to an audience in a way that resonates, inspires, and spurs action. A presentation delivers value to the audience in the form of key points and supporting evidence. The message is presented in ways that are meaningful to the audience, using methods that enhance memory and employing strategies that motivate the audience to attend, learn, engage, and take action.

2 When organizing content for a presentation, maintain focus on the overall goal, SOCO and key message points, and learning objectives. Select content and organize it based on the needs of the audience. Determine what audience members know and what they need to know, and present content to make connections between concepts and ideas in ways your audience can understand. The structure of a presentation can assist the communicator in making meaningful connections and help an audience put knowledge into practice.

3 Once the purpose for a presentation is determined and the content is organized to present the information to be meaningful and useful to an audience, it is time to select specific strategies for learning and application of content. These strategies should be chosen to gain and maintain attention and to promote learning and application based on research and best practices. Understanding the way audience members prefer to learn and how they engage with learning and each other can assist communicators in selecting optimal presentation strategies.

RESOURCES

Multiple intelligences test: www.literacynet.org /mi/assessment/findyourstrengths.html

VARK learning style: http://vark-learn.com

Kolb's learning styles:
- www.researchgate.net/profile/David_Kolb /publication/303446688_The_Kolb_Learning _Style_Inventory_40_Guide_to_Theory _Psychometrics_Research_Applications /links/57437c4c08ae9f741b3a1a58/The-Kolb -Learning-Style-Inventory-40-Guide-to-Theory -Psychometrics-Research-Applications.pdf
- http://med.fau.edu/students/md_m1_orientation /M1%20Kolb%20Learning%20Style%20Inventory .pdf
- www.bunbury.wa.gov.au/pdf/environment/u472 /Appendix%2019%20U472%20Community %20Facilitator%20Kolb%20Questionnaire%20Final .pdf

Felder and Soloman's learning styles index: www4.ncsu.edu/unity/lockers/users/f/felder/public /ILSdir/styles.htm

Index of learning styles questionnaire: www.engr.ncsu.edu/learningstyles/ilsweb.htm

Myers-Briggs Type Indicator: www.myersbriggs.org /my-mbti-personality-type/mbti-basics

Four Tendencies quiz: https://gretchenrubin.com/take-the-quiz

Tools for organizing presentations: https://extremepresentation.com

Learning styles assessment: http://www.educationplanner.org/students/self -assessments/learning-styles.shtml

REFERENCES

1. Anderson C. *TED Talks: The Official TED Guide to Public Speaking.* Houghton Mifflin Harcourt; 2016.
2. Stephens GL, Silbert LJ, Hasson U. Speaker–listener neural coupling underlies successful communication. *Psychol Cogn Sci Neurosci.* 2010;107(32):14425-14430.
3. Port M. *Steal the Show.* Houghton Mifflin Harcourt; 2015.

4. Munter M, Russell L. *Guide to Presentations.* Prentice Hall; 2002.

5. Abela AV. *Advanced Presentations by Design: Creating Communication That Drives Action.* 2nd ed. Wiley; 2013.

6. LeFever L. *The Art of Explanation.* John Wiley and Sons; 2013.

7. Ausubel DP. *The Acquisition and Retention of Knowledge: A Cognitive View.* Springer Science and Business Media; 2000.

8. Novak JD. *Learning, Creating, and Using Knowledge: Concept Maps as Facilitative Tools in Schools and Corporations.* Routledge; 2010.

9. Getha-Eby T, Berry T, Xu Y, O'Brien B. Meaningful learning: theoretical support for concept-based teaching. *J Nurs Educ.* 2014;53(9):494-500.

10. Schnotz W. Integrated model of text and picture comprehension. In: Mayer RE, ed. *The Cambridge Handbook of Multimedia Learning.* 2nd ed. Cambridge University Press; 2014:72-103.

11. Ayres P. State-of-the-art research into multimedia learning: a commentary on Mayer's *Handbook of Multimedia Learning. Appl Cogn Psychol.* 2015;29:631-636.

12. van Merrienboer J, Kester L. The four-component instructional design model: multimedia principles in environments for complex learning. In: Mayer RE, ed. *The Cambridge Handbook of Multimedia Learning.* 2nd ed. Cambridge University Press; 2014:104-148.

13. Zak PJ. Why inspiring stories make us react: the neuroscience of narrative. *Cerebrum.* 2015:2.

14. Medina J. *Brain Rules.* Pear Press; 2008.

15. Fink L. *Creating Significant Learning Experiences: An Integrated Approach to Designing College Courses.* Jossey-Bass; 2013.

16. Nilson LB. Understanding your students and how they learn. In: *Teaching at Its Best.* 3rd ed. Jossey-Bass; 2010:3-15.

17. Novak JD. *A Theory of Education.* Cornell University Press; 1977.

18. Cousineau TM, Goldstein M, Franko DL. A collaborative approach to nutrition education for college students. *J Am Coll Heal.* 2004;53(2):79-84.

19. Fisher R. The curse of knowledge. *New Sci.* 2011;211(2823):39-41.

20. Gardner H. *Multiple Intelligences: New Horizons in Theory and Practice.* Basic Books; 2006.

21. Pashler H, McDaniel M, Rohrer D, Bjork R. Learning styles: concepts and evidence. *Psychol Sci Public Interes.* 2008;9(3):106-116.

22. Fleming ND, Mills C. Not another inventory, rather a catalyst for reflection. *To Improv Acad.* 1992;11:137-146.

23. Kolb DA. *Experiential Learning: Experience as the Source of Learning and Development.* 2nd ed. Pearson Education; 2015.

24. Myers IB, Myers PB. *Gifts Differing: Understanding Personality Type.* 2nd ed. Davies-Black Publishing; 1995.

25. Rubin G. *The Four Tendencies.* Harmony Books; 2017.

26. Kirk J, MacDonald A, Lavender P, Dean J, Rubin G. Can treatment adherence be improved by using Rubin's Four Tendencies Framework to understand a patient's response to expectations? *Biomed Hub.* 2017;2(1)(suppl):239-250.

27. Dale E. *Audiovisual Methods in Teaching.* 3rd ed. Holt, Rinehart, and Winston; 1969.

28. Dale E. *Audiovisual Methods in Teaching.* 2nd ed. Dryden Press; 1954.

29. Lalley JP, Miller RH. The learning pyramid: does it point teachers in the right direction? *Education.* 2007;128(1):64-79.

30. Norris J. *From Telling to Teaching.* Learning by Dialogue; 2003.

31. Artino A. Academic self-efficacy: from educational theory to instructional practice. *Perspect Med Educ.* 2012;1(2):76-85.

32. Gardner B, Lally P, Wardle J. Making health habitual: the psychology of "habit-formation" and general practice. *Br J Gen Pract.* 2012;62(605):664-666.

CHAPTER 17

Deliver Strong Openings and Closings

Barbara J. Mayfield, MS, RDN, FAND
and Sonja Kassis Stetzler, MA, RDN, CPC

"Looking for the secret to capturing an audience's attention? Hook them from the start and create a desire to learn. A strong opening grabs the audience's attention and sets the stage for what follows. The end of the presentation is just as important. It is a critical opportunity to emphasize the main point and promote taking action."

> *"Begin with the end in mind."*
> —STEPHEN R. COVEY

Introduction

Looking for the secret to capturing an audience's attention? Hook them from the start and create a desire to learn. A strong opening grabs the audience's attention and sets the stage for what follows. The end of the presentation is just as important. It is a critical opportunity to emphasize the main point and promote taking action. In fact, it may be the most memorable part of a presentation if well planned and executed.

This chapter answers six questions:

- What is the purpose of the opening or introduction?
- What are the components of an effective opening or introduction?
- What are effective introduction strategies?
- What is the purpose of the presentation closing?
- What are the components of an effective closing?
- What are effective closing strategies?

Research suggests that the opening and closing of a presentation may be the most memorable parts of an entire presentation. As far back as the 1880s, beginning with Hermann Ebbinghaus's famous "forgetting curve," research regarding what information is most easily recalled has led to a body of research supporting what are known as the *primacy* and *recency effects*, which are covered later in this chapter, and the U-shaped *serial position memory curve*.[1]

This classic curve was created using research in which subjects were presented with a list of words to remember.[1,2] This fascinating phenomenon suggests that what is presented in the opening (primacy effect) and closing (recency effect) of a presentation is remembered more than what is in the middle. This does not discount what is presented in the middle, but it does underscore the importance of making what is presented first and last, the opening and closing, meaningful and impactful.

What Is the Purpose of the Opening or Introduction?

Just as the first scene in a play or first few lines in a magazine article are designed to engage and prime an audience for the rest of the show or article, the opening or introduction of a presentation has a similar purpose. First impressions count in presentations, too, and the first few lines will either invite an audience to stay with the presenter for the rest of the speech or make them decide to tune out. Another reason for putting effort into an opening is the *primacy effect*, which is the tendency to recall the first things seen or heard in sequenced information.[2] The primacy effect means that an audience will remember what happens first in a presentation.

The opening or introduction of a presentation serves several critical purposes. These include creating a desire to attend, establishing the presenter's credibility, and setting the stage for what follows. Accomplish each one to be effective.

Create Desire to Attend

A presenter's first objective is to gain and sustain an audience's attention. The results of a survey of individuals from a wide variety of professions reveal that the top-ranked skill in preparing and delivering a speech is keeping an audience's attention.[3] If an audience isn't paying attention, the presenter loses the ability to share a message and have an impact. Therefore, the primary goal of an opening is to capture the audience's attention and engage them. To "capture" an audience's attention means drawing it away from distractions, including distracting thoughts, and getting the audience focused on the message.

Capturing an audience's attention requires both perceptual arousal and inquiry arousal.[4] *Perceptual arousal* can be attained with a sudden, unexpected voice change, a surprising piece of information, or humor. *Inquiry arousal* can be attained by creating a problem situation in which the resolution is gained by seeking the knowledge that the presentation is going to provide. For example, a presentation could open this way: "Nearly 40% of the food purchased in the United States is wasted. In today's presentation you will learn three practical ways you can significantly decrease your household's food waste. Let's learn how to reduce, reuse, and recycle."

Many specific techniques can be employed to effectively gain attention, and they will be described later in the chapter.

Establish Credibility

Grabbing attention without credibility is like using "click-bait," a headline that makes an outlandish claim that is unfounded or built on anecdotal evidence. The impact in this case will be short-lived and may result in a negative outcome. Credibility refers to a person's qualifications to communicate about a topic. Presenters' credibility is based on their knowledge of a topic, their experience with the topic (whether it's firsthand experience or information they have researched), and how they relate the topic to their audiences' needs. An audience will perceive credibility based on those factors. As presented in Chapter 10, a communicator must establish *ethos*, the word Aristotle used for *credibility*, in addition to *pathos* (emotion) and *logos* (logic). To be heard, a presenter must be trusted and credible.

Prior to a speaker taking the stage, it is likely that someone else (usually an event presider or moderator) will provide an introduction. One of the main purposes for a speaker introduction is to establish the speaker's credibility and build audience interest in hearing the information the speaker will share. Presenters can assist presiders or moderators in making successful introductions by providing accurate information about themselves and the topic of the presentation.

Confidence and delivery also play a role in how an audience perceives credibility. Credibility is an attitude that exists not in the speaker, but in the minds and perceptions of the audience.[5,6] A speaker's credibility is largely determined by two factors: competence and character. Competence comes about when the speaker has knowledge and expertise on the subject being discussed, and character describes the speaker's sincerity, trustworthiness, and concern for the audience's well-being. The higher the audience regards the speaker's competence and character, the more likely they will believe and trust the messages they receive from the speaker.[5]

There are several ways to enhance and establish credibility. The first is for speakers to explain or share their experience, research, or background as it relates to the topic on which they are speaking. Second, common ground can be established with an audience by identifying ideas that are consistent with their values and beliefs. Speakers who demonstrate empathy and caring toward their audience's well-being are more likely to be trusted. Third, a presentation should be delivered with preparedness and enthusiasm.[6]

Set the Stage for What Follows

Audiences are more likely to stay with a presenter when they know where the presentation is going. Give an audience a road map so they know where a presentation is taking them. A good introduction previews the speech by giving the audience the central idea and the key points that will be covered. This chapter will discuss several successful approaches for setting the stage.

The emotional tone of a speech is also established during the opening. Be certain that it matches the purpose and message. An audience will mirror the speaker's emotions. Presenters must set the tone so the audience feels what the presenter wants them to feel.

Chapter 34 describes how to give a professional introduction.

What Are the Components of an Effective Opening or Introduction?

See Chapter 11 for how to complete an audience assessment.

Several components characterize an effective opening or introduction that gains the attention of the audience, builds credibility, and tells them where the presentation is going. A good opening creates a positive impression, demonstrates the speaker's knowledge of the audience, and introduces the key messages.

Make a Good First Impression

One of Will Rogers's famous quotes is, "You never get a second chance to make a first impression." This applies not only during the opening of a presentation but during the time leading up to it. First impressions can even be influenced by the description of a talk in a conference brochure or from the speaker's reputation mentioned by a colleague. Presenters should consider that an audience sees them before they hear them. A first impression forms spontaneously within 34 milliseconds of seeing a person's face.[7,8] First impressions also form based on a person's tone of voice, actions, and word choice. From the first contact with an audience, everything a speaker does and says is helping create a positive impression or a negative impression.[9]

No matter what a presenter's intentions, it is the audience's perception that counts. A negative impression is harder to change than a positive one.[10] People are quick to generalize, and once a generalization is formed, further observations and information tend to confirm their generalization.[11,8] If a presenter gets off on the wrong foot, it will take considerable effort to change a negative impression. First impressions are difficult to erase.[8] Make them positive.

The opening of a presentation is an opportunity to make a good impression and build rapport with an audience. Relating a topic to an audience's needs and interests helps to build a positive relationship with them. Speakers must show they know their audience.

Demonstrate Knowledge of the Audience

Knowing an audience is a recurring theme throughout this book. Likewise, an effective introduction acknowledges the needs and wants of the audience. Good presenters do their homework and know who their audience is and what is important to them. Knowing the audience allows the communicator to begin where the audience is and build on that knowledge in a meaningful way. It allows speakers to acknowledge what they share in common, build rapport, and convey the benefits the audience will receive as a result of listening to the message.

BEGIN WHERE THE AUDIENCE IS

An audience will be prepared to take in new information and accept new ideas if the new information and ideas are anchored to existing knowledge or experiences.[12,13] Help an audience recall what audience members already know about a subject. Provide a starting point for what the presentation will teach them. Demonstrate knowledge about what they already know (having assessed it), and check whether that is correct. Many opening strategies help an audience connect the topic to previous knowledge and experience and establish a good starting point for acquiring new knowledge and adopting new behaviors. Several effective strategies are explored in the section that follows.

BUILD RAPPORT

By tailoring a presentation to an audience's needs, wants, and values, a presenter is connecting with the members of that audience and building rapport. The English word *communication* comes from the Latin word *communis*, which means "common." As pastor and author Rick Warren said, "You can't communicate with people until you find something you have in common with them." Or as Abraham Lincoln said, "If you would win a man to your cause, first convince him that you are his friend."

One way to connect with others is through sharing emotions. A presenter's emotions are contagious—enthusiasm, competence, and caring will be mirrored back by an audience through "mirror neurons" located in the brain.[14] Recall from Chapter 3 the principle of empathy. If a speaker appears relaxed and confident, the audience will feel relaxed and confident. If a speaker appears uneasy, they will be uneasy. If a speaker smiles, they will perceive the speaker as a friendly person and smile back. If a speaker frowns, audience members will frown back. If a speaker doesn't make eye contact, they will feel excluded. If a speaker fidgets and appears nervous, they will lose confidence in the speaker and the message. If a speaker appears sincere and trustworthy, they will pay attention to the message.

Another element of building rapport with an audience is composure. Audiences tend to be influenced by and develop empathy with speakers who are emotionally stable and who are confident and in control of themselves.[15] Audiences want to feel secure, and speakers who share emotional, sensitive, or challenging content will want their audiences to know that the challenges and experiences being shared have been overcome or are being taken care of. Speakers who can pick up on signals sent by their audiences and adapt their presentation style accordingly will be more successful in having their message received by their audiences.

SHOW THE AUDIENCE "WHAT'S IN IT FOR ME?"

Audience members will be asking themselves (though a presenter may never hear this), "What's in it for me?," commonly known as *WIIFM*. Effective presenters know they are in service of their audience and strive to answer the WIIFM question for them. People want to know how they will benefit from what a presenter says. The better the presenter knows the audience, the better they can answer this question. Mary Munter and Lynn Russell, in their *Guide to Presentations*, suggest using benefit statements, following these three steps[16]:

1. Identify features about the idea or message being presented.

   For example, in a presentation on healthy eating for a corporate wellness program, a speaker could discuss the benefits of packing a lunch vs going out to eat: Packing a lunch saves money, permits control over portion size, and takes less time during the lunch hour.

2. Apply an audience filter by examining the features from the audience's perspective.

   For an audience who is trying to reduce calories, focus on the portion size feature.

3. Create a targeted benefit statement that explains WIIFM.

   For example, the benefit statement could be "Pack your lunch to control portion size."

Introduce Key Messages

An audience wants and needs a road map to know where a speech is going. Give them a glimpse by giving them a preview of the content. A century-old formula for describing the three parts of a speech, attributed to British preacher J. H. Rowett

in 1908,[17] as printed in the *Sunday Strand*, is this:

> *Tell them what you're going to tell them. Tell them.*
> *Tell them what you told them.*

In the opening of a presentation, a presenter "tells them what you're going to tell them." Share what the audience will learn, the main points that will be covered, or the questions that will be answered. Pique the audience's interest so they will want to hear more.

This road map can become the structure for a presentation. As described in Chapter 15, a presentation is best organized around key message points. By introducing this structure in the opening, the presenter can help the audience to organize the information as well.

What Are Effective Introduction Strategies?

There are many ways to begin a presentation, depending on the audience, the message, and the context in which a presenter is speaking. An effective opening draws the audience in, focuses them on the topic, and forms the basis for what follows. The audience will be hooked and waiting for more.

Tell a Story

Humans are hard-wired to listen to stories.[18] Storytelling has been part of human social interaction throughout history and across cultures. Stories allow people to practice empathy as they walk in the shoes of a character. Stories can be effective at any point in a presentation as well as broken down and told in parts, beginning in the opening and wrapping up at the end. Stories can come from personal experience or the experience of others. Stories make an emotional connection with an audience. Be sure a story is relevant to the core idea or main point of the presentation.

Use Little-Known Facts or Statistics

According to neuroscience, human brains like novelty, so an unexpected statistic or little-known fact can interest an audience and engage them with a topic.[19] Just make sure the provocative statistic or fact relates to the topic or core idea.

For more on the power of stories, see Chapter 18.

Begin with a Quote

The development of presentation content may reveal an intriguing statement or thought that would be an ideal beginning of the speech. Quotes can come from reference sources, a song, or even a movie. A quote can help build a speaker's credibility if it comes from someone the audience is familiar with. Always be sure to give attribution to the source of the quote.

Ask the Audience a Question

Asking a question can interest and engage audience members because it gets them to think about the topic. A question is most effective when a speaker pauses after asking it to allow the audience to answer it mentally.[5] Also consider asking a series of questions related to the topic to draw the audience deeper into the presentation.

Ask the Audience to Imagine

The word *imagine* is powerful because it moves audience members from being passive listeners to active listeners.[20] Asking them to imagine an outcome or result can help a speaker to make a case while supporting the key points throughout the speech.

Refer to the Place or Occasion of the Speech

If there is significance to the presentation's place or event, making reference to it can make an emotional connection with the audience and draw them into a speech.

Best Practices for Speech Openings

In addition to effective techniques, keep in mind the following best practices:

KEEP THE SPEECH OPENING BRIEF

A speech introduction or opening should only be about 10% of a speech. Too long of an introduction might lose the audience.

PLAN THE OPENING AFTER DEVELOPING THE BODY OF THE SPEECH

The key points have to be known before they can be introduced.

NEVER APOLOGIZE IN AN OPENING

Self-deprecation makes a speaker less credible, and an audience really doesn't want to know that the speaker is nervous, has not been able to practice, or whatever else he or she may be apologizing about.

START A SPEECH BY DIVING IN

Rather than starting a presentation by saying something perfunctory such as, "Today, I'm going to talk about …" or "I'm going to tell you a story …," just begin. Those phrases do not engage an audience and are not an effective way to start, as it gives the audience an opportunity to tune out.[21] Instead, take advantage of an audience's attention first thing and dive in to a story, statistic, quote, or question.

MEMORIZE THE OPENING

Memorizing will help reduce speech anxiety and make a speaker appear more confident. Remember, there's never a second chance to make that great first impression!

 **BOX 17.1**

Begin a Presentation with PUNCH

P = Personal. Starting with content that is personal and relevant to an audience grabs their attention from the very start.

U = Unexpected. Reveal or do something that is unexpected to get an audience's attention.

N = Novel. Human brains love novelty, and an audience will respond positively to something that is new and different.

C = Challenging. Challenge an audience intellectually to keep them engaged during a presentation. Tap into their natural curiosity.

H = Humor. An audience that laughs together becomes more connected with the speaker and with each other. Laughter builds positivity in and rapport with an audience.

One of the best ways to remember how to start a presentation comes from Garr Reynolds in his book *The Naked Presenter*.[22] Reynolds uses the acronym *PUNCH* to remember key points for starting a presentation. See Box 17.1 for the meaning of *PUNCH* as applied to effective speech openings.

The Words of Experience box illustrates the use of an opening delivered with PUNCH for a preschool presentation about trying new foods. The opening connected the topic to each child's *personal* food tasting experiences. It revealed items that were *unexpected*. The foods were *novel* and gave the children an opportunity to try something new. The opening created anticipation for exploring foods in fun and exciting ways and *challenged* their ideas about trying new foods. Most children respond negatively when asked if they want to try new, unfamiliar food. To counter this tendency, the opening culminated with a fun reading of Dr Seuss's *Green Eggs and Ham*, replacing anxiety about food tasting with *humor*. A strong opening is like a good first impression: It opens the audience to a favorable impression of what is coming. Reluctance turns into anticipation, active engagement, and a willingness to explore. At the conclusion of the presentation, an interactive puppet show reviewed what was learned and children joyfully expressed their willingness to explore and try new foods in the future.

What Is the Purpose of the Presentation Closing?

Recall from the beginning of this chapter the primacy effect, which emphasizes that what is presented at the beginning of a presentation may be better recalled than what follows. Similarly, at the end of a presentation, the recency effect is observed. This phenomenon describes how what is presented at the end is remembered better than what comes in the middle. Together, the primacy and recency effects create a U-shaped memory curve.[1] A closing that is well planned and executed will enhance learning and memory and promote taking action and achieving the desired outcomes.

Summarizes the Key Points

The closing is the final opportunity to state the key messages and the single overriding communication

WORDS OF EXPERIENCE

Surprise and Delight

by Barbara J. Mayfield, MS, RDN, FAND

If you're looking for a proven way to open a presentation with young children, you can't beat a Wonder Box. All it takes is a large shoe box covered with colorful wrapping paper or foil and fun stickers. Inside the box, hide something related to the topic of the presentation that you will reveal after building suspense. To create maximum anticipation, demonstrate your own excitement with vivid facial expressions and vocalized enthusiasm.

I created a nutrition curriculum for teaching young children and featured the Wonder Box in the opening of each lesson. I titled the opening Assessment and Anticipation to emphasize the purpose, which gained audience members' attention and helped me find out what the children already know about the topic (assessment), as well as building excitement for what they'll be learning about (anticipation).

You can easily build your own Wonder Box. Inside the Wonder Box, place one or more items that relate to the topic of the presentation. For example:

- In a presentation about trying new foods, place foods that the audience members might not have seen before, such as a kiwi, star fruit, horned melon, and a mango. *Assess*: "Do you know what each food is?" *Build anticipation*: "Won't it be fun to explore new foods?"
- In a presentation about cooking, place the kitchen utensils you will be using. *Assess*: "Do you know what each one is used for?" *Build anticipation*: "Are you excited to start cooking?"
- In a presentation about physical activity, place a TV remote and a small ball. *Assess*: "Can you tell me which one is for being active and which one is for sitting still?" *Build anticipation*: "Are you ready to get moving?"

To locate copies of preschool lessons using the Wonder Box, see the resources at the end of the chapter.

objective, or SOCO, so make them stick. Repetition is a powerful memory technique.[16] Don't worry about the audience hearing the key points too often. In fact, the more complex the message, the more important it becomes to deliver a summary.[21] Presenters often err on the side of not saying them enough. If the key messages are well written and well presented, the audience appreciates being reminded of what is most important.

In some settings, having the audience repeat the key messages during and at the end of a presentation is appropriate and effective. Doing so can work well not only with children and youths but also adults. Think of ways to help an audience learn the key messages and allow them to show off what they learned at the end.

This can be as simple as putting a key message that has been reinforced throughout a presentation on a slide at the end, but rather than writing it out in its entirety, delete one or two key words or phrases and ask the audience to say them out loud together. For example, the words *realistic goals* are missing in the following key message:

> Behavior change results when we set
> _____ _____ to overcome real
> challenges and concerns with practical,
> workable solutions.

To place the emphasis on "practical, workable solutions," delete that phrase instead. Since "testing" is an effective method for remembering what one has learned, this technique is effective for multiple reasons.[23]

Gives a Take-Home Message and Call to Action

To learn for learning's sake is good, but to act on that learning is better. Even with "pure learning" in a classroom setting, the call to action can be further study to reinforce learning—learning that promotes content mastery and testing success.

Adult learners are self-directed and like to be given autonomy for how to put a message into action.[24-26] Rather than telling them what they *should* do with the information, share what they *can* do and provide plenty of helpful and practical tips for how to do it. Present the call to action in positive terms that make it seem possible even if it is challenging. Promote self-efficacy. Help learners anticipate success and not expect failure. Using

Chapter 21 describes aspects of a presentation to include in an evaluation

the goal-setting example, a closing statement could be: "As you reach your goals, each success will motivate further achievement."

Provides an Opportunity to Assess Changes in Knowledge, Attitudes, and Behavioral Intentions

Chapter 15 demonstrated how to write measurable and descriptive learning objectives. A presentation closing provides an optimal opportunity to assess these objectives. Several approaches to testing are described later in this chapter. Whatever method is chosen, make sure all objectives are assessed, including knowledge gains, changes in attitudes, and behavioral intentions.

A closing also provides an optimal time to collect feedback about the presentation. Plan an approach to assessing objectives and gathering feedback into a closing so that they are not forgotten or cut short. Allow time for audience members to complete a brief assessment or evaluation, which can be administered via paper and pencil, electronically, or with a discussion or activity. An assessment form sent home with an audience is less likely to be returned.

What Are the Components of an Effective Closing?

"Well, that's all we have time for …" is *not* an effective closing. That leaves the audience with the impression that the speaker has run out of time and left things unsaid. It implies that the speaker did not plan or rehearse enough to be able to finish on time and finish strong, with all key messages fully delivered. An effective closing gives the audience a feeling of closure, a sense that the presenter finished what was started and all is complete. Let's explore three components of an effective closing.

Flows Logically from the Opening and Body of the Presentation

A well-organized presentation has a logical flow from beginning to end. In Chapter 16, this was described as the foundation that holds the entire presentation together. The closing should be presented with the same style or theme as the opening and the body.

An effective presentation has a rhythm and a closing in harmony with the rest of the speech. Like a great musical score, a presentation should change key or tempo to provide contrast, as described in Chapter 16, but the changes are designed to be pleasing and intriguing, not startling or unsettling. Does the planned outline for a presentation indicate a good flow and a unifying feel from the opening all the way to the closing?

What does a logical and unifying flow look and feel like? If a presentation has humor interspersed throughout, feel free to include a cartoon in the closing that goes along with the theme. If the presentation is more serious, a cartoon may fall flat.

If audience participation was included throughout the presentation, it's appropriate to include an activity or audience sharing as part of the closing. In fact, this can be a great way to confirm that the audience "got it" by having participants talk about what they learned or how they plan to use what they learned. If there were no audience activities, one added at the end may be less effective than in a presentation that warmed them up to involvement throughout.

There is no one formula for an effective closing, but overall it will flow from the entire presentation, complementing and completing all that came before.

Assures the Story Is Finished and the Questions Posed Are Answered

A good closing can be compared to fitting the final piece into a jigsaw puzzle—it gives the audience a satisfying sense of completion.

If a presentation teased the audience at the opening that it would answer three questions, make sure all three were answered. Review the answers, which ideally are the key points, as part of the closing.

If a presentation opened with a problem, make sure to provide the solution. If the solution isn't known, describe possible solutions and potential areas for future research to help provide answers. Prepare and practice to end a presentation cleanly.

Is Memorable and Motivating

A presenter wants an audience to not only pay attention but also to remember the message, share it with others, and take action to achieve the desired outcomes after the presentation ends. The recency effect does not guarantee a closing will be memorable. Prepare what to say and how to say it to make a lasting impact.

The closing is the final opportunity to call an audience to action. In planning the closing, review the presentation to make sure it has provided compelling evidence and practical, actionable ideas for steps to take. In closing, inspire the audience to put what they learned into practice. Bring in personal descriptions of moving forward to fully achieve the same things being taught and make a personal commitment to continued progress. Be authentic and human.

Give an audience a vision of what is possible if what has been presented is implemented. Could it reduce risk of …? Could it improve … or help prevent …? Great achievements begin with a vision. Help an audience see what to strive for.

What Are Effective Closing Strategies?

As with effective openings, there are many ways to end a presentation. The technique that is chosen should be appropriate for the audience, the message, and the context in which the presentation is happening. Effective closing strategies often mirror the opening and provide the audience with a satisfying assurance that they got what they came for.

Form a Bookend with the Opening

Take another look at the list of effective speech openings. An effective speech closing can be the bookend that parallels the opening. If a presentation began with a quote, it could end with another quote. If a presentation opened with a question, answer the question. If the audience was asked to "imagine" at the beginning, the end can describe or illustrate the potential for the future based on what was presented. One of the most effective bookend approaches is to begin and end with a story.[21]

Provide the "Rest of the Story"

If the presentation opened with a story, finish it. As longtime radio personality and storyteller Paul Harvey used to do, give an audience "the rest of the story." A factual story, or one based on real life, gives the content of a presentation a personal, relatable context.

The opening story draws the audience in and provides a rationale for the "problem" to be solved during the presentation. Providing the "rest of the story" during the closing gives the solution and offers an opportunity to discuss practical applications of the content.

Engage the Audience in Sharing Goals and Ideas

When asking an audience to take action based on what has been presented, give them an opportunity to formulate goals and verbalize their intentions. Writing down goals and sharing them with others can be a powerful tool for bringing about positive change.[27] Writing and sharing goals is no guarantee they will be fulfilled, but it increases the likelihood that they will. Inviting an audience to consider how they will put the content to practical use and allowing them time to share their goals and ideas with others in the group can inspire audience members with ideas they may not have considered but find appealing. Chapter 20 describes several audience interaction activities that can be used for sharing goals and planned action steps.

"Test" the Audience in an Engaging and Memorable Way to Enhance and Measure Learning

Some types of presentations require an assessment to determine whether the audience achieved the desired learning objectives or outcomes. In some situations, a pretest is required as well as a post-presentation assessment. The assessment can be administered at the same time as feedback is collected about the presentation. A survey tool can be used to ask audience members what they gained from the session and to rate the presenter and presentation.

Consider replacing a traditional "paper and pencil" assessment with an alternative approach. Play a game such as Jeopardy or bingo using questions that "test" whether participants have learned the content presented. Many game show formats can be adapted for a fun approach to assess learning. Create a crossword puzzle with clues that test the audience's knowledge of the key concepts presented. Free online tools are available to create puzzles. Fun, competitive quizzes with participants broken into teams are also fun and effective for assessing learning.

Another approach is to have participants do a reflection activity to answer thought-provoking questions about what they learned. Ideally, allow time after reflection for sharing between partners and then a whole-group discussion. For a record of their answers, collect the papers or have audience members take a picture of their answers and upload the photo to a designated site. See Box 20.5 in Chapter 20 for a list of possible reflection activities.

"Teach-back" is a learning assessment technique used extensively in counseling, but with applications in group learning situations.[28] In counseling, practitioners tell their patients they want to make sure they explained everything clearly and ask their patients to describe what was talked about in their own words, as if they were explaining it to a friend or family member. To use teach-back in group learning situations, ask participants to present information learned in the session to the group or demonstrate how they would explain it to others. This method is especially useful in longer sessions such as workshops.

If the presentation was structured around a series of questions that were answered, a potential assessment is to ask the audience to answer the questions in the closing rather than stating the answers as a summary. This provides the audience with an opportunity to test what they learned and clarify any misunderstandings that may still exist. Just be sure to ask the questions in a nonthreatening way and provide encouragement and support as participants respond.

Whatever approach is used, allow plenty of time. Assessment can be a valuable way to reinforce learning if done well. A participant who didn't catch something earlier may "get it" when it becomes the answer to a question in a game.

Follow the Question-and-Answer Session

Allowing an audience to ask questions is an expected part of presentations. How to manage a question-and-answer (Q&A) session effectively is the topic of Chapter 36. Questions can potentially be taken at any time during a presentation. It is ultimately up to the presenter to decide whether to hold them to the end or allow them earlier. Ideally, schedule a Q&A before the final closing so that what sticks in the audience's mind drives home the main point. Things may be "wrapped up" before the Q&A, but if it must be at the end of a talk, plan as a minimum to make a closing statement after the Q&A is over. The SOCO can be a succinct and effective closing statement that takes little time to say but can leave a big impact.

The goal in a Q&A is to strengthen the message and build on what has been presented. However, if the Q&A goes off on a tangent, an audience may remember the unrelated discussion rather than the intended message. Follow the advice in Chapter 36 to steer the conversation back to the key points. A well-run Q&A can enhance a presentation and deliver additional content in a way that meets the audience's needs.

End on Time

A well-prepared speaker finishes by or before the scheduled ending time. An audience begins to tune out even the best speaker when they are feeling cheated out of getting the time allotted for the next presentation, or when they think their refreshment or restroom break will be cut short, or worst of all, when they are worried about missing their on-time departure to return home.[29] To keep an audience fully focused on a message rather than the clock, stick to the time limit.

An ill-prepared speaker may omit the closing to end on time, which may leave the audience feeling unsatisfied. Rehearse the closing enough to ensure that the presentation can be adapted to fit within the time constraints that may be encountered at the speaking event. Below is a useful checklist for effective openings and closings.

Make the closing strong. It is the last opportunity to reinforce the key message, make that final impression, deliver a call to action, and give a simple "thank you," if appropriate, to the host or meeting planner.

✓ Opening Checklist

____ Have you gained the attention of your audience by using one of the techniques discussed in the chapter?

____ Does your speech opening relate to the audience and its needs?

____ Have you established your credibility to speak on your topic?

____ Have you introduced your key messages?

____ Is the opening of your speech approximately 10% of your speech time?

____ Have you rehearsed your opening so you can present it flawlessly?

✓ Closing Checklist

____ Have you summarized and rehearsed your key messages in your conclusion?

____ Is there a call to action in your closing?

____ Did you choose an effective closing strategy to end your speech?

____ Did you remember to include a Q&A session before your closing remarks?

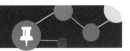

Deliver Strong Openings and Closings

1 Well-organized communication includes a strong opening that captures the audience's attention and sets the stage for what follows. The end of the presentation is a critical opportunity to reiterate the main point and promote taking action. Research suggests that the opening and closing may be the most memorable parts of an entire presentation.

2 The opening, or introduction, of a presentation serves three critical purposes: It creates a desire to attend; it establishes the speaker as a credible source; and it sets the stage for what follows. Do all three to be effective.

3 Several components characterize an effective opening that captures the attention of the audience, builds credibility, and tells them where the presenter is going. A good opening creates a positive impression, demonstrates the speaker's knowledge of the audience, and introduces the key messages.

4 There are many ways to begin a presentation. The technique that is chosen will depend on the audience, the message, and the context of the speech. An effective opening draws the audience in, focuses them on the topic, and forms the basis for what follows. An audience will be hooked and waiting for more.

5 When a closing is well planned and executed, it will enhance learning and memory and promote taking action and achieving the desired outcomes. Effective closings summarize the key messages, provide a take-home message and call to action, and assess whether desired outcomes were achieved.

6 An effective closing gives the audience a feeling of closure, a sense that the speaker finished what was started and all is complete. The three components of an effective closing are that it flows logically from the rest of the presentation, finishes the story and answers any questions, and is memorable and motivating.

7 As with effective openings, there are many ways to end a presentation. The technique should be appropriate for the audience, message, and context of the speech. Effective closing strategies often mirror the opening and provide the audience with a satisfying summary of the key message of the presentation.

RESOURCES

Preschool lessons: www.nutritioncommunicator.com/kids
-club-lessons-and-songs

REFERENCES

1. Azizian A, Polich J. Evidence for attentional gradient in the serial position memory curve from event-related potentials. *J Cogn Neurosci.* 2007;19(12):2071-2081.

2. Ebbinghaus H. Human memory. Accessed February 5, 2018. Dr Bruce Abbot Homepage website. http://users.pfw .edu/abbott/120/Ebbinghaus.html

3. Engleberg IN. Presentations in everyday life: linking audience interest and speaker eloquence. *Am Commun J.* 2002;5(2). http://ac-journal.org/journal/vol5/iss2/special /engleberg.pdf

4. Keller J. *Motivational Design for Learning and Performance: The ARCS Model Approach.* Springer Science; 2010.

5. Lucas S. *The Art of Public Speaking.* 10th ed. McGraw-Hill; 2009.

6. Engleberg I, Daly J. *Think Public Speaking.* Pearson; 2013.

7. Over H, Cook R. Where do spontaneous first impressions of faces come from? *Cognition.* 2018;170:190-200.

8. Ambady N, Skowronski JJ, eds. *First Impressions.* Guilford Press; 2008.

9. Kostos C. Brain friendly first impressions. *Train Dev.* 2013;40(6):14-15.

10. Mann TC, Ferguson MJ. Reversing implicit first impressions through reinterpretation after a two-day delay. *J Exp Soc Psychol.* 2017;68:122-127.

11. Todorov A, Olivola C, Dotsch R, Mende-Siedlecki P. Social attributions from faces: determinants, consequences, accuracy, and functional significance. *Annu Rev Psychol.* 2015;66(5):519-545.

12. Ausubel DP. *The Acquisition and Retention of Knowledge: A Cognitive View.* Springer Science and Business Media; 2000.

13. Getha-Eby T, Berry T, Xu Y, O'Brien B. Meaningful learning: theoretical support for concept-based teaching. *J Nurs Educ.* 2014;53(9):494-500.

14. Pfeifer J, Iacoboni M, Mazziotta J, Dapretto M. Mirroring others' emotions relates to empathy and interpersonal competence in children. *Neuroimage.* 2008;39:2076-2085.

15. Rothwell J. *Practically Speaking.* 2nd ed. Oxford University Press; 2017.

16. Munter M, Russell L. *Guide to Presentations.* Prentice Hall; 2002.

17. Tell 'em what you're going to tell 'em; next, tell 'em; next, tell 'em what you told 'em. Quote Investigator website. Published 2017. Accessed September 3, 2018. https://quoteinvestigator.com/2017/08/15/tell-em

18. Hsu J. The secrets of storytelling: our love for telling tales reveals the workings of the mind. *Sci Am Mind.* 2008;19(4):46-51.

19. Medina J. *Brain Rules.* Pear Press; 2008.

20. Meyers P, Nix S. *As We Speak: How to Make Your Point and Have It Stick.* Simon and Schuster; 2011.

21. Osborn M, Turner K. *Public Speaking: Finding Your Voice.* Pearson; 2015.

22. Reynolds G. *The Naked Presenter.* New Riders; 2011.

23. Roediger H, Karpicke J. The power of testing memory: basic research and implications for educational practice. *Perspect Psychol Sci.* 2006;1(3):181-210.

24. Cercone K. Characteristics of adult learners with implications for online learning design. *AACE J.* 2008;16(2):137-159.

25. Vella J. *Learning to Listen, Learning to Teach.* Jossey-Bass; 2002.

26. Norris J. *From Telling to Teaching.* Learning by Dialogue; 2003.

27. Study demonstrates that writing goals enhances goal achievement. Dominican University of California website. Published January 5, 2017. Accessed September 6, 2018. www.dominican.edu/dominicannews/study-demonstrates -that-writing-goals-enhances-goal-achievement

28. Osborne H. Confirming understanding with the teach-back technique. Health Literacy Consulting website. Published November 20, 2007. Accessed March 9, 2018. https://healthliteracy.com/2007/11/20/teach-back

29. Dlugan A. Presentation timing: 5 tips to stay on time and avoid audience wrath. Six Minutes: Speaking and Presentation Skills website. Published December 2, 2012. Accessed September 20, 2018. http://sixminutes.dlugan .com/presentation-timing

Utilize Visual Aids to Enhance Communication

Barbara J. Mayfield, MS, RDN FAND
Sonja Kassis Stetzler, MA, RDN, CPC
and Angie Hasemann Bayliss, MS, RDN, CSP

"Combining visual depictions of information along with or in place of verbal descriptions can more effectively convey key messages. Visual aids assist audiences in understanding content, storing it in long-term memory for future use, and putting knowledge into practice."

> "Well-designed visuals do more than provide information; they bring order to the conversation."
> —DALE LUDWIG

Introduction

Combining visual depictions of information along with or in place of verbal descriptions can more effectively convey key messages. Visual aids assist audiences in understanding content, storing it in long-term memory for future use, and putting knowledge into practice. An audience may understand visual images even when they don't understand written or spoken language.[1]

This chapter answers four questions:

- What is the evidence for using visual aids?
- How can complex concepts be conveyed so that they enhance audience understanding?
- What visual aids and strategies are most likely to achieve the speaker's objective?
- What are best practices for using presentation software as a visual aid?

The food and nutrition professional who expends the time and resources to design and construct effective visual aids, ones that enhance the audience's understanding and memory of the content the speaker delivers, will be a more effective communicator. This chapter discusses not only why to use visual aids but how to use visual aids for maximum effect.

One of the most overused and ineffectively used visual aids is presentation software, such as PowerPoint. When used effectively, it can improve a presentation. When used improperly, it can lead to what has been coined "death by PowerPoint." Similarly, any poorly designed presentation visual aid will not enhance a presentation but rather take away from the message's effectiveness. Do not use visual aids for the sake of using them; use visual aids to help convey a message and improve understanding and retention. The communicator who uses visual aids well will stand out from the crowd.

What Is the Evidence for Using Visual Aids?

Recall from the discussion of memory in Chapter 16 that information is conveyed in two basic ways: descriptions and depictions. If descriptions are the words chosen to convey a message, depictions are the visuals. The term *visual aid* encompasses many things: still or moving pictures, props and displays that are fixed or manipulated, and skits and demonstrations—all used to illustrate information and enhance an audience's understanding of the content that is presented. A visual can even include helping an audience create an image in their mind's eye. This section will explore the evidence for choosing visual techniques that best align with increasing attention, deepening meaning, improving retention, increasing persuasion, and promoting taking action. All of these enhance the presentation experience for the audience.

Evidence for Increasing Attention

The human brain is exposed to a multitude of stimuli at any given moment. Selective attention is used to focus on what is important and filter out what is unnecessary or unimportant. An effective presenter uses every means available to assist an audience in maintaining focused attention.

As discussed in previous chapters, an audience maintains attention for limited periods of time unless the presenter

> "If I tell you the truth, I tell it with a story, and if I tell that story with pictures, I can keep you glued to your seat."
> —DAN ROAM, *SHOW AND TELL*[2]

changes delivery with structural, emotional, or delivery contrast. Using visual aids can be an effective method for providing structural contrast. However, for a visual to provide a needed change, it must attract the attention of the audience *and* add value to the content that is being delivered. For this reason, it's best not to use too many visuals, or too many similar visuals. One well-selected visual can be more effective and attention-getting than a barrage of poorly designed ones.

According to the cognitive theory of multimedia learning, working memory has a cognitive capacity of five to seven chunks of information at one time.[1] Therefore, to improve attention and enhance learning, visuals must be clear and uncluttered, focused on ideally one main idea, and include no more than five to seven pieces of information. Extraneous information that does not assist in learning must be eliminated to prevent distracting an audience from a presentation's main message. Do not split an audience's attention—focus it.

Evidence for Enhancing Meaning

Visuals can convey meaning faster and more effectively than words. Imagine trying to explain the human digestive tract without a picture or image for an audience to grasp the function and placement of digestive organs.

The *multimedia principle* is based on research of Richard Mayer and others that demonstrates that learning is enhanced through the use of words and pictures compared to words alone. Multimedia learning includes not just text and images but visual combined with verbal, as in a presentation, as well as animation combined with narration. Research using validated assessments indicates learners create more accurate mental models and have deeper understanding, greater problem solving, enhanced ability to apply knowledge in new situations, and greater acquisition of psychomotor skills from multimedia learning.[3]

The manner in which the words and pictures are conveyed is critical to see these benefits. This includes clearly labeling diagrams and determining the complexity of design to match the knowledge level of the audience.[3] The depth of the learners' existing knowledge determines the complexity or simplicity of visual images to use. For novice learners, simplified visual representations are best with nonessential details omitted.

For expert learners, more complex diagrams work well. For audiences between novice and expert, determine the appropriate degree of complexity. Make visuals no more complex than needed to convey the information. Compare the diagrams in Figure 18.1. Consider which one would be appropriate for an introductory lesson on digestion and which one for a more advanced lesson.

Evidence for Improving Retention

The picture (or visual) superiority effect is based on brain research that shows that when information is presented in text only, people remember only about 10% (when they are tested 72 hours after exposure). When relevant and interesting images are used in addition to the text, people remember 65% of the information.[4] Visuals enhance memory.

Research by Hale[5] found that adults are much better than children at processing and retaining information learned via audio channels or by hearing alone. Hale proposes that an adult's cognitive maturity and greater capacity for symbolic thought allows for superior auditory retention. Children retain more information when received via visual channels. Hale's research emphasizes the importance of an effective combination of audio and visual.

Evidence for Improving Persuasion

A classic study, often referenced to support the benefits of visual aids, is the 1986 Persuasion and the Role of Visual Presentation Support: The UM/3M Study.[6] In this study, nine test groups of undergraduate business students viewed videotaped presentations given with and without visual support. The type of visual support was also examined. This research found that presentations with visual aids were overall 43% more persuasive than presentations without visual support.

Aspects of effective visual aids included the use of color as well as clear, well-selected graphics. Presenters who used visual aids were perceived as more prepared, concise, interesting, professional, and persuasive. The researchers compared "typical" presenters with more polished presenters and found that typical presenters using visuals were perceived as well as, or even more favorably than, "better" presenters who did not use visuals.[6]

FIGURE 18.1 **Simple and complex diagrams of the digestive system**

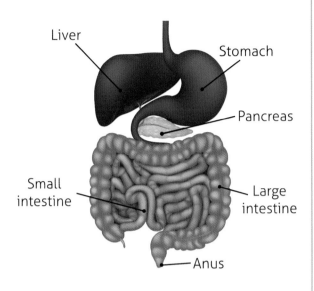

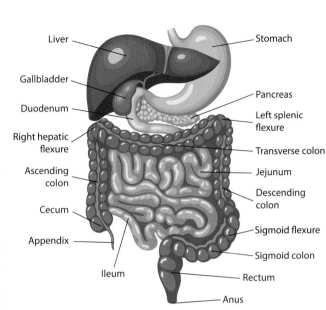

Evidence for Promoting Taking Action

A study by Shu and Townsend[7] illustrates that attractive visuals may promote taking action, especially in instances that require people to change a firmly held point of view. They found that showing people images that affirm positive aspects of their prior decisions along with very attractive images of proposed behaviors increased their likelihood to accept the proposed option.

In a health education context, another study found evidence that visual aids help promote desirable behaviors. A study by Garcia-Retamero and Cokely[8] found that when health messages promoting sexually transmitted disease (STD) prevention and detection behaviors (condom use and screening) were combined with high-quality visual aids, the gain- and loss-framed messages were equally effective. A gain-framed message is one in which a positive outcome or benefit is promoted. A loss-framed message is one in which avoiding a negative consequence or cost is promoted. Without visuals, gain-framed messages were more effective in promoting prevention behaviors and loss-framed messages were more effective in promoting detection behaviors. The addition of visual aids promoted both prevention and detection.

Evidence for Benefits to the Presenter

Creating visual aids can be costly and time-consuming. Manipulating them on a stage can be a challenge. Technology and other best-laid plans can fail. How could using visual aids provide benefits to the presenter? For all of the reasons just discussed.[1,3-8]

Visual aids can save time in getting a point across and increase a presenter's effectiveness, more likely leading to an attentive audience that is following every word rather than looking at their smartphones. Well-delivered content using visual aids is satisfying to present. An engaged audience is fun to present to and stimulates presenters to even greater effectiveness.

No matter what other visual aids are chosen, recognize that the most important visual in any presentation is the presenter. Consider that at least one-third of the most-viewed TED talks use no slides.[9] The presenter is the focus, not the slides or any other type of visual aid. A presenter can connect with an audience, while a slide or prop cannot. Presenters must not allow visual aids to distract an audience from the presenter or the message. Use visual aids for their intended purpose, to make a message *more* effective and to help an audience understand subject matter, especially when it is complex or confusing.

Chapter 21 will describe how to most effectively utilize visual aids.

How Can Complex Concepts Be Conveyed Effectively?

In nutrition and other sciences, the challenge of teaching complicated models and complex concepts can be daunting. A key role of a nutrition communicator is to break down complex concepts into digestible bites. Visual aids play a vital role in this process. Imagine learning the citric acid cycle (also called the TCA cycle or Krebs cycle) without a diagram. Imagine hearing about international cuisine without seeing a picture of the dish or meal being described. If the foods are unfamiliar, there is no context for creating a visual image. Visual aids can connect an audience to a topic. They can help an audience understand important details as well as see the big picture. Visual aids can explain the pieces and illustrate how they fit into the larger puzzle of a topic.

Teach-back is explained in Chapter 17.

Information is often conveyed as answers to the five *W*'s and one *H*: who, what, where, when, why, and how. These can also serve as useful frameworks for how information is presented visually. Dan Roam, in *Back of the Napkin: Solving Problems and Selling Ideas with Pictures*, refers to this as the 6×6 Rule of Visual Thinking.[10] He suggests that each problem or question can best be illustrated with a specific type of visual image, as shown in Box 18.1.

In contemplating various types of complex ideas and concepts, consider which type of visual aid is best suited to convey meaning and help an audience see both the forest (big picture) and the trees (details).

Conveying Key Ideas

Remember that the purpose of a presentation is to convey one or more key ideas to an audience. When a participant leaves a presentation, or for that matter, a reader finishes a blog post or a patient exits a counseling session, the hope is that they leave with the key ideas or messages the communicator intended to provide. While teach-back (a learning assessment technique used extensively in counseling) is one way to confirm that, retention of core ideas can be proactively encouraged by engaging the visual learner, appealing to other senses, and utilizing visual aids to help ensure the goals for the communication are met.

A communicator educating elementary school children on healthful eating can show a visual poster of a rainbow of fruits and vegetables, which not only teaches colors but can also leave a visual impression

BOX 18.1 Types of Visual Images Using the 5 *W*'s and 2 *H*'s[10]

Type of Question	Type of Representation	Example of Visual
Who? or What?	Qualitative representation	Portrait
How much?	Quantitative representation	Chart
Where?	Position in space	Map
When?	Position in time	Timeline
How?	Cause and effect	Flowchart
Why?	Deductions, predictions, interactions	Multiple-variable plot

of a key message: Eat a variety of colors. In looking at the 6×6 chart in Box 18.1, this is an example of using a portrait to answer "*What* should I eat?" The answer: Eat a variety of colors of fruits and vegetables.

Similar to a portrait, a prop can provide a qualitative representation of a key idea. In nutrition, one of the most effective props is food. For example, at a cooking demonstration, participants may remember more about the food displayed, and ideally sampled, than the information presented. However, using food as an aid to share main points (such as "Whole grains can taste like other grains"; "Low-fat foods can be flavorful"; or "Substituting sweet potatoes for oil in brownies doesn't change the flavor profile much but does improve nutrient density") may be the most effective messaging tool. In any setting, while an audience is viewing a visual aid, it provides the presenter the opportunity to drive home the main points.

See the Words of Experience box for practical and creative examples of conveying key ideas.

Defining Terms

An effective way to define a term is to provide visual information in addition to a verbal or written meaning. For example:

- Pictures are essential in teaching the definition of *malnutrition*. Nutrition-focused physical exam training includes numerous pictures that assist in defining terms and classifications.
- Clear jars filled with whole grains will give audiences a better understanding of the similarities and differences between the grains than will simply reading or hearing about them.
- The definition of *phytochemicals* may make more sense when audience members can see, touch, and taste foods that feature properties imparted by phytochemicals.

Illustrating How Things Work

The popularity of YouTube home improvement videos illustrates the value of video as a type of visual aid in demonstrating how things work. It would be difficult to understand the process of dialysis without seeing a drawing of a dialysis machine, or even better, standing next to a machine as a patient is connected to it for treatment. It can be challenging to understand the process of food production from a textbook, but firsthand

WORDS OF EXPERIENCE

Conveying Key Ideas: Vitamin and Mineral Presentations

by Angie Hasemann Bayliss, MS, RDN, CSP

Reviewing the vitamins and minerals—their food sources, their functions, and their risks for deficiency and toxicity—can be a lot for students to process and remember. It is quite a bit more tangible when the learning method becomes more hands-on. In an introductory nutrition course I taught for undergraduate students, I asked groups of two to three students to choose a vitamin or mineral to teach the rest of the class about. The key part of their grade was based on creativity and usefulness in helping the audience remember the information.

This activity inspired a variety of creative ideas, including a song about magnesium accompanied by a ukulele; a *Fear Factor*-type eating challenge to learn food sources of niacin; an interactive song about folic acid ("If you're pregnant and you know it, clap your hands"); a science experiment to show vitamin K sources and the vitamin's role in coagulation (featuring glue bottles labeled as green leafy vegetables); and several game-show inspired quizzes. Conveying key ideas with creative approaches and hands-on visual aids was quite memorable for the class.

experience with a 40-gallon steam-jacketed kettle gives a whole new meaning to large-scale cooking. Visual aids have a nice way of showing multiple steps in a concise manner and providing an enhanced view of how the steps fit together.

Illustrating Data Effectively

Numbers can be a challenge to remember, compare, and assess in verbal or even written communication. Visually communicating comparisons and contrasts can ease the translation process. Tables, graphs, and charts can summarize large amounts of data in a simple image. Shading positive results in green and missed targets in red will allow an audience to process the information more quickly and more readily understand the bigger picture. Circling, highlighting, or bolding key numbers can draw an audience to the primary data findings.

See Chapter 7 for information about the science of visualizing data for optimal meaning.

Making Comparisons

Visual aids can be effective tools for comparing similarities and differences. For example, a table of the amounts of vitamins and minerals needed by adolescent patients following bariatric surgery versus adult patients following bariatric surgery would provide a quick representation of the differences and also show which recommendations are the same for both age groups.

Visual aids can also compare a tangible object to one that is abstract or hidden. For example, a fist can illustrate the size of the heart. A deck of cards is an accurate reference for 3 oz of meat, the appropriate serving size for an adult. Carbohydrate counting of fruits becomes less complicated and more memorable when the reference of a tennis ball or baseball is used to show the size of fruit that has 15 g of carbohydrate.

Connecting Concepts

It may be relatively easy for an audience to grasp single concepts, but understanding how they all relate may prove more challenging. Visual aids can show the process of digestion of carbohydrates, fats, and proteins. Recognizing the progression of poorly managed diabetes becomes more tangible when visuals of affected body parts are shown. A review of the comorbidities associated with obesity can be better understood and remembered when a picture of the human body is included in the education.

What Visual Aids and Strategies Are Effective?

As stated earlier, there is a fine balance between using visual aids to engage an audience and having visual aids become a distraction. While creativity can lead a presenter down many paths of developing visual aids, the right visual will capture the audience's attention to provide key understanding of a presentation's content and help them remember it longer.

The Power of Story— Audience Visualizes, Relates, Remembers

Storytelling has likely been a form of communication since humans began controlling the use of fire, which allowed for an extension of daylight hours and time for human socialization.[11] Stories have been recognized and used for millennia to illustrate, inform, inspire, and entertain.

A common story arc used in presentations includes a character who needs to solve a problem (and is therefore experiencing some type of pain, mental or physical) and must overcome hardship and hurdles before he or she eventually succeeds. The more the audience can relate to the character and his or her struggles, the more effective the story will be in illustrating the presentation's points.

Stories convey ideas in ways that captivate and inspire. Maya Angelou once said, "I've learned that people will forget what you said, people will forget what you did, but people will never forget how you made them feel." This quote illustrates the potential of a story to elicit emotion from an audience. It draws them into what is being shared. Stories provide a "human wrapper" to the ideas and facts a presenter wants to convey to an audience.[12] Teaching about celiac disease is more relatable when a person with this condition shares his or her experience with an audience. An audio recording of a nurse or dietitian teaching about diabetes from the 1970s quickly illustrates just how far technology has come.

In addition to using storytelling in presentations, listening to patient stories is a practice used in narrative medicine. Physicians and health care providers are taught to use storytelling techniques in their patient interactions. This can result in improved communication between provider and patient, improved cognitive and affective outcomes, and enhanced care.[13]

When crafting a story, make sure it conveys the intended point. Consider the audience members and how they will relate to the main characters. Are the struggles the characters must overcome ones the audience members have experienced as well? Stories can be fact or fiction. Be sure to tell an audience whether a story is personal, based on real life, or fictional.

A story doesn't require visual aids to be effective. If a story is told well, listeners "picture" the story without visuals. However, visual aids can be used to help tell a story and may allow an audience to better visualize and remember what they learned. For example, speakers who share their stories of successful dietary change might be more memorable when they bring the many bottles of medication they no longer need thanks to positive lifestyle changes.

In storytelling, include sufficient detail without slowing the story down or distracting the listener from the main point. Practice telling a story until it is just right. A well-told story can have a lasting impact.

A Picture Is Worth a Thousand Words

Using pictures in place of or in addition to words may benefit any type of nutrition communication. Learning about wound healing becomes more realistic when students or interns see what they are trying to help rebuild; visuals serve as a helpful reminder of the severity of the nutrition needs for such patients. A quick Google search of "milk builds strong bones" produces countless images that convey the role of milk and calcium in building strong bones. Using a picture instead of a thousand words shortens the time it takes an audience to process a longer or more complex verbal description and therefore gives a speaker more time to discuss other topics.

Props and Demonstrations

Props will grab the attention of an audience and provide a stage for expanded learning. Added sugar content in food is more tangible when the concept is shown as sugar cubes or sugar being poured into a bowl. See the Words of Experience box for an example of using pictures and props to help convey a message.

Demonstrating a technique in a presentation can be a very effective way to teach anything a presenter wants the audience to put into practice. Cooking demonstrations, whether in person or on television or YouTube, are a popular method that has been shown to involve audiences in greater depth than other nutrition education venues.[14] For more on this effective strategy, see Chapter 25.

Smiley-Face Plate

by Angie Hasemann Bayliss, MS, RDN, CSP

Want to know how to teach children and adults how to balance meals, focus on fruits and veggies, and eat appropriate portions in a simple, easy-to-remember way? Try out this simple "Make Your Hands Smile" trick to teach clients of any age in under 5 minutes. Although it is not a complete nutrition education program, it may just be the most effective tool you've ever learned.

Place your hands palms up, side by side. Your meal should be just enough food to cover your hands (accounting for children of different ages). One palm is a lean protein; the other is a whole grain. Fingers are filled with fruits and veggies. Your hands are filled, but what if you're still hungry? Spread out your fingers to fit more fruits and veggies (the best options for seconds). Recognize the shape of the smiley face, with the most important part (the mouth) being fruits and vegetables—the best part to eat first! Using numerous photos of actual meals demonstrating this concept to encourage balance and portion control and to focus on fruits and veggies is the perfect teaching tool for clients, students, and other health professionals. Family tested and dietitian approved, this simple technique I developed for teaching the very basics of nutrition in a fun and creative way has helped to promote learning and positive behaviors with children of all ages and is regularly used with overweight and obese children in the University of Virginia's Children's Fitness Clinic.

Posters and Infographics

Posters have long been used to summarize scientific research. They can also feature pictures, graphs and tables, or flow sheets. Infographics gather numbers and details and display them in a visually appealing and concise manner. Online tools (eg, Canva or Snappa) allow for easy formatting and development of infographics for a variety of purposes. See an example infographic in Figure 18.2.

Displays and Bulletin Boards

Bulletin boards and other displays are still used to communicate reminders and streamline messages to others. A simple area displaying nutrition-related volunteer opportunities in a busy hallway can easily pass that message along to the intended audience. A bulletin board featuring pictures of high-fiber foods or tips to drink more water may be an effective tool in a weight management clinic.

Videos

See Chapter 24 for more on using and creating video.

With many media sources competing for the attention of students and patients, brief video footage may be the most interesting to this audience. Not only can this strategy better engage an audience but it allows the education to be captured for multiple uses.[15]

What Are Best Practices for Using Presentation Software as a Visual Aid?

When thinking of visual support for a presentation, PowerPoint likely comes to mind, or some other presentation software tool designed for creating computer-generated slides to convey images, words, and embedded videos via projection equipment. To be most effective, think of a slide deck as an indoor billboard: An audience must process the message on each slide in about 3 seconds.[16] This gives audience members time to quickly process the message and turn their attention back to the speaker. Another assessment is the squint test, in which a viewer squints at each slide and determines if the main message is clear even with the text blurred.[17] The design of the slide should effectively introduce the key idea. Using the 3-second

FIGURE 18.2 **Infographic example**

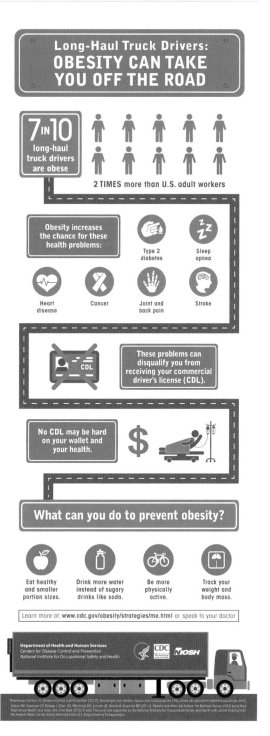

Reproduced from the National Institute for Occupational Safety and Health. Long-haul truck drivers. Centers for Disease Control and Prevention website. Published March 13, 2018. Accessed November 22, 2019. https://www.cdc.gov/niosh /topics/truck/infographic.html

guideline and the squint test as rules for slide design can help communicators create slides that enhance the content being delivered. This section will clarify how to best use slideware and how to avoid common mistakes.

Keep the Focus on the Presenter, Not the Slides

No matter what presentation software is used—PowerPoint, Keynote, Google Slides, or Prezi—the most important point to remember is that the presenter and the message are the presentation, not the slides.

Delivering a presentation with slideware has many benefits. Studies have shown that audiences find presentations more interesting, grasp the information more readily, and remember the content longer when there are visuals.[18] Well-designed slides can attract and hold an audience's attention, add clarity to the words that are delivered by the presenter, and save time when graphics are used to summarize complex material, such as processes or statistics. A good rule of thumb to use when designing slides is to ask: Does it help the audience *understand* or *remember* a point being made? Good design principles, which will be discussed next, can help accomplish the objectives set for an audience.

SLIDES PROVIDE VISUAL SUPPORT

Well-designed slides can be used to create many of the visual effects described in the previous section on visual aids. An image can be projected much larger on a slide (as opposed to being placed on a poster or other display). Slides can be used to embed a video and have it ready for showing within a presentation. Slides can also be used in combination with other visuals, such as props or live demonstrations.

A word of caution on slide use, though: An overuse or dependency on slides can minimize the speaker-audience connection, distract the audience, and damage the speaker's credibility, which reduces the speaker's impact.[19] Strive for balance with slides and audience interaction. Changing delivery modes within a presentation is the key to maintaining audience interest and engagement.

MAXIMIZE USE OF VISUAL IMAGES, MINIMIZE USE OF WORDS

If a slide contains 50 or more words, it is no longer a visual aid. Instead, it becomes a "docuslide" or a teleprompter,[16] and audience members become readers instead of listeners. When text is read to an audience, communication is less effective because the text and the presenter's voice are competing for the audience's attention. This has been termed the redundancy principle.[17]

For presentation slides to be effective, visual images should be maximized and words minimized. Before building a presentation (sometimes called a slide deck), keep these key points in mind:

- Ensure that messages are clear and structured. Create a slide deck *after* creating content.
- Use only one idea per slide.
- Keep the representation of an idea on a slide simple.[20,21]

A best practice to optimize slides is to *not* use the presentation software's templates. Take a different approach and start with a blank slide with no template. Most venues now project slides on a wide screen with a 16:9 (widescreen) dimension. Most presentation software opens in 4:3 (standard) mode. Check with the meeting planner to find out if the speaking venue has a 4:3 or a widescreen projector, and remember to change the software settings to match.

Ensure that images on slides are "full bleed," meaning that the image covers the entire slide if needed. If an image cannot be enlarged without distorting it, use a black background on the slide. This will leave a border that is unobtrusive, and the image will still have the intended impact.

A situation that often occurs for conference speakers is the requirement of the conference to follow uniform PowerPoint guidelines and submit PowerPoint files well in advance of the conference. The conference then takes the PowerPoint decks and creates handouts for the attendees. This results in slide decks that are subpar and may not provide the best visual support for a speaker's live presentation. Garr Reynolds, a leading authority on presentation design and author of *Presentation Zen Design*, calls this practice "Slideumentation."[21] An alternative for handouts is to create a separate one with the main points or a fill-in-the-blank handout that audience members fill out during the presentation. It is more work for the presenter; however, the handout may contain more useful information, including the presenter's contact information, and will anyone really use the conference-produced handout if it contains mostly images?

Many stock photo websites offer images for slides. A few paid sites include iStock (www.istock .com), Shutterstock (www.shutterstock.com), and DepositPhotos (www.depositphotos.com). Sites that offer free images include Pexels (www.pexels .com), Unsplash (www.unsplash.com), and Pixabay (www.pixabay.com). Always be aware of the licensing agreement on the photos that will be used, as some photos may require that attribution be given to the photographer. Best practice is to not copy and paste photos from Google images, as many of those photos are copyrighted and may bring a fine if they are used for commercial purposes. Unlike commercial use, educators may use copyrighted material and images for certain educational purposes under the Fair Use law. More information about copyrights and fair use can be found through the US Copyright Office (www.copyright.gov/fair -use/more-info.html).

Use minimal text on slides. In most cases, no text is needed because the image conveys the message. There are no hard and fast rules about these, though many follow the 6×6 rule for bullet points or the 7-word rule per slide. The consensus among top slide designers is to use good design sense to create a visually interesting slide.

APPROPRIATE USE OF FONT CHOICE, SIZE, COLOR, AND ANIMATION

Fonts When choosing fonts, a general guideline is not to use more than two different fonts for slides. Fonts come in two varieties: serif and sans serif. Serif fonts have a little tail on the end of each letter, which increases the readability of the text in printed form, especially when there is a lot of text to read. Sans serif fonts do not have a tail at the end of each letter and provide a cleaner look. (See Figure 18.3.) Sans serif fonts are preferred for slides because they are more easily read on screens where the audience sits at various distances from the screen.[21]

The best font choice fits the tone of a presentation and can be seen clearly from the last row in the room. Consider that fonts or typefaces subconsciously communicate to an audience information expressed through associations in the style of type—formal or informal, serious or playful, modern or traditional. Decide what font or typeface best suits the presentation content.

Size When it comes to font size, the bigger the better. Audiences will become annoyed if they can't read type from the back of the room. A guideline to determine if a font size is too small is to print a slide on an 8.5 × 11-inch piece of paper. Place the paper on the floor, and while standing with the paper on the floor, read the text on the slide. If it isn't readable, the font size is not large enough.[22]

Another technique to determine whether a font is too small involves using a tape measure to take a diagonal measurement of a computer screen. For example, if the diagonal measurement of a computer screen is 15 inches, mark off 15 feet from where the computer sits. Put the presentation in slideshow mode. If the text on a slide cannot be seen from the 15 feet away, audience members in the back of the room will most likely have difficulty seeing it as well.[16]

Text tips If text is being placed on an image on a slide, be sure to place the text in a space where the audience can read it. On a busy slide, add a black bar at the bottom of the slide and add white text on top.

Typically, the text entered on a slide will be horizontal. Consider tilting the text at an angle. Using this technique (with discretion) adds emphasis, draws attention, and gives a new dimension to the words on a slide.

Avoid using italics or underlining, as these make text harder to read.

FIGURE 18.3 **Font examples**

Serif	Sans Serif
Caslon	Arial
Courier	**Helvetica**
Garamond	Futura
Georgia	Franklin Gothic
Times New Roman	Tahoma

Color Color is an important element in a slide presentation, as it sets the tone and mood of the presentation as well as representing the presenter's brand or company.[16] Color can grab viewers' attention, direct their eyes, and even evoke emotion. Most presentation software offers color combinations to help slide creators with color choices. At the time of this writing, a good online tool for help with creating color themes is available through Adobe (http://kuler.adobe.com). The most important guideline for using color in slides is to use *contrast*, as it is most appealing to people's eyes. Dark text on a white background or white text on a black background are easy to read because they contrast.

Speaking of color, approximately 8% of men and about 0.5% of women suffer from color vision deficiency (CVD), or color blindness.[23] If there are concerns or requirements regarding accessibility for audience members with CVD, check the slides with an online tool for this specific issue (www.color-blindness.com/coblis -color-blindness-simulator).[24]

For international audiences, keep in mind that colors may represent something different from what's traditional in the presenter's own country. For instance, Americans associate the color green with money and prosperity; however, the Chinese associate red with prosperity.

The bottom line is that simplicity and contrast are two design principles to consider when choosing slide and font colors. Proper usage is dependent on knowing the audience, alignment with the presentation's message, and consistency with the presenter's brand.

Animation Animation can be used on a slide *if it creates a focal point.*[25] Too often, however, animation is misused. Common examples of misuse include movement that distracts the audience from the presenter, an animation that startles the audience, animation that was used because it was available and does not add value to the presentation, or too many animations that dilute the purpose of the message.[16] Animation creates movement, and the best use of animation is to help in transitions, sequences, or interrelatedness of the information being presented. According to Garr Reynold, use animation (1) to emphasize a particular part of a visual, (2) to draw attention to or clarify a relevant point on a visual, (3) to visually build a point, or (4) to create a change to move a point forward.[21] Before adding animation,

ask why it is being used. If it does not support the point being made, delete it. Use animation sparingly to maximize its effectiveness.

Box 18.3 (page 300) illustrates principles of effective slide design. Consider ways to improve slides by minimizing text and maximizing the use of images.

BLANK SLIDES ARE A USEFUL TOOL TO REDIRECT AUDIENCE TO PRESENTER

There may be times during a presentation where no slides are needed, such as during a question-and-answer period. The best practice here is to use the "B" key on the keyboard to black the screen. The "W" on a keyboard will turn a screen all white. If the Q&A is scheduled in a presentation (rather than having impromptu questions arise), a better option is to format a slide with a black background so that the audience will focus their attention on the presenter. Also, most remote controls will have a key to make the screen black.

Used Wisely, Slides Can Help Presenters and Audiences Stay on Track

Slides can provide helpful structure to a presentation that both the presenters and the audience can use to follow along. Used wisely, they can keep a presenter on track. For example, slides can help assure that key content is presented. However, this is only successful when the presenter is well prepared and practiced. Without practice, many presenters prepare too many slides for the time allowed and end up going over their time limit, speeding through the slides, or skipping content.

Remember, presentation slides are a visual aid, not the presentation. Do not use them as a crutch for remembering content. This often leads to the presenter turning his or her back to the audience and reading the slides. Last, if technology does not work as intended, the presenter who is depending on the slides is stuck.

A presentation slide deck can be used to make handouts, which the audience can use to follow along, make notes on, and refer to later. Handouts can help the audience remember the information that has been provided. The most effective handouts are generally *not* copies of PowerPoint slides but are created specifically as written support for a presentation.

See Chapter 23 for more on creating effective presentation handouts.

BOX 18.3 # Principles of Effective Slide Design

① This slide is a typical type used in presentations. There are no images, the text covers more than one idea, the type is small and in different colors, and the overall design is confusing and hard to read. An audience will spend time reading and discerning the information on the slide rather than listening to the speaker.

② This slide features noticeable improvements: There is less text, the type is larger and easier to read, the image on the slide conveys an emotion, the design makes it easier for the audience to understand the concepts, and it would enhance the speaker's content.

③ This slide is well designed because it conveys a single message and the emotions of calmness and stability. The type is large, bold, and clear; the image covers the entire slide; and the speaker would maintain the audience's attention because they will not be reading while viewing the slide.

Notice that attributions for the images used in slides 2 and 3 are located unobtrusively on the edge of the image. Even though both images were obtained from Pexels, which grants commercial use of the images because they are not copyrighted, attribution was given as a courtesy to the site or the photographer.

Slides Are Ideally Used Along with Other Effective Strategies

Using presentation software in conjunction with other visual aids, audience participation, and embedded videos can elevate a presentation and make it memorable for an audience. In considering how to present information most effectively, don't assume slides are the only option. In addition to the visual aids described previously, consider incorporating discussions and audience participation, as described in Chapters 19 and 20, and above all, keep in mind that a compelling presenter *is* a visual aid and nothing additional may be needed.

In summary, these are practical strategies for using presentation software:

1. Plan and create content before developing slides. Use sticky notes, draw sketches, or create a storyboard for ideas as content is developed.
2. Choose presentation software that best fits the needs and style of the presentation.
3. Feature one idea or point per slide.
4. Use an outline and key points to create slides that tell a story.
5. Proofread and review the slides to ensure there are no spelling or grammar mistakes, type is large enough, and images are aligned.
6. Rehearse, rehearse, rehearse to ensure familiarity with the material in the event of technical glitches at the event.

Evaluation Checklist for Presentation Slides

_____ Have I chosen the appropriate presentation software for the audience and my topic?

_____ Have I chosen appropriate images to enhance what I am going to say?

_____ Does each image cover the entire slide? If images were cropped or reduced to fit on the slide, are they still understandable for my audience?

_____ Did I obtain my images from an appropriate stock photo website, and have I given attribution when needed?

_____ Does each slide address just one point or key message?

_____ Have I limited slide text?

_____ Is the slide text large enough to be read from the last row?

_____ Did I use fonts that are easy to read?

_____ Did I use colors that work well together, and did I use sufficient contrast between the text and slide background?

_____ Have I used animation appropriately?

_____ Have I rehearsed my presentation so that I can move through my slides without turning my back to the audience?

_____ Have I rehearsed so that I am comfortable with the animation and blacking out of slides when necessary during my presentation?

_____ Does embedded video work in my slides?

_____ Have I proofread my slides to ensure there are no misspelled words or grammatical errors?

Travel tip If traveling to deliver a presentation, always have a backup. Even if the slides were sent to the meeting organizer, email a copy of the presentation to yourself, have it on a flash drive, add a copy to a file-sharing app (such as Dropbox), or save a PDF of the slides to your computer. Nothing is worse than spending the time to create beautiful slides to support a presentation and not being able to use them!

See the checklist provided to evaluate presentation slides. For a humorous look at common PowerPoint mistakes, see the TED Talk link in the resources section at the end of the chapter.

Jim Endicott, in an article published in the trade periodical _Presentations_,[26] said it well:

> _In presentations, as in other designed products, our message doesn't have to be defined by the tools we use. It's defined by the clarity of our story, the passion with which we tell it and its relevance to our audience._

Though Endicott made this statement in 1999, this will be true for decades to come, no matter what technologies are invented to create visual aids.

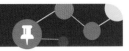

Utilize Visual Aids to Enhance Communication

1 Combining visual depictions of information along with or in place of verbal descriptions can more effectively convey key messages. Visual aids assist audiences in understanding content, storing it in long-term memory for future use, and putting knowledge into practice. Visual images may be understood even when written or spoken language is not.

2 Visual aids enhance communication in numerous ways. They increase attention, enhance meaning, improve retention and persuasion, promote taking action, and enrich the presentation experience.

3 Visual aids play a vital role in breaking down complex concepts and making them understandable. Visual aids can be used to connect to an audience and to help explain a variety of important pieces to understanding the larger puzzle of a topic.

4 There is a fine balance between using visual aids to engage an audience and having visual aids become a distraction. The most effective visual aids capture the audience's attention long enough to provide key understanding. These include the use of stories, pictures, props, demonstrations, posters and infographics, displays and bulletin boards, and videos.

5 Delivering a presentation with slides created using presentation software can have many benefits. Well-designed slides can attract and hold an audience's attention. Using presentation software is most effective when it is used to enhance a presentation, with slides designed to help an audience *understand* or *remember* a point.

RESOURCES

TED Talk video by Don McMillan, "Life After Death by PowerPoint": https://ed.ted.com/on/vox3XepQ

Adobe color wheel: http://kuler.adobe.com

Color blindness simulator: www.color-blindness.com/coblis-color-blindness-simulator

REFERENCES

1. Mayer R. Cognitive theory of multimedia learning. In: Mayer R, ed. *The Cambridge Handbook of Multimedia Learning.* 2nd ed. Cambridge University Press; 2014:43-71.
2. Roam D. *Show and Tell.* 2nd ed. Portfolio/Penguin; 2016.
3. Butcher K. The multimedia principle. In: Mayer R, ed. *The Cambridge Handbook of Multimedia Learning.* 2nd ed. Cambridge University Press; 2014:174-205.
4. Medina J. *Brain Rules.* Pear Press; 2008.
5. Hale JJ. The visual superiority effect: retention of audiovisual messages. *Int J Instr Media.* 2009;36(3):275-286.
6. Vogel DR, Dickson GW, Lehman JA. *Persuasion and the Role of Visual Presentation Support: The UM/3M Study.* University of Minnesota; 1986.
7. Shu S, Townsend C. Using aesthetics and self-affirmation to encourage openness to risky (and safe) choices. *J Exp Psychol Appl.* 2014;20(1):22-39.
8. Garcia-Retamero R, Cokely E. Effective communication of risks to young adults: using message framing and visual aids to increase condom use and STD screening. *J Exp Psychol Appl.* 2011;17(3):270-287.
9. Anderson C. *TED Talks: The Official TED Guide to Public Speaking.* Houghton Mifflin Harcourt; 2016.
10. Roam D. *Back of the Napkin: Solving Problems and Selling Ideas with Pictures.* Portfolio/Penguin; 2009.
11. Gowlett JAJ. The discovery of fire by humans: a long and convoluted process. *Philos Trans R Soc Biol Sci.* 2016;371(1696). doi:10.1098/rstb.2015.0164
12. LeFever L. *The Art of Explanation.* John Wiley and Sons; 2013.
13. Hurwitz B, Charon R. A narrative future for health care. *Lancet.* 2013;381(9881):1886-1887.
14. McKnight L, Doolittle N, Stitzel K, Vafiadis D, Robb K. Simple cooking with heart: nutrition education and improving diet quality through culinary skill-based education. *J Nutr Educ Behav.* 2013;45(4S):S23. doi:10.1016/j.jneb.2013.04.063
15. Brame CJ. Effective educational videos: principles and guidelines for maximizing student learning from video content. *CBE Life Sci Educ.* 2016;15(4):1-6. doi:10.1187/cbe.16-03-0125
16. Duarte N. *Slide:ology the Art and Science of Creating Great Presentations.* O'Reilly Media; 2008.
17. Abela AV. *Advanced Presentations by Design: Creating Communication That Drives Action.* 2nd ed. Wiley; 2013.
18. Mayer R. *The Cambridge Handbook of Multimedia Learning.* Cambridge University Press; 2005.
19. Osborn M, Turner K. *Public Speaking: Finding Your Voice.* Pearson; 2015.
20. Lucas S. *The Art of Public Speaking.* 10th ed. McGraw-Hill; 2009.
21. Reynolds G. *Presentation Zen Design.* New Riders; 2010.
22. Engelberg I, Daly J. *Think Public Speaking.* Pearson; 2013.
23. Facts about color blindness. National Eye Institute website. Published 2015. Accessed August 2, 2018. https://nei.nih.gov/health/color_blindness/facts_about
24. Coblis—color blindness simulator. Colblindor website. Accessed August 2, 2018. www.color-blindness.com/coblis-color-blindness-simulator
25. Williams R. *The Non-Designer's Presentation Book.* Peachpit Press; 2010.
26. Endicott J. A strong template identity creates powerful impressions. *Presentations.* 1999:28-29.

CHAPTER 19

Facilitate Discussions to Generate Ideas and Solutions

Barbara J. Mayfield, MS, RDN, FAND
and Angie Hasemann Bayliss, MS, RDN, CSP

"*Facilitated discussions are interactive and audience focused. They can enhance learning more than lecture-style presentations and have greater potential to promote cooperation and consensus as well as applied learning and behavior change.*"

> "The aim of argument, or of discussion, should not be victory, but progress." —JOSEPH JOUBERT

Introduction

Creating high-impact presentations involves more than a solid central message, logical organization, a strong opening and closing, and effective use of visual aids. All of these approaches can occur in a traditional lecture-style presentation. Moving beyond lecturing to more interactive presentation approaches is the focus of this chapter and the next.

As Mortimer Adler, the Aristotelian philosopher, said: "Lecturing is the transfer of information from the notes of the lecturer to the notes of the student without passing through the minds of either." Of course, using the attention-getting strategies discussed in the first three chapters of this section will help lecture-style presentations effectively engage an audience and promote learning. However, to elevate learning to the application of knowledge and problem solving, presentations benefit from a greater degree of audience engagement.

The facilitated discussion is an effective communication strategy that is inherently audience focused, which leads to promoting learning and adopting healthful behaviors. This chapter answers three questions:

- What are the benefits of facilitated discussions vs conventional presentations?
- How are facilitated discussions planned and implemented?
- What practical strategies for facilitated discussion enhance success?

Facilitated discussions are a practical approach in numerous settings, from staff meetings and in services to community education to breakout sessions at a professional conference. Discussions can be inserted within a more traditional presentation or training workshop or be the format used for the entire session. Facilitated discussions work with small groups or larger groups that have broken into small groups. This chapter explains why facilitated discussions are an important and necessary tool in a nutrition communicator's tool kit and gives the steps for being an effective discussion facilitator.

This chapter is an introduction to the field and not a preparation for certification as a professional facilitator. Recognize that certification programs are available for those interested in pursuing this area at an advanced level. See the resources section at the end of the chapter for information.

What Are the Benefits of Facilitated Discussions vs Conventional Presentations?

Facilitated discussions are interactive and audience focused. They can enhance learning more than lecture-style presentations and account for the characteristics of adult learners much better than lectures do.[1] They have greater potential to promote cooperation and consensus[2] as well as applied learning and behavior change.[3] Facilitated discussions are often preferred over conventional presentations.[4]

"In the modern world, the original function of the classroom, simple information transfer, has been replaced by books and the Internet. The classroom has now become the best opportunity for students to practice the desired thinking while getting timely feedback to support learning. This feedback comes from interactions with their fellow students and teachers."

—C. WEIMAN AND S. GILBERT. "TAKING A SCIENTIFIC APPROACH TO SCIENCE EDUCATION, PART II: CHANGING TEACHING," *MICROBE*[5]

A *discussion* is a conversation with one or more people, generally for the purpose of sharing ideas or reaching a decision. Without direction, discussions can easily get off-track or even turn into arguments. A facilitated discussion is just what the term implies—it is facilitated. A facilitator (the nutrition communicator) leads and directs the discussion. This does not imply that the facilitator does most of the talking or instructs people in what to think or say. Rather, they *facilitate* talking and the free-flowing exchange of ideas.

To *facilitate* is to make a process easier. A discussion facilitator (often called a moderator) gets the conversation started and keeps it moving. Facilitators prevent participants from getting off on tangents or getting into unproductive arguments. They assure participants engage with respect, listen well, and are listened to. They help groups get comfortable with sharing, solicit input and feedback, help make connections among participants and between ideas, and summarize outcomes.

Facilitated Discussions Have a Breadth of Potential Uses

Discussion as a means for learning dates back to the time of Socrates, but the concept of facilitated discussion is a more recent trend. The first documented use in a nutrition setting was in the Special Supplemental Nutrition Program for Women, Infants, and Children (WIC) in New Mexico in the 1990s.[6] Since then, it has been widely used as a means for nutrition education in community settings throughout the United States.

Facilitated discussions are useful in small-group settings in which the sharing of ideas among participants will result in the greatest amount of ideation, problem solving, or learning.

In addition to community settings like WIC, examples include a college classroom, a work setting among staff, a volunteer organization, or a variety of patient or client education settings, such as nutrition classes sponsored by a clinic or hospital or group weight management classes like the Diabetes Prevention Program. With an adequate number of facilitators, these discussions can also be used in larger settings, such as a conference of professionals, in which the group is broken into smaller discussion groups.

Facilitated Discussions Are Audience Focused

A challenge for nutrition communicators in a traditional presentation is tailoring the message to a specific audience. A benefit of the facilitated discussion approach is the ability to learn about an audience in real time and adjust the direction of learning to best meet the audience's wants and needs.

Within a broad topic area selected by the discussion facilitator, audience members generate the specific topics discussed and get their questions answered and problems solved. The information shared focuses on the audience's needs and interests because it is generated by the audience itself. The facilitator's goals are to[7,8]:

- help the group establish the desired outcomes or purpose of the discussion,
- set the tone (creating a climate of respect and openness),
- initiate the conversation and keep it moving,
- gently correct inaccuracies or direct participants to credible sources,
- maintain focus and structure, and
- encourage taking action, all while being as unobtrusive as possible.

Facilitated discussions are an ideal approach for adult learners, including college students. Recall from Chapter 14 that adults are self-directed, experts on themselves, skeptical, pragmatic and problem-centered, internally motivated, and autonomous. The facilitated discussion takes into account all of these characteristics.

Facilitated Discussions Build Community and Fully Engage Audience Members

Facilitated discussions allow relationships to build between the teacher and learners and among learners much more efficiently than lecture-style presentations. By creating a comfortable atmosphere in which participants feel safe sharing, ideas will flow and the conversation will be productive. Strategies for building community are described later in the chapter.

Facilitated discussions are considered a "power-with" setting rather than a "power-over" setting. A power-over setting is one in which the professional plays the role of an expert who provides advice that participants are expected to follow. A power-with setting is one that allows for a partnership between a professional and the participants, encourages mutual sharing and decision making, and empowers participants to solve problems.[6,9]

The process of group development has been described in a variety of ways. One of the best-known models is Tuckman's stages of group development,[10] which started with four stages when first published in 1965; a fifth stage was added in 1977. Tuckman's five stages are: forming, storming, norming, performing, and adjourning. Another model, called the process model of group discussion, describes its four stages as orientation, conflict, consensus, and group decision.[2] In these and other models, groups begin with building community before generating ideas or making decisions.

Recall from Chapter 1 the relational component of communication, and from Chapter 3 the role of empathy in building relationships—both between the communicator and the audience and among audience members. Effective group processes promote empathy, build relationships, and in turn create community. In community, audiences can generate ideas and solve problems.

Facilitated Discussions Promote Creative Problem Solving

Facilitated discussions provide an optimal setting for creative problem solving. This process occurs in four stages, as described by the Creative Education Foundation[11,12]:

1. Clarify: Explore the vision, gather data, and formulate questions to challenge the audience.
2. Ideate: Generate ideas to answer the challenge questions.
3. Develop: Formulate solutions.
4. Implement: Formulate a plan by identifying resources and actions to take.

Creative problem solving (CPS) recognizes that everyone is creative and that creativity is a skill that can be learned and enhanced.[11,12] CPS is based on four core principles[11,12]:

1. Balancing divergent and convergent thinking (in other words, promoting both the spontaneous generation of ideas and solutions as well as a logical and systematic approach to determining the best answer)
2. Asking problems as questions
3. Deferring judgment until ideation is complete
4. Supporting the generation of ideas and solutions with statements of "yes, and" rather than "no, but"

Facilitated Discussions Promote Goal Setting and Application of Learning

Discussions offer numerous benefits over conventional lecture-style presentations.[13] Discussions promote deeper examination of personal beliefs, attitudes, values, and behaviors. They allow for greater exploration of new ideas and increase the potential for applying knowledge in new situations. Discussion participants are empowered to set goals and solve problems. Facilitated discussions are an effective audience-centered approach to reaching communication goals.

The emphasis on using group intervention strategies, including facilitated discussion, in the National Diabetes Prevention Program, specifically promoting autonomous goal setting and problem solving in a supportive environment, is considered instrumental in the successful outcomes seen in this program.[14]

How Are Facilitated Discussions Planned and Implemented?

Facilitated discussions can achieve the benefits described when well planned and properly implemented. This section will describe how to prepare for and lead a facilitated discussion that accomplishes its intended purpose.

Determine the Purpose and Goals—Promote Win-Win for Everyone

Planning a facilitated discussion may take more time than preparing for a traditional lecture because the facilitator will not be in full control of the path the conversation takes. However, that is potentially one of the greatest strengths of this communication tool, as participants are empowered and trusted to generate ideas and solutions.[8]

The first step is outlining the purpose of the discussion, which should help both the facilitator and the audience to understand why the facilitated discussion method was chosen for the topic. If the purpose of communication is simply knowledge transfer about policies or rules, a discussion might not be appropriate. In contrast, to explore nutrition myths perpetuated by the media, a facilitated discussion allows the audience to share their experiences with the topic while also asking for the facilitator's guidance on how to assess and address their concerns. This proves to be a win-win for all involved.

The goals of a facilitated discussion are best met when the values of brainstorming, sharing both sides of a conversation, and tapping into the current knowledge and experiences of an audience are recognized. Goals of this type of communication tool may not be driven by results, but rather by the process of engaging in dialogue. Specific goals can help determine if tangible results are needed and expected at the end of the conversation and serve as guides to measure efficacy and progress.

Determine the Target Audience

A facilitated discussion is not appropriate for every audience. Young children or highly emotional stakeholders may be unable to effectively contribute to a discussion in a productive manner. Negative emotions can be contagious and unproductive in group settings.[15] Once an audience has been deemed to be appropriate for this tool, it is imperative to define the audience in detail. Questions to consider include:

1. How comfortable are audience members with each other?
2. How much prior knowledge do they have on this topic?

Malnutrition Work Group Uses Facilitated Discussion

As nutrition-focused physical examination has become more familiar in clinical nutrition, it has led to more thoughtful conversations about how to diagnose malnutrition accurately and consistently in the nutrition profession. At the University of Virginia Health System, clinical nutrition manager Kate Willcutts used a facilitated discussion to cover this intricate topic with her inpatient registered dietitian nutritionist (RDN) team. First, she gave team members a survey outlining four patient cases and asked them to diagnose the degree of malnutrition in each case. Then, Kate used the baseline data to highlight inconsistencies with the interpretation of malnutrition guidelines and to establish the consensus on the need for a group discussion.

Prior to beginning the discussion, Kate reviewed the group rules and the general goal of the conversation with the team—to review guidelines and make notes or adjustments to help build consistency in interpretation among team members. A notetaker was identified for each session, and a projector showed both guidelines and notes during the conversation. After two sessions of contemplative and productive discussion, the group established additional details for more consistent interpretation, and just as important, they engaged in thoughtful dialogue on patients who were less-than-straightforward cases. This led to more conversations among team members for future challenging cases.

3. How do they like to learn (eg, read the material themselves, receive a lecture, discover through interactive communication)?
4. What is the best way to get everyone involved?

An audience composed of individuals who are too familiar with each other may be distracted from the conversation, while a group of strangers may hesitate to share opinions and engage in dialogue until they warm up to each other. Their prior knowledge base of the topic will determine the starting point in the discussion. Knowing the audience serves as a great benefit when determining the facilitation style and any preparatory information to share.

Recognizing general demographics (eg, age, gender, socioeconomic status, education level) may assist in better understanding the broader questions. This may also allow for anticipation of the audience's needs and frustrations related to the topic, as well as how they typically access information, all of which will help to provide more effective facilitation.

Box 19.1 illustrates the use of facilitated discussion for a malnutrition work group. Consider the wide variety of potential uses for facilitated discussions.

Develop Engaging Open-Ended Questions, Probe for Deeper Understanding, Plan Backup Questions

A facilitator must steer the bus while someone else pushes on the gas. A prepared list of questions can engage the audience and guide the group to either dive deeper into topics or move on to the next area of discussion. There is an art to knowing when to probe for deeper thought and when to redirect conversation. These skills come with practice and prove easier with a more familiar audience.

Preparation for a facilitated discussion involves determining the goal and the process to achieve it.[16] Prepare an outline and open-ended questions that encourage dialogue. Planning follow-up questions, for clarification as well as to promote deeper thought, will increase the depth of the discussion. Recognizing that an audience may interpret questions differently than intended necessitates the creation of potential backup questions. These rephrased questions can be planned ahead of the discussion as well as during the discussion when it

becomes clear that the facilitated questions have been misinterpreted.

If a facilitated discussion reaches a lull, additional questions can help to reignite thought sharing. For example, if a group of teenagers has been gathered to discuss their needs and ideas for a community exercise class, they may quickly come to a consensus about a basketball club. Probing questions about what other activities they and their friends enjoy, what other physical activity resources are nearby, and what activities could be done year-round may help drive the discussion to broader ideas and considerations for next steps.

Box 19.2 (page 310) shows general principles for writing effective discussion questions. The examples illustrate the principles using potential questions for a facilitated discussion about family meals. Use them as a guide to write new questions.

Plan an Opening Activity That Breaks the Ice and Sets the Stage

Especially when audience members do not know each other well, it is vital to build a comfortable space. Prior to the arrival of the group, set up an inviting physical environment. Arrange chairs to allow for an open discussion in which no one is blocking another participant's view and everyone has an equal status in the room. Before the discussion begins, engage the audience with appropriate and friendly introductions. Introductions can be part of an opening activity that provides some fun and sets the stage for the rest of the session.

While it's common to break the ice by asking participants their names and other pertinent information, such as their year in school or where they live, the discussion topic often suggests other appropriate questions. With nutrition topics, participants can be asked to share their favorite food, the best meal their family makes at home, or the weirdest food they've tried as fun additions to the basic introduction. For a more serious audience or discussion, ask participants what they would like to get out of the discussion or what motivated them to attend.

Traditional icebreakers can also work well to open a facilitated discussion. Entering "icebreakers for [teens, adults]" into a search engine will reveal dozens of ideas. Depending on the total time available, select icebreakers that build community without taking too much time. Those

BOX
19.2

Sample Questions for a Discussion about Family Meals

- **Open with a safe question that warms up the group to the topic. A question about personal experience is good; make sure it is something everyone can answer, and do not judge the responses. For example:**

"Our discussion topic is family meals. I'd like to start with asking this: How often did your family eat dinner together during a typical week when you were in elementary school?"

(At the start, be specific; general questions are harder to answer.)

- **Follow up:**

"How often did you eat together when you were in high school?"

- **The next question should probe a bit deeper:**

"What do you think are the major barriers to eating together more often as a family, especially as children get older?"

- **Follow up with a question that gives personal relevance:**

"Did you experience any of these barriers in your family?"

(If the group answers a planned question before it is asked, omit the question, or it will seem like attention wasn't paid to the earlier answers.)

- **Ask questions using phrases like "What have you heard?" to find out what they know about a topic:**

"What have you heard are benefits of families eating together?"

Compare that to a question that asks about knowledge, which feels harder to answer:

"What do you know about the benefits of family meals?"

- **Make sure that most, if not all, people answer each of the questions, not just one or two people. If that is not happening, turn to another person and ask a question such as:**

"[Name], what else have you heard are benefits ...?"

- **Make sure group members have fully answered all they know:**

"Are there any other benefits you can think of?"

- **Write lots of potential follow-up questions:**

"Which benefit(s) do you believe are the strongest motivators to promote family meals?"

"What have you heard are the potential *negative* outcomes for families who don't eat together on a regular basis?"

"What do you think it is about eating family meals, or *not* eating family meals, that leads to these outcomes?"

"In your opinion, should families be encouraged to eat together more, or does that just produce guilt?"

"What do you think families need the most help with to succeed at having family meals?"

that encourage some movement (eg, standing up when in agreement with questions, using the scale method to show interest in or familiarity with topics by moving more or less along a line, or moving into groups based on personal attributes) can add energy to the group, while also showing similarities among the audience members.

An effective opening activity provides a sincere welcome for group members and allows them to begin to feel at ease with each other. One of the primary goals of an icebreaker activity is for every participant to contribute. A person who has talked once may be more likely to do it again if the environment is safe, supportive, and welcoming.

Establish Ground Rules, Such as Confidentiality and Free-Flowing Conversation Where Everyone Contributes

While the ground rules for an appropriate discussion may seem straightforward, it is helpful to communicate explicit expectations and general guidelines.[16] This may include a statement about confidentiality (eg, all information shared will remain confidential and not be shared outside of the facilitated group). Outlining the desire for a free-flowing conversation may help encourage open sharing of information. Encouraging contributions from everyone and providing some guidance to avoid interruptions may be helpful when going over ground rules. Consider limiting individual responses to a set number of minutes and stating that only one person is to speak at a time. It is also important to establish an environment of respect and open opportunity for all viewpoints to be shared.

Discussion of the ground rules may also be a good time to share general announcements to promote the comfort of participants. Reviewing the timeline for the discussion, as well as room information (eg, location of food, drink, restrooms), can assist in making group members feel relaxed and ready to participate fully. Unless cell phones are being used to provide information, ask that group members put them away or silence them.

Prepare Methods to Keep on Track

As in any conversation, it may be easy to fall down "rabbit holes." The facilitator's role is to recognize these distracting conversations and adjust the course. Staying true to the outline and prepared questions will allow for an easy transition back to the discussion topic. Recognizing the use of motivational interviewing skills in redirection can make these transitions feel more natural and comfortable for all involved. Some key phrases that may come in handy include the following:

- Let's hold that thought for now and wrap up our discussion on _____ first.
- I like where this is going, but for the sake of time, let's move on to _____.
- It's great to see your interest and passion on this topic. For now, let's move on to _____, and if we have extra time at the end, we'll come back to this.
- Thank you for sharing so freely about this. If you don't mind, let's transition to hearing your thoughts on _____.

Plan How the Discussion Will End, Be Summarized; Provide Next Steps

Participants like to feel a sense of progress and closure just as much as the facilitator does. Planning time to summarize key findings, review next steps, and thank the group members for their contributions is a vital piece of an effective facilitated discussion. While it may seem natural for the facilitator to cover these items, allowing time for the audience to share what they heard as key messages may help them to feel further engaged in the process. This is also a good time to review future opportunities for participation. Next steps may include this information, as well as how the notes from the initial discussion will be utilized in the future.

What Practical Strategies Enhance Success?

While the previous section covered some of the basics of an effective facilitated discussion, the following information will review key tactics to help ensure success in this communication style. These practical strategies are good guidelines for first-time facilitators, as well as good reminders for seasoned facilitators.

Facilitate and Speak Less Than 25% of the Time

The facilitator may be the expert on the topic and may be tempted to lead the discussion and participate regularly. However, that is not the purpose of this type of communication. For a truly effective facilitated discussion, the leader must be comfortable with taking a back seat and allowing the audience to lead. Aiming to speak less than 25% of the time is a nice rule of thumb for the facilitator, with most verbal communication serving to drive the conversation deeper or into a new area. Excessive time spent with the audience listening to the facilitator's views on the topic diminishes the role of the group and could sway the discussion and monopolize the results.

Build Rapport and Trust and Promote Safe Involvement

Building rapport is a key feature of the facilitator's role. Showing appreciation for the group's time, attendance, and input is an important step toward this goal. Addressing hostile or confrontational moments with consideration for both sides, expressing curiosity for better understanding, and transitioning to the next topic, as appropriate, can help to promote safe involvement for all group members. The leader is responsible for smoothing over disputes or awkwardness that can come with multiple people sharing thoughts and opinions openly.

Promote Sharing and Balanced Contributions

Guiding the conversation to ensure that all participants have the opportunity to share is vital to the strength of facilitated discussions. Many would attest to the challenge of balancing those who are eager to contribute with those who are hesitant to speak up, both of which are addressed in detail in Chapter 35. Balanced contributions will not only allow each member to feel a part of the process but will also lead to better feedback and information sharing.

Present Well-Designed Questions in Logical Sequence to Provide a Framework, Be Responsive to Discussion, and Adapt

Although a facilitator may have spent hours developing an outline that builds the discussion, it is imperative that a facilitator function like a TV interviewer. The primary role of a facilitator is to listen first and build off the information received by asking questions related to the previous response given. It is easy to have an agenda, but being comfortable following the discussion and adjusting accordingly is key. Responsiveness and adaptability are easier with adequate preparation, with expectations for the directions in which the conversation may flow, and with greater experience facilitating group discussions.

Address Misconceptions and Misinformation

It is likely that during the course of a discussion, a participant will share information that is inaccurate or could be considered a misconception. Rather than taking the role of expert and dispelling the myth with a knowledgeable explanation, consider ways to assist the participant and the group explore the accuracy of the information and discover for themselves what is true.[17]

For example, a common misconception is that cutting out gluten can help people lose weight. The facilitator could ask if someone knows what gluten is, followed by questions to see if the group is aware of who should avoid it and why. Ask if anyone is aware that many gluten-free foods are higher in calories than their gluten-containing counterparts. Acknowledge that the belief is common, and like many other diet misconceptions, people who have experienced success in avoiding gluten and losing weight are successful due to something else, such as eating fewer calories from grain-based desserts.

Implement a Recording Strategy to Provide Opportunities for Further Discussion and Summarize Ideas

Discussions can happen quickly, where thoughtful and important information is rapidly being shared. Therefore, using a strategy to record key information helps the facilitator remember where the conversation traveled, provides opportunities to note where further discussion is needed, and allows for a summary of what progress was made. These notes are helpful in the wrap-up portion of the discussion, in communicating general findings with broader teams, and for following up.

Designating one note taker can be an effective strategy for recording a conversation. Alternatively, some groups have effectively used a dry-erase board or large notepad for recording ideas in a method visible for the group to immediately reflect upon. Others have taken creative steps to illustrate the conversation as it occurs (see, the Academy of Nutrition and Dietetics Second Century Nutrition Impact Summit drawing: https://eatright foundation.org/why-it-matters/second-century /nutrition-impact-summit/). The most important point here is to establish the method before the discussion starts and to stick to a simple strategy the first few times you lead a facilitated discussion.

Stay on Task and End on Time

Staying on task and ending on time go a long way toward establishing appreciation of and respect for participants' time. When developing a discussion outline, setting time frames can help to ensure all topics are addressed. While it may be difficult to guess an appropriate discussion length for each topic, general structure and timing guidance can ensure that there is sufficient time to complete all of the planned topics. Leaving sufficient time at the end for final thoughts and a wrap-up will allow participants to not feel rushed at the end of the group meeting. Allowing a pleasant closure can go a long way in building further rapport for future conversations.

After the discussion ends, use the evaluation checklist provided to reflect on what went well and what could be improved.

Evaluation Checklist for Facilitated Group Discussions[a]

_____ Did the purpose fit the group's needs and concerns?

_____ Did I begin with a check-in: introductions, purpose, rules, and so on?

_____ Did I begin with an icebreaker: every member shared?

_____ Did I deliver the first open-ended question and then allowed silence?

_____ Did I use open-ended questions and keep the conversation flowing?

_____ Was the conversation guided and kept on topic?

_____ Was everyone encouraged to participate?

_____ Did I practice active listening (make eye contact, lean forward, nod, remain quiet)?

_____ Did I make sure I clarified (made points clearly, probed, reflected) when necessary?

_____ Did I accept people as they are (respected feelings, didn't judge)?

_____ Did I deal with misinformation and misconceptions (assist participants in discovering accurate information by involving them in the reasoning process)?

_____ Have I summarized the discussion?

_____ Did I have fun (laughter, relaxed)?

[a] Adapted from Facilitated Group Discussion Workshop Training Manual for Indiana WIC Program 2001.

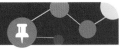

Facilitate Discussions to Generate Ideas and Solutions

1 Facilitated discussions are inherently audience focused, which leads to promoting learning and adopting healthful behaviors. They are a practical approach in numerous settings, from staff meetings and in-services, to community education, to break-out sessions in a professional conference. Facilitated discussions work in small-group settings or in larger groups that are broken into small groups.

2 Facilitated discussions enhance learning and account for the characteristics of adult learners. They have great potential to promote applied learning and behavior change. They are interactive and audience focused. Audiences often prefer facilitated discussions over conventional presentations.

3 Facilitated discussions can be very effective when well planned and properly implemented. The first step is outlining the purpose of the discussion, which should help both the facilitator and the audience to understand why the facilitated discussion method was chosen for the topic. The goals of a facilitated discussion are best met when the values of brainstorming, sharing both sides of a conversation, and tapping into the current knowledge and experiences of an audience are recognized. Preparation for a facilitated discussion often involves an outline and questions that can help encourage dialogue.

4 Practical strategies begin with the facilitator recognizing that he or she must be comfortable with taking a back seat and allowing the audience to lead; facilitators should speak less than 25% of the time. Building rapport is a key feature of the facilitator's role and is shown by respecting the participants' time, attendance, and input. Guiding the conversation to ensure that all participants have the opportunity to share is vital to the strength of facilitated discussions. Balancing flexibility with staying on task is a necessary skill.

RESOURCES

Examples of advanced training and certification programs for professional facilitators:

- www.iaf-world.org/site/professional/cpf
- www.td.org/education-courses/facilitation-skills-certificate

Creative problem solving:

www.creativeeducationfoundation.org/creative-problem-solving/the-cps-process/

REFERENCES

1. Vella J. *Learning to Listen, Learning to Teach.* Jossey-Bass; 2002.
2. Meleady R, Hopthrow T, Crisp R. The group discussion effect: integrative processes and suggestions for implementation. *Personal Soc Psychol Rev.* 2013;17(1):56-71.
3. Lamb H, Lamb S. Leading effective discussions in the classroom. Accessed May 11, 2020. http:// unitar.org/hiroshima/sites/unitar.org.hiroshima/files/9.AF06_WSII_Leading_Effective_Discussions.pdf
4. Birkett D, Johnson D, Thompson J, Oberg D. Reaching low-income families: focus group results provide direction for a behavioral approach to WIC services. *J Acad Nutr Diet.* 2004;10:1277-1280.
5. Weiman C, Gilbert S. Taking a scientific approach to science education, part II: changing teaching. *Microbe.* 2015;10(5):204.
6. Abusabha R, Peacock J, Achterberg C. How to make nutrition education more meaningful through facilitated group discussion. *J Acad Nutr Diet.* 1999;99(1):72-76.
7. Smith M, Chilcote M. What is a facilitator? Essential skills for effective facilitation. The Training Clinic website. Accessed September 22, 2018. https://thetrainingclinic.com/articles/what-is-a-facilitator
8. McFadzean E. Developing and supporting creative problem solving teams: part 2—facilitator competencies. *Manag Decis.* 2002;40(6):537-551.
9. Labonte R. Health promotion and empowerment: reflections on professional practice. *Heal Educ Behav.* 1994;21(2):253-268.
10. Tuckman BW. Developmental sequence in small groups. *Psychol Bull.* 1965;63:384-399.
11. Creative Education Foundation. The CPS process. Published 2018. Accessed September 22, 2018. www.creativeeducationfoundation.org/creative-problem-solving/the-cps-process
12. Creative Education Foundation. *Educating for Creativity Level 1 Resource Guide.* Creative Education Foundation; 2015.
13. Nilson LB. Leading effective discussions. In: *Teaching at Its Best.* 3rd ed. Jossey-Bass; 2010:127-135.
14. Trief P, Cibula D, Delahanty L, Weinstock R. Self-determination theory and weight loss in a Diabetes Prevention Program translation trial. *J Behav Med.* 2017;40:483-493.
15. Luoma-aho V. Emotional stakeholders: a threat to organizational legitimacy? Paper presented at: 60th Annual Conference of the International Communication Association; June 22 2010; Singapore. Accessed May 11, 2020. www.academia.edu/245892/Emotional_stakeholders_A_Threat_to_Organizational_Legitimacy
16. McFadzean E, Somersall L, Coker A. A framework for facilitating group processes. *Strateg Chang.* 1999;8:421-431.
17. Galindo JH. Revealing and dealing with misconceptions. Harvard University website. Accessed September 22, 2018. https://ablconnect.harvard.edu/revealing-and-dealing-misconceptions

Engage Audiences with Participation Strategies

Barbara J. Mayfield, MS, RDN, FAND
and Kayle Skorupski,
MS, RDN-AP, CSG, CNSC, FAND

"*Audience interaction and engagement are more than just a current trend in education and communication; they are features of a proven approach to increasing attention, enhancing learning and understanding, improving retention and application of learning, strengthening enjoyment of learning, and promoting behavior change.*"

> "I hear and I forget,
> I see and I remember,
> I do and I understand."
> —CONFUCIUS

Introduction

It's a common enough experience—the boring lecture where listeners are wondering if the presenter even noticed they were in the room, let alone considered soliciting their involvement. The most memorable part of that experience is how unmemorable it is. Contrast that experience with one in which listeners feel drawn into the presentation from the moment it begins. The presenter asks questions, gets the audience talking and possibly even moving, to connect them with the topic and each other. What is memorable about that presentation is not only the content but how enjoyable the presentation is. Audience members leave the presentation motivated to emulate the interactive strategies with their audiences.

Audience interaction and *engagement*—these are two buzzwords in education and communication. However, they are more than just a current trend; they are features of a proven approach to increasing attention, understanding, enjoyment, and application of learning. In addition to facilitated discussions, there are numerous strategies to involve audience members. Why and how to involve audiences is the focus of this chapter.

This chapter answers three questions:

- Why include audience participation in presentations?
- What are effective approaches to incorporating audience participation?
- What practical strategies for participation enhance success and avoid problems?

The beauty of most audience participation strategies is their wide applicability. Most activities can be employed with a wide variety of groups in all types of settings and can be adapted to almost every topic imaginable. Be creative. Take the ideas listed in this chapter and use them in multiple ways. Seek out additional ones; they are plentiful and easy to find. Create new ones. Audiences will be grateful! Speakers and audiences alike will be rewarded with improved outcomes.

Why Include Audience Participation in Presentations?

Why is audience participation recommended for effective presentations—presentations that lead to an audience attending, learning, and applying knowledge; presentations that meet their desired outcomes? Because participation engages the audience. To *engage* means to attract and maintain attention, to come together, and to take part or participate.[1] *Participation*, *engagement*, and *involvement* are synonyms. No matter what it is called, audience participation promotes attention, which is necessary for achieving all subsequent communication outcomes.

The thought of attending a presentation may automatically conjure the image of a lecture hall, with a stage in front, where the presenter commands the attention of the crowd through lecturing. However, "lectures have an infamous reputation for being utterly forgettable."[2] Nutrition communicators want to be memorable, impart knowledge, and encourage their audiences to make healthy lifestyle changes. Audience participation can help make the educational session memorable, not forgettable. Chapter 16 addressed how learning occurs best by doing.

Capture and Maintain Attention

When planning an educational presentation, it is relatively easy to think of all the topics and facts to share with an audience. But, it's also important to remember that an audience's attention span is about 10 minutes.[3] Additionally, the human brain has the most difficulty maintaining focus when learning is passive rather than active.[2]

What can be done to keep an audience's attention while providing an educational experience? Intersperse audience participation activities throughout a presentation to allow the audience to reflect on what they are learning, practice performing a new task, or apply the content.[2,4] Include activities that gauge whether the audience is meeting the learning objectives. Specific ways to engage audiences are covered later in this chapter.

Enhance Learning

According to the *interactivity principle*, "interactivity encourages the processing of new information" by engaging participants "in an active search for meaning."[5] Audience participation is most effective when designed for multimodal learning and engagement. Recall from Chapter 16 the various learning style preferences represented in an audience. For most people, learning is more effective when they learn by doing (experiential) rather than by reading or attending a lecture.[6] There are many types of audience participation: answering questions, discussion, teaching others, applying techniques, trying things out, solving problems, reflection, evaluating ideas, and conducting experiments.

Incorporating multiple learning strategies and participation methods can allow a communicator to appeal to all types of learners.[2] For example, active learners prefer group work, discussions, application, and experiential activities. Reflective learners prefer to process information and solve problems internally. Providing opportunities for experiential activities (doing and observing) as well as reflection enhances learning.[7] Both can serve as audience participation and are considered forms of active learning rather than passive learning, which is simply receiving information and ideas.[7]

See Chapter 15 for more on learning objectives.

Consider the taxonomies of learning objectives described in Chapter 15.

Incorporating a variety of participation strategies can help accomplish a variety of learning objectives.[8] To advance from lower-level objectives to higher levels, such as evaluating and creating, requires the learner to more actively engage with the material.

Increase Retention

Lecture, though a popular way to educate, has an established "forgetting curve."[9] Research shows that the average person can recall 62% of material just presented, 45% of material 3 to 4 days later, and only 24% of material 8 weeks later.[2,9] In other words, over one-third of material presented through lecture is forgotten in minutes. This is certainly a call to enhance retention by replacing passive instruction with various methods of audience participation during presentations. Research on incorporating audience participation strategies, such as the use of audience response technology, demonstrates increased retention over instruction without participation.[10-12]

In Chapter 16, Edgar Dale's Cone of Experience[13,14] was presented (see Figure 16.7 on page 271), which illustrates that people remember much less of what they merely see or hear (what takes place during a lecture) compared to what they say, write, or do (what occurs during audience participation). For nutrition communicators, planning for audience participation can improve learning and retention.

Promote Self-Efficacy, and Potentially, Behavior Change

What is it about participation that impacts an audience? According to Fink, "significant learning" makes a difference in how people live, results in lasting change, and promotes learning that is valued. Fink proposes that significant learning requires audience engagement and a high-energy learning environment.[7]

In terms of promoting behavior change, active learning by doing or observing can increase an individual's self-efficacy.[15] Self-efficacy is the "belief in [one's] ability to make a behavior change."[16] Active learning approaches that may promote self-efficacy and enhance behavior change include performing experiments, direct practice, service learning, and case-study discussions. Even if audience members can't do the activity themselves, observing someone modeling the activity can help increase self-efficacy.[16] Food demonstrations are an example of modeling and have been shown to result in adopting the desired behaviors.[17] Modeling is most likely to be successful if the person being observed is similar in age, gender, and culture to the audience. Taking into account the needs assessment of an audience can help to plan who might be used as a volunteer from the audience or who to cast in a case presentation. Make the example fit the audience for the greatest impact.

An interactive presentation can lead audience participants to have a positive change in self-efficacy, increasing the probability that they can make a lasting behavior change.

What Are Effective Approaches to Incorporating Audience Participation?

The previous section discussed the potential benefits of active audience participation. This section discusses several approaches for incorporating audience participation in presentations.

Questions, Quizzes, and More

Asking a question is a common method for engaging an audience. Through questioning, a presenter can learn more about the audience, what they currently know (ie, prior knowledge), and what might have the potential to make the most impact throughout the presentation. Questions can also be used to help launch a meaningful discussion. Take advantage of the following tools to aid in asking questions and learn how to develop the best types of questions to use in presentations.

SURVEYS, QUIZZES, AND THE LIKE

Options for surveying an audience's response to a question can be as low-tech as asking them to raise their hands or as high-tech as having them use a computer, phone, or portable device as a clicker. Asking for a show of hands is easy to do but has its weaknesses. In a large audience, it is hard to know whether everyone is participating, and unless there is an abundant amount of time, counting all the hands is out of the question. It may give a

glimpse at the distribution of responses to a question or inquiry, but it does not provide a record of responses, and since hand raising isn't anonymous, audience members "may mindlessly change their answers just to follow the crowd."[2] On the other hand, if the goal is only to get a rough estimate, raising hands can be efficient and effective.

A step up from raising hands is having the audience use flash cards of different colors, where each color signifies an answer. Another option is using one sheet of paper (a voting card), which is folded to show the preferred response choice (A, B, C, or D) when held in the air (see Figure 20.1). This allows audience members to be anonymous, if they would like, by holding their choice in front of their face. However, this method does allow others to potentially poll the room before making their choice, instead of following their instincts. Just as with raised hands, flash cards don't provide a record of the responses, unless the group is small. Additional low-tech polling techniques include thumbs up and thumbs down to indicate agreement or disagreement and secret answer, in which audience members indicate their choice of numbered answers by holding up one, two, or three fingers close to their chests. Another polling possibility is to ask participants to stand in response to choosing an option. As will be discussed later, standing can be a participation technique that enlivens an audience.

See Chapter 11 for information on needs assessment.

FIGURE 20.1 **Voting card**

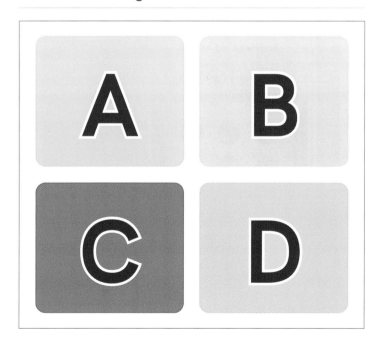

Using clickers, also known as response or voting systems, is a higher-tech method for quizzing and polling. Other options include phone applications (eg, Turning Technologies, Top Hat; see Figure 20.2) and online tools that use the texting feature on cell phones (eg, Poll Everywhere). These response systems record answers from the audience, immediately tally the responses, and can display a histogram (a graphical display of data similar to a bar graph) on a screen or monitor for the audience to see.[2] Using clickers to answer questions enhances student learning, but even the use of lower-tech flash cards produces learning gains that are equally impressive as those achieved via clicker.[18] This is encouraging news for the nutrition communicator who doesn't have the resources to use high-tech techniques. Even old-fashioned paper and pencil can effectively be used to record answers to questions throughout a presentation and be collected at the end.

What do quizzing and surveying the audience offer as a learning experience? They[2]:

- provide a break in the lecture;
- allow time for the audience to participate;
- allow audience members to interact with each other;
- allow practice with higher-ordered thinking;
- give the audience time to critically examine and defend their thinking;
- improve the formative assessment of learning (assessment during the learning process as opposed to waiting for an end-of-instruction quiz or test);
- provide instant feedback on understanding and retention;
- heighten attention and alertness during the presentation;
- enhance engagement with the material; and
- develop metacognition (the ability to think about one's learning, understanding, and performance).

Even if a presentation is low-tech, asking good questions will have an impact on learning.

Tips for effective questioning through clickers

- Have a clear idea of the goals to be achieved with clickers, and design questions to improve audience engagement and interactions with each other and the presenter.
- Focus questions on particularly important concepts.
- Use questions that have multiple plausible answers and will reveal audience confusion.
- Use questions that will generate spirited discussion.
- Take care that clicker questions are not too easy. Audiences will learn more from challenging questions and often learn the most from questions they get wrong.
- Give the audience time to think about the clicker question on their own and then discuss as a group.
- Listen in on the discussions about clicker questions to understand how the audience thinks and to address misconceptions on the spot.

Note that these tips apply to other response approaches in addition to clickers. The benefit of this technology is the ability to collect and share the data with the audience.[19]

Asking for hands or using flash cards or "clickers" is only the first step in engaging audiences

FIGURE 20.2 **Types of clickers from Turning Technologies**

Reproduced with permission from Turning Technologies.

with questions. Follow-up these responses with further audience reflection or interaction to encourage higher-level thinking.

One way to continue to engage the audience after asking a question is through engagement in peer instruction. After the audience replies with their initial answers, have the audience members discuss with their neighbors and explain the reasoning behind their answers. This encourages the audience members to explain their thinking, listen to other audience members' reasoning, and then try to reach a consensus—and encourages a collaborative learning experience for the audience.[20] For nutrition communicators, it is key to interact with an audience during this time, as they work to understand the concept. Then, before moving on, poll the audience again by repeating the question. This helps identify whether there continues to be any confusion or questions and allows the presenter to adjust the presentation on the spot to clarify misunderstandings or to address unresolved questions.[20] It is imperative to give adequate feedback because abundant feedback strengthens retention.[6]

The use of questions, quizzes, and surveys is an easy way to engage a large audience; however, the quality of the questions is important for learning. Questions that are too easy only "ensure at some minimal level the audience is awake."[20] The following tips will help to prepare quality questions and learn the types of questions to avoid.

ASKING QUESTIONS

Learning can be enhanced through using questions, but learning also depends on the types of questions used. Questions can be used to gauge how well the audience is learning—for example, "Do we need to review a topic?" or "Are we ready to move on in the presentation?" It's also important to ask quality questions in order to engage the audience and impact learning. McKeachie's fruitful, challenging questions can help to determine what types of questions to prepare, based on what type of engagement and learning is envisioned for a presentation.[21] See Box 20.1 for a list of these four types of questions and descriptions of what each type entails.

Another good resource is Brookfield and Preskill's seven momentum questions—seven questions that help sustain the momentum of discussion.[2] See Box 20.2 on page 322.

Gale and Andrew's high mileage–type questions[2] (see Box 20.3) are those that will encourage

 BOX 20.1

McKeachie's Fruitful, Challenging Questions[21]

Types of Questions	Characteristics
Comparative questions	Ask audience to compare and contrast different theories, research studies, and so on
	Help audience identify the important dimensions for comparison
Evaluative questions	Extend comparisons to judgments of the relative validity, effectiveness, or strength of what is being compared
Connective and causal effective questions	Challenge audience to link facts, concepts, relationships, theories, and so on that are not explicitly integrated and might not appear to be related
	This is particularly useful in cross-disciplinary settings/audiences.
	Ask audience to draw and reflect on their personal experiences, connecting these to evidence-based practices and research findings
	When the audience understands these links, material becomes more meaningful to them.
Critical questions	Invite audience to examine the validity of a particular argument or research claim
	Foster careful, active reading and good listening skills

the audience to participate in answering questions and in discussion.

While all of these are examples of good types of questions to engage the audience, there are also questions that are best to avoid (see Box 20.4).

QUESTION AND ANSWER

Adding a question-and-answer (Q&A) session to a presentation is another way to engage the audience.

For more information regarding Q&A techniques and best practices, see Chapter 36.

Brookfield and Preskill's Momentum Questions[2]

Types of Questions	Characteristics
Questions requesting more evidence	Ask audience members to defend their positions
Clarifying questions	Invite audience members to rephrase or elaborate on ideas to make them understandable
Cause-and-effect questions	Make the audience consider the possible causal relationship between variables and events
Hypothetical questions	Ask "What if?" and require creative thinking
Open questions	Have multiple respectable answers
Linking or extension questions	Ask the audience to think about the relationship between responses
Summary and synthesis questions	Ask the audience to summarize/synthesize important ideas as a wrap-up

 # Gale and Andrew's High Mileage–Type Questions[2]

Types of Questions	Characteristics
Brainstorming questions	Invite audience members to generate many conceivable ideas
Focal questions	Ask audience members to choose a viewpoint or position and support their choice with reasoning or evidence
Playground questions	Challenge the audience members to select or develop their own themes and concepts for exploring, interpreting, and analyzing

 # Good-for-Nothing Questions[21]

Types of Questions	Characteristics
Fuzzy questions	Too vague and unfocused for the audience to know how to approach them
Chameleon and shotgun questions	Series of weakly related questions fired off one after the other
Programmed-answer questions	Indicate that the presenter has only one specific answer in mind
Put-down questions	Imply that the audience ought to know the answer and shouldn't have any more questions
Ego-stroking questions	Assume the superiority of the presenter to the disparagement of the audience
Dead-end questions	Quiz-show questions with yes or no answers

Audience Engagement

Audience engagement benefits the participants through enhanced attention, learning, retention, and behavior change.[2,6,7,12,15] Additionally, it benefits the presenter by providing ongoing and real-time audience assessment, assistance in presentation tasks, and a break from being the focus of attention. Possibly most important, it promotes connection with the audience.

Audiences need to feel a connection with presenters before they trust them and what they are saying.[22,23] One of the best ways to connect and build rapport and trust with an audience is through audience engagement. Rather than being passive observers, the audience participates, allowing more free-flowing, two-way communication between the presenter and audience members. A nutrition communicator who is listening and responding to audience members is demonstrating empathy and facilitating effective communication.

Audience engagement can take many forms. Several approaches that engage an audience as individuals, with no need to partner or form small groups, will be covered next.

VOLUNTEER PARTICIPATION TO DEMONSTRATE OR FACILITATE

Why should a presenter do something if an audience member can do it as well? Consider these uses for audience volunteers:

- Need to write lists on a flip chart or white board? Solicit a volunteer from the audience. It allows the presenter to keep facing the audience.
- Need to chop ingredients in a food demonstration? Ask for a volunteer. It shows the rest of the audience how easy it is to prepare the dish and frees up the presenter to begin another task or more easily talk about the food.
- Demonstrating a skill? Invite someone to do it at the same time.
- Need help with a prop? Ask for an assistant.

There are many ways to utilize volunteers. An audience is likely to include people who enjoy the limelight or love to serve. Either type can assist a presenter and engage members of an audience.

Consider activities that include many audience members in simple, nonthreatening ways.

For example, in a discussion of heart disease, it may be helpful to define some important terms. Rather than showing a boring slide with terms and definitions, show only the terms on the slide and have the definitions written on cards that can be drawn out of a basket. In this exercise, a volunteer pulls out a card, reads it out loud to the group, and decides which term it defines, asking for assistance from the audience as needed. Conversely, one definition at a time could be up on a slide and the terms written on cards, and the volunteers could decide whether they are holding the card with the right term. Simple, yet effective. What in a presentation could be done by or with an audience member instead of only the presenter?

BRAINSTORMING

Brainstorming uses the brains of the entire group to "storm" a problem with creative ideas, according to the originator of the technique, Alex Osborn, who described it in his book *Your Creative Power*, published in 1948.[24] Brainstorming is a useful collaborative activity when searching for solutions to problems that affect the entire group. It is also referred to by other names, such as *ideation*, a creative process for generating ideas.

Brainstorming uses several of the same principles that make improvisational theater so effective: trust, spontaneity, accepting offers, and listening and awareness.[25] *Trust* tells the audience they are safe to share ideas without condemnation. *Spontaneity* frees them to share ideas without analyzing them first. *Accepting offers* encourages lots of ideas—the more the better. *Listening and awareness* pays attention to what is shared and encourages more.

The best ideas may appear crazy and foolish when initially shared. Write them down and keep them coming. To be productive, brainstorming does not judge responses as they are given but saves that task for later. Brainstorming inspires collaboration and builds community when done in a spirit of openness. Establishing ground rules for a brainstorming session is recommended.

Consider fun ways to brainstorm. Toss a soft ball among audience members. Each time a participant has the ball, they share another idea. To employ an improvisational theater technique, have participants begin each new idea with the phrase, "Yes, and …" to accept and build on the idea that came before.

See Chapter 19 for more on discussion ground rules.

SPEAKING, SINGING, MOVING TOGETHER

A simple way to involve an audience is to have them say something together. It could be one word, a key message, or a longer reading. In teaching a new term, have the audience repeat it out loud. They will appreciate the practice in learning how to pronounce it. A presenter might prompt the audience to repeat a key message in response to a question that is asked several times during a presentation. It bears repeating: Repetition is a powerful memory technique … pun intended.[26] Although this approach, sometimes referred to as *choral response*, is used frequently with children, it can also be effective with adults if not done in a juvenile manner. Consider the willingness of adults at a concert or sporting event to respond in unison and with great enthusiasm.

Singing is not only fun, it is a great way to learn, and music enhances memory.[27] The rhythm and melody of a song help people remember the lyrics. Advertisers use music because it sticks in people's heads. Imagine memorizing the 26 letters of the alphabet without singing them to "Twinkle, Twinkle, Little Star." Check out the Section 4 showcase starting on page 252 to see how music can captivate audiences and teach about food and nutrition. For a fun activity, ask an audience to put what has been taught to music and teach the rest of the group.

Movement is a surefire way to wake up an audience. Even for audience members who don't consider themselves kinesthetic learners, movement is a successful audience engagement strategy. Try body voting to poll an audience. For example, ask people who know someone with cancer to stand. Standing will be less intimidating when the number of people who will stand is greater than the number who will remain seated. Voting can also involve moving around the room. Have people who prefer abc move and stand in one corner of the room and those who prefer xyz move to the opposite corner. Substitute any number of comparisons in the blanks. Use this technique to better understand an audience and illustrate similarities and differences. Although an effective method to drive home a point, movement can be incorporated simply to enliven the audience. In a longer session, have the audience stand up, stretch, or jog in place for 30 seconds just to get moving.

Remind yourself about the cognitive domain and Bloom's taxonomy in Chapter 15.

REFLECTION AND APPLICATION

Reflection and application activities help an audience personalize their learning and consider how to make a message meaningful to their lives. With reflection activities, learners pause and think about what they learned and what it means to them. With application activities, learners practice what they learned.

The *reflection principle* states that participants learn better when provided with opportunities to reflect as they process meaning from a message.[5] The *personalization principle* states that messages that can be personalized enhance attention and learning.[5] Interactive discussion and other activities allow for personalizing information to an audience.

See Box 20.5 for easy-to-implement reflection activities. These ideas are widely used in education and other group settings and are available from a variety of sources. Select one or more to complete during a presentation. As a minimum, include one on a handout provided after the presentation. Ideally, allow time during the presentation, possibly with time to share with a partner or the entire group.

Application activities are more content specific than reflection activities: for example, doing a calculation, creating a menu, or reading a Nutrition Facts label. The objective is to provide the audience with an opportunity to put knowledge gained into practice. Taking an audience beyond the first levels in Bloom's taxonomy of educational objectives requires application to demonstrate achievement. The verbs listed in Figure 15.2 suggest potential types of activities, such as experiment, plan, and solve. After teaching a concept, allow time and provide guidance for the audience to apply the knowledge. An action completed under a presenter's direction is more likely to be practiced later than one that is simply talked about or observed.[15]

Application activities that individuals can complete include worksheets, experiments, demonstrating a skill, writing assignments, and case studies. Many application activities can be done with partners or in groups as well as individually.

Partner and Group Activities

Working together in groups promotes learning, interpersonal relationships, and mental health. Most studies find group work superior

Audience Reflection Activities

3-2-1 reflection
Write down three facts or ideas you learned in this session.

Write down two questions you still have that you'd like to look up and learn about later.

Write down one opinion you have about what was covered in this session.

Most important
Write down three new ideas you learned in this session. Put a star by the most important.

One sentence
Write one sentence explaining what you learned in the last ___ minutes.

One question
Write one question about what you've learned.

These could be collected for a question-and-answer session at the end.

Muddiest point
Write down what is most confusing about what was just learned.

These can be collected and redistributed among audience members to read out loud and try to answer.

Wow and How About
Before this activity, the presenter provides all participants with two sticky notes. Afterward, the two groups of notes are posted on two labeled flip charts and participants debrief as a group.

On one sticky note write a Wow statement—what you learned that was most intriguing. On the other write a How About question or idea—another question or idea stimulated by the discussion.

Personal reflection
You've just completed a group brainstorming activity. Now reflect on which idea you are most inclined to support, do first, and so on.

One-word splash
Write down one word that describes something you learned or experienced in the session.

Participants can submit their words on index cards or slips of paper or upload them using an interactive tools such as Poll Everywhere to create a word cloud.

1-minute paper
In 1 minute, write down what you learned or experienced in this session.

The presenter can specify what the audience writes about. Time for 1 minute.

Look back and bridge forward
Ask participants to individually answer a series of questions that involve reflecting on past, current, and future practices.

Participants can also share answers with a partner or group.

Goals and action steps
Based on what you learned, what is one goal and one or more specific action steps you intend to achieve in the next ___ (week, month)?

Three applications
Write down three ways you can apply what you learned. Circle what you plan to do first.

---

to working individually in promoting critical thinking, self-esteem, and prosocial behaviors.[28] The old adage "Two heads are better than one" applies to partner and group activities. When audience members work with partners or in groups, the role of presenter switches to that of coach or facilitator.

PARTNER ACTIVITIES

Partner activities are easily employed in nearly any type of group or setting, as long as audience members are in close proximity to a neighboring participant. If the group consists of an odd number of participants, presenters can create one group of three or themselves join with a partner. If audience members are spreading themselves out as they take their seats, encourage them to sit more

Learn more about facilitated discussions in Chapter 19.

BOX 20.6 Partner Activities

Think-pair-share
Give the audience 30 seconds to answer a question or write down at least one idea in their notes (*think*). Then ask them to discuss what they wrote with the person sitting next to them (*pair*). Finally, ask for volunteers to share their answers or ideas with the entire group (*share*).

Pair-share-repeat
After a think-pair-share activity, ask participants to find new partners to share what the original partners discussed.

Wisdom of another
Adapt think-pair-share to require participants to share their partner's ideas with the entire group.

Partner—most important
Following the individual "most important" reflection activity (see Box 20.5), ask participants to share their lists with a partner and negotiate which two ideas listed they agree are important. Call on sets of partners to share their two most important ideas.

Pro-con
In pairs, audience members discuss two sides of an issue or two ways to solve a problem, with one partner taking one side and the other taking the opposite side.

300-year gap conversation25
Break participants into pairs and designate one person in each pair as A and the other as B. The A in each pair portrays a modern-day person with the task of explaining the use and value of a modern-day object or idea to B, who portrays someone from 300 years ago. B can ask questions to help him or her understand. This activity works well for discussions of technological advances—how we treat disease, how we prepare food, ways we communicate.

Partner interviews
One person is designated as the interviewer and the other the interviewee. Provide potential questions that relate to the presentation topic. After a few minutes, partners switch roles. This activity encourages participants to discuss what they found interesting and what they intend to try as a result of learning.

Role-playing
Provide a scenario and designate roles. Give a time limit for portraying the roles followed by a time to debrief as partners or as an entire group. Role-playing is effective in practicing counseling and teaching skills.

---

closely together, or ask them to move to new seats before starting the activity.

Depending on the group and the topic, partner activities may work better when the partners already know each other well and are likely sitting next to each other. In other situations, activities may work better when partners are unfamiliar with each other, which may require participants to move around and find a new partner. Base the decision of how to form partnerships on the situation and desired outcomes.

A benefit of partner activities over large-group activities is the potential for people to feel safe and comfortable to share. Partner activities work well with both introverts and extroverts. See Box 20.6 for a list of partner activities widely used in various settings and that can be adapted to many situations.

In addition to the ideas listed in Box 20.6, many activities performed individually can be done as pairs. This includes many audience reflection activities as well as most types of application activities, such as problem solving, performing experiments, and analyzing case studies.

SMALL-GROUP ACTIVITIES

What is a small group? There is no definition of how few or many people make up a small group. It is larger than a pair of two, but other than that, the number depends on the total size of an audience, easily divisible subgroups, room configuration, table size, and type of activity. Groups with more than 10 or 12 members limit individual involvement. Create groups small enough for each member to participate fully and large enough to promote diversity of ideas and the contribution of knowledge and skills. See Box 20.7 for a list of potential small-group activities that are applicable to many settings and types of groups.

LARGE-GROUP ACTIVITIES

With large-group activities, the whole group participates together rather than splitting into smaller groups. Team games, debates, panel discussions, simulations, and gallery walks are examples of large-group activities. See Box 20.8 (page 328) for a description of widely used strategies for using these techniques.

What Practical Strategies Enhance Success and Avoid Problems?

Audience interaction is most successful when participants feel the learning environment is safe, when clear directions are provided, and when cooperation is encouraged and supported.[29,30]

Create a Safe Learning Environment

Audiences learn best in an environment that is nonthreatening and feels safe.[29] They feel welcomed and appreciated for being present and for participating. They don't fear speaking up *or* remaining silent. Audience involvement builds gradually, and time is provided to warm up and get acquainted. Two features of a safe learning environment are trust and voluntary participation.

BUILD TRUST

It's easier for audience members to participate when they know the presenter and their fellow participants. What's scary to do in front of strangers can be fun in front of friends. Presenters must allow time for an audience to get to know them and each other. Do an icebreaker to warm them up and prepare to participate further. As people build connections and recognize similarities and commonalities they share, they are more receptive to learning, sharing, and participating.[23] Convey a nonjudgmental attitude and a caring demeanor. Build trust through what is said and how it is said. People are more willing to participate for people

Small-Group Activities[25]

Icebreakers
Get-acquainted games and activities work well in small groups. Numerous types of icebreaker activities can be found in books and online.

Brainstorming
Ideally, brainstorming occurs in small groups, even if ideas are later shared in a larger group.

Flip-chart summary
Provide each small group a piece of flip-chart paper and allow them 5 minutes to summarize the key points learned. Specify whether they should use pictures only or pictures and words. All should contribute.

Showtime summary
Assign each small group a different topic that was covered, and ask them to prepare a short, creative presentation summary of what they learned.

Role-playing
For role-playing scenarios that involve more than two players, form small groups. Allow extra members to serve as a director, an observer who comments on what is done well or could use improvement, and a group member to video record the action and play it back for a group discussion.

One-word-at-a-time stories
Position participants in a circle. Provide a topic or title. Have them tell a story one word at a time, with each person adding the next word. The second time around, have them add two words at a time. The third time around, have them add three words at a time. Then ask them to reverse back down to one word.

Small-group marketing
Provide each group with a flip chart and markers. Allow them about 10 to 15 minutes to come up with a group name, logo, tagline, and ad campaign that relates to a topic covered in a session. All group members must participate in sharing results.

they trust. People hesitate when they aren't sure whether to trust or not. People may refuse when there is a lack of trust.

Make the first audience participation activity one that is easy, is fun, and helps audience members feel confident and knowledgeable. Acknowledge their contributions to encourage more. An

BOX 20.8 # Large-Group Activities

Team games

Team games, such as Jeopardy, are used to assess learning, as described in Chapter 17. Other examples are relay races to perform a skill or complete a sorting activity, and team quizzes.

Debates

Split the group in half and assign each team to support one side of an issue. Examples: Low-fat vs low-carb diets. Causes of obesity—which one is strongest (pick 2): genetics, lifestyle, diet and exercise, or environment? Organic vs conventional farming. Vegan vs omnivore. Moderation vs abstaining.

Panel discussion

In a setting in which small groups have discussed a topic or generated ideas, use a panel discussion format to present back to the entire group. This allows for questions and whole-group interaction about each topic.

Simulations

This large-group activity requires significant planning and preparation, but the outcomes are worth the resource and time investment. Examples are poverty simulations, which allow participants to experience what it is like to live in poverty, and simulations to experience living with a disability, being elderly, or traveling to another part of the world.

Gallery walk

This activity simulates walking around an art gallery—participants walk around the room and look at words or pictures displayed on the walls that link to the issue or topic. Activities may be completed at each display. It can involve group members moving to stand next to a word or picture in response to a question. For example, participants can stand next to the visual or word depicting their preferred learning style, favorite physical activity, or favorite cuisine.

Live barometer

This activity is a type of body voting used to assess audience members' opinions, practices, or beliefs. It requires a large, open space. A facilitator gives two options and audience members move to one side of the room or the other to show their preferences or practices. If neutral is an option, they can stand in the center. Example questions include, Would you rather do something challenging or do something convenient? Would you rather get a bonus or get a vacation? Would you rather have a day free from routine or keep to a schedule? Would you rather save time or save money?

---

activity that connects the audience to the topic, reminds them of their current knowledge and experiences, and builds anticipation for what is ahead will be most successful. For example, a presentation about smart grocery shopping might open with an activity asking participants to share what they like least about shopping for food. If the group is large, do this activity as think-pair-share, allowing for enough audience members to share with the entire group to give a good idea of common frustrations. Wrap up the activity by stating that after the presentation, they will be armed with new ideas that can help them overcome many of these challenges.

MAKE PARTICIPATION VOLUNTARY

Unless the situation requires all audience members to perform an activity, make participation voluntary. Even in those instances, solicit volunteers to give the first responses before calling on others to contribute. To be truly voluntary, ask for participants to indicate willingness to participate by signing up ahead of time or by raising their hand in response to "Who would like to …?"

In situations where there are more volunteers than available jobs, pick volunteers by using a method that prevents selection bias. Examples include:

- the person with the birthday closest to today's date,
- people with a green sticker under their chair, and
- names of willing volunteers dropped in a hat or bucket and drawn at random.

Use a variety of approaches for selecting volunteers—switch it up. When the activity is desirable and presented enthusiastically, people will volunteer.

Provide Clear Directions

Audiences of all ages like to know what to expect and what is expected of them. Clearly describe expectations, directions, and rules for audience participation activities. Ideally, pilot test directions with a test group or ask a potential audience member or a colleague to review the directions and suggest alternative wording or illustrations if clarity is needed.

Provide directions in more than one way. These are some potential ways:

- Describe each step one at a time, checking for understanding.
- Show the directions on a slide, a poster, a handout, or a combination of materials.
- Use an audience participation activity in which members take turns reading the directions as the presenter or another audience member follows them.

PROVIDE STEPS AND DEMONSTRATE

Break down more complex activities into manageable steps and demonstrate how to do each one. Examples include using a new computer program, mastering a new culinary technique, or using a new piece of equipment. Allow time for audience members to ask questions and, ideally, to follow the demonstration by trying out each step. Before moving on to the next step, confirm that everyone is caught up and not two steps behind. An audience that is rushing to keep up with the presenter may grow frustrated and quit.

MAKE PARTICIPATION EASY AND CONVENIENT

Greater audience participation will be achieved when it is easy and convenient for members to join in, especially early in a presentation or if the goal is for everyone to participate. Allow participation to take place without getting up on stage, talking to a stranger, or taking the risk of looking foolish. As participation activities progress, the difficulty or risk involved can be increased. For example, in a food tasting experience, begin with having a volunteer just smell or describe a new food before asking someone to taste it.

Enhance Cooperation

Cooperation—the process of working together to achieve the same end[31]—is enhanced when the audience feels a sense of community and a desire to meet group goals, when the audience is properly managed and each participant demonstrates individual responsibility to the group, and when participants feel recognized and appreciated. In the context of promoting successful audience participation, focus on avoiding tangents and take-overs and on recognizing the efforts of the audience.

AVOID TANGENTS AND TAKE-OVERS

A tangent occurs when a discussion, role-play, or activity veers from the key messages or task at hand. For example, a tangent occurs when a nutrition communicator is leading a workshop on kitchen safety and a group wants to portray a skit about reducing sugar in recipes. Good topic, but misplaced. Direct the audience back on course.

A take-over is when a participant takes center stage without being invited and the presenter loses control. This can happen when group sharing turns into a mini-speech or when a question becomes a speech or an attack on the presenter or another participant. Other audience members will get nervous and look to the presenter to maintain control. Well-established ground rules and directions are keys to avoiding take-overs through prevention. If one still happens, graciously stepping in will bring a collective sigh of relief from the audience.

RECOGNIZE PARTICIPANTS

Recognition comes in two ways—acknowledging who people are and appreciating them for what they do and say. To recognize them for who they are is to see them, to make eye contact and smile, to show an appreciation for them and gratitude that they are there. To the extent possible, call audience members by name. If the venue doesn't supply name tags, bring some, or ask a contributor

Chapter 35 discusses how to successfully create an environment that promotes learning and engagement.

for their name and use it. Using names builds a sense of community in a group and helps people get acquainted, further promoting audience participation.

Finally, acknowledge the contributions of an audience. When someone provides assistance, thank the person. Invite others to applaud when an audience member or small group performs or gives an especially insightful answer. Vary recognition approaches—words of thanks, applause, high fives, cheers—and make sure they are heartfelt and sincere.

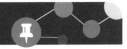

KEY POINTS

Engage Audiences with Participation Strategies

1. Audience interaction and engagement are more than just a current trend in education and communication; they are features of a proven approach to increasing attention, enhancing learning and understanding, improving retention and application of learning, strengthening enjoyment of learning, and promoting behavior change.

2. There are numerous approaches to engaging an audience and promoting participation, including questions, quizzes and surveys, question-and-answer sessions, volunteer participation, brainstorming, moving together, reflection and application activities, and games. Activities can be done individually or with partners, in small groups, or in large groups.

3. Audience interaction is most successful when participants feel the learning environment is safe, when clear directions are provided, and when cooperation is encouraged and supported.

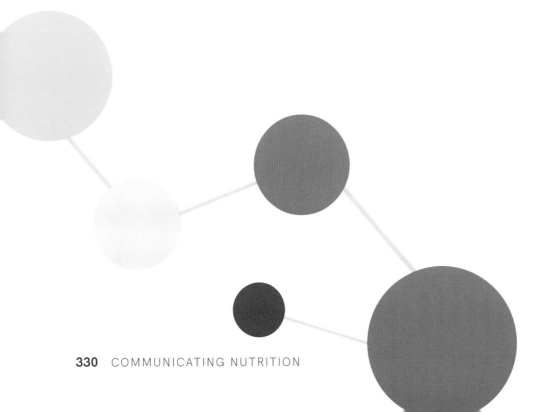

REFERENCES

1. Engage. *Merriam-Webster Dictionary*. Published 2018. Accessed July 6, 2018. www.merriam -webster.com/dictionary/engage

2. Nilson LB. *Teaching at Its Best: A Research-Based Resource for College Instructors.* 3rd ed. Jossey-Bass; 2010.

3. Medina J. *Brain Rules*. Pear Press; 2008.

4. Vandenberg L. Facilitating adult learning: how to teach so people learn. Accessed December 2, 2019. www.canr.msu.edu/od/uploads/files/PD /Facilitating_Adult_Learning.pdf

5. Abela AV. *Advanced Presentations by Design: Creating Communication That Drives Action.* 2nd ed. Wiley; 2013.

6. Brown P, Roediger H, McDaniel M. *Make It Stick: The Science of Successful Learning*: Belknap Press of Harvard University Press; 2014.

7. Fink L. *Creating Significant Learning Experiences: An Integrated Approach to Designing College Courses.* Jossey-Bass; 2013.

8. Krathwohl DR, Bloom BS, Masia BB. *Taxonomy of Educational Objectives: The Classification of Educational Goals. Handbook II: Affective Domain*. David McKay; 1964.

9. Menges R. Research on teaching and learning: the relevant and the redundant. *Rev High Educ.* 1988;11:259-268.

10. Simonson S. Modifying the Monte Carlo Quiz to increase student motivation, participation, and content retention. *Coll Teach.* 2017;65(4):158-163. doi:10.1080/87567555.2017.1304351

11. Dhaliwal H, Allen M, Kang J, Bates C, Hodge T. The effect of using an audience response system on learning, motivation and information retention in the orthodontic teaching of undergraduate dental students: a cross-over trial. *J Orthod.* 2014;42(2):123-135. doi:10.1179/14653133 14Y.0000000129

12. Developing training to involve the audience. *Prof Saf.* 2013;58(1):55.

13. Dale E. *Audiovisual Methods in Teaching.* 3rd ed. Holt, Rinehart, and Winston; 1969.

14. Dale E. *Audiovisual Methods in Teaching.* 2nd ed. Dryden Press; 1954.

15. Fook C, Dalim S, Narasuman S, Sidhu G, Fong L, Keang K. Relationship between active learning and self efficacy among students in higher education. *Int Acad Res Soc Sci.* 2015;1(2):139-149.

16. Bauer K, Sokolik C. *Basic Nutrition Counseling Skill Development: A Guideline for Lifestyle Management.* Wadsworth/Thomas Learning; 2002.

17. McKnight L, Doolittle N, Stitzel K, Vafiadis D, Robb K. Simple cooking with heart: nutrition education and improving diet quality through culinary skill-based education. *J Nutr Educ Behav.* 2013;45(4S):S23. doi:10.1016/j.jneb.2013.04.063

18. Lasry N. Clickers or flashcards: is there really a difference? *Phys Teach.* 2008;46:242-244.

19. Weiman C, Perkins K, Gilbert S. Clicker resource guide: an instructor's guide to the effective use of personal response systems (clickers) in teaching. Carl Weiman Science Education Initiative at the University of British Columbia website. Published 2017. Accessed February 26, 2018. www.cwsei. ubc.ca/resources/clickers.htm

20. Kober N. *Reaching Students: What Research Says About Effective Instruction in Undergraduate Science and Engineering.* National Academies Press; 2015.

21. McKeachie W. *Teaching Tips: Strategies, Research, and Theory for College and University Teachers.* 11th ed. Houghton Mifflin; 2002.

22. Hogan K. The surprising persuasiveness of a sticky note. In: *Emotional Intelligence: Influence and Persuasion.* Harvard Business Press; 2018:115-124.

23. Alda A. *If I Understood You, Would I Have This Look on My Face?* Random House; 2017.

24. Osborn AF. *Your Creative Power: How to Use Imagination.* C. Scribner's Sons; 1948.

25. Koppett K. *Training to Imagine.* 2nd ed. Stylus Publishing; 2013.

26. Munter M, Russell L. *Guide to Presentations.* Prentice Hall; 2002.

27. New York Academy of Sciences. *The Neurosciences and Music IV: Learning and Memory.* Overy K, Peretz I, Zatorre RJ, Lopez L, Majno M, eds. Blackwell Publishing; 2012.

28. Nilson LB. Learning in groups. In: *Teaching at Its Best.* 3rd ed. Jossey-Bass; 2010:156.

29. Norris J. *From Telling to Teaching.* Learning by Dialogue; 2003.

30. Vella J. *Learning to Listen, Learning to Teach.* Jossey-Bass; 2002.

31. Cooperation. Dictionary.com. Published 2018. Accessed September 11, 2018. www.dictionary .com/browse/cooperation?s=ts

CHAPTER

21

Deliver Clear, Compelling Presentations

Barbara J. Mayfield, MS, RDN
and Sonja Stetzler, MA, RDN, LDN

"One of the main benefits of building presentation skills is enhanced confidence, which in turn enhances a speaker's effectiveness. The confident speaker is considered trustworthy, believable, and persuasive."

> "The only thing that truly matters in public speaking is not confidence, stage presence, or smooth talking. It's having something worth saying."
>
> —CHRIS ANDERSON, IN *TED TALKS: THE OFFICIAL TED GUIDE TO PUBLIC SPEAKING*

Introduction

The food and nutrition professional has the expertise to deliver accurate, up-to-date, and practical food and nutrition information to a wide variety of audiences. In addition to well-planned and researched content, clear objectives, well-written key messages, and interactive and audience-centered presentation strategies, effective presentation skills are essential for the successful delivery of a message. The nutrition communicator can learn and practice presentation skills to improve effectiveness and increase confidence.

This chapter answers three questions:

- Why are presentation skills essential?
- What presentation skills are essential?
- How can nutrition professionals enhance presentation skills?

There are multiple ways to deliver an effective presentation; the key is to apply timeless presentation principles using a personal, unique style. Don't try to imitate another speaker. Be yourself.

Why Are Presentation Skills Essential?

Employers rated verbal communication skills the top skill they consider when assessing a candidate's skills and qualities, according to the National Association of Colleges and Employers *2016 Job Outlook Report*.[1] Additionally, according to the results of a survey conducted collaboratively by Prezi, a cloud-based presentation platform company, and Harris, a communications equipment company, 70% of employed Americans say that presentation skills are critical to their success.[2] Being able to clearly present complex ideas, keep an audience's attention, and move an audience toward learning and behavior change are essential skills for success in today's world of work.

Is Effectiveness 10% Content and 90% Delivery?

Presentation skills include "any time speakers use verbal and nonverbal messages to generate meanings and establish relationships with audience members, who are usually present at the delivery of a presentation."[3] Are these skills more important to a presenter's success than the content that is delivered? No. Quality content is critical; however, excellent content should not fail because the delivery is too difficult for the audience to attend to or puts them to sleep. To be truly successful, the content *and* the delivery must be excellent. This chapter focuses on how to apply excellence in presentation delivery skills.

There's a common notion that 90% of a presenter's success depends on delivery and only 10% on content. Where did that idea originate? Is that oft-quoted statistic true? Is there evidence to support it? Well, sort of. This statement is based on research that has been misrepresented so often that the investigator himself cringes each time he sees or hears it misquoted. See Box 21.1 (page 334) for the truth behind the viral statistics of 1967. What do these statistics reveal about presentation content vs delivery?

When a person communicates, the aspects of delivery—voice tone, nonverbal expressions, and body language—must work together with the

Chapters 16 through 20 addressed how to create excellent presentation content.

The Viral Statistics of 1967[4,5]

In studying nonverbal communication, a reader is likely to come across the 7/38/55 formula. Where did it come from? How did it go viral decades before the internet?

In 1967, Albert Mehrabian, PhD, professor of psychology at the University of California at Los Angeles, conducted two experiments on nonverbal communication that resulted in what became known as the Mehrabian rule, or 7/38/55 formula. The numbers represent the relative contributions of verbal and nonverbal factors to the meaning of a message: 7% of meaning comes from the actual meaning of the words, 38% from how the words sound (voice inflection, tone, volume, and speed), and 55% from facial expressions (often extrapolated to body language). The last two percentages are generally considered nonverbal and add up to over 90%.

In the first study, participants were asked to judge the feelings portrayed by a speaker toward the listener. They listened to a recording of a speaker saying nine single words with varying tones of voice—positive, neutral, and negative. When the word and voice intonation were inconsistent—that is, when a positive word, such as *thanks*, was spoken with a negative tone, or a negative word, such as *terrible*, was spoken with a positive tone—the feeling expressed by the vocal intonation was perceived over the feeling expressed by the word itself.

In Mehrabian's second experiment, in addition to listening to the recording of a word spo-

ken with varying vocal intonations, pictures of different facial expressions were shown to the participants. Only one word was used, *maybe*, which was selected as a neutral word. The study compared the influence of vocal tone with nonverbal facial expression on determining the feeling of the speaker toward the listener. They found that nonverbal expressions were 1.5 times more influential in judging the feeling of the speaker than tone of voice. The researchers combined the findings of the two studies to suggest the relative contributions of verbal (words), vocal (tone of voice), and facial (body language) factors.

However, in the half century since Mehrabian's research was conducted, the widespread misinterpretations of his research have taken it way beyond its limited applicability, which is this: In artificially created settings in which the audience hears one word recorded in a voice tone that doesn't match the word, or is shown a picture of the speaker's face with a facial expression that is inconsistent with the word spoken, the audience will perceive the feelings of the speaker less from the word and more from the way it is presented. Can these findings be extrapolated to natural settings where speakers are present with listeners and speak more than one word? Is it possible that the words used—the content—contribute only 10%, or less, of the perceived meaning and the tone of voice and body language account for greater than 90%? Probably not.

---

spoken words to convey the same message. If they are incongruent, the meaning of the words can be overtaken and misrepresented by vocal intonations and facial expressions. Mehrabian's experiments, as described in Box 21.1, were designed to create inconsistencies, whereas in natural settings verbal and nonverbal communication work in concert to convey a consistent message. Communication researchers Jones and LeBaron proposed an integrated approach to studying nonverbal and verbal communication, because the two phenomena are inseparable.[6] In combination, verbal and

nonverbal skills are the means by which messages are conveyed and are only effective when they work together. It bears repeating: To be truly successful, the content *and* the delivery must be excellent.

Presentation Skills Enhance Confidence, Which Enhances Effectiveness

One of the main benefits of building presentation skills is enhanced confidence, which in turn enhances a speaker's effectiveness. The confident speaker is considered trustworthy, believable, and persuasive.[7] A speaker expresses confidence through tone of voice, with intensity that's not too soft and pitch that's not too high; through speaking at a speed that's not too fast or slow; and by using speech that is varied and interesting, not monotonous. Confident speakers pause instead of using filler words and express confidence and clarity through word choice—for example, saying *certainly* instead of *perhaps*. Conversely, speakers who appear anxious will not be perceived as confident or knowledgeable.

Some believe that the fear of public speaking is many people's number-one fear, worse than the fear of death. Although the fear of public speaking is common, it is not number one, according to a 2017 survey of the top fears of Americans.[8] Out of 80 choices, death was ranked number 48 and public speaking was ranked number 52. However, it makes for a good joke, as comedian Jerry Seinfeld puts it[9]:

> I saw a thing, actually a study that said speaking in front of a crowd is considered the number one fear of the average person. I found that amazing—number two was death. Death was number two. This means to the average person, if you have to be at a funeral you would rather be in the casket than doing the eulogy.

Regardless of the accuracy of the statistic about the fear of public speaking, an anxious speaker is not as effective as a confident speaker. Nervousness can impact the ability to speak well. Nervous speakers often speak too fast, or too softly, or forget what they intend to say.[10] Audiences more readily attend to confident speakers, trust their knowledge, and follow their lead. As a result, confident speakers will achieve their desired outcome—audiences that listen, learn, and apply what they learn to their lives—which is the ultimate measure of presentation effectiveness.

To gain confidence, speakers need two attributes: confidence in their knowledge of the subject matter and confidence in their presentation skills. Presenters can take care of the first attribute by speaking on topics within their areas of expertise. The information that follows will help to build confidence in presentation skills.

What Presentation Skills Are Essential?

An effective presenter possesses a set of skills that are acquired and built over time. Becoming a proficient presenter requires practice as well as knowledge of presentation skills. This section covers how to overcome nervousness, how to effectively use body language to enhance a message, and the importance of the speaking voice.

Overcoming Nervousness

Standing in front of an audience of any size generally raises uncertainty for presenters. It triggers the primal reaction of flight, fight, or freeze, the physiological response that comes from perceived threats to safety. The following recommendations can help to counter the effects of the additional adrenaline people's bodies produce during times of stress. This dose of adrenaline is what causes a faster heartbeat, sweaty palms, a churning stomach, and a dry mouth.

Noted American radio and television news broadcaster Edward R. Murrow said, "Stage fright is the sweat of perfection." This is a perfection that is inwardly focused—focused on "looking good" rather than excelling to benefit the audience. Instead, when presenters focus on the audience rather than themselves, they are more likely to reduce their level of nervousness. Before a presentation, visualize the audience as engaged and interested, and picture delivering an engaging talk. Know that the audience wants the presenter to succeed—that's what they came for. During a presentation, continue to turn attention outward by focusing on serving the audience rather than focusing on the performance. This will reduce nervousness.

Ralph C. Smedley, founder of Toastmasters, said, "The unprepared speaker has a right to be scared." Proper preparation can minimize nervousness, so know the audience, the topic, and the message. Allow plenty of time to learn, rehearse, and refine a presentation. This will enhance relaxation and confidence and allow for the delivery of a more effective presentation that is clear and compelling.

Don't be rushed on the day of a presentation. Arrive early to set up, and become familiar with the room, stage, podium, and equipment. Check technical equipment to ensure it works. Being prepared when the audience arrives gives time to meet, greet, and get acquainted with early arrivers. Throughout a presentation, continue to connect with audience members as though having a one-on-one conversation, using eye contact and a smile. If the audience feels familiar, which results when the speaker becomes acquainted with some of the audience members before the presentation, the level of relaxation will be much greater. When nerves strike, looking at a friendly face of an audience member met prior to the presentation will help to reduce nerves.

Create a prespeech routine that enhances relaxation and reduces the symptoms of the flight, fight, or freeze response. See Box 21.2 for a list of ideas to try.

During a presentation, stand confidently but relaxed, with an open, expansive posture. Place feet shoulder-width or hip-width apart, with one foot slightly in front of the other and weight balanced on the balls of the feet, body leaning slightly forward, and knees unlocked. This posture should prevent rocking and encourage moving and gesturing without appearing frozen in place.

If nerves take over at the start of a presentation, it may be calming to start with an audience participation activity. This type of activity takes the focus off of the presenter and shifts it on to the audience, where it belongs.

Above all, adopt a can-do attitude. Decide there's nothing better to be doing than giving this presentation and demonstrate that attitude to the audience. Reframe *stage fright* from a negative term into a positive term indicating excitement and motivation. Some nervous anticipation can work to good advantage when the adrenaline is channeled into enthusiasm.

Body Language, Eye Contact, Gestures, Body Movement

Chapter 18 discussed the importance of visual aids to learning. The most important visual aid in a presentation is the presenter. While the audience is the presenter's primary focus, remember that audience members will be focusing on the presenter. Compelling presentation delivery requires awareness of body language. A person's body speaks through stance, body movement, gestures, facial expressions, and eye contact with everyone in the room.

STANCE AND MOVEMENT

In addition to taking a stance that appears relaxed and avoids rocking, where to stand is another consideration. A podium may provide a place for a laptop or notes; however, it can be a barrier between the presenter and the audience. For an audience to get the full visual effect of the speaker's body language, step away from the podium—even if only occasionally.

Make body movements purposeful. Due to mirror neurons, audiences mimic presenters in order to connect on an emotional level. Presenters who pace or display symptoms of the flight, fright, or freeze response will have audiences who experience a similar nervous response.[12] Well-planned, purposeful movement on the stage can help a presenter make a point. Coming closer to the audience attracts their attention. When making a key point, stop moving and say it. A step back can look reflective. Often, a good time to move is during transitions from one point to the next. Purposeful movement enhances the message. Practice body movements when practicing a speech.

BOX 21.2 Prespeech Routines[11]

Do stretching exercises.

Take a walk.

Do progressive relaxation exercises to loosen up tense muscles by tensing each muscle group for 5 to 7 seconds, then quickly releasing, one muscle group at a time.

Make funny faces if your face feels tense. (Do this in a private spot, not in front of your audience!)

Do a vocal warm-up. Hum or sing to warm up your voice.

Practice deep breathing—your abdomen should move, not your shoulders.

Drink plenty of water to keep hydrated. (Many voice and speech coaches recommend reducing caffeine intake, but recent research has shown that caffeine does not adversely affect voice production. Tolerance levels for caffeine vary among individuals and consumption should be evaluated on an individual basis.)

GESTURES

Talking with hand gestures can also enhance or distract depending on whether the gestures support what the presenter is saying or are nervous mannerisms. When gestures align with the spoken words, they strengthen the impact of a message, even if the audience doesn't consciously notice them.[13] For instance, spreading arms wide helps to convey something large, while holding the thumb and forefinger close together conveys something small; both help the audience visualize meaning. Gestures can dramatize an action, such as stirring an imaginary pot or illustrating numbers by holding up fingers. Gestures can convey emotion, such as giving or receiving with an open palm, or being perplexed with a shoulder shrug. Gestures can prompt an audience to applaud, raise their hands, or come forward. Gestures are also more visible to a large audience than facial expressions.

Make gestures an extension of the message. Do them naturally. Gestures should fit the size of the audience—smaller and more contained in a smaller space and larger and more expansive in a larger space. Gestures should also fit the audience itself. Know what certain gestures mean to other cultures. A gesture that is acceptable to one may be obscene or insulting to another.

Eliminate distracting gestures, movements, and mannerisms: rocking, swaying, pacing, gripping or leaning on the podium, crossing arms, clutching the upper arm with one hand, clasping hands nervously, holding arms behind the back, tapping fingers, biting or licking the lips, jingling pocket change, playing with a remote, excessive finger pointing (instead, use the whole hand with a sideways palm to point), playing with hair, or adjusting clothing. These are generally done unconsciously and are often due to nerves, so presenters may not even be aware they are doing them. Presenters can record and watch a videotape or ask an observer to point out nervous habits; this can help them become aware of these habits and monitor their progress on eliminating them.

FACIAL EXPRESSIONS AND EYE CONTACT

Certain facial expressions can help enhance a message. Begin a presentation with a warm, genuine smile and direct eye contact. Throughout a presentation, vary facial expressions naturally to align with the information being conveyed. For instance, when discussing an unpleasant topic, such as disease risk, a serious, concerned look is appropriate, while a pasted-on grin is not. Use the same expressions as in a face-to-face conversation. The larger the room, the more expressive a presenter needs to be for the audience to read their face.

The eyes are the first part of the face looked at during human interaction and what hold people's attention the most. More than any other non-verbal behavior, eye contact connects a presenter with an audience. Eye contact enhances communication by capturing and holding the audience's attention, enhancing audience self-awareness, improving memory, activating prosocial behaviors, and increasing the audience's positive perception of the presenter.[14] Eye contact signifies confidence and honesty to American audiences.[15] A lack of eye contact demonstrates nervousness or dishonesty.[16]

Eye contact involves the audience and helps them feel important and included. It makes a presentation more personal and conveys sincerity—the presenter appears more credible and friendly. Eye contact increases the audience's attention and acts as a mirror—when the presenter pays attention to the audience, the audience pays attention to the presenter.

Eye contact invites feedback. Presenting involves not only sending information but also receiving it. A presenter can glean valuable feedback by making eye contact with the audience. As mentioned previously, eye contact helps presenters overcome nervousness because it focuses attention on the audience.

To effectively make eye contact, don't look over the audience's heads, but rather select a few friendly faces in each section to connect with. Nearby attendees will also feel this gaze. The smaller the audience, the easier it is to look at everyone over the course of a speech. Vary looking around the room without darting the eyes nervously or moving the gaze in a repetitive pattern.

To be natural and conversational, hold eye contact long enough with each person to complete a thought. Don't stare—looking at one person too long can make them feel uncomfortable.

Making eye contact can sometimes be a challenge. If the house lights are down and the faces of the audience are not visible, use imagination to picture their faces and make mental eye contact. In a larger room, the audience members in the front row are easily overlooked, so make sure to look at those in front as well as those in the back. Connect with the entire audience.

Speaking Voice: Vocal Variety, Speed, Articulation, Filler Words

Voice quality affects credibility and how well a message is received.[17] Along with body language, the voice is the channel that conveys a message in a presentation. An effective speaking voice is pleasing, is easy to listen to, and conveys the meaning behind words. Speak in a natural voice and make it expressive by varying speech rate, volume, and pauses. A dynamic voice is more effective than a monotonous voice lacking emotion. Let's take a closer look at a good speaking voice.

VOCAL VARIETY

According to Toastmasters International: "Vocal variety is the way you use your voice to create interest, excitement, and emotional involvement."[18] It consists of pitch, volume, and projection. A raised pitch, or inflection, adds emphasis to a word. A change in inflection can alter the entire meaning of a sentence. Try saying, "I am a registered dietitian nutritionist" three times. Each time, use inflection on a different word—first "I," then "am," and finally "registered." Notice how the meaning of the sentence changes.

Pitch is largely determined by anatomy—most men speak at lower pitches than women due to their larger and longer larynx. While higher pitches signal empathy and excitement, lower pitches signal authority, integrity, strength, and competence.[19] There is no right or wrong pitch; however, even a pleasant pitch gets monotonous if it never varies. Consistently speaking with a high pitch can annoy an audience, while speaking consistently with a low pitch will convey a lack of warmth. Varying pitch to align with the meaning of words helps the audience stay interested in what they are hearing.

Projection is the ability to send the voice from the speaker's mouth to an audience's ears. A good rule of thumb to use is to speak loudly enough for the back row of an audience to hear you. If using a microphone to amplify the voice, speak normally and allow the equipment to project the voice. Generally speaking, using a microphone is optimal for audiences of greater than 50 people. If no microphones are available, use an "outdoor" voice to be heard by the audience members farthest away. Clarity is the key to projection, not volume. Articulating the consonants and vowels in words enables more energy to be put into delivery (see more on articulation later). Varying volume also adds interest and emphasis and aids in maintaining an audience's attention.

SPEED

Speaking rate influences how well an audience can pay attention, understand meaning, and retain information in memory. How fast or slow a person speaks is influenced by their culture, dialect region, personality, and demographic factors, such as gender and age. Younger people speak more quickly than older people. Native speakers talk more quickly than nonnative speakers. Speaking rate also varies by situation and by the topic of conversation.[20] Research on the ideal speaking rate for radio, which does not have the advantage of nonverbal or visual cues to enhance attention and learning, finds that for English the ideal rate of speech is 160 to 180 words per minute, with a sufficient number of pauses to assist listeners in understanding. The average English speaker talks at a rate of between 150 and 190 words per minute.[21]

Vocal variety is varying speed while speaking, but it's best to avoid speaking too fast or too slowly overall. When a presenter speaks too quickly, listeners may struggle to follow and end up tuning out. Talking too fast can make it difficult to articulate words and can alter voice quality. Speed is often caused by nerves. Concentrate on connecting with an audience by making eye contact and eliciting feedback. Take note of audience reaction: Speaking speed is probably good if they appear to be following along, but too fast if they appear lost.

People can process what is heard up to three times faster than what is spoken, so speaking too slowly might lose the audience's attention.[3] Speaking slowly is associated with voice tone that lacks intensity, volume, and pitch. In other words, slow speech is more apt to lose an audience. Strive for an optimal rate of speech and vary the rate to reflect emotion and emphasize key points.

ARTICULATION

Speaking clearly requires proper articulation, which is how distinctly words are formed when speaking. Articulation includes pronunciation and enunciation. Proper pronunciation is using the correct sequence of sounds in a word. If the pronunciation of a particular word is uncertain, look it up in an online dictionary that sounds it out and practice saying it several times. If it's difficult to pronounce a word, use a synonym or take a deep breath before saying the word. Enunciation refers to the fullness and clarity of speech sounds. With formal enunciation, each syllable of a word is clearly pronounced. Informal enunciation is less stiff sounding and uses words like *gonna* instead of *going to*.[15] Use the level of formality that fits the audience.

To speak clearly, take time to breathe correctly, open the mouth sufficiently, and make sure each sound is completed accurately. If a speaker's voice trails off at the end of a word or a sentence, listeners will have difficulty following. Make sure to finish all words and to pronounce each consonant, especially at the end of words.

To practice speech articulation, voice coach D'Arcy Webb,[22] professor of voice and speech at the University of the Arts in Philadelphia, recommends practicing a portion of a speech with the forefinger and middle finger in the mouth. Then practice the same part of the speech without fingers in the mouth. The difference in how well words can be articulated may be surprising. The lesson: It is important to open the mouth wide enough to properly articulate words.

Practice vocal variety by reading children's books out loud; practice articulation by saying tongue twisters out loud. Make a voice recording and analyze it for any problems in articulation, speed, or vocal intonation. Another option for improving voice modulation and vocal variation is to practice with a presentation app called Orai (www.oraiapp.com). The app monitors speech rate, use of filler words, and articulation. For further assistance, consult a speech pathologist or voice coach.

See the listing in the resources section of this chapter for speech pathologist Cheryl Dolan's unconventional approach to practicing articulation with a stability ball.

PAUSING WITHOUT FILLERS

Pauses are brief periods of silence between words and phrases. They provide grammatical organization, allow speakers to breathe, and give listeners time to absorb information. They separate ideas, hold attention, and can build suspense.[23]

Purposeful pauses are associated with truthful speech.[24]

Avoid filling pauses with filler words such as *um, ah, so, okay, you know, like*, or any repetitive word or phrase. And don't fall into the trap of using a filler like *um* before even uttering the first word. To eliminate fillers from speech, pay attention to when and which ones are used and practice pausing without fillers. A purposeful pause is helpful to the listener to process the message being delivered, while a filler word is distracting. Vary transitional phrases, and practice, practice, practice so that thoughts will flow without fillers. Fillers are less common the more prepared a presenter is.[23] One more reason to rehearse.

Speakers who convey their message with strong presentation skills—appropriate body movement, gestures, eye contact, facial expressions, and speaking voice—powerfully impact an audience. Presentations allow for human connection, empathy, and engagement that can surpass other forms of communication. It pays to improve these skills.

How Can Nutrition Professionals Enhance Presentation Skills?

Presentation skills are an area of professional practice that can be continually improved. Make it a goal in a professional development portfolio. Seek out continuing education opportunities to learn best practices, allow plenty of time to rehearse and refine presentations, work with a mentor or speech coach, participate in skill-building opportunities, and above all, keep presenting—and welcome evaluation and feedback for improvement.

Learn Better Practices

Chris Anderson, the head of TED, writes in his book, *TED Talks: The Official TED Guide to Public Speaking*, "There are hundreds of ways to give a talk, and everyone can find an approach that's right for them and learn the skills necessary to do it well."[25]

Similarly, Garr Reynolds, author of *Presentation Zen Design*, writes that one should "approach a task with a beginner's mind."[26] By starting with a beginner's mind, a presenter is not saddled with fear but brings fresh eyes and a new perspective. A beginner's mind-set is often one of openness and an enthusiasm for trying something new.

Each speaking opportunity will present its own set of challenges; however, with the knowledge of best practices, a presenter is better equipped to overcome these challenges and act to inform or inspire audiences in the way that best fits their needs. Just as a person can't learn to swim without getting in the water, effective presentation skills can't be developed without practice. The learning is in the doing.

WORDS OF EXPERIENCE

A Rehearsal Story

by Sonja Kassis Stetzler, MA, RDN, CPC

I was hired to coach several speakers for a supply chain industry's executive summit. The speakers I worked with were subject matter experts, not professional speakers. I worked with one speaker in particular to craft his content and adapt it to the executive audience that would hear his presentation. This client knew his material well but did not spend much time rehearsing.

During the dress rehearsal the day before his presentation, he forgot his lines, paced nervously on stage, and did not clearly articulate his words. I knew the real presentation would not be successful if I did not intervene. Speech anxiety is common before presentations, especially when the stakes are high. My client's reputation, his company's reputation, and his career would be impacted by his performance. I suggested to my client that we continue to rehearse that afternoon and evening.

That night, this speaker skipped the speakers' dinner and we rehearsed multiple times. The next day, when it was his turn to take the stage, he walked out calmly, took a deep breath (as we had practiced), and delivered a flawless presentation. He was an unpaid speaker (his company sponsored him), yet he received higher speaker scores than the professional speaker at the event, who commanded a $10,000 fee. The host organization is still talking about my client's amazing speech!

Practice. Rehearse. Receive Feedback. Repeat.

As a rule of thumb, devote half the time of creating a presentation to content development and the other half to rehearsing. The late Steve Jobs, founder of Apple Computers, was renowned for his speeches during Apple's new product launches and how effortless he made it look. "Steve would rehearse endlessly and fastidiously," according to Schlender, Tetzeli, and Andreessen, authors of *Becoming Steve Jobs*.[27] See the Words of Experience box for an example of the impact of rehearsals on the final performance.

Rehearsing as part of presentation preparation helps the presenter to learn the material and provides an opportunity to make any necessary changes. Author and speaking coach Michael Port provides a protocol of best practices for rehearsing a presentation[28]:

- Table read. After scripting content, sit at a table or desk and read the script out loud. Table reads are useful because people typically write differently from the way they speak. Reading a script out loud helps to detect words or phrases that don't fit a natural manner of speaking.
- After a few table reads, begin to mark up the script and underline the words that should be emphasized; make a slash mark behind words where a pause should occur, and mark contrasts with how different parts of the presentation are delivered.
- Stand up and plan how to move during the presentation. Movement influences how the audience sees the presenter. Planning movements ahead of time will prevent wandering aimlessly on stage, shifting weight from one foot to the other, or giving any other nonverbal signs that suggest lack of confidence or poor preparation.
- Rehearse. Practice the presentation in front of small groups of people to get their feedback. These rehearsals can be live performances or through virtual platforms, such as Skype or Zoom. Ask for specific feedback about what works well and what could be improved. Figure 21.1 provides a feedback form presenters, rehearsal audiences, mentors, or coaches can use to evaluate practice performances and provide useful feedback.

Without a live audience to rehearse with, consider using virtual reality presentation software programs. Two available options are Presentation Simulator (www.presentationsimulator.com/presentation-software) and Virtual Orator (https://virtualorator.com).

Videotaping during rehearsal is a useful tool for identifying areas that need improvement. Watch and reflect on what is being done well and not just on areas to change. It's common for people to be their own worst critic. If a slide deck is included in the presentation, practice with the slides until they can be used without looking at them. A flawlessly executed presentation shows professionalism!

Work with a Mentor

Working one-on-one with a mentor or speech coach is another way to improve presentation skills. As discussed in Chapter 2, a mentor or coach who specializes in speech preparation can provide guidance, knowledge, and support in content creation and in speech delivery. A mentor can respond to ideas, offer tips based on experience, and help to accelerate progress in becoming a more polished and effective speaker.

Participate in Skill-Building Opportunities

As mentioned in Chapter 2, the best way to improve a skill is to continue practicing to develop it. Continue learning. Formal public speaking courses are available through colleges and universities. Many Academy of Nutrition and Dietetics Practice Groups offer events for continuing education focused on building and improving presentation skills.

Form a live or virtual rehearsal group with peers who are interested in elevating their presentation performances. Each participant can rehearse parts of upcoming presentations and receive valuable feedback.

FIGURE 21.1 **Rehearsal feedback form**

CONTENT

Was the main message of the speech clear?	YES NO
Was the speech organized?	YES NO
Was the content adapted for the audience?	YES NO
Was there a balance in the use of data, statistics, and story?	YES NO
Was the opening of the speech intriguing?	YES NO
Did the closing of the presentation summarize the speech or contain a call to action and leave the audience satisfied?	YES NO
Did the speaker include audience interaction techniques during the presentation?	YES NO
Were the audience interaction techniques effective?	YES NO

DELIVERY

Did the speaker vary the rate, pitch, and volume when speaking to maintain audience engagement?	YES NO
Did the speaker repeatedly use filler words?	YES NO
Did the speaker use pauses appropriately?	YES NO
Did the speaker move with purpose?	YES NO
Did the speaker exhibit nervousness through distracting movements or pacing?	YES NO
Did the speaker use appropriate eye contact?	YES NO
Did the speaker read too often from notes?	YES NO
Did the speaker use visuals that were appropriate?	YES NO
Were visuals well prepared?	YES NO
Did the visuals enhance the presentation?	YES NO

Other Notes/Observations:

Reproduced with permission of Sonja Kassis Stetzler, MA, RDN, CPC.

Join a Toastmasters club. Toastmasters is an international organization that offers a step-by-step approach to developing public speaking skills. Clubs meet weekly or every other week, and meetings provide a consistent forum for practicing and evaluating public speaking skills.

Attend local National Speakers Association (NSA) meetings. Most local NSA chapters allow guests to attend their meetings. The opportunity to network and learn from professionally paid speakers is invaluable. See the resources section for where to find more on these organizations.

Keep Presenting

To keep improving presentation skills, seek opportunities to speak. If an organization has a speaker's bureau, volunteer to become a participant. There are many community organizations looking for speakers for their meetings. Meet-up groups often host speakers for their events. Network with other speakers. There is a saying in the professional speakers' world that "speakers get other speakers work." Refer colleagues to speak at events, and the favor will likely be returned.

Have Audiences Evaluate

It's common practice for audiences to evaluate a speaker's performance and content after a presentation. Use this feedback to improve future presentations. Ask the meeting planner to share the evaluations, or better yet, create a unique evaluation tailored to a particular audience. Create a tracking system to record presentation factors that could be improved. As management guru Peter Drucker stated, "What gets measured, gets improved."

In closing, consider this final message from Chris Anderson, the head of TED:

I want to persuade you of something: That however much public speaking skills matter today, they're going to matter even more in the future. Driven by our growing connectedness, one of humankind's most ancient abilities is being reinvented for the modern era. I've become convinced that tomorrow, even more than today, learning to present your ideas live to other humans will prove to be an absolutely essential skill ... for anyone, period.[25]

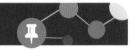

KEY POINTS

Deliver Clear, Compelling Presentations

1. Effective presentation skills are essential to the successful delivery of a message. The nutrition communicator can learn and practice presentation skills to improve effectiveness and increase confidence.

2. Employers rate verbal communication skills the top skill they evaluate when assessing a candidate's skills and qualities. Additionally, 70% of employed Americans say that presentation skills are critical to their success. The ability to clearly present complex ideas, keep an audience's attention, and move an audience toward change is essential for success in today's world of work.

3. An effective presenter possesses a body of skills acquired and built over time. To become proficient requires practice as well as knowledge. Effective presenters know how to overcome nervousness, how to effectively use body language to enhance a message, and the importance of their speaking voice.

4. Presentation skills are an area of professional practice that can continually be improved. Participate in continuing education to learn best practices. Allow plenty of time to rehearse and refine presentations, work with a mentor or speech coach, participate in skill-building opportunities, welcome evaluation and feedback for improvement, and above all, keep presenting.

RESOURCES

From speech pathologist Cheryl Dolan: An unconventional way to reduce nerves and become more articulate—bounce on a stability ball: http://cheryldolan.com/as-the-ball-bounces

Toastmasters International: www.toastmasters.org

National Speakers Association: www.nsaspeaker.org

REFERENCES

1. National Association of Colleges and Employers. Employers: verbal communication most important candidate skill. Published 2016. Accessed March 9, 2018. www.naceweb.org/career-readiness/competencies/employers-verbal-communication-most-important-candidate-skill

2. Gallo C. New survey: 70% say presentation skills are critical for career success. *Forbes.* September 25, 2014. Accessed March 9, 2018. www.forbes.com/sites/carminegallo/2014/09/25/new-survey-70-percent-say-presentation-skills-critical-for-career-success/#1ac60b7b8890

3. Engelberg I, Daly J. *Think Public Speaking.* Pearson; 2013.

4. Mehrabian A, Wiener M. Decoding of inconsistent communications. *J Pers Soc Psychol.* 1967;6(1):109114.

5. Mehrabian A, Ferris S. Inference of attitudes from nonverbal communication in two channels. *J Consult Psychol.* 1967;31(3):248-252.

6. Jones SE, LeBaron CD. Research on the relationship between verbal and nonverbal communication: emerging integrations. *J Commun.* 2002;52(3):499-521.

7. Jiang X, Pell MD. The sound of confidence and doubt. *Speech Commun.* 2017;88:106-126.

8. America's top fears 2017: Chapman University survey of American fears. Wilkinson College of Arts, Humanities, and Social Sciences blog, Chapman University website. Published October 11, 2017. Accessed March 4, 2018. https://blogs.chapman.edu/wilkinson/2017/10/11/americas-top-fears-2017

9. Seinfeld, J. "I'm telling you for the last time." YouTube website. Published 2014. www.youtube.com/attribution?v=yQ6giVKp9ec

10. Atkinson M. *Lend Me Your Ears: All You Need to Know About Making Speeches and Presentations.* Oxford University Press; 2005.

11. Erickson-Levendoski E, Sivasankar M. Investigating the effects of caffeine on phonation. *J Voice.* 2011;25(5):e215-e219.

12. Bowden M. *Winning Body Language: Control the Conversation, Command Attention, and Convey the Right Message—Without Saying a Word.* McGraw-Hill; 2010.

13. Toastmasters International. *Gestures: Your Body Speaks.* 2011. Accessed December 3, 2019. www.toastmasters.org/-/media/files/department-documents/education-documents/201-gestures.ashx

14. Conty L, George N, Heitanen J. Watching Eyes effects: when others meet the self. *Conscious Cogn.* 2016;45:184-197.

15. Munter M, Russell L. *Guide to Presentations.* Prentice Hall; 2002.

16. Lucas S. *The Art of Public Speaking.* 10th ed. McGraw-Hill; 2009.

17. Osborn M, Turner K. *Public Speaking: Finding Your Voice.* Pearson; 2009.

18. Toastmasters International. *Your Speaking Voice: Tips for Adding Strength and Authority To Your Voice.* 2011. Accessed December 3, 2019. www.toastmasters.org/~/media/B7D5C3F93FC3439589BCBF5DBF521132.ashx

19. Anderson R, Klofstad C. Preference for leaders with masculine voices holds in the case of feminine leadership roles. *PLoS One.* 2012;7(12):e51216. doi:10.1371/journal.pone.0051216

20. Waller S, Eriksson M, Sorqvest P. Can you hear my age? Influences of speech rate and speech spontaneity on estimation of speaker age. *Front Psychol.* 2015;6:978.

21. Rodero E. A comparative analysis of speech rate and perception in radio bulletins. *Text Talk.* 2012;32(3):391-411.

22. Webb D. Your 15-minute warm-up: heroic public speaking. Speech presented at: Arden Theater; February 6, 2017; Philadelphia, PA.

23. Zandan N. How to stop saying "um," "ah," and "you know." *Harv Bus Rev.* August 1, 2018. https://hbr.org/2018/08/how-to-stop-saying-um-ah-and-you-know

24. Benus S, Enos F, Hirschberg J, Shriberg E. Pauses in deceptive speech. Published 2006. Accessed December 3, 2019. www.cs.columbia.edu/nlp/papers/2006/benus_al_06.pdf.

25. Anderson C. *TED Talks: The Official TED Guide to Public Speaking.* Houghton Mifflin Harcourt; 2016.

26. Reynolds G. *Presentation Zen Design.* New Riders; 2010.

27. Schlender B, Tetzeli R, Andreessen M. *Becoming Steve Jobs: The Evolution of a Reckless Upstart into a Visionary Leader.* Crown Publishing Group; 2015.

28. Port M. *Steal the Show.* Houghton Mifflin Harcourt; 2015.

SECTION 5

Designing and Delivering Communication via Print, Video, and Demonstrations

Web-Based Communication Provides Maximum Impact on a Minimal Budget

Alice Henneman, MS, RDN

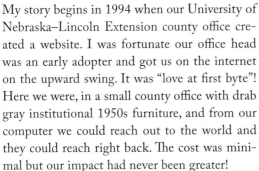

Alice Henneman,
MS, RDN

My story begins in 1994 when our University of Nebraska–Lincoln Extension county office created a website. I was fortunate our office head was an early adopter and got us on the internet on the upward swing. It was "love at first byte"! Here we were, in a small county office with drab gray institutional 1950s furniture, and from our computer we could reach out to the world and they could reach right back. The cost was minimal but our impact had never been greater!

Our organization's mission is to help people in our state "enhance their lives through research-based education." With more people using the internet, it was important to include web-based strategies as a method of outreach.[1] Our state extension office selected me, because of my county website work, to coordinate the creation of a new university-wide food website. I recruited a team of dietetics and food-related professionals that wished to use web-based communications as one of their ways of reaching the public and with related *multiplier groups*, which included dietitians, family and consumer science teachers, and people in food-related media activities. Together, our team grew the website to become our state extension's largest website and the third most visited website at our university (more than 2.6 million page views per year by people in more than 200 countries).

Web-based communication is surprisingly easy. Thanks to the emergence of content-management systems (CMS), most basic web work can be quickly learned from a colleague,

community class, online tutorial, or web-based directions that come with the system. CMS software helps create and manage online content and can make producing basic web-based content comparable to using a word-processing system. Social media sites offer help sections on getting started. Or, there may be opportunities to submit information to others who will post content on the web.

An added benefit of web-based communication is the ease of having a voice on the internet, communicating loud and clear to a wide audience, even if public speaking seems intimidating. In addition, there is time to compose your thoughts and check your work before sharing it with the world.

Why Bother?

George Berkeley, an 18th-century Anglo-Irish philosopher, said, "If a tree falls in a forest and no one is around to hear it, does it make a sound?"[2] When nutrition and dietetics practitioners don't amplify their message through web-based communication, how much of their message is heard?

Section 5 explores several channels of communication that are among the most commonly used by food and nutrition professionals: writing (including newsletters and handouts), video, food demonstrations, and food photography. Each of these forms of communication can be delivered in multiple ways, with one of the most prevalent and cost-effective being the internet. Handouts that once could only be copied and passed out in person are now available online, with audience members choosing to read on their screen or download and print. A food demonstration can reach one roomful of audience members or be made into a video and broadcast across the globe via the internet. Section 6 continues with a focus on communicating via mass media channels, in which internet-based channels play a major role.

The popularity of various web-based platforms changes over time. The Pew Research Center, a nonpartisan, nonadvocacy fact tank collects research on issues, attitudes, and trends that shape the world.[3] Check the Internet and Technology research area of their website to obtain recent statistics on social media usage and other types of web-related issues, as these are constantly changing, with new and different platforms gaining in prominence (www.pewinternet.org/internet).

Up until my retirement in 2018, I was still sitting in that office with the drab gray furniture; however, my influence was now global rather than local. In addition, I have web-based communication materials that are available every day, at any hour, wherever there is an internet connection.

It isn't necessary to reinvent the wheel to get started with web-based communication. Most practitioners probably have several original works (handouts, reports, instructional videos, and the like) that can be repurposed for sharing on the internet.[4] If these materials have been created for an employer or someone else, check with them before putting the content on the web.

Below are some low-cost to no-cost things our team did that can be used to help you get started. *Experiment and pick one, two, or a few that are effective.* Continue to monitor and drop, add, or adapt as times change.

Begin by exploring and trying various channels of communication. As the former president of the Academy of Nutrition and Dietetics Judith Dodd said, "Look before you leap, but do leap!"[5] We can only imagine the channels future food and nutrition professionals will have available for communication!

Helpful Ideas to Get Started

WEBSITE OR BLOG

A website serves as a home base for posting materials and information. A blog is a good alternative to a website (see Chapter 30). Several services offer blog hosting for free, or a customized domain name can be obtained for a small annual fee.

> TIP: Explore the blog platforms used by colleagues for valuable insights and assistance.

FACEBOOK

This is the most popular social media platform, and a page can be created for free. A page differs from a profile, which is a personal account. A page can represent such entities as a company, organization, brand, cause, or community. A Facebook page can be managed as a shared responsibility with colleagues, with a designated role for each person. Post regularly to build a following. Invite friends to "like" the page. When a post is especially popular, boost it to a designated target audience. This has helped us grow our followers. In fact, Facebook is the biggest driver for getting people to our website. Use a personal Facebook profile account to join Facebook groups. Groups are a great way to network and seek assistance from others with a similar interest. More information can be found on the Facebook website (www.facebook.com/help).

> TIP: There are numerous Facebook groups for nutrition and dietetics practitioners dedicated to specific interests. Enter the word *dietitian* into Facebook's search feature to find them.

TWITTER

A Twitter account is free. Hashtags (#), such as #FNCE, provide a way to interact and share information by using a common category. Bring items to someone's attention by directing a tweet to their Twitter handle, the Twitter name they use that is preceded by @. When possible, add a photo or video to draw attention to a tweet. More information is available on Twitter's website (https://help.twitter.com).

> TIP: Include a photo and enough personal details in an account profile, especially if you have a common name, so people can identify who is who.

PINTEREST

A photo can be saved from a webpage to a Pinterest board, which in turn directs people back to the webpage. Or, a photo can be uploaded with a webpage address associated with the photo. There is no charge for this basic use of Pinterest. More information is on the Pinterest website (https://help.pinterest.com).

> TIP: Pinterest entries come up in web searches, so include a description with words that people are likely to search for.

LINKEDIN

Create at least a basic, free account on LinkedIn. People may search LinkedIn for information if considering a practitioner for a job, speaking engagement, committee position, and so on. Explore relevant LinkedIn groups for sharing information and networking. More information is on the LinkedIn website (www.linkedin.com/help/linkedin).

> TIP: Remember to keep all profiles updated! See Chapter 29 for more about these and other social media platforms.

EMAIL NEWSLETTERS

Email newsletters are still going strong and can build an ongoing constituency of readers.[6] An internet search will yield several free services. The limiting factor is the number of emails, subscribers, and features available without paying for more.

> TIP: Some email newsletter providers have a reduced rate for nonprofit and educational institutions.

REFERENCES

1. Pew Research Center. Internet/broadband fact sheet. Published February 5, 2018. Accessed September 3, 2018. www.pewresearch.org/internet/fact-sheet/internet-broadband
2. George Berkeley. Goodreads website. Accessed September 3, 2018. www.goodreads.com/quotes/334037-if-a-tree-falls-in-a-forest-and-no-one
3. Smith A, Anderson M. Social media use in 2018. Pew Research Center website. Published March 1, 2018. Accessed September 3, 2018. www.pewresearch.org/internet/2018/03/01/social-media-use-in-2018
4. Franzen-Castle L, Henneman A, Ostdiek, D. "Reduce" your work load, "re-use" existing extension print materials, and "recycle" to new digital platforms. *J Extension*. 2013;51(4). Accessed September 3, 2018. www.joe.org/joe/2013august/tt2.php
5. Dodd, JL. Look before you leap—but do leap! *J Amer Diet Assoc*. 1999;99(4):422-425. Accessed August 30, 2018. https://jandonline.org/article/S0002-8223(99)00103-0/abstract
6. Henneman A, Franzen-Castle L, Wells C, Colgrove K. Are you overlooking the power of email newsletters? *J NEAFCS*. 2016;11:83-92. Accessed September 3, 2018. www.neafcs.org/assets/documents/journal/2016%20jneafcs.pdf

Write to Be Read, Understood, and Remembered

Barbara J. Mayfield, MS, RDN, FAND
and Milton Stokes, PhD, MPH, RD, FAND

"Quality writing forms the foundation for all types of communication and is essential for success. It is audience focused, clear and concise, accurate and well supported, and it creates visual imagery. Successful writers choose meaningful words that resonate with the audience's needs and values."

"Start writing, no matter what. The water does not flow until the faucet is turned on." —LOUIS L'AMOUR

Introduction

Quality writing forms the foundation for all types of communication and is essential for success. It is audience focused, clear and concise, accurate and well supported, and it creates visual imagery. Successful writers choose meaningful words that resonate with the audience's needs and values. Quality writing can build knowledge, inspire positive attitudes, and promote behavior change.

Poor writing is a major cause of miscommunication and damages the credibility of the writer. It lacks focus, is riddled with grammatical errors, and is easily misunderstood. However, poor writing skills are not a life sentence—education and practice improve writing skills.

This chapter answers three questions:

- Why communicate in writing?
- What are the characteristics of quality writing?
- How can food and nutrition professionals become better writers?

Strong writing skills enable the food and nutrition professional to write for all types of channels: newsletters, handouts, scripts for video, podcasts, oral presentations, newspapers, magazines, social media, blogs and web-based articles, educational curriculums, scholarly research articles, books, and more. Writing is the basis for all types of communication. This chapter covers foundational writing principles, while subsequent chapters cover specific types of writing.

Why Communicate in Writing?

Communication is the sharing of ideas. Writing plays a role throughout the communication process, from planning through delivery and evaluation. Written words form the basis for all communication, support other types of communication, provide a record of communication, and allow for review and retention of information.

Written Words Form the Basis for All Communication and Enhance Other Types of Communication

Humans communicate with words, images, music, body language, emotion, and tone of voice. For example, a video may include all of the above without a single written word onscreen, but written words are instrumental in a video's planning and production. Words are written in scripts and lyrics before they are spoken or sung. Even the production of a silent movie employs written words, such as those instructing the videographer about which images to capture. In all types of communication, some type of writing generally comes first. Clear writing ensures the desired result.

Writing is an essential component of planning communication as well as all subsequent stages of creating and delivering messages. Food and nutrition communicators must write proficiently regardless of the communication channels they use. Communicators tend to craft written

Transcripts Allow for Later Reference and Silent Viewing

From the *Sound Bites* podcast

James O. Hill, PhD: We are pretty good at losing weight, but not so great at keeping it off. Weight loss maintenance requires sustained behavior change—but how do we achieve that? Transformative weight management is the key to sustainable behavior change and it's the biggest game changer I've seen in 35 years of working in this field. When you align the life you want to live with your life purpose and values, you have a very powerful internal motivation—not to stay on a diet, but to keep living a healthier lifestyle.

From the *Healthy Under Pressure* podcast

Amber Pankonin: My name is Amber Pankonin. I'm a registered dietitian and I've been surrounded by entrepreneurs my entire life. I was raised by entrepreneurs. Many of my friends are entrepreneurs, and I even married an entrepreneur. This podcast highlights the stories and struggles of entrepreneurs and busy people learning to live healthy under pressure.

Excerpts from podcast transcripts reproduced with permission from Melissa Joy Dobbins and Amber Pankonin. For more information about how Pankonin uses text for her first podcast episode, visit the Healthy Under Pressure website (www.healthyunderpressure.com/episode-1-tiffany-verzal).

content to inform other types of communication, such as audio and video productions and speaking engagements.

Written words also enhance other types of communication. In fact, no matter how a message is conveyed, providing key components of a message in writing provides an audience with essential information that might otherwise be forgotten or remembered incorrectly. Examples of this include a speaker providing handouts to help the audience follow along and take notes to use as a reference later. A culinary demonstration provides recipes along with helpful shopping and cooking tips. A video provides captioning for those who are hearing-impaired. A podcast includes a transcript for easy reference at a later date (see the examples in Box 22.1). Text overlay is often used on videos on social media so the audience can watch a video and get the gist without having to turn on their sound (which can be helpful in a public place). The text overlay may also enhance the message of the video.

Publications—both in print and online—remain one of the primary delivery systems for information even in an electronic age. Writing provides the means to retain and review communication.

Writing Provides a Record of Communication

The written word provides documentation of the communicated message. The food and nutrition professional in a clinical setting recognizes the importance of clear and accurate documentation. In other settings, written words are an equally important record of the information communicated.

When words are merely spoken, a person might say, "That's not what I meant" or even "That's not what I said" if there is a misunderstanding. But when words are written down, they provide evidence of the message that was conveyed, and clear writing maximizes the potential for understanding. Choose words the audience will understand. Use proper grammar and punctuation. See Box 22.2 (page 352) for examples of how punctuation matters.

The written word is a permanent record, whether retained on paper or electronically. Long before technology allowed for recording speeches electronically, speeches delivered centuries ago were transcribed. Writing has long been viewed as a main means for transmitting ideas, well before other channels became available. Writing will continue to be a primary means for communicating.

Writing Allows for Review and Retention of Information

Food and nutrition communicators are in the business of conveying messages that enhance knowledge and motivate health-promoting behaviors. Helping people to accurately learn and remember those messages is possibly the most important reason to put the information in writing. Even when the primary form of communication is spoken, written words allow a practitioner to give specific instructions, provide additional detail, list scholarly references, and suggest sources for further information. Written text is superior to spoken information when it comes to serving as a permanent record and allowing for later review.[1]

Numerous studies have examined how well information is remembered and recalled, including research on patients provided with medical information regarding their health and necessary regimens for treatment.[2] The results paint a discouraging picture. In general, when people are asked to recall information provided verbally, they remember less than 25% to 50% of the information

See Chapter 18 for more on visual aids.

communicated.[3-5] Visual aids, while imperfect, improve retention during instruction, but providing information in a form that can be reviewed later, whether written or as an audio or video recording, greatly increases the potential for accurate recall.

This chapter will look at the issues of low literacy and health literacy, which require special attention to word choice and the use of visual support in creating written materials. Poorly written materials are unlikely to enhance learning, whereas quality writing will.

What Are the Characteristics of Quality Writing?

Quality writing has a number of key features.

- Quality writing is written with the audience in mind. It is focused and has a clear purpose and overriding message. It is well supported with adequate evidence and relevant illustrations that provide context and enhance meaning.
- Quality writing is logical, flows well, and is clear and concise, with appropriate brevity. Words are understandable to the target audience, based on their literacy level. Quality writing is easy to read. Every word counts.
- Quality writing uses the modern style with active voice while avoiding jargon (see Box 22.3), clichés, and vague modifiers, such as *very* and *so*. It is free of spelling and grammatical errors. It has undergone editing, proofreading, and ruthless revision. A first draft is not quality writing. Write, review, revise, and repeat.

Writing with the Audience in Mind (Audience Focused) Based on Needs Assessment

Effective writing speaks to its audience. To accomplish this, the food and nutrition communicator benefits from completing a needs assessment of the target audience. Refer to Section 3 for strategies for assessing and understanding audiences.

In *Write Now*, Russell[6] identifies audience characteristics to account for, which are listed in Box 22.4. For example, when the audience's age

---

BOX 22.2 Punctuation Matters: What's Up with Emily?

What's up with Emily? With the right punctuation, she's just fine; without it, tread lightly.

Example 1
Emily finds joy in cooking her family and her dog.
Emily finds joy in cooking, her family, and her dog.

Example 2
Emily is working twenty four-hour shifts.
Emily is working twenty-four-hour shifts.

Example 3
Emily likes to cut and paste kids.
Emily likes to cut and paste, kids.

Example 4
Emily is having her favorite sandwich, coleslaw and chocolate cake.

Emily is having her favorite sandwich, coleslaw, and chocolate cake.

---

bracket is known, it is possible to write in a way that relates to what they know and how the topic may be pertinent to them. Consider an audience's experience and knowledge in order to focus writing on aspects of the topic they care about. Education and literacy level are two important characteristics that should influence the words that are used and how much information is included. While these are just a few characteristics, the more thoroughly these factors are considered, the more focused and effective a message will be.

With the knowledge provided by a needs assessment, a communicator can write with the audience in mind. What is audience-focused writing? It is writing that addresses needs and concerns identified in the target audience. For example, an article promoting eating more fruits and vegetables could focus on seasonal recipes for an audience that likes to cook, ways to satisfy picky eaters for parents of young children, or ways to use canned fruits and vegetables when fresh are not in season.

Audience-focused writing provides evidence pertinent to the target audience. Share statistics that are relevant to them or those they care for. A 10th-grade health class, required for all 10th graders at their high school, needs to know about general nutrition recommendations for their growth stage, while an audience of high school wrestlers needs more specific information and tactics to enhance their athletic performance. The specific information and tactics for wrestlers are not relevant for all 10th graders and thus wouldn't be included in the health class presentation.

Audience-focused writing uses meaningful examples. Would a sports analogy work, or would an example from classical literature resonate more? Find out what an audience cares about. For example, different generations will remember historical references that occurred in their lifetimes.[7] Choose examples wisely. See Box 22.5 for more ideas.

Writers who identify what their audience wants and needs to know can write with the audience in mind. For a refresher on how to write for an audience, review Section 3 before moving on.

Written Logically with a Key Idea at the Center

Quality writing is focused, with a clearly stated purpose and main idea. If the overriding message cannot be conveyed clearly and concisely, work on

Save Jargon for Other Practitioners

Any group communicates with jargon. For example, registered dietitian nutritionists (RDNs) who practice inpatient medical nutrition therapy use jargon when documenting patient care in the medical record. Health professionals possess their own language for expediency in peer-to-peer interaction—for example, writing "MI" to indicate that the patient had a myocardial infarction, which is another word for heart attack.

However, using jargon when speaking to patients may pose a barrier to effective communication. Most patients are likely to know what a heart attack is, but the term *myocardial infarction* would be foreign to them. In some cases, jargon can provide teachable moments. Depending on the situation, explaining that *myocardial infarction* is another word for *heart attack* may help the average listener feel more included. Either way, use jargon sparingly and appropriately, with your target audience in mind.

Audience Characteristics to Consider When Writing[6]

Age	Reading ability
Experience	Education level
Opinions	Knowledge of the subject
Beliefs	
Gender	Religion
Political views	Ethnicity
Cultural background	Occupation
Interests	Socioeconomic status

it until it can. If needed, review Chapter 15 for how to write key messages.

Before beginning to write, have a plan and develop an outline. The main, overriding message—the big idea, or the SOCO (single overriding communication objective)—must stand out at the center of the writing. When someone reads the text, they should quickly and easily be able to identify the main idea. In fact, a good way to evaluate whether

For more on effectively communicating with audiences of different ages and generations, review Chapter 14.

this has been accomplished is to ask someone unfamiliar with the writing to read it and identify the key message. See Box 22.6 for information from the Center for Plain Language. Professionals from other countries may think Americans all understand what the US government publishes. Unfortunately, much governmental writing is less clear than it could be.

Focused and logical writing is evident from beginning to end. Create an opening or introduction, a body, and a summary or conclusion. The main idea should be clear from the start, supported throughout, and restated in closing. Make it memorable and actionable.

Each paragraph is ideally centered on one main point or concept, with a strong topic sentence positioned in the paragraph for maximum impact. Each sentence flows logically and supports the main idea with evidence, context, illustrations, or supporting examples. The paragraph may end with a summary statement or a suitable transition to the next paragraph.

Organize writing around key messages. Help the reader identify them with clear headings showcasing the key messages. Repeat key ideas, and provide a summary list at the end.

Written Using Modern Style and Active Voice

The modern style of writing encompasses several best practices. It reads clearly and concisely in an active voice. The author avoids vague or confusing language. The reader will easily visualize the subject of the sentence rather than struggle with an abstract idea.

Active voice means that the subject does the action. Passive voice means the subject receives the action. Consider these two examples:

A: The revision of the article will be completed by the intern.

B: The intern will revise the article.

Which one is clearer? B is written in the modern style and uses active voice. "Old" writing (A) uses passive voice and sounds wordy. Notice the subject in B is stated at the start of the sentence, helping the reader grasp the meaning and comprehend the conveyed idea more quickly.

Modern-style writing recognizes that readers prefer clarity. Replace vague words, like *very* or *slightly*, with specific or precise descriptions. Instead of saying, "Portion sizes are becoming very large," for example, say, "Portion sizes are 50% larger than they were 20 years ago." Providing specificity and adequate detail creates more persuasive communication.[9]

Readers desire brevity. Eliminate words that contribute little to the message. Make each word count. The Gettysburg Address contained just over 250 words, fewer than the number that fit on one typed page. No more were needed. In reviewing and revising, look for ways to cut extraneous content.

Vary sentence length between longer and shorter sentences, with an average length of between 10 and 15 words. Variety in sentence length gives writing a pleasing rhythm.

Modern-style writing is conversational and uses common, everyday words. Avoid clichés, and use wording that is clear and direct. When writing for lay audiences, use contractions, personal pronouns, and words that elicit emotion. Avoid acronyms (or if they are used, explain their meaning). Include a call to action. (See Box 22.7 for a summary of the characteristics of modern style.)

Written at an Appropriate Reading Level for the Audience

It's true: Many writers enjoy transcribing their thoughts into words on paper, and those thoughts make sense to the writer. But what happens when there's an audience beyond the writer? Operating under the assumption that the writer plans to increase knowledge, or intends to impact attitudes and beliefs, the writer must consider the audience. Is it homogeneous or mixed? Will the audience tolerate jargon or require plain English? Does the medium call for a scholarly and detached style or a friendly and familiar style? Answering these questions will help determine the best approach to maximize comprehension. Baker, in *The Practical Stylist*, writes, "Your written language, in short, will be respectful toward your subject, considerate toward your readers, and amiable toward human failings."[10]

Food and nutrition professionals may work with individuals, communities, and populations to enhance health. Because individual learning styles and preferences vary, best practices dictate that written educational materials are provided to reinforce the message—something documented for future reference when clients are working to implement some of the new information. However, despite food and nutrition professionals' best intentions of helping, it's common to encounter clients who consume and process information differently from the way they do. Predominant language, literacy level, and communication style help shape health literacy.[11] Nutrition communicators are tasked with writing and designing all communication at the appropriate audience level.

Writers may use readability tools (see Box 22.8) to help shape written content based on the audience reading level. Many tools exist, but writers are cautioned not to rely on them too heavily. In fact, these tools are not flawless: They do not measure reading ease, check comprehension, or demonstrate consistency across multiple tools. Consider these resources as additional

Modern Style of Writing

Use …

Active voice

Clear structure

Just the right number of words needed to convey the message

Variable sentence length

Conversational style

Readability Tools

Writers may employ readability tools to assess the reading level of their writing. Several of the most common are listed below, along with URLs for websites providing background and calculators to assess reading levels using each formula.

- **SMOG (Simple Measure of Gobbledygook):** www.readabilityformulas.com/smog-readability-formula.php
- **The Flesch Reading Ease Readability Formula:** www.readabilityformulas.com/flesch-reading-ease-readability-formula.php
- **The Fry Graph Readability Formula:** www.readabilityformulas.com/fry-graph-readability-formula.php

information but not guarantees of readability.[12,13] Many word-processing software programs have built-in readability tests, a feature found under the grammar and spelling menus. Additional tools, including checklists to assess readability, are listed in the resources section at the end of the chapter.

Supported with Graphics, Charts, Tables, and More

Words form the basis for communication. Written words, in report form, concretely capture the writer's thesis and supporting ideas. In an information-rich environment with time-crunched readers, condensing and repackaging content as visuals can facilitate understanding. Photos and drawings help expand attention and translate ideas. A variety of tools exist online to help create informational

BOX 22.9

Infographic Tools

To create infographics, visit any of the following free tools online:

- Visme (www.visme.co)
- Canva Infographic Maker (www.canva.com)
- Google Charts (https://developers.google.com /chart)
- Piktochart (www.piktochart.com)
- Infogram (www.infogram.com)
- Venngage (www.venngage.com)
- Easelly (www.easel.ly)

See Chapter 18 for more on including visuals in presentations and written materials.

graphics, or infographics (see Box 22.9).

For example, the International Food Information Council (IFIC) communicates nutrition science and health for the public good. To do this, they create infographics, which combine imagery with smaller amounts of text, to tell the story gleaned from a significantly longer report or scientific study. IFIC covers a variety of topics in food, food safety, and nutrition, including agriculture and food production. See the resources section at the end of the chapter for where to find examples of the infographics IFIC has created.

Some communicators also use presentation software, such as PowerPoint, to create infographics. Communicators with design experience can utilize design software, such as Adobe Illustrator or InDesign (paid software) or Adobe Spark (free), to create their own infographics from scratch.

Infographics are used to portray information in a readable and useful format for all types of topics. Figure 22.1 illustrates an infographic listing common writing mistakes.

In addition to infographics, memes transmit ideas in condensed form using imagery and text. *Memes* are visuals that transmit ideas and language usage over social media, often using humor; good memes can go viral and spread rapidly via social media platforms. See Figure 22.2 for an example of a nutrition meme.

FIGURE 22.1 **Sample infographic: 10 Writing Mistakes Even Book Lovers Make**[a]

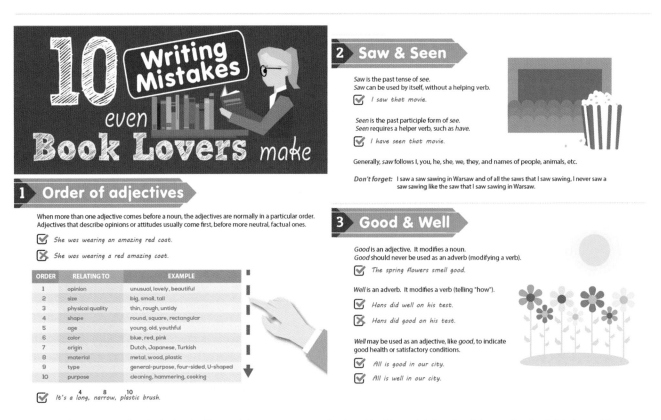

[a] Image has been cropped to fit the book. Please visit www.grammarcheck.net/writing-mistakes-book-lovers for the full infographic. Reproduced with permission from Grammarcheck.net. 10 writing mistakes even book lovers make. Published May 17, 2018. Accessed June 18, 2020.ww.grammarcheck.net/writing-mistakes-book-lovers for the full infographic[14]

FIGURE 22.2 **Sample nutrition meme**

Reproduced with permission from the Sarcastic Nutritionist.

As written content is developed, the writer or designer will make decisions about the layout, the lettering, graphics, and other elements of design. In some settings, all of the design decisions will already be made, and the writer will only be responsible for the content. In other settings, the writer will work with a professional graphic designer and be asked to provide input or feedback. In still other situations, a writer will be on his or her own. Some types of writing require no design per se, only neat and organized writing. When design decisions *are* needed, understand the terminology and characteristics of quality design.

A well-designed layout is like a well-composed photograph or painting. The same design concepts that apply to art can be used to create a visually appealing document. For the purposes of this chapter, what follows serves as an overview of layout and design terms and principles.

FORMAT

Design includes the overall format. For a print document, what will be the size and shape? Will it be a folded brochure, a booklet, or a flat page? Will text be laid out across the full page or in columns? Columns are considered easier to read, having fewer than 40 characters per line. When appropriate, break up text with images and other graphics that complement the text. Choose ones that have the same feel as the text and are appropriate to the audience. All design decisions relate to the type of publication or writing, the purpose, and the audience.

ASYMMETRY

A photographer is trained to position the subject off-center. In the same way, avoid centering large portions of text. Human eyes are trained to read along a hard edge, making center alignment more difficult to read. Layout can feel balanced without being symmetric.

ALIGNMENT

Alignment means that everything is lined up with something to provide organization, a polished appearance, and strong design. For example, bullet points are left aligned as well as indented from the remaining text to set them apart and provide organization. Information should be provided in such a way that the reader can easily follow it and understand the meaning.

PROXIMITY

Proximity creates relationships between groups of text or images. Headings are placed near the text they introduce. Captions are placed near the images they describe. Items in lists are placed in proximity to show they go together.

FONTS

Choose fonts suitable to the medium and the message. Design contrast can be achieved by combining a serif font with a sans serif font. (See Figure 18.3 on page 298 for examples.) Serif fonts are those with strokes (or little tails) at the end of letters. Serif fonts are recommended in text-heavy documents that will be read on paper. Serifs assist the reader in moving the eye across the page. These are often paired with a sans serif font used for the heading or title. Sans serif fonts require extra space between lines. Online, sans serif fonts are primarily used because serifs can appear blurry and pixelated on a screen. Serif fonts can be used for larger titles in online materials. A rule of thumb in graphic design is to avoid using two serif fonts or two sans serif fonts—instead, use one of each. This book uses a serif for body text and a sans serif for headings. When selecting fonts, also consider the following: Italics and use of all capital letters slow down the reader. Use them sparingly.

DESIGN ELEMENTS

When in doubt about design, remember that clean and simple is always better than busy and messy, or no design at all. Also use specific design elements to enhance visual appeal. Balance imagery with words and "white" (unused) space to convey a sense of harmony.

Most organizations have what is called a style guide to maintain their brand. The style guide usually contains preferred fonts, specific colors, logo usage guidelines, and more. If creating content for an organization, refer to their style guide for these elements. If creating content for a personal business or freelance work, practitioners should consider creating a style guide that aligns with

their brand—this will help with continuity across all work and make that work recognizable. Even a small business or organization can benefit from working with a professional to create a suite of templates that align with their branding (eg, a logo, word-processing template, and slide template).

The layout and design of a communication depends on the audience and the context. Scholarly manuscripts are written for a standard 8.5 × 11-inch white sheet of paper using word-processing software. Margins run about 1 inch all the way around. Font style is either Times New Roman or something comparable, with a 10- or 12-point font size. But today's food and nutrition communicator writes more than manuscripts: There are client education materials; blogs for online readers; short, catchy phrases for imprinting marketing materials, such as T-shirts and other collateral; and so forth. Professionals in food and nutrition may find themselves in positions at marketing and advertising agencies where the task is to create copy for consumer promotion. The possibilities are so vast that college courses, majors, and professions specialize in these areas. Know when it's time to consult a professional or invest in further educational courses.

Good with Grammar

Grammar is a system for sentence structure. It includes agreement between subject and verb, matching pronouns, proper punctuation, person and number agreement, and so forth. Teaching grammar is beyond the scope of this text, but there are several reliable resources that address grammar: Purdue University's Online Writing Lab (https://owl.english.purdue.edu/owl); Baker's *The Practical Stylist*; Strunk and White's *The Elements of Style*; and Truss's *Eats, Shoots and Leaves*.

It's Just a Typo

by Barbara J. Mayfield, MS, RDN, FAND

The students in Purdue University's Nutrition Communication course work all semester to prepare for a final presentation to a real audience. Years ago, a set of partners presented a food demonstration featuring healthy soup recipes to a community group. They had worked hard to modify and perfect old family recipes to share with their audience. They had found helpful nutrition information, shopping tips, cooking tips, and fun facts about the ingredients and recipes. To accompany their presentation, they created a full-color brochure complete with recipes and photographs. They invested their own money to have lovely color copies printed. It wasn't until the presentation that one very small typo was found in a recipe. The instructions were supposed to tell the reader to "add" the next ingredient. However, the letter to the left of *d* on the keyboard, the letter *s*, was used instead and the word *add* became *ass*. Not an appropriate word choice for the elderly audience served by the local extension office. A spellchecker doesn't find mistakes that form real words; only careful proofreading does. Uncorrected typos can make you feel like an ...

Checked to Be Grammatically Correct and Free of Typos

When it comes to grammar, many people may have flashbacks to elementary school and diagramming sentences. While teaching grammar is beyond the scope of this text, several resources address grammar, and some are highlighted in Box 22.10. Grammar is an incredibly important component of written communications—the most insightful blog post will have its credibility affected and its message lost if it is filled with poor grammar. Brushing up on grammar, proofreading all content, and including a third-party editor (whether a spouse, a friend, a family member, a colleague, or a professional) are all good practices when it comes to producing error-free content.

Check spelling and ensure the appropriate words have been selected. Homonyms, such as *to*, *too*, and *two* or *their*, *there*, and *they're*, are commonly confused with each other. Remember, a first draft is just a draft. Write. Review. Revise. Repeat. Take a break between writing and revising, ideally at least overnight. After a break, return to the writing, read it out loud, and edit as necessary. Then ask someone else to review it. It can be hard for writers to edit

Writing Quality Checklist

_____ Audience is clearly identified and writing shows evidence of audience assessment.

_____ Theme is consistent and unified.

_____ Thesis is clear—focused on a central key message or SOCO (single overriding communication objective).

_____ Writing is organized with an introduction, body, and conclusion.

_____ Transitions assist with flow.

_____ Evidence and illustrations support message.

_____ Grammar, punctuation, and spelling are accurate.

_____ Extraneous content is trimmed.

their work, but it invariably results in a better product. See the Words of Experience box for an example of the importance of proofreading one's work.

The Writing Quality Checklist can be helpful for evaluating written work, whether it is the writer's own work or another author's.

How Can Food and Nutrition Professionals Become Better Writers?

Writing is work that's hard for some and easy for others. But one thing is for sure—being a capable writer is an essential skill for all food and nutrition professionals. Regardless of skill level, all practitioners can become better writers. Continually seek to improve writing skills. Take a writing class. Access one of the online resources listed at the end of the chapter to assess skills. Work through the online tutorials to correct problem areas. Work with a writing mentor or coach. Seek to grow, to stretch, to improve.

Step one is putting pen to paper—or fingers to keyboard—and starting someplace. Protect writing time by scheduling it. When the time comes, all a writer has to do is write. First drafts rarely pass for the most intelligible content. First drafts may never

see the light of day. Writing begets better writing.

Embrace the editing process. Published works pass through rounds of editing, including the writer's own edits and possibly the edits of editorial teams and reviewers who help refine the content. Allowing others to view one's work is an opportunity for feedback and improvement. The most critical editors are those who will help a writer grow the most. Constructive criticism helps stretch skills. Select colleagues and friends to serve as readers. Challenge them to provide support for improvement. Listen to the comments of an audience—before writing, while writing, and after publishing. Write. Review. Revise. Keep writing.

Good writers read as much as possible. Whatever the genre of writing, read anything and everything. Others' writing provides examples of how to approach topics—some approaches will appeal, and some won't. It helps writers to read media where they aim to publish. For example, if a target is national glossy magazines that cover men's health, read those magazines regularly. This will reveal the publisher's preferred tone and style, as well as provide inspiration for ideas. Keep notes of observations. Capture ideas for future stories, such as in a smartphone app like Evernote.

Food and nutrition communicators write to be read. Compel audiences to pay attention—draw them in with an opening statement and motivate them to stay to the final sentence. Communicators write to be understood. Learn an audience's language. Teach the audience a new language. Write clearly. Communicators also write to be remembered. Use best practices in crafting the written word to be memorable as well as accurate. Use principles of design and layout to best deliver the written message. Write to be read, understood, and remembered.

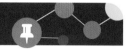

KEY POINTS

Write to Be Read, Understood, and Remembered

1. Written words form the basis for most communication. For example, speeches are first born as manuscripts. Sketching out remarks helps speakers focus their messages to remain on point. A transcript of the speech then serves as a written record for the future.

2. Writers best serve readers by keeping a focus on what the reader expects. Based on audience assessment, writers declare the thesis, or the point of their writing, and ideas flow with logical support in a modern style and active voice. Sometimes, however, the passive is appropriate and expected (eg, in scholarly writing). Regardless, writers transmit ideas from their minds to the written word, understanding that others will consume those ideas and attempt to make sense of them. Keep an audience top of mind. Since readers are as busy and distracted as everyone else, they expect succinct content that is appropriately accompanied by graphics and wrapped in an appealing design aesthetic.

3. Proofread all work to avoid spelling and grammatical errors. Solicit feedback from critical reviewers. Learn as much as possible from them; revise. Keep writing.

4. Work to consistently improve as a writer. Establish a writing routine. Review all your writing and invite others to review and critique your work. Assess current skill levels and take steps to become a better writer.

RESOURCES

General Writing

Cron L. Story genius: http://wiredforstory.com/story-genius-1

Dennard S. Resources for writers: http://susandennard.com/for-writers

Guide for writing easy-to-read health materials: https://medlineplus.gov/etr.html

Northern Illinois University Online Writing Tutorial: www.niu.edu/writingtutorial

Purdue University's Online Writing Lab: https://owl.english.purdue.edu/owl

Grammar

Capital Community College interactive grammar and writing quizzes: http://grammar.ccc.commnet.edu/grammar/quiz_list.htm

Fogarty M. Grammar Girl: www.quickanddirtytips.com/grammar-girl

Strunk W, White EB. *The Elements of Style.* Pearson Education Limited; 2014. Online version. www.bartleby.com/141

Yale Center for Teaching and Learning: https://ctl.yale.edu/writing/resources-multilingual-writers/downloadable-english-grammar-tutorials

Infographics

International Food Information Council: www.foodinsight.org/tags/infographic-0

Readability

Centers for Disease Control and Prevention, Clear Communication Index: www.cdc.gov/ccindex/index.html

Centers for Disease Control and Prevention, Guide for Creating Easy-to-Understand Materials: www.cdc.gov/healthliteracy/pdf/Simply_Put.pdf

Readability checklist: www.plainlanguage.gov/resources/checklists

SAM (Suitability Assessment of Materials) criteria to assess readability beyond just reading level: http://aspiruslibrary.org/literacy/sam.pdf

Tool Kit for Making Written Materials Clear and Effective: www.cms.gov/Outreach-and-Education/Outreach/WrittenMaterialsToolkit/index.html?redirect=/WrittenMaterialsToolkit

Publishing Resources

Brewer RL. *Writer's Market 2018: The Most Trusted Guide to Getting Published*: F + W Media; 2017.

Just for Fun

Taylor Mali's poem about proofreading: https://taylormali.com/poems/the-the-impotence-of-proofreading/www.youtube.com/watch?v=OonDPGwAyfQ

REFERENCES

1. Ayres P. State-of-the-art research into multimedia learning: a commentary on Mayer's *Handbook of Multimedia Learning*. *Appl Cogn Psychol.* 2015;29:631-636.
2. Watson P, McKinstry B. A systematic review of interventions to improve recall of medical advice in healthcare consultations. *J R Soc Med.* 2009;102:235-243.
3. Margolis R. What do your patients remember? *Hear J.* 2004;57(6):10,12,16-17.
4. Ley P, Whiworth M, Skilbeck C, et al. Improving doctor-patient communication in general practice. *J R Coll Gen Pract.* 1976;26:720-724.
5. Sandberg E, Sharma R, Sandberg W. Deficits in retention for verbally presented medical information. *Anesthesiology.* 2012;117:772-779.
6. Russell K. *Write Now.* 2nd ed. McGraw-Hill; 2016.
7. Pew Research Center. Americans name the 10 most significant historic events of their lifetimes: modern historic events by generation. Pew Research Center U.S. Politics and Policy website. Published December 14, 2016. Accessed May 18, 2018. www.people-press.org/2016/12/15/americans-name-the-10-most-significant-historic-events-of-their-lifetimes/pp_12-15-16_history-new-01
8. Pew Research Center. Americans name the 10 most significant historic events of their lifetimes. Pew Research Center U.S. Politics and Policy website. Published December 15, 2019. Accessed December 5, 2019. www.people-press.org/2016/12/15/americans-name-the-10-most-significant-historic-events-of-their-lifetimes
9. Abela AV. *Advanced Presentations by Design: Creating Communication That Drives Action*. 2nd ed. Wiley; 2013.
10. Baker S. *The Practical Stylist.* 7th ed. Harper Collins Publishers; 1990.
11. Boehl T. Linguistic issues and literacy barriers in nutrition. *J Acad Nutr Diet.* 2007;107(3):380,383.
12. US Department of Health and Human Services Agency for Healthcare Research and Quality. Be cautious with readability formulas for quality reports. Published 2015. Accessed December 3, 2017. www.ahrq.gov/professionals/quality-patient-safety/talkingquality/resources/writing/tip6.html
13. Wang L, Miller M, Schmitt M, Wen F. Assessing readability formula differences with written health information materials: application, results, and recommendations. *Res Soc Adm Pharm.* 2013;9(5):503-516.
14. Grammarcheck.net. 10 writing mistakes even book lovers make. Published May 17, 2018. Accessed June 18, 2020.ww.grammarcheck.net/writing-mistakes-book-lovers for the full infographic

Reach Target Audiences with Newsletters and Handouts

Erin E. Healy, MS, RDN
and Heidi Katte, MS, RDN, CD, FAND

"Clear and focused messaging is essential when formulating a newsletter or handout. Use an objective approach and keep the message clear and concise."

> "The writer who breeds more words than he needs is making a chore for the reader who reads." —DR SEUSS

Introduction

Section 3 addressed message development and audience-focused communication. Newsletters and handouts are print or electronic documents that deliver key messages to target audiences. Upcoming chapters will discuss other tools, such as videos, culinary demonstrations, and photography.

Think of these documents as tools in the nutrition communicator's tool kit, much like utensils in a chef's kitchen. The desired outcome is shared, but the means of achieving the goal are different. For example, chefs will use a variety of utensils to cook one dish. They will use a knife to slice vegetables and a wooden spoon to stir them into the sauce. The same is true for newsletters and handouts. The shared intent is to inform or persuade audiences, but newsletters and handouts serve different functions in the pursuit of that intention.

This chapter answers three questions:

- What role do newsletters and handouts play in nutrition communication?
- What are best practices for communicating via newsletters and handouts?
- What are practical strategies for communicating via newsletters and handouts?

The answers to these questions will provide an understanding of the similarities and differences between newsletters and handouts, as well as the appropriate use of each. Much like skilled chefs, successful nutrition communicators know the appropriate tool to use for the design and delivery of effective communication.

What Role Do Newsletters and Handouts Play in Nutrition Communication?

Newsletters and handouts are communication tools that provide written support for informing or persuading target audiences for particular purposes. Nutrition communicators use these tools in different ways to achieve that common goal. Each plays a unique role in nutrition communication.

Newsletters Educate and Update Audiences

Newsletters can serve as a central location for the most current and accurate information on a specific topic, or from a particular organization, that is of interest to a targeted audience.[1,2] These communication tools offer a full range of articles, success stories, helpful hints, calls to action, details on upcoming events or opportunities, award recognitions, and additional resources. Newsletters can also include links to blog posts or other online content that drives readers to the nutrition communicator's personal or organization website and social media accounts for more information. Distribution of newsletters should be on a regular and ongoing basis in either print or digital format, or both.

The role newsletters play in nutrition communication is varied. Nutrition communicators use these tools to form relationships, establish credibility, and generate opportunities to inform or persuade audiences. By consistently engaging with audience members, newsletters create an allegiance. That sense of loyalty keeps current audience members coming back for more and builds name recognition among new members. Because newsletters contain recent and sourced information, audiences rely on these tools to stay informed and up to date. Newsletters allow audience members to quickly and easily access information. This builds trust and authenticates the nutrition communicator as a subject matter expert in his or her field.[1] In turn, expert status can open the door to new clients, speaking engagements, or partnership opportunities, which enables the nutrition communicator to reach a broader audience and expand his or her area of influence.

Take a moment to review *Ventures*, the newsletter of the Nutrition Entrepreneurs dietetic practice group (DPG) of the Academy of Nutrition and Dietetics (see Figure 23.1). This sample newsletter will be referred to throughout the chapter.

Handouts Provide Written Support to Enhance Learning

Handouts are complementary documents that accompany a presentation, speech, workshop, counseling session, or other audience interaction. They help audience members remember and use the information provided during those interactions.[3,4] Handouts are typically one page (single- or double-sided) in length; however, if the topic is highly technical or detailed, a longer format might be needed.

The role handouts play in nutrition communication differs from that of newsletters. Nutrition communicators use handouts to emphasize key messages, expand on current themes, provide how-to guides, and reach new audience members. Handouts also serve as written takeaways. Whether created for a presentation or a counseling session, handouts are a physical reminder of the information discussed to review later. Many handouts also offer additional information to extend the conversation.[3] This continues the learning experience beyond the initial interaction, which helps to further inform or persuade audiences. Finally, these tools can be used to connect with a broader audience when individuals who participated in the initial interaction share the handouts with others.

Take a moment to review the National Dairy Council's Power of Protein: Quality Matters! handout (Figure 23.2). This sample handout will be referred to throughout the chapter.

What Are Best Practices for Communicating via Newsletters and Handouts?

The best practices presented in this section will provide direction to and assist nutrition communicators in writing newsletters and handouts. Focusing on the audience, delivering clear messages, using calls to action, and following a uniform layout and design are the four best practices discussed.

Focus on the Audience

The more a nutrition communicator knows about an audience (what motivates them, how to reach them, where they obtain information, and so on), the easier it will be to inform and persuade them. Review Chapter 11 for how to conduct a needs assessment to learn more about an audience. Review Box 22.4 on page 353 for audience characteristics to consider when writing newsletters and handouts.

Audience focus involves understanding the audience's perspective. Each person has a collection of personal experiences that impacts that person's worldview. Realize this when writing for a group. Use the terms and jargon that best relate to a particular audience. In *Write Now*, Karen Russell reminds the writer to "keep in mind the needs and interests of your primary audience, but realize others (your secondary audience) might also read your document."[5] An example of a secondary audience would be a family member of a patient who reads the information.

Deliver Clear Messages

Clear and focused messaging is essential when formulating a newsletter or handout. Use an objective approach and keep the message clear and concise. If the communicator's personal opinions and bias are infused, the message can become skewed and its credibility decreased.

As discussed in Chapter 15, when creating and organizing messages, begin with identifying the purpose. Because the role of a newsletter or handout is primarily to inform or persuade, the purpose will be to provide useful information or to teach the audience how to do something. State the purpose clearly so readers understand what message will be conveyed.

Nutrition Entrepreneurs

a dietetic practice group of the

eat right. Academy of Nutrition and Dietetics

Ventures

Enterprising News & Ideas for Nutrition Entrepreneurs

Spring 2018
Volume XXXVI
Number 4

Branding: Discovering Your Unique Voice

A Brand New You

Rosanne Rust, MS, RDN, LD
Chair

Springtime is a time of renewal. Rebirth. Rejuvenation.

As an entrepreneur it's always a good idea to do a yearly check-up on your work, whether you are an established brand or are still working on it. I recently read Mel Carson's (delightfulcommunications. com) "10 Steps to a New Professional You" at Entrepreneur Magazine's website. I've listed his 10 Steps here and detailed some of my own thoughts and recommendations:

1. Get a great headshot. This is often the first perception a potential client will have of you. A good image of you smiling and dressed sharply makes you more competent, likeable and influential in the person's eyes. I prefer a real picture of yourself. While in some cases a humorous or cartoon-like picture is appropriate, you want to have a real, up-to-date photo somewhere too (not of a random mountain or sunset, nor a photo that's 15 years old).

2. Be discoverable online. We live in an ever-increasing digital world. Do an internet search of your name and see what the results are. Being discoverable isn't just about SEO; it's now about credibility. While imposters supporting nutrition pseudo-science may not be credible, they appear credible in internet searches, so put yourself (and your credentials) out there.

3. Have a professional purpose. Bring your passion. The excitement you have for your niche should shine through in your online presence.

4. Learn to listen and practice empathy. Work on your listening skills to learn from others. Hear people out and effectively share your views with empathy.

5. Practice writing. I understand that everyone isn't a writer, but everyone has to be able to communicate clearly and professionally in written form. Work on it. The more you write, the better you'll get. Hire a writer or editor to review your work, and proofread your own writing (including social media comments) so you come through professionally in every setting.

6. Re-engineer your digital presence. Review all your pages and profiles at least twice a year to be sure they are consistent across the board. Update photos or taglines, links, contact info, etc.

7. Analyze your competitors. Check out what other people in your niche are doing so you can provide a unique service.

8. Craft your personal branding statement. Include your audience, mission and values.

9. Embrace and expound your experience. Start talking about your experiences. Not everyone is reading your CV. By sharing your background and story, you can reach more like-minded clients and customers.

10. Be social by design. Look for new ways to use various platforms to make the most out of your social media. Be friendly and engage - add comments, ask questions and offer answers.

I'm so glad you are here and can enjoy the ride with your fellow entrepreneurs at NEDPG!

In This Issue:

Rosanne Rust, MS, RDN, LDN, is the owner of Rust Nutrition Services, and blogs at Chew the Facts. She's written a few books and works as a nutrition communications consultant. Her passion is fact-finding and translating nutrition data into well-reasoned dietary advice, so people can enjoy eating for good health. As an adventurous mom of three sons, she considers herself a boy expert. She's been there, done that, and is almost done with that. If you call and say "let's go," she's ready, especially if it's to hop a plane to her happy place in Venice, Florida.

Power of Protein: Quality Matters!

Protein is naturally found in a variety of animal and plant foods. But did you know not all protein is created equal?

- High-quality proteins are those that provide all the essential amino acids the body needs to function properly. Foods vary in their protein quality as not all proteins are equivalent sources of essential amino acids.

- Whey protein, a high-quality protein naturally found in milk, is one of the best sources of essential amino acids for a relatively modest amount of calories.

- Some experts recommend eating 20-30g of high-quality protein at each meal to help build a higher protein diet to support weight management, active lifestyles and healthy aging.[1-4] Research shows that ~10-15 grams of essential amino acids per meal, including ~2-3 grams of leucine, can help rebuild muscle.

Dedicated U.S. dairy farmers provide enough milk to make the U.S. the largest single country producer and exporter of whey in the world.*

Consider how 25g of protein stacks up across a variety of sources[†]:

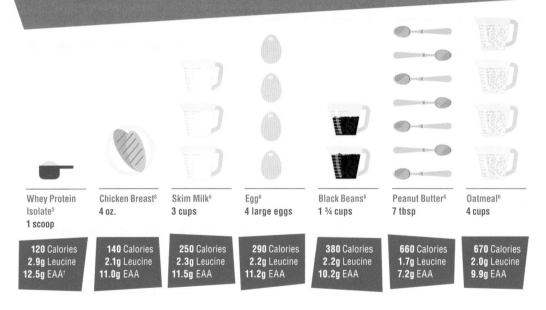

Whey Protein Isolate[5] 1 scoop	Chicken Breast[6] 4 oz.	Skim Milk[6] 3 cups	Egg[6] 4 large eggs	Black Beans[6] 1 ¾ cups	Peanut Butter[6] 7 tbsp	Oatmeal[6] 4 cups
120 Calories 2.9g Leucine 12.5g EAA[†]	**140** Calories 2.1g Leucine 11.0g EAA	**250** Calories 2.3g Leucine 11.5g EAA	**290** Calories 2.2g Leucine 11.2g EAA	**380** Calories 2.2g Leucine 10.2g EAA	**660** Calories 1.7g Leucine 7.2g EAA	**670** Calories 2.0g Leucine 9.9g EAA

* U.S. production data from USDA Economics, Statistics, and Market Information System (April 2017). European production data from *Annual Production Series of Dairy Products*, Eurostat Agriculture and Rural Development (Jan 2017). U.S. export data from U.S. Census Bureau Trade Data (2016). Global export data obtained from Global Trade Atlas® (September 2017).

† Examples of the amount of food needed for ~25 grams of protein are for illustrative purposes only. Consult a registered dietitian to help build a meal plan that meets your individual goals. The recommended amount of protein per day for adults is 0.8 g/kg body weight or 10-35% of energy intake.

1 Leidy HJ, et al. The role of protein in weight loss and maintenance. Am J Clin Nutr. 2015;101 (Suppl):1320S-9S.

2 Thomas DT, et al. Position of the Academy of Nutrition and Dietetics, Dietitians of Canada, and the American College of Sports Medicine: Nutrition and Athletic Performance. J Acad Nutr Diet. 2016;116(3):501-28.

3 Bauer J, et al. Evidence-based recommendations for optimal dietary protein intake in older people: a position paper from the PROT-AGE Study Group. J Am Med Dir Assoc. 2013;14(8):542-59.

4 Paddon-Jones D, et al. Protein and healthy aging. Am J Clin Nutr. 2015;101(Suppl):1339S-45S.

5 Whey Protein Isolate Nutrition Panel. Available at http://www.gnc.com/whey-protein/GNCProPerfornace-100WheyIsolate.html

6 USDA National Nutrient Database for Standard Reference, Release 28. 2016. Available at https://ndb.nal.usda.gov/ndb/.

Visit wheyprotein.nationaldairycouncil.org to learn more about high-quality protein and whey protein benefits and recipes.

Planning and organizing is the next step in creating a focused message. Break down a message into several key points and use them to organize the writing. Follow a logical sequence in presenting information. Place key points at the beginning, followed by details and supportive evidence, and close with practical tips and motivation to apply the information.

Choosing a title can be daunting or it can be fun. Titles and subtitles must communicate the main points. Depending on the audience, make it fun by choosing titles that are catchy and concise. For example, use "Eating for Your Heart" and "Go Nuts for Nuts" versus "The Cardiovascular Benefits of Consuming Complex Carbohydrates" and "Diets High in Almonds Increase High-Density Cholesterol." Titles and headings are key tools for organizing writing, and they can help the reader interpret the information. It is important that titles, email subject lines, and headings are engaging and draw a reader in. In an email newsletter, consider that if the subject line doesn't grab a reader's attention immediately, they may not click to open or read it at all.

When compiling ideas, bring similar concepts together and place them in a logical order. Selecting subtitles and distinct topics to cover are ways to organize. Good organization can help the reader interpret the information. When considering the length of the newsletter or handout, remember that less is more: Do not overwhelm the reader. Offer the information and get to the point concisely.

Use Direct Calls to Action

An element of persuasion must be used to call the reader to action. In the area of nutrition, audiences are free to make their own choices. Therefore, the information must be presented in a way to encourage action toward change. Refer to Chapter 12 for the behavioral elements of making decisions surrounding nutrition and health choices. Write calls to action using motivational messaging.

Russell offers tips for effective persuasive writing,[5] which will be summarized here. The examples provided to illustrate each tip could be from a newsletter article or handout encouraging registered dietitian nutritionists (RDNs) to promote urban gardens and farmers markets to limited-resource audiences as an approach to reduce the risk of chronic inflammation.

- Support the message with evidence-based research. Offering an explanation using information resulting from research lays the groundwork for the persuasive messaging.

  Example: "According to the *Journal of the Academy of Nutrition and Dietetics* in June 2018, the results from the NHANES suggest that 'food security status may be associated with dietary inflammatory potential, which is hypothesized to play a role in multiple chronic health conditions.'[6] Therefore, understanding where clients' food is coming from is essential when discussing menu planning."

- Make a strong claim about the subject, making certain to keep a third-person point of view.

  Example: "Creative menu planning can be an option when considering the availability of food banks, pantries, and soup kitchens in the area."

- Support the claim with evidence that appeals to the audience.

  Example: "Finding fresh fruits and vegetables at a neighborhood farmers market can be helpful for increasing nutrients in the diet."

- Ensure the messaging is logical.

  Example: "More fresh foods are becoming available in urban areas where they hadn't been before."

- Avoid deceiving or making big promises. The reader is more likely to agree with a claim if it is reasonable.

  Example: "Good health comes from healthful habits. Clients have what it takes to improve health right in their neighborhood."

- Organize supporting evidence effectively to clearly state such information.

  Example: "Inflammation can lead to chronic health problems. Local urban gardens and farmers markets have fresh fruits and vegetables that can decrease inflammation."

Follow a Uniform Layout and Design

Employ a uniform layout and design that helps the reader of the newsletter or handout, whether published online or in print, locate and read the information provided.

Elements to consider are:

- format;
- images and graphics;
- fonts and colors;
- white space;
- bullets and numbers;
- boxes and borders;
- headings and subheadings; and
- logos.

Consider the visual appeal of a layout. The elements listed can all enhance the appearance of a document when artfully designed.

Layout can also enhance the interactivity of a piece of writing. In a handout, consider whether space should be left to add notes, to fill in blanks, or to give short answers. This can increase retention and learning. In digital formats, create clickable links to promote accessing further information. Make sure the documents are readable on a variety of devices and formats.

The Academy of Nutrition and Dietetics Foundation, along with Feeding America and the National Dairy Council, created the Developing and Assessing Nutrition Education Handouts (DANEH) checklist (Figure 23.3).[7] See the resources section at the end of the chapter for where to find the full checklist, which incorporates 22 constructs identified as quality indicators to be included in nutrition education handouts. The constructs are categorized into five main topic areas: content, behavior focus, cultural sensitivity, written word, and organization/readability. Upon completion of the checklist, a score can be calculated to determine the handout's acceptance or approval score.

Refer to Chapter 22 for further descriptions of various elements of layout and design.

FIGURE 23.3 Introduction to the Developing and Assessing Nutrition Education Handouts checklist

Developing & Assessing Nutrition Education Handouts (DANEH) Checklist

The Developing & Assessing Nutrition Education Handouts (DANEH) checklist was created by the Academy of Nutrition and Dietetics Foundation as part of the Future of Food (FOF) project. The purpose of the DANEH checklist is twofold: 1) to screen existing nutrition education handouts in order to establish the inclusion/exclusion of important quality components, and; 2) as a tool to use in developing quality nutrition education handouts. The checklist incorporates 21 constructs identified as quality indicators to be included in nutrition education handouts, based on a literature review. The constructs are categorized into five main topic areas: content; behavior focus; cultural sensitivity; written word; and organization/readability.

Results of DANEH validation testing proved that DANEH is a valid tool and has good interrater reliability for handouts for a general low-income audience when RDNs are the reviewers. It is recommended that a score of 18 out of 21 possible points (86%) by two reviewers is the cutpoint for handouts to be considered high quality handouts. For handouts with a score of 17, it is recommended that a 3rd reviewer rates the handout using DANEH. It is recommended that handouts with a score of 16 or less are not considered high quality.

What Are Practical Strategies for Communicating via Newsletters and Handouts?

Many factors go into developing a successful strategy intended to inform or persuade an audience. Aligning message, audience, and communication tools allows nutrition communicators to determine the best approach. Keep in mind that not all communication tools serve the same function; therefore, the plan of action for each tool differs as well. The following are practical strategies for communicating via newsletters and handouts that have been tested and proved effective by nutrition communicators.

Four Guidelines for Effective Newsletters

Newsletters provide the most current and accurate information on a specific topic or from a particular organization that is of interest to a target audience. The role of newsletters in nutrition communication is to educate audience members and form relationships with them while establishing the communicator as a credible resource.[1] The best strategies for fulfilling those functions are to:

- be organized,
- stay consistent,
- always inform, and
- partner with others.

Nutrition communicators who apply these strategies when communicating via newsletters will more effectively reach their goals.

Newsletters are designed to be one-stop shops for information on a particular topic. A practical strategy for communicating via newsletter is to ensure that the newsletter is organized. That means that each issue should follow a similar layout and design.

BE ORGANIZED

Organized newsletters help nutrition communicators inform or persuade audiences in several ways. Based on best practices, the structured format establishes a sense of familiarity and brand identity, which can breed trust.[1] Over time, audience members come to know exactly what to expect from the

Be Organized

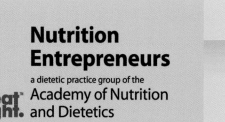

Notice the Nutrition Entrepreneurs dietetic practice group logo in the upper right-hand corner, which brands the newsletter, and the "In This Issue" sidebar, which quickly orients readers to the newsletter's contents. An article from the chairperson is always featured on the front page, and information on mini-meetings is always on the back page. An organized strategy for communicating via newsletters establishes a sense of familiarity that audience members come to rely on.

newsletter and where to find certain information. By quickly and easily accessing the information that they need, when they need it, audience members save time and leave satisfied. This keeps them coming back for more, which creates additional opportunities for interaction. Organized newsletters also provide a professional appearance, which adds to the credibility of nutrition communicators and expands their field of influence. See Box 23.1.

Tips for implementing an organized strategy:
- Use a template to ensure a uniform layout.
  - Work with a graphic designer to develop a custom template; learn how to develop a custom template; or download a free version online.
- Identify colors, fonts, logos, and images that will resonate with audience members and align with your brand.
- Incorporate headings and subheadings to clearly delineate sections and increase readability.
- Integrate call-out boxes and sidebars to add visual interest and draw attention to certain

information, such as award recognitions or upcoming events.

STAY CONSISTENT

Another practical strategy for communicating via newsletters is to maintain consistency. To be effective, newsletters must be reliable in terms of timing and quality.[1,2]

Newsletters should be circulated on a set schedule, such as weekly, monthly, or quarterly. This form of consistency can build trust as audience members come to rely on receiving the newsletter on a particular date. It can also breed loyalty as some members may begin to set aside time to read the newsletter on, or shortly after, the day it is scheduled for release.

Ensure that each newsletter follows the appropriate guidelines for excellence in writing, as outlined in the previous section on best practices. Content is presented in simple, common terms that are appropriate for the audience and purpose of the newsletter. Acronyms are spelled out and technical jargon is typically avoided. Key messages are clearly articulated and repeated for emphasis. This

form of consistency enhances readability, which increases audience members' use and retention of those messages. It also contributes to the nutrition communicator's credibility and can open the door to future audience interactions. See Box 23.2.

Following are tips for staying consistent:

- Assess resources, schedules, and availability of staffing before identifying a distribution date and frequency.
- Once a date is set, develop a production schedule that accounts for the various elements needed to produce a single issue, such as research, content development, editing, graphic design, printing, and shipping if using a print version.
- Conduct regular check-ins during the production schedule to ensure that the schedule is being met and adjust as needed.
- Develop standards for writing and design to create a cohesive newsletter.
- Allocate time in the production schedule for peer review, proofreading, and copy editing.

ALWAYS INFORM

By definition, newsletters should be informative. The content should be both current and of value to the audience. If newsletters are seen as an ongoing conversation with audience members, then each issue must advance the dialogue in some way. This is done by including articles on the most recent research or developments; tips that are based on contemporary, evidence-based practices; and announcements about upcoming events.

Successful newsletters include timely topics and, when possible, get out ahead of the issues that are of interest to audience members.[1] Nutrition science is constantly evolving, and the dietetics industry is constantly changing, so it is important to stay abreast of the latest research and the newest technology. This establishes nutrition communicators as subject-matter experts in their field and results in audiences viewing these experts as the go-to source for information. This helps maintain existing interactions and creates openings to inform or persuade future audience members. See Box 23.3.

Implement these ideas for informative strategy:

- Read journals and professional publications associated with the newsletter's topic.
- Connect with experts in the nutrition field through professional associations to stay abreast of the latest scientific advancements.

BOX 23.2

Stay Consistent

Spring 2018
Volume XXXVI
Number 4

Branding: Discovering Your Unique Voice

The Nutrition Entrepreneurs dietetic practice group newsletter is distributed on a quarterly basis. The consistent strategy for communicating via newsletters builds trusts among audience members.

BOX 23.3 # Always Inform

1. Get a great headshot. This is often the first perception a potential client will have of you. A good image of you smiling and dressed sharply makes you more competent, likeable and influential in the person's eyes. I prefer a real picture of yourself. While in some cases a humorous or cartoon-like picture is appropriate, you want to have a real, up-to-date photo somewhere too (not of a random mountain or sunset, nor a photo that's 15 years old).

2. Be discoverable online. We live in an ever-increasing digital world. Do an internet search of your name and see what the results are. Being discoverable isn't just about SEO; it's now about credibility. While imposters supporting nutrition pseudo-science may not be credible, they appear credible in internet searches, so put yourself (and your credentials) out there.

3. Have a professional purpose. Bring your

In the article "Let Consistency Be Your Guide," the author offers actionable advice on how to build a branding style guide to help nutrition entrepreneurs clarify their business's identity. The informative strategy for communicating via newsletters establishes nutrition communicators as the go-to source for valuable information.

- Connect with experts in other fields, such as business and marketing, to identify common trends.
- Interact with members of an audience to gauge their interest in and knowledge about a particular topic.
- Monitor traditional news outlets and social media platforms.

PARTNER WITH OTHERS

Newsletters that are organized, consistent, and informative can build credibility among audiences. In

BOX 23.4 # Partner with Others

 ## RDN's Who Have Mastered Branding

Toby Amidor
Specialty Group Leader: Authors and Writers

Branding is a way that clients and readers get to know you. It helps promote recognition of your company, sets you apart from the competition, and builds credibility and trust. Branding also helps generate referrals so you can get more business. Whether you're starting a new brand or decide it's time to rebrand your business, it's important to do your research to see who's got it right. These three dietitians are diverse in what they do, yet they all have mastered the branding of their company

Melissa Joy Dobbins, MS, RDN, CDE

Melissa's brand is The Guilt Free RD® and website is Sound Bites® (SoundBitesRD. com) where she promotes "sound science, smart nutrition and good food." Her popular Sound Bites® podcast includes guests such as SciBabe Yvette d'Entremont, Ellie Krieger and Dr. Michael Roizen.

Melissa's advice to finding your brand: Spend lots of time thinking about "who" you are. Get some advice from a branding expert, or someone who has created a strong brand, so you can explore the different areas of your personality, attributes and core values. Don't rush the process – it could take months.

Sharon Palmer, RDN

You've probably seen Sharon's brand, *The Plant Powered Dietitian* (sharonpalmer.com), online, at FNCE® or in publications. Sharon combined her love of food and writing and focuses her expertise in plant-based nutrition. Her work includes authoring several books, working as a spokesperson with plant-based brands and creating mouth-watering, plant-based recipes for her blog.

Sharon's advice on developing brand identity: When my first book was about to come out (*The Plant-Powered Diet*), my publisher and PR person were discussing various titles and we decided on "The Plant-Powered Diet." We did a Google search and at that time no one was using it. I got the domains and then they suggested using the name as my byline: *The Plant Powered Dietitian.* Now, EVERYONE is using the term *plant-powered!* So, it's really important to jump on something when you have the idea.

Jessica Levinson, MS, RDN

Jessica (jessicalevinson.com) is a culinary nutrition expert focusing on childhood nutrition. Her tagline is "nutritious and delicious recipes for the entire family," and you'll see her cooking together with her beautiful kids in many of her social media posts. Although Jessica has been around for quite some time, she decided it was time to rebrand her website.

Jessica's advice on rebranding: Think through your target audience and get some feedback from people in that audience to see what resonates for them. It's also important to look at what is already trademarked before coming up with a brand name. I decided to switch to using my name rather than a specific brand because I wanted my site to have a longer shelf life. I can always update pictures down the road, but if your focus is too narrow you can box yourself into one area without room to grow.

In the *Ventures* article "Three RDNs Who Have Mastered Branding," the author teams up with three different dietitians who share their firsthand knowledge of how to brand a business with nutrition entrepreneurs. The partnering strategy for communicating via newsletters takes a collaborative approach to educating audience members, which enhances the nutrition communicator's credibility.

turn, audience members may begin to trust nutrition communicators. Once they have the audience's confidence, nutrition communicators can inform or persuade audience members. See Box 23.4.

What happens when a current issue that is of interest to audience members is outside the nutrition communicator's area of expertise? A practical strategy is to enlist the help of a subject-matter expert who is familiar with the issue. A nutrition communicator may partner with a knowledgeable source to provide audience members with accurate and up-to-date information.[2] This can be done by asking an expert to author an article, provide an interview, develop a list of helpful hints, or identify relevant upcoming events to highlight in the newsletter. By doing so, the nutrition communicator maintains audience trust, enhances credibility, and builds relationships with other professionals.

When partnering with others, consider the following:

- Join professional associations to connect with other experts in and out of the nutrition field.
- Establish formal and informal collaborations with like-minded professionals to share expertise and exchange intellectual capital.
- Include professional contact information and an open invitation to reach out with questions, comments, or collaboration ideas.

Four Guidelines for Effective Handouts

Handouts are complementary documents that help audience members recall and use the information provided during a presentation, speech, workshop, counseling session, or other audience interaction. The role of handouts in nutrition communication is to echo key messages, expand on current themes, and reach new audiences. The best strategies for fulfilling those functions are to:

- reinforce lessons learned,
- include supplemental information,
- make the handout stand alone, and
- deliver the handout at the appropriate time.

BOX 23.5 Reinforce Lessons Learned

- High-quality proteins are those that provide all the essential amino acids the body needs to function properly. Foods vary in their protein quality as not all proteins are equivalent sources of essential amino acids.

- Whey protein, a high-quality protein naturally found in milk, is one of the best sources of essential amino acids for a relatively modest amount of calories.

- Some experts recommend eating 20-30g of high-quality protein at each meal to help build a higher protein diet to support weight management, active lifestyles and healthy aging.[1-4] Research shows that ~10-15 grams of essential amino acids per meal, including ~2-3 grams of leucine, can help rebuild muscle.

"The Power of Protein: Quality Matters!" handout provides a brief, three-bullet summary of key points and serves as an attractive visual reminder of the event. The supportive strategy for communicating via handouts helps audience members retain information and encourages them to use it.

Nutrition communicators who apply these strategies when communicating via handouts will more effectively reach their goals.

REINFORCE LESSONS LEARNED

Handouts are written takeaways that capture the themes addressed during a presentation, speech, workshop, counseling session, or other audience interaction. The intent is for audience members to revisit and use the material at a later date.[3,4] For this reason, a practical strategy for communicating via handouts is to reinforce the lessons learned. This is done by developing a professional document that summarizes content as opposed to duplicating it. See Box 23.5.

Nutrition communicators utilize supportive handouts in two ways. First, the brief synopsis is a concise, easy-to-read document that audience members can read and reread. This creates additional opportunities to reinforce key messages. Second, this review sheet serves as a physical reminder of the original discussion.[3,4] The visual prompt helps audience members retain information and encourages them to use or act on it. Together, these efforts help to inform or persuade audiences beyond the initial interaction.

Tips for implementing a supportive strategy:
- Recap, but do not repeat content verbatim.
- Create handouts in conjunction with presentation slides, talking points, or session outlines, not as an afterthought.
- Prepare handouts with the same level of professionalism and quality used to develop presentation slides and other materials.
- Ensure handouts have the same look and tone as presentation slides and other materials to solidify brand identity.

INCLUDE SUPPLEMENTAL INFORMATION

In addition to summarizing content that was discussed during the initial audience interaction, handouts can also be used to expand on those themes.[3] This is done by including new information in the handout that was not provided at the time of the interaction.

Effective handouts offer more detailed data or a fresh perspective to advance the topic and further engage audience members.[3] This supplemental information continues the learning experience beyond the initial interaction, which helps to further inform or persuade audiences. It also gives

Include Supplemental Information

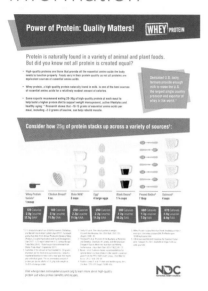

During a speech or counseling session, a presenter may use general terms, such as *high-quality protein* and *recommended amounts per meal*. The presenter may also offer a handout, such as "The Power of Protein: Quality Matters!" handout, which identifies specific sources of high-quality protein and the amount of food needed to meet the recommendations. The supplemental strategy for communicating via handouts gives audience members a reason to keep the handout and refer back to it after the event.

audience members a reason to keep the handout or share it with others. The longer a handout remains in circulation, the more opportunities there are for reexamination. See Box 23.6.

Here are some tips for implementing a supplemental strategy:

- Collect all pertinent information related to the topic.
- Taking into account audience interest and time constraints, determine the amount of information to include in the interaction.
- Identify pieces of information to withhold from the interaction.

Make It Stand Alone[a]

"The Power of Protein: Quality Matters!" handout is an example of a stand-alone handout. It offers an independent synopsis of the topic as well as additional facts. The stand-alone strategy for communicating via handouts appeals to both audience members and other individuals who did not participate in the initial event.

[a] Refer to Figure 23.2 for a larger image.

- Present the new information in the handout as a continuation of the material discussed during the initial interaction.

MAKE THE HANDOUT STAND ALONE

Handouts are designed with two audiences in mind. Nutrition communicators first consider the interests and needs of those attending a speech, presentation, workshop, counseling session, or other audience interaction. Then they consider the interests and needs of those who did not participate in the initial interaction but received the handout from someone who did. These combined considerations allow the nutrition communicator to develop an independent and universally beneficial handout.

The stand-alone strategy for communicating via handouts is critical because it allows nutrition communicators to extend their area of influence.[3] While it is difficult to determine the motivations of unknown audience members, the fact that they received the handout from a current audience member indicates that they share a common interest. Where they differ is in their needs. Those who participated in the audience interaction may need reinforcing and reminding. Those who are new to the discussion need to be brought up to speed. Skilled nutrition communicators develop content that addresses all these needs in one handout, thereby informing or persuading a larger audience. See Box 23.7.

Tips for implementing a stand-alone strategy include the following:

- Consider the initial audience and a broader audience simultaneously.
- Do not assume the audience member has participated in the initial interaction or has background knowledge of the issue.
- Have someone who is not familiar with the topic or interaction review the handout for clarity.

Deliver the Handout at the Appropriate Time

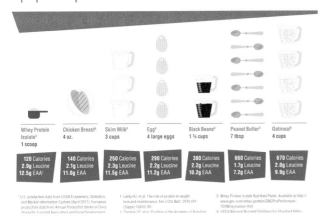

Whey Protein Isolate[5] 1 scoop	Chicken Breast[6] 4 oz.	Skim Milk[6] 3 cups	Egg[6] 4 large eggs	Black Beans[6] 1 ¾ cups	Peanut Butter[6] 7 tbsp	Oatmeal[6] 4 cups
120 Calories 2.9g Leucine 12.5g EAA[7]	**140** Calories 2.1g Leucine 11.0g EAA	**250** Calories 2.3g Leucine 11.5g EAA	**290** Calories 2.2g Leucine 11.2g EAA	**380** Calories 2.2g Leucine 10.2g EAA	**660** Calories 1.7g Leucine 7.2g EAA	**670** Calories 2.0g Leucine 9.9g EAA

* U.S. production data from USDA Economics, Statistics, and Market Information System (April 2017); European production data from *Annual Production Series or Dairy Products; Eurostat Agriculture and Rural Development*

1. Leidy HJ, et al. The role of protein in weight loss and maintenance. Am J Clin Nutr. 2015;101 (Suppl):1320S-9S.
2. Thomas DT, et al. Position of the Academy of Nutrition

5. Whey Protein Isolate Nutrition Panel. Available at http://www.gnc.com/whey-protein/GNCProPerfornace-100WheyIsolate.html
6. USDA National Nutrient Database for Standard Refer-

"The Power of Protein: Quality Matters!" handout is an example of a handout that could be distributed after interacting with audience members. The chart identifying different sources of protein serves as a good reminder of the material discussed. The timely strategy for communicating via handouts keeps audience members focused on the presentation.

- Avoid abbreviations, acronyms, and technical jargon.
- Provide additional resources.
- Include contact information, if appropriate.

DELIVER THE HANDOUT AT THE APPROPRIATE TIME

There is some debate among nutrition communicators over the best time to distribute handouts to audience members.[3,4] Should it be before, during, or after a speech, presentation, workshop, counseling session, or other audience interaction? The answer may depend on the intent of the handout. Is it a traditional handout meant to remind audience members of the material discussed during the interaction along with some additional facts as food for thought? Or is it an interactive worksheet meant to be analyzed and completed during the event? Consider the pros and cons of distributing handouts before, during, and after an audience interaction.

There are several reasons nutrition communicators distribute handouts before interacting with audience members: the handout may be intended to be an interactive worksheet requiring audience members to respond to questions, develop a list of priorities, or record their thoughts; the material to be discussed may be highly technical or detail-oriented; or the planned interaction may be long, such as a full- or half-day seminar.[3]

The pros of distributing handouts *before* interacting include the following:

- It gives audience members something to take notes on.
- It allows audience members to relax and listen.
- It prevents disruptions to the flow of the presentation.

The cons of distributing handouts before interacting include:

- It may cause distraction due to shuffling of paper.
- Audience members may pay more attention to the handout than to the presenter.

There are different reasons nutrition communicators may wait to distribute handouts until needed during an audience interaction. For example, a presenter may wait if the handout is intended to be an interactive worksheet and he or she wants to draw specific attention to that material.[3]

The pros of distributing handouts *during* an interaction include the following:

- It keeps audience members focused on the material being discussed prior to receiving the handout.
- It alerts audience members to the fact that the material in the handout is noteworthy.
- It intentionally breaks up the presentation to help keep audience interest and focus, particularly during long presentations.

The cons of distributing handouts during interaction include:

- It may disrupt the flow of the presentation.
- It may cause distraction due to shuffling of paper.
- It may be difficult to regain the audience's attention.

Finally, there are several reasons nutrition communicators distribute handouts after interacting with audience members: the handout may be a written takeaway that serves as a reminder of what was discussed during the audience interaction; the nutrition communicator may want to incorporate an element of surprise in the presentation; or the nutrition communicator may view the handout as a parting gift or thank you to audience members for participating in the event.[3]

The pros of distributing handouts *after* an interaction include the following:

- It prevents disruptions to the flow of the presentation.
- It eliminates distractions due to shuffling of paper.
- It reduces the temptation to read the handout instead of listening to the presenter.
- It allows the presenter to reveal information throughout the interaction as opposed to all at once.

The cons of distributing handouts after interaction include:

- It may cause audience members to focus more on note-taking than on listening.

Regardless of when a handout is distributed, there are a few key points about distribution that are universal. It is essential that nutrition communicators know their audience so that the handout can go beyond what audience members already know about a topic and provide what they need to know about a topic. It is also important for nutrition communicators to understand their audience's preferred learning style. Do audience members prefer to learn by listening or reading? Are they easily distracted? Do they have the ability to focus on the presentation? The answers to these questions may assist in determining the ideal timing for handout distribution. See Box 23.8.

Here are some tips for implementing a timely strategy:

- Know the audience's preferred learning style.
- Identify the intent for the handout. Is it intended to be a postinteraction recap and reminder? Or will it be used as an in-session interactive worksheet?
- If distributed before the interaction, consider leaving blank spaces where audience members can take notes and fill in missing information during the interaction to hold their attention.
- If distributed during the interaction, do not cover new material while distributing the handout; tell a story that reinforces an earlier point until audience members have returned their attention to the presentation.
- If distributed after the interaction, let audience members know at the beginning of the interaction that they will be given a handout at the end to decrease note-taking and increase listening. Alert the audience throughout to what is included in the handout as well as what they may want to write down.

See Chapter 16 for more on learning styles.

KEY POINTS

Reach Target Audiences with Newsletters and Handouts

1 Newsletters and handouts are communication tools that provide written support for informing or persuading target audiences for particular purposes. Nutrition communicators use these tools in different ways to achieve that common goal.

2 Newsletters and handouts are most effective when they are audience-focused, deliver clear messages, use direct calls to action, and follow a uniform layout and design.

3 Newsletters and handouts serve different functions; therefore, the strategies for communicating via these tools differ as well. Newsletters, which provide information on a specific topic to a target audience, should be organized, consistent, informative, and collaborative. Handouts, which are complementary documents distributed to audience members, should reinforce lessons learned, provide supplemental information, exist as stand-alone documents, and be delivered at the appropriate time.

RESOURCES

Nutrition Entrepreneurs dietetic practice group—Ventures newsletter (Spring 2018): https://drive.google.com/file/d/1VQRLcQRtGpcbthcmpye8X9DW62An4oXQ/view

National Dairy Council, Power of Protein: Quality Matters!" handout: www.nationaldairycouncil.org/content/2017/power-of-protein-quality-matters

Developing and Assessing Nutrition Education Handouts (DANEH) checklist: http://hungerandhealth.feedingamerica.org/wp-content/uploads/2013/12/Nutrition-Education-Handout-Checklist-rev-10-17-13.pdf

REFERENCES

1. Teixeira S, Cardoso P, Pimenta N. The newsletter in the context of public relations and digital communication: the sector of services of health care and wellbeing in Portugal. *Int J Market Comm New Media.* 2015;3(5):107-132.
2. Luke K. 10 makeover tips for your newsletter. *J Fin Plan.* 2011;January/February:16-17.
3. Kroenke K. Handouts: making the lecture portable. *Med Teach.* 1991;13(3):199-203.
4. University of Texas at Austin, University of Texas Libraries. Handouts. Accessed September 4, 2018. http://legacy.lib.utexas.edu/services/instruction/tips/tt/tt_handout.html
5. Russell K. *Write Now.* 2nd ed. McGraw-Hill; 2016.
6. Bergmans RS, Palta M, Robert SA, et al. Associations between food security status and dietary inflammatory potential within lower-income adults from the United States National Health and Nutrition Examination Survey, cycles 2007 to 2014. *J Acad Nutr Diet.* 2018;118(6):994-1005.
7. Academy of Nutrition and Dietetics Foundation, Feeding America, National Dairy Council. Developing and Assessing Nutrition Education Handouts (DANEH) checklist. Hunger and Health website. Accessed September 22, 2018. http://hungerandhealth.feedingamerica.org/wp-content/uploads/2013/12/Nutrition-Education-Handout-Checklist-rev-10-17-13.pdf

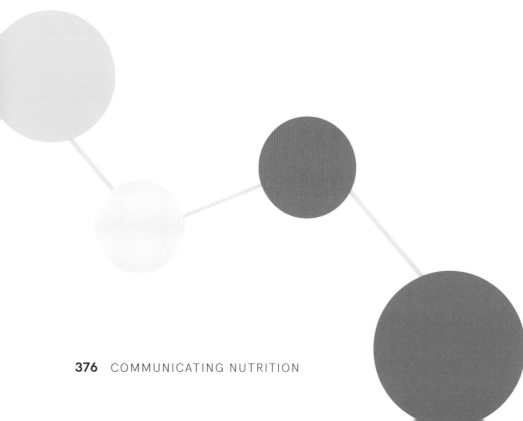

CHAPTER 24

Create Video to Maximize Impact

Betsy Ramirez, MEd, RDN
and Ann Gaba, EdD, RD, CDN, CDCES, FAND

"Video is a valuable communication tool that allows the nutrition professional to captivate and connect with an audience through a multisensory experience that can be shared with others."

"A picture is worth a thousand words ... and a video is worth a thousand pictures!" —ANKALA V. SUBBARAO

Introduction

Why is video important? Is it just moving pictures or something more? Video goes beyond the written word. It is a powerful tool that allows viewers to experience the message as if they were there. This experience can be more effective than words alone. Video can bring difficult concepts to life and has the power to change behaviors. It engages and ignites emotions, becoming a great tool for learning. Video allows for storytelling and creates an opportunity for engagement with an intended audience. It is impossible to ignore the impact video can make, and it has become easier than ever for people to produce their own videos, even as amateurs.

This chapter answers four questions:

- What are the benefits of communicating with video?
- What types of video can food and nutrition professionals utilize?
- What are the steps for planning a quality video?
- What are the components of video setup and production?

Consider ways to implement the use of video in nutrition communication to maximize the impact of a message. Video creation is no longer only feasible for professional videographers. With knowledge and practice, a nutrition communicator can create videos to effectively show and tell messages to audiences compellingly and creatively.

What Are the Benefits of Communicating with Video?

"Tell me and I forget, teach me and I may remember, involve me and I learn." The words of Benjamin Franklin ring true with the power of video. Video has the ability to create connections through a multisensory experience that can impact any audience.

Promotes Multisensory Learning

With the surging popularity of video, registered dietitian nutritionists (RDNs) have a prime opportunity to inform, influence, and inspire people through this digital medium. It can bring nutrition messages alive to the intended audience. It's a multisensory experience that can promote behavior change. As nutrition experts, RDNs have a unique opportunity to embrace video and share healthy recipes or evidence-based messages. As easy as it is to pick up a camera and record, it's important to understand how an audience learns and how to hook the ideal audience.

A primary goal of any video is to capture the intended audience's attention and promote learning. Video supports learning and retention through a multisensory experience. As described in Chapter 16, a number of educational theories and models support the concept that multisensory learning improves retention of the content presented. Recall that Edgar Dale was one of the progenitors of experiential learning. As illustrated in Figure 16.7 on page 270, Dale's Cone of Experience[1] suggests that watching a video promotes greater retention of information than simply reading or hearing. Refer to Box 24.1 for six ways to improve learning and retention with video.

Cognitive load theory was developed by John Sweller.[5] According to this theory, sensory inputs are first processed in the working memory, which has a very limited capacity, prior to being encoded into long-term memory. Because of the limits of working memory, the audience is selective about the information presented. Receiving information from multiple senses, such as visual and auditory, can increase the capacity of working memory, thus enhancing learning.[6] Video communications target working memory with visual and auditory messaging that can be viewed repeatedly and even shared.

Allows Replicability

The replicability of video content is an immense benefit. It allows a communicator to do the work once and share it with multiple audiences on many different platforms, whether in a classroom or on social media. Video allows for audiences across time, place, and format to experience the exact same information, taught in the exact same way. Research has shown the efficacy of incorporating video content into education for dental students,[7] medical students,[8-10] nursing students,[11] and patients.[12-14] Use of video has also been shown to be valuable in populations with limited literacy.[15,16]

Uses Storytelling to Connect

Storytelling is an essential part of captivating an audience. A nutrition story may be thought of as being like a children's fairy tale, with characters, a plot, a conflict, and a happily-ever-after ending. Storytelling can be an effective strategy for nutrition communication when an audience's problem is solved and a potential happily-ever-after ending is provided, with evidence-based messaging that can positively impact their lives.

Video provides the opportunity to humanize content. When a nutrition communicator tells the audience about personal experiences, they are engaged on an emotional level. It creates the opportunity to develop trust. That trust can convert viewers into new clients or social media followers.

 ## Ways to Improve Video Retention[2,3,4]

Eliminate distractors: Include only content that is essential for the target audience. Content should be age and skill-level appropriate. More advanced learners will be able to process more material than those learners for whom the topic is entirely new.

Use signals: Use on-screen indicators (eg, arrows or highlighted words) to point out key information.

Segment content: Break down information into segments or steps, and place these into a logical sequence. Pause filming in between each step to ensure the information is being shared at an appropriate pace.

Match up music or audio: Music or audio should work together with the video content. Any music added should not overpower the visual content. It should complement it.

Ask and answer questions: Anticipate questions that an audience is likely to have, and then provide answers to those questions. Polling an audience beforehand is a great way to engage the audience and answer their questions directly.

Engage emotions: When hearing a story or a personal experience, an audience becomes engaged when they have empathy and experience the story with the speaker. The recording of memories by the human brain is influenced by emotional states.

The trust built from effective video communications can increase a food and nutrition professional's online presence and authority. Refer to Box 24.2 (page 380) for storytelling concepts to consider.

What Types of Video Can Food and Nutrition Professionals Utilize?

After choosing to incorporate video into nutrition communications, determining which type of video to create is the next decision. While the options may be overwhelming, it's essential to understand what type of video should be used.

BOX 24.2 # Storytelling Concepts

Video is a perfect platform for telling a narrative. Whether solving a dinner problem or guiding viewers through a gluten-free diet, a story requires essential elements.

Characters: Who is involved in the story?

Setting: Where does the story take place?

Plot: What is the main idea? What are the beginning, middle, and end of the entire story?

Problem: What is the problem that needs to be solved?

Resolution: How is the problem solved?

Food Videos

Food is a primary focus within the nutrition profession, so it's no wonder that food videos would be popular among RDNs. Food videos, also called recipe videos, do not require a team of people to film or really expensive equipment. They are often called hands-in-pans videos because only the cook's hands are shown in the video, which is recorded from a stationary and overhead position. These are videos of an actual preparation of a recipe condensed into a brief, generally 1-minute-long demonstration, showing the viewer a visual breakdown of the steps involved. The visual representation of the recipe entices viewers to make the recipe or share it with others on social media platforms. Refer to Box 24.3 to see what preparing for a food video entails.

Cooking Shows

Since the days of Julia Child, cooking show formats have been the most commonly viewed video format in the food arena. When the Food Network came on the scene in 1993, cooking shows became widely popular. They continue to flourish as additional channels appear, such as the Cooking Channel, which was started in 2010. Although not everyone with a passion for food and cooking can be on a major television network, anyone can potentially garner a wide viewership with the advent of online channels, such as YouTube. Online platforms give everyday, stay-at-home cooks the opportunity to have their own web-based cooking show.

A cooking show format allows a food and nutrition professional to develop a relationship with an audience. It provides more opportunity than a food video to elaborate on food and nutrition topics throughout the cooking demonstration. It also requires more preparation and planning than a food video. A cooking show requires an on-air appearance and a structured recipe with talking points. Making a worthwhile cooking video requires a kitchen, equipment, lighting, attention to appearance, and practice. While it is possible to do this solo, it does involve a bigger time commitment. There are pros and cons to this format, especially as regards to time and consistency, but cooking show videos can allow a food and nutrition professional to create a community and a following.

Informational or Educational Videos

Informational or educational videos are one of the most popular types of videos. People look for this type of video for information and instruction. They allow for a variety of formats, such as a question-and-answer session that helps solve a problem. Informational or educational videos should be quick, easy, and useful. These videos focus on the basics of teaching and learning—providing the what, why, and how behind a topic to help build foundational knowledge. A food and nutrition professional can build trust and credibility with an audience using this format.

Equipment needed for these videos can be minimal. Preparation for will require researching and practicing various talking points. Appearance and a background setting with good lighting will also need to be planned before filming.

Educational videos can be created for use in an academic setting. A description of video case studies is featured in the Words of Experience box. Consider ways to create videos to enhance experiential learning. Even better, involve students in the video-creation process to expand learning further.

Promotional Videos

A promotional video has an end goal in mind. It can be a video in which a practitioner introduces himself or herself and explains his or her services. It can also be an opportunity to tell a story or give testimonials. Promotional videos are more likely to play on the viewers' emotions and drive them to action. Before choosing to make a promotional video, knowing the goal and audience is critical for success. A promotional video can be as complex or as simple as desired. Equipment for this type of video depends on what picture will be painted for the viewer.

Livestream Videos

Livestreaming is the newest platform for video. Livestreamed videos allow a communicator to demonstrate and speak in real time to an audience while interacting with them. Audiences love these videos for the suspense and behind-the-scenes look they get while participating. Livestreamed videos boast more engagement than recorded videos. Another advantage of these videos is that they require only one piece of equipment: a phone. They are easy to create and can be downloaded once they are over. Livestreaming has become a viable marketing strategy and one that dietitians should not overlook while promoting their events or businesses.

What Are the Steps for Planning a Quality Video?

High-quality video is well planned, is well composed, and fits the intended audience. Before a video can be made, it is essential to decide what the objective of the video is and to plan content to meet that objective. A well-developed content plan is the core of a quality video. Use the storytelling elements to help with the development of a plan by answering who, what, when, where, and why in the video.

1. Know the Audience

If a practitioner has a blog or a private practice, the target audience is probably clear. If not, the practitioner needs to think about whom to target. Is the target audience male or female? What are their interests? How old are they? What do they want? What social media platforms are they using? How will their needs be met? Where do they go for information? The answers to these questions can help to pinpoint a target market and provide the necessary information to create a quality video that makes an impact.

Planning for a Food Video

1. Choose a tried-and-true recipe that is simple to make.
2. Make a list of ingredients, equipment, and utensils needed for the recipe.
3. Select a location with an appropriate background.
4. Make a list of steps needed to demonstrate the recipe and decide what shots will work based on the steps.
5. Choose a day and time to shoot based on natural light available. Use artificial light if needed.
6. On the day of filming, have all ingredients, equipment, and utensils set up and ready for shooting. Also, have a prepared dish available for "beauty shots" to save time.

 WORDS OF EXPERIENCE

Student Education: Video Case Studies Support Experiential Learning

by Ann Gaba, EdD, RD, CDN, CDCES, FAND

The nutrition profession has increasingly recognized the value of experiential learning in developing nutrition students' practice skills.[17] The more realistic a simulated experience is, the more effective the education provided can be. Yet simulated practice settings, and actors portraying standard or typical patients, can be too costly to provide a realistic option for many educational programs. However, if patient portrayals and likely scenarios in caring for them can be preserved on video, students can have a close approximation of the "live" simulation at a fraction of the cost. Once created, a video can be used over and over and provide consistency in the educational experience. Video case studies are relatively easy to create and do not have to include professional actors. The patients and staff portrayed can even be animated characters, produced with commercially available software. Animated characters eliminate any concerns about patient privacy and allow for easy addition of diverse characters and situations that may not be readily available otherwise. Closed-captioning should be included on all video exercises to ensure compliance with the Americans with Disabilities Act.[18]

Review Chapter 11 for how to learn about an audience with a needs assessment.

2. Choose a Video Platform

Where will the video live? This will depend on where the target audience is found. Are they on Instagram, Facebook, Twitter, or YouTube? Social media platforms have different requirements for video, which can make an impact on the amount of time available on the production end. For example, a food video can be on many of the platforms, such as Instagram, Facebook, Twitter, or YouTube. The 1-minute time frame makes it possible to carry across platforms. A cooking show or an informational or educational video would be better suited for YouTube. A promotional video can be any length, depending on where it will appear. Livestreaming can be used on Facebook, Instagram, and YouTube. See Table 24.1 for the allowed lengths on each platform.

3. Assemble Equipment

Cameras, lighting, backdrops, editing software, microphones, props, and food all count as equipment in food video production. Keep in mind there isn't a one-size-fits-all equipment package. Budgets and filming experience are both considerations when it comes to equipment. However, spending more money on equipment doesn't mean a video will be better. All of the components need to fit together synergistically.

CAMERA

A camera is the one piece of equipment that is crucial for video production. It can be as simple as a cell phone or tablet. Phones and tablets with video capabilities are popular options for livestream video, especially when on the go. They can also be used for all other types of video. Drawbacks of using a phone or tablet include an inability to focus, variable lighting, storage limits, and limited battery life. However, if operating on a tight budget, it's the best choice until video production becomes a comfortable option.

A digital single-lens reflex (DSLR) camera is a more flexible option than a phone or tablet. Quality, focus, and lighting make DSLR video better for filming. Shutter speed and frame rate can be adjusted for the best video outcome. DSLR batteries also last longer, and memory cards can hold more video footage. Lenses can also be switched to suit different needs. It's advantageous that DSLR cameras can take incredible photos as well as video.

TRIPOD

For best results, a tripod is an essential component of video equipment. There are many examples of videos that look like they were filmed during an earthquake. That is exactly what a tripod prevents—shakiness. Video that is hard to watch is video that won't be watched. In a sense, the tripod may be the most important purchase in video equipment. Tripods can range in price and size depending on needs. They may require additional attachments in order to hold a phone, tablet, or DSLR camera. Keep in mind that a tripod must be able to hold the weight of a camera and be the appropriate height.

MICROPHONE

Microphones are a necessary part of an equipment package for making videos (except for food videos). Bad audio can ruin an entire video. Cameras have microphones built in, but they are not optimal. The quality can vary depending how far away a presenter is from the camera and if there is background noise. Lavalier, wireless, directional, and audio recorders are all options to explore for better audio for video. Prices can vary to fit any budget.

TABLE 24.1 **Amount of Time Allowed on Popular Video Platforms**

Platform	Time
Instagram	Up to 1 minute in the feed; up to 10 minutes for IGTV (videos on Instagram)
Facebook	Up to 45 minutes
YouTube	Up to 15 minutes without a verified account; up to 12 hours with a verified account
Twitter	Up to 140 seconds (2 minutes 20 seconds)

This list was accurate as of July 2018. These times are subject to change by the platforms.

FIGURE 24.1 **Three-point lighting**

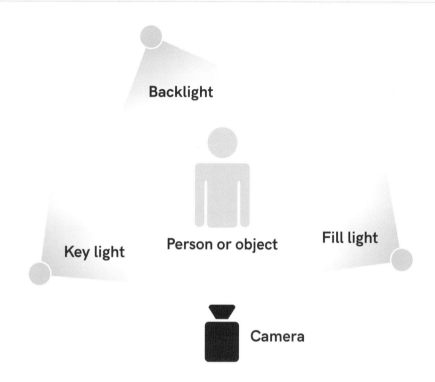

4. Consider Lighting

When it's difficult to see the subject, as in a dark or overexposed video, people won't continue to watch. Having a solid lighting plan makes for a well-lit video. Natural light is free and can be perfect for video. Consider the time of day for filming and, if filming inside, access to windows. If the sun is really bright, it may be helpful to diffuse the light with a sheer curtain. Using a reflector or white board can help redirect the light onto a subject.

If natural light is not an option, artificial light can prevent dark video. Three-point lighting is a system used by photographers and videographers. It involves a key light, a fill light, and a backlight (see Figure 24.1). Lighting systems range in price and style.

Key light The key light is the strongest light and is placed in front of the subject, to the side of the camera.

Fill light The fill light is softer than the key light and helps balance the shadows that the key light creates. It sits opposite the key light.

Backlight The backlight sits behind or to the right of the person or object. Its purpose is to illuminate from behind and create depth.

5. Use Backdrops

Whether filming a food video or an informational video, an appealing background is a fundamental component of the video process. Food videos use more food photography–type backgrounds to demonstrate the recipe. Cooking show formats require a kitchen or kitchen setup. For informational or promotional videos, a more neutral backdrop may be more appropriate. Whether filming in a kitchen, office, or living room, think about whether there is anything that could be distracting to the viewers of a video. Too much going on around the communicator can take away from the message.

6. Choose Editing Software

Deciding on editing software can be an overwhelming choice. Food and nutrition professionals are generally not trained in videography, so finding an intuitive platform is crucial. Choices range from free to expensive. Of course, more bells and whistles may result in better quality. The moderate to expensive versions will allow for the use of more techniques, such as transitions, special effects, and even lighting adjustments. Starting on a free platform can give novice videographers an opportunity to get familiar with video editing. Look for a platform that allows for easy uploading and editing of footage, adding and animating of text, and uploading of audio.

What Are the Components of Video Setup and Production?

Once the type of video has been chosen, it's time to step into production mode. This process is the behind-the-scenes component of video. The time and effort involved in this part of video production will determine the outcome of the video. Taking the time to be meticulous in the planning and production will make the process easier.

Create a Storyboard

The first part of production involves outlining a video using a storyboard. Imagine using still photographs to convey a message. How would it be broken down? When those shots are lined up in a row, do they tell the intended story? Bring to mind a memorable commercial television show. What was attention-catching? What stood out about the story? Was it the flow or the emotions it elicited? Now, take that experience and use it to select essential components to include in a story.

Storyboards are basically a graphic organizer for a video. The process begins by writing down a list of what to include in a video. Then, the list is broken down into shots to capture, and the storyboard is used to describe what each shot should look like. Refer to Figure 24.2 for an example of a storyboard.

FIGURE 24.2 **Storyboard example**

PROJECT NAME: Fruit Salad

Shot: landscape, overhead
Action: cutting a mango

Shot: close up, 45 degrees
Action: washing strawberries

Shot: side shot, close up
Action: blueberries drying

Shot: side shot, close up
Action: zesting and juicing limes

Shot: landscape, 45 degrees
Action: combining ingredients in a bowl

Shot: beauty shot
Action: put fork in salad and lift toward camera

EQUIPMENT NEEDED:
cutting board, knives, bowls, spoons, fork, dish towel, zester, extra fruit for shots, lighting, background, DSLR camera

Reproduced with permission from Betsy Ramirez, MEd, RDN.

One of the easiest traps to fall into when storyboarding is trying to put too much into one video. Be more specific and leave viewers wanting more, especially when shooting an informational or educational video. Break the topic into parts by creating a series of short videos. For instance, if the series theme is "Going Gluten-Free," the first video might define gluten and identify what ingredients to avoid. The second video could be titled "Shopping for Gluten-Free Foods" and provide tips on how to read food labels. The third video could be "Dining Out Gluten-Free." Instead of piling information into one video, breaking it down creates more opportunities for the audience to retain the information and also leaves them wanting more information.

Write a Script

A well-written script has a beginning, a middle, and an end. Open with a compelling first line. An effective opening can be a question: "Are you going gluten-free and confused about what to eat?" Clearly state the problem in the opening so the audience knows what to expect. The middle of the video will contain the content or action that answers the question or solves the problem stated at the beginning. The ending of the video should summarize the information presented in a memorable way. It may even include a call to action.

Working from a script requires practice and some memorization, which makes the production process more time-consuming, but it can better regulate content and timing. To make sure a script works well, read it out loud. Rehearse it in front of people to see if it flows. Make sure it is clear and concise. Communicators should script what is said to allow their personality to shine through. A stoic performance won't gain video views. Science-based practitioners often use scientific terms. If a scientific word, such as *polyphenols*, is used, make sure it is pronounced correctly and then define it for the viewer. Do not assume viewers will understand the term: have the word appear on the screen.

Plan Setup

It's filming day! After all the planning and preparation, it's time to get all the equipment set up and ready for shooting. The type of video being created will determine the setup for production. Camera and lighting positions, backgrounds, and equipment will vary. Refer to Box 24.5 for a "four-corner check."

BOX 24.5 Four-Corner Check

When setting up to film, check all four corners of the image frame to ensure everything is included. Adjust to keep out anything that does not belong.

FOOD VIDEO SETUP

A food video requires far less planning time-wise than the other types of video commonly used by RDNs. Setup includes the following considerations.

- A background is an essential asset to food video production. Depending on the desired look, a solid-color background can be appealing in a food video. Many people use a wooden or marble-type background. Whatever the choice, it shouldn't compete with the food and be distracting. A painted 24- by 24-inch piece of plywood is an inexpensive background option for food videos.
- If using natural light, position the work station by big, open windows. If the light is too bright, filter it with a sheer curtain. If using artificial light, position the lighting using the three-point lighting system (see Figure 24.1).
- Position the camera overhead or at a side angle depending on the position planned in the storyboard.
- Make a checklist of all the ingredients, bowls, and utensils needed for the recipe and have those ready alongside the work station.
- Practice positioning bowls and utensils before filming to see how the movement will flow.
- Check the four corners of the image frame to ensure only what is wanted appears in the frame.
- Begin filming, using the storyboard for guidance.
- It may be helpful to do the first task, stop, and replay the footage to make sure the look and feel are right before going any further. It's a way to double-check the plan and ensure quality.

Once the video has been filmed and the beauty shots have been captured, it's time for the editing. See Box 24.6 for an important food video tip.

Box 24.6 Food Video Tip

Ensure the cook's hands are clean and well manicured if they will be shown in the video.

COOKING SHOW SETUP

When creating a cooking show video, not only does the food need to be prepared, but the script or talking points need to be remembered as well. Setup requires a kitchen or a kitchen-type setting. Artificial lighting, like a three-point lighting system, will be needed unless there are enough windows to bring in the necessary light. Audio will be a key piece of the video, so test the microphone before starting to film. A storyboard is a crucial step in preparing for a cooking show to ensure a good flow. If filming solo, it may be necessary to film the food separately in order to get the shots and angles needed. The food will be a primary focal point to capture and maintain an audience's attention, so these types of shots can make or break a video. Take time to check and double-check the appearance of everything that will appear in the video.

INFORMATIONAL OR EDUCATIONAL VIDEO SETUP

As with the cooking show format, audio, lighting, and appearance will be of utmost importance. However, informational and educational videos may not require food or even a lot of face time, depending on whether still pictures and text are incorporated into the video. Informational and educational videos allow for greater freedom of format, whether that ends up being all on-camera personality or a mix of pictures, text, B-roll (see Box 24.7), and on-camera speaking. If the presenter will talk throughout the entire video, it may help to record it all with an on-camera appearance. The audio can be detached during editing and the desired pictures, text, or B-roll can be cut in.

Box 24.7 What Is B-Roll?

B-roll is the extra footage captured on camera that can enrich a final video to help tell the story.

PROMOTIONAL VIDEO SETUP

Promotional videos can utilize a variety of formats. The most important determinant of format comes from understanding the audience and knowing what can be provided for them, whether as a service or a product. Testimonials make great promotional videos and require filming someone else. Good audio, three-point lighting, and appearance are all required for this type of format. B-roll can also be used for promotional videos. For example, a practitioner can film someone using their products or create B-roll showing the practitioner counseling or providing a service. Using a storyboard is a crucial piece of putting together a promotional video, since a picture is being painted for the audience. Creating a promotional video can be like a puzzle pieced together in editing. It may require a lot of different footage to tell a story.

LIVESTREAM VIDEO SETUP

Livestreaming video is the cheapest and easiest to produce. Only one piece of equipment is really needed, a phone or tablet. If livestreaming for professional reasons, a small tripod can stabilize the filming device. It's important to prepare for the topic before livestreaming and to look professional. Try to use natural light to livestream to keep it simple, but if that's not an option, set up some lighting to improve the quality. The background can vary, since it's a more behind-the-scenes peek into the presenter's life. Film settings can include the office, living room, backyard, or kitchen. The beauty of livestreaming is no editing is required! It is filmed live, and then it is done.

Prepare for Editing

Intuitive editing software will help create the desired video to convey to an audience. Each software program has the same basic components, even though they are set up differently. Listed here are the basic elements to use on any editing platform.

IMPORT

Import all the clips that will be made into a video. Once they are imported, they can be dragged and dropped into a video timeline. Keep the storyboard available to reference while working in the editing software.

AUDIO DETACH

Once the clips are imported into the timeline, detach the audio from the video. If speaking parts are in the video, separating will keep the audio intact as you are cutting and pasting the clips together.

CUTTING

Cutting down the video is part of the editing process. Whether it was a mistake or an unnecessary scene, parts of the video will get cut.

SPEED DURATION

Speed duration or playback speed is utilized many times in food videos. The video can be sped up or slowed down to meet the desired time duration.

SAVE AND UNDO

Save the video often while working in the editing software. Do not rely on autosave. If the program crashes, all the work goes with it. "Undo" is a tool of preference to undo cuts or edits that didn't line up correctly.

TRANSITIONS

Transitions are a valuable asset in video editing. A transition can take two separate clips and make them flow within the video. These are used in food videos often due to the multiple steps used in recipes. It helps with the flow and feel of the video.

TEXT

Adding text is one of the last steps in video editing. Once all the cutting, transitions, and flow are set, text is the next element that will add interest and information. With educational videos especially, text may be a key element within the video. Small and light-colored text won't show up well because video moves quickly.

MUSIC

Background music is used in most videos, but especially in food videos. Software has the ability to manipulate the volume of the music or to taper up or out in the beginning and end of the video. Plenty of royalty-free music is available online, but it's important to remember to give proper credit. Check the terms of use on royalty-free music websites for proper citing. Music can also be purchased to use without citing it.

EXPORT

When the video is complete, it's time to export the video file. Save the video with a clear, descriptive name. When exporting it, make sure it is in the correct dimensions. Common dimensions are 16:9 (rectangle), 1:1 (square), and 9:16 (portrait). Some software programs allow dimensions to be selected before the clips are even imported. Ensure the video is set to its maximum render settings or best quality when exporting. Choose to export it as a MP4 file.

Branding and a Call to Action

Branding is a fundamental marketing strategy. Video creates an opportunity to get more eyes on branding and create trust and credibility for a business, product, or service. With any video, having a logo or name on a video throughout and at the beginning and end provides powerful marketing to the audience without saying a word.

A call to action is another marketing strategy to utilize in video. Asking open-ended questions to engage in dialogue or inviting viewers to subscribe to a YouTube channel, "like" a Facebook page, or sign up for a newsletter gently reminds the viewers to come back for more.

Outsourcing Video Production

Video production has an intensive learning curve. If it isn't interesting or seems too difficult, consider outsourcing. However, setup, filming, possibly cooking, and editing can require a lot of time and expense. Look for someone who is experienced in the type of video that is desired. Ask for references and examples of their work, as well as what editing program they use.

Knowing video basics is essential, whether self-creating video or outsourcing it to a professional. More knowledge allows a practitioner to better assist a crew in creating an optimal product on time and on budget.

Measuring Return on Investment with Video

After all the time and effort put into a video, it's time to see a return on the investment. What video metrics have value? While that depends on the objective, there are some metrics to watch to determine the success or value of a video. Look for the total view count, engagement, comments, shares, or subscriptions on social media channels. If it went out in a newsletter, look at open rates (the percentage of people that received the email and opened it). Since video is a multisensory experience, it will be remembered more than a written word or picture.

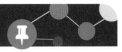

KEY POINTS

Create Video to Maximize Impact

1 Video is a valuable communication tool that allows the nutrition professional to captivate and connect with an audience through a multisensory experience that can be shared with others.

2 Nutrition professionals can incorporate several different types of video into their communications strategy, including food videos, cooking show videos, informational or educational videos, promotional videos, and livestream videos.

3 A well-executed video has an effective plan in place before production begins. The target audience, the type of platform desired, and the types of equipment needed must be known and organized in advance before the video can be produced.

4 Video setup and production bring the plan together using a storyboard and script. The setup of equipment and lighting follows, ending in editing in the chosen video editing software.

RESOURCES

YouTube Creator Academy: https://creatoracademy.youtube.com

Stockman S. *How to Shoot Video That Doesn't Suck.* Workman Publishing Company; 2011.

Jackman J. *Lighting for Digital Video and Television.* 3rd ed. Elsevier; 2010.

Jago M. *Adobe Premiere Pro CC Classroom in a Book.* Adobe Press; 2018. www.adobepress.com/store/adobe-premiere-pro-cc-classroom-in-a-book-2018-release-9780134853239

Hubspot—video production quality: http://blog.hubspot.com/blog/tabid/6307/bid/29075/12-Tips-to-Instantly-Enhance-Video-Production-Quality.aspx

Hubspot—video marketing: https://blog.hubspot.com/marketing/video-marketing

REFERENCES

1. Dale E. *Audio-Visual Methods in Teaching.* Dryden; 1969.
2. Berk RA. Multimedia teaching with video clips: TV, movies, YouTube, and mtvU in the college classroom. *Int J Teach Learn.* 2009;5(1):1-21.
3. Ramsay SA, Holyoke L, Branene IJ, Fletcher J. Six characteristics of nutrition education videos that support learning and motivation to learn. *J Nutr Educ Behav.* 2012;44(6):614-617.
4. Brame CJ. Effective educational videos: principles and guidelines for maximizing student learning from video content. *CBE Life Sci Educ.* 2016;15:e6:1-6.
5. Sweller J. Cognitive load theory, learning difficulty, and instructional design. *Learn Instr.* 1994;4:295-312
6. Mayer RE. Applying the science of learning: evidence-based principles for the design of multimedia instruction. *Cogn Instr.* 2008:19:177-213.
7. Chi DL, Pickerell JE, Riedy CA. Student learning outcomes associated with video vs. paper cases in a public health dentistry course. *J Dent Educ.* 2014;78(1):24-30.
8. Jang HW, Kim KJ. Use of online clinical videos for clinical skills training for medical students: benefits and challenges. *BMC Med Educ.* 2014;(14):56.
9. Pan M, Haracharik S, Luber A, Bernardo S, Levitt J. Instructional video for teaching venepuncture. *Clin Teach.* 2014;(11):436-441.
10. McCoy L, Petit RK, Lewis JH, et al. Developing technology-enhanced active learning for medical education: challenges, solutions, and future directions. *J Am Osteopath Assoc.* 2015;15(4):202-210.
11. Salina L, Ruffinengo C, Garrino L, et al. Effectiveness of an educational video as an instrument to refresh and reinforce the learning of a nursing technique: a randomized controlled trial. *Perspect Med Educ.* 2012;1:67-75.
12. Arterburn DE, Westbrook EO, Bogart TA, et al. Randomized trial of a video-based patient decision aid for bariatric surgery. *Obes.* 2011;19(8):1669-1675.

13. Wang DS, Jani AB, Sesay M, et al. Video-based educational tool improves patient comprehension of common prostate health terminology. *Cancer.* 2015;121:733-740.

14. Szeszak S, Man R, Love A, et al. Animated educational video to prepare children for MRI without sedation: evaluation of appeal and value. *Pediatr Radiol.* 2016;46:1744-1750.

15. Greenberg CJ, Wang L. Building health literacy among an urban teenage population by creating online health videos for public and school health curriculum use. *J Consum Health Internet.* 2012;16(2):135-146.

16. Joventino ES, Ximenes LB, da Penha JC, Andrade LC, de Almeida PC. The use of educational video to promote maternal self-efficacy in preventing early childhood diarrhea. *Int J Nurs Pract.* 2016;23:e12524.

17. Thompson KL, Gutschall MD. The time is now: a blueprint for simulation in dietetics education. *J Acad Nutr Diet.* 2015;115(2):183-194.

18. US Department of Justice Civil Rights Division. Americans with Disabilities Act Title III regulations: part 36 nondiscrimination on the basis of disability in public accommodations and commercial facilities. ADA.gov website. Published January 17, 2017. Accessed September 28, 2018. www.ada.gov/regs2010/titleIII_2010/titleIII_2010_regulations.htm

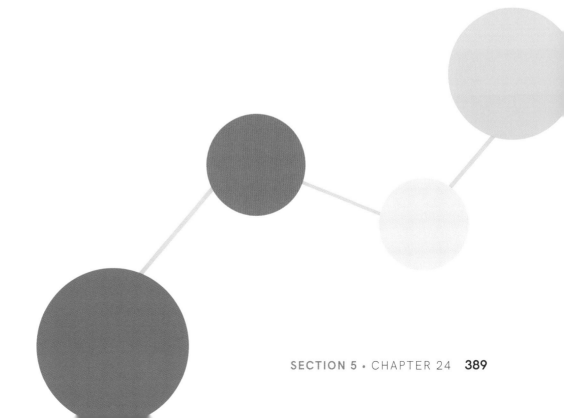

Entertain and Educate with Food Demonstrations

Jen Haugen, RDN, LD and
Martine I. Scannavino, DHSc, RDN, LDN, FAND

"People associate food with pleasure. Nutrition professionals can use food demonstrations to support a healthy and positive relationship with food."

> "This is my advice to people: Learn how to cook, try new recipes, learn from your mistakes, be fearless, and above all have fun." —JULIA CHILD

Introduction

Food and nutrition practitioners may only get one opportunity to positively influence the nutritional health of a target audience. Therefore, nutrition communicators need to integrate strategies that can have the greatest impact. Food demonstrations are an effective multimodal approach to introducing skill sets, stimulating motivation, explaining food preparation concepts, and enhancing food literacy.[1] In addition to being a means for sharing food and nutrition knowledge, they are "how-to" presentations that instruct and engage participants in selecting ingredients, following each step in a recipe, and learning new food preparation skills and tips.[2] Tasting the finished product is the ultimate motivator in audience acceptance of the recommended recipe or cooking strategy.

Food demonstrations enable nutrition practitioners to engage an audience and teach healthy eating approaches using methods that integrate the three primary learning styles: auditory, visual, and kinesthetic.

This chapter answers these three questions:

- What is the purpose of a food demonstration?
- What are the characteristics of quality food demonstrations?
- What practical tools for food demonstrations enhance success?

Nutrition professionals who employ the knowledge provided in this chapter will be able to effectively plan, implement, and assess food demonstrations, and in turn influence positive food and nutrition behaviors among their target audiences.

What Is the Purpose of a Food Demonstration?

People associate food with pleasure. Nutrition professionals can use food demonstrations to support a healthy and positive relationship with food. Demonstrating new ways to prepare family and personal favorites can offer a target audience bountiful opportunities to connect or reconnect with meal preparation in an enjoyable way.

Nutritious eating behaviors support positive health outcomes by helping to reduce risk factors associated with chronic disease and promoting overall well-being.[3] Behavior change is a complex process. When it comes to what, how, and why people eat, it becomes even more complicated. Positive changes in dietary intake have a significant impact on the health of individuals and populations throughout the life span. Therefore, finding a method of educating while simultaneously motivating the individual has the promise of making a greater, lasting impact.

A lecture on healthy eating may be informative and address the learning style of the auditory learner, but when the visual and kinesthetic components of demonstrations are added, plus the olfactory benefits of food, an audience becomes truly engaged.

Review Figure 16.7 on page 271, which depicts Edgar Dale's Cone of Experience. This figure illustrates how active learning approaches, such as demonstrations, improve retention of information when measured 2 weeks after exposure.[4]

The demonstration method of teaching is primarily used to enhance the learning of applied practical skills. There are many advantages to this teaching method. In particular, demonstrations enable the nutrition communicator to[5]:

- efficiently share food preparation techniques and the application of cooking skills;
- focus the learner's attention on the tasks at hand;
- effectively use the "power of observation";
- motivate the learners to try, and to increase acceptance of, healthier food choices; and
- effectively reach both individuals and groups of varying size.

While hands-on cooking classes have documented better outcomes when assessed for skill development and later application of new skills,[4] research supports the efficacy of the food demonstration as a means of enhancing one's effectiveness in the kitchen. The literature also supports that food demonstrations increase the likelihood that participants will try the new cooking skills observed.[6-9] Food demonstrations can accomplish a great deal at a much lower cost and with fewer resources than cooking classes, which may require costly space, equipment, supplies, and more ingredients.

Research has shown that food demonstrations offer nutrition communicators a cost-effective method of engaging target audiences in a way that teaches skills, reduces the audience member's barriers to changing their food choices, and helps them implement healthier behaviors.[9]

Food demonstrations can accomplish a number of goals. They can[10]:

- provide a multimodal approach to educating groups about food and nutrition;
- demonstrate food preparation techniques;
- provide food samples to introduce new foods, healthier options for familiar foods (eg, low-fat or low-sodium choices), and healthy cooking methods (eg, crispy oven-baked potato wedges instead of fried potatoes);
- engage a target audience to improve their attention to topics;
- introduce kitchen "hacks" (or shortcuts) that make cooking easier;
- motivate target audiences to prepare specific food items and meals;
- demonstrate portion control and appropriate portion sizes; and
- introduce new products to make healthy meals easier to prepare, such as quick-cooking whole grains, low-sodium broths and soups, and oven-ready lean meats and fish;

Food demonstrations can be of varying lengths, formats, and degrees of culinary difficulty. A very quick demo as part of a media interview might simply show the ingredients, demonstrate one or two quick preparation techniques, and then show off the finished product: Voilà! Although a longer demonstration can provide more culinary instruction and depth, don't allow a limited time frame to prevent creating an effective food demonstration and fulfilling any of the purposes outlined next.

Demonstrate a Food Ingredient or Product

Individuals may not include more healthful food choices in their diet for many reasons. One reason may be a lack of *food literacy*, which can be defined as "a set of functional skills (including literacy and numeracy) as well as social and critical abilities which are needed to select and prepare food in a perspective of well-being enhancement."[11] Food demonstrations provide the registered dietitian nutritionist (RDN) with a chance to introduce new foods that make meals more interesting, as well as teach exciting new ways to prepare old favorites.

New products arrive on the market at a rapid rate. According to the Economic Research Service, a branch of the US Department of Agriculture, over the period spanning 2011 to 2016, more than 19,000 new food and beverage products entered the marketplace each year.[12] This presents a dizzying array of food products for consumers to navigate. Product labels and claims can also be a source of frustration and confusion for consumers. The food demonstration offers the perfect opportunity to educate target audiences on how to choose and use healthier products.

Consumer expectations of existing products in the marketplace greatly influence acceptance of newly introduced food products.[13] When introducing new, healthier versions of products during a food demo, it is essential to be fair and honest about flavor and quality, especially when comparing the products to the original versions. Claiming that a low-sodium or low-fat product is identical to the full-sodium or full-fat version can backfire and may inadvertently jeopardize the trust a practitioner hoped to build to foster healthier eating behaviors and food choices. Introducing food samples through taste-testing may increase

Bake	To cook surrounded by hot air in an oven
Broil	To cook directly under a high heat or flame
Grill	To cook directly over a high heat or flame
Steam	To cook over or surrounded by steam heat
Braise	To cook food partially covered by liquid
Stew	To cook food completely covered by liquid
Chop	To cut into very small, random-shaped pieces
Dice	To cut into small pieces of even size and shape

More cooking terms can be found on the Academy of Nutrition and Dietetics website (www.eatright.org /food/planning-and-prep/cooking-tips-and-trends/culinary-lingo).

acceptance of new foods.[14] Fostering acceptance of unfamiliar foods through sampling and user-friendly recipe ideas can increase consumption of healthier food choices in the diet.[5,14,15] Therefore, when developing a demonstration to introduce new products or preparations:

- be sure that the recipes are well tested to ensure preparation success;
- keep in mind the skill level of the participants so that the demonstrated product or preparation method is not intimidating;
- taste-test foods with an untrained panel (remember, opinions about food taste and appearance may vary); and
- think about brand recognition, which can increase acceptance of and preference for some food items.[16]

When planning demonstrations for sampling new products and preparation methods, it is vital that the nutrition communicator carefully consider consumer acceptability in terms of taste, cost, cultural appropriateness, and appearance.[5,15] Acceptance of food items increases when food is presented in a visually attractive manner.[17]

Demonstrate a Cooking Technique

The literature describes how a "lack of cooking knowledge, confidence, and skills can limit at-home preparation of healthy meals and may explain some of the trend towards decreased cooking."[18] Food

demonstrations can teach audience members basic cooking techniques and recipe modifications, which may build confidence and motivate them to apply new skills in the kitchen. Demonstrating cooking shortcuts can alleviate some of the time constraints felt by audience members who believe preparing meals is too time-consuming.

The demonstration is an opportunity to showcase healthy approaches to popular foods that are traditionally prepared in less-than-healthful ways. Introducing healthy cooking methods—such as starch-thickened soups versus cream-based soups and steam-sautéing in place of sautéing in butter and oil—will introduce new options for personal and family favorites while reinforcing healthy, nutritious eating habits. The added persuasive feature is the taste test throughout the event.

Food demonstrations provide an opportunity to educate the audience about cooking terminology. Participants will be more likely to apply newly learned skills when they use recipes at home if they understand the "language of cooking."[19] Refer to the Terms to Know box for a glossary of common cooking terms. Don't assume an audience knows the jargon of cooking. See the Words of Experience box (page 394) for an example of how demonstrating easier ways to prepare foods can make them more accessible.

Discussing and presenting safe food-handling techniques is an essential part of any food demonstration. Discuss time and temperature considerations, cross-contamination, and proper storage throughout the demonstration. Demonstrate good food-handling practices, such as appropriate

> "Once you have mastered a technique, you hardly need to look at a recipe again and can take off on your own." —JULIA CHILD

Demonstrating Simple and Safer Ways to Handle Foods Makes Them More Accessible

by Martine I. Scannavino, DHSc, RDN, LDN, FAND

Food demonstration WFMZ: Sunrise Chef October 2016.

Early one autumn, I was contacted to do a short food demonstration segment on our local news station. When I sent my menu, which included butternut squash, to my presentation partner, she asked if I should do something different since butternut squash is so hard to cut and may not go over so well. I assured her I would demonstrate a simple and safer way to manage the squash and she agreed to give it a go.

That morning, while on live TV, I pulled out my simple stainless-steel potato peeler and instructed the news host to peel off the hard skin. Once peeled, the squash was easy to slice for the roasted squash recipe.

A daunting task made simple opens up the opportunity for adding this nutrient-rich, affordable, and delicious vegetable to meals.

handwashing (in fact, always begin a demonstration by modeling how to wash hands) and eliminating the risk of cross-contamination by using different cutting tools and boards for meats, vegetables, and ready-to-eat foods.

When demonstrating food preparation, a presenter should be sure to wear clean and appropriate covering, such as an apron and a hat or hairnet (or at least have their hair pulled back). Presenters must also avoid jewelry, nail polish, open-toed shoes, and scented products or perfumes.

Make use of the many food-safety support materials available from reputable sources, such as the US Department of Health and Human Services, the US Department of Agriculture's Food Safety and Inspection Service, and the Centers for Disease Control and Prevention (relevant websites are provided in the resources section at the end of the chapter).

Demonstrate Menu Ideas

When planning meals, it's important to include nutrient-rich foods from all food groups (a variety of vegetables; fruit; low-fat or fat-free dairy foods or fortified vegetarian milk substitutes; protein foods, such as lean meats, poultry, seafood, eggs, and legumes; and healthy fats, such as olive oil, nuts, and seeds). It is also important to limit sodium, saturated fats, and added sugars.[20]

Promoting balance in meal planning is a skill and an art, and with a little help and direction, one that program participants can acquire. Present a well-planned menu to participants to clearly illustrate the menu-planning techniques and tips introduced in the demonstration.

Introduce program participants to basic concepts for healthy, balanced meal planning using reputable guidelines, such as those found on the Nutrition.gov and Academy of Nutrition and Dietetics EatRight.org websites. These resources offer ideas and supporting materials to help develop a demonstration customized to any audience, as well as tools for incorporating concepts such as culture-specific foods, meals for families on a budget, cooking for one, and special diets for diseases and conditions. Assist audiences in learning efficient, economical, nutritious, and time-saving food-preparation techniques.

Planning a demonstration should also address the aesthetic design of menu items. Capture the attention of an audience by presenting a visually engaging menu in terms of colors, textures, and shapes. Don't underestimate the olfactory component, as there are few, if any, better ways to grab and hold the attention of an audience than with the aroma of delicious food.

Demonstrate Recipe Modifications

Recipe modification—making changes to existing recipes to improve the nutrient profile, simplify preparation, or adjust seasonings to meet individual preferences—is an effective method for introducing more healthful food-preparation methods. A presenter needs a comprehensive understanding of food science to successfully modify recipes. Communicating the basics of foundational food-science principles to an audience can enable them to modify their favorite meals and menu items at home.

An example of a common recipe modification is to reduce salt or fat while enhancing flavor by using herbs and spices. For some populations, modifications may require enhancing recipes with added protein, fiber, calories, or other key nutrients (such as folic acid for pregnant women).

The resources section at the end of the chapter provides sources for modified recipes. Recipes for people with special dietary needs are offered by several organizations: the American Heart Association (www.heart.org), the American Diabetes Association (www.diabetes.org), and the National Kidney Foundation (www.kidney.org).

One of the valuable contributions credentialed food and nutrition professionals can provide to their food-demo audiences is not only modified recipes but also accurate nutrition facts about all recipes being prepared. Be sure to discuss nutrition facts in demonstrations and include pertinent nutrition facts on any written recipes provided to an audience. The resources section at the end of the chapter includes sources for assistance in calculating nutrition information.

What Are the Characteristics of Quality Food Demonstrations?

A high-quality food demonstration will leave an audience both inspired and educated because it is fun! The experience should be fun for the presenter as well, because when the presenter is having fun, so is the audience. When the audience leaves the demonstration, they should feel empowered to make the healthy changes illustrated in a recipe, try a tip that was shared, incorporate a kitchen technique that was showcased, or experiment with a new food they've tasted and plan to purchase.

There are several best practices for a successful and quality food demonstration to consider while planning and preparing. These best practices include the following:

- Keep the audience focused and engaged.
- Plan key messages in advance and articulate them well.
- Prepare, plan, and organize the demonstration and the stage.
- Make the demonstration "edu-taining."
- Emphasize helpful tips throughout the demonstration.

When these best practices are in place, the demonstration will be more engaging and more inspiring and will leave the audience feeling empowered to make changes. And don't forget, it's important to practice the demonstration at least once or twice before going live in front of an audience. Mistakes made in practice can be avoided in the demonstration, and lessons learned can be shared with the audience.

Best Practice: Keep the Audience Focused and Engaged

What keeps audience members engaged? Often, it's not just the information shared, but the *way* it is shared. Information can be shared by telling a compelling story or recent experience, adding an amusing observation or humorous anecdote, providing real-life tips or hacks that simplify food-planning strategies or preparation techniques, asking the audience questions, and encouraging dialogue to keep the demonstration moving forward. Perhaps

Refer to Chapter 13 if demonstrating global cuisine.

most important, presenters should be authentic without letting nerves get in the way. It will allow the demonstration to flow in a natural way. Here are some tips for engaging an audience:

USE COMPELLING PERSONAL STORIES OR RECENT EXPERIENCES

Come up with 10 personal experiences that relate to food or health that can be shared with an audience to prove a point or provide a learning opportunity. To speak confidently, keep this tip in mind from Stacey Hanke, author of *Influence Redefined*: Make statements bullet points. Presenters who speak in short phrases and get right to the point are much more influential.[21]

SHARE FUNNY OBSERVATIONS AND HUMOR

Audience members love to laugh, but keep the humor professional and light, as it isn't a stand-up comedy act. An easy way to add humor to a demonstration is to find humor in everyday life, according to Toastmasters International.[22] This can include everyday experiences in the kitchen, work, or life; these can allow a presenter to relate to the audience. Pick out one to three funny anecdotes and add them to a demonstration to keep it lively.

OFFER REAL-LIFE HACKS

Audiences love hacks, or simple tricks that streamline a technique or process. Think about personal tips you've developed as a nutrition expert in the kitchen or details learned from an article or a website. Keep in mind—the hack should be safe to implement, make sense as part of the demonstration, and be realistic in nature.

SHARE THE STAGE

The best demonstrations include audience participation, whether that's in the form of a dialogue around a topic, questions from the audience, or audience members being invited to the staging area to participate in the demonstration. Audiences love to see nonexperts participating in a demonstration, so use that as an advantage. Coaching an audience member through a technique may inspire observers to think, "I could do that too."

MOVE THE DEMONSTRATION FORWARD

Stagnant demonstrations, or those that lack action, are hard to watch and cause audience members to lose attention. To prevent that, the presenter needs to keep things moving by speaking clearly, being enthusiastic, and eliminating or skipping small steps that don't offer a benefit or value to the audience. In preparing and practicing a demonstration, take the audience's point of view. Is the demonstration interesting, engaging, and useful?

BE AUTHENTIC

When a presenter shares their authentic self with an audience they become relatable. The audience should get to know not only the topic being presented but also the presenter, as the presenter's influence increases when an audience knows, likes, and trusts him or her. Share a struggle or a challenge and the solution. Be vulnerable with a compelling story. Sharing personal stories will keep the audience engaged and curious to learn more.

See Figure 25.1 for a visual summary of these strategies for engaging an audience. In addition, see the Words of Experience box for an example of the value of engaging the audience.

FIGURE 25.1 **Strategies for keeping audiences focused and engaged**

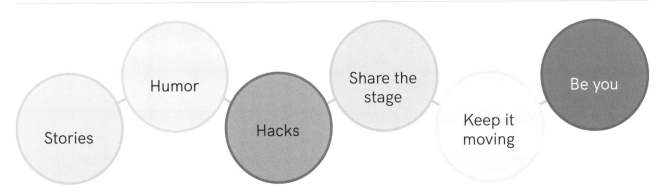

Best Practice: Focus on Key Messages

Effective, engaging, and inspiring demonstrations must have key messages. A key message is a strong statement or point that a communicator wants to get across to the audience. That key message might relate to a technique the audience can learn or to a recipe modification to support better health or to a specific product or food to entice the audience to prepare during mealtime in their own kitchens. It might also involve a strategy, a tip, or a key health point.

While many types of key messages relate to health and nutrition, what's most important is that the key message for the event is clearly defined. Well-defined key messages help to distinguish exactly what the presenter is trying to convey through the demonstration being delivered. A well-defined key message takes the audience on an organized journey toward better understanding of the topic being presented and supports the likelihood of their making healthful changes.

Great presenters engage an audience, whether they have just a few moments with them or an hour or more. They develop key messages that leave the audience feeling inspired and better educated. When defining key messages, ask these three key questions, viewing them from the perspective of the audience:

- At the end of the demonstration, what is something the audience should be able to **do**?
- At the end of the demonstration, what should the audience **think**?
- At the end of the demonstration, what should the audience **feel**?

As an example, consider the topic of increasing vegetable intake during dinner. The goal might be to have the audience spiralize vegetables and add them to a fettuccine recipe, believe spiralized vegetables taste good, use them frequently in main entrees or as a salad at dinner, and feel confident in the ability to incorporate other spiralized vegetables into recipes. The words *do*, *think*, and *feel* describe the learning objectives for the demonstration. Write key messages to correspond with the objectives. In fact, transform the objectives into memorable key messages.

How are objectives transformed into memorable key messages for the audience? There are a number of ways, and creativity plays a role. The best

Dynamic Demonstrations

by Jen Haugen, RDN, LD

Not long ago, I walked into a healthy-recipe demonstration where there was pure silence. It was deafening silence. The dietitian/chef presenter was cracking an egg for a recipe but wasn't talking at all. This uncomfortable pause would have been the perfect time to share information about the nutrient profile of eggs or a tip about what to do with eggshells to reduce food waste or maybe a funny story about a mess in the kitchen with eggs. As I observed the audience, they were disengaged, and, quite frankly, they were bored. I felt bad for the presenter but worse for the audience, who would leave with a bad taste in their mouths. I was in that audience and had hoped to gain a new tip or cooking technique and instead left without anything to inspire or empower me in the kitchen. In fact, I walked out because it felt like a waste of time.

Contrast that with another presentation I had the opportunity to attend, with an audience of about 500. That is a lot of people to engage! But this presenter did a fabulous job of taking the same mundane task of cracking an egg and turning it into a time to share a trick for making the fluffiest scrambled eggs. She even enlightened the audience with a childhood memory that involved cooking eggs with her dad every Saturday morning. This presenter articulated key messages easily as they flowed with the recipe steps. She shared memories in the kitchen through stories and added humorous anecdotes to bring the recipe to life. Not by accident, I still have my recipes and notes from that demonstration because it was so well done, and it made me walk away thinking, "I can do that!" That's the goal—to get the audience believing at the end of the presentation, "I can do that too!"

bet is to create short, simple key messages that focus on the main point. These key messages should be easy to repeat and memorize, both from the presenter's point of view as well as the audience's point of view. They must be easy to say during the demonstration, and the audience should leave the demonstration repeating them. Consider the topic of spiralizing vegetables and how to apply the previous objectives to creating memorable key messages for a demonstration. Here are some examples:

- Spiralizing is easy, from *p* to *z*! (Transform your favorite *p*asta recipe with zucchini.)
- Serve salads at every supper. (Make it easy with spiralized vegetables.)
- Know the nine that are divine! (Meet nine vegetables that are easily spiralized.)

The number of key messages needs to fit the time slot for the demonstration, keeping in mind that three key messages are probably the maximum to integrate. If a presentation will last for an hour, having three key messages is reasonable. However, if a presentation is only a few minutes long, one key message is more appropriate. Match the key messages to the topic, and the audience will leave feeling empowered to make a change.

For more on writing objectives and key messages, review Chapter 15.

Best Practice: Plan, Be Prepared, and Be Organized

Having a plan, being fully prepared and practiced, and being organized means that a demonstration will be more effective for an audience and more fun for the presenter. Following these steps will convey energy and enthusiasm. The audience will leave feeling eager and excited to implement what they have learned because of it. Figure 25.2 lists essential tips and strategies for planning, preparing, practicing, and organizing a demonstration.

When making an equipment list, don't forget these items:

- pot holders
- timer
- food thermometer
- spoons and knives
- cutting board
- serving equipment
- extension cords
- sampling materials (utensils, plates, cups)—if sampling is allowed; check state regulations
- tablecloth
- paper towels
- food-safe gloves
- tub for dirty dishes
- bucket for capturing compostable food
- garbage bowl
- wet wipes or damp paper towels
- handwashing and sanitation supplies

Use clear bowls and pans if possible to make it easier for the audience to see what is being done. Be sure to keep the table or presentation area as neat and tidy as possible to help keep the demonstration organized. An easy way to keep things organized is to use trays to group supplies for a recipe or steps in a recipe. These grouped supplies could also correspond with key messages to help keep the demonstration on track. Using a tray also makes it easier to move grouped items onto and off the demo table as needed.

Practicing sometimes seems like an easy step to skip, but don't risk it. A well-rehearsed presentation is essential. With practice, actions and speech become more natural. The energy spent struggling through an unrehearsed presentation can be redirected to the enthusiasm that will be brought to the event, making it a more personal and satisfying experience for the audience. When practicing, pay attention to posture, grammar, vocabulary, and even facial expressions. Videotaping practice sessions as well as the actual presentation (when possible) will allow for a critique of the performance and overall approach—and a chance to set goals for personal improvement.

Following these best practices of planning, preparing, and practicing before the demonstration, and staying organized throughout the demonstration will lead to success.

Best Practice: Keep It Edu-Taining

The definition of *edutainment* is entertainment that is designed to be educational. In other words, make the demonstration fun and memorable—exactly what a food demonstration should be! What is the best way to ensure a demonstration is edu-taining?

Begin with a great hook. As described in Chapter 17, a presentation's beginning will either draw the audience in or cause them to tune out and miss everything else the presenter has to say. Think about how to open a demonstration. Saying, "Can you hear me now?" isn't the most dynamic way to capture an audience's attention. Instead, hook the audience right away.[23] Make a provocative statement. Tell a story. Ask a question. Be authentic.

Once the audience's attention is captured, how can it be kept? Simply, make it about them. Hold the audience's attention by talking about their goals, aspirations, and anxieties. In other words, use a demonstration to help them with a struggle, challenge, or pain point. Keep them engaged by using audience interaction techniques,

PLAN	PREPARE & PRACTICE	ORGANIZE
• Ask crucial questions to understand the space and the event • Know where access is to water, electricity, and appliances • Choose a theme and recipe • Write your key messages	• Make grocery lists • Make equipment and tool lists • Make copies of handouts or recipes • Prepare and pack everything you need • Select your props, if using • Conduct a dry rehearsal with setup • Conduct a dress rehearsal with food	• Measure everything in advance • Layout the demo ingredients in the order you will use and talk about them • Ensure that all appliances and electricity work • Have notes for key messages and tips • Remember food safety techniques (for both role modeling as well as sampling)

such as asking a question to poll the audience, asking them to share their ideas or tips about the topic, or inviting an audience member to participate in the demonstration.

Conclude a demonstration by issuing a call to action and asking the audience to take a specific step. This helps attendees leave feeling empowered that they can use what they've learned. Some example calls to action include:

- purchasing a specific food or product,
- purchasing a cookbook or downloadable ebook,
- signing up for a newsletter (which brings weekly or monthly inspiration and ideas),
- sharing tips learned at the demo on social media with a hashtag,
- referring to another organization or colleague for another demonstration, and
- participating in a contest or mini-challenge to keep momentum going.

Make the call to action clear and direct and encourage the audience to act quickly, with low barriers to action. The action should be simple to accomplish and require minimal energy or time. It is important to highlight benefits for the audience and explain clearly how the call to action will help them take action, make a change, or improve a behavior.

Start with a hook, make the presentation about the audience, and leave the audience with a call to action. These simple strategies will leave audience members feeling confident about their next steps to improve their health.

Best Practice: Sharing Tips Brings Value

Much of the value of a food demonstration to an audience member comes in the form of tips that are provided throughout the presentation. These tips can cover cooking, food safety, saving time or money, improving health, or reducing food waste. If providing frequent food demonstrations, start a tip list. Begin pulling tips together from sources, such as cooking shows, articles, podcasts, and cookbooks. Whether these tips are written in a notebook or stored in a cloud-based application, such as iCloud or Google Drive, they will save time when pulling a demonstration together, as the tips can be easily identified and incorporated throughout a presentation. The following are examples of tips or information that could be used when presenting a particular food, dish, or cooking technique:

- how the food might be used in an alternate recipe
- history of the food
- agricultural perspective or story
- how to store the food or preserve the food for future use

- food-safety guidelines
- what to do with scraps or how to reduce food waste
- what other foods work well for the cooking technique that's being demonstrated
- kitchen hacks that save time and money
- how to cook the dish in an alternate way in less time
- nutritional highlights and benefits
- ingredient substitutions

The best tips are practical in nature and delivered in short sound bites. They should be delivered in a way that can be easily incorporated throughout the demonstration. In fact, using tips can be one way to interact with the audience, as many are willing to share their best tips on a topic. One thing to note: Tips shared should be from a reputable source, be based on current science, and convey positive information to the audience. There are a number of resources for tips, which are listed at the end of the chapter. Box 25.1 summarizes five best practices for educational and inspirational food demonstrations.

What Practical Tools Enhance Success?

The recipe demonstration planning worksheet and the demonstration flow worksheet (see Figures 25.3 and 25.4) that follow can help to plan, organize, and present a demonstration in the best way possible. Box 25.2 summarizes seven practical stratagies for achieving a quality food demonstration.

Putting It All Together

The steps for designing and delivering an entertaining and educational food demonstration include clearly defining goals, creating well-written key messages, doing research to establish a solid evidence base and provide background, pretesting recipes, defining desired outcomes, and then implementing the plan. If you plan to offer samples of the finished recipe, be sure to check local health department guidelines on food sampling.

Clearly Define Goals and Write Messages

When preparing for a food or cooking demonstration, the best place to start is to assess the needs of the target audience. This can be done through a comprehensive needs assessment, but it can also be accomplished with a simple survey to provide background for planning a relevant presentation. If a survey is not possible, then gather as much information about the target audience from a contact person. This information will prove invaluable for developing the program's goals and message.

The message must be applicable to the target audience, aligning with the audience's (1) health concerns or areas where dietary improvements can be made; (2) socioeconomic needs, ensuring that the food products and equipment needed are appropriate to the target group; and (3) literacy and language abilities and level of comprehension.

BOX 25.1 Five Best Practices for Educational and Inspirational Demonstrations

- Keep the audience focused and engaged.
- Focus on key messages.
- Plan, prepare, and practice to be organized and polished.
- Keep it edu-taining.
- Add value by sharing tips.

BOX 25.2 Seven Practical Strategies for a Successful Food Demonstration

1. Clearly define goals and messages.
2. Support the messages with science.
3. Pretest the recipes.
4. Practice, practice, practice.
5. Be very organized before and during the event.
6. Visualize the stage prior to being on it.
7. Make the demonstration interactive.

FIGURE 25.3 **Recipe demonstration planning worksheet**

Date of event: _____   Location of event: _____

Notes about space/stage: _____

_____

Topic/Theme: _____

Audience: _____

Key Messages:

- _____
- _____
- _____

Opening:

- _____
- _____
- _____

Recipe(s):

- _____
- _____
- _____

Recipe Planning:

Ingredient List	Equipment List

Tips to offer during demonstration:

- _____
- _____
- _____
- _____
- _____
- _____

How will I engage the audience?

- _____
- _____
- _____

What's my call to action? _____

_____

Props/handouts: _____

_____

Food safety essentials: _____

_____

_____

FIGURE 25.4 **Demonstration flow worksheet**

Key Messages:
- _____
- _____
- _____

Opening:
- _____
- _____
- _____

Steps of Recipe:
- _____
- _____
- _____
- _____
- _____
- _____
- _____
- _____
- _____
- _____

Closing Summary:
- _____
- _____
- _____

Support Messages with Science

The RDN is the food and nutrition expert and is responsible for presenting information to the public that is evidence-based. The public is barraged with nutrition messages and relies on the RDN to navigate this complex field. The following principles for content credibility and for responsible information sharing apply well to food demonstrations[24]:

- Always provide accurate and truthful information.
- Distinguish between science-based facts and a personal point of view.
- Share only information from credible sources.
- Include the source of nutrition studies or claims cited.
- Place the results of new studies in context.
- Correct misinformation and respond to inaccuracies.

The RDN is charged with providing food and nutrition information during the demonstration that is reliable, credible, and evidence-based. These standards of practice are important when choosing products to demonstrate and promote. The RDN has a duty to explain and clarify nutrient claims on products, misinformation in the media, and fads or unsubstantiated food or health trends and recommendations.

Pretest Recipes

Demonstrating how to do something requires all components of the demonstration to be tested and retested to ensure success. There is nothing worse than demonstrating a food product or preparation technique to an audience and having it fail.

When choosing recipes that support the goals and messages of a presentation, begin by focusing on recipes that use mastered preparation techniques. Over time, new skills and an expanded repertoire can be added, but until then, stick with what is known.

When testing a recipe, be sure to address the following:

- Are the ingredients available and affordable to the target audience? Check with a few grocery stores in the area to be sure.
- Never assume it is possible to simply remove or reduce an ingredient and have the recipe still be successful. Pretest and retest all recipe modifications and be sure to get sensory feedback on the new version prior to using it.
- Does the recipe yield meet defined needs? The only way to verify this is to prepare the recipe and measure final yield.
- Does the recipe cooking time change when using the equipment that will be available on-site? Here again, the only way to know this is to cook the recipe on the equipment that will be used. (This is especially important when using hot plates or other mobile cooking gear.)

Once each of these considerations has been addressed, be sure to make all necessary adjustments and test the recipe again.

Define Outcomes

Outcomes are central to the purpose and implementation of food demonstrations. During the planning phase, it is essential for the nutrition communicator to identify the intended outcomes and design an appropriate method for collecting data. Outcome data can be used to validate best practices, establish the value of the intervention, and provide evidence of the impact on the community served. As the Academy of Nutrition and Dietetics recommends, "Research forms the backbone of dietetics practice and the basis for the Academy's work in education and policy."[25]

To achieve an outcomes-oriented program, the learning outcomes or behavior changes for the participants must be clearly identified. A program can begin with a simple pretest of knowledge and practices and end with a post-test of what was learned. The results can provide the evaluation needed to plan, apply, and check if a program is meeting the expected goals and outcomes. At the conclusion of a program, perform a summative evaluation, and develop a program improvement plan to implement the next time the program is given.

Food and cooking demonstrations are widely used methods for educating the public. However, there is limited research that addresses their efficacy as a means of improving nutritious food intake, health outcomes, or changes in perceptions and acceptance of healthier food choices. With planning and support, food demonstration programs can offer opportunities for research and provide evidence needed in this area of practice.

For more on evaluation, refer to Chapter 38.

KEY POINTS

Entertain and Educate with Food Demonstrations

1 Do the homework. Ensure that the planned demonstration meets the needs of the audience being served.

2 Follow these five best practices for successfully providing an effective and high-quality cooking demonstration: keep the audience engaged and focused; plan and articulate the key messages; be prepared and organized; use edutainment to make the demonstration informative and fun; and deliver useful tips to the audience. Audiences that leave feeling "I can do this!" will make the necessary changes to positively impact their health.

3 Use the practical strategies to enhance success outlined in Box 25.2 for a demonstration that is organized, engaging, and fun—for both the presenter and the audience.

4 Test all recipes to ensure they work, taste good, and look delicious.

5 Focus on and use well-known preparation methods; then, rehearse the demonstration from start to finish.

Resources for Cooking and Recipe Tips:

Academy of Nutrition and Dietetics—cooking tips and trends: www.eatright.org/resources/food/planning-and-prep/cooking-tips-and-trends

Academy of Nutrition and Dietetics—planning and prep: www.eatright.org/resources/food/planning-and-prep

Cooking tips and trends: www.eatright.org

Home food safety: www.homefoodsafety.org

Nutrition education materials: https://hungerand health.feedingamerica.org/healthy-recipes

Nutrition:

- www.nutrition.gov
- www.nutrition.gov/subject/shopping-cooking-meal-planning

Duyff R. *Academy of Nutrition and Dietetics Complete Food and Nutrition Guide.* 5th ed. Houghton Mifflin Harcourt; 2017.

What's Cooking USDA Mixing Bowl: https://whatscooking.fns.usda.gov

Resources for Calculating Nutrient Facts:

Centers for Disease Control and Prevention, food safety education resources: www.cdc.gov/foodsafety/index.html

Powers C, Dolven CL. *Recipe Nutrient Analysis: Best Practices for Calculation and Chemical Analysis.* Culinary Nutrition Publishing; 2015.

Tufts Calorie Computations for Meals: https://hnrca.tufts.edu/flipbook/resources/restaurant-meal-calculator

Resources for Food Safety

US Department of Health and Human Services: ww.foodsafety.gov

US Department of Agriculture, Food Safety and Inspection Service: www.fsis.usda.gov/wps/portal/fsis/topics/food-safety-education

Resources for Interesting Presentations

Toastmasters International—rules for using humor: www.toastmasters.org/Magazine/Articless/Six-Rule-of-Humor

Presentation hooks used by the best TED presenters: http://blog.visme.co/how-to-start-a-presentation

1. Campbell L, Olan E, Puig E. A multimodal approach to health literacy in an urban food desert. Paper presented at: European Conference on Educational Research 2016; August 2016; Dublin, Ireland.

2. Champions for Change, Network for a Healthy California. Food demonstration training kit. Published 2007. Accessed May 31, 2018. www.eatsmartmovemorenc.com/HealthyFoodRetail/texts/Network-FV-RP-FoodDemoTrainingKit-2007-10.pdf

3. Dietary Guidelines Advisory Committee. *Scientific Report of the 2015 Dietary Guidelines Advisory Committee.* US Department of Agriculture; 2015. https://health.gov/dietaryguidelines/2015-scientific-report/PDFs/Scientific-Report-of-the-2015-Dietary-Guidelines-Advisory-Committee.pdf

4. Dale E. *Audio-Visual Methods in Teaching.* 3rd ed. Holt, Rinehart and Winston; 1969.

5. Kuznesof S, Brownlee IA, Moore C, Richardson DP, Jebb SA, Seal CJ. WHOLEheart study participant acceptance of wholegrain foods. *Appetite.* 2012;59(1):187-193. doi:10.1016/j.appet.2012.04.014

6. McKnight L, Doolittle N, Stitzel K, Vafiadis D, Robb K. Simple cooking with heart: nutrition education and improving diet quality through culinary skill-based education. *J Nutr Educ Behav.* 2013;45(4S):S23-S23. doi:10.1016/j.jneb.2013.04.063

7. Burg T, Lenders C, Sharifi L, et al. A hospital-based food pantry and demonstration kitchen: a unique role for the dietitian. *J Acad Nutr Diet.* 2016;116(9):A67. doi:10.1016/j.jand.2016.06.238

8. Birlson O, Singleton M. The demonstration kitchen: gauging participant learning in cooking demonstrations. *J Acad Nutr Diet.* 2017;117(10):A139. doi:10.1016/J.JAND.2017.08.076

9. Contento IR. *Nutrition Education—Linking Research, Theory, and Practice.* Jones and Bartlett; 2007.

10. Garcia AL, Reardon R, McDonald M, Vargas-Garcia EJ. Community interventions to improve cooking skills and their effects on confidence and eating behaviour. *Curr Nutr Rep.* 2016;5(4):315-322. doi:10.1007/s13668-016-0185-3

11. Palumbo R. Sustainability of well-being through literacy: the effects of food literacy on sustainability of well-being. *Agric Agric Sci Procedia.* 2016;8:99-106. doi:10.1016/j.aaspro.2016.02.013

12. US Department of Agriculture. New products. US Department of Agriculture Economic Research Service website. Updated April 5, 2017. Accessed November 15, 2017. www.ers.usda.gov/topics/food-markets-prices/processing-marketing/new-products

13. Meiselman H, Schutz H. History of food acceptance research in the US Army. *Appetite.* 2003;40(3):199-216. doi:10.1016/S0195-6663(03)00007-2

14. Hughes L, Cirignano S, Fitzgerald N. Fruit and vegetable tastings in schools offer potential for increasing consumption among kindergarten through sixth grade children. *J Acad Nutr Diet.* 2016;116(9):A19. doi:10.1016/j.jand.2016.06.054

15. Micheelsen A, Holm L, O'Doherty Jensen K. Consumer acceptance of the new Nordic diet: an exploratory study. *Appetite.* 2013;70:14-21. doi:10.1016/J.APPET.2013.06.081

16. Bimbo F, Bonanno A, Nocella G, et al. Consumers' acceptance and preferences for nutrition-modified and functional dairy products: a systematic review. *Appetite.* 2017;113:141-154. doi:10.1016/j.appet.2017.02.031

17. Zellner DA, Loss CR, Zearfoss J, Remolina S. It tastes as good as it looks! The effect of food presentation on liking for the flavor of food. *Appetite.* 2014;77:31-35. doi:10.1016/J.APPET.2014.02.009

18. Smith LP, Ng SW, Popkin BM. Trends in US home food preparation and consumption: analysis of national nutrition surveys and time use studies from 1965–1966 to 2007–2008. *Nutr J.* 2013;12(1):45. doi:10.1186/1475-2891-12-45

19. Academy of Nutrition and Dietetics. Culinary lingo. eatright website. Published December 4, 2017. Reviewed August 2018. Accessed June 28, 2019. www.eatright.org/food/planning-and-prep/cooking-tips-and-trends/culinary-lingo

20. US Department of Health and Human Services; US Department of Agriculture. *2015–2020 Dietary Guidelines for Americans.* 8th edition. December 2015. Accessed December 11, 2019. https://health.gov/dietaryguidelines/2015

21. Hanke S. *Influence Redefined.* Green Leaf Press; 2017

22. Honaker G. Six rules of humor. *Toastmaster.* June 2015. Accessed December 11, 2019. www.toastmasters.org/Magazine/Articles/Six-Rules-of-Humor

23. Chibana N. 12 presentation hooks used by the best TED presenters. Visme Visual Learning Center website. Accessed December 11, 2019. https://visme.co/blog/how-to-start-a-presentation

24. Helm J, Jones R. Practice paper of the Academy of Nutrition and Dietetics: social media and the dietetics practitioner: opportunities, challenges, and best practices. *J Acad Nutr Diet.* 2016;116(11):1825-1835. doi:10.1016/j.jand.2016.09.003

25. Academy of Nutrition and Dietetics. Research. eatrightPRO website. Accessed December 11, 2019. https://eatrightpro.org/research

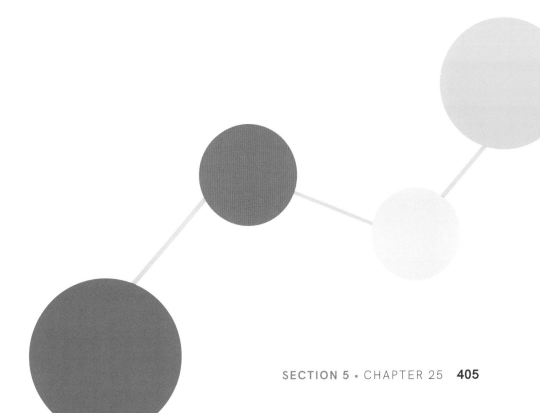

Inspire Audiences with Food Styling and Photography

Lynn Dugan, MS, RDN
and Trinh Le, MPH, RD

"The beauty of food photography is its power to sell a recipe, food product, or idea. A quality food photo is as important as a quality recipe."

> "Of all our inventions for mass communication, pictures still speak the most universally understood language." —WALT DISNEY COMPANY

Introduction

Quality food photography is an essential tool in the nutrition communicator's arsenal. Consumers today expect recipes to be accompanied by a food photo. Food photos can enhance food and nutrition writing in print and digital media. An effective food photo can inspire the audience to make the food for themselves.

This chapter answers three questions:

- What is the purpose of food photography?
- What are the characteristics of quality food photography?
- What are practical strategies for creating "tasty" food photos?

Like any form of communication, food styling and photography are skills anyone can learn. This chapter will describe the characteristics of quality food photography and offer practical strategies for creating appealing food photos.

The Words of Experience stories at the opening and close of this chapter share the authors' journeys with food photography, with the hope that the reader, too, will be inspired to take photographs of food.

What Is the Purpose of Food Photography?

There is a famous saying that a picture is worth a thousand words, and this is most certainly true for food photography. A food photo can provide more information than is possible with the written word and in a much more impactful way. A brief search on the internet for a recipe will likely turn up a food photo that captures the searcher's attention: the soft interior of homemade bread, the caramelized flesh of roasted butternut squash, or the juiciness of a

fresh grapefruit section tossed onto a bed of mixed baby greens—all noticed in an instant from the photo. It catches the eye and prompts the consumer to want to read the recipe and consider making it at home.

The beauty of food photography is its power to sell a recipe, food product, or idea. Consumers have come to expect food photographs when they make decisions about food and food preparation. These consumer decisions are often based on what is seen, which creates demand for good food photography. In turn, quality food photography is important for nutrition communicators, as it enhances their writing about food and nutrition in both print and digital media as well as increases its shareability across social media platforms.

Effective food photography begins with determining the components of the food or recipe that are important to highlight. A photo can illustrate the finished dish, as found in a variety of traditional publications: cookbooks, magazines, newspapers, and newsletters. Without food photos in these publications, it is difficult to visualize the end product. The same is true for recipes found in digital media. Good food photography communicates to consumers what they can expect when preparing that item. Cooking equipment or a specific cooking skill can also be highlighted. A photo can include a pasta machine cranking out smooth homemade noodles, the angle of a whisk used to create an emulsion for a sensational salad dressing, or the beautiful tagine used to make aromatic Moroccan stew.

Food photography can be used to illustrate the use of a food or recipe by painting a mood or story that is aligned with the intended publication's brand or goal. Different ambiance and background in a food photograph can communicate if that recipe or food is intended for a dinner party or casual brunch, an after-school snack or a family meal.

Food photography can also illustrate quantity. The recipe in its entirety can be highlighted: a pot of chicken noodle soup, a sizzling vegetable stir fry, or chilled chia

My Journey in Food Photography

by Lynn Dugan, MS, RDN

Roasted Butternut Squash Soup (2012). www.myplate2yours .wordpress.com

Roasted Butternut Squash Soup (2017). www.myplate2yours .com

Same soup, different photos. Same recipe, different response. I posted the photo on the left on my original WordPress blog in 2012. I even took the photo with an expensive digital single-lens reflex (DSLR) camera. Yikes! When I transitioned to a new website three years later, this photo screamed at me to replace it. The updated photo on the right, which I took with an iPhone 6S, was successful because of a few simple enhancements: The soup was in focus (very important!), I chose a better surface for the photo's background, I added common warm props for balance, and I shot the photo in natural light. These few changes yielded a higher-quality image and a much better consumer response.

My photography has been a journey, and my skill continues to evolve and improve. My old blogging self was more focused on the quality of the recipe. And for good reason, as I was working to build my repertoire of recipes at the time. Typically, I would make a dish for family dinner, ask my family to wait to eat it until I had a chance to photograph the food, and then settle for the photo I quickly snapped without much planning, staging, or thought. Now, when I'm trying a new recipe that I want to capture with a photo, I make sure I have time to properly stage and capture the image, or I set aside a serving to stage and shoot when I'm not rushed. Now, I would never post a photo if it didn't sell my recipe. I have learned that a quality food photo is as important as a quality recipe. It is truly a synergistic relationship!

pudding. Or, the dish may be divided up into individual portions so that the photo can also communicate serving size. Showing the portion size may be important, especially if nutrition information is included.

There are many aspects of food photography to consider in the initial stages of planning a photo shoot. Determine what to capture in a food photograph, such as any special or specific:

- cooking equipment,
- cooking procedures or techniques,
- eating occasion or holiday, and
- portion size.

These factors are the foundation for selling the food or recipe with food photography and ultimately grabbing the attention of the consumer.

What Are the Characteristics of Quality Food Photography?

The art of capturing the consumer's attention with food photography includes planning the photo as well as the quality of the finished product. The ultimate goal of the photo is to grab the consumer's interest and achieve the response: "I can make that!" This can be portrayed with a single photo: Think of Instagram, Pinterest, Twitter, and food websites. The finished food photos on these social media platforms convey a consumer's aspirations. If space allows, a series of photos can communicate the necessary cooking stages involved in making the recipe. Many food bloggers use a series of photos to illustrate procedural steps in a highlighted recipe. A photo series inspires consumer confidence with each step and offers images that more closely mimic a detailed food video.

Colors, textures, shapes, and sensory cues all contribute to the overall quality of the food photo. Colors of the food, props, background, and place setting can work together in the finished photo. If the food or finished dish contains inherent and contrasting color, it naturally stands out, as with salads, vegetable wraps, and fruit desserts. Conversely, if the food or finished dish has a bland or muted appearance, simply adding a colorful garnish can help achieve the desired look: a lemon wedge with a poached white fish, fresh berries with a warm bowl of oatmeal, and cilantro and colorful bell peppers with a steak taco.

Colorful plates and bowls or place mats and tablecloths can also help with color. It does require a special balance of colors and contrast to achieve the desired aesthetic value without distracting too much from the highlighted food. Textures and sensory cues are harder to highlight but important to overall quality. Showing the oozing center of a sliced grilled cheese sandwich, the rugged surface of whole-grain toast spread with mashed avocado, or the glistening surface of a freshly cut watermelon brings the message of authenticity.

The farm-to-table trend is evident in some of the current trends of food photography. These photos have a real, local, even organic look and feel. Place settings and props can contribute to this natural look: rugged, worn, and shabby surfaces (think of an old barn-door table, a worn wooden cutting board, and tableware with patina). But a clean, bright, "real food" trend is also popular in food photography. Whatever the desired look, it will take practice with different place settings, dishware, and props to discover the most effective way to make the food stand out in a photo.

Digital photography has made this process easier. Instant feedback with digital photography assists in achieving the desired outcome. It may take a few attempts to get the correct placement and visual appeal of dishes and table accessories, but that investment is worth the response desired from consumers: "I want to make that and eat it, too." Effective food photography incorporates a sensory appeal and contributes to this confident consumer response.

What Are Practical Strategies for Creating "Tasty" Food Photos?

Getting good-quality, mouthwatering shots of food doesn't happen by chance. A photographer needs to plan for success! If shooting food photos for personal use, as is the case with many personal blogs, there is more leeway with the strategies that follow. If contracted to shoot for a brand or second party, however, then there are more factors to consider. (See the Words of Experience box

WORDS OF EXPERIENCE

A Note on Working with Brands

Marie Ferguson, graphic designer, photographer, and food enthusiast, DM Creative Design, Eyota, MN

Planning is the key to success when working with a second party. Communicate a solid vision and budget early. Find out whether the brand desires historical consistency (in other words, all photos adhere to a set standard for the brand). Consider every aspect of the planned photo to achieve this vision: style, lighting, background (including textures and colors), and props. This planning needs to happen well before the food or recipe is prepared for the shoot, because, despite our best efforts, the fresh look of the food does fade (soufflés fall, baked macaroni and cheese dries out, and even fresh garnishes wither). The background, lighting, and props must all be in place and ready for the shoot to best guarantee success. Food photography is artistry with one click. I track my success with photos of the setup and a journal of measurements to keep a record of what did and did not work; it is a valuable resource.

on what to consider when working with a second party.) In either case, anyone can adapt the strategies presented here to suit their individual needs.

Focus on the following six components of food photography to create food photos and recipes to be proud of. The basics of each of these components are covered in this chapter, recognizing that full-length books, advanced training, and coursework are available to fully address each of these areas:

- Developing and testing recipes
- Food styling tips and tricks
- Photo equipment options
- Adequate lighting
- Photo composition
- Soliciting feedback

For more on writing recipes see Box 42.4 on page 656.

Developing and Testing Recipes

Recipe development is truly an art. Recipes can be developed from scratch, but inspiration can also be found by browsing recipes from different sources. Recipe inspirations can come from cookbooks, food magazines, online media outlets, other food bloggers, and even relatives. From a legal standpoint, recipes are not protected under copyright law. According to the US Copyright Office[1]:

Copyright law does not protect recipes that are mere listings of ingredients. Copyright protection may, however, extend to substantial literary expression—a description, explanation, or illustration [food photo], for example—that accompanies a recipe or to a combination of recipes, as in a cookbook.

Regardless of copyright law, however, it is professional courtesy to credit the recipe's original source, even if several changes are made. If publishing in print media, add a byline in the recipe. If publishing in digital media, link back to the original recipe somewhere in the blog post or article. Even when a recipe looks and tastes different from the one that inspired it, it is appropriate to credit the original recipe with "adapted from X" or "inspired by Y."

Once a list of possible recipes has been identified, it's time to test them—at least twice! Skipping recipe testing can lead to unhappy customers, especially if they do not achieve the correct finished product after following the recipe. The first test is critical because it indicates whether the ingredients and directions produce the desired result. This test will help to make:

- **ingredient adjustments** to get the desired taste (sweet, salty, sour, bitter, savory), sensory appeal (aroma, texture), and yield;
- **direction adjustments** to get optimal cooking time, temperature, technique, and equipment.

Additionally, the first test can help inform the next step: food styling. If a dish is rather drab and monotone, such as turkey with gravy, it may be helpful to add color with garnishes and props.

The purpose of the second test (and beyond) is simple: to ensure the adjustments made in the first (or previous) test will lead to good results. If all goes well, the recipe made the second time can be used for the food photo.

Food Styling Tips and Tricks

A professional food photo shoot is usually carried out by a team that includes an art director, photographer, food stylist, and prop stylist.[2] This can make food photography seem very intimidating to those just starting out and working as a one-person team. However, many amateur and solo photographers have been able to create high-quality food photos for personal and professional use. And if this is a first attempt, results will naturally improve with practice. The goal is to get gorgeous shots of food using what is already in the kitchen pantry.

An effective food photo highlights the main dish and stimulates the viewer's imagination. Consider an untouched stack of pancakes compared to a stack of pancakes with a wedge cut out, as if someone has taken a bite. If a viewer sees a stack of fluffy pancakes with a wedge cut out, he or she may start to imagine who began eating the hearty breakfast, and in doing so, will make a more intimate connection to the food. Creative food styling involves experimenting with food, settings, and backgrounds to create a desired mood or story.

Nonfood and food props help achieve a desired look. Food props typically include ingredients used to cook up a dish, such as the main ingredients, herbs, spices, and garnishes. Salt and pepper shakers, a butter dish, or any other condiments that commonly accompany a dish can be included. Even human elements can add interest to any scene. A hand holding a utensil or a hand grasping a cup or glass can be very effective. Box 26.1 describes the effective use of nonfood props.

Once the appropriate props have been selected, it's time to style the food. Being a good food stylist means having a keen eye for detail. When starting out, it's helpful to make extra servings of food in case there's an issue with the photo shoot. How food appears on camera is a direct result of how much time and effort is put into it off camera. Before styling, it's helpful to visualize how the shot will look. Will the shot be horizontal or vertical? Straight on or overhead? Will the entire dish be visible or just a fraction of it? Everyone has their own personal flair for food styling, but check out Box 26.2 for technical tips to help build a beautiful plate. Pick up an extra tip in the Words of Experience box on page 412 for a note on selecting backgrounds and settings for food photography.

Photo Equipment Options

Having the right equipment is important, but it does not guarantee the best food photos. Equally important is learning how to use equipment and becoming comfortable and adept with whatever camera is chosen. This section will describe

BOX 26.1 Nonfood Props 101

Five Quick Tips for Prop Selection

Your foods should be the star in your photography, but props play an important supporting role. When selecting props, keep in mind that they should complement, not compete, with your food and its story. Here are some quick tips for effectively using props.

- **Keep the mood in mind.** Are you going for rustic, casual, light and bright, or dark and dramatic? This is driven by the creative direction of your particular project.
- **Simple is better.** Steer clear of distracting shapes, patterns, textures, and colors; examples include bold checkered patterns, large polka dots, or high-contrast colors. White, beige, black, gray, pastel, and muted colors work best because they won't outdo most foods. A matte finish is less distracting than a shiny finish.
- **Downsize your plate and bowls.** This is a well-known styling trick! Using smaller tableware makes your food look larger and more appealing to the viewer.
- **Build authenticity with backgrounds and surfaces.** Natural textures like wood, stone, marble, and metal are best. Scratched baking sheets and distressed wood are popular because they lend an air of authenticity to your food's story.
- **Use contrast for visual interest.** Your props should be a different color and texture than your food. Layer a tablecloth, napkin, and plate to add interest.

Common Nonfood Props

- Plates
- Bowls
- Serving dishes
- Silverware
- Serving utensils
- Chef knives
- Spatulas and tongs

- Pots and pans
- Cooling racks
- Linens
- Napkins
- Tablecloths
- Cutting boards or pastry boards
- Wood surface

- Water pitchers
- Colanders
- Herb and spice jars
- Cheese graters
- Glasses and mugs
- Mason jars

- Measuring cups and spoons
- Salt and pepper shakers
- Wooden bowls
- Rolling pins

---

equipment options, beginning with digital cameras. The two types of digital cameras are point-and-shoot and digital single-lens reflex (DSLR). See the resources section at the end of the chapter for a recommended book to learn more about DSLR photography.

POINT-AND-SHOOT VS DIGITAL SINGLE-LENS REFLEX CAMERAS

Point-and-shoot cameras are small, palm-sized cameras that take the guesswork out of photography. The exposure and focus cannot be fully adjusted. The point-and-shoot camera does the calculations and makes the decision for the photographer. Pretty food photos can be attained from a point-and-shoot camera, but it's hard to get the highest-quality photos because there is less control over the settings that allow light into

the camera. A point-and-shoot camera is a good option for beginners. To advance food photography skills, invest in a DSLR camera.

DSLR cameras are more complex. For example, it is possible to purchase a camera body that works with a variety of interchangeable lenses. There are also more modes to shoot in, which allows for control of the amount of light entering the camera. As with a point-and-shoot camera, the camera can make all the decisions in "automatic" mode, but for more photographic control and customizable quality, transitioning over to "manual" mode may be best. Manual mode allows for control of the exposure by adjusting aperture, shutter speed, and ISO speed (all defined next) in what's known as the "exposure triangle"[3]:

Food Styling Technical Tips

Some professional food stylists concoct mashed potato "ice cream" and use WD-40 to make food glisten for that perfect shot. While these strategies may work, it may be just as desirable to have food that can be eaten after the shoot. Here are a few food-styling technical tips that allow for just that:

- **Brush cut fruit with lemon juice.** The citric acid prevents it from browning.
- **Undercook vegetables.** This helps them hold their color and firmness for longer.
- **Wrap herbs and leafy greens in a damp paper towel.** It keeps their delicate leaves from wilting during a shoot.
- **Spritz whole fruits and veggies with water.** This will give them a just-picked look, if that's what is desired.
- **Brush oil on grilled and roasted meats.** It helps them appear juicier and more enticing.
- **Use mashed potatoes to bulk up soups and stews.** Add mashed potatoes to the bottom of bowls before ladling on the soup. Don't skimp on adding more soup solids (eg, chunks of potatoes, cut carrots, cooked meat) to each bowl. This makes the soup look heartier and more abundant.
- **Use a spoon to texturize thick dips and spreads.** Creating spirals on the surface of hummus, guacamole, spinach dip, and other similar dishes adds visual interest.
- **Meats should be cooked rare, sliced, and cooled before shooting.** Rare meat looks juicier. Slicing and cooling allows extra juices to escape so they won't dribble out onto the plate during the shoot.
- **Spritz baked goods with butter-flavored cooking spray.** This enhances the golden appearance of buns, rolls, breads, and more.
- **Lightly toss cooked pasta in oil.** It keeps individual pieces of pasta from drying and sticking together and gives the pasta an appetizing sheen.
- **Don't be afraid to get messy.** Food spilling out over the bowl or even onto the surface makes the scene more realistic and authentic.
- **Garnish savory dishes with herbs, cheese, or nuts.** Chopped mint, basil, cilantro, or onion can enhance color contrast. Chopped nuts and shredded cheese can add texture. Use a pair of tweezers to position these items.
- **Sprinkle sweets and baked dishes with confections.** A dusting of powdered sugar or shaved chocolate gives cakes, cookies, and pies another dimension.
- **Drizzle extra sauce.** Chocolate sauce, Sriracha, pesto, and olive oil can be dispensed into a squeezable bottle so the drizzle can be controlled.

WORDS OF EXPERIENCE

A Note on Choosing a Background

Ashley Zaher, photo production coordinator, Williams-Sonoma Inc, San Francisco, CA

A marble surface or counter is an excellent background because it captures light nicely and helps highlight the natural colors of the food. A dark slate also works well because it can help provide just the right amount of contrast to the overall look of the image, especially when using white or light-colored dinnerware or service ware. It also helps to provide a bit more drama. Make sure to always be thinking of the type of food being photographed and play toward that theme. For example, comfort food may work better on a darker surface, and fruit or a breakfast item may look better on a marble surface or a light wood—bright and clean. It's important to find props and surfaces that are relatable to potential followers and viewers so they can imagine themselves replicating that recipe and having the end product turn out the same.

Aperture controls the amount of light that enters a camera. Light enters the camera through a hole that's measured by the f-stop—for example, f/1.2, f/1.4, f/4.0, f/10, and so on. The smaller the number, the bigger the f-stop, meaning the bigger the hole, which allows more light to enter the camera. This results in a shallow depth of field and a blurry background that's common in many food photos (see Box 26.3 for more information).

Shutter speed controls how long light has to enter a camera. It's measured in fractions of a second—for example, 1/45, 1/90, 1/180, and 1/500. A slow shutter speed lets in more light and is good for dim environments. A fast shutter speed lets in less light but is better at capturing quick motions without blur. With food photography, the subject is more forgiving than kids or pets. Lighting can be controlled and the subject will stay in one place. Because of this, adjusting shutter speed is less of an issue. Depending on what aperture is picked, adjust the shutter speed to let in appropriate light. Use a faster shutter speed to offset shaky hands and lack of a tripod.

ISO speed controls how sensitive a camera's sensor is to light. The higher the number, the more sensitive the sensor is to light. Examples of ISO (which stands for International Standards Organization) numbers are 100, 200, 400, and 800. High ISO may help in dimmer environments, but it comes at the cost of graininess and "noise" in the photo. A low ISO leads to better image quality, but the ISO may need to be increased if photos are being taken in the evening.

A NOTE ON DIGITAL SINGLE-LENS REFLEX CAMERA LENSES

For new DSLR camera owners, it's important to get a lot of practice and learn the full capabilities of the camera. Practice taking photographs with the lens that comes with the camera. This will help to clarify its limitations. It may or may not be necessary to upgrade to another lens. If getting another lens, keep in mind that aperture is important for food photography. Look for a lens that allows for the use of the desired f-stop. Finally, if it is too difficult to get close enough to the food to achieve a larger-than-life photo, try looking into macro lenses.

What's Bokeh?

A digital single-lens reflex (DSLR) camera's lens is like the iris of a human eye. It controls how much light enters by dilating or contracting. An f-stop such as f/1.8 will result in a smaller focus area than f/16. This allows the photographer to artistically focus on a segment in the photo while throwing the foreground and background out of focus. This blurry, out-of-focus area is known as bokeh.

TIP: Bokeh can be achieved by shooting manually with a DSLR camera or by opting for "aperture" mode. In aperture mode, the photographer selects the f-stop and the camera chooses the shutter speed and ISO. An aperture of f/1.8 to f/3.0 is good for food photos, but experiment with it. Keep in mind that a camera's lens must be able to accommodate an aperture of f/1.8 to f/3.0 to have bokeh in the photographs.

Bokeh with f/1.8   Bokeh with f/4.5   Bokeh with f/16

Photos reproduced with permission from Trinh Le, MPH, RD, from Fearless Food RD (www.fearlessfoodrd.com).

SMARTPHONE CAMERAS

The camera on a smartphone can be used for food photography. The mere convenience of a smartphone camera is a huge advantage. Photos can be taken, edited, and uploaded to blogs, websites, and social media platforms directly from the phone. And since technology continues to advance, camera features improve with every phone update. In addition, the development of photography apps and accessories also aids in making smartphone cameras—both iPhone and Android—a viable option for food photography.

There are some basic differences between a DSLR and a smartphone camera. See Figure 26.1 for an example of image quality from an iPhone.

There is significantly less control of the photo taken with a smartphone than with a DSLR camera. This fact makes it necessary to control the environment. Natural light is optimal for smartphone photography. Artificial lighting can give an unwanted yellow or orange hue to a photo. Because of this, using a flash is not ideal for smartphone food photography. Use the tips described in Working with a Natural Light Source on page 415 to achieve the optimal environment.

There is a main feature on smartphones that gives the user some control of the photo: The exposure on the camera can be adjusted. For example, when snapping a photo on an iPhone, start by tapping the screen to set focus on what is desired to appear sharp. Then slide a finger up or down on the screen. Sliding up will increase the exposure, making the image brighter. Sliding down will decrease the exposure and make the image darker. On Android phones, this line appears horizontally, and tapping along the line increases or decreases exposure. It is best to take multiple pictures since sometimes the images look good at first glance but then appear blurry upon closer inspection or when uploaded to a computer for editing.

There are literally hundreds of apps and accessories to aid smartphone photography, such as apps that help to achieve the bokeh effect described in Box 26.3. One example, the Big Lens app, allows a photographer to add depth of field, like using a DSLR camera, in order to achieve a similar effect for photos taken with an iPhone or iOS device. It

FIGURE 26.1 **Food photograph taken with an iPhone**

Reproduced with permission from Lynn Dugan, MS, RDN, from MyPlate2Yours (www.myplate2yours.com).

is best to do research on available apps to determine what will work best for any particular needs or situation. YouTube videos, Google searches, and iPhone Photography School are resources for making these decisions. Available accessories for smartphones include external lenses, tripods, and lighting systems. It is best to work with the inherent features of the phone and try a few low-cost apps first before investing in expensive equipment.

Basic photo editing, like cropping, enhancing, and adjusting brightness and color, can be done on the phone. More advanced apps can also be used for editing directly on the phone. There are many apps for this purpose, so it is wise to search and review these apps to find the one that suits a given skill level and desired outcome. It is also easy to upload photos for online editing, as would be done with photos from DSLR cameras.

Adequate Lighting

Good lighting is essential for high-quality food photography. Even a well-plated meal will look unappetizing if it's poorly lit or marred by shadows. When it comes to lighting, choose between a natural light source, such as sunlight, and an artificial light source. Natural light is beautiful and familiar, but it can be unreliable. The time of day and season of the year can affect the quality and availability of natural light. Artificial light helps with this challenge. However, either source can provide adequate light for the perfect food photo.

WORKING WITH A NATURAL LIGHT SOURCE

Natural light is free but less predictable. If using natural light, do a few test shots on the camera near various windows in the home or office. Depending on the home or office layout, the kitchen or dining room may not be the best locations. Some say to consider north- and south-facing windows since the light source is more diffuse. Even so, sunlight can be strong and harsh, so it will need to be softened by placing a sheer white drape across the window. This acts as a diffuser to scatter the light. Ideally, use natural light about 2 hours before sunset. The sun's intensity at that time has softened to provide better photographic quality.

Be creative and look for ways to shape the natural light. A large white poster board or card can reflect or channel the direction of natural light. Try placing the poster board opposite a

WORDS OF EXPERIENCE

A Note on Working with Reflective Surfaces

Kelly Swartz, president/owner and photographer, Kelly Swartz Photography, Chicago, IL

While your culinary masterpiece is the hero of the shot, food photography also means you're shooting glassware, dishes, and silverware, and they have highly reflective surfaces. Many times, when looking closer at what initially seems like a great shot, you'll notice reflections of the camera, the photographer, lights, or things used to prep the shot. Make sure you zoom in and take a look! It's much easier to make that correction and adjustments before you complete the photo session than when you edit it after the session. More often than not, simply tilting an angle, moving a fork, or adjusting a light placement eliminates unwanted reflections. Light tents and reflective cards can also help block out distracting environments on highly reflective surfaces.

direct-lighted window with the food to be photographed in between the window and the board. The board will act to balance the light and reflect it back onto the food. Sometimes two boards can be positioned opposite each other to reflect the light in different directions. There will be reduced shadows since the light will be reflected on opposing sides.

WORKING WITH AN ARTIFICIAL LIGHT SOURCE

Artificial light is reliable, but it will require investing in more equipment since the artificial light inherent to a home or office is not photo quality. There are a variety of light boxes and lighting kits on the market at different price points. Decide which is right for a given situation, but don't get too bogged down by all these gadgets. To keep it simple, use one light box to be a light source, or two maximum. These light boxes should come with their own diffuser, but if not, placing a sheer white drape over them will do the trick. (See the Words of Experience box for lighting tips and how to work with reflective surfaces.) Alternatively, there are some great guides online for how to build a light box for a fraction of the cost.

SETTING UP A SHOOT

Once the primary light source is established, it's time to arrange the table or shooting surface in relation to the light source. Prioritize sidelight or backlight for food photography. Move the table or surface so that the light source(s) illuminates the food from the back or side. This creates interesting shadows, making the food appear more natural. Avoid applying frontlighting to the food because it creates a boring, flat look. Frontlighting means the light source is placed in front of the food, or the same direction that the camera is facing.

What about the side or sides that don't receive much light? Certain areas may have too many shadows. If that's the case, a reflector can lighten these shadows. A reflector is usually made of gold, white, or silver that can bounce light back onto the food. A dark reflector (usually black) can also be used if there's a need to absorb extra light from bright areas, but this is uncommon.[4] Please note that it isn't necessary to purchase expensive reflectors. A medium to large white poster board works really well as long as it's propped up correctly. Try a white, trifold foam board (found very reasonably priced at a local craft store). Once the setup is complete, it's time to plate the food and start shooting.

Photo Composition

Get creative with photo composition and practice, practice, practice! One of the benefits of digital photography is that it is possible to take as many shots as desired—keep the best and delete the rest. This section will cover camera angles, wide and tight shots, and the rule of thirds.

THREE COMMON CAMERA ANGLES

Three traditional camera angles used in food photography are discussed here. Figure 26.2 shows visual examples of each angle.

Diner's Angle This angle shows what would be seen from the viewpoint of a diner. The view is slightly above the food, looking down at it. It's an inviting gaze, between 20 and 55 degrees, with lower angles allowing space for background props.

Straight On This angle puts the viewer at the same height as the food. It highlights the food's height and is often used with pancake stacks, tiered cakes, and tall sandwiches or burgers.

Top Down As the name suggests, this angle involves shooting directly above the food, with the camera held level to the shooting surface. Shooting farther out allows more space to showcase component ingredients in the dish or to set the context of the meal. However, there won't be much depth to the food.

WIDE VERSUS TIGHT SHOTS

A wide shot is zoomed out and shows the whole (or close to whole) food subject along with props and any background elements. Wider shots put food in context—for example, a wide shot may show a plate of cookies along with the glass of milk and linen napkin it is being served with. On the other hand, a tight shot is zoomed in and shows more details of the food. Tighter shots magnify details, such as a cookie with a bite taken out and crumbly edges. Try to capture both wide and tight photos of food for more variety. Wide and tight shots are shown in Figure 26.3.

THE RULE OF THIRDS

Finally, no photography discussion is complete without bringing up the rule of thirds.[5] This rule can be used to frame all photos, not just food photos. It involves using lines to divide a shot into three equal parts horizontally and vertically. This creates four intersection points. The sharpest, most visually interesting components in photography should ideally be placed at any of these four points. See Figure 26.4 for examples.

Soliciting Feedback

After shooting a few food photos, gather feedback to help improve various photography skills. Share the photos with family, friends, or colleagues or on social media channels such as Snapchat, Instagram, and Pinterest.

FIGURE 26.2 **Common camera angles in food photography**

Photos reproduced with permission from Trinh Le, MPH, RD, from Fearless Food RD (www.fearlessfoodrd.com).

FIGURE 26.3 **Wide versus tight shots**

Photos reproduced with permission from Trinh Le, MPH, RD, from Fearless Food RD (www.fearlessfoodrd.com).

FIGURE 26.4 **Rule of thirds in action**

Photos reproduced with permission from Trinh Le, MPH, RD, from Fearless Food RD (www.fearlessfoodrd.com).

On Finding Your Niche in Nutrition

Trinh Le, MPH, RD, food and nutrition blogger, www.fearlessfoodrd.com

As nutrition professionals, we are lucky to work in such a vast and ever-changing field! There are tons of opportunities, so finding your niche can be challenging. I found mine by combining my formal training as a dietitian with two of my favorite hobbies: writing and photography. I started my Fearless Food RD blog (www.fearlessfoodrd.com) at the start of 2017 after working for a few years as a content marketing manager for MyFitnessPal.

This blog became my outlet for sharing recipes, stories, and advice with friends and family. It also taught me the power of pictures and words in nutrition communication. Over time, I honed my food styling and photography skills, one recipe at a time. On the left is a photo of my salmon burger shot for fun in 2015, and on the right is the same salmon burger restyled and reshot in 2017. Both images were taken with a digital single-lens reflex (DSLR) camera, so you can see how my photography skills have changed over the years. I like looking back on my progress, and there is value in both photos. If you're new, don't be too hard on yourself because you will get better!

Salmon Burger (2015)

Shot under dim lighting with no real focus point. Prop selection isn't thought through.

Salmon Burger (2017)

Shot under bright lighting with good focus on the burger patty. A straight-on composition is used to emphasize the burger's height.

KEY POINTS

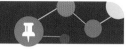

Inspire Audiences with Food Styling and Photography

1 Quality food photography is important for nutrition communicators, as it enhances food and nutrition writing in both print and digital media and makes online recipes and articles shareworthy.

2 A special balance of colors and contrast is important to achieving the desired aesthetic value without distracting from the highlighted food.

3 Food styling and photography are learned skills. More practice equals better food photos.

RESOURCES

Black B. *DSLR Photography for Beginners: Take 10 Times Better Pictures in 48 Hours or Less! Best Way to Learn Digital Photography, Master Your DSLR Camera, and Improve Your Digital SLR Photography Skills*. Brian Black; 2013.

REFERENCES

1. US Copyright Office. Works not protected by copyright. Accessed June 30, 2019.www.copyright .gov/circs/circ33.pdf
2. Ferroni L. *Food Photography: Pro Secrets for Styling, Lighting and Shooting*. Pixiq; 2012.
3. Cambridge in Colour. Camera exposure. Accessed December 10, 2017. www.cambridgeincolour.com /tutorials/camera-exposure.htm
4. Parks-Whitfield A. Lighting equipment needed for food photography. Dummies website. Accessed December 10, 2017. www.dummies .com/photography/digital-photography/types-of -photography/lighting-equipment-needed-for -food-photography
5. Parks-Whitfield A. How to frame images in food photography. Dummies website. Accessed December 10, 2017. www.dummies.com /photography/digital-photography/types-of -photography/how-to-frame-images-in-food -photography

SECTION 6

Designing and Delivering Communication via Mass Media

A Podcasting Journey: How I've Recorded More Than 300 Episodes over a Decade

Liz Weiss, MS, RDN, host of *Liz's Healthy Table* podcast and blog

Liz Weiss, MS, RDN

I'm at my laptop with my headphones on, waiting for Sandor Katz to answer my Skype call. In a few seconds, I'll be talking with one of the world's foremost experts on food fermentation for my podcast, *Liz's Healthy Table*. Soon thousands of people will hear our conversation. Am I nervous? Maybe a little. But it's not too bad. I've done this hundreds of times before.

Podcasting has gone from being a way to promote my platform (business) to being one of my foremost tools for reaching and teaching people about planning and prepping healthful family meals. I can't imagine my life or my business without it. It has helped to build and grow my online brand, establish me as an expert in the family nutrition arena, and bring in new partnerships via sponsored blog posts and podcast episodes, speaking engagements, and sponsored TV segments. It's a powerful tool available to a small business owner, and I have fantastic news: Getting your own podcast off the ground isn't as daunting as it may seem.

Podcasting is still relatively new and can be a bit perplexing, with some people saying, "What's that?" and some ready to launch into their 20 must-listen shows. For those of you among the former, here's Apple's definition: "Podcasts are episodes of a program available on the Internet. Podcasts are usually original audio or video recordings, but can also be recorded broadcasts of a television or radio program, a lecture, a performance, or other event."[1]

Now you're all caught up.

Millions of Downloads

When I began podcasting, it was all new territory. Before I began my current website, blog, and podcast, *Liz's Healthy Table*, I co-owned an online platform with fellow dietitian Janice Newell Bissex called *Meal Makeover Moms*. Together, we wrote cookbooks and created a food and nutrition blog.

In 2007, Janice and I heard from two fellow bloggers who also happened to host a wildly successful podcast called *The Manic Mommies*. They invited us to join them on their podcast as guests, and after being on their show, we were hooked. We knew they had a huge audience with thousands of mom listeners, so we decided to start a podcast of our own to reach a similar audience.

At the time, there weren't too many registered dietitian nutritionists (RDNs) who were podcasting, so we saw an opportunity to jump into the game early. We created *Cooking with the Moms*, a podcast available on our website and on iTunes.

Our gamble on this new form of media paid off enormously. Over 9 years, we had millions—literally millions!—of downloads and heard from listeners with thanks, praise, topic ideas, and personal stories of how our show was changing family eating habits and mealtime dynamics for the better. Those communications with our audience kept us going. We created a dynamic and engaged community that has stayed with me to this day.

We recorded an astonishing 297 episodes featuring just about every topic imaginable: Picky Eater Pointers, Healthy Holiday Baking, Tips for Reducing Food Waste, Egg Nutrition, Smart Snacking, Lunchbox 101—and the ever-popular Brussels Sprouts Show!

The Next Chapter

When it was time for Janice and I to part ways and pursue our own passions, I knew I wasn't ready to give up podcasting, so I created *Liz's Healthy Table*, where I serve up wholesome, flavorful recipes with a tasty side of science, good nutrition, and fun. As a mom of two grown boys, my focus is on the family. Since I no longer have a sidekick to cohost the show with, I invite fellow dietitians, cookbook authors, and chefs onto the show. As of August 2018, I'm 35 episodes into *Liz's Healthy Table*, and I'm busy planning out the next few dozen! I'm covering topics like Cooking on a Budget, Going Meatless More Often, Eating Sustainably, Freezer Cooking, the Art of Fermentation, Managing Food Allergies, Cooking with Pulses, and so much more. My shows provide practical advice and recipe ideas, and it's fun for listeners to get to know my guests and hear their mealtime stories. I have a closed group on Facebook, which I call Liz's Podcast Posse, that anyone can join. The beauty of the group is that I'm able to crowdsource show topic ideas and encourage members to ask my guests questions, which we then answer on the show.

Make Your Own Podcast

Does all this sound great to you? Then maybe you should consider starting your own podcast. Here are some tips that will make the process much smoother:

- Determine your niche. What are you passionate about? What can you talk about for hours on end?
- Listen to lots of other shows to figure out how your show can add to the content out there.
- Decide if you'll record the show alone or whether you'll invite guests to join you. In other words, figure out the format.
- Figure out the dos and don'ts of recording, editing, and uploading. I recommend hiring a podcast consultant to work out the kinks and assist you with the start-up phase and possibly

implementation. I use Skype to record my interviews. I hire TeamPodcast.com to edit each episode and to write the first draft for my companion show notes, and I make my show available for download on my website as well as on iTunes, Stitcher Radio, Google Play, iHeartRadio, and a few more!

Spreading the Word

I've been in the podcasting trenches for a decade, and I now realize that producing and recording the shows is the easy part. The challenge is spreading the word so the world can discover you. One thing I love to do is pitch myself as a guest on other parenting podcasts. Being a guest on someone else's show introduces me to a new audience and enables me to forge new relationships with fellow podcast hosts. Just like with blogging, where it's important to build community with other bloggers, podcast hosts do the same thing. I'm in a Podcast Mastermind Group and a closed Facebook group with fellow RDN podcasters. The benefits: We avoid isolation, promote each other's shows, and are a resource for one another.

I ♥ Podcasting!

For me, podcasting isn't a last resort because I "can't get placement" anywhere else—in fact, I have a huge amount of experience in traditional media, including producing and reporting on nutrition at CNN for 5 years. Communicating to the public via mass media is in my DNA. For me, though, podcasting is my favorite way to do it. I have complete control. I get to decide on the topics, guests, and featured recipes, and I'm able to share my life with my listeners. There's a level of intimacy and authenticity I achieve that resonates with listeners and just feels right to me.

Embracing new technologies may seem daunting, but there are resources out there to help you get started. Search the internet, network with fellow podcasters, and consider hiring a consultant when you're getting started. I love the challenge of podcasting, hearing from listeners, and getting to know my guests, and I look forward to the day I hit 400 shows!

REFERENCE

1. For podcast fans: frequently asked questions. what is a podcast? Apple Inc. website. Accessed December 16, 2019. www.apple.com/itunes/podcasts/fanfaq.html

Nutrition Communicators Have Greater Reach via Mass Media

Melissa Joy Dobbins, MS, RDN, CDCES
Anna Busenburg, RDN, CSP, LD, CLC
Carolyn O'Neil, MS, RDN, LD
and Jaime Schwartz Cohen, MS, RD

"Positioning the registered dietitian nutritionist as the nutrition expert via mass media is critical for maximizing reach, sharing messages quickly, and countering inaccurate information."

"Three minutes in front of the camera is worth more than three years behind the desk."

—JEAN REGALIE-CARR, RDN

Introduction

Communicating via mass media allows food and nutrition professionals to reach the widest possible audience quickly and efficiently. Never before have so many media channels existed to reach audiences around the world. To reach people effectively requires nutrition communicators to be savvy with technology and mass media. Those with the greatest reach do so using various media outlets. Nutrition communicators have important messages to share. Optimize the use of mass media channels to spread messages farther and faster.

This chapter answers three questions:

- What is the rationale for communicating via mass media?
- What are best practices for communicating via mass media?
- What are practical strategies for communicating via mass media?

After reading this chapter, readers will have a better understanding of why mass media is an essential and effective tool for nutrition communicators, how to use various media outlets to share messages, and practical strategies for successfully communicating via mass media.

What Is the Rationale for Communicating via Mass Media?

Communicating via mass media is important for two main reasons: Mass media expands the reach of the nutrition communicator's message, and, equally important, the nutrition communicator provides the media with an accurate and reliable source for news and information about food and nutrition. It's a win-win-win for the media, the communicator, and the consumer.

Food and nutrition professionals play a vital role in the media. The media is looking for experts to comment on nutrition news and provide expertise and context. If registered dietitian nutritionists (RDNs) aren't available, less-informed and underqualified interviewees may be chosen, perhaps spreading nutrition misinformation on a topic. RDNs are the most prepared professionals to speak on nutrition topics to lay audiences because of their knowledge of food and nutrition science and experience with sharing practical consumer guidance.

In turn, the media provides the nutrition communicator with access to the widest audience. In fact, to reach the largest possible audience, nothing is more efficient than mass media. Every potential audience member has access to one or more forms of mass media: web-based channels, traditional television and radio, podcasting, print media, and social media. However, figuring out how various platforms work and how best to use them can seem overwhelming. Begin by taking the time to learn about different mass media channels and determine how to present and share a message.

Nutrition communicators have an obligation to be present on mass media to provide evidence-based information for people seeking answers to nutrition-related questions. Positioning the RDN as the nutrition expert via mass media is critical for maximizing reach, sharing messages quickly, and countering inaccurate information.

Maximize Reach!

Mass media provides an opportunity to concisely share a message with hundreds, thousands, possibly millions of people all over the world. No other means of communication comes close to maximizing reach. Using a mass media platform to share an idea has the potential to reach people not only locally but globally, making it a powerful form of communication. For example, on Twitter, that tweet of up to 280 characters is on the internet for not only followers but potentially the more than 300 million other users to see (depending on privacy settings).[1]

Various forms of mass media have differing levels of impact. A tweet could reach people all over the world, compared with a newspaper interview in a small town that is likely to be seen only by local subscribers. However, if someone tweets a link to the online newspaper article, it increases the reach of that local interview. The chosen mass media platform determines the potential size of the target audience.

Craft nutrition messages to fit the potential target audience and the media platform. Create clear and memorable key points and takeaway messages. To provide additional information, a 280-character tweet might contain a link to a newspaper article, research abstract, or a blog post on the topic. Every mass media platform reaches a particular audience and delivers messages using a specific format (eg, words and photos for a newspaper, or video for television).[2] Make the message match the medium.

Tailoring the message to each audience and mass media platform will help maximize a message's reach. For example, if sharing a blog post on Twitter, Facebook, and LinkedIn, write different introductions for each one. Tailor the introductory comments to fit each platform's audience. Taking that extra step to personalize the message for each media platform will help users effectively share their message.

Maximize Speed

Consumers today expect instant information. A message sent via text, email, or post on social media has the potential to reach an audience within seconds. But just because a message reaches a follower's Twitter feed seconds after hitting Tweet, that doesn't mean the message will be seen or read. If a post appears while someone is off-line, it will be buried below more recent posts, which will be viewed first. Speed helps reach an audience but doesn't guarantee engagement.

Using various mass media platforms can help get the nutrition message out to a broader audience. The goal is to share information in real time and have people read what is shared. Determine whom to reach with each media post. If the same message is appropriate for a wide audience, it can be shared quickly to more people by linking to multiple mass media platforms. For example, on Instagram, users can share a picture post via Twitter and Facebook. If RDNs are at a professional conference and share their experience on one platform, they can also share that post simultaneously via the other social media platforms.

Mass media is dynamic. News outlets are constantly seeking the latest information to share with the public. For nutrition communicators to be involved in mass media requires them to be able to quickly share their nutrition expertise. When a news reporter contacts a nutrition professional for an interview, the professional is expected to be well versed on the requested topic. When asked to speak on a topic that is not within their expertise, communicators must know when to refer the reporter to a colleague. Staying up to date on nutrition research and current nutrition trends helps nutrition communicators be prepared to speak on a variety of topics. Resources for keeping current follow later in this chapter; Chapter 32 discusses preparing for media interviews. The Words of Experience box illustrates how to prepare scientific evidence–based information in a timely manner for a media interview.

Counter the Competition of Misinformation

The public will often turn to public figures, celebrities, or web-based influencers for advice on nutrition and health. When the public wants answers to nutrition-related questions, they are likely to search the internet via their computer, smartphone, or tablet. A potential audience member may or may not have the skills to separate fact from fiction on the internet. To counter misinformation from less-than-credible sources, credentialed food and nutrition professionals need to be present on mass media platforms providing accurate information.

Refer to Chapter 29 for more on personalizing a message for various social media channels.

For example, many consumers want an easy fix to better their health and may seek out information about the latest supplement, detox, or cleanse. People reading, viewing, or listening to a media article or segment about a popular supplement may wonder whether it will help them lose weight or make them look and feel younger. What they really need to know is whether it's effective from an evidence-based standpoint. The nutrition communicator can provide evidence-based information in a clear and compelling manner that consumers can understand.

The media looks to experts to provide input on a story, but if a credentialed professional is not available, they may call on people who are not nutrition experts to give nutrition advice, potentially resulting in misinformation. A nutrition professional's role is to present evidence-based information. When asked about a fad diet or an unsubstantiated food or nutrition trend, the nutrition expert needs to be ready to address why a diet trend may not be scientifically validated. Nutrition professionals have the training and tools to present evidence-based nutrition information in a way that is relatable and easy to understand. Changing jargon into everyday language and providing context the general public can relate to can effectively combat misinformation.

The goal for the nutrition communicator is to proactively share credible nutrition information to elicit positive dietary behaviors.[3] Nutrition communicators who use mass media are able to reach more people in a timely manner, present evidence-based nutrition messages, and counter nutrition misinformation. When pseudoscience circulates on talk shows and the internet, nutrition communicators can provide evidence-based information to help consumers discern between falsehoods and evidence-based recommendations. To help counter misinformation, consult the most recent Academy of Nutrition and Dietetics position papers on current topics (see the resources section at the end of the chapter).

Position the Dietitian as the Nutrition Expert

The media, whether print, online, or broadcast, relies on subject matter experts who can provide background information and quotes. This provides a great opportunity for RDNs to be *the* resource that the media turns to for expertise when they cover nutrition and health-related topics.

WORDS OF EXPERIENCE

Quick Turnaround

by Anna Busenburg, RDN, CSP

As a clinical dietitian, I have worked in a hospital throughout my career. A common goal of each hospital where I have been employed is for the hospital to serve as a nutrition resource for the community. I wanted to be involved in providing this service and represent the hospital at public speaking events. To get started, I began with cultivating a positive relationship with the hospital's public relations department. I got to know the staff in the public relations office and checked in with them on a regular basis to see if they needed someone to speak about nutrition-related topics. Whenever the public relations department was contacted by a local media outlet to address a nutrition topic, they would call me and I was happy to put together a story.

Often these media requests require a fast turnaround. Working with mass media requires a communicator to be flexible and to use resources to quickly put together a segment that contains evidence-based recommendations. As a nutrition expert, whatever I say on television needs to be accurate and easy to understand. Developing the skills to quickly write an outline for the segment, remember the key points, and then deliver that message to the media takes practice. The first outlines that I put together took me a while. I spent a long time trying to figure out how I would organize my thoughts. As time went on and I did more and more media interviews, I became more efficient with my outline writing. My skills increased with experience and practice.

One of the joys of working with mass media is that push for a fast turnaround. It provides a slight adrenaline rush to have 1 or 2 hours to put together a 3- to 5-minute segment that will air that evening on the news. Being willing to serve as that nutrition resource for the hospitals where I have worked has been such a rewarding and fun experience. I pushed myself to never turn down a public speaking opportunity. Being available, at a moment's notice, to give that evidence-based viewpoint is one of the attributes of a good nutrition communicator.

An effective nutrition communicator exemplifies what the media looks for in a subject matter expert, namely:

For more information on how to effectively communicate scientific research with the public, refer to Chapter 7.

- a reliable source who responds in a timely manner with respect to the media professional's deadlines;
- a skilled communicator who responds to questions succinctly with easy-to-understand and quotable comments;
- a source willing to introduce the reporter to another expert if he or she is unable to make a deadline or feels unqualified to comment on a particular subject;
- a source that discloses any business relationships with brands or other monetary conflicts of interest related to the topic of the query; and
- a source that will share the final published article on his or her personal or professional social media channels.

What Are Best Practices for Communicating via Mass Media?

Best practices for communicating via mass media include understanding the media landscape, taking advantage of available channels, knowing the audience, and building media-specific communication skills.[4]

The variety of available media channels allows nutrition communicators to specialize in the types of media they are more comfortable with or more skilled in, such as writing versus on-camera appearances. Fundamentally, nutrition professionals are educators, and subsequently communicators. However, communication skills need to be learned and continually honed. These skills are transferable to different media channels and outlets; for example, a good writer can use his or her writing skills to prepare effective talking points. However, certain skills may be less familiar and, therefore, require more formal training, such as doing live television interviews or making cooking demo videos.

Refer to Chapter 32 for more on preparing for interviews.

Review Chapter 25 for more on food demonstrations.

Understand the Media Landscape

The media landscape continues to evolve as traditional media is joined by ever-expanding digital media alternatives. Beyond traditional television, radio, and print media, there's a plethora of web-based options for communicating via videos, podcasts, online articles, and social media platforms. Understanding the available channels and taking advantage of the options that are best suited to specific topics and skills can increase the audience reach and impact. This section will introduce some options, and subsequent chapters go into greater depth.

Begin with gaining a basic understanding of the media landscape, which includes local, national, and international media outlets.[5]

Each type of media, traditional or new, national or local, can potentially reach millions. For example, each one of the top 20 local television media markets in the United States reaches more than one million TV households.[6] The New York City market alone reaches more than 7 million viewing households, the Los Angeles market reaches more than 5 million, and the Chicago market more than 3 million. Additionally, local news stories can be picked up by affiliated national outlets and reach an even wider audience.

Even though new media, such as blogs, have become popular sources of news in recent years, a survey conducted by the Pew Research Center in 2017 shows that Americans still rely on traditional media to get news. And while only about 20% of Americans consume news from physical newspapers, the online sites of these publications reach many more.[6]

National and local network shows typically report each news update in 4,000 words or less, the equivalent of four columns in a standard-sized newspaper. A major story gets an average of 58 seconds of airtime.[5] Experts might be interviewed live or taped, the latter of which will be edited down to fit within the allocated time segment. It is important for nutrition communicators, especially those appearing on television, to deliver messages in sound bites. Sound bites are succinct, catchy statements that meet the short attention span of the audience.[5]

There are different formats of newspapers, such as daily, weekend, weekly, semiweekly, and Sunday. Daily newspapers tend to reach international audiences, while weeklies typically report on local news. On average, newspapers devote about 50% of their space to editorial content; the rest is advertising, with some unpaid public service announcements. Newspapers produced in local communities are indigenous to those communities, and these local connections give newspapers a perceived credibility.[5] When RDNs become a resource for national and local media, it provides an opportunity for professional brand-building and visibility that can attract clients and business.

Magazines provide more targeted information than newspapers, and readers turn to magazines for in-depth treatments of their special interests. Magazines commonly have both print and digital formats, while some magazines have ceased print editions completely and are only available online. Magazines have editors and staff writers, but also contributors and freelance writers.[5] Dietetics professionals can not only serve as expert resources to magazine staff but can also pitch their own story ideas as well, building relationships with editorial staff and becoming regular contributors or freelancers.

Take Advantage of Available Channels

For all forms of media, opportunities exist for dietetics professionals to be subject matter experts. There are a few things RDNs should consider about different types of media and the opportunity to deliver nutrition information to the public.

TRADITIONAL BROADCAST: TELEVISION AND RADIO

Broadcast media is television and radio transmitted by an established media outlet. In most cases, the nutrition communicator appears as a guest on a show or segment, either live or taped. Typically, the nutrition communicator pitches the story idea to the producer or is sought out by the TV or radio station because of his or her area of expertise on the topic or spokesperson status. Nutrition communicators who wish to work with broadcast outlets should build these skills:

- story-idea pitching
- on-air or on-camera verbal skills
- key-message and supporting-point development
- food and prop display

TRADITIONAL PRINT: NEWSPAPERS AND MAGAZINES

Print outlets include newspapers and magazines. Typically, a nutrition communicator is interviewed for a story and quoted in the story. However, more and more nutrition communicators are pitching stories to or writing regular columns for these outlets. Nutrition communicators who wish to work with print outlets should build these skills:

- story-idea pitching
- written skills
- verbal skills
- key-message and supporting-point development

Chapter 32 explores preparing for media interviews.

Chapter 28 covers newspaper and magazine articles in depth.

DIGITAL: WEB-BASED CHANNELS, ONLINE ARTICLES AND BLOGS, PODCASTS, VIDEOS

The digital media landscape is ever-evolving and includes web-based channels, such as YouTube, and a variety of online magazine articles and blogs, as well as digital audio (podcasts) and video. The skills needed for these channels vary but may include the following:

- written skills
- on-air or on-camera verbal skills
- key-message and supporting-point development
- food and prop display

SOCIAL MEDIA

Social media plays an important role in nutrition communications as well as in the marketing of programs and ideas. Social media includes various channels or platforms geared toward different audiences and communication styles. Some channels are more image-based, while others allow for more text and links to information. The skills needed for social media vary depending on the channel.

Know the Audience

Although it can be more challenging to know the characteristics of an audience reached through mass media (vs one that is reached in person), knowing the audience remains an essential starting point for effective communication. In mass media communications, the audience will naturally be broad. However, there are some characteristics to determine based on the media outlet (eg, television station) and type of show or column. For example, is it traditional media or social media? Local or national? Is it a weekday, evening, or weekend show or column? Is the target audience likely to be younger or older? Are they predominantly male or female? What is their socioeconomic status or education level? This information may be obtained online or from the contact person at the media outlet (eg, the reporter, producer, or editor). When audience characteristics are considered, communication efforts can be focused in a relatable and meaningful way.

Build Effective Skills

Continually building communication skills is crucial to being an effective communicator. Being comfortable in front of an audience and sharing credible content is a good start; however, there is much more to being an effective communicator. Build skills in communicating clearly, concisely, and compellingly. Being *clear* means avoiding jargon and using familiar words, sharing evidence-based information in a relatable manner. Being *concise* means getting to the point directly and succinctly, focusing more on solutions instead of problems. Being *compelling* means effectively using stories, statistics, examples, analogies, and visuals to bring these messages to life.

It's imperative that nutrition communicators seek opportunities to learn communication skills through workshops, trainings, webinars, and other programs. In addition, it's crucial to practice communication skills through writing, speaking, and media interviews. The more communicators learn and practice, the greater their skills and confidence level will be. Every experience brings opportunities for learning, growth, and development. See the Words of Experience box for a real-life story of being willing to say yes to an opportunity to build media skills.

What Are Practical Strategies for Communicating via Mass Media?

Being able to communicate and utilize mass media to get nutrition messages to target audiences clearly, succinctly, accurately, and in a timely manner is the goal. These are skills that can be refined and improved over time. Following these practical strategies will make the task of using mass media much less overwhelming and help to get nutrition messages to target audiences.

Chapter 30 covers blogging and web-based writing.

Chapter 24 discusses the use of video.

Chapter 29 explores the best practices and strategies for this area of social media communications.

Chapter 2 discusses ways to improve communication effectiveness through continuing education, experience, and other opportunities.

Chapter 11 explores the skills and strategies involved in needs assessments for audience focus.

Develop Relationships to Become a Media Resource

In a home market, pay attention to which reporters, editors, or producers cover food- and nutrition-related stories. For local TV, radio, and newspapers, it's often the consumer reporter or the health reporter. But when a story breaks, such as a food-borne illness outbreak or a headline-making nutrition study, the newsroom assignment editor is the one often charged with quickly finding an expert to interview on the topic. Contact these news professionals ahead of time (via phone, email, or social media messaging) to offer services as a food and nutrition expert. Include your name, credentials, contact information, and brief biography. If called to do an interview, make sure to follow up with a thank-you note offering to help again. Make producers' and reporters' jobs easier by helping them identify reliable, credentialed experts.

Here are four practical ways RDNs can develop relationships and become media resources:

1. Read local, national, and even international newspapers (print or digital editions) to determine who typically covers nutrition and health topics. Write an email, letter, or short message via social media to writers or editors introducing yourself and your expertise and offering to be a resource. Stories often include the email address of the writer or editor. Provide some ideas for future stories related to upcoming health observances (eg, Heart Health Month, National Nutrition Month) and a brief overview of how this would be of interest to their readers or followers. Identify the editor's email address and send a note with a subject line such as "Introduction to nutrition subject matter expert."

2. If you read an article online about a topic in your area of expertise, write a tailored note to the writer introducing yourself and your expertise and offering to be a resource for similar articles. Here is a good tip: Mention what you liked about the article, what resonated with you, and anything else that would help to develop the relationship (eg, note something in the writers Twitter profile that you have in common).

3. Follow health and nutrition media on social channels, including Twitter, LinkedIn,

Saying Yes! Jump, and the Net Will Appear

by Melissa Joy Dobbins, MS, RDN, CDCES

After being employed in my first job as a clinical dietitian in Chicago for 3 years, I took my dream job as an outpatient dietitian and diabetes educator in 1995. The very first day on this new job, I found myself volunteering to do a live television interview. The camera crew was on its way, and the topic was men's health—not my area of expertise! What was I thinking? I had been interviewed for print articles while I was in graduate school and working for the Missouri State Extension office, but I had never done a television interview.

Under the guidance of my clinical manager, I did some research on the topic, including calling the Academy of Nutrition and Dietetics (then named the American Dietetic Association) and asking them to fax over some information. I studied the topic and pulled together the most compelling facts to share during the interview. I had no idea what questions the reporter would ask, and I had no idea what bridging was (bridging is a technique used to bring an interview from off-topic back to the topic), so I was not prepared to handle any tough questions. Thankfully, the interview was very straightforward and I was able to share some credible, meaningful tips for the viewers.

At the end of the day, I was glad I took the risk to learn new skills (such as gathering data, organizing and prioritizing the information, and considering a call to action) and communicate evidence-based information to the masses. After all, being on television in Chicago could reach hundreds of thousands of viewers in just a few minutes, whereas my one-on-one counseling and group classes could reach approximately 2,000 people in 1 year. Over the next 5 years, I continued to work closely with the public relations department at the hospital and conducted many more television, radio, and print interviews. This media experience helped me land a coveted supermarket dietitian job in 2000, in which the majority of my responsibilities focused on media, namely weekly television, radio, and print interviews. Over the next few years, I conducted hundreds of media interviews and gained invaluable experience, learning important lessons with every single interview.

and Instagram. Engage with contributors by commenting on their posts, sharing their posts, and tagging them in your posts. This helps them recognize you as a thought leader and potential contact when they need a subject matter expert.

4. Subscribe to platforms that connect members of the media with subject matter experts, such as Help a Reporter Out (HARO) and Prof-Net. After subscribing, participants receive daily queries via email from media seeking specific types of experts for their articles.

Be Prepared to Cover Nutrition Topics for Lay Audiences

News is often categorized as hard news and soft news. Think of it as a spectrum: On one end is serious, breaking, hard news events, such as a food-borne illness outbreak or new research linking diet and risk of death. On the other end of the spectrum are light and less urgent soft stories, such as how to buy the best fresh produce or health benefits of an oatmeal cookie recipe. Before a media interview, consider the seriousness of the story and be aware of the big picture.

As health professionals, RDNs have the education and experience to accurately summarize research and to help add perspective to a food recall, food-borne illness outbreak, or diet-related disease story. Somber stories where death and disability are involved should be handled with a solemn tone, with respect for the seriousness of the health issue. Stick to the facts and offer firm advice on how this issue can be prevented or treated.

The style for a soft news interview can be more casual, friendly, and even comical but should always demonstrate expertise and confidence. The RDN can offer actionable everyday advice grounded in a foundation of evidence-based research. A light tone does not mean light on information. Consumers look to financial experts for guidance on buying a home mortgage. Likewise, they rely on the RDN to provide tips and advice on buying healthful foods.

Most commonly, RDNs are called upon to be experts in a feature story. Food and nutrition topics aren't just found in the food and health sections of media platforms. Sports reporters may want information on performance nutrition for athletes. Business reporters may want information on food product trends. Travel reporters may want information about special diets at wellness retreats.

Feature stories cover many topics but generally fall into these categories: food, health, lifestyles, home and garden, science and technology, and entertainment. Food and nutrition angles can be identified in each of these categories. For instance, a story in the entertainment section might feature tips for healthful dining out or how to choose the healthiest movie popcorn.

Keep Up to Date on Nutrition News and Trends

Having information at the ready is invaluable when a communicator needs to respond quickly to a media request. RDNs are likely familiar with the latest research and news in their area of expertise, but it's important to stay abreast of developments in other areas, such as popular diets and consumer food trends.

A simple way to organize resource files is to create physical or electronic files in broad major topic areas, including key contacts, recent research studies, nutrition news, food trends, food and nutrition consumer surveys, food safety news, culinary trends, and recipe ideas. Keep physical files to a minimum by scanning or photographing print materials and filing them electronically in the appropriate category.

"I like to stay up to date on the topics being touted on magazine and tabloid newspaper covers. All you have to do is scan the covers in the supermarket checkout line and take a photo with your smartphone if it's something that seems particularly newsworthy or troubling." —CAROLYN O'NEIL, MS, RDN, LD

The amount of nutrition-related information available can be overwhelming. Build a resource list of trusted sources that is routinely used to navigate this information. Make a habit of reading through sources, such those featured in Box 27.1, which provides a recommended list to help keep nutrition professionals informed on the most recent nutrition research and information.

The Academy of Nutrition and Dietetics has a daily email newsletter called *Nutrition and Dietetics SmartBrief*. It contains links to research articles, nutrition-related media stories, and journal reviews. This is a helpful resource to reference for pertinent nutrition topics that are making headlines around the world. As noted at the end of each newsletter, the news and editorial content for the daily listing is curated by SmartBrief editors and is not selected by the Academy of Nutrition and Dietetics, with the exception of the Academy News section.

There are electronic mailing lists (EMLs) that nutrition professionals can subscribe to and follow to have information sent directly to them. Dietetic practice groups (DPGs) of the Academy of Nutrition and Dietetics have EMLs or web-based forums for members and offer additional ways for professionals to connect. These are potential avenues for connecting with fellow nutrition communicators around the country, getting questions answered, and obtaining credible information.

Using mass media as a tool to stay up to date on relevant nutrition information is another practical resource. Following other nutrition communicators and researchers on social media is a simple way to see what other professionals are sharing. When a researcher shares a published study or research findings, this is an easy way to quickly see the information and use it for a pitch to mass media outlets. Navigating mass media can serve to keep nutrition communicators current on the newest nutrition information available. Additionally, if they regularly search for research articles on PubMed in a particular topic area, they can set up automatic searches and email alerts.

Be Familiar with the Latest Research on Topics of Interest

When talking about a specific topic, aim to share the most relevant and current information. Effective nutrition communicators incorporate scientific research into their reference base and use that

 Potential Resources: Online Sources and Electronic Mailing Lists

Food and Nutrition Updates:
www.nal.usda.gov/fnic-nutrition-talk

Academy of Nutrition and Dietetics *Nutrition and Dietetics SmartBrief*:
www2.smartbrief.com/signupSystem/subscribe.action?pageSequence=1&briefName=eatrightpro

Food and Nutrition Professionals Who Educate the Public (FNSPEC through Purdue University):
https://lists.purdue.edu/mailman/listinfo/fnspec (for exchange of resources and information)

Obesity and Energetics Offerings (OEO):
https://obesityandenergetics.org/subscription

Dietetics resources from the Academy of Nutrition and Dietetics: www.eatrightpro.org/resources/practice/practice-resources

Complete list of the dietetic practice groups of the Academy of Nutrition and Dietetics:
www.eatrightpro.org/resources/membership/academy-groups/dietetic-practice-groups

Reporting on current nutrition research:
www.sciencedaily.com/news/health_medicine/nutrition

A site for medical news: www.medicalnewstoday.com

Office of Disease Prevention and Health Promotion:
https://health.gov/our-work/food-nutrition

research, along with additional evidence-based information, to provide background about the topic presented. For example, if a nutrition professional is asked to talk about intermittent fasting, he or she should be ready to define what fasting entails and what the research says about the effect of intermittent fasting on metabolism. As the nutrition communicator, share this information in an easy-to-understand way. Provide relevant examples and explanations tailored to the audience.

Doing additional research and getting data to support a message takes time. However, supporting talking points with evidence-based information helps the audience make informed decisions based on credible information.

Refer to Section 2 for more information on accessing and understanding research.

Chapter 15 delves into the topic of talking points.

Chapter 15 discusses in depth how to write key messages.

Chapters 15 and 16 discuss organizing information so that it flows well.

Chapter 17 discusses strong openings and closings.

Prepare Talking Points

Regardless of the media channel, prepare talking points (also known as key message points or key messages). First, identify the audience's needs and the focus of the topic. Consider the amount of time you will be on air or the length of the article, and choose the main points to convey. In many situations, such as a 3-minute television segment or short radio interview or video, three main points are sufficient. However, it's possible that certain situations might lend themselves to just one or two talking points, or even perhaps five.

Once the main talking points have been determined, organize the information so that the most important point is shared first, the information flows well and builds on each point, and the communication ends with a specific, motivating call to action, such as "Try these budget-friendly tips for getting more produce in your diet."

Prepare Supporting Evidence and Examples

Once the talking points have been created, add supporting evidence, statistics, examples, stories, and actionable tips to bring the points to life. Each talking point should have several supporting points to help communicate the concept more clearly. For example, if preparing a media story or interview on National Soup Month, the key messages may be as follows:

> **Point 1:** Simply start with a can of soup and boost the nutrition by adding more vegetables, protein, or whole grains; food waste can also be decreased by adding leftovers to the soup.

> **Point 2:** Do a recipe makeover—this recipe for broccoli cheddar soup cuts the calories and fat in half.

> **Point 3:** Plan ahead and "shop the kitchen" to use ingredients that are already on hand. For example, lasagna soup uses lean ground beef and canned tomatoes, which are easy to have on hand, and makes a hearty dinnertime soup.

The points might include the following:

1. Statistics: National Soup Month, family dinnertime, and food waste
2. Personal experiences: what the nutrition communicator's family likes
3. Credibility: credentials and areas of expertise

4. Examples and tips: easy recipes to try, cooking utensils that save time
5. Word pictures: savor the flavor, secret ingredient, recipe for success

It's important to note that the preparation of key messages and supporting points, such as in the example just given, is a best practice not only for media interviews but also for writing an article or a blog or preparing for a presentation.

Pitch Stories to the Media

The RDN doesn't always have to wait for the media to make the first move. Food and nutrition professionals can also pitch stories to the media. See the Words of Experience box on pitching to the media with three suggested steps. And always submit the pitch to the appropriate person.

Recognize the Limits of One's Expertise

Speaking knowledgeably about many food and nutrition topics requires specific expertise. These topics may include advice for a specific population, such as nutrition support for a pediatric disease, or commentary on a field that nutrition professionals are aligned with but not directly involved in, such as agriculture. If a nutrition professional is not equipped to answer questions on a topic and does not have the time to fully research the topic, it's acceptable and preferable to decline the interview and help the news professional find a credible expert to interview or suggest a credible organization to contact. There are RDNs working in just about every area of the food, nutrition, and agricultural world.

Convey Information Accurately and in Context

While nutrition and dietetics professionals always want their responses to media queries to be evidence-based, it's important to deliver the information in a format that is easily digestible to media. Here is a simple format to follow:

1. Indicate your name and affiliation.
2. Address their questions in short sound bites.
3. Provide links to research and resources that support the responses.

To be a preferred resource for the media, be aware of their needs and respect the demands of their profession. The strength of the RDN's message is built on a foundation of evidence-based information with the expertise to translate scientific findings into relatable nutrition advice to support optimal health for broad or specific populations.

Create a System for Tracking Media Contacts

Whatever channel is used—newspaper, magazine, social media, television—keep track of media contacts. Tracking will help to keep up with deadlines, make new pitches, follow up with leads, and measure the rate of success in delivering a message. The chapters that follow in this section provide useful tips and strategies for each type of media channel. An additional resource is the Academy of Nutrition and Dietetics *Working with the Media* handbook (see the resources section at the end of this chapter).

Box 27.2 provides a useful tool for tracking media contacts. It helps to note important contact information as well as summarize the content covered and list details about the actual story or interview. It ends with a useful suggestion to record ideas for future interviews—for example: "Interviewer mentioned her mother was just diagnosed with type 2 diabetes. Follow up on (date)

Pitching to the Media: Three Steps

by Anna Busenburg, RD, CSP

Step 1: What is the story? Often a media pitch is based on a single topic or story. Base a media pitch on a specific topic such as the latest diet trend or a new research study.

Step 2: Find research to support the topic. Find additional research to support a topic, and include it in the talking points.

Step 3: Write a pitch to the media. Put together a short summary of a topic or story, what evidence supports this claim, and how it would impact the target audience. This summary is what would be sent to the media outlet to pitch an idea for a nutrition-related segment.

to pitch story on diabetes and high-fiber diets (or another appropriate story angle)." Create an electronic or paper copy for filing.

Bottom line: Reach out to the media. Say "yes" when they call. Increase both reach and impact!

See Write an Effective Query Letter in Chapter 28.

FIGURE 27.1 **Media contact log**

Name of outlet (newspaper, magazine, radio, TV station, social media channel):	
Reporter's name and title:	
Contact information:	
What is the story about?	
What do they want me to write or talk about?	
Who else is being interviewed?	
What's the deadline?	
When and where will the story run or air?	
Dates of contact(s):	
Link to interview or story:	
Ideas for future interviews:	

KEY POINTS

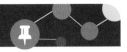

Nutrition Communicators Have Greater Reach via Mass Media

1 Food and nutrition professionals play a vital role in the media. Serving as a nutrition expert via mass media is critical for sharing messages quickly, countering inaccurate information, and maximizing reach.

2 Best practices for communicating via mass media include understanding the media landscape, taking advantage of available channels, knowing the audience, building effective skills, and positioning the registered dietitian nutritionist as the nutrition expert.

3 Practical strategies for communicating via mass media include building a list of trusted sources in order to keep up to date on nutrition news and research; being ready to translate current research in understandable ways and share nutrition knowledge; and preparing talking points and supporting evidence and examples to communicate in a clear, concise, and compelling manner. Building relationships with members of the media, pitching stories, and tracking media contacts enhance visibility and help position the RDN as a reliable resource.

RESOURCES

Nielsen ratings for media markets:
www.nielsen.com/content/dam/corporate/us
/en/public%20factsheets/tv/2017-18%20TV
%20DMA%20Ranks.pdf

Academy of Nutrition and Dietetics *Working with the Media* handbook:
www.eatrightpro.org/-/media/eatrightpro-files/career
/career-development/workingwiththemedia.pdf

Academy of Nutrition and Dietetics position papers:
www.eatrightpro.org/practice/position-and
-practice-papers/position-papers

REFERENCES

1. Statista. Number of monthly active Twitter users worldwide from 1st quarter 2010 to 1st quarter 2019 (in millions). Published August 4, 2019. Accessed December 16, 2019. www.statista.com /statistics/282087/number-of-monthly-active -twitter-users

2. Bergstrom G. Why news audiences are fragmented. The Balance Small Business website. Published 2017. Accessed January 9, 2018. www.thebalance.com/why-audiences-are -fragmented-and-what-you-can-do-about-it -2295929

3. Rayner M. Nutrition communication from theory to practice: some future perspectives. *Forum Nutr.* 2003;56:129-131.

4. Academy of Nutrition and Dietetics Strategic Communications Team. *Working with the Media: A Handbook for Members of the Academy of Nutrition and Dietetics.* Academy of Nutrition and Dietetics; 2018. Accessed December 17, 2019. www.eatrightpro.org/-/media/eatrightpro-files /career/career-development/workingwiththemedia

5. Broom G, Sha B. External media and media relations. In: *Cutlip and Center's Effective Public Relations.* 11th ed. Pearson; 2013:233-260.

6. Pew Research Center. State of the news media. Published 2017. Accessed February 18, 2018. www.pewresearch.org/topics/state-of-the-news -media

Nutrition Topics Make Popular Newspaper and Magazine Articles

Jodie Shield, MEd, RDN, LDN
and Anne Elizabeth Cundiff, RD, LD, FAND

"Why write for the popular press? Because it helps position the registered dietitian nutritionist as the nutrition expert and provides an effective tool for communicating evidence-based nutrition information to the public."

> *"You don't write because you want to say something, you write because you have something to say."* —F. SCOTT FITZGERALD

Introduction

You may think you'll never be approached to write an article for a newspaper or magazine. Or, maybe writing articles sounds appealing but it isn't clear how to reach editors with story ideas. Consider these potential scenarios:

- School begins soon, and a local newspaper asks you to write a story about packing a healthy lunch. Do you accept the assignment?
- As a diabetes educator, you spend countless hours evaluating glucose monitoring apps. You would like to share your findings with some popular health magazines but are not sure how to approach them.
- You started a blog because you love to cook and are passionate about experimenting with cuisines from many cultures. You would like to expand your audience and write for digital newspapers and magazines, but how do you get started?

For the past 20 years, maverick registered dietitian nutritionists (RDNs) without formal journalism training forged ahead to become prominent nutrition writers and food editors. Today several RDNs enjoy lucrative freelance careers writing for popular magazines like *Self*, *Family Circle*, *Men's Health*, and *Reader's Digest*, just to name a few. Some RDNs write syndicated columns for national newspapers, such as the *Baltimore Sun* and *USA Today*. Why write for the popular press? Because it helps position the RDN as the nutrition expert and provides an effective tool for communicating evidence-based

nutrition information to the public. How did these RDNs launch their writing careers? More importantly, how can RDNs get started writing for newspapers and magazines?

This chapter answers four questions:

- What is the popular press, and what is its role in nutrition communication?
- What are best practices for communicating via popular press?
- What are practical strategies for communicating via popular press?
- What are best practices for getting started?

Whether RDNs are interested in writing as a public service for patients and clients or as full-time, bylined authors, this chapter will help RDNs transform their interest in writing about food and nutrition into news consumers can use to improve their health.

What Is the Popular Press, and What Is Its Role in Nutrition Communication?

The term *popular press* refers to print and online media channels that publish articles written for the general public—newspapers and magazines are the most common examples. This is different from scholarly peer-reviewed articles written for an academic or research audience, or trade articles written for a specific industry audience that are not peer reviewed.

The popular press includes reading material customers would pick up while in line at the grocery store checkout, in a waiting room, at the airport terminal while waiting for a flight, or in digital form on a smartphone. Take a moment and think about the articles you read. What draws you to an article? Is it the headlines? Are the articles you choose from a certain brand, company, or product you trust and identify with? Is it the content and variety of contributors you enjoy? These are the same questions the general public thinks about when they read the popular press.

The Popular Press Includes Newspapers and Magazines

If RDNs are interested in writing, the popular press is a place to get started. Submitting articles for the popular press will teach the writer more about the process of pitching, editing, and publishing written articles for print and online. Submitting articles for the popular press will also help the writer to develop a personal style of writing in the niche the writer is passionate about. Refer to Box 28.1 for examples of popular press publications versus what would be considered trade and peer-reviewed publications.

Press Can Be In Print or Digital and May Reach Millions

Articles published in print and online may reach millions of people a day. The demand for online content is increasing, which includes nutrition and health-related information. Nutrition articles are found in a variety of magazines from *Women's Health* to *Time* magazine. The public influences popular press content, and this is why nutrition information can even be found in *Popular Mechanics*,[2,3] a magazine about popular technology. The public is exposed to a variety of nutrition and health information, and the RDN is uniquely qualified to provide evidence-based content.

Changes in technology have resulted in a shift in how people obtain information from the popular press. Between 2013 and 2016, the percentage of American adults who regularly got their news from print newspapers dropped from 27% to around 20%. Decreases occurred across all age groups, although there were large differences among age groups: Only 5% of 18- to 29-year-olds regularly got their news from a print newspaper,

 # Examples of Popular Press, Trade Journals, and Scholarly Publications[1]

Popular Press

Newspapers:

- *New York Times*
- *USA Today*
- *Wall Street Journal*
- *Washington Post*
- *Chicago Tribune*

Magazines:

- *Women's Health*
- *Shape*
- *Prevention*
- *Good Housekeeping*
- *Food and Wine*
- *Travel and Leisure*
- *Family Circle*
- *Cooking Light*
- *Parents*
- *Better Homes and Gardens*

Trade Journals

- *Today's Dietitian*
- *Beverage Industry*
- *Advertising Age*
- *Progressive Farmer*
- *Food Processing*
- *Education Week*

Scholarly Journals

- *Journal of the Academy of Nutrition and Dietetics*
- *American Journal of Clinical Nutrition*
- *Pediatrics*
- *Journal of the American Medical Association*
- *New England Journal of Medicine*

whereas about half (48%) of those aged 65 and older did.[4,5] The largest shift in popular press usage was reflected in the 28% of adult Americans who got their news digitally via website or app versions of newspapers and magazines.[6] In 2017, print newspaper circulation decreased by 11% for weekday papers and 10% for Sunday papers.[7]

According to the Academy of Nutrition and Dietetics *Change Drivers and Trends Driving the Profession: A Prelude to the Visioning Report 2017*[8]:

> *Twenty years into the technology revolution, the acceptance and spread of digital products and services have been historically unparalleled. In 1997, only 18% of US households had access to the internet; 74% had internet access and 63% had smartphones in 2013. In 2014, 4 in 10 US households had cell phones only, which is double the number from 2009. Technology is transforming the way we learn, work, and live.*

The audience that RDNs wish to write for will help determine the form of media they plan to use. For example, an RDN who enjoys sharing nutrition expertise with older populations should pitch ideas to print media rather than digital media. An RDN who wants to write about evidence-based food innovations may find that digital platforms best reach the target audience. Many newspapers and magazines share articles in both print and digital formats and have digital platforms in the form of websites and apps. There are also many digital platforms that exist without a print media source. Keep in mind that digital media adds new published articles more quickly than traditionally printed media. Consequently, digital media has created many more opportunities for RDNs to pitch articles and can increase their chances of getting an article published.

Nutrition and Health Are Trendy Topics for Popular Press Audiences

In today's era of preventive medicine, people are hungry for nutrition stories to help them lose weight, lower blood pressure, and eat foods that will help them stay healthy, among other nutrition-related information. According to the Pew Research Center, Americans frequently visit the internet for health information.[5] About 6 in 10 (59%) say they did so in the past year, and nearly 8 in 10 (77%) say they began at a search engine, such as Google. Another 13% say they began at a site specializing in health information, like WebMD.[5]

Now more than ever, the popular press is open to publishing articles to address current, trendy, and relevant nutrition and health topics. RDNs are ideal authors for writing these stories. In the 2018 Food and Health Survey, 76% of older Americans (over 65 years of age) and 65% of younger adults (younger than 35 years of age), designated an RDN as a source they trust to provide accurate information about what to eat and food safety.[9]

In order to write for the popular press, a nutrition professional must stay current on what is happening in nutrition and health. Be a media monitor by answering queries with clients and people in the community and by following headlines and trends online and in print media to stay current and to see what the general public is searching for. One tool to consider is Google Trends (https://trends.google.com), where readers are able to search daily, weekly, and yearly topic trends. Also, popular press outlets focused on web-based publishing, such as *Food & Nutrition Magazine* and *Nutrition and Dietetics SmartBrief,* cover trending nutrition and health topics as they are being released. Staying current on the evidence-based research on a variety of nutrition topics, including trends, can help position RDNs as experts who can write articles with substance and appeal to audiences.

What Are Best Practices for Communicating via Popular Press?

Both newspapers and magazines approach their audiences from a unique perspective and with different publication guidelines and production schedules. Before RDNs write a nutrition story, they need to have a firm understanding of how the popular press operates. This will help them brainstorm hot nutrition topics and tailor their messaging so that they can reach the target audience and write compelling, evidence-based nutrition stories.

Know the Audience Targeted by a Particular Channel

Newspapers Newspapers publish a collection of relatively brief news stories that provide updates on current events and are typically published daily, weekly, or biweekly. Originally newspapers were printed on paper (newsprint), but many news publications are phasing out print editions and providing their newspapers electronically or on websites as online publications, often with a subscription fee for full access to articles.

All newspapers are typically divided into sections (eg, national and international news, food and health, business, sports, politics, lifestyle and fitness) and provide content with a specific news angle of interest to their corresponding reader-audience. Each section has an editor who determines the editorial calendar, which is a schedule for keeping track of stories and articles from concept to development to publishing. Each section operates on a beat system, with reporters responsible for covering stories pertaining to certain topics. Larger papers, such as the *New York Times*, *Wall Street Journal*, and *USA Today* (see Box. 28.1), have more specialized reporters and syndicated columnists, while smaller or local papers often have reporters who cover a variety of sections.

Given the decline in newspaper circulation, many editors employ a lean staff and frequently use wire services (eg, Reuters, Associated Press) or freelance writers to provide news stories. This presents an excellent opportunity for the nutrition and dietetics practitioner to pitch stories. Keep in mind that newspapers have shorter publication deadlines than magazines, and the editorial calendar for most daily newspapers is set about 2 weeks in advance.

Here is an example of how an RDN might pitch a story for National Nutrition Month (March) to a specific newspaper audience. Assume that the target audience is parents and the RDN wants to pitch a story idea about five easy ways to get kids to love their veggies. First, the RDN should identify which section of the paper covers this type of story (eg, food; lifestyle and fitness). Then, the RDN should pitch a story by writing a query letter to that section's editor. All of this would need to happen in mid-January to attract the editor's attention and allow for enough time to write the story if assigned. For more on writing pitch, or query, letters, see the Words of Experience box on page 235 and the Academy's of Nutrition and Dietetics *Working with the Media* handbook listed in the resources section at the end of this chapter, which includes tips for writing pitch letters as well as sample letters.

Magazines Magazines offer a collection of articles on a wide variety of topics and are published in two basic formats: general news (eg, *Time*, *US News and World Report*) and special interest (eg, *Weight Watchers*, *Parents*, *Cooking Light*). Generally, magazines are published monthly, bimonthly, or quarterly. While most magazines are published both on paper and digitally, the online digital content tends to differ from the print version to appeal to a more tech-savvy audience and encourage online subscriptions. For example, *Cooking Light,* which is published exclusively online, features certain recipes paired with video cooking demonstrations.

Each magazine has a managing editor and, typically, assistant, associate, and contributing editors who determine the editorial calendar, write articles, and work with freelance writers. As a general rule, print and online publications employ different editorial staffs.

The audience for a magazine will depend on the publication format (eg, general news, special interest) and types of articles featured. As part of their business plan, magazines conduct market research to gather reader demographics (age, gender, geographic location, education level, income), which are shared with writers and marketing departments to help generate advertising. Magazines have a longer publishing timeline than newspapers and tend to work at least 3 to 6 months in advance.

Using the National Nutrition Month example from before, here is how to craft a story about five easy ways to get kids to love their veggies for a specific magazine audience. The first thing is to identify the target audience. Since the readership of magazines tends to be more focused than that of newspapers, be more specific in choosing an audience. If the audience is parents of infants and preschoolers, for example, think of articles for *American Baby* or *Parents*. Finally, write a query letter pitching the story to the editor in charge of nutrition or health articles. Because magazines have longer publishing timelines than newspapers, writers should want to pitch their stories from September through December for publication in the following calendar year. See Figure 27.1 on page 435 for a useful contact log for tracking stories that have been pitched as well as those that are in process.

Write in the Tone Used by the Channel

Good writers "speak" to a specific type of reader. They narrow the nutrition topic to meet the interests of the audience and use consumer-friendly language and audience-specific examples to make their writing relevant and relatable. For example, if an RDN is writing a story about caffeine for *Fit Pregnancy*, it will be useful to include how caffeine may impact the health of both mom and baby and offer tips about how to limit foods and beverages with caffeine. If an RDN is writing a caffeine story for *Runner's World*, the focus might be on the performance-enhancing aspects of caffeine, with suggestions on how to safely consume more caffeine-containing foods and beverages.

Chapter 3 and Section 3 cover the importance of defining the audience and learning about their needs, concerns, interests, and preferences in order to communicate effectively.

One of the ways to connect with an audience is to become familiar with the publication's tone. The best way to understand the tone of a newspaper or magazine is to thoroughly read it and get a feel for the writing style and the types of nutrition and health stories covered. To help conduct and organize research, use the Media-Monitoring Checklist provided. Look for trends in topics, writing style, word choice, formatting, advertising, reader feedback, and anything else that will help to understand an audience.

Writers do not have to be part of a target audience to write for it. For example, men can write for *Fit Pregnancy,* even though the audience is pregnant women. A good writer knows how to investigate the needs of the audience and write from their perspective. This is similar to what RDNs do when they counsel clients by tailoring their dietary needs to their unique lifestyles.

Provide Accuracy and Context for Information Presented and Give Credit to Sources

How often is a new study reported incorrectly, out of context with the body of research, or with key details missing? Newspapers and magazines employ food editors and health reporters trained in journalism, and most are very good at their jobs. While they know how to thoroughly investigate nutrition topics, they need credible and knowledgeable sources to verify their research and to help them identify hot nutrition topics. This reinforces the importance of working with the media to promote nutrition messages that are accurate, evidence-based, and able to reach large audiences. RDNs who are interested in writing for newspapers or magazines should brush up on research interpretation skills. The following recommendations feature resources that are easily accessed by RDNs[10]:

- Read the *Journal of the Academy of Nutrition and Dietetics,* available online.
- Know the Academy of Nutrition and Dietetics official views by reading its position and practice papers.
- Visit the Evidence Analysis Library for nutrition research.
- Stay current on studies published in other health and medical journals.
- Keep up on Academy of Nutrition and Dietetics news and topics of interest by reading *Food & Nutrition Magazine* and by subscribing to *Eat Right Weekly, Nutrition and Dietetics SmartBrief,* and dietetic practice group (DPG) and affiliate newsletters.
- Attend continuing education meetings and scientific conferences.

Chapter 6 covers research interpretation in depth.

Media-Monitoring Checklist

____ What is the title of the newspaper or magazine?

____ Who are the editors?

____ Who are the key reporters covering nutrition stories?

____ Who is the target audience?

____ What topics have been covered and when?

____ What sections or columns feature food and nutrition articles?

____ What types of headlines do they use?

____ How to they begin articles and what type of ledes (also spelled *leads*) do they use?

____ How do they conclude articles?

____ What types of sources (eg, academic, celebrity, ordinary people) do they quote?

____ How many sources are quoted in an article?

____ What type of research is cited?

____ Do they include recipes?

____ Do they provide photos?

____ What types of advertisements (if any) do they allow?

Understand What Makes a Story Newsworthy

Once the writer identifies the audience and channel (eg, newspaper, magazine), it is time to adapt the nutrition message. While RDNs are uniquely qualified to write evidence-based nutrition stories, those stories must be interesting and entertaining to an audience. How does a writer develop nutrition story ideas that are also newsworthy, entertaining, and something an editor will want to publish? The key is remembering that newspaper and magazine editors look for stories that provide new information to their readers, such as new nutrition and health studies, food products, or recipes. In addition to being new, a story is newsworthy if it is[10]:

- interesting,
- timely,
- relevant,
- informative,
- educational, and
- locally oriented.

Most people don't know that January 19 is National Popcorn Day or that September is National Breakfast Month. In addition to new nutrition topics, editors are always looking for a fresh angle or new approach to covering seasonal stories (eg, back to school, summer grilling, Thanksgiving) or evergreen topics (eg, reducing food waste, mindful eating, swapping excess sodium for herbs and seasonings). For writing inspiration, many successful nutrition writers develop a creative calendar and look for unique holidays to tie in to nutrition topics for their stories (see the examples in Figure 28.1). Websites such as Holiday Insights (www.holidayinsights.com) and Time And Date (www.timeanddate.com) post calendars featuring all kinds of interesting days, weeks, and months to serve as a springboard for nutrition stories.

Use the Inverted Pyramid Style

The inverted pyramid style of writing is commonly used to pitch stories to editors in the popular press (see Figure 28.2). Journalists are trained

FIGURE 28.1 **Sample creative calendar**

Month and Event	Nutrition Topic	Media Audience
January 3: Festival of Sleep Day	Four Foods to Help You Sleep Better	*Mindful Magazine*
February: Canned Food Month	Tomatoes: Getting Canned Is Good	*Men's Health*
March 1: Peanut Butter Lovers Day	Discovering the Truth About Peanut Butter and Allergies	Lifestyle section of local paper
April 19: Garlic Day	How Much Garlic Should You Eat to Lower High Blood Pressure?	Food section of local paper
May: National Hamburger Month	How to Build a Healthy Burger	*Shape*
June 1–7: Fishing Week	Go Fish! 5 Tips for Getting Kids to Take a Bite	*Family Circle*
July: National Ice Cream Month	Ice Cream vs Gelato: What's the Difference?	*Food & Nutrition Magazine*
August: National Picnic Month	How to Prevent 7 Picnic Food-Safety Mistakes	Lifestyle section of local paper
September 16: Working Parents Day	Freezer-Friendly Family Meals	*Working Mother*
October 31: Halloween	Trick or Treat? What Can My Gluten-Free Child Eat?	Food section of local paper
November: National Diabetes Awareness Month	5 Foods to Help Fight Diabetes	*Health*
December 18: Bake Cookies Day	Should You Eat Raw Cookie Dough?	*Good Housekeeping*

to write and report the news using the structure of the inverted pyramid, and it is important that writers understand the underlying concepts.

The inverted pyramid style of writing involves placing the most important information a reader needs to know in the story's lede (sometimes spelled *lead*), or opening paragraph. All of the other information is funneled down into other paragraphs based on the order of importance. The five *W*'s represent the most important information to report:

- Who is the story about?
- What is the story about?
- Where does it take place?
- When does it take place?
- Why, or who cares?

Thanks to modern technology, there has been a scholarly debate about the need for using the inverted pyramid. The origins of the inverted pyramid trace back to the telegraph. At that time, news outlets transferred information over the wire, and to avoid interruption, they transmitted the important information first.[11] Fast-forward to today: We are using computers, tablets, cell phones, and the internet. Audiences are bombarded with information, making it vital to capture readers with an attention-grabbing lede (eg, one that presents a statistic, anecdote, story, or definition). And the lede must include keywords that are search engine optimization (SEO)–friendly, meaning they can be picked up by search engines so they increase the likelihood of keywords or stories turning up in a reader search. Nonetheless, journalism schools continue to teach the inverted pyramid style of writing. Many editors often cut copy from the bottom of an article when space is limited, so the inverted pyramid continues to be widely used in newswriting.

For more information about pitching, see Chapter 32.

What Are Practical Strategies for Communicating via Popular Press?

This section explores strategies to help writers pitch their stories to newspapers and magazines and potentially land themselves a byline as the expert author to write them.

FIGURE 28.2 **Inverted pyramid style of writing**

Who, what, when, where, why: the most important information

Supporting information and key quotes

Additional facts, information, and quotes

Background and alternative explanations

Least important information

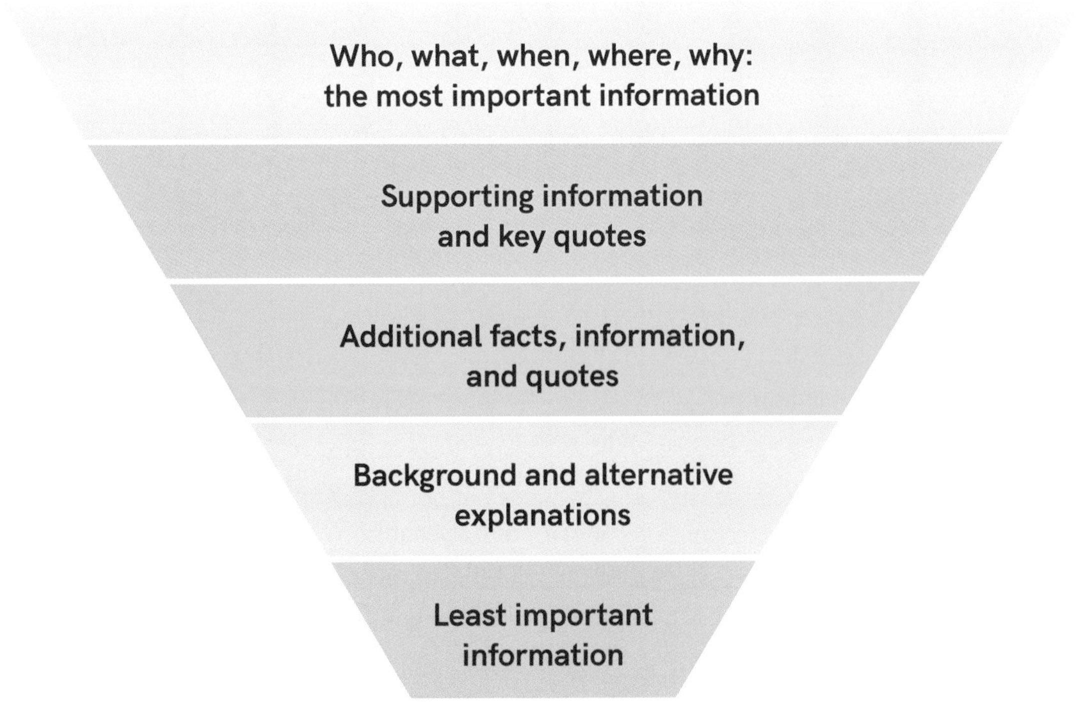

Follow Author Guidelines

Before typing a single word of the query letter or story, consult the publication's author guidelines. Author guidelines provide information about the current managing and department editors and what the magazine is looking for, such as word count for articles, referencing requirements, artwork expectations, pay rates, and how to submit query letters. Every year thousands of magazines publish their guidelines in books such as *Writers Market*. Also, most magazines and newspapers provide author guidelines on their websites.

Write an Effective Query Letter

Query letters are brief, formal letters sent to a specific editor describing a story idea, the plan to develop the story, and the writer's qualifications for writing it. A well-written query letter is the first step in getting a foot in the door and landing a popular press writing assignment. The query letter is considered an exclusive, meaning the writer is giving that editor the first chance to publish a story. The writer should not pitch the story elsewhere before hearing back from the editor. It is acceptable in a query letter to let the editor know a time frame as to how long the story will be exclusive. Writers must be familiar with recent food and nutrition articles so they don't pitch something the outlet just ran. A guideline for the length of a query letter is one page maximum. Here are four steps to follow when writing a query letter.[12,13]

Know the editor Address a query letter to the editor who seems most appropriate for the specific type of story, such as the food editor for a recipe-based story idea. Pay careful attention to details, such as the correct spelling of the editor's name, correct title, and correct gender. Job changes are common in the publishing industry, and the period of 3- to 6-months between manuscript submission and publication means current issues of magazines do not always reflect current staff. Take time to verify the editor's position and name by placing a quick phone call or email to the publication's section editor.

Hook the editor Query letters begin with a *hook*, a catchy opening paragraph that succinctly conveys the story idea and leaves the editor wanting to read more. Statistics, surprising facts, personal anecdotes, questions, and wordplay can be useful in baiting an opening hook. A good hook often becomes the lede in a story.

Provide story details The query letter's second paragraph should describe the story idea. This description includes a summary of the proposed idea, how the story will be conveyed, and suggestions for supporting highlights, such as a chart or sidebars and potential resources. Include a clever title that will grab the editor's attention. This is an easy way to demonstrate creativity.

Explain qualifications The final paragraph usually supplies a brief summary of the writer's background, including writing credits and qualifications unique to writing this particular story. As-yet-unpublished writers can highlight relevant experience and expertise, such as specific areas of practice, research, or special interest.

Have a Flexible Plan for Telling the Story

When editors contact writers, they may want to discuss changes to the story idea. They may think the story would fit better in a different column or section or at a different time of year. The idea may need fine-tuning to meet the needs of the publication. For example, if a writer pitched a newspaper food editor a summer salad recipe story called "Seven-Layer Salads Seven Different Ways," the editor may want more visual variety for photography, may ask the writer to change the story to "Seven Cool Summer Salads," or may request recipes beyond seven-layer salads, such as for three bean salad, potato salad, and pasta salad. Going back and forth with a publication is a normal part of the pitching process, so be prepared to work with the editor to finalize the story idea.

Be a Resource and Follow Up Promptly

Following up with editors is one of the most important things writers can do to establish themselves as professional nutrition communicators. Be patient and give the publication time to respond to a query letter. Wait at least a week before following up via email. If a writer doesn't hear back after a specified time frame from the initial query letter, as a professional courtesy, the writer may choose to send the publication an email thanking them but stating that the article will be pitched to another publication. The following suggestions can help an RDN build a good reputation as a writer.[12]

Be persistent "No" might just mean "not now." Ideas can be reworked and resubmitted to the same publication or reformulated for a different publication.

Deliver the goods Writers who submit their articles on time are more likely to get repeat assignments. The writer who fails to deliver on time creates chaos, especially at deadline-driven publications, such as daily newspapers.

Be dependable Editors tend to assign articles to writers who can deliver articles that are timely, well researched, and written in a style compatible with their publication. A dependable writer is also available for rewrites and gives editors enough notice if he or she will be unavailable for a period of time. Every time writers make the editor's job easier, they increase their value.

What Are Best Practices for Getting Started?

Writing for the popular press helps position the RDN as the food and nutrition expert, a reliable resource for popular press publications, and RDNs posses effective tools for communicating evidence-based food and nutrition messages. As noted earlier in this chapter, nutrition topics are highly sought after by the popular press because of the large variety of the population it caters to. If someone is just starting out as a writer, it is important for him or her to know what to expect in terms of compensation for services and to understand what a writer's rights are. Networking with colleagues will help writers explore various writing opportunities and launch a writing career.

Get Compensated and Know the Author's Rights

Freelance authors receive payment in a variety of ways: by the project, the hour, the word, or the page. The Editorial Freelancers Association has an online guide,[14] and payment can vary from $40 to $100 per hour or $0.20 to $2.00 per word for unspecified writing for newspapers or magazines. Use these guidelines as a starting point in determining compensation. For a writer who is just starting out and needs to obtain published writing samples, it might be useful to consider writing for free and receiving compensation in a different way. For example, a short biographical note or photo could be included, the article could be shared on the publication's website or social media sites, multiple writing opportunities could be provided by expanding the article as a series, or a product or small monetary compensation could be offered. Establishing a contract is a starting point in determining the compensation that is desired and feels acceptable for the writing that is produced.

A writer who is hired to write for a publication will sign a contract both the writer and the company has agreed upon, explaining the writer's rights to the material submitted. A writer has copyright of the material when he or she starts typing and will retain copyright ownership of the article unless the publication negotiates the contract to include complete copyright ownership. Once the article is complete, the writer may have additional rights to the final product if he or she owns the copyright, and the writer may sell the article in the future by reprinting the article in a different publication market at a later date. This gives writers the opportunity to make additional money on the same article as well as to attain greater reach to additional audiences.

TERMS TO KNOW: Important Rights-Related Terms for Freelancers to Know[15]

One-time rights or first North American serial rights	This is the right to publish your story once, or the right to publish your story for the first time in North America.
All rights	You lose the ability to resell your written material. The publisher can reprint and resell, without compensating the original author.
Electronic rights	This is the right to publish your article online or on CD-ROM. "Online" includes email newsletters.
Reprint or second rights	This is the right to publish your material a second time.

The Terms to Know box defines the various rights a publication has with respect to written articles.

Look for Writing Opportunities

Many beginning freelance writers start out with local publications. Locally, writers can achieve success by being recognized as a food and nutrition expert in the community, collecting published writing samples along the way. The local popular press will be more open to using a familiar face or name within the community to their advantage and may ask an RDN to write for their publication. The Academy of Nutrition and Dietetics is also a resource, with publishing opportunities via *Food & Nutrition Magazine*, *Stone Soup* blog, and eatright For Kids (www.eatright.org/for-kids).

The Words of Experience box illustrates how an RDN obtained writing opportunities by identifying local popular-press publications.[16]

Network and Identify Resources

When considering writing for the popular press, find other RDNs working with the media and popular press and reach out to them for advice. Think of other dietetic professionals currently writing for the popular press, either respected work peers or professionals on social media. The world of dietetics is composed of professionals inclined toward helping one another. This is an opportunity to exchange ideas, brainstorm, share resources, and gain insight from what they have learned. The Nutrition Entrepreneur DPG's Authors and Writers specialty group maintains an online forum for sharing ideas and answering questions.

A state affiliate of the Academy of Nutrition and Dietetics may also have a media chairperson and group of media spokespersons who are active with local media. They are educated and comfortable with many types of media, including writing for local magazines and newspapers, and may have contacts to whom RDNs can pitch.

When considering local resources, contact the local chamber of commerce to inquire about popular press contacts within the organization. Chambers focus on the growth of businesses they support and have multiple avenues for connecting the community by breakfast and luncheon gatherings, presentations, leadership trainings, and round tables.

Getting Started with the Popular Press[a]

by Evelyn Tribole, MS, RD

I started working with the popular press by approaching a local company, the Tidee Didee Diaper Service, and pitching my services and expertise to offer practical information to their customers. My first daughter had just been born, and as a new parent I could relate to their customer base. This was my first opportunity to demonstrate my talent on a regular basis. Even though it was unpaid, it allowed me to determine if I enjoyed writing and to create a portfolio with consistent content. I then started writing a monthly column for a local paper, which added to and enhanced my writing portfolio.

Knowing your audience is the first and most important factor in writing for the popular press. Discovering local outlets is a great place to begin your writing career because you are familiar with your audience. When you know the reader, then you know what topics you can write about to make a difference. It is important to take a real practical angle and make it relatable to you, your passions, and the audience you are writing for. As my personal and professional life changed, so did the popular press entities I pitched to and wrote for. For me, working with people made a significant difference in how I wrote for different audiences because my writing was based on my own personal experiences.

Evelyn Tribole is an award-winning registered dietitian nutritionist (RDN) with a nutrition counseling practice in Newport Beach, CA, specializing in eating disorders, intuitive eating, and celiac disease. She has written nine books, including the bestsellers Healthy Home-style Cooking *and the coauthored* Intuitive Eating. *Tribole has had an extensive career and provides realistic insights into writing for the popular press.*

[a] See reference 16 for information on working with the popular press.

KEY POINTS

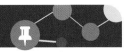

Nutrition Topics Make Popular Newspaper and Magazine Articles

1. The popular press includes print and digital newspapers and magazines written for a general audience. Technology paired with consumer interest in health has increased the demand among various newspapers, magazines, and their respective websites for nutrition stories. Registered dietitian nutritionists are the ideal authors for writing evidence-based nutrition articles for the popular press.

2. Know how the popular press operates and what writing tone is used. Read past issues or articles written on similar topics. Notice whether a publication is written mostly by staff or by freelance writers.

3. Understand what makes a story newsworthy and how to develop audience-specific topics. Stay up-to-date on current evidence-based research by reading professional journals, attending conferences, reading trade journals, and networking. Track what topics are popular by doing online searches of key nutrition words, talking with friends and patients or clients, and following social media.

4. Tailor evidence-based, entertaining messages, and story ideas to specific popular press audiences. Develop a creative calendar to help develop story ideas relevant to specific newspaper and magazine audiences.

5. Become familiar with author guidelines and what publications are looking for in authors. Use the guidelines to write a query letter. Rejection is common, so be persistent and continue to submit query letters with interesting story ideas.

6. A query letter is a short letter addressing the editor with an enticing sentence at the beginning to capture interest. It should also include who the writer is, what the writer wants to write about, why it is a great idea, and a short paragraph describing the idea. Include links or an attachment of sample articles previously written and keep the query letter in the tone of the publication.

7. Never give up. Give the publication time to respond. If there has been no response after a week, send a professional follow-up email to the editor. Some publications will list the guidelines for queries submitted on their website, which may include how the editor will respond to receiving a query. Look for those guidelines to become familiar with a particular publication to determine the process before submitting a query.

RESOURCES

Academy of Nutrition and Dietetics, *Working with the Media* (handbook for members): www.eatrightpro .org/-/media/eatrightpro-files/career/career-development /workingwiththemedia.pdf

REFERENCES

1. Walden University. What are the "popular press articles" and how can I find them? Walden University Quick Answers website. Published 2017. Accessed October 10, 2018. http:/ /academicanswers.waldenu.edu/faq/72688

2. Feltman R. Why don't we have food replacement pills? *Popular Mechanics*. March 21, 2013. Accessed October 10, 2018. www.popularmechanics.com/science/health/a8787 /why-dont-we-have-food-replacement-pills-15248871

3. Detwiler J. I hacked my body so you don't have to. *Popular Mechanics*. June 25, 2018. Accessed October 10, 2018. www.popularmechanics.com/science/health/a21272160 /biohacking

4. Mitchell A, Gottfried J, Barthel M, Shearer E. Pathways to news. Pew Research Center Journalism and Media website. Published July 7, 2016. Accessed January 18, 2018. www .journalism.org/2016/07/07/pathways-to-news

5. Pew Research Center. Majority of adults look online for health information. Published February 1, 2013. Accessed January 18, 2018. www.pewresearch.org/fact-tank/2013/02 /01/majority-of-adults-look-online-for-health-information

6. Bialik K, Matsa K. Key trends in social and digital news media. Pew Research Center website. Published October 4, 2017. Accessed January 18, 2018. www.pewresearch.org/fact -tank/2017/10/04/key-trends-in-social-and-digital-news -media

7. Pew Research Center. State of the news media. Published 2017. Accessed February 18, 2018. www.pewresearch.org /topics/state-of-the-news-media

8. Academy of Nutrition and Dietetics. *Change Drivers and Trends Driving the Profession: A Prelude to the Visioning Report 2017.* Updated September 2016. Accessed December 17, 2019. www.eatrightpro.org/~/media /eatrightpro files/leadership/volunteering/committee leader resources/changedriversandtrendsdrivingtheprofessionreport .ashx

9. International Food Information Council Foundation. 2018 food and health survey. Food Insight website. Published 2018. Accessed October 5, 2018. www.foodinsight.org/2018 -FHS-Report-FINAL.pdf

10. Academy of Nutrition and Dietetics Strategic Communications Team. *Working with the Media: A Handbook for Members of the Academy of Nutrition and Dietetics.* Academy of Nutrition and Dietetics; 2018. Accessed December 17, 2019. www.eatrightpro.org /-/media/eatrightpro-files/career/career-development /workingwiththemedia.pdf

11. Scanlan C. Writing from the top down: pros and cons of the inverted pyramid. Poynter Institute website. Published June 20, 2003. Accessed January 15, 2018. www.poynter .org/reporting-editing/2003/writing-from-the-top-down -pros-and-cons-of-the-inverted-pyramid

12. Tribole E, Herrmann M. Writing for the lay press. In: Chernoff R, ed. *Communicating as Professionals.* American Dietetic Association; 1994:105-110.

13. Tyson W, Zemsky R. *Pitch Perfect: Communicating with Traditional and Social Media for Scholars, Researchers, and Academic Leaders.* Stylus Publishing; 2010.

14. Editorial Freelancers Association. Editorial rates. Published 2018. Accessed January 17, 2018. www.the-efa.org/rates

15. Schaefer L. How freelance magazine writing works. How Stuff Works: Money website. Accessed January 17, 2008. https://money.howstuffworks.com/magazine-writing.htm

16. Tribole E. Evelyn Tribole: The Original Intuitive Eating Pro website. Accessed February 1, 2018. www.evelyntribole.com

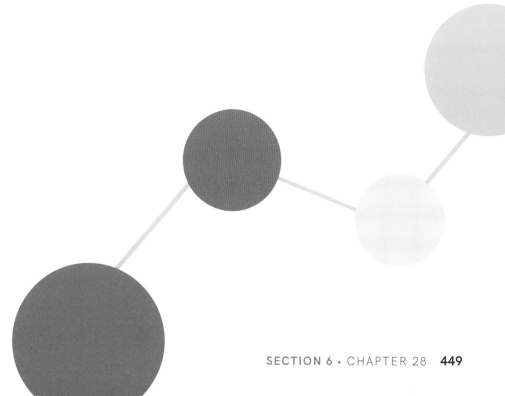

Social Media Is a Powerful Tool for Nutrition Communication and Professional Marketing

Janet Helm, MS, RDN

"Everyone can have a voice with social media. This is why it is critical for nutrition and dietetics practitioners to have a thorough understanding of social media and incorporate online technologies into nutrition communication activities and business plans."

> "Social media is changing the way we communicate and the way we are perceived, both positively and negatively. Every time you post a photo, or update your status, you are contributing to your own digital footprint and personal brand."
>
> —AMY JO MARTIN, FOUNDER OF DIGITAL ROYALTY AND AUTHOR OF *RENEGADES WRITE THE RULES*

Introduction

Social media comprises a set of communication and collaboration tools that empower and enable interactions and opportunities that were previously unavailable to the nutrition profession. Blogging, podcasting, video blogging, and all the various social media platforms (such as Facebook, Instagram, and Twitter) have become effective ways for nutrition and dietetics practitioners to communicate credible information to large audiences.

Social media has not only become a primary source of information and news—it has allowed anyone to be a publisher. Brian Solis, a digital analyst, anthropologist, and futurist, says social media represents the democratization of information and the equalization of influence.[1] In other words, everyone can have a voice with social media. This is why it is critical for nutrition and dietetics practitioners to have a thorough understanding of social media and incorporate online technologies into nutrition communication activities and business plans.

The world is increasingly connected—with rapidly expanding devices, platforms, and channels. So, it is imperative that the profession becomes digitally literate and seizes these new tools for 21st-century communications.

Social media can help nutrition and dietetics practitioners efficiently reach large audiences to deliver credible information and increase their own digital influence, which can translate into new clients and new opportunities. Social media allows professionals to connect directly to consumers, extending the reach of nutrition communication or public health activities and providing venues to market their services.

This chapter answers three questions:

- What is the role of social media in nutrition communication?
- What are best practices for communicating nutrition information via social media?
- What are practical strategies for using social media?

The goal is to provide readers with the rationale for engaging in social media and the confidence to build online strategies into nutrition communication and marketing activities.

The emphasis of this chapter is on social media platforms and social networking, including Facebook, Instagram, Twitter, Pinterest, and You-Tube (Box 29.1 features a list of major social media platforms). This chapter includes an approach to introduce social media tactics for beginners and ideas to increase social media engagement for more experienced users.

What Is the Role of Social Media in Nutrition Communication?

Since social media has become a dominant source of information and news—especially related to food and health[3]—dietetics practitioners can use social media to communicate credible

Chapter 30 focuses on blogging, a major part of a social media strategy.

BOX
29.1 # Social Media Platforms[2]

The most popular social media platforms used by marketers are Facebook (94%), Instagram (66%), Twitter (62%), LinkedIn (56%), YouTube (50%), Pinterest (27%), and Snapchat (8%).

Facebook: The largest social network, with more than 2 billion daily active users. A Facebook profile is typically for personal use, and a Facebook page is for businesses, organizations, and public figures. Facebook groups have become a popular forum to communicate about shared interests with certain people. Registered dietitian nutritionists (RDNs) are using closed Facebook groups, such as Dietitians on the Blog, to interact with clients or lend support to colleagues. Facebook Live allows livestreaming video, which RDNs are using for cooking demonstrations and on-location tours when traveling.

To get started: www.facebook.com/help

Twitter: A real-time social networking site that allows users to share short messages called tweets. Users can retweet or like the tweets of other users and engage in conversations via Twitter chats or using @mentions, replies, and hashtags.

To get started: https://help.twitter.com

LinkedIn: A business-oriented social networking site that is primarily used for professional networking. It enables users to publish a profile, connect and share content with other professionals, and join relevant groups. LinkedIn has more than 500 million members.

To get started: www.linkedin.com/help

Instagram: A visual social network (owned by Facebook) with over 800 million monthly users. Instagram photos and videos with captions can be posted to a user's feed. Instagram stories are typically real-time photos and videos that can be strung together to tell a story. Instagram stories only last for 24 hours unless they are reposted to a feed. Like Facebook, Instagram differentiates personal profiles and business accounts. Instagram business accounts allow for promotional ads, shoppable posts, and account insights. IGTV allows for longer-form video content on Instagram.

To get started: https://help.instagram.com

YouTube: A video-sharing website (owned by Google) that has become the internet's second-largest search engine. YouTube has over 1 billion users and reaches more people in the United States than any TV network. Cooking demonstrations and how-to's are popular videos on YouTube.

To get started: https://support.google.com/youtube

Pinterest: A social curation or visual bookmarking site that allows users to organize and share online images and videos. Pinterest has more than 200 million monthly users and 1 billion Pinterest boards. The Food and Drink category is one of the most popular.

To get started: https://help.pinterest.com

Snapchat: A social app that allows users to send and receive time-sensitive photos and videos known as snaps. A Snapchat story is a series of snaps that lasts for 24 hours.

To get started: https://support.snapchat.com

nutrition information, correct misinformation, and respond to inaccuracies via the internet. Unfortunately, not all nutrition content online is reliable or science-based, and some social media posts have been reported to aggravate disordered eating and poor body image.[4-6] By actively engaging in social media, nutrition and dietetics practitioners can help shift the balance of accurate nutrition information online.

Many nutrition and dietetics practitioners are using social media (primarily blogs and Facebook) to promote healthy eating, physical activity, or lifestyle behavior change. This social media usage is often combined with other activities, such as emails, text messages, and face-to-face meetings.[7] Social media has not only become an effective tool for communicating with the public and engaging with patients or clients, it is being used to communicate with students, collaborate with colleagues, and network with other health care professionals.

Social media has also become a major component of advocacy campaigns and public health interventions, including programs to impact weight management, diabetes, heart health, pregnancy, physical activity, and smoking cessation.[8-10] Dietetics practitioners are using social media to change perceptions on nutrition topics, advocate for an issue, champion a cause, and even start a movement (Figures 29.1–29.3).

Share Information and Ideas to a Wide Audience

Social media is the ultimate illustration of mass media—it allows information and ideas to reach broader, more diverse audiences and facilitates conversations or a two-way dialogue.[1] Social media has become a part of everyday life for a large part of the population and is heavily relied on by certain segments of the population, which allows targeted communication to specific audiences.

A Pew Research Center survey of US adults found that about three-quarters of the public (73%) regularly use more than one of the eight social media platforms measured in the survey: Facebook, YouTube, Instagram, Twitter, Pinterest, Snapchat, LinkedIn, and WhatsApp.[11] While the typical (median) American uses three of these sites, younger adults tend to use a greater variety of social media platforms.

As illustrated in Figure 29.4, Facebook and YouTube are the primary platforms for most

FIGURE 29.1 Kara Lydon shares body kindness and intuitive movement messages on Instagram

FIGURE 29.2 Dayle Hayes created School Meals That Rock on social media to showcase successful school lunch and breakfast programs

FIGURE 29.3 Kate Scarlata used social media to launch her #IBelieveinyourStory campaign to support IBS sufferers

Americans. About two-thirds of US adults (68%) report that they use Facebook, and roughly three-quarters (74%) of those users access Facebook on a daily basis. With the exception of adults 65 and older, a majority of Americans across a wide range of demographic groups now use Facebook. Nearly three-fourths of US adults (73%) use YouTube.[11]

Young adults ages 18 to 24 are more likely to use Snapchat and Instagram compared to other age groups. For instance, 78% of people aged 18 to 24 years are Snapchat users, but that share falls to 54% among those aged 24 to 29. Pinterest remains substantially more popular with women (41%) than with men (16%), and the messaging service WhatsApp, which is popular in Latin America, is primarily used in the US by Hispanics (49% report they are users).[11]

Engage Audiences to Change Behavior

The growth of social media provides an unprecedented opportunity to implement nutrition education and health promotion programs. Digital health strategies to promote behavior change are an integral part of programming for the Centers for Disease Control and Prevention[12] and are

FIGURE 29.4 **Percentage of US adults who use social media**

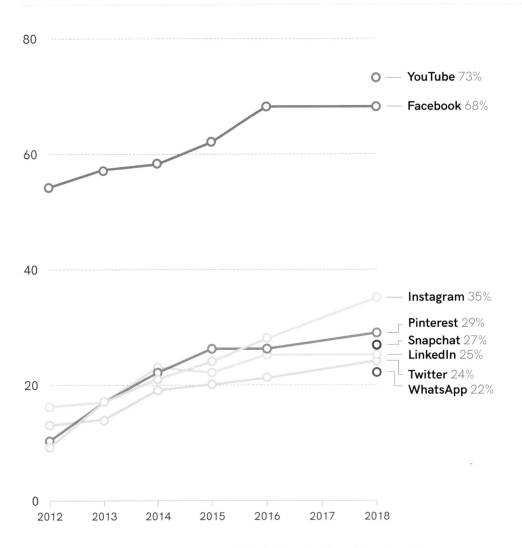

Note: Pre-2018 telephone poll data is not available for YouTube, Snapchat, or WhatsApp.

Adapted with permission from the Pew Research Center. Smith A, Anderson M. Social Media Use in 2018. Pew Research Center Website. Published March 1, 2018. Accessed December 18, 2019. www.pewresearch.org /internet/2018/03/01/social-media-use-in-2018[11]

FIGURE 29.5 Danielle Omar created a Facebook Group to interact with her Fearless Cooking community

FIGURE 29.5 Danielle Omar created a Facebook Group to interact with her Fearless Cooking community

increasingly used by dietetics practitioners and other health care professionals.[7,13] In addition to the potential scalability of interventions, social media helps reduce the in-person time burden of traditional interventions, such as individual or group consultations, is cost-effective, and provides social support and interactivity.[12]

Two reviews of health-related social media interventions found modest benefits, although the authors admit that the field of research is still in its infancy.[10,13] Maher and colleagues conclude: "Further research is needed to determine how to maximize retention and engagement, whether behavior change can be sustained in the longer term, and to determine how to exploit online social networks to achieve mass dissemination."[13]

A meta-analysis of 22 social media-based interventions about weight-related behaviors found that Facebook, Twitter, and Instagram activations resulted in statistically significant reductions of body weight and an increase in the number of daily steps taken.[14] A six-week nutrition intervention delivered solely through social media (Twitter) resulted in increased knowledge, reduced fat intake, and decreased body mass index in student athletes.[15]

A social media–based program for beginner runners delivered via a Facebook Group produced sizable and sustained changes in weekly physical activity compared with the same running program delivered in a self-administered format.[16] The Facebook Group format received strong engagement, high compliance, and favorable feedback from participants. Social media and mobile game-based nutrition interventions, including virtual reality, were also found to be useful for young adults, ages 18 to 35 years.[17]

Some dietetics practitioners have created Facebook Groups (Figure 29.5) to offer more personalized interactions, share resources, and build a community. The Facebook Groups provide a venue for asking questions and sharing recipes or health-focused strategies.

Public health campaigns frequently use social media to disseminate messages to specific target audiences to inspire behavior change. A campaign called "You're the Mom" (Figure 29.6; www .yourethemom.org) created by Tufts University and ChildObesity 180 used social media tactics to empower moms to help make simple changes to their children's eating habits.

Promotion of Programs and Services

Beyond nutrition communication and public health education, social media is an effective tool to promote products and services and engage with

FIGURE 29.6 "You're the Mom" social media campaign

YOU'RE THE **mom**

A CAMPAIGN TO EMPOWER MOMS TO MAKE HEALTHIER CHOICES FOR THEIR KIDS IN RESTAURANTS.

current clients, including through virtual counseling and text messaging that often complement in-person consultations. Dietetics practitioners are using social media to attract new clients, support book sales, and promote products—including online classes, e-book and curricula, meal plans or other fee-based content, nutrition-related merchandise, and food products. Figures 29.7 through 29.9 illustrate how nutrition and dietetics practitioners are using social media to promote their books, nutrition merchandise, and food products.

A strong digital presence has helped many dietetics practitioners become social media influencers, which has led to incremental income and new business opportunities. A large or highly engaged social media following can be attractive to food companies, ingredient suppliers, agricultural commodities, food-service organizations, and other potential sponsors who want to leverage the authority, credibility, and online communities of registered dietitian nutritionists (RDNs).

These marketing partnerships include sponsored blog posts, recipes, food videos, and Instagram posts featuring a specific brand or food product. Social media partnerships may also involve advocacy of an issue, translating science, or providing practical context around a product, ingredient, or technology. All of these sponsored social media activities are considered endorsements, and this marketing relationship must be adequately disclosed, which is covered more extensively in the best practices section of this chapter.

What Are Best Practices for Communicating via Social Media?

As nutrition and dietetics practitioners engage in social media, it is critical to maintain professional and ethical standards, understand social media etiquette, and remain respectful and civil. It is also important to establish social media goals and strategies, track and measure success, and learn techniques to be efficient and effective. Refer to the Terms to Know on page 458 for a glossary of social media terms.

Maintaining Professional and Ethical Standards

When using social media, nutrition and dietetics practitioners should remember they remain governed by the same Code of Ethics that guides all other aspects of practice.[18] For instance, the Code of Ethics reinforces integrity in personal and organizational behaviors and practices. Nutrition and dietetics practitioners shall adhere to the following:

- Disclose any conflicts of interest, including any financial interests in products or services that are recommended.
- Refrain from accepting gifts or services that potentially influence or that may give the appearance of influencing professional judgment.
- Respect intellectual property rights, including citation and recognition of the ideas and work of others, regardless of the medium (eg, written, oral, electronic).

The Academy of Nutrition and Dietetics practice paper on social media identifies the major professional and ethical issues governing social media, which include privacy and confidentiality, professional liability, professional boundaries, content credibility, intellectual property and copyright, transparency and disclosure, and personal conduct.[8]

Social media transparency is not only a matter of professional ethics: It is mandated by the Federal Trade Commission (FTC), which has published rules requiring disclosure of all paid endorsements in social media.[19,20] That means disclosing if payment was received to create a recipe, appear in a video, host a Twitter chat, post on Instagram, or share any sponsored content on social media platforms.

The FTC does not mandate specific wording, although suggested social media disclosures include #ad, #sponsored, and #paid (hashtags are frequently used but are not required to accompany the disclosure). Rather than using #advisor, #partner, #client, or #ambassador, which could be ambiguous or confusing to a consumer, the FTC recommends either combining these words with #paid and the

FIGURE 29.7 Tanya Zuckerbrot promotes her book on Instagram

FIGURE 29.8 Sound Bites Nutrition promotes nutrition merchandise for dietetics practitioners on Instagram

FIGURE 29.9 Mitzi Dulan uses Facebook to promote the protein balls she created

name of the client or adding "I'm a paid consultant to X" or "I'm working with X brand."[21]

For example, a paid consultant to a food or ingredient company, brand, or organization must disclose this relationship in a related social media post, even if the consultant is not being paid for that specific post. A member of an advisory board for a company or organization must disclose this relationship if reposting relevant articles or leaving comments on a blog or a social networking site. A paid spokesperson sharing a video clip from a TV appearance must include a form of disclosure in a social media post. Even if products were given for free, disclosure is required, such as "Company X gave me this product to try." Similarly, sponsored travel, events, and other gifts must be disclosed. Refer to Figure 29.10 for an example of disclosure used on Instagram.

Tagging the client, using the name of a promotion or campaign, or thanking the sponsoring company is not adequate for sponsored posts. The material connection must be clear to the

TERMS TO KNOW: Glossary of Social Media Terms

Algorithm	A computer-based formula used by a social media platform, such as Facebook, Twitter, and Instagram, to determine what content will be shown to users
Analytics	Collecting and analyzing data from social media platforms and blogs, including reach (number of people who see posted content) and engagement (number of interactions people have with posted content)
Avatar	A visual representation of a user online, such as a social media profile picture
Clickbait	Web content with a sensational or misleading headline that entices readers to click through to the full story
Direct message	A private message between Twitter, Facebook, or Instagram users
Engagement	Likes, shares, comments, and other ways people interact with a social media post
Geotag	Mappable coordinates that can be associated with a social media post; allows social media sites to index content by geography
GIF	Graphics interchange format—an image file format that allows users to create short, animated images for sharing on social media
Handle	A person's identity on social media platforms, such as @yourname or @yourbrand
Hashtag	The # symbol and a keyword or phrase written together without spaces to index and make a topic more searchable, such as #nutrition or #nationalnutritionmonth
Influencer	A social media user who can reach a significant audience and drive awareness
Live-tweet	Real-time tweeting at a conference or event (eg, #FNCE)
Meme	A visual representation of a theme, often containing a comedic element, shared widely online
Podcast	A digital or audio file that can be saved for playback on a smartphone or computer; also referred to as an online radio show
Retweet	Sharing a tweet from another user on Twitter, typically preceded by the letters *RT*
Thread	A continuous discussion of a specific topic on a blog or social media site
Twitter chat	A scheduled conversation on Twitter that is followed by hashtags (eg, #foodchat, #NEchat)

consumer and conspicuous, meaning the disclosure cannot be buried in a string of other hashtags, deep within an Instagram caption, or at the bottom of a blog post.

PROFESSIONAL CIVILITY

Maintaining professional standards in social media includes respect and civility. Social media should not be used to publicly criticize colleagues and attack their points of view if different from one's own. Dietetics practitioners who question the content posted by a colleague should do so in a private message and not disrupt the relationship colleagues have with their communities.

Every individual has a right to participate in social media and should be able to do so without the threat or fear of being ostracized by a colleague. However, it remains critical to fact-check posts and only share science-based information on social media. If there is not time to fully read a post by a colleague or dig deeper than the headline of a nutrition article, do not share it.

To reinforce the importance of respectful social media engagement, the Academy of Nutrition and Dietetics *Food & Nutrition Magazine* developed a Pledge of Professional Civility (Figure 29.11) and guiding principles for positive social media engagement.[22] To take the pledge, visit the *Food & Nutrition Magazine* website (www.foodandnutrition.org/professionalcivility).

Consistent and Efficient Engagement

Frequent and consistent posting on social media is one of the best ways to grow an audience in order to reach even more people with credible nutrition information. Social media can be time-consuming, so consider using automation software and apps to be more efficient. Each tool may have unique features, but they all essentially allow RDNs to manage multiple social profiles in one place, schedule posts in advance, and track analytics (including audience reach and engagement)

FIGURE 29.10 **An example of social media disclosure by Toby Amidor on Instagram**

tobyamidor • Follow

tobyamidor #SPONSORED Snacks are mini-meals that should provide nutrients that you may fall short on throughout your regularly scheduled meals. To meet three servings of dairy each day, it's simple to include milk or dairy foods in my snacks. In honor of National Nutrition Month this March, I'm sharing my top dairy snack picks (and a few recipes, too!). #UndeniablyDairy

24 likes

MARCH 28, 2018

Add a comment...

FIGURE 29.11 The Pledge of Professional Civility

The Pledge of Professional Civility

- I pledge to demonstrate respect to my colleagues and all others.
- I pledge to support constructive dialogue and positive engagement.
- I pledge to discourage the public belittling of my colleagues, even when we do not agree.
- I pledge to model professional conduct in all my public communications and actions.

FOOD & NUTRITION MAGAZINE®
Pledge of Professional Civility

#PROcivility
FoodandNutrition.org/**ProfessionalCivility**

Reproduced with permission from Professional civility. *Food & Nutrition Magazine*. Accessed March 3, 2018. https://foodandnutrition.org/professionalcivility[22]

> Refer to Chapter 9 for a more detailed view of the Pledge of Professional Civility.

across platforms. Many of these tools have a social listening feature that will alert users when someone mentions their name or leaves a comment.

Some of the most popular tools include:

- Buffer (https://buffer.com)
- CoSchedule (https://coschedule.com)
- Hootsuite (https://hootsuite.com)
- HubSpot (www.hubspot.com)
- Later (https://later.com)
- MeetEdgar (https://meetedgar.com)
- Social Oomph (www.socialoomph.com)
- SproutSocial (https://sproutsocial.com)
- Social Flow (www.socialflow.com)
- Tailwind (www.tailwindapp.com)

Bloggers can use plug-ins, tools that allow them to automatically post on their social media channels whenever they publish a new article, which can be a significant time saver. Sharing a new blog post, YouTube video, or podcast on all social channels is one of the best ways to drive visitors back to a blog. Examples are shown in Figures 29.12 and 29.13.

Remember, social media is not just about sharing one's own content. It is also about sharing other people's content, including content from other nutrition and dietetics practitioners (Figure 29.14). Curating or identifying relevant content is easier with the help of social media automation tools. For example, Hootsuite gives users the option to find suggested content based on keywords,

such as *food* and *nutrition*. Buffer allows users to create a posting schedule based on updates from their network. TweetDeck helps users view multiple timelines in a dashboard, which can make it easier to view users to retweet. TweetDeck is also helpful for managing multiple Twitter accounts and scheduling tweets for posting in the future.

Creative and Effective Outreach

Social media is changing rapidly, with new platforms and features constantly being introduced. Video is an increasingly popular format, especially live video on Facebook and Instagram. Many nutrition and dietetics practitioners have their own YouTube channel and promote their videos across all of their social media platforms (Figure 29.15). Podcasts and Facebook Live shows are also increasingly used by dietetics practitioners to communicate about nutrition and inspire a healthy lifestyle (Figures 29.16 through 29.18).

Social media tools, such as Canva (www.canva.com), PicMonkey (www.picmonkey.com), Pablo (www.pablo.buffer.com), MemeGenerator (www.memegenerator.com), and Recite (www.recite.com), are available to help create photo collages, graphics, quotes, and other images for social media posts. Giphy (www.giphy.com) is a free collection of animated GIFs that can be used in social media. Research indicates that social media posts with images get the most engagement, including likes and shares. For example[23]:

FIGURE 29.12 Regan Miller Jones of This Unmillenial Life promotes her new blog posts on Twitter

FIGURE 29.13 Jenny Shea Rawn uses Twitter to share a new recipe post on her blog

FIGURE 29.14 Laura Chalela Hoover of Smart Eating for Kids retweets a meal planning post from Sally Kuzemchak's *Real Mom Nutrition* blog

FIGURE 29.15 Mary Donkersloot created a weekly video series called the *Smart Eating Show* that she promotes on social media

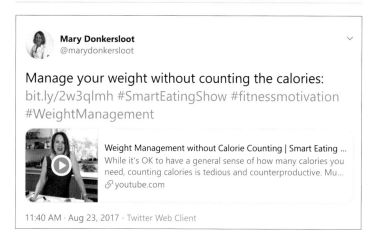

FIGURE 29.16 Liz Weiss promotes her podcast *Liz's Healthy Table* on her social media channels

FIGURE 29.17 Jill Castle hosts *The Nourished Child* podcast and uses social media to attract listeners

- Articles containing images receive 94% more views than articles without images.
- Tweets with images are retweeted 150% more than those that are text only.
- Facebook posts with images receive three times more engagement than posts without images.
- Infographics are liked, shared, and retweeted three times more than other types of content on social media platforms.
- Four times as many consumers prefer to watch a video about a product than to read about it.

Due to algorithms introduced by many social networking sites, including Facebook and Instagram, not all posts will be seen by all followers. That is why these sites have increasingly become paid platforms. That means paid support is needed (such as promoted posts and display ads) to be sure the content reaches the intended audience. Investing money to extend the reach of social media posts is typically only important if social media is being used to generate income.

Strategically using hashtags can help users be more discoverable, especially on Twitter and Instagram, where users can now follow hashtags in the same way they follow other users. Food is also especially popular on Instagram, and many food-related hashtags, such as #instafood, #feedfeed, #huffposttaste, and #buzzfeedfood, have millions of followers. Use a mix of hashtags that reflect the keywords in a post combined with popular food hashtags. Research what hashtags other dietetics practitioners and food bloggers are using and test out related hashtags. When users type a hashtag into Instagram's search bar, they can find related hashtags in a scroll-down menu.

Social media analytics can tell users what their audience prefers and the types of content that performs best. Test a few approaches—for example, ask questions, host a contest, or share a personal story—to see how engagement changes. Consider a reader survey to gain insights on what the audience prefers. The Words of Experience box provides some ideas about finding success using Instagram.

What Are Practical Strategies for Using Social Media?

Social media can seem overwhelming at first, so it is helpful to observe how other nutrition and dietetics practitioners are engaging in social media and learn from these colleagues. When RDNs start using social networking sites personally, they can begin to identify ways to benefit professionally from social media.

RDNs should identify what they hope to gain by using social media and be realistic about the time and resources they can devote to it. Rather than using multiple platforms all at once, they should start by choosing one or two that best represent their focus and intended audience.

Identify Social Media Goals

Begin by identifying the end goal. What do you want to achieve by engaging in social media? Is it primarily to network with colleagues and connect with family and friends? Or do you want social media to help build a business or become established as an authority on a specific topic. Is your social media goal to attract clients, advocate for an issue, or become a social media influencer?

FIGURE 29.18 **Ellie Krieger created a weekly Facebook Live show and uses social media to drive viewers**

Ellie Krieger ✓ was live.
May 30, 2018 · ⊙

Live From My Test Kitchen: Unexpected Ways To Use Wasabi

6K Views

117 Likes 77 Comments 21 Shares

↪ Share

RDNs should have a vision of what success looks like and put it in writing. The ultimate goal will determine the amount of time and resources the RDN will need to devote to social media. In addition, consider who will be reached, such as millennials, moms, athletes, or fellow health care professionals. The intended audience will determine what social channels to prioritize, the type of content to create, and the approach of the writing. For instance, if an RDN wants to reach teenagers, Snapchat or Instagram will be more effective than Facebook.

Seek Inspiration from Colleagues

Start by following other nutrition and dietetics practitioners on Twitter, Instagram, Facebook, and Pinterest and observe what they share on their channels to gain insights. Look at the type of content they post and how they engage with their audiences. Some RDNs are primarily recipe focused (Figure 29.19), while others are using their channels to promote weight management and fitness (Figures 29.20 and 29.21). When visiting

 WORDS OF EXPERIENCE

Finding Success on Instagram by Rachel Paul, PhD, RD

Instagram has become one of the most popular social media platforms for nutrition and dietetics practitioners to visually showcase their expertise and build their personal brands. I chose @collegenutritionist for my Instagram handle because it helps position me as a nutrition expert for college students. I started by surveying my target audience, which helped me develop the description of my Instagram profile and shape my content strategy, which is primarily focused on weight management and meal prep for one.

Here are some techniques I used to build an audience on Instagram:

FLOUR TACOS   LETTUCE WRAPS

4 small tortillas: 240 cals   4 lettuce shells: 5 cals

Inspire with Organization. Show snacks or meal prep ideas that are organized in eye-catching ways or interesting containers.

Color Wins. Use contrasting or complementary colors to help photos stand out. When editing photos with an app (I use VSCO), I have found that the brighten and contrast functions can highlight color differences.

Compare and Contrast. Feature comparisons between two or more items, such as "try this, not that"; "precooked vs cooked"; and "healthy swaps."

Aim for visual consistency with an Instagram feed because it allows users to easily recognize that content when scrolling and helps build a professional brand. In addition to the feed, try Instagram stories, which are a series of videos or photos that expire after 24 hours. I post stories when finding new food products or share tips that are relevant for my audience. When followers see the poster's face and hear his or her voice in Instagram stories, they get to know the person in a more personal way than through captions in a feed. When followers interact with a person's stories via liking or commenting, they are more likely to discover that person's posts in their feeds.

their social media platforms, note whom they follow to identify others to follow yourself. To gain inspiration from experienced bloggers, visit Nutrition Blog Network (www.nutritionblognetwork.com), which is an aggregator of blogs written by registered dietitian nutritionists. Nutrition Blog Network is also on Facebook and Twitter.

Evaluate the Return on Investment

If RDNs are devoting significant time and resources to social media, they should be sure they are building in some way to measure success. Social media return on investment (ROI) will depend on the overall goals, which may be financial (new clients, product sales, or brand sponsorships) or related to professional reputation and thought leadership, such as speaking invitations or media interview requests.

Start by setting specific goals, such as a number of email list sign-ups, contact form inquiries, or downloads of e-books, and then regularly assess user actions. Google Analytics (www.google.com/analytics) is a valuable tool to help track and measure results against user goals.

Evaluating social media activities will allow RDNs to identify where they can improve their efforts, determine which social media channels are performing best, and determine how specific changes can impact their social media results.

Remember, not every nutrition and dietetics practitioner will want or need to use social media to connect with an audience or build a business. Yet, digital strategies are increasingly important for all types of professionals. When choosing to engage in social media, it is important to establish goals, recognize best practices, track metrics, and measure success.

FIGURE 29.19 **The Real Food Dietitians share recipes from their blog on Instagram**

therealfoodrds Follow

2,956 posts   **190k** followers   **347** following

Dietitians, Jess & Stacie
Food & Lifestyle blog that will inspire you to:
 Eat well
Live well
Be well

⊞ POSTS   ⊙ IGTV   🔲 TAGGED

FIGURE 29.20 Emily Field shares her nutrition counseling philosophy and client feedback on Instagram

FIGURE 29.21 Jim White features fitness and lifestyle tips on Instagram

KEY POINTS

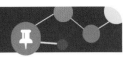

Social Media Is a Powerful Tool for Nutrition Communication and Professional Marketing

1. Social media has become an effective way for nutrition and dietetics practitioners to broadly communicate nutrition messages to the public, extend support to patients and clients, attract new clients, communicate with students, collaborate with colleagues, and network with other professionals. Increasingly, digital approaches are used to implement nutrition education and health promotion programs, advocate for an issue, champion a cause, and build thought leadership.

2. Nutrition and dietetics practitioners who engage in social media must maintain professional and ethical standards, identify social media goals and strategies, track and measure activities, understand social media etiquette, and remain respectful and civil with colleagues and other social media users.

3. Social media can seem overwhelming at first, so it is helpful to observe how other nutrition and dietetics practitioners are engaging in social media and learn from the best practices of these colleagues. Using social networking sites personally or just for fun can help registered dietitian nutritionists identify ways to benefit professionally from these channels.

RESOURCES

Food & Nutrition Magazine, Professional Civility: https://foodandnutrition.org/professionalcivility

Journal of Medical Internet Research—the leading peer-reviewed journal for digital medicine, health, and health care in the internet age: www.jmir.org

Nutrition Communications Academy: Achieving Online Excellence through Education and Coaching: https://reganmillerjonesinc.teachable.com

eMarketer—a website that provides insights and trends on digital marketing, media, and communications: https://emarketer.com

Mashable—a global, multiplatform, media and entertainment company that covers technology and digital culture: https://mashable.com

Social Media Examiner—articles, expert interviews, and research on social media marketing: www.socialmediaexaminer.com

Social Media Explorer—tools and tips for using social media: https://socialmediaexplorer.com

Social Media Today—resource on social media and digital strategy: www.socialmediatoday.com

TechCrunch—online publisher of technology news: https://techcrunch.com

REFERENCES

1. Solis B. Defining social media: 2006–2010. Brian Solis website. Published January 7, 2010. Accessed March 26, 2018. www.briansolis.com/2010/01/defining-social-media-the-saga-continues

2. Stelzner M. 2018 social media marketing industry report: how marketers are using social media to grow their businesses. Social Media Examiner website. Published May 7, 2018. Accessed August 21, 2018. www.socialmediaexaminer.com/social-media-marketing-industry-report-2018

3. Jacobs W, Amuta AO, Jeon KC. Health information seeking in the digital age: an analysis of health information seeking behavior among US adults. *Cogent Social Sciences*. 2017;3:1-11.

4. Raggatt M, Wright CJC, Carrotte E, et al. "I aspire to look and feel healthy like the posts convey": engagement with fitness inspiration on social media and perceptions of its influence on health and wellbeing. *BMC Public Health*. 2018;18(1):1002.

5. Saunders JF, Eaton AA. Snaps, selfies and shares: how three popular social media platforms contribute to the sociocultural model of disordered eating among young women. *Cyberpsychol Behav Soc Netw*. 2018;21(6):343-354.

6. Cohen R, Newton-John T, Slater A. The relationship between Facebook and Instagram appearance-focused activities and body image concerns in young women. *Body Image*. 2017;23:183-187.

7. Dumas AA, Lapointe A, Desroches S. Users, uses, and effects of social media in dietetic practice: scoping review of the quantitative and qualitative evidence. *J Med Internet Res.* 2018;20(2):e67.

8. Helm J, Jones RM. Practice paper of the Academy of Nutrition and Dietetics: social media and the dietetics practitioners: opportunities, challenges, and best practices. *J Acad Nutr Diet.* 2016;116(11):1825-1835.

9. Yeung D. Social media as a catalyst for policy action and social change for health and well-being: viewpoint. *J Med Internet Res.* 2018;20(3):e94.

10. Williams G, Hamm M, Shulman J, et al. Social media interventions for diet and exercise behaviours: a systematic review and meta-analysis of randomized controlled trials. *BMJ Open.* 2014;4:e003926.

11. Smith A, Anderson M. Social media use in 2018. Pew Research Center website. Published March 1, 2018. Accessed March 4, 2018. www.pewinternet .org/2018/03/01/social-media-use-in-2018

12. Centers for Disease Control and Prevention. CDC social media tools, guidelines and best practices. Accessed March 21, 2018. www.cdc.gov/socialmedia /tools/guidelines/socialmediatoolkit.html

13. Maher CA, Lewis LK, Ferrar K, et al. Are health behavior change interventions that use online social networks effective? A systematic review. *J Med Internet Res.* 2014;16(2):e40.

14. An R, Ji M, Zhang S. Effectiveness of social media-based interventions on weight-related behaviors and body weight status: review and meta-analysis. *Am J Health Behav.* 2017;41(6):670-682.

15. Coccia C, Fernandes SM, Julinar A. Tweeting for nutrition: feasibility and efficacy outcomes of a 6-week social media–based nutrition education intervention for student-athletes. *J Strength Cond Res.* Published online February 22, 2018. doi:10.1519/JSC.0000000000002500

16. Looyestyn J, Kernot J, Boshoff K, Maher C. A web-based, social networking beginners' running intervention for adults aged 18 to 50 years delivered via a Facebook group: randomized controlled trial. *J Med Internet Res.* 2018;20(2):e67.

17. Nour M, Yeung SH, Partridge S, Allman-Farinelli M. A narrative review of social media and game-based nutrition interventions targeted at young adults. *J Acad Nutr Diet.* 2017;117(5):735-752.

18. Academy of Nutrition and Dietetics. Committee on Dietetic Registration. Code of ethics for the nutrition and dietetics profession. eatright website. Effective June 1, 2018. Accessed August 19, 2018. www.eatrightpro.org/-/media /eatrightpro-files/career/code-of-ethics /coeforthenutritionanddieteticsprofession.pdf

19. Federal Trade Commission. Guides concerning the use of endorsements and testimonials in advertising federal acquisition regulation; final rule. *Fed Regist.* 2009;74(198):53123-53143. Accessed December 19, 2019. www.ftc.gov /sites/default/files/documents/federal_register _notices/guides-concerning-use-endorsements -and-testimonials-advertising-16-cfr-part-255 /091015guidesconcerningtestimonials.pdf

20. Federal Trade Commission. *.com Disclosures: How to Make Effective Disclosures in Digital Advertising.* March 2013. Accessed March 28, 2018. http://business.ftc.gov/documents/bus41 -dot-com-disclosures-information-about-online -advertising

21. Federal Trade Commission. The FTC's endorsement guides: what people are asking. Published September 2017. Accessed March 28, 2018. www.ftc.gov/tips-advice/business-center /guidance/ftcs-endorsement-guides-what-people -are-asking#SocialNetworkingSites

22. Professional civility. *Food & Nutrition Magazine.* Accessed March 3, 2018. https://foodand nutrition.org/professionalcivility

23. Price C. 6 types of visual content that get the most links and shares. *Search Engine J.* Published November 13, 2017. Accessed April 10, 2018. www.searchenginejournal.com/visual-content -types-links-shares/223277

Blogging and Web-Based Writing Establishes the Nutrition Communicator as an Expert Resource to a Wide Audience

Janet Helm, MS, RDN
and Rachel Meltzer Warren, MS, RDN

"Blogs and other online platforms have ushered in a new era to help nutrition and dietetics practitioners reach much larger audiences and connect with other health care professionals, the media, and the public."

Teach Your Teen about Nutrition Facts Panels

If decoding the information on a food package is a challenge for adults, think of how hard it is for teens who are just beginning to make choices for themselves.

"The greatest paradox surrounding the internet is that as much as it allows us to isolate and limit ourselves only to what we believe is immediately relevant to our specific needs, so does it allow us to connect at unprecedented levels and extend ourselves beyond our farthest horizons."

—GARY VAYNERCHUK, AUTHOR OF *CRUSH IT! WHY NOW IS THE TIME TO CASH IN ON YOUR PASSION*

Introduction

In many ways, digital media has transformed the practice of dietetics. It has helped reinvent the ways nutrition and dietetics practitioners can educate the public and engage with clients. It has served as a powerful communication tool—a platform for showcasing expertise, sharing nutrition messages, and connecting with diverse audiences. Digital media has also been a valuable way for entrepreneurial dietetics practitioners to establish a business and build a brand.

Blogs (derived from the word *weblog*) are a core element of digital communication. Writing for blogs and websites should follow the same principles of quality writing addressed in other chapters, while recognizing several key differences in how people consume content online.

This chapter answers three questions:

- What is the role of blogging and web-based writing in nutrition communications?
- What are practical strategies for starting and maintaining a blog?
- What are blogging best practices?

The answers to these questions will help readers understand the benefits and challenges of blogging and arm them with strategies for developing engaging and share-worthy online content. This chapter addresses quality web-based writing, editorial planning, search engine optimization, content socializing, blog analytics, and the ethical and legal issues governing digital media.

What Is the Role of Blogging and Web-Based Writing in Nutrition Communications?

Blogs and other online platforms offer new avenues for nutrition and dietetics practitioners to reach large audiences and connect with the public, media, and fellow health care professionals.[1] Digital media can be an effective way to amplify credible nutrition messages and correct misinformation using the extensive reach of the internet.

Public Education

Blogging provides an efficient platform from which to educate the public on food and nutrition, as consumers increasingly turn to the internet to learn more about health topics, what to eat, and how to shop for food.[2,3] If dietetics practitioners are not familiar with how to use digital technologies to communicate food and nutrition information, it is a missed opportunity that others will seize.

Unfortunately, blogging allows individuals without nutrition credentials to broadcast messages to large audiences without gatekeepers to check for accuracy. The volume of nutrition and health information online makes it difficult for the public to discern what is reliable and science-based. Misleading and potentially harmful nutrition advice provided by some digital influencers and bloggers has been frequently documented.[4-6]

Blogs written by dietetics professionals may be particularly valuable in helping the public make healthier food choices, according to Bissonnette-Maheux and colleagues, who conducted a study with French-Canadian women to explore the impact of nutrition blogs.[7] Study participants valued the credibility of blogs written by registered dietitian nutritionists (RDNs) and cited several benefits—including the personal connection with a nutrition professional and access to trusted information about new foods, nutrition trends, and healthy recipes. Researchers concluded that RDN blogs may be important nutrition knowledge translation tools for preventing chronic disease.

In a follow-up study, the same research team found that the most useful characteristics of RDN blogs were recipes, hyperlinks, and references.[8] Images, videos, ease of navigation, and well-structured posts that were not overloaded with text were preferred characteristics.

Blogs written by nutrition and dietetics practitioners may be especially helpful in balancing the negative or "pathogenic" framing of food that is frequently found in health and fitness magazines, suggest researchers at the University of Toronto.[9] In a yearlong study, 141 health and fitness articles in US magazines were compared to 459 healthy-living posts from six blogs, including one written by an RDN. The magazine articles tended to view food through the lens of obesity and demonized certain foods that were worthy of restriction, while the blogs predominantly framed food in a more positive way—as capable of promoting health and well-being, along with pleasure and enjoyment. Figures 30.1, 30.2, and 30.3 are examples of RDN blogs that combine nutrition advice, recipes, and positive food messages.

Extended Reach

Growing numbers of dietetics practitioners have created food and nutrition blogs or websites and are using social media to communicate nutrition to a broad audience. (Box 30.1 includes a list of where to find food and nutrition blogs.) Many of these blogs serve as an online resume or storefront—helping to attract new clients for in-person or virtual nutrition counseling. Some blogs are directed at the general public, while others are focused on a specific segment of the population, such as pregnant women, moms with young children, adults with diabetes, college students, or older adults.

Blogging has become a valuable way for dietetics practitioners to translate scientific research, provide perspective on current nutrition issues, and elevate a specific expertise—from feeding children and gluten-free cooking to sports nutrition, digestive health, and intuitive eating.

Many RDNs have built large online followings and a digital presence, becoming sought-after resources for the media. Many are also getting paid to write for other websites and attracting advertisers to their blogs. Others have turned their blogs into books or have used their digital platforms and online influence to launch new businesses.

More Discoverable

Compared to a static website, a blog is continually updated, which increases the likelihood that people will find it through internet searches. Search engines, such as Google, track content on blogs differently from how they track website content, and this difference helps blog content appear higher up in a list of search results. A blog thrives on new content, and the more it is updated, the more attention it will get. Blog content also travels—often showing up in people's Facebook newsfeeds and Twitter timelines. A blog is all about two-way communication or participating in conversations, and it is going where consumers (or potential clients) are—not waiting for them to find it.

BOX 30.1 Where to Find Food and Nutrition Blogs

The Nutrition Blog Network (www.nutritionblog network.com) aggregates and promotes blogs written by registered dietitian nutritionists (RDNs).

Food & Nutrition Magazine (https://foodandnutrition.org/blogs) features four different blogs: *Stone Soup*, *The Feed*, *The Cutting Board*, and *Student Scoop.*

Healthy Aperture (https://healthyaperture.com) is a visual recipe discovery site and multiauthor blog showcasing the work of RDN bloggers and other food bloggers.

An RDN who already has a website may want to consider adding a blog element to it, either as a subdomain or a page to make it more discoverable online. Some dietetics practitioners who previously had websites to promote their private practices or consulting businesses have added blog components. Guest posting on other RDN blogs or writing for established websites can also help RDNs communicate nutrition messages to a broad audience and increase their online exposure.

Professional Resource

Not all blogs are targeted to the general public. Depending on a blog's focus and mission, it can be a valuable resource for nutrition colleagues and other health care professionals—as with blogs on science, public health, agriculture, or food policy. Some professional blogs provide consumer education handouts, tool kits, and presentations, or feature skill-building tools—such as how to start a blog or podcast and tips for improving food photography or media interviews. Some of the content is free, yet more in-depth resources and virtual coaching on media training, blogging, and social media require a fee. Other professional blogs are focused on helping colleagues build successful school food-service programs or community-based nutrition initiatives. Many supermarkets, hospitals, universities, organizations, and government agencies have blogs. Some are written for the public, while others target a professional audience. For RDNs who work for one of these institutions, there may be opportunities to contribute to these blogs or be featured as a nutrition expert.

The RDN blogger community is rapidly growing, and RDN blogs continue to serve as inspiration, idea starters, and valuable resources for nutrition and dietetics practitioners, as well as other professionals. One of the best ways to succeed at blogging is to follow RDN blogs and join some of the Facebook groups dedicated to RDNs in social media. There is a large, supportive group of RDN bloggers who can serve as mentors. Refer to the Terms to Know box for a glossary of popular blogging terms.

Financial Benefits

Blogging can be financially beneficial, although that should not be the primary reason for starting a blog. It will take some time to begin making

FIGURE 30.1 *Food Heaven Made Easy* blog created by Jessica Jones and Wendy Lopez

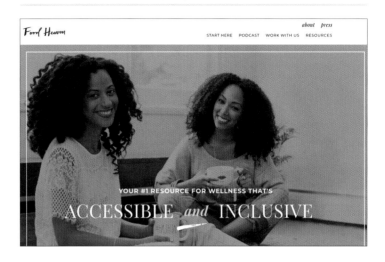

FIGURE 30.2 Chris Mohr maintains a blog called *Mohr Results* that focuses on vibrant living

FIGURE 30.3 Holley Grainger created a blog on "cleverful living" that often features creative lunchbox ideas

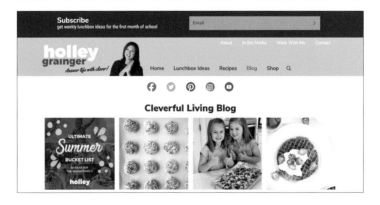

money, and it will not likely replace a full-time income. Bloggers can make money through e-commerce, such as book sales or downloadable e-books, online courses, and other resources. Some dietetics practitioners have a section of their blog that is fee-based only. That means payment is required to access the more advanced information, including meal plans, customized nutrition strategies, or interactive video coaching.

Other ways to monetize a blog include sponsors who want to place advertisements or pay for sponsored blog posts or videos. Affiliate links are additional revenue-generating opportunities for bloggers. An affiliate link is a hyperlink to an affiliated organization that is placed on a blog for the purpose of generating commissions on books and other products purchased by blog visitors. All marketing relationships, including sponsored posts and affiliate links, must be adequately disclosed on the blog and in social channels. Learn more about transparency and disclosure in the best practices section: Be professional and ethical.

Beyond the direct income, blogging may lead to new referrals or speaking opportunities. Having an online presence may encourage someone to book an appointment for nutrition services (see Figure 30.4) or lead to other opportunities, such as consulting or paid media spokesperson contracts.

Chapter 9 addresses the Code of Ethics for the nutrition and dietetics profession.

What Are Practical Strategies for Starting and Maintaining a Blog?

Digital technologies may seem intimidating, but it is easier to start a blog than it may seem at first. If an RDN wants to establish himself or herself as an authority on a specific topic, reach a broad audience with a point of view, promote a private practice, or pursue entrepreneurial opportunities, then starting a blog might be a good idea. However, the RDN will need to learn a new lexicon,

TERMS TO KNOW: Glossary of Blogging Terms

Affiliate	A company who partners with a blogger to sell products or services (Blog visitors click on hyperlinks to affiliate sites placed on the blog, and the blogger earns commissions for each sale.)
Anchor text	The clickable text in a hyperlink
Blog	Derived from weblog, a website that is regularly updated and written in an informal or conversational style
Content	Any creative element on a blog, such as text, images, and video
Disclosure	The practice of revealing marketing relationships or relevant affiliations in blog posts that may pose a conflict of interest (This type of transparency is required by the Federal Trade Commission.)
e-book	Electronic version of a book that can be downloaded from a blog
e-commerce	The use of blogs or websites to sell products or services
HTML (hypertext markup language):	Coding used to display certain elements on a webpage, such as fonts, line spacing, and layout
Hyperlink	Clickable content on a blog that takes the user to an external site or another page on the blog (internal link)
Keywords	A highly used and relevant word related to a blog post; typically, keywords people type into search engines that allow them to find a blog
Meta keyword	A specific type of meta tag in the HTML code of a webpage that tells search engines what the page is about
Meta tag	A snippet of text that describes the content of a webpage
Mobile-friendly	The quality of being easily readable on mobile devices, achieved by optimizing design for smaller displays and touch control; *responsive* design will automatically reformat blogs for all screen sizes
Monetize	To use a blog as a source of profit through advertising, sponsored posts, affiliate links, sales of digital products such as eBooks, and virtual coaching

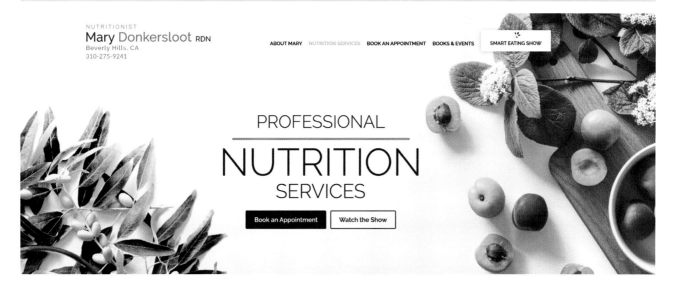

Page ranking	The use of an algorithm (computer formula) used by Google and other search engines to measure authority of a webpage
Page views	The number of times a webpage or post is viewed or visited
Permalink	In the context of blogging, the URL for a particular post published on a blog vs the blog's main URL
Pingback	A notification that one's blog post has been linked to by another site
Plug-in	A piece of software that contains a group of functions that can add new features to a blog, such as a recipe plug-in that make it easy to format, publish, and print recipes
Podcast	A downloadable or streamable audio or visual file on a blog or website, such as an online radio show
Referral traffic	Users who visit a blog by clicking on a link from a different website
RSS (really simple syndication)	Allows subscribers to get continuously updated content or feeds from their favorite sites
SEO (search engine optimization)	The process of optimizing a blog to achieve better ranking in search engine results to improve the volume of traffic; one SEO method involves finding and searching for keywords
SERP (search engine results page)	The listing of results that are displayed by search engines such as Google in response to typing in keywords
Site map	The directory or index of a blog or website; search engines use site maps for "crawling" and ranking sites
Tag	A word or short phrase attached to a blog post that helps make the post more findable online
Unique visitor	A distinct, individual visitor to a blog or website who is only counted once, regardless of how many times or webpages he or she visits
URL (uniform resource locator)	A blog or website's address on the internet; frequently referred to as a web address (eg, www.eatrightpro.org and www.choosemyplate.gov)

recognize what it takes to build a community, and invest sufficient time in maintaining a blog.

Secure Domain Name, Blogging Platform, and Host

Starting a blog takes three major steps.

DOMAIN NAME

The domain is the URL (uniform resource locator) or web address for a blog, such as eatright.org or google.com. Choose a memorable name for the blog and register the domain at GoDaddy.com, Register.com, Name.com, or another accredited domain registrar (where users can check to see if the name is available). Whenever possible, choose the more popular dot-com (.com) extension for the URL, instead of the .net, .blog, .xyz, .in, or other domain extensions. Some people run blogs without registering their own domain. However, to build a professional social media platform, it's best to own the domain name so the site is easier to find and the owner is freed from depending on any one blogging platform, such as having to use a subdomain like myblog.wordpress.com.

BLOGGING PLATFORM

A blogging platform is the software or service that a blogger uses to create and publish a blog. The most popular and customizable platform is WordPress, which has a large community behind it and resource sites dedicated to users. Other frequently used platforms include Blogger, Tumblr, Typepad, and Squarespace. Factors to consider when choosing a blogging platform are ease of use, flexibility to allow growth, features (design themes, available plug-ins, or blog apps), and service.

BLOG HOST

A blog or web host is what enables blogs to be posted on the internet. While there are free blog hosts, the paid hosting options will provide greater flexibility for customization and will give bloggers more control if they want to monetize a blog with ads. Bluehost is one of the most popular hosting services; other options include iPage, HostGator, SiteGround, and InMotion Hosting. Factors to consider when choosing a blog host are cost, speed, uptime, and technical support.

Refer to Box 30.1 to find online destinations where RDNs can learn more about how to start a blog, blogging best practices, and tips for maximizing or monetizing their blogs.

Create Theme and Design

Blog layouts are known as themes, and blogging platforms have various design themes users can select to give the blog the desired look and feel they want. Consider hiring a designer to create a logo and customize the blog design. Unless an RDN has strong technology and design skills, it is best not to attempt to do it all solo. A contemporary, highly visual, and eye-catching blog is essential to promote a professional image, break through the crowded "blogosphere," and gain followers.

Read other blogs for inspiration and design ideas. Look at the different elements featured on the blog, including the top navigation bar, pages, footer, and sidebars. Ask colleagues who they worked with to create their blogs or look for design credits on popular blogs. To find a local designer, do an online search for area social media consultants or designers specializing in popular blogging platforms.

Develop a Content Strategy

Spend time thinking about the mission of the blog and how it will be perceived. Consider ways the content can stand out from other bloggers' content. Target a specific niche and develop a focus. Instead of a general food or nutrition blog, pick an angle or approach that plays to individual strengths, unique expertise, and passions. Determine where the blog can fulfill a need online.

Identify the topics to blog about, the approach, and the type of content to create. Think about the categories or content pillars to cover on the blog, from recipes and meal planning to trend spotting and myth busting. Will the blog primarily feature posted articles and photos, or will it include videos or a podcast? Increasingly, bloggers are podcasting and vlogging (video blogging) from their blogs.

Include a section on the site that articulates the philosophy and the focus of the blog to let readers know what to expect when they visit the blog (see Figure 30.5). Be sure to write several posts before it is officially launched. There is only one chance to make a good impression. If new readers arrive at the blog and find a single "Welcome to my blog" posting and little other content of value, they won't know enough about the blog to come back or subscribe.

BODYKINDNESS®
"Simple and True" — *The New York Times Book Review*

ABOUT   SHOP   PODCAST   BLOG   GET STARTED   LOGIN   Q   ✉   MORE ☰

Create a *Better* life

Body Kindness

Transform your health
—from the inside out—
and never say diet again.

Establish an Editorial Calendar

As stated in Chapter 22, the first step in writing is putting pen to paper—or, in the case of a blogger, fingers to keyboard—and getting started. Blogging is like exercise—it helps to make an appointment to make it happen. Mapping out a monthly editorial calendar with planned topics can help writers stick with a regular routine.

Consistency in posting is the best way to help grow a blog's audience. Adding content regularly will let Google and other search engines know that the blog is alive. If it's not an active blog, search engines will visit it less often (digital robots constantly "crawl" and index web content), which could negatively impact its ranking. Some bloggers post daily, but it may be more realistic to aim for weekly, twice monthly, or another schedule that works. Just make sure to stick with it so that posts are consistent and readers know when to expect new content.

Tailor Writing for Online Readers

Blog writing follows the same guidelines as those for excellence in any written communication, but the style is typically more informal and conversational. It's also a format that benefits from personal storytelling by bringing in personal perspectives and experience. Because the content is read online rather than in a print publication, there are other techniques to help increase readability and engagement.

BE SCAN-FRIENDLY

Eye-tracking studies show that people read only about 20% of an online post on average.[10] When reading screens instead of paper, people have a greater tendency to scan pages rather than read them word for word. It helps to break up long blocks of copy; even 300 uninterrupted words tend to look overwhelming online. Using lists, bullet points, short paragraphs, subheads, bold font, visuals, and open space in posts will help improve the scanability of blog posts.

KEEP IT CLEAR AND CONCISE

Be sure the writing doesn't sound like an academic paper. Write in a natural speaking voice and avoid jargon or clichés. If using technical words, be sure to define and explain. Delete extra words; long, complicated sentences; and vague modifiers, such as *very*, *a lot*, or *slightly*.

FIND A VOICE

The more a writer blogs, the easier it will be for him or her to develop a unique blogging voice, or a personality to convey in writing. Use a tone that is professional yet personable. Dietetics professionals can be authoritative and still have their personality

See Chapter 22 for more on written communication.

shine through. Social media engagement will increase if the audience can connect with the person behind the post. Read the writing out loud to help ensure the post sounds like the writer is explaining the topic to a friend. But whether using humor, sarcasm, or simply a bit of sass, just stay authentic.

USE VIBRANT, ACTIVE WORDS

Let the writing show enthusiasm for the topic and use an active voice. Think of it as *who* is doing *what*? For instance, "The children ate the food" is active, while "The food was eaten by the children" is passive. Sentences written with a passive voice tend to be wordy, vague, and ineffective.

CREATE STRUCTURE FOR THE POST

Every blog post should have an introduction, a main section featuring the key messages, and a conclusion or call to action. Start by outlining this structure and then fill in with writing. If you have written related posts, add those links to further inform the reader and make the post appear stronger to search engines because it shows authority on the subject. If citing a study, news article, or another blog or website, include a link and reference to the source.

Write Strong Headlines

An information-packed, engaging blog post will not reach its full potential without an irresistible, clickable headline. Make blog headlines work harder so the writing can reach even more people by following these tips:

USE NUMBERS AND LISTS

Start a headline with a number, as in "7 Protein-Packed Vegan Breakfasts" or "5 Easy Ways to Reduce Sugar." Headlines starting with numbers grab readers more than other types of headlines.[11] The number 10 has been found to be the highest performing headline number, followed by 5, 15, and 7.[12] Organizing a post as a list gives readers a clearer idea of what to expect and promises a quick, scan-friendly read.

BE DESCRIPTIVE

Use keywords in the headline that summarize the main objective of the post. It makes it clear to readers what will be discussed in the post and helps the blog post rank better with Google and other search engines. Keywords are the descriptive words that someone may type into a search bar if they're seeking information on the topic of the blog post.

"WHAT'S IN IT FOR ME?"

Tease with words that let readers know they have something valuable to gain by clicking. For example, use words such as *reasons, facts, how-to's, ways, tips, tricks, secrets, ideas,* and *strategies*. Research by BuzzSumo found that "will make you" was the most popular word combination in headlines.[12] "This is why" and "the reason is" were other popular three-word combinations in headlines.

OFFER A SURPRISING TWIST

Take an approach that suggests readers may not have all the facts on a subject. For instance, try "5 Myths About Weight Loss You Probably Still Believe." Use words like *myths, lies, truth, wrong, surprising,* and *shocking*.

ASK QUESTIONS

Asking readers a question will draw them in, and the question mark helps catch the eye in a similar way that numbers do.[12] Try headlines such as "What's the Best Cooking Oil?" or "Are You Getting Enough Iron?"

KEEP IT TIGHT

The ideal length of a headline is between 40 and 50 characters.[13] If it's longer than 70 characters, Google and other search engines will start truncating the headline in searches.

Think Visually

Include images in a blog posts to help them get noticed (blog posts with images get 94% more total views than content without images)[14] and to make them easier for readers to share. Remember, no one can pin a post to Pinterest without an image.

If bloggers are not taking their own photographs, they can explore free and inexpensive stock photos or identify photos with a Creative Commons license. Creative Commons (www.creativecommons.org) is a nonprofit organization devoted to expanding the free use of creative works, including photos. Under a Creative Commons license, photographers can give others permission to use and share their work, based on conditions the owner specifies—such as proper credit and links back to a website. Flickr (www.flickr.com) is a major source of free, downloadable Creative Commons–licensed photos.

When bloggers upload photos, they should tag them with keywords in the file name and fill out the alternate text (alt text) field with a brief

SARA HAAS – CULINARY DIETITIAN

Let me guide you through cooking and the benefits of thoughtful, healthful eating.

CHECK OUT MY YOUTUBE CHANNEL

▶ YouTube

I've got a new YouTube Channel! Head on over and subscribe now!

HOME   RECIPES   ABOUT ME   PRESS   COOKBOOKS

Mushroom Beef Burger Sliders

in beef and pork / dinner july 25, 2018 4 comments

When I was pregnant with the little sous chef I craved 3 things – guacamole, milk shakes and burgers! The first two made perfect sense to me, but the burgers were a big surprise. I don't remember ever really getting excited about burgers any time before that, what made pregnancy so different? But here's the deal, I only wanted BEEF burgers. So weird! Well, ironically, that craving still exists even 5+ years after the sous chef was born! And it was about time I shared a burger recipe with you. Let's talk about these Mushroom Beef Burger Sliders!

keyword-rich description of the photo; these are sections in the blogging platform when writing and editing a post. Photos should also be properly sized. Typically, a photo should be the same width as the article in which it appears, as a smaller image that will look dwarfed on the page (see Figure 30.6).

What Are Blogging Best Practices?

Bloggers are their own publishers. Content needs to provide value to the audience, and it needs to benefit the blogger—raising an RDN's profile as a nutrition expert, advancing public health, and meeting business or marketing objectives. Here are a few blogging best practices to maximize time and investment.

Know the Target Audience

Keep audience in mind when creating content. Unless a blog is specifically targeting food and nutrition colleagues or other health care professionals, readers will likely be the general public. Think about who the consumer audience will be. Is the blog targeting moms, men, or millennials? Or is it directed to athletes, college students, or baby boomers? Adjust the writing style and content to appeal to the target audience.

Gather feedback from the audience to help provide content of interest to them. For example, ask questions to help guide future content, or conduct a survey to find out what topics or recipes they most want to see on the blog. End posts with a question to spark conversations. When readers leave comments on the blog, respond in a timely manner and encourage feedback. Tools like Google Analytics (www.google.com/analytics) can help bloggers learn what performs best on the blog and support them in creating content the audience is looking for and values.

If a particular post gets a good response, the blogger may want to consider turning it into a weekly series or regular feature that keeps readers coming back for more. (Figure 30.7 is an example of a series.)

Socialize the Content

Providing quality content remains the best way to build a blog following, but an audience is unlikely to discover blog posts if the writer is not using social media to promote the content. Each time a writer writes a new blog post, he or she should use Facebook, Twitter, Pinterest, and other social media platforms to share the post and drive viewers back to the blog. Consider these platforms as part of a syndication plan to extend the reach of the posts. Social media management tools, such as HootSuite, TweetDeck, Seesmic Desktop, Hubspot, and Buffer, can help schedule and manage posts across several social networks.

Include a prominently placed RSS (really simple syndication) button on the blog and offer readers the ability to subscribe to the posts via email. Be sure to give readers the tools to promote the blog on social media, such as a "pin it" button for Pinterest and "share" buttons for Facebook, Twitter, LinkedIn, and other channels.

To make it easier for people to find a blog, writers can leave thoughtful comments on other blogs, including RDN blogs. This gives the blogger an opportunity for more exposure and additional places for consumers and other bloggers to discover the blog. Set up Google alerts (www.google.com/alerts) to track mentions of the blog. If traffic from an unfamiliar blog comes in, check it out and thank the blogger for the link.

Optimize for Search Engines

After a writer starts blogging, he or she will learn that a significant amount of traffic comes through searches. That means readers are using a search

More information on social media tools and how to socialize blog content is found in Chapter 29.

FIGURE 30.7 Katie Morford created a meal-planning series called *Weeknight Rescue* on her blog, *Mom's Kitchen Handbook*

engine, such as Google or Bing, to look for information on a specific topic and the blog pops up. The goal is to get a blog to appear higher on the search engine results page (SERP) to increase the chances that someone will click on the blog page.

The strategies to get a higher ranking are part of search engine optimization (SEO). There are several aspects of SEO, but many of the tips are related to keywords. Every time a blogger writes a new post, he or she should think about the words someone would likely type into a search bar to look for information on the topic. The writer will want to use those keywords throughout the post so search engine "crawlers" will take note when indexing the content. Use keywords in the title, subheads, introduction, concluding paragraph, anchor text (the text that is hyperlinked to other related pages on the site), and the title tags and meta descriptions. This process will be prompted by the blogging platform when writing and editing the post.

When bloggers are writing about a particular topic, they will likely automatically choose relevant keywords that will help with online searches. They can also use special tools and techniques for finding keywords related to the blog post, such as Google's keyword planning tool (https://adwords.google.com/home/tools/keyword-planner). Google Trends (https://trends.google.com/trends) is helpful for learning more about trending words in food and nutrition so bloggers can write about those topics.

If a blog features recipes, it is important to include recipe metadata to tell search engines there is a recipe on the page. This recipe metadata will help improve search engine rankings. Tools or plug-ins are available to help optimize recipes, such as WP Recipe Maker, Easy Recipe, and Total Recipe Generator.

There are other factors important for SEO: Make sure the blog is mobile-friendly (easy to read on a smartphone); link internally to other relevant pages on the blog, link externally to authoritative sources; and consistently create quality content. For some blogging platforms, bloggers can install content analysis tools, such as the Yoast SEO plug-in, to help them write SEO-friendly blog posts.

Dig into the Data

Once a blogger has a blog, it is helpful to track traffic and learn how content is performing. Google Analytics is the leading analytics tool for gaining these insights. It is free and provides valuable details about readers, what they're looking for, and how the writer can better serve them. The data can also help identify the social platforms that are most responsive to the content to help the writer customize outreach and maximize reach. These are the types of questions Google Analytics can help answer:

- How many people visit a blog?
- Where do the readers live?
- Should the blog be more mobile-friendly?
- What websites send traffic to the blog?
- Which posts on the blog are most popular?
- What type of headlines perform the best?
- What type of content do readers like the most (eg, recipes, articles, product roundups)?

Include Critical Elements

Be sure to include these elements or features on a blog.

"ABOUT ME"

Create a biographical page with a picture and identify yourself as a RDN. This is an opportunity to showcase expertise, credentials, and experience—along with personality and unique perspective on the world. Readers want to know about the person behind the blog. See Figure 30.8 for an example. Be sure to include a way to be contacted via email and feature links to connect on social media.

DISCLOSURE STATEMENT

This page should contain a written statement or policy informing blog readers of any relationships with products, brands, and partners mentioned on the site. It shares the RDN's material connections or monetary partnerships. RDNs should adopt a disclosure policy to guide all communication efforts, including blog articles, social media posts, and traditional media interviews. For guidance, read the disclosure statements on other blogs, including RDN blogs, or visit DisclosurePolicy.org to find sample statements and best practices for disclosure.

PRIVACY POLICY

This page tells visitors about the type of information that is collected about them when they are visiting a blog or website, such as name, email address, shipping address, credit card details, or other means of identifying a returning user. Typically linked in the footer of a blog, the privacy policy discloses the use of internet cookies (text files

FIGURE 30.8 The "About Me" page from Marisa Moore's blog

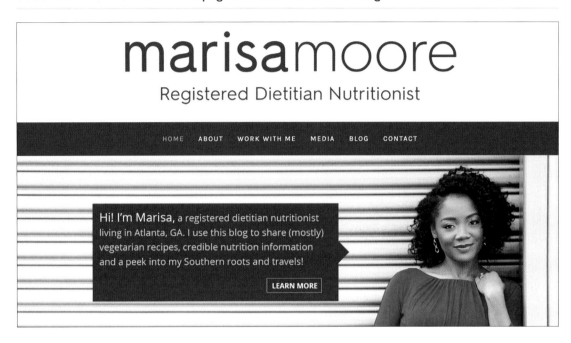

on a website that track user online behavior) and reinforces the blogger's commitment to protecting personal information. This is especially important for those dietetics practitioners who monetize their blogs with advertisements. Many companies and ad networks, such as Google AdSense, will not do business with bloggers who do not have a privacy policy page. See the resources list at the end of the chapter to find sample privacy policies.

TERMS AND CONDITIONS

Also known as terms of service or terms of use, this statement details the rules a user must follow when visiting a blog. Often described as a disclaimer, this statement can help limit liability from errors on the blog and protect the rights to the content on a blog. The statement typically includes information on copyrighted property, limitations of liability, and the termination policy for unacceptable behavior of visitors. See the resources list to find sample terms and conditions statements.

CALL TO ACTION

Consider what people should do after they visit the blog. Should they sign up for an email newsletter, download an eBook, make an appointment, or order a book? Including some type of email sign-up with an incentive is a good way to be sure the nutrition content makes a regular appearance in people's inboxes without relying on them to

find the blog (see Figures 30.9 and 30.10). If collecting emails, a privacy policy is essential.

Be Professional and Ethical

The professional and ethical issues related to blogging include privacy and confidentiality, transparency and disclosure, and intellectual property or copyright. The Academy of Nutrition and Dietetics practice paper on social media identifies the major professional and ethical issues governing digital media.[1] Additional resources include the Academy of Nutrition and Dietetics Ethics Opinion on the impact of social media on business and ethical practices in dietetics[14] and the Ethics in Action paper on blogging and social media.[15]

TRANSPARENCY AND DISCLOSURE

Blogs provide nutrition and dietetics practitioners with new opportunities to generate income and build a business with food companies, brands, organizations, publishers, and agencies. However, once writers enter into a marketing relationship, they become subject to truth-in-advertising laws and are required to disclose all material connections.

Disclosing these marketing relationships is not only a matter of professional ethics,[16,17] it is mandated by the Federal Trade Commission (FTC).[18] The FTC, whose mission is to prevent fraudulent, deceptive, and unfair practices in the marketplace,

FIGURE 30.9 Dawn Jackson Blatner offers a sign-up for her weekly *Nutrition WOW* emails

FIGURE 30.10 Sally Kuzemchak of *Real Mom Nutrition* offers an email course to readers who sign up on her blog

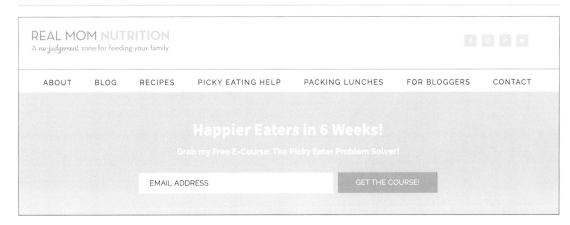

outlines in its endorsement guides that bloggers and individuals using social media are considered advertisers once they endorse a product in exchange for any type of payment or in-kind compensation, such as free samples and sponsored travel.[19]

The FTC requires that all disclosures be clear, conspicuous, and made in close proximity to where the endorsement is made. This means that simply including a general disclosure statement on the blog is not sufficient by the FTC's standards. Disclosures must be made in the blog post (such as "This post is sponsored by X company"), and all tweets, Facebook updates, and other social media posts must include some type of disclosure, such as #ad or #sponsored. See Figure 30.11 on page 482 for an example of a blog disclosure.

Common activities that require disclosure include:

- being paid to create a recipe, photo, video, or blog post;
- linking to a product's or company's website and receiving a commission;
- receiving payment, free products, coupons, or gifts in exchange for mentions on social media;
- serving as a consultant or advisory board member and writing a blog post on a related topic, even if not compensated for that specific post; and
- receiving free travel and experiences from a company, brand, or organization.

COPYRIGHT

Copyright law protects an individual's intellectual property, such as articles, photos, designs, and other creations. Do not assume that photos found through a Google image search are available to add to a blog. Unless a photo or image is clearly in the public domain, such as works from the federal government, assume it is covered by copyright. Providing attribution and citing a source is not sufficient to avoid infringement.

Copyright law permits short quotations of other materials for the purpose of criticism, commentary, news reporting, teaching, and research under fair use. Copyright law also allows the use of facts and ideas reported in articles or websites; however, the expression of these facts and ideas—the exact language and structure of the piece—is protected.

Similarly, copyright does not protect recipes or the listing of ingredients.[20] However, it can extend to the literary expression of a recipe, such as the description, explanation, or illustration that accompanies a recipe. Even if recipes are not protected by copyright, writers should not copy and republish someone else's recipe without permission and attribution. It's important when citing any work by another blogger to provide adequate credit and link back to the blog.

In conclusion, blogging can be fun, rewarding, impactful, and even lucrative—but it's not for everyone. Even though increasing numbers of nutrition and dietetics practitioners have blogs, it takes a commitment. Writers may choose to communicate nutrition through other channels, write for established blogs or websites, or be active in social media without maintaining their own blog. Responding to the constant need for new content can take tremendous discipline. Either way, it is important to recognize the changing communications landscape and be familiar with the multiple opportunities to communicate nutrition via digital channels.

FIGURE 30.11 Example of disclosure for a sponsored blog post by Liz Weiss of *Liz's Healthy Table*

KEY POINTS

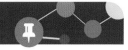

Blogging and Web-Based Writing Establishes the Nutrition Communicator as an Expert Resource to a Wide Audience

1 Blogs and other online platforms have ushered in a new era to help nutrition and dietetics practitioners reach much larger audiences and connect with other health care professionals, the media, and the public. Digital media offers an effective way to amplify credible nutrition messages, promote products and services, strengthen thought leadership, and build a professional brand.

2 Starting a blog requires securing a domain name, a blogging platform, and a host. Choose a premade theme or enlist a designer to give the blog the desired look and feel. Developing a mission for the blog, establishing an editorial calendar, learning to tailor writing for online readers, writing strong headlines, and thinking visually are strategies that will help the blog stand out.

3 Blogging best practices include tailoring content to a target audience, syndicating to social media channels, focusing on search engine optimization (SEO), and using analytics to gain audience insights.

4 Ethical and legal issues governing digital media involve transparency and intellectual property or copyright. Disclosing all marketing relationships on a blog and in social media is not only a matter of professional ethics, it is mandated by the Federal Trade Commission.

RESOURCES

Sites offering free articles and resources on how to create, grow, and monetize a blog

ProBlogger: https://problogger.com

The Blog Starter: www.theblogstarter.com

Copyblogger: https://copyblogger.com

Fee-based sites providing tutorials and online coaching for food and nutrition bloggers

Food Blogger Pro: www.foodbloggerpro.com

Nutrition Communications Academy: https://reganmillerjonesinc.teachable.com

Resources for creating disclosure statements, privacy policies, and terms and conditions for blogs

Privacy Policies: www.privacypolicies.com

Free Privacy Policy: www.freeprivacypolicy.com

Privacy Policy Online: www.privacypolicyonline.com

Shopify: www.shopify.com/tools/policy-generator

TermsFeed: www.termsfeed.com

Termly: https://termly.io

GetTerms: https://getterms.io

REFERENCES

1. Helm J, Jones RM. Practice paper of the Academy of Nutrition and Dietetics: social media and the dietetics practitioner: opportunities, challenges, and best practices. *J Acad Nutr Diet.* 2016;116(11):1825-1835.
2. Lee K, Hoti K, Hughes JD, Emmerton LM. Consumer use of "Dr Google": a survey on health information-seeking behaviors and navigational needs. *J Med Internet Res.* 2015;17(12):e288.
3. Lee XJ, Ha S. Consumer use of the internet for health management. *J Cons Health Internet.* 2016;20:1-18.
4. Freeman H. Green is the new black: the unstoppable rise of the healthy-eating guru. *Guardian.* June 27, 2015. Accessed January 19, 2018. www.theguardian.com/lifeandstyle/2015/jun/27/new-wellness-bloggers-food-drink-hadley-freeman
5. Boepple L, Ata RN, Rum R, et al. Strong is the new skinny: a content analysis of fitspiration websites. *Body Image.* 2016;17:132-135.

6. Boepple L, Thompson JK. A content analysis of healthy living blogs: evidence of content thematically consistent with dysfunctional eating attitudes and behaviors. *Int J Eat Disord.* 2014;47(4):362-367.

7. Bissonnette-Maheux V, Provencher V, Lapointe A, et al. Exploring women's beliefs and perceptions about healthy eating blogs: a qualitative study. *J Med Internet Res.* 2015;17(4):e87.

8. Bissonnette-Maheux V, Dumas AA, Provencher V, et al. Women's perceptions of usefulness and ease of use of four healthy eating blog characteristics: a qualitative study of 33 French-Canadian women. *J Acad Nutr Diet.* 2018;118(7):1220-1227.

9. Rodney A. Pathogenic or health-promoting? How food is framed in healthy living media for women. *Soc Science Med.* 2018;213:37-44.

10. Nielsen J. How little do users read? Nielsen Norman Group website. Published May 6, 2008. Accessed January 23, 2018. www.nngroup.com /articles/how-little-do-users-read

11. Safran N. 5 data insights into the headlines readers click. Moz website. Published July 17, 2013. Accessed January 18, 2018. https://moz.com /blog/5-data-insights-into-the-headlines-readers -click

12. Rayson S. We analyzed 100 million headlines. Here's what we learned (new research). BuzzSumo website. Published June 26, 2017. Accessed January 23, 2018. http://buzzsumo.com/blog/most -shared-headlines-study

13. Ezra RB. Which ad headlines and images catch your readers' attention? Outbrain website. Published May 16, 2018. Accessed January 23, 2018. www.outbrain.com/blog/outbrain-amplify -headline-image-best-practices

14. Ayres EJ. The impact of social media on business and ethical practices in dietetics. Ethics Opinion. *J Acad Nutr Diet.* 2013;113(11):1539-1543.

15. Bullas J. 6 powerful reasons why you should include images in your marketing. *Jeff Bullas* blog. Accessed January 18, 2018. www.jeffbullas.com /6-powerful-reasons-why-you-should-include -images-in-your-marketing-infographic

16. Helm J. Ethical and legal issues related to blogging and social media: ethics in action. *J Acad Nutr Diet.* 2013;113(5):688-690.

17. Academy of Nutrition and Dietetics Commission on Dietetic Degistration. Code of ethics for the nutrition and dietetics profession. eatright website. Effective June 1, 2018. Accessed August 19, 2018. www.eatrightpro.org/-/media /eatrightpro-files/career/code-of-ethics /coeforthenutritionanddieteticsprofession.pdf

18. Federal Trade Commission. Guides concerning the use of endorsements and testimonials in advertising federal acquisition regulation; final rule. *Fed Regist.* 2009;74(198):53123-53143. Accessed January 15, 2018. www.ftc.gov/sites /default/files/documents/federal_register _notices/guides-concerning-use-endorsements -and-testimonials-advertising-16-cfr-part-255 /091015guidesconcerningtestimonials.pdf

19. Federal Trade Commission. *.com Disclosures: How to Make Effective Disclosures in Digital Advertising.* March 2013. Accessed January 18, 2018. http://business.ftc.gov/documents/bus41 -dot-com-disclosures-information-about-online -advertising

20. Bailey J. Recipes, copyright and plagiarism. Plagiarism Today website. Published March 24, 2015. Accessed January 25, 2018. www .plagiarismtoday.com/2015/03/24/recipes -copyright-and-plagiarism

Online Education Is an Effective Tool for Nutrition Communicators

Devon L. Golem, PhD, RD, LDN

"Online education serves many roles in the field of nutrition and dietetics. From blog posts to online learning modules, online education provides a gateway for nutrition communicators to spread their message."

> *"We need to bring learning to people instead of people to learning."* —ELLIOT MASSIE

Introduction

Online education is an effective way for nutrition communicators to teach to a variety of audiences. Like all education, online education must be well planned and designed for a specific audience using evidence-based content that is relevant and practical. Although many traditional pedagogical strategies apply, lack of face-to-face interaction means that online education must be designed to ensure students are learning effectively.

Well-planned online education delivers a learning experience that improves learner knowledge or skills.[1-4] Because online education is ubiquitous, it can reach many different target audiences. Technology advances at a more rapid pace than nutrition information, so it is crucial that nutrition communicators continually hone their technological skills.

This chapter answers three questions:

- What is the role of online education in nutrition communication?
- What are best practices for online education?
- What practical strategies enhance the success of online education?

The answers to these questions will help nutrition communicators effectively use online education.

What Is the Role of Online Education in Nutrition Communication?

The use of e-learning and online education in traditional academic programs is well established. Preprofessionals—better known as dietetics and nutrition students—have access to online courses, web-based modules, and online resources. However, the role of online education does not stop at the preprofessional level. Nutrition professionals often rely on online education for their own continuing professional education as well as for teaching their clients, patients, and the public. This section will discuss the roles of online education in each of these arenas.

Continuing Professional Education

The purpose of continuing professional education (CPE) is to help professionals maintain competency in their field and provide up-to-date nutrition information to disseminate and apply to their nutrition practice.[5]

Credentialed food and nutrition professionals have many choices when it comes to continuing their education. They can attend conferences, workshops, seminars, and in-person trainings.[5] Yet, these options can be expensive and inconvenient if they require time off from work, schedule rearrangement, professional memberships, or travel. Food and nutrition professionals can also learn from case presentations, exhibits, posters, professional publications, and self-study materials.[5] However, these may be unstructured, unguided educational experiences where the learner proceeds without learning objectives, activities, or assessments.

Since the turn of the 21st century, online education has provided an alternative to traditional opportunities. There are many sources of webinars and online courses that address the educational needs of nutrition professionals in an efficient and effective manner.

Online education is a popular continuing education option for nutrition professionals. An online poll conducted in 2016 by the Institute of Continuing Education for Nutrition Professionals (ICENP) examined the education practices and preferences of 240 nutrition professionals across the United States. Over 30% of the respondents claimed to rely exclusively on online education to earn their continuing professional education units (CPEUs), while nearly 70% relied on a mix of online and in-person CPEU opportunities. Online live webinars and self-study opportunities were the most preferred modes of continuing education.[6]

Although live webinars are popular, recorded online education, in the form of courses (also referred to as modules), is becoming more available. These online courses differ from live webinars in that they contain recorded presentations paired with learning assessments such as quizzes, exams, and activities. Using recorded presentations eliminates the need for the presenter/educator and the learners to be online at the same time, as with live webinars. The inclusion of learning assessments provides methods for determining whether the learner achieved the learning objectives and has actually learned from the educational experience.

Online professional education courses offer an autonomous, flexible learning environment. Nutrition professionals can select the topic, timing, and sometimes even the rate and depth of their education. Those selecting the online mode of continuing education prefer to work independently, learn at their own pace, and complete modules with a mix of audiovisual interactions.[6] Food and nutrition professionals can more conveniently fit online continuing education into their schedules because they can complete it at any time and place. Some online modules provide functions that enable the learners to rewind, replay, fast-forward, skip, listen, or read to help them learn at their own pace. Many online CPE providers also offer nutrition education topics at varying levels of depth. For example, a Food Allergy Bundle course worth 14 CPEUs provides a more in-depth educational experience than a Food Allergy Basics course, worth 2 CPEUs. Food and nutrition professionals seeking a quick review and update on food allergies will select the latter online course.

There are limitations to online professional education programs. The cost can range from $20 to $200 depending on the course and the number of CPEUs offered. The typical cost is about $20 to $25 per CPEU.[6] Another limitation is the inability for learners to ask questions and obtain answers as they complete the education. This lack of Q&A also means that learners cannot learn from the questions or comments of other learners. In order to ask questions or provide comments to the presenter, learners must contact the presenter via email or phone call. Then they must wait to receive the answers. This is an inefficient way to communicate. Despite these limitations, online education continues to be a popular option.[6]

Food and nutrition professionals are not the only beneficiaries of online professional nutrition education. Other health-related professional organizations, such as the American Academy of Pediatrics, invite experts in the dietetics field to provide webinars or prerecorded online modules to their members.[7] Other health care professionals, including physicians, nurses, pharmacists, dentists, radiologists, and respiratory therapists, use online education to better understand the role of nutrition in their practice and focus on their preferred topics of interest while saving money, time, and effort. As examples, the following organizations offer online continuing education courses about nutrition: Nutrition in Medicine (www.nutritioninmedicine .org), University of Pittsburgh Medical Center Physician Resources (www.upmcphysicianresources .com/cme-courses/nutrition-assessment-parenteral -nutrition-and-venous-access), and Medline University (www.medlineuniversity.com courses/course -categories/dietary-nutrition).

Patient and Client Education

As technology becomes more commonplace, people have learned to rely on the internet for information, including nutrition information. Online education confers the benefit of increased access and exposure to nutrition information. Nutrition professionals can share online nutrition information and education with clients between nutrition counseling sessions to provide an introduction, pique interests, and prepare patients and clients for more in-depth nutrition counseling sessions. Digital tracking information (eg, pedometer tracking, dietary intake tracking) and online resources (ie, credible, reliable websites) can be incorporated into online education modules to better meet the needs of patients and clients. This section will discuss the utility of online education in nutrition counseling as well as the incorporation of other online resources and tools within online nutrition education for the patient and client. See Box 31.1.

In the past, most nutrition counselors had to wait until they were face-to-face with patients and clients to provide nutrition education. Typically, this did not occur until the second or third session, since assessment and tracking took precedence.[8] Instead of using paper handouts and

pamphlets, which previously accompanied nutrition education in the last 10 to 15 minutes of counseling sessions, nutrition professionals are now developing online courses and modules that are easily shared via text or email.[8]

Providing education in this manner allows the nutrition professional to prepare patients and clients for upcoming sessions by introducing information in advance. This information can then be reinforced during nutrition counseling sessions. Obtaining education on a specific nutrition topic prior to a nutrition counseling session enables patients or clients to spend time thinking about aspects that specifically align with their personal situation. By answering the follow-up questions at the end of the online module, patients or clients can communicate these aspects, through their answers, to the nutrition professional prior to the meeting. Clients' answers will also reveal the level of their understanding of the information within the online nutrition course. With this information, the nutrition professional can better prepare a targeted counseling session.

One significant advantage of online education is that it can be prepared once and provided numerous times. For instance, the online course provided to the patient Doris in the example from Box 31.1 can be provided to any other patients having issues managing their blood glucose levels. Nutrition professionals can create online education courses and save them in a database or library that includes other online nutrition courses on a variety of nutrition-related topics. Providing access to libraries or databases filled with a variety of online nutrition education courses empowers patients and clients to select topics that align with their needs and to complete the education at their own pace. Online education can range from hour-long learning modules to minute-long educational videos. Sometimes brief educational pieces can encourage patients and clients to make behavior changes and learn more. For an example, see NutritionFacts.org (https://nutritionfacts.org).

Other online applications can be integrated by the nutrition professional into the design of online nutrition education. This can include the integration of mobile apps, software programs, and online tools that patients may already use to track their dietary intake, physical activity, anthropometric measurements, and other health indicators. For example, a nutrition professional can design an online education module about nutrition and

Example of Online Nutrition Education for Patients and Clients

Online Nutrition Education
Between Face-to-Face Nutrition Counseling Sessions

Doris has a hard time managing her blood glucose levels and has elevated hemoglobin A1c. Her dietitian emails her the link to an online module that reviews the common causes of increased blood glucose levels. At the end of the module, Doris answers a few questions and indicates that one of the common causes that often applies to her is use of steroid medication. Doris did not see the connection until she completed the online education. She indicates in her answer that about 30 minutes after taking her afternoon dose, she finds it difficult to control her blood glucose level with diet and insulin. Doris's dietitian reviews this answer prior to their next counseling session, discusses this discovery with Doris's physician and endocrinologist, and develops an action plan to discuss with Doris during their upcoming visit. Without online education, the nutrition care process would have been delayed by up to two more sessions.

exercise habits in which there are questions asking the clients about their activity the prior day (eg, "How many steps did you take?" "How many minutes were you moderately active?"). The clients engaging in the online education would be able to input the data from their own activity monitor. Additionally, instead of having patients manually enter their own dietary information from a tracking app, such as MyFitnessPal, into a worksheet in an online nutrition course, they could automatically upload this information to the worksheet if MyFitnessPal was integrated into the online nutrition course. This is similar to the way that MyFitnessPal integrates activity tracker apps into its platform, enabling data sharing from one app (eg, Garmin Connect or Fitbit) to another app (MyFitnessPal). With this type of integration, nutrition professionals can provide opportunities to clients or patients to apply their own tracking information to an educational context in which it will be compared to goals and standards and incorporated into nutrition care plans.

Additionally, nutrition professionals can easily incorporate online information resources into online patient education, which makes it easier for the patients to practice using the resource immediately at the time of introduction. For example, the LactMed database (https://toxnet.nlm.nih.gov/newtoxnet/lactmed.htm) can be incorporated into nutrition education for lactating women. This website, published by the National Institutes of Health (NIH), contains information on the safety of common drugs and chemicals to which nursing mothers may be exposed. Not only can this website be discussed in an online course, but the nutrition professional can develop an activity that requires patients or clients to navigate the website and find specific information. Since they are already online for the online nutrition education, a resource-navigating activity is a convenient and easy way to help them become more familiar with an online resource.

Public Education

Nutrition professionals can provide online nutrition education directly to the public. By increasing their online presence, many nutrition professionals are providing clear and reliable information in an entertaining manner to those seeking it. Online education can include videos, whiteboard animations, recorded presentations, blog posts, e-newsletter articles, and more.

The general public tends to respond to shorter, less verbose nutrition education.[9,10] The main goal for nutrition professionals is to provide reliable information that is engaging and thought-provoking. Ten- to 15-minute webinars or 2-minute annotated videos can answer common questions surrounding a popular nutrition topic while directing viewers to reliable information resources. Online educational material can deliver vital public health nutrition messages and summarize nutrition interventions meant for the masses.

Additionally, online education can provide interactive activities and games that engage the public while helping them manipulate the information (ie, repeatedly see the information, contemplate the information, apply the information to themselves, and practice using the information in different scenarios) to a greater degree. Refer to Box 31.2 on page 490 for a list of online educational resources for children and adults.

Appending video demonstrations to online education activities can encourage the public to apply the information that is being presented. These types of activities may help increase self-efficacy, which is the belief in one's own ability to complete a task, by teaching the audience *how* to apply—not just *what* to apply. For example, refer to BuzzFeed's Tasty[11] and Tasty Vegetarian[12] channels, which feature fast-motion cooking demonstration videos. These entertaining and enticing online videos can be part of a quick nutrition education module focusing on specific foods to incorporate into the diet. It has yet to be determined whether viewers have changed their behaviors to incorporate these recipes in their life, yet the large following on Facebook (greater than 10 million followers) suggests increased interest in cooking healthy foods.

What Are Best Practices for Online Education?

Effective online education is targeted, follows pedagogical traditions, and involves the learner.[1-4,9,13,14] As opposed to simply providing information, online education should improve the learner's knowledge or skills. Learners should be able to demonstrate the way(s) in which they improved after completing the education. The best practices

BOX
31.2 Online Educational Resources

For Children

Activities and Games

- www.fns.usda.gov/tn/blast-game
- www.choosemyplate.gov/browse-by-audience/view-all-audiences/children/kids
- www.bcm.edu/cnrc-apps/healthyeatingcalculator/eatingCal.cfm
- www.fns.usda.gov/track-and-field
- www.fueluptoplay60.com
- www.cdc.gov/bam/index.html
- www.girlshealth.gov
- https://kidshealth.org/en/kids/interactive/#cat20918
- www.nourishinteractive.com
- www.ncagr.gov/cyber/kidswrld/foodsafe/bbq/Bbqhome.htm
- www.girlshealth.gov/about/best-bones/best-bones.html
- www.fda.gov/food/nutrition-education-resources-materials/snack-shack-game
- https://choosemyplate-prod.azureedge.net/sites/default/files/printablematerials/Food_Critic_508 .pdf
- https://choosemyplate-prod.azureedge.net/sites/default/files/printablematerials/Bingo_508.pdf
- www.fsis.usda.gov/shared/PDF/Mobile_Coloring_Book.pdf

For Adults

Activities and Games

- http://extension.oregonstate.edu/nep/nutrition-links
- https://fsnep.ucdavis.edu/curriculum/Adult%20Materials
- www.health.ny.gov/prevention/nutrition/resources/games.htm
- www.healthyeating.org/CC
- www.nhlbi.nih.gov/health/educational/wecan/portion/index.htm

Blogs

- www.nutritionblognetwork.com
- https://blogs.webmd.com/food-fitness/default.htm
- http://dietitians-online.blogspot.com
- https://health.usnews.com/health-news/blogs/eat-run
- www.health.com/nutrition
- www.joybauer.com
- https://nutritiontwins.com/blog
- https://urockgirl.com
- http://blogs.bu.edu/salge
- https://rachelbegun.com/blog
- www.eastewart.com/blog

Videos

- www.eatright.org/videos
- www.uwhealth.org/nutrition-wellness/nutrition-and-health-education-informational-videos/13731
- https://nutritionfacts.org/videos
- www.watchknowlearn.org
- https://ed.ted.com/lessons?category=nutrition
- www.etr.org/store/categories/topics/nutrition-weight-fitness
- www.facebook.com/tastyvegetarian/

for online education are rooted in the design of the education and will be discussed in this section.

Design Online Education for a Target Audience

It is crucial that online education is designed with a specific audience in mind. Information about the target audience is used to clarify the content and make decisions about the delivery of the education. Cultural aspects, as well as the knowledge and skill levels, of the target audience will shape the development of the online education.

Beyond demographic data, cultural aspects include groups living with the same health condition, practicing the same lifestyle behaviors, or working toward the same health goals. For example, Hispanic pregnant women may share the cultural aspects of ethnicity, gender, and a health condition. A needs assessment of this target audience may reveal the desire to learn more about n-3 fatty acid intake during pregnancy and its role in fetal neurological development. Refer to Chapter 11 and Chapter 13 to learn more about needs assessments and cultural competency, respectively.

Determining the gaps in knowledge and skills of a target audience is important, but it should not be the sole determinant of the content of the online education. Learning needs should be paired with the learning interests of the target audience. Online education will not be successful if the audience is not interested in learning about the topic. For instance, online education about vitamin C intake may not be effective if it is targeted to uninterested middle-aged men who smoke cigarettes, even though the dietary recommendations for vitamin C intake are increased for this group.[11] It is important to learn what an audience needs and wants.

When learning about the target audience, address the following questions:

- What nutrition education topics address both the audience's learning interests and needs?
- What are the frequently asked questions regarding each topic?
- What aspects need to be considered to make the education culturally appropriate?
- What should the target audience be able to achieve at the end of the nutrition education?

The answers to these questions will provide information about the target audience that will shape the content and delivery of the nutrition education.

Base Online Education on Learning Objectives

The ultimate outcome of online education is to improve the knowledge or skill level of the audience. To do this, a registered dietitian nutritionist should ask, "What exactly do I want the audience to be able to do once they complete the education?" The answer to this question will help identify the learning objectives. This strategy is often referred to as "backwards design" as the developer begins by determining the desired end result and works backward to develop education that leads to achievement of that end result.

Learning objectives are outcomes that learners will aim to achieve by the end of the education. They clarify the main aspects of the education, and they are phrased in a manner in which their achievement can be measured. For example, the learning objectives for an educational activity on nutrition and heart disease might be that, by the end of the activity, learners will be able to do the following:

- Describe the three most common symptoms of a heart attack.
- Explain the two most important roles of diet in heart disease.
- List eight risk factors for heart disease.
- Name three heart-healthy dietary changes that they are willing to make over the next 3 months.

Learning objectives not only clarify the main aspects of the education but also provide explicit instruction for how their achievement can be measured. Notice the phrase that introduces these learning objectives ("by the end of this educational activity, learners will be able to …"). It indicates the time at which these objectives should be achieved. Each objective begins with a verb that can be assessed (ie, *describe*, *explain*, *list*). Verbs such as *understand* or *learn* are too broad, and objectives formed with such verbs are not easily assessed.

It is important to remember that the learning objectives represent the bare minimum of learning achievement and are often accompanied by the sentiment "If nothing else, the learners will be able to achieve…." Keeping this in mind will help ensure that there are not too many learning objectives. Typically, there are three to seven learning objectives for each online course or module. These are the most important aspects and can be used as the initial outline of the educational activity. Once the learning objectives are developed, the creation of the online education content can begin. For more information on developing learning objectives, refer to Chapter 15.

Ensure the Content Is Engaging, Interactive, and Evidence-Based

Information is at the core of the content, but the audience must feel engaged. This occurs using various strategies that are best described by the AIMES model (watch a video about this model from ICENP on YouTube: https://youtu.be /zc-ig1rf8Ws). Th AIMES model indicates that the five most important aspects of education are affirmation, information, motivation, engagement, and self-efficacy—AIMES (Figure 31.1).

Learners like being *affirmed* in their preconceived notions, experiences, and reasons for learning more about the topic. See Box 31.3 on page 494 for an example. Nutrition communicators must develop online education with this in mind by determining the general consensus, the misconceptions, and the reasons that learners elect to pursue education on the particular topic. Usually, people decide to learn more about a topic because they believe it is important, and they believe that learning more will help them progress.

Beyond being affirmed, learners want to gain new information. They want to be *informed*. The information has to be novel to the learner in order for learning to take place. As with all credible nutrition education, information provided through online education must be evidence-based. Obtaining information from scientific literature and reliable sources is the key to ensuring that it is evidence-based. Examples of reliable sources of nutrition evidence include studies published in peer-reviewed journals, Academy of Nutrition and Dietetics position papers, the US Dietary Guidelines for Americans, and publications from other credible health organizations (eg, the American Heart Association, American Diabetes Association, or American Cancer Society). Reviewing the entire scope of a topic, so as not to overemphasize atypical research evidence, is crucial. One of the biggest challenges nutrition communicators face involves negating skewed information that gets disseminated whenever the media highlights outlying results or misinterprets research findings. For examples, see the "Headline vs Study" subhead on the home page of the Obesity and Energetics Offerings website (www.obesityand energetics.org), an informational service provided by obesity experts from Indiana University

FIGURE 31.1 **AIMES Model of Educational Objectives**

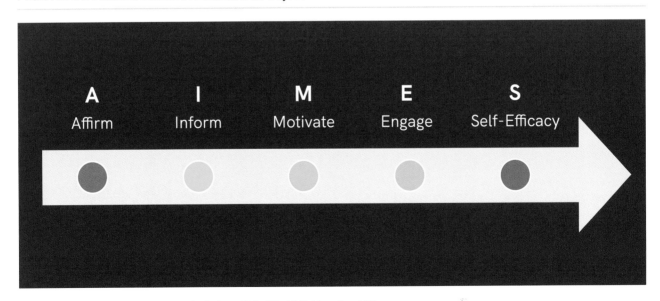

Adapted with permission from Devon L. Golem, PhD, RD, LDN, Novedgo, LLC.

and the University of Alabama at Birmingham. The site gives weekly listings (offerings) of current information on obesity and energetics, and the "Headline vs Study" section provides links to a media article that reports the findings of a study and the peer-reviewed published study that is mentioned in the media article. It is up to the reader to evaluate whether the news media story accurately represents the evidence from the study. Refer to Chapters 5 and 7 for more details on delivering evidence-based information.

Motivation to learn stems from the learner's emotional attachment to the topic (engagement) and the anticipation of improved skills or application of knowledge (self-efficacy). *Self-efficacy* is the belief in one's own ability to complete a task or achieve an outcome. Patients and the public are motivated to learn when they believe they will be able to solve a problem or resolve an issue that is important to them. Professionals are motivated to learn when they believe they will improve the outcomes of their practice. Online education can motivate people to learn by including practical applications to improve their self-efficacy.[15] For example, an online continuing professional education module about gut microbiome genetic screening kits could include three case scenarios in which the learners apply the information they just learned to evaluate and incorporate the screening results into separate nutrition care plans for each of the three cases. The more opportunities the learners have to apply the presented information to real-life scenarios, the more likely they will feel confident in applying it in the future. Interactions such as answering questions, pondering situations, applying the information to case studies and fictitious scenarios, practicing using resources, and more, will allow learners to become more familiar with the information and feel confident in their ability to retain and apply the information in the future.

To *engage* learners, think of them as an audience that wants to be entertained. Engagement extends beyond audiovisual components and media, as it also involves forging an emotional bond between the learners and the material to be mastered. Humor, empathy, and fear are often great ways to gain learners' investment in education. Eliciting an emotional response from learners is challenging, yet a clear sign of effectively engaging them.[16] Some strategies are consistent across all modes of education, whether in person or online. For example,

including a joke or a heartfelt story within an online education presentation might connect learners with the teacher and topic. The nutrition communicator must remember that online education usually has an audience of one. This means that the teacher should speak as if addressing a single listener, as opposed to a lecture hall full of students.

One of the best ways to improve a learner's *self-efficacy* is to provide interactive opportunities within the online education.[17] The more a person manipulates (ie, hears, reads, reviews, ponders, evaluates, applies, and recalls) the information, the more likely they will feel confident in their ability to retain and apply the information in the future.[18] After presenting the information, provide activities and interactions that allow learners to implement that information. Interactions could include answering questions, pondering situations, applying the information to case studies and fictitious scenarios, practicing using resources, and more.

For example, the online sleep and weight course described in Box 31.3 is accompanied by a workbook that allows learners to take notes in a fill-in-the-blank fashion while watching the presentation. An assignment that requires learners to develop a nutrition care plan that incorporates sleep management accompanies this course. They can refer to the course information and the resources to practice this skill. After completing this assignment and receiving feedback, learners feel more confident in their ability to apply this newly acquired knowledge.

Promote Learner Reflection

There are two reasons to include learner reflection within online education: to provide learners with more opportunities to think about the information being presented and to allow them to assess their own learning.

Learner reflection includes self-reflections such as "How would I feel?" and "What would I do?" It may seem narcissistic, but people learn more from content that they can apply to themselves.[1-4,9,13,14] For example, when discussing a study, an instructor could ask the simple question "Can you imagine collecting your own urine every day for 28 days?" to get learners to consider this information in a new light by empathizing with the subjects. This can also apply to dietary interventions. For example, a teacher may ask, "Which of these foods rich in n-3 fatty acids would you include in your daily diet?"

BOX 31.3 AIMES Applied to Online Education

I have provided education regarding my research on the connection between sleep and weight. What follows is an example of one way I applied the AIMES model to an online nutrition course.

A needs assessment revealed that most nutrition professionals wanting to learn about the link between sleep and weight recognize that many people, maybe even themselves, do not sleep enough, and they have good ideas as to why. They also agree that sleep and weight are connected, although they may not know the ways and reasons this holds true. These nutrition professionals are interested in addressing both poor sleep and body weight in their practice but may not know how to do so.

Affirm: The learners want affirmation that most of their preconceived notions about societal lack of sleep and the connection between sleep and weight are correct. This is achieved by reviewing the related evidence and including phrases such as "as you probably suspected." The course directs learners to ask themselves if they agree with each of the reasons people do not sleep enough: stress, work, media, physical inactivity, time demands, and so on. They receive affirmation that they were wise to select this online course. Learners may not only encounter the sleep-weight connection frequently in their lives and practices but also want to learn how to address it. The course clearly affirms their beliefs and makes them feel justified in their engagement.

Inform: To inform learners, the course provides the evidence that supports the affirmations just described (ie, that the sleeping status of Americans is poor and that poor sleep is associated with increased body weight). It also provides new information about sleep interventions within weight management programs, methods for assessing sleep quality, and techniques for improving sleep.

Motivate: The course motivates the audience by discussing the success of the application of sleep intervention to weight management programs. It provides results and conclusions of studies indicating that specific sleep-promotion techniques assist in weight loss. The course specifically indicates how they can apply this in their practice to get similar results.

Engage: When presenting in person and online, I have found that starting with humor lightens the mood and relaxes the audience. With a statement as simple as, "Before I begin, I invite you to get up from your seat and stretch a little bit … because as much as I am a proponent of sleep (pause and chuckle), I'd prefer if you did not sleep right now." (Follow with a smile.) Later in the lecture, I include a video clip featuring Cookie Monster singing a song about self-regulation (www.youtube.com/watch?v=9PnbKL3wuH4). Although this information is indirectly related, it is cute, entertaining, and elicits a laugh. Again, it is important to recognize that an online audience needs to be treated the same as an in-person audience when it comes to eliciting an emotional response. However, it is much more personal online, as each audience member is often alone when engaging in the education and is unaware of other learners. The presenter directs comments to each online audience member individually, not to a group.

Self-efficacy: The course promotes self-efficacy by providing not only specific, practical methods of sleep intervention but also online activities within supporting materials that allow audience learners to practice applying the new strategies. They complete fill-in-the-blank worksheets during the presentation, assess their own sleep, find a local sleep specialist, and develop sleep interventions based on the information provided in the presentation.

Applying the AIMES model has made this my most popular online course.

Learners need to made aware of their achievement of the learning objectives, retention of content, and ability to apply the knowledge. All online education needs to include this type of learner reflection. It allows the nutrition communicator to assess and improve the education and allows learners to conclude their educational experience by summarizing their learning achievements.

What Practical Strategies Enhance the Success of Online Education?

The success of online education depends upon several practical strategies: using reliable technology, maintaining ethical practices, providing support materials, and marketing to the target audience. Each of these strategies will be discussed.

Select Reliable Online Platforms and Tools

The learning curve for online education continues to steepen, even for experts in the field. This is mainly due to the growing availability of new technologies. From interactive software to novel data storage, the number of applications and platforms available to nutrition communicators is vast. Online learning platforms are websites that manage delivery of and access to online education. One of the most challenging aspects of providing online education is selecting appropriate platforms and tools.

For example, an online lecture to nutrition students could provide a copy of the slides, a webinar, an audiovisual recorded lecture, an interactive module, or some combination of these methods. To do this, a nutrition communicator would need software to create the lecture materials and recording and a learning management system (LMS) to deliver the lecture. The LMS would also provide data storage and enable communication between the students and teacher. Although universities and colleges often provide a universal LMS such as Sakai, Canvas, or Blackboard, there are countless LMS options available to nutrition communicators.

Although PowerPoint is the traditional software used to deliver educational information and lectures, there are numerous other programs and applications that can be used to organize and present online. Webinar platforms are commonly used in professional and patient education. See Box 31.4 (page 496) for features to consider, as well as examples of online education platforms and presentation tools.

Although novelty and usefulness need to be considered, the reliability of online platforms and tools must be high for online education to be successful. Reliability is a function of a service's long-term market stability and ability to function consistently over time. While the number of potential software solutions out there is vast, not all products will continue to be viable in the future. To avoid investing time, resources, and energy into a platform that will not exist in a year or two, ensure that the vendor is well-funded, has a strategy for the future development of the platform, and has a broad base of clients or users.

A unique educational presentation is not useful if it cannot be reliably relayed to the audience. When selecting platforms, determine the features that are most relevant to the educational situation and use them to create a rubric for evaluating platforms and tools. See Box 31.4 for example features to consider.

Ensure the Online Education Is Ethical and Accessible

When it comes to ethical practices online, plagiarism tends to be of utmost concern. It is very easy to cross ethical boundaries online since all published content is considered copyright protected even if a copyright symbol is not visible. US copyright law (www.copyright.gov/title17) protects original authorship of all online publications, including online education. This means that online education produced by nutrition communicators cannot be used by others, and vice versa, without paying attention to applicable copyright laws. Most people are aware of this when it comes to typed content, but they need help when it comes to images and pictures.

There are legal exceptions to copyright laws: fair use and permission. *Fair use* is a term that describes the permission that content developers provide to allow others to use their work. There are fair use databases with a wealth of images that can be used freely. See Box 31.5 (page 498) for examples.

Online Education Platforms and Tools[a]

BOX 31.4

Platforms—Learning Management Systems

Features to Consider

- Learning type: visual, auditory, read/write, kinesthetic, blended
- E-commerce: ability to charge for access to education
- Gamification: incorporation of game principles and design elements
- Mobile learning: ability to use mobile devices such as smartphones and tablets
- Social learning: ability to develop relationships and learn from others online
- Video conferencing: real-time communication through transmission of audiovisual signals

Learning Management System Examples

- Absorb: www.absorblms.com
- Atrixware: www.atrixware.com
- Bridge: www.getbridge.com/learning-management-system
- Canvas: www.canvaslms.com
- Cornerstone LMS: www.cornerstoneondemand.com/learning
- Digital Chalk: www.digitalchalk.com
- Edmodo: www.edmodo.com
- eLeap: www.eleapsoftware.com
- Gnosis Connect LMS: https://lms.gnosisconnect.com/home/index.php
- Grovo: www.grovo.com
- Litmos: www.litmos.com
- Moodle: https://moodle.com/moodle-lms
- Schoology: www.schoology.com
- SmarterU: www.smarteru.com
- Teachable: https://teachable.com
- Thought Industries: www.thoughtindustries.com
- Torch: www.torchlms.com

Platforms—Webinar Software

Features to Consider

- Attendee management: ability to manage registration, open invite, audio capabilities, and more
- Email marketing: option to provide e-newsletters and announcements
- Chat: ability to enable real-time discussions or chat boards
- Presenter sharing: ability to share presenter capabilities
- Online payments: ability to charge attendees
- Polls/voting: ability to obtain feedback from attendees in poll or voting format
- Question-and-answer sessions: shared communication in question-and-answer session format
- Reminders: ability to develop automated reminder emails to attendees, host, and presenters
- Recordings: ability to record, store, and share webinar or webcasts
- Social sharing: ability to post announcements and recordings on social media sites

Webinar Software Examples

- Adobe Connect: www.adobe.com/products/adobeconnect/webinars.html
- AnyMeeting: www.anymeeting.com
- Business Hangouts: https://business-hangouts.com
- ClickMeeting/ClickWebinar: https://clickmeeting.com
- EasyWebinar: http://easywebinar.com
- FreeConferenceCall.com: www.freeconferencecall.com
- GoToWebinar: www.gotomeeting.com/webinar
- GlobalMeet: www.pgi.com/products/globalmeet/webcast
- Join.Me: www.join.me
- MegaMeeting: www.megameeting.com
- omNovia: www.omnovia.com/webinars
- ON24: www.on24.com
- PeekTime: www.peektime.com
- ReadyTalk: www.readytalk.com
- Skype: www.skype.com/en
- WebEx: www.webex.com
- MyLeadSystemPRO: www.myleadsystempro.com
- Webinars On Fire: http://webinarsonfire.com
- Webinato: www.webinato.com
- Zoom Video Webinar: https://zoom.us/webinar

Permission can be obtained from original authors to publish their work within online education by contacting them or by purchasing the rights to use the content. Some publishing platform services include template designs and images that are legal for customers to use in their online publications. For example, WordPress (https://wordpress.com) provides stock images that can be included in blog posts that are published using their platform. Nutrition communicators can include these images in their nutrition education posts.

The other main aspect of ethical practice regarding online education is accessibility. Nutrition communicators need to take efforts to make online education easy to view, navigate, and understand. This is achieved by focusing on the organization of content, paying attention to the specificity of instructions, and considering special populations.

ORGANIZATION OF CONTENT

Learners with varying technological skill levels need to be able to easily navigate online education platforms. Avoiding overly sensitive drop-down menus and clearly mapping the online content are examples of strategies used to ease navigation. Additionally, the information must be organized in a manner that is easy to digest. Using consistent fonts and letter sizes for headings and content is necessary to organize typed content. Colors can be manipulated to ease navigation and learning. The higher the contrast between text color and background color, the easier it is to read. Similar information and related images should be placed into groupings to help learners understand the conceptual connection of the information. To learn more about website accessibility, visit WebAIM (https://webaim.org). The more organized the information, the better the learning environment. See the University of California

 Online Education Platforms and Tools[a] (continued)

Tools—Presentation and E-Learning Software

Features to Consider

- Real-time collaboration: allows learners to work together on the same document at the same time
- Mobile editing: ability to edit on mobile devices
- Audio: options to include audio tracks and sounds into presentations
- Operating system: ability to accommodate Mac, PC, or Unix environment
- Animation: ability to engage audience with animated details on a slide
- Import/export abilities: ability to universally apply and share presentations
- Online sharing: allows presentation to be published on the web
- Technical support: to assist with technical problems, new features, and system updates
- Template availability: ability to apply professional templates

Presentation and E-Learning Software Examples

- Articulate: https://articulate.com
- Camtasia: www.techsmith.com/video-editor.html
- CustomShow: www.customshow.com
- Emaze: www.emaze.com
- FlowVella: https://flowvella.com
- Genial.ly: www.genial.ly
- Google Slides: https://docs.google.com/presentation/u/0
- Haiku Deck: www.haikudeck.com
- Impress: www.libreoffice.org/discover/impress
- iSpring: www.ispringsolutions.com
- Keynote: www.apple.com/keynote
- Prezi: https://prezi.com
- PowToon: www.powtoon.com/home
- Slidebean: https://slidebean.com
- SlideDog: https://slidedog.com
- Slides: https://slides.com
- Visme: www.visme.co
- Vyond: www.vyond.com

[a] Developed January 22, 2018.

CalFresh Nutrition Education website (http://fsnep.ucdavis.edu/curriculum/Adult%20Materials) to review each of these organizational aspects in exemplary form.

SPECIFICITY OF INSTRUCTIONS

Some learners need specific instructions to locate, navigate, and engage in online education. These instructions should be placed at the beginning of the nutrition education. Instructions must be updated with the platform to make the education more accessible to online learners. The challenge for the nutrition communicator is that it is easy to generalize one's own familiarity with a platform onto other people. Providing specific instructions helps users focus on the substance, not the form, of the educational experience.

SPECIAL POPULATIONS

All educational content must always consider the needs of hearing-impaired and visually impaired learners. The Americans with Disabilities Act, Title II, states that communications with persons with disabilities must be "as effective as communications with others."[19] Captions and transcripts must accompany all audiovisual content. Additionally, descriptions of images and resizing options must be available to visually impaired learners.

Provide Support Materials

It is well known that learners must be exposed to information multiple times in a variety of ways in order to learn.[16] However, in order for learners to feel engaged, content must be provided in a succinct and concise manner.[1,3,4,9,13] Nutrition professionals include support materials within online nutrition education to provide repeat exposure to the information in different forms and to meet the learning preferences of different learners. For example, some learners prefer to write and take notes during a presentation. Providing a worksheet or notes page as support material will indulge this preference.

Support materials include workbooks, resource lists, and practice activities. These materials allow the nutrition communicator to provide further details, references, additional examples, and application activities that can deepen the educational experience without overshadowing the main content in a given context. Support materials allow nutrition communicators to meet the needs of learners seeking different educational experiences.

Support materials are an essential component of online education.[1,3,4] Learners can typically access these materials as an attachment at the beginning of an online course or module. These materials enable learners to be exposed to the conceptual information in another manner, provide necessary repetition of information, enable learners to practice applying the information, and allow them to refer to other resources on the topic.

Market Online Education to the Target Audience

Online education designed for a target audience needs to be marketed to that audience. Marketing is a practical strategy that contributes to the success of online education by matching potential learners with content that meets their educational aims. Refer to Chapter 37 for details about marketing.

Of the 4 C's of marketing[20]—consumer, cost, convenience, and communication—the latter two appear to be the most relevant to online education. Convenience is thought to be inherent in online education as learners can gain access at any time and from any place. Convenience also includes ease of finding the education as well as information about the education online.[21] Communication refers to education promotion. The aim is to create a dialogue with potential learners based on their needs and wants.[22]

Nutrition professionals promoting online education to target audiences must determine *where* on the internet an audience may be reached. Studying the online behavior of the target audience will help determine the best places and strategies to advertise. For example, nutrition professionals may place a promotion for childhood diabetes education on Children with Diabetes Forums (https://forums.childrenwithdiabetes.com). They may also advertise on the Parents of Type 1 Diabetes Facebook page (www.facebook.com /Parents-of-Type-1-Diabetes-126365504087562). They could develop their own groups on social networking platforms or create discussion forums and recruit learners to follow them online (also known as creating a following). They may create their own blogs and e-newsletters to build stronger, more intimate relationships with their target audiences. Through posted articles in the daily feed, audience members can be redirected to a nutrition education website where they can decide to join the newsletter list and obtain regular educational articles in their inbox.

After the target audience is located, it is important to advertise the targeted information in a manner that will capture the interest of consumers and encourage them to explore the available nutrition education. Well-designed imagery and clever, yet clear, article titles are necessary to appeal to the target audience. Consider using a graphic tool such as Canva (www.canva.com) or Stencil (https://getstencil.com) to create an image to introduce and market online education. See examples of marketing materials in Figure 31.2.

The audience can also be visually stimulated with videos clips. For examples, see the following videos on YouTube: "Nutrition Professionals Who Love Their Job" (www.youtube.com/watch ?v=_brZckMfoY0), "Early Life Protein Intake JAND Article Review 08/2017" (www.youtube .com/watch?v=E0vqy4rgCAw&t=172s), and "Palliative Care JAND Article Review" (www.youtube .com/watch?v=9IFIALymAy0&t=71s).

FIGURE 31.2 Examples of online education marketing materials

Clockwise from left: A flyer advertisement for a webinar on homemade tube feeding; an image for a blog post about the Pomodoro technique for time management titled "How a Fruit Can Help You Manage Your Time"; an image for a LinkedIn article titled "Dive Deeper into the Dietetics Field"; an image for a blog post titled "Why Some People Choose Fad Diets Over Nutrition Counseling; an image for a blog post titled "5 Myths Uncovered About Nutrition & ADHD."

Most likely, the mind-set of the target audience members as they come across an advertisement for online education is different from their mind-set while they are engaging in education. While perusing a social media website or their email inbox, the ad will be only one of hundreds of potential opportunities that they could click on or skip. With this in mind, the advertisement must be brief, entertaining, and essential. It is a "hook" that should entice the consumer to want to click to learn more. Consider the following tips when developing content and a title or subject line for an online education advertisement.

TIPS FOR CONTENT AND TITLES

Here are some tips for creating content and titles for your writing[8]:

- Provide a solution to a problem.
- Reveal the value. *What is in it for the reader?* The title must indicate that valuable information is only a click away.
- Show evidentiary support. Use facts and statistics supporting that the information is based on evidence.
  - Use a statistical fact that supports the value of the content—for example, "Lower Your Blood Pressure by 10% in One Week."

- Use keywords and search engine optimization (SEO). Refer to Chapter 30 for more details.
- Use title tools and templates (see Box 31.6). Refer to Chapter 30 for more information on blogs.

For more information on developing marketable content, consult the following:

- "The Ultimate Guide to No-Pain Copywriting" by Joanna Wiebe[23]
- "10 Sure-Fire Headline Formulas That Work" by Brian Clark[24]
- "5 Headline Templates That Grab Readers" by Ray Edwards[25]
- "43 Data-Driven Headline Ideas from 1,000 of the Most Popular Posts" by Nathan Ellering[26]

Practice Technological Flexibility

It is no secret that technology swiftly changes. From updates to existing products to the emergence of new tools, technological advances shape the way online education is designed and distributed. When it comes to technology, nutrition professionals need to maintain a flexible attitude and continually optimize online education.

Even if a product appears to be stable in the market, vendors frequently update their platforms. This is generally a good thing; updates illustrate that the vendor is committed to the long-term development of their product and demonstrate that the vendor values user feedback. However, be aware that certain features and functionalities that users enjoy in the current version of a platform may be substantially modified or even removed when a new version is released. Good vendors will try to minimize the amount of disruption that occurs between updates and support multiple versions for users who prefer not to upgrade their software.

Successful online educators recognize which aspects of technology to master and which aspects should be delegated to experts. There is generally no need to learn how to code or program, but it is important to learn how to explore different templates and platforms. Since different target audiences may respond to different technology, it may be necessary to become proficient in numerous platforms and programs.

BOX 31.6 Blog Title Tools and Templates

SEOPressor's Blog Title Generator:
https://seopressor.com/blog-title-generator

Portent's Content Idea Generator:
www.portent.com/tools/title-maker

CoSchedule's Headline Analyzer:
https://coschedule.com/headline-analyzer

Impact's BlogAbout: www.impactbnd.com/blog-title-generator/blogabout

Gooyaabi Templates: https://gooyaabitemplates.com

Colorlib's blog templates:
https://colorlib.com/wp/free-blogger-templates

Envato Market's blog templates:
https://themeforest.net/category/blogging

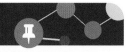
Online Education Is an Effective Tool for Nutrition Communicators

1 Online education serves many roles in the field of nutrition and dietetics. From blog posts to online learning modules, online education provides a gateway for nutrition communicators to spread their message. Online education can be used to educate nutrition and other health care professionals, clients and patients, and the general public.

2 Online education is similar to in-person education in that it is designed with evidence-based content for a target audience, and it follows basic pedagogical strategies. Online education is different from in-person education in that it has a broader reach, is more convenient, and provides learners with more autonomy in their learning schedule and pace.

3 Online education must be engaging and interactive. Since the audience has more autonomy, they must be intrigued by the content to pursue and complete the education. Online education should **A**ffirm, **I**nform, **M**otivate, **E**ngage, and improve the **S**elf-efficacy of the learners—AIMES. Nutrition communicators must ensure that the content for their online education is ethically obtained and accessible to all audience members. Providing support materials is a practical way to enhance online education.

4 Online education must be marketed to the target audience. Develop blog posts, video clips, polls, and infographics to advertise online education. Use social media and other online networks as pathways to advertise.

5 Online education is most successful when presented on reliable platforms using reliable tools. Nutrition communicators must be flexible and adaptable when it comes to technological advances and changes.

REFERENCES

1. Devedzic V. Introduction to web-based education. In: *Semantic Web and Education.* Springer US; 2006:1-28. doi:10.1007/978-0-387-35417-0_1
2. Pelz B. (My) three principles of effective online pedagogy. *J Asynchronous Learn Networks.* 2010;14(1):103-116.
3. *Best Practices in Online Teaching Strategies.* Hanover Research Council; 2009. Accessed May 21, 2020. https://q8rkuwu1ti4vaqw33x41zocd-wpengine.netdna-ssl.com/academics/files/2015/05/Best-Practices-in-Online-Teaching-Strategies.pdf
4. Ragan LC. 10 principles of effective online teaching: best practices in distance education. *Fac Focus.* July 12, 2009. Accessed May 21, 2020. www.facultyfocus.com/free-reports/principles-of-effective-online-teaching-best-practices-in-distance-education

5. Commission on Dietetic Registration. Professional development portfolio. Accessed November 3, 2017. www.cdrnet.org/pdp/professional-development-portfolio-guide
6. Institute of Continuing Education for Nutrition Professionals. Online CPEU survey. Published 2016. Accessed October 17, 2017. SurveyMonkey website. www.surveymonkey.com/collect/?sm=lJCmnyBmz-Pnh9MuHAvXKQWC4WuXr1BJftvSIMDm-STd0Q6ROdcEHmkYAx2DlI9YdV
7. EPIC Pediatric Obesity website. www.epicobesity.org. Accessed January 17, 2018.
8. Marketing-Schools.org. Viral marketing: explore the strategy of viral marketing. Published 2012. Accessed January 5, 2018. www.marketing-schools.org/types-of-marketing/viral-marketing.html
9. Ramsay SA, Holyoke L, Branen LJ, Fletcher J. Six characteristics of nutrition education videos that support learning and motivation to learn. *J Nutr Educ Behav.* 2012;44(6):614-617. doi:10.1016/j.jneb.2011.10.010

10. Pew Research Center: Journalism and Media Staff. *You Tube and News: A New Kind of Visual News.* Pew Research Center Project for Excellence in Journalism; July 16, 2012. www.journalism.org/2012/07/16/youtube-news

11. Tasty Buzz Feed Facebook page. Accessed January 18, 2018. www.facebook.com/buzz feedtasty

12. Tasty vegetarian Facebook page. Accessed January 17, 2018. www.facebook.com/tastyvegetarian

13. University of Florida, University of Idaho, Iowa State University, University of Missouri-St. Louis, Texas A&M University, Texas Tech University. Roadmap to effective distance education instructional design: differences between distance and traditional education. Accessed December 16, 2019. http://umsl.edu/services/ctl/DEID /destination1dedifferences/differences.pdf

14. Means B, Toyama Y, Murphy R, Bakia M, Jones K. *Evaluation of Evidence-Based Practices in Online Learning: A Meta-Analysis and Review of Online Learning Studies.* US Department of Education; 2010. Accessed May 21, 2020. https://eric.ed.gov/?id=ED505824

15. Cook DA, Artino AR. Motivation to learn: an overview of contemporary theories. *Med Educ.* 2016;50(10):997-1014. doi:10.1111/medu.13074

16. Cavanagh SR. *The Spark of Learning: Energizing the College Classroom with the Science of Emotion.* West Virginia University Press; 2016.

17. Dinther M, Dochy F, Segers M. Factors affecting students' self-efficacy in higher education. *Educ Res Rev.* 2011;6:95-108.

18. Bandura A. *Self-Efficacy: The Exercise Control.* Freeman and Company; 1997.

19. Department of Justice. Americans with Disabilities Act Title II Regulations: Nondiscrimination on the Basis of Disability in State and Local Government Services. September 15, 2010. Accessed May 21, 2020. www.ada.gov/regs2010 /titleII_2010/titleII_2010_regulations.pdf

20. Lauterborn B. New marketing litany: four P's passe; C-words take over. *Advert Age.* 1990;61(41):26. http://rlauterborn.com/pubs /pdfs/4_Cs.pdf

21. Acutt M. Marketing mix—convenience. The Marketing Mix website. Accessed October 16, 2017. http://marketingmix.co.uk/convenience

22. Schultz D, Schultz H, Tannenbaum S, Lauterborn B. *Integrated Marketing Communications.* McGraw-Hill; 1993.

23. Wiebe J. The ultimate guide to no-pain copywriting (or, every copywriting formula ever). Copyhackers website. Published 2015. Accessed January 17, 2018. https://copyhackers .com/2015/10/copywriting-formula/#Headline _formulas_for_use_on_lead-gen_pages_for _marketing_ebooks_or_for_blog_posts

24. Clark B. 10 sure-fire headline formulas that work. Copyblogger website. Published July 30, 2006. Accessed January 17, 2018. www.copyblogger .com/10-sure-fire-headline-formulas-that-work

25. Edwards R. 5 headline templates that grab readers. Michael Hyatt website. Published 2013. Accessed January 17, 2018. https://michaelhyatt .com/headline-templates

26. Ellering N. 43 data-driven headline ideas from 1,000 of the most popular posts CoSchedule website. Published 2015. Accessed January 18, 2018. https://coschedule.com/blog/headline-ideas

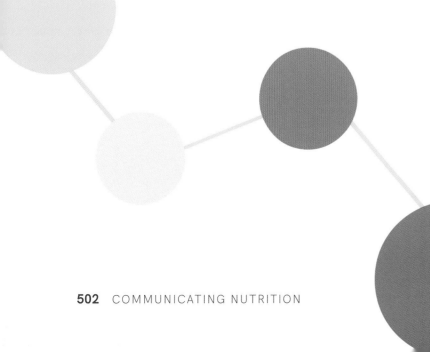

CHAPTER 32

Master Media Interviews to Be a Reliable and Relatable Expert

Melissa Joy Dobbins, MS, RDN, CDCES
and Carolyn O'Neil, MS, RDN, LD

"The food and nutrition professional who learns successful interview techniques will effectively communicate and become a valuable resource to the media."

> "The profession of journalism ought to be about telling people what they need to know, not what they want to know." —WALTER CRONKITE

Introduction

The food and nutrition professional who learns successful interview techniques will effectively communicate and become a valuable resource to the media.[1] Registered dietitian nutritionists (RDNs) are uniquely qualified to translate media headlines into bottom-line takeaways and nutrition science into sensible strategies for the public.

This chapter answers three questions:

- What role do media interviews play in nutrition communications?
- What are best practices for media interviews?
- What are practical strategies for media interviews?

After reading this chapter, readers will have a better understanding of how nutrition communicators can provide expertise on timely topics as both a host and an interviewee. Readers will learn professional behavior and best practices for media interviews, tips for conducting media interviews, and practical strategies including preparing key messages, honing skills to help control the interview, and conveying messages effectively with visual aids.

What Role Do Media Interviews Play in Nutrition Communication?

All forms of media—from traditional print, television, and radio to websites, blogs, and news aggregators—need a constant stream of content to attract an audience. Food is a popular topic and can be presented in a wide variety of subtopics, including nutrition and health. The registered dietitian nutritionist (RDN) can be one of the best interviewees on food topics because of the profession's academic training in nutrition science and food service. The RDN is a credible source of practical advice to help translate scientific principles into action with recipes, shopping tips, cooking tips, and food safety information. RDNs can help shape media headlines and present the bottom line so consumers can put information into practice.

Media Interviews Provide Expertise on Timely Topics

Credentialed food and nutrition professionals such as RDNs are uniquely qualified to communicate evidence-based nutrition information in the media. When RDNs are featured, the media provides the opportunity for professional insight and interpretation of timely topics such as new scientific research, breaking nutrition news, or seasonal food and nutrition topics. Nutrition communicators are able to take sensational headlines and translate the information into essential advice for the public.

Media interviews are a valuable communication tool for many reasons. One reason not often considered is how the interview is much more than the interview. When conducting a media interview, whether it is live or taped, always consider that the actual interview is not the only time comments will be shared because the media outlet may share them multiple times on multiple platforms, including in their website archives and on social media channels. This means an interview is "searchable" on the web and in that sense lives on forever. That means professionals must make sure they know what they are saying and that the information is evidence-based and "shareable." To be shareable, the message should be relatable, with actionable examples to translate good nutrition advice into tips for shopping, cooking, and other food choice behaviors.

Registered Dietitian Nutritionists Can Be Hosts or Interviewees

Traditionally, dietitians have primarily been guests on television and radio shows and quoted in print articles. However, more RDNs have become hosts or reporters themselves, interviewing others for their stories, such as Joy Bauer, MS, RDN, on the *Today* show. This has become more common with the popularity of Facebook Live and Instagram TV, where anyone with an account can interview an expert or be interviewed as the expert and share with audiences. See the Words of Experience boxes for Carolyn O'Neil's story and Melissa Joy Dobbins's story.

What Are Best Practices for Media Interviews?

This section addresses situations where the RDN is being interviewed. Keep in mind this could be by a television or newspaper journalist or by a social media influencer. These guidelines are important for all media platforms.

Be on Time

Show up not just on time, but ahead of time. There are always going to be glitches, and this will allow

I'm a Dietitian, but I Didn't Play One on CNN

by Carolyn O'Neil, MS, RDN, LD

During my tenure of almost 20 years on CNN, my role was to cover the news beat of food, nutrition, and cuisine. As a correspondent and executive producer, it was not my job to give advice as a registered dietitian using my personal voice. It was my job to be a journalist interviewing nutrition experts and choosing the stories and issues to cover for the CNN audience. With an educational background in nutrition science, I was able to review new nutrition research more quickly, and, arguably more accurately than a general assignment reporter could. If it was reporting on research about a nuance of nutrition support of patients with diabetes, I didn't need to review the basics on diabetes—I could jump ahead to what's new and help translate that for a consumer audience. I'm sure the researchers appreciated this too because I got the story right!

I often had to defend my belief that reporters and producers hired to cover the food and nutrition beat should have at least some educational background in the health sciences. Some argued that anyone can cover the food beat "because we all eat food." I would counter with this: "Can you imagine someone who knows nothing about baseball history and statistics covering the World Series? Can you imagine someone who doesn't know about price-to-earnings ratios or small cap vs large cap covering Wall Street news?" I rest my case. Registered dietitian nutritionists are uniquely qualified to report food and nutrition news.

the interviewee to be ready to respond. Whether it's a live television interview or a telephone interview, be prepared ahead of time. It will help the RDN be calmer as well.

Look the Part

Food and nutrition professionals don't always have to wear a business suit to look like an expert. For men, a fashionable sports coat is a good look, but a tie might be too formal. If unsure of what to wear for the interview, look at the website for the program and see what others have worn. A good idea is to go on Pinterest and search suggestions for "professional yet casual" clothing ideas.

For television, consider where the audio person will clip the microphone. Turtleneck sweaters are a problem. Dresses are a problem unless someone does not mind the audio person reaching down the back of a dress to secure the battery pack on her bra strap. (Yes, that's what they do!) Wear a V-neck sweater or a blouse that's not too flimsy or low-cut and a skirt or pants so the

microphone can be secured near the neckline and the battery pack on the waistline of a skirt or pants. For a cooking demo, it's usually easy to attach the microphone to an apron. Avoid long, loose sleeves that might get into the mixing bowl.

Bottom line: Comfortable clothes mean the interviewee will be more comfortable during the interview and can concentrate on delivering the message. (See Box 32.1 on page 511 for more about being camera-friendly.)

Attend to the Interviewer

When there are cameras all around, it can be hard to know where to look. It may be tempting to look at the camera, but the rule is to focus attention on the interviewer unless directed otherwise. The main exception to this is when the interviewer is remote; then the interviewee will be expected to look directly at the camera. In an interview, make eye contact with the person asking the questions to demonstrate attention. A sure giveaway that an interviewee is not paying attention is when they don't answer the question that was asked. Listen carefully, and if unsure of a question ask for clarification, or rephrase the question and confirm that the content is understood correctly.

Paying attention to the interviewer is just as important as paying attention to anyone else having a conversation. But remember, this is not a cocktail party. There is limited time to get to key messages, so listen to the questions carefully and respond in such a way as to provide an answer that emphasizes a key point or supporting information prepared in advance.

It is important to be aware of time constraints. If the interviewer is going on and on, avoid interrupting and demonstrate engagement by acting excited about what they're saying, and as soon as there is a pause, agree with style: "Oh! Yes, I know what you're saying! That's why...."

Respond to Questions in Sound Bites

A sound bite is a succinct but complete response. This means it's best to respond to questions in full sentences that may be used without the audience ever hearing the questions. For instance, if the interviewer asks, "What are examples of probiotic foods?" Don't respond, "Yogurt, sauerkraut, and kefir." Respond, "Probiotic foods that may help improve our gut health include foods you may

The Other Side of the Mic

by Melissa Joy Dobbins, MS, RDN, CDCES

After 20 years of traditional media experience, primarily television and radio interviews, I launched my own "radio show" and became the host of my *Sound Bites* podcast. It was a bit of an adjustment to ask the questions instead of answering them, but it was refreshing to choose a topic and a guest that was credible and meaningful instead of the sensational hype I often heard on local radio stations.

My traditional media experience taught me that "bridging" (see page 509) was the most important skill I could possess because the reporters often knew little or nothing about the topic and therefore usually didn't ask very good questions. Now, as the host of my own show, I draw on that experience to guide me in interviewing my guests with more insight and preparation on the topic. In addition, I help my guests prepare by letting them know what to expect and how to bring their best self forward during the interview.

> *"People are interesting. You just have to ask them the right questions."* —JOHN TRAVOLTA

already be eating, such as yogurt, but they also include sauerkraut and kimchi, as well as drinkable yogurt-like beverages such as kefir." This technique allows a taped interview to edit out the question, making the interviewee's comments more likely to be in the final cut.

Provide Context and Clear Meaningful Examples

When preparing for a media interview, think about how to provide context and clear examples the audience will understand and find relatable. Lead with the science first, addressing the interviewer's question about a nutrition research finding or a current hot topic. But, always have at least two or three actionable tips for the consumer. Always take science to the supermarket.

Here's an example. If the interview is about consuming more n-3 fatty acids for good health, develop a memorable message using the number three: "Here are the three reasons you want to eat more omega-3s and three examples of foods that contain them."

Tips for Conducting Media Interviews

Conducting a media interview takes skill and concentration to guide the interviewee to share the best information and insight within a specific time frame. RDNs who work in broadcast reporting may routinely conduct television and radio interviews. But increasingly RDNs are conducting interviews for their personal or company websites, blogs, and podcasts. The same rules apply for successful interviewing.[2]

SETTING UP THE INTERVIEW

Do the homework. Become familiar with the topic. While most RDNs have studied nutrition and food science, they are not necessarily experts in the nuances of specialties in nutrition science or food production, for example. Decide upon the best source and, if there are strong opinions on an issue, balance the story with interviews offering multiple opinions and insights.[2]

PREPARING FOR THE INTERVIEW

The more the interviewer understands the subject matter, the more productive an interview will be. Don't waste people's time forcing them to explain basic stuff an audience should already know; instead, use the interview to collect details, insights, and specific tips. Prior to the interview, do background research on the topic to assist in formulating an angle and preparing a list of interview questions.[2]

DURING THE INTERVIEW

Relax and be friendly and curious. Make the interviewee feel comfortable. At the same time, don't forget that as the interviewer, you are the one in charge and asking the questions.[2]

Budget time and get right to the meat of the matter if there are only a few minutes. Focus the questions. Rather than asking "What's the Mediterranean diet like?" be more precise: "What are the top three foods that make up the Mediterranean diet?"[2]

Keep it simple. Avoid long, rambling two- or three-part questions. Long questions are often the result of interviewers trying to impress the audience with their knowledge. Keep in mind that the interview is about finding out what an interviewee thinks.[2]

Avoid yes and no questions, such as, "So, your research shows that replacing saturated and trans fats in the diet with monounsaturated and polyunsaturated fats leads to improved cholesterol levels?" Be more open-ended to allow the interviewee to reveal more: "Which of your research findings related to fat in the diet are important for consumers to understand to protect their heart health?"[2]

Ask follow-up questions: "How did you determine those findings?" "Can you give me an example?" "What excited you the most about that finding?"

Don't worry about asking "dumb" questions. Often these are the questions on the public's mind. Research frequently asked questions (FAQs) on a topic via the web and ask those questions to make sure not to miss a point that needs emphasizing or clarifying.[2]

Stay flexible. Sometimes an interview takes a turn that was never predicted. Go with the flow; some of the best material results from these diversions. Strive to balance the potential for unexpected but beneficial material with staying on point.[2]

For audio- or video-recorded interviews: Find a location free of disturbing background noise and distracting visuals. Avoid "stepping on" sound bites with the next question or reactions (like "uh-huh") as subjects are speaking.[2]

CONCLUDING THE INTERVIEW

Review notes before the end of the interview. Recap to fill in gaps, correct errors, or clarify confusion. Ask, "Who else should I contact?" Often an interviewee will share a link to a better source or a source with even more expertise on another aspect of the topic. Finally, thank the person. The interviewee has just given his or her time and expertise.[2]

What Are Practical Strategies for Media Interviews?

When being interviewed by the media, being prepared is crucial. Contrary to popular belief, "thinking on your feet" is not a reliable strategy and should not replace careful preparation. Practical strategies for media interviews begin with drafting key messages and supporting points; knowing how to "control" the interview through techniques such as hooking, bridging, and flagging; and using visual aids (eg, food and props) to effectively enhance messages.

Prepare Key Messages and Supporting Points

The topic of a media interview is the starting point and foundation for creating key messages and supporting points to convey during the interview. Reporters for print or online interviews sometimes send questions ahead of time, but that is rarely the case in television or radio interviews. However, the nutrition communicator may want to send the reporter a list of "suggested questions" to ask—with the understanding that the reporter may or may not use them. Another best practice is to send copy for on-screen graphics that emphasize messages or tips.

Preparing key messages and supporting points is necessary to organize information and determine the best way to communicate it to an audience. Chapters 10, 11, and 15 discuss assessing audience needs and preparing key messages and supporting points in general. However, for media interviews, give extra consideration to the amount of time allotted for the interview. A typical television segment may last only 3 minutes, while radio interviews may range from a few minutes up to an hour. Time spent on a print interview may vary, and oftentimes only one of the points makes it into the story as a quote. In all of these situations, brevity is essential, so "frontloading" the key messages and repeating them in various ways by using stories, examples, comparisons, and other techniques helps bring these points to life while keeping the interview focused and memorable. In addition, a strong opening statement and a closing call to action will help the audience better understand the information and put it into practice. Chapter 17 explores this concept further.

Practice Interview Skills

In addition to preparing key messages and supporting points, it's important to learn and practice three proven interview skills: hooking, bridging, and flagging. Mastering these skills gives food and nutrition professionals the confidence to handle any interview situation.

HOOKING

Hooking leads the interview in the direction the interviewee wants it to go. Think of it as "bait" that irresistibly lures the interviewer to ask a question and allows the RDN to emphasize a key point or provide examples to illustrate a point. These are a few examples:

- Hook: "If you remember just four steps to food safety, you will avoid spreading foodborne illness." In response, the interviewer will ask, "What are the four steps?" or possibly, "What is one step?"
- Hook: "You may be interested in learning what we found." In response, the interviewer will ask, "What did you find?"
- Hook: "That isn't the only way to get more fiber." In response, the interviewer will ask, "What are some other ways?"

Even if the interviewer doesn't take the hook and ask another question, the hook can provide important information, such as stating that food safety involves four steps, or that the example already discussed isn't the only way to get fiber.

BRIDGING

Bridging takes the interview from off-topic back to the topic, and ideally to a key message. It is likely the most useful technique to master because it helps an interviewee stay on topic, handle difficult questions, and reiterate important information. There are many different ways a reporter can take the interview off topic, and subsequently, many different reasons to bridge back to a key message. The reporter may ask a question that the interviewee does not know the answer to or doesn't want to spend valuable time answering, or a question that is controversial, unclear, or misleading. Being able to bridge back to key messages with a transitional statement allows the interviewee to address the question or comment, yet communicate what is most important for the audience to know. These are a few examples:

- "I don't know about that, but what I do know is …"
- "I can't speculate on that, but what I can tell you is …"
- "Actually, the opposite is true …"
- "_____ has not been proven to result in _____, but what has been shown to _____ is …"

To be effective, the bridge must begin by answering, or at least addressing, the question asked and then transitioning to the key message. A well-executed bridge shows both respect to the interviewer and expertise in the subject matter.

FLAGGING

Flagging draws attention to and emphasizes the importance of a key message. These are a few examples:

- "The most important thing to remember is …"
- "The bottom line is …"
- "The real issue is …"
- "What this means for you is …"

Being prepared also means practicing delivery before the interview, managing nerves, speaking clearly, having good eye contact, and using positive body language. Chapter 21 discusses these skills in depth.

Consider Visual Aids to Illustrate Messages

If the interview format is on camera, such as television or video, it's important for the food and nutrition professional to consider how visual aids, such as food, props, or on-screen graphics, can illustrate the messages. Using visuals effectively can make the difference between a good interview and a great one, and they should be carefully chosen to enhance messages. Following are some tips to consider.

Get Organized

Select visuals to coincide with key messages. If there are three key messages, prepare three main visuals, or groups of visuals, one for each message. Make sure the audience can easily see and identify visuals. If an interview is in the studio, find out where the cameras are filming from to determine which direction to face the food or props. The point of using visuals is to make it easier for the audience to understand the messages, not to confuse them.

SHOWCASE THE FOOD

The display will look much more appealing if the food itself is shown instead of the package. If there is a specific reason to show the package, such as highlighting label information or grab-and-go products, then it's acceptable to use it. Avoid brand-name products if possible. When displaying food, use white or clear dishes so it's more visible. Colored dishes also work for holiday themes.

Most television studios do not have a kitchen set, and even those that do often do not have a working sink. Bring paper towels and bottled water or disposable wipes in case there is a need to "clean something" quickly before going on camera. Also bring a garbage bag to dispose of food after the segment. Do not leave garbage at the studio.

TAKE IT TO THE NEXT LEVEL

Adding a little height to the display makes it more visually appealing. Get creative with dishes and other props. For example, a cake stand can be used for any food, not just cake. Also, sometimes having signs with words or numbers on them can help viewers better understand and remember the points. This is especially true when sharing many numbers, like nutrition facts or prices. For example, when talking about carbohydrate counting, show a sign with the grams of carbohydrate to reinforce the message.

See Figure 32.1 for an example of using foods as visuals and elevating a display for more visual appeal.

GIVE FOOD SOME PROPS

If the segment has a theme, think of props that help tell the story.

For instance, in a segment on which summer foods to choose and which to cut back on, having a few bright-yellow, classic tape measures winding like a ribbon around the least calorie-dense dishes gives the visual clue on camera that these foods are ones to choose more often. On the other side of the table, yellow caution tape can be used as a ribbon around the higher-calorie summer food choices, which gives a visual clue that these foods should be enjoyed in moderation. Figures 32.2 and 32.3 illustrate creative approaches to showcasing foods that help drive home a key point.

Have a little fun. For example, a Twister game mat could serve as a tablecloth, and the host could spin the Twister color wheel to choose healthy toppings for a pizza night segment. "You got red! Add some sliced red bell peppers."

Finally, it's important to consider what the food and props look like on camera. Practice ahead of time. As described previously, check with the camera person or floor director about the camera setup. What angle is the camera filming from? Does the food or prop need to be turned to face in that direction? Is there more than one camera?

Chapter 26 discusses food styling and photography, and Chapter 25 discusses conducting food demos, which are skills that can be utilized for on-camera interviews as well. See Boxes 32.1 and 32.2 for more specific tips that may be helpful for planning and giving media interviews.

Mastering media interviews is crucial for nutrition communicators to be seen as reliable and relatable. Even in this digital age, traditional interview skills are essential to nutrition communications and can be leveraged in many different ways. Understanding the role of media interviews, adopting best practices, and learning practical strategies for media interviews creates a foundation to build upon. The Academy of Nutrition and Dietetics *Working with the Media* handbook[1] is an online resource available to members of the Academy of Nutrition and Dietetics and includes information about media interviews as well as other topics such as pitching and social media.

FIGURE 32.1 **Melissa shares tips for food and props on camera in a YouTube video**

How to Be Camera-Friendly by Melissa Joy Dobbins, MS, RDN, CDCES

- Keep it simple. Clothes, makeup, and jewelry should *not* be more interesting than you!
- Solid colors are better than prints and patterns. White can appear too bright and tends to "glow." Green may be a problem if filming in front of a green screen.
- Wear makeup—that goes for men too! High-definition foundation can be purchased at any department store or makeup store. A little more blush than usual and light-colored lipstick helps avoid looking washed-out.
- Make sure there is a place to clip the microphone, such as on a collar or V-neck top.
- Keep hair off your face. Otherwise, if the camera is coming from a side angle, your face may be hidden completely.

- Avoid wearing jewelry that makes noise or moves around a lot—no bangle bracelets or large dangling earrings. Be careful with necklaces because they can interfere with the microphone.
- Avoid picking up any food or props during the interview—only point or gesture to them. If something is picked up, it may inadvertently be taken out of the camera shot. Hosts may do this, but they are skilled at checking the monitor and knowing where the camera is focused.
- Don't look directly at the camera unless instructed to do so. Instead, keep good eye contact with the host. This may feel awkward, but it looks good. Nothing is more awkward than looking at the wrong camera.

FIGURE 32.2 **Carolyn O'Neil, the Lady of the Refrigerator on *Good Eats,* knows that sometimes you have to put on a costume to communicate food and nutrition messages.**

FIGURE 32.3 **Make food props the star with movement on visual media to draw attention to your message; Carolyn O'Neil drizzles honey during live TV segment.**

BOX 32.2

Tips from TV's "The Lady of the Refrigerator"

by Carolyn O'Neil, MS, RDN, LD

Follow these tips to prepare for a media interview:

Choose the "broad content area":

Example: "The farm-to-table trend isn't automatically a healthy menu choice."

Create a catchy "lead-off sentence":

Example: "Sure we want to eat more farm-fresh foods from local growers and enjoy them in season … but farm fresh items such as butter, bacon, and cream call for some culinary caution."

Identify key messages (three is a good number):

- Benefits of the farm-to-table trend: local, seasonal, affordable, fresh
- Culinary cautions for the farm-to-table trend: fat calories, saturated fats, sodium
- Best ways to enjoy the farm-to-table trend: low-fat or fat-free dairy, portions

Come up with tips and props to use in the interview to illustrate the key messages:

- Examples of healthy farm-to-table dishes
- Examples of farm-to-table dishes that are high in fat and saturated fat

Identify a bottom line or concluding statement for a strong finish:

Example: "Just because something is sustainable, organic, local, and seasonal doesn't automatically make it good for heart health and weight management. Choose a bounty of fresh seasonal produce, enjoy cheese and butter in moderation, and seek out low-fat or fat-free dairy. Make sure your farm-to-table food choices are fabulous for taste and health!"

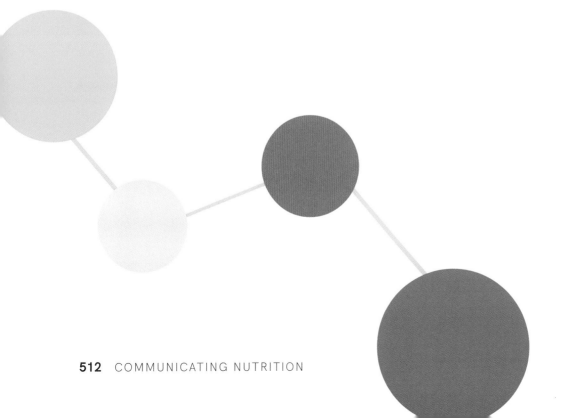

KEY POINTS

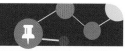

Master Media Interviews to Be a Reliable and Relatable Expert

1. Registered dietitian nutritionists and other credentialed food and nutrition professionals are uniquely qualified to communicate evidence-based nutrition information in the media, providing professional insight and interpretation of timely nutrition topics so consumers can put information into practice.

2. Arriving to media interviews on time, looking and acting professionally, having good eye contact, and displaying listening skills are best practices for media interviews.

3. Communicating in sound bites, or complete sentences, increases the chances of being understood and being quoted.

4. Preparing key messages and supporting points is key to a successful media interview that is clear, concise, and compelling.

5. Interview skills such as hooking, bridging, and flagging are effective ways to control the interview, stay on track, and handle questions confidently.

6. Utilizing visuals to enhance messages is an important aspect of on-camera interviews.

RESOURCES

Working with the Media: A Handbook for Members of the Academy of Nutrition and Dietetics: www.eatrightpro.org/-/media/eatrightpro-files/career/career-development/workingwiththemedia.pdf

Food and Props 101: On-Camera Tips for Effective Visuals (blog post): www.soundbitesrd.com/food-props-101-on-camera-tips-for-effective-visuals

Food and Props 101: On-Camera Tips for Effective Visuals (video): www.youtube.com/watch?v=ocwptn1dHzc

REFERENCES

1. Academy of Nutrition and Dietetics Strategic Communications Team. *Working with the Media: A Handbook for Members of the Academy of Nutrition and Dietetics.* Academy of Nutrition and Dietetics; 2018. www.eatrightpro.org/-/media/eatrightpro-files/career/career-development/workingwiththemedia.pdf

2. Harrower T. *Inside Reporting: A Practical Guide to the Craft of Journalism*, 3rd ed. McGraw-Hill Education; 2013.

SECTION 7

Practices That Can Make or Break Success in Designing and Delivering Communication

Effective Leadership Communication Promotes Success

Lucille Beseler, MS, RDN, LDN, CDE, FAND, Academy of Nutrition and Dietetics President 2016-2017, and Donna S. Martin, EdS, RDN, LD, SNS, FAND, Academy of Nutrition and Dietetics President 2017-2018

As you delve into Section 7, think about effective leadership communication. What is it? Why is it important, and how do you prepare for it? In this section opener, we share our thoughts and experiences as Academy of Nutrition and Dietetics Presidents.

When we embarked on our leadership journeys, we understood that effective leadership communication not only helps to create effective teams but also inspires, prevents crises, and finds solutions for problems. During our terms, we were confronted with many situations that would challenge our communication skills and our overall success. It was imperative to map out a solid plan to maintain focus on accomplishing our predetermined goals and desired outcomes. Since the role of an Academy of Nutrition and Dietetics President is to serve the membership, our vision was to deliver messages that would move our profession forward and provide members with tools for success. We each had unique and individual views of how we wanted to approach our communication platform and leadership roles as Academy of Nutrition and Dietetics Presidents.

When we are asked what influenced our individual communication platforms, the answer is simple: The Academy of Nutrition and Dietetics 100-year vision and mission formed the blueprint for all messaging. The Board of Directors solidified the vision and mission with a strategic plan that was the road map to successful outcomes. Armed with this vision and the support of the board, staff, and colleagues, we had a strong foundation from which to launch our communication platforms.

Donna S. Martin, EdS, RDN, LD, SNS, FAND, and Lucille Beseler, MS, RDN, LDN, CDE, FAND

We believed in our messages, and we believed in ourselves. But simply believing in yourself is not enough to ensure successful communications. As Academy of Nutrition and Dietetics Presidents, we had expectations for conducting successful meetings and developed solid guidelines to ensure them. Members of the board and individual committees were expected to do their homework, just as we did when developing our plan of work. Inviting feedback and constructive ideas is also essential. Board members and committee members were encouraged to provide ideas for improvement, just as the membership was invited to provide feedback to us during and after our presentations as Presidents of the Academy of Nutrition and Dietetics.

However, we had to do more than engage members at presentations and meetings; we needed to expand communication and allow the membership to provide direct input to the Academy of Nutrition and Dietetics. And so, the Academy of Nutrition and Dietetics newly developed membership engagement zone was born. This membership engagement zone uses email as the platform for our members to share their ideas. This has been successful in giving Presidents, the board, and executive staff a better platform to gather and understand diverse opinions from our members in a timely manner. The member engagement zone uses technology to successfully bridge the communication gap for our diverse membership.

So, what are effective communication strategies that can promote effective leadership? Countless business articles and books have checklists for

Lucille's Vision for Motivating by Lucille Beseler, MS, RDN, LDN, CDE, FAND

My vision was to motivate members to get involved, think outside of the box, and develop visionary skills. To achieve this, I knew I needed to inspire and motivate. When addressing my audiences, I introduced myself as the "chief motivating officer," hoping to stimulate excitement and motivation in members who would, in turn, share their motivation with their colleagues.

Health care is changing so rapidly, and unless we change with it, we will be replaced by other health professionals. My role as a leader is to educate our members on the business of nutrition and encourage members to secure their future while looking at new and creative ways to be part of the changing health care landscape. If I don't motivate them to do so, I haven't been an effective leader.

Donna's Vision for Motivating by Donna S. Martin, EdS, RDN, LDN, SNS, FAND

My motto during my year as Academy President was "Teamwork makes the dream work." I focused on the Academy's powerful and ambitious new strategic plan and vision: "To transform the health of the world through the power of food and nutrition." My message to every audience was to support each other and make sure that whatever we do should advance our strategic plan.

My job as a leader is to make sure we work as a team so that we are accelerating improvements in health. It is also vitally important that we become part of the interdisciplinary health care team. We have so much to contribute, and our skill sets have prepared us to take a leadership role on these teams.

effective leadership communication.[1,2] Here are some simple tips that sum it up well, from an article by Dan Scalco in *Success* magazine[1]:

- Know yourself.
- Know your audience.
- Be direct, specific, and clear.
- Pay attention to nonverbal communication.
- Listen more than you speak.
- Be positive and respectful.

Remember that the opportunity to communicate successfully happens everywhere—in large-group presentations, small-group presentations, committee meetings, and even individual conversations. The six chapters in Section 7 discuss all the various communication skills we use to work successfully in our role as Academy of Nutrition and Dietetics leaders. At every step in the communication process, we are planning, executing, evaluating, and revising as needed. This process makes our messaging stronger and more collaborative.

As Presidents, we knew that one of our most difficult challenges was getting up in front of very large and diverse audiences. How does one practice speaking in front of thousands of people? Unique skills must be developed, including an engaging delivery style, effective audience management, and the ability to field questions. Some people can get up in front of an audience and immediately connect. They make it look easy. It can be labeled charisma, or the "it" factor. We call it hard work and a skill to be developed and fine-tuned. For both of us, getting up in front of a large audience was a skill we had to hone to feel confident, poised, and engaging.

Our tips are fairly simple, whether you're speaking to a small or a large audience:

- Believe in your message and ensure it reflects who you are and what you want the audience to know.
- Practice, practice, and then practice some more. There are teleprompter apps that can help you practice your speech. Gather

a friendly audience to provide you with feedback.

- Remember to smile, be enthusiastic, and communicate the passion you have for what you are presenting, and you will be believable. Adding a little humor to your presentation will help break the tension everyone is feeling when it is a large audience.
- Do not let difficult questions sidetrack you. If you do not know an answer, admit it, and you can get back to them at a later time and then follow through.

The work is not completed once a speech or any piece of communication is launched. Take the time for thoughtful contemplation. Ask, "What effect did the communication have on my audience? Did it resonate? Did it create good dialogue and the desired outcomes?" Honestly critique yourself and ask for feedback from colleagues.

To answer the question we first posed, "What does effective leadership communication look like, and how do you achieve it?"—in summary, we approach communication as we approach our relationships as leaders. It starts with building confidence in ourselves, in our colleagues, and in our audiences. We do our homework and take the time to know our colleagues and our audiences. Only then can you truly understand how to make these relationships work. When communicating, you are developing a relationship, albeit sometimes a brief relationship. Connecting to your audience in a respectful and inspiring way ensures that you are doing your job. Do your job, and the audience will appreciate it.

There is not one simple recipe for achieving success through effective communication. It is certain that effective leadership communication requires hard work, dedication, thoughtful reflection, and sometimes sheer will, but when success is achieved, it looks, feels, and sounds great.

We each have quotes we live by that inspire us....

"Life is a big canvas; throw all the paint on it you can."

—**DANNY KAYE**

LUCILLE'S FAVORITE QUOTES

"It's not who you are that holds you back from being a leader. It's who you think you're not that holds you back." —**AUTHOR UNKNOWN**

DONNA'S FAVORITE QUOTE

"Leadership is not about a title or a designation. It's about impact, influence, and inspiration. Impact involves getting results, influence is about spreading the passion you have for your work, and you have to inspire teammates and customers." —**ROBIN S. SHARMA**

REFERENCES

1. Scalco D. 6 communication skills that will make you a better leader. *Success*. May 1, 2017. Accessed October 9, 2018. www.success.com/6-communication-skills-that-will-make-you-a-better-leader
2. Sanborn M. *You Don't Need a Title to Be a Leader: How Anyone, Anywhere, Can Make a Positive Difference*. Doubleday; 2006.

CHAPTER

33

Attention to Logistical Details Promotes Successful Communication

Barbara J. Mayfield, MS, RDN, FAND

"Careful preparation helps an event to come off with minimal problems and allows a nutrition communicator to concentrate on the reason for being there—to communicate effectively."

> "Give me six hours to chop down a tree and I will spend the first four sharpening the axe." —ABRAHAM LINCOLN

Introduction

Logistics is "the handling of the details of an operation."[1] Details include far more than preparing content, a slide deck, and audience activities. They include working with the organization hosting the event, and for event planners, making arrangements regarding the location, equipment, supplies, registration, and more. Logistical planning anticipates potential problems and seeks to prevent them and prepare backup plans. Attending to the details involved in an event or program eliminates many potential problems.

This chapter answers three questions:

- What is the rationale for planning logistics?
- What are the components of logistical planning?
- What are practical strategies for avoiding logistical problems?

This chapter is written for the nutrition communicator speaking at an event or serving as the coordinator for a smaller event. Planning and coordinating large events is beyond the scope of this chapter. Although logistical planning may be delegated to someone other than the communicator, to ignore its significance or fail to attend to requests for input in making decisions or providing information will lead to potential problems. The saying "the devil is in the details" applies to logistical planning. It is often the smallest missed detail that can become a major annoyance and get in the way of effective communication. Plan. Prepare. Prevent.

What Is the Rationale for Planning Logistics?

Careful preparation helps an event to come off with minimal problems and allows a nutrition communicator to concentrate on the reason for being there—to communicate effectively. A well-planned and well-executed event or program is a pleasure for all involved—the organizers and the participants.

Preventing Problems

Problems cannot be totally avoided, but they can largely be prevented through preparation. A problem that is averted or overcome fails to remain a problem. In fact, it can become an opportunity for achieving even greater success. Demonstrating preparation for dealing with problems communicates an added value to an audience. A problem that is handled with professionalism and a calm demeanor will be remembered not for the problem but for the solution.

Problems can include situations involving program personnel, the location, presentation details and supplies, attendees, and even natural disasters. Throughout each step in preparation, consider the potential for something to not go as planned. Take steps to prevent problems and have a backup plan in place. As Benjamin Franklin wisely said, "An ounce of prevention is worth a pound of cure."

Improving the Audience Experience

An audience will have greater confidence in the speakers and event organizers when the event runs smoothly. Glitches in any aspect of an event can undermine confidence and lead to an unsatisfied audience.

The audience experience begins with the first communication about an event. Has it arrived in plenty of time to allow for attendance? Are important details accurately and clearly conveyed? Is the registration process easy to follow? Will attendees be able to locate the venue, find parking, and get to the room without difficulty? Once there, is the room comfortable, with adequate seating, good lighting and temperature, and an unblocked view of the speaker? Is the equipment operating as intended? Will everyone be able to see and hear? Are there enough handouts for everyone in attendance? Are breaks and restrooms adequate for audience comfort?

When everything goes well, the audience may not notice or appreciate the advance planning that took place. But, when problems occur, the audience experience suffers.

Allowing the Communicator to Focus on Communicating

Advance attention to details means the communicator won't have to worry about them during the event and can focus on giving an effective presentation. Communicators who can rest assured everything should go as planned can connect with the audience and convey their message effectively.

Logistical planning is generally a shared responsibility. The role of the speaker may be minimal, but it is important that everyone involved knows who is handling what task, and whom to contact if problems arise. Refer to page 528 for a checklist of logistical details to consider. If not personally responsible for a task, list the name of the person who is responsible. Whether serving as event coordinator, committee member, or presenter, consider the details of the role in making sure logistics are in place for a successful event.

> "There is a rhythm and flow to every event that must be carefully orchestrated. All must be organized ahead of time—everything in its place and ready to go."
> —JUDY ALLEN, *EVENT PLANNING*[2]

What Are the Components of Logistical Planning?

Logistical planning encompasses a wide array of factors. It begins with making all of the necessary arrangements and considering who is involved, what must be provided, and when and where an event takes place. It includes all of the preparations for creating, assembling, and copying visual aids, handouts, and other supplies. It makes certain that equipment is reserved and in working order. It builds in backup plans for potential disasters.

Making Necessary Arrangements

Events and programs don't happen by themselves. They are projects that require people to fill every role, a suitable location, adequate supplies, well-functioning equipment, and an audience ready to participate. Allow plenty of time before the event to make all arrangements, with a built-in buffer of time to handle unforeseen glitches. National events begin initial planning more than a year in advance to select dates and locations. Speakers are selected 6 to 9 months ahead of the event, with solicitations for speakers several months before that. A local or regional program can be planned within a shorter time frame, but allowing more time results in less stressful planning. Event planners or coordinators should create a timeline and task list that identifies designated personnel to fill each role and complete each task. Make sure everyone knows who is responsible for what. Presenters at an event should make note of who is the direct contact and what the presenter is responsible for.

LOCATION, DATE, TIME, PARKING, AND MORE

One of the first decisions is where and when an event will take place. For example, the locations for the Academy of Nutrition and Dietetics Food & Nutrition Conference & Expo (FNCE) are reserved years in advance, before themes or speakers are selected. When selecting a location for an event, account for travel distance for audience members, cost, space and accommodations available, and suitability for the occasion and audience. For example, a state park or retreat center may be ideal for certain types of programs, whereas a university conference center may be appropriate for others.

When selecting a date, consider conflicts with other events that will compete for attendance, or events that will pose a challenge for travelers. For example, avoid hosting an event in Indianapolis the same weekend as the Indy 500 or in Boston the weekend of the Boston Marathon, unless the plan is to attract the same audience. Recurring events, such as FNCE or state affiliate meetings that occur at roughly the same time each year, have the advantage of being planned for by potential attendees.

The larger the event, the more likely an event planner will handle logistical arrangements regarding location, housing, transportation, and parking. For smaller events, the presenter may fill this role. If responsible for this aspect of logistical planning, step into the shoes of the audience members and consider all of the details of attending that will make their participation enjoyable and hassle-free. The last thing a planner needs is to run out of hotel rooms, parking spaces, box lunches, or auditorium seats.

Timing for a professional, educational event is a balancing act. Plan adequate time for attendees to arrive, park, and register. Provide a location that is conducive to networking while waiting for the event to begin. This time can also be an opportunity for visiting an exhibit area or poster sessions. Participants will appreciate using this time constructively. Consider the availability of refreshments and beverages during registration, such as breakfast items served during an early morning registration. Attendees may have traveled several hours and will welcome nourishment before beginning the meeting.

In planning the timing of sessions throughout the event, provide a balance of sessions and breaks that gives adequate time for transitions between sessions, comfort breaks, and visiting with fellow attendees and that also prevents running behind if one speaker talks for a few extra minutes or participants linger after a presentation. Larger venues generally build in 30-minute breaks, whereas smaller venues often allow for 10- to 15-minute breaks. If different speakers require setup between sessions, allow a minimum of 10 to 15 minutes for a smooth transition. If timing is cut too close, it can result in later speakers being short-changed. If the breaks are too long, this can limit the hours of continuing education available to attendees.

LOCATION-SPECIFIC ARRANGEMENTS

Different types of settings or venues require specific arrangements. Both speakers and event organizers should refer to the following lists to prepare for various settings.

Youth Settings Youth settings include early childhood centers, schools, after-school programs, camps, and community programs. When working in a youth setting, it is best to consider the following:

- Ensure that a staff member will remain in the room during the presentation to maintain discipline and handle emergencies (eg, student injuries, fire drills, intruder drills).
- Ask about any special needs of students (eg, disabilities, literacy level, English language proficiency) and assist with planning appropriate accommodations.
- Identify participants with food allergies that would prohibit bringing particular foods or food packaging.
- Discuss policies regarding food preparation and food service and what facilities are available for food preparation and storage.
- Find out what technology is available, such as interactive whiteboards, and if assistance in their use will be available.
- Find out what supplies will be available and what may need to be provided (such as markers for name tags or supplies suitable for a craft, such as crayons or scissors).
- Arrange for the safe and legal capture of photos or video of the presentation. Many locations will have permissions on file or request that permission forms be supplied.
- Inform and help the presenter comply with the site's security protocol for entry as a guest.

Academic and Professional Settings These settings include seminars and colloquiums on university campuses, medical round tables, professional meetings, workshops, symposiums and conferences, and online versions of these events, such as webinars and video conferencing. Below are some suggestions for planning a meeting in an academic or professional setting:

- Although most settings for professional meetings are equipped for technology—with a computer, projection and sound equipment, internet, microphones, and so on—check with the venue to be sure.
- Determine whether the audience will receive copies of the presentation slides or additional handouts, and whether they will be provided in print or electronically.
- For event planners, the venue will likely have a conference-planning staff to work with. Work with the conference planner well ahead of the event to determine deadlines and responsibilities.
- Know whom to check in with to obtain information and assistance at the event.
- Work with technical support staff to set up and trouble-shoot potential problems.

Community and Recreational Settings These settings include programs hosted at community centers, fitness centers, libraries, faith-based organizations, assisted living facilities, farmers markets, retail stores, parks, or public health events or health fairs. Here are some things to keep in mind when planning an event at a community or recreational setting:

- Settings within the community vary greatly and may or may not be equipped for technology; determine available resources for presentations before content development. Presenters should find out what will be available. Event coordinators should communicate with presenters what is available or make arrangements to accommodate their needs. If using on-site technology, who is available to assist? Who has technology pass codes?
- Always consider the space and setup. Is there room to move, tables for note-taking, or facilities to keep foods safe for a demonstration or taste-testing?

- Arrive at the venue early to set up, and ensure resources and space are functional prior to a presentation.
- Confirm with the location who is responsible for room setup, cleanup, and key access.
- Identify logistical information such as resources, budget, setup, parking, and flow prior to the day of presentation.

Workplace Settings Workplace settings include small and large businesses and offices (eg, a local real estate company, a power plant, a Fortune 500 company), hospitals or doctor's offices, and corporate wellness programs. Keep the following in mind when planning a presentation at a workplace:

- Workplace settings vary greatly. Determine available resources at the worksite, such as:
  - access to technology (ie, computer, projector, internet, electrical outlets);
  - space (ie, auditorium, classroom, break room) and setup and teardown for the presentation;
  - presenter aids, such as a whiteboard or chalkboard; and
  - space for audience movement, note-taking, and taste-testing.
- Arrive at the venue early to set up and ensure that resources and space are functional prior to the presentation.

SPEAKER ARRANGEMENTS

Arranging for speakers should take place well in advance of an event. Speakers should expect to be invited months in advance. As mentioned previously, national events begin this process nearly a year ahead. State or local programs operate about 6 months ahead. To find out about presenting for an organization, check their website for a call-for-speakers announcement and meet all deadlines. Provide potential titles and learning objectives that support their planned theme and audience needs and preferences.

When asked to be a speaker, request a timeline and task list related to contracts, travel arrangements, providing handouts, and other requests. Work with the event organizers to make their jobs easier and more enjoyable. An organized speaker who meets deadlines will get more speaking engagements than one who does not. Work with event organizers to make all of the necessary arrangements related to the presentation, such as determining the presentation time slot and making travel plans.

It is not unusual to have speakers cancel on short notice, in which case the event organizers may need backup speakers. A nutrition communicator who has more than one suitable presentation ready can offer to fill in a gap and save the day.

ROOM SETUP, LIGHTING, AND COMFORT

A room's physical setup can support a presentation or make it more challenging for audience members to participate as planned. Various room arrangements lend themselves to different types of presentations. See Figure 33.1 for typical room arrangements and their uses. Work with the facilities team to determine the best room setup possible. If the room cannot be arranged as requested, adjust plans to best fit the room. As a minimum, find out in advance what the room arrangement will be in order to plan accordingly. A meeting-room space calculator is listed in the resources section at the end of the chapter to assist in determining room size and setup to accommodate an audience.

Arrange chairs so that everyone in the room can easily see the speaker and screen. If possible, place the podium to the left of the screen from the audience's perspective. People who read left to right are accustomed to looking left to right, so looking from a speaker to the screen is most comfortable and natural when speakers are to the left of the screen. When speakers move away from the podium while speaking, they should make sure their body does not block the screen. In advance of a presentation, sit in various places in the room to check out the field of vision to the screen.

Lighting can enhance or detract from a presentation. Lighting that is too bright makes it difficult to see images and words on a screen. Lighting that is too dark makes it hard to see the audience, limits eye contact, and can promote sleepiness. Work with the facility's technology support crew to set up the lighting to best fit specific needs. Adjust it to enhance the audience's ability to see the speaker and the speaker's ability to see the audience. Dim the lighting enough for slides to show up well, but don't make it so dim that it's difficult for the audience to take notes. Windows can also impact lighting. Depending on time of day and the availability of shades, glare through windows can make it difficult

for audience members to see. Position the speaker and audience to minimize the impact.

The temperature in a room can be a tricky issue. Often, an empty room will feel cold before an audience arrives. If the temperature is increased, the room can become uncomfortably hot once filled with warm bodies. One approach is to have someone available to make adjustments after the audience has arrived and a comfort check can be made. Avoid making people too hot or too cold. Presenters should select an outfit that provides the most comfort, taking into account a personal tendency to get warm or cold.

TECHNOLOGY NEEDS AND MICROPHONES

Standard equipment provided for presentations generally includes a podium with standing microphone, a screen, a laptop computer, and a projector. It may be necessary to request additional requirements, such as Wi-Fi, speakers for showing a video with sound, a lavalier or handheld microphone, flip charts, and additional tables.

If bringing personal equipment for a presentation, such as a laptop and projector, also bring a heavy-duty extension cord and power strip in case electrical outlets are far from where the presentation will be set up.

Plan to use a microphone in a setting that is large enough for an audience of 50 or more people, or if the group may be hard of hearing, such as an elderly audience. Practice using the microphone before the presentation to make sure there is no feedback and that the sound level is just right. If using a lavalier microphone, plan for clothing to include a pocket, waistline, or belt for the transmitter and a collar or neckline for attaching the microphone.

If the room is not occupied right before the presentation, go in ahead of time to set up and make sure all equipment is functioning properly. Get to know the technology support crew and how to contact them if a problem arises.

ONLINE PRESENTATION ARRANGEMENTS

Online presentations, such as webinars, allow for participants to attend from remote locations and are often recorded and made available for later viewing. Logistical planning includes arranging for a platform for delivery (eg, GoToWebinar or Zoom), securing one or more speakers, finding a host, and establishing a method for participants

FIGURE 33.1 **Room arrangements for presentations**[a]

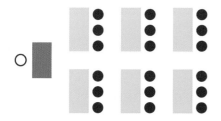

Classroom Style
(16 square feet per person)

Classroom style is appropriate for presentations in which participants will be expected to take notes or to work with partners.

Conference Style
(20 square feet per person)

Conference or boardroom style is appropriate for small discussion groups or meetings.

Auditorium Style
(8 square feet per person)

Auditorium or theater style fits the most audience members into a space. However, it limits movement and makes it more difficult to take notes or break into groups.

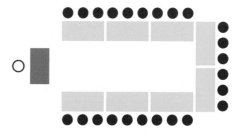

Horseshoe or U-Shape
(20 square feet per person)

A horseshoe or U-shape works well for demonstrations or small-group discussions.

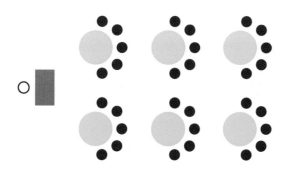

Buzz Style
(20 to 24 square feet per person)

Herringbone Style
(20 square feet per person)

The buzz style and herringbone style, also called V style, are ideal for group activities.

[a] Adapted from references 3 and 4.

See Chapter 34 for information about the presider role.

to register. The host serves as presider. A run-through with the host and speaker a few days before the event is a wise practice to eliminate potential problems. Designate a person to monitor technology during the webinar.

Preparing and Procuring Supplies

No matter what role is being filled in an event, keep a running list of supplies needed. This includes everything from name tags and handouts to an extra roll of tape, a pair of scissors, and safety pins just in case. Do a mental run-through and note every supply that might be needed. When preparing to be a presenter, practice with visual aids and props during rehearsals to make sure everything that will be needed has been accounted for and can be comfortably used.

VISUAL AIDS AND PROPS

Visual aids and props can greatly enhance learning. Make sure they are an appropriate size for the room and the number of people in the audience. For example, if a prop is too small for people in the back to see, the presenter will need time to walk to the back so they can. Instead, use a larger prop that is easy to see.

See Chapter 18 for more on props and visual aids.

It may also be necessary to create props or items for audience members to use during an activity—for example, small cards with icebreaker questions in a small basket, or the response (or voting) card illustrated in Figure 20.1 on page 319. Keep the design simple and easily replicated. Audiences appreciate activities they can easily replicate and reuse. Be prepared to share templates and directions. Know how many people are expected to attend in order to provide adequate supplies for each audience member or group. Plan in advance how to break people into groups to best use the space available.

Logistics for food demonstrations, including a food demo planning worksheet, can be found in Chapter 25.

Many food and nutrition presentations require food and cooking equipment, including equipment for proper storage during transport and on-site.

HANDOUTS CREATED AND DUPLICATED

Chapter 23 discusses how to create effective handouts.

Handouts are a tool for audiences to take notes on and preserve information for later reference. Handouts can be provided to audience members electronically before a presentation or afterward. For electronic handouts to be useful during a presentation, audience members must know how to access

them or print copies in advance, if desired. Hard copies of handouts can also be provided during or after a presentation. If providing hard copies of handouts that are also being sent to the audience electronically before the event, let them know in advance that hard copies will be available at the presentation. Plan the most efficient way to distribute handouts and make sure to have enough copies.

Preparing Speeches, Having Notes, and Backing Up Slides

Speech preparation is not a logistical preparation per se, but preparing to have more than one copy available as a backup is. Many conference organizers will ask speakers to submit their presentation slide deck as an electronic file ahead of time. It is also wise to bring a copy of the presentation on a flash drive, to send the file to a personal email, or to have a copy stored in the cloud. That way a copy will be available in case the original version doesn't work or is misplaced at the venue.

As a precaution, bring a hard copy of the presentation notes to refer to in case technology breaks down. Be prepared to give a talk with or without the slides. When traveling, keep a copy of the presentation and notes in a carry-on, not packed in a checked bag.

What Are Practical Strategies for Avoiding Logistical Problems?

Although it is impossible to prepare for every potential problem, most can be prevented through careful planning and having systems in place to assure all plans are followed. Keeping good records, tracking details and deadlines, and confirming all arrangements are problem-prevention strategies. When disaster strikes despite the best efforts, implement plan B and maintain a positive attitude. The audience will remember how the situation was handled, so make that memory a positive one.

Keep Good Records of All Correspondence and Arrangements

Record keeping has never been easier thanks to both electronic and paper files. Keep all records and materials for one event, project, or trip in a dedicated folder, including both electronic and paper versions. Electronic files go in a folder of computer documents labeled clearly by the event name, and paper files are kept securely in a manila folder for hard copies. Have a system for tracking that correspondence has been read and responded to. Rather than deleting emails related to an event or project, file them in a dedicated folder within an email program until it is certain they'll no longer be needed. For larger projects, create subfolders for various aspects of the project, such as travel arrangements, presentation handouts, and so on. A small initial time investment to organize files can help prevent wasted time later to track down information or, worse, missed obligations and deadlines.

Putting expectations and arrangements in writing can take the form of a formal agreement or contract, or for more informal events be listed in an email or letter. To avoid misunderstandings, it is imperative to document all arrangements. Information to document may include:

- names and contact information for both speaker and host or event planner;
- date and location of event or presentation;
- title, description of presentation, and learning objectives;
- speaker biography or introduction;
- travel arrangements;
- audiovisual requirements and supplies;
- honorarium and fees;
- policies for handling cancellations, photos, book sales, and so on; and
- signatures.

A communicator who speaks professionally on a regular basis benefits from having an agreement template ready for situations in which one is not provided by the organization. Even a volunteer or local event merits a detailed letter or email to clarify all expectations and prevent misunderstandings.

Keep Track of Details and Meet Deadlines

As stated earlier in the chapter, create a master timeline and task list (unless provided by an event planner). Schedule deadlines in a calendar as well as plan reminders for when to begin tasks and a timed-based strategy for completion.

Check and double-check that all times, dates, and locations have been correctly entered. This is especially important for travel arrangements. Arriving one day late is a problem that cannot be remedied, only apologized for.

Strive to meet deadlines in advance. This allows for situations beyond personal control, such as a website that goes down on the deadline for uploading a file or registering for an event. A speaker who meets deadlines early or on time is more likely to receive invitations for future speaking opportunities.

Confirm All Arrangements

Confirming arrangements with other key players involved in a project or event helps ensure that everyone has the same details in the same order. For presenters, these individuals include the event coordinator, session presider or moderator, and potentially others who may assist with travel, such as a person designated to pick up a speaker at the airport or hotel and provide transport to the venue. Just because a presenter has kept careful track of arrangements doesn't mean everyone else has as well. Confirmation may prevent a disaster if someone else forgot or if there was a change of plans.

Confirming arrangements takes many forms, such as double-checking the confirmation notices sent or received or checking times on an online agenda. It may require contacting key people. For example, if there was an initial notification with session details but no response or follow-up, initiate a follow-up. Know whom to contact for any last-minute questions and have a method for reaching them while en route. If someone else reaches out to confirm arrangements, reply promptly.

Have a Backup Plan for Disasters

As a general rule, expect the unexpected. Flights are delayed, so avoid taking the last one available. Luggage occasionally gets lost, so wear an outfit for traveling that could also be worn for the presentation. Parking lots can be full, so allow plenty of time to park farther from the venue than expected. Meeting rooms can change and speakers and participants show up in wrong locations, so be prepared to move. Technology can fail, so be prepared to speak without slides. Fire alarms can go off and an entire audience has to evacuate the room. Be prepared to shorten a presentation to allow for unexpected interruptions.

Once on-site, know whom to contact for help and how to reach them. This includes the session moderator or event organizer if there is one. Notice if the room has a number to call for help posted on a wall or the podium. Larger organizations, such as universities, have building deputies who can assist with facility-related problems. A contact name and number also may be available for technology-related issues. If these aren't provided, ask for them before beginning the event or starting a presentation. Keep these phone numbers in two places—in your phone and also on your person.

The more presentations nutrition communicators give, the more disasters they will encounter. These may be stressful in the moment, but they make great stories for future presentations. Each one can be a learning opportunity for steps to take in the future to prevent or deal with problems. See the Word of Experience box for an example of lessons learned from a day of disasters.

Keep calm, which leads to the most important advice of all: Maintain a positive attitude.

Maintain a Positive Attitude

When the unexpected happens, it can be a challenge to remain positive, but doing so is essential for maintaining composure. When presenters take the stage, they communicate not just with their words, but by the way they present themselves. Nothing tests that like the stress of something going awry. When unforeseen events occur, communicate professionalism and confidence. Diffuse the stress with calm. This response will be contagious. If a presenter is upset, the audience will become upset. If a presenter remains calm, so will they. If appropriate, display a sense of humor.

In many situations, the disaster is relatively short-lived, even though it feels like an eternity while in the middle of it. Consider how the audience will remember the experience when discussing the incident later. Display an attitude and behaviors that would be a source of pride if later posted on social media. Keep in mind that everyone is affected and try to create the best possible outcome for all. Maintain a positive attitude.

Checklist of Logistical Details

Before the event:

___ Confirm date, time, and location.

___ Take care of contracts and paperwork; meet deadlines.

___ Prepare and procure supplies.

___ Have a backup of your speech and notes.

___ Confirm travel arrangements and last-minute details.

___ Identify the location contact (to ensure access to venue, room, and electronics).

At the event:

___ Arrive early, and meet others who are part of the event.

___ Work with the technical support crew to test equipment.

___ Make any necessary adjustments to the room setup, lighting, and temperature.

___ Organize supplies and handouts.

___ Run through timing and assistance needed.

___ Start and end on time.

After the event:

___ Confirm who is responsible for cleanup, room arrangement, and locking doors.

___ Submit requested paperwork.

___ Thank those who helped.

A Day of Disasters

by Amy L. Habig, MPH, RDN, LD

When we started planning a training session for paraprofessional nutrition educators for our newly adopted curriculum, Eating Smart • Being Active (developed by Colorado State University Extension), we were eager to devote an entire day of hands-on training to food preparation and knife skills. Three people from our state and regional staff brainstormed what we thought would be a fun and enriching agenda.

We invited a professional chef to lead a knife-skills training in the morning to give our staff the opportunity to properly cut a variety of fruits and vegetables used in the recipes in our new curriculum. For the food preparation portion of the training, we developed a PowerPoint presentation and recruited several individuals to facilitate and model food preparations at the training.

I worked diligently to practice my presentation, plan logistics, coordinate with my colleagues, and pack everything on my checklist. I was feeling good. I arrived to the training site eager to start the day. Then, as I was walking into the training site, my phone rang. A colleague was calling to tell me our grocery order had been canceled. She was at the store scrambling to find all the items on our list (including about 10 different fruits and vegetables for each of the 30 attendees to cut in the morning, and ingredients for five food preparations). I called several other colleagues and asked them to help her shop.

The first agenda item required the fruits and vegetables, so several of us at the training site devised a new plan for the day. One person set up the cooking stations for several of the afternoon food preparations, while another set up the audiovisual equipment. After talking with the chef, we decided to do part of our PowerPoint presentation while we waited for the groceries. When the groceries arrived, several people carried them in on carts and then washed, sorted, and distributed the produce among the tables at the training site so the chef could start the knife-skills training.

We got through the grocery disaster and then started the food preparation section of the training. One recipe was for oven-fried fish, which, as the name implies, requires an oven. Much to our surprise, the oven at the training site did not work. We tried to improvise by cooking the fish in an electric skillet. Fortunately, it worked and the fish was saved!

When it was time to start the next food preparation activity, a huge storm rolled in and killed the power to the room for about 10 minutes. We obtained help from the event staff, who were able to get everything working again. To avoid wasted time, we set up for the remaining food preparations while we waited for the power to come back on.

After the training, I created a list of suggestions for improvement. We were going to implement the same training again in a few months and *did not* want to relive the same disasters. We utilized my list of suggestions and feedback from attendees when planning and implementing the next training. It went *much* smoother! Helpful strategies included expanding our committee to include a few more individuals (including our professional development coordinator, who could help with some of the logistics), purchasing the food and setting up the room the day before the training, using a more familiar training site, testing equipment ahead of time, and converting the PowerPoint presentation into online modules completed ahead of the training to allow more flexibility in the agenda, keep presenters available to deal with unexpected issues, and eliminate the potential for technical difficulties in showing a PowerPoint.

Although we encountered several disasters, everything worked out in the end. We even ended the day on time! I wanted to cry at times, but I resisted and remained positive. These experiences—albeit stressful—taught us valuable lessons that have helped us offer better trainings for our staff. Moreover, participants were inspired with strategies for dealing with the inevitable disasters they face with their audiences—the importance of working together to improvise, stay calm, and creatively seek solutions.

Amy L. Habig, MPH, RDN, LD, is the program specialist, EFNEP at the Ohio State University.

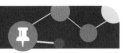

KEY POINTS

Attention to Logistical Details Promotes Successful Communication

1 *Logistics* is "the handling of the details of an operation." It includes working with the organization hosting the event, making arrangements, preparing supplies, and following through on plans. Logistical planning anticipates potential problems and seeks to prevent them and prepare backup plans. Plan. Prepare. Prevent.

2 Careful preparation allows for an event to come off with minimal problems and allows the presenter to concentrate on the reason for being there—to communicate effectively.

3 Logistical planning encompasses a wide array of factors. It begins with making all of the necessary arrangements for an event: Consider all the details of the who, what, when, and where. It includes all of the preparations for creating, curating, and copying visual aids, handouts, and other supplies. It makes certain that equipment is reserved and in working order. It builds in backup plans for potential disasters.

4 Although it is impossible to prepare for every potential problem, most can be prevented through careful planning and having systems in place to assure all plans are followed. Keeping good records, tracking details and deadlines, and confirming all arrangements are prevention strategies. When disaster strikes in spite of best efforts, implement plan B and maintain a positive attitude.

RESOURCES

Meeting-room space calculator:
www.meetings.com/Meeting-Room-Capacity-Calculator

Examples of event and conference planning resources:
- https://blog.bizzabo.com/the-directory-of-event-planning-resources
- https://meetingtomorrow.com/blog/conference-planning-resources

Event planning using function analysis:
https://inldigitallibrary.inl.gov/sites/sti/sti/5025986.pdf

Event planning books for conference planners:
www.wiley.com//legacy/products/worldwide/canada/event_planning/

REFERENCES

1. Logistics. *Merriam-Webster Dictionary*. Published 2018. Accessed April 17, 2018. www.merriam-webster.com/dictionary/logistics
2. Allen J. *Event Planning: The Ultimate Guide to Successful Meetings, Corporate Events, Fundraising Galas, Conferences, Conventions, Incentives, and Other Special Events.* 2nd ed. John Wiley and Sons, Canada; 2009.
3. Conference Place. 8 meeting room setup styles and how to choose the best. Published 2016. Accessed September 30, 2018. www.conference.place/tips/meeting-room-setup-styles
4. Carnegie Mellon University Conference and Event Services. Meeting room set-ups and styles. Published 2016. Accessed September 30, 2018. www.cmu.edu/conferences/facilities/meeting/uc/room-styles.html

An Effective Presider Sets the Stage

Marianne Smith Edge, MS, RDN, LD, FAND, FADA
and Barbara J. Mayfield, MS, RDN, FAND

"The role of a presider or moderator is more important than it may initially seem; the outcome of a meeting or session can depend on the moderator's effectiveness. Be prepared, be polished, know the audience, and anticipate the unexpected."

> "A good host can establish a friendly atmosphere in the room, make the speakers feel authentically welcome, and go a long way toward ensuring that interesting questions are asked and a solid discussion ensues."

—LINDA K. KERBER, "CONFERENCE RULES: HOW TO LEAD A PANEL DISCUSSION," *THE CHRONICLE OF HIGHER EDUCATION*[1]

Introduction

A presider or moderator plays an important role in an event or presentation. This person serves as host, moderator, and overall problem solver and essentially sets the tone of a session or event. A presider or moderator welcomes the audience, handles logistical details and announcements, establishes the credibility of the speaker through a well-planned introduction, makes sure the speaker stays on time, moderates the question-and-answer session, and brings closure to the event. At times a speaker will need to fill these roles, so knowing what is entailed will help the speaker know what to do and when. At larger events and those where the speaker is a guest, there is generally someone who serves specifically as presider or moderator.

This chapter answers three questions:

- What is the role of a presider or moderator?
- What are the components of a professional introduction?
- What practice strategies enhance a moderator's effectiveness?

A new professional is likely to be asked to introduce a speaker or to serve as a moderator for an event before ever being asked to be a main speaker. Learn how to do it well. The role is an important one and can make the difference between a successful event that runs smoothly and one with less-than-optimal outcomes.

What Is the Role of a Presider or Moderator?

The role of a presider or moderator is more important than it may initially seem; the outcome of a meeting or session can depend on the moderator's effectiveness. Be prepared, be polished, know the audience, and anticipate the unexpected.

Serves as Host and Facilitates an Effective Session or Event

Imagine sitting in a room full of colleagues waiting for a presentation or discussion to begin. Everyone knows it's time to start, but who is going to start the meeting? What are the ground rules? Who will introduce the speaker or facilitate discussion? The answers to these questions lie within the duties of a presider or moderator. An effective moderator is a host or emcee of the meeting or specific presentation and is in charge of ensuring the event runs smoothly. This includes starting and finishing on time, maintaining orderly conduct among the audience, facilitating questions for the speaker, and keeping questions relevant to the subject matter. The moderator is in charge and must accept the accompanying responsibilities.

Understands Venues and Events That Require a Moderator or Host

Regardless of the size of the event or venue, a moderator or designated host is required to initiate action. Meetings, virtual or in person, don't start on their own. Formal dinners have hosts, parades have grand marshals, and webinars have hosts—without them, chaos would reign. However, the size and venue of the event will determine the responsibilities of a moderator or host. For small events or meetings, the host may play multiple roles as program planner, speaker, and logistics coordinator, while in larger settings a moderator is a designated individual for a particular forum or speaking engagement.

For virtual meetings or events, a host's responsibilities may go beyond the basic duties to include monitoring participants' social media postings and coordinating logistics. When logistics are part of the role as a moderator, whether in a live or virtual setting, it's important to know what the expectations are. For live events, logistics may include coordinating technology equipment, setting up the room, securing hosts, and keeping time. For virtual events, operating the web platform, announcing the start of the webinar, and fielding questions are typical examples of logistic coordination.

Welcomes the Audience and Orients Them to the Event

The tone and tenor with which a moderator welcomes the audience to an event or presentation sets the stage. If the moderator shows enthusiasm and energy (and even a little humor), the audience will absorb this energy and be open to listening to the speakers. Remember that tone of voice is extremely important in a virtual setting, as it's the only means by which the audience hears enthusiasm. Smiling while speaking causes voice tone to automatically reflect the warmth of the introduction.

In addition to introducing a speaker, the moderator provides the ground rules for the event or presentation, including use of social media, the setup of the question-and-answer segment (Q&A), logistics for any technology used during the presentation, and access to handouts or evaluations, if applicable. At formal venues

or professional conferences, the event planner or organizer usually gives the moderator written guidelines covering these areas. However, at times, the event planner expects the moderator to know the guidelines without written notes. In either case, confirm the details with the organizer prior to moderating the session. Be prepared.

Introduces the Speaker to Establish His or Her Credibility and Build Anticipation

As described in more detail in the next section, establishing a speaker's credibility is one of the primary functions of an introduction and is the most important function of a moderator. How the speaker is introduced can make or break a session. Speakers are asked to present information or viewpoints based on their expertise. Moderators are responsible for connecting the speaker's expertise and topic of the presentation with the audience. They establish why the audience should want to listen. The more the speaker is established as an expert, the better. Audiences like to think they are listening to a winner.[2]

Moderates All Aspects of a Session to Run Smoothly and on Time

"Timing is everything" goes the saying, and this is especially true for moderating a successful session. A moderator is responsible for starting and ending a session or webinar on time. It sounds like a simple task, but there is actually more involved than just starting or stopping a timer. Prior to introducing a session, the moderator needs to know the time allotted to the speaker and to the Q&A session so an introduction and closing can be planned accordingly to fit the time frame. Remember, a moderator is *not* the speaker, so remarks should simply set the stage. A moderator is remembered by how efficiently a session was run within the allotted time … or not.

When serving as the moderator during a virtual presentation, it's important to check the web platform operating system prior to the start of the event for sound quality and presentation functionality. Be sure the system is tested with the speaker 1 day prior or at least 30 minutes before the start of the event to avoid any presentation problems. When beginning the webinar, speak distinctly

Chapter 33 discusses logistics of presentations.

and directly into a phone or microphone, not a computer, as clarity is better. Muting the audience during a virtual presentation is preferred to avoid potential logistical issues and ensure the planned time is available for Q&A.

What Are the Components of a Professional Introduction?

A well-prepared and well-delivered professional introduction serves to connect an audience with the speaker, establishes the speaker's credibility, and builds anticipation and enthusiasm in the audience so they pay attention to the presentation. A quote from the *Tips for Presiding Officers Handbook* (now out of print) of the former American Dietetic Association, now the Academy of Nutrition and Dietetics, summarizes this well:

> *Mastering introductions is mastering an art. An introduction sets the tone for the speech, and often determines the audience's interest and response.*

Address the Audience

To make an introduction, stand at the front of the room so as to be easily seen and heard by the audience. Stand at the podium (or standing microphone) or next to the speaker, if he or she wishes to be at the podium from the beginning rather than coming up after being introduced. Follow the protocol of the event or organization, or ask speakers for their preferences.

Begin with a warm welcome to the audience. Depending on the time of day, this can be as simple as "Good morning [or afternoon or evening]!" Other greetings include "Welcome to …" or "Greetings.…" Extend the greeting with genuine enthusiasm and enough volume to gain the audience's attention and quiet them as needed. If they are not quiet after the first time, repeat the greeting. "It's time to begin" may be commonly used, but it is not an ideal welcome. If it's necessary to say "Please take your seats," first extend a greeting.

Addressing the audience is often a part of the greeting, or it may be necessary to gain attention later in the presentation. Consider ahead of

time what a suitable name for audience members could be. An older, more formal audience may feel comfortable being called *ladies and gentlemen*, but in general, make it a rule to use a gender-neutral title instead, such as *all* or *everyone*. One option is to address them by the location or name of the group, such as "Greetings residents of Central City." If the group is an organization of which you are a member, addressing the audience as "fellow [Rotarians, Toastmasters, Academy of Nutrition and Dietetics members, alumni, and so on]" is a suitable approach. If moderating an event at a place of employment, using the terms *fellow colleagues* or *coworkers* is appropriate.

A group of children could be addressed as *class*, *students*, *friends*, *campers*, *Scouts*, or by the title of their group mascot or school nickname. A group of young children might be addressed by saying, "Hello, friends, I'm so excited to be in your classroom!" A group of teens could be addressed by saying, "Good afternoon, class" or "Welcome to the camp cooking demo, cadets."

Addressing an audience may be necessary at various points throughout a presentation. Avoid calling a professional group "you guys." The older the audience, the more likely they will be offended by this, especially if it is used repeatedly. In its place, simply say *you* or use one of the titles suggested above, whichever best fits the situation.

Introduce Yourself, the Event, the Speaker, and the Topic

After a brief welcome, tell the audience who you are. Introduce yourself before introducing the speaker: "I am …" or "My name is …" The only exception is when it is certain that everyone in the group knows you. If in doubt, tell them. It may be appropriate to also provide your title or the role you play in the program or in the organization represented, such as "I am serving as chair of the spring conference planning committee." As described previously, at the start of an event, in addition to introducing yourself, introduce the event and provide information the audience may need before introducing the first speaker.

Finally, it is time to say, "I have the pleasure of introducing …" or "Our first speaker is …" Provide the speaker's full name, and then throughout the rest of the introduction, refer to the speaker the way he or she prefers to be addressed. For example, an introduction to Jane Smith could be, "It is

Chapter 35 covers additional methods for gaining the attention of an audience.

my pleasure to introduce Dr Jane Smith, professor of nutrition at [X] State University. Dr Smith will be speaking about …" Alternatively, the speaker may want to be referred to as Jane. Then, before giving more background about the speaker, briefly introduce the topic of the presentation. If the title of the speech is self-explanatory, it can be used to introduce the topic, but be sure to elaborate further, as will be discussed, after telling the audience more about the speaker.

Provide Accurate Information About the Speaker

Establishing a speaker's credibility is one of the primary functions of an introduction. Therefore, before delving into more about the topic of the speech, the audience needs to know why the presenter is qualified to speak on the topic. The best source of this information is the speaker. It is common practice for a speaker to provide a short biography (bio) to be used in the introduction, so if one is not available, request one. Speaker profiles may be available from LinkedIn or from professional or personal websites, but confirm the accuracy with the speaker prior to using it.

Select enough background about the speaker to build the person's credibility without going overboard. Consider what the audience may already know and seek to provide new information. If appropriate, make a personal connection with the speaker. Share the facts that will be most relevant to the audience as well as to the topic of the speech.

Relate the Speaker and the Audience to the Topic

Speakers generally present about topics with which they have a personal connection or expertise. Perhaps it is their area of research, or they might have personal experience related to the topic. Talk with the speaker ahead of time to determine how to relate him or her to the topic. However, avoid stealing a story the speaker plans to share as part of the presentation.

In addition to relating the speaker to the topic, try to connect yourself and the audience to the topic when appropriate. For example, saying something like, "Regardless of our place of work, everyone is asking us about the validity of ketogenic diets, so we look forward to hearing …" becomes a way to connect. This will emphasize interest in the presentation and will build interest among the audience.

Again, make sure what is said in the introduction won't take away from the speaker's presentation. The moderator is not there to give the speech, only to introduce it and build excitement.

Invite the Audience to Applaud

An introduction should be completed in less than 2 minutes. If it goes much longer, the audience (and speaker) may get restless. Close with a phrase that includes the speaker's name and invites the audience to applaud, such as, "Now join me in welcoming …" Continue to applaud until the speaker reaches your side at the podium. Shake his or her hand, if extended, and return to a seat. Once seated, be prepared for the unexpected. A speaker may need assistance with the computer or audiovisual controls. In virtual situations, invite the audience to listen after finishing the introduction and turn the webinar system control function over to the speaker.

At the close of a presentation, the speaker will turn the podium back to the moderator. This is a signal to rise and again invite the audience to applaud if they are not already doing so. In an informal setting, you can thank the speaker by standing up at your seat, but in a more formal setting, return to the podium. In a virtual setting, the speaker will end the presentation and turn the hosting function back to the moderator. In this case, thank the speaker and begin the Q&A session.

The Q&A session may take place after the official end of the speech or before the closing remarks. Coordinate the timing with the speaker and event planner (if applicable) before the session starts.

Strategies for effectively moderating a Q&A session are described in the next section as well as in Chapter 36.

What Practical Strategies Enhance a Moderator's Effectiveness?

Being a moderator comes with responsibility. How an introduction is delivered and how well allotted time is maintained within the session will convey to the audience and the speaker the importance the moderator placed on the responsibility.

Prepare an Introduction for the Speaker in Advance

Prepare in advance are the three most important words to remember in this chapter. To set the correct tone and tenor of a session, the moderator needs to be familiar with the speaker's credentials and communicate with the speaker prior to the event regarding the desired information to be highlighted.

Remember, a speaker may submit a bio that would take longer than 2 minutes to deliver; it's the moderator's job to review, summarize, and highlight those accomplishments most appropriate to the intended audience. If the speaker is an acquaintance, add a personal insight to the introductory remarks. If not, contact the speaker and ask how he or she would like to be introduced. Let the speaker's personality shine through the introduction.

Practice Pronouncing the Speaker's Name, Title, and Difficult Words

Each person is a unique individual—with a name that is a reflection of that individuality—making someone's name an important part of an introduction. It is essential to pronounce the speaker's name correctly in an introduction. If the pronunciation of a speaker's name is difficult for you, ask the speaker for the correct pronunciation and write it out phonetically if necessary. Each of us may have words or vowels that we find difficult to pronounce. If a title of a presentation or a speaker's bio includes one of these tongue twisters for you, practice, write it out phonetically, or find a synonym (as long it doesn't change a research or publication title). Correct pronunciation reflects careful preparation.

The speaker is the best source for not only the proper pronunciation of a name but for all aspects of the introduction. Don't hesitate to ask a speaker for assistance in getting it right. Speakers may prefer the use of gender-neutral terms, such as "our speaker," when they are not being referred to by name. Also, asking speakers their preferred pronouns shows respect.

"Every name is real. That's the nature of names."

—JERRY SPINELLI

Show Enthusiasm While Keeping Focus on the Speaker

A moderator has the opportunity to set the stage for the speaker. A moderator's warm smile and friendly voice will help make the speaker feel welcomed and reduce any potential stress as they start their presentation. But remember, the moderator is *not* the speaker, and overshadowing the speaker will only dim the moderator's professionalism. At the end of the introduction, invite the speaker to the podium with a smile and applause.

Assist with Timekeeping, Technology, and Handouts

The role of the moderator may extend beyond the introduction of the speaker, so be prepared for additional responsibilities. Keeping a session or an event within the time scheduled is one of the hardest responsibilities of moderating, but it is most appreciated by the audience and other program participants. If responsible for maintaining the time, consult with the speaker or event planner before the session begins regarding the time allocation for the presentation and Q&A session so everyone is aligned. It is also important to inform the speaker how the end of the session will be communicated if an electronic timer is not available. For some venues, raising one or two fingers signifying remaining minutes works as long as the speaker knows where the moderator is sitting.

A moderator may also be responsible for assisting with technology, such as microphones or computers, and with distribution of handouts. If so, get familiar with the technology in order to help the speaker set up the presentation and to provide emergency help if a glitch occurs during the presentation. In today's world, printed handouts are less common because more organizations post them on their websites or via a mobile app. When printed handouts are provided, coordinate with the speaker about the desired distribution method and timing. It's usually easiest to provide handouts at the back of the room for attendees to pick up as they enter or leave, but at times, it's more appropriate to place a copy at each individual seat.

Moderate Questions and Answers

Moderating a Q&A session involves more than just recognizing a participant with a hand raised to ask a question. Whether the setting is virtual or in person, establishing the ground rules of the Q&A session is the first step. Review these basic guidelines with the audience:

1. You must identify yourself prior to asking a question.
2. You must ask the speaker a question, not give your personal opinions.
3. Your questions must relate to the topic discussed.
4. Ask only one question to allow time for other audience members.[2]

When an audience member goes outside the question guideline boundaries, it's the role of the moderator to maintain control of the Q&A session. If a personal opinion is expressed, the moderator can politely interrupt by asking, "Do you have a question to ask? If not, thank you for your interest." If an audience member starts to ask another question or a question unrelated to the speaker's topic, the moderator has the authority to politely interrupt and remind, "Only one question, please, so others can have theirs answered" or "Please keep your question related to the information presented." It may feel uncomfortable initially to stop an audience member from speaking, but it will be viewed by the majority of the participants as fair and professional. Being consistent is important, as it will help keep the Q&A session under control, especially if a contentious issue is being discussed.

One final reminder when moderating an in-person session: Carefully observe when audience members raise their hands or come to a microphone. It's important to recognize the individuals who have raised their hands first (whether they are seated in the first or the back row). When floor microphones are used, alternate between microphones to acknowledge the order in which audience participants are standing at each.

Depending on the setting and the size of the audience, participants may be instructed to submit written questions either on index cards or via mobile apps. In these cases, the moderator has significant influence on the type of questions being asked. Screening inappropriate questions that are not relevant to the subject matter is within the moderator's guidelines, but it is important to ask a variety of questions to show balance in the dialogue and discussion. Last, regardless of the Q&A session format, closing the session on time

and announcing how additional questions may be answered by the speaker are the final steps to successful Q&A moderation.

Special Considerations for Moderating Panels and Other Events

Moderating a panel involves more preparation time before the event than the introduction of a speaker. A moderator controls the flow of the panel discussion and the engagement of the audience. When moderating a panel, the moderator may be responsible for the logistics of the panel setup, including placement of chairs, speakers' name cards, providing water for the panel members, and seating arrangement of the panel.

Once the logistics are in place, the focus should be on the flow and content of the panel discussion. There is no one way to manage the flow of a panel, but typically the following format is used:

- Introduce yourself as the moderator and state your connection to the panel discussion.
- Explain the format and flow of the panel to the audience.
- Introduce each panel member and start the dialogue by asking the panel members a planned question.
- Allow each panelist to provide a response within the established time frame.[2]

As with other moderator responsibilities, keeping panelists within their allotted time is essential to allowing adequate time for the Q&A segment among panelists and with the audience. At the end of the panel discussion, provide several closing statements that summarize the discussion and thank panel members for participating.

Being a moderator requires not only preparation but the ability to make decisions in the moment and be professional and diplomatic. See the Words of Experience box (page 538) for a real-life example.

The role of moderator can extend beyond educational sessions and panel discussions. Whether the responsibility is emceeing an awards banquet at a workplace or hosting an organization's monthly or annual meeting, the basic principles remain unchanged. Be prepared, be polished, know the audience, and expect the unexpected. For a handy guide, see the Checklist for Moderators on page 540.

Moderating a Panel—When Knowing the Background and Bias of Panel Members Is Important

by Marianne Smith Edge, MS, RDN, LD, FAND, FADA

A moderator needs to know the backgrounds of the panel members and the general content of presentations: this is definitely a rule to live by, as it will help diffuse difficult situations.

A few years ago, I was asked to moderate a session titled the "Sugar Controversy—Taxes, Soda and Public Health" at the National Food Policy Conference in Washington, DC. Knowing that the topic, as well as the panelists, would make it a lively discussion, preparation as the moderator was key. Before the meeting, two calls were convened with all panelists to discuss the content each was presenting and the format for the panel. Following the calls, bios were sent to the conference organizer and me.

During the presentation, panel members provided a balanced viewpoint of the topic by representing the beverage industry, nongovernmental organizations (NGOs), and academia, and set the stage for a potentially lively discussion. All panelists conducted themselves professionally and delivered insightful comments within the established time frames. However, the Q&A segment provided some "spark" to the panel! When answering an audience question about what the beverage industry was doing to reduce soda consumption, the beverage industry representative responded with a comment about "diet soda as a good replacement," which hit a nerve with the NGO panelist.

Knowing the NGO panelist's bias (along with his whispering in my ear, "I have to respond"), I acknowledged his desire to speak, which resulted in a couple of exchanges of opinions about diet sodas and artificial sweeteners between the two panelists. However, after each panelist responded, I interjected politely (and with a little humor), stating, "It's obvious artificial sweeteners is a topic that demands its own panel, but since this panel is about the sugar controversy, let's redirect our attention back to the topic. Are there any more questions from the audience?"

The dialogue among panelists was defused, and audience participation continued until the end of the session. The question may be asked, "Why did you allow the diet soda or artificial sweetener comment in the first place when it was off topic?" Sometimes, a moderator has to weigh the risks and benefits of the immediate situation and make the best judgment call. In this case, if I had not acknowledged the panelist's comment, he would have likely interrupted the discussion and perceived there was general bias against "telling the whole story." By acknowledging his desire to speak yet redirecting the conversation back to the panel topic, I, as the moderator, kept control of the situation, and the panelists felt their issues had been heard. Moderators need to always "stay in the moment," sensing as well as hearing the conversation.

Checklist for Moderators

Before the event:

___ Know the time and the place of event or session.

___ Understand the duties and responsibilities of the moderator.

___ Have introductions and bios of speaker(s).

___ Review and modify the introduction script.

___ Practice and time the introduction to make sure it is 2 minutes or less.

___ Check your ability to pronounce names and all words within the introduction.

___ Schedule a time to meet the speakers in advance of the presentation.

___ Review session logistics of session with the program planner and speaker to ensure that all know the timing of the presentation and Q&A.

During the event:

___ Check in with the program planner or organizer at least 1 hour before the event or presentation.

___ Review the time allocation for remarks and Q&A with the speaker(s) again.

___ Establish a timekeeping system for the notifying speaker if an electronic timer is not available.

___ Check the technology and seating arrangements for the session.

___ Use notes to introduce the presentation, logistics of the session, and speaker.

___ Keep time and notify the speaker within a predetermined time frame when to finish.

___ Provide the audience with ground rules for the Q&A session.

___ Maintain a neutral position during the Q&A session regardless of the questions or topic.

___ Read audience questions or solicit questions from the audience.

___ Foster a cohesive and meaningful dialogue during the Q&A session.

___ Close the Q&A session on time.

___ Provide closing comments and thank the speaker and audience.

KEY POINTS

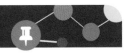

An Effective Presider Sets the Stage

1. **Be ready.** The tone and tenor of the moderator sets the stage for the success of an event or meeting. Know the logistics and flow of the event. A smile and confidence will put the audience and speakers at ease.

2. **Be prepared.** Whether it's your first or 50th time moderating or hosting a session, prepare introductions and remarks in advance and keep on script. This is not the time to ad lib. Practice the pronunciation of all names. If a mistake is made, apologize and proceed.

3. **Know the audience.** Typically, a moderator will be familiar with the audience at the event or session, but it's important to know any potential interest, bias, or hot buttons that may exist among the audience. By understanding the composition of the audience, a moderator can help promote goodwill or defuse any potential tensions.

4. **Expect the unexpected.** Regardless of the preparation or organization by the moderator, the unexpected can happen, from the absence of a speaker to full failure of the technology. How the moderator handles the situation affects how the audience will respond. Maintain composure, work with organizers to create a smooth transition, and above all, add a little humor and smile.

5. **Respect time.** This is the most important rule of moderating a session. Preparation and work will go unnoticed if the session or event extends beyond the allotted time.

RESOURCES

How to moderate a panel effectively: www.fripp .com/how-to-effectively-moderate-a-panel

How to be a great moderator: https://guykawasaki .com/how_to_be_a_gre

REFERENCES

1. Kerber LK. Conference rules, how to lead a panel discussion. *Chronicle of Higher Education.* March 14, 2008. Accessed March 27, 2018. www.chronicle.com/article/Conference-Rules -Part-1/45729
2. Detz J. *Can You Say a Few Words?* St. Martin's Press; 1991.

Successful Audience Management Promotes Communication

Barbara J. Mayfield, MS, RDN, FAND

"When an audience and communicator are in sync with each other, effectively connecting and exchanging ideas and information, the potential to achieve the desired communication outcomes is maximized."

> "Example is not the main thing in influencing others. It is the only thing." —ALBERT SCHWEITZER

Introduction

The goal of audience management is for nutrition communicators to build and maintain an atmosphere of mutual respect that is conducive to effective communication and promotes learning. Audiences of all types can become disengaged, distracted, or disruptive. Learn how to prevent these negative behaviors and promote positive audience attention and engagement.

This chapter answers three questions:

- Why is audience management important?
- What are strategies for audience management?
- How can disruptive audiences be managed?

Audience management doesn't just happen—it is planned for and executed deliberately. Learn principles and practices to help stay focused and aware of the audience and prevent disruptions and disrespectful behavior.

Why Is Audience Management Important?

As stated in Chapter 3, successful communication begins and ends with the audience. When an audience and communicator are in sync with each other—effectively connecting, exchanging ideas, conveying and sharing emotions—the potential to achieve the desired communication outcomes is maximized. Conversely, when an audience and communicator are not attending to one another and are failing to connect, miscommunication is likely. Keep reading to compare situations when audience management succeeds and fails.

An Audience That Is Not Engaged Is Not Learning and Distracts Others

Imagine an experience in which an audience is not engaged with the presentation and has potentially become disruptive. No one seems to be listening or paying attention. They may have been engaged in an audience activity and ignored directions to regroup and focus on the presenter again. They may have been distracted by side conversations, electronic devices, or something taking place through a window or doorway. If any audience members *are* interested in learning, they would have to make extra effort to *not* be distracted by other audience members. This situation is not conducive to learning.

In these situations, the presenter will appear to have lost command of the audience. The presenter may appear oblivious to the audience's lack of attention or may display frustration in attempting to regain attention—if the presenter ever had it to begin with. The audience may also exhibit frustration as audiences naturally expect presenters to gain and maintain attention. Audience members will lose confidence in the presenter and tune out. The desired communication outcomes will not be realized.

Effective Communication Occurs When Both Speaker and Audience Are Listening to One Another

Now imagine an optimal situation in which the presenter and the audience are clearly paying attention to one another. The speaker is tuned in to the audience and responsive to their feedback. The speaker uses effective techniques to gain and maintain attention. Expectations for behavior are clearly communicated. The environment is conducive to listening and learning.

The audience is focused on the speaker and fully participating. Intent on paying attention, the audience blocks out potential distractions and demonstrates respect to the presenter and to one another. The audience is confident the presenter is in charge, leading to greater trust in the presenter's message and greater willingness to follow their lead.[1]

A presenter with strong audience management skills can interact with an audience, direct activities, and maintain attention. Audiences appreciate presenters who create an environment characterized by respect and open communication.[1] The potential for achieving the desired communication outcomes is maximized.

Rudeness and Unprofessional Behavior in Person or Online Undermines Communication Effectiveness

The greatest potential for failed audience management occurs when rudeness or unprofessional behaviors are exhibited. These behaviors can be exhibited in person or online. Examples include snide, sarcastic, or inappropriate comments; put-downs; rude facial expressions or gestures; displays of temper; physical violence; and walking out. These behaviors are less likely to occur when an environment of respect has been achieved and the presenter is modeling professionalism.

The potential for problems is increased when anonymity is allowed.[2] Identifying people by name can help prevent unprofessional behavior both in person and online. This is one reason requesting people to provide their name when making a comment or asking a question is a common practice. Additionally, providing guidance on expected behaviors, such as the pledge of civility described in Chapter 29, can serve as a preventive measure. (See the resources section at the end of this chapter for where to find this pledge.) Responding professionally can prevent escalations in negative behaviors.

Presenters should never exhibit rude or unprofessional behaviors themselves, nor should they allow them in audience members. Civility and professionalism are necessary to build and maintain respect.[1,2] The next section outlines strategies for successful audience management.

What Are Strategies for Audience Management?

Audience management is successfully achieved when a presenter clearly understands what it entails, expectations are clearly defined and communicated, positive behaviors are modeled, and expectations are consistently enforced.[3,4] Acceptable behaviors can vary depending on the setting. A more formal setting will suggest more reserved behaviors. A more casual setting will have more relaxed expectations while still achieving attention, respect, and learning.

The Communicator Is Aware of the Environment and Responsive to the Audience

The person presiding over an event sets the tone and establishes the atmosphere. To be an effective communicator, whether serving as moderator or presenter, it is essential to be aware of everything that is going on in the environment of the presentation and with the audience. Presenters and moderators should sense the mood and respond to it, adapting and adjusting words and actions to create and maintain a productive atmosphere.

Make eye contact purposefully and read the nonverbal feedback from an audience. Are they attentive? Do they appear to understand? Do they seem to be agreeing or disagreeing? Are they distracted by something on their phone or laptop? Read their body language. Are they frowning, with arms crossed? Or are they smiling and nodding in agreement? Respond accordingly. If there is negative feedback, address it respectfully:

"It appears that many of you aren't sure you agree with what I just said. Let's look at the issue from several angles and the evidence for each." Or, "It appears many of you may be confused. Let me explain it another way." The larger the audience, especially in a setting where the lighting makes it difficult to see their faces, the more challenging it will be to perceive audience feedback. It may be necessary to use another approach to solicit their level of engagement. Consider using a polling feature, as described in Chapter 20.

Be open to making adjustments to what is being said and how in order to engage an audience and ensure they understand the message. Asking questions can be an effective method to check in with an audience and find out what they think and if they are following.

Focus on connecting with an audience. Be fully present—focused on reaching the audience with the message—rather than distracted by thoughts of appearance or performance, or worse yet, a totally unrelated task or issue. The next section explores what it means to be fully present and why it is critical for communication success.

Suggested questions to help judge presentation efficacy can be found in Chapter 20.

The Fully Present Communicator Is Able to Control the Environment Without Being Controlling

Effective communicators are fully present. They are actively aware of everything in their presentation environment and seek to fully engage with their audience. To be fully present is to be focused, to be giving full attention. As a presenter, it means being completely focused on presenting a message to an audience. The audience can perceive the presenter's full attention, meaning the presenter is not distracted or multitasking. Imagine watching a speaker who is simultaneously texting on a phone, typing on a laptop, or looking distracted by other thoughts.

When a presenter is fully present, the audience feels confident of the presenter's control of the situation, from the beginning to the end of the presentation, even when they are involved in an activity. Being in control means exercising a responsive type of control, not creating a harsh, controlling type of atmosphere. The communicator who is fully present conveys a sense of authority by demonstrating that he or she is aware of what is going on, confident, and engaged.

To accomplish this goal goes beyond practicing a confident stance and effective eye contact. It requires planning and preparation so the entire presentation time is accounted for, everything is organized to function smoothly, and ground rules are established as needed. Adults and children both respond positively to an organized, structured environment.[4] The speaker who is prepared and organized will also make a good first impression, which promotes audience attention and engagement.

Expectations for Acceptable Behavior Are Established Clearly and Enforced Consistently

All audiences benefit from clearly defined expectations.[4] *Ground rules* is a common term for expectations, but the word *expectations* is more positive than *rules* and is therefore recommended.[5] Rules are generally written with the word *don't*, and expectations tell what to *do*. Young children may need more reminders, but even adults are instructed to silence their cell phones and take noisy children to the lobby at the movie theater. It is wise not to assume that an audience will know what is expected.

How can expectations be conveyed? Going over the expectations or ground rules can be a task of the moderator, if there is one. If announcements are printed in a handout or posted on slides, expectations can be included.

Keep expectations as simple and few as possible. Communicate both expectations and consequences clearly and then follow through if they are violated. As soon as an expectation is not followed or enforced, it ceases to be effective.

EXAMPLES OF EXPECTATIONS WITH GROUPS OF CHILDREN

There are two key expectations for maintaining control with an audience of children:

- Be quiet and pay attention when someone else is talking.
- Request permission to talk by raising a hand.

There may be occasions for additional expectations, such as "Stay seated unless instructed to stand or move." In general, these can be discussed when preparing for a specific activity.

As a guest in a classroom or with a group of children, find out what rules and expectations the teacher has and use the same ones. If possible, observe the group in advance and notice how the teacher or leader enforces the rules.

At the beginning of a presentation, review expectations. One effective approach when using expectations that are already in place is to call on the students to state the expectations out loud. During the presentation, expect the expectations to be followed. If they are not, gently correct the students. For example, if someone starts talking without raising their hand, stop them and say, "Please raise your hand if you wish to answer a question." At times it may be appropriate to diverge from that rule and allow a group of children to answer without raising their hands. If so, say so: "If you know the answer to the next question, you can say it out loud without raising your hand."

EXAMPLES OF EXPECTATIONS WITH ADULTS

With adults, note that expectations apply to both presenters and audience members. For example, communicating that the session will start and end on time is essentially an expectation for the presenter, but it tells audience members to show up promptly if they don't want to miss out. Appropriate expectations may include any combination of factors from this list[6]:

- starting and ending on time
- silencing electronic devices
- saving texting for breaks
- respecting the contributions of others
- maintaining confidentiality
- being open to new ideas
- giving everyone a chance to participate
- resolving differences respectfully
- staying on topic

Select expectations that fit the situation and help prevent anticipated problems. Recall from Chapter 19 the expectations that are important for facilitated discussions, such as confidentiality and giving everyone a chance to participate. At the start of a presentation, it might only be necessary to mention the expectations regarding silencing cell phones and refraining from texting. Add others if needed before starting an activity. Don't overwhelm an audience with expectations; keep it simple.

The best way to enforce expectations with adults is for the presenter to practice them as well and to provide friendly reminders. For example, if

someone's phone rings during a presentation, the presenter could say, "If anyone else still needs to silence their phones, please do so now. And if you need to take a call, please feel free to excuse yourself to the lobby." In a later section in the chapter, we will discuss more ways to handle typical disruptions.

EXAMPLES OF EXPECTATIONS FOR ONLINE COMMUNICATION

Follow the guidelines of professional civility outlined in Chapter 29. Determine whether to allow only comments from people who identify themselves and provide an email address. Post expectations for commenting, such as: "Please keep comments clean, constructive, and respectful." A helpful resource is the Centers for Disease Control's social media public comment policy, which lists potential ideas to implement (see the resources section at the end of this chapter). Respond to all comments in a professional manner, but especially negative comments.

Use a Signal That Audience Members Can Easily Learn to Quiet a Group and Gain Attention

Gaining the attention of an audience that is engaged in an activity or talking while settling into their seats at the beginning of a presentation can be a challenge. In a setting with a stage and a microphone, simply speaking into the microphone can be enough to quiet the group, especially at the start, when they are expecting the program to begin. Later in a presentation, when it is necessary to signal for an activity or discussion to end and for the audience to redirect their attention, select a signal that fits the group, the occasion, and the location. Here are some effective approaches that work with different age groups:

- For all ages: Play music, ring a bell, sound chimes, make a sound with another musical instrument, or set a timer (such as one embedded in PowerPoint) that makes noise when it goes off.
- For all ages: Use hands—raise a hand and everyone in the audience raises their hand and is silent.
- For children: Use hands—say, "Clap three times if you can hear me," or use a clapping

rhythm that the audience responds to by finishing or repeating the rhythm.

- For children: Use a spoken signal, such as: "1, 2, 3, look at me," to which the children reply, "1, 2, I see you." Use the single overriding communication objective, or SOCO, or a key message as a spoken signal by splitting it in half, and when you say the first half, the audience responds with the second half.
- Look for more ideas online (search for "attention signals"). Be creative!

Whatever signal is chosen, practice it before using it. With adults, it is sufficient to tell them what it will be: "When the timer goes off, we'll stop and turn our attention to the front again."

Revisit the idea of SOCO in Chapter 15.

Use Names with Both Children and Adults

Calling people by name gains attention and solicits participation better than pointing or using a description (such as "the person wearing green in the back row"). Using names creates an intimate atmosphere and helps form connections among audience members and with the presenter. If audience members' names aren't known, provide name tags, use table-tent name cards, or ask people to identify themselves before participating. Make it a point to say a person's name when responding to him or her; this helps reinforce it in memory and acknowledges that person's contribution.

Chapter 34 included a discussion of ways to address an audience using gender-neutral titles. (Refer to "What Are the Components of a Professional Introduction?" and "Practice Pronouncing the Speaker's Name, Title, and Difficult Words.") This section will look at how that might be achieved throughout a presentation, when engaging in activities or answering questions. Recall that terms such as *everyone* and *all* are appropriate. For example, imagine the audience has been engaged

in table discussions and it is time to direct them to the next part of the activity: "If everyone would please turn their attention to the table in the front. The first group is ready to share their ideas."

Ideally, address audience members by calling them by name: "Thank you. Did everyone hear what Brenda said?" Relevant gender-neutral pronouns for children include terms such as "your friend" or "your classmate." Using a child's first name, when known, is ideal—for example, when referring to a comment a student made, "Jessie, your classmate shared an excellent idea," or when asking for the class's attention, "Second graders, can you please turn your eyes and ears to our friend John, who is talking?" Use names whenever possible. See the Words of Experience box for an illustration of using name tags to assist in calling people by name.

When referring to people who have a disease or a disability, use what is referred to as people-first language. People-first language recognizes the individual's personhood rather than classifying people by their condition. Say "Mary has diabetes" rather than "Mary is diabetic." If having diabetes isn't relevant, just say Mary. Speaking of names, presenters must also consider what the audience should call them. If the audience should use the presenter's title and surname, be sure those are detailed in the introduction. If they can be less formal, extend permission to use a preferred name: "Good evening, my name is Barbara Mayfield, but please call me Barb." With a group of children, follow the protocol of the organization. When speaking to a school group, a presenter will usually be referred to as Miss, Ms, Mr, Mrs, or Dr and their surname. When speaking to a preschool audience, the presenter may be Miss, Ms, or Mr and their first name.

Provide Clear Instructions When Leading Activities

Prepare clear instructions for any activity involving audience participation. This includes assisting the audience when following along on a handout by directing them to the page and the location on the page where they should focus their attention. When engagement and participation are desired, provide directions for how to contribute or participate in an orderly fashion. It is much easier to describe in advance what an audience should do than to try to regain control later when no directions have been given.

"Remember that a person's name is to that person the sweetest and most important sound in any language." —DALE CARNEGIE

Plan an efficient method for handing things out, getting in line, coming to the front, taking turns, or completing an activity. Take the audience step-by-step through the plan. Write out instructions as needed and include them in printed materials or post where all can see. Ask colleagues or potential audience members to review the instructions ahead of time to see if they are understandable and easily followed.

The younger the audience, the more clarity will be needed in instructions. Plan transitions between activities, plan how to involve everyone so no one is left out or waiting around, and have alternative plans if the original plan doesn't work. Be flexible.

How Can Disruptive Audiences Be Managed?

Ideally, prevent the need to manage an unruly audience by captivating them so effectively that paying attention and participating is easy. Add to that clear expectations that are effectively enforced, and problematic situations will be minimized, but the potential cannot be eliminated.

Recognize the potential for audience members to pose a challenge for the presenter. These challenges range from nonparticipation to taking over and monopolizing the stage. Audience members can disengage, refuse to interact, become distracted or distracting, be belligerent, be whiny, or exhibit any number of undesirable behaviors. The communicator's goal is to maintain a positive atmosphere, respect the individual, and never lose control over the situation. With a little tact, patience, and practice, the most challenging audience member can be handled.

Preventing and Handling the Improper Use of Technology

A technology-free presentation is becoming less and less common. In most settings, expect technology to be present. *Technology* refers to personal cell phones, tablets, laptops, and other types of electronic devices. These devices may be used to follow along with electronic handouts, take notes, look up information, post to social media about the event, or answer polling questions during a speech.

WORDS OF EXPERIENCE

Hello, My Name Is ...

by Barbara J. Mayfield, MS, RDN, FAND

I love name tags! I try hard to learn people's names, but using name tags is a tremendous help. Find out what a person wants to be called—formal title and surname, full name, first name, or nickname. Please call me Barb.

I am a huge proponent of having name tags whenever I give a speech, even going so far as to have larger name cards if I am incorporating discussions and participation activities. I provide blank sheets of paper and markers and instruct the audience to write their first name in large print and then hold up their name card whenever they wish to be called on or if they have a question. It eliminates pointing. A card is raised and their name is called.

My first year of teaching at Purdue, I had a class of over 450 students in a large lecture hall. On the first day of class, I instructed the class to create name cards with their names printed large enough for me to read easily from the front of the room. The students kept them inside their binders or backpacks and got them out during class discussions. Over the semester, I learned about 50 names of students who contributed most often. Rather than feeling like a large, impersonal class, it had an intimate, friendly atmosphere.

In lecture classes I taught with 50 to 100 students, I asked everyone to select a permanent seat so I could create a seating chart, allowing me to call students by name as well as easily identify who was absent. In the smaller lab-based course I taught in nutrition communication, the students created "name tents" that included a personal logo. Students often commented that they appreciated getting to know their classmates by name in my classes. I was asked to write numerous letters of recommendation due to the students' belief that I "knew them better than any other instructor." What contributed to that belief? Calling them by name.

The next time you speak to a group, use their names. See if you notice a difference.

Technology can be useful, but it can also be distracting both to the person using it and others around them. If an audience member is distracted by funny videos on Facebook or is answering a text or email, they are not paying attention and may distract others. It can be disconcerting to the presenter to see audience members looking down at screens rather than paying attention to the presentation. The goal is for technology to enhance the experience, not detract from it.

GUIDELINES FOR ALLOWED USE OF PHONES, TABLETS, AND LAPTOPS

If in a position of authority, consider prohibiting the audience from using electronic devices, or limit it to uses related to the presentation, such as for note-taking. However, if the presenter is a professional peer of the audience, prohibiting use of electronic devices could appear presumptuous. As a minimum, request that electronic devices be silenced and request that calls be taken outside the room.

The presenter will be competing for the attention of the audience if they become distracted by their devices for other purposes. Acknowledge approved uses of their devices and possibly even encourage their use for those purposes. For example, encourage audience members to post tweets about the presentation to their followers, or ask them to look up the answer to a question by giving them an appropriate source. Involve them in a survey using a polling app. Directing the use of devices to those that enhance engagement and understanding may minimize their use for distracting purposes.

DEALING WITH DISRUPTIONS AND DISTRACTIONS

Despite a presenter's best efforts, there will be situations where a cell phone rings or someone's device pings each time they receive an incoming message. A polite reminder to silence cell phones may not even be needed when this happens. Generally, the offender is embarrassed and others will quickly check to be sure their phones are off.

Less easily addressed are situations in which the offender is purposefully being distracting or is oblivious to being the source of a disruption. Moving closer to their area of the room and getting their attention with direct eye contact can refocus their attention. Without appearing frustrated, simply stop talking. Silence can be an effective method for regaining attention. If an audience is one with which the presenter has recurrent encounters, it might be possible to speak to the offender privately between sessions to discuss how to encourage acceptable behaviors.

Avoid calling someone out in front of others, especially adults.

Preventing and Handling Talkative Audience Members

Audience members talk during a presentation for a variety of reasons. A side conversation may occur when someone missed or did not understand what was presented. If this appears to be happening, ask the audience if the information should be repeated or explained in a different way. The more tuned in to the audience, the better the presenter will be at interpreting their reasons for talking.

Audience members may talk during a presentation because they want to express an opinion about the topic. To prevent this from being a distraction, build in times for reflection and discussion. Provide opportunities for the audience to ask questions or state their viewpoints. Suggest in advance that audience members jot down their thoughts as they arise so they will be prepared for an activity.

Preventing and Handling Audience Members Who Challenge the Speaker, Take Over the Floor, or Know It All

One of the more challenging situations for a presenter is handling an audience member who takes over, often during a group discussion or a question-and-answer session. Practice the following guidelines to regain control during this situation:

- Recognize the audience member by name. Identifying the individual often prevents escalations in temper or further challenges, due to being recognized and the subsequent potential for repercussions, such as negative social media postings, feedback to colleagues, and so on. If the person's name is not known, ask for it.
- Acknowledge the individual's contribution and thank them for their viewpoint. Be gracious. Avoid sarcasm, unkind remarks or expressions, or being defensive. Be attentive.
- Determine whether to address what the person said or to move on.
- Strive to keep on topic.
- If necessary, cut the person off in the interest of time: "Thank you for your perspective. In the interest of time, we need to take the next question."

- Maintain a positive and professional demeanor. If the offender is acting hostile in any way, do not match his or her behavior, but remain calm and pleasant.
- Offer to speak to the person later.

An audience will appreciate a presenter for maintaining composure and preventing an unpleasant exchange during the presentation.

Preventing and Handling Late Arrivals and Those Who Walk Out

In some settings, audience members may come and go, which can be distracting to the presenter and others. This is most common at larger conferences, where people may be trying to attend more than one session or may be meeting with others before or after a session. Assume the best about their reasons for arriving and departing rather than taking it personally. In most cases, try to ignore their coming and going.

In some instances, late arrivals will stand in the back rather than move forward to an empty seat. If possible, welcome them and invite them forward without disrupting the flow of the talk. They are more likely to remain for the session and fully participate. This is especially appropriate during natural breaks, such as after an introduction or before beginning an activity. Some locations prohibit people from standing or sitting in aisles or in the back. This makes it essential to help people find empty seats. If this is the case, pause and announce that there are many people standing in the back and if anyone has a vacant seat next to them to raise their hand. It won't take long and it demonstrates respect for the audience.

If presenting to a particular audience frequently, speak privately to anyone who is routinely tardy or leaves early. Contact them via email, phone, or text if they are not around before or after a presentation. They may have a situation that prevents them from being on time or necessitates leaving before the session ends. If not, becoming aware that the presenter notices may prevent future interruptions. To account for this type of situation, at the onset of a series of sessions ask if anyone will have a conflict with arriving on time or need to leave early. This will let everyone know the reason and it won't be viewed as disrespectful.

Dealing with Audience Members Who Refuse to Participate

At times, an audience member may refuse to participate in a group activity. One solution is to create various levels of participation and assign the reticent member the role of observer. An observer can acknowledge whether participants followed directions or provide encouragement. Give the person something specific to observe rather than saying, "You can just watch." Consider ways to involve audience members that are nonthreatening. Invite people to work together.

Refusing to participate may be more common with young children who are shy or who lack confidence in their ability to do an activity. In these situations, provide an easy way for them to be involved. For example, you or someone else could do the activity and ask them to state whether it is being done correctly. Many children enjoy participating vicariously through others. Or, do the activity with them. Often, once they have completed something with another person, they are ready to do it on their own. Avoid pressuring or shaming someone into participating. Opting out of participation may also happen in settings with audience members for whom English is not their first language. Similar to the aforementioned advice, consider ways to help them participate, such as partnering with someone who can provide assistance.

Dealing with Audience Members Who Complain or Whine

If an audience has chosen to be there, as in a conference session, they are less likely to complain or whine. However, in settings like classrooms, these behaviors may be more common. When comments such as "Do we have to …?" or "This is so boring …" are expressed, what can a presenter do? Remain patient and tactful. If appropriate, offer such individuals a choice to sit out and watch others, but don't allow them to get out electronic devices. If full participation is in order, mention how quickly an activity will occur and what will take place next if everyone stays on task. Invite complainers to meet later and ask them to provide more details for their complaint and suggested alternatives. Complainers are often silenced when they are given an ear. The goal is to prevent others from joining their chorus.

See the resources section at the end of this chapter for additional suggestions for dealing with difficult audience members.

Effective audience management can be summarized in three words: *Be fully present*. When communicators are fully present—focused on connecting with the audience—they are more likely to engage their audience in ways that prevent problem behaviors and will be able to respond quickly and effectively to any situations that arise. When an audience is fully present, they will not be distracted or distracting. They will attend and listen, participate and provide feedback, and contribute to the achievement of the desired outcomes. As a communicator or an audience member, strive to be fully present. Use the checklist provided to prepare for effective audience management.

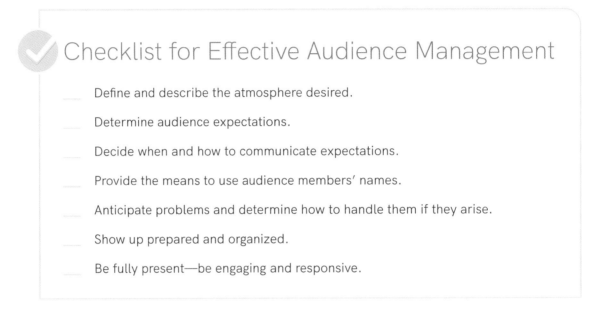

Checklist for Effective Audience Management

___ Define and describe the atmosphere desired.

___ Determine audience expectations.

___ Decide when and how to communicate expectations.

___ Provide the means to use audience members' names.

___ Anticipate problems and determine how to handle them if they arise.

___ Show up prepared and organized.

___ Be fully present—be engaging and responsive.

KEY POINTS

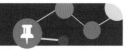

Successful Audience Management Promotes Communication

1 The goal of audience management is to build and maintain an atmosphere of mutual respect that is conducive to effective communication and promotes learning. Audiences of all types can become disengaged, distracted, or disruptive. Prevent these negative behaviors and promote positive audience attention and engagement.

2 When an audience and communicator are in sync with each other, effectively connecting and exchanging ideas and information, the potential to achieve the desired communication outcomes is maximized. Conversely, when an audience and communicator are clearly not attending to one another and are failing to connect, miscommunication is likely.

3 Audience management is successfully achieved when it is clearly defined, expectations are communicated, positive behaviors are modeled, and expectations are consistently enforced. Acceptable behaviors can vary depending on the setting. A more formal setting will suggest more reserved behaviors. A more casual setting will have different, less restrictive expectations while still achieving attention, respect, and learning.

4 At times audience members will pose a challenge for the presenter. These challenges range from nonparticipation to taking over and monopolizing the stage. The communicator's goal is to maintain a positive atmosphere, respect the individual, and never lose control over the situation. With a little tact, patience, and practice, a presenter can handle the most challenging audience member.

RESOURCES

Pledge of Professional Civility: https://foodandnutrition.org/professionalcivility/pledge

Centers for Disease Control social media public comment policy: www.cdc.gov/socialmedia/tools /CommentPolicy.html

Ideas for handling difficult audience members and situations: www.thoughtco.com/manage -disruptive-behavior-in-classroom-31634

Audience management slides, examples of disruptive audience members: www.slideshare.net /KristjanoMonka/audience-management-61828331

Dealing with audiences and devices: https://blog .powerspeaking.com/topic/audience-management

Presenting to a difficult audience: https://peterstark.com/presenting-difficult-audience

REFERENCES

1. Weiss M. *Presentation Skills: Educate, Inspire and Engage Your Audience.* Business Expert Press; 2015.
2. Maia R, Rezende T. Respect and disrespect in deliberation across the networked media environment: examining multiple paths of political talk. *J Comput Commun.* 2016;21(2):121-139.
3. Sabatine J. Managerial effectiveness: a quick guide to setting clear expectations. *Am Med Writ Assoc J.* 2012;77(2):77.
4. Skiba R, Ormiston H, Martinez S, Cummings J. Teaching the social curriculum: classroom management as behavioral instruction. *Theory Pract.* 2016;55(2):120-128.
5. Meador D. Classroom strategies for improving behavior management. ThoughtCo. Published 2017. Accessed April 14, 2018. www.thoughtco .com/classroom-strategies-for-improving -behavior-management-3194622
6. Peterson D. Manage disruptive behavior in the classroom. ThoughtCo. Published 2017. Accessed April 14, 2018. www.thoughtco.com/manage -disruptive-behavior-in-classroom-31634

CHAPTER 36

Strengthen Communication by Effectively Responding to Questions

Marianne Smith Edge, MS, RDN, LD, FAND, FADA
Katie McKee, MCN, RDN, LD
and Barbara J. Mayfield, MS, RDN, FAND

"An effective presentation will stimulate audience questions, and a well-run question-and-answer session is an excellent opportunity for a speaker to make sure content is understood and to reinforce key messages."

> "You can tell whether a man is clever by his answers. You can tell whether a man is wise by his questions." —NAGUIB MAHFOUZ

Introduction

An effective presentation will stimulate audience questions, and a well-run question-and-answer (Q&A) session is an excellent opportunity for a speaker to make sure content is understood and to reinforce key messages. A presentation that sparks the audience's curiosity is likely to prompt the most questions. If an audience is unresponsive to a call for questions, it may be a signal they aren't interested in learning more rather than a sign that all of their questions were answered. Encourage questions and help the audience formulate good ones. Learn how to answer even the most difficult questions.

This chapter answers four questions:

- What is the role of the Q&A?
- How does a nutrition professional effectively call for and respond to questions?
- How does a nutrition professional deal with difficult questions?
- What are practical strategies to ensure successful Q&A?

Don't shy away from the Q&A in presentations. Questions are a sign that an audience is interested and wants to learn more. This chapter will discuss the Q&A and how to effectively call for, listen to, and respond to questions.

> "It is better to ask some of the questions than to know all the answers." —JAMES THURBER

What Is the Role of the Question-and-Answer Session?

The Q&A session following a presentation is just as important as the planned presentation and can be a way to highlight key points. As a speaker, preparing for a Q&A session is equally as important as preparing the remarks. Understanding the audience and anticipating their questions will help frame responses to potential questions.

Demonstrates the Audience's Interest in the Topic and a Desire to Learn

Questions following a presentation should be viewed as a positive response to the topic presented, as they can demonstrate the audience's interest in the topic and promote engagement. The Q&A can be an excellent opportunity to reinforce a message, so embrace it and be prepared. A speaker may even stimulate an audience to ask questions by providing the moderator or program planner with a few typical questions before the presentation, which can then be asked if the audience remains silent after the presentation. When serving as a moderator, being prepared with a question or two at the conclusion of the presentation is good practice.

Provides the Opportunity to Clear Up Confusion

During a presentation, time restraints can limit thorough explanations of complex thoughts or ideas. The Q&A session serves as an opportunity to provide more in-depth explanation about these concepts. An observant speaker can usually tell if the audience is confused about a point being presented, and so will further explain it even if the audience doesn't ask. The greater detail or context provided by the explanation can result in a grateful audience that feels more confident in their knowledge and views the presentation more favorably.[1]

Provides the Opportunity to Expand on Information Provided

The Q&A session allows the speaker to provide more background on an issue or subject matter mentioned in the presentation. If statistics were used in the presentation to highlight a key point, the Q&A session can be used to provide more detail about how they were derived. Use of personal stories or examples can also give needed context to the presented information, improving the audience's understanding of the information. The additional detail provided by speakers reflects their knowledge base of the subject matter and reinforces their credibility.

Provides the Opportunity to Reinforce Key Messages

The Q&A session is also an opportunity for the speaker to reinforce the main points or key messages of the presentation. Think about key messages in the context of "What would you want to see on Twitter?" Whether the questions asked by the audience address the key messages or not, it is important for a speaker to summarize and emphasize the key concepts. An audience should be able to leave a presentation and communicate the main points to a colleague. The final 30 seconds of a presentation leave a lasting impression with the audience. It's vital for the speaker to be prepared to make that positive impact.

How Does a Nutrition Professional Effectively Call for and Respond to Questions?

The Q&A is an opportunity to field questions, which is the intentional act of calling for, listening to, and providing impromptu answers to questions from an audience. It conjures up images of a press conference but fits many scenarios—taking questions during or at the end of a conference presentation, during an online webinar, in a classroom setting, or during a meeting.

Questions can be posed in a variety of ways. They can be delivered verbally or in writing. They may come in person in real time or be delivered electronically, either in the moment or delayed. In larger venues, submitting questions via an app on participants' smartphones is becoming commonplace. Audience members can view and score questions they are most interested in having answered. This method has both benefits and drawbacks. It promotes asking and endorsing questions as well as helps speakers or moderators determine which questions are most popular. However, it does pose a potential distraction to both speakers and audience members. Focusing on what is being presented can be more difficult if paying attention to a stream of questions.

Likewise, questions can be answered multiple ways: verbally or in writing, in real time or later. The principles for fielding questions effectively are largely the same no matter the setting or how they are posed.

To answer questions most effectively requires more than simply knowing the right answer. It also involves listening, making sure the question is clearly stated, and demonstrating respect for the questioner or individual who is seeking information. The steps for effectively fielding questions, which are outlined next, can be applied in most settings and to answering questions from an individual as well as from members of a larger audience.

Listen (or Read) the Question Fully Without Formulating an Answer

The first step in responding to a question is to listen. Really listen. Pay attention to the question, the entire question, without formulating an answer. If an answer is formulated before the questioner is finished, the wrong question may be answered. To listen carefully demonstrates respect to the questioner and the audience. It can also provide the presenter with a more complete understanding of the question. As further described shortly, make sure to understand the question. If the answer doesn't match the question, the presenter will be considered the poor communicator.

In addition to listening well, fully observe the person asking, looking for nonverbal cues. These can include facial expressions, where the person is looking, crossed arms or hands on their hips, and fidgeting or shifting motions. Even if the person can't be seen, listen for their tone of voice. If the question is in writing, observe the overall tone of writing. Is the audience member confused about, or in disagreement with, something that was said? An effective response accounts for the tone conveyed as well as the question itself.

Recognize the possibility of a hidden, unasked question. This is when an unspoken question is what the questioner is most interested in getting answered. The nutrition communicator should consider whether a question is the actual question or is disguising an unspoken question. People can be hesitant to share their true questions due to fear, insecurity, or intimidation. Good listeners look beyond what's being asked and discern the questioner's motive and intent. For example, a questioner may simply ask, "What is …?" and appear to be requesting a straightforward definition, but that person may actually be asking, "Why should I care about …?" By responding with more than a definition, the nutrition communicator can help the questioner understand the bigger picture and recognize the value of understanding the subject. As described later, ask follow-up questions to help understand not only the question, but the context.

Pause Briefly to Organize Your Thoughts

Take a moment to organize your thoughts and prepare an answer. There is power in silence. It demonstrates respect to the audience member that his or her question is worthy of thought. Unless the pause goes on for a long time, it does not make the presenter appear ignorant. A brief pause makes a communicator appear thoughtful, wise, and considerate.

In Person, Repeat the Question

Repeating the question is not a hard-and-fast rule, but it is important in many settings. For example, if other audience members did not hear the question, repeating it demonstrates a desire to involve and share information with everyone and eliminates the appearance that the answer is solely for the questioner. Repeating the question also clarifies that the presenter heard and understood the question correctly, and gives more time to formulate a good response. When repeating the question, it can even be upgraded to a better question—not a different question, but a question more in line with the key messages. In the section that follows on answering difficult questions, this technique will be further discussed.

A question can be repeated either as a question or as the beginning of the answer. For example: "The question was what foods are the best sources of …" To include the question in the answer, the nutrition communicator could say: "To answer the question of which foods are the best sources of …, they include …" The answer can also include enough of the question without repeating it, by simply stating: "The foods that are the best sources of … include …." The last approach is recommended in media interviews and other settings that may be quoted. It allows the quote to be complete without including the question. Note how much more effective all three of these responses are compared to answering the question without repeating it and only giving a list of foods. Audience members who missed the question may not know what the answer referred to.

Summarize the Answer

Begin a response with a one- or two-sentence summary of the answer. If possible, tie the response back to a key point. Using the example just discussed, the answer could begin with, "The foods that are the best sources of beta carotene are primarily bright red or orange fruits and vegetables. As we discussed, a plant food's color can serve as a clue to which nutrients it contains." This could be followed with specific examples.

Provide Supporting Evidence or an Example

When answering a question, if only the most direct, concise response is provided, the opportunity is lost to improve understanding by providing context and a more complete explanation.[1] Skilled communicators recognize the intent of the question and seek to meet the questioner's need to know not just what, but possibly who, or how, or when, or why. Focus on enhancing understanding.

When providing additional explanation in the form of evidence or an example, a good guideline is to provide a brief answer and add one supporting piece of evidence—a statistic, an example, a reason, a fact, even an opinion or quotation (if clearly indicated as such). This suggests that although just one main piece of support is being given, more details could be provided if the questioner, or others, wish to know more. Making it clear that further explanation is an option avoids boring the audience with more than they want to know. Let someone ask for more information.

The supporting evidence may emphasize what was already shared in the presentation, or even better, provide additional depth or context. The nutrition communicator in our example could share that beta carotene is a pigment that gives plants their orange color. To suggest that there's more to say, the communicator could follow that with, "Carrots and sweet potatoes aren't the only food sources high in beta carotene." This might solicit a follow-up question: "What are other sources?" As discussed in Chapter 32, this technique is called *hooking*. Use it to express an openness to furthering the conversation without rambling on with an answer.

Summarize the Answer or Key Point

In closing, an answer can be made stronger by restating the initial response or by emphasizing a related key point—for example, "Remember to eat many different-colored fruits and vegetables to get a variety of nutrients."

Don't end with a statement that weakens the response, such as, "I don't know if that answered your question," or, "I really don't know any more than that." Just end. Smile and turn to the audience to demonstrate an openness to more questions.

In summary, answer a question following these steps: Listen, pause, repeat, summarize, elaborate, and end with a restatement of the response or a key point. Be complete, but answer as briefly as possible. For a handy reminder of the steps for effectively fielding questions, see Box 36.1.

 Steps for Fielding Questions Effectively

1. Listen to (or read) a question fully without formulating an answer.
2. Pause briefly to organize your thoughts.
3. Repeat the question, as needed, to allow all to hear it and to ensure that the question was understood correctly.
4. Summarize the answer.
5. Elaborate on the answer with *one* piece of supporting evidence or an example.
6. End by repeating the summary or by tying the answer to a key point.

If time runs out, provide a means for the audience to ask further questions, such as meeting during the break or emailing questions. End on a positive note and in control of the closing remarks.

How Does a Nutrition Professional Deal with Difficult Questions?

When someone asks a difficult question, such as one that is long and complex, confusing, not well thought out, intended to intimidate, or inappropriate to the time or place, what can a presenter do? Try to get a better question: Ask for the question to be repeated, ask for clarification, or ask for a definition. Or, ask a question in return to help the questioner focus the question. This section will explore a variety of common difficult questions and potential ways to deal with them professionally.

Off-the-Subject or Limited-Interest Questions

These questions take the discussion off the focus of a presentation or meeting. For the question that is off the subject or unrelated to the topic, politely ask

Refer to Chapter 17 for how to close a presentation following a Q&A.

the questioner to rephrase the question so it is more related to the topic, or request to discuss the answer later privately unless it is possible to respond quickly and move on. If there is a way to relate the question to the subject, it is a win-win for all. For example, suppose that following a presentation about healthy aging, an audience member asks about the connection between obesity and high-fructose corn syrup. A response may be, "Are you asking about the obesity rate of older adults and potential causes? If so, this is what we know …"

A limited-interest question is similar to an off-subject one. Before assuming it is of limited interest, find out if it does interest others: "Does anyone else have this concern?" Don't ask it as if they don't; it will be reflected in your tone of voice and appear condescending. It may turn out the question is not as limited as it first appeared. When answering, try to bridge the response to the bigger picture. An example of a limited-interest question following a presentation on healthy aging could be, "What percentage of adults over the age of 75 are currently residing in long-term care?" A response could be, "The majority of adults over the age of 75 live independently, underscoring the importance of healthy aging. I do not know the exact number, but it's less than …"

Within this category of off-subject or limited-interest questions is the question that seems off the wall or a bit crazy. It may be asked to stump, embarrass, or test the presenter. Even these questions merit respect to the asker and a professional response.

The "Stupid" Question

There is an old saying: "There is no such thing as a stupid question." Certainly, don't say a question is dumb—avoid even thinking it. The best example of a stupid question is one that is fairly obvious, but that just means it's obvious to you. Probe, because this might reveal a deeper question that provides insight to the questioner and might help to clarify one of the key messages.

To put it into the context of this book, a stupid question asked after reading the 35 previous chapters might be, "What is a needs assessment?" However, if that question was asked at the beginning of reading the book, it wouldn't seem like a stupid question at all. Now, its answer should be something the reader is familiar with and understands. It's the kind of question that might make

everyone else in an audience groan because they all know the answer.

Help the questioner save face. Respond with something like: "Let's look at the answer to that together." Maybe probe the questioner for what is unclear or pose the question to the entire audience, or break it up into parts that provide for a quick review that obviously the questioner needs and could benefit everyone. Avoid the temptation to make a sarcastic comment about sleeping during the session.

Rambling or Long-Winded Questions

A question that goes on and on is most likely a mini-speech rather than a question. The audience will appreciate it when the presenter says, "I'm sorry, but I must interrupt you in the interest of time." or "I appreciate your perspective; did you have a question?" In response, rephrase the main idea briefly and give an answer.

Multiquestions

At times, people will ask two or more questions, even when requested to ask only one. There are several options for how to handle this. Remember each question, and answer them quickly. If that is too difficult or time-consuming, ask the questioner which question they want answered, or select one to answer. Preface the answer with something like, "Allow me to answer your last question…" If there is time to answer all of them, ask that they be stated one at a time and answer them individually.

I-Don't-Know Questions

This is the question everyone dreads. Nutrition communicators will never know the answer to every question, but they should know how to answer most questions related to the content of a presentation. Preparing ahead of time and anticipating potential questions should eliminate the potential for having to say "I don't know" very often.

If the presenter does not know the answer, he or she should be honest. There are several ways to handle this type of question effectively:

- Depending on the audience, defer to them: "Is there someone who can answer this question?" This works only if the presenter is comfortable that audience members are knowledgeable and willing to share. Base this decision on the makeup of the audience. Be certain the answer that is received will be accurate and evidence-based. An example of an audience where this approach works well is a university seminar with researchers in the audience who are knowledgeable about the topic.

- Ask the audience member to send the question in an email later, allowing some time for researching the answer. This response is appropriate when a presenter is not capable of giving an on-the-spot answer but has confidence in being able to find the answer. Make sure to follow through with a reply.
- If a partial or related answer is possible, say: "I don't know …, but I do know … and …" Use this technique if the answer helps summarize a key point.
- Also consider times when no one knows the answer to the question posed. The answer may be that further study is needed before the answer is known.

Hostile Questions

When questioners are angry or upset, have them identify themselves and call them by name—it will soften the hostility. Try to determine the reason for their hostility. Allow them to briefly state their opinions, since that is likely what they want to do. Thank them for their input and state, "I respect your opinion," as that may be the only appropriate response. If there is a commonly known factual response to a question, give it objectively, without emotion. Or, agree to discuss the subject in private later. In this situation, any specific answer by the speaker will not usually calm the questioner. Do not match their hostility. Acknowledge and respect them.

Questions About Controversial Topics

When someone asks a question about a controversial topic, begin by identifying the reason behind the question. What prompted the person to ask? Probe with a return question, such as, "Did you recently read or hear something that sparked your interest in this topic?" The better the presenter understands the questioner's viewpoint, the better the odds of formulating a suitable response.

People often hold strong differing viewpoints on controversial topics. Look for common ground. This allows for an identification of areas of agreement and helps in the formulation of a response that is less likely to become an argument. Provide solid evidence and examples for context. Don't overwhelm the questioner with too much information. Recognize the differences of opinions and acknowledge that agreeing to disagree may be the best course. See the Words of Experience box for an example of handling a difficult question.

What Are Practical Strategies to Ensure A Successful Question-and-Answer Session?

Effectively answering questions is key to being an effective communicator. Q&A sessions may feel like entering the unknown, but with skill they can be used to successfully communicate. It's all about knowing the audience, anticipating questions, listening well, and thoughtfully formulating and delivering responses. Practice may or may not make perfect, but it does lead to increased skill and confidence. It may not be possible to predict the future, but it is possible to prepare for it.

Practice and Prepare

Just like practicing key messages, take time to practice responses to anticipated questions. Many presenters dread the Q&A session because they fear the loss of control. The more presenters prepare, the more at ease they'll feel. Feeling at ease may help to maintain control and answer questions effectively while reinforcing the main points.

Typical audience questions may be familiar from previously presenting on a topic. If this is a first time presenting on the topic, think about your own questions. Likely many of them have been answered, but an audience member may want more context or clarification. Another strategy is to seek feedback from colleagues, friends, and family about potential questions. They may ask something that hasn't yet been considered.

Focus on feeling confident and prepared when practicing and when presenting. Remember that audience questions can be a positive sign. In most cases, it means an audience was engaged in the presentation and wants to know more.

The Toastmasters website offers helpful references for speakers, from tips about Q&A

A Limited-Interest Question Meets the Hostile and Controversial Question by Marianne Smith Edge, MS, RDN, LD, FAND, FADA

"Expect the unexpected" is a quote that was never more appropriate than at an annual Academy of Nutrition & Dietetics Food & Nutrition Conference & Expo (FNCE). Several years ago, the International Food Information Council (IFIC) Foundation submitted a Chemicals in Food educational session for FNCE during the time I was part of their senior management team. It was approved through the normal professional development process, with subject-matter expert speakers confirmed. Understanding that the subject matter could be viewed as controversial by some, the IFIC Foundation knew it was important to give speakers autonomy when preparing their presentations. During the presentations, it was obvious that some of the speakers' remarks were not received well by all audience members. When the presentations were finished, I, in my role as moderator, opened the Q&A session, with a long line of audience members waiting at the microphones. In accordance with procedure, audience members were recognized and questions were asked of speakers. However, when one of the audience members was recognized, her question started with, "This is a question for the moderator. I want to know if IFIC funded this session and how it was approved." Hearing the tone and tenor of the question and knowing that the individual asking the question was not a fan of IFIC, I repeated the question and responded in a balanced tone, citing the facts that the presentation went through the same procedure as all others and that the speakers' expenses were paid according to policy but with no involvement in subject matter by the IFIC Foundation. This was definitely a limited-interest question, but due to the sensitivity of the question and subject, it was important to be transparent. It was apparent that the answer was not satisfactory to the questioner, but it was appreciated by the silent majority. When intentionally hostile questions are asked, the presenter's answer will probably never satisfy the questioner, but transparency and truth will be appreciated by most.

sessions to Table Topics. *Table Topics* are questions or prompts about a particular theme posed during a Toastmasters meeting, which allow practice with impromptu speaking to help build skill and comfort level with answering questions.[2-4] For Toastmaster resources, see the resources section at the end of this chapter.

Experience is another valuable tool. The more Q&A sessions are engaged in, the more prepared a presenter will be for future questions. Common questions on a topic are referred to as FAQs, or frequently asked questions. See the Words of Experience box titled "Anticipate the Question" on page 560 for an example of knowing the FAQs about a topic.

Make Sure Everyone in the Audience Hears the Question and Feels Involved in the Response

Clearly restating the question asked is important. It allows everyone in the room to hear the question, allows a few moments for gathering one's thoughts, and makes everyone feel included. Restating the question also saves time from having to answer the same question twice.

Maintain Professional Delivery

A Q&A session can be tense. Everyone eats; therefore, everyone has opinions about food and nutrition. This chapter has given tips for addressing many types of questions, ranging from those that are off the subject to those that are hostile. These are a few tips for successfully addressing questions:

- Answer each question as best as possible. If needed, ask for some clarifications of what the questioner is really asking.
- Know that it may not be possible to answer every question to someone's satisfaction.
- Share what answers are known and offer to find the answers that aren't immediately available.

- End with a final thought. Decide when to end the Q&A session. Take one last question. Close the session with the statement the audience should remember once they've left the presentation.

Responding to Panel Question-and-Answer Sessions

Refer to Chapter 34 when serving in the moderator role.

When participating in a panel presentation, the Q&A session is a planned component of the allotted time and will be coordinated by the moderator of the session. The guidelines of fielding questions during a panel Q&A are the same, with a few additional nuances. During the Q&A session, the moderator may begin with a planned question for each panelist prior to opening the session to the audience. What follows are guidelines for panelists.

WORDS OF EXPERIENCE

Anticipate the Question

by Katie McKee, MCN, RDN, LD

As a registered dietitian nutritionist working for the local dairy council, my world is all things milk, cheese, and yogurt. It may seem that dairy foods is a limited topic, but it's really quite diverse. I've presented on high-quality protein, culinary modifications for allergies and intolerances, Dietary Approaches to Stop Hypertension (DASH), and the journey of milk from farm to fridge. The Q&A session offers valuable feedback for what the audience learned as well as what piqued their interest.

Many times, the Q&A session becomes the FAQs—or frequently asked questions—session. Health professionals and consumers want to know more about where their food comes from, and for dairy, that means they want to know more about the farm. Before each presentation, I know the audience is likely to ask about animal care, antibiotic use in animal agriculture, and artificial hormones in cows. In addition, I'm usually asked about dairy's nutrient profile compared to other foods. It isn't always possible to know the questions that will be asked, but it is possible to prepare for the questions that may be asked. Knowing the FAQs is important. Plus, already knowing the answers will boost confidence while tackling this portion of the presentation.

When audience participation begins, *listen* is the key word to remember. An audience member may direct their question to a particular panelist or open with "This question is for any of the panel members." When a question is open to all panelists and you have insights to share, state, "I can respond to that" when the questioner is finished posing the question. If another panel member provides an answer, add a comment by stating, "I can also add …" If you have no comments to add, it's appropriate to remain silent or respond, "I have no additional comments."

In addition to taking questions from the audience, there will be times that panel members ask each other a question for clarification of a position. Regardless of the manner in which the question is asked, respect should be shown to fellow panel members by acknowledging in a clear, balanced tone, "Thank you for asking. As I mentioned previously …" or "I recognize there may be a difference of opinion, but my position is based on …" Likewise, if asking a question of another panel member, the same courtesy needs to be extended. The value of a panel is the diversity of opinions and backgrounds. Participation in panel Q&A sessions can be one of the most beneficial learning experiences for developing good skills in responding to questions.

Responding to Virtual Question-and-Answer Sessions

Webinars are a great way to engage an audience virtually. Technology can have its challenges, and participating in a successful webinar Q&A session is all about planning and preparation. Before the webinar begins, determine how questions will be handled. Will a moderator collect them throughout the presentation or open it up to the audience at the end? Will participants raise hands or add questions to the chat? Being comfortable with the moderator can be the key to success. Many presenters are nervous about what could go wrong with technology. Knowing that there is a plan to answer questions at the end of the webinar can ease anxiety. Here are a few additional tips for handling Q&A during a virtual presentation:

- Establish a defined time allotment with the moderator prior to the start of the webinar. Webinars are usually scheduled for an hour. Depending on the topic, plan on 10 to 15 minutes to answer questions.

- Create a system for fielding questions that come in. Many times the moderator will collect the questions that come in via the chat function or by email. If a significant amount of questions are anticipated, or if questions can be asked via multiple venues, seek additional support to help flag questions as they are asked and pass them along to the moderator.
- Offer to answer questions off-line. Often there are more questions to be answered when the webinar finishes. Provide contact information for participants to follow up if their questions were not answered.

If acting as a virtual moderator, here are a few items to ensure success:

- Set the stage: Provide instructions to the audience regarding submission of questions during the webinar.
- Be prepared: Brainstorm a few questions ahead of time with the speaker in case the audience is slow to ask questions or asks many of the same questions.

- Be proactive: Collect comments throughout the session. Use a flagging feature if available in order to easily access questions at the end of the presentation.
- Ask out loud: Verbally relay questions to the speaker. This prevents the speaker from sorting through the written questions and informs the audience about what's been asked.

End by Emphasizing the Key Message

Before beginning a presentation, know the ending. Closing statements when leaving the stage or finishing a webinar may be the main information the audience remembers. If answering a question via email, the reader may only pay attention to the first line. Be as effective in communication as possible. Consider closing with a summary of key points and any relevant points covered during the Q&A to help reinforce the most important information communicated.

KEY POINTS

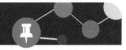

Strengthen Communication by Effectively Responding to Questions

1. View the question-and-answer (Q&A) session as an opportunity to end a presentation effectively. When answering questions, be clear, concise, and complete. Also take the opportunity to reinforce key messages before finishing.

2. The presenter is in control of the Q&A session. When responding to questions, it is important to really listen to the question. Repeating the question back to the audience ensures that everyone has heard it and is anticipating the answer. If necessary, take a moment to collect your thoughts before responding. When answering, make sure to elaborate on a key piece of evidence and share the information the audience should remember.

3. Embrace difficult questions. Develop a strategy for reducing any potential fear of a difficult question. Answer the question briefly and move on to take another one, or seek to have a more answerable question by asking for clarity.

4. Practice makes perfect. While it isn't possible to anticipate every question that will be asked, it is possible to plan for potential questions and practice appropriate responses. This will lead to stronger confidence and a feeling of being in control during the Q&A session.

RESOURCES

Toastmasters International:
- http://toastmasters.wikia.com/wiki/Question -and-Answer_Session
- www.toastmasters.org/Magazine/Articles/Table -Topics-Workout
- www.toastmasters.org/resources/public-speaking -tips

Fearless Presentations: www.fearlesspresentations .com/handling-questions-answers/

REFERENCES

1. LeFever L. *The Art of Explanation.* John Wiley and Sons; 2013.
2. Mitchell O. How to prepare for your Q&A session. Accessed April 20, 2018. https://speakingaboutpresenting.com/audience /how-to-prepare-for-a-qa-session
3. Question-and-answer session. Toastmasters Wiki. Accessed April 20, 2018. http://toastmasters.wikia .com/wiki/Question-and-Answer_Session
4. Zappala M. A table topics workout. Toastmasters International website. Accessed April 20, 2018. www.toastmasters.org/Magazine/Articles/Table -Topics-Workout

Market Products, Programs, and Messages to Maximize Response

Ilene V. Smith, MS, RDN
and Wendy H. Weiss, MA, RD

"*Effective marketing successfully drives awareness, engagement, and action.*"

> "Managing your marketing approach can be defined as the analysis, planning, implementation, and control of programs designed to bring about desired exchanges with target audiences for the purpose of personal or mutual gain. It relies heavily on the adaptation and coordination of product, price, promotion, and place for achieving effective response." —**PHILIP KOTLER**[1]

Introduction

It may not seem like there is a need to understand marketing principles as a food and nutrition professional. Not true. For nutrition communicators with something to share, effective marketing helps to ensure that the target audience takes notice and responds as desired. Aligning social marketing principles with behavior change theories, which were covered in Chapters 10 and 12, can help to increase the likelihood of meeting objectives and desired responses, which may include increased awareness, observed behavior change, greater program attendance, or new referrals and work streams. Identify and engage with a target audience, raise awareness of an issue or opportunity, express value, address barriers to participation, and most important, drive a desired action in order to maximize the desired response.

All nutrition communicators, no matter what they are promoting, can improve their expected outcomes by understanding and implementing marketing strategies.

This chapter answers three questions:

- What is the role of marketing in nutrition communications?
- How does one develop a marketing strategy that ensures success?
- What are potential methods for marketing?

Equipped with the answers to these questions, nutrition communicators will more effectively reach audiences and deliver effective messages.

What Is the Role of Marketing in Nutrition Communications?

Put simply, the ultimate role of nutrition communication is to promote positive behaviors. Whether the goal is to have someone eat a more balanced diet, reduce their sodium intake, get adequate vitamin C, or consume a specific food because of its nutritional properties, it involves human behavior. The same is true when nutrition communicators take on a marketing role. In marketing, influencing behaviors ultimately depends on the target's mind-set. This may mean building awareness, shifting attitudes, developing a relationship with the audience, or engaging in activities that facilitate behavior change.

Build Awareness

The stages of change model[2] pictured on page 179 illustrates the role of nutrition communication along the path to behavior change. For example, someone may be at the first stage, precontemplation. In the behavior change model, that phase is when the person does not yet acknowledge that a behavior change is needed.

This is when building awareness is critical. The marketing techniques used to build awareness will vary depending on the established goals. For example, the goal may be to make an audience aware of a practice, a business or organization, a service, or a product. There may be a specific nutrition message, such as raising awareness of a shortfall nutrient. The task may be to raise awareness that the audience needs to consume more of a certain food group, like whole grains, or to consume a certain product because it belongs in that food group (eg, eat oats more often). The nutrition communicator's role may be to raise awareness of the nutritional benefits of a specific brand or family of brands (eg, Grandma's Oats contain 16 g of whole grains per serving). Case Study 1[3,4] in Box 37.1 is an example of a scenario where raising awareness is the goal.

Shift Attitudes

Target audiences who are further along in the stages of change may be well aware of their need to change behavior but, for various reasons, have an attitude or belief that prevents them from making that change. Using an example of fiber and whole grains, consumers may know they should consume more fiber and whole grains but don't eat whole grains because they think they don't taste as good as refined grains. In that case, the nutrition communicator's task is to shift the belief to either "Whole grains have a great nutty flavor that I can enjoy in my diet more often" or "Grandma's Oats are a great-tasting way to add more whole grains and fiber to my diet." Using a different example, see Box 37.2 for Case Study 2,[5] a nutrition communications program that shifted attitudes.

Facilitate Engagement

The rise in social media and the subsequent opportunity to connect with an audience more frequently and more personally than before has pushed marketers to engage with their target audiences. Social marketers define engagement in myriad ways, but the purpose is to create sufficient interest among an audience that they want to enter a two-way conversation with the communicator or to share the communicator's message with their online circle.[7] In the days before social media, this might have been considered relationship marketing, which has been defined as establishing, maintaining, and enhancing relationships with customers and other partners, and is achieved by a mutual exchange and fulfillment of promises.[6]

Case Study 1: Tropicana Takes Nutrition to Heart[3,4]

When orange-juice-maker Tropicana successfully petitioned the US Food and Drug Administration in 2000 to allow it to put a health claim on its Pure Premium orange juice linking potassium to a reduced risk of hypertension and stroke, the juice maker wanted to leverage the claim to make national news and drive sales. It faced one problem: Not only were consumers unaware of the research indicating the benefits of potassium but so were the majority of health professionals. In addition, despite containing 227 mg of potassium per 4-oz serving, orange juice usually failed to make lists of good sources of potassium. A survey revealed that more than 95% of adults were unaware of the mineral's role in controlling blood pressure or stroke and 94% did not know that orange juice is a good source of potassium. An integrated campaign that included public relations, advertising, and marketing was developed to drive awareness of potassium's benefits.

Case Study 2: Cans Get People Cooking[5]

Addressing a decade-long decline in the sale of canned foods, the Can Manufacturers Institute launched an expansive campaign to shift consumer attitudes toward canned foods and increase industry sales. They looked to generate more positive conversation about canned foods among consumers by amplifying lesser-known benefits, including freshness and flavor, a diverse role in homemade meals, optimal nutrient content, and environmental and economic sustainability. The campaign involved a comprehensive, media-driven strategy that used television, social media, and digital influencers to deliver the message. The results showed an 11% increase in volume of conversation around the benefits of canned foods on social media, a shift from net neutral to net positive conversation, and a 17.1% all-commodity volume at retail.

Promote Behavior Change

As already mentioned , a common goal among nutrition communicators is to change behavior. The goal may be to have an audience make a dietary change (eg, adding more whole grains to the diet), take a physical action (eg, exercise more often), buy a category of products (eg, purchase more whole grain foods), purchase a specific brand (eg, buy Grandma's Oats), attend a presentation, read an article, or visit the nutrition communicator's practice. Nancy Schwartz, PhD, RD, explains that nutrition and dietetics professionals' role in nutrition communications is to direct traffic for consumers by balancing the different messages they receive from multiple sources of nutrition information in a way that accelerates the shift toward a healthier diet. The ultimate goal or outcome criteria of these efforts, however, should be sustained behavior change.[7]

How Does One Develop a Marketing Strategy That Ensures Success?

To understand whether or not the purpose of a marketing initiative is to raise awareness, shift attitudes, facilitate engagement, or change behavior, it is necessary to begin by determining the goals and objectives, getting to know the target audience, and understanding the barriers to success for the nutrition communicator or target audience. This knowledge allows for the creation of a marketing strategy that meets expressed goals and objectives and has a clear, concise, and action-oriented tactical plan. Once designed, the plan can be implemented, assessed, and refined.

Chapter 15 discusses developing communication strategies.

See Figure 15.1 on page 242 for more about SMART goals and objectives.

Define Goals and Objectives

An important first step in developing any communications strategy is to define goals and objectives. If the desired results aren't known, it's difficult to set up a successful approach for achieving them. That means setting a clearly defined set of goals and objectives.

There is some debate among marketing communications experts as to whether goals and objectives are one and the same. Ron Smith, in his book *Public Relations: The Basics*, describes a *goal* as a "global indication of how an issue should be resolved," while an *objective* is "a statement of a specific outcome expected for a public, indicating a way to more precisely conceptualize the goal."[8] For those who distinguish between the two, goals are the general direction, while objectives are measurable end points. According to Kent Huffman, founder of DigiMark Partners, "a goal is a broadly defined, observable, and desired end result." While goals may be aligned with objectives, goals aren't necessarily measurable: "They are 'whats,' not 'hows.'"[9]

Objectives, meanwhile, are the specific measurable benchmarks that must be achieved to reach the goals. A common approach to setting objectives is the SMART approach, where each objective is not only *specific* and *measurable* but also *achievable*, *relevant*, and *timely*.[10]

Objectives should answer the questions of *what*, *who*, *how much*, and *when*. *What* is the desired output or outcome, *who* is the specific target audience, *how much* is the magnitude of the change needed to be considered successful, and *when* is the time frame in which the objective should be achieved.[11] By this definition, an example of an objective in a nutrition communications program would be to increase consumption of whole grains among 20% of the target audience by one serving per day within 3 months of the start of the campaign.

THE DIFFERENCE BETWEEN BUSINESS GOALS AND COMMUNICATIONS GOALS

It's also important to understand the difference between business or organizational goals and communications goals. Sometimes, marketers and communicators launch into a communications initiative without considering what the business or organization really wants to achieve from that initiative. Grandma's Oats may want to increase awareness about the health benefits of oats, but why? It's likely because they want to increase sales of their products or, perhaps, they want to gain market share from a competitor. This is the goal that should be driving not only the communications strategy but all other areas of the business or organization as well. Understanding the business objectives can help to better formulate communications goals and the strategy or strategies that will get there.

Identify—and Get to Know— the Target Audience

When asked to define the target audience for a communication program aimed at dispelling some of the nutrition myths around a company's products, the chief marketing officer of a major food company responded: "It's simple: everybody." It may seem logical for the head marketer of a food company to encourage everyone to eat their products. It may also seem logical to name everybody as the audience for a nutrition communications activity. After all, don't we want everyone to eat a healthy, balanced diet? Don't we want everyone to eat more whole grains? While that's the ideal, in real life, it isn't that simple.

For one thing, reaching everybody would be an extremely expensive proposition, even for the most profitable of companies or the most prolific nutrition communicator. Second, as described in the stages of change model, everyone might not be at the right stage to hear and act on a message.[2] Third, a message may be targeted to the wrong audience. For example, a marketing message from a company that makes food products with conventionally grown ingredients is less likely to be effective with a consumer who exclusively buys certified organic products. Instead of trying to reach every person with the same message in the same way, identify what marketers like to call the low-hanging fruit (in other words, the consumers who are easiest to reach).

This phase of the strategic planning process often takes place before or during the goal- or objective-setting phase. If it isn't clear who the target audience is, it's hard to gauge what a communicator will be able to accomplish. Communicators must know their target before they decide on the best approach to reach it. Start by learning more about the target audience in a few key areas:

- demographics (age, gender, education, income, geographic location)
- psychographics (attitudes, opinions, interests, values)
- behaviors (media habits, purchasing habits, brand loyalty)
- influencers (social media, friends and family, health professionals)

 ## Resources for Audience Information

US Census Bureau (www.data.census.gov) is a free and easy-to-use tool provided by US Census Bureau for key demographic information for specific populations.

SurveyMonkey (www.surveymonkey.com) is a software tool that allows for the creation of surveys to identify the psychographics of a target audience; free and paid subscription services available.

Talkwalker (www.talkwalker.com) is an online listening and analytics company that tracks consumer conversations and online discussions both relevant and specific to a particular brand.

International Food Information Council Foundation (https://foodinsight.org) conducts an annual survey of information on food trends, consumer attitudes, and consumer buying habits.

Food Marketplace Inc (www.fmi.org) conducts an annual study on consumer purchasing habits.

Mintel (www.mintel.com) is a market research company offering market intelligence reports for purchase, with comprehensive analysis and expert insight across various markets, including food and retail.

Facebook Analytics (https://analytics.facebook.com) is a paid social media analytics tool that helps marketers discover a target audience's online engagement.

Twitter Analytics (http://analytics.twitter.com) is a paid social media analytics tool that helps marketers discover a target audience's online engagement.

Pixlee (www.pixlee.com) is a free analytics tool for Instagram that helps identify relevant influencers to a target audience as well as potential followers.

Crowdfire (www.crowdfireapp.com) is a free analytics tool for Instagram that helps identify relevant influencers to a target audience as well as potential followers.

The more information that is known about an audience, the better prepared a nutrition communicator will be to develop a communications campaign. Box 37.3 provides some resources for identifying answers to those questions. Box 37.4 includes some of the questions to ask about an audience.

See Chapter 11 for more about completing an audience needs assessment.

Get to Know an Audience

- What is the age range of the audience? Do they fall into a generational category like baby boomers or millennials? Or do they cover a broad age range, like ages 25 to 54?
- Is the audience well educated, either in general or about a specific product, campaign, message, or issue?
- What is the audience's race and ethnic background? What is their primary language?
- What is the audience's average household income?
- What is the average size of the audience's household? Does it include parents or single people without children?
- Where does the audience live? Are they urban, suburban, or rural home dwellers? Do they live in a specific region of the country?
- What are the audience's attitudes toward a product, a campaign, a message, or an issue?
- What else is the audience interested in? Do they have hobbies? Are they engaged politically or involved with their local church?
- What are the audience's shopping habits? Do they buy products online, in stores, or both?
- What is the audience's lifestyle like? Do they exercise regularly? If so, what types of exercise do they do?
- Does the audience have dietary restrictions?
- Is the audience's diet affected by cultural or religious practices (eg, kosher or halal)?
- Does the audience follow a vegan or vegetarian diet?
- Are there any allergy or diet-related restrictions among the audience (eg, gluten, nuts, or dairy)?
- Is there a prevalence of medical or health issues that affect the audience's diet?

- What types of foods does the audience consume regularly? What types of foods does the audience avoid?
- Does the audience follow any diet trends? If so, what are they?
- Are there any misconceptions about diet and nutrition topics among the audience and within their community?
- Does the audience want to modify or improve their diet? Do they believe they should modify or improve their diet? If so, in what ways?
- How often does the audience prepare meals at home?
- Does the audience like to cook with fresh ingredients? Do they have access to fresh ingredients? Do they use canned or prepackaged foods in addition to or in place of fresh ingredients when cooking?
- What types of products does the audience purchase? Do they buy products with conventionally grown ingredients, organic products, or a mix of both? Are they brand-loyal, or do they like to try new things?
- What are the audience's media habits? Do they get all of their news through social media, or do they go to traditional sources like television news and newspapers?
- How influential are the audience's friends and family? Are they more likely to listen to social media influencers? Do they listen to health professionals, and if so, which ones have the most influence?
- How has the media covered a particular product, campaign, issue, or message? Has it been favorable or unfavorable? How much of that point of view needs to be shifted?
- How has the audience or the people who influence them talked about a particular product, campaign, issue, or message on social media?

Understand the Barriers to Success

Just as it is necessary to understand an audience, it is also important to consider the environment surrounding a client, program, product, or educational effort. This will help to reveal factors that might impede the ability to reach goals and objectives. Some things to pay attention to include some of the ideas listed here.

TIMING

Does the launch of an activity coincide with anything that could distract an audience? For example, public relations practitioners try to avoid making any big announcements in the weeks leading up to Election Day, particularly if it's a presidential race or if there is a hotly contested local race in a market where efforts are being focused.

COMPETITIVE ACTIVITY

Are competitors waging a big campaign at the same time? If so, are they spending more? What are they saying? Make use of tools like Google Alerts and Hootsuite to monitor whether or not a competitor suddenly appears in traditional and social media (see more on these tools in the resources section at the end of the chapter). In some cases, it may be useful to speak out and be heard, but it may also work to wait until the stage is free. For example, if a competitor is doing interviews espousing a point of view different from your own, then there is an opportunity to insert your view into the discussion. However, if launching a new product or book or making any big announcement, make sure that it will be impossible to steal the spotlight.

NEGATIVE NOISE

Is there a high level of negative news in the marketplace that might impact efforts? For example, has a study come out touting the benefits of a ketogenic diet just when you are launching a book on whole grains? If so, this might not be the right time to promote the book. Or, perhaps, the timing will give an opportunity to address any faults or errors in the study. It's important to closely monitor traditional and social media to understand anything that could affect marketing efforts.

IS IT NEWS?

One of the biggest questions is whether or not anyone else will think what is being offered is news. All too often, marketers will want to make an announcement, expecting strong results but are disappointed when the news isn't perceived to be big by others or interests only a small, specific audience. Research how similar campaigns fared in the past to get a sense of whether or not this will indeed get the attention that's expected.

Create a Strategy That Meets Goals and Objectives

Once goals, objectives, audience, and research are established, it's time to start planning a strategy. The first step is to understand what a marketing strategy is and what it isn't. All too often, when people develop a strategy, it sounds more like a tactical plan. Other times, it's written as a restatement of the goals.

Put simply, a strategy is the *how*—how to achieve goals and objectives. In other words, a strategy is a plan of action.[12] *Adweek* describes strategy as how a person thinks about something before doing it. Strategy is "a larger, overall plan that can comprise several tactics, which are smaller, focused, less impactful action items that are part of the overall plan. Without a great strategy, there are no good tactics." Public relations consultant and author Ron Smith says, "Strategy deals with planning that focuses on the desired outcomes and the conceptual ways of achieving them. It's not about specific tools of communication but rather deciding where to go and how to get there."[8]

One way to think about strategy is to take the stance of a general in the military. The general's job in a time of war is to think about how to win the *war*, not how to win a given *battle*. The strategy, in that situation, is to understand the units or branches of the military that need to be engaged, where they need to be deployed, and how they're going to confront the target. Estimate how long the war will take. The battles fought along the way are tactics. It's important to win those battles, but they all lead up to winning the war.

Thankfully, nutrition communications is a much more peaceful process. Box 37.5 provides examples of simple nutrition communications strategies versus tactics. Box 37.6, with Case Study 3, provides a real-world example of how tactics were used to execute the strategy of the US Highbush Blueberries Council.[13]

BOX 37.5

Examples of Strategies Versus Tactics

Goal: Increase whole grain consumption among all consumers.

Objective: Increase whole grain consumption of culinary-minded consumers by one serving per day after 1 year.

Strategy: Demonstrate practical ways consumers can add whole grains to their diets by working with a culinary organization.

Tactic: Partner with the James Beard Foundation to conduct a series of culinary demonstrations and dinners with menus featuring whole grains; create new recipes and 30-second video demonstration to post on the James Beard website.

Goal: Increase whole grain consumption among all consumers.

Objective: Increase consumption of whole grains among children aged 4 to 6 years by one serving every day after 1 year.

Strategy: Use influencers, social media, and shareable content to drive awareness and trial of the benefits of whole grains among moms with children aged 4 to 6 years.

Tactic: Work with 20 social media influencers that match the target to post recipes, photos, and tips three times per month over the next year.

Goal: Increase whole grain consumption among all consumers.

Objective: Increase mentions of whole grains by registered dietitian nutritionists on traditional and social media by 20% over 1 year.

Strategy: Engage registered dietitian nutritionists as ambassadors to share information with consumers about the health benefits of whole grains.

Tactic: Arm registered dietitian nutritionists with an electronic tool kit of resources, including fact sheets, research studies, and infographics that they can use while counseling patients and clients.

Create a Clear, Concise, and Action-Oriented Tactical Plan

The tactical phase of the plan is when the vehicles and methods that will be used to tell the story are chosen. As Ron Smith explains it, "If the strategy is the skeleton and muscles for your communication program, tactics are the flesh."[1] Tactics can involve a single approach or multiple approaches, as shown by the US Highbush Blueberry Council case study (Box 37.6). The next section outlines some of the most important tactical approaches for nutrition communications.

Implement the Plan

In marketing, there isn't a uniform way to accomplish a tactical plan. However, it's advisable to create a detailed timeline that outlines every task in the plan and a deadline to complete each one. If working with a team, make sure everyone understands their role for this particular plan and the tasks involved.

Assess Success of the Plan and Refine as Needed

The next chapter addresses measurement tools and techniques. However, most measurement methods focus on the results at the end of a program rather than during the program's execution. As with the formative evaluation methods described in Chapter 38, it will be necessary to assess along the way how well the plan is doing against key performance indicators (KPIs), which help to clarify how the strategy is performing against the goals and objectives. This assessment can be conducted at various points in the program, such as when a tactic has been completed or, if it's a yearlong program, after each quarter. For example, if the goal is to raise awareness by a certain percentage over the course of a year, then a KPI against the awareness goal might be the amount of media coverage that has been received. If, a few weeks or few months into the program, the media KPIs are not being met, then it may be time to course-correct and identify additional ways to expand that coverage. Perhaps it's necessary to increase activity, employ different tactics, or make a slight alteration in tactics. See Box 37.7 (page 572) for examples of KPIs for different marketing disciplines.

BOX 37.6 Case Study 3: Driving Demand for Frozen Blueberries[15]

When the US Highbush Blueberry Council tapped marketing agency Padilla in 2016 to launch the first-ever, frozen-only marketing campaign, "Goodness Frozen," the overall goal was to increase consumer demand for frozen blueberries, and the objectives were to increase volume sales and get more berries out of suppliers' storage facilities and onto store shelves. The strategy was three-pronged: (1) Use online video to create a connection with women and moms and increase the appeal of frozen blueberries; (2) provide digital content to generate engagement, increase consideration, and encourage trial; and (3) use the authority and credibility of registered dietitian nutritionists (RDNs), as well as parenting and lifestyle influencers, to validate the health benefits, convenience, and great taste of frozen blueberries.

The tactics the agency employed against those strategies included:

- Creating a Goodness Frozen online video series of 30-second spots showcasing all the benefits of frozen blueberries, including taste, convenience, versatility, and health.
- Creating 11 new frozen blueberry recipes that demonstrate versatility, health, convenience, and great taste and that were promoted via social media; creating

the GoodnessFrozen.com content hub featuring all campaign videos, recipes, a downloadable frozen blueberries eBook, and an infographic.
- RDNs to participate in three broadcast segments in the top 15 markets, including Atlanta, Chicago, and Minneapolis; sampling frozen blueberries at the Food & Nutrition Conference & Expo (FNCE); and sending an email blast to supermarket RDNs to generate interest in promoting frozen blueberries in stores.
- Collaborating with four nutrition and parenting bloggers who reach moms and women aged 25 to 44 to create recipes featuring frozen blueberries and share the convenience and health benefits; working with two top-tier parenting influencers (Momma's Gone City and Laura Fuentes) to create content featuring and recommending frozen blueberries.

The strategy and tactical plan allowed the US Highbush Blueberry Council to achieve its objectives. Frozen blueberry volume sales increased 7.3% over 2015, and the movement of frozen blueberries out of cold storage during the months of the campaign was 17% higher than in the same time period in 2015.

Jim Macnamara, the author of *Public Relations Handbook*, cautions that leaving measurement until the end can have negative consequences:

> What is the strategic value of finding out after you have published your newsletter for a year that it has not been read or well received by readers? Who wants to go to their boss's office and admit: "You know that newsletter we did. Well it didn't work."

Macnamara compares KPIs to the indicators that gauge a car's performance. Although thousands of functions could be measured, usually only a few indicators appear on a car's dashboard that help a driver know when to add oil, refuel, or check tire pressure.[14]

What Are Potential Methods for Marketing?

As the world's largest organization of food and nutrition professionals, the Academy of Nutrition and Dietetics serves to "accelerate improvements in global health and well-being through food and nutrition."[15] Academy of Nutrition and Dietetics members and nutrition professionals with similar goals need marketing to drive that acceleration. They need to ensure messages are heard, programs are attended, services are utilized, and offerings are purchased. Many nutrition professionals don't know where to begin to make that happen, while

Establishing Key Performance Indicators[16]

Key performance indicators (KPIs) differ widely, depending on the business and the marketing activities. The following are some KPIs for various marketing activities.

Blog Posts

- **Unique visitors:** the number of people who have visited a blog over a certain period of time
- **Shares:** the number of times content was shared on social media
- **Average time on page:** a metric from Google Analytics that tracks the amount of time the average visitor spends on a particular page
- **Return visitors:** people coming to the blog who have previously been tagged as having been on the site

Media Outreach

- **Impressions:** an estimate of the number of people who have seen a mention of a person, a product, or a company in the media
- **Share of voice:** percentage of coverage compared to competitors
- **Sentiment:** tone of articles published

Social Media

- **Total engagement:** shares, comments, likes, retweets (RTs), replies, direct messages, and so on
- **Engagement rate:** number of people who actively engaged with posts (RTs, likes, and so on) divided by the total number of followers per channel
- **Mentions:** number of times a company was mentioned by name on a social network
- **Sentiment:** tone of articles published and social media posts

others may be quite marketing-savvy. This section provides a variety of marketing suggestions for all to consider.

Before jumping in, it is essential to reiterate the ethical principles covered in Chapter 9 that help govern the dietetics profession. Marketing methods, in particular, can be highly scrutinized by authoritative groups (eg, the Ethics Committee of the Academy of Nutrition and Dietetics or the US Federal Trade Commission), which serve to maintain the credibility, validity, and value of the work of nutrition professionals. In this aspect, it is critical that marketing messages containing nutrition information be accurate, substantiated, and rooted in sound science. There are penalties for false representation of the science or for being misleading. In addition, it is important to be fully transparent about funding sources and sponsors in all materials, including self-promotion, and to disclose all bias or conflict of interest. Enlisting legal counsel and professional support to ensure

that outreach meets the necessary guidelines is an option. See the resources section at the end of the chapter for more detail.

Traditional and Social Marketing Methods

Philip Kotler, widely regarded as the father of modern marketing, outlines the varying ways that marketing has been defined—some see it as a business activity, others as a frame of mind, yet others as an integrative approach to policy making.[17,18] This demonstrates the wide applications for marketing, including the traditional marketing of goods (eg, a food or nutritional supplement, recipe collection) and services (eg, nutrition seminars, weekly menus, home-delivery meal kits), as well as the social marketing of nutritional changes (eg, learning about portion control, supporting blood glucose control through diet) and campaigns to foster greater change (eg, promoting healthful lunch offerings in school settings).

Though these applications are different in nature, they generally use the same marketing mix, including advertising, public relations, and promotion.[1] Additionally, this mix has developed over time to include influencer outreach, social media, technology, and elements described below.

ADVERTISING

Advertising refers to any paid placement that calls attention to a product, service, or need.[19] Paying for placement guarantees control over who sees it, what it says, where and when it runs, and how it looks. Advertising is one of the most common tools companies use to direct persuasive communications toward buyers.

Advertising formats are vast, but all aim to put key messages in front of the right audience. Some of the most well-known formats include television and magazine placements. Other examples include a paid ad placement on the social media feed of an influential person, a banner ad on a popular website, a mailing or email directed to a specific group of people, a public service announcement on the radio, or native advertising, which shares content in a natural form and function for the space in which it is placed. Native advertising is commonly used in social media, but it can also be used in print, such as with a "listicle" or "advertorial," both of which appear like an article but contain the copy of an advertisement. See Box 37.8 for a sample listicle, which ran in print media, including *SF Gate*, the *Houston Chronicle*, and the *Chicago Tribune*.[20]

PUBLIC RELATIONS

Public relations (PR) largely focuses on putting a client's messages in the hands of a credible third party. This is generally referred to as earned media. A message from an independent third party (eg, popular columnist, contributing broadcast health enthusiast, dietitian working in the media, or influential blogger) is often considered more persuasive than a message delivered directly through an advertisement.

Envision the target consumer for a new healthful food delivery service. Consider the impression that consumer might have after reading an advertisement about it and the health benefits associated with obtaining a subscription. The person might be interested enough to look into it but wonder if anyone had tried it and has an opinion about it. Now, imagine if a *New York Times* food

BOX 37.8 Excerpt from a Listicle

5 mouthwatering ways to keep the feeling of summer

Leaves are beginning to change colors, kids are back in school and you're probably wearing more layers than you did a few weeks ago. Like it or not, the signs are all there: autumn is coming. But that does not mean the favorite flavors of summer have to go away.

Hold off on covering the grill or putting away seasonal spices. Keep that perfect summer feeling alive with these five delicious recipe ideas that capture the best of what summer has to offer, no matter the time of year.

Photos and recipe ideas at https://www.zespri.com/en-US/recipes.

Reproduced with permission from Zespri Kiwifruit. Article by Ketchum 2017 on behalf of Zespri Kiwifruit.[21]

columnist or national morning television talk show host touted their experience with the same service, describing how it not only taught them to manage a healthier eating pattern but also helped them lose weight and feel great as a result. The consumer might be more inclined to try it. There is great PR value in opinion leaders telling their audience about a positive personal experience or offering an implied endorsement through their mention.

Some additional approaches for getting attention for a product or program include an organizing partnership, such as with a contracted spokesperson or social media influencer. This might include working with public-facing registered dietitian nutritionists or recipe developers, mom bloggers, vloggers, podcasters, radio announcers, and more to deliver messages in a controlled medium.

TRADITIONAL MEDIA OUTREACH

Traditional media generally refers to nondigital media, such as print and broadcast outlets that are focused on delivering news and information, which makes them an optimal place to have a person, a brand, or particular work recognized. These can be local, regional, national, or international outlets and include newswires, newspapers, newsletters, magazines, radio, television, and relevant news generated by health professionals, contributors, and bloggers. Generate a list of media that reach a designated target. Then prepare to introduce messages through a pitch that will demonstrate why their specific audience should or would want to know more about these messages. See Box 37.9 for a stepwise approach and the resources section at the end of this chapter for more direction.

INFLUENCER OUTREACH

The ability and motivation to engage in any behavior is influenced by personal, structural, and social variables.[21] Registered dietitian nutritionists (RDNs) strive to be seen as the most trusted source of reliable nutrition information. Statistics from the International Food Information Council Foundation's 2018 Food and Health Survey confirm that the RDN is the most trusted source regarding which foods to eat or avoid, with 70% of those surveyed rating RDNs as highly trusted. The next most trusted source was respondents' personal health care professional. Only 26% listed friends or family members as highly trusted sources about food and nutrition.[22]

Social media influencers are also a major source of information, despite the fact that some influencers are more credible than others. Therefore, if RDNs want to reach their audience, they also need to educate the people who are influencing that audience. Adjust messages accordingly and find ways to include these audiences within the scope of educational outreach to drive the desired change or behavior. Additionally, consider reaching out to people within the following areas who may influence behavior change in an audience through recommendations and referrals[23]:

- health care professional associations
- community networks
- commercial sector
- decision makers
- faith communities
- family and peer groups
- government and regulatory groups
- health professionals (including special interest subgroups)
- key opinion thought leaders
- nongovernmental organizations and civil societies

BOX 37.9 Media Outreach

1. **Develop a priority media list.** Develop a list of all the places a target audience looks for information and news.
2. **Identify optimal contacts.** Agencies usually maintain databases that keep and update this information, but in the absence of this, research an independent contact list by looking or listening for names and making calls to outlets for preferred contact information (phone, email, Contact Me page, and so on). In marketing nutrition programs or products, aim to identify writers, producers, and other influencers at those media outlets that cover specific subject matter. These might include health, nutrition, and food writers, bloggers, reporters, or contributors. Additionally, local calendar listing editors can provide an effective place to post local events open to the public.
3. **Do the homework.** Read previous work written by these contacts on similar subjects to recognize their stance on relevant issues. As it is typical for some topics, such as those related to food and nutrition policy or human welfare, to spark controversy, it is generally best to target media contacts that are open and receptive to a particular message rather than opposed to it.
4. **Prepare the pitch.** Plan to customize outreach for each contact—which could include a note, a call, a delivery, an invitation, or other options—suggesting reasons why they should share information about you and your program, product, or offering with their readers.
5. **Reach out.** Decide on a plan for reaching out and then begin, being considerate of the recipients' time and closing the conversation with a gauge of their interest in pursuing coverage of the pitch. Follow up as appropriate.

- policy makers
- volunteer groups and advocates

Reaching some of these audiences may simply require providing information and education. In other cases, true infrastructure change might be necessary to make changes happen. For example, improving school breakfast and lunch provisions for students would require intervention at the government level.

PROMOTION

For many nutrition communicators, promotion is where there is an opportunity to express themselves; use key messages; raise awareness that a product, program, or concept exists; and convince people that it's something they need to have or to do. Using this communication-persuasion strategy and effort can make the product, program, or message familiar, acceptable, and even desirable to an audience. How promotion is handled will depend on the available budget and the size and scope of what is being worked on, and may include some of the tools and activations discussed next.

PRINT MATERIALS

Classic among promotional tools, the well-designed print advertisement, brochure, fact sheet, sell sheet, poster, and flyer can be effective pieces to help market a program or product when used in the right venues. Consider optimal distribution points in physical places, including your own location and related health care offices, settings, or fairs; marketing booths; waiting places; targeted mailings; and bulletin boards.

SOCIAL MEDIA

Social media presence, often across multiple social and professional networks, is a critical component of expanding a professional network, connecting with customers and driving opportunities to get health and nutrition messages out into the world. Social media provides easily accessible tools for entrepreneurs, small business owners, and large brands alike to establish credibility and build a following. But per John Hall, CEO of Influence & Co, this needs to be more than just shameless self-promotional marketing and driving traffic. Rather, communicators should promote content that is meant to educate, entertain, provoke questions, and drive behavior.[24]

 ## Social Media Applications for Marketing Communication

To hear about effective social media applications within nutrition communications, we met with fellow nutrition communicator Serena Ball, MS, RD. She and her work partner Deanna Segrave-Daly, RD, talk about nutrition through the enjoyment and celebration of food through their company, Teaspoon Communications, and blog, *Teaspoon of Spice* (https://teaspoonofspice.com).

They often work with food companies to promote their products using a combination of different social media platforms that include short or long posts, blog articles, photos, videos, newsletters, live-streaming, and links to relevant news, promotions, or selling opportunities.

Serena explains, "For us, these various vehicles are part of selling our brand. They showcase our credibility, our character, our passion and inspiration, and most of all, our personal voice." In her experience, she says, "High-quality content with consistent messaging is king and drives a strong follower base, which in turn drives more revenue-generating sales and assignments."

She reports, "Online analytics can also tell you about opportunities in the marketplace. Find trends that are in line with your brand messaging and then fill those gaps."

Refer to Box 37.10 for further insights into social media applications for marketing in nutrition communication.

An article in *AdAge* describes how the Kraft Heinz Company has used social media marketing to launch Mayochup, a combination of mayonnaise and ketchup.[25] Through Kraft Heinz social media channels, they posted a poll asking consumers, "Want #mayochup in stores? 500,000 votes for 'yes' and we'll release it to you saucy Americans."[26]

Based on the positive feedback the product received, this product was brought to market with a built-in audience, media buzz, and social chatter around the product. See Figure 37.1 on page 576.

See Chapter 29 for an in-depth look at social media.

FIGURE 37.1 **Social media marketing launch**

Reproduced with permission from H.J. Heinz Company Brands LLC.[26]

SPECIAL EVENTS

Special events can provide an opportunity for nutrition communicators to introduce themselves, their brands, and their products with the people who matter most, oftentimes an exclusive list of media, influencers, or end users. Prepare an invitation list, develop a relevant set of speakers and messages, and theme the event around a timely topic that will draw the desired audience. Special events take many forms but may include some of the following:

- Conferences: Targeted conferences can help to reach thousands in a target audience. Conference opportunities include booth exhibition, sponsored symposiums, networking sessions, receptions, and specialty marketplaces.
- Property tours: Factory or farm tours can provide a prime opportunity to introduce foods and goods alongside their health and nutrition messages. These could even be done

virtually—with cameras and tour guides on one end and attendees watching from the comfort of their office desks on the other.
- Culinary experiences: Food and nutrition messaging often goes hand in hand with a culinary experience or demonstration and the chance to learn, handle, and taste what is being offered.
- Outings: Conducting a seminar or learning experience on-site in a desirable location can draw a crowd and earn valuable time to host and network with guests.

TECHNOLOGY

The expansive growth rate of technology, hand-held smartphones, computer interfaces, electronic devices, and applications will continue to offer new and innovative ways to market to a target audience. Popular marketing tools at this time include the following:

- Applications (or apps): These provide a medium for connection with peers, followers, and customers and offer a powerful way to put essential subjects like nutrition, diet, and fitness management literally at people's fingertips.
- Chatbots: Chatbots allow a communicator to connect with an audience with preprogrammed messaging, information, and programming. Forksy is a nutrition-focused chatbot that communicates with users via Facebook Messenger. The bot asks users what they've had to eat that day and responds with calorie amounts and a breakdown of macronutrients. The bot also keeps a food diary, making it easy for users to keep track of their food intake throughout the day.[27] Consider how a program might benefit from this type of 24/7 customer engagement.
- Virtual reality: This rapidly developing technology allows people to use special lenses to virtually step into another world and a simulated life experience. Nutrition students utilized this technology by creating content for the Academy of Nutrition and Dietetics annual Food & Nutrition Conference & Expo (FNCE) by filming in a grocery store with a 360-degree camera. Editors take it from there, preparing a virtual world that could be useful for virtual grocery

store tours, reading food labels, and cooking demonstrations.[28] The Society for Nutrition Education and Behavior agrees that virtual reality can be part of future classroom learning in their webinar course "Making VR a Reality: Virtual Reality in Nutrition Education."[29]

- Augmented reality: This tool integrates technology with reality through the lens of a smartphone or device. Many programs are in use already; many more are in development, and technology reporters envision programs that will be able to tell users the nutritional value of a food simply by viewing it through their screen.[30]
- Digital assistants: Digital assistants can provide the time, weather, local restaurant suggestions, and movie times while also controlling a home's lights, temperature, and security systems. These can also be programmed with skills that allow consumers to interact with a brand, get information about foods, or obtain nutrition advice.

SOCIAL PROOF

Robert Cialdini, PhD, is often regarded as the godfather of influence. In his national best seller, *Influence: The Psychology of Persuasion*, he states that people look to others for cues to determine what is correct, termed *social proof*.[31] Examples of social proof include reviews people read when deciding whether to purchase a product, eat at a restaurant, or book a vacation. Similarly, nutrition programs, products, and practitioners can receive reviews as evidence of social proof of excellent service or effective outcomes.

Within a specific area of expertise, a nutrition professional may regularly conduct several core programs that are customized for particular clients or groups. Program repetition can be valuable in a marketing approach, since it provides social proof of the efficacy of a product, and thereby the opportunity to obtain testimonials and referrals from within an established customer or client pool.

Sonja Kassis Stetzler, MA, RDN, CPC, and coauthor of several chapters in this book, is a professional speaker and communications coach. She shares the simplicity and application of securing an evaluation at the conclusion of a program or presentation: "Testimonials share someone's experience. They demonstrate that someone tried your program,

applied your techniques, and they worked. This is a social proof point that strengthens your credibility."[32] She adds, "It is relatively simple to obtain if you just ask for it, and with permission, can be used within your promotional literature, professional media platforms, and marketing materials." With each evaluation form, she suggests tweaking questions (avoiding yes-or-no questions) to receive a variety of useful responses, including questions, such as[32]:

- What did you think of [X]'s presentation?
- How would you describe the presentation?
- What would you say was the greatest value of this presentation?
- What will you use as a result of the presentation you've just heard?

Evaluation responses can also guide future work leads, using questions, such as[32]:

- Who else do you know that I can help?
- Please name another group that might also benefit from or enjoy this program.
- Whom would I contact to discuss future opportunities?

Given recent movement toward video capture, Stetzler recommends shifting some paper testimonials to short video clips to use in digital marketing. Testimonials provide valuable social proof to help establish expertise and market what is being offered. Testimonials, such as the following, can become invaluable tools for marketing a nutrition professional as an expert[32]:

Excellent presentation! This was the missing key for me in delivering effective nutrition presentations. I learned take-home, usable skills for my nutrition presentations. —Lisa Phillian, RD

Nutrition communicators have plenty of value to offer, but they need to effectively reach their target audience to drive the audience's interest and foster the changes they are recommending. After all, as an unknown sage said, "It isn't nutrition unless it is consumed." Applying that concept to marketing nutrition programs, products, and messages means that nutrition communicators can share all they want about better nutrition practices, prepare and present lectures, and promote new offerings—but if no one hears their messages or is motivated to take steps to improve their nutritional habits, even the best efforts will be ineffective.

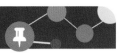
Market Products, Programs, and Messages to Maximize Response

1 Effective marketing successfully drives awareness, engagement, and action. The most successful programs align with social marketing principles by engaging a target, raising awareness of an issue or opportunity, expressing value, addressing barriers to participation, and most important, driving a desired action.

2 In marketing, changing consumer behavior depends on changing the consumer's mind-set. In some cases, it may be necessary to first build awareness, shift attitudes, develop a relationship with the audience, or engage in activities that facilitate the behavior change.

3 The strategy that ensures communications success begins with determining goals and objectives, getting to know a target audience, and understanding the barriers to success. This knowledge allows a nutrition communicator to create a marketing strategy that meets goals and objectives and has a clear, concise, and action-oriented tactical plan. Once designed, the plan can be implemented, assessed, and refined.

4 Marketing tactics help bring a product, program, or idea to market. They help to deliver messaging in way that helps people understand that they want to do something, change a behavior, step out of their comfort zone, or buy a product.

5 It is critical that marketing messages containing nutrition information be accurate, substantiated, and rooted in sound science. There are penalties for falsely representing science or for being misleading. In addition, it is important to be fully transparent about funding sources and sponsors in all materials, including self-promotion, and to disclose all bias or conflict of interest.

RESOURCES

Marketing and Public Relations

- Academy of Nutrition and Dietetics Member Online Marketing Center: www.eatrightpro.org /practice/career-development/marketing-center
- American Marketing Association: www.ama.org
- Public Relations Society of America: www.prsa.org

Media Lists

- Mondo Times: www.mondotimes.com
- Easy Media List: www.easymedialist.com
- LinkedIn: www.linkedin.com
- Agility PR Solutions: www.agilitypr.com

Ethics, Regulations, and Legal Advice

- Academy of Nutrition and Dietetics Code of Ethics: www.eatrightpro.org/-/media/eatrightpro -files /career/code-of-ethics/coeforthenutritionand dieteticsprofession.pdf
- Public Relations Society of America Code of Ethics: www.prsa.org/ethics/resources

- US Food and Drug Administration: www.fda.gov /Food/LabelingNutrition
- Agricultural Marketing Service (AMS): www.ams .usda.gov/rules-regulations
- American Health Lawyers Association (AHLA): www.healthlawyers.org

REFERENCES

1. Kotler P. *Marketing Management: Analysis, Planning and Control.* 2nd ed. Prentice Hall; 1972.
2. Stages of change. Paper presented at: Governor's Conference on Children's Services Transformation; December 16-17, 2009; Richmond, VA. Accessed April 21, 2018. www.cpe.vt.edu/gttc/presentations /8eStagesofChange.pdf
3. Public Relations Society of America. Tropicana Takes Nutrition to Heart; 2001. Accessed April 21, 2018. http://apps.prsa.org/SearchResults /Download/6BW-9305A/0/Tropicana_Takes _Nutrition_To_Heart

4. McGill C. Tropicana Pure Premium and the potassium health claim: a case study. In: Hasler C M, ed. *Regulation of Functional Foods and Nutraceuticals: A Global Perspective.* IFT Press, Blackwell Publishing; 2007: 101-108.

5. Public Relations Society of America. Cans Get You Cooking. Accessed October 10, 2018. https://apps.prsa.org/Awards/SilverAnvil/Search?sakeyword=-Canned%20Food&saoutcome=&sayear=All&sacategory=&pg=1&saindustry=

6. Digiday. How brands define engagement. Published 2018. Accessed April 21, 2018. https://digiday.com/marketing/how-brands-define-engagement

7. Schwartz N. Communicating nutrition and dietetics issues. *J Am Diet Assoc.* 1996;96(11):1137-1139. doi:10.1016/s0002-8223(96)00292-1

8. Smith R. *Public Relations: The Basics.* Routledge; 2014.

9. Huffman K. Marketing and branding goals vs. strategies vs. objectives vs. tactics. Published 2018. Accessed April 22, 2018. http://kenthuffman.com/marketing-and-branding-goals-vs-strategies-vs-objectives-vs-tactics

10. Chaffey D. How to define SMART marketing objectives. Smart Insights Website. Published May 1, 2018. Accessed April 22, 2018. www.smartinsights.com/goal-setting-evaluation/goals-kpis/define-smart-marketing-objectives

11. Anderson FW, Hadley L, Rockland D, Weiner M. *Guidelines for Setting Measurable Public Relations Objectives: An Update.* Institute for Public Relations; 2009. http://painepublishing.com/wp-content/uploads/2014/04/Setting_PR_Objectives-1.pdf

12. Watkins MD. Demystifying strategy: the what, who, how, and why. *Harvard Business Review.* September 10, 2007. Accessed April 22, 2018. https://hbr.org/2007/09/demystifying-strategy-the-what

13. US Highbush Blueberry Council Padilla. *Goodness Frozen: Warming Consumer Appetites to Frozen Blueberries*, Silver Anvil award winner. Public Relations Society of America website. Published 2017. Accessed April 26, 2018. https://apps.prsa.org/Awards/SilverAnvil/Search?sacategory=&pg=2&sayear= 2&sayear=All&sakeyword=&saindustry=Food-Beverage&saoutcome=

14. Macnamara J. PR metrics: how to measure public relations and corporate communication. Published 2005. https://amecorg.com/wp-content/uploads/2011/10/PR-Metrics-Paper.pdf

15. Academy of Nutrition and Dietetics. Academy mission, vision and principles. Accessed April 26, 2018. www.eatrightpro.org/about-us/academy-vision-and-mission/mission-and-vision-statements

16. Adapted from Ritz B. Proving marketing ROI: the metrics you should report. Meltwater. Published January 6, 2017. Accessed September 17, 2018. www.meltwater.com/blog/setting-the-right-marketing-kpis-metrics-you-should-keep-track-of

17. Kotler P, Zaltman G. Social marketing: an approach to planned social change. *J Mark.* 1971;35(3):3-12.

18. Marketing Staff of the Ohio State University. A statement of marketing philosophy. *J Mark.* 1965;29:43.

19. Advertising. Merriam-Webster Dictionary. Accessed August 19, 2019. https://www.merriam-webster.com/dictionary/advertising

20. 5 mouthwatering ways to keep the feeling of summer. BrandpointContent. Published September 13, 2017. Accessed May 3, 2018. www.brandpointcontent.com/article/31596/5-mouthwatering-ways-to-keep-the-feeling-of-summer

21. Patterson K, Grenny J, Maxfield D, McMillan R, Switzler A. *Influencer: The Power to Change Anything.* McGraw-Hill; 2008.

22. International Food Information Council Foundation. 2018 Food & Health Survey. Published 2018. Accessed August 19, 2019. www.foodinsight.org/2018-FHS-Report-FINAL.pdf

23. Lefebvre RC. *Social Marketing and Social Change: Strategies and Tools for Improving Health, Well-Being, and the Environment.* John Wiley and Sons; 2013.

24. Hall J. 5 Business goals of content marketing. Forbes website. Published October 20, 2013. Accessed May 29, 2020. www.forbes.com/sites/johnhall/2013/10/20/5-business-goals-of-content-marketing/#53b63b5043af

25. Wohl J. From "Mayochup" to potential mayhem: Kraft Heinz and social media. *AdAge.* Published April 24, 2018. Accessed April 25, 2018. http://adage.com/article/cmo-strategy/kraft-heinz-dishes-social-media-approach/313247

26. Heinz Ketchup (@HeinzKetchup). Want #mayochup in stores? 500,000 votes for "yes" and we'll release it to you saucy Americans. Twitter. Accessed April 25, 2018. https://twitter.com/HeinzKetchup_US

27. Forksy Facebook Page. Accessed September 14, 2018. www.facebook.com/forksybot

28. Otto E. Virtual reality: the new frontier in dietetics? *Food Nutr.* February 9, 2017. Accessed January 14, 2010. https://foodandnutrition.org/blogs/student-scoop/virtual-reality-new-frontier-dietetics

29. Cuales M, Dunnagan C, Cooke N. Making VR a reality: virtual reality in nutrition education. Society for Nutrition Education and Behavior Website. Published September 8, 2016. Accessed April 25, 2018. www.sneb.org/products/technology/making-vr-a-reality-virtual-reality-in-nutrition-education/?back=products

30. Gallagher J. Learn what your food is made of using augmented reality. Next Reality Website. Published July 18, 2017. https://mobile-ar.reality .news/news/apple-ar-learn-what-your-food-is -made-using-augmented-reality-0178874

31. Cialdini R. *Influence: The Psychology of Persuasion.* William Morrow; 1993.

32. Stetzler S. Testimonials. Published 2018. Accessed April 14, 2018. www.effective connecting.com/testimonials

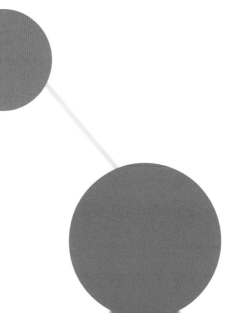

CHAPTER 38

Measure Success with Testing and Evaluation

Virginia Quick, PhD, RDN

"Testing and evaluating messages or projects improves the effectiveness of the communications, engages the target audience, and more wisely allocates investments."

> "Do not measure success by today's harvest. Measure success by the seeds you plant today." —ROBERT LOUIS STEVENSON

Introduction

No one wants to travel a long distance, spend a fortune, and then end up in the wrong place. The journey taken along the course of any project can present road blocks, but appropriate planning and evaluation make it easier and more efficient to successfully reach a communication's final destination.

Evaluation of communication messages and programs should be an ongoing process throughout the 10 stages of nutrition communication development and implementation. Well-designed tests and evaluation methods will improve communication activities and success.

This chapter answers three questions:

- What is the purpose of testing and evaluating communication?
- What approaches can be utilized for testing and evaluating communication?
- What are practical strategies for testing and evaluating communication?

The answers to these questions provide a solid foundation for successfully applying measurement techniques to nutrition communication. Nutrition communicators who apply the strategies described in this chapter will increase their chances of successfully reaching their communication goals and objectives.

See Chapter 3 for more on the stages of nutrition communication.

What Is the Purpose of Testing and Evaluating Communication?

Effective nutrition communications facilitate learning and behavior change.[1,2] How can it be determined if the audience accurately interprets and understands messages? How can it be determined if the audience can use these messages to improve their behaviors? Testing and evaluation can help answer these questions and more.

Nutrition communication should have carefully thought out testing and evaluation methods for intended audiences. Here are the reasons why.

Improve Effectiveness of Communications

A well-planned and well-executed evaluation strategy helps assess whether communications are working or whether they need adjustments.[3] Nutrition communications can be assessed through data collection methods that identify communication messaging strengths and weaknesses and determine whether the communications are likely to produce desired progress toward outcomes. Identified weaknesses or problem areas can be adjusted and refined to increase audience understanding and reach. Ultimately, this leads to improvements in communications and helps audiences reach the overall outcomes sought.[4] Thus, the data gathered during evaluation allow nutrition and dietetics practitioners to advance their evidence-based practice by creating messages that resonate with intended audiences and promote improved health.

Effectively Engage Target Audience

To ensure that messaging resonates with an audience, include an evaluation strategy during the planning phase, not after the project development has begun or is completed. From the beginning of the development phase, baseline research should be conducted to help better understand an audience's priorities and values (otherwise known as a needs assessment). That is, communication strategies for the target audience need to be considered, modified, and tailored accordingly. During the development phase, formative evaluation research strategies can be used to gather feedback from an audience and learn how they respond to messages.[4] During the implementation phase, outcome evaluation research can provide the evidence and justification needed to reveal how effective the message is at educating an audience and motivating positive behavior change in the short- and long-term.[4]

More Wisely Allocate Resources

If on a tight budget, examining cost-benefit ratios may help in determining whether communication investments need to be redistributed more effectively to achieve similar results. For example, a brief video may be more effective than written materials for those with low reading levels or those who have limited interest in reading. Using the most effective communication mode is especially important for projects that require evaluation by external mandates, authorizers, or others to help justify the need for further funding and support. Additionally, evaluating nutrition communication helps ensure that finances are not wasted on ineffective projects or programs.[5]

What Approaches Can Be Utilized for Testing and Evaluating Communication?

A systematic approach is commonly used to evaluate communications, including testing projects and learning objectives and evaluating communication strategies, and is built into all phases of project planning, implementation, and management. Formative, outcome, and process evaluations are three types of evaluations commonly used when testing objectives and evaluating strategies.[6] Each type of evaluation has a specialized purpose and must link to the communication goals and objectives described in Chapter 15.

Formative Evaluation

Evaluative activities that are undertaken to furnish information that will guide program and project improvement are known as formative evaluation.[4,6] Formative evaluations can occur before message delivery or program implementation,[7] such as during a needs assessment. They can also occur during delivery or implementation for the purposes of testing concepts or product or message design and to pretest materials with a target audience. Typically, formative assessments are qualitative in nature and use strategies, such as focus groups and observation, which may address the following types of questions:

- What are participants' thoughts, ideas, and opinions of the message?
- Will the mode of communication be applicable and well received by the target audience?
- What are the target audience's likes and dislikes regarding the material being developed?

As nutrition messages and educational materials are developed and implemented, formative assessments, such as focus groups, can be used with the target audience to better understand their thoughts, ideas, and opinions. Feedback from the target audience also provides information on whether they are likely to ignore, reject, or misunderstand the message. Hence, formative evaluation is necessary because it can identify problems with the communication's effectiveness to teach and the participant's ability to learn, thus allowing for revision of plans, methods, techniques, or materials.[7] See the Word of Experience box on page 584 for an example of a formative assessment.

Outcome Evaluation

Evaluative activities undertaken to obtain a summary judgment on certain aspects of the program's

Read more about needs assessment in Chapter 11.

See Chapter 11 for more on focus groups and needs assessments.

or project's performance, such as determining whether specific goals and objectives were met, are defined as *outcome evaluation* or *summative evaluation*.[4,6] This type of evaluation is usually administered at the end of a term, course, campaign, blog post, or learning activity to determine if the communication was successful. Outcome evaluation is important because it assesses how well the message or project met its objectives and provides guidance in areas that need to be changed or improved to be more effective in the future. Outcome assessments tend to be quantitative in nature, such as surveys or tests, and may ask the following types of questions:

Formative Assessment in Action by Virginia Quick, PhD, RDN

As a graduate assistant, I assisted colleagues on a research study where we created a series of 30- to 60-second short videos to promote improved food safety behaviors of middle school youth (sixth to eighth graders). From the beginning, we conducted formative testing using a wide range of formative evaluation, including focus group discussions, informal one-on-one discussions, and observations, blogs, and video closet confessionals (a technique with which students independently recorded and shared their thoughts on video).

By conducting the formative evaluations, we were able to make suggested changes and revisions to the videos (eg, better voice quality and graphics, film environment more personally relatable) so they would be more receptive to our target audience (middle school youth). After making some suggested revisions based on student feedback, we were able to further confirm they liked the video story lines, personality and look of the characters, technological interface design features, qualities of the environment or setting of the videos, musical styles, and messaging at the end of the video (eg, Don't Be Gross, Wash Your Hands!). On average, most students said they were likely to share the videos with their social network. This allowed us to better tailor our education materials to our audience in making sure that the materials would be well received.

- Were the outcome goals and objectives achieved?
- Do the communication activities have beneficial or adverse effects on the recipients?
- Are some recipients affected more than others by the communication?
- Has the problem or situation the communication intended to address improved?

ESTABLISH A BASELINE

Outcome evaluations should be preplanned and tightly linked to communication goals and objectives.[3] Establishing a baseline, the initial data that will serve as a starting point, is critical for a good evaluation.[3,8] Media coverage, website or blog traffic, public opinion surveys, and feedback or requests received via email, letters, or phone calls are all examples of tools that can be used to determine baselines. During implementation of the nutrition communication activities, it will be possible to compare the baseline with new data gathered over time (eg, via posttest or follow-up test) to assess progress, make course corrections, and measure success.

For example, in a nutrition presentation focused on improving fruit and vegetable behaviors targeted to school-aged children, the goal and objectives described in Figure 38.1 were tied to the outcome evaluations (pretest and posttest surveys). See Figure 38.1 for sample questions asked on pretest and posttest surveys to assess whether the objectives of the presentation were met. Paired t-tests revealed students ($N = 100$) significantly ($p < .05$) increased their attitudes, knowledge, self-efficacy, and intentions toward eating more fruits and vegetables after receiving the nutrition education presentation.

USE PROFESSIONAL OBSERVERS

Using professional observers is another method for evaluating a communication.[9] For example, if a presentation on healthy snacking was given by a nutrition communicator in a classroom setting to school-aged children, the teacher of the classroom could act as the observer in providing feedback about the overall presentation and teaching style of the nutrition communicator. The feedback provided by the professional observer could be survey-based or verbally given to the nutrition

Goal: To improve fruit and vegetable intake behaviors of fourth- and fifth-grade students in the Montville Township Public School District after they received a nutrition education presentation focused on the benefits of eating fruits and vegetables.

Objectives: By the end of the presentation (posttest), school-aged children will have:

- increased positive **attitudes** toward eating fruits and vegetables;
- increased **knowledge** about the benefits of eating fruits and vegetables;
- increased **self-efficacy** in the ability to increase fruit and vegetable intake; and
- increased intentions to eat more fruits and vegetables.

Survey for Students:

We would like to know what you think. Please select the answer that best describes you by placing an "X" in the appropriate cell for each question.

	Strongly disagree	Disagree	Neither agree or disagree	Agree	Strongly agree
1. I really enjoy eating fruits and vegetables. (Attitude)					
2. I know a lot about the health benefits of eating fruits and vegetables. (Knowledge)					
3. I plan to eat five or more fruits and vegetables each day. (Behavior)					
4. I really want to improve my fruit and vegetable intake. (Behavioral Intention)					
5. I feel confident in my ability to eat more fruits and vegetables. (Self-efficacy)					

communicator at the end of a project. Often, rating scales and checklists are used to evaluate teacher effectiveness.[7] Categories or attributes are listed and, for clarity, should be defined in detail. Figure 38.2 (page 586) shows sample survey questions to ask a professional observer who is evaluating a lesson given by a nutrition and dietetics professional.

DO A SELF-EVALUATION

A self-evaluation is a thoughtful reflection and written review of one's own performance. This involves rating established goals, competencies, and overall performance. To self-assess means to become an active participant in evaluation. This enables a nutrition communicator to honestly assess personal strengths and areas of improvement. The presenter can do a self-evaluation after giving the presentation to school-aged children by reflecting

upon and responding on paper to a set of open-ended questions, such as the following:

- What are some things that I did well?
- Are there areas that I need to improve upon?
- How can I learn from this project?

When used in combination with other evaluation methods, self-evaluation can enhance a nutrition communicator's skills.

Process Evaluation

Process evaluation monitors and documents project implementation to examine whether the project was carried out as planned.[4,10] This type of evaluation is increasingly being incorporated into health promotion and intervention studies because it can help identify problem areas in a program or project.[10] For example, in a social media campaign to reduce sugar-sweetened beverage intake, a process evaluation may ask the following types of questions:

- How much media coverage was received?
- What was the tone of that coverage (positive or negative)?
- Which media outlets was the coverage in? Where in those outlets? What is the audience of those placements?
- Were the desired visuals achieved?
- Did the audience pick up the key messages?
- How many visitors saw the content?
- How long did they spend on the website?
- What webpages did they visit?

- What was their bounce rate and conversion rate?

Common dimensions of process evaluation that are assessed include fidelity, dose, and reach[10]:

- *Fidelity* refers to the extent to which the project is delivered as intended.
- The project *dose* refers to how much of the intended project activities is delivered to participants.
- *Reach* refers to the proportion of intended recipients who actually participate in the project.

FIGURE 38.2 **Sample questions for an evaluation conducted by a professional observer**

Please rate the presenter on the characteristics below on a scale of 1 (needs improvement) to 5 (accomplished professionally).

Lesson Preparation	SCORE
Evidence of sufficient and up-to-date research and preparation	
Well organized	
Able to answer questions easily	
Communication	**SCORE**
Professionalism	
Eye contact, gestures, facial expressions	
Enthusiasm	
Self-confidence	
Audience	**SCORE**
Good rapport	
Able to gather audience attention, interest, involvement	
Lesson Content and Delivery	**SCORE**
Teaching method was appropriate for audience	
Lesson content was tailored appropriately for audience	
Visual aids: appropriate, well prepared, used effectively	
Time management	
Discussion and reinforcement methods	
Comments for areas of improvement:	
Other comments:	

Fidelity, dose, and reach can be tracked and documented using various forms of monitoring, including observations, surveys, and media metrics. The barriers and facilitators of successful project implementation are typically assessed using qualitative methods such as focus groups and interviews. Overall, information from process evaluation is useful for understanding how project impact and outcomes were achieved and for project replication. Figure 38.3 can be used as a helpful guide in listing the steps to take for evaluating communications.

GUIDE FOR EFFECTIVE NUTRITION INTERVENTIONS AND EDUCATION (GENIE) CHECKLIST

The Guide for Effective Nutrition Interventions and Education (GENIE) is an online resource designed to help nutrition and dietetics professionals design, modify, or compare effective nutrition programs.[11] GENIE is an evidence-based checklist of quality criteria (nine categories with 35 quality criteria) that has been validated based on reliable scientific evidence. Nutrition communicators can benefit from using GENIE during the design process in building nutrition education programs with a higher likelihood of achieving their outcomes.[12] Additionally, funders can use the GENIE checklist as a way to compare and score a number of proposals and use the results to guide funding decisions.

GENIE is an easy-to-use tool that can be used by nutrition communicators when evaluating nutrition education programs.[11] More information on the tool and other resources are on the GENIE website (https://genie.webauthor.com /public/partner.cfm).

Visit Chapter 11 to learn more about focus groups and interviews.

FIGURE 38.3 **Five stages of nutrition communication development and related evaluation types and functions**

Stage of Nutrition Communication Development	Question to Be Asked	Evaluation Type and Function
1 Assessment of communication problems and needs	Are the target audience's needs and standards being met?	Needs assessment; problem description (using primary and secondary data)
2 Determination of communication goals and objectives	What needs to be done to meet those needs and standards?	Formative evaluation; service needs (use of SMART objectives that support goals)
3 Design of communication message, project, or program	Which communication activities would be the best to achieve the desired change(s)?	Formative evaluation; pilot testing (using focus groups, interviews, survey research)
4 Communication implementation and operation	Is the communication project or program operating as planned?	Process evaluation; program monitoring (fidelity, dose, reach), media metrics
5 Communication outcomes	Is the communication project or program having the desired effects?	Outcome evaluation (pretest and posttest surveys, games to test knowledge gains, media metrics oral questions, professional observer, self-evaluation)

SMART goals are smart, measurable, achievable, relevant, and time bound. See pages 241 and 242 for more information.

Adapted from Rossi P, Lipsey M, Freeman H. *Evaluation: A Systematic Approach.* 7th ed. Sage Publications; 2004.[6]

What Are Practical Strategies for Testing and Evaluating Communication?

There are myriad testing and evaluation methods that can be utilized during formative and outcome processes. The choice of which to use will depend on a number of factors, such as the intended audience and project design. For example, using a paper-and-pencil questionnaire may be more appropriate for a senior population not accustomed to or technologically savvy enough to complete online questionnaires.

It is important to choose the instrument or technique that best fits the communication design to help ensure objectives and goals can be statistically and appropriately assessed. Additionally, any evaluation method used, such as a paper-and-pencil survey, should be pretested (otherwise known as pilot-tested) with a smaller group before actual use to ensure that it is the appropriate tool for an audience.[7] It is also important to note that some evaluation methods, such as being a moderator for focus groups, may require working with professional evaluators or training staff to ensure uniform application and accurate data interpretation.

In general, most nutrition communication projects use more than one method to get a comprehensive and accurate picture of the audience. Both qualitative and quantitative testing and evaluation methods of projects can be used. What follows is a summary of qualitative and quantitative methods along with practical strategies that can be used when assessing nutrition communication projects.

Qualitative Versus Quantitative Testing and Evaluation Methods

Qualitative research is defined as an approach that produces findings not derived from standard statistical procedures or other means of quantification. Qualitative methods, such as focus groups and semistructured interviews, use a naturalistic approach that seeks to understand phenomena in which data are not numbers; rather, data are text, audio, or visual.[13] In essence, qualitative research

is an effort to better understand people's interpretation of their experiences.[14] On the other hand, quantitative testing and evaluation methods, such as written or online surveys with closed-ended questions are more objective and are commonly used to assess nutrition communication projects.

WRITTEN AND ONLINE SURVEYS

Written surveys and online surveys can be used to test and evaluate projects. Surveys are, for the most part, inexpensive to conduct and the most commonly used strategy due to ease of creating and implementing for a wide variety of audiences.[13] Often, it is possible to adapt and modify surveys that have been tested and used before with a similar audience. However, give careful consideration to the phrasing and interpretation of questions to ensure accurate responses from survey participants. For example, if the plan is to collect survey data among a low-income population with low reading levels, the data collected on the overall project will not be reliable if the audience being tested does not understand the questions on the survey. Thus, the survey should be checked for its readability and understandability before implementation.

GAMES

At times, written and online surveys may not be the most appropriate to implement due to time limits and the cognitive or physical abilities of an audience. Other strategies, such as the use of games,[15,16] can be employed to test knowledge gains of an audience as part of the overall project. The use of games, such as playing nutrition Jeopardy with youth and bingo with senior citizens during a lesson, can be a less arduous task for participants who may have short attention spans and low cognitive and physical abilities. Additionally, audience members can have fun playing the game while the nutrition communicator gauges whether or not the audience understands the lesson material by observing how they respond to the game. Box 38.1 provides an example of how a game was implemented to test knowledge gains of middle school youth on the topic of food safety.

MEDIA METRICS

In evaluating nutrition communications on various media channels (eg, publications, blogs, Facebook, Twitter), there are a number of website

Chapter 11 describes the various types of qualitative and quantitative methods in more detail.

Chapter 11 also discusses how to develop and implement a survey.

traffic metrics that can be utilized to assess the engagement, reach, and quality of a media platform.[8,17]

The total count of followers, fans, and page likes represents the number of people who have taken an interest in nutrition communication content, such as a blog. Examining click-rate metrics can help to understand how followers are engaged, why they are engaged, and what's making them click on different page links. For example, Facebook provides a detailed analysis of the number of page likes as well as gains and losses of likes over a designated time period. This helps to monitor an audience's reactions to certain posts or determine which time periods are better for engaging new people. Replies and comments on posts can also help to gauge how interesting or engaging a topic is. These direct-response metrics can help to reevaluate any uninteresting nutrition communication content on a social media page.

Content-share metrics are important to examine as well because they reflect how an audience may perceive the value of nutrition communication content.[8] Highly shared posts indicate that an audience found the nutrition communication content particularly helpful or had a strong emotional or psychological connection to it. Additionally, the more often it is shared, the greater the reach. Overall, monitoring nutrition communication content via media channels using the above metrics is vital because it allows for creating better targeted, customized nutrition content that improves engagement with audiences.[8,17] Figure 38.4 (page 590) provides a summary of key questions and indicators to assess nutrition communications using various media channels.

OTHER QUALITATIVE EVALUATION METHODS

Other qualitative testing and evaluation methods, such as interactive activities and oral questions, may be more appropriate for certain audiences and situations. For example, for young children, written surveys may not be the most developmentally appropriate type of evaluation technique.[7] However, using other forms of qualitative methods, such as a fun drawing activity or asking oral questions about what a child learned may be more effective for assessing the project.[7] The example that follows provides some context into other types of strategies used to test and evaluate communication projects.

 ## Use of Games to Test Knowledge Gains[18]

A food-safety educational game called Ninja Kitchen was used to educate middle school youth on the importance of food safety in the classroom. Ninja Kitchen is a web-based food safety education video game that has 15 levels. Each level has key food-safety concepts (eg, preventing cross-contamination, hazards of leaving food in the danger zone) and is appropriate for middle school youth. The game is set in a modern-day diner where the Ninja receives food safety wisdom from the Sensei, takes customer orders, then prepares and serves the food. Players earn points by practicing safe food handling and lose points if players serve customers contaminated food. Players can use their points to buy more advice and supplies to help boost their score. Students played the game as part of their classroom curriculum.

The game allowed middle school youth to learn about the topic of food safety in a fun and interactive manner. It also enabled the nutrition communicator to evaluate the participants' knowledge gains about food safety as evidenced by advancing to higher game levels. Additionally, classroom teachers, as the professional observers, felt the game helped to create a positive learning environment where both teamwork and good-natured competition were observed between students.

Preschool students (ages 4 and 5 years) example In a nutrition education lesson given to preschool-aged students at a day care facility in New Jersey, an interactive action story (15 minutes in length) was presented by nutrition educators. The goal of the lesson was to encourage children to incorporate new foods into their diet by making them aware of a variety of fruits and vegetables. A few objectives were that by the end of the lesson:

- at least 50% of preschoolers would be able to recall and associate at least one new fruit or vegetable with its appropriate color;
- 50% of preschoolers would be more familiar with foods they do not typically consume, as evidenced by their ability to illustrate such foods in a drawing; and

- students would feel excited about the new foods they plan to try at home with their families, as evidenced by the enthusiasm generated by the lesson activities and verbal affirmations.

Throughout the lesson, nutrition educators asked the audience questions to assess whether they were understanding the content and were engaged in the learning process (eg, Do you remember …? What have you learned today?). At the end of the lesson, students received a handout and were asked to draw a new fruit and vegetable that they learned about during the lesson. They were also encouraged to color food items in the appropriate color. The drawing activity allowed the nutrition educators to evaluate whether students learned something new by having students recall what they were taught during the lesson. Additionally, classroom teachers of the students were asked to evaluate the overall presentation by responding

FIGURE 38.4 **Key questions and indicators that assess the reach and quality of nutrition communications in various media channels**[a]

Key Questions	Potential Indicators	Purpose of Indicators
Is my audience growing?	Publications or blogs: • number of page views in a time period • number of downloads in a time period • number of clicks to download from the page Social media: • number of shares or clicks	Assess the most popular nutrition communication content Estimate of how many people viewed the content (If downloads) Increase the chances the audience read the content and didn't just look at the webpage Indicates success of the landing page if tracking clicks
How are users interacting with my nutrition communications?	Time spent on a webpage Number of times nutrition content was mentioned in digital newspapers, in blogs, on social media, on or other media platforms	Indicates if users were reading more of a particular publication or blog Gives an indication as to the range of the audience type
Were my nutrition communications shared by audiences or reproduced in any way?	Number of times nutrition content was cited or referred to Number of social media retweets, shares, comments, or other user actions Number of shares to social media via website share buttons Number of requests to reproduce or cite information	Discover other platforms where the nutrition communications are available Assess whether the nutrition content is reaching audiences beyond the initial target audience Gives an indication of quality (if the audience perceived the nutrition content to be high quality and considered it useful for others)
Did I receive feedback from my users on my nutrition communications?	Social media tweets or comments Comments received (eg, blog, Facebook post)	Tells the quality of the nutrition communications through audience feedback

[a] Adapted from reference 8.

to open-ended questions (eg, What did you like about the presentation? What areas could use improvement?). The comments from classroom teachers (the professional observers) provided feedback for the nutrition educators on areas of needed improvement and helped to gauge how well the presentation was received.

A variety of testing and evaluation methods can be used to determine whether a communication's goals and objectives are met. The type of method chosen will depend on the research question (goals and objectives) to be answered, the nature of the materials, the intended audience, and the amount of time and resources available for testing and evaluating. Careful mapping of the journey (start to finish) that includes proper testing and evaluation methods will support success as a nutrition communicator. The questions in Box 38.2 will assist in performing a useful evaluation.

 # Questions to Consider When Testing and Evaluating Nutrition Communications from Start to Finish

Nutrition Communication Needs (Formative Evaluation)

- What nutrition communications are needed in the target population?
- What are the target audience's thoughts, ideas, and opinions?
- Which media channel(s) would be most appropriate for the target audience?

Nutrition Communication Implementation (Process Evaluation)

- Are there a sufficient number of people utilizing the nutrition communications (eg, program, project, media traffic on blog)?
- Are the intended nutrition communications being delivered to the intended people?
- Is the intended audience satisfied with the nutrition communication?
- If applicable, are administrative, organizational, and personnel functions handled well?
- How much media coverage was received?
- What was the tone of that coverage (positive or negative)?
- Which media outlets was the coverage in? Where in those outlets? What is the audience of those placements?
- Were the desired visuals achieved?

- Did the audience pick up the key messages?
- How many visitors saw the content?
- How long did they spend on the website?
- What webpages did they visit?
- What was their bounce rate and conversion rate?

Nutrition Communication Outputs and Resource Costs (Outcome Evaluation)

- Was a baseline established?
- What type of evaluations (eg, professional observer, self-evaluation, media metrics, and survey) will be used to measure the success of the nutrition communication?
- Are the outcome goals and objectives of the nutrition communications being met?
- Do the communication activities have beneficial or adverse effects on the recipients?
- Are some recipients affected more than others by the communication?
- Is the problem or situation the communication intended to address improved?
- Were resources used efficiently?
- Is the cost reasonable in relation to the magnitude of the benefits (cost-benefit ratio)?

KEY POINTS

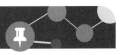

Measure Success with Testing and Evaluation

1 Nutrition projects should have carefully planned testing and evaluation methods throughout the nutrition communication development and implementation stages. Testing and evaluating messages or projects improves the effectiveness of the communications, engages the target audience, and more wisely allocates investments.

2 Formative, outcome, and process evaluations are three types of evaluation commonly used in nutrition communication projects and programs. Each type of evaluation has a specialized purpose and can provide valuable feedback about the project content, audience, and nutrition communicator.

3 Qualitative and quantitative methods are often used in formative, outcome, and process evaluation of nutrition communication projects. Qualitative methods may include games, interactive activities, and oral questions, while quantitative methods may include written and online surveys with closed-ended questions and media metrics. One or more method types can be used for testing and evaluating nutrition communications, but the choice of the method will more than likely vary depending on the audience, time, and resources available.

RESOURCES

Rossi PH, Lipsey MW, Freeman HE. *Evaluation: A Systematic Approach.* 7th ed. Sage Publications; 2004.

GENIE tool: https://genie.webauthor.com/public /partner.cfm

US Department of Health and Human Services Centers for Disease Control and Prevention. *Introduction to Program Evaluation for Public Health Programs: A Self-Study Guide.* Centers for Disease Control and Prevention; 2011. www.cdc.gov /eval/guide/cdcevalmanual.pdf

Social media metrics: www.socialmediaexaminer .com/10-metrics-to-track-for-social-media-success

REFERENCES

1. Whitehead K. Changing dietary behaviour: the role and development of practitioner communication. *Proc Nutr Soc.* 2015;74:177-184.
2. Whitehead K, Langley-Evans S, Tischler V, Swift J. Communication skills for behaviour change in dietetic consultations. *J Hum Nutr Diet.* 2009;22:493-500.
3. Asibey E, Parras T, van Fleet J. Are we there yet? A communications evaluation guide. 2008. Accessed January 14, 2020. www.lumina foundation.org/files/resources/arewethereyet.pdf
4. US Department of Agriculture. *Nutrition Education: Principles of Sound Impact Evaluation.* US Department of Agriculture; 2005:10.
5. US Department of Health and Human Services; Centers for Disease Control and Prevention; Office of the Director, Office of Strategy and Innovation. *Introduction to Program Evaluation for Public Health Programs: A Self-Study Guide.* Centers for Disease Control and Prevention; 2011.
6. Rossi P, Lipsey M, Freeman H. *Evaluation: A Systematic Approach.* 7th ed. Sage Publications; 2004.
7. Holli B, Beto J. *Nutrition Counseling and Education Skills for Dietetics Professionals.* 6th ed. Lippincott Williams and Wilkins; 2014.
8. Cassidy C, Ball L. Communications monitoring, evaluating and learning toolkit. Oversees Development Institute website. Published January 2018. www.odi.org/sites/odi.org.uk/files /long-form-downloads/odi_rapid_mel_toolkit _201801.pdf
9. Centers for Disease Control and Prevention. Data collection methods for program evaluation: observation. Updated August 2018. Accessed January 14, 2020. www.cdc.gov/healthyyouth /evaluation/pdf/brief16.pdf
10. Saunders R, Evans M, Joshi P. Developing a process-evaluation plan for assessing health promotion program implementation: a how-to guide. *Health Promotion Practice.* 2005;6:134-147

11. Academy of Nutrition and Dietetics. Guide for effective nutrition interventions and education. eatright website. Published 2015. Accessed January 16, 2020. https://genie.webauthor.com /public/partner_content.cfm?code=about

13. Abram J, Hand R, Parrott J, Brown K, Ziegler P, Steiber A. What is your nutrition program missing? Finding answers with the Guide for Effective Nutrition Interventions and Education (GENIE). *J Acad Nutr Diet.* 2015;115:122-130.

14. Harris J, Gleason P, Sheean P, Boushey C, Beto J, Bruemmer B. An introduction to qualitative research for food and nutrition professionals. *J Acad Nutr Diet.* 2009;109:80-90.

15. Hartman J. Using focus groups to conduct business communication research. *Int J Bus Comm.* 2004;41:402-410.

16. Ariffin MM, Oxley A, Sulaiman S. Evaluating game-based learning effectiveness in higher education. *Procedia—Soc Behav Sci.* 2014;123:20-27.

17. Akl E, Kairouz V, Sackett K, et al. Educational games for health professionals. *Cochrane Database Syst Rev.* 2013;28:CD006411.

18. Quick V, Corda K, Chamberlin B, Schaffner D, Byrd-Bredbenner C. Evaluation of a food safety education game for middle school youth. *Br Food J.* 2013;115:686-699.

19. McKay B. The six most effective social media metrics to understand your campaign's success. *Forbes.* July 14, 2017. www.forbes.com/sites /forbesagencycouncil/2017/07/14/the-six-most -effective-social-media-metrics-to-understand -your-campaigns-success/#5083d07d64cb

SECTION 8

Designing and Delivering Professional Communications

Improving Communication Skills Requires Broad Shoulders

David H. Holben, PhD, RDN, LD, FAND

David H. Holben, PhD, RDN, LD, FAND

During my senior year of college, I took a literature class that stretched me. As part of the general education, I was required to deviate from my science-based curriculum. I remember thinking, "What? Do I have to read T. S. Eliot's *Old Possum's Book of Practical Cats* and then critique the poem 'The Rum Tum Tugger'?" Yikes.

As a dietetics student, I was more comfortable dryly stating the results from an experimental foods project than I was analyzing a sonnet or narrative. But, in the end, you know what? I loved that literature class, in spite of it being at 8:00 AM, on Fridays even. I eagerly looked forward to the comments from my literature instructor. His feedback was helpful, and it fostered my growth not only as a writer but also as a problem solver and critical thinker. In fact, years later, I find myself applying the analytical, critical thinking, and storytelling skills learned in that course to my professional writing.

Virtually any vocation requires writing, and nutrition and dietetics is no exception. Our profession is diverse, and it requires professionals to employ equally diverse strategies of communication. As such, over the last three decades, I have endeavored to hone my professional communication skills so that I can effectively communicate with a wide range of stakeholders—dietitians, donors, and countless others.

I have spent the majority of my career in academia. Consequently, I utilize a wide range of communication skills, especially written communication skills. You may not have the same career path, but I would hazard a guess that you, too, have to write reports, manuscripts, or grant proposals to accomplish your goals. What is my advice to you, as you embark upon reading Section 8 of this volume? As a writer, I learned early on that *broad shoulders* are needed to strengthen professional writing (and other professional communication) skills. In a nutshell, you must learn to take criticism when developing these skills, and then you must take personal responsibility for improving them.

My Career Path

Allow me to take you on a quick jaunt down my own career path. At the start of this journey were adult and pediatric major medical centers, where I had to effectively author manuscripts centered on clinical research findings. From there, I moved on to elite academic institutions that required me to effectively author a dissertation and countless peer-reviewed manuscripts. Along the way, I have been steered to funding agencies or industry partners that required me to craft a vision for them—one that centered on my research and how they fit into it. Each stop along the way has also included individuals, like Instructor Patrick from my literature class, who have helped me to sharpen my professional communication skills. For that, I am very thankful.

There is one other aspect of my professional career that I want to highlight as an illustration—the military. My career has included being a registered dietitian in the Reserve Component of the United States Army. Now, the military *did* teach me the concept of "bottom line up front"—clearly communicating vital information at the beginning of the communication to facilitate rapid decision making—but that is not what I want to highlight here. Indulge me for a minute while we talk about military fitness. Why? I think that it is a parallel to becoming an expert professional communicator in nutrition and dietetics.

Army dietitians, like all soldiers, must meet physical fitness standards that measure, at a minimum, muscular strength and cardiorespiratory fitness. Essentially, soldiers must pass a three-event test that includes running, sit-ups, and push-ups. When you put on the uniform, you don't magically run faster or do more push-ups, however. You have to work at it. Officers must take personal responsibility for their fitness. You have to be committed to doing physical activity almost every day, and, eventually, with instruction and critique from committed colleagues, you develop stronger lungs, faster legs, and tougher muscles—*broader shoulders*. It is my view that professional communication is the same. You have to work at it and take personal responsibility for its development.

Personal Development and Responsibility

As a young dietitian, I had no idea that I would author a textbook centered on community nutrition. I had no idea that I would publish peer-reviewed articles that help to clarify our understanding of aspects of nutrition. And, I had no idea that I would utilize grant proposals to convince donors and agencies to fund the work that I do.

Similar to accepting instruction and critique for development of physical endurance and strength, professional communication requires development of *broad shoulders* through feedback. Drafting and redrafting professional communications, after effective feedback from colleagues whom you trust, is vital. In the end, I think that "nutrition and dietetics soldiers" will hone their professional communication skills to effectively communicate with a wide range of stakeholders only when they learn to take criticism well and personal responsibility seriously.

Broad shoulders.

CHAPTER 39

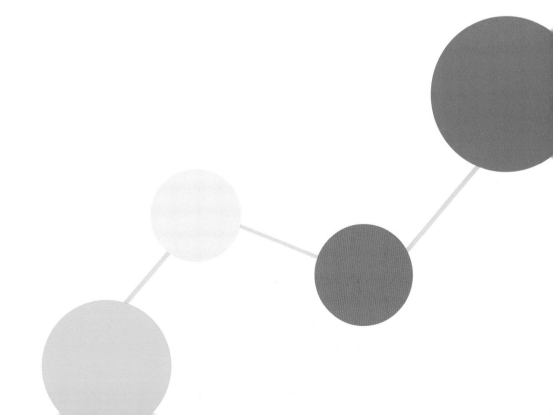

Business Communication Demonstrates Professionalism

Nicci Brown, MS, RDN
Laura Goolsby, MS, RDN, LDN
Lori A. Kaley, MS, RDN, LD, MSB and
Lisa Ann Jones, MA, RDN, LDN, FAND

"Practical strategies for success in business communication include listening first, making connections and building relationships, allowing time to complete the work, and seeking to be of service to others."

"Professional is not a label you give yourself—it's a description you hope others will apply to you." —DAVID MAISTER

Introduction

Effective business communication, whether in health care, business, media, or other settings, is an essential skill for nutrition communicators to maintain integrity and professionalism and effectively convey messages and receive feedback.

This chapter answers three questions:

- What is included in business communication?
- What are best practices in business communication?
- What are practical strategies for success in business communications?

Effective business communication also sets up the communicator to be a more organized professional, and as Alton Brown, US television personality, chef, and host of the Food Network show *Good Eats*, notes, "Organization sets you free."[1] Ultimately, effective communication enables better teamwork, results in higher quality work, and better supports professional relationships.

What Is Included in Business Communication?

In today's business world, a majority of communication is electronic, whether it is written or spoken. Email dictates to-do lists, and social media is ever present as a marketing or educational tool. Although face-to-face interactions have decreased

with technological innovations, presenting oneself in a professional manner remains paramount—whether in person, on the phone, via email, during video conferencing, or on social media platforms. Additionally, materials used to introduce and represent a professional, such as business cards and resumes, must exemplify strong communication skills. All business communication needs to reflect competence and professionalism.

Business Correspondence

Correspondence refers to communication via the written word. In the past, business correspondence primarily consisted of formal letters sent by regular mail. Although traditional paper correspondence is still used, electronic forms of business communication are now the norm.

EMAIL

Electronic mail—commonly known as email—is a primary business communications tool in all areas of nutrition and dietetics. Depending upon job choice, email may be the driving force that helps to determine daily tasks. Email overcomes time and space constraints in our fast-paced, online world.[2] Since colleagues and business associates receive many emails to and from multiple accounts daily, it is prudent to adhere to the following guidelines for effective email correspondence:

- Use an appropriate greeting. If unsure of the name or title of the addressee, use "Good morning," "Good afternoon," or "Good evening."
- If the addressee's name and title are known, use them in the greeting for introductory

and formal communications: "Dear Ms Smith," "Good morning, Dr Smith," or "Good evening, Mr Smith."

- In professional communications, it is essential and respectful to research an addressee ahead of time in order to properly address them. For example, additional research may be required for gender-neutral names (eg, Taylor Smith) or to confirm titles. If the recipient *is* a doctor (medical or academic), it is most appropriate to use the title *Dr*. Google, LinkedIn, and the website of the addressee's organization are good tools for this purpose.

- If communicating with an acquaintance or colleague, it is acceptable to be more informal while still maintaining professionalism: "Hi, Jane," or "Good morning, John."

- Send (alternatively termed copy) only those who need the information. Do not unnecessarily copy those who may receive a negative impression of the addressee from the email or who have no need for the information. Use the blind carbon copy (bcc) function to send to others who need the information but when it is best to keep the transmission private.

- Do not reply to all unless everyone on the email thread needs the information.

- Identify the purpose of the email in the subject line. Be as specific, compelling, and succinct as possible.

- Be as concise in the body of the email as possible. Get to the point quickly and refrain from including too much information in one email. Consider attaching a document rather than including excess detail within an email, and consider using bullet points to list items or ideas.

- Be polite. Email communication cannot convey body language or verbal tone, so make sure the subtext of the message is appropriate. Reread emails before sending and consider if the wording and tone convey the intended meaning. Revise as needed.

- Use proper grammar, punctuation, and spelling. Avoid slang, jargon, text language (such as LOL for "laugh out loud"), emojis (digital icons used to express emotions), and uncommon acronyms and abbreviations.

(See Box 39.1.) Avoid overusing exclamation points in professional communications.

- Use logical formatting so that the email is easy to read on both a computer and a mobile device:
  - Include spacing between paragraphs.
  - Break up large chunks of text into multiple, shorter paragraphs.
  - Use bulleted lists when appropriate.

- Always proofread and spell-check emails before sending.

- Include a signature with contact information.

- Close the email politely and appropriately: *Sincerely* and *Kind regards* are common closing words. Consider including an expression of gratitude as a last sentence before the closing. Possible ending thoughts include: "Thank you for your time," "Thank you for your guidance," "I welcome further discussion," and "I look forward to working together."

- If an email does not receive a response, follow up. Generally, follow up on time-sensitive matters every 1 to 2 days. Sometimes, follow-up is in the form of another email. At other times, the subject matter may be more complex and require a phone call or face-to-face meeting. Controversial subjects may be better suited to verbal communication. Always respect the busy schedules of colleagues and request scheduling of any phone calls or face-to-face meetings.

- Follow up on less time-urgent matters every 1 to 2 weeks. Many professionals receive hundreds of emails daily and may not see the first message or have had time to respond. Courteous follow-ups are often welcomed reminders.

SOCIAL MEDIA

When using social media to communicate professional information, keep the following in mind:

- Refrain from mixing personal and professional information. Consider having separate accounts for personal and professional use. Be professional on all accounts.

- Manage social media accounts regularly.
  - Be a two-way street: Check content that followers add and interact with them as appropriate.
  - Regularly add evidence-based content to keep followers engaged.

- Use good grammar, punctuation, and spelling.
- Practice integrity online.
  - Interact with followers and other users in a professional and respectful manner, especially if they disagree with a post.
  - Share evidence-based information.
  - Disclose any paid or sponsored content. It's the law.
  - Note when an opinion is being shared rather than evidence-based facts.

Meetings

Meetings are an important part of professional life. Common reasons to hold meetings are to generate a discussion among a group of people, to communicate information simultaneously to group members, and to make decisions that impact the group.

Today, many group meetings include individuals who are not physically in the room. Meetings can occur in real time in a number of ways: in person, on the phone, or via a conference call, which can include audio only, video, or web conferencing for both audio and video. When possible, it is preferable that a newly formed group meet in person so group members can develop a rapport.

Preparation is the key to ensuring a productive meeting, one in which the goals and objectives of the meeting are met. Best practices for administering a meeting include the following:

- Determine the meeting goals, objectives, and desired outcomes.
- Identify the meeting leader and facilitator.
- As needed, assign other roles, such as scribe and timekeeper.
- Identify the date, time, location, and method(s) for the meeting.
  - If participants have diverse schedules, the meeting leader or host may use an electronic poll program, such as Doodle, to identify the best date and time. Be cognizant of time zones when coordinating a meeting with members across the country or world.
  - For in-person meetings, make sure the location can accommodate all physical attendees and provide other communication methods, such as

 Emojis: Helpful or Harmful?

Using emojis in professional communications is a matter of personal preference, and many professionals feel strongly one way or the other about their use. Often, preference varies among generations, as well as with the intent and context of the message. While younger people may rely on emojis to help convey tone, older people may view emojis as frivolous and inappropriate. When in doubt, follow these tips:

- At their most basic, emojis are not considered professional, so err on the side of caution. For example, do not use emojis:
  - in a first professional communication with a new contact;
  - when pitching yourself; or
  - in formal business communications (eg, to authority figures within an organization, the head of a department, or a new professor who does not yet know you).
- Never use emojis in designed materials, such as resumes, business cards, or cover letters.
- Using emojis may be acceptable with colleagues who are frequent correspondents (eg, exchanging emails multiple times a day). However, assess each correspondence individually to determine whether the situation is appropriate.
- If authority figures use them first—for example, if a boss sends the occasional smiley face—it is probably okay to use them occasionally too. Never use more than one or two emojis in a single correspondence.

speaker or videoconference technology for remote attendees.
  - When planning to use technology or a software program to share critical information, host a trial run or recommend that participants try out the technology before the meeting to ensure compatibility with their electronic devices.
- Schedule sufficient time to include introductions, the required number and type of agenda items, discussion, decision making, next steps, and wrap-up.

Chapter 29 covers effective social media communication in depth, including a civility pledge.

- To guide the meeting, create an agenda that incorporates the outcome and objectives and an outline with timing and an assigned speaker or facilitator for each section. At the top of the agenda, include the name of the meeting, date, time, location, and instructions for participating via conference call or video or web conference, if applicable.
- If appropriate, gather agenda items from meeting participants beforehand or add them during the meeting, allowing sufficient time in the agenda to incorporate additional topics.
- When possible, at least 1 week before the meeting, the leader or host should send out a calendar invitation to meeting participants with the agenda, instructions for how to participate, and a means to respond with their availability. Send out email reminders leading up to the meeting, especially if tasks need to be completed prior to the meeting.
- On the day of the meeting, take a few moments to make sure that electronic connections are working properly, if necessary. Start the meeting on time. Welcome and thank participants for attending and, if necessary, do a roll call or ask each participant, including remote attendees on the phone or web, to introduce themselves by stating their name and affiliation.
- If participation during the meeting is limited, ask the group why. There could be multiple reasons for limited participation, including that the issue has been resolved or that it is too charged to discuss in a group. Once the reason for limited participation is identified, take appropriate steps to address it.
- If unanticipated conflict arises during the meeting, acknowledge the conflict, request that participants remain respectful, and ask the group if there is time during the meeting to address the conflict. Follow the consensus of the group to either handle the conflict at that time or reconvene specifically to address the conflict with those who have an interest. If the conflict is handled during the meeting, then in the interest of time other agenda items may need to be addressed at a subsequent meeting.
- Similarly, when the meeting goes off on a tangent, ask participants if they want to spend time on the tangent issue that has come up or get back on track with the meeting agenda.
- Conflicts or other issues can also be put into a "parking lot" to be addressed at future meetings.
- Remember to involve any remote attendees by asking for their input or if they have any questions. Allow 10 seconds of silence for them to respond before moving on.
- End the meeting on time.

Identify a scribe, or notetaker, to capture the names of meeting participants who are present and absent, highlights of discussions, action items, decisions made, next steps, and who is responsible for any action items and deadlines. Have the scribe provide notes to the meeting leader, who will review and complete the notes and distribute them to group members within 1 week of the meeting. In some situations, it may be appropriate for the meeting leader to ask the group to provide any additions or corrections to the notes.

Meeting recurrences and timing recommendations can vary depending on how frequently a particular group meets and the culture of the particular field.[2]

As a meeting attendee, it is good professional courtesy to respond promptly to meeting requests for availability and agenda items, as well as to RSVP to the scheduled meeting. Participant feedback and participation is critical to the success of meetings. Prepare by reviewing the meeting method instructions and agenda ahead of time. When attending an online meeting, refrain from multitasking in order to keep attention on the meeting and be ready to be an active participant. To share something during an online meeting, wait for a quiet moment in the discussion or for the meeting leader to ask for participation to avoid talking over others.

Networking

According to the *Merriam-Webster Unabridged* dictionary, networking is "the exchange of information or services among individuals, groups, or institutions."[3] The word *networking* may seem exciting or scary. Just watching a networking session may be daunting, as it is a skill that comes naturally to some but is alien to others. The Academy of Nutrition and Dietetics Food & Nutrition Conference & Expo (FNCE) is a great example of a diverse

Tips for Perfecting an Elevator Speech

An elevator speech is a 20- to 30-second introduction of a person's background and why they are attending a particular event. Named for the time it takes to ride an elevator (20 to 30 seconds), it can be used in any networking situation.

Sample Elevator Speech: "I'm a registered dietitian nutritionist who helps postmenopausal women develop healthier eating habits and successfully manage their weight. Do you know any women in this age group that would be interested in discovering and developing these new habits?"

Use the following tips to help perfect an elevator speech:

- Prepare. Define the audience and potential scenario before crafting the words.
- Make the message memorable. Open with a hook. A hook is something engaging that draws the audience in and makes them want to continue listening.
- Help the audience visualize what is being said. Use descriptive language to help formulate the situation and provide a solution to put the issue into perspective.
- Finalize the speech. It should be no longer than 90 words.
- Practice, practice, practice!
- Leave the audience with a call to action that will inspire them to act and follow up.

offering of networking sessions in which attendees can participate over the course of the conference. The advantages of networking are numerous and are rooted in all of the relationship-building opportunities that result. Though it may not come naturally, effective networking is a skill that can be learned, practiced, and applied in every business setting. How can a nutrition communicator be a better networker?

Know your strengths Create a list of your best qualities, contributions, expertise, experiences, training, and, if applicable, an overview of your business or company. Prepare a brief "elevator speech" as an introduction. See Box 39.2 for tips on crafting an effective elevator speech and Box 39.3 (page 604) for how to be a good conversationalist.

Role-play Practicing ahead of time will increase comfort in new situations and provide support to accomplish networking goals. Role-play an elevator speech with friends and family and record their interactions to review.

Stay focused This is a twofold goal. First, have a clear picture of what the goal is. Second, listen attentively and focus on how to meet the needs of new acquaintances. Keep in mind that even when a connection is made through networking but the person does not currently need help or offer help that is immediately useful, making the connection is still valuable.

Networking can be done online or in person. While online networking gives the opportunity to make more connections, face-to-face connections are often deeper, since they avoid technical barriers and provide in-person communication. LinkedIn is the largest online social networking site for business. However, in examining the quality of those connections, it may turn out that they include many individuals whom you have never met in person. Examples of in-person networking events include local chamber of commerce events, Toastmasters meetings, and state dietetics affiliate get-togethers. Meetup, an online platform connecting like-minded individuals, lists networking events in most areas of the country.

Materials: Business Cards, Resumes, Cover Letters, and LinkedIn

Just as emails and meeting agendas should be professional, so should all of the materials that reflect a person as a professional. This includes business cards, resumes, cover letters, and LinkedIn profiles.

BUSINESS CARDS

Never leave home without business cards, especially if attending a professional event or meeting. Consider keeping a few cards in a purse or wallet

Good-Conversationalist Checklist

BOX 39.3

Being a good conversationalist is essential for successful networking. Use the checklist below to assess skills:

- **How is your body language?** Relax and keep your arms open at your sides. Crossed arms may signal anger or boredom to the other person. Look people in the eye when speaking to them and when listening to them.
- **Are you understandable?** Avoid filler words like *um, like, uh,* and *you know.* Filler words are not necessary, and speakers seem more confident without them. Refer to Chapter 21 for ways to eliminate fillers.
- **Are you engaging?** Never interrupt. Reflect what the other person has said back to them and ask questions. The best way to know if someone is receiving a message is if they mirror what you are saying and ask further questions to learn more.
- **Are you focused?** Avoid distractions and really listen. Put the smartphone away so there's no temptation to check the time or laugh at a funny text. It shows the listener you are interested and engaged in the conversation.
- **Are you concise?** Be succinct and prepared. Planning is everything! Be prepared with a message, and be as succinct as possible.
- **Is what you are saying compelling?** Incorporate stories; everyone loves a great story, and stories help the listener remember the storyteller and the message.

at all times. There are many situations that may arise where it would be useful to share business cards, such as at networking events, professional meetings, events, conferences, or an everyday situation when an individual expresses an interest in your business or services.

Larger organizations or companies may provide their employees with business cards with a set template and style. Include personal credentials and, when possible, the name you use to introduce yourself. For example, if you go by Rob Smith rather than Robert Smith, use that name on the business card to help people remember the meeting.

For nutrition communicators who are self-employed or have a side business, it's essential to create and print business cards. There are many free, well-designed templates available through Microsoft Office or companies like FedEx or Staples. Business cards can also easily be designed online, such as through Vistaprint or a similar vendor, or a designer can create them. Best practices for business cards include the following:

- Include first and last name, credentials, title, and contact information, including email address and phone number.
- If applicable, also include social media handles, website address, company name,

logo, and additional relevant contact information, such as address and fax number. A headshot can be appropriate for professionals who are promoting speaking or media work. For others, a photo may be viewed as presumptuous.
- Ensure that the business cards are:
  - readable (don't make text too small or too tightly spaced);
  - visually interesting (use a splash of color or a unique design, such as vertically oriented rather than the standard horizontal orientation); and
  - professional and polished (ensure printing is high quality and cards are cut evenly).

RESUMES

A resume or curriculum vitae (CV) is often the first impression potential employers, colleagues, and partners have of a professional. It should be a positive and accurate reflection of the professional and tell a story about his or her background, skills, and expertise. A CV will provide a complete list of professional experiences, whereas a resume will include information pertinent to the reason it is being shared. Either one should be carefully proofread and free of errors.

Always tailor a resume to the specific opportunity at hand, which means some experience is relevant in certain cases but should be left out of other versions of the resume. For example, when applying for a clinical dietetics job, include clinical experience details. When applying for a communications job, abbreviate the clinical experience and highlight communications-related experience. Consider keeping a master version of a resume with a full list of experiences and skills that can easily be customized.

Most job openings receive dozens if not hundreds of applications, so a resume should be visually compelling and easy to read. Below are some tips for creating a resume:

- Use a professional-looking serif or sans serif font and a legible font size: 11-point is considered readable.
- Limit a resume to two pages. A CV can be as long as needed, but brevity is appreciated.
- Format a resume appropriately, including appropriate spacing, bullets, and indentation. Include adequate white space so it is easy to read.
- Make the flow logical. List experience in chronological order, with the most recent job first.

A resume should stand out from the crowd. Here are some tips:

- A subtle splash of color goes a long way in the design. Consider using a readable color for a few elements of a resume, such as name, divider lines, or headers.
- Look beyond the standard resume templates, which may produce a resume that comes across as dated and boring. Microsoft Word and other programs offer alternative templates, and Google offers nontraditional resume templates. See the resources section at the end of this chapter for links.
- Consider including the following design elements:
  - a personal logo
  - a sidebar to highlight skills, certifications, or professional development
  - modular boxes to highlight unique skill sets
- Design your resume online. It isn't necessary to be a trained graphic designer to design a

resume. Free websites, such as Canva, can help to produce attractive resumes that get noticed.
- Consider a resume a sales tool. Ask whether it effectively sells you and your skills.
- List current position title first, followed by the organization and location.
- Use strong power verbs, such as *executed, managed, coordinated, designed, developed, founded, pioneered, spearheaded, launched, advanced, amplified, expanded, maximized, revitalized, cultivated, facilitated, fostered,* and *investigated.*
- Consider including a section with unique skills or areas of expertise, such as social media marketing, creative writing, and website management.

Following are tips to avoid in resume writing:

- Don't use clichés, slang, jargon, or overused terms, and avoid words like *passionate, love,* and *go-getter.*
- Don't include an objective. When applying for a position, the objective is understood, so including one only takes up valuable space.
- Do not include references; if an employer wants them, they will ask.
- Make sure the resume is free of mistakes. Carefully proofread a resume to catch misspellings, grammatical errors, inconsistent formatting, and details, such as using the present tense to describe a past job.
- Don't include grade point average (GPA). Except for new graduates with a GPA of about 3.7 or higher, GPA is irrelevant and, in some cases, a turnoff for potential employers.

COVER LETTERS

A cover letter should complement a resume and continue to tell the story. Tailor it to the opportunity by showcasing how specific skills meet the potential employer's needs.

Where a resume is objective, the cover letter should be more subjective and paint a picture of background, skills, and expertise. Cover letters can include professional qualities (eg, "I enthusiastically embrace challenges" or "I thrive under pressure") and passions. They can also include specific examples of experiences relevant to the opportunity.

One way to format the flow of a cover letter is to include buzzwords from the job posting and discuss how you meet or demonstrate the criteria required for the position.

LINKEDIN

LinkedIn is a professional social networking site where users can create an online resume and connect with other professionals. An online presence is often required to find new opportunities—or to let them find you. It's also a great way to network and meet others with similar professional interests.

A LinkedIn profile should be very similar to a resume, and it can include all past experiences, expertise, and skills. The online integration also allows for the creation of links from a profile to organizations you have worked with, publications you contributed to, and projects you were involved in.

What Are Best Practices in Business Communication?

The goal is to communicate effectively within whatever format is chosen. To ensure success, it is helpful to have a best practices guide for a reference. The following guide to best practices covers professionalism, teamwork, respect, clear and open communication, and written documentation. This guidance should prove helpful to anyone who aspires to be a better communicator. The key to success is to be consistently striving for the highest standards of excellence and integrity.

Professionalism

Professionalism in business communications means that the communication focuses on the reason for the communication without delving into irrelevant or personal issues. While there may be occasion to address a personal issue, it is handled in a way that is appropriate and brief, while maintaining the focus of the business communication on the matter at hand. To be professional in business communication is to convey competence as well as respect, empathy, and consideration for the audience.

Review Chapter 2 for more background on professionalism.

WRITTEN WORD

When putting business communications in writing, follow the basic principles outlined below, whether the communication is a letter, memo, or email. Email is a common method used in business communications, and letters and memos are often electronic and attached to email instead of being sent as hard copy through regular mail.

When addressing others in a new professional situation, err on the side of formality, using an appropriate salutation (ie, Dr, Ms, Mr, or Mrs) and full first and last names. In a known professional setting, follow the culture of that setting to address others, unless someone requests otherwise. Should an individual request the use of a less formal address, take their lead and do so.

For hard-copy letters, use company letterhead and include the recipient's full name, credentials, title, position, business name, and mailing address in the upper left. Include the date. Be sure to sign the letter with a full name and include contact information (this may be part of company letterhead). At the bottom of the letter under the signature, include who will receive copies of the letter, if anyone, by adding cc: (stands for "carbon copy") and list each individual's name and position under the cc: heading. (See Figure 39.1 for an example.) This translates to email format, where a signature can be created that is added automatically at the end of each email. Including others in email communications is accomplished by adding their email addresses at cc: in the recipients section.

Use correct spelling and grammar. Review all writing at least once to ensure that it conveys the intended communication in an appropriate tone. Do not put anything in writing that you would not want attributed to you (ie, published on the front page of the newspaper or sent all over the internet). Refrain from maligning or complaining about others.

When possible, conduct important or difficult conversations in person rather than by email; use the telephone as a second choice. If it is necessary to document substandard behavior, do so in writing (either hard copy or electronic) and include the date, time, place, who was present, and what occurred. If a human resource professional is available, obtain their counsel and follow through.

Respond to email in a timely fashion, preferably within one to two business days or whatever time frame is standard for a particular business. A timely email reply can be simply to acknowledge receipt of the email and promise to follow up after completing further action. If you will be unavailable for an unusual period of time during regular business hours or while on vacation, create an automatic out-of-office reply that includes the best way to find help in the case of an urgent situation.

FIGURE 39.1 **Hard copy letter example**

[Your Company Letterhead]

Date of Letter

Recipient Name, Credentials

Recipient Title/Position

Business Name

Business Street Address

Business City, State, Zip Code

Dear Recipient Name,

[Body of letter]

Sincerely,

Your Signature

Your Name

Your Contact Information

cc:

Your Company Colleague's Name, Position

Additional Company Colleague's Name, Position

SPOKEN WORD

When someone answers your telephone call, state your name and affiliation first, whom you are trying to reach, and briefly what the call is about. For example, "Hello, this is Chris Caller. I am the dietitian at Regional Hospital, and I am calling to speak with Dr Best about one of her patients. Is Dr Best available?" If calling unannounced, ask the person who answers if they have time for the call or if it is possible to set up a date and time that better meets their availability. You want the content of a call to receive attention from the person you are calling. If a call reaches a voicemail box, be prepared to leave a message with your name, affiliation, whom you wish to speak with, the reason for the call, date of the message, and a telephone number where you can be reached.

When answering your telephone, say hello or use a similar greeting and state your first name. Check voicemail regularly, and strive to respond to phone calls within one to two business days. If you will be unavailable for an unusual period of time during regular business hours or on vacation, leave an outgoing voice message that states your availability and the best way to reach someone else in an urgent situation.

IN GROUPS

In meetings, encourage equal participation from all attendees when serving as leader, and be an active and respectful participant when an attendee. If attendees participate by phone, include them by asking for their input. If participating via conference call, call in on time, announce your presence, be an active participant, and mute the phone when not speaking to limit background noise. If working from home, maintain professionalism by being prepared and ready for work, and be clear when speaking.[4] Be mindful of the timing on the agenda and the total time allocated for the meeting when participating to allow time for others to participate.

To maintain professionalism in all business communications, be on time, be prepared, be present, be considerate, be responsive, and be positive.

Teamwork

Refer to Chapter 3 for more on effective teamwork.

Effective communication is required for teams to work well together. In any business setting, there are many opportunities for employees to work together in team environments. Teams are at their best when there are no impediments to clear communication. Additionally, clear communication contributes a sense of accomplishment to a group and may lead to a better distribution of responsibilities. For some, working in teams can be a source of stress and anxiety when the group is not communicating clearly. For effective communication, all team members must have an open mind, listen actively, and have a clear understanding of the work that needs to be accomplished.

Consider the example described in the Words of Experience box. Notice that teamwork is essential when working in this type of environment—if the team is to produce the results they need in a way that addresses and acknowledges the contributions of the entire group.

Respect

IN CORRESPONDENCE

Communication should always reflect respect for others' opinions and beliefs. This requires cultural competence, which is important for success whether dealing with people in a home country or abroad. When the only communication is electronic, it is imperative that correspondence strikes the right tone. Treating others how you wish to be treated is the best way to convey respect. When communicating about a difficult, controversial, or emotionally charged topic, write a draft and reread it before sending it. If possible, also ask a trusted colleague or mentor to read it and provide feedback.

IN MEETINGS

Many of the above considerations also apply to in-person or virtual meetings. In addition, respectful interactions that occur in a meeting setting include not interrupting others, providing meeting agendas so all participants are prepared, and giving credit for important contributions.

Clear and Open Communication

Clarity, honesty, and transparency in business communications are important for building trust, understanding, and acceptance. These practices apply to written and spoken communications. Clarity can be accomplished by stating what is true or describing the circumstance in an objective manner. Be as open as possible. When there is information that cannot be shared, stating that fact openly can be helpful.

Be open to feedback and questions, as this can help to clarify what is being communicated. Remember that others may have different understandings of issues and different "filters" for how they receive information and for how much information they can process, so it may take more than one communication or more than one method of communication to be understood. It is also helpful to ask others what their preferred method of communication is (ie, verbal vs visual). The path of communication goes both ways, and the more open communicators are, the more it allows others to be open. Ask for feedback from others to make sure communications are understood. Address all questions and concerns. Being open also includes listening to what others ask or say. Ask others to explain or clarify themselves, if necessary. When written communication is received, read it thoroughly, and then read it again.

When communicating in writing, review what has been written at least once before sending. This takes some patience, but it's worth the effort because it improves the chances that others will understand the message.

As part of being clear and open, it is especially important to communicate when you:

- need clarification or don't understand something,
- will not be able to do what you said you would do,
- need help,
- will miss a deadline,
- will be late, or
- have made a mistake.

These are opportunities to learn more about yourself, learn and accept assistance from others, or renegotiate a time frame or scope of work.

Displaying integrity in communications will build a professional reputation more than trying to be perfect or hiding when something does not go as planned. Attempt to maintain calm in the face of seemingly negative feedback, harsh criticism, or difficult questions. Continue to be clear, open, and objective and handle questions and concerns as well as possible. Honesty, clarity, and a willingness to be open are valuable attributes that come through to others in professional communications.

Documenting in Writing

Taking notes is valuable when communicating verbally. Whether having a one-on-one conversation

Silos by Lisa Ann Jones, MA, RDN, LDN, FAND

As a nutrition communications consultant for the past 15 years, I have seen firsthand how ineffective teamwork can keep people from achieving great business results and how working in a team environment often does little to empower individuals to improve their communication skills.

When I worked in one particular corporate environment, one of my tasks was to lead several different department areas in improving processes that affected the entire company. I quickly realized that the team members selected from each department all had a different process from what was documented. Or rather, their processes were documented—but in their heads rather than on paper. Our first task was to create and document a process that included all of the stakeholders. The group worked collectively on the process, and the different departments realized they had been reinventing the wheel when they could have been collaborating all along.

This experience spurred the team to create a communication task force to improve the communication skills of the entire company and break down the existing silos. If these silos had not been acknowledged and addressed, it would have been difficult, if not impossible, for communication to be effective and great teamwork to come to fruition.

or a group meeting, and whether meeting in person or via phone or conference technology, documenting what was said is essential in professional settings.

As mentioned in the Meetings section earlier, assigning a scribe or notetaker for group meetings, either ahead of time or at the start of the call, is imperative. That way, there is no confusion about who is documenting what's discussed. When taking notes, use an outline format or other shorthand that avoids full sentences and uses accepted acronyms. As a meeting participant, even if someone else is officially taking notes, it may be helpful to jot down a few reminders to use for future reference, to keep track of any assigned responsibilities, or to remember important deadlines. In many business settings, the scribe also sends the draft notes out to the meeting participants and asks for any corrections or feedback before circulating the final notes.

In one-on-one situations, one person can still fill the scribe role. Of course, taking notes may not be so important in this situation. Regardless, jotting down deadlines, responsibilities, project details, and timelines is always a good practice. Having a dedicated notebook, electronic file, or app, such as Microsoft OneNote, Evernote, or Google Keep, can help to keep track of these notes.

Taking notes, regardless of the setting, helps increase effective communication by maintaining a record, decreases inefficiency by preventing revisiting questions that were already answered or rehashing topics that were already discussed, and keeps team members accountable. It may be the case that notes from months or even years ago are useful. Further, having a written record may be especially important in the event of conflict, when controversial or sensitive topics are being discussed, or when there are legal ramifications.

What Are Practical Strategies for Success in Business Communications?

The consummate food and nutrition professional strives for professionalism in all business communications. There are practical strategies to support success in this area. While incorporating the individual professional's contribution in business communications, these strategies include a focus on others with the intent of improving the quality of communication through collaboration. This section will cover four practical strategies for success in business communication: Listen first; make connections and build relationships; allow time for writing, reviewing, and responding; and, above all, seek to be of service to others.

"Most people do not listen with the intent to understand; they listen with the intent to reply."

—STEPHEN R. COVEY[5]

Listen First

Registered dietitian nutritionists and other nutrition communicators spend a lot of time hearing from patients, clients, customers, and key opinion leaders, but does that mean they always understand what they are hearing? Are they really listening? According to Stephen R. Covey, renowned author of *The 7 Habits of Highly Effective People*, people should use empathic listening to communicate effectively. In fact, Habit 5, "First seek to understand, then to be understood," highlights the importance of empathic listening. In essence, empathic listening is the task of really feeling what the person speaking is saying. However, this type of listening takes time and practice. About 70% to 80% of daily life is spent engaged in some form of communication, and about 55% of that time is spent listening. Humans can listen to about 450 words per minute, but they process only about 17% to 25% of what is heard.[6]

Here are several tips to help improve listening skills:

- **L = Learn:** Keep an open mind and consider every conversation an opportunity to learn something new and to engage fully.
- **I = Interest:** Eliminate distractions and give the speaker full attention. Do not look at a phone, watch, or the next person who will be speaking.
- **S = Show**: Demonstrate attention by acknowledging what the other person is saying; smile, nod, and use positive facial expressions.
- **T = Turn:** Patiently wait a turn and do not interrupt or talk over the other person speaking.
- **E = Empathic:** Practice reflective listening, a technique that helps to establish mutual understanding—where both people understand what the other is trying to say—and leads to providing an appropriate response.
- **N = Now:** Resist the urge to think about what needs to be done later, like the next item on a to-do list, cooking dinner, or whatever big project might be underway. Instead, focus on the present and the conversation that is happening now.

Make Connections and Build Relationships

When engaging with others in professional settings, connections are forged with colleagues, co-workers, and peers. Welcome and cultivate these connections because building relationships can improve trust, respect, and mutual understanding. Positive connections and relationships in the workplace can also be beneficial for mental health.[7]

Practicing the professional attributes discussed throughout this chapter can help to make connections and build relationships. Other tips include these:

- Be reliable and accountable: Do what you say you will do, and if you don't, apologize and accept responsibility.
- Be reciprocal: Don't always ask others for something—also offer to help when needed.
- Be genuine: Being yourself can help make meaningful connections.

Allow Time for Writing, Reviewing, Responding

Two heads are better than one, goes the old saying, and when it comes to communicating, working with others can create a better product. Working with others also has the potential to add time to the process, which is why it requires organization to work efficiently and effectively.

When working with one or more individuals to create communications, such as written documents, start by reviewing the timeline for when the final draft is due and create a calendar with specific dates, agreed upon by the group, that includes:

- time to write or draft the communication,
- time for each member of the group to review and provide feedback,
- time for authors to create a revised draft, and
- time for final review and additional revisions to develop a final copy.

Another strategy is to determine ahead of time how many drafts the group plans to do, with one iteration consisting of each group member reviewing and providing feedback on the product. This may also be determined by the type of product that is being written. It is helpful to use the track-changes feature in a program like Microsoft Office Word or to use a document-sharing program that has a track-changes function, such as Google Docs. The group can determine which program they prefer to use track changes for edits and comments that are attributable to each author for follow-up, as needed.

See Box 39.4 for an example of a timeline and key activities used by four authors who collaborated to write a book chapter.

Utilize the various methods of communication available (meetings, email, and so on) to determine how the group plans to delve into the process and the timing of writing, reviewing, and responding to create the desired product within the time provided for the assignment.

BOX 39.4 Six Weeks Until Due Date: Sample Timeline and Activities for Four Coauthors of a Chapter

First drafts due from all authors to first author on January 17 (6 weeks before due date).

First author consolidates all drafts, reviews using track-changes tool, and sends to second author on January 24 (each author has 1 week to review and provide tracked changes, which adds up to 4 weeks).

Second author reviews using track-changes and sends to third author on January 31.

Third author reviews using track-changes and sends to fourth author on February 7.

Fourth author reviews using track-changes and sends back to all authors on February 14 (leaves 2 weeks for final review with any additional writing, editing, or other details to be completed before due date).

All authors review full draft with all track-changes on conference call on February 16; discuss and determine next steps for revising document, which author(s) will do final revisions, and which author(s) will draft the chapter introduction (in some cases, designate a primary author who makes decisions on final drafts).

Final revisions due February 23 and sent out to all authors.

All authors provide final review and sign-off on final draft by February 27.

Determine which author will provide final draft of chapter to editor by March 1 due date.

Seek to Be of Service

The foundation of effective business communication is a desire to serve customers or clients, colleagues and coworkers, and anyone else a person comes into contact with professionally. Helping to satisfy the needs of others goes a long way to solidifying positive working relationships. Communication should reflect the desire to achieve positive outcomes for everyone a nutrition communicator is entrusted to serve. Being self-serving may tarnish a nutrition communicator's reputation and diminish opportunities for future projects.

KEY POINTS

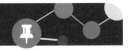

Business Communication Demonstrates Professionalism

1 Business communication includes correspondence, social media, meetings, networking, business cards, resumes, and other materials. Professionals maintain high standards throughout all forms of communication to reflect their best selves and foster mutual respect with colleagues and teammates.

2 Best practices in business communication include professionalism, teamwork, respect, clear and open communication, and documenting communications in writing.

3 Practical strategies for success in business communication include listening first, making connections and building relationships, allowing time to complete the work, and seeking to be of service to others.

RESOURCES

Templates for creating resumes:
- Google Template Library: https://docs.google.com/document/u/0/?ftv=1&tgif=c
- Microsoft Office: https://templates.office.com/en-us/resumes-and-cover-letters
- Canva: https://www.canva.com/templates/resumes

REFERENCES

1. Brown A. *EveryDayCook*. Ballantine Books; 2016.
2. Kelsey D, Plumb P. *Great Meetings! Great Results*. Hanson Park Press; 2004.
3. Networking. Merrian-Webster Unabridged. Accessed January 15, 2020. http://unabridged.merriam-webster.com/unabridged/networking
4. Benton D. *The Virtual Executive: How to Act Like a CEO Online and Offline*. McGraw-Hill; 2012.
5. Wilson B. The role of listening in Stephen Covey's *The Seven Habits of Highly Effective People*. businessLISTENING.com website. Accessed April 4, 2018. www.businesslistening.com/seven-habits_covey.php
6. Janusik L. Listening facts. International Listening Association website. Accessed April 4, 2018. www.listen.org/Listening-Facts
7. Hellebuyck M, Nguyen T, Halphern M, Fritze D, Kennedy J. *Mind the Workplace*. Mental Health America; 2017. Accessed January 16, 2020. www.mentalhealthamerica.net/sites/default/files/Mind%the%Workplace%-%MHA%Workplace%Health%Survey%2017%FINAL.pdf

Quality Communication in Grant and Project Proposals Is Rewarded

Amy R. Mobley, PhD, RD
and Elizabeth Yakes Jimenez, PhD, RDN, LD

"Writing high-quality grant and project proposals is an important skill set in many areas of nutrition practice, especially public health and research."

"You can have brilliant ideas, but if you can't get them across, your ideas won't get you anywhere." —LEE IACOCCA

Introduction

Obtaining grant or project funding is an inherently competitive process. Anything that can be done to more effectively communicate the ideas and plans in a grant or project proposal will improve the chances that it will be selected for funding. This chapter provides an introduction to writing strong grant or project proposals. In light of the competition for grants in today's funding climate, important considerations include doing preliminary reading about the granting agency and applicant eligibility, reviewing criteria and grant instructions thoroughly, writing clearly and concisely, developing a strong project design and plan, and consulting mentors before submitting the proposal.

This chapter answers three questions:

- Why is it important to hone grant-writing skills?
- What are best practices for writing competitive grant and project proposals?
- What are practical strategies for writing competitive grant and project proposals?

Overall, successful grant writing takes planning, time, and often failure before success. A checklist of summary guidance is provided at the end of the chapter.

Why Is It Important to Hone Grant-Writing Skills?

Some areas of nutrition practice commonly depend almost entirely on grant and project funding, including public health nutrition and nutrition research. To succeed in these practice areas, it is important to develop effective grant- and project-proposal writing skills.

Competition for grants, and especially federal grants, has increased over the past few decades. Overall, the National Institutes of Health (NIH), the most prominent federal funder of nutrition research, awarded funding to only 17.2% of grant applicants in the 2008 to 2017 time frame.[1] The US Department of Agriculture (USDA), which also commonly funds nutrition research and projects, recommended 32.8% of grant applications for funding in fiscal year 2015 but awarded funding to only 21.1% of applicants, primarily due to lack of available funds to support all high-ranked proposals.[2] Thus, the pressure and expectation to produce a strong, well-written proposal are high.

Funding rates for foundations and nonprofit organizations are more variable than for federal agencies. For example, funding rates for most American Heart Association grants and fellowships are similar to or even more competitive than those for the NIH and USDA.[3] Foundation funding rates generally depend on how well the foundation is known, the number of proposals received, and the funding available.[4]

One thing is for certain: Poor-quality, hastily written proposals are unlikely to be funded. This chapter provides an overview of strategies to strengthen a grant or project proposal, as well as additional resources that may be helpful to consult during the proposal-writing process.

What Are Best Practices for Writing Competitive Grant and Project Proposals?

This section covers steps for preparing a strong grant or project proposal, including identifying the right funding opportunity, following instructions, seeking out examples and scoring criteria, and ensuring that all aspects of a proposal are concise, consistent, clear, and complete.

Identify The Right Funding Opportunity

There are numerous potential sources of funding for nutrition research and projects, including federal agencies; corporate and private foundations; global, national, and local nonprofit organizations; local and state governments; and industry funders. Box 40.1 (page 616) identifies potential sources of federal, foundation, and nonprofit funding for nutrition research and projects. There are also websites that will allow users to search for and subscribe to opportunities across multiple funders, such as Grants.gov (www.grants.gov), Foundation Directory Online (https://fconline.foundationcenter .org; requires a subscription), and Pivot (https:// pivot.proquest.com; designed for researchers; and may require affiliation with a university).

An important first step in developing a successful proposal is to identify the right funding agency and funding opportunity. For a proposal to be competitive, there must be a strong match between the funding agency's request for proposal or stated priorities and the grant or project objectives and plan. It is important to understand whether a funder focuses on projects or program delivery versus research, domestic versus global work, and specific areas of nutrition practice.

Another consideration is the total budget and amount of indirect—that is, facilities-related and administrative—costs allowed by grants. Indirect

"If you don't qualify, don't apply."
—FOUNDATION CENTER

costs are also known as overhead expenses, or general or administrative expenses. Examples of indirect costs include building rent, utilities, and administrative staff salaries. These costs are difficult to assign to a specific program or project, so each program or project usually allows a certain proportion of its budget to go toward covering indirect costs. In some cases, indirect funds are vital to the financial health of an organization or institution, and there may be specific policies requiring that only grants that provide a certain proportion of the budget as indirect costs be applied for. Generally, federal grants provide the largest overall budgets and the highest indirect funds, and foundations and nonprofit organizations limit total budgets and indirect funds more strictly. If the scope of a planned grant or project does not match the funds available, it can be difficult to convince funders and reviewers that the project can actually be accomplished. If funding is obtained and there is a sizable shortfall in budget, it may not be possible to deliver what was promised in the proposal, which can affect relationships with both the funder and the collaborators and community, as well as the ability to obtain future funding. All grant and project proposals involve a substantial investment of time and effort. Time and effort are best maximized by applying only to opportunities that are a good fit for the planned project and institution or organization.

At times, it may be possible to obtain feedback about whether an idea is a good fit for the funder before submitting a full proposal. Some funders may first require a letter of intent or inquiry (LOI). Usually a LOI is short, no more than one to two pages. In some cases, funders use LOIs to prepare for grant application reviews. In other cases, LOIs are competitive, and only some applicants will be invited to submit a full grant proposal. When writing a LOI, it is important to closely follow the directions regarding required content. This will be specific to the funder and may include details, such as investigator names and contact information; the proposed study or project title, objectives, justification, timeline, brief methods, and expected outcomes; an estimated budget; and an explanation of how the project or study meets the sponsor's mission or funding priorities. Remember that this is a first chance to make a good impression with the grant sponsor. Be sure to avoid common downfalls, such as forgetting to include required content, using technical jargon, being too wordy, or adding irrelevant information. Be sure to have someone else proofread the letter to assess clarity and identify spelling and grammatical errors.

In some cases, it may be possible to seek input on a grant or project plan from the designated contact person for the funding opportunity announcement. Sometimes the designated contact person will be willing to review the project objectives to provide feedback. Grant funders sometimes host webinars or meetings before a grant submission deadline, which gives the opportunity to ask questions and hear questions from other applicants related to eligibility, funding priorities, and the grant process.

BOX 40.1 Potential Sources of Federal, Foundation, and Nonprofit Funding for Nutrition Research and Projects

Federal Agencies

- **National Institutes of Health**—National Cancer Institute; National Heart, Lung, and Blood Institute; National Institute of Diabetes and Digestive and Kidney Disorders; National Institute on Aging; National Center for Complementary and Integrative Health; National Institute of Child Health and Human Development

  https://grants.nih.gov/grants/grants _process.htm

- **Maternal and Child Health Bureau, Health Resources and Services Administration**

  www.hrsa.gov/grants/apply-for-a-grant

  https://mchb.hrsa.gov/find-funding

- **National Institute of Food and Agriculture, US Department of Agriculture**

  https://nifa.usda.gov/grants

- **Centers for Disease Control and Prevention**

  www.cdc.gov/grants/index.html

- **Agency for Healthcare Research and Quality**

  www.ahrq.gov/funding/index.html

- **National Science Foundation**

  www.nsf.gov/funding

- **Grants Learning Center**

  www.grants.gov/web/grants/learn -grants.html

Foundations

- **Robert Wood Johnson Foundation**

  www.rwjf.org/en/how-we-work/grants-and -grant-programs.html

- **Wellcome Trust**

  https://wellcome.ac.uk/funding

- **W.K. Kellogg Foundation**

  www.wkkf.org/grantseekers

- **Bill and Melinda Gates Foundation**

  www.gatesfoundation.org/How-We-Work /General-Information/Grant-Opportunities

- **Academy of Nutrition and Dietetics Foundation**

  https://eatrightfoundation.org /scholarships-funding/Grants

Nonprofit Organizations

- **American Cancer Society**

  www.cancer.org/research/we-fund-cancer -research/apply-research-grant.html

- **American Heart Association**

  https://professional.heart.org/professional /ResearchPrograms/AwardsPolicies /UCM_475340_Awards.jsp

- **American Diabetes Association**

  https://professional.diabetes.org /research-grants

Follow Instructions

One of the most important pieces of advice received at any grant-writing workshop or from any expert grant writer is: Be sure to read the entire grant opportunity announcement and carefully note all the directions. Most requests for proposals, calls for proposals, or requests for applications contain a comprehensive set of instructions, including information on funding priorities, funder goals, eligibility, formatting, content and submission requirements, and deadlines.

First, carefully review deadlines. Grant writing takes time, often several months, depending on the complexity of the project and budget and the size of the project team and number of organizations and institutions involved. It is helpful to construct a timeline that works backward from a deadline of 1 week before the final due date, and to establish deadlines for each component of the grant or project proposal up to that deadline. Particularly for electronic submissions, be ready to submit at least a few days before the deadline in case of technical issues or problems with the uploading or transmission process.

Make sure to follow directions related to formatting, content, and submission requirements. Funders often receive many more proposals than they can fund, and may reject proposals, without review, on technicalities. Few things are more painful than spending months of effort on a grant or project proposal and having it rejected based on a small detail or an error during a last-minute submission.

Write Clearly with Focus

Once a promising potential funder has been identified, review successfully funded projects, if possible. This will help to further determine if the opportunity is a good fit, as well as identify effective writing strategies in funded proposals. Information on previously funded projects may not be available from all funding sources, but many organizations provide some details. The National Institute of Allergy and Infectious Diseases (NIAID), for example, posts examples of well-written components of grant applications in the public domain (www.niaid.nih.gov /grants-contracts/sample-applications). These may be helpful even if the proposal being written is not for an NIAID grant.

Before beginning to write, review the grant evaluation or peer review criteria. Usually the proposal review criteria are available early in the process. Make sure to have a clear understanding of how the proposal will be evaluated and scored. Be certain to address all items that will be scored or considered in the decision to fund the grant or project application. Pay close attention to any areas or items that are more heavily weighted in the scoring criteria.

Overall, a grant or project application needs to be focused, clear, and concise. Follow page or word limits specified in the proposal guidelines. Project and grant reviewers are often busy experts volunteering their time and expertise, which makes succinct writing essential. Explain concepts at the level of an intelligent layperson, because project and grant reviewers may or may not share a particular specialty area. Avoid using technical jargon and minimize use of acronyms. Some funding agencies now require that an abstract or project summary be written in lay language.

Beyond good writing, the proposal document(s) should be visually appealing and reader-friendly. Consider using figures and tables to summarize key points, pilot data, and planned outcome assessments or to illustrate the planned intervention. Reading through lines and lines of crammed text is hard on the eyes and not aesthetically pleasing, so allow some white space in the document, with appropriate margins and font style and size per the proposal guidelines. Use headings and subheadings to clearly label required sections of the proposal.

It is important to spend extra time on certain elements of a proposal, as they may be the only elements that some reviewers see. These elements include the title, abstract, and specific aims or objectives. Ideally, these three elements should catch the reviewers' attention, be memorable, and convey the significance of the proposal while keeping to any word, character, or page limits. For the title, start by listing relevant keywords for the grant subject matter and then carefully arrange the words into an impactful and attractive title; many people try to create titles that contain relevant acronyms to make them more memorable. Write the abstract last so that it accurately captures the content of the proposal.

Write Clear Objectives That Match the Intention of the Grant

As mentioned in the previous section, sometimes the only page or component of a grant proposal that is reviewed is the page containing the objectives (sometimes called Specific Aims, Study, Project Aims, or Objectives). On some grant review panels, certain panel members may only review the summary page or aims page. Thus, spend extra time ensuring that objectives or aims are well written.

Clearly relate the objectives to the funder's priorities, mission, and vision. If the grant sponsor's priorities, mission, and vision are not clearly stated in the request for proposals, review their website and other available materials, such as annual reports.

The objectives should also speak to a clear need. For research, the need is generally related to filling an identified gap in knowledge. For project and program implementation, the need may be related to translating promising research findings into practice or responding to a community needs assessment that identifies gaps in services or populations served. As part of the objectives page, review and summarize relevant literature and available data, highlighting and summarizing the unmet need. Above all, reviewers and the funder should understand the significance of the proposal to scientific progress, to translational or implementation science, or to a community or population with unmet needs.

Generally, grant proposals include one to three objectives. Ideally, objectives should be SMART—Specific, Measurable, Achievable, Relevant, and Time-Bound, as described in Figure 15.1 on page 242. In other words, it should be possible to clearly evaluate whether the objectives are being accomplished during and at the end of the project. If there are multiple objectives, each should stand alone; objectives can build upon each other but should not be dependent on each other. The primary reason for avoiding dependent objectives is that if the first objective fails, it will not be possible to complete the overall project. Dependent objectives are an unnecessary risk for the funder. The following is an example of a dependent objective (without a successful objective 1, objective 2 cannot be tested):

> Objective 1: To determine the impact of the All 4 Kids 40-week nutrition education program on fruit and vegetable intake in preschool-aged children.

> Objective 2: To determine how increased fruit and vegetable intake mediates improvements in body mass index z-score in preschool-aged children participating in the All 4 Kids program.

Refer to Chapter 38 for more on GENIE.

Objectives are often followed by a hypothesis, particularly if a research project is being proposed. Sometimes, the objectives are preceded by an overarching project goal or even long-term goal. This will depend on the funder's requirements.

A logic model is a useful tool for planning a project and especially for considering the relationship between the grant or project objectives and outcomes. This type of model is a pictorial representation linking a project's objectives, activities, and outcomes. In fact, some federal agencies, such as the USDA and the National Science Foundation, require logic models for certain grant applications. If a logic model is not required, it is still important to communicate the relationship between elements of a proposal in a table, diagram, or figure by clearly linking project aims to outcomes that will be used to evaluate them. See Figures 10.3 and 10.4 on pages 153 and 154 for examples of logic models from the University of Wisconsin Program Development and Evaluation team.[5]

Make Sure the Project Is Novel and Well Designed

While the ability to communicate a grant idea in a well-written application is critical, if the research or project approach is poorly designed, it is unlikely to be funded. Therefore, allow adequate time to identify current research methods that are valid and reliable or project approaches that are evidence-based. An example of a resource available to nutrition professionals for developing well-designed nutrition education programs is the Guide for Effective Nutrition Interventions and Education (GENIE) tool (https://genie.web author.com/public/partner.cfm). This online tool provides a checklist of quality indicators for nutrition education programs.

Ensure that the proposal conveys both feasibility (eg, the team has the appropriate skills and resources, the timeline is reasonable) and sustainability (eg, it includes a plan for what will happen to continue the work when the funded project ends). All projects will have limitations and potential difficulties, and these should be acknowledged and, ideally, addressed. For example, if it seems that it may be difficult to recruit research study or project participants, it may be helpful to outline multiple recruitment strategies along with a plan for how they will be sequentially implemented to ensure that the sample size for the research project or the target number of participants for the program is achieved.

Develop a Realistic and Carefully Justified Project Budget

A grant or project budget must accurately reflect the costs of properly executing a project; in particular, it should reflect the planned methods, a timeline, and an outcome evaluation plan. The budget should at minimum consider costs related to personnel (including employee salaries and fringe benefits), professional services and contract costs, office supplies, computer software, copying, printing, postage, telephone or teleconference lines, travel, equipment, and indirect costs. If possible, review the budget with an experienced colleague or fiscal agent from the institution or organization who may identify important budget categories that have been inadvertently omitted or overestimated or underestimated.

Writing a careful justification of a budget can also help to more realistically estimate costs; many funders require that a budget justification be included. The following are example budget justifications, along with sample information that would be included:

- The translator (consultant) will be responsible for translating all study intervention materials into Chinese.

   40 hours x $35/hr = $1,400

- We will purchase database and statistical analysis software to assist us with collecting and analyzing evaluation data.

   10 licenses (2 for each clinic site) @ $250/license = $2,500

Experienced grant reviewers and funders can easily detect inadequate or inflated budgets. They may rate a grant lower based on the assumption that the grant writer does not have a clear grasp of how much a project or program truly costs to execute. Proposals that attempt to accomplish too much in too little time with too little funding are unlikely to receive funding because of concerns that the work plan cannot be fulfilled.

Provide Supporting Evidence and Documents

The grant guidance from the funding organization should specify what can and cannot be included as additional evidence or supporting documents. At minimum, many grant applications require preliminary or pilot data or documentation of previous success to convince reviewers that a project will likely be successful. If working collaboratively with other experts or community partners, it will be necessary to demonstrate the collaborators' willingness of those parties to work together, usually through letters of support. A letter of support from a collaborator should generally outline the collaborator's role in the project and why they are interested in participating. The grant applicant may draft letters of support, but each collaborator should tailor and edit their own version. A sample letter of support can be found on the Center for Public Health Practice at the Colorado School of Public Health website (www.publichealthpractice.org /sites/default/files/Letter%20of%20Support%20 Template_0.pdf) or within a full sample proposal shared by the NIAID (www.niaid.nih.gov/sites /default/files/parrishfull.pdf).

Proposals also may include supporting documents, such as relevant publications or reports, evidence of institutional review board submission or approval (for research projects), the applicant's resume or curriculum vitae (if not already part of the standard required documents), and an outline of an intervention curriculum or examples of educational materials, to name a few. Follow specific guidelines regarding supporting documents (eg, they may be required, optional, or encouraged) and any page limits. These guidelines can change, so even if a grant has previously been submitted to the same organization, double-check what is allowed for the current application.

What Are Practical Strategies for Writing Competitive Grant and Project Proposals?

The previous section addressed best practices for writing high-quality grant and project proposals. In this section, some additional practical strategies are provided that will help in getting a grant or project proposal submitted and funded, including setting a reasonable timeline, identifying a mentoring team, volunteering to serve on grant review panels, viewing a proposal from funder and reviewer perspectives, and refining a proposal through additional submissions.

Allow Adequate Time for Quality Work and Revision

Generally, grant deadlines are inflexible, and most funders will automatically reject proposals submitted after the stated deadline. As emphasized earlier in the chapter, it is essential to allow adequate time to prepare, review, and revise a proposal before submission. It may be possible to write shorter proposals with limited partners or collaborators in 1 to 3 months, but larger, more complex proposals generally take at least 6 to 12 months to prepare, review, revise, and submit. The ability to gauge how much time is needed for writing a grant comes from practice and experience, or initially from consulting with experienced collaborators or mentors.

Allow enough time for at least one internal colleague or collaborator (or partner), and ideally multiple individuals, to review all work. Internal reviewers should use the grant peer review criteria and focus on identifying areas that are missing, underdeveloped, or inconsistent. They can help to vet the research or program design and implementation plan as well as proofread for errors in spelling, grammar, and reference citation; clarity issues related to symbols and abbreviations; and issues related to the numbering of tables and figures. Applicants should also carefully proofread their own work, ideally when they are well rested and have stepped away from the proposal for a while.

Identify Mentors Who Can Provide Early and Ongoing Input and Review

While it is helpful to have multiple colleagues or collaborators (or partners) review a grant proposal draft, new grant writers can benefit from identifying an appropriate mentoring team early on during the grant development process. Regular involvement from experienced mentors can improve the quality of a grant submission. An ideal mentoring team would, at minimum, include an expert in the content area or methods included in the proposal, individuals to advise on statistical and fiscal considerations, and someone who has successfully obtained grants from the identified funding agency. Experienced mentors can help to develop a realistic writing timeline, review and provide early feedback on sections of the grant, assist with troubleshooting problems that arise, and provide key insights into strategies for succeeding with submissions to a particular funder.

Volunteer to Serve on Grant Review Panels

Volunteering to serve on a grant review panel can provide invaluable experience in understanding a funding agency's priorities and expectations. Grant reviewers are provided an opportunity to closely critique grant applications and can gain insight into what it takes to write a competitive proposal in the context of that funding agency. The review process also provides perspective into how ideas are best communicated and organized. It should be noted that issues related to conflict of interest are closely considered and evaluated; therefore, grant reviewers may not serve on panels at agencies where they have a current grant submission or on panels that are reviewing any grant submissions from current or recent collaborators.

Review the Proposal from the Funder's and Reviewers' Perspectives

An experienced mentor can also help to carefully review a proposal from the funder's and reviewers' perspectives. Generally, funders are interested in wisely investing their money to make the greatest impact. So, clearly and prominently feature the significance of a proposal in the title, abstract, and objectives. Reviewers have a different role—their goal is to identify weaknesses and inconsistencies that make a proposal infeasible or cause it to be ranked lower than other proposals. Reviewers are often busy and potentially bored or overwhelmed from reading several proposals at once. Consider a proposal from a reviewer's perspective and think about whether it is concise, compellingly written, easy to read, well organized, well justified, and well aligned with the funder's priorities. Does the proposal merit funding?

Don't Give Up

Don't get discouraged if a grant or project proposal is not funded. As noted at the beginning of this chapter, obtaining grant funding is a very competitive process. If a proposal is rejected, address themes in reviewer feedback before resubmitting the grant to the same funder or submitting it to a new funder. Some funders may have policies around resubmissions. For example, resubmission may be allowed only once, or it may be necessary to include a summary of how reviewer feedback was addressed in a resubmission. Aim to resubmit in a timely manner so that the work and momentum that were put into the initial submission are not lost, particularly if working with a team of partners and collaborators.

See the checklist provided to prepare for a grant submission.

 Summary Checklist to Prepare for a Grant Submission

Have you:

___ volunteered to serve on grant review panels or attended grant writing workshops or trainings?

___ closely reviewed the grant sponsor's guidelines, including funding priorities, funder goals, eligibility, formatting, content and submission requirements, and deadlines?

___ given enough time to prepare the grant proposal?

___ identified a mentoring team?

___ developed a novel and well-designed approach?

___ arranged for colleagues to review the proposal and provide feedback?

___ proofread the proposal?

___ incorporated reviewer feedback before resubmitting the grant?

KEY POINTS

Quality Communication in Grant and Project Proposals Is Rewarded

1 Writing high-quality grant and project proposals is an important skill set in many areas of nutrition practice, especially public health and research.

2 Pay careful attention to grant or proposal guidance provided by the funding organization and any supplemental materials, such as example grants or scoring criteria, that are available from funders; submit a grant or proposal that is well written and well designed, responds to all guidance, carefully addresses all scored areas, and is an excellent fit for funder goals and priorities.

3 Allow enough time to do quality work; it is difficult to write a high-quality grant or project proposal on a short timeline.

4 Do not become discouraged if a grant or project proposal is not funded on the first try. Everyone's first few proposals are a learning process. Seek out mentorship from experienced proposal writers to shorten the learning curve.

RESOURCES

US Department of Agriculture—government grant information: https://www.nal.usda.gov/fnic/government-and-non-government-grant-information

National Institutes of Health—grant writing advice and sample applications:
- https://nccih.nih.gov/grants/resources/grantwrite-advice.htm
- www.niaid.nih.gov/grants-contracts/sample-applications

National Institutes of Health—videos about the peer review process: http://public.csr.nih.gov/NewsAndPolicy/PeerReviewVideos

US Department of Agriculture—grant-writing resources: https://nifa.usda.gov/grant-training

Grant Writers' Seminars and Workshops website: www.grantcentral.com

Purdue Extension, Purdue University—Writing a Successful Grant Proposal: www.extension.purdue.edu/extmedia/EC/EC-737.pdf

REFERENCES

1. US Department of Health and Human Services, National Institutes of Health, Research Portfolio Online Reporting Tools (RePORT). Funding success rates. January 2014. Accessed March 1, 2018. https://report.nih.gov/success_rates
2. US Department of Agriculture, National Institute of Food and Agriculture. Agriculture and Food Research Initiative (AFRI) 2016 annual review: tables 1 and 2. Accessed March 1, 2018. https://nifa.usda.gov/tables-1-and-2
3. American Heart Association. Success rates 2016–2017. Accessed March 1, 2018. https://professional.heart.org/professional/ResearchPrograms/AwardeesResearchAccomplishments/TopAdvancesInResearch/UCM_444458_Success-Rates.jsp
4. GrantSpace. What is the percentage of grant proposals that foundations actually fund? Accessed March 1, 2018. http://grantspace.org/resources/knowledge-base/percentage-of-funded-grant-proposals
5. University of Wisconsin-Extension, Program Development and Evaluation. Logic model worksheet. Accessed March 1, 2018. https://fyi.uwex.edu/programdevelopment/files/2016/03/LM_UW-Coop-Ext-Logic-Model_WorksheetTableformat.pdf

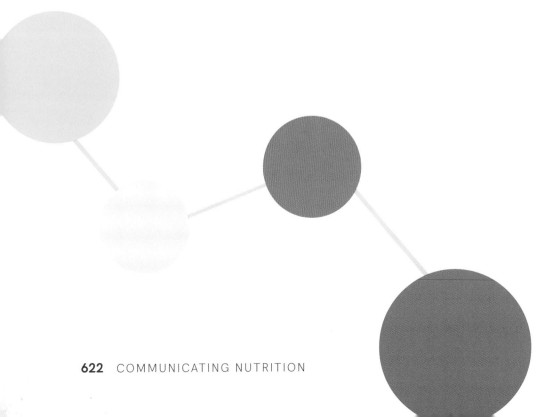

Nutrition Communicators Publish Research in Peer-Reviewed Journals

Elizabeth Yakes Jimenez, PhD, RDN, LD
Ann Gaba, EdD, RD, CDN, CDCES, FAND
and Virginia Quick, PhD, RDN

"Publishing research is an important way to contribute to the scientific field that can advance evidence-based practice guidelines and policies."

> *"To get to know, to discover, to publish—this is the destiny of a scientist."* —FRANÇOIS ARAGO

Introduction

Why write for a peer-reviewed journal?

By its very nature, nutrition science is an incremental process, with scientists reviewing and building on the work of others to advance the field and nutrition treatments, interventions, and practices in all settings.[1,2] Publishing in peer-reviewed journals allows nutrition communicators to inform the work of other scientists in their area and contribute to scientific progress.[3] In addition, they can potentially influence nutrition practice and outcomes for populations served by nutrition practitioners. The translation of nutrition science into practice recommendations currently occurs through evidence-based practice guidelines[4] and practice and policy statements, which are often informed by periodic systematic reviews of the literature.

By definition, evidence-based practice is the integration of individual-level expertise in a field with the best external evidence available to make decisions about how to proceed.[5] Timely publication of research in peer-reviewed journals allows a nutrition communicator to contribute to the body of knowledge that informs practice guidelines.

This chapter answers four questions:

- What are best practices for preparing a scientific manuscript for a peer-reviewed journal?
- What are key considerations for selecting a peer-reviewed journal for a submission and submitting a manuscript?
- What are strategies for successfully navigating the manuscript review and revision process?
- Beyond the basics, what else is useful to know about publishing a peer-reviewed journal article?

The advancement of nutrition science requires nutrition professionals to publish their research in peer-reviewed journals. The journey to getting published in scientific journals follows a similar path to that outlined in Chapter 22 on writing: Write, review, revise, repeat. Quality research combined with quality writing results in well-communicated nutrition science.

What Are Best Practices for Preparing a Scientific Manuscript for a Peer-Reviewed Journal?

The preparation of a comprehensive and well-organized manuscript is a slow and steady process that includes not only writing but also extensive review and revision, resulting in quality work that will be accepted for publication and contribute to the scientific literature.

Write a Comprehensive and Well-Organized Manuscript

This section includes practical suggestions for effectively preparing a scientific manuscript based on original research, including guidance to ensure that manuscript content is comprehensive and well organized. Starting a manuscript is often the hardest part—take it step by step, making steady progress, and a manuscript will come together.

REVIEW PROFESSIONAL GUIDANCE ON KEY ELEMENTS

Several sets of professional reporting standards and checklists are available to guide nutrition communicators in drafting the sections of a manuscript. The EQUATOR Network (Enhancing the Quality and Transparency of Health Research) compiles reporting guidelines for all main study types, along with other relevant resources, on their website (www.equator-network.org). Examples of available reporting standards for study designs that are common in nutrition research are included in Box 41.1. Using these reporting standards can improve the quality, organization, and coherence of a manuscript and potentially save time during the review phase. Most journals also provide specific author guidelines, which will be further discussed later in this chapter.

UPDATE THE LITERATURE REVIEW

After identifying and reviewing appropriate reporting guidelines, the next step is to update the review of the relevant literature. A literature review was likely done when planning the project, but it is important to update it when starting to write the manuscript if significant time has passed. Think about summarizing what is known about the topic area, identifying key gaps in knowledge, and understanding the context of the research findings. It can be helpful to systematically extract information regarding author and year of publication, population characteristics, setting, study design, elements of the intervention (if applicable), key findings, and limitations from the relevant articles into a table, to assist with synthesizing findings across studies.

CHOOSE AN APPROPRIATE TITLE, KEYWORDS, AND ABSTRACT

The title is generally the shortest part of a manuscript, but it is important because it will often be

Reporting Standards for Study Designs Common in Nutrition Research[6-11]

Randomized controlled trials: CONSORT (Consolidated Standards of Reporting Trials)

Cluster randomized trials: CONSORT extension for cluster trials

Cohort, case-control, and cross-sectional studies: STROBE (Strengthening the Reporting of Observational Studies in Epidemiology)

Evaluations with nonrandomized designs: TREND (Transparent Reporting of Evaluations with Nonrandomized Designs)

Quality Improvement Studies: SQUIRE (Standards for Quality Improvement Reporting Excellence)

Qualitative research: COREQ (Consolidated Criteria for Reporting Qualitative Research)

used to index the article, and it is the main result that people see when they search for research articles in a database like PubMed. Aim for a title that is specific and accurately reflects the purpose, issues addressed, design, and results of the study. A good title should clearly convey the manuscript's contribution to the field.[12] Jamali and Nikzad describe four common formats for journal article titles[13]:

- **Declarative titles** include the main conclusions of the study. For example: "Adipose Gene Expression Prior to Weight Loss Can Predict Dietary Carbohydrate Responders."
- **Descriptive titles** describe the subject of the article without mention of the main outcome or conclusion. For example: "Food Insecurity in Urban Versus Rural Counties in the United States."
- **Interrogative (question) titles** indicate the subject of the article in the form of a question to appeal to the curiosity of readers. For example: "Does Birth Order Predict Probability of Disordered Eating?"
- **Compound titles** may start with a short question followed by a subject statement, or

start with a noun phrase followed by a colon and a declarative sentence or a question (or vice versa). For example: "Maternal Choline Supplementation Positively Affects Infant Development: A Randomized Controlled Trial" or "Education for Food Safety: Can Early Childhood Interventions Prevent the Spread of Infectious Disease?"

Shah[14] suggests a stepwise process of revisions to craft the most impactful title. First, consider the following questions: What was studied? What study design was used? Who or what was studied? How was it done? Where was it done? What were the results? From the list of answers, choose key phrases or words to include in the title.

Having a clear and concise title for a paper is also likely to yield a greater number of downloads and citations. Jamali and Nikzad's[13] study of open-source publications found that articles with longer titles were downloaded less frequently than articles with shorter titles, and titles with colons in them received fewer downloads and citations. Paiva and colleagues reported similar results,[15] finding that not only did short-titled articles have higher viewing and citation rates than those with longer titles, but that titles containing a question mark or that used a colon or a hyphen were associated with a lower number of citations. They further note that short titles presenting results or conclusions were independently associated with higher citation counts. To shorten a title, remove unnecessary waste words that do not alter the meaning, such as "a study of," "an investigation of," or "observation of," as well as excessive details about the intervention, population, and location where the study was conducted.

Keywords help people find published research when they search a database. Many journals request keywords that are Medical Subject Headings (MeSH) compliant; MeSH is the National Library of Medicine (NLM) controlled vocabulary for indexing and cataloguing biomedical literature. The NLM has several resources available to help authors identify MeSH-compliant keywords, including MeSH on Demand, which automatically identifies keywords from a block of text, such as an abstract, and the MeSH Browser, which allows authors to directly search for MeSH terms.[16]

The abstract is a summary of an article that can be accessed through databases like PubMed. Potential readers will use the abstract to decide if they will seek out the full text of the article. Although the abstract is the first section of a manuscript, it usually will be the last section that is written, as it should accurately reflect the full content of the manuscript and convey its major purpose, findings, and implications. Generally, abstracts are limited to 150 to 300 words, with standard structure including the study background or purpose, objectives, methods, results, and conclusions.

WRITE AN INTRODUCTION

The article introduction has three major purposes, which should be succinctly covered in approximately one to two pages: briefly summarizing what is known about the topic area from the relevant literature, identifying key gaps in knowledge, and outlining the research questions, objectives, and hypotheses of the study. When discussing what is known about an issue, consider including more information, such as the prevalence of a disease or condition and its impact on health and economic or other relevant outcomes. It may be useful to make the case to the reader that this problem or issue is important and needs to be addressed. Then, emphasize that this article is adding something new to what is known about this problem or issue. So, ideally, the study objectives should aim to address a key gap in knowledge, and this should come across strongly in the introduction.

The introduction should *not* be an extensive review of the literature in the area. Other commonly encountered issues in the introduction section include not identifying the study objectives and hypotheses (particularly for exploratory or observational studies) and presenting study results or conclusions. Results and conclusions should be saved for the results and discussion sections of the manuscript.

DESCRIBE THE METHODS

The goal of the methods section is to give readers enough details about what was done so that they could replicate the study. Replication of findings is an essential part of the scientific process.

The methods need to be set out in a clear and complete way, with a separate subheading for each required step. The reporting standards and checklists mentioned earlier in the chapter are a good place to start when developing the subheading outline for the methods section. This will help to avoid the common error of leaving out key elements or information. Key general elements of the methods section include descriptions of the study design; the study setting and participants, including the study eligibility criteria; ethical review, informed consent, and participant recruitment and enrollment; any interventions that were implemented; and information about how data were collected and analyzed and how the study sample size was determined. In some cases, it is important to describe methods for randomization and blinding. The rationale for any decisions that were made related to the protocol or analysis should be included. For example, it may be useful to explain why individuals from a specific age range, sex, race, or ethnicity were included as participants; why certain elements were included in the intervention; why specific instruments were used for data collection; or why certain biomarkers were collected.

SHOW RESULTS THROUGH TABLES AND FIGURES

The results section presents the findings from the data analysis. There should be a clear connection between the methods and results sections, in that the outcomes of all of the data collection and analysis procedures described in the methods section are reported in the results. Present the results in the same order in which the data collection and analysis methods are described in the methods section. Avoid describing data collection and statistical methods in the results section; be sure to

describe *what* was done in the *methods* section and the *outcome* of the analysis in the *results*. Be sure to summarize and highlight both positive and negative results.

The results section usually includes tables and figures that concisely summarize the findings from the data analysis and enhance reader comprehension of the study findings. It may be helpful to prepare the tables and figures first, then write the text of the results section. That way the key findings shown in the tables and figures can be highlighted in the text. Do not repeat all of the information provided in the tables and figures again in the text.

A reader should be able to review a table or figure and understand it without reading the text. To facilitate this, include footnotes for tables and figures that define abbreviations and briefly describe data collection and statistical methods.

A table is best used to concisely present many numerical values and compare and contrast them by study group or participant characteristics.[17] For example, most manuscripts have a Table 1 that summarizes descriptive characteristics of the study participants. See Figure 41.1 for an example of a table that summarizes the characteristics of research study participants.

Figures, such as graphs and diagrams, can be useful to show visual trends and patterns in data (rather than specific numeric values) and to explain certain aspects of the study design.[17] For example,

FIGURE 41.1 Example of a table summarizing the characteristics of research study participants

Child and Maternal Baseline Characteristics by Study Group

	Intervention Group (n = 59)	Control Group (n = 52)
Child characteristics		
Age (months), mean ± SDa	4.3 ± 0.4	4.1 ± 0.6
Girls, n (%)	28 (47)	26 (50)
Exclusively breastfeeding, n (%)	25 (42)	20 (38)
Maternal characteristics		
Age (years), mean ± SD	28.6 ± 7.4	29.0 ± 8.1
BMIb (kg/m2), mean ± SD	24.7 ± 5.1	25.2 ± 4.7
College graduate, n (%)	42 (71)	38 (73)

a = SD, standard deviation
b = BMI, body mass index

many manuscripts include a flow diagram to visually depict study recruitment and retention.[18] See Figure 41.2 for an example of a graph illustrating an interaction between initial length and change in length for children participating in a cluster-randomized intervention trial[19] and Figure 41.3 for an example of a study flow diagram.[19]

Several practices can help to make tables and figures clear and understandable. Consider using subheadings in tables to identify important categories and splitting tables that are long (more than one page) into multiple tables. For figures, use a standard font and ensure that all aspects of the figure are legible and labeled for ease of interpretation. For both tables and figures, specify units for all quantities to aid in interpretation. In preparing tables, graphs, and figures for publication, remember that they will probably be in smaller print when published. Always double-check the results section for errors and inconsistencies prior to submitting a manuscript. This includes verifying that results in the text are consistent with results in the tables and figures.

WRITE THE DISCUSSION

The main goal of the discussion section is to consider the study findings related to the larger context of the research area, and to highlight the implications of the study in that area and next steps in research or practice. Box 41.2 (page 630) contains a suggested outline for organizing the discussion section, which should generally be about four to six pages long.

There are several key questions that should be answered in the discussion section: What has been discovered? What does it mean, and what are the implications for research or practice? How do the results of the study compare with what has been found by previous studies? If there are differences between this study's findings and those of others, how are these differences explained? Some points to consider in making these comparisons are differences in study design, sample size, population demographics, study setting, data collection or analysis methods, time or duration, and specific interventions, if any, for each study. Avoid just listing the other studies and their outcomes.

FIGURE 41.2 **Example of a graph illustrating study results**

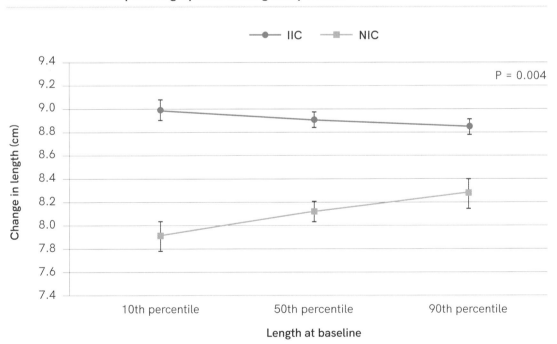

Fig 2. Change in length by initial length in young children in Burkina Faso. IIC = Intervention cohort. NIC = Non-intervention cohort

Reproduced with permission from Hess SY, Abbeddou S, Jimenez EY, et al. Small-quantity lipid-based nutrient supplements, regardless of their zinc content, increase growth and reduce the prevalence of stunting and wasting in young Burkinabe children: a cluster-randomized trial. *PloS One*. 2015;10(3):e0122242. doi:10.1371/journal.pone.0122242[19]

FIGURE 41.3 **Example of a study flow diagram**

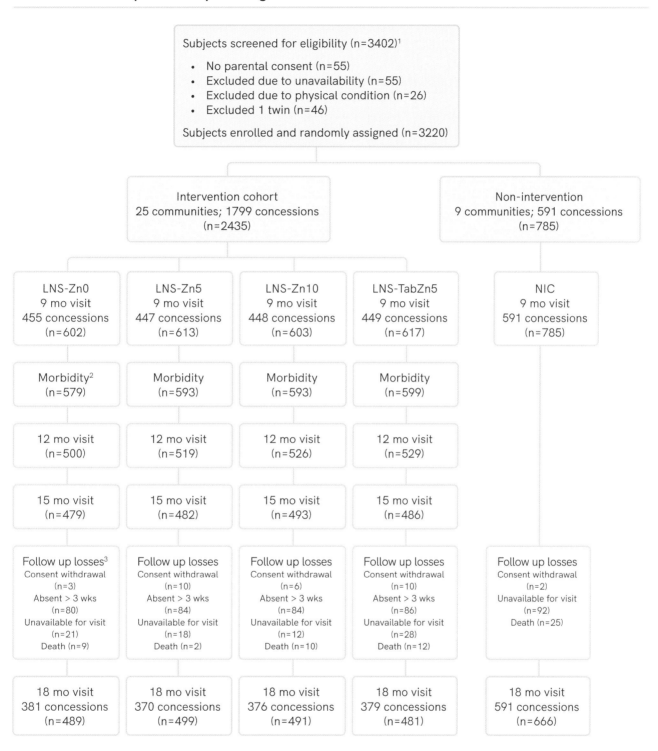

¹Eligibility was determined at the level of the child
²Children with >30 d of morbidity surveillance
³Number of children who dropped out between enrollment and 18 months visit

Fig 1. Flow diagram of clusters and participant progression through the iLiNS-ZINC trial

Reproduced with permission from Hess SY, Abbeddou S, Jimenez EY, et al. Small-quantity lipid-based nutrient supplements, regardless of their zinc content, increase growth and reduce the prevalence of stunting and wasting in young Burkinabe children: a cluster-randomized trial. *PloS One*. 2015;10(3):e0122242. doi:10.1371/journal.pone.0122242[19]

Potential Outline for the Discussion Section

1. Paragraph summarizing the major results of the study; this should synthesize the results section, rather than repeat it, and highlight important findings.
2. Paragraph comparing this study's findings to the results of studies with similar findings.
3. Paragraph comparing the findings to the results of studies with different findings, with some explanation for why the results might be different.
4. Paragraph highlighting the strengths and limitations of the study, and the implications for study interpretation and generalizability.
5. Paragraph discussing implications for clinical practice, public health, management, public policy, education, research, or other relevant areas, and next steps.
6. A conclusion statement (two to three sentences), which should briefly summarize key findings, implications, and next steps; for some journals, the conclusion may be a separate section.

A final important question is: What is the level of confidence in the findings? It is important to be clear about the strengths and weaknesses of the study and how they affect the interpretation of the study findings. Internal factors to consider include the study design, sample size, and data collection and analysis methods, as well as the study's quality control procedures, including training and ongoing monitoring of study staff, data management procedures, efforts to ensure that the study interventions were delivered as intended (fidelity), and assessment of participant completion of the intervention (retention, participation, and adherence). Also consider the extent to which the study lends itself to being applied in other populations or settings; this requires careful consideration of participant characteristics and the setting where the study was conducted. Lead with the strengths to help readers understand why the study was done the way it was and how that helped to improve its validity or generalizability. When presenting weaknesses, explain how the weakness might affect the interpretation of the study or the ability to generalize it to other

settings or populations, and comment on the extent of the impact.

Carefully consider the strengths and weaknesses of a study when drawing conclusions about its implications. Be conservative about what the results of the study mean in the larger world. It is inappropriate to make claims that go beyond what is actually supported by the data, or to make unsubstantiated statements about what is now known.

SHOW REFERENCES AND CITATIONS

Failure to properly cite the work of others mentioned in a manuscript is considered plagiarism and constitutes a serious threat to the credibility of any work. When providing statistics or quoting or paraphrasing from material written by others, a citation is necessary. It is also necessary to cite your own previously published works to avoid self-plagiarism. Each mention of the same work, by the same author(s), should be cited to the same reference. References should be listed at the end of the manuscript. It can be helpful to use reference software, such as EndNote, Mendeley, or Zotero, to organize and manage references and citations while writing.

Plan to Revise the Article Several Times Before Submission

Seek out feedback from colleagues who are experienced in publishing peer-reviewed articles and are experts in the content area and in statistics; these internal reviewers can help to anticipate feedback from reviewers and address concerns before submission. Make sure to build adequate time for revisions into the overall writing timeline.

What Are Key Considerations for Selecting a Peer-Reviewed Journal and Submitting a Manuscript?

This section includes practical suggestions for finding the right peer-reviewed journal for submitting a manuscript. Every manuscript submission involves time and effort spent formatting the manuscript to the journal specifications and waiting for editorial and peer review. Deciding where to submit a manuscript can be a challenging decision, but investing time in this step can save a lot of effort in the long run.

Choose an Appropriate Journal

If a journal is a poor fit (ie, the research theme is not suitable for the content or audience of the journal), there may be immediate rejection or significant delays in manuscript publication related to the journal's struggle to find appropriate reviewers. Submitting to the most suitable journal for the manuscript's content can make the difference between successful and timely publication and disappointing frustration. It also ensures that research reaches the most appropriate target audience.

Refer to Box 41.3 for tips on how to navigate journal selection. Become familiar with journals that report on nutrition and other related fields. A quick glance at the manuscript's reference list may identify journals that are a good fit for a particular topic area. It is also possible to search for similar topics in PubMed and note where those studies were published. The Journal/Author Name Estimator (JANE; http://jane.biosemantics.org) is a freely available web-based tool that, on the basis of a sample text (eg, title and abstract of a manuscript), can suggest appropriate journals.[20] JANE also examines some aspects of journal quality that are discussed later in this chapter.

Once several potential journals have been identified, examine the journal homepages, which should include the journal aims and scope (likely in the About the Journal section of their website) and author guidelines. If it is still unclear whether a manuscript would be appropriate for a journal, submit a presubmission inquiry to the editor. Presubmission inquiries should include at minimum the title and abstract of the manuscript as an attachment.

Once the possibilities have been narrowed to a few journals, consider additional factors like publication fees, length of time from acceptance to publication, and indicators of journal quality.

Information about publication fees should be clearly listed on the journal's webpage. Some journals charge an article fee, while others charge by

BOX 41.3

Tips for Selecting a Journal for Publication[21]

Identify the audience for which your research is most relevant.

Determine the type of journals your audience reads.

Determine the various journals that publish your line of work by reviewing recent issues.

Identify a journal that best serves your purpose by examining the journal aims and scope.

Carefully read the instructions to authors (author guidelines) to verify a good fit.

Be aware of publication fees for the journals that you are considering.

Consider indicators of journal quality and the length of time from acceptance to publication for a typical article in that journal.

the page. In some cases, journals may only charge a fee if the article will be open access, or available online for anyone who wishes to download and read it. There may also be additional charges for color figures or photos. In the interest of timely publication, authors should investigate the timeline for an average paper that is published in a journal under consideration. This information may be summarized on the journal website, but if it is not, look at published articles from the journal to see the dates that the articles were received, revised, accepted, and published (online and in print, if applicable).

It is normal for the process from acceptance to publication to take about 6 months to 1 year. Significantly shorter or longer timelines may be a red flag regarding the quality or management of the manuscript review process at the journal. Both peer review policies and publication fees should be clearly available on the journal's website. If not, question the legitimacy of that journal.

Another indicator of journal quality is the journal's impact factor, which is usually available on the journal's website. An impact factor is based on how many times articles in that journal are cited; it is widely considered to be a measure of the overall quality of the journal. A high impact factor is often considered a hallmark of prestige for a journal, as is publishing in those journals. However, journals with high impact factors receive more submissions and usually accept only a small proportion of manuscripts submitted. Impact factors can change over time and are calculated annually by the number of citations as listed in the Web of Science database. Journals that are not indexed in Web of Science do not have impact factors. It should be noted that there are some factors independent of quality that influence impact factor. For example, since review articles are cited more frequently than articles describing individual studies, journals publishing a high number of review articles are more likely to have a high impact factor. Older, more established journals are also more frequently cited, and thus have higher impact factors than newer journals. Journals with a narrow focus tend to have a lower impact factor. Impact factors can also vary greatly across different disciplines; therefore, impact factors should be compared to those of other journals in the same disciplinary category. Many nutrition-related journals will report their ranking within the Nutrition and Dietetics category. Some examples of impact factors of journals of interest to nutrition communicators are shown in Box 41.4. There are also a few more recently developed indicators of journal quality to consider, including the h5-index (Google Scholar Metrics),[22] Eigenfactor,[23] and Article Influence score.[23]

A final consideration is whether a manuscript will be indexed (ie, included in advanced search engine services, such as PubMed and Medline) by one or more leading databases. Publishing in a peer-reviewed journal that has a wider network for abstracting and indexing will increase readership and citation of the work. Information about where the journal indexes articles can be found on the journal's website, usually under the heading Abstracting and Indexing. Following are a few common search engine services in the nutrition- and health-related fields:

 ## Nutrition-Related Journals—Impact Factors for 2017

Journal	Impact Factor
New England Journal of Medicine	79.3
Lancet	53.3
Journal of the American Medical Association	47.7
American Journal of Clinical Nutrition	6.5
Nutrition Reviews	5.8
Journal of Nutrition	4.4
Journal of Parenteral and Enteral Nutrition	4.2
Journal of the Academy of Nutrition and Dietetics	4.0
Nutritional Neuroscience	3.3
Appetite	3.2
Journal of Nutrition Education and Behavior	2.6
Public Health Nutrition	2.5
Journal of Renal Nutrition	2.7
Nutrition and Cancer	2.3

- PubMed indexes biomedical literature from life science journals and online books. It also accesses the Medline bibliographic database of references and abstracts.
- Scopus indexes journals from the fields of science, technology, medicine, social sciences, and arts and humanities. It can also provide research analysis and tracking tools.
- EBSCO Information Services database includes titles compiled by the company as well as journals from other databases and publishers, such as Medline.

OPEN ACCESS VERSUS PROPRIETARY JOURNALS

Open access publishing makes it easier for individuals outside of academic settings to access a nutrition communicator's work and can increase citations of that work.[24] Some funders, such as the National Institutes of Health and the Gates Foundation, require results of their funded work to be published in an open access format. Open access publications are usually copyrighted under a Creative Commons license, with copyrights being retained by the author(s). This form of copyright allows others to copy, distribute, and make noncommercial use of the work. There are various versions of this type of license, so prospective authors should check the terms and be sure they are acceptable before submitting a manuscript as a prospective open access publication. Authors usually pay a publication fee to the journal to cover the expenses of publishing open access manuscripts, since the journal does not recoup publishing costs via subscription fees.

There is some controversy about open access publishing. Beall[25] has written extensive critiques of open access publishing, labeling a significant number of open access journals as "predatory"[26] for aggressively soliciting articles from authors, charging steep publication fees, and lacking a rigorous peer review process (see Box 41.5 for an example of a solicitation from a potentially predatory journal). Be suspicious of a journal that sends an unsolicited email using excessively flattering and enthusiastic language or odd grammar (as shown in Box 41.5), or that promises publication in an unrealistically short time frame, such as days instead of several months.

Articles in proprietary, or subscription, journals are only available to subscribers. Authors usually transfer the copyrights to the journal where

BOX 41.5 Example of a Solicitation Email from a Potentially Predatory Journal

Dear _____,

Greetings from XYZ Journal of Health Issues!

As we have gone through your profile which is quite impressive and appropriate to our journal. So we would like to cordially invite you to be a part of the Editorial Board for our journal.

XYZ Journal of Health Issues is interested to associate with eminent scientists such as you are to increase the reach in the scientific community and request you to kindly accept our invitation for being an honorable Editor in our Journal.

We also hope you may have an eminent work of scholarship to submit for our next issue, which is due for publication in just 30 days. XYZ Journal of Health Issues aspires to bring spectacular eminent original findings of research information across the globe into light and aims to build an efficient platform for the researchers/readers all over the world. It is the platform to bring the highest quality research over advance topics.

Hope our Journal will offer you an enriching experience and hope to achieve great successful endeavors. If you are interested to be a part of our EB, Kindly submit: Present CV, Research interest, Short biography (about 250 words) and Recent photograph.

Hope you accept our invitation and look forward to receive article from you at the earliest!

Have a great day!

Ira Editor
XYZ Journal of Health Issues

the manuscript will appear. Proprietary journals are supported by subscriptions, and therefore authors usually do not have to pay to publish their work. Some authors believe that criticism of open access publishing is being driven by proprietary publishers' concerns for loss of market revenue.[27,28] Recently, many proprietary journals have added open access options for authors who want to make their work more widely available for an additional fee.

Ultimately, the decision regarding open access or proprietary publishing is determined by the goals, preferences, financial resources, and funders of the prospective authors. Box 41.6 highlights some journal evaluation resources for authors.

Review and Follow the Author Guidelines

Once the authors have selected a journal, it is essential that the authors carefully review the journal's author guidelines and format the manuscript accordingly. In particular, authors should pay attention to guidance regarding preferred section headings and organization, page or word limits, citation and reference style, figure or table specifications, and other journal preferences. Guidelines can vary significantly for different article types and from one journal to the next. The author guidelines will also generally provide instructions regarding supplemental materials to submit with a manuscript, such as a cover letter to the editor, title page, conflict of interest statements, and contributors' statement. Meticulously following the author guidelines will save time and help to avoid an immediate rejection based on formatting issues or missing documents.

Write a Cover Letter to the Editor

The author guidelines of most journals outline expectations for a cover letter to the editor. In general, the cover letter should be concise (no more than one page) and include a brief summary of the study and its potential implications, a short summary of why the article will be of interest to the journal's readers, and any required statements related to funding sources, author contributions, conflicts of interest, and exclusivity of submission. Most journals want assurance that the article is only under consideration by one journal at a time; the author must wait for the article to be rejected before submitting it to another journal, unless the submission is withdrawn.

Journal Evaluation Resources for Authors

Journal/Author Name Estimator (JANE): http://jane.biosemantics.org

Think. Check. Submit.: http://thinkchecksubmit.org

Ryerson University Library, Faculty Research Guide on Scholarly Communication: http://learn.library.ryerson.ca/scholcomm/journaleval

Committee on Publication Ethics (COPE): https://publicationethics.org/about

Directory of Open Access Journals, Principles of Transparency and Best Practice in Scholarly Publishing: https://doaj.org/bestpractice

Creative Commons, Frequently Asked Questions: https://creativecommons.org/faq

How Open Is It? A Guide for Evaluating the Openness of Journals, Scholarly Publishing and Academic Resources Coalition (SPARC): https://sparcopen.org/wp-content/uploads/2016/01/hoii_guide_rev4_web.pdf

Open Access Overview, by Peter Suber: http://legacy.earlham.edu/~peters/fos/overview.htm

Directory of Open Access Journals (DOAJ): https://doaj.org

What Are Strategies for Successfully Navigating the Manuscript Review and Revision Process?

Successfully navigating the review process requires an understanding of the process, being responsive to the reviewers' suggestions, and making the necessary revisions. This process of peer review is designed to result in the highest-quality publications.

Understand the Review Process

When a manuscript is submitted to a journal, an editor or associate editor will review it to decide if it should be sent out to reviewers, and the submitter will be informed of this decision. If it is sent to reviewers, expect that it will take 1 to 4 months to receive the results of the reviews; some journals may be faster or slower, depending on their policies and reviewers.

There are several possible outcomes once the reviews are received. Outright acceptance of a manuscript after the first round of reviews is a relatively rare occurrence. More likely outcomes are a request to resubmit after minor or major revisions or a rejection.

Respond to Reviewers' Suggestions and Make Corrections

An invitation to resubmit is an encouraging sign and an opportunity to improve the manuscript. The time frame to submit a revision will be specified by the editor and should be observed unless an extension is requested; extensions will usually be granted. Generally, there will be a bulleted list of suggestions for improvement, referencing specific lines or sections of the manuscript. Prepare a response to the editor that explains how each suggestion was addressed in a politely worded, respectful way. Also plan to submit a revised version of the manuscript that incorporates any changes that were made; some journals will request that changes be indicated using the track-changes feature.

It is not unusual to have an emotional reaction to critical feedback on a piece of work that represents a significant investment of time and effort, so wait to respond to reviewers and the editor until it is possible to review the feedback objectively and respond calmly and systematically. It may be helpful to discuss the reviewer comments with coauthors or other colleagues to get an unbiased perspective.

In most cases, make the improvements and changes to the article suggested by reviewers and editors. In some cases, it may be necessary to reanalyze data in a different way or rewrite sections of text. Ignoring a reviewer's comments because it requires a significant amount of work to address them is not a productive strategy. Rarely, it may seem that the reviewer misunderstood an aspect of the article or the reviewer may be requesting a change that is not possible, such as analyzing data that were not collected. If so, it may help to clarify the misunderstanding or acknowledge that the suggestion is valid but not possible to address.

When the revised manuscript is returned, it may be sent back to the original reviewers or to different reviewers for a second review. Two rounds of peer review are not unusual, and additional revisions may be required after the second round of reviews.

Above all, do not be discouraged by rejection, as this happens to everyone at least a few times

(and sometimes many times!) during the publishing process. If one journal rejects a manuscript, submit it to another journal. Make sure to consult the aims, scope, and author guidelines for the new journal to ensure that it is a good fit and that all formatting requirements have been met, as these can vary substantially among journals. If reviewer feedback is received as part of a rejection, consider making improvements to the article before submitting it to another journal, rather than just making formatting changes. As long as a study is well designed and well reported, it should be possible to get the manuscript published.

Beyond the Basics, What Else Is Useful to Know About Publishing a Peer-Reviewed Journal Article?

The previous sections discussed best practices for writing a manuscript, selecting a journal, submitting a manuscript, and navigating the review process. This section includes some additional advice on how to succeed in publishing a journal article in team research settings.

Publish in a Timely Way

Often it is tempting to wait to write the manuscript until a research study is complete. This can be problematic, however, as many research studies are grant-funded, and once the grant ends, everyone moves on to new grants and other activities while manuscripts on completed research languish. This can lead to long delays in publishing the results of a study, with potential negative consequences:

- Research can quickly lose relevance if it takes years to publish. A research question that was initially compelling may be answered several times over if there is a long delay in publishing results.
- Funders may question the productivity of the research team. Funders look for active and timely dissemination of results when they make funding decisions.

There are strategies that can help prevent long publication delays. For instance, discuss a plan for publishing early in the process with the research team. Identify writing activities that can occur as the study is in progress. For example, generally it is possible to write study methods while developing the protocols and revise them during implementation of the study. It may even be desirable to publish the study protocol.

Navigate Writing a Manuscript with Coauthors

Team science, research work by interprofessional teams, is becoming increasingly common and offers many advantages, such as shared knowledge and resources. However, it can create challenges when it comes to publication and granting credit for the work done. This section contains concrete advice for how to successfully handle publishing in a team science setting.

BEST STRATEGIES FOR WRITING AS A TEAM

The most important strategy for success in publishing a manuscript with one or more coauthors is to be sure that everyone understands their role in the undertaking. Delegation of manuscript tasks is usually managed by the primary investigator for the study, but everyone on the team should have the opportunity to discuss who will be responsible for which aspects of the process. Be sure that each person will have enough time and resources to carry out their share of the tasks on the agreed-upon timeline. Manuscripts that are prepared by a team of authors take at least 3 to 6 months to complete. As the work begins and moves forward, clear communication among coauthors is vital for success. Have a plan to communicate on a regular basis to share progress and any problems that need to be worked out.

One person is designated as the corresponding author. The corresponding author does the actual submission of the manuscript and follows up with the journal editor throughout the review and publication process. This author is also usually identified on the published paper as the person to contact with any questions about the publication. The corresponding author ensures that the journal's administrative requirements, such as providing details of authorship and gathering conflict of interest forms and copyright statements, are properly completed. The corresponding author should be available throughout the entire process to respond to editorial queries and should update the journal regarding any important contact information that changes. The corresponding author does not necessarily have to be listed as the first author on the manuscript.

CRITERIA FOR AUTHORSHIP

Who should be included as an author on the manuscript? Authorship implies responsibility for the published work. Courtesy authorship, or the practice of including someone as an author as a reward for some other favor, is not appropriate. Likewise, simply having a position, such as department chair, does not necessarily justify being listed as an author. Actual substantive contributions to the work are necessary. Some journals require that the contributions of each author be described as part of the article submission process. These reported contributions may also be published in the article.

The International Committee of Medical Journal Editors (ICMJE)[29] has identified four criteria that should be met in order for a person to be included as an author of a journal article, which can be summarized as follows:

1. The person has made substantial contributions to the conception or design of the work or acquisition, analysis, or interpretation of data.
2. The person has drafted or revised the manuscript based on that work.
3. The person reviewed and approved the final manuscript being submitted.
4. The person is willing to be publicly and professionally responsible for the work being reported in the manuscript.

Contributors who do not meet all four criteria should not be listed as authors but should be acknowledged. Consult author guidelines for instructions on where acknowledgments should be listed in a manuscript. Because being included in the acknowledgments can imply public endorsement by these individuals of a study's data and conclusions, the corresponding author should obtain permission for inclusion from all acknowledged individuals.

AUTHOR ORDER

The order in which authors' names appear in the published article is considered to be significant in terms of their relative contributions to the research and production of the manuscript. However, there are no hard-and-fast standards for order of authors; standards can also vary among disciplines.[30] It is a good practice to discuss plans for order of authorship early in the publication process to avoid misunderstandings.

The first author listed is usually the person who did the most work on the research study and drafted most of the manuscript. If this role was shared equally between two or more people, then the order of authors may be determined by consulting with a senior colleague, or first authorship may be shared (co-first, or equal, authorship). Co-first authorship is only allowed by some journals.

After the first author, the remaining authors should be listed in order of the significance of their contributions to the manuscript.[31] The major exception in some fields (often including nutrition) is the senior author, who is listed last and generally considered responsible for conceptual design and overall oversight for the research. In cases where several authors contributed equally to the manuscript, list them alphabetically by last name.

STUDENTS AS AUTHORS OR COAUTHORS

A student is usually listed as first author on a multiauthored article that is based primarily on the student's dissertation or thesis. These works, by definition, consist of original work by the student. In most cases, it would be unethical for a faculty advisor to be first author on this type of article.[32] In other situations, such as when a student is assisting on a research project, consider their contributions and the amount of supervision and support they required from the research advisor. As with any other prospective coauthors, discuss with students in advance the division of labor, responsibility, and anticipated author order.

Publishing Your Study

See the summary checklist below when preparing a manuscript for submission.

Summary Checklist for Publishing a Manuscript

___ Has a plan for publishing the research been discussed with the study team?

___ Has appropriate professional guidance been reviewed on key elements to include in sections of the manuscript?

___ Do the title and abstract accurately and compellingly reflect the content of the manuscript?

___ Does the introduction briefly summarize what is known about the topic area, identify key gaps in knowledge, and outline the objectives and hypotheses of the study?

___ Has the methods section been checked against appropriate professional guidance to avoid omitting important elements or information?

___ Is there good consistency between the methods and results sections?

___ Have the results section and tables and figures been double-checked for errors and inconsistencies?

___ Has repetition been minimized between the results section text and tables and figures?

___ Do the tables and figures "stand alone"?

___ Does the discussion place the results of the study into context and highlight the importance of the study and next steps, without overreaching?

___ Has the manuscript been proofread and revised to try to anticipate reviewer comments?

___ Has an appropriate journal been selected?

___ Have the author guidelines been reviewed and followed?

___ Have reviewers' suggestions been addressed, point by point, in a polite and systematic way?

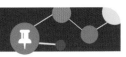

Nutrition Communicators Publish Research in Peer-Reviewed Journals

1 Publishing research is an important way to contribute to the scientific field that can advance evidence-based practice guidelines and policies.

2 Several strategies can help to save time and effort in publishing work, including selecting an appropriate journal, carefully following the journal author guidelines and professional guidance relevant to the study design, and seeking feedback early and often.

3 It is important to not get discouraged by harsh feedback or rejection of a manuscript submitted to a peer-reviewed journal, as everyone's first few manuscripts are a learning process. Over time, the nutrition communicator will learn and improve by engaging fully with the publication process.

REFERENCES

1. Jha KN. How to write articles that get published. *J Clin Diagn Res.* 2014;8(9):XG01-XG03.
2. Kotz D, Cals JWL, Tugwell P, Knottnerus JA. Introducing a new series on effective writing and publishing of scientific papers. *J Clin Epidemiol.* 2013;66(4):359-360.
3. Knottnerus JA, Tugwell P. Communicating research to the peers. *J Clin Epidemiol.* 2007;60(7):645-647.
4. Academy of Nutrition and Dietetics, Evidence Analysis Library. Policy and process overview. Accessed March 1, 2018. www.andeal.org/evidence-analysis-process-overview
5. Sackett DL, Rosenberg WM, Gray JA, Haynes RB, Richardson WS. Evidence based medicine: what it is and what it isn't. *BMJ (Clinical research ed).* 1996;312(7023):71-72.
6. CONSORT Statement. Accessed March 1, 2018. www.consort-statement.org
7. Campbell MK, Piaggio G, Elbourne DR, Altman DG. Consort 2010 statement: extension to cluster randomised trials. *Br Med J.* 2012;345.
8. STROBE Statement: STROBE checklists. Accessed March 1, 2018. www.strobe-statement.org/index.php?id=available-checklists
9. Centers for Disease Control and Prevention. Transparent Reporting of Evaluations with Nonrandomized Designs (TREND). Reviewed September 26, 2018. Accessed March 1, 2018. www.cdc.gov/trendstatement
10. SQUIRE 2.0 Guidelines. Accessed March 1, 2018. www.squire-statement.org/index.cfm?fuseaction=Page.ViewPage&pageId=471
11. Tong A, Sainsbury P, Craig J. Consolidated criteria for reporting qualitative research (COREQ): a 32-item checklist for interviews and focus groups. *Int J Qual Health Care.* 2007;19(6):349-357.
12. Mensh B, Kording K. Ten simple rules for structuring papers. *PLOS Comput Biol.* 2017;13(9):e1005619.
13. Jamali HR, Nikzad M. Article title type and its relation with the number of downloads and citations. *Scientometrics.* 2011;88(2):653-661.
14. Shah JN. Writing good effective title for journal article. *J Patan Acad Health Sci.* 2014;1(2):1-3.
15. Paiva CE, Lima JP, Paiva BS. Articles with short titles describing the results are cited more often. *Clinics (Sao Paulo, Brazil).* 2012;67(5):509-513.
16. National Library of Medicine. Suggestions for finding author keywords using MeSH tools. Accessed March 1, 2018. www.nlm.nih.gov/mesh/authors.html
17. Rodrigues V. Tips on effective use of tables and figures in research papers. Editage Insights website. Published November 4, 2013. Accessed November 7, 2018. www.editage.com/insights/tips-on-effective-use-of-tables-and-figures-in-research-papers
18. CONSORT flow diagram. Accessed November 7, 2018. www.consort-statement.org/consort-statement/flow-diagram
19. Hess SY, Abbeddou S, Jimenez EY, et al. Small-quantity lipid-based nutrient supplements, regardless of their zinc content, increase growth and reduce the prevalence of stunting and wasting in young Burkinabe children: a cluster-randomized trial. *PloS One.* 2015;10(3):e0122242. doi:10.1371/journal.pone.0122242

20. Schuemie MJ, Kors JA. Jane: suggesting journals, finding experts. *Bioinformatics.* 2008;24(5):727-728.

21. Macdonald NE, Ford-Jones L, Friedman JN, Hall J. Preparing a manuscript for publication: a user-friendly guide. *Paediatr Child Health.* 2006;11(6):339-342.

22. Google Scholar. Google Scholar metrics. Accessed November 7, 2018. https://scholar.google.com/intl/en/scholar/metrics.html#metrics

23. Cornell University Library. Measuring your research impact: Eigenfactor and Article Influence. Updated May 1, 2019. Accessed November 7, 2019. http://guides.library.cornell.edu/c.php?g=32272&p=203396

24. Björk B-C, Solomon DJ. Open access versus subscription journals: a comparison of scientific impact. *BMC Med.* 2012;10(1):73.

25. Beall J. Predatory publishing is just one of the consequences of gold open access. *Learn Publ.* 2013;26(2):79-84.

26. Beall J. Criteria for determining predatory open-access publishers. 3rd ed. Published January 1, 2015. Accessed November 7, 2018. https://beallslist.weebly.com/uploads/3/0/9/5/30958339/criteria-2015.pdf

27. Larivière V, Haustein S, Mongeon P. The oligopoly of academic publishers in the digital era. *PLoS One.* 2015;10(6):e0127502.

28. Schimmer R, Geschuhn K, Volger A. Disrupting the subscription journals' business model for the necessary large-scale transformation to open access. Published April 28, 2015. Accessed November 7, 2018. https://pure.mpg.de/pubman/faces/ViewItemOverviewPage.jsp?itemId=item_2148961

29. International Committee of Medical Journal Editors. Defining the role of authors and contributors. Accessed November 7, 2018. www.icmje.org/recommendations/browse/roles-and-responsibilities/defining-the-role-of-authors-and-contributors.html

30. Tscharntke T, Hochberg ME, Rand TA, Resh VH, Krauss J. Author sequence and credit for contributions in multiauthored publications. *PLOS Biol.* 2007;5(1):e18.

31. Akhabue E, Lautenbach E. "Equal" contributions and credit: an emerging trend in the characterization of authorship. *Ann Epidemiol.* 2010;20(11):868-871.

32. Fine MA, Kurdek LA. Reflections on determining authorship credit and authorship order on faculty-student collaborations. *Am Psychol.* 1993;48(11):1141-1147.

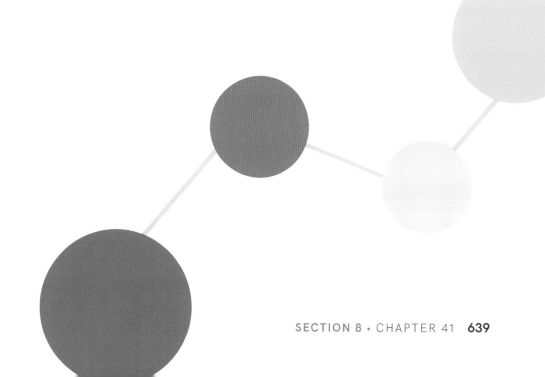

CHAPTER 42

Nutrition Communicators Write Books to Make a Difference

Roberta Larson Duyff, MS, RDN, FAND, FADA

"A book is a lasting platform to communicate important nutrition information to target readers."

"My own self. At my very best. All the time."

—AMERICAN YOUTH FOUNDATION MOTTO

Author note: Insights, encouragement, and practical publishing information in this chapter come mostly from my 40 years of authoring and editing traditionally and self-published books for children, teens, and adults and from my "The Write Approach to Nutrition" presentations to professional groups.

Introduction

Books can be lasting sources of valuable, credible, and relevant nutrition information. Their content may be *life-changing* for readers. Becoming a published author can be *career-changing* for nutrition professionals.

Throughout this book, different chapters have addressed how to effectively communicate food, nutrition, and health expertise. Writing one book (or more) may be another avenue. But before starting on the path to publishing, reflect on these questions:

- Why should *you* write a food and nutrition book? What are your goals and vision?
- What are ten best practices for successful authors?
- What are the steps to getting a book written, published, and marketed? Is traditional, hybrid, or self-publishing the best option?

Birthing a book is often likened to becoming a parent: first pondering the possibility; then experiencing the emotional, financial, and lifestyle ups and downs that come along the way; and finally, celebrating the exhilaration (perhaps forgetting the challenges) of an amazing outcome!

Why Should *You* Write a Book?

Because you have something to say! Authoring a book provides another platform for leveraging the food and nutrition expertise nutrition communicators train for and hone throughout their career. Before plunging into authorship, however, do the homework. Think first about what the motivation is. Consider the many positives. Ponder the realities too.

First, a reality check: A title will likely not sell a quarter million copies. Few titles in any publishing genre or for any topic ever do, even best sellers (although some books written by registered dietitian nutritionists [RDNs] have). Book sales probably will not make an author a lot of money—not when weighed against the resources that are allocated and redirected for research, writing, and marketing—or make the author really famous. Authorship will likely not provide an easier, more flexible lifestyle than a traditional job. Check with other authors: Most would say that authoring a book is a far more demanding professional and personal commitment than they ever realized.

Consider, too, the occupational hazards. Book writing can be lonely, with looming deadlines, endless days sitting at a computer, and perhaps no encouragement other than a signed contract. Writing itself isn't always easy, either. Author David McCullough notes, "Writing is thinking. To write well is to think clearly. That's why it's so hard."[1]

That said, if you're passionate about a topic and decide to add "book author" to your resume, be clear about goals, realistic with expectations, and smart about the process. Then enjoy the satisfaction of sharing your expertise. Many rewards truly do come with authorship! If the writer is fulfilled by the journey, the readers likely will be as well.

Your Expertise Matters!

Thousands of books, including many about nutrition, food, and health, are published yearly. Many make unfounded promises; their advice may delay proper health care.

The publishing world needs well-written, evidence-informed food and nutrition-focused books written for the general public. Academic and professional publishers, including the Academy of Nutrition and Dietetics and the American Diabetes Association, also need authors for professional development and higher-education titles. Your expertise matters!

Strategies for Writing About Science for the General Public[2,3,4]

BOX 42.1

Provide enough background information to help readers understand what they want to know.

Respect what readers know already.

Present scientific information from the familiar to the unfamiliar.

Simplify evidence and implications to the level that's adequate for readers' needs and purposes.

Explain technical terms, but don't oversimplify.

Illustrate and explain technical terms and concepts with anecdotes, visuals, and analogies (eg, "Like letters of the alphabet, amino acids are arranged in countless ways, and some combinations are used more often than others. The same … twenty-six letters of the alphabet form thousands of words in many languages, each word with its own meaning."[a]

Keep the message relevant to hold readers' interest. Answer the question: "What's in it for me?"

[a] This quote was taken from Hamlin A, Rubio C, DeSilva M. Ethics in technical writing. In: *Technical Writing.* Press Books; 2020. https://coccoer.pressbooks.com[4]

If you like to write, why not address what you know best in a book? You communicate your expertise daily through counseling; teaching; meetings with colleagues; posting on social media; advising patients, consumers, friends, or family members—and by being an example yourself.

A Book Can Translate Complex Science into Practical Guidance

Knowing the complex science of nutrition is one thing. Putting that information in context and translating it into practical terms are quite another. RDNs have—and can develop and strengthen—the skills to convey scientific information and evidence through concrete, concise, and meaningful guidance. See Box 42.1 and review Chapter 7.

A Book Can Serve as a Lasting, Impactful Resource

Authors have consequential responsibilities. A nutrition book may influence food decisions over time and thereby significantly influence readers' health and well-being. Books for academic and professional audiences may influence professional practice or public policy.

A book's impact may extend beyond its readers. Books and their authors are often quoted and referenced, multiplying their reach. A well-written nutrition book may even become part of historical legacy. Consider: When the Academy of Nutrition and Dietetics celebrates a milestone year, your book could represent today's key food and nutrition issues!

Research for a Book Keeps the Author Current

Call it lifelong learning. The rigors of authoring, publishing, and book marketing extend professional skills. Researching the content, target audience, and marketplace does more:

- It keeps the author's finger on the pulse of emerging and evolving science, public policy initiatives and changing regulations, health issues and controversies, current nutrition practice, hot topics, and food, nutrition, and lifestyle trends.

- It informs of current consumer beliefs, needs, and behavior.
- It helps shape messages by broadening the context.

Writing a book can also organize and clarify expertise that's already in the author's head and files. American writer Flannery O'Connor recognized, "I write to discover what I know."

A Book Can Be a Career Ticket

Writing a book can take the author in new, unexpected directions, generate attention, and promote what is already being done or produced:

- Writing a book provides recognition. Chances are, sales from a single book can't replace income from a day job or a successful consulting practice. However, the book can nevertheless get attention. The authority, credibility, and attention from authorship may help launch a new endeavor or market an established one.
- Writing a book differentiates your expertise, expands your influence and platform, and builds your professional brand. A book can establish a food and nutrition niche or specialty. For example, *Gluten Free: The Definitive Resource Guide* helped establish author Shelley Case, BS, RD, as a leading international authority on gluten-free diets.
- Writing a book creates connections. Research and fact-checking grow a network. Visibility from book marketing can expand a network further.
- Writing a book launches career opportunities. Authorship can open doors: to spokesperson and media appearances, consulting opportunities, and speaking engagements. Beyond that, one successful book can beget another. Traditional publishers look for successful authors.

A Book Reflects Its Author

Self-expression, personal satisfaction, and passion for a topic are worthy motivations. So are desires to inform, motivate, and impact others. A book is also a published record of the writer's perspectives, the quality of his or her work, and what matters to that writer.

What Are Ten Best Practices for Authors?

Before taking pen to paper, or fingers to keyboard, it is necessary to have a firm idea of *why* and *for whom* the book is being written. There also must be commitment to the best practices of authorship.

One: Respond to Inspiration

Thomas Edison is credited with this adage: "Genius is 99% perspiration and 1% inspiration." Good writers are typically 24-hour-a-day idea people. Ideas come when least expected. Aspiring writers can follow the advice here:

- Record inspirations. Have notepaper and pen handy. Use a voice recorder or the note app on a smartphone. Take a photo. Send yourself an email, text, or phone message with an idea or interesting fact. Don't expect that same inspiration to knock twice.
- Keep a personal journal. It may provide anecdotes, examples, or insights that support a manuscript later.
- Write when feeling inspired. Take advantage of spontaneity. While research uncovers or confirms content, freewriting can help to explore thoughts. Freewriting, often a technique for generating ideas, is continuous writing without regard for grammar, spelling, or content.
- Generate inspiration. Track the ever-evolving world of food and nutrition. Read food and nonfood publications. Follow digital and social media sites such as Facebook, Instagram, Twitter, and podcasts. Attend nutrition and non-nutrition conferences.
- Keep things that are inspiring within eyesight. Without creating clutter, display family photos, honors for work, travel trinkets, or flowers. Play inspiring music.
- Experience something new! Inspiration comes from experiences.

Two: Learn to Write Well; Edit Rigorously

Good writing shows. Within the first few pages of a proposal or manuscript, book editors and agents will determine if the author's writing style, tone, clarity, format, and word usage are worth their effort.

To hone writing skills:

- Practice, as skilled athletes, painters, and dancers do. Paid or not, write for different genres, not only to develop skills but also to build a portfolio and get noticed.
- Enroll in a writing class. Enlist a writing coach or freelance editor.
- Read to explore different writing styles, gather ideas, know what others write about, and broaden overall knowledge.

To quote the 18th-century writer Samuel Johnson, "The greatest part of a writer's time is spent reading in order to write; a [person] will turn over half a library to make one book."

Skilled authors write "tight, light, and bright," as addressed in Chapter 22 and noted here.

Show, don't just tell Use graphics, statistics, analogies, anecdotes, and stories that clarify and support a message.

Edit out unneeded words For example:

- Change modifying phrases to adverbs and adjectives: "crisp, deep-green lettuce," not "lettuce that is deep-green and crisp."
- Use strong nouns and action verbs, requiring few adjectives and adverbs: "intensifies," not "made more forceful."
- Bullet for brevity. Bulleted copy requires fewer connecting words.

Use active voice, which is more powerful, engaging, and concise. Verbs in passive voice start with *is*, *are*, *were*, or *was*: "This newsletter provides gluten-free recipes," not "Gluten-free recipes are provided in this newsletter."

Check grammar, punctuation, and spelling Use tools of the literary trade: dictionary, thesaurus, stylebooks, and readability (reading level and human interest) scoring. Many are built into word-processing programs.

That said, *use* a spellchecker. But don't *count on* a spellchecker, as illustrated here: "Pork with geek and garlic" (leek and garlic) and "kindly beans" (kidney beans) would both pass a program's spellcheck. (See the resources section at the end of this chapter for stylebooks.)

Write to express, not impress Complex writing doesn't mean complex thinking. Nutrition jargon can confuse and separate nutrition communicators from their readers. For the general public, write "everyday food choices," not "dietary pattern," and "beneficial plant compounds," not "phytochemicals."

Three: Find Your Voice

Is your writing authoritative and scholarly? Snappy and fun? Warm and nurturing? Voice is the style and quality that makes a person's writing distinctive. It reflects that person's attitudes, personality, and values. Consider it a signature that can sell a book proposal to a publisher and make readers eager for more.

Voice in writing is like paralanguage for speaking. It's more than word choice, sentence length, and sentence structure; more than active or passive voice; and more than first, second, or third person. It's also cadence, tone, melody, and perhaps story. Like paralanguage, voice conveys more than literal meaning.

Writing for different audiences may require different voices. For example, an academic book reads differently from a trade book for the general public or children.

To develop a unique voice, try freewriting (no thinking or editing) without concern for topic. Experiment, perhaps by writing in ways that seem unconventional or feel uncomfortable. Write from a passion about what matters most to you. Read how other writers express themselves; to learn, try to match their voices. Eventually, a voice will emerge that best expresses you and the readers who will listen to you.

Four: Make Research a Habit

Good research goes beyond digging into journal articles, position papers, and professional presentations. Popular media, news, and public conversations are treasure troves too.

Research to gather fresh ideas, new information, and supportive context; to verify accuracy; and to know the marketplace. Research also:

- fosters unique perspectives, so a book won't simply rehash another title;
- helps clarify and organize thinking—the more you know, the better you'll write;
- deepens messages, even if not everything that is learned is used;
- promotes a balanced, unbiased perspective and helps avoid omissions that impact a message;

See Chapter 22 for more on readability scoring.

- respects readers so that writing is neither too lofty nor too simple; and
- serves as an investment, because keeping updated doesn't stop when a book heads to the printer. New knowledge may become a hook for book promotion, a future edition, or another book.

Five: Write for Readers—First and Always

A successful book speaks to target readers; it addresses their needs, not the writer's, and discusses what they want to buy, not what the writer wants to sell.

While gathering ideas, developing a proposal, and writing a first draft, envision the readers. Have *their* interests been captured? Will *they* learn or better understand? Will this book help empower *them* to make healthier food and nutrition decisions? Does the writing show that you understand and respect *their* challenges, perhaps to lose weight, succeed with breastfeeding, or provide healthy meals on a limited budget? Will the book help *them* sort through headlines and tweets? Does the reading level, style, tone, format, and genre match *them*? Try these tips:

- Find out what target readers want to know and read. Talk in person or through social media. Invite them to react to a topic, outline, and perhaps a sample chapter. Be realistic: This book concept may not be right for them.
- Read books published for them. Include those by other RDNs. Talk to booksellers and librarians to learn what sells. Check *Publishers Weekly* (see the resources section). Read book reviews on websites, such as Amazon.
- Learn from other nutrition professionals. Join the Authors and Writers specialty group within the Academy of Nutrition and Dietetics Nutrition Entrepreneurs dietetic practice group. Check its *Ventures* newsletter and website, attend its webinars and conference sessions, follow the listserv, and check books authored by RDNs on its website.
- For lay readers, write like you are talking with them, with a one-on-one frame of mind. Consider the readers as people you spend time with, *not* simply as readers.[5] While it is necessary to provide enough clearly stated scientific context for the *why*

of nutrition and health guidance, most readers aren't interested in all you know. Instead, they want to know what you think and what they can do.

Six: Gather a Team

Putting words on paper is a solitary endeavor. However, a book proposal and manuscript will be stronger if the writer connects with others from the start for ideas, as sounding boards, and for psychological support.

- Seek out other authors. Learn from their breadth of experience and advice. Being with other book authors helps identify you as an author too. Benefit from the resources and mentorship of the previously mentioned Authors and Writers specialty group. Other organizations, such as the International Association of Culinary Professionals, have authors, agents, and editors as members.
- Join a local writers' group; take writing classes. Ask a local library or community college for recommendations.
- Engage potential readers, content experts, and peers. Welcome their critiques and reviews. Blog posts (for writers with blogs) can garner insights.
- Seek support from "cheerleaders" (coworkers, friends, family). Mr Rogers from children's television once said, "There's always someone who thinks you can do more than *you* think you can."
- Give back. Acknowledge, celebrate, and review the books of your colleagues and mentors on social media, Amazon, and other platforms. With success, become an author mentor too.

Seven: Test Content in Other Platforms

Do you write for a healthy-eating blog, magazine, newspaper, or newsletter? Do you teach a cooking class, give supermarket tours, or present wellness seminars? Like focus groups, these platforms offer opportunities to test topics, approach, and writer's voice—and they help create an audience of eager book buyers. Book concepts evolve by addressing content on other platforms.

Refer to Chapters 10 through 15 to learn about communicating with different audiences.

Eight: Reflect Evidence; Double-Check Facts

Professional credibility and trust depend on content accuracy and fastidious fact-checking. Even a minute error can irritate readers and erode their faith in the author. With today's social media and online reviews, a single mistake, noticed by a single reader, can reach thousands of potential book buyers and negatively affect book sales. Moreover, many readers make food- and nutrition-related decisions based on what authors write. Follow these tips when writing:

- Use primary sources of evidence, such as professional journals and the Academy of Nutrition and Dietetics Evidence Analysis Library, whenever possible. Seek credible secondary sources, such as Academy of Nutrition and Dietetics position papers and practice papers. Google Scholar, PubMed, and ScienceDirect are among other credible web-based databases of health and nutrition research. (Wikipedia isn't a primary source.)
- Document sources while writing to avoid omitting them. Cite the author's name and perhaps publication year. For online sources, take a screenshot or create a PDF file with the online address; it could disappear.
- Keep documentation on file. Whether with hard copies, cloud storage, or a memory stick, organize for fact-checking later.
- Make checking and double-checking habitual. Even when a fact or value seems obvious—perhaps a nutrient's Recommended Dietary Allowance or the safe internal temperature for roasted turkey—a quick check avoids an unintended error. Small details can be overlooked under deadline pressures.
- Embrace peer review. Unlike magazine publishers, most book publishers don't have fact-checkers to catch errors or omissions.

See Chapter 8 for referencing sources.

See Chapters 4 and 5 for credible sources and scientific research, and Chapters 6 and 7 for interpreting and conveying research evidence to the public.

See Chapters 8 and 9 for more on plagiarism and ethics.

Nine: Stay Disciplined

Success takes personal discipline. With editorial deadlines to meet, it may be necessary to write even when words don't flow. To cultivate discipline:

- Make time, rather than finding time, to write. Determine when thoughts flow best; keep writing commitments made with yourself.

Become accountable to someone else, perhaps another author, a literary agent, a colleague, or a family member. Establish a schedule.
- Assess your writing location; limit whatever provides a distraction. Designate a private space where your brain goes into writing mode. Clear away competing projects and clutter. Close email and social media sites. Silence your phone.
- Create ways to relieve writing stress. Try upbeat or soothing music, a favorite view, the aroma of a candle, or a pet for company. Save and back up computer files regularly to avoid stress if a technology glitch happens.
- Set small, reasonable writing goals: what needs to be written, by when, to meet deadlines. Writing a big book may seem daunting. Approaching each section or chapter as a short magazine article makes it manageable. Stick to interim deadlines to avoid stress later. Factor in second- and third-draft deadlines.
- Stay flexible. If thoughts won't flow, set the writing aside. Factor in physical activity time as a refocusing strategy. See Box 42.2.

Ten: Always Make Ethics a Top Priority

Ethics are imperative to credibility. Writing factual and balanced content, avoiding plagiarism, giving proper credit, and disclosing conflicts of interest are obvious ethical practices. Conveying information so that target readers understand, recognize, and judge its relative importance contributes to ethical writing too. That's where writing to accurately convey evidence-informed messages comes in.

Ethics in nutrition and health writing means reflecting research and communicating objectively, clearly, and completely. Resist highlighting evidence that supports a position without giving the full context. Avoid suppressing relevant information or over-extrapolating its message; and don't limit research to bias a message or misrepresent data with statistics, charts, and tables. Even unintentional oversights can result in ethics violations.[4]

Follow these tips to make ethics a top priority in your writing:

- Be clear about the ethics of authorship. The Academy of Nutrition and Dietetics Code of Ethics, listed in the resources, addresses

Writer's Block: Try This!

Writer's block happens, even among successful, productive authors. A short break or location change may be enough to get things back on track. Even an afternoon or few days off from writing pressure works. Consider these reasons for writer's block, with tips to overcome it:

- **Too much time between writing sessions**

  Long breaks can break the rhythm of writing. Waiting until the "perfect" time means writing may not happen.

  Tip: Try to write daily, even if only a paragraph or two, a journal entry, or a thought for an idea file. The natural flow of writing benefits from routine.

- **Believing that inspiration must come first**

  Not true. The very act of writing is thinking and often inspiring.

  Tip: Talk it out through freewriting. Capture thoughts on a computer or paper, where it's easier to juggle ideas. Refrain from evaluating, correcting, or rearranging. Writing and editing simultaneously often creates writer's block.

- **Concern that the writing won't be good enough**

  Most books aren't perfect—even when completed. Striving to write perfectly from the start will sabotage a book. Writing is a process of arranging and rearranging, inserting and deleting, and writing and rewriting. Good news: Editors and peer reviewers only see the finished draft.

  Tip: Just start, perhaps with stream-of-conscious thinking. Rearrange thoughts. Polish the writing later when thinking is fresh.

- **Thinking a book must start at its beginning**

  Again, not true.

  Tip: With a good outline, a writer can start anywhere: beginning, middle, end.

- **Fatigue and stress**

  Writing nearly 24/7 with insufficient sleep, stress, and a sedentary work style can be serious barriers to good thinking, good writing, and good health.

  Tip: Step away. A mental break relieves writing pressure.

---

nutrition communications. Employment or volunteer organizations may as well. Many professional writers' organizations share codes of ethics online; among these groups are the Society for Technical Communication, the National Association of Independent Writers and Editors, and the Alliance of Independent Authors.

- Check the publishing contract. It will likely require authors to sign an ethics agreement, and many publishing contracts have indemnification clauses. Breaching a contract (by committing ethics violations) may terminate a book contract and even lead to costly litigation.

- Safeguard your work from potential legal action. A book's copyright page can carry a disclaimer, such as this one in the *Academy of Nutrition and Dietetics Complete Food and Nutrition Guide*[6]:

  This book presents the research and ideas of its author. It is not intended to be a substitute for consultation with a professional health care practitioner. Consult with your health care practitioner before starting any diet or

Visit Chapter 7 for more on developing skills for clear communication.

Work that is potentially vulnerable to lawsuits can be protected by writer's professional liability insurance against allegations of copyright and trademark infringement and of personal damages to others (eg, defamation, libel, and plagiarism). Errors and omissions insurance can also protect against allegations of negligence or inadequate work.

See Chapter 9 for ethical communication practices.

What Are the Practical Steps to Publishing a Book?

Writers only get published if they run with their ideas! So, if you have a book concept in mind, it may be time for the next steps. Among the first considerations:

- What type of book do you envision? Books are written for many genres and subgenres. They're defined as nonfiction or fiction; by content, such as health or self-help; by literary technique, such as a reference book; and by tone or length. Books are classified in categories too: for example, trade (general public); elhi (elementary–high school textbooks); college, professional, or business; age category (children, young readers, adult); and format (how-to book, cookbook, picture book, and others).
- Who do you want to publish it, and how? Will this be a print or electronic book (eBook) or both? Will you pursue a traditional (large or small press) publisher? Or will you consider hybrid publishing? Or self-publishing?
- Will you be *the* author or collaborate as a coauthor? Have you been approached to be a ghostwriter or contributor with a work-for-hire contract? ("Work-for-hire" authors generally are paid a flat fee for contracted writing; they don't receive royalties or own editorial rights.)
- What are the steps from concept to successful book sales? Read on.

Determine the Publishing Approach

Prospective authors have publishing options.

TRADITIONAL PUBLISHERS

Traditional publishers handle all steps in editing, design, production, distribution, and marketing. The publisher assumes the costs and risks and retains some rights. Large publishing companies often have imprints (or trade names), which market books for different consumer segments.

For published book authors or those with a strong platform and a significant social media presence, traditional publishing is a good option.

SELF-PUBLISHING

Self-publishing is do-it-yourself. The author takes responsibility for everything: writing, editing, design, production, distribution, and marketing. Self-publishing is a good option for a niche (narrow topic or narrow audience) book, for a book targeted at a local market, for first-time authors, and for those wanting a resource or tool for their work or business. Self-publishing can be faster and may lead to a traditional publishing deal.

Self-publishing may be easier for those with experience and skill in writing, editing, print or online production, and self-marketing. Julie Beyer, MA, RDN, author of the self-published *You CAN Write a Book*, notes that self-publishing is well suited for many RDNs. Among the benefits, content can be updated and improved easily with each printing; the author can parlay the work into many income streams.[7]

HYBRID PUBLISHING

Hybrid publishing, also called vanity or partner publishing, is a middle ground between traditional and self-publishing, but without the selection criteria generally required of authors by traditional publishers. Authors are often the main buyers, using their book as an educational tool or promotional item. A book published to market a product, company, or trade association may use hybrid publishing.

Hybrid publishing gives independence to the author, but with more support than self-publishing. The author pays the publisher for editorial work, design, production, marketing, and distribution. Hybrid publishing is usually faster than traditional publishing but offers limited distribution. A hybrid book may lead to a traditional publishing deal.

Find Publisher Information

The Literary Marketplace and *Writer's Market* (listed in the resources) provide information about publishers: their editorial mission, number of titles published yearly, percentage of books from first-time authors, royalty terms and advances, recent titles, and what they look for. If an author has a literary agent (discussed later in this chapter), the agent will identify appropriate publishing houses for a proposal. Note that having an academic job isn't required to publish with an academic publisher.

To find potential publishers for a book proposal and concept, check a bookstore for titles on a similar subject. A book's copyright page identifies its publisher.

The steps outlined in the next sections address traditional trade publishing, but many steps are similar for other publishing routes. Editorial, marketing, and distribution steps for textbooks, academic books, and professional books, as well as acquisition and contracts, often differ from those for trade books.

See Figure 42.1 on page 650 to compare traditional and self-publishing.

Start with a Book Proposal

A proposal is a business case for a book. It tells prospective publishers what a book is about, why they should publish it, why it will interest readers, and why *you* should write it. It needs to be persuasive, with a clear concept of the book and its audience and the reasons why it is marketable and worth the publisher's investment.

What goes into a successful nonfiction book proposal? While there is no single format or set number of pages, a typical proposal is 20 to 30 pages.[8] Despite this length, a publisher often decides to offer a contract after reading only the first few pages.

OVERVIEW OF A BOOK CONCEPT

A successful, strong case for a book starts with an overview that immediately hooks a potential publisher.

Book concept, vision, and need A brief overview or summary (two to three pages) of the concept, not a deep dive into the content, provides the general idea. As important is the vision: why this concept is unique or why the topic is trending, and why the content will benefit and matter to target readers and perhaps a broader audience. Include an attention-grabbing working title and a proposed book trim size and page count. (Trim size is the dimensions of the printed book.)

Author's platform This is where you sell yourself as the right author for this book. Your platform shows your credibility, expertise, and experience; professional network; and the social media platforms and other channels that give visibility and a sales network. For example, seven cookbooks by Ellie Krieger, MS, RDN, such as *Whole in One: Complete Healthy Meals in a Single Pot, Skillet or Sheet Pan,* are spokes in her marketing platform, which includes television, social media, and a newspaper column.

Major publishers may want to know the statistics and analytics behind an online following (eg, websites, blogs, podcasts, social media accounts), an offline following (eg, speaking, teaching, leadership, and memberships), traditional media (eg, regular engagements, features, coverage), a network, and past book sales.[9] (If it's necessary to build a platform and social media presence, self-publishing may be a better option than traditional publishing, at least for now.)

Target readers Publishers want to know about the potential market (eg, adult consumers, health professionals, athletes, new parents) that will find the book compelling enough to buy. Provide demographic statistics on target buyers and potential sales numbers.

Competitive analysis Publishers want a competitive analysis of published books that address similar issues. This analysis differentiates the book and justifies why it's needed.

Each competitive title should include these basics: author, publisher, page count, publication date, price, format, ISBN,[10] and edition (if more than one), along with a content description and constructive analysis.

No competition? A publisher may view that as an opportunity—or instead as no interest in a concept or a topic that is too specialized to sell.

Marketing A publisher wants specifics about how you will promote the book, including your current platforms and networks. After signing a contract, you'll be asked to complete a detailed author questionnaire, which you and the publisher will use for marketing plans.

TABLE OF CONTENTS

A proposed table of contents or outline shows the intended flow, depth, and range of content. For each chapter, provide an engaging title and description that summarize its key ideas and points. Keep them brief, focused, and clear. If features or sidebars seem possible, such as self-assessments, infographics, or recipes, indicate them. Proposing a cookbook? Provide recipe concepts for each chapter.

SAMPLE CHAPTER(S)

One or more sample chapters show the author's writing style, voice, and skill. They also show how the concepts, vision, and benefits in a proposal's overview are conveyed and how chapters are introduced, how they bridge to content, and how conclusions are presented. The sample chapter doesn't need to be the first chapter of the book, nor should it be the introduction. Choose the chapter(s) that show the best writing.

See Chapter 15 for organizing content.

FIGURE 42.1 Traditional publishing vs self-publishing: Weighing the benefits

	Traditional Publishing	Self-Publishing
Author platform	• Traditional publishers typically require that authors have a strong book-marketing platform. • Publishing with a major or well-recognized publishing house gives credibility and prestige to an author.	• No barriers exist to self-publishing. • A self-published book gives an author a platform, credibility, and recognition.
Finances	• An advance against royalties is often paid to an author. An advance is payment, based on predicted earnings as a percentage of sales. A royalty is what the publisher is legally required to pay the author for actual earnings from copyrighted work. (Work-for-hire contracts usually don't pay royalties.) • No up-front publishing costs are charged to the author. • Selling price is set by the publisher. • Income depends on royalties from books sold after returns and after the advance is earned out. (To "earn out," earned royalties equal the advance.) Traditional book selling is a returns-based business where booksellers can return unsold books. • A percentage of the royalty is typically paid to the literary agent. • Traditional publishing can result in wider distribution, often to national store chains. • The publisher pays for and acquires the book's ISBN[a] and registers the copyright.	• No advance is paid. • The author pays all costs for publishing (graphics or photography, design, perhaps editing and proofreading, and formatting), distribution, and marketing. • The author has control over costs, which are variable and based on design and outsourced services. • Selling price is determined by the author, after publishing costs and the price of competitive books are considered. • Printed cost per book to the author may be low; a large initial print order may be required to keep the price down. Print-on-demand, such as CreateSpace from Amazon, may keep the price low. • All income after expenses goes to the author. • Profit depends on publishing (editorial, production), distribution, and marketing costs against the book sales. • The author pays for and acquires the book's ISBN and registers the copyright.
Editorial input and control	• The publisher's team handles the editorial work, including editing, design and art direction, copy editing, and indexing. • The author controls the book content, with possible changes required by the editors. • The author has less control over the title, cover art, graphics, and book design. • The schedule for revisions and corrections depends on the publisher.	• The author is responsible for, and is in full control of, editorial work. • A custom publishing service may be contracted for paid editorial services. • The author has full creative control and responsibility over the title, content, cover art, graphics, and design. • The author can make revisions, fix errors, and change formats more easily, especially if the first print run is small, or if the book is an eBook or printed on demand.

For a cookbook proposal, include sample recipes with recipe headnotes. If a book concept requires illustrations, infographics, or photographs (perhaps for a children's book or step-by-step cookbook), provide sample page spreads (a page spread is two facing pages).

AUTHOR BIO

An biographical sketch (bio) provides an extensive opportunity to share professional expertise and credentials, more about platforms, and relevant volunteer or personal experiences. For example, if proposing a book on feeding children, publishers would be interested to know that you teach a kids' cooking class, that you've mastered feeding challenges with your own children, or that you bring your passion and skills, such as theater or athletics, to reaching youth.

For health, self-help, or parenting books that are meant to impart useful information or benefit readers' lives, the author bio establishes credibility and professional expertise. That in turn will convey authority and instill confidence with readers. With an author bio:

- provide published writing samples (originals or scans), preferably reflective of the book concept, if available;
- include published recipes if proposing a cookbook; and
- include testimonials from others, if possible.

The proposal is ready. The literary agent (discussed next) may submit it to one publisher or several simultaneously. If several, potential publishers need to know. If a book has a niche, or narrow audience, a small press publisher may be the

FIGURE 42.1 Traditional publishing vs self-publishing: Weighing the benefits (continued)

	Traditional Publishing	Self-Publishing
Timeline to book launch	• The process is generally slower (often 2 years or more) from query to book launch (includes finding an agent; submitting a proposal; contracts; writing, editing, production, and distribution; fitting into an editorial or catalog calendar).	• The process can be faster (sometimes within 6 months) once the book concept and publishing plan are complete. • A quick turnaround (if published as an eBook) is more likely than with traditional publishing.
Production, distribution, marketing, accounting	• The publisher manages the design and electronic file preparation, production, printing, and warehousing. • The publisher manages the distribution, which likely results in a greater distribution, to sales outlets, as well as libraries, schools, and other venues. • Online booksellers broaden distribution; deep discounts are required. • The publisher handles initial marketing and listings in publishing databases; the author is typically responsible for most ongoing marketing efforts. • The publisher manages all accounting: sales and returns, requests for book copy, reprint, permissions, and royalties.	• Total responsibility and control for design and electronic file preparation, production, printing, warehousing, and distribution is with the author. *Print-on-demand* (printing one or small book orders only after an order is received) can be a wise option. • Self-publishing services, contracted for a fee, may get books listed in publishing databases but not sold into sales outlets. • For a fee, online booksellers can broaden distribution. Distribution of self-published books generally is limited and mostly through online sources. • The author handles all marketing, unless these services are contracted. • The author manages and tracks all accounting: costs, sales, returns, earnings, and permission requests.
Author rights	• Control over rights is negotiated in the publishing contract. Some rights are given over to the publisher, such as foreign and exclusive electronic rights.	• The author owns and controls all rights, with the direct ability to sell spin-offs and foreign rights.

ᵃ ISBN (International Standard Book Number) is a product identifier used by publishers, booksellers, libraries, internet retailers, and others in the supply chain for ordering, listing, sales records, and stock control. The ISBN identifies the registrant, title, edition, and format.8

best bet. A literary agent will do the follow-up. Allow 2 or 3 months. Will there be a response if the proposal is rejected? That depends. Rejected authors may or may not be notified. Today publishers generally respond electronically.

A self- or hybrid-published book concept doesn't need a book proposal. Neither do many work-for-hire contracts, since publishers typically seek authors on their own. A work-for-hire author may need to develop concepts and an outline (and for a cookbook, a list of recipes) before or after a contract is signed.

Get a Literary Agent

Is it worth contracting with an agent? Major trade (consumer) publishers generally won't consider a proposal without an agent. Small press, academic, and specialty or niche publishers may. Although their services require a fee, an agent can sell a proposal and negotiate a favorable contract. A literary agent isn't needed for self- or hybrid publishing.

A literary agent typically handles these tasks:

- helps shape a book proposal
- submits the proposal to appropriate publishing houses that have an imprint and line of books that match the book's concept
- negotiates a fair book contract and monitors adherence to it
- may review the accuracy of royalty statements
- may suggest a topic for a next book

Finding the right agent takes research. The *Literary Marketplace*, published annually, is one resource, or you may want to subscribe to Publishers Marketplace (see the resources section). Other approaches include the following:

- Check the acknowledgments in similar food and nutrition books, ask other book authors, or meet agents at conferences, such as the International Association of Culinary Professionals.
- Send a potential agent a short, concise, and well-written query letter with the book's concept, objectives (for the reader and marketplace), and a bio that's relevant to the book. While many agents prefer to work with published authors, a unique book idea with broad appeal and a strong platform and promotion plan can make a proposal

attractive to literary agents, even as a first-time author.

If a literary agent agrees to represent an author, the contract likely will include the length of time for representation, tasks the agent will perform, the fee based on a percentage of the royalties, perhaps monies earned from book promotion events, and whether the agent has first rights to represent the author for a subsequent title. An agent typically earns 15% of the book advance and royalties.[8]

If choosing to self-publish, a mentor or writing coach, rather than an agent, can help with manuscript development. Check the Authors and Writers specialty group of the Academy of Nutrition and Dietetics Nutrition Entrepreneurs dietetic practice group to find a mentor.

Learn from Rejection

Proposal rejected? No response to a proposal? Try again! Continue to work on a social media platform. Or self-publish. Becoming a published author takes persistence and perseverance. Proposals, even from successful, established authors, get rejected, possibly several times. That doesn't mean the proposal was poor. Perhaps the book didn't fit within the publisher's book line (catalog). The timing may be off. A competing title may already be on a publisher's list or in the works. Or the publisher may not choose to take a risk on the book or on committing the resources required. To learn from your rejection, do the following:

- Read the rejection letter. It may state why the proposal was rejected. Ask for constructive feedback from the literary agent or, if possible, from the publisher's acquisition editor, who decides what proposals to accept.
- Turn lemons into lemonade; learn from the process. Barry Farber, author of *Diamond in the Rough*, once noted: "When the 27th publisher bought my book, I was not getting a manuscript that had failed 26 times. I was getting a manuscript that had benefited from the advice of 26 talented, knowledgeable professionals."[11]
- Rewrite the proposal if needed. Keep it circulated. Send it to different publishers. A book proposal is rejected only if it is never submitted again.

- Build online and offline platforms and visibility. Then refocus, revise, and recirculate the proposal. Rejection often results from a limited author platform.

Self-publishing is another option if an interested publisher isn't turning up. Weigh the benefits, as noted in Figure 42.1, of a self-publishing route.

Negotiate a Contract

Congratulations! A publisher is interested in your book. That said, landing the contract may require modifying the proposed outline, target readership, or length. Be flexible without sacrificing the book's integrity. Contract negotiation is the next step, typically handled by the publisher's acquisition editor and you, and a literary agent if there is one.

A book contract is a legal document. It addresses the responsibilities of both author and publisher. An *author* is to submit an acceptable (original, accurate) manuscript with revisions, on agreed-upon deadlines; to secure (and often pay for) permissions of copyrighted material; and perhaps to provide and pay for graphics, illustrations, or photographs. The *publisher* is responsible for editing, proofreading, designing, indexing (which may be charged to the author), typesetting, printing, binding, warehousing, distribution, and accounting. Both the *author and publisher* have marketing responsibilities.

For royalty authors, contract terms also may include, but are not limited to, book size; deadlines; royalty rates; book advance; payment schedule; charges for indexing, artwork, and author alterations once in production; publisher rights; author approval rights; author discounts; author copies; and limitations for writing a similar, competitive book with a different publisher.

Among other contract terms, publishing contracts typically include provisions that protect the publisher and help ensure author ethics, such as requiring delivery of original work and work that isn't encumbered by other contracts; avoidance of infringement on intellectual property and proprietary content; avoidance of libelous or defamatory content; avoidance of errors and omissions that may cause harm; and more.

A work-for-hire contract is simpler. The terms typically include, but are not limited to, deadlines for manuscript submission, book length, fee to the author with no royalty, all rights to the publisher, payment schedule, and perhaps the number of free author copies. See the Words of Experience box on page 654 for personal insights and lessons learned throughout the journey of writing a book.

Work with the Editorial Team

Although writing is a solo activity (except for co-authors), authors aren't alone. If a contract is with a traditional or hybrid publisher, an editorial team will take the manuscript from draft to a print-ready or online-ready book. Taking constructive criticism well is an asset in collaboration.

MANAGING EDITOR

From start to finish, the managing editor coordinates editorial and production steps, establishing deadlines for each. In large publishing houses, a separate production editor will likely handle the printing, eBook, or print-on-demand processes.

DEVELOPMENTAL OR GENERAL EDITOR

The developmental editor and author work closely and creatively throughout manuscript development. *Developmental editing* shapes the manuscript with a format, voice, and flow that appeals to buyers. At this stage, features, such as sidebars, infographics, charts, boxes, and graphics or photography, are specified. This editor may address how tone, clarity, and meaning are expressed.

COPY EDITOR

Copy editing happens before a manuscript goes to production. The copy editor checks for correct grammar, punctuation, spelling, and syntax and for consistency internally and with the publisher's stylebook.

PEER REVIEWERS

The author is usually responsible for peer review. Peer feedback—noting what might be added, deleted, or reframed; catching unintended errors; and helping to clarify content—improves a manuscript. For books published by the Academy of Nutrition and Dietetics, the publisher facilitates peer review by technical experts, including RDNs.

RECIPE TESTERS

Writing a cookbook? The author is usually responsible for recipe testing and retesting. This includes outside testers, who often work for hire. Testers evaluate whether the recipes work, assess flavor and appeal, ensure a complete ingredient list with correct amounts, and check for clearly written directions, temperatures, timing, yields,

Writing a Book: The Journey by Roberta Larson Duyff, MS, RDN, FAND, FADA

"The pages all started like this ..

*... and then came
the WORDS
and the days
and nights
and the WORDS
and more WORDS
and the pages filled
and finally, finally
a BOOK!"*

*—Carl Hermann,
graphic designer and
longtime friend*

The proposal was accepted. The contract was signed. The editorial team is supportive. Thankfully the vision and book outline were well crafted. Thankfully the agent secured a good contract after lively bidding by several publishers. And thankfully I'm an experienced and enthusiastic writer. Now where do I start the *Academy of Nutrition and Dietetics Complete Food and Nutrition Guide*? How can I, as the author, provide practical, sound, healthy-eating guidance to the general public and, equally important, best represent the then-named American Dietetic Association in its many pages? A daunting but exciting opportunity!

Book publishing wasn't new to me. Before signing the contract for the book, I'd had 15 years of experience—as an author in elhi (elementary–high school) publishing for McGraw-Hill for several high school–level food and nutrition textbooks; as a contributing author to a college nursing text; as coauthor of an early childhood nutrition textbook; and as editor, contributor, and peer reviewer for several health and nutrition titles. I'd ghostwritten a trade book on nutrition, contributed to cookbooks with work-for-hire contracts, and written traditionally and self-published children's books. But, as with every book, the *Complete Food and Nutrition Guide* came with somewhat different steps, different expectations, and different challenges, arguably benefiting from my range of publishing experiences.

The many insights and steps shared throughout this chapter reflect what I learned along the way. Here are several other experiences from my publishing journey and their lessons:

*Photo credit:
Beverly Bajus*

The joy of a book signing! The first edition of the award-winning American Dietetic Association Complete Food and Nutrition Guide, a practical guide to healthy eating for every age and stage of life, was launched in 1996. This trade book is now in its fifth edition. As a category best-seller, it received a 2018 Gold National Health Information Award and a Best in Show among all Gold Awardees.

Experience: Early on, the publisher of a high school textbook I was authoring greeted my first chapters positively, but with a seemingly impossible task: to shorten them by 50%—without cutting any content.

Lesson: Write tightly for clarity and impact. Good editing is a learning opportunity for better writing.

Experience: Four years of writing a weekly column for the *St. Louis Post Dispatch* offered a treasure trove of book content.

Lesson: Repurpose and refocus great content that is already reader-tested.

Experience: A stolen laptop resulted in a stolen chapter and stolen time for the Academy of Nutrition and Dietetics book. Fortunately, the recreated chapter was even better than my original.

Lesson: Back up and save your work, over and over. Keep the backup in a separate place to protect carefully crafted content.

Experience: Starting with a blank computer screen was daunting, but only at first.

Continued ▶

Lesson: Write each chapter as a short article. Writing the first paragraph of the *Complete Food and Nutrition Guide* last—after the content and flow of all 26 chapters was finished—allowed me to write an impactful opening more easily.

Experience: My consumer books, textbooks, and children's books have had similar themes about fruits and vegetables but were written with very different voices, for different reading levels, and with different designs and graphics. For example, *All Our Fruits and Vegetables* for preschoolers spoke in rhyme and iambic pentameter; a comic book for grade schoolers for the Florida Citrus Commission delivered content through illustrations and dialogue; my *Food, Nutrition, and Wellness* textbook taught practical skills to teens; and several consumer trade books wove science-based context into how-to content.

Lesson: Know your readers, read what they read, and test your manuscript and graphics. Writing with fewer words for young readers has unique challenges! Beyond that, illustrations deliver messages that words alone cannot.

Experience: *The Complete Food & Nutrition Guide* in early editions was translated and distributed in Chinese, Greek, and Turkish, with portions also sold for Arabic-language distribution.

Lesson: Be clear about foreign rights in your book contract. Know that intellectual property can't be protected everywhere.

Experience: Responsibility to my readers and profession has meant countless hours of fact-checking and of honing my ability to write with sensitivity and without ambiguity or misunderstanding.

Lesson: Always seek and value insights from peer reviewers, editors, outside experts, and the target readers who make your book a lasting, impactful success.

The full title for the first through fourth editions is *American Dietetic Association Complete Food and Nutrition Guide*, and for the fifth edition, *Academy of Nutrition and Dietetics Complete Food and Nutrition Guide*, a trade book from a traditional publisher.

safety notes, and doneness signs. See Box 42.3 on page 656 and Chapters 25 and 26 for more about recipe development.

ART DIRECTOR OR DESIGNER

Every successful book has a look, designed to grab attention, allow ease of reading, and distinguish it on a bookshelf or in an online catalog. Design decisions may include choice of ink color(s), typefaces and type size, cover art, graphics, illustrations, and the look of chapter openers. The author might not have a say in these decisions, depending on the contract. However, the author is entitled to an opinion; ask to discuss the design if it is of concern.

INDEXER

A detailed index that includes keywords enables a reader to navigate the book with ease. Self-published authors should note that indexing software for the layperson generally doesn't work well.

PROOFREADER

Proofreading is one last manuscript check, done before transmission to production.

If you are self-publishing, consider hiring someone with editorial expertise to help through the design and editing stages.

Family members, friends, and colleagues also can provide invaluable editorial support. Bounce ideas off them. Involve them as another set of eyes during revision and proofreading. (And include them in the acknowledgments.)

Remember that editors are your friends who believed in the title and in you as an author from the start. You'll get to know them quite well. Editors guide authors through the process and serve as sounding boards for ideas and content before manuscripts are submitted. Editors may be your toughest critics, but they also can help make your writing stronger!

Make a Plan and Begin Writing

Plan, plan, plan … whatever publishing route is taken. For traditional publishing, author contracts generally specify the deadline for first draft submission, with a general date for book launch. The editorial team generally sets due dates throughout the process. For a self-published or hybrid-published book, the author determines the launch date and the deadlines in between.

Create a spreadsheet to track writing tasks and deadlines as they're accomplished. These tasks may include outline development, first draft, peer review and subsequent revisions, revisions after copy editing, proofreading of final pages, and permissions. For a cookbook, include recipe development and writing, recipe testing and retesting, and perhaps photography and nutrition analysis.

Regardless, the process requires discipline. See Nine: Stay Disciplined earlier in this chapter.

Write

Staring at a blank computer screen or paper isn't easy. Writing the first page can be the hardest. It may not be necessary to start there. With a well-articulated outline, a book starts to write itself. Keep this in mind:

- Study the publisher's author guidelines, such as the font and type size, line spacing, margins, chapter headings, manuscript length, and file management.
- Obtain the publisher's stylebook or find out which published style guide is used. A stylebook or guide provides standards for the writing and design of documents. If self-publishing, consider using the *Chicago Manual of Style* or the *Associated Press Stylebook*. For a cookbook, decide what form recipes will take, usually a standard, narrative, or action form. Refer to The Recipe Writer's Handbook noted later in the resources section.
- For terms and meanings unique to the manuscript, create a unique style sheet of terms that are repeated—for example, *ceviche* or *seviche* or *breastfeeding* or *breast-feeding*. Be consistent with word usage, spelling, and meanings.
- Use the final outline as a writing map. Stay flexible in case the manuscript needs to take a different direction.
- Keep graphics, sidebars, infographics, and other features in mind while writing. Perhaps provide notes for the design team to show how to create these features.
- Make note of permissions needed for copyrighted content. If used in the final draft, secure permission. Ask for the permissions form from a traditional publisher. If self-publishing, create a permissions form. See the resources section for a source.
- Keep track of references for footnotes, resource lists, and attributions. Organize them for future reference. Keep track, too, of people to acknowledge.
- Double-check numbers, such as nutrient values, Recommended Dietary Allowances, recipe amounts, cooking times and internal temperatures, and food storage times.

BOX 42.3 From Kitchen to Keyboard

Most recipes are written in one of three forms: standard, narrative, or action. The standard form first lists ingredients, then directions. The narrative form puts ingredients and their amounts within the directions and is often used on packaging or in short recipes with few ingredients. The action form is a cross between the two, as used in the classic cookbook *Joy of Cooking* (most recent edition published by Scribner in 2019).

A well-written recipe is more than the sum of its parts. First and foremost, it is accurate, complete, and straightforward.

Short sentences with clear, concise directions reduce ambiguity and make recipes easier to follow and less daunting at first glance.

Successful recipes match a cook's culinary literacy and skills. For the less kitchen savvy, simpler terms are often better. Consider writing "simmer, covered" instead of "braise" or "cut into $\frac{1}{8}$- to $\frac{1}{4}$-inch cubes" instead of "dice."

A good recipe also follows a logical workflow for efficiency, avoids food waste, and uses handling methods that ensure food safety.

Consistency adds clarity. A publisher or food company may have a recipe stylebook that dictates its wording or punctuation. If not, creating your own stylebook standardizes your recipes and helps give voice to your culinary creativity.

Whether it's new or a makeover, a written recipe anticipates a cook's questions and is only finished when tested, retested, and carefully proofread. Remember the ultimate goals: a confident cook and a successful dish.

Adapted with permission from Duyff RL. From kitchen to keyboard. *Food & Nutrition Magazine*. November-December 2013. Accessed January 17, 2020. https://foodandnutrition.org/november-december-2013/from-kitchen-to-keyboard[12]

- Polish your work before submitting a first draft. Check for consistency. Rewrite for clarity, brevity, and readability. Run a readability score. Remove repetition. Smooth transitions. Add examples and anecdotes for interest and understanding. The cleaner the manuscript, the more efficient the editing process. See Two: Learn to Write Well; Edit Rigorously in this chapter.
- Before submitting a manuscript, read it aloud. That's often the best way to spot a missing word, an incomplete sentence, poor grammar, clumsy wording, or lack of clarity. It is possible to hear mistakes that aren't seen. Ask someone, perhaps a target reader, to read it too.

Revise

Revise, revise, revise to submit the best effort. Follow these tips:

- Collaborate with editors. Accept constructive criticism as a positive. They'll check for clarity, organization, and tone. Accuracy is the writer's responsibility; most book publishers don't employ fact-checkers.
- Respond to editor queries and copy editing. Revise accordingly. Has research turned up new regulations or guidelines since the first draft? Now is the time for editorial changes that keep the book current. Once a print book is transmitted to production, changes can be impossible or costly.
- Learn and use standard copy editing and proofreading marks for any editing on paper.
- Organize peer review or recipe testing (for a cookbook) unless handled by editors. Consider recommendations. Revise as needed, or explain why they're rejected, perhaps with a note to the editor in the manuscript's electronic file.

Proofread

The production team is nearly ready to print the book or complete its readiness as an electronic book, or both. There is one more step: proofreading.

- Proofread the composed (typeset) pages carefully. This is the last chance to fix an error.
- Read the book aloud again. Double-check numbers again.
- If the book has hyperlinks or websites, make sure they work.

Market the Published Book

Finally, you hold your published book in your hands or click into the eBook. You see it on bookstore shelves and listed by online booksellers. But your work isn't over. All authors must be marketers too. As Catharine Powers, MS, RDN, LD, coauthor of *Recipe Nutrient Analysis*, a self-published reference, notes, "Publishing is more about marketing than publishing."

Marketing starts while a book is still in the writing stage. Before and after book launch, execute the marketing plan:

- Complete the publisher's author questionnaire, where the available marketing channels are detailed. Compile a contact list.
- Take time to develop an online (eg, website, blog, Instagram, Facebook) and offline presence. Arrange speaking engagements, cooking classes, guest writing on others' blogs, and book signings for the book launch and beyond. They offer opportunities for back-of-room sales (books marketed with author seminars and speaking events), as successfully done by Nancy Clark, MS, RDN, CSSD, author of *Nancy Clark's Sports Nutrition Guidebook*, now in its sixth edition.
- Initiate a prepublication review from experts; ask for quotes for the cover or inside page. This is generally done once a final manuscript can be shared, allowing time to include quotes during production.
- Plan and market through social media, speaking, media appearances, workshops or cooking classes, book award entries, and announcements in professional, community, and university publications. Post positive reviews on your website. Refer to the author questionnaire.
- Add the title to the author list of the Academy of Nutrition and Dietetics Nutrition Entrepreneurs dietetic practice group.
- Link to the Goodreads Author Program (noted in the resources section), which has ways to reach a target audience.

Marketing a book is a shared responsibility, with the completed author questionnaire serving as a tool. Traditional publishers market books to distributors and major book buyers through their catalogs, press releases to trade publications (eg,

Publishers Weekly), and book expos. They target key publications and organizations with press releases and book samples to potential buyers. Unlike in the past, most no longer send authors on multicity media tours. Self-published or not, authors need to schedule their own tours or hire a publicist to do so.

Marketing for school and college books differs and depends on contractual requirements with the publisher. For example, textbook marketing is generally handled *only* by the publisher.

Work-for-hire authors may join marketing efforts if allowed by the contract, especially if the visibility of authorship contributes to their personal brand.

See Chapter 37 for more on marketing and Chapters 27 to 32 for marketing through mass media.

See Chapters 4 and 5 for how to identify credible sources.

Prepare for an Update

Many books, especially reference books, aren't finished once published. If another edition is likely, files for the next edition start when a book goes to press. Even if a book only has one edition, publishers may do a small print run first to allow for corrections or updates in subsequent printings; online books are revised more easily. Updates in dietary guidance, nutrition science, and government regulations make updates especially important for nutrition books.

Some smart practices for a next edition:

- Keep current with professional reading; follow daily or weekly postings on the Academy of Nutrition and Dietetics *SmartBrief* (subscribe through eatrightpro@smartbrief.com), *Eat Right Weekly,* and credible non–Academy of Nutrition and Dietetics resources.
- Continue to attend professional meetings and webinars, such as the Academy of Nutrition and Dietetics Food & Nutrition Conference & Expo (FNCE), its many state and local conferences, and webinars of its dietetic practice groups.
- File articles, ideas, and reviews. Keep reviews and comments from peers and readers in a file too.
- Mark up one of the books with revision notes. For an eBook, print it out to use for mark-ups and revise as possible.

The book publishing process can be lengthy, requiring countless hours of work, significant effort, and the passage of years to a successful book launch. If you have an important, perhaps unique message to share, the effort is well worth it. With so many publishing options today, it is possible to find a viable pathway to publishing!

KEY POINTS

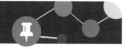

Nutrition Communicators Write Books to Make a Difference

1 A book is a lasting platform for communicating important nutrition information to target readers. It's a place to share expertise. A book can translate complex nutrition science into sensible guidance. The content can serve as an ongoing resource that impacts the food decisions, health, and well-being of readers.

2 Research for a book provides valuable benefits. As a learning experience, it helps an author keep current on food and nutrition issues, trends, and more and provides a way to polish editorial skills. Because a book reflects the author, research also can leverage career opportunities. Before embarking on the journey of authorship, nutrition professionals should consider their motivation and ponder the realities.

3 The best practices for publishing begin with a firm idea. Why write this book and for whom? Beyond that, successful authors respond to inspiration, write well, edit rigorously, and write with their distinct voice. They make research a habit, write for their readers first and always, gather a support team, test their content through other platforms, reflect evidence and check facts, stay disciplined, know how to overcome writer's block, and always make ethics a priority.

4 Whether a book is published through a traditional or hybrid publisher or self-published, its journey from concept to publication is a multistep process. Prospective authors need to compare different publishing pathways for the best approach. Whichever route is taken, authors need a plan and the discipline to write, revise, and proofread the manuscript and its composed book pages before printing. Once a book is published, marketing and perhaps preparing for updates are the next steps.

RESOURCES

Books

Associated Press Editors. *The Associated Press Stylebook and Briefing on Media Law.* Hachette Books; 2017.

Beyer J. *You CAN Write a Book: The No-Nonsense Guide to Self-Publishing.* NutraConsults; 2009.

Brewer RL. *Writer's Market 2019: The Most Trusted Guide to Getting Published.* Writer's Digest Books; 2018. (This is published annually.)

Brown University Science Center. *Quick Guide to Science Communication.* May 2014. www.brown .edu/academics/science-center/sites/brown.edu .academics.science-center/files/uploads/Quick_Guide _to_Science_Communication_0.pdf

Burke F. *Online Marketing for Busy Authors: A Step-by-Step Guide.* Berrett-Koehler Publishers; 2016.

Friedman J. *Publishing 101: A First-Time Author's Guide to Getting Published, Marketing and Promoting Your Book, and Building a Successful Career.* Jane Friedman; 2014.

Ostmann BG, Baker JL. *The Recipe Writer's Handbook.* John Wiley Sons; 2001.

Powers C, Dolven CL. *Recipe Nutrient Analysis.* Culinary Nutrition Publishing; 2015.

Perelman LD, Paradis J, Barrett E. Writing for laypersons. In: *The Mayfield Handbook of Technical and Scientific Writing.* McGraw-Hill; 2001.

University of Chicago Press Editorial Staff. *The Chicago Manual of Style.* 17th ed. University of Chicago Press; 2017.

Other Resources

Academy of Nutrition and Dietetics, Nutrition Entrepreneurs dietary practice group Authors and Writers specialty group: *Ventures* newsletter.

Academy of Nutrition and Dietetics. What is the Code of Ethics?: www.eatrightpro.org/resources /practice/code-of-ethics/what-is-the-code-of-ethics

Ackermann B, Glossary of Publishing Terms: http://aaupwiki.princeton.edu/index.php/Glossary_of_Publishing_Terms

Alliance of Independent Authors, Code of Standards: www.allianceindependentauthors.org/code-of-standards

CreateSpace (Amazon publishing sites): www.createspace.com

Friedman J. Jane's writing advice archive (blog): www.janefriedman.com/writing-advice-archive

Goodreads Author Program: http://goodreads.com/author/program

Independent Book Publishers Association: www.ibpa-online.org

Literary Marketplace: www.literarymarketplace.com

National Association of Independent Writers and Editors, Code of Ethics: https://naiwe.com/ethics

New York Book Editors: https://nybookeditors.com (many articles, including "How to Find Your Writers Voice")

Publishers Marketplace: www.publishersmarketplace.com

Publishers Weekly: www.publishersweekly.com

Society for Technical Communication. Ethical Principles: www.stc.org/about-stc/ethical-principles

University of Chicago Press, Author's Permission Guidelines: www.press.uchicago.edu/infoServices/permissions.html

Writers Digest: www.writersdigest.com

Writers Services, Publishing Glossary: www.writersservices.com/resources/publishing-glossary

REFERENCES

1. Cole B. Interview. *Humanities*. July/August 2002;23(4).
2. Brown University Science Center. Quick guide to science communication. Published May 2014. Accessed August 22, 2019. www.brown.edu/academics/science-center/sites/brown.edu.academics.science-center/files/uploads/Quick_Guide_to_Science_Communication_0.pdf
3. Perelman LD, Paradis J, Barrett E. Writing for laypersons. In: *The Mayfield Handbook of Technical and Scientific Writing.* McGraw-Hill; 2001.
4. Hamlin A, Rubio C, DeSilva M. Ethics in technical writing. In: *Technical Writing.* Press Books; 2016. Accessed January 17, 2020. https://coccoer.pressbooks.com
5. Helping scientists translate their work for the lay public: Q&A with Jane Nevins, author of *You've Got Some Explaining to Do.* The Dana Foundation website. Published April 8, 2014. Accessed March 14, 2018. www.dana.org/publications/NevinsQA
6. Duyff RL. *Academy of Nutrition and Dietetics Complete Food and Nutrition Guide.* Houghton Mifflin Harcourt; 2017.
7. Beyer J. Easy, fast, and inexpensive: why self-publishing was made for dietitians! *Ventures: Enterprising News & Ideas for Nutrition Entrepreneurs.* 2017;33(5).
8. Friedman J. Start here: how to write a book proposal. Published May 28, 2017. Accessed January 18, 2020. www.janefriedman.com/start-here-how-to-write-a-book-proposal www.isbn-international.org/content/what-isbn
9. Gonzales G. The path to publishing. Webinar for Siggi's Dairy. Presented September 20, 2018.
10. International ISBN Agency. What is an ISBN? Published 2014. Accessed January 18, 2020.
11. Farber B. *Diamond in the Rough: The Secret to Finding Your Own Value—and Making Your Own Success.* Berkley Books; 1995.
12. Duyff RL. From kitchen to keyboard. *Food & Nutrition Magazine.* November-December 2013. Accessed January 17, 2020. https://foodandnutrition.org/november-december-2013/from-kitchen-to-keyboard

Continuing Professional Education

This edition of *Communicating Nutrition: The Authoritative Guide* offers readers 14 hours of Continuing Professional Education (CPE) credit. Readers may earn credit by completing the interactive online quiz at: https://publications.webauthor.com /communicating-nutrition

APPENDIX:
Example of Dietetics Research Published in a Scholarly Journal

RESEARCH

Original Research: Brief

Prevalence of and Differences in Salad Bar Implementation in Rural Versus Urban Arizona Schools

Michelle Blumenschine; Marc Adams, PhD, MPH; Meg Bruening, PhD, MPH, RD

ARTICLE INFORMATION

Article history:
Submitted 12 October 2016
Accepted 10 September 2017
Available 30 November 2017

Keywords:
Fruits and vegetables
Rural
Salad bars
Schools

2212-2672/Copyright © 2018 by the Academy of Nutrition and Dietetics.
https://doi.org/10.1016/j.jand.2017.09.004

ABSTRACT

Background Rural children consume more calories per day on average than urban children, and they are less likely to consume fruit. Self-service salad bars have been proposed as an effective approach to better meet the National School Lunch Program's fruit and vegetable recommendations. No studies have examined how rural and urban schools differ in the implementation of school salad bars.

Objective To compare the prevalence of school-lunch salad bars and differences in implementation between urban and rural Arizona schools.

Design Secondary analysis of a cross-sectional web-based survey.

Participants/setting School nutrition managers (N=596) in the state of Arizona.

Main outcomes measured National Center for Education Statistics locale codes defined rural and urban classifications. Barriers to salad bar implementation were examined among schools that have never had, once had, and currently have a school salad bar. Promotional practices were examined among schools that once had and currently have a school salad bar.

Statistical analyses performed Generalized estimating equation models were used to compare urban and rural differences in presence and implementation of salad bars, adjusting for school-level demographics and the clustering of schools within districts.

Results After adjustment, the prevalence of salad bars did not differ between urban and rural schools (46.9%±4.3% vs 46.8%±8.5%, respectively). Rural schools without salad bars more often reported perceived food waste and cost of produce as barriers to implementing salad bars, and funding was a necessary resource for offering a salad bar in the future, as compared with urban schools ($P<0.05$). No other geographic differences were observed in reported salad bar promotion, challenges, or resources among schools that currently have or once had a salad bar.

Conclusions After adjustment, salad bar prevalence, implementation practices, and concerns are similar across geographic settings. Future research is needed to investigate methods to address cost and food waste concerns in rural areas.
J Acad Nutr Diet. 2018;118:448-454.

FRUIT AND VEGETABLE (F/V) CONSUMPTION IS PROtective against chronic diseases such as diabetes, heart disease, and some cancers.[1-3] Most youth do not meet the recommendations for F/V consumption,[4] and F/V consumption decreases throughout adolescence.[5] Eating patterns established in childhood often play a role in nutrition habits in adulthood.[6]

Concomitantly, individuals living in rural settings are increasingly at risk for health disparities.[7] Rural populations in the United States experience a disproportionate burden of chronic conditions and public health challenges, including obesity,[8-11] diabetes, and tobacco use.[12] Rural children also consume more calories per day on average than urban children, and these additional calories typically come from sugarsweetened beverages and low-fiber foods.[13]

Few studies have described school nutrition environments in rural areas; however, several state-specific studies have provided analogous data. For example, in Minnesota, urban schools supported healthier food environments for students compared with rural schools, often as a result of more resources and fewer challenges with staffing.[9] A study of school nutrition and F/V availability in schools across 28 states showed significantly higher likelihood of F/V availability at suburban schools than at town/rural schools.[10]

Schools can be useful venues for serving F/Vs and encouraging intake so that students develop healthy habits for a lifetime. The National School Lunch Program (NSLP) serves 31 million students daily and provides opportunities to improve F/V intake.[1] In accordance with the Healthy, Hunger-Free Kids Act, starting in 2012, NSLP-participating schools were required to help students meet new dietary recommendations through increased F/V variety in cafeterias, stipulating a weekly minimum of five different nutrient-rich F/Vs.[4] Schools are required to compose meals of a greater proportion of F/Vs (minimum of half cup fruit or half cup vegetable daily) to receive federal reimbursement for qualifying students. Serving additional F/Vs is costly.[14] Given the limited amount of federal contributions, schools are eager to identify methods to efficiently and effectively increase F/V intake.

Providing F/Vs that meet NSLP standards and appeal to students is an ongoing challenge. Self-service salad bars have been proposed as an effective approach to better meet the NSLP F/V recommendations.[15] In 2015, the Centers for Disease Control and Prevention reported that an average of 30% of schools have salad bars, including 29% of elementary schools, 31% of middle schools, and 35% of high schools.[16] Few peer-reviewed studies that have examined the dietary impact of school salad bars exist, and these studies provide limited evidence that salad bars increase F/V intake,[17,18] suggesting that contextual factors such as number of items offered may influence intake[15,19,20] and creating room to explore potential promotion methods and barriers that might enhance and/or constrain implementation. In a recent study, investigators examined differences in salad bars across metro vs nonmetro areas in the United States and found no differences in students' reported access.[21] To date, no studies have examined differences in prevalence or implementation of salad bars in urban vs rural schools as reported by school nutrition managers. Research is needed to elucidate potential differences in salad bar implementation in urban vs rural locales and to identify challenges and sources of support involved in implementation of school salad bars. The purposes of this study were to compare the prevalence of school-lunch salad bars across urban and rural Arizona schools and to assess the differences in implementation practices, including distinct challenges and sources of support for these populations. It was hypothesized that prevalence of salad bars would differ between urban and rural settings, with urban schools having a greater prevalence of salad bars and fewer challenges in salad bar implementation.

METHODS

This secondary analysis used data from a Web-administered survey[22] distributed during the 2013-2014 academic year to school nutrition managers via e-mail in Arizona. The Arizona Department of Education provided school-level contact information (names and e-mail addresses) of school nutrition managers participating in the NSLP (1,799 schools). If the nutrition manager's information was not listed or the information was outdated (eg, e-mail undeliverable), district nutrition directors and schools were contacted for the e-mail addresses of school nutrition managers. Researchers obtained valid contact information for 863 school nutrition managers who were then invited to take the survey. Managers were e-mailed reminders up to seven times with various prompts. Of these managers, 648 completed the survey (75.1%), meeting the power required to assess the prevalence of having a salad bar (primary aim of original study).[22] For the purposes of this study, the existing survey data were merged with data on locale of participating schools from the National Center for Education Statistics (NCES).[23] Of those 648 surveys, 52 were from schools not included in the NCES urban-centric locale categories and were excluded from the study. A total of 596 schools from 207 districts were included in the analytical sample. Participants provided informed consent by means of

an online check box and received a $5 gift card and entry into a raffle for a $50 or $100 gift card for completing the survey. The Arizona State University Institutional Review Board approved the study protocol.

Urban and Rural Classification

More than two dozen federal definitions of rural exist, and the various classifications of rural areas in the United States include a range of 17% to 49% of the population.[20] The NCES is the primary federal entity that collects and analyzes data on schools. The NCES locale codes are a measure of geographic status on an urban continuum. With data from the Census Bureau, the NCES revised its definitions of school locale types in 2006 to create the current classification system. Their definitions rely less on population size and county boundaries and more on proximity of an address to an urbanized area.[24] The system has four major locale categories: city, suburb, town, and rural; each of these is further subdivided into three subcategories. City and suburb are divided into large, midsize, and small; and town and rural are divided into fringe, distant, and remote. Fringe is defined as a territory inside an urban cluster, less than or equal to 10 miles from an urban area; distant is more than 10 miles but less than or equal to 35 miles from an urban area; and remote is more than 35 miles from an urban area.[25] Locales in the present study were combined into one of two groups: urban or rural. Urban comprised city, suburb, and town (fringe, distant). Rural comprised town (remote) and rural. These designations were based on both the number of schools listed in each locale subcode and the geographical characteristics of Arizona. Arizona public school distribution is 83% urban and 16% rural.[26]

Instrumentation

The 68-item survey was developed by reviewing existing items in the gray literature (not peer-reviewed) and consulting with state and national content experts on salad bars. The previous literature included the Food and Farming Foundation Salad Bar survey,[27] a previous survey conducted by the Arizona Departments of Education and Health Services,[28] and the Food and Fitness survey from Bridging the Gap.[29] Nutrition and public health content experts judged the face validity of developed items and refined existing items as necessary. More information about the instrumentation has been published elsewhere.[22]

Having a Salad Bar. Participants were asked to respond "yes" or "no" to the following question developed for this survey: "Does your school currently offer a self-service salad bar (also known as produce bars, fresh fruit and vegetable bars, fruit and vegetable bars, condiment bars, etc) to students in your cafeteria/multipurpose room?" If "no" was chosen as the answer to this question, participants were asked to respond "yes" or "no" to the following question: "Have you ever had a self-service salad bar (also known as produce bars, fresh fruit and vegetable bars, fruit and vegetable bars, condiment bars, etc) for students in your school?" Use of these questions resulted in a coding of "currently have a salad bar", "once had a salad bar", and "never had a salad bar".

Salad Bar Promotion. For schools that once had a salad bar or currently have a salad bar, participants were asked what practices their school used to promote salad bars. Response choices included posters, morning announcements/promotions, multimedia, newsletters/parent folders, school website, classroom education, carrot chaser, F/V of the day, meal tray color, and matching salad bar offerings to entrée.

Barriers to Having a Salad Bar. Participants at schools that had never had a salad bar were asked what barriers to having a salad bar they experienced. Response choices included not having enough staff, cost of produce, lack of space, sanitation/food safety concerns, concern with reimbursement from federal agency, time to get through lines, difficulty ordering F/Vs, unsupportive administrators, children's dislike of salad bars, food waste concerns, no budget for future maintenance, outside caterer/vendor, new regulations, and clean-up concerns. Respondents could also enter other reasons/barriers beyond the listed response choices. Participants were asked to identify, by choosing from a list, the top three resources that might be helpful in offering a salad bar in the future. Response options included training and conference sessions, sharing listserv, blog, Facebook, funding, and support from school administration. Participants at schools that currently have salad bars were asked to name the challenges they faced in implementing salad bars. Answer choices offered were identical to the options for schools without salad bars.

School-Level Sociodemographic Covariates. A *grade-level* variable was created by asking respondents to list all grades in the school; and grade level was classified as elementary, middle, or high school.[22] To minimize participant burden, survey data were combined with state data on school-level *free/reduced price lunch* and *enrollment* data using school and district codes.[30] Given that many school-level policies and practices are influenced at the district level, a *district* variable was created to adjust for the clustering of schools within districts. A *years in position* variable was created with the question directed to nutrition managers ("How many years have you been in this position at this school?") and was kept as a continuous variable for analyses.

Analysis

Data were cleaned after examination for irregularities and omissions had been conducted. As noted previously, 52 schools were excluded because of a lack of NCES urban-centric locale categories. Descriptive statistics, normality, collinearity, and nonindependence were reviewed before analyses for those that completed the survey; no concerns were found. Differences in the presence of salad bars in urban vs rural areas were examined by school level, years in current position, free/reduced price lunch rates, and enrollment rates. General estimating equation methods for binomial regression models—controlling for school grade level, years in current position, free/reduced price lunch rates, and enrollment rates—were used to examine the adjusted prevalence of salad bars by locale. For the purpose of assessing factors (eg, salad bar promotion, barriers to having a salad bar) associated with having a salad bar by locale (dependent variable), general estimating equation models were examined, adjusting for school level, free/reduced price lunch rate, school enrollment,

years in position of respondent, and district clustering. Statistical significance was assessed at $P<0.05$. All analyses were done by using Stata Statistical Software (Release 13, 2013).[31]

RESULTS

Table 1 presents results from 596 surveys included in this study with 462 (77.5%) surveys from urban schools and 134 (22.5%) surveys from rural schools. The average free and reduced price lunch eligibility was 64% among urban schools and 67% in rural schools. School nutrition managers reported having held their positions in urban schools for an average of 6.2 years vs 7.8 years in rural schools.

The unadjusted prevalence of schools with salad bars was 67.3% urban and 51.1% rural (Table 1). The prevalence of having a salad bar after adjusting for school level, free/reduced price lunch rate, school enrollment, years in position of respondent, and district clustering was 46.9%±4.3% in urban schools and 46.8%±8.5% in rural schools ($P=0.974$; data not shown). In adjusted models, the only statistically significant association with having a salad bar was free and reduced-price lunch eligibility rate (data not shown: odds ratio=0.66; 95% CI: 0.50, 0.87): the odds of having a salad bar were 34% lower among schools with a 50% or higher free/reduced price lunch eligibility rate.

Challenges and Barriers

Among schools that have never had salad bars, twice as many rural as urban schools reported cost of produce as a barrier to implementing salad bars ($P=0.009$, Table 2). Rural schools without salad bars also listed food waste as a barrier more

Table 1. Demographics and prevalence of having a salad bar in a sample of Arizona schools by rural vs urban locale (n=596)

Demographics	Rural	Urban
	←———n (%)———→	
Schools surveyed	134 (22.5)	462 (77.5)
	←———mean±SD[a]———→	
Free/reduced lunch rate	67.2±20.0	63.1±26.0
Years of nutrition manager employment at site	7.8±6.9	6.2±5.8
Enrollment	806.5±25.9	437.4±20.0
	←———n (%)———→	
School level		
Elementary	73 (54.8)	311 (67.3)
Middle	8 (60.8)	46 (10.0)
High	53 (39.5)	105 (22.7)
Salad bar prevalence		
Schools with a salad bar	68 (51.1)	310 (67.3)
Schools once with a salad bar	19 (14.2)	49 (10.6)
Schools who never had a salad bar	47 (35.1)	103 (22.3)

[a]SD=standard deviation.

Table 2. Adjusted prevalence of challenges and barriers in salad bar implementation in a sample of Arizona schools (n=596)[a]

Survey question	Rural adjusted prevalence (%)	Urban adjusted prevalence (%)	P value
Never had a salad bar: *What are the barriers to having a salad bar in your school?*			
Cost of produce	43.6	22.1	0.009[b]
Lack of space	36.8	42.8	0.49
Sanitation/food safety concerns	42.1	32.3	0.21
Not enough staff	27.7	18.6	0.07
Concern with reimbursement	17.3	19.2	0.78
Time to get through the lines	38.7	30.4	0.29
Difficulty procuring fruits and vegetables	6.5	3.2	0.30
Unsupportive administration	1.5	5.8	0.19
Kids don't like salad bars	9.0	8.5	0.92
Food waste concerns	58.2	38.7	0.024[b]
Children serving themselves	9.0	8.5	0.92
No budget for future maintenance	16.7	10.7	0.32
Other. Please specify	19.8	8.2	0.17
None of the above	5.0	4.5	0.86
Once had a salad bar: *What contributed to you discontinuing your salad bar?*			
Not enough staff	19.0	11.0	0.13
Cost of produce	7.6	5.7	0.66
Lack of space	2.5	2.7	0.97
Sanitation/food safety concerns	11.7	17.3	0.41
Concern with reimbursement	3.2	8.0	0.29
Time to get through the lines	7.9	6.6	0.74
Unsupportive administration	7.2	3.5	0.44

(continued)

Table 2. Adjusted prevalence of challenges and barriers in salad bar implementation in a sample of Arizona schools (n=596)[a] *(continued)*

Survey question	Rural adjusted prevalence (%)	Urban adjusted prevalence (%)	P value
Other. Please specify	7.9	6.2	0.67
None of the above	8.4	6.8	0.75
Currently have a salad bar: *What have been the challenges for your school in implementing a salad bar?*			
Not enough staff	12.1	7.9	0.16
Cost of produce	17.8	13.4	0.33
Lack of space	3.2	8.7	0.08
Sanitation/food safety concerns	6.6	7.8	0.66
Concern with reimbursement	2.7	2.5	0.93
Time to get through the lines	11.8	12.8	0.82
Unsupportive administration	2.9	0.60	0.19
Kids don't like salad bars	5.7	8.7	0.33
Food waste concerns	13.3	20.6	0.09
Children serving themselves	15.2	17.8	0.57
No budget for future maintenance	2.7	0.78	0.14
Outside caterer/vendor	1.4	2.0	0.69
Other. Please specify	7.2	2.6	0.05
None of the above	10.6	13.3	0.53

[a]General estimating equation binomial regression models adjusting for school level, free/reduced rate, years in position of respondent, and district clustering.
[b]Statistical significance was assessed at $P<0.05$.

often than urban schools, a statistically significant difference ($P=0.024$). Among schools that once had salad bars, no statistically significant differences in the percentages of these reasons (ie, barriers) for discontinuation were observed between urban and rural schools. In other words, nutrition managers did not respond differently to having or not having a specific barrier. In schools that currently have salad bars, affirmative responses to food waste concerns as a challenge to implementation were not statistically significantly different between urban and rural schools at the $P<0.05$ level. Urban schools reported waste concerns 21% of the time compared with rural schools, which reported waste concerns 13% of the time ($P=0.096$). "Other" barriers schools listed

Table 3. Adjusted prevalence of practices used by a sample of Arizona schools to promote salad bars (n=596)[a]

Survey question	Rural adjusted prevalence (%)	Urban adjusted prevalence (%)	P value
Once had a salad bar:			
Did your school ever use any of the practices listed below to specifically promote your salad bars?			
Posters	19.4	25.7	0.24
Morning announcements/ promotions	8.8	11.7	0.47
Multimedia	2.5	1.9	0.44
Newsletters/parent folders	8.3	9.6	0.72
School website	15.5	17.8	0.63
Classroom education	4.2	9.0	0.14
Fruit and vegetable of the day	6.0	11.0	0.29
Match salad bar offerings to the entrée	11.8	13.0	0.74
Change meal tray color	2.3	3.7	0.53
Other (please specify)	10.4	4.3	0.037
Currently have a salad bar:			
Does your school use any of the practices listed below to specifically promote your salad bars?			
Posters	37.4	45.0	0.32
Morning announcements/ promotions	16.5	19.6	0.64
Newsletters/parent folders	15.6	17.0	0.82
Classroom education	8.4	15.1	0.21
Fruit and vegetable of the day	12.2	19.4	0.31
Match salad bar offerings to the entrée	24.2	25.0	0.89
Change meal tray color	4.7	6.3	0.71
Other. Please specify	17.4	6.6	0.025

[a]General estimating equation binomial regression models adjusting for school level, free/reduced rate, years in position of respondent, and district clustering.

were getting students to be aware of and to stop at the salad bar and facing unsupportive staff, teachers, and administrations.

Promotion

Except for the "other category," there were no statistically significant differences in the affirmative answers to the promotion approaches used by urban or rural schools that currently have salad bars or once had salad bars (Table 3). The most popular approach to salad bar promotion across all school levels was posters. More than 10% of rural schools that once had a salad bar and 17% of rural schools that currently have a salad bar reported using an "other" strategy; most reported using menus to promote the salad bar. Other examples included using window clings, stickers, and a "roving chef."

Resources

Among schools that never had salad bars, 71% of rural schools listed funding as one of the top three most needed resources, and 44% of urban schools indicated funding in the top three (P=0.001; data not shown). Among schools that currently have salad bars, rural and urban schools were equally likely to list increased funding as a necessary resource in offering salad bars. (There was no statistically significant difference).

DISCUSSION

This study assessed the prevalence of school-lunch salad bars across urban and rural locales and examined differences in implementation practices for and barriers to salad bars in Arizona. Results demonstrated that no significant differences exist in the prevalence of salad bars between urban and rural Arizona schools. The findings from this study suggest that urban and rural school nutrition managers experience similar challenges in implementation. However, rural schools without salad bars are more likely than urban schools without salad bars to report barriers, such as cost of produce and food waste.

The adjusted prevalence of salad bars was not significantly different across locales, contrary to our expectations of rural inequalities that are typically seen in many environmental evaluations[32] and health outcomes studies.[33] The results of this study are consistent with those of VanFrank and colleagues[21] who report no statistically significant differences in students' reported access to salad bars across metro and nonmetro areas (source and definition of metro/nonmetro not provided) in 2011 or 2014.[21] Students' reports (from the study by Van Frank and colleagues[21]) and school nutrition managers' reports from this study support the absence of urban/rural inequality for salad bars, even after methodological differences across these two studies have been considered. However, the present study showed that higher free/reduced price lunch eligibility rates were related to a lower prevalence of salad bars after adjusting for all other variables.

Few significant differences emerged in reported implementation practices across schools in urban and rural locales in Arizona. These findings suggest that most intervention approaches may not need to differ by locale, because rural school nutrition managers reported similar benefits, and once rural schools have a salad bar, approaches to implementation are similar to those used in urban schools. However, more research is needed to confirm these results. An exception is that more rural schools reported higher cost and waste concerns. School nutrition managers in rural schools have noted smaller staffs, increased food costs, and increased waste concerns as barriers to implementing changes put forth by the Healthy, Hunger-Free Kids Act.[34] In the present study, we did observe a lower adjusted odds of having a salad bar with higher rates of free and/reduced price lunch enrollment. In addition, funding for salad bars was reported as a barrier by both rural and urban schools; rural schools were more likely to list increased funding as a necessary resource. If rural schools are faced with fewer resources and a higher cost of produce, these schools may be more likely to perceive barriers related to cost and food waste. Additional financial support may be needed to address cost and waste barriers to implementation of salad bars in rural schools.

Future research may include an objective evaluation of F/V intake or examination of other factors associated with salad bars such as demographic factors, barriers, and facilitators of adoption and/or use. Given that this study revealed that the association of salad bars was lower in schools with greater free/reduced price lunch eligibility rates, nutrition professionals could assist lower-income schools interested in a salad bar by directing them to resources that support implementation, such as Let's Move Salad Bars to School.[27,35]

Strengths and Limitations

Assessing associations with outcomes at the school level is a strength of this study. Many school environment studies are conducted at the district level and report on school-level factors. Additional strengths are the relatively large sample size with a high response rate and inclusion of elementary, middle, and high schools. This study was limited by its cross-sectional nature and the resulting nonprobability sample. Even though 36% of all schools across Arizona were sampled, it is unknown whether findings are generalizable to all schools or grade levels in Arizona or those outside of Arizona. However, the urban/rural locale of participating schools in this study reflected the Arizona public school distribution, 83% urban and 16% rural, with an average Arizona eligibility rate for free/reduced price meals of 67%.[34] This study did not assess how salad bars affected consumption of F/Vs among students. Although items were adopted from existing measures and content experts judged the face validity of the survey, the survey was not otherwise validated. The study spanned 2 academic years; however, given the climate in Arizona, it is unlikely that seasonal differences in produce availability affected the results. Finally, 52 schools were excluded from the study because of missing NCES locale codes. Many of these were parochial (religious) schools and may have been smaller or perhaps more rural, limiting the sample size when compared with urban schools.

CONCLUSIONS

No significant differences in prevalence of salad bars were observed between rural and urban schools, but school nutrition managers at rural schools that never had salad bars reported cost and food waste barriers more often than those at urban schools. No other barriers or implementation

practices appeared to differ by locale. In the future, researchers might consider investigating methods to address cost and waste concerns in rural areas and might evaluate the impact of salad bars on F/V consumption by urban and rural locale.

References

1. US Department of Agriculture. National School Lunch Program Fact Sheet. http://www.fns.usda.gov/cnd/lunch/aboutlunch/NSLPFactSheet. pdf. Published September 2013. Accessed October 2015.

2. Daniels SR, Arnett DK, Eckel RH, et al. Overweight in children and adolescents. *Circulation.* 2005;111:1999-2012.

3. Larson NI, Neumark-Sztainer D, Hannan PJ, et al. Trends in adolescent fruit and vegetable consumption, 1999-2004: Project EAT. *Am J Prev Med.* 2007;32(2):147-150.

4. US Department of Agriculture and the US Department of Health and Human Services. *Dietary Guidelines for Americans 2010.* 7th ed. Washington, DC: US Government Printing Office; 2010.

5. Adams M, Bruening M, Ohri-Vachaspati P, et al. Location of school lunch salad bars and fruit and vegetable consumption in middle schools: A cross-sectional plate waste study. *J Acad Nutr Diet.* 2016;116(3):407-416.

6. Larson NI, Neumark-Sztainer D, Hannan PJ, Story M. Family meals during adolescence are associated with higher diet quality and healthful meal patterns during young adulthood. *J Am Diet Assoc.* 2007;107(9):1502-1510.

7. Hartley D. Rural health disparities, population health, and rural culture. *Am J Public Health.* 2004;94(10):1675-1678.

8. Gamm LD, Hutchinson LL, Dabney BJ, Dabney BJ, Dorsey AM, eds. *Rural Healthy People 2010: A Companion Document to Healthy People 2010.* Volume 1. College Station, TX: The Texas A&M University System Health Science Center, School of Rural Public Health, Southwest Rural Health Research Center; 2010.

9. Caspi CE, Davey C, Nelson TF, et al. Disparities persist in nutrition policies and practices in Minnesota secondary schools. *J Acad Nutr Diet.* 2015;115(3):419-425.

10. Nanney MS, Davey CS, Kubik MY. Rural disparities in the distribution of policies that support healthy eating in US secondary schools. *J Acad Nutr Diet.* 2013;113(8):1062-1068.

11. Cohen JFW, Rimm EB, Bryn Austin S, et al. A food service intervention improves whole grain access at lunch in rural elementary schools. *J Sch Health.* 2014;84(3):212-219.

12. Lutifiyaa MN, Change LF, Lipsky MS. A cross-sectional study of US rural adults' consumption of fruits and vegetables: Do they consume at least five servings daily? *BMC Public Health.* 2012;12:280.

13. Liu J, Jones SJ, Sun H, et al. Diet, physical activity, and sedentary behaviors as risk factors for childhood obesity: An urban and rural comparison. *Child Obes.* 2012;8(5):440-448.

14. US Department of Agriculture. *Implementation Plan: Healthy, Hunger-Free Kids Act of 2010. Food and Nutrition Services.* Washington, DC: US Department of Agriculture; 2012.

15. Adams MA, Pelletier RL, Zive MM, et al. Salad bars and fruit and vegetable consumption in elementary schools: A plate waste study. *J Am Diet Assoc.* 2015;105(11):1789-1792.

16. Merlo C, Brener N, Kann L, et al. School-level practices to increase availability of fruits, vegetables, and whole grains, and reduce sodium in school meals—United States, 2000, 2006, and 2014. *MMWR Morb Mortal Wkly Rep.* 2015;64:905-908.

17. Adams MA, Bruening M, Ohri-Vachaspati P. Use of salad bars in Schools to increase fruit and vegetable consumption: Where's the evidence? *J Acad Nutr Diet.* 2015;115(8):1233-1236.

18. Wordell D, Daratha K, Mandal B, Bindler R, Butkus SN. Changes in a middle school food environment affect food behavior and food choices. *J Acad Nutr Diet.* 2012;112(1):137-141.

19. Slusser WM, Cumberland WG, Browdy BL, et al. A school salad bar increases frequency of fruit and vegetable consumption among children living in low income households. *Public Health Nutr.* 2007;10(12):1490-1496.

20. McCormack LA. Diet and physical activity in rural vs urban children and adolescents in the United States: A narrative review. *J Acad Nutr Diet.* 2016;113(3):467-480.

RESEARCH

21. VanFrank BK, Onufrak S, Harris DM. Youth access to school salad bars in the United States—2011 to 2014 [published online ahead of print October 21, 2016]. *Am J Health Promot*. 2016. https://doi.org/10.1177/0890117116671645.

22. Bruening M, Adams MA, Ohri-Vachaspati P, Hurley J. Prevalence and implementation practices of school salad bars across grade levels [published online ahead of print February 19, 2017]. *Am J Health Promot*; 2017. https://doi.org/10.1177/0890117116689159.

23. National Center for Education Statistics. https://nces.ed.gov/ Accessed December 2016.

24. Office of Management and Budget. Standards for defining metropolitan and micropolitan statistical areas; Notice. *Fed Regist*. 2000;249(65).

25. "Identification of Rural Locales." https://nces.ed.gov/programs/edge/geographicLocale.aspx. National Center for Education Statistics. Accessed December 2016.

26. National Center for Education Statistics. https://nces.ed.gov/surveys/ruraled/tables/a.1.a.-2.asp. Published 2014. Accessed March 5, 2017.

27. Chef Ann Foundation. Salad Bars to Schools. 2015. http://www.chefannfoundation.org/programs/salad-bars-to-schools/. Accessed June 15, 2017.

28. Arizona Department of Health Service, Arizona Department of Education. Salad Bars in Arizona: Survey Results. 2012. http://www.azdhs.gov/phs/bnp/nupao/saladbars/index.php?pg=survey. Accessed June 15, 2017.

29. Bridging the Gap. Food and Fitness: School Health Policies and Practices Questionnaire. 2012. http://www.bridgingthegap research.org/_asset/41v3cv/ES_2012_survey.pdf. Accessed June 15, 2017.

30. Arizona Department of Education. http://www.ade.az.gov/wizard/default.asp. Published 2014. Accessed September 5, 2015.

31. *Stata Statistical Software* [computer program]. Version 13. College Station, TX: StataCorp LP; 2013.

32. Andreson TJ, Saman DM, Lipsky SM, Lutfiyya MN. A cross-sectional study on health differences between rural and non-rural U.S. counties using the county health records. *BMC Health Serv Res*. 2015;15:441.

33. Lutfiyya MN, Lipsky MS, Wisdom-Behounek J, Inpanbutr-Martinkus M. Is rural residency a risk factor for overweight and obesity for U.S. children? *Obesity*. 2007;15(9):2348-2356.

34. Cornish D, Askelson N, Golembiewski E. "Reforms looked really good on paper": Rural food service responses to the Healthy, Hunger-Free Kids Act of 2010. *J Sch Health*. 2016;86(2):113-120.

35. Let's Move Salad Bars to Schools. http://www.saladbars2schools.org/. Published 2017. Accessed August 18, 2017.

AUTHOR INFORMATION

M. Blumenschine is a medical student, University of Arizona College of Medicine, Phoenix. M. Adams is an assistant professor and M. Bruening is an assistant professor, School of Nutrition and Health Promotion, Arizona State University, Phoenix.

Address correspondence to: Meg Bruening, PhD, MPH, RD, School of Nutrition and Health Promotion, Arizona State University, 550 N 5th St, Phoenix, AZ 85004. E-mail: meg.bruening@asu.edu

STATEMENT OF POTENTIAL CONFLICT OF INTEREST

No potential conflict of interest was reported by the authors.

FUNDING/SUPPORT

This study was funded by the Virginia G. Piper Charitable Trust ZBS-0019.

ACKNOWLEDGMENTS

We would like to thank the participants for taking the time to participate in this study and for all of their tireless efforts in feeding Arizona's schoolchildren. In addition, we would like to acknowledge Cara Alexander, RD, SNS, Gayle McCarthey, MPH, RD, Cynthia Melde, Amal Hammoud, RD, and Dianne Harris, PhD, MPH, CHES, for contributing to the survey development.

INDEX

alphanumeric outline, 248
AMA. *See* American Medical
    Association citation style
American Academy of Pediatrics,
    487
American Cancer Society, 122, 616*b*
American College of Cardiology,
    Guidelines on Lifestyle
    Management to Reduce
    Cardiovascular Risk, 59
American Diabetes Association, 57,
    58, 395, 616*b*, 642
        Nutrition Therapy
            Recommendations for the
            Management of Adults with
            Diabetes, 59
American Dietetic Association.
    See Academy of Nutrition and
    Dietetics
American FactFinder, 567*b*
American Heart Association, 57, 58,
    395, 616*b*
        grants, 614
        Guidelines on Lifestyle
            Management to Reduce
            Cardiovascular Risk, 59
*American Journal of Clinical
    Nutrition*, 60
American Management Association,
    31
American Marketing Association,
    145
American Media Institute, 69
American Medical Association
    (AMA) citation style, 119–120
American Press Institute, 68, 69
American Psychological Association
    (APA) format, 121
American Sign Language (ASL),
    204
American Society for Nutrition, 59
Americans with Disabilities Act, 498
American Translators Association,
    214
Amidor, Toby, 459*f*
analytic learners, 268
analytic research study, 80, 89
anchor text, 472
AND function, 62
anecdotal evidence, 73, 109
animal studies, 108
animation, slides, 299

APA. *See* American Psychological
    Association format
aperture, 413, 413*b*
apologies, in presentation openings,
    280
application activities, in
    presentations, 324
applications (apps), 339, 359, 414,
    489, 554, 576, 610
applications (research article), 81,
    91, 93
Arab female population, 53
Area Health Education Center
    programs, 33
Aristotle, 147, 149
art director/designer, 655
Article Influence Score, 632
articulation, presenter, 338–339
artificial light, for photos, 414, 415
arts, 252–253
ASL. *See* American Sign Language
assignment editor, 431
assimilation theory of meaningful
    learning, 258
Associated Press Stylebook, 656
asymmetry, written document, 357
attention of audience, 542
        attention of speaker and
            audience to one another, 543
        and audience participation, 318
        gaining, 545–546
        during presentations, 259–260,
            277
        and visual aids, 289–290
attitudes
        audience, 47, 168, 171
        and behavior change, 184
        changes, assessment of, 282
        and marketing, 565, 565*b*
        audience, 37–38, 142. *See also*
            audience participation, in
            presentations
        addressing, 534
        attention. *See* attention of
            audience
        attitudes, 47, 168, 171
        behaviors/practices, 168–169,
            171
        beliefs, 168
        blogs, 477
        characteristics, 352–353, 353*b*
        and choice of channels, 39,

47–48
        clear instructions for, 546–547
        collaboration with, 43–44
        and communication design, 16
        and communicators, connection
            between, 46–47, 146, 164, 323
        and compelling communicators,
            29–30
        and creativity of communicators,
            30–31
        demographics, 169
        education/updation of, 363–364
        and evaluation, 583
        experience, improving, 521
        facilitated discussions, 306–307,
            308–309
        identification of, 41, 42, 116,
            166–167, 567, 568*b*
        information, resources for, 567*b*
        inputs, 13, 15
        interest in topic and desire to
            learn, 553
        inviting to applaud, 535
        knowledge, assessment of, 168,
            171
        language of, 265
        learning, understanding,
            267–272
        and learning objectives, 241
        magazines, 441
        and marketing, 567, 568*b*
        mass media, 425, 430
        motivators, barriers, and
            readiness to change, 169
        multiple intelligences/learning
            styles, 267–269, 267*b*, 268*f*
        needs assessment. *See* needs
            assessment
        needs of, 145–146, 157
        newspapers, 440–441
        online education, 491
        personalities/tendencies,
            269–270, 270*f*
        popular press, 440, 447
        quieting, 545–545
        relating to topic, 535
        relational communication,
            13–14, 15
        resonation of messages with,
            146–148
        secondary, 364
        size of, 37

and audience participation,
318–319
influencers, 183–188, 183*f*
and marketing, 566
and social media, 454–455
behavior change theories, 15, 178
audience stage of change,
question to determine, 182*f*
behavior change influencers,
183–188, 183*f*
decision-oriented, 188–191
effective strategies for using,
191–194
health belief model, 188–189,
190*f*
integrated behavioral model,
189–190, 191*f*
polytheoretical framework, 192,
192 f–193*f*, 194
precaution-adoption process
model, 181, 181*f*, 182*f*
progress of behavior change,
178–179
putting knowledge into practice,
183*b*, 186*b*, 187*b*, 188*b*, 191*b*,
194*b*
social cognitive theory, 190–191
stage of change, 194
theory of planned behavior, 189
theory of reasoned action, 189
transtheoretical model, 179–182,
179*f*
behavior modification theories,
266
behaviors
acceptable, expectations of,
544–545
audience, 168–169, 171
desirable, and visual aids, 291
generational, 231
and progress, 178–179
beliefs
audience, 168
and behavior change, 184
beneficence, 128, 129, 131, 135
bias
and disclosure, 133
in needs assessment, 167
observer, 174
of panel members, and
moderation, 538
in research study, 101

unconscious, 207
Big Lens app, 414
Bill and Melinda Gates Foundation,
616*b*, 633
Bing, 72, 479
Bingo (game), 284, 588
bioethics, 128
biology, and behavior change, 185
blank slides, 299
Blatner, Dawn Jackson, 481*f*
blind carbon copy (bcc) function,
600
Blogger, 474
blogs/blogging, 347, 418, 428, 430,
460, 461*f*, 469
About Me section, 479, 480*f*
audience, 477
best practices, 477–482
call to action, 480, 481*f*
content, socializing, 478
content strategy, 474, 475*f*
copyright, 482
data, 479
disclosure statement, 479
discoverability of, 470–471
domain name, 474
editorial calendar, 475
financial benefits, 471–472
headlines, 476
host, 474
images, 476–477, 477*f*
online readers, tailoring writing
for, 475–476
platform, 474
practical steps for starting/
maintaining, 472, 474–477
privacy policy, 479–480
professional and ethical issues,
480–482
as professional resource, 471
and public education, 469–470
reach of, 470
role in nutrition communication,
469–472
search optimization, 478–479
structure of posts, 476
terms, 472
terms and conditions, 480
theme and design, 474
tile tools and templates, 500*b*
transparency and disclosure,
480–481, 482*f*

weekly series, 477, 478*f*
Bloom's taxonomy, 243–245,
244*f*, 324
Bluehost, 474
body movement, 204, 336
bokeh, 413*b*
book concept, 649, 651, 652
book contract, 647, 652, 653
book proposal, 649
books, 641. *See also* authorship
best practices for authors,
643–648
and career, 643
citing, 120
and disclosure, 133–134
and expertise of authors, 642
and lifelong learning, 642–643
practical steps for publishing,
648–658
reasons for writing, 641–643
as reflection of author, 643
as resource, 642
translating of complex science
into practical guidance, 642
writing, journey, 654–655
boolean operators, 62, 63*f*
bots
chatbots, 576
and search engines, 72
brainstorming, 156, 258, 323, 327*b*
branding, videos, 387
brands, and food photography, 409
brevity of communication, 157
bridging, 509
Briggs, Katherine Cook, 269
Briggs Myers, Isabel, 269
broadcast media, 429
B-roll, 386*b*
bubble chart, 112, 115*f*
budget, grant, 615, 619
budget justification, 619
Buffer, 478
bulletin boards, 296
business cards, 603–604
business communication, 599
best practices, 606–610
business correspondence,
599–601
clear and open communication,
608–609
documentation in writing,
609–610

listening, 610

making connections and relationship building, 611

materials, 603–606

meetings, 601–602

networking, 602–603

practical strategies, 610–612

professionalism in, 606–608

respect, 608

service, 612

teamwork, 608, 609

writing, reviewing, and responding, 611

business goals, vs communication goals, 566

BuzzFeed, 489

C

CAB Abstracts, 60

calendar invitation, for meetings, 602

CalFresh Nutrition Education, 497–498

callouts, 81, 92

calls for proposals, 617

calorie labeling, 111

cameras

angles, photography, 416, 417*f*

photo, 411, 413

video, 382

Can Manufacturers Institute, 565*b*

canned foods, 565*b*

Canva, 460, 498, 605

cartoons, giving credit to, 121*f*

case reports, 81, 89

case series, 81, 89

case studies, 81, 88, 381

Castle, Jill, 461*f*

causal inferences, 81

causation, 72–73, 109

CBPR. *See* community-based participatory research

CDC. *See* Centers for Disease Control and Prevention

CDR. *See* Commission on Dietetic Registration

Center for Plain Language, 354*b*

Centers for Disease Control and Prevention (CDC), 8, 57, 69, 89, 152, 170, 454, 616*b*

Food Safety Education Resources, 394

Healthy Weight website, 59

certainty messaging, 146

Chamber of Commerce, 447, 603

change agents, 10

channels, 39, 170

availability and affordability of, 39

choosing, 166

definition of, 9

effectiveness of, 47–48

and generations, 231

identification of, 41

and mass media, 429–430

popular press, 440–442

traditional vs nontraditional media channels, 12

character, of presenters, 277

charts, 112, 115*f*, 355–357

chatbots, 576

checklists, 90

cherry picking, 72

Chicago Manual of Style, 656

children, communication with, 223, 224*f*

and cultural differences, 235

MyPlate, 224, 225*b*

school and extracurricular settings, 234

tailoring goals and strategies to child development, 223

translation of principles into practice, 224

Children with Diabetes Forums, 498

ChooseMyPlate, 58, 154

choral response, 324

CINHAL Plus, 60

circular communication, 205

citations, 630, 646

citation styles, 119–120, 121

civility, in social media communication, 459

clarity in communication, 157, 430, 608–609

in blogging, 475

in grant writing, 617

classroom lecture to college students, referencing sources during, 121

clickbait, 458

headlines, 72

clickers, 320, 320*f*

click-rate metrics, 589

client education, and online

education, 487–489, 488*b*

clinical significance, 100

closed-ended questions, 87

closings, presentation, 276, 561

answering questions, 283

assessment, 284

bookends, 283

changes in knowledge, attitudes, and behavioral intentions, 282

checklist, 283

components of, 282–283

ending time, 285

key points, summary of, 281–282

logical flow, 282–283

memorable and motivating, 283

purpose of, 281–282

questions and answers, 285

rest of the story, providing, 284

strategies, 283–285

take-home message and call to action, 282

writing and sharing goals/ideas, 284

clothing, for media interviews, 505–506

CMS. *See* content-management systems

coaches

speech coach, 341

working with, 33

coauthors, writing a manuscript with, 636

author order, 636–637

best strategies, 636

criteria for authorship, 636

students as authors/coauthors, 637

Cochrane Library, 61, 69

Code of Ethics for the Nutrition and Dietetics Profession, 70, 128, 129*f*, 135, 136, 457, 646–647

accurate/truthful information, providing, 134

autonomy of patients/clients, respecting, 135

competence and professional development, 130–131

confidentiality of patients/clients, safeguarding, 135

integrity in personal and organizational behaviors/

content-share metrics, 589
context
    for information, popular press, 442
    presentation, 266
context (communication), 204
    high-context communication, 204
    low-context communication, 204–205
context, putting research findings into, 105
    body of knowledge on the topic, examining, 106–107
    dose and total diet, 108
    environmental factors, 108
    evolving nature of research, recognizing, 106
    individual differences, 107–108
continuing education, 33, 341
continuing professional education (CPE), 33, 486–487, 493
continuous improvement of communicators, 30
    collaboration, 31
    commitment, 31–32
    creativity, 30–31
    curiosity, 30
contract(s)
    book, 647, 652, 653
    negotiation of, 653
    for writers, 446
controversial topics, questions about, 558, 559
convenience, and online education, 498
convenience sampling, 167
conversationalist checklist, 604*b*
cookbooks, 651, 653, 656
cooking
    demonstrations, 12, 295, 351, 506
    technique, demonstration of, 393–394
    terms, 393
Cooking Channel, 380
Cooking Light, 441
cooking shows, 380, 382, 383
    setup of, 386
Cooking Together for Family Meals, 14
Cooking with the Moms, 422

cooperation, and audience participation, 329–330
Coordinated Programs (CPs), 23
    competencies for RDNs for, 25*f*
    coping capacity, and behavior change, 185
copy editor, 653
copyright, 134, 410
    blogs, 482
    and online education, 495
Copyright Act (1976), 134
copyright laws, 495
copyright page, in books, 647–648, 649
COREQ (Consolidated Criteria for Reporting Qualitative Research), 625*b*
correlation, 72–73, 109
correspondence, business, 599–601, 608
corresponding author, 636
counseling, 13, 284, 488
County Health Rankings, 57, 58
    Explore Health Rankings, 57
    Take Action to Improve Health, 57
courses, communication, 32–33
courtesy authorship, 636
cover letter, 605
    to journal editor, 634
CPE. *See* continuing professional education
CPS. *See* creative problem solving
CPs. *See* Coordinated Programs
CRDNs. *See* competencies for RDNs
creative calendar, 443*f*
Creative Commons, 134, 476, 498*b*, 633
Creative Education Foundation, 307
creative problem solving (CPS), and facilitated discussions, 307
creativity, 18–19, 30–31, 307, 397
    and skills, 19
credentials
    and ethics, 74
    reputable vs fake, 67–68
    using appropriately, 131–132
credibility of communicators, 28, 370
    clues to credibility, 69
    integrity, 29

    and moderators, 533
    and presentation openings, 277
    and professional introduction, 534, 535
    professionalism, 29
credible sources, 67. *See also* sources, referencing
    author, examination of, 75
    claims, examination of, 76
    credentials/training, reputable vs fake, 67–68
    defining, 67–68
    and disclosure, 69–71
    ethical standards, 68
    history, 68
    professional organizations as, 68–69
    questionable source, identification of, 71–74
    red flags, 68, 69*f*, 72
    teaching consumers to discern the difference, 75–76
    website, examination of, 75
credit to sources. *See* sources, referencing
cross-cultural communication, 205
    barriers, overcoming, 213, 214*f*, 215*f*
    collaboration with culture, 211, 213
    communication plan, 213
    team, 212
    translations, 214, 216–218
cross-sectional studies, 81, 89
crossword puzzles, 284
Crowdfire, 567*b*
cultural appropriation, 217*b*
cultural awareness, 207*f*
cultural competence, 131, 199, 202, 204, 205, 207–208, 207*f*
    Bennett model of, 206 f
    and business communication, 608
cultural competence continuum, 131
cultural exchange, 217b
cultural immersion, 208, 210
cultural informants, 210, 211, 218
cultural knowledge, 207*f*
cultural sensitivity, 207*f*
culture, 199–200, 491
    and behavior change, 186
    and cognitive style, 203

domain name, blog, 474
Donkersloot, Mary, 461*f*, 473*f*
Doodle, 601
dose (project), 586–587
dose, of experimental treatment, 108
downward messaging, 146
DPDs. *See* Didactic Programs in Dietetics
DPGs. *See* dietetic practice groups
drawings, 355, 590
DSLR cameras, 382, 411, 413
Dulan, Mitzi, 457*f*
dynamic learners, 269

E

EAL. *See* Evidence Analysis Library
early adulthood, 227*f*
earned media, 573
Easy Recipe, 479
EatRight.org, 394
Eat Right Weekly, 442, 658
eBooks, 472
EBSCO Information Services, 633
e-commerce, 471, 472
economic costs of poor communication, 11
economic environment, and behavior change, 187
Edelman Trust Barometer Global Report (2018), 71
editing
    book, 643–644
    photo, 415
    written communication, 359
editing, video, 386
    audio detach, 387
    cutting, 387
    export, 387
    import, 386
    music, 387
    save and undo, 387
    software, 383–384
    speed duration, 387
    text, 387
    transitions, 387
editorial calendar, blogs, 475
Editorial Freelancers Association, 446
editorial team, 653, 655
educational videos, 380, 381, 382, 385
    setup, 386

edutainment, 398–399
effectiveness, communication, 32
    coaches/mentors, working with, 33
    communication courses, 32–33
    continually learning and practicing skills, 33
    continuing education opportunities, 33
    external opportunities, 33
    and presentation skills, 334–335
EFNEP. *See* Expanded Food and Nutrition Education Program
Eigenfactor, 632
electronic mailing lists (EMLs), 433
electronic rights, 446
elementary school-age audiences, 224*f*, 225*b*
elevator speech, 603*b*
email, 599–600, 606
email newsletters, 348
EMLs. *See* electronic mailing lists
emojis, 601*b*
emotional contrast, 259–260
emotional intelligence, 29
emotions
    addressing in messages, 147
    in presentations, 278, 280
empathic listening, 610
empathy, 29, 47, 278, 279, 307
employment, and communication skills, 11
EndNote, 630
engagement (social media), 458
enthusiasm of communicators, 30
enunciation of presenter, 338–339
environment, 9
    factors, and research findings, 108
    physical environment sphere, 187–188, 188*b*
    safe learning environment, 327–329
    social environment sphere, 186, 187*b*
equality messaging, 146
EQUATOR Network, 625
equipment
    photo, 410–415
    presentation, 524
    video, 382
ERIC (Education Resources

Information Center), 60
errors and omissions insurance, 648
Essential Practice Competencies for CDR Credentialed Nutrition and Dietetics Practitioners, 22–23
ethics, 70, 128
    authorship, 646–648
    blogs, 480–482
    commitment, 31–32
    and credentials, 74
    definition of, 128
    dilemmas, obligations for considerations in, 130*b*
    evidence-based information, 130–131
    foundational principles, 128–132
    integrity, 29, 131, 132–135
    marketing, 572
    online education, 495, 497
    principles of greatest concern, 132–135
    promotion of ethical practice, 135–136
    respect for individuals, 131
    and social media communication, 457–459
    standards, 68
ethnocentrism, 205
ethnorelativism, 205–206
ethos, 147, 277
European Social Marketing Association, 151
evaluation, 41, 577, 582
    approaches, 583–587
    effectiveness of communications, improving, 582–583
    engaging target audience, 583
    formative, 583, 584
    outcome, 583–585
    practical strategies, 588–591
    process evaluation, 585–587
    purpose of, 582–583
    qualitative and quantitative, 588–591
    questions, 591*b*
    and resource allocation, 583
    type and function, 587*f*
evaluation (research), 81, 86
Evernote, 610
Evidence Analysis Library (EAL), 60–61

evidence-based information, 130–131, 492, 646

evidence-based medicine pyramid, 73, 73*f*

evidence-based nutrition communication, 17–18, 17*f*

evidence-based practice, 18, 624

exact phrases, 62, 63*f*

examples, selection of, 166

Expanded Food and Nutrition Education Program (EFNEP), 16

experiential learning, 267–268, 268*f*, 381

experimental research designs, 81, 89, 92, 106

experts, quoting, 124

exposure triangle, 411

extracurricular settings, 234

extrinsic motivators, 169

eye contact, 543
    during media interviews, 506
    of presenter, 337–338

F

Facebook, 12, 137*f*, 347, 382, 387, 426, 451, 452*b*, 453–454, 455, 457*f*, 460, 462, 464, 478, 489, 498, 589, 643

Facebook Analytics, 567*b*

Facebook Groups, 455, 455*f*, 471

Facebook Live, 460, 462*f*, 505

face-to-face interviewing, 172

facial expressions, of presenter, 337

facilitated discussions, 305
    backup questions, 309
    and community building, 307
    vs conventional presentations, 305–307
    and creative problem solving, 307
    ending, summary, and next steps, 311
    and engagement of audience, 307
    evaluation checklist for, 313
    facilitation role of leader, 312
    focus on audience, 306–307
    and goal setting/application of learning, 307
    ground rules, 311
    for malnutrition workgroup, 308*b*

methods to keep on track, 311

misconceptions/misinformation, dealing with, 312

open-ended questions, 309, 310*b*

opening activity, 309, 311

planning and implementation of, 308–311

practical strategies, 311–313

purpose/goals, determining, 308

rapport/trust building, 312

recording answers, 312–313

responsiveness and adaptability, 312

safe involvement of group members, 312

sharing and balanced contribution of group members, 312

staying on task and ending on time, 313

target audience, determining, 308–309

wide breadth of potential uses, 306

facilities and administration costs, grants, 615

fact-versus-fiction filters, 74, 76

fair use databases, 495, 498*b*

falsehoods, 71–72

FAQs. *See* frequently asked questions

farm-to-table, 408

FastStats, 57

fear-based marketing, 72

Fearless FoodRD, 418

fears
    addressing in messages, 147, 148
    fear of public speaking, 335

federal agencies, funding for nutrition research and projects, 616*b*

Federal Grants Learning Center, 616*b*

Federal Trade Commission (FTC), 457, 480–481

FedEx, 604

feedback, 16, 43, 558, 609
    audience, 543–544, 583
    definition of, 9
    and eye contact, 337
    food photography, 416

informal, 167
    during internships, 32
    on journal article, 630
    meetings, 602
    about presentation, 282, 342
    during presentations, 321
    rehearsal, 340, 341*f*
    reviewer, grants, 620–621
    for writing, 359

Feeding America, 368

feelings
    addressing in messages, 147, 148
    and behavior change, 184

fidelity, project, 586–587

Field, Emily, 465*f*

figures, 81, 92–93, 627–628, 628*f*
    giving credit to, 121, 121 f

fillers, pauses without, 339

fill light, 383

financial benefits of blogging, 471–472

first impression, in presentation openings, 276, 278

first North American serial rights, 446

flagging, 509

flash cards, 319, 319*f*, 320

Flesch Reading Ease Readability Formula, 355*b*

flexibility, 231, 235

Flickr.com, 476

flip-chart summary, 327*b*

flow diagram, 628, 629*f*

FNCE. *See* Food & Nutrition Conference & Expo

foam board, 415

focus groups, 81, 88, 173–174

fonts
    size, 298
    slide, 298, 298*f*
    written document, 357

Food and Agriculture Organization, 213

Food and Drug Administration, 565*b*

Food and Health Survey, 3, 170, 440, 574

Food and Nutrition Science Alliance, 76

food demonstrations, 12, 319, 347, 358*b*, 391
    advantages of, 391–392

immigrants, and culture, 202

impact factor, 60, 631–632, 633*b*

implications (research article), 81, 91, 93

incentives for surveys, 171

independent t test, 84

independent variables, 82, 90, 95, 98

in-depth interviews, 171

indexation of manuscript, 632–633

indexer, 655

indirect communication, 205

indirect costs, grants, 615

indirect observations, 174

individual differences, and research findings, 107–108

individualism, and culture, 202

influencer (social media), 458

influencer outreach, 574–575

infographics, 112, 296, 296*f*, 356, 356*b*, 356*f*

informal feedback, 167

informants, cultural, 210, 211, 218

informational videos, 380, 382, 383, 385

    setup, 386

information environment, and behavior change, 188

ingredient adjustments, recipes, 410

InMotion Hosting, 474

in-person surveys, 172*b*

inputs, communication, 15

    audience, 15

    communicator, 15–16

inquiry arousal, 277

inspirational messages, 148

inspirations, and book writing, 643

Instagram, 12, 382, 408, 416, 426, 432, 451, 452*b*, 453*f*, 454, 455, 457*f*, 459*f*, 460, 462, 463, 464*f*, 465*f*, 643

Instagram TV, 505

Institute of Continuing Education for Nutrition Professionals (ICENP), 487

Institute of Education Sciences, 60

Institute of Medicine, Who Will Keep the Public Healthy? report, 11

instructional objectives, 241

instrumental dimension of communication, 13, 16

instruments/instrumentation, 82, 90, 91–92, 98–99

integrated behavioral model, 189–190, 191*f*

integrity in personal and organizational behaviors and practices, 131, 132–135

integrity of communicators, 29

intellectual property rights, respecting, 134, 482

intentional plagiarism, 123

intentions, and behaviors, 169, 190

interactivity principle, 318

interference, definition of, 9

internal motivation, of adult learners, 226

internal resources, and behavior change, 184–185

International Association of Culinary Professionals, 645, 652

International Committee of Medical Journal Editors (ICMJE), 636

International Food Information Council (IFIC), 2, 3, 142, 170, 356

    Message Development Model, 143, 149–150, 149*f*, 247

International Social Marketing Association, 151

internet, 56–57, 71, 346, 439, 440

    and plagiarism, 122, 123

interpreters, 216–218

interrogative titles, 625

intervening process, 16

intervention, study, 91–92

interview guide, 82, 88, 171

interviews, 82, 88, 171–173. *See also* media interviews

    partner, 326*b*

    tips for interviewer, 173

intrinsic motivators, 169

introduction (presentation). *See* openings, presentation

introduction (research article), 82, 91, 95, 96*f*, 626

inverted pyramid style of writing, 443–444, 444*f*

iPage, 474

iPhone, 414, 414*f*

iPhonePhotographySchool.com, 415

ISO speed, 413

iStock, 298

iStock Photo, 498*b*

"It's All About You" campaign, 3, 3*f*

J

JANE. *See* Journal/Author Name Estimator

jargons, 147, 166, 265, 353, 644

JBI. *See* Joanna Briggs Institute

Jeopardy (game), 284

Joanna Briggs Institute (JBI), 61

Jones, Jessica, 471*f*

Jones, Regan Miller, 461*f*

Journal/Author Name Estimator (JANE), 631

journalism, 68. *See also* popular press professional organizations, 69

Journal of Enteral and Parenteral Nutrition, 60

Journal of Hunger and Environmental Nutrition, 60

Journal of Nutrition and Dietetics, 442

Journal of the Academy of Nutrition and Dietetics, 60, 120, 134, 442

Journal of the International Society of Sports Nutrition, 60

journals, 59–60, 59*f*, 73, 439 b. *See also* research articles

Jump with Jill, 253–254

Jung, Carl, 269

junk science, red flags of, 76, 76*f*

justice, 128, 129

K

key light, 383

key messages, 256–258. *See also* messages

    checklist for creating, 249

    and clarity/focus, 241–242

    food demonstrations, 397–398

    identification of, 41

    mass media, 434

    media interviews, 508, 509

    and outlines, 248–249

    in presentations, 279, 281–282

    purpose of, 240–242

    and Q&A session, 554, 561

    structure of, 242–247

    succinct and memorable, 246–247

    and writing, 354, 354*b*

key performance indicators (KPIs), 570, 572*b*

keywords (blogging), 472
keywords (research article), 626
keywords (search), 64
Kids Eat Right, 447
kinesthetic learning, 324
knowledge
    audience, 264, 278–279, 353, 491
    audience, assessment of, 168, 171, 265
    and behavior change, 184, 185
    changes, assessment of, 282
    connecting new knowledge to prior knowledge, 265
    gains, games for testing, 589b
    objective, 168
    perceived, 168
knowledge requirements for RDNs (KRDNs), 23, 24f
Kolb's model of learning styles and experiential learning, 267–269, 268f
KPIs. See key performance indicators
Kraft Heinz Co., 575, 576f
KRDNs. See knowledge requirements for RDNs
Krieger, Ellie, 462f
Kuzemchak, Sally, 461f, 481f

L

LactMed, 489
language use
    and culture, 203
    in presentations, 265
laptop use, guidelines for, 548
large-group activities, 327, 328b
latchkey kid, 229
late adulthood, 227f, 228
lateral messaging, 146
lavalier microphone, 524
lay audiences
    nutrition topics for, 432
    and source referencing, 124–125
layout
    handouts/newsletters, 368, 368f
    written documents, 357–358
leadership communication, 516–518
learning
    adult, 225–226
    application, and facilitated discussions, 307
    and attention of audience, 542

audience, understanding, 267–272
    and audience engagement, 260
    and call to action, 282
    Cone of Experience, 270, 271f, 391
    enhancement, and audience participation, 318
    experiential, 267–269, 268f
    and handouts, 364
    kinesthetic, 324
    learner reflection, 493, 495
    meaningful, 258
    multimedia, 290
    multisensory, 378–379
    observational, 184
    and Q&A session, 553
    safe learning environment, 327–329
    significant, 318
learning management system (LMS), 495, 496b
learning objectives, 241, 243
    affective domain, 244–245, 245f
    assessment of, 282
    cognitive domain and Bloom's taxonomy, 243–245, 244f
    online education, 491–492
    psychomotor domain, 245, 246f
    tool for creating, 145f
    learning styles, 169, 213, 267–269, 267b, 268f
letter of intent or inquiry (LOI), 615
letter of support, 619
life experience
    of adults, and learning, 226
    generational, 231
lifelong learning, 33, 642–643
lifestyle factors, 107
    and behavior change, 185
lighting
    food photography, 414, 415–416
    room, 524
    video, 383, 383f
limitations, study, 93, 98, 100–101, 107
limited-interest questions, 556–557, 559
linear communication, 205
line graph, 112, 115f
LinkedIn, 348, 426, 431, 452b, 478, 603, 606

listening, 29, 543
    business communication, 610
    definition of, 29
    empathic, 610
    to question, 554–555
literary agent, 652
Literary Marketplace, 649, 652
literature review, 82, 86, 95
    updation of, 625
live barometer, 328b
live-stream videos, 381, 382
    setup, 386
live-tweet, 458
Liz's Healthy Table, 423, 461f, 482f
LMS. *See* learning management system
local media, 428, 429
location
    event, 522–523
    meeting, 601
logical flow
    and outlines, 249
    in presentations, 282–283
logical writing, 353–354
logic model, 152, 618
    background and rationale, 152–153
    example, 153f, 154f
    message development using, 153–154
logistical planning, 520
    audience experience, improving, 521
    backup plan for disasters, 527–528
    checklist, 528
    components of, 521–526
    confirming arrangements, 527
    focus on communication, 521
    handouts, 526
    keeping track of details and meeting deadlines, 527
    location, date, time and parking, 522
    location-specific arrangements, 522–523
    necessary arrangements, 521–526
    online presentation arrangements, 524, 526
    positive attitude, maintaining, 528

models, for effective messages,
148–149
  IFIC Message Development
    Model, 149–150, 149*f*
  logic model, 152–154, 153*f*, 154*f*
  PRECEDE-PROCEED
    model, 154–156, 155*f*
  social marketing, 150–152, 152*f*
moderator guide, 82
moderators, 532, 553
  assisting with timekeeping,
    technology, and handouts, 536
  checklist, 539
  enthusiasm, 536
  establishing speaker's credibility
    and building anticipation, 533
  hosting and facilitation of
    session/event, 532
  moderating panels and other
    events, 537–538, 560
  preparing introduction in
    advance with input from
    speaker, 535–536
  professional introduction,
    534–535
  pronouncing name, title, and
    difficult words, 536
  Q&A session, 536–537
  role of, 532–534
  timely management of sessions,
    533–534
  understanding of venues/events,
    533
  welcoming and orienting
    audience, 533
moderators (focus groups), 82, 173
Modern Language Association
  (MLA) format, 121
modern style of writing, 354–355,
  355*b*
modular organization, presentations,
  262
Mohr, Chris, 471*f*
Mohr Results blog, 471*f*
momentum questions (Brookfield
  and Preskill), 321, 322*b*
Mom's Kitchen Handbook, 478*f*
Morford, Katie, 478*f*
mosaic plagiarism, 121*b*
most important (activity), 325*b*
motivation
  and goals/objectives, 242–243

and messages, 259
and online education, 493, 494*b*
for parents, 228
motivators
  audience, 169
  internal, 226
movement
  of audience, 324
  of presenter, 336
MTV generation. *See* Generation X
  (Gen X)
muddiest point activity, 325*b*
multidimensionality of culture, 201
multimedia learning, 290
multimedia principle, 290
multiple intelligences (Gardner),
  267–269, 267*b*
multiquestions, 557
multisensory learning, and videos,
  378–379
music, 324
  -based health programs,
    253–254
  in videos, 387
Myers–Briggs Type Indicator
  (MBTI), 269
MyFitnessPal, 489
MyPlate, 58, 143, 224, 225*b*
MyPlate Message Toolkit, 158

N

names
  pronouncing, 536
  using, 534, 546
name tags, 547
narrative recipe form, 656
National Academies of Sciences,
  Engineering, and Medicine, 4
    Committee on the Science of
    Science Communication, 10
National Agricultural Library, 60
National Association for Media
  Literacy Education, 225*b*
National Association of
  Broadcasters, 69
National Association of Colleges
  and Employers, 333
National Association of
  Independent Writers and Editors,
  647
National Cancer Institute, 8, 57
  fruit and vegetable screener, 171

National Center for Complementary
  and Integrative Health, 57
National Center for Education,
  Statistics Common Core of Data,
  234
National Center for Health
  Statistics, 57
National Communication
  Association, 33
National Council on Disabilities
  (NCD), 57
National Dairy Council, 364, 366*f*,
  368
National Disability Rights Network
  (NDRN), 57
National Health and Nutrition
  Examination Survey (NHANES),
  89, 170
National Institute of Diabetes and
  Digestive and Kidney Diseases,
  Health Information website, 57
National Institutes of Health (NIH),
  11, 57, 131, 489, 616*b*, 617, 619,
  633
    grants, 614
    Health Information website, 57
National Kidney Foundation, 395
National Library of Medicine, 57, 62
national media, 428, 429
National Newspaper Association, 69
National Press Club, 69
National Science Foundation, 616*b*,
  618
National Soup Month, 434
National Speakers Association
  (NSA), 33, 342
native advertising, 61, 573
natural light
  for photos, 414, 415
  for videos, 383
NCD. *See* National Council on
  Disabilities
NDRN. *See* National Disability
  Rights Network
NDTR. *See* nutrition and dietetics
  technician, registered
needs assessment, 41, 42, 44, 150,
  157, 163, 213, 231, 265, 400
    breadth/depth of topics, 166
    channels, choosing, 166
    communicators and audience,
    connection between, 164

conducting, 166–174

data collection and analysis, 163–164

for driving decisions, 165–166

focusing on message, 165

formal, 166

identification of audience, 166–167

information to collect, determining, 167–170

involvement and interest of audience, 164

online education, 491

primary data collection, 170–174

purpose of, 163–164

secondary data, sources/uses of, 170

for understanding generations, 230*b*

waste of time/resources, prevention of, 164

words/examples, selection of, 166

and writing, 353

needs of audience, 145–146, 157

negative framing of messages, 247

negative news, and marketing, 569

nervousness, overcoming, 335–336

nesting, 62, 63*f*

networking

business communication, 602–603

and writing for popular press, 447

new media, 428, 429

New Nutrition Conversation with Consumers, 142–143

news articles, 61

newsletters, 363, 365*f*, 433, 442

consistency, maintaining, 370, 370*f*

delivering clear messages, 364, 367

direct calls to action, 367

education and updation of audience, 363–364

effective, guidelines for, 369–372

focus on audience, 364

informative content, 370–371, 371*f*

organized, 369, 369*f*

partnering, 371–372, 371*f*

uniform layout and design, 368

newspapers, 428, 429, 431, 438, 439

accuracy and context for information, 442

audience, 440–441

author guidelines, following, 445

following up with editors, 445

formats, 428–429

inverted pyramid style of writing, 443–444, 444*f*

network and identification of resources, 447

newsworthiness of story, 443

print, 439

query letters, 445

reputation of writer, 445–446

storytelling, flexible plan for, 445

tone, 442–443

writing opportunities, 447

news sources, credible, 69

newsworthiness of story, 443

New York Times, 441

NHANES. *See* National Health and Nutrition Examination Survey

NIH. *See* National Institutes of Health

Ninja Kitchen (game), 589*b*

NLM. *See* US National Library of Medicine

noise, definition of, 9

nonmaleficence, 128, 130–131, 132

nonprobability sampling, 167

nonprofit organizations, funding for nutrition research and projects, 616*b*

nonstudy document, referencing, 124

nontraditional media channels, 12

nonverbal communication, 334*b*

nonverbal cues, and culture, 203–204

norms, 185–186, 200

notes

meeting, 602, 609

presentation, 526

notetaker, 602, 609–610

NOT function, 62

Nourished Child, The, 461*f*

NSA. *See* National Speakers Association

numbered list, 262

Nutrition and Dietetic Educators and Preceptors, 26

nutrition and dietetics technician, registered (NDTR), 23

Nutrition Blog Network, 464, 470*b*

nutrition communication, 2, 7

activities, 11

as both art and science, 17–19

building diverse perspectives into practice, 2

definition of, 8

development, stages of, 587*f*

effectiveness, improvement of, 32–33

essentialness of communication, 10–12

evidence-based, 17–18, 17*f*

forms of, 12–13

framework, 14*f*, 15–17, 18

goals of, 10

listen and learn, 5

models and theories, 13–17

purposes of, 8

research systems and thinking, 3–4

self-explanatory nature of, 7–8

and skills/creativity, 18–19

as team effort, 2

Nutrition Communication Development Strategy, 40–41, 41*f*, 42*b*, 148

nutrition counseling, 488

nutrition education, definition of, 8

Nutrition Entrepreneurs, 26, 33, 364, 447

Authors & Writers Specialty Group, 645, 652

nutrition facts, in food demonstrations, 395

Nutrition.gov, 394

nutrition information and guidelines, 56–59

Nutrition in Medicine, 487

Nutrition Jeopardy (game), 588

Nutrition Therapy Recommendations for the Management of Adults with Diabetes, 59

O

obesity, 53

Obesity and Energetics Offerings (Indiana University/University of Alabama), 492–493

positive attitude, maintaining, 528

positive framing of messages, 247

positivity of communicators, 29–30

poster board, 415

posters, 296

postmillennials. *See* Generation Z

Power of Protein: Quality Matters handout, 366*f,* 372*f,* 373*f,* 374*f*

power-over setting, 307

PowerPoint, 289, 296, 297, 301, 356, 495, 529

power-with setting, 307

PR. *See* public relations

practicality, and adult learning, 226

practice competencies. *See* competencies, communication

precaution-adoption process model, 179, 181, 181*f,* 182*f,* 192

PRECEDE-PROCEED model, 154, 155*f*

    background and rationale, 154–155

        message development using, 156

predatory journals, 60, 633, 633*b*

predispositions, 9, 15–16

prepublication review, 657

preschool audiences, 224*f,* 225*b*

preschool students, qualitative evaluation methods for, 589–591

presentation literacy, 256

presentations. *See also* closings, presentation; openings, presentation; visual aids

    active engagement, promotion of, 270–272

    application experiences, 271

    autonomy of audience, 272

    connecting new knowledge to prior knowledge, 265

    content, organization of, 260–263

    content, presentation of, 263–266

    context, 266

    dialogue approach, 270–271

    discussions. *See* facilitated discussions

    evaluation. *See* evaluation

    foundations, analogies for, 257*b*

    interactive activities in, 42

    key points and supporting evidence, 256–258

    language of audience, 265

meaningful messages, 258

memorable messages, 258–259

motivating messages, 259

and multiple intelligences/ learning styles, 267–269, 267*b,* 268*f*

offering suggestions/options, 272

oral, citing, 120–121

and oral interpretations, 218

and personalities/tendencies, 269–270, 270*f*

purpose of, 256–260

relevant and useful information, 265–266

skills, 18

software, 497*b*

strategies that promote attention/engagement, 259–260

travel tips, 301

to varied audiences, 12

Presentation Simulator, 341

presentation skills, 333

    better practices, learning, 339–340

    and confidence/effectiveness, 334–335

    content vs delivery, 333–334

    definition of, 333

    enhancement of, 339–342

    evaluation by audiences, 342

    facial expressions and eye contact, 337–338

    gestures, 337

    mentors, working with, 341

    nervousness, overcoming, 335–336

    rehearsal, 340–341, 341*f*

    seeking opportunities to speak, 342

    skill-building opportunities, participation in, 341–342

    stance and body movement, 336

    voice, 338–339

presiders, 532

    assisting with timekeeping, technology, and handouts, 536

    checklist, 539

    enthusiasm, 536

    establishing speaker's credibility and building anticipation, 533

hosting and facilitation of session/event, 532

moderating panels and other events, 537–538, 560

preparing introduction in advance with input from speaker, 535–536

professional introduction, 534–535

pronouncing name, title, and difficult words, 536

Q&A session, 536–537

role of, 532–534

timely management of sessions, 533–534

understanding of venues/events, 533

welcoming and orienting audience, 533

prespeech routines, 336, 336*b*

presubmission inquiries, 631

primacy effect, 276, 281

primary data, definition of, 170

primary data collection, 170–174

primary research. *See* original research

print materials, marketing using, 575

print media, 429

    newspapers, 439, 440

privacy policy, blogs, 479–480

Private School Universe Survey, 234

probability sampling, 167

probability value. *See* P value

problem-centered learning, 226

problem solving

    creative, and facilitated discussions, 307

    structure, presentations, 261–262

process evaluation, 585–587

pro-con activity, 326*b*

professional development, 130–131, 132

professional guidance, for scientific manuscripts, 625, 625*b*

professional introduction, 277, 534

    accurate information about speaker, 535

    addressing audience, 534

    introducing self, event, speaker, and topic, 534–535

    inviting audience to applaud, 535

summarizing the answer, 555,
556
virtual, responding to, 560–561
questions
asking, 321, 321*b*, 322*b*
audience participation, 319–321,
321*b*, 322*b*
closed-ended, 87
evaluation, 591*b*
facilitated discussions, 309, 310*b*
good-for-nothing, 322*b*
media interview, 507
open-ended, 87, 88, 171, 309,
310*b*
in presentation closings, 283
in presentation openings, 280
quizzes, 319–321
quotes, use in presentations, 280

R

radio, 429
rambling questions, 557
randomized controlled trials (RCTs),
73, 89, 106
avoiding bias in, 101
rapport with audience
and audience participation, 312
in facilitated discussions, 312
in presentations, 278–279
Rawn, Jenny Shea, 461*f*
RCTs. *See* randomized controlled
trials
RDNs. *See* registered dietitian
nutritionists
reach
of blogs, 470
of mass media, 426
of popular press, 439–440
project, 586–587
readability tools, 355, 355*b*
readers
blog, 475–476
book, 645, 649
readiness to change, audience, 169,
182*f*
reading level of writing, 355
Reading the Mind in the Eyes test,
46
Real Food Dietitians, 464*f*
realistic messages, 148
real-life hacks, in food
demonstrations, 396

Real Mom Nutrition blog, 461*f*, 481*f*
receiver, definition of, 9
recency effect, 276, 281, 283
recipe demonstration planning
worksheet, 400, 401*f*
recipes
development, 409–410, 656
modifications, demonstration of,
395
pretesting, 402–403
sharing, 464*f*
testing, 409–410
recipe testers, 653, 655
recipe videos, 380, 381*b*
Recipe Writer's Handbook, The, 656
reciprocal determinism, 183, 183*f*,
190
Recite, 460
recognition of audience, 329–330
and generations, 231
recognition programs, 231
record keeping, 526–527
recreational settings, 234–235, 523
red flags, credible source, 68, 69*f*, 72,
76, 76*f*
redundancy principle, 297
references, 630. *See also* sources,
referencing
referral traffic, 473
reflection activities, in presentations,
284, 324, 325*b*
reflection principle, 324
reflective learners, 318
reflective surfaces, 415
reflector, 383, 415
registered dietitian nutritionists
(RDNs), 10, 23, 67, 75, 76, 80, 378,
402, 438, 504, 574
competencies for, 23, 25*f*
as hosts and interviewees, 505,
505*b*, 506*b*
knowledge requirements for, 24*f*
as media resources, 431–432
quoting, 125
as subject matter experts,
427–428, 432
understanding of research
articles, 90–91
use of jargons, 353
rehearsal of presentation, 340–341,
341*f*

relational dimension of
communication, 13–14, 15, 16
relationship marketing, 565
relationships, building, 14, 43, 307
business communication, 611
and cultural competence, 210–211
and mass media, 431–432
and networking, 603
reliability of online tools and
platforms, 495
repetition, in presentations, 282, 324
replicability of videos, 379
reporting
research, 83, 86
standards for study designs, 625,
625*b*
reprint rights, 446
requests for applications, 617
requests for proposals, 617
research, 3–4, 17–18, 43, 80, 165. *See
also* scientific research
abstracts, 80, 83, 84, 95
and authorship, 644–645
bias, 101
evidence, strength of, 100
interpretation of, 99–101
latest research on topic of
interest, 433
message, 41
principles, 84–90
putting findings into context,
105–108
skills, 18
statistical significance vs clinical
significance, 100
study, referencing, 124
research articles, 90–91
discussion, conclusion, and
applications, 93, 98, 109
introduction and background,
91, 95, 96*f*
methods and data analysis,
91–92, 98–99
questions to ask of, 91
results, tables, and figures,
92–93, 97*f*, 98, 99
sections, common information
included in, 94*b*
source of, 95
strategies for understanding/
critically reading, 93, 95,
96*f*–97*f*, 98–99

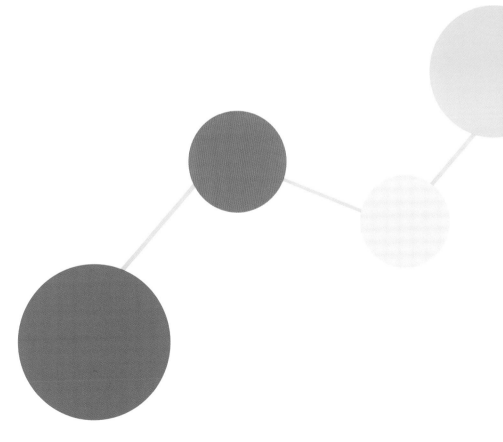